A Flexible Organization for Instructors

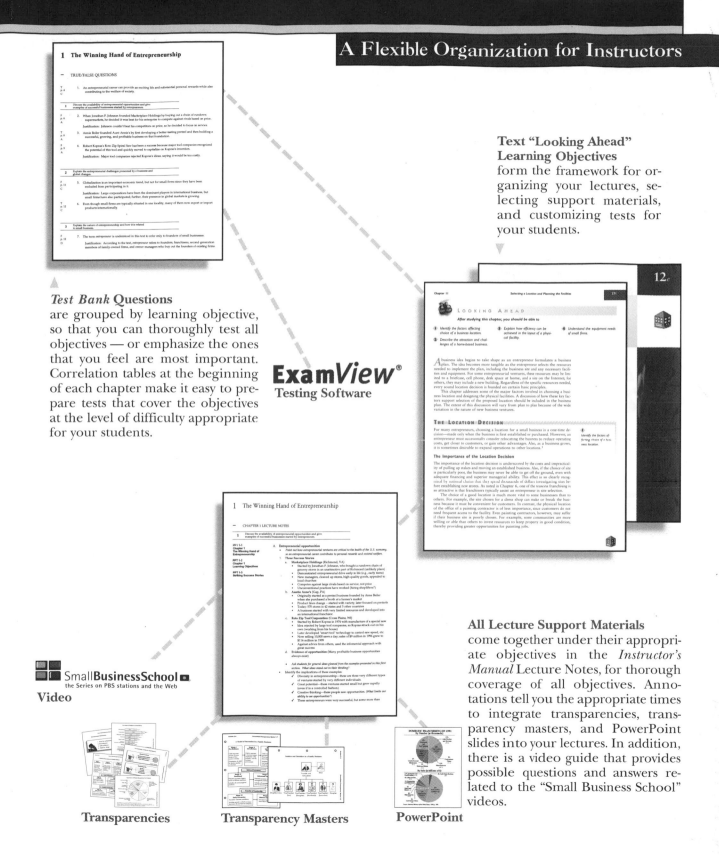

1 The Winning Hand of Entrepreneurship

— TRUE/FALSE QUESTIONS

T p. 4 C — 1. An entrepreneurial career can provide an exciting life and substantial personal rewards while also contributing to the welfare of society.

1 Discuss the availability of entrepreneurial opportunities and give examples of successful businesses started by entrepreneurs.

F p. 6 A — 2. When Jonathan F. Johnson founded Marketplace Holdings by buying out a chain of rundown supermarkets, he decided it was best for his enterprise to compete against rivals based on price.

Justification: Johnson couldn't beat his competitors on price, so he decided to focus on service.

T p. 8 A — 3. Annie Beiler founded Aunt Annie's by first developing a better-tasting pretzel and then building a successful, growing, and profitable business on that foundation.

F p. 9 A — 4. Robert Kopras's Roto Zip Spiral Saw has been a success because major tool companies recognized the potential of this tool and quickly moved to capitalize on Kopras's invention.

Justification: Major tool companies rejected Kopras's ideas, saying it would be too costly.

2 Explain the entrepreneurial challenges presented by e-business and global changes.

F p. 11 C — 5. Globalization is an important economic trend, but not for small firms since they have been excluded from participating in it.

Justification: Large corporations have been the dominant players in international business, but small firms have also participated; further, their presence in global markets is growing.

T p. 12 C — 6. Even though small firms are typically situated in one locality, many of them now export or import products internationally.

3 Explain the nature of entrepreneurship and how it is related to small business.

F p. 12 D — 7. The term *entrepreneur* is understood in this text to refer only to founders of small businesses.

Justification: According to the text, *entrepreneur* refers to founders, franchisees, second-generation members of family-owned firms, and owner-managers who buy out the founders of existing firms.

***Test Bank* Questions**
are grouped by learning objective, so that you can thoroughly test all objectives — or emphasize the ones that you feel are most important. Correlation tables at the beginning of each chapter make it easy to prepare tests that cover the objectives at the level of difficulty appropriate for your students.

Text "Looking Ahead" Learning Objectives
form the framework for organizing your lectures, selecting support materials, and customizing tests for your students.

Chapter 11 — Selecting a Location and Planning the Facilities — 271

LOOKING AHEAD

After studying this chapter, you should be able to

1. *Identify the factors affecting choice of a business location.*
2. *Describe the attraction and challenges of a home-based business.*
3. *Explain how efficiency can be achieved in the layout of a physical facility.*
4. *Understand the equipment needs of small firms.*

A business idea begins to take shape as an entrepreneur formulates a business plan. The idea becomes more tangible as the entrepreneur selects the resources needed to implement the plan, including the business site and any necessary facilities and equipment. For some entrepreneurial ventures, these resources may be limited to a briefcase, cell phone, desk space at home, and a site on the Internet; for others, they may include a new building. Regardless of the specific resources needed, every sound location decision is founded on certain basic principles.

This chapter addresses some of the major factors involved in choosing a business location and designing the physical facilities. A discussion of how these key factors support selection of the proposed location should be included in the business plan. The extent of this discussion will vary from plan to plan because of the wide variation in the nature of new business ventures.

THE LOCATION DECISION

For many entrepreneurs, choosing a location for a small business is a one-time decision—made only when the business is first established or purchased. However, an entrepreneur must occasionally consider relocating the business to reduce operating costs, get closer to customers, or gain other advantages. Also, as a business grows, it is sometimes desirable to expand operations to other locations.[1]

1 *Identify the factors affecting choice of a business location.*

The Importance of the Location Decision

The importance of the location decision is underscored by the costs and impracticality of pulling up stakes and moving an established business. Also, if the choice of site is particularly poor, the business may never be able to get off the ground, even with adequate financing and superior managerial ability. This effect is so clearly recognized by national chains that they spend thousands of dollars investigating sites before establishing new stores. As noted in Chapter 6, one of the reasons franchising is so attractive is that franchisors typically assist an entrepreneur in site selection.

The choice of a good location is much more vital to some businesses than to others. For example, the site chosen for a dress shop can make or break the business because it must be convenient for customers. In contrast, the physical location of the office of a painting contractor is of less importance, since customers do not need frequent access to the facility. Even painting contractors, however, may suffer if their business site is poorly chosen. For example, some communities are more willing or able than others to invest resources to keep property in good condition, thereby providing greater opportunities for painting jobs.

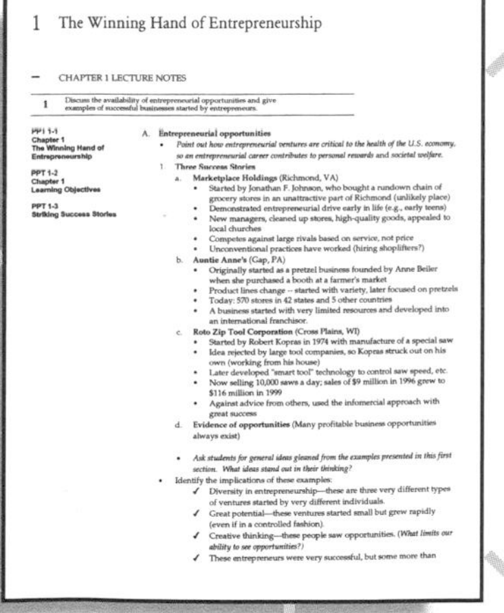

1 The Winning Hand of Entrepreneurship

— CHAPTER 1 LECTURE NOTES

1 Discuss the availability of entrepreneurial opportunities and give examples of successful businesses started by entrepreneurs.

PPT 1-1 Chapter 1 The Winning Hand of Entrepreneurship

PPT 1-2 Chapter 1 Learning Objectives

PPT 1-3 Striking Success Stories

A. **Entrepreneurial opportunities**
- *Point out how entrepreneurial ventures are critical to the health of the U.S. economy, so an entrepreneurial career contributes to personal rewards and societal welfare.*

1. **Three Success Stories**
   a. **Marketplace Holdings** (Richmond, VA)
      - Started by Jonathan F. Johnson, who bought a rundown chain of grocery stores in an unattractive part of Richmond (unlikely place)
      - Demonstrated entrepreneurial drive early in life (e.g., early teens)
      - New managers, cleaned up stores, high-quality goods, appealed to local churches
      - Competes against large rivals based on service, not price
      - Unconventional practices have worked (hiring shoplifters?)

   b. **Auntie Anne's** (Gap, PA)
      - Originally started as a pretzel business founded by Anne Beiler when she purchased a booth at a farmer's market
      - Product lines change -- started with variety, later focused on pretzels
      - Today: 570 stores in 42 states and 5 other countries
      - A business started with very limited resources and developed into an international franchisor.

   c. **Roto Zip Tool Corporation** (Cross Plains, WI)
      - Started by Robert Kopras in 1974 with manufacture of a special saw
      - Idea rejected by large tool companies, so Kopras struck out on his own (working from his house)
      - Later developed "smart tool" technology to control saw speed, etc.
      - Now selling 10,000 saws a day; sales of $9 million in 1996 grew to $116 million in 1999
      - Against advice from others, used the infomercial approach with great success

   d. **Evidence of opportunities** (Many profitable business opportunities always exist)

   - *Ask students for general ideas gleaned from the examples presented in this first section. What ideas stand out in their thinking?*

- Identify the implications of these examples:
  ✓ Diversity in entrepreneurship—these are three very different types of ventures started by very different individuals.
  ✓ Great potential—these ventures started small but grew rapidly (even if in a controlled fashion).
  ✓ Creative thinking—these people saw opportunities. (*What limits our ability to see opportunities?*)
  ✓ These entrepreneurs were very successful, but some more than

SmallBusinessSchool
the Series on PBS stations and the Web
Video

Transparencies

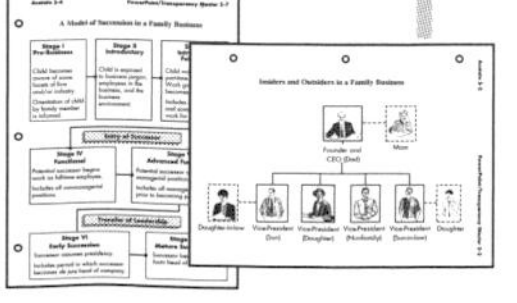

Transparency Masters

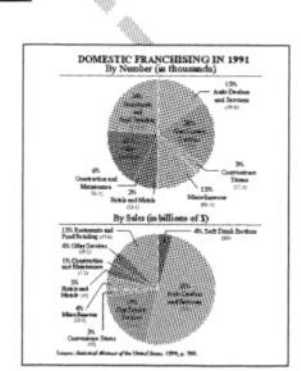

PowerPoint

All Lecture Support Materials
come together under their appropriate objectives in the *Instructor's Manual* Lecture Notes, for thorough coverage of all objectives. Annotations tell you the appropriate times to integrate transparencies, transparency masters, and PowerPoint slides into your lectures. In addition, there is a video guide that provides possible questions and answers related to the "Small Business School" videos.

12e

Small Business Management

An Entrepreneurial Emphasis

Justin G. Longenecker
Baylor University

Carlos W. Moore
Baylor University

J. William Petty
Baylor University

THOMSON SOUTH-WESTERN

Australia · Canada · Mexico · Singapore · Spain · United Kingdom · United States

Small Business Management: An Entrepreneurial Emphasis, 12th Edition

Justin G. Longenecker, Carlos W. Moore, J. William Petty

VP/Editor-in-Chief:
Jack Calhoun

VP/Team Director:
Michael Roche

Executive Editor:
John Szilagyi

Developmental Editor:
Theresa Curtis

Marketing Manager:
Rob Bloom

Production Editor:
Robert Dreas

Production House:
Lifland et al., Bookmakers

Manufacturing Coordinator:
Rhonda Utley

Compositor:
Parkwood Composition Service, Inc.

Printer:
R.R. Donnelley & Sons
Willard, Ohio

Design Project Manager:
Michelle Kunkler

Cover and Internal Designer:
Jennifer Lambert/Jen2Design
Cincinnati, Ohio

Cover Photographer/Illustrator:
©Todd Joyce
www.joycephotography.com

Photography Manager:
Deanna Ettinger

Photo Researcher:
Susan Van Etten

Printed in the United States of America
2 3 4 5 05 04 03 02

For more information contact South-Western, 5191 Natorp Boulevard, Mason, Ohio 45040.
Or you can visit our Internet site at:
http://www.swcollege.com

Library of Congress Cataloging-in-Publication Data
Longenecker, Justin Gooderl, [date]
Small business management : an entrepreneurial emphasis / Justin G. Longenecker, Carlos W. Moore, J. William Petty. -- 12th ed.
p. cm
Multi-media instructional materials are available to supplement the text.
Includes bibliographical references and index.
ISBN: 0-324-06554-X (hc)
1. Small business--Management.
I. Moore, Carlos W. II. Petty, J. William, [date] III. Title

HD62.7 .L66 2002
658.02'2--dc21 2002018885

BRIEF CONTENTS

CONTENTS

PART 7

A Guided Tour

What We Do and How We Do It

Before you open the door and step inside this new edition of *Small Business Management: An Entrepreneurial Emphasis* turn over the next few pages. See the work, hear the stories, meet the people, and get a sense of what small business is all about. Our history is rich and eventful. Our door is your point of entry. Our goal is to transfer our knowledge to you.

Integrated Learning System

Beginning with the "Looking Ahead" learning objectives that open each chapter, we organize information into distinct, focused, and comprehensible bites. What are the central ideas of the chapter on family business opportunities? Go to page 167. We identify five ideas, which we state at the chapter outset as learning objectives, repeat at the beginning of the section where the applicable content is discussed, and recap in the chapter-end "Looking Back" summary. How well have you mastered chapter topics and how well can you apply them? Our "Looking Back" summaries provide a great way to review chapter content and a perfect tool for assessing if you're ready to take on chapter exercises and cases.

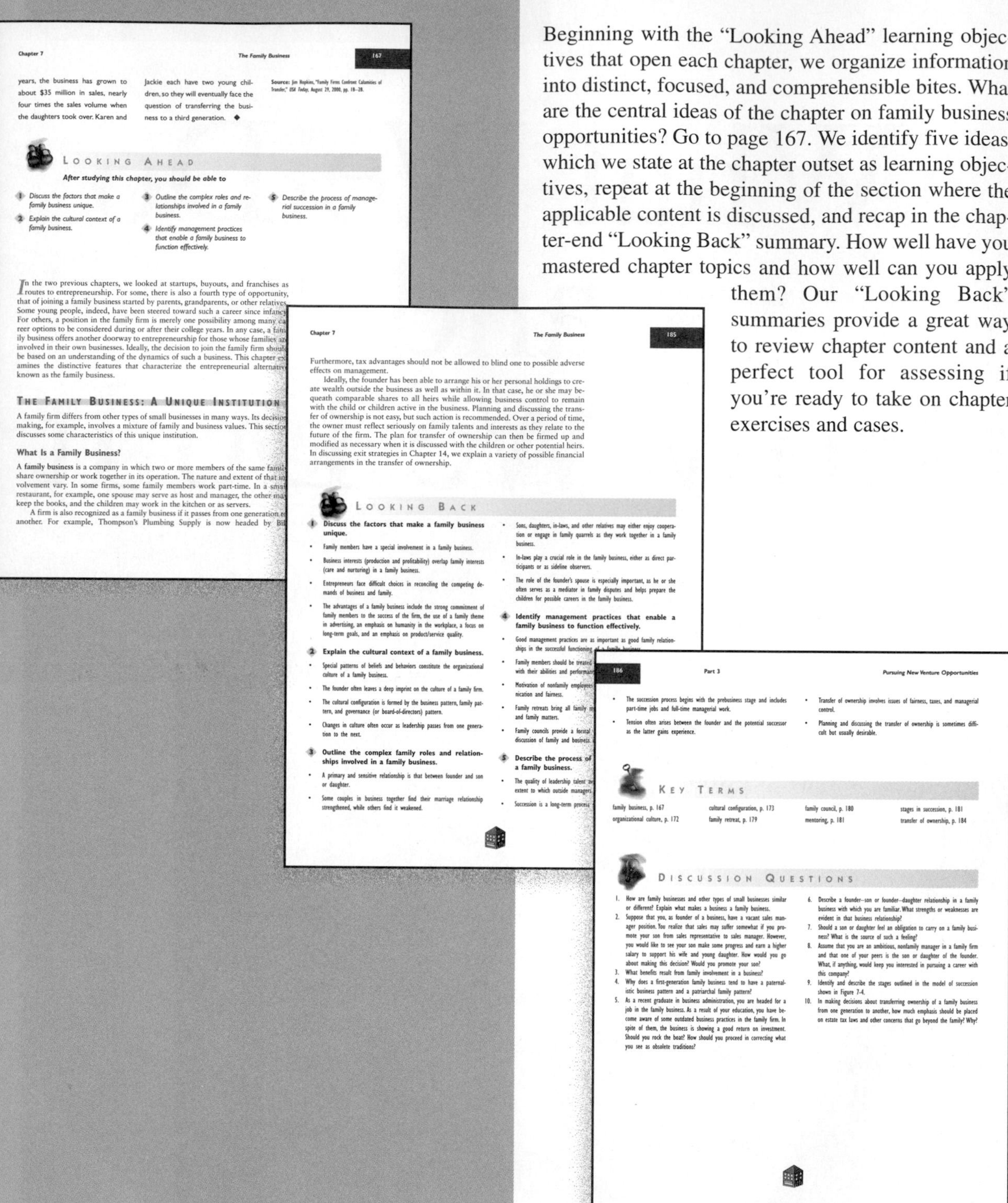

Chapter 7 | The Family Business | 167

years, the business has grown to about $35 million in sales, nearly four times the sales volume when the daughters took over. Karen and Jackie each have two young children, so they will eventually face the question of transferring the business to a third generation. ◆

Source: Jim Hopkins, "Family Firms Confront Calamities of Transfer," *USA Today*, August 29, 2000, pp. 1B–2B.

LOOKING AHEAD

After studying this chapter, you should be able to

1. *Discuss the factors that make a family business unique.*
2. *Explain the cultural context of a family business.*
3. *Outline the complex roles and relationships involved in a family business.*
4. *Identify management practices that enable a family business to function effectively.*
5. *Describe the process of managerial succession in a family business.*

In the two previous chapters, we looked at startups, buyouts, and franchises as routes to entrepreneurship. For some, there is also a fourth type of opportunity, that of joining a family business started by parents, grandparents, or other relatives. Some young people, indeed, have been steered toward such a career since infancy. For others, a position in the family firm is merely one possibility among many career options to be considered during or after their college years. In any case, a family business offers another doorway to entrepreneurship for those whose families are involved in their own businesses. Ideally, the decision to join the family firm should be based on an understanding of the dynamics of such a business. This chapter examines the distinctive features that characterize the entrepreneurial alternative known as the family business.

THE FAMILY BUSINESS: A UNIQUE INSTITUTION

A family firm differs from other types of small businesses in many ways. Its decision making, for example, involves a mixture of family and business values. This section discusses some characteristics of this unique institution.

What Is a Family Business?

A **family business** is a company in which two or more members of the same family share ownership or work together in its operation. The nature and extent of that involvement vary. In some firms, some family members work part-time. In a small restaurant, for example, one spouse may serve as host and manager, the other may keep the books, and the children may work in the kitchen or as servers.

A firm is also recognized as a family business if it passes from one generation to another. For example, Thompson's Plumbing Supply is now headed by Bil

Chapter 7 | The Family Business | 185

Furthermore, tax advantages should not be allowed to blind one to possible adverse effects on management.

Ideally, the founder has been able to arrange his or her personal holdings to create wealth outside the business as well as within it. In that case, he or she may bequeath comparable shares to all heirs while allowing business control to remain with the child or children active in the business. Planning and discussing the transfer of ownership is not easy, but such action is recommended. Over a period of time, the owner must reflect seriously on family talents and interests as they relate to the future of the firm. The plan for transfer of ownership can then be firmed up and modified as necessary when it is discussed with the children or other potential heirs. In discussing exit strategies in Chapter 14, we explain a variety of possible financial arrangements in the transfer of ownership.

LOOKING BACK

1 **Discuss the factors that make a family business unique.**

- Family members have a special involvement in a family business.
- Business interests (production and profitability) overlap family interests (care and nurturing) in a family business.
- Entrepreneurs face difficult choices in reconciling the competing demands of business and family.
- The advantages of a family business include the strong commitment of family members to the success of the firm, the use of a family theme in advertising, an emphasis on humanity in the workplace, a focus on long-term goals, and an emphasis on product/service quality.

2 **Explain the cultural context of a family business.**

- Special patterns of beliefs and behaviors constitute the organizational culture of a family business.
- The founder often leaves a deep imprint on the culture of a family firm.
- The cultural configuration is formed by the business pattern, family pattern, and governance (or board-of-directors) pattern.
- Changes in culture often occur as leadership passes from one generation to the next.

3 **Outline the complex family roles and relationships involved in a family business.**

- A primary and sensitive relationship is that between founder and son or daughter.
- Some couples in business together find their marriage relationship strengthened, while others find it weakened.
- Sons, daughters, in-laws, and other relatives may either enjoy cooperation or engage in family quarrels as they work together in a family business.
- In-laws play a crucial role in the family business, either as direct participants or as sideline observers.
- The role of the founder's spouse is especially important, as he or she often serves as a mediator in family disputes and helps prepare the children for possible careers in the family business.

4 **Identify management practices that enable a family business to function effectively.**

- Good management practices are as important as good family relationships in the successful functioning of a family business.
- Family members should be treated ... with their abilities and performan...
- Motivation of nonfamily employees ... nication and fairness.
- Family retreats bring all family m... and family matters.
- Family councils provide a formal ... discussion of family and business ...

5 **Describe the process of ... a family business.**

- The quality of leadership talent av... extent to which outside managers ...
- Succession is a long-term process ...

186 | Part 3 | Pursuing New Venture Opportunities

- The succession process begins with the prebusiness stage and includes part-time jobs and full-time managerial work.
- Tension often arises between the founder and the potential successor as the latter gains experience.
- Transfer of ownership involves issues of fairness, taxes, and managerial control.
- Planning and discussing the transfer of ownership is sometimes difficult but usually desirable.

KEY TERMS

family business, p. 167
organizational culture, p. 172
cultural configuration, p. 173
family retreat, p. 179
family council, p. 180
mentoring, p. 181
stages in succession, p. 181
transfer of ownership, p. 184

DISCUSSION QUESTIONS

1. How are family businesses and other types of small businesses similar or different? Explain what makes a business a family business.
2. Suppose that you, as founder of a business, have a vacant sales manager position. You realize that sales may suffer somewhat if you promote your son from sales representative to sales manager. However, you would like to see your son make some progress and earn a higher salary to support his wife and young daughter. How would you go about making this decision? Would you promote your son?
3. What benefits result from family involvement in a business?
4. Why does a first-generation family business tend to have a paternalistic business pattern and a patriarchal family pattern?
5. As a recent graduate in business administration, you are headed for a job in the family business. As a result of your education, you have become aware of some outdated business practices in the family firm. In spite of them, the business is showing a good return on investment. Should you rock the boat? How should you proceed in correcting what you see as obsolete traditions?
6. Describe a founder–son or founder–daughter relationship in a family business with which you are familiar. What strengths or weaknesses are evident in that business relationship?
7. Should a son or daughter feel an obligation to carry on a family business? What is the source of such a feeling?
8. Assume that you are an ambitious, nonfamily manager in a family firm and that one of your peers is the son or daughter of the founder. What, if anything, would keep you interested in pursuing a career with this company?
9. Identify and describe the stages outlined in the model of succession shown in Figure 7-4.
10. In making decisions about transferring ownership of a family business from one generation to another, how much emphasis should be placed on estate tax laws and other concerns that go beyond the family? Why?

A Truly Integrated Network

Student Learning Guide

Our integrated learning system offers students and instructors a truly integrated network of solutions, designed to help you tackle small business issues and study efficiently. Our *Student Learning Guide,* a supplement to the text, is organized around the text's learning objectives, letting you isolate and focus attention on just that material most troublesome to you before moving ahead. If, after working through the learning guide's summaries of key concepts and exercises, you still feel a little shaky about some concepts, you can easily locate all applicable chapter content by simply looking for the appropriate numbered objectives in the text. Like the in-text "Looking Back" summaries, the *Student Learning Guide* provides a useful indicator of lessons learned versus lessons not quite mastered. Then it gives you any extra help you may need to overcome hard-to-digest material by testing and re-testing content knowledge across a variety of formats: true/false, multiple choice, fill-in, and essay.

1 The Winning Hand of Entrepreneurship

LEARNING OBJECTIVES

1 Discuss the availability of entrepreneurial opportunities and give examples of successful businesses started by entrepreneurs.

- Where a business idea is often a concept in search of an application, an entrepreneurial opportunity is a desirable and timely innovation that creates value.
- Successful entrepreneurs pursue opportunities by first identifying value-creating innovations with market potential.
- Marketplace Holdings, the largest supermarket chain owned by an African-American in the United States, became successful through offering innovative services.
- Auntie Ann's, an example of a successful franchise, grew from humble beginnings to provide business opportunities to hundreds of others.
- Roto Zip Tool Corporation, a company typical of an inventor-based business, grew out of a frustration with a type of tool needed for the inventor's own use.
- No matter what a person's background may be, opportunities for successful entrepreneurial ventures must be recognized and grasped with enthusiasm.

2 Explain the entrepreneurial challenges presented by e-business and global changes.

- Two powerful forces at work in the business community are e-business and globalization.
- Entrepreneurs can be founders of business firms, active owner-managers, or even second-generation members of family-owned firms.

TRUE/FALSE QUESTIONS

Mark each statement with a T, if it is true, or with an F, if it is false.

1 Discuss the availability of entrepreneurial opportunities and give examples of successful businesses started by entrepreneurs.

_____1. Some individuals begin their entrepreneurial careers because of disappointing experiences as employees.

_____2. A successful entrepreneur must be able to recognize opportunity and act on it.

2 Explain the entrepreneurial challenges presented by e-business and global changes.

_____3. Two powerful forces at work in the business community are globalization and innovation.

3 Explain the nature of entrepreneurship and how it is related to small business.

_____4. Small business has little economic impact on employment in the United States.

_____5. Small business is usually financed by a small group of owners.

_____6. The marketing function of a small business is usually geographically localized.

_____7. Typically, the number of employees in a small business is fewer than 100.

4 Identify motivators or rewards of entrepreneurial careers.

_____8. Many entrepreneurs use their independence to achieve flexibility in their personal lives and work habits.

_____9. Foreign refugees are individuals who escape the political, religious, or economic constraints of their homeland by crossing national boundaries.

_____10. Individuals who leave small firms to join the bureaucratic environment of big business are called corporate refugees.

5 Describe the various types of entrepreneurs and entrepreneurial ventures.

_____11. Founders may be inventors who initiate a business on the basis of new or improved products or services.

_____12 Franchisees differ from general managers in the degree of their independence.

_____13. Firms that have great prospects for growth are called gazelles.

_____14. Microbusinesses provide very large profit returns to their owners.

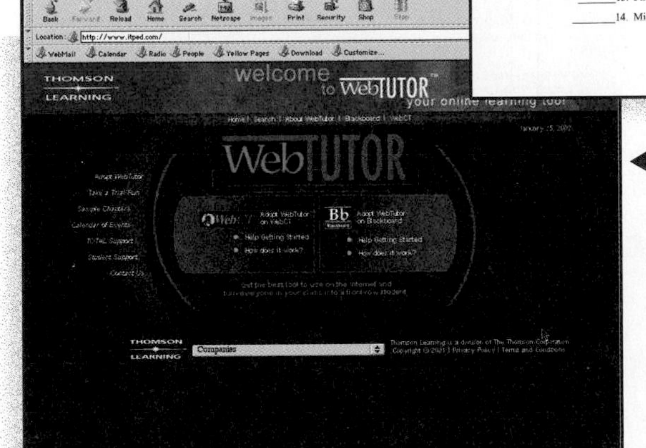

WebTutor™ on WebCT and on Blackboard

WebTutor™ on WebCT or WebTutor™ on Blackboard complements *Small Business Management* by providing interactive reinforcement that helps students grasp key concepts. WebTutor's online teaching and learning environment brings together content management, assessment, communication, and collaboration capabilities for enhancing in-class instruction or delivering distance learning. For more information, including a demo, visit **http://webtutor.swcollege.com**.

Build Your Own Business Plan

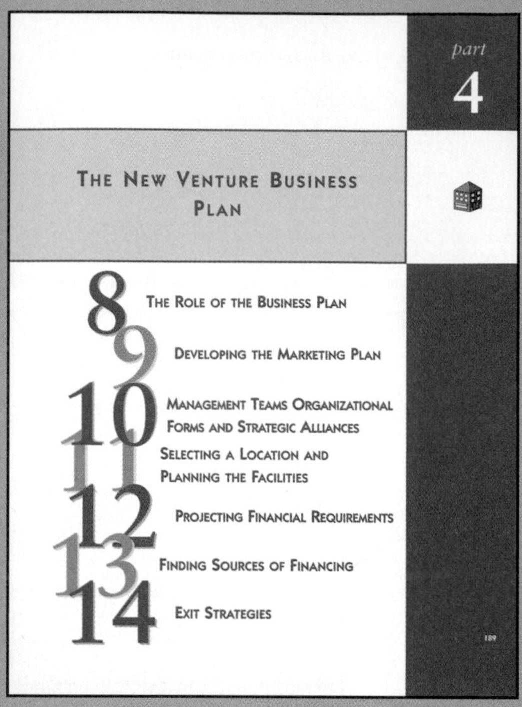

part 4

THE NEW VENTURE BUSINESS PLAN

189

The New Venture Business Plan
A fundamental task in getting a business opportunity off the ground is developing a sound and detailed business plan. Each chapter in Part 4 of the text covers a major component in building a business plan, giving you not only ample opportunity to pull the pieces of your own plan together but also a comprehensive model on which to base your decisions.

Business Plan Tools
New to this edition is a collection of author-prepared planning tools to supplement in-text coverage of the fundamentals. These tools are available on the CD-ROM accompanying your textbook.

The Business Plan: Laying the Foundation
Designed around a series of questions, end-of-chapter exercises lead you through the process of building a business plan by prompting you to reflect on critical issues that impact small businesses. What is your company's distinctive competence? How do you plan to forecast sales for your product or service? What types of research must be conducted to collect the information you need? Who are the members of your management team? These questions, and others that we document for you, may be difficult to answer, but by thinking through your responses to them you will increase immeasurably your understanding of a business opportunity and thereby strengthen your resolve to succeed.

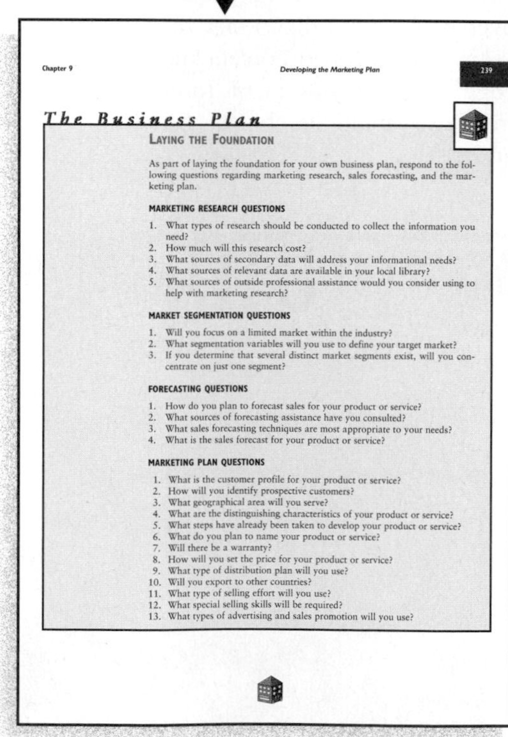

Chapter 9 Developing the Marketing Plan 239

The Business Plan

LAYING THE FOUNDATION

As part of laying the foundation for your own business plan, respond to the following questions regarding marketing research, sales forecasting, and the marketing plan.

MARKETING RESEARCH QUESTIONS

1. What types of research should be conducted to collect the information you need?
2. How much will this research cost?
3. What sources of secondary data will address your informational needs?
4. What sources of relevant data are available in your local library?
5. What sources of outside professional assistance would you consider using to help with marketing research?

MARKET SEGMENTATION QUESTIONS

1. Will you focus on a limited market within the industry?
2. What segmentation variables will you use to define your target market?
3. If you determine that several distinct market segments exist, will you concentrate on just one segment?

FORECASTING QUESTIONS

1. How do you plan to forecast sales for your product or service?
2. What sources of forecasting assistance have you consulted?
3. What sales forecasting techniques are most appropriate to your needs?
4. What is the sales forecast for your product or service?

MARKETING PLAN QUESTIONS

1. What is the customer profile for your product or service?
2. How will you identify prospective customers?
3. What geographical area will you serve?
4. What are the distinguishing characteristics of your product or service?
5. What steps have already been taken to develop your product or service?
6. What do you plan to name your product or service?
7. Will there be a warranty?
8. How will you set the price for your product or service?
9. What type of distribution plan will you use?
10. Will you export to other countries?
11. What type of selling effort will you use?
12. What special selling skills will be required?
13. What types of advertising and sales promotion will you use?

We've Assembled All the Tools

Appendix: Sample Business Plan
The appendix shows you a real business plan. Use this example to see how the pieces come together. Refer to it as you build your own plan—either now as a class project or, later, when you are ready to go into business!

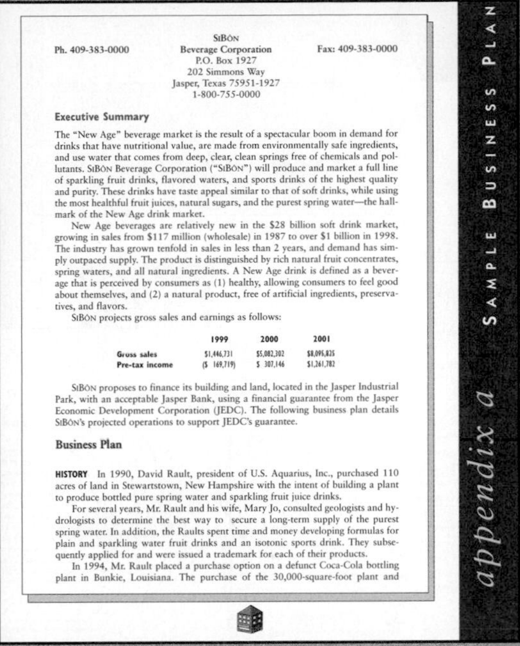
appendix a Sample Business Plan

SiBôn
Ph. 409-383-0000 Beverage Corporation Fax: 409-383-0000
P.O. Box 1927
202 Simmons Way
Jasper, Texas 75951-1927
1-800-755-0000

Executive Summary

The "New Age" beverage market is the result of a spectacular boom in demand for drinks that have nutritional value, are made from environmentally safe ingredients, and use water that comes from deep, clear, clean springs free of chemicals and pollutants. SiBôn Beverage Corporation ("SiBôn") will produce and market a full line of sparkling fruit drinks, flavored waters, and sports drinks of the highest quality and purity. These drinks have taste appeal similar to that of soft drinks, while using the most healthful fruit juices, natural sugars, and the purest spring water—the hallmark of the New Age drink market.

New Age beverages are relatively new in the $28 billion soft drink market, growing in sales from $117 million (wholesale) in 1987 to over $1 billion in 1998. The industry has grown tenfold in sales in less than 2 years, and demand has simply outpaced supply. The product is distinguished by rich natural fruit concentrates, spring waters, and all natural ingredients. A New Age drink is defined as a beverage that is perceived by consumers as (1) healthy, allowing consumers to feel good about themselves, and (2) a natural product, free of artificial ingredients, preservatives, and flavors.

SiBôn projects gross sales and earnings as follows:

	1999	2000	2001
Gross sales	$1,446,731	$5,082,302	$8,095,825
Pre-tax income	($ 169,719)	$ 307,146	$1,261,782

SiBôn proposes to finance its building and land, located in the Jasper Industrial Park, with an acceptable Jasper Bank, using a financial guarantee from the Jasper Economic Development Corporation (JEDC). The following business plan details SiBôn's projected operations to support JEDC's guarantee.

Business Plan

HISTORY In 1990, David Rault, president of U.S. Aquarius, Inc., purchased 110 acres of land in Stewartstown, New Hampshire with the intent of building a plant to produce bottled pure spring water and sparkling fruit juice drinks.

For several years, Mr. Rault and his wife, Mary Jo, consulted geologists and hydrologists to determine the best way to secure a long-term supply of the purest spring water. In addition, the Raults spent time and money developing formulas for plain and sparkling water fruit drinks and an isotonic sports drink. They subsequently applied for and were issued a trademark for each of their products.

In 1994, Mr. Rault placed a purchase option on a defunct Coca-Cola bottling plant in Bunkie, Louisiana. The purchase of the 30,000-square-foot plant and

Tools for Preparing a Simplified Business Plan
With the twelfth edition, we are excited to introduce "Tools for Preparing a Simplified Business Plan." This multimedia resource on CD-ROM offers additional information, guidance, and opportunities to try out assumptions that build on the concepts covered in Part 4, "The New Venture Business Plan." Included on this CD are short and engaging articles from respected business publications that provide additional insights into the planning process. Video clips from the popular television series "Small Business School," which airs weekly on most PBS member stations, daily on Worldnet, and always on the Web, are available to provide the link between theory and practical, real-world approaches to the planning process. Business plan templates in Microsoft® Word and Excel give you a navigational path to follow. If you find you need more information, use the list of Web addresses to start your search for leading resources on business plans.

A View from the Trenches

With this edition of *Small Business Management: An Entrepreneurial Emphasis,* we invite you to get into the trenches with some very interesting and compelling small businesses. Each chapter opens with an "In the Spotlight" profile, designed to provide context for the material you are about to read. Then, throughout each chapter, "In the Trenches" boxes provide examples of how real companies face real issues. A catalog of inspiration and innovation, our "In the Trenches" boxes track the ups and downs of small businesses. Read a few of our reports from the trenches. By telling us what they've been through, an incredible variety of entrepreneurs and small business owners give us valuable insights into what motivates and sustains them.

chapter 9

DEVELOPING THE MARKETING PLAN

In the Spotlight

BBH Exhibits, Inc.

Finding a market and then developing a marketing plan to meet customer needs are essential steps in developing a successful business venture. Consider BBH Exhibits Inc. and the marketing strategy of its founder, president, and CEO, Stacy F. King. Her company, based in San Antonio, Texas, was started in 1992 and after nine years is already a premier provider of traveling museum exhibits. How did her firm become so successful so quickly? She had a marketing plan.

After college and a brief stay at Neiman Marcus in Dallas, Texas, where King was the youngest buyer in the store's history, she left to pursue her entrepreneurial dream. King believed that there was a market for educational exhibits providing high-quality, multisensory experiences and that she could meet those needs. Her plan was to quickly grab hold of the exhibits market—and she did, beginning with her first brainchild exhibit, Backyard Monsters.

King promotes her exhibits to corporate sponsors, such as Ford, IBM, and Hertz, who pay for some of the up-front development costs associated with producing the museum exhibits. In return, the companies receive name recognition and positive goodwill. Her firm reports that over 60 million people have

http://www.bbhinc.net

In the Spotlight opening vignette

Chapter 9   Developing the Marketing Plan   233

IN THE TRENCHES   ENTREPRENEURSHIP TODAY

KNOW YOUR COMPETITORS

Frequently, entrepreneurs ignore the competition until their own ventures are under way, when it may be too late. A better strategy is to evaluate competitors before beginning a business.

This is the strategy entrepreneur Amy Ratekin followed before launching Little Elf, an event décor and gift service, in 1996. "I wanted to learn from the best," she says. "By discovering what other businesses in the industry do, finding out what works in other parts of the country and even other parts of the world, and using the ideas in my business, I have become very successful."

For example, before opening her business, Ratekin visited two local balloon companies and learned how they assembled their baskets and bouquets. Her husband then reproduced some of the ideas in their own shop design. Studying the competition also helped her learn that many existing businesses were not educating customers about how this type of service could be used. She says, "People don't know what's available. By teaching them, you increase your business."

Her home-based business operates in West Des Moines, Iowa, with 4 family members as part-time employees and 16 others as "per-needed" employees who help prepare event decorations and balloon sculptures for corporations and special events.

Source: Personal communication with Amy Ratekin, July 31, 2001; and Jacqueline Lynn, "Know the Enemy," *Entrepreneur,* http://www.entrepreneur.com, December 1999.

casting, they should be minimized. The forecasting method should be described and supported by empirical data wherever feasible.

The Competition

Frequently, entrepreneurs ignore the reality of competition for their new ventures, believing that the marketplace contains no close substitutes or that their success will not attract other entrepreneurs. This is simply not realistic.

Existing competitors should be studied carefully, and their key management personnel profiled. A brief discussion of competitors' overall strengths and weaknesses should be a part of this section of the plan. Also, related products currently being marketed or tested by competitors should be noted. An assessment should be made of the likelihood that any of these firms will enter the entrepreneur's target market.

Many competitors can be monitored by visiting their Web sites. Ann Blakeley, president of Orlando, Florida–based Earth Resources Corporation, a hazardous materials technology firm, uses search engines like AltaVista to check out her competitors. "I check every couple of months just to make sure nothing has changed," Blakeley says. "If any competitors have new products, odds are they'll put it on their Web pages."[6]

In the Trenches: Entrepreneurship Today

In the Trenches: Utilizing New Technology

222   Part 4   *The New Venture Business Plan*

UTILIZING NEW TECHNOLOGY   IN THE TRENCHES

WEB CUSTOMERS VOICE OPINIONS

Dale Bathum's idea for a nontraditional golf shoe has taken his firm, Bite Footwear, from a startup in 1996 to a successful manufacturer with over $4 million in sales in the first half of 2001. With its 35-year-old entrepreneur at the helm, the Preston, Washington company now sells sporting shoes and apparel to over 2,000 retail customers worldwide.

Bathum has always gathered research information prior to introducing new products. As an example, he cites a proposed design for a shoe named Reverse Pivot, which Bite hoped would be a smash hit. Before committing to its introduction, the firm posted a photo of and information about the shoe on its Web site and e-mailed 50 loyal customers for comments regarding the shoe's style and price. Although many golfers liked the Reverse Pivot style, most retail buyers didn't and were hesitant to say that they would order the shoe—so the design was scrapped.

Later, in 1998, while developing a design for the bowling-shoe market, Bite again displayed prototypes online to gather buyer feedback. "Before the Web, we flew in key buyers from all over the country to see the line," says Bathum. "That was super-expensive."

After receiving buyers' e-mail responses to prototypes, company representatives always telephone respondents. "You have a reason to call them up, other than trying to sell them something," Bathum says. "Plus, they feel as if they are a part of the process."

This entrepreneur understands how to use the Web as both a marketing channel and a research tool.

Source: From material from http://www.bitefootwear.com, July 31, 2001; and Anne Marie Borrego, "Will They Bite?" http://www.inc.com, November 15, 1999.

http://www.bitefootwear.com

http://www.sudburysoup.com

method of observational research has been devised by Jean Sullivan, who experiments with new soup ideas for her Sudbury Soup Company, located in Concord, Massachusetts. She arranges tastings in most of the supermarkets where her soups are sold and closely observes shoppers' reactions to the samples she cooks for them.[2]

Observational methods can be economical. Furthermore, they avoid the potential bias that can result from a respondent's contact with an interviewer during questioning. Observation—for example, counting customers going into a store—can be conducted by a person or by mechanical devices, such as hidden video cameras. The cost of mechanical observation devices is rapidly declining, bringing them within the budget of many small businesses. When Scott Semel and Reed Chase wanted to learn more about their competitors and customers after buying a candy-importing company, Cody-Kramer Imports, in Blauvolt, New York, what did they do? They attended several major industry trade shows and checked out competitors' booths. They also wandered the aisles of candy retailers, observing whatever they could about candy-buying customers.[3]

Questioning Methods Surveys and experimentation are both questioning methods that involve contact with respondents. Surveys can be conducted by mail, telephone, or personal interview. Mail surveys are often used when target respondents are

To help you identify and explore a full range of issues facing today's entrepreneur, the following categories are utilized in this feature: Entrepreneurship and Ethics, Building Customer Loyalty, Entrepreneurship Today, Living in a Diverse World, and Utilizing New Technology.

In the Video Spotlight, Courtesy of "Small Business School" ▶

In this edition, half of our chapter-opening Spotlights are video enriched, drawing on the experiences of business owners whose unique insights into how to start, run, and grow a business have been captured on video by the producers of the popular television series "Small Business School." This program airs weekly on most PBS member stations, daily on Worldnet, and always on the Web. We are delighted that our exclusive partnership with "Small Business School" allows us to provide these video counterparts. With this unparalleled access to today's entrepreneurs, you gain a substantial boost up and over the learning curve. Their stories will inspire you and, more important, leave you with the expert advice needed to achieve your goals.

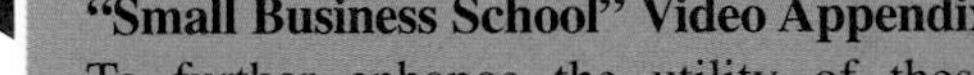

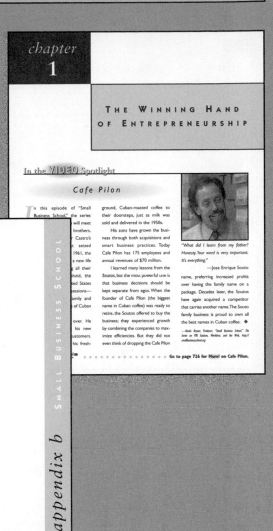

◀ **"Small Business School" Video Appendix**

To further enhance the utility of these video-enhanced Spotlights, we have provided a companion study guide in an appendix at the end of the text. There you'll find additional information on the companies and business owners featured in each video segment, as well as critical-thinking questions related to chapter topics.

Learning by Doing

To be a successful small business manager, you need to practice. Without giving you opportunities to act as a decision maker, *Small Business Management: An Entrepreneurial Emphasis* would just whet your appetite without bringing you any closer to the table. Practical information ready to be put to use is presented in every chapter, but to ensure active learning, each chapter concludes with application exercises designed to put you to the test.

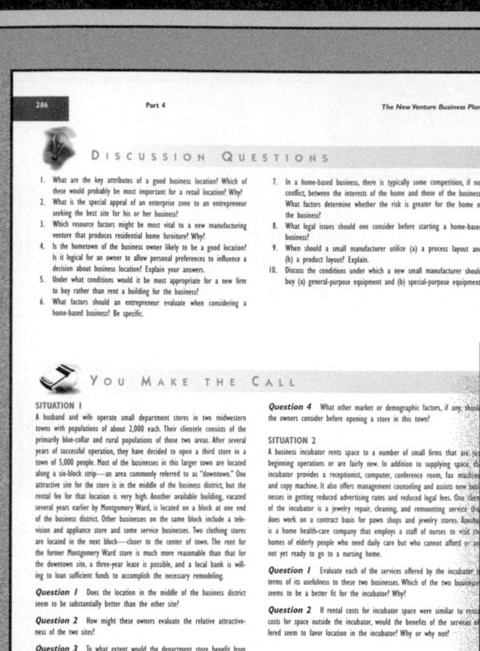

Discussion Questions

1. What are the key attributes of a good business location? Which of these would probably be most important for a retail location? Why?
2. What is the special appeal of an enterprise zone to an entrepreneur seeking the best site for his or her business?
3. Which resource factors might be most vital to a new manufacturing venture that produces residential home furniture? Why?
4. Is the hometown of the business owner likely to be a good location? Is it logical for an owner to allow personal preferences to influence a decision about business location? Explain your answers.
5. Under what conditions would it be most appropriate for a new firm to buy rather than rent a building for the business?
6. What factors should an entrepreneur evaluate when considering a home-based business? Be specific.
7. In a home-based business, there is typically some competition, if not conflict, between the interests of the home and those of the business. What factors determine whether the risk is greater for the home or the business?
8. What legal issues should one consider before starting a home-based business?
9. When should a small manufacturer utilize (a) a process layout and (b) a product layout? Explain.
10. Discuss the conditions under which a new small manufacturer should buy (a) general-purpose equipment and (b) special-purpose equipment.

You Make the Call

SITUATION 1

A husband and wife operate small department stores in two midwestern towns with populations of about 2,000 each. Their clientele consists of the primarily blue-collar and rural populations of those two areas. After several years of successful operation, they have decided to open a third store in a town of 5,000 people. Most of the businesses in this larger town are located along a six-block strip—an area commonly referred to as "downtown." One attractive site for the store is in the middle of the business district, but the rental fee for that location is very high. Another available building, vacated several years earlier by Montgomery Ward, is located on a block at one end of the business district. Other businesses on the same block include a television and appliance store and some service businesses. Two clothing stores are located in the next block—closer to the center of town. The rent for the former Montgomery Ward store is much more reasonable than that for the downtown site, a three-year lease is possible, and a local bank is willing to loan sufficient funds to accomplish the necessary remodeling.

Question 1 Does the location in the middle of the business district seem to be substantially better than the other site?

Question 2 How might these owners evaluate the relative attractiveness of the two sites?

Question 3 To what extent would the department store benefit from having the service businesses and the television and appliance business in the same block?

Question 4 What other market or demographic factors, if any, should the owners consider before opening a store in this town?

SITUATION 2

A business incubator rents space to a number of small firms that are just beginning operations or are fairly new. In addition to supplying space, the incubator provides a receptionist, computer, conference room, fax machine and copy machine. It also offers management counseling and assists new businesses in getting reduced advertising rates and reduced legal fees. One client of the incubator is a jewelry repair, cleaning, and remounting service that does work on a contract basis for pawn shops and jewelry stores. Another is a home health-care company that employs a staff of nurses to visit the homes of elderly people who need daily care but who cannot afford or are not yet ready to go to a nursing home.

Question 1 Evaluate each of the services offered by the incubator in terms of its usefulness to these two businesses. Which of the two businesses seems to be a better fit for the incubator? Why?

Question 2 If rental costs for incubator space were similar to rental costs for space outside the incubator, would the benefits of the services offered seem to favor location in the incubator? Why or why not?

case 1

Steve's Olympic Tees

Jump-Starting a Business

"I thought it was a great idea. After all, how often do the Olympics come to town?" mused Steve, as he pondered his decision to open a tee-shirt shop. Steve opened Steve's Tees in March 1996, a few months before the start of the 1996 Summer Olympic Games in Atlanta, Georgia.

Several years earlier, just after the announcement had been made that the Summer Olympic Games would be held in Atlanta, entrepreneurs began to make plans to capitalize on this monumental event. The Atlanta Olympic Committee had projected that more than 1.4 million people would come to the area over a 17-day period. The economic impact of the Olympics was estimated at more than $5.1 billion—the economic equivalent of 31 Super Bowl games! Further, an impact study, commissioned by the Atlanta Committee for the Olympic Games, projected that the economic benefit would be diffused into the surrounding region because many of its Olympic venues were in other areas of the state, including the cities of Athens, Buford, Conyers, and Savannah.

A major event like the Olympics has the potential to attract less-than-scrupulous business operators hoping to get rich quick. Therefore, prospective Olympic vendors had to complete an application and agree to meet specific requirements, as well as pay the required fees for retail space within a defined Olympic area. Vendors selling products with the Olympic logo were also required to obtain permission and to pay a fee for use of the logo.

Steve had no desire to go through the Olympic bureaucracy to become an official Olympic vendor. However, he thought that he could still capitalize on the games—that they would provide a good chance for him to start a business. Why should big businesses, and people from outside the state, be the only ones to benefit from this once-in-a-lifetime opportunity? After all, a native—like Steve—should be in a better position than others to begin a business in the area.

Steve's Background and Qualifications

Steve had grown up in the north Georgia town of Dahlonega, a small historic settlement in the foothills of the Appalachian Mountains. Atlanta, the state capital, was only about 55 miles to the southwest. In addition to being a thriving community, Dahlonega was also a favorite vacation spot for campers and hikers. The town was adjacent to the Chattahoochee National Forest, an area replete with wildlife, waterfalls, and native plants and trees. The first gold rush

Source: This case was prepared by Elisabeth J. Teal of Baylor University.

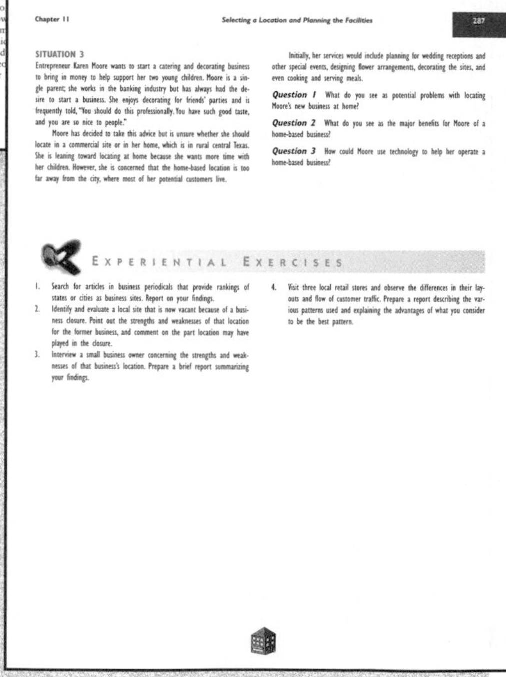

SITUATION 3

Entrepreneur Karen Moore wants to start a catering and decorating business to bring in money to help support her two young children. Moore is a single parent; she works in the banking industry but has always had the desire to start a business. She enjoys decorating for friends' parties and is frequently told, "You should do this professionally. You have such good taste, and you are so nice to people."

Moore has decided to take this advice but is unsure whether she should locate in a commercial site or in her home, which is in rural central Texas. She is leaning toward locating at home because she wants more time with her children. However, she is concerned that the home-based location is too far away from the city, where most of her potential customers live.

Initially, her services would include planning for wedding receptions and other special events, designing flower arrangements, decorating the sites, and even cooking and serving meals.

Question 1 What do you see as potential problems with locating Moore's new business at home?

Question 2 What do you see as the major benefits for Moore of a home-based business?

Question 3 How could Moore use technology to help her operate a home-based business?

Experiential Exercises

1. Search for articles in business periodicals that provide rankings of states or cities as business sites. Report on your findings.
2. Identify and evaluate a local site that is now vacant because of a business closure. Point out the strengths and weaknesses of that location for the former business, and comment on the part location may have played in the closure.
3. Interview a small business owner concerning the strengths and weaknesses of that business's location. Prepare a brief report summarizing your findings.
4. Visit three local retail stores and observe the differences in their layouts and flow of customer traffic. Prepare a report describing the various patterns used and explaining the advantages of what you consider to be the best pattern.

You Make the Call
These scenarios place you in the role of decision maker and ask you, as the owner/operator of a small business, what you would do.

Cases
The twenty-five cases located at the end of the book are brief but substantive. Designed to give you practice in analyzing, evaluating, and making recommendations to resolve real business problems, these cases, as you will discover, delve into a wide variety of issues that impact small businesses, providing lots of opportunity to sharpen problem-solving skills.

Experiential Exercises
Designed to connect "book learning" to the real world, these exercises often send you into your community to gather information and ideas from small business managers. They also encourage you to draw on your own experiences to flesh out chapter concepts.

With a Special Emphasis on the Internet

- URLs where you need them, right alongside text discussion, tie Web sites to businesses and organizations featured in the text.
- The role that technology, including Internet technology, is playing in the lives of small businesses is integrated throughout the text, as is practical advice about the advantages that technology offers small firms. How can a small business use technology to deliver better customer service, expand a home-based operation, manage its operations, and find sources of financing? All these questions, and more, are posed and answered.
- At http://longenecker.swcollege.com, we provide free access to a robust support site. On this site, you will find links to dozens of useful Web sites to further your exploration of the exciting topics introduced in the text. For those looking for extra practice questions, interactive quizzes are provided for each chapter. PowerPoint slides are available as a learning tool, as are Web exercises, self-assessments, and more!

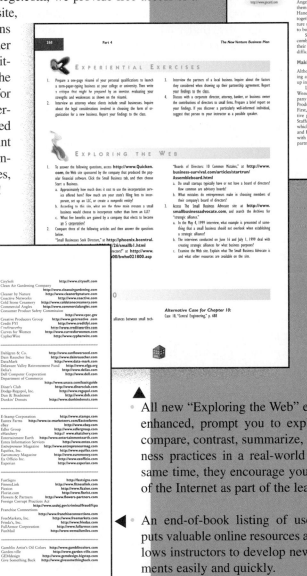

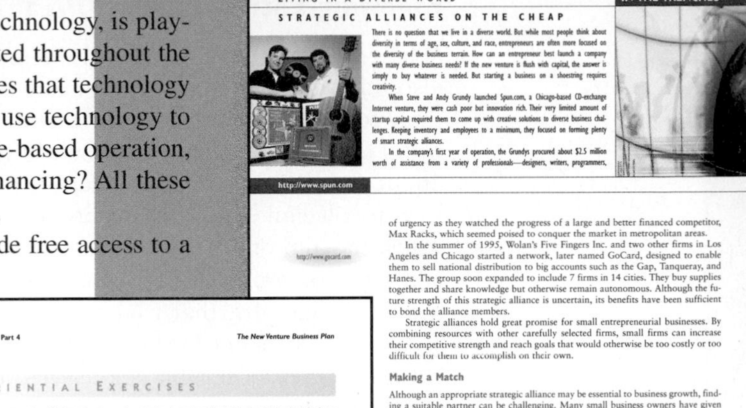
256 Part 4 The New Venture Business Plan

LIVING IN A DIVERSE WORLD — IN THE TRENCHES

STRATEGIC ALLIANCES ON THE CHEAP

There is no question that we live in a diverse world. But while most people think about diversity in terms of age, sex, culture, and race, entrepreneurs are often more focused on the diversity of the business terrain. How can an entrepreneur best launch a company with many diverse business needs? If the new venture is flush with capital, the answer is simply to buy whatever is needed. But starting a business on a shoestring requires creativity.

When Steve and Andy Grundy launched Spun.com, a Chicago-based CD-exchange Internet venture, they were cash poor but innovation rich. Their very limited amount of startup capital required them to come up with creative solutions to diverse business challenges. Keeping inventory and employees to a minimum, they focused on forming plenty of smart strategic alliances.

In the company's first year of operation, the Grundys procured about $2.5 million worth of assistance from a variety of professionals—designers, writers, programmers,

http://www.spun.com

http://www.gocard.com

of urgency as they watched the progress of a large and better financed competitor, Max Racks, which seemed poised to conquer the market in metropolitan areas.

In the summer of 1995, Wolan's Five Fingers Inc. and two other firms in Los Angeles and Chicago started a network, later named GoCard, designed to enable them to sell national distribution to big accounts such as the Gap, Tanqueray, and Hanes. The group soon expanded to include 7 firms in 14 cities. They buy supplies together and share knowledge but otherwise remain autonomous. Although the future strength of this strategic alliance is uncertain, its benefits have been sufficient to bond the alliance members.

Strategic alliances hold great promise for small entrepreneurial businesses. By combining resources with other carefully selected firms, small firms can increase their competitive strength and reach goals that would otherwise be too costly or too difficult for them to accomplish on their own.

Making a Match

Although an appropriate strategic alliance may be essential to business growth, finding a suitable partner can be challenging. Many small business owners have given up in frustration after months—even years—of trying to establish such connections.

Launched in 1999, Staffcentrix is an Internet outsourcing company based in Woodstock, Connecticut. Despite having only $10,000 in first-year sales, the company was able to form alliances with Microsoft, the United Nations, and Waterside Productions. How did co-founders Christine Durst and Michael Haaren pull it off? First, they identified potential e-mail contacts by scouring the Web sites of prospective partners and taking note of anyone associated with any projects parallel to Staffcentrix's interests. Using this information, they created a "contact profile," which detailed each contact's personal involvement with these projects. Then Durst and Haaren sent personal e-mail messages to these contacts, promoting an alliance with Staffcentrix. Within months, the company was up and running with big-name partners.[14]

268 Part 4 The New Venture Business Plan

EXPERIENTIAL EXERCISES

1. Prepare a one-page résumé of your personal qualifications to launch a term-paper-typing business at your college or university. Then write a critique that might be prepared by an investor, evaluating your strengths and weaknesses as shown on the résumé.
2. Interview an attorney whose clients include small businesses. Inquire about the legal considerations involved in choosing the form of organization for a new business. Report your findings to the class.
3. Interview the partners of a local business. Inquire about the factors they considered when drawing up their partnership agreement. Report your findings to the class.
4. Discuss with a corporate director, attorney, banker, or business owner the contributions of directors to small firms. Prepare a brief report on your findings. If you discover a particularly well-informed individual, suggest that person to your instructor as a possible speaker.

EXPLORING THE WEB

1. To answer the following questions, access **http://www.Quicken.com**, the Web site sponsored by the company that produced the popular financial software. Click the Small Business tab, and then choose Start a Business.
   a. Approximately how much does it cost to use the incorporation service offered here? How much are your state's filing fees to incorporate, set up an LLC, or create a nonprofit entity?
   b. According to this site, what are the three main reasons a small business would choose to incorporate rather than form an LLC?
   c. What five benefits are gained by a company that elects to become an S corporation?
2. Compare three of the following articles and then answer the questions below.
   "Small Businesses Seek Directors," at **http://phoenix.bcentral.** ... **/26/smallb1.html** ... rectors?" at **http://www.** ... **00/bwho021800.asp**
   "Boards of Directors: 10 Common Mistakes," at **http://www.business-survival.com/articles/startrun/Assembleboard.html**
   a. Do small startups typically have or not have a board of directors? How common are advisory boards?
   b. What mistakes do entrepreneurs make in choosing members of their company's board of directors?
3. Access The Small Business Advocate site at **http://www.smallbusinessadvocate.com**, and search the Archives for "strategic alliance."
   a. In the May 4, 1999 interview, what example is presented of something that a small business should not overlook when establishing a strategic alliance?
   b. The interviews conducted on June 16 and July 1, 1999 deal with creating strategic alliances for what business purposes?
   c. Examine the Web site. Explain what The Small Business Advocate is and what other resources are available on the site.

... alliances between small tech-

Alternative Case for Chapter 10:
Case 18, "Central Engineering," p. 688

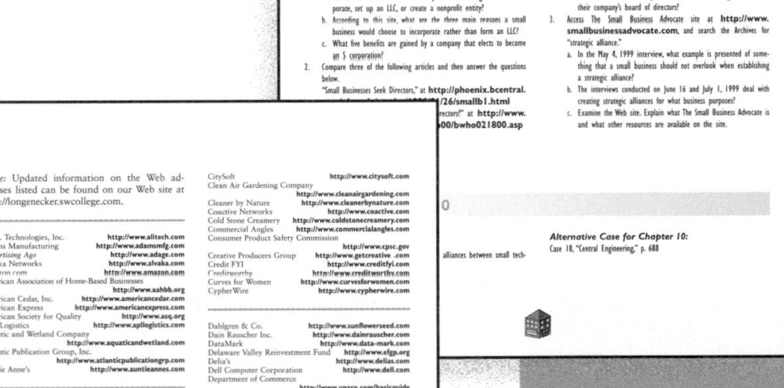
USEFUL URLS

Note: Updated information on the Web addresses listed can be found on our Web site at http://longenecker.swcollege.com.

A.L.L. Technologies, Inc. http://www.alltech.com
Adams Manufacturing http://www.adamsmfg.com
Advertising Age http://www.adage.com
Alvaka Networks http://www.alvaka.com
Amazon.com http://www.amazon.com
American Association of Home-Based Businesses http://www.aahbb.org
American Cedar, Inc. http://www.americancedar.com
American Express http://www.americanexpress.com
American Society for Quality http://www.asq.org
APL Logistics http://www.apllogistics.com
Aquatic and Wetland Company http://www.aquaticandwetland.com
Atlantic Publication Group, Inc. http://www.atlanticpublicationgrp.com
Auntie Anne's http://www.auntieannes.com

Baazee.com http://www.baazee.com
Basic Guide to Exporting, A http://www.unzo.com/basicguide
BBH Exhibits, Inc. http://www.bbhinc.net
Benolds http://www.benolds.com
Best Cellars, Inc. http://www.bestcellars.com
Better Business Bureau http://www.bbb.org
Big Dog Motorcycles http://www.bigdogmotorcycles.com
Big Emerging Markets, U.S. Department of Commerce http://www.ita.doc.gov/bems
Bite Footwear http://www.bitefootwear.com
Blue Marlin Corporation http://www.bluemarlincorp.com
Blue Note http://www.bluenote.net
Bo Peep Productions http://www.bopeepproductions.com
BooksonBiz.com http://www.booksonbiz.com
Boston Book Company http://www.rarebook.com
Bplans.com http://www.bplans.com
British Franchising Association http://www.british-franchise.org
Build-A-Bear Workshops http://www.buildabear.com
Business Incubation Group http:// www.bizincu.com
Business Marketing Group, Inc. http://www.bmginc.com
Business Mediation Associates http://www.business-mediation.com

Cambria Environmental Technology http://www.cambria-environment.com
CareerBuilder, Inc. http://www.careerbuilder.com
Carmelo's Italian Restaurants http://www.carmelositalrest.com
CCI Triad http://www.ccitriad.com
Celestis http://www.celestis.com
Certified Business Brokers http://www.certifiedbb.com
Certified Fraud Examiners http://www.cfenet.com
Chicago Manufacturing Center http:// www.cmcusa.org
Chick-fil-A http://www.chick-fil-a.com
Cindy Rowe Auto Glass http://www.cindyrowe.com
City Laundry and Drycleaning Company http://www.citylaundry.com

CitySoft http://www.citysoft.com
Clean Air Gardening Company http://www.cleanairgardening.com
Cleaner by Nature http://www.cleanerbynature.com
Coactive Networks http://www.coactive.com
Cold Stone Creamery http://www.coldstonecreamery.com
Commercial Angles http://www.commercialangles.com
Consumer Product Safety Commission http://www.cpsc.gov
Creative Producers Group http://www.getcreative .com
Credit FYI http://www.creditfyi.com
Creditworthy http://www.creditworthy.com
Curves for Women http://www.curvesforwomen.com
CypherWire http://www.cypherwire.com

Dahlgren & Co. http://www.sunflowerseed.com
Dain Rauscher Inc. http://www.dainrauscher.com
DataMark http://www.data-mark.com
Delaware Valley Reinvestment Fund http://www.efgp.org
Delia's http://www.delias.com
Dell Computer Corporation http://www.dell.com
Department of Commerce http://www.unzco.com/basicguide
Diner's Club http://www.dinersclub.com
Dodge-Regupol, Inc. http://www.regupol.com
Dun & Bradstreet http://www.dnb.com
Dunkin' Donuts http://www.dunkindonuts.com

E-Stamp Corporation http://www.stamps.com
Eastex Farms http://www.tx-marketeers.com/Eastexfarms
eBay http://www.ebay.com
Edler Group http://www.edlergroup.com
eHatchery http:// www.ehatchery.com
Entertainment Earth http://www.entertainmentearth.com
Entex Information Services http://www.entex.com
Entrepreneur Magazine http://www.entrepreneurmag.com
Equifax, Inc. http://www.equifax.com
Euromoney Magazine http://www.euromoney.com
Ex Officio Inc. http://www.exofficio.com
Experian http://www.experian.com

FastSigns http://fastsigns.com
FitnessLink http://www.fitnesslink.com
Fizzion http://www.fizzion.com
Florist.com http://www.florist.com
Flowers & Partners http://www.flowers-partners.com
Foreign Corrupt Practices Act http://www.usdoj.gov/criminal/fraud/fcpa
Franchise Connections http://www.franchiseconnections.com
FreeMarkets, Inc. http://www.freemarkets.com
Frieda's, Inc. http://www.friedas.com
FullArmor Corporation http://www.fullarmor.com
FunMail http://www.wemailsmiles.com

Gamblin Artist's Oil Colors http://www.gamblincolors.com
Garden-ville http://www.garden-ville.com
GEMdesign http://www.gemdesign.bigstep.com
Give Something Back http://www.givesomethingback.com

- All new "Exploring the Web" exercises, expanded and enhanced, prompt you to explore, explain, describe, compare, contrast, summarize, and analyze small business practices in a real-world context online. At the same time, they encourage you to make extensive use of the Internet as part of the learning process.

- An end-of-book listing of useful Internet addresses puts valuable online resources at your fingertips and allows instructors to develop new Internet-based assignments easily and quickly.

Welcome to the twelfth edition of *Small Business Management: An Entrepreneurial Emphasis!* This edition continues to focus on that large segment of the economy represented by small business and the entrepreneurial process that gives it life and vitality.

Following Entrepreneurial Dreams

While this text treats the knowledge needed to lead and manage small businesses, it also reflects a much broader concern—the pursuit of entrepreneurial dreams. More than routinely managing people and situations, entrepreneurs build businesses to fulfill dreams for themselves, their families, and their communities. When we write about small business, therefore, we are writing about individuals whose business lives involve and impact their broader family and community roles and aspirations. Thus, the aim of *Small Business Management: An Entrepreneurial Emphasis,* 12th edition is to provide instruction and guidance for successful entrepreneurial journeys. It is our hope that what we have written will contribute to that goal for those seeking independent business careers, either directly or indirectly through the wise counsel of a teacher who has selected this book.

Today, you can find exciting opportunities for operating your own business if you are committed strongly enough to a dream to overcome the obstacles you will encounter. New ventures can create personal value for both owners and investors who devote their time and money.

New ventures can also improve and protect our way of life by creating jobs and providing new products and services. In the aftermath of September 11, 2001, it was an entrepreneurial firm that produced the equipment needed to treat anthrax-tainted mail. In 1981, Gene Ray and Ed Knauf sketched a business plan for Titan Corporation on a napkin in a restaurant. Subsequent development of their product line led to machines that can irradiate food and also kill bacteria such as anthrax.

Entrepreneurs need to dream, to see opportunities where others see only failures. Benjamin Franklin was admonished to stop experimenting with electricity. What an absurd waste of time, trying to improve on the fabulous oil lamp! Thomas Edison discouraged his friend Henry Ford from pursuing his fledgling idea of building a motorcar. Convinced of the worthlessness of the idea, Edison invited Ford to come and work for him. Ford, however, remained committed and tirelessly pursued his dream. Although his first attempt resulted in a vehicle without a reverse gear, Ford knew he could make it happen—and, of course, he did. Thank goodness Ford and Franklin dreamed dreams and believed they could accomplish them. We all benefit from their achievements.

Exciting New Content

When we undertook this revision of *Small Business Management,* currency and relevancy, as always, were at the heart of our endeavor. And, as always, we found many interesting ideas, trends, people, and companies to write about. With an abundance of real-world examples to keep both veterans and new readers totally engaged, this edition of *Small Business Management* offers plenty that's new:

- Chapter 2, "Strategies That Capture Opportunities," has been reorganized and refocused to demonstrate, with ringing clarity, the importance of strategies that will remain as relevant in the years ahead as they are today.
- A new chapter on e-commerce (Chapter 3, "E-Commerce Opportunities") has been added. Clearly, some products and some business models are better suited to living online than others. We help you sort through the critical issues, providing a balanced treatment of strategies and tactics.

- Chapter 4, "Global Opportunities," is entirely new, and we have expanded global examples throughout the text. The challenges of competing in a global economy are huge for small and big businesses alike.
- A new video feature, courtesy of the popular television series "Small Business School," which airs weekly on most PBS stations, daily on Worldnet, and always on the Web, has been added. Accordingly, special "In the Video Spotlights" appear at the beginning of 12 chapters and a video portraying the same companies and business owners can be shown in the classroom. Appendix B: Video Appendix provides further information on these businesses and questions to generate critical thinking on chapter topics.
- A new epilogue has been added on the neglected issue of conflict between building a business and building a life, ensuring that personal interests as well as business interests are addressed in entrepreneurial dreams and careers.
- Because concepts related to financial planning are not mastered easily, we have put special emphasis on simplifying all financial presentations.
- With the twelfth edition, we introduce a new multimedia resource on CD-ROM: "Tools for Preparing a Simplified Business Plan." Among a host of special resources, templates in Microsoft® Word and Excel give you a navigational path to follow for generating a take-it-to-the-bank plan.

Features That Enhance Learning

A number of unique features in the twelfth edition make substantial contributions to the learning process. Offering a variety of experiences, these features deliver hands-on learning that captures student interest and leads to practical knowledge.

- ***Unique Support for Building a Business Plan.*** In preparing business plans, small business owner-managers often use software specifically designed for this purpose. This edition includes a CD-ROM that contains a number of useful tools for preparing business plans. Microsoft® Word and Excel templates designed in conjunction with the seven chapters of Part 4, "The New Venture Business Plan," form an integral part of learning how to develop workable plans. These templates provide an obvious advantage over commercially available planning aids: The experience they offer in preparing a plan is closely aligned with the particular approaches to planning that we present in the book.
- ***Integrated Learning System.*** We have retained the integrated learning system that structures the text and the teaching supplements around learning objectives. The numbered objectives are identified in the "Looking Ahead" section, and each is precisely addressed in the "Looking Back" section at the end of the chapter. These same objectives introduce related exercises in the *Student Learning Guide.* If students are having trouble with certain concepts, they can easily locate related materials in the text and in the *Student Learning Guide* simply by looking for the appropriate objective.

  The integrated learning system also makes lecture and test preparation easier. The lecture notes in the *Instructor's Manual* are grouped by learning objective and identify the appropriate acetates, masters, and PowerPoint slides that relate to each objective. Questions in the *Test Bank* are grouped by objective as well. A correlation table at the beginning of each *Test Bank* chapter permits selection of questions that cover all objectives or that emphasize objectives considered most important.

- *Exploring the Web.* Structured Internet exercises appear at the end of every chapter. Designed to familiarize students with the best online resources for small business on the Internet, "Exploring the Web" exercises send students to specific Web sites, prompting them to perform targeted searches, analyze the effectiveness of what they find, and theorize about what could be done better. The future of technology in small businesses is wide open; these exercises go a long way toward ensuring that students stay informed about the trends to watch. All are new to this edition.
- *You Make the Call.* "You Make the Call" incidents at the end of each chapter present realistic business situations that require examining key operating decisions. Give your students a leg up in addressing the concerns of small businesses by having them take on the role of a small business owner.
- *Cases.* Twenty-five cases, seven of which are new to this edition, provide opportunities for students to apply chapter concepts to realistic entrepreneurial situations. These brief cases call for careful analysis of real business problems and ask for recommendations to solve specific problems.
- *In the Spotlight and In the Trenches.* Practical examples from the world of small business and entrepreneurship carry both instructional and inspirational value. "In the Spotlight" profiles (12 of which are video enhanced) open each chapter on a high note. "In the Trenches" boxes appear at critical junctures throughout the chapters, refueling and refreshing chapter concepts with additional examples that are straightforward and honest.

Updated and Enhanced Supplements

All of the supplements that accompany *Small Business Management: An Entrepreneurial Emphasis,* 12th edition are designed to fit a variety of teaching methods, learning styles, and classroom situations.

- *Student Learning Guide.* Prepared by Rosemary Shields of the University of Texas at El Paso, this valuable student supplement contains key points, brief definitions of chapter terms, and a variety of self-testing materials, including true/false, multiple-choice, fill-in-the-blank, and essay questions.
- *Instructor's Manual.* Written by Leslie E. Palich, of Baylor University, this manual contains annotated lecture outlines, with special discussion prompts related to the use of PowerPoint slides, transparency acetates, and transparency masters; answers to "Discussion Questions" and "Exploring the Web" exercises; comments on "You Make the Call" situations; and teaching notes for the cases. A guide to the use of the "Small Business School" video and a selection of transparency masters are also included.
- *Test Bank.* Thoroughly revised by Leslie E. Palich, of Baylor University, the *Test Bank* includes true/false, multiple-choice, and discussion questions. A correlation table at the beginning of each chapter enables the instructor to select questions most appropriate for particular classes.
- *ExamView® Testing Software.* All questions from the printed *Test Bank* are available in South-Western's testing program, ExamView. It is an easy-to-use test-creation program, compatible with Windows and Macintosh operating systems.
- *Microsoft® PowerPoint®.* A complete set of 500 full-color images, including key figures from each text chapter has been developed by Charlie Cook, of the University of West Alabama, to accompany the textbook.

- *Transparency Acetates.* A selection of must-have PowerPoint images is also available in the form of overheads.
- *Instructor's Resource CD-ROM.* Get quick access to all instructor ancillaries from your desktop. This easy-to-use CD lets you electronically review, edit, and copy what you need.
- *"Small Business School" Video.* Available in two volumes, selections from the popular television series on PBS stations let you in on some very big ideas at work in a variety of interesting and innovative small businesses. Want to know how to recruit the best people? Curious about the Internet strategy of a well-positioned provider of travel services? Use these videos to bring the real world into your classroom and let your students learn from the experts.
- *Web Site.* This textbook has its own home page at http://longenecker.swcollege.com. At this site, resources for both instructors and students can be located and utilized. You can also find links to additional case material, chapter quizzes, additional "Exploring the Web" exercises, downloadable ancillaries, and more.
- *WebTutor™ on WebCT and on Blackboard.* WebTutor™ on WebCT or WebTutor™ on Blackboard complements *Small Business Management* by providing interactive reinforcement that helps students grasp key concepts. WebTutor's online teaching and learning environment brings together content management, assessment, communication, and collaboration capabilities for enhancing in-class instruction or delivering distance learning. For more information, including a demo, visit http://webtutor.swcollege.com.
- *WebTutor™ Advantage.* More than just an interactive study guide, WebTutor™ Advantage delivers innovative learning aids that actively engage students.
- *Something Ventured Telecourse Videos.* Available from INTELECOM, a not-for-profit producer of distance-learning courseware, this set of 26 video segments covers a range of topics, from acquiring startup capital to franchising, risk management, and marketing. For more information, visit http://www.intelecom.org or call (626) 796-7300.

  A *Telecourse Guide* to accompany this series, including learning objectives, assignments, video viewing questions, and self-tests, is available from South-Western.

Special Thanks and Acknowledgments

There are numerous individuals to whom we owe a debt of gratitude for their assistance in making this project a reality. In particular, we thank our friends at South-Western/Thomson Learning. We are especially indebted to John Szilagyi and Judy O'Neill, of South-Western; Jeanne Yost, of Lifland et al., Bookmakers; and Theresa Curtis, of Ohlinger Publishing Services. They are true professionals!

Special thanks go to Dr. Les Palich for his preparation of Chapter 4 and revision of Chapters 2 and 10. Also, we thank Emily Ketchum for her assistance in developing the "Exploring the Web" exercises, and Elizabeth Vaughn and Karen Moore for their excellent word-processing skills. Rosemary Shields, of the University of Texas at El Paso, prepared the *Study Learning Guide,* and Charlie Cook, of the University of West Alabama, created the PowerPoint images. And, again, we appreciate the understanding and support of our wives—Frances, Karen, and Donna—during this process.

For their helpful suggestions during our preparation of this edition, we are especially grateful to the following individuals:

Lon Addams
Weber State College

Samuel Adekunle
Albany State College

Hal Babson
Columbus State Community College

Richard E. Baldwin
Cedarville University

Peter Banfe
Ohio Northern University

Ann Barnitz
Ashland Community College

Tom Bergman
University of Central Oklahoma

John D. Boos
Ohio Wesleyan University

Marvin Borgelt
University of Mary

Martin Bressler
Thomas College

Rochelle Brunson
Alvin College

Terry Burbey
Silver Lake College of the Holy Family

Richard Butler
Alverno College

Joe Cannon
Oral Roberts University

Jack Cichy
Davenport University

Harry A. Domicone
California Lutheran University

Bonnie Dowd
Palomar College

Tony Enerva
Lakeland Community College

Ivan Figueroa
Miami Dade Community College

Howard Foster
Adams State College

David W. Frantz
Indiana University East

Glen Gelderloos
Grand Rapids Community College

Jutta Green
New River Community College

Jeff Hardesty
Owens Community College

Brenda Harper
Calhoun Community College

Donald Howard
Augusta State University

Nabil A. N. Ibrahim
Augusta State University

Judith Kizzie
Clinton Community College

Mary Beth Klinger
College of Southern Maryland

Les Ledger
Central Texas Community College

Randolph Manning
Suffolk County Community College

K. Michael Matthews
The College of Saint Rose

Larry McDaniel
Alabama A&M University

Pat McInturff
California State University

Len Middleton
University of Michigan

Marla Miller
Oregon Institute of Technology

Julie Mobley
Rowan-Cabarrus Community College

John Nader
Grand Valley State University

Karen Nagle
Herkimer County Community College

Terry W. Noel
Witchita State University

Cliff Olson
Southern Adventist University

Diane Sinkinson
Cape Fear Community College

Barry Van Hook
Arizona State University

Max Wortman
Iowa State University

As a final word, we express our sincere thanks to the many instructors who use our text in both academic and professional settings. Ultimately, it is your evaluation that is important to us. We want to know what you think. Please contact any of us as questions or needs arise; our telephone numbers, fax numbers, and e-mail addresses are provided below. We view ourselves as partners with you in this venture, and we wish to be sensitive to your wishes and desires whenever possible. We thank you for letting us serve you.

Justin G. Longenecker
Tel.: (254) 710-4258
Fax: (254) 710-1093
E-mail:
Justin_Longenecker@baylor.edu

Carlos W. Moore
Tel.: (254) 710-6176
Fax: (254) 710-1068
E-mail:
Carlos_Moore@baylor.edu

J. William Petty
Tel.: (254) 710-2260
Fax: (254) 710-1092
E-mail:
Bill_Petty@baylor.edu

About the Authors

JUSTIN G. LONGENECKER, *BAYLOR UNIVERSITY*

Justin G. Longenecker's authorship of *Small Business Management: An Entrepreneurial Emphasis* began with the first edition of this book and continues with an active, extensive involvement in the preparation of the present edition. He has authored a number of books and numerous articles in such journals as *Journal of Small Business Management, Academy of Management Review, Business Horizons,* and *Journal of Business Ethics.* Active in a number of professional organizations, he has served as president of the International Council for Small Business.

Dr. Longenecker grew up in a family business and attended Central Christian College of Kansas for two years. He earned his bachelor's degree in political science from Seattle Pacific University, his M.B.A. from Ohio State University, and his Ph.D. from the University of Washington.

CARLOS W. MOORE, *BAYLOR UNIVERSITY*

Carlos W. Moore is the Edwin W. Streetman Professor of Marketing at Baylor University, where he has been an instructor for more than 30 years. He has been honored as a Distinguished Professor by the Hankamer School of Business, where he teaches both graduate and undergraduate courses. Dr. Moore has authored articles in such journals as *Journal of Small Business Management, Journal of Business Ethics, Organizational Dynamics, Accounting Horizons,* and *Journal of Accountancy.* His authorship of this textbook began with its sixth edition.

Dr. Moore received an Associate Arts degree from Navarro Junior College in Corsicana, Texas, where he was later named Ex-Student of the Year. He earned a B.B.A. degree from The University of Texas at Austin, an M.B.A. from Baylor University, and a Ph.D. from Texas A&M University.

Besides his academic experience, Dr. Moore has business experience as co-owner of a small ranch and as a partner in a small business consulting firm.

J. WILLIAM PETTY, *BAYLOR UNIVERSITY*

J. William Petty is Professor of Finance and the W. W. Caruth Chairholder in Entrepreneurship at Baylor University. He holds a Ph.D. and an M.B.A. from The University of Texas at Austin and a B.S. from Abilene Christian University. He has taught at Virginia Tech University and Texas Tech University and has served as the dean of the business school at Abilene Christian University. His research interests include corporate restructuring, acquisitions of privately held companies, shareholder value-based management, the financing of small and entrepreneurial firms, and lender-borrower relationships. He has served as co-editor for the *Journal of Financial Research* and editor of the *Journal of Entrepreneurial and Small Business Finance.* He has published articles in a number of finance journals and is the co-author of two leading corporate finance textbooks—*Basic Financial Management* and *Foundations of Finance.* Dr. Petty has worked as a consultant for oil and gas firms and consumer product companies. He also served as a subject matter expert on a best-practices study by the American Productivity and Quality Center on the topic of shareholder value-based management. He has served on a research team for the Australian Department of Industry to study the feasibility of establishing a public equity market for small- and medium-size enterprises in Australia.

To the Student

As authors of *Small Business Management: An Entrepreneurial Emphasis,* we must measure our success by the effectiveness of our presentation to you. Although you may not be involved in selecting this textbook, we still consider you our customer and wish to be sensitive to your needs in learning the material presented. For this reason, we have made every effort to make it understandable and relevant. We have also tried to consider your viewpoint in each chapter we have written.

We extend our best wishes to you for a challenging and successful course.

part

1

Entrepreneurship and Small Business

1 The Winning Hand of Entrepreneurship

chapter 1

THE WINNING HAND OF ENTREPRENEURSHIP

In the VIDEO Spotlight

Cafe Pilon

In this episode of "Small Business School," the series on PBS stations, you will meet Enrique Souto and his brothers, Alberto and Angel. After Castro's communist government seized their father's business in 1961, the family fled Cuba to make a new life in Miami, Florida. Leaving all their worldly possessions behind, the Soutos came to the United States with their greatest possessions—their integrity, love of family and friends, creativity, and love of Cuban espresso coffee.

Mr. Souto started over. He went door to door in his new neighborhood to find customers. Soon he was delivering his fresh-ground, Cuban-roasted coffee to their doorsteps, just as milk was sold and delivered in the 1950s.

His sons have grown the business through both acquisitions and smart business practices. Today Cafe Pilon has 175 employees and annual revenues of $70 million.

I learned many lessons from the Soutos, but the most powerful one is that business decisions should be kept separate from egos. When the founder of Cafe Pilon (the biggest name in Cuban coffee) was ready to retire, the Soutos offered to buy the business; they experienced growth by combining the companies to maximize efficiencies. But they did not even think of dropping the Cafe Pilon name, preferring increased profits over having the family name on a package. Decades later, the Soutos have again acquired a competitor that carries another name. The Souto family business is proud to own all the best names in Cuban coffee. ◆

"What did I learn from my father? Honesty. Your word is very important. It's everything."

—Jose Enrique Souto

—Hattie Bryant, Producer, "Small Business School," The Series on PBS Stations, Worldnet, and the Web, http://smallbusinessschool.org

SmallBusinessSchool
the Series on PBS stations and the Web

Go to page 726 for More! on Cafe Pilon.

LOOKING AHEAD

After studying this chapter, you should be able to

1. *Discuss the availability of entrepreneurial opportunities and give examples of successful businesses started by entrepreneurs.*
2. *Explain the entrepreneurial challenges presented by e-commerce and global changes.*
3. *Explain the nature of entrepreneurship and how it is related to small business.*
4. *Identify three motivators or rewards of entrepreneurial careers.*
5. *Describe the various types of entrepreneurs and entrepreneurial ventures.*
6. *Identify ways to gain a potential competitive edge for small entrepreneurial firms.*
7. *Discuss factors related to readiness for entrepreneurship and getting started in an entrepreneurial career.*

Welcome to the world of entrepreneurship and small business! At one time or another, many people reflect on the possibility (or maybe the impossibility) of some day operating their own business. Occasionally, this inspiration starts early in life as happened with this entrepreneur:

I started my first business at age 5. It was a restaurant. My partner (my 3-year-old sister, Susan) and I worked tirelessly to offer a comprehensive casual dining experience.

Our marketing campaign was simple—we posted a very colorful handcrafted sign on the front porch, and we waited. Sales were dismal. By 8 p.m. that first day, after consuming a good portion of our inventory, we shut down. Patience, perseverance and experience are not inherent virtues of a 5-year-old CEO, but time was on our side. Our careers could recover.[1]

Time is on your side, too, because you are about to embark on a course of study that will prove invaluable if you elect to pursue a career in entrepreneurship or small business. An entrepreneurial career can provide an exciting life and substantial personal rewards while also contributing to the welfare of society. This book is designed to give you an understanding of entrepreneurship and to help prepare you for the life of an entrepreneur.

Entrepreneurs in various industries serve the economy by providing jobs and producing goods and services for customers around the world. Although giant corporations attract more public attention and make more headlines in the news media, small businesses and entrepreneurial endeavors constitute a less-visible part of the economy that is equally important to the world's economic and social well-being.

ENTREPRENEURIAL OPPORTUNITIES

1 *Discuss the availability of entrepreneurial opportunities and give examples of successful businesses started by entrepreneurs.*

An entrepreneurial opportunity is more than just a good business idea. Insightful entrepreneurs have interesting ideas all the time—concepts for new products, ingenious technologies, and inventive services. The difference between a successful and an unsuccessful venture is often the difference between an intriguing business idea and a truly promising opportunity. Whereas a business idea is often a concept in search

entrepreneurial opportunity
a value-creating innovation with market potential

of an application, an **entrepreneurial opportunity** is a desirable and timely innovation that creates value for interested buyers or end users.

Building a better mousetrap holds little promise in a world without mice. And such an innovation is unlikely to sell if an ordinary mousetrap can catch as many or more mice at a fraction of the cost. Clearly, successful entrepreneurs pursue opportunities by first identifying value-creating innovations with market potential. Great ideas alone are simply not enough.

Our working definition distinguishes between entrepreneurial opportunities and business ideas. It is important to note, however, that a given opportunity will not be equally attractive to everyone. Because of differences in experiences and perspectives, one person may see an opportunity where others do not. But, in any case, a true opportunity exists only for the entrepreneur who has the interest, resources, and capabilities that are required to succeed.

Entrepreneurial opportunities exist today in a business world that differs markedly from the business world of yesterday. In this section, we will discuss the paths to successful entrepreneurial ventures taken by some present-day entrepreneurs.

Three Success Stories

From the following three examples of entrepreneurial success, you may receive inspiration. Perhaps you also may soon be part of a success story—one to be written in the days ahead! In addition, you will see that entrepreneurship takes many forms. These stories suggest a few of the numerous possibilities you can consider for your own career. Some of your opportunities, of course, may be drastically different from those described.

MARKETPLACE HOLDINGS (RICHMOND, VIRGINIA) Jonathan F. Johnson operates a chain of supermarkets in what has been called the "rough and tattered Church Hill neighborhood" of Richmond, Virginia.[2] Johnson's highly successful business in an unlikely business environment has been described as follows:

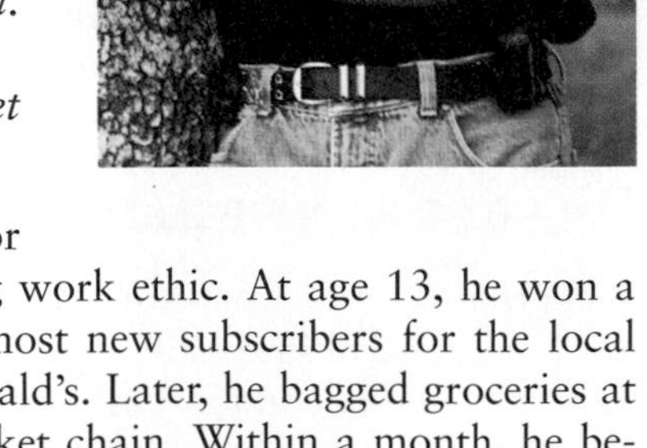

This is a place where unemployment hovers like smog at 13%. It's also a place where Johnson makes his money in the grocery business. Food stamps are the currency used in 90% of purchases. "They're better than checks," says Johnson. "They don't bounce."

At 36, Johnson owns the largest supermarket chain of any African-American in the country.[3]

Johnson's early employment prepared him for his entrepreneurial career and reflects his strong work ethic. At age 13, he won a trip to Spain and Portugal for signing up the most new subscribers for the local newspaper. At one point, he worked for McDonald's. Later, he bagged groceries at a store owned by Farm Fresh, a local supermarket chain. Within a month, he became the night manager, and eventually he ran 42 Farm Fresh stores.

Another well-established supermarket owner, impressed with Johnson's work, tried to hire him and, when that failed, agreed to back him in his own business. By

borrowing on his home and IRA and borrowing from his business backer, Johnson was able to raise $300,000 as a down payment on four rundown stores in downtown Richmond. Rather than starting from scratch, Johnson became an entrepreneur by purchasing an existing business.

Johnson did not operate the stores in the same way they had been run in the past, however. He brought in his own managers, cleaned up the stores, and replaced low-quality goods with higher-quality products. He hired from the community and made appeals at local churches.

Since he couldn't beat his competitors on price, Johnson decided to outdo them on service.

One evening he offered a lift to a shopper loaded down with two heavy bags. She accepted, but ordered him back to the store. "She bought fifty bucks more worth of stuff," he says. Then it clicked. Taking out a second mortgage on his home to buy five vans, Johnson gave free rides home to anyone who purchased more than $40 worth of groceries. "My sales went from [an annualized] $13 million to $19 million in five months," he says.[4]

Johnson's business has prospered. After losing money for a few years, Johnson expected to net $1.3 million on more than $100 million in revenues from his business in 1999. The business now includes six Community Pride stores in Richmond's downtown area and three RackNSack stores in the suburbs.

In operating his business, Johnson has displayed a real entrepreneurial spirit, changing what needed to be changed by using innovative methods. He takes an unusual perspective in dealing with shoplifters.

"If they steal steaks, I'll arrest them," he says. "If they steal bologna and bread, I'll give them $50 and a job application." He claims that since 1992 he's hired hundreds of shoplifters and at least 60 have stayed with the company for more than three years.[5]

He has also hired from city welfare rolls—300 employees since 1997, out of a total staff of 1,030. Turnover is low; only 2 of 47 core managers have left.

This success story started with the purchase of a very marginal business. Many businesses offered for sale, however, are well managed and profitable. Although the circumstances under which a business is bought vary widely, any purchase can launch an entrepreneurial career.

AUNTIE ANNE'S (GAP, PENNSYLVANIA) In the late 1980s, a Pennsylvania housewife started a pretzel business that grew so quickly it soon stretched across the United States.[6] The rapid growth was accomplished through franchising, another type of entrepreneurship.

http://www.auntieannes.com

Anne Beiler grew up in a Mennonite family in Lancaster County, Pennsylvania, and viewed the world from the back of a horse-drawn buggy for the first years of her life. She was married at 19 to a man who shared her commitment to faith and community service.

After living for several years in Texas, the Beilers and their two daughters moved back to Pennsylvania in 1987, with the dream of opening a free counseling center for couples and families. In order to help realize this dream, Beiler found a job paying $200 a week managing a concession stand at a Maryland farmers' market.

When a booth came up for sale at another farmer's market in Downington, Pennsylvania, Beiler borrowed $6,000 from her father-in-law and purchased it, sight

unseen. She sold pizza, stromboli, ice cream, and hand-rolled soft pretzels. Eventually, the strong demand for pretzels eliminated other products. After an experience with a disappointing batch of pretzels, Beiler began experimenting with a recipe of her own. Her husband suggested adding a few additional ingredients, and soon the great-tasting Auntie Anne's pretzel was born.

In February of 1988, Beiler christened her fledgling company "Auntie Anne's," a term of endearment used by her 30 nieces and nephews. The popularity of Auntie Anne's pretzels grew by word of mouth, and, before long, people began contacting Beiler with the request to start their own Auntie Anne's business. As a result, she began franchising in early 1989.

Today, with more than 570 store locations in 42 states and 6 countries—including Indonesia, Singapore, Malaysia, Thailand, and the Philippines—Beiler's entrepreneurial talents have been recognized by *Inc.* magazine, which named her "Entrepreneur of the Year" twice. She has been featured on the "Oprah Winfrey Show" and on CNN's "Managing with Jane Hopkins." The firm has been consistently ranked in *Success* magazine's "Franchise Gold 100" list.

The Auntie Anne's success story features a young woman with limited resources who developed a better tasting pretzel and built a successful, growing, and profitable business on that foundation. In addition, Auntie Anne's has created business opportunities for hundreds of others. Franchisees receive 6 to 11 days' training at the company's headquarters, store design assistance, and rights to use Auntie Anne's logos and trade names. This business relationship involves another type of entrepreneurship—owning a business as a franchisee and operating it in cooperation with the franchisor.

http://www.rotozip.com

ROTO ZIP TOOL CORPORATION (CROSS PLAINS, WISCONSIN) Robert Kopras, a young journeyman carpenter, started Roto Zip® Tool Corporation in 1974 in order to manufacture a special type of saw he had designed.[7] Today, the firm, sometimes described as a privately held family business, produces one of the top-selling power tools in the country.

The saw was born out of Kopras's frustration. As a carpenter doing drywall work, he needed a time-saving technique for making rectangular holes for electrical boxes, windows, and doors. After experimenting with several designs, he came up with a rotating bit that could be drilled into the wall and then directed in a linear fashion to produce a box-shaped cut, thereby combining the functions of a drill and a saw. Called the Roto Zip Spiral Saw, the tool can enter material much like a drill and then slice clean freehand cuts in any direction. These features have made it a favorite of both hobbyists and professionals.

When Kopras took his invention to major tool companies, they rejected the idea as too costly—but Kopras knew its value! He managed to raise about $20,000, putting a second mortgage on his home and using the retirement savings of his wife, Becky. Working out of their home, Kopras refined and eventually patented the tool.

He also added bits that could cut through wood, Plexiglas, tile, aluminum, and marble. Today, he holds the patents on the Sabrecut bits that enable the tool to work like a saw.

As a later refinement, the company's electronic engineers added a computer chip to create a smarter tool, one that automatically adjusts power to maintain preselected speeds. Using the same computer technology found in laptops and cell phones, the saw monitors rotational speed, automatically increasing or decreasing power to produce the cleanest cut. This "smart" saw permits both professionals and amateurs to make clean, precise cuts through a variety of materials, regardless of their skill levels and work techniques.

The company also used some unique promotional methods to introduce this revolutionary product.

"Everyone told us not to do an infomercial," says son Jason Kopras, the company's vice president, who created the spot. "But we wanted to demonstrate how the tool worked." So they put together a 30-minute tape, a knockoff of Home Improvement's "Tool Time" segment, complete with a tool-belt-wearing, buxom blonde assistant and a contest between some trades guy using his equipment and Bob [Kopras] with the Spiral Saw. Sales spiked again—particularly among women, who now represent 45% of Roto Zip buyers.[8]

Roto Zip Tool Corporation ships an average of 10,000 saws daily to companies like The Home Depot, Sears, Lowe's, and Ace Hardware. Sales jumped from $9 million in 1996 to $116 million in 1999.

The highly successful entrepreneurial venture arose from the pioneering efforts of a young carpenter who had just graduated from high school. He was not afraid to use his ingenuity and to strike out on his own when established companies were unable to see his vision of a tool of the future. Also note that Roto Zip Tool Corporation is a family-run business—it was Jason Kopras, son of the founder, who created the very effective Roto Zip Saw infomercial. Many young people have similar opportunities to seek an entrepreneurial career within the family business.

EVIDENCE OF OPPORTUNITIES In a private enterprise system, any individual is free to enter into business for himself or herself. In the video spotlight and three examples, we have described four very different people who took that step—a Cuban refugee, a hard-working employee/manager of a supermarket chain in Virginia, a homemaker/farmers' market worker in Pennsylvania, and a journeyman carpenter in Wisconsin. In contrast to many others who have tried and failed, these individuals achieved outstanding success.

At any given time, many potentially profitable business opportunities exist in the environment. But these opportunities must be recognized and grasped by individuals with abilities and desire strong enough to assure success. The startups just presented were successful in a big way; they were chosen to show the impressive opportunities that exist. In contrast to these examples, many individuals achieve success on a more modest level in business endeavors far different from those described here.

Special Opportunities in a Changing World

2

Explain the entrepreneurial challenges presented by e-commerce and global changes.

Entrepreneurial opportunities do not exist in a vacuum. They must be found in a rapidly and continuously changing environment that affects not only businesses but many aspects of society at large. In this section, we identify two powerful forces currently at work in the business community.

E-COMMERCE In the last half of the 20th century, businesses throughout the world entered the Information Age. Obviously, computers and related aspects of modern technology have permanently changed and will continue to change the way people do business. Companies of all sizes use information technology to become more effective.

Yogi Berra has been quoted as saying, "You can observe a lot by watching," and you will do some watching and analyzing of e-businesses in Chapter 3, E-Commerce Opportunities. That chapter describes changes occurring in the new economy and identifies some of the opportunities opening up for entrepreneurship and small business.

One specific example of an e-business is provided by the Buch Spieler Music Store in Montpelier, Vermont, which established a Web site and advertised "music of all kinds from around the world for all kinds of people." The site produced the store's first out-of-state sales in 27 years and pushed the store's overall sales up 5 percent in only 8 months.[9]

GLOBALIZATION Another important economic change is the trend toward a global economy, which creates a new kind of competition and also opens up business opportunities. Although large corporations have been the dominant players in international business, the growing presence of small firms in the global market has modified the traditional image of small businesses as strictly domestic.

Auburn Farms, Inc., a small Sacramento, California snack foods company, started importing products from South Africa.[10] The company, whose annual sales volume is $15 million, has become the exclusive U.S. importer of Beacon Sweets & Chocolates of South Africa, a candy maker that exports to 23 other countries. The strategy is meant to broaden Auburn Farms' line of fat-free snack foods and to help make the company a more general supplier of specialty foods.

Although the majority of small firms are still not directly involved in international business, the number of small firms functioning as importers and exporters is growing, along with the overall volume of international business. Such business opportunities, which are becoming more widely available, are discussed in detail in Chapter 4, Global Opportunities.

Entrepreneurship and Small Business

Explain the nature of entrepreneurship and how it is related to small business.

Thus far, we have discussed entrepreneurship and small business opportunities in a very general way. However, it is important to note that, despite many similarities, the terms *entrepreneur* and *small business manager* are not synonymous. One reason for this is that, although most entrepreneurial endeavors begin as small businesses, a few are quite substantial in size even when they begin or quickly grow into large businesses, requiring extensive managerial skills.

entrepreneur
a person who starts and/or operates a business

WHO ARE THE ENTREPRENEURS? **Entrepreneurs** are those individuals who discover market needs and launch new firms to meet those needs. They are risk takers who provide an impetus for change, innovation, and progress in economic life. (In contrast, salaried employees receive some specified compensation and do not assume ownership risks.)

In this book, we consider all active owner-managers to be entrepreneurs. We do not limit the term *entrepreneur* only to founders of business firms; we also apply the

FIGURE 1-1 *The Independent Entrepreneur*

term to second-generation operators of family-owned firms, franchisees, and owner-managers who have bought out the founders of existing firms. Our definition, however, does exclude salaried managers of larger corporations, even those sometimes described as entrepreneurial because of their flair for innovation and their willingness to accept risk.

WHAT IS SMALL BUSINESS? What does it mean to talk about "small business"? A neighborhood restaurant or bakery is clearly a small business, and General Motors is obviously not. But among small businesses, there is great diversity in size.

Being labeled a "small business" may convey the impression that a business is inconsequential or unimportant. That impression, however, would be totally incorrect. The U.S. Small Business Administration has assessed the economic impact of small businesses as follows:

As we enter the 21st century, America's 25 million small businesses continue to be a potent force in our dynamic economy. They employ more than 52 percent of the private work force. They are the principal source of new jobs in the country: more than 20 million since 1993. And they generate more than 51 percent of the private sector gross domestic product.[11]

There have been many efforts to define the term *small business,* using such criteria as number of employees, sales volume, and value of assets. There is no generally accepted or universally agreed-on definition. Size standards are basically arbitrary, adopted to serve a particular purpose. For example, legislators sometimes exclude firms with fewer than 10 or 15 employees from certain regulations, so as to avoid imposing a financial burden on the owner of a very small business.

In this book, primary attention is given to businesses that meet the following criteria:

1. Financing of the business is supplied by one individual or a small group of individuals. Only in rare cases does the business have more than 15 owners.
2. Except for its marketing function, the business's operations are geographically localized.
3. Compared to the biggest firms in the industry, the business is small.
4. The number of employees in the business is usually fewer than 100.

Obviously, some small firms fail to meet all of the above standards. For example, a small executive search firm—a firm that helps corporate clients recruit managers from other organizations—may operate in many sections of the country and thereby fail to meet the second criterion. Nevertheless, the discussion of management concepts in this book is aimed primarily at the type of firm that fits the general pattern outlined by these criteria.

Thus, small businesses include tiny one-person firms—the kind you may decide to start. They also include small firms that have up to 100 employees. In most cases, however, they are drastically different in their structure and operations from the huge corporations that are generally featured in the business media.

The Payoff of Entrepreneurship

Identify three motivators or rewards of entrepreneurial careers.

What might cause you to think about operating your own business? Individuals are *pulled* toward entrepreneurship by a number of powerful incentives (see Figure 1-2). Some are especially attracted by one particular incentive, while others are drawn to entrepreneurship by a blend of potential rewards. These rewards may be grouped into three basic categories: profit, independence, and personal fulfillment.

Make Money (Profit)

Like any other job or career, entrepreneurship provides for one's financial needs. Starting one's own business is a way to earn money. Indeed, some entrepreneurs

FIGURE 1-2

Entrepreneurial Incentives

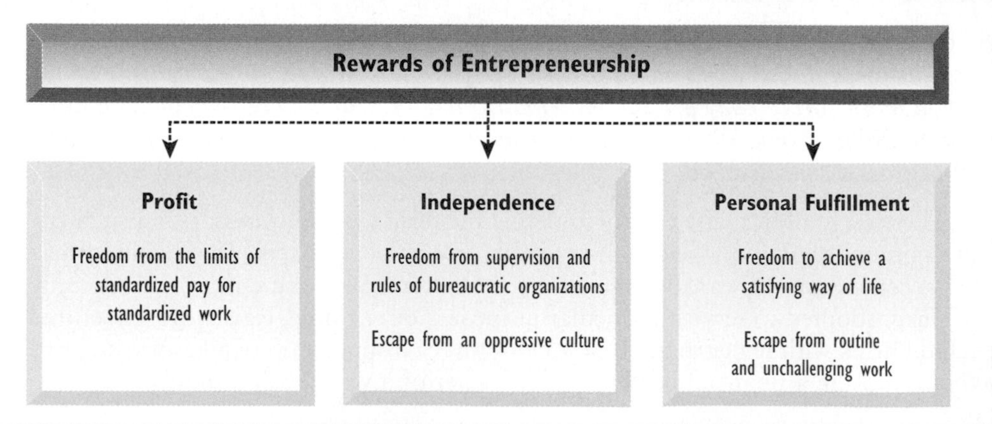

earn lots of money. In *The Millionaire Next Door,* Stanley and Danko conclude that self-employed people are four times more likely to be millionaires than are those who work for others.[12] The profit motive, then, is one reason, although not the only reason, for operating one's own business.

The financial return of any business must compensate its owner for investing personal time (a salary equivalent) and personal savings (an interest and/or dividend equivalent) before any true profits are realized. Entrepreneurs should expect a return that will not only compensate them for the time and money they invest but also reward them well for the risks and initiative they take in operating their own businesses. Indeed, some profit is necessary for a firm's survival.

Some entrepreneurs, no doubt, are highly motivated by the prospect of profits. They have heard the stories about young people who launched dot.com companies and quickly became multimillionaires. Seemingly, there are big bucks out there for those with innovative ideas, provided the business is economically viable.

Most startups, however, involve entrepreneurs with more modest expectations. For some, profits are a way of "keeping score." Such entrepreneurs may spend the money they make on themselves or give it away, but most are satisfied with what they consider to be a reasonable profit.

Be Your Own Boss (Independence)

Freedom to operate independently is another reward of entrepreneurship. Its importance is evidenced by results of a survey of small business owners.[13] Thirty-eight percent of those who had left jobs at other companies said their main reason for leaving was that they wanted to be their own boss. Like these entrepreneurs, many people have a strong desire to make their own decisions, take risks, and reap the rewards. Being one's own boss seems an attractive ideal.

The smallest businesses (i.e., part-time businesses and one-person firms), of which there are millions in the United States, probably offer the greatest flexibility to entrepreneurs. Many are the type of business that can hang a "Gone Fishing" (or the equivalent) sign on the door when the entrepreneur feels the urge to engage in nonbusiness activities.

Obviously, most entrepreneurs don't carry their quest for flexibility to such lengths. But entrepreneurs in general appreciate the independence inherent in their chosen careers. They can do things their own way, reap their own profits, and set their own schedules.

Of course, independence does not guarantee an easy life. Most entrepreneurs work very hard for long hours. But they do have the satisfaction of making their own decisions within the constraints imposed by economic and other environmental factors, including undesirable working conditions.

Some people, at various ages, enter entrepreneurship in order to escape a bad situation. As an escape hatch, then, entrepreneurship provides independence for such people, whom Professor Russell M. Knight of the University of Western Ontario has labeled **refugees.**[14] Knight has identified a number of factors that serve as external motivators for refugees. Some individuals, for example, emigrate to escape the political, religious, or economic constraints of their homeland. Frequently, such **foreign refugees** face discrimination when seeking salaried employment in the new country. As a result, many of them go into business for themselves.

refugee
a person who becomes an entrepreneur to escape an undesirable situation

foreign refugee
a person who leaves her or his native country and becomes an entrepreneur in a new country

Living in a Diverse World

IN THE TRENCHES

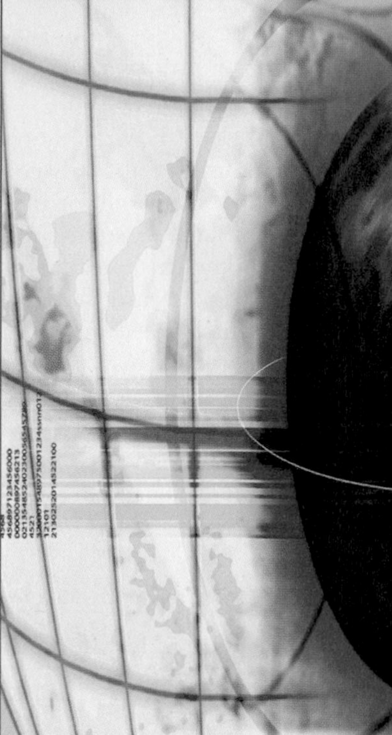

FOREIGN REFUGEES BECOME GLOBAL ENTREPRENEURS

To escape a bad situation (or take advantage of a good one), some emigrants (foreign refugees) become entrepreneurs in the United States.

The entrepreneurial, creative spark is probably randomly distributed around the world. But opportunities for that spark to burst into flame are not evenly distributed.

The same tinder that is available to native entrepreneurs here is available as well to foreign entrepreneurs who come here—which explains why so many of them do and explains why there are now 22 foreign-born people on the Forbes 400. For example: John Kluge from Germany, George Soros from Hungary, David Sun from Taiwan, John Tu from China, Charles Wang from China (see photo), Fayez Sarofim from Egypt and Michel Fribourg from Belgium.

Together these entrepreneurs have accumulated net assets worth some $39 billion. In one generation. In no other country in the world can you find immigrants making such strides.

Just as the chance for cheap farmland once attracted to America the hardiest and most ambitious among Europe's poor peasants, so do entrepreneurial opportunities now attract here many of the best entrepreneurs from other societies. Their continuous flow—the self-selection of vital talents from around the world—enriches an already healthy supply of home-bred talent.

Source: Reuven Brenner, "Land of Opportunity," *Forbes 400,* Vol. 162, No. 8 (October 12, 1998), pp. 66–68.

corporate refugee
a person who leaves big business to go into business for himself or herself

Individuals who flee the bureaucratic environment of large (or even medium-size) firms by going into business for themselves are identified by Knight as **corporate refugees.** Employees of large corporations often find the corporate atmosphere and/or the relocations required by their jobs to be confining and undesirable. Entrepreneurship provides an attractive alternative for many such individuals.

Knight identified five additional types of refugees:

- The *parental (paternal) refugee,* who leaves a family business to show the parent that "I can do it alone"
- The *feminist refugee,* who experiences discrimination and elects to start a firm in which she can operate independently without the interference of male co-workers
- The *housewife refugee,* who starts her own business after her children are grown or at some other point when she can free herself from household responsibilities
- The *society refugee,* who senses some alienation from the prevailing culture and expresses it through such entrepreneurial activity as a soil conservation business or an energy-saving business
- The *educational refugee,* who tires of academia and decides to go into business

Enjoy a Satisfying Life (Personal Fulfillment)

Entrepreneurs frequently speak of the satisfaction they experience in their own businesses; some even refer to their work as fun. Part of their enjoyment may derive from their independence, but some of it reflects an owner's personal fulfillment in working with the firm's products and services—the pleasure, for example, that a ski shop operator gets from talking to other skiers about the sport and equipment related to it. An entrepreneur may also enjoy being the boss, attending Rotary Club, and serving as a civic leader in the community.

The role of entrepreneur in even a one-person business can often bring to an individual a sense of dignity or significance that makes life worth living. Lynn Cabral operates a hot dog stand along a bike trail in Arlington, Massachusetts.[15] In 1993, a car accident left her permanently disabled and ended her career as producer for a cable channel in Boston. Even though she wears a leg brace from hip to toe and walks with a cane, she opened her snack cart business in 1998.

"Before this I spent about 90% of my mental energy trying to deal with chronic pain," says Cabral, whose disability once kept her from going out in public. "People used to point and say, 'There's the girl with the bad leg.' Now it's, 'There's the hot dog lady.' That's a big change."[16]

The reward, then, may derive from a pleasurable activity, from enjoyable associations, from respect in the community, or from some other aspect of the business. For many entrepreneurs, the life satisfaction they receive is much more important than money or independence.

THE MANY VARIETIES OF ENTREPRENEURSHIP

5

Describe the various types of entrepreneurs and entrepreneurial ventures.

Entrepreneurship is marked by diversity—that is, there is great variety in the people and the firms termed entrepreneurial. As a potential entrepreneur, you can be encouraged by the diversity embodied in the dissimilarities between founder entrepreneurs and administrative entrepreneurs or between artisan entrepreneurs and opportunistic entrepreneurs.

Founder Entrepreneurs Versus Administrative Entrepreneurs and Franchisees

founder
an entrepreneur who brings a new firm into existence

Generally considered to be "pure" entrepreneurs, **founders** may be inventors who initiate businesses on the basis of new or improved products or services. They may also be artisans who develop skills and then start their own firms. Or they may be enterprising individuals, often with marketing backgrounds, who draw on the ideas of others in starting new firms. Whether acting as individuals or as part of a group, founders bring firms into existence by surveying the market, raising funds, and arranging for the necessary facilities. The process of starting an entirely new business is discussed in detail in Chapter 5.

administrative entrepreneur
an entrepreneur who oversees the operation of an ongoing business

At some point after a new firm is established, it may be purchased or taken over by a second-generation family member or another entrepreneur who acts as administrator of the business. Thus, we recognize another group of entrepreneurs called **administrative entrepreneurs,** who preside over the operation of successful ongoing business firms. The distinction between founders and administrators is often hazy. In some cases, well-established small firms grow rapidly, and the entrepreneur's

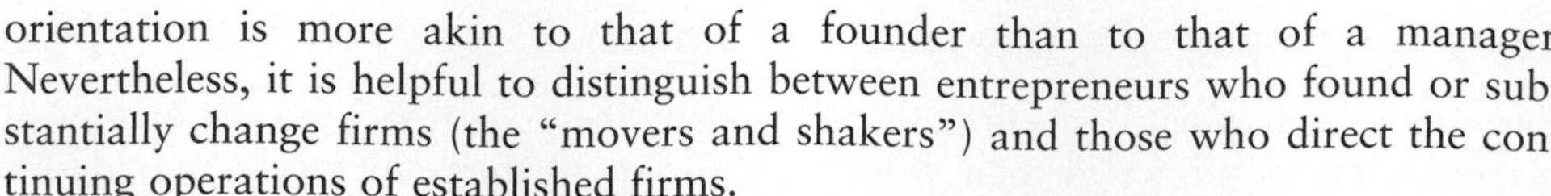

orientation is more akin to that of a founder than to that of a manager. Nevertheless, it is helpful to distinguish between entrepreneurs who found or substantially change firms (the "movers and shakers") and those who direct the continuing operations of established firms.

franchisee
an entrepreneur whose power is limited by a contractual relationship with a franchising organization

Another category of entrepreneurs comprises franchisees. **Franchisees** differ from administrative entrepreneurs in the degree of their independence. Because of the constraints and guidance provided by contractual relationships with franchising organizations, franchisees function as limited entrepreneurs. Chapter 6 presents more information about franchisees.

High-Potential Ventures Versus Attractive Small Firms and Microbusinesses

high-potential venture (gazelle)
a small firm that has great prospects for growth

Small business ventures differ greatly in their potential for growth and profits. Some create millionaires, while others produce much less spectacular results. Fast-track entrepreneurs are those with the brightest prospects. A few businesses have such glowing prospects for growth that they are called **high-potential ventures,** or **gazelles.** Even within this group, there is variation in styles of operation and approaches to growth. Some are high-tech startups—the kind that have made Silicon Valley in California famous. The success stories have often featured a technology wizard with a bright idea, backed by venture capitalists eager to underwrite the next Microsoft. When such companies prosper, they usually grow at blinding speed and make their founders wealthy by being sold or going public.

Other high-potential ventures are privately held and grow in a less spectacular fashion. They begin with a much smaller initial capital investment and remain under private ownership. These less noticeable, privately held companies also provide opportunities for people to get ahead, while creating jobs and helping the economy. And some get ahead very well indeed! Wendell Murphy of Warsaw, North Carolina has become a billionaire as a pig farmer.[17] By using a systemized management approach, he developed a successful agricultural business, which now has 275,000 sows and 6,000,000 hogs at various stages between birth and the packing house.

attractive small firm
a small firm that provides substantial profits to its owner

In contrast to high-potential ventures, **attractive small firms** offer substantial financial rewards for their owners. Entrepreneurial income from these ventures easily may range from \$100,000 to \$300,000 or more annually. They represent a strong segment of small businesses—solid, healthy firms that can provide rewarding careers.

microbusiness
a small firm that provides minimal profits to its owner

The least profitable types of firms, including many service firms such as dry cleaners, beauty shops, gas stations, and appliance repair shops, provide only very modest returns to their owners. They are called **microbusinesses,** and their distinguishing feature is their limited ability to generate significant profits. Entrepreneurs who devote personal effort to such ventures receive a profit return that does little more than compensate them for their time. Part-time businesses typically fall into the category of microbusinesses.

Plural Entrepreneurs

entrepreneurial team
two or more people who work together as entrepreneurs

Our discussion thus far has focused on entrepreneurs who function as individuals, each with his or her own firm. And this is usually the case. However, entrepreneurial teams are becoming increasingly common, particularly in ventures of substantial size. An **entrepreneurial team** consists of two or more individuals who combine their

efforts to function in the capacity of entrepreneurs. In this way, the talents, skills, and resources of two or more entrepreneurs can be concentrated on one endeavor.

Artisan Versus Opportunistic Entrepreneurs

Because of their varied backgrounds, entrepreneurs display differences in the degree of professionalism and in the management styles they bring to their businesses. The ways in which they analyze problems and approach decision making may differ radically. Norman R. Smith has suggested two basic entrepreneurial patterns, exemplified by artisan (or craftsman) entrepreneurs and opportunistic entrepreneurs.[18]

According to Smith, the education of the **artisan entrepreneur** is limited to technical training. Such entrepreneurs have technical job experience, but they typically lack good communication skills and managerial training. Artisan entrepreneurs' approach to business decision making is often characterized by the following features:

artisan entrepreneur
a person with primarily technical skills and little business knowledge who starts a business

- They are paternalistic—they guide their businesses much as they might guide their own families.
- They are reluctant to delegate authority.
- They use few (usually only one or two) capital sources to create their firms.
- They define marketing strategy in terms of the traditional components of price, quality, and company reputation.
- Their sales efforts are primarily personal.
- Their time orientation is short, with little planning for future growth or change.

A mechanic who starts an independent garage and a beautician who operates a beauty shop are examples of artisan entrepreneurs.

IN THE TRENCHES ENTREPRENEURSHIP TODAY

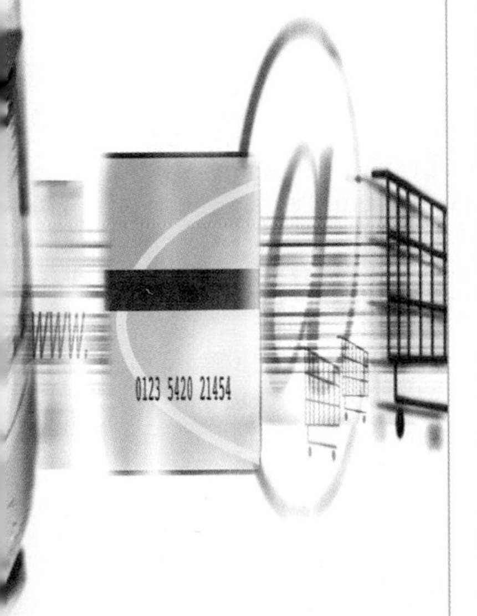

AN ARTISAN BECOMES A FASHION DESIGNER

Adrienne Landau exemplifies both the woman entrepreneur and the artisan entrepreneur. Granted, she is a notch or two above an auto mechanic in her role as an artisan entrepreneur. Even so, she started a business based on her artistic talents in an industry where she lacked experience.

Landau, 52, was a painter and stumbled into her business while trying to barter some artwork for a coat. The business began as she obtained scraps of material and designed purses with the scraps. Her product line grew to include scarves, wraps, and other accessories.

The deficiencies in her business experience quickly became apparent. She soon learned, the hard way, that cash flow must be monitored and that careful assessment is needed in hiring personnel. Through difficult learning experiences, she gradually acquired some business expertise to supplement her artistic abilities.

In the early days of her business, Landau lost money, but profits appeared as revenues later grew to $6 million. Her products have been well received and have been worn by such customers as Nancy Reagan and Elizabeth Taylor.

Source: Richard C. Morais, "An Artisan Discovers Cash Flow," *Forbes*, Vol. 164, No. 10 (October 18, 1999), pp. 150–152.

opportunistic entrepreneur
a person with both sophisticated managerial skills and technical knowledge who starts a business

In contrast to the artisan entrepreneur, an **opportunistic entrepreneur** is one who has supplemented his or her technical education by studying such nontechnical subjects as economics, law, or English. Opportunistic entrepreneurs avoid paternalism, delegate authority as necessary for growth, employ various marketing strategies and types of sales efforts, obtain original capitalization from more than two sources, and plan for future growth. An example of an opportunistic entrepreneur is a small building contractor and developer who adopts a relatively sophisticated approach to management, including careful record keeping and budgeting, precise bidding, and systematic marketing research.

Smith's model of entrepreneurial styles illustrates two extremes: At one end is a craftsperson in an entrepreneurial position, and at the other end is a well-educated and experienced manager. The former "flies by the seat of the pants," and the latter uses systematic management procedures and something resembling a scientific approach. In practice, of course, the distribution of entrepreneurial styles is less polarized than that suggested by Smith's model, with entrepreneurs scattered along a continuum of managerial sophistication. This book is intended to help you move toward the opportunistic and away from the artisan end of the continuum.

Women Entrepreneurs

Although entrepreneurship and business in general have been male dominated for decades, the scene is rapidly changing. There are now about 9.1 million businesses owned by women, representing 38% of all firms in the United States. Since 1992, the number of people employed nationwide by female-owned firms has grown 108%.[19]

http://www.cindyrowe.com

Women are not only starting more businesses than they did previously but also establishing them in nontraditional industries, with ambitious plans for growth and profit. Not too many years ago, female entrepreneurs confined themselves, for the most part, to operating beauty shops, small clothing stores, and other establishments catering especially to women. Though most startups by women are still focused on providing services, women's ownership of construction firms and similar businesses is growing rapidly.

Cindy Rowe-Taylor, who launched Cindy Rowe Auto Glass in Harrisburg, Pennsylvania, is an example of a woman entrepreneur in a nontraditional field.[20] A registered nurse, she left her profession in 1980 to start repairing dings in car windshields. She attended a school in Minneapolis where she learned to repair windshields and then launched her business from the trunk of a Chevrolet Vega.

"A part of me said, 'You're crazy,'" says Rowe-Taylor, 52. "But I wanted to do something different on my own. Every time I fixed a windshield, it felt like a little success."[21]

The daughter of a surgeon, Rowe-Taylor was more familiar with operating rooms than with operating profits. However, she recognized that there was no glass ceiling in the windshield repair business, although her father was at first disappointed with her choice. Today, this over $7 million enterprise repairs or replaces more than 40,000 windshields a year at 10 locations in central Pennsylvania.

Female entrepreneurs obviously face problems common to all entrepreneurs. However, they must also contend with difficulties associated with their newness in entrepreneurial roles. Lack of access to credit has been a frequent problem for women who enter business. This is a troublesome area for most small business owners, but women often carry the added burden of discrimination. Loan officers point out that many times female applicants lack a track record in financial management and argue that this is what creates problems in loan approval. Women entrepreneurs have found, however, that some male loan officers still have stereotypical ideas of what women can accomplish.

Another barrier for some women is the limited opportunity they find for business relationships with others in similar positions. It takes time and effort to gain full acceptance and to develop informal relationships with others in local, mostly male, business and professional groups. Women are dealing with this problem by increasing their participation in predominantly male organizations and also by forming networks of their own—the female equivalent of the "old boy network."

Competitive Advantages of Entrepreneurial Firms

Identify ways to gain a potential competitive edge for small entrepreneurial firms.

Small entrepreneurial firms need not be weaklings. Indeed, a look at the structure of the U.S. business community reveals small, entrepreneurial businesses to be a robust part of the total economy. The important role of small firms is documented by the research of David Birch, president of Cognetics Inc., an economics research firm in Cambridge, Massachusetts, who has argued persuasively that almost all new jobs in the United States are created in small businesses.[22]

How is it that small and entrepreneurial firms can hold their own and often gain an edge over successful, more powerful businesses? The answer lies in the ability of new and smaller firms to exploit opportunities.

In this overview, we'll take a look at some areas in which new firms can gain a competitive edge. In Chapter 2, we will define the term *competitive advantage* and discuss specific strategies for capturing business opportunities.

Customer Focus

Business opportunities exist for those who can produce products and services desired by customers. If a business can make its product or service especially attractive, its prospects will brighten considerably.

Good customer service can be provided by a business of any size, of course. However, small firms have a greater potential than larger businesses do for achieving this goal. If properly managed, small entrepreneurial firms have the advantage of being able to serve customers directly and effectively, without struggling through layers of bureaucracy or breaking corporate policies that tend to stifle employee initiative. In many cases, customers are personally acquainted with the entrepreneur and other key people in the small business.

The first step toward creating customer satisfaction and getting customer loyalty is to earn it. Michael Barrier offers a simple explanation of the process:

In large part, cultivating customer loyalty means doing what good businesses always do—meeting customer needs—but with a shift of emphasis away from sales and marketing, in particular, and toward customer service.[23]

Not all small firms manage to excel in customer service, but many realize their potential for doing so. Having a smaller number of customers and a close relationship with those customers makes customer service a powerful tool for entrepreneurial businesses. For further discussion of this subject, see Chapter 15, Customer Loyalty, Product, and Distribution Strategies.

Quality Performance

There is no reason that a small business needs to take a back seat in achieving quality in operations. Many small firms, for example, have applied for the distinguished Baldrige National Quality Award, a process that involves developing quality programs and undergoing detailed examination of these programs. Some outstanding businesses have been granted this recognition.

In service businesses, quality performance is closely linked to customer service. Think of your favorite restaurant, for example. What distinguishes it from other dining places? It may be the atmosphere, the freshness and taste of the food, or the attentiveness of servers who are quickly aware of your needs and who promptly refill your beverage glass or coffee cup. These elements of dining quality can be found in a very small restaurant. In fact, the owner of a small establishment can insist on high levels of quality without experiencing the frustration of a large-company CEO who may have to push a quality philosophy through many layers of bureaucracy.

Many small firms excel in performing quality work, whether it is in auto repair, hair styling, financial audits, candy production, computer services, or clothing retailing. In quality management, entrepreneurial firms have a tool that enables them to compete effectively, not only with their peers but also with large corporations.

BUILDING CUSTOMER LOYALTY

IN THE TRENCHES

A SMALL OFFICE SUPPLY STORE COMPETES WITH SUPERSTORES

Providing good customer service is an important tool of small firms in meeting the challenge of giant retailers. Business as Usual, a 1,500-square-foot office supply store in Ketchum, Idaho, must compete with national office supply chains in Twin Falls, 70 miles away, and also with online sellers. Owner Bradford Roos usually meets or beats the prices charged by his competitors.

How does he do it? By linking up with United Stationers, the largest office products wholesaler in the country.

[Roos] can tap into an inventory of 35,000 United Stationers products from more than 500 manufacturers—from a single Bic pen to a 325-pound fireproof safe, and all kinds of computer ware in between. "I order something by 4 p.m., and it gets here the next day," Roos says. "I'm in the boonies. That's fantastic." Even better, he can ask United Stationers to pack the order with his return label and ship it directly from one of 66 distribution centers to his customer. "It looks like I warehoused it and sent it, but I never touched it."

By purchasing effectively, this ingenious entrepreneur has found a way to remain competitive even in the age of big-box retailers and the Internet.

Source: Ashlea Ebeling, "Paper Tiger," *Forbes*, Vol. 165, No. 4 (February 21, 2000), pp. 71–74.

Integrity and Responsibility

The future is particularly bright for firms that add to excellent product quality and good customer service a solid reputation for honesty and dependability. Customers respond to evidence of integrity because they are aware of ethical issues. Experience has taught them that advertising claims are sometimes not accurate, that the fine print in contracts is sometimes detrimental to their best interests, and that businesses sometimes fail to stand behind their work.

A small business that is consistently ethical in its relationships can earn the loyalty of a skeptical public. For example, consider the case of a small diesel-engine service business that performed a major overhaul on an engine for a large construction company. Such an overhaul is expensive, generally costing from $20,000 to $25,000. Soon after the initial overhaul, the engine malfunctioned again. At considerable expense to itself, the small business performed the necessary repair work at no additional charge. The customer was so impressed with this firm's dependability that it often sends equipment more than 200 miles, past other repair centers, to the firm that demonstrated trustworthiness in a very practical way. A major customer was won through quality work and integrity in customer relationships.

Innovation

One might think that large companies would be the primary source of important inventions, but that isn't necessarily true. Many entrepreneurs are innovators, who see different and better ways of doing things. On the basis of several studies by the U.S. Department of Commerce, Jeffrey A. Timmons suggested that 50 percent of all innovations and 94 percent of all radical innovations since World War II have come from new small firms. Timmons provided as examples the microcomputer, the pacemaker, overnight express delivery, the quick oil change, fast food, and oral contraceptives.[24]

Research departments of big businesses tend to emphasize the improvement of existing products. Creative ideas may be sidetracked because they are not related to existing products or because they are unusual. Unfortunately, preoccupation with an existing product can sometimes obscure the value of a new idea. The jet engine, for example, had difficulty winning the attention of those who were accustomed to internal combustion engines.

Entrepreneurs can compete with firms of all sizes through the use of innovative methods. Such innovations include not only new products but also new ways of doing business.

Low-Cost Production

In many industries—auto manufacturing, for example—large corporations are the low-cost producers. However, big business does not always have the advantage of lower operating costs.

In many situations, small firms can find ways to operate that give them a cost advantage. As a simple example, think of a retail business firm that serves the local community in a very small town. Wal-Mart is not a threat, because Wal-Mart requires a larger minimum customer base than exists in a remote location.

Getting Started

7 *Discuss factors related to readiness for entrepreneurship and getting started in an entrepreneurial career.*

Starting any type of business career is exciting. Launching one's own business, however, can be absolutely breathtaking because of the extreme risk and great potential in such a venture. Let's think for a moment about some special concerns of individuals who are ready to get their feet wet in entrepreneurial waters.

Age and Entrepreneurial Opportunity

One practical question is, What is the right age to become an entrepreneur? As you might guess, there is no simple answer to this question. Most businesses require some background knowledge. In addition, most prospective entrepreneurs must first build their financial resources in order to make the necessary initial investments. A certain amount of time is usually required, therefore, to gain education, experience, and financial resources.

Though there are no hard-and-fast rules concerning the right age for starting a business, some age deterrents do exist. As Figure 1-3 shows, young people are discouraged from entering entrepreneurial careers by inadequacies in their preparation and resources. On the other hand, older people develop family, financial, and job commitments that make entrepreneurship seem too risky; they may have acquired interests in retirement programs or achieved promotions to positions of greater responsibility and higher salaries.

The ideal time for entrepreneurship, then, appears to lie somewhere between the mid-20s and the mid-30s, when there is a balance between preparatory experiences on the one hand and family obligations on the other. Research conducted by Paul Reynolds shows that the highest percentage of startups is in the 25- to 35-year age group.[25] Obviously, there are exceptions to this generalization: Some teenagers start their own firms, some 50- or 60-year-olds walk away from successful careers in big business when they become excited by the prospects of entrepreneurship.

One teenage entrepreneur, Jayson Meyer of Daytona Beach, Florida, went into home schooling at the age of 15 so that he could manage the growth of his business.[26] By the time he was 16, Meyer had graduated from high school. His firm, Meyer Technologies, Inc., got its start building business computer systems from a

http://www.meyertechnologies.com

FIGURE 1-3

Age Concerns in Starting a Business

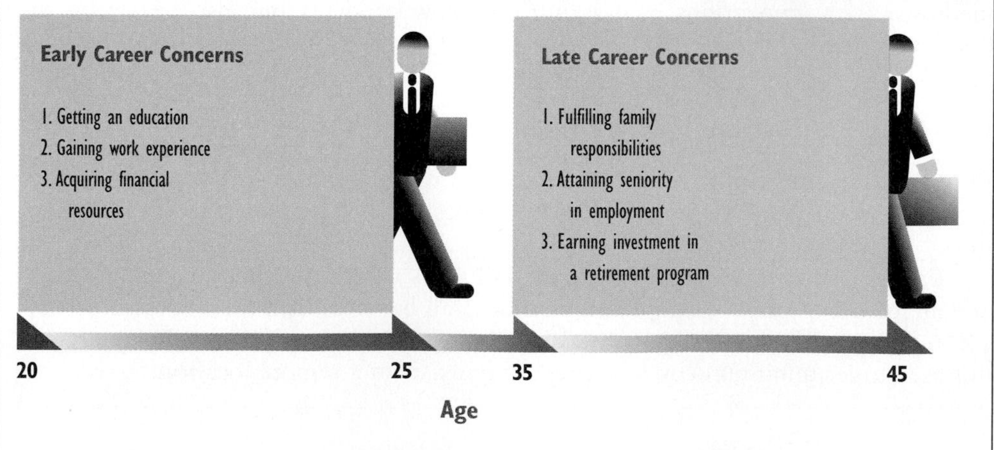

booth in the Daytona Beach flea market; it now develops online software for various vertical markets. In 1997, the business's revenue was $4,000; in 2001, it had reached $1.5 million! Meyer's explanation for his entrepreneurial success: "Anything is possible when you set your mind to it."[27]

Characteristics of Successful Entrepreneurs

What kinds of people become successful entrepreneurs? It is not surprising that no well-defined entrepreneurial profile exists. Individual entrepreneurs differ greatly from each other. This should give you encouragement if you wish to start your own business; you do not need to fit some prescribed stereotype.

Some qualities are common, however, among entrepreneurs and probably contribute to their success. One of these characteristics is a strong commitment to or passion for the business. It is an attitude that results in tenacity in the face of difficulty and a willingness to work hard. These entrepreneurs do not give up easily.

Such individuals are typically confident of their ability to meet the challenges confronting them. This factor of self-confidence was described by psychologist J. B. Rotter as an **internal locus of control**—a feeling that success depends on one's own efforts.[28] In contrast, an **external locus of control** reflects an attitude of dependence on luck or fate for success. Though an extreme degree of self-confidence can lead to a destructive egotism that negatively affects the business, reasonable self-reliance and a passion for the work are factors that contribute to success.

internal locus of control
a belief that one's success depends on one's own efforts

external locus of control
a belief that one's life is controlled more by luck or fate than by one's own efforts

Entrepreneurs are also portrayed as risk takers. Certainly, they do assume risk. By investing their own money, they assume financial risk. If they leave secure jobs, they risk their careers. The stress and time required to start and run a business may place their families at risk. By identifying closely with a new venture, they may also assume psychic risk as they face the possibility of failure. Even though entrepreneurs assume risk, they are what we might term moderate risk takers—accepting risks over which they have some control—rather than extreme risk takers, who accept outcomes depending purely on chance.

Growing and Managing the Business

An airplane pilot not only controls the plane during takeoff but also flies it and lands it. Similarly, entrepreneurs not only launch firms but also "fly" them; that is, they manage their firm's subsequent operation. In this book, you will find a discussion of the entire entrepreneurial process, including strategy, business startup and operations, and even life after entrepreneurship.

- *Part 2, Entrepreneurial Strategy (Chapters 2–4).* These chapters discuss the basic issues relative to a firm's choice of products, types of service, and market segments. Decisions regarding these important topics are referred to as entrepreneurial strategy. The discussion includes consideration of today's e-commerce world and international business.

- *Part 3, Pursuing New Venture Opportunities (Chapters 5–7).* By following any one of the various routes to entrepreneurship described in these chapters, an individual can become an independent business owner. As noted earlier, the term *entrepreneur* is sometimes restricted to those who build entirely new businesses, in which case the only real entrepreneurial career opportunity is starting a new firm. When the concept is broadened to include various independent business options, launching an entirely new business becomes one of four alternatives: (1) buying an existing business, (2) starting a new business, (3) opening a franchised business, or (4) entering a family business.
- *Part 4, The New Venture Business Plan (Chapters 8–14).* The safest way of starting a business is to first create a business plan. These chapters explain how to prepare a plan that deals with marketing, human resources, financing, and other critical elements. Exit strategies are also discussed.
- *Part 5, Small Business Marketing (Chapters 15–17).* As a going concern, a business is vitally concerned with marketing and its relationships with customers. These chapters deal with decisions concerning pricing, credit extension, advertising, and other aspects of the interface between the firm and its customers.
- *Part 6, Small Business Management (Chapters 18–21).* Managers of going concerns must act as decision makers in various areas of business operations. They must, for example, decide whom to hire and how much to pay in salaries. They must direct the operating system of the firm and make choices based on ethical values. These chapters discuss the full range of issues involved in a firm's managerial process.
- *Part 7, Financial Management in the Entrepreneurial Firm (Chapters 22–24).* This section of the book explains some of the ongoing financial realities of every entrepreneurial business. Each entrepreneur, for example, faces the sobering task of meeting the company payroll—that is, having enough dollars in the bank on pay day. Questions of cash flow, working capital management, and risk management are featured.
- *Epilogue, Visualizing the End: What's Next?* The final stage in the life of a business is somewhat comparable to landing a plane. For a landing to be good, the pilot must be able to walk away from the plane. Similarly, the entrepreneur should at some point be able to walk away from the business. In the epilogue, therefore, we discuss life after entrepreneurship and the planning needed for a successful "landing."

Taking the Plunge

precipitating event
an event, such as losing a job, that moves an individual to become an entrepreneur

In starting a business, there comes a point at which the entrepreneur must "take the plunge." It may be scary because of the risks, but entrepreneurship is not for the fearful. For many people, the right time for beginning a business is hastened by some special circumstance, described as a **precipitating event.** The individual may be fired, for example, or discover an unusual opportunity with strong potential.

Criticizing management has the potential for creating change—especially in the life of the critic! Consequently, it can lead to a precipitating event. Dave and Annette King, a husband-and-wife team, were avid weekend players of slow-pitch softball.[29] While playing in a tournament in a small Colorado town, they made critical com-

ments about the poor management of the event. The event manager asked them to leave and told them that if they thought they could do it better, they should try it. This was their precipitating event. The Kings' response was to do just that by creating Triple Crown Sports, and today they profitably run approximately 400 events a year in softball, baseball, soccer, and basketball.

http://www.triplecrownsports.com

Many other types of experiences also serve as catalysts, hastening the plunge into entrepreneurship. Some individuals become refugees, disenchanted with formal academic programs or exasperated with rebuffs or perceived injustices at the hands of superiors in large organizations. In a more positive vein, other entrepreneurs unexpectedly stumble on business opportunities.

It is difficult to say what proportion of new entrepreneurs actually make their move because of some particular event. Whether propelled by a precipitating event or not, all who wish to enter the world of independent business ownership must eventually summon their courage and take the plunge.

LOOKING BACK

1 Discuss the availability of entrepreneurial opportunities and give examples of successful businesses started by entrepreneurs.

- An entrepreneurial opportunity is a desirable and timely innovation that creates value for interested buyers and end users.
- Exciting entrepreneurial opportunities exist for those who recognize them.
- Marketplace Holdings, Auntie Anne's, and Roto Zip Tool Corporation are examples of highly successful businesses started by entrepreneurs.

2 Explain the entrepreneurial challenges presented by e-commerce and global changes.

- The rapid growth of e-commerce and computer-based technology provides both challenges and opportunities for small entrepreneurial firms.
- As the marketplace becomes increasingly global in scope, entrepreneurial firms find opportunities to do business abroad and also experience competition from distant competitors.

3 Explain the nature of entrepreneurship and how it is related to small business.

- Entrepreneurs are individuals who discover market needs and launch new firms to meet those needs.
- Owner-managers who buy out founders of existing firms, franchisees, and second-generation operators of family firms may also be considered entrepreneurs.
- Definitions of small business are arbitrary, but this book focuses on firms of fewer than 100 employees that have mostly localized operations and are financed by a small number of owners.
- Most entrepreneurial firms are small when they begin, but a few quickly grow into large businesses.

4 Identify three motivators or rewards of entrepreneurial careers.

- Entrepreneurial rewards include profit, independence, and personal fulfillment.
- Entrepreneurs who are escaping a bad situation are sometimes called refugees.

5 Describe the various types of entrepreneurs and entrepreneurial ventures.

- Founders of firms are "pure" entrepreneurs, but administrators or franchisees may also be considered entrepreneurs.
- A few fast-track entrepreneurs start high-potential ventures (gazelles); other entrepreneurs operate attractive small firms and microbusinesses.
- Plural entrepreneurs are teams of two or more individuals who combine their efforts to function as entrepreneurs.
- Based on their backgrounds and management styles, entrepreneurs may be characterized as artisan entrepreneurs or opportunistic entrepreneurs.

- The number of women entrepreneurs is growing rapidly, and they are entering many nontraditional fields.

6 Identify ways to gain a potential competitive edge for small entrepreneurial firms.

- Entrepreneurial managers have an opportunity to know their customers well and to focus on meeting their needs.
- By emphasizing quality in products and services, small firms can build a competitive advantage.
- Independent business owners can build an internal culture based on integrity and responsibility in relationships both inside and outside the firm, and such a culture will give a firm strength in a competitive environment.
- Many small firms and individual operators have demonstrated a superior talent for finding innovative products and developing better ways of doing business.
- Small firms that find a way to become the low-cost producer gain a competitive advantage.

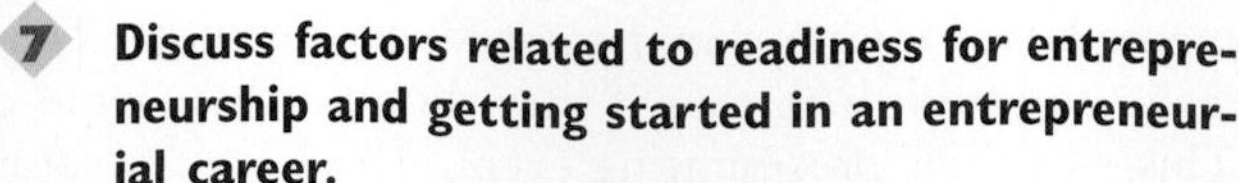

7 Discuss factors related to readiness for entrepreneurship and getting started in an entrepreneurial career.

- The period between the mid-20s and mid-30s appears to be when a person's education, work experience, and financial resources are most likely to enable him or her to become an entrepreneur.
- There is no well-defined entrepreneurial profile, but many entrepreneurs have such helpful characteristics as a passion for their business, strong self-confidence, and a willingness to assume moderate risks.
- Routes to entrepreneurship include entering a family business, opening a franchise, starting a new business, and buying an existing business.
- Once a business is launched, the entrepreneur must manage growth of the business and issues related to its ongoing operation.
- Entry into entrepreneurial careers is often triggered by a precipitating event, such as losing a job.

Key Terms

entrepreneurial opportunity, p. 4
entrepreneur, p. 8
refugee, p. 11
foreign refugee, p. 11
corporate refugee, p. 12
founder, p. 13
administrative entrepreneur, p. 13
franchisee, p. 14
high-potential venture (gazelle), p. 14
attractive small firm, p. 14
microbusiness, p. 14
entrepreneurial team, p. 14
artisan entrepreneur, p. 15
opportunistic entrepreneur, p. 16
internal locus of control, p. 21
external locus of control, p. 21
precipitating event, p. 22

Discussion Questions

1. The outstanding success stories at the beginning of the chapter are exceptions to the rule. What, then, is their significance in illustrating entrepreneurial opportunity? Are these stories misleading?
2. What is meant by the term *entrepreneur?*
3. Consider an entrepreneur you know personally. What was the most significant reason for his or her deciding to follow an independent business career? If you don't already know the reason, discuss it with that person.
4. The rewards of profit, independence, and personal fulfillment attract individuals to entrepreneurial careers. What problems might be anticipated if an entrepreneur were to become obsessed with one of these rewards—that is, have an excessive desire for profit, independence, or a particular lifestyle?
5. What is the advantage of using an entrepreneurial team?
6. Distinguish between an artisan entrepreneur and an opportunistic entrepreneur.
7. Explain how customer focus and innovation can be special strengths of small businesses.
8. Why is the period from the mid-20s to the mid-30s considered to be the best time in life for becoming an entrepreneur?
9. Explain the term *internal locus of control* and its significance for entrepreneurship.
10. What is a precipitating event? Give some examples.

You Make the Call

SITUATION 1

In the following statement, a business owner attempts to explain and justify his preference for slow growth in his business.

I limit my growth pace and make every effort to service my present customers in the manner they deserve. I have some peer pressure to do otherwise by following the advice of experts—that is, to take on partners and debt to facilitate rapid growth in sales and market share. When tempted by such thoughts, I think about what I might gain. Perhaps I could make more money, but I would also expect a lot more problems. Also, I think it might interfere somewhat with my family relationships, which are very important to me.

Question 1 Should this venture be regarded as entrepreneurial? Is the owner a true entrepreneur?

Question 2 Do you agree with the philosophy expressed here? Is the owner really doing what is best for his family?

Question 3 What kinds of problems is this owner trying to avoid?

SITUATION 2

Nineteen-year-old Kiersten Berger, now in her second year at a local community college, has begun to think about starting her own business. She has taken piano lessons since she was seven years old and is regarded as a very good pianist. The thought has occurred to her that she could establish a piano studio and offer lessons to children, young people, and even adults. The prospect sounds more attractive than looking for a salaried job when she graduates in a few months.

Question 1 If Kiersten Berger opens a piano studio, will she be an entrepreneur?

Question 2 Which type of reward(s) will be greatest in this venture?

Question 3 Even though she is an artisan, she will need to make decisions of a business nature. What decisions or evaluations may be especially difficult for her?

SITUATION 3

Dover Sporting Goods Store occupies an unimpressive retail location in a small city in northern Illinois. Started in 1935, it is now operated by Duane Dover—a third-generation member of the founding family. He works long hours trying to earn a reasonable profit in the old downtown area.

Dover's immediate concern is an announcement that Wal-Mart is considering opening a store at the southern edge of town. As Dover reacts to this announcement, he is overwhelmed by a sense of injustice. Why should a family business that has served the community honestly and well for 60 years have to fend off a large corporation that would take big profits out of the community and give very little in return? Surely, he reasoned, the law must offer some kind of protection against big business predators of this kind. Dover also wonders whether small stores such as his have ever been successful in competing against business giants like Wal-Mart.

Question 1 Is Dover's feeling of unfairness justified? Is his business entitled to some type of legal protection against moves of this type?

Question 2 How should Dover plan to compete against Wal-Mart, if and when this becomes necessary?

Experiential Exercises

1. Analyze your own education and experience as qualifications for entrepreneurship. Identify your greatest strengths and weaknesses.
2. Explain your own interest in each type of entrepreneurial reward—profit, independence, and personal fulfillment. Point out which of these is most significant for you personally and tell why.
3. Interview someone who has started a business, being sure to ask for information regarding the entrepreneur's background and age at the time the business was started. In your report of the interview, indicate whether the entrepreneur was in any sense a refugee, and show how the timing of her or his startup relates to the ideal time for startup explained in this chapter.
4. Interview a woman entrepreneur about what problems, if any, she has encountered in her business because she is a woman.

EXPLORING THE WEB

1. Go to the home page for your textbook, *Small Business Management: An Entrepreneurial Emphasis,* at **http://longenecker.swcollege.com**.
   a. Follow the link to Student Resources. List the chapter materials available to students online.
   b. List the learning aids that will assist you in studying.
   c. Under Learning Aids, follow the link under Self Assessments. Then click on the link to Can You Succeed in a Small Business? and take the quiz. Report your score and what your deficiencies probably are.
2. Of the Web sites sponsored by nonprofit or government agencies, the best ones for small businesses are the Kauffman Center's site, the Edward Lowe Foundation's Entrepreneurial Edge, and the Small Business Administration (SBA) site. According to a review by *Inc.* magazine (April 2000), each of these sites has specific strengths you should know about.
   a. Access the Kauffman Center's site at **http://www.entreworld.org**. Print the site map. Under what major categories is this site arranged?
   b. Check out the Entrepreneurial Edge **(http://edge. lowe.org)**. One of the best features is Business Builders, a digital library that *Inc.* says is a "good place to begin research on many startup topics." Choose Browse All, and print the list of topics.
   c. Go to the SBA's site at **http://www.sba.gov**. Under Starting Your Business, select Success Series; then click on Stories and summarize the information provided there about one of the successful startups.
3. Many Web sites offer useful information targeted to women entrepreneurs. One of the best sites is the SBA's Women's Business Center online. You can access the site at **http://www.onlinewbc.org**.
   a. Look under About Us to find some statistics on women's business ownership. Jot them down.
   b. Write down the function of Women's Business Centers and the address of the one nearest you.
   c. Examine the resources listed on the site. Which ones are specific to women business owners?
   d. Also check out **http://www.discoverbusiness.org** for some resources for young female entrepreneurs. In your opinion, what parts of this site are most attractive to young people?
   e. Access *Entrepreneur* magazine's site at **http://www.entrepreneur.com**. Search for "women" and note how many different articles address women's issues. Print one of interest to you.

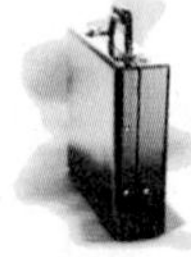

CASE 1

STEVE'S OLYMPIC TEES (p. 637)

This case describes the problems faced by an entrepreneur who saw an opportunity and made the decision to act on it.

Alternative Cases for Chapter 1:

Case 6, "Universal Business Brokers," p. 652
Case 16, "EBC Computers, Inc.," p. 683
Case 19, "Gibson Mortuary," p. 691

part

2

ENTREPRENEURIAL STRATEGY

chapter 2

Strategies That Capture Opportunities

In the VIDEO Spotlight

Record Technology

In this episode of "Small Business School," the series on PBS stations, you will meet Don MacInnis, the owner of Record Technology, a producer of top-quality vinyl albums. For over 100 years, the primary way to listen to recorded music was by playing vinyl albums on a turntable. In the early 90s, the CD was introduced and was completely embraced by the average consumer of recorded music.

Though initially concerned about the CD revolution, Don was either prescient or extremely optimistic. He predicted that once people tried CDs some would tire of the metallic sound and return to vinyl. He was right. Record Technology is growing and now has 37 employees with annual sales headed toward $5 million.

From day one, Record Technology's competitive advantage has been quality. The company has cultivated audiophiles, who consider listening to music a very serious hobby and will spend thousands of dollars to purchase the equipment necessary to create the optimum experience.

"We keep a very close watch on our market and in constant contact with our customers. And we do make the best grooves in the world."

—Don MacInnis

These people want high-quality albums, and Don delivers. Some in-

Go to page 728 for More! on Record Technology.

dustry experts consider Record Technology to be the best maker of vinyl albums in the world. With a world-class product and global recognition, the company has been able to not only survive but grow. And, about the time that the CD was bulldozing his competitors, customers were asking Don to come up with a heavier product, which is now his best seller. The HQ-180 is a high-quality, 180-gram record that thousands pay up to $30 per record to own.

While Don is not an audiophile himself, he sure is happy that the world is full of people who want to listen to music the old-fashioned way. ◆

—Hattie Bryant, Producer, "Small Business School," The Series on PBS Stations, Worldnet, and the Web, http://smallbusinessschool.org

LOOKING AHEAD

After studying this chapter, you should be able to

1. *Define* competitive advantage.
2. *Describe the factors that comprise external environments.*
3. *Describe the factors that comprise internal environments.*
4. *Identify and compare broad-based strategy options for the entrepreneurial venture.*
5. *Explain the focus strategy concept and its importance to small business.*
6. *Discuss the importance of the sustainability of competitive advantage.*

Great companies always start from great ideas, right? Not necessarily. Recent research has shown that some of the world's most impressive firms—such as Hewlett-Packard, Sony, 3M, and Wal-Mart—did not sprout from the seeds of spectacular ideas; rather, they grew from a grand vision of building a world-class company.[1] When Sam Walton founded Wal-Mart Stores, Inc., his goal was to build the finest retailing company possible—period! Although Walton was not the first to pursue the discount department store concept, bargain shoppers have declared his enterprise the champion among low-price contenders.

http://www.walmart.com

While people marvel at Wal-Mart's accomplishments, many of the greatest stories of success in business are yet to be written—perhaps yours will be one of them. In this textbook you will find a number of critical insights that can guide you in starting or acquiring a venture and realizing your entrepreneurial vision. This chapter highlights the value of identifying a promising entrepreneurial opportunity (one that is right for you!) and outlines a process for matching that opportunity with a winning strategy.

The Path to Competitive Advantage

Define competitive advantage.

If great companies do not always start from great ideas, does this mean that the task of selecting the right business opportunity is unimportant? Not at all. Identifying a good business opportunity is a great place to begin, but it is just that—a starting point. Many entrepreneurs have squandered good opportunities by relying on an attractive business concept to carry the day and neglecting the task of crafting an effective strategy to exploit that concept.

After an opportunity has been identified, the entrepreneur must come up with a strategy that will help to sustain the competitive advantage of the business (see Figure 2-1). A **strategy** is defined as a plan of action that coordinates the resources and commitments of an organization to achieve superior performance; a **competitive advantage** exists when a firm offers a product or service that is perceived by customers to be superior to those of competitors. The variety of competitive strategies may be as great as the number of firms in operation. (However, specific strategies are derived from a few broad-based strategy options, which will be described later.) A well-planned strategy promotes competitive advantage and leads to desirable outcomes such as venture growth and profitability.

strategy
a plan of action that coordinates the resources and commitments of an organization to achieve superior performance

competitive advantage
a benefit that exists when a firm has a product or service that is seen by its target market as better than those of competitors

Sometimes a competitive advantage just happens, but entrepreneurs are far more likely to gain an edge in the marketplace when they are careful and deliberate in identifying an entrepreneurial opportunity and designing a strategy to exploit it. Unfortunately, the failure of many entrepreneurs to understand the strategic management process leaves them with little or no sense of direction and no clear competitive advantage for their ventures. As a result, these individuals find it difficult to describe the strategy of their enterprise, even when pulling together an initial business plan. A venture that lacks a strategy is like a rocket without a guidance system—it may be rising under full thrust, but there is no telling whether the craft will reach a desired target.

Though the types of competitive advantage are numerous, some of the more common approaches are based on price/value, unique service features, notable product attributes, customer experience, and customer convenience (see Figure 2-2). The following examples illustrate these bases for competitive advantage:

- ***Price/Value.*** Fredrick Bozin launched the Watermarket Store, in Fallbrook, California to sell purified water to value-conscious consumers. Using an efficient purification system and controlling costs through streamlined operations, Bozin was able to offer high-quality, good-tasting tap water for 25 cents a gallon, compared to 50 cents or more at the supermarket and $1.50 delivered to the home.[2]

FIGURE 2-1

The Path to Competitive Advantage

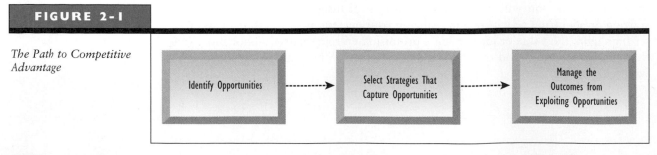

Identify Opportunities → Select Strategies That Capture Opportunities → Manage the Outcomes from Exploiting Opportunities

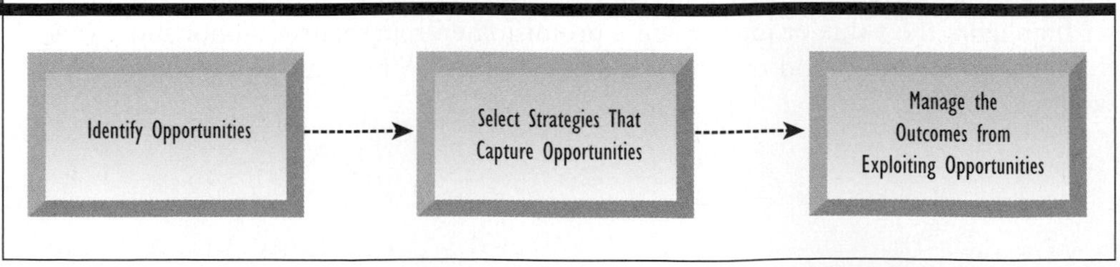

- ***Unique Service Features.*** In their small pharmacy in New York City, John and Abby Fazio compete successfully with area drug store chains by emphasizing customer service. For example, they greet patrons by name at the store entrance, offer exceptional consultation services at the pharmacy counter, fill same-day special orders, and even accept IOUs from needy patients. In response, sales increased 9 percent in a recent year, yielding $240,000 in profits.[3]
- ***Notable Product Attributes.*** Vincent Yost formed Intelligent Devices, Inc. in Harleysville, Pennsylvania after he developed a "smart" parking meter that automatically resets to zero when a car leaves (capturing revenue that would otherwise be lost) and records data useful in studying parking usage. The unique features of the product allow Yost to demand higher prices than those charged for a standard meter.[4]
- ***Customer Experience.*** A Tipton, Pennsylvania firm called New Pig Corporation sells solutions for industrial clean-ups, but it does so in a way that allows customers to "feel" each contact with the company. For example, a customer can visit the firm at One Pork Avenue or call 1-800-HOT-DOGS. Even while on hold, clients can get into the spirit of the business by listening to "Kiss a Pig," a Ray Stevens tune.[5]

http://www.newpig.com

- ***Customer Convenience.*** The demand for convenient access is driving the trend toward mobile businesses. Bobby Thigpen of Hewitt, Texas recently quit his job to start American Fast Lube, which will come to a customer's home or office to perform automotive services ranging from changing the oil to light engine work. This convenience is greatly appreciated by those whose daily planners leave no time for the drive to and wait at a typical auto service center.[6]

When entrepreneurial ventures provide distinctive products or services that customers value, they achieve competitive advantage and enjoy superior profitability.

Even if they recognize the importance of competitive advantage, many entrepreneurs conclude that they cannot achieve this edge in the marketplace. This misperception comes from two common myths. The first is that most of the good business opportunities are already gone. The other is that small firms cannot

FIGURE 2-2

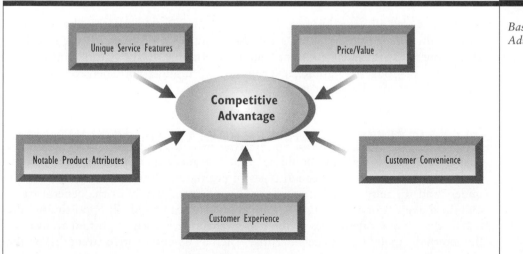

Bases for Competitive Advantage

Unique Service Features → Competitive Advantage
Price/Value → Competitive Advantage
Notable Product Attributes → Competitive Advantage
Customer Convenience → Competitive Advantage
Customer Experience → Competitive Advantage

ENTREPRENEURSHIP AND ETHICS

IN THE TRENCHES

EARNING THE POSTAL SERVICE'S STAMP OF APPROVAL

In founding E-Stamp Corporation, Salim Kara turned an ethical dilemma into an entrepreneurial opportunity. Kara used new technology as an entry wedge into the metered mail business where rigged machines were metering up to $100 million a year in unpaid postage.

Since 1920, Pitney Bowes, Inc. has dominated the postage-meter business, controlling as much as 85 percent of this $20 billion market. But unfortunately, its mechanical meters can be rigged to print postage that goes unrecorded.

Using new software and hardware, E-Stamp developed a system that is more convenient to use and reduces the problem of postage theft. With this new technology, small businesses and home offices can buy, download, and print stamps from the firm's Web site, calculate the weight of parcels, determine postage costs, and track usage. The system is convenient, since customers can purchase postage online; it reduces fraud by including sophisticated security hardware that verifies the authenticity of each stamp.

The U.S. Postal Service granted E-Stamp approval to sell stamps online in 1999. By year's end, the startup had 157 employees and $1.3 million in sales (an astounding annual sales growth rate of 1,200 percent!). Despite early successes, E-Stamp recently announced that it is exiting the online postage business to focus on its Web-based shipping and logistics operations. This shift in strategy will require the company to lay off 30 percent of its staff and perhaps even change its name, but its future is promising. In fact, the firm's shares rose nearly 50 percent following the announcement.

Source: Rodney Ho, "Postage-Meter Firms Seek Market's Stamp of Approval: Start-Ups Are Challenging Pitney Bowes's Tight Lock on the Industry," *The Wall Street Journal,* February 10, 1997, p. B2; and Khahn T. L. Tran, "E-Stamp Will Exit Web Postage to Focus on Shipping, Logistics," *The Wall Street Journal,* November 28, 2000, p. B8.

http://www.stamps.com

compete well with big companies. Neither of these assumptions is true! Nevertheless, existing companies, large and small, do not typically welcome competitors. As one well-respected author, Karl H. Vesper, puts it,

Established companies do their best to maintain proprietary shields . . . to ward off prospective as well as existing competitors. Consequently, the entrepreneur who would create a new competitor to attack them needs to have some sort of "entry wedge," or strategic competitive advantage for breaking into the established pattern of commercial activity.[7]

An entry wedge allows a business to enter an industry (for example, by offering a new product or service, copying a successful business, or participating in a franchise), but it is also likely to shape long-term strategy. Early victories in the marketplace can lead to significant growth and more comprehensive strategies, including strategic alliances with large partners.

IDENTIFYING ENTREPRENEURIAL OPPORTUNITIES

A small company's strategy should be guided by more than blind instinct. Making good choices requires two general types of evaluation. Entrepreneurs first need to understand the nature of the external environment. A study of the general trends and the dynamics of competition within an industry can highlight opportunities that match the unique capabilities of the entrepreneur. It is then important to evaluate the internal capabilities of the enterprise (such as its competitive strengths) so that

these can be matched with market needs and other external opportunities. In other words, analysis of the external environment helps the entrepreneur to determine *what business potentials exist,* whereas internal analysis reveals *what the venture is able to do.* Figure 2-3 shows a model of competitive advantage that outlines the essential relationships discussed throughout this chapter.

Assessing Potentials in the External Environment

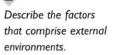

Describe the factors that comprise external environments.

general environment the broad environment, encompassing factors that influence most businesses in a society

industry environment the combined forces that directly impact a given firm and its competitors

Recent research has confirmed that the external environment impacts the growth and profitability of firms.[8] Entrepreneurs benefit when they search the external environment to find opportunities and to identify threats that call for protective measures. This external analysis should cover both the general environment and the industry environment. The **general environment** is very broad, encompassing factors that influence all—or at least most—businesses in a society. In comparison, the **industry environment** is defined more narrowly as the combined forces that directly impact a given firm and its competitors. Within both the general environment and the industry environment, the search for opportunities should focus on change.

THE GENERAL ENVIRONMENT The general environment has a number of critical segments, shown in Figure 2-4 on page 34. Forces in the *macroeconomic segment* include changes in the rate of inflation, interest rates, and even currency exchange rates, all of which promote or discourage business growth. Included in the *sociocultural segment* are societal trends that may affect consumer demand, opening up new markets and forcing others into decline. In the *political/legal segment,* changes in tax law and government regulation (such as safety restrictions) may pose a threat to businesses or render an inventive business concept unworkable. The *technological segment* is perhaps most important to small businesses, since it is developments in this segment that spawn—and make obsolete—many new ventures. The *global segment* encompasses

FIGURE 2-3

A Model of Competitive Advantage

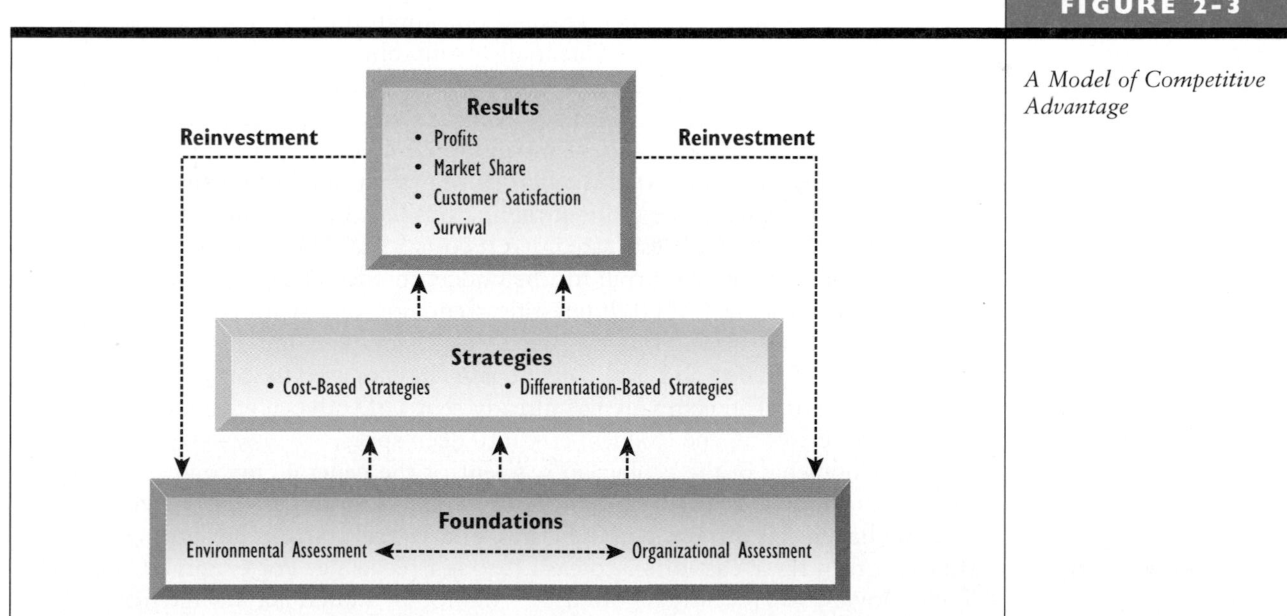

FIGURE 2-4

Segments of the General Environment

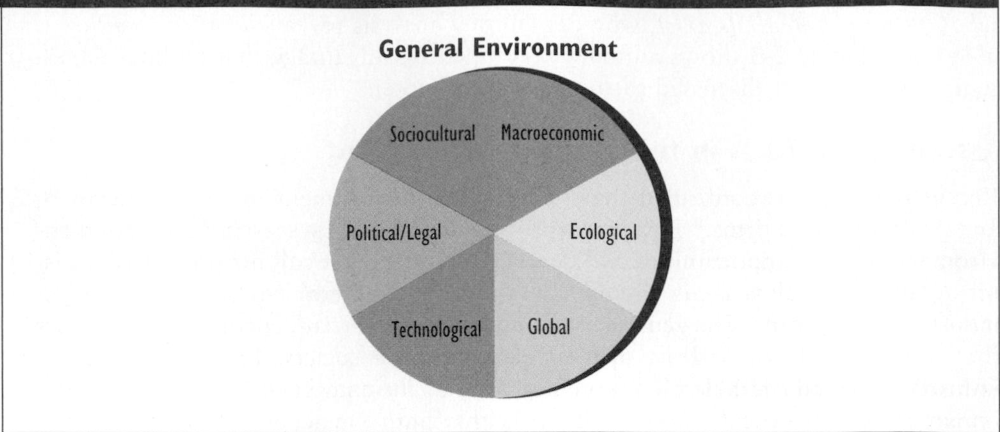

critical international developments that create new opportunities to expand markets, outsource internationally, and invest abroad. For example, the Chinese government recently lowered trade barriers to foreign professional services providers, allowing U.S. law firms to open offices there. If a small law firm is aware of this opportunity to tap the largest market in the world, it can gain an advantage by being among the first to set up an office in China. Finally, recent emphasis on environmental issues has grown to the point where the *ecological segment* of the general environment merits separate consideration. The general environment is obviously a two-edged sword that can open up new opportunities to the small firm—or threaten its existence.

Some people believe that evaluation of the general environment is appropriate only for large firms that have the support of a corporate staff to manage the process, but in fact small businesses can also benefit from this type of analysis. Consider the findings in a recent report on technological developments in the general environment. It outlined ideas about markets that could open up if the cost of launching payloads into space were greatly reduced. Potentially profitable business concepts described included the predictable (selling space novelty items) as well as the "far out" (establishing orbiting business parks for firms whose laboratories would benefit from zero or variable gravity). There was even mention of marketing space to incapacitated earthlings who, once freed from the burden of gravity, might find space living more accommodating. One of the more intriguing business opportunities was in the area of space burials. The study estimated that it costs $50,000 to send one pound of cremated remains into eternal orbit; for the budget-minded client, a less-enduring orbit could cost as little as $3,000. Interestingly enough, one small company is already marketing such a service. Houston-based Celestis markets burials in space at prices ranging from $5,300 to $12,500; satellite launches are used to carry the cremated remains into orbit. The company has already sent LSD advocate Timothy Leary and "Star Trek" creator Gene Roddenberry into deep space.[9]

http://www.celestis.com

Developments in the ecological segment of the general environment have also opened the door to many new and creative small businesses. One current environmental challenge is disposing of used tires, and several startups have recognized that they can turn these cast-offs into cash through recycling. For example, GreenMan Technologies, Inc. recently reported $4.7 million in annual net income from sales of tire-derived fuel to power plants, paper mills, and cement kilns. The company an-

http://www.greenman-tech.com

ticipates shredding more than 17 million tires a year into small "fuel chips," each of which contains the equivalent of more than two gallons of fuel oil. RB Rubber Products, Inc. recognized the same environmental development, but responded with a very different strategy. The company's 90 employees transform used tires into rubber mats that are sold as playground surfaces, liners for horse stables, commercial flooring, and other products. Dodge-Regupol, Inc. turns old tires into "crumbs" and then converts these fragments into products such as flooring and automotive parts. Employing 150 workers, the company transforms more than two million tires each year.[10] With very different strategies, these three firms are responding to developments in only one segment of the general environment. And all of the companies described in this section have demonstrated how analysis of the general environment can lead small businesses to potent opportunities.

http://www.rbrubber.com

http://www.regupol.com

THE INDUSTRY ENVIRONMENT Besides general environmental influences, an entrepreneur also faces the more direct influences of his or her industry. According to Michael Porter in his book *Competitive Advantage,* five forces determine the nature and degree of competition in an industry:

- Threat of new competitors
- Threat of substitute products or services
- Intensity of rivalry among existing competitors
- Bargaining power of suppliers
- Bargaining power of buyers

IN THE TRENCHES — UTILIZING NEW TECHNOLOGY

WHEN TOO MUCH HIP IS ANYTHING BUT HIP

Technological innovations do not always tap opportunities as anticipated. Levi-Strauss uses body scanning to provide a custom fit for its jeans customers. In its New York Niketown store, the athletic footwear giant Nike uses foot scanning to provide perfect-fitting shoes for its customers. Recently, catalogue favorite Lands' End and upscale clothier Brooks Brothers contracted with Image Twin Inc., a small firm located in Cary, North Carolina, to develop body-scanning kiosks that are being placed in shopping malls.

Image Twin hopes to make fitting rooms obsolete by determining the exact dimensions of an individual's body through scanning, taking over 200,000 micro-measurements. The venture had introduced 50 scanning kiosks before the end of 2001, storing scanned measurements for future use in a secure database on the Web. This is promising new technology with the potential to offer great convenience to customers.

But using cutting-edge technology can be risky. Just ask Lands' End. Rebecca Quick, a reporter for *The Wall Street Journal,* used an Image Twin scanner (a virtual dressing room) to try on Lands' End apparel. The results were less than accurate and far from flattering. Lands' End software read as hip dimensions the measurements taken from a larger and more rounded part of the body, creating an expanded "pear shaped" figure for the reporter. This produced a shocking image that did not exactly promote a sale and certainly provided something less than a perfect fit. Lands' End has since fixed the computer glitch, but Quick is slow to forget the distorted image she saw.

Source: Rebecca Quick, "As Our Reporter Said, This Apparel Web Site Was Just Way Too Hip," *The Wall Street Journal,* October 25, 2000, p. B1; and "Body Scanning Kiosks May Improve Clothes' Fit," *The St. Louis Post-Dispatch,* October 18, 2000, p. C1.

Figure 2-5 depicts these five factors as weights that offset the attractiveness of a target market. Generally speaking, the profitability of firms in an industry is inversely related to the strength of these competitive forces—strong forces yield weak profits, whereas weak forces yield strong profits.

Because of differences among industries, the impact of a given force will vary from one situation to the next. Collectively, however, the contribution of these five market forces to the dynamics of the industry environment is widely recognized.

Entrepreneurs who understand competitive forces can better assess market opportunities and guard against threats to their ventures. Obviously, the forces dominating competition in an industry will depend on its unique circumstances. Therefore, the entrepreneur must recognize and understand these forces to position the venture in a way that makes the most of what the industry offers. In other words, analyzing the five industry forces provides a good overview of the "lay of the competitive land."

The extent to which new competitors pose a threat is determined by *barriers to entry,* which include obstacles such as limited access to necessary raw materials, control of proprietary technologies, and restricted access to channels of distribution. High barriers discourage the entry of new rivals and thus protect market space from competition, which translates into higher profits for firms in the industry. Threat of entry is also influenced by such factors as the uniqueness of competing products, switching costs (what it would cost customers to change vendors), and government policies.

FIGURE 2-5

Major Factors Offsetting Market Attractiveness

While barriers to entry prevent new competitors (outsiders) from entering an industry, *mobility barriers* keep rivals (insiders) from competing in protected segments within the same industry. In other words, high mobility barriers discourage competition by turning back potential rivals from other segments of the industry, thus shielding profits in the protected market niche.

Like the threat of new competitors, the threat of substitute products or services can impact potential profits in an industry by placing a ceiling on prices. That is, if prices rise too high, consumers are likely to turn to substitutes, especially if the cost of switching is low.

More than 50 companies entered the airline industry in the 1980s, but only one of these was still in operation by 2001. Why? In some cases, these startups lost business when passengers turned to cheaper substitutes (primarily buses and automobiles), which cut into market demand. And, they faced an even greater challenge when more established airlines took advantage of weak mobility barriers to open service on the same routes. By offering lower fares and better service in these niche markets, the major airlines drove profits down and forced newcomers from the industry.

Along with the threat of new competitors and product substitutes, Porter identifies competitive rivalry as a critical industry force. The intensity of rivalry within an industry is determined by factors such as the number and size of competitors, the market demand for the product or service, and forces called *exit barriers,* which can keep rivals in an industry even after they become unprofitable. Rivalry is intense (and profits are usually low) when the industry is populated by a large number of firms of similar size, demand for the product or service is stable or declining, and barriers deter rivals from exiting the industry. These linkages of competitive rivalry with profits and opportunity are sometimes easy to see. For example, the landscaping industry is very fragmented, consisting of a large number of small companies. As a result, no single company dominates the competition, rivalry is usually intense, and profits in the industry tend to be razor thin.

Thus, as part of the industry analysis, it is important to determine the strength, positioning, and likely response of rivals. In fact, experts insist such analyses are critical to effective business plans. William A. Sahlman of Harvard University contends that every business plan should answer several questions about competitors:[11]

- Who are the new venture's current competitors?
- What resources do they control?
- What are their strengths and weaknesses?
- How will they respond to the new venture's decision to enter the industry?
- How can the new venture respond?
- Who else might be able to observe and exploit the same opportunity?
- Are there ways to co-opt potential or actual competitors by forming alliances?

This analysis helps an entrepreneur to "size up" the nature and extent of competition and to fine-tune future plans. It can also help to identify business opportunities based on the competitive terrain, such as untapped market potentials, successful differentiation options, and strategies to open up new market space.

Big Dog Motorcycles knows the value of understanding the competition when crafting a strategy. In the heavyweight segment of motorcycle manufacturing, Harley-Davidson is the undisputed champion. However, despite increased production at Harley, demand for its cruisers continues to outstrip the firm's capacity to

http://www.bigdogmotorcycles.com

produce, leading to high dealer markups and two-year delays in the delivery of some models. Enter Big Dog Motorcycles. Sheldon Coleman founded this startup in 1995 to respond to excess demand for Harleys, and it generated more than $400,000 in sales the first year. Given untapped market potential, Big Dog has focused on providing highly customized cruisers at a premium price. As for the effectiveness of the strategy, the results speak for themselves. The company achieved profitability during the first six months of 2000, posting a 30 percent increase in sales over the $18 million generated in 1999 (representing the fifth straight year of double-digit growth).[12] The success of Big Dog Motorcycles shows that knowing the weaknesses of competitors can reveal business opportunities and shape a strategy that yields competitive advantage.

Finally, Porter cites the power of suppliers and buyers as factors influencing the prices charged for inputs and those paid for outputs, respectively. The bargaining power of these firms is determined by such factors as the number and size of alternative suppliers/buyers, the level of differentiation of their products or services, and the cost of switching between them. Their bargaining power declines as the number of alternative suppliers or buyers grows, the products or services become more similar, and unfavorable changes in switching costs occur. This explains why California businessman Dennis Tito had to pay the Russian space program $20 million for the privilege of becoming the first space tourist. The high fare was a result of NASA's refusal to take Tito into space; hence, the Russians ended up with a monopoly on commercial space travel. The price would surely have been lower if NASA had bid against the Russian program; additional suppliers would have generated even more intense bidding and an even lower fare.

Strategy expert Gary Hamel points out an additional step in analyzing the industry environment—identifying the conventional wisdom that constrains behavior in the industry. One example of this kind of thinking is that students assume they must buy a textbook rather than "rent" it for a semester. These insights, when combined with a thorough grasp of changes occurring in the general environment (such as emerging technologies with market potential, changes in lifestyles that clear the way for new products or services, or political shifts that open foreign markets), can shed light on the path that leads to competitive advantage.[13]

CHANGE-BASED SOURCES OF OPPORTUNITY Change may be the most important source of entrepreneurial opportunities. Shifts in the general and industry environment are likely to be more challenging to large firms, since they tend to be more bureaucratic and less flexible and have profited from the way things were before. Often, large firms prefer things to remain the same. In contrast, entrepreneurs are much more likely to recognize change as an opportunity and to have the creativity and flexibility to exploit it. Peter Drucker recommends that entrepreneurs consider seven sources of opportunity in the environment as they prepare to launch or extend their enterprises.[14] Drucker's change-based sources of opportunity are outlined in Table 2-1.

Drucker has suggested that innovation is "the means by which the entrepreneur either creates new wealth-producing resources or endows existing resources with enhanced potential for creating wealth."[15] In other words, entrepreneurship harnesses the power of creativity to provide innovative products and services. Since change inspires innovation, recognizing shifts in the factors outlined in Table 2-1 expands the range of entrepreneurial opportunities.

TABLE 2-1 *Change-Based Sources of Entrepreneurial Opportunities*

Change Factor	Definition	Illustration
Industry factors		
The unexpected	Unanticipated events lead to either enterprise success or failure.	Pet pharmaceuticals have been very successful, with more than 30% of dogs and cats now taking medication.
The incongruous	What is expected is out of line with what will work.	Low-fat ice cream was developed for those trying to lose weight.
Process needs	Current technology is insufficient to address an emerging challenge.	Carmakers offer gas-electric hybrid cars to deal with rising energy costs.
Structural change	Changes in technology, markets, etc., alter industry dynamics.	Growth in the use of the Internet for e-commerce has been dramatic.
Human and economic factors		
Demographics	Shifts in population size, age structure, ethnicity, and income distribution impact product demand.	Baby boomers are now in their prime income earning years and are saving for retirement, promoting an increase in the need for financial planning.
Changes in perception	Perceptual variations determine product demand.	Perceived security threats have led to development of gated communities.
New knowledge	Learning opens the door to new product opportunities with commercial potential.	Increased knowledge of the Internet has fueled the growth of online investment firms.

When small firms engage in change-based analysis to uncover entrepreneurial opportunities that might otherwise be overlooked, they must keep in mind the **paradox of attraction:** An industry opportunity that is attractive to one entrepreneur will also draw others, and their combined efforts to exploit it may destroy the appeal of that industry for all newcomers. In other words, the very feature of an industry that makes it attractive to one entrepreneur (that is, the lack of competition) also makes it attractive to others. Thus, the opportunity vanishes as several entrepreneurs move to capitalize on it. For example, when online merchants experienced inadequate storage and delivery support during the 1999 Christmas season, several new companies rushed in to fill the void. Within one year, what these startups had seen as a profitable business turned into a crowded industry with scant profits.[16]

paradox of attraction
the concept that an attractive industry opportunity is likely to draw multiple new entrants, diminishing its attractiveness

One entrepreneur who had the foresight to anticipate the competition is Louis Brown, Jr. of Beltsville, Maryland. Brown started a new company called MICROS Systems, Inc. to sell a "smart" cash register he had developed. The sophisticated device enables managers to compare sales data and crosscheck information against inventory records, among other functions. Customers were sure to be interested in this advanced technology. But in order to be successful, MICROS Systems had to consider more than the general environment (the technology segment, in this case)—it also had to factor in industry forces. Brown recognized the challenges of competing head on with industry Goliaths like NCR Corporation and IBM, so he decided to design his registers for restaurants, a market segment where profit potential was great and the threat of competitive retaliation was relatively low. This attention to the general and industry environments paid dividends in competitive advantage and

http://www.micros.com

remarkable performance. In fact, with 2,500 employees worldwide and more than $350 million in revenues, the company has been so successful that it can no longer be called a *small* business.[17]

OTHER LEADS ON OPPORTUNITIES If a change-based analysis does not reveal the specific entrepreneurial opportunity that is right for you, other sources of leads include the following:

- Personal contacts with potential customers and suppliers, professors, patent attorneys, former or current employees or coworkers, venture capitalists, and chambers of commerce
- Visiting trade shows, libraries, production facilities, universities, and research institutes
- Reading trade publications, bankruptcy announcements, commerce department publications, and business classifieds

UTILIZING NEW TECHNOLOGY

IN THE TRENCHES

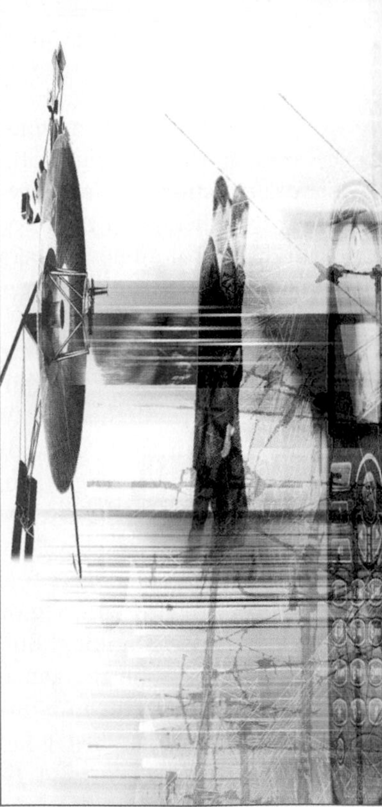

TURN ON ANOTHER APPLIANCE AND SAVE ELECTRICITY

The television commercials go something like this. A young couple is on vacation, enjoying a playful day at the beach, when it suddenly dawns on them that they are hundreds of miles from home and they forgot to turn off the oven. Panic builds until one of them pulls out a wireless device and turns off the offending appliance. With their peace of mind restored, fun at the beach resumes.

One of the companies seizing an opportunity in this rapidly emerging "computerized gateway" industry is Coactive Networks®, whose 60 employees labor quietly at the firm's low-profile Sausalito, California headquarters. The company markets a technology that enables users to control home appliances from any distance via the Internet, using cell phones, laptops, and other devices. Coactive markets its $200 Coactive Connector as a convenience whose time has come, and other firms have also recognized the commercial potential of such devices. Competing products in the works include a high-end, $400 gateway device by Swedish giant Telefon AB L. M. Ericsson and a system that Xanboo Inc. of New York plans to offer through retailers, telephone and utility companies, and other distributors. The competition will certainly be stiff.

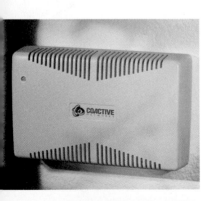

But Coactive's timing is excellent, given the trends emerging in a completely different industry—energy. Shortages resulting from energy deregulation in California set off rate increases, as soaring demand outpaced available supply, fueling interest in energy-saving devices like the Coactive Connector. With power costs rising, analysts predict that consumers will flock to gadgets that will allow them to take energy-saving measures (like leaving lights and air conditioning off until shortly before they return home), and small businesses will be drawn to features allowing them to program and monitor energy usage. The convenience offered by the wireless feature of this technology will sweeten consumer interest. So, as the cost of electricity rises, it might be good to think about turning on another appliance—a gateway device like the Coactive Connector.

Source: Jim Carlton, "Coactive Gives Users Remote Control of Homes," *The Wall Street Journal,* October 11, 2000, p. B10.

http://www.coactive.com

- Observing trends related to materials and energy shortages, emerging technologies, recreation, fads, pollution problems, personal security, and social movements

In addition, the Internet provides ready and convenient access to a wealth of Web sites that are helpful in identifying opportunities.

The options within the listed sources are unlimited, so the search will need to be restricted. Karl Vesper's study of approximately 100 successful entrepreneurs found that a random search for entrepreneurial opportunities does not provide as much benefit as one that is guided by the entrepreneur's education, work background, or hobbies. Most of the entrepreneurs studied generated their business ideas from personal expertise rather than external sources, and most of the new ventures were inspired by prior work experience.[18]

Assessing Potentials in the Organization

Identifying opportunities by analyzing the external environment is only the first step. Finding promising business concepts also requires a systematic assessment of the firm's internal potentials. In other words, the entrepreneur's understanding of available business opportunities must be wedded to insight regarding what the firm is able to do. The latter is best determined by conducting a thorough analysis of the strengths and weaknesses of the firm, an exercise called *organizational assessment.*

Describe the factors that comprise internal environments.

ORGANIZATIONAL RESOURCES AND CAPABILITIES In order to assess the organizational potentials of a business, it is important to understand the difference between resources and capabilities. **Organizational resources** are those basic inputs that a firm uses to conduct its business; they include such factors as capital, technology, equipment, and employees. Organizations have both tangible and intangible resources. **Tangible resources** are visible and easy to measure. Plants and equipment, cash reserves, and the firm's borrowing capacity are all tangible resources. They differ fundamentally from **intangible resources,** which are invisible and therefore difficult to quantify. Intangible resources include intellectual property rights such as patents and copyrights, as well as endowments from brand recognition and firm reputation.

organizational resources basic inputs that a firm uses to conduct its business

tangible resources those organizational resources that are visible and easy to measure

intangible resources those organizational resources that are invisible and difficult to quantify

Though the terms are often used interchangeably, resources technically are not the same as capabilities. Like a keyboard, which is of no practical value until it is integrated into a system of computer components, organizational resources cannot provide competitive advantage until they are bundled into some useful configuration. Thus, whereas resources are singular in nature, **organizational capabilities** are best viewed as the integration of several resources that are deployed together to the firm's advantage.

organizational capabilities the integration of several organizational resources that are deployed together to the firm's advantage

CORE COMPETENCIES Once entrepreneurs have an accurate view of an organization's resources and capabilities, they are ready to identify its core competencies. **Core competencies** are those resources and capabilities that provide a firm with a competitive advantage over its rivals—such as the superior customer service through which a fast food restaurant gains sales. Core competencies emerge when a company learns over time to use its resources and capabilities in unique ways, establishing patterns that reflect the "personality" of the enterprise. Entrepreneurs who can identify core competencies and apply them effectively can help their firms achieve a competitive advantage and superior performance.

core competencies those resources and capabilities that provide a firm with a competitive advantage over its rivals

Matching Environmental and Organizational Potentials

SWOT analysis
a type of assessment that provides a concise overview of a firm's strategic situation

Establishing a solid foundation for competitive advantage requires matching the strengths and weaknesses of an organization with a profile of current or probable opportunities and threats. This integration is best implemented through **SWOT** (*S*trengths, *W*eaknesses, *O*pportunities, and *T*hreats) **analysis,** which provides a concise overview of the firm's strategic situation. Table 2-2 lists a number of factors that can constitute strengths, weaknesses, opportunities, and threats; however, these are merely representative of the innumerable possibilities a given firm may encounter.

In practice, a SWOT analysis is often a static summarizing of a firm's current situation. This is unfortunate, since firms achieve higher performance when they view their strategic setting as dynamic. That is, firms with superior profitability are forward-thinking, leveraging current capabilities to position themselves for anticipated business opportunities. In short, the best performing firms in the future will be those that improve on today's capabilities to meet the challenges of tomorrow.

Determining the Best Opportunity

Analyzing both the environment and the organization and bringing these observations together in the SWOT analysis should help an entrepreneur identify opportunities for which a venture may be well suited. Then the entrepreneur can determine the *best* opportunity by asking a few important questions:

- Will the opportunity selected lead to others in the future?
- Will the opportunity help build skills that open the door to new opportunities in the future?

TABLE 2-2

Examples of SWOT Factors

	POSITIVE FACTORS	NEGATIVE FACTORS
	Strengths	**Weaknesses**
INTERNAL FACTORS	• Important core competencies • Financial strengths • Innovative capacity • Skilled or experienced management • Well-planned strategy • Effective entry wedge • Protection from competitive threats • Positive reputation in the marketplace • Proprietary technology	• Inadequate financial resources • Poorly planned strategy • Lack of management skills or experience • Inadequate innovation • Negative reputation in the marketplace • Inadequate facilities • Distribution problems • Inadequate marketing skills • Production inefficiencies
	Opportunities	**Threats**
EXTERNAL FACTORS	• Untapped market potential • New product or geographic market • Favorable shift in industry dynamics • Potential for market growth • Emerging technologies • Changes allowing foreign market entry • Deregulation • Increasing market fragmentation	• New competitors • Rising demands of buyers or suppliers • Sales shifting to substitute products • Increased government regulation • Adverse shifts in the business cycle • Slowed market growth • Changing customer preferences • Adverse demographic shifts

- Will pursuit of the opportunity be likely to lead to competitive response by potential rivals?

Obviously, the most promising opportunities are those that lead to others (offering value and profitability over the long run), promote the development of additional skills that will allow the firm to pursue new prospects, and yet do not provoke competitors to strike back.

Hugh Kenneth Holyoak certainly understands how one business can lead to another and how new skills can open the floodgates of opportunity. The 63-year-old owner of Ken's Hatchery and Fish Farms, two commercial lakes, and a wild-pig hunting business has introduced a number of fishy innovations over the years, including Ken's Floating Raceway Fish Factory, the Scale-O-Matic Electric Fish Scaler, the E-Z Floating Fish Cage, and his own hybrid fish called the Georgia Giant. Noting that rising demand and disappearing wetlands have created a serious shortage of free-range frogs for dining and dissecting, he has set his sights on the frog farming business, offering an indoor frog-raising system that promises to generate substantial profits. Future prospects are bright indeed, given current demand. And because most frog farms are located in low-wage countries and use labor-intensive methods, competitive retaliation is unlikely.[19] By setting his sights on frog farming, Holyoak found a way to match external developments (rising demand for frogs) and internal capabilities (fish-raising know-how). With virtually no competition at the moment, related opportunities are sure to open up, and the skills Holyoak learns from frog farming are likely to benefit his fish-related operations as well.

http://www.kens-fishfarm.com

Conducting environmental and organizational analyses and integrating their results builds a solid foundation for competitive advantage. Working from this platform, the entrepreneur can begin to craft a strategy to achieve competitive advantage and superior financial performance.

Selecting Strategies That Capture Opportunities

As stated earlier, a strategy is, in essence, a plan of action for coordinating the resources and commitments of an organization in order to achieve superior performance. Strategy selections should be guided by the firm's situation, rather than the momentum of past choices, the latest industry fad, or whatever "feels" right at the moment. Choosing strategies that make sense for a particular entrepreneur and his or her enterprise is a critical step on the path to superior performance.

Broad-Based Strategy Options

Identify and compare broad-based strategy options for the entrepreneurial venture.

Firms competing in the same industry can adopt very different strategies. Consider two of the major players in the suction cups market: Presto Galaxy Suction Cups, Inc. of Greenpoint, New York and its archrival, Adams Manufacturing of Portersville, Pennsylvania. In order to achieve competitive advantage in this industry, these two firms wield the potent weapons of price, quality, and even "smiley faces."

These competitors could not be more different, and that is by design. Bill Adams, president of Adams Manufacturing, sums up the essence of his firm's product strategy.

http://www.suctioncupsinc.com
http://www.adamsmfg.com

"The suction cups should be as invisible as possible," he says, "They're not gaudy, they're not decorative. They're there to do a job. . . . If Martha Stewart were going to buy a suction cup, she'd buy ours."[20]

In contrast to Adams, Presto caters more to children and other focused interests. For example, Presto's glow-in-the-dark, rotating, and hologram suction cups have all been hits. Presto also offers decorator suction cups with "Susie Stuckup" and "Sun Smiley" faces and others with sport and holiday themes.

Though the firms differ in size, their strategies seem to be working. Both claim to be profitable, with Presto reporting annual sales of $1.4 million and Adams reporting revenues of $3.5 million. These two firms have created a competitive advantage in the industry by carefully crafting different strategies that lead to success. Based on knowledge of the competition, each has established a unique market approach, one by stressing the functional features of the product and the other its creative and decorative adaptation.[21] The experiences of these two firms illustrate how competitive advantage can be traced back to broad-based strategy options—creating an advantage related to cost or establishing a differentiated product or service.

cost-based strategy
a plan of action that requires a firm to be the lowest-cost producer within its market

http://www.integrityindustries.com

COST-BASED STRATEGY A **cost-based strategy** requires a firm to be the lowest-cost producer within the market. The sources of cost advantages are quite varied, ranging from low-cost labor to efficiency in operations. Many people assume that cost-based strategies will work only for large corporations; however, cost-advantage factors are so numerous and varied that, in many cases, small businesses may be able to use them with greater success. For example, Max Duncan, founder of Integrity Industries, Inc. in Kingsville, Texas, created a cost advantage by locating his new chemical-blending operation in a vacant facility whose owner he persuaded to sign on as a partner.

[Then] he found an experienced sales manager willing to take another third of the company in lieu of a year's salary. Duncan bought used equipment for "pennies on the dollar"; he ordered free samples from chemical companies for his initial raw materials. . . .

Duncan quickly found customers. The reason was simple: His costs were so low that he could charge 10 percent to 20 percent less than the competition. . . . "We're able to make healthy profit margins and keep prices low by maintaining extreme efficiency in operation," he explains.[22]

Integrity Industries continues to grow but has not abandoned its key cost advantage.

differentiation-based strategy
a plan of action designed to provide a product or service with unique attributes that are valued by consumers

DIFFERENTIATION-BASED STRATEGY The second general option for building a competitive advantage is creating a **differentiation-based strategy,** an approach that emphasizes the uniqueness of a firm's product or service (in terms of some feature other than cost). A firm that can create and sustain an attractive differentiation strategy is likely to be a successful performer in the marketplace. For the strategy to be effective, the consumer must be convinced of the uniqueness and value of the product or service—whether real or perceived. A wide variety of operational and marketing tactics, ranging from promotion to product design, can lead to product or service differentiation.

Inventor Henry Artis entered the home composting market by creating a competitive marketing advantage through product design. A composter is a device that turns organic waste into soil-enriching matter called humus. Traditional models were designed as fixed rectangular bins. These stationary designs require periodic stirring to introduce oxygen into the leaves, grass clippings, and discarded food. Other designs use elevated tubes that are rotated with a hand-operated crank. Artis's idea, called TumbleBug, features a giant hollow plastic ball that can be rolled across the

yard to achieve the necessary agitation to create compost. Though more expensive than competing designs, Artis's product provides "better looks, no odors, higher temperatures, and faster composting."[23] In other words, this venture relies on product differentiation rather than low cost to maintain its competitive advantage.

Focus Strategies

5

Explain the focus strategy concept and its importance to small business.

If one firm controlled the only known water supply in the world, its sales volume would be huge. This business would not be concerned about differences in personal preferences concerning taste, appearance, or temperature. It would consider its customers to be one market. As long as the water product was wet, it would satisfy everyone. However, if someone else discovered a second water supply, the first business's view of the market would change. The first business might discover that sales were drying up and take measures to modify its strategy. The level of rivalry would likely rise as competitors vied for position in the industry.

If the potential for water sales were significant, small businesses might eventually become interested in entering the market. However, given their limited resources and lack of industry experience, these companies would be more likely to succeed if they avoided head-to-head competition with established industry giants and sought a protected market segment instead. In other words, they could be competitive if they implemented a **focus strategy,** adapting their efforts to concentrate on the needs of a specific niche within the market. To gain entrance, these businesses might focus their attention and resources on a fragment of the market that was small enough to escape the interest of major players (for example, filtered water delivered to individual homes) or perhaps employ an entry wedge to permit access without immediate competitive reprisals (for example, filling market gaps resulting from supply shortages).

focus strategy
a plan of action that isolates an enterprise from competitors and other market forces by targeting a restricted market segment

Focus strategies represent a market approach in which entrepreneurs try to isolate themselves from market forces, such as competitors, by targeting a specific market segment (sometimes called a *market niche*). The strategy can be implemented through any element of the market mix—price, product design, service, packaging, and so on. A focus strategy is particularly attractive to a small firm that is trying to escape direct competition with industry giants while building a competitive advantage.

The two broad options for a marketplace that is relatively homogeneous, or uniform, in nature—a cost-based strategy and a differentiation-based strategy—can also be used when focusing on a limited market within an industry. Although fewer entrepreneurs adopt a cost-based focus strategy, it certainly does happen. For example, Fredrick Bozin's Watermarket Store is following a cost-based focus strategy by using an efficient purification system to offer high-quality, good-tasting water to price-sensitive customers at a fraction of the price charged by competitors (see p. 30).

Bozin's strategy varies greatly from the differentiation-based focus strategy implemented by Elias and Gaynell Hendricks when they started Wee Care Academy, Inc. in Birmingham, Alabama. They wanted to fill a void in the education market by providing a preschool that would appeal to parents who were looking for an education featuring "a challenging, fun curriculum that incorporates African and African American viewpoints." Today, Wee Care Academy owns or operates 11 facilities in the Birmingham area, and the program continues to grow.[24] Both of these small businesses serve a limited market niche with a focus strategy, but the Watermarket Store competes on price whereas Wee Care Academy competes on unique service attributes.

http://www.weecareinc.com

ADVANTAGES/DISADVANTAGES OF FOCUS STRATEGIES Focus strategies can be effective in both domestic and international markets. Noted author John Naisbitt foresees a huge global economy with smaller and smaller market niches. He believes that success in those niches "has to do with swiftness to market and innovation, which small companies can do so well."[25] This suggests that small firms will see rich opportunities in the future, at home and abroad.

New ventures often fail because of poor market positioning or lack of a perceived advantage in the minds of customers in their target market. To minimize the chance of failure, an entrepreneur should consider the benefits of exploiting gaps in a market rather than going head to head with the competition. Focus strategies can be implemented in any of the following ways:

- Restricting focus to a single subset of customers
- Emphasizing a single product or service
- Limiting the market to a single geographical region
- Concentrating on superiority of the product or service

Many entrepreneurs have focused on market niches, and their creative efforts illustrate just how well these strategies can work. For example, realizing that most magazines are designed to appeal to upscale markets, Arthur Schiff decided to take a different approach. In 1989, he introduced a quarterly publication called *City Family,* which offers content targeted to the poor and is priced accordingly. In the years since, the magazine's annual circulation has climbed from 10,000 to 250,000 copies, offering clear evidence of the potential of focus strategies.[26]

http://www.atlanticpublicationgrp.com

Another success story in the publishing industry comes from Atlantic Publication Group, Inc. (APG). During its first four years of existence, this small publishing business offered only broad-based, general-interest magazines. Then, in 1989, Marvin Jenkins, president of APG, began developing products for specific niche markets. Today, this small company in Charleston, South Carolina produces more than three dozen publications, including *South Carolina Commerce Magazine, Charleston Area Golf Guide,* and *The Lehigh Valley Real Estate Report,* for a variety of organizations. Characteristic of a niche player, APG develops each product in response to a particular need.[27] Once that need has been identified, the firm differentiates the publication in ways that customers value. Owing to their flexibility, small companies may actually have an operational advantage over large corporations when it comes to achieving success via niche-oriented strategies.

strategic decision
a decision regarding the direction a firm will take in relating to its customers and competitors

By selecting a particular focus strategy, an entrepreneur decides on the basic direction of the business. Such a choice affects the very nature of the business and is thus referred to as a **strategic decision.** A firm's overall strategy is formulated, therefore, as its leader decides how the firm will relate to its environment—particularly to the customers and competitors in that environment. One small business analyst expresses a word of caution about selecting a niche market:

Ventures that seek to capture a market niche, not transform or create an industry, don't need extraordinary ideas. Some ingenuity is necessary to design a product that will draw customers away from mainstream offerings and overcome the cost penalty of serving a small market. But features that are too novel can be a hindrance; a niche market will rarely justify the investment required to educate customers and distributors about the benefits of a radically new product.[28]

Selection of a very specialized market is, of course, not the only possible strategy for a small firm. But focus strategies are very popular because they allow a small firm to operate in the gap that exists between larger competitors. If a small firm chooses to compete head to head with other businesses, particularly large corporations, it must be prepared to distinguish itself in some way—for example, by attention to detail, highly personal service, or speed of service—in order to make itself a viable competitor.

http://www.zanescycles.com

Consider the extraordinary customer service of Zane's Cycles. Chris Zane has considered numerous modern business ideas to give his entrepreneurial venture the edge it needs to survive in the competitive world of bicycle dealerships. He has examined the merits of continuous learning, the benefit of surprise derived from guerrilla marketing, and the advantages of community-relations marketing. But the 31-year-old has determined that "doing anything to attract and keep customers" will continue to be the mainspring that drives the success of Zane's Cycles, the largest independent bicycle dealership in the New Haven, Connecticut market. Zane gains and holds customers' loyalty by maintaining contact with them over time.

He offers free coffee and soft drinks to waiting customers. "A lot of our customers will now come in on Saturday mornings to have coffee, hang out for 15 or 20 minutes, read the paper, and leave," says Zane. Where Zane differs from many business people is that he thinks of such customers in terms of relationships, not transactions. The transaction-minded business person might look at the Saturday-morning coffee drinkers and see only freeloaders; Zane sees people who have bought from him in the past and will buy from him again.

Zane does much more to encourage long-term relationships than offer free coffee; he offers free lifetime service for each bicycle purchased at the store. He does that not to sell a bike . . . but to get purchasers of bikes to send their friends to Zane's, too.[29]

Zane has been growing his business at 25 percent a year, with recent sales reaching $5 million. His advantage begins with a unique point of view. As Zane puts it, "The attitude [must change] from 'The customer is inconveniencing you and preventing you from doing your job' to 'The customer *is* your job.'"[30]

MAINTAINING THE POTENTIAL OF FOCUS STRATEGIES Firms that adopt a focus strategy tread a narrow line between maintaining a protected market and attracting competition. If their ventures are profitable, entrepreneurs must be prepared to face competition. In his book *Competitive Advantage,* Michael Porter cautions that a segmented market can erode under any of four conditions:[31]

1. The focus strategy is imitated.
2. The target segment becomes structurally unattractive because the structure erodes or because demand simply disappears.
3. The target segment's differences from other segments narrow.
4. New firms subsegment the industry.

The experience of Minnetonka, a small firm widely recognized as the first to introduce liquid hand soap, provides an example of how a focus strategy can be imitated. The huge success of its brand, Softsoap, quickly attracted the attention of several giants in the industry, including Procter & Gamble. Minnetonka's competitive advantage was soon washed away. Some analysts believe this happened because

Building Customer Loyalty

IN THE TRENCHES

STARTUPS THAT WINE AND DINE—AT 30,000 FEET

The history of the airline industry is replete with stories of failed competitors. Well-known investor Warren Buffett sums up his assessment of the airline industry and its potential with the following comments:

I like to think that if I'd been at Kitty Hawk in 1903 when Orville Wright took off, I would have been far-sighted enough, and public-spirited enough . . . to shoot him down. I mean, Karl Marx couldn't have done as much damage to capitalists as Orville did.

His remarks are obviously offered in humor, but his observation is painfully accurate. Over the years, the airline industry has yielded scant returns on investors' capital. But despite discouraging profits and the domination of large firms, enterprising entrepreneurs continue to enter the market with startups operating on shoestring budgets.

Recently, the strategy of entrants seems to have shifted in a big way. The startups of yesterday attempted to attract passengers by offering low fares, which translated naturally to no-frills service. Squeezing costs wherever possible, these low-cost contenders were forced to fly less convenient, secondary routes and to serve peanuts in place of the complete meals to which many seasoned air travelers were accustomed. Approximately 51 startups entered the market in the 1980s, but only one, America West Airlines, has survived—after emerging from bankruptcy protection in 1994. The results for companies en-

the company focused too much on the advantages of liquid soap in general and not enough on the particular benefits of Softsoap.

Sometimes it is difficult to anticipate the exact source of competition. Before Bob Lindberg started his upscale apparel shop in Tustin, California, he felt that he had adequately researched the market, including potential competition. "The only other upscale retailer, as far as I know, [had] no plans to expand here," said Lindberg, whose research showed him customers weren't worried about price—they simply wanted quality-brand merchandise and good service. Lindberg opened A.J. & Co. Big and Tall in October 1993, and a steady flow of customers began to patronize his business. Shortly thereafter, Lindberg realized that other upscale retailers were not his only competitors. Several catalog retailers were offering similar merchandise, and Lindberg had failed to anticipate the impact on his sales. "Catalogs offer convenience retailers find hard to match—especially for men who have experienced a lot of shopping frustration in the past. Almost everyone who comes into my store has purchased something from a catalog," he says.[32] A.J. & Co. Big and Tall offers competitive pricing and maintains its competitive advantage by providing a wide selection, accurate sizing, and—most importantly—personalized service. This strategy enables the firm to compete effectively, even against catalog retailers.

Clearly, focus strategies do not guarantee a sustainable advantage. Small firms can extend their success, however, by developing competitive clout.

So far, we have looked at two of the three major components of the competitive advantage model (see Figure 2-3)—building a solid foundation through sound environmental and organizational assessments and determining which strategy will be best for the firm. We turn next to the third element of the competitive advantage model: the performance outcomes of competitive advantage.

tering the market during the 1990s were not much better. Except for Southwest Airlines (started in 1971), no low-fare startup has thrived in this competitive market. It can be argued that the cause of the widespread failure of new entrants is grounded in strategy. Those firms that compete by the sword of price will likely perish by the same.

More recent startups are taking a different approach. Gone are the days of low-cost, no-frills air service. Instead, new entrepreneurial players such as National Airlines and JetBlue Airways are offering upscale service, including newer and cleaner planes, appetizing meals served on real china, in-flight satellite television, and leather seats throughout the aircraft. Passengers find the strategy appealing because such upgrades are offered at fares that meet or beat those of the major airlines. These small entrants hope their emphasis on superior service will generate long-term customer loyalty.

Of course, more serious challenges now face the entire airline industry—among them, the public's heightened safety concerns and fear of flying in the wake of recent terrorist activity.

Source: Melanie Trottman, "Now Available on Start-Up Airlines: Leather Seats, Wine, Satellite TV," *The Wall Street Journal,* October 25, 2000, p. B1.

Managing for Results

6 *Discuss the importance of the sustainability of competitive advantage.*

From a menu of strategy options, entrepreneurs generally choose the one they believe will lead to the most desirable outcomes. The relevant outcomes are not necessarily limited to sales revenue and profits. For example, a decision may be made to relocate a business halfway across the country just to place it near the owner's favorite golf course in Florida! Such decisions are not as uncommon as you may think. But if it is to produce results, a strategy must be designed to generate outcomes such as superior profitability, increased market share, improved customer satisfaction—or even simple survival (see Figure 2-3). These are the "fruits" of competitive advantage, all of which contribute to the value of the firm.

No competitive advantage lasts forever.[33] Research has emphasized the importance of **sustainable competitive advantage,** a value-creating industry position that is likely to endure over time.[34] To plan sustainability into strategy, the entrepreneur should use the unique capabilities of the firm in a way that competitors will find difficult to imitate. Sooner or later, however, rivals will discover a way to copy any value-creating strategy.[35] Therefore, it is also important to think of new ways to reinvest performance outcomes (financial returns, customer goodwill, etc.) so that the basis of competitive advantage can be renewed over the long run.

sustainable competitive advantage a value-creating industry position that is likely to endure over time

Competitive advantage follows a consistent pattern. Building a competitive advantage requires resource commitments that lead to a performance payoff. However, returns from that competitive advantage will always diminish over time. Figure 2-6 illustrates the competitive advantage life cycle, which has three stages: develop, deploy, and decline. Simply put, a firm must invest resources to *develop* a competitive advantage, which it can later *deploy* to boost its performance. But that position will eventually *decline* as rival firms build these advantages into their own strategies.[36]

FIGURE 2-6

The Competitive Advantage Life Cycle

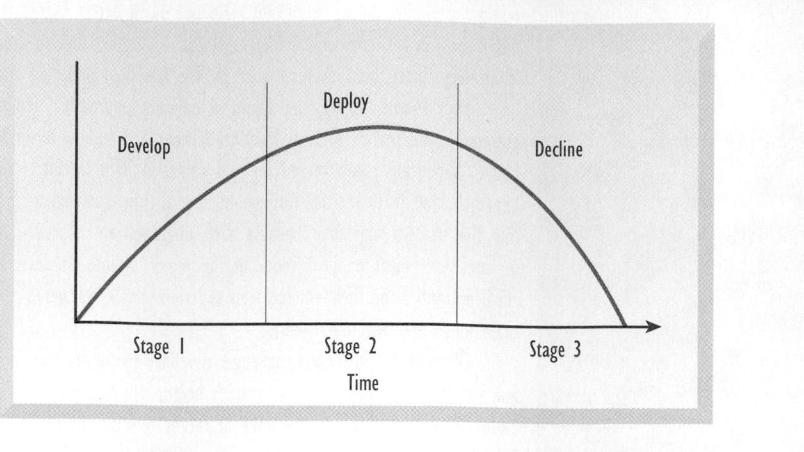

In order to maintain performance over time, firms must produce a continuous stream of competitive advantages in order to keep performance from falling off. That is why the model (shown in Figure 2-3) features arrows that redirect performance outcomes back into foundations for advantage. It is tempting to ride the wave of success too long—to relax and enjoy the fruits of previous efforts. However, tomorrow's performance can be maintained only if it is supported by today's surplus resources. In other words, a firm must launch a new competitive advantage *before* the current strategy has run its course (see Figure 2-7). Entrepreneurs are more likely to maintain venture performance if they keep an eye on the future.

Thinking of the future requires that entrepreneurs design and implement their ventures with the risk of litigation in mind. Clearly, a lawsuit is a huge threat to the sustainability of a strategy. For example, consider the suit filed by San Antonio–based Mexican restaurant chain Taco Cabana against upstart Two Pesos for copying the look and color scheme of its restaurants. Although generic restau-

FIGURE 2-7

Sustaining Competitive Advantage

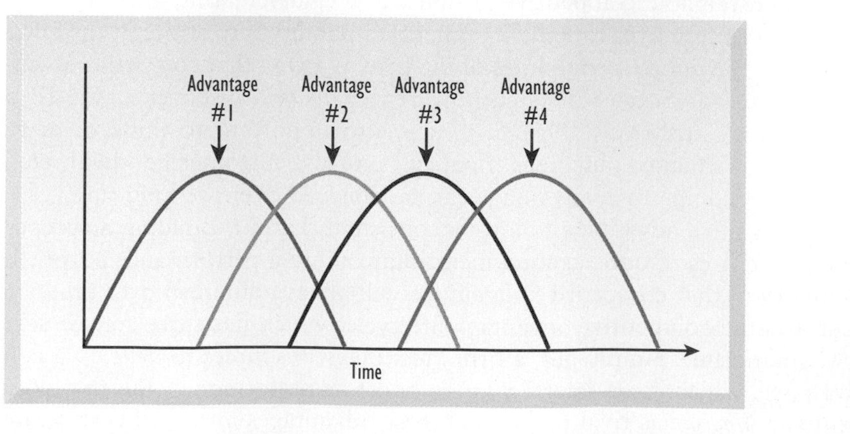

rant features would not have been protected under law, the U.S. Supreme Court ruled in favor of Taco Cabana's contention that the imitated features were not generic, thereby sealing the fate of Two Pesos. Similarly, Ty Inc. of Oak Brook, Illinois, maker of Beanie Babies, has charged HolyBears, Inc. with copyright infringement. Ty alleges that the patterns for HolyBears' 25 religious-themed bears are virtually identical to its patterns. HolyBears is putting up a fight, but just the legal costs may be prohibitive, in which case the strategy will not be sustainable.[37]

http://www.tacocabana.com
http://www.ty.com
http://www.holybears.com

Best Cellars, Inc. operates three wine stores designed to make wine buying simpler and less intimidating. Recently, Joshua Wesson, founder of the firm, sued Grape Finds, Inc. for copying his business and design approach (a concept known as *trade dress*). The judge issued a decision favoring Best Cellars, though he did not exclude the use of practices that simplify the wine-buying experience.[38]

http://www.bestcellars.com

These cases illustrate just how difficult it can be to satisfy the requirements of the law and how important careful planning is. Few hazards can ruin a successful enterprise faster than legal challenges.

Of course, sustainability involves more than legal planning. For example, Chris Zane (see p. 47) built a competitive hedge around his bicycle business by carefully managing product quality and customer service. He spent $200,000 setting up a system for fast delivery and meticulous assembly-and-shipping for his corporate premiums business (that is, his contract with large firms to distribute high-end bicycles to their employees as performance incentives). This was an expensive proposition for Zane, but he believes that the huge capital investment required will prevent competitors from imitating his approach.[39] If Zane is right, his finely tuned order fulfillment system will help to insulate his business from competition and thus promote the sustainability of its competitive advantage.

Patrick Kelly understands how a small business must evolve over time if it is to maintain its competitive advantage and survive. He and his partners started Physician Sales and Service, Inc. (PSS) in an effort to exploit a limitation in the services of most medical supply companies at the time. The industry norm was to stock medical services facilities by delivering supplies such as sterile bandages and syringes once every couple of weeks. In order to create a competitive advantage, PSS introduced next-day service for medical supply orders, charging slightly higher prices for this preferred service. Business boomed, but this attracted the attention of displaced competitors. Since the competitive advantage at PSS was easy to duplicate, rival firms quickly mobilized to offer their own next-day service. So, the company raised the bar again by providing laptop computers and mobile communications to field reps so that they could take orders in the morning and fill them that same afternoon. However, it was only a matter of time before others followed suit, so Kelly set new goals, expanding the business to reduce costs and offer even more attractive service. The plan worked, but Kelly is still on the move.[40] *A small business is more likely to survive if it is a moving target.*

http://www.pssd.com

This stage brings the model full circle. Well-planned foundations are more capable of supporting advantage strategies that work, and advantage strategies ultimately yield desirable outcomes. But the cycle must not be broken. Sustainable competitive advantage can be achieved only when the entrepreneur continuously assesses the external environments and upgrades organizational capabilities to find creative combinations that will support strategies that create value and sustain the firm's competitive position in the industry.

chapter 3

E-Commerce Opportunities

In the VIDEO Spotlight

Le Travel Store

In this episode of "Small Business School," the series on PBS stations, you will meet Joan and Bill Keller, founders of Le Travel Store. In 1976 the couple invested $3,000 they received as a wedding gift and borrowed another $3,000 to open a travel agency. Their first big seller was a low-cost plane ticket to Europe, which in 1976 was novel.

They built a loyal following, and in 1985 Joan and Bill left their funky Pacific Beach location and moved into an upscale mall in downtown San Diego. Then in 1994 they took a leadership position in the effort to revive San Diego's downtown historic business district. The couple bought a building, then worked to bring its original 1907 personality back to life. Just two years later, they put up the cash to build a location in the world's newest location, cyberspace.

Joan and Bill always seem to be in the right place at the right time. While their physical location is a lovely large shop full of great travel gear, books, and maps—all dedicated to the independent international traveler—as I write this, 60 percent of their sales are coming from http://letravelstore.com. They hired a team to design and deploy the first site, and over the years Joan and a staff person have learned HTML coding and how to shoot, crop, and post photos on the site. Without the help of "the pros," Joan launched a shopping spot at Yahoo.com; location, location, location continues to be critical to success. You will meet Joan and Bill Keller via video tape but, to fully appreciate their e-commerce success, have a look at the site for yourself. ◆

"We've always been investors rather than consumers. We like to take what we earn and reinvest it in growing the business."

—Joan Keller

—Hattie Bryant, Producer, "Small Business School," The Series on PBS Stations, Worldnet, and the Web, http://smallbusinessschool.org

SmallBusinessSchool
the Series on PBS stations and the Web

Go to page 730 for More! on Le Travel Store.

Looking Ahead

After studying this chapter, you should be able to

1. *Explain how the Internet developed and how it supports e-commerce activity.*
2. *Understand the benefits of e-commerce to small firms.*
3. *Describe the different business models followed by e-commerce firms.*
4. *Identify the initial considerations in launching a dot.com business.*
5. *Discuss criminal and ethical issues related to e-commerce.*

How many hits did you get this month? What is being done about the virus that is infecting our community? Did you get the firewall set up? How many cookies did we deliver today? Are these questions posed by baseball fans, medical doctors, firefighters, and bakers? Not necessarily. They may simply be questions posed by e-commerce entrepreneurs, speaking the language of cyberspace about their business operations.

We currently live in a digital economy fueled by the tremendous growth of the Internet. Access to the Internet is rapidly transforming the way we live and the way business is conducted. It is important for aspiring entrepreneurs to learn as much as they can about cyberspace because *there's opportunity online.*

What is the Internet, and how does it support e-commerce? What benefits does e-commerce offer small firms? What business models reflect an e-commerce strategy? What initial considerations confront an Internet startup? What are some of the criminal and ethical issues related to e-commerce? These are the primary questions we address in this chapter. We hope that our discussions will help you understand both the opportunities and the limitations associated with today's digital economy. Additional e-commerce topics are discussed in later chapters.

The Internet and E-Commerce

Since e-commerce is predicated on the Internet, let's begin with a brief history lesson.

Explain how the Internet developed and how it supports e-commerce activity.

What Is the Internet?

In 1957, the Russians launched *Sputnik,* the first unmanned satellite, into space. Their success in this first lap of the space race spurred a chain reaction in the United States. One of the charges given to the U.S. Department of Defense, in response to the fears raised by *Sputnik,* was to develop a communication system that could survive a nuclear war. So the department began intense and secret research on developing a different way to transmit information over communication channels. One of the results is what we now know as the Internet.

Internet
a huge, loosely connected computer network that links smaller networks all over the world, through modems, phone lines, satellite links, and other communication channels

The **Internet** is one huge, loosely connected computer network that links smaller networks all over the world through modems, phone lines, satellite links, and other communication channels. It enables people to communicate with other connected computer users via electronic mail (e-mail) and real-time (typed) conversation. In addition, it provides access to huge amounts of data, stored on computers all over

the world, that can be read or downloaded. And it allows people at one physical site to use the processing power of computers located at a different physical site. The Internet is a phenomenon that has significantly changed, and will continue to change, the way people communicate in the new millennium.

How the World Wide Web Works

World Wide Web (WWW)
a system of Internet servers accessible with browsers, which navigate via hypertext links

The **World Wide Web (WWW)** is a system of Internet servers accessible with browsers, which navigate via hypertext links. The World Wide Web was conceived and initiated in 1992 at the European Laboratory for Particle Physics, commonly known as CERN, in Switzerland. The idea was to expand the types of media used to convey information—to use not only text but also sound, video, animation, and hyperlinks. Today, information is posted on Web "pages," just as it is on printed pages in a book, and the interface is graphical.

Servers store information and process requests from clients. Using HyperText Transfer Protocol, or HTTP, the servers send the requested information and instructions on how to display that information (formatted in HyperText Markup Language, or HTML) back to the clients. The clients then handle the chore of displaying the information for the end user. In order to display the information, clients use a special type of program called a Web browser.

Using the Internet for E-Commerce

e-commerce
the paperless exchange of business information via the Internet

What does the term *e-commerce* really describe? **E-commerce** means electronic commerce, or the paperless exchange of business information via the Internet. It is a means of conducting business transactions that traditionally have been carried out by telephone, by mail, or face to face in brick-and-mortar establishments. As Table 3-1 shows, the growth of the Internet and e-commerce has been dramatic, despite a crash in Web-based stocks in 2000.

brick-and-mortar store
the traditional physical store from which businesses have historically operated

Although the Internet, like the telephone, is merely a tool that parties use to communicate with each other, it is a communication medium unlike any previously available to business. It is reshaping the way firms conduct business while also providing an alternative to the **brick-and-mortar store**—the traditional physical store from which businesses have historically operated. E-commerce has even found its way into the board games we play at home. In the new dot.com edition of the

TABLE 3-1 *E-Business Growth and Projections*

	1996	1999	Projected 2002–2003
Internet hosts (domains)	12.9 million	56.2 million	More than 100 million
Web users	28 million	65 million (U.S.) 163 million (worldwide)	83 million (U.S.) 175 million (worldwide)
Percent of Web users who buy goods or services	25%	39%	46%
Business-to-consumer Web commerce	$2.6 billion	$13 billion	$108 billion
Business-to-business Web commerce (includes transactions over extranets)	Less than $43 billion	$109 billion	$1.3 trillion (9% of U.S. sales)
Advertising revenue	$236.5 million	$2 billion	$7.7 billion

Source: Brad Alan Kleindl, *Strategic Electronic Marketing, Managing E-Business* (Cincinnati, OH: South-Western, 2001), p. 9.

world's most successful board game, Monopoly, brick-and-mortar utilities and real estate have been replaced by Internet-based properties like eBay and Lycos.

Myths About E-Commerce

Though e-commerce is a young industry, several myths have already developed about opportunities in the digital marketplace. To avoid confusion, we will briefly examine and dispel each myth.

First, some believe that the technical nature of the Internet makes e-commerce too expensive for small firms. This simply isn't true. Many e-commerce sites have been successfully launched with relatively small budgets. Consider the Web site of entrepreneur Deb Edlhuber's Prairie Frontier seed company, based in Waukesha, Wisconsin. Launched in 1997 after Edlhuber completed a course of self-instruction about the Web, the site had an original cost of only $400. "We put our Web address on our packaging and our displays. People would buy the seeds at garden centers and see the URL and go to the site to get information," says Edlhuber.[1] In 1999, her Web site was named by *Inc.* magazine as one of the 20 best small business Web sites. And, so, the first myth is dispelled: Small firms with limited budgets *can* be successful online.

http://www.prairiefrontier.com

A second myth is that e-commerce is nothing more than a new way of taking orders, supplementing the capabilities of the telephone or fax machine. True, customers can place orders on a Web site—but e-commerce offers much more to both customers and firms, and it requires business savvy and sound planning. For example, Data-Link Associates, a computer supplies company, began in a traditional fashion; owners Buddy and Helene Stone prospected for customers over the phone, making sales calls and so forth from their North Bellmore, New York home. Then,

IN THE TRENCHES UTILIZING NEW TECHNOLOGY

WHO'S RUNNING THE ONLINE STORE?

Many e-commerce firms begin as one-person operations, often resulting in an overwhelming experience for the entrepreneur. Outsourcing is one approach to lightening the workload. An entrepreneur who recognized the benefits of outsourcing is Lars Hundley, who launched the Clean Air Gardening Company online in 1998. This online store sells environmentally responsible lawn and garden products—push mowers, composters, etc. Hundley saw very early that he needed help with daily business operations, so he included outsourcing as part of his business model.

Hundley's success—the company reported profits of $100,000 in 2000—has hinged on knowing what to outsource and what he can best do himself. For a monthly fee of $100, Yahoo! Store processes orders and payments. And to expedite payment to suppliers, the business uses an automated accounting program offered by Wells Fargo Internet banking system. "I don't have to mess with licking envelopes," Hundley says. Also, a company named Personalized Communications handles initial orders and also compiles marketing information for the firm at a cost of $350 a month.

Using these services gives Hundley time to concentrate on decisions about what new products to offer and time each day to make a trip to the warehouse—a 10-by-17-foot ministorage unit—where he picks up the merchandise necessary to fill the day's orders.

Outsourcing saves Hundley time, but it does cost money. However, Hundley believes that having himself as the company's sole employee is the best way to keep expenses low and profits high—at least for now.

Source: Jill Hecht Maxwell, "One Man, One Computer, 1,431 Lawn Mowers," *Inc. Technology,* Vol. 23, No. 9 (2001), pp. 46–50.

http://www.cleanairgardening.com

in 1997, the Stones launched their first Web site, where they posted their product list. As the Stones' Internet business savvy improved, sales increased—to $1.5 million in 2000. E-commerce has changed their entire relationship with their customers. Customers are now finding them and asking questions. Their marketplaces are as far away as Australia, and credit card buying has increased from 1 percent of sales to almost 20 percent, improving credit collection.[2] Is e-commerce effective? Yes. Is it simply a means of taking orders? No.

The last myth we dismantle is that being first is the only way to be successful online. Innovators do, of course, have an extra edge in defining and developing a market, but the "earliest bird" doesn't automatically have a monopoly on success. An entrepreneur interested in entering a market can learn many important lessons from watching innovators. For example, marketing clothing online is no longer novel, but still provides opportunities for success. Adventure travel clothing firm Ex Officio Inc., founded in 1986 and based in Seattle, uses its Web site to offer visitors more than just an online clothing store. Ex Officio launched the site in 1999 to provide travel information as well as clothing items. "We want it to be a virtual community for travelers," says marketing manager Janine Robertson. In fact, four screens of travel information are provided to customers before they even encounter a garment for sale.[3] This clothing store is successful, even though it certainly wasn't the first to go online, perhaps because navigating its site is an enjoyable experience for both consumers and travelers.

http://www.exofficio.com

Benefits of E-Commerce to Small Firms

2 *Understand the benefits of e-commerce to small firms.*

Electronic commerce benefits small firms in a number of ways. Basically, it offers a firm the opportunity to compete with bigger businesses on a more level playing field. Limited resources frequently restrict the ability of small firms to expand beyond local markets. Confined to their brick-and-mortar world, small firms typically serve a small geographic area. But the Internet blurs geographic boundaries. E-commerce allows any business to access customers almost anywhere. The Internet is proving to be the great equalizer, giving small firms a presence comparable to that of the giants in the marketplace.

An e-commerce operation can help small firms with cash flow problems by compressing their sales cycle—that is, reducing the time between receiving an order and converting the sales to cash. E-commerce systems can be designed to generate an order, authorize a credit card purchase, and contact a supplier and shipper in a matter of minutes, all without human assistance. The shorter cycle translates into quicker payments from customers and improved cash flows to the business.

Electronic Customer Relationship Marketing (eCRM)
an electronically based system that emphasizes customer relationships

E-commerce also enables small firms to build upon one of their greatest strengths—customer relationships. The Internet has brought new life and technology to bear on the old-fashioned notion of customer service. **Electronic Customer Relationship Marketing** (**eCRM**) is an electronically based system that emphasizes customer relationships. At the heart of eCRM is a customer-centric data warehouse. A typical eCRM system allows an e-commerce firm to integrate data from Web sites, call centers, sales force reports, and other customer contact points, with the end goal of building customer loyalty. To appreciate the possibilities, consider this hypothetical example posed by Professor Thomas W. Leigh of the University of Georgia, as he discusses how an existing dot.com retailer might use eCRM:

IN THE TRENCHES

UTILIZING NEW TECHNOLOGY

DOGGIE SNACKS GO GLOBAL

The Internet offers small firms the opportunity to expand beyond local markets. This is exactly the approach used by Dan Dye and Mark Beckloff of Kansas City, Missouri, founders of Three Dog Bakery. Back in 1989, they began baking dog biscuit treats in their kitchen and selling them to local pet owners. The premise for their venture was that dog owners, who spend billions of dollars each year just to feed their pets, would buy them high-quality (and high-priced) doggie snacks.

Sales were so good that two years later Dye and Beckloff rented an old storefront for $750 a month and began diversifying. Later, they launched their first Internet site, hoping to sell snack treats online. It worked! Their electronic store has provided access to customers around the world. "We ship to Japan and Jakarta, and we never would have had the resources to reach [those customers] otherwise," Beckloff says. Their Web page racks up more than a million hits a month and the average sale is $40, more than twice the average sale at the bakery counter.

With their click-and-mortar strategy, Beckloff and Dye have created a $10 million-a-year business. Clearly, these two entrepreneurs seized the opportunity to use e-commerce to grow their business.

Source: From material from http://www.threedog.com; and Dina Temple-Raston, "Canine Cuisine Fetches Success," *USA Today*, February 17, 2000, p. 12B.

http://www.threedog.com

Consider my local flower and gift retailer, or even a larger firm such as flowers.com and garden.com. With my permission, they can build a personalized database on Thomas W. Leigh. You can think of this database as a folder, hypercard, or line of code. The data may be collected from a variety of sources. Checkout line bar codes detail my purchases. Warranty cards and survey responses suggest my interest and preferences. Telephone calls indicate my interest in certain information or problem resolution. And, very importantly, if the firm has my trust, the eCRM system can be managed by an ongoing dialogue that allows me to help the flower retailer understand and manage my flower and gift needs.

Let's see, that means that flower retailer can develop an annual gift plan for me. Imagine, I could plan all my gifts on January 1 instead of merely making a pledge "to do better in 2001." The retailer would then remember my wife's and mother's birthdays. And our anniversary. I could choose a set of pre-selected gifts, perhaps modified at the suggestion of the retailer if something new hit the market. The retailer could schedule appropriate delivery dates. No more late gifts and apologies. The retailer would then send me a reminder and a timely payment plan. No surprises when I get home. Just a happy family! Sounds pretty good, doesn't it? Oh, by the way, they can suggest new products to fit my needs without asking me. Why? Because I gave them permission to track my purchases. They can begin to anticipate my needs, making my life even simpler and better.[4]

There are, of course, innumerable other benefits that small firms can reap from e-commerce; space does not allow us to discuss them all here. And as e-commerce continues to evolve, additional benefits will emerge.

Building Customer Loyalty

WHERE DOES YOUR LOYALTY LIE?

Dealing with the American farmer over the Internet is a big challenge. Several dot.com firms are slowly taking root among farm customers. However, many traditional agricultural retailers are uneasy about the growth of e-commerce in their industry.

Some companies, such as Gempler's, have served farmers directly with catalogs for years and are now experiencing a smooth transition into e-commerce. Over 9,000 catalog items can now be bought online. However, firms like QuickFarm Incorporated, an online input exchange dealing in seed, fertilizer, and chemicals, are facing resistance because they are hurting local retailer outlets. "The retailer is the most threatened entity out there," says a board member of QuickFarm.

Brian Lindsay is a farmer near Masonville, Iowa who has purchased farm chemicals online. However, he is unsettled about the purchases because he knows his local retailer is aware of the lost business and isn't happy about it. "It worked out fine, but we do want to do business with our current suppliers. They're local," says Lindsay. Getting customers to change this loyalty is not easy for e-commerce businesses.

Trust is a major issue for farmers who are lured to the Internet by lower prices. Gerald Warren Farms in Newton Grove, North Carolina recently saved $8,000 by buying on the Internet. But the transaction was not stress-free.

He had to pay for the product before it was shipped. Once it arrived, he was on his own. It is a no-frills way of doing business, he says. "They don't buy you supper, and you won't get a free cap or jacket," adds Warren.

E-commerce firms serving farmers will undoubtedly grow, and many local retailers will probably close their doors. But others will adapt.

Source: Dan Miller, "The Lure of the Net," *Progressive Farmer,* Vol. 115, No. 11 (October 2000), pp. 24–26.

http://www.quickfarm.com

E-Commerce Business Models

Describe the different business models followed by e-commerce firms.

business model
a group of shared characteristics, behaviors, and goals that a firm follows in a particular business situation

The dictionary defines an opportunity as a "combination of circumstances favorable for a chance to advance oneself." Thus, it is logical to study the circumstances surrounding e-commerce in its current state in order to uncover e-commerce opportunities. Let's begin by examining some existing e-commerce business models.

The term **business model** describes a group of shared characteristics, behaviors, and goals that a firm follows in a particular business situation. Online business firms differ in their decisions concerning what customers to serve, how best to become profitable, and what to include on their Web sites. Figure 3-1 shows some possible alternatives for business models. None of these models can currently be considered dominant, and some Internet businesses cannot be described by any single model. The real world of e-commerce contains endless combinations of business models.

Can a poorly devised business model be a major factor in business failure? Yes, it can! Appendix 3A discusses the reasons for three dot.com failures.

FIGURE 3-1

E-Commerce Business Models

- **Type of Customers Served**
  - Business-to-Business (B2B)
  - Business-to-Consumer (B2C)
  - Auction Sites
- **Approach to Profitability**
  - Revenue-Based
  - Expense-Based
  - Growth-Based
- **Degree of Online Presence**
  - Content/Information-Based
  - Transaction-Based

Type of Customers Served

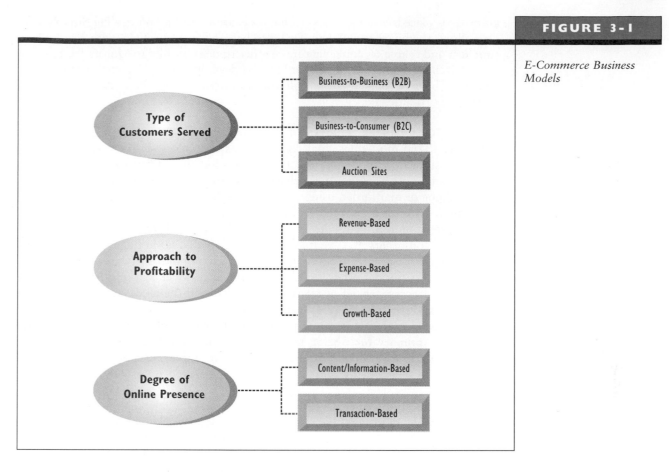

Marketing theory classifies traditional brick-and-mortar firms as manufacturers, wholesalers, or retailers, depending on the customers they serve. E-commerce businesses also are commonly distinguished according to customer focus. There are three major categories of e-commerce business models: business-to-business (B2B), business-to-consumer (B2C), and auction sites. In this section, we examine some strategies used by e-commerce firms within these three categories.

business-to-business (B2B) model
a business model based on selling to business customers electronically

BUSINESS-TO-BUSINESS MODELS Notice in Table 3-1 that the dollar amounts listed for firms using a **business-to-business (B2B) model** (selling to business customers) are significantly greater than those listed for firms with a business-to-consumer (B2C) model (selling to final consumers). Because B2B success stories generally receive less publicity than B2C ventures do, the potential of a B2B opportunity may be missed. Aspiring entrepreneurs should be sure to consider the B2B model.

All B2B firms do not look alike. One form of B2B strategy emphasizes sales transactions. By using online capabilities, a B2B firm can create greater efficiency in its selling and buying. Dell Computer Corporation is a good example. By dealing directly with its corporate customers online, it is able to build computers to specifications *after*

an order is placed. Storage and carrying costs are reduced, and dealing directly with Dell allows the buyer to pay less. Dell also has online connections with hundreds of suppliers and is able to implement more efficient delivery of parts for its factories.

http://www.dell.com

As B2B e-commerce models continue to develop and evolve, new versions will emerge. The wise entrepreneur will continue to monitor these changes to learn where opportunities lie.

business-to-consumer (B2C) model
a business model based on selling to final consumers electronically

BUSINESS-TO-CONSUMER MODELS In contrast to a B2B model, a **business-to-consumer (B2C) model** has final consumers as customers. In the traditional retail setting, customers generally approach a business location (a brick-and-mortar store) with the intent of shopping or purchasing. Alternatively, customers might purchase via telephone or mail order, using a printed catalog. The B2C model introduces another alternative for consumers—buying online.

http://www.amazon.com

Amazon.com represents the classic B2C firm, which is directly focused on individual final consumers. B2C ventures are extremely diverse in the products they sell, with products ranging from clothing to pet items, computer software, toys, and groceries. The B2C model offers three main advantages over brick-and-mortar retailing: speed of access, speed of transaction, and round-the-clock access to products and services, often referred to as **24/7 e-tailing.**

24/7 e-tailing
electronic retailing providing round-the-clock access to products and services

On the negative side, many final consumers avoid online shopping for several reasons, the primary ones being reluctance to send credit card data electronically and to purchase a product without first seeing it. Table 3-2 summarizes concerns mentioned by respondents in a recent survey conducted by a major Internet consulting firm.

http://www.delias.com

Many B2C firms offer an electronic environment where customers can experience a sense of community. For example, Delia's sells fashionable clothing to young girls but also devotes a part of its Web site to something called The Lounge. It's a chat room where young girls can talk about their summer plans, music, the prom, or whatever. It creates a feeling of community that builds customer loyalty.[5]

TABLE 3-2

Why Consumers Didn't Buy Online

	Percentage of Online Households That Didn't Purchase via the Web
1. Uncomfortable sending credit card data across Net	97%
2. Preferred to see product before purchased	53%
3. Couldn't talk to a sales representative	18%
4. Couldn't get enough product information to make decision	16%
5. Product too expensive relative to alternatives	15%
6. Couldn't get information or products suited to needs	13%
7. Couldn't talk to other buyers of product about their views	12%
8. Process too long	11%
9. Had to download software	11%
10. Web site was hard to navigate through	10%
11. Process was too confusing	8%
12. Product information or products were not current	6%

Source: "The Second Annual Ernst & Young Internet Shopping Study," sponsored by the National Retail Federation, 1999, p. 11.

B2C dot.com businesses have the ability to quickly change merchandise mixes and prices, as well as the appearance of their "store" (their Web site). Traditional merchants find such changes very costly and time-consuming.

AUCTION SITE MODELS Some entrepreneurs sell their wares over the Internet without either a Web site or a storefront, by means of e-commerce sites based on the auction site model. Internet **auction sites** are Web-based businesses offering participants—primarily final consumers, but also businesses—the ability to list products for bidding by potential buyers. Revenues to the auction site are derived from listing fees and commissions on sales.

auction sites
Web-based businesses offering participants the ability to list products for bidding

The earliest e-commerce auction sites dealt with collectibles, but now such sites are conduits for almost any kind of product. EBay is one of the largest e-commerce businesses using this model. Yahoo!, the largest search engine on the Internet, also has an auction site, which offers free postings and no commissions.

Partners Michael O'Harro and Charles Shoup operate a profitable small business called Champions Stuff, which uses eBay to sell its vintage photographs. Without a storefront or Web site, Champions Stuff sells about a thousand photos per week. The company interacts with buyers via e-mail and offers a money-back guarantee.[6]

At sites geared exclusively to businesses, suppliers compete online for manufacturers' orders in live open auctions. Such business giants as General Motors, Raytheon, and Quaker Oats report saving more than 15 percent on parts, materials, and even services at Internet auctions sponsored by FreeMarkets, Inc.[7]

http://www.freemarkets.com

Approach to Profitability

Despite the many exciting changes brought about by the electronic age, one issue remains of concern to both traditional and e-commerce firms: profitability. E-commerce firms seek profitability in a variety of ways. *Revenue-based models* emphasize revenue enhancement, while *expense-based models* focus on expense reduction. *Growth-based models* concentrate on growing the customer base.

REVENUE-BASED MODEL Like more traditional businesses, e-commerce ventures must generate revenues in order to survive. **Revenue-based models** are focused on generating, maintaining, and increasing revenues. However, these revenues may be derived in many different ways. In the early days of the Internet, the only sources of revenue for online sites were charges to access online content and user subscription fees. As e-commerce grew, other sources of revenue were identified.

revenue-based model
a business model that focuses on generating, maintaining, and increasing revenues

For example, Web site owners learned that they could sell advertising on their sites, with the fee tied to the number of **hits,** or Internet connections made to the site. First used in 1994, banner advertising has become an important source of revenue for Web site owners. Fees may be charged, or revenue may be derived from commissions on sales resulting from the advertising appearing on the site.

hits
Internet connections made to a Web site

"Good banners are billboards on the Internet," says Edward Ziv, a business technology consultant with Flash Creative Management, in Hackensack, New Jersey. "They're short, with just a few words, and offer a clear message. And you'll increase your results if two of those words are 'Click Here,'" he says.[8]

A popular form of site linkage today is called **affiliation.** In a formal agreement with the sponsoring firm, other Web site owners contract to include on their sites an icon that allows visitors quick access to the site of the sponsoring firm. Such a

affiliation
a form of Web site linkage whereby other Web sites gain visitors from the sponsoring firm

relationship can be a substantial source of revenue for small firm affiliates. Amazon.com, for instance, pays affiliates up to a 15 percent commission for sales generated by traffic originating from their sites. In late 2000, Amazon.com had over 460,000 Web sites in its network.

http://www.florist.com

Online flower store Florist.com features links to dozens of affiliated gift-related Web sites on its site. Affiliation is "a way for us to expand what's sold on our site, at no cost to us," says Aaron Benon, who runs the retail flower shop in Beverly Hills. "These are products we don't have to fulfill or ship, yet we get a commission on them," he says.[9]

Of course, the essence of e-commerce is the generation of revenue from selling products and services online. Transaction sales are the fastest-growing source of revenue for online businesses. Once a firm commits its Web site to transaction revenues, the performance of the site becomes extremely important.

expense-based model
a business model that focuses on reducing costs

EXPENSE-BASED MODEL Expense reduction is the factor motivating many small firms to enter cyberspace. Lowering costs always increases profitability, and **expense-based models** focus on reducing costs.

A number of business functions can be conducted more economically over the Internet. One costly process that can often be performed more cheaply online is providing information to customers in a timely manner. For example, airlines have found that they can provide updated scheduling and pricing information via the Internet at far less cost than is required to support a call center or mail brochures. Many small firms have discovered that they can save time and money by incorporating a Frequently Asked Questions (FAQ) feature on their Web site, thereby reducing the number of individual customer inquiries they have to answer.

B2B firms, in particular, use e-commerce to reduce costs associated with sales force management. In fact, some industries are seeing a reduction in the size of their sales force because Web sites are handling much of the selling activity more efficiently.

growth-based model
a business model that focuses on customer growth for profitability

GROWTH-BASED MODEL At first glance, the **growth-based model,** which focuses on customer growth for profitability, appears to be out of focus. This is because many of the more established e-commerce firms are not yet making a profit or do not appear to be approaching profitability. These firms are concentrating on growth that they assume will eventually bring profits. The growth model partially explains the survival of firms like Amazon.com. Expenditures on marketing and technology have kept Amazon.com in the red. Although stock prices are falling, they are still relatively high, and the company is viewed as a leader in e-commerce.

Apparently, Amazon.com and other firms like it are establishing customer relationships on the Web with the hope of cashing in at a later date. The term *monetizing* is used to describe the essence of this e-commerce model. How long these firms can continue to survive without showing a profit is unclear.

By early 2001, the business morgue was filling with dot.coms, in part because of business models that didn't bring in sufficient revenues. Pets.com, for example, was losing about 20 cents on every dollar of revenue at the time of its failure—the more it sold, the more it lost.

Degree of Online Presence

A third broad way of categorizing e-commerce models relates to the firm's intended level of online presence. The role of a Web site can range from merely offering content and information to enabling complex business transactions.

CONTENT/INFORMATION-BASED MODEL In a **content/information-based model** of e-commerce, a Web site provides access but not the ability to buy or sell products and services. During the early days of e-commerce, the *content model* was the model of choice. For example, America Online (AOL) began with this model. Originally, revenue for AOL came from fees paid by users for the privilege of connecting and gaining access to its content. Today, content models are found mostly in countries where Internet usage by small firms is less developed.

content/information-based model
a business model in which the Web site provides information but not the ability to buy or sell products and services

A slight variation of the content model is the *information model.* A Web site built on this model contains information about the business, its products, and other related matters but doesn't charge for its use. It is typically just a complement to an existing brick-and-mortar store. For example, a small business named Duck Soup, located in Sudbury, Massachusetts, launched its Web site in June of 1999 after its retail store completely burned. The goal of the site was "to create an environment that's . . . inviting and [as] much an expression of the owners' personalities as the real store was."[10] The site told the story of the fire and kept customers informed of the company's plans. A new brick-and-mortar store opened in early 2000. The company is now experimenting with the sale of coffee from its online store.

Another example of an information model is FunMail's Web site. Betty Jo Houck, of Cuyahoga Falls, Ohio, operates this home-based business that sells lawn ornaments. Information regarding the products is available on the site, but orders can be placed only by phone or fax.

http://www.wemailsmiles.com

TRANSACTION-BASED MODEL In a **transaction-based model** of e-commerce, a Web site provides a mechanism for buying or selling products or services. The transaction-based model, which is at the very heart of e-commerce, calls for Web sites to be online stores where visitors go to shop, click, and buy.

transaction-based model
a business model in which the Web site provides a mechanism for buying or selling products or services

Many dot.com stores sell a single product or service. For example, Huber and Jane Wilkinson, based in Waco, Texas, market their reading comprehension program, Ideachain, through their MindPrime, Inc. Web site. Similarly, Todd Green of Santa Monica, California sells his HeadBlade shaving device only from his Web site (see Case 3).

http://www.mindprime.com
http://www.headblade.com

Other ventures are direct extensions of a brick-and-mortar store, creating a click-and-mortar strategy. For example, if you were interested in purchasing a new printer, you might research options on Office Depot's Web site and then choose to either buy your selection online or drive to the neighborhood Office Depot store and pick up the printer there. Gradually, a small firm can add to and improve its Web site store until all of its products are available online.

Preparing to Launch a Dot.Com Business

Numerous decisions must be made prior to launching a dot.com business. Many of these, such as financing, are beyond the scope of this chapter. However, three critical startup tasks related to Web sites are discussed here: (1) creating and registering a site name, (2) building a user-friendly site, and (3) promoting the site.

4
Identify the initial considerations in launching a dot.com business.

Creating and Registering a Site Name

Selecting the best name for a dot.com business is an important decision. Contrary to general opinion, plenty of Web site names remain available. Currently, a domain name can have a maximum of 67 characters preceding the final domain

Utilizing New Technology

WEB SITES CAN CREATE CHANNEL CONFLICT

Does cyberspace marketing significantly impact traditional distribution policy? It can. Just ask Bob Duncan, owner of American Leather, a nine-year-old furniture company based in Dallas, Texas. He remembers what happened when one of his retailers went online.

American Leather set up a Web site in 1997 to serve as an online brochure only. Retailers carrying the branded furniture were happy with this policy. One day, a retailer in another state began offering a "lowball" price for American Leather furniture over its Web site to shoppers not located in its geographic market area. The retailer in one buyer's local area was irate, considering the sale to be a violation of dealer exclusivity, which was a practice of American Leather. Duncan's reaction was as follows:

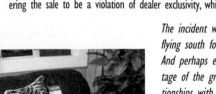

The incident was a wake-up to me: with retailers flocking to cyberspace like birds flying south for the winter, how could we enforce our policy of dealer exclusivity? And perhaps even more challenging: how could American Leather itself take advantage of the growth opportunities offered by the Internet without destroying its relationships with its 600-plus retailers—the very heart of the distribution channel that we at the company had spent our entire careers developing?

American Leather has since redesigned its Internet site to include more detailed product information and a dealer locator to encourage customers to find the American Leather retailer nearest to them.

Duncan is also considering selling products directly over the Internet with the delivery and after-sale support handled by the dealer closest to the buyer. If he decided to implement this policy, Duncan says, "We would then pay the dealers the approximate margin that they would have made on the sale if it had taken place in their showroom."

Source: Bob Duncan, "First Do No Harm," *Inc. Technology,* Vol. 22, No. 4 (2000), pp. 29–30.

designation. Given all the letters, numbers, and hyphens that domain names can contain, it is estimated that 99 percent of all possible dot.com domain names are still available.

http://www.namelab.com

Since a domain name gives a small business its online identity, it is desirable to select a descriptive and appealing name. "It's no harder to make up names for dot.coms than for colas," says Ira Bachrack of San Francisco's NameLab.[11]

Obviously, some of the shorter, more creative names have already been taken. But, like real estate, Web site names can be bought and sold. Marc Ostrofsky, former CEO of Information Publishing, owns more than 100 domain names. He purchased the name "business.com" in 1997 from a British Internet service provider for $150,000 and later sold it for $7.5 million.[12]

http://www.icann.org

Once a desired name has been selected, it should be checked for availability and then registered. The Internet Corporation for Assigned Names and Numbers (ICANN) is the nonprofit corporation currently overseeing the global Internet. Recently, it approved seven new domain designations, including ".biz" for businesses, in response to a need to make available valuable addresses taken in existing domains. However, the rollouts of the new domain designations have encountered problems. Some companies complain that the planned application process is flawed,

IN THE TRENCHES

BUILDING CUSTOMER LOYALTY

KEEP IT SIMPLE

Walkabout Travel Gear sells products through its Web site to adventure travelers. Its site lists products ranging from an all-terrain money belt to insect repellent. Located in a recreational vehicle in Moab, Utah, the business has been operated by entrepreneurs Brad and Gia Boyle since its launch in 1996.

Brad's hint for other small businesses building an online business is to keep it simple. "We never treated the Internet as a place to use flashy advertising, but see it as a tool," Brad says. Most of Brad's time in maintaining the Web site is spent adding new items for sale and creating links to travel information sites. The site also has a message board for people looking for travel partners.

"We wanted our Web site to be a reference source as well as sell things," Brad says. "We focus on the customer, and the site is a forum for them." The company grew 45 percent in 1999 and averaged almost $250,000 from commissions on the products it sold. With no permanent employees, these entrepreneurs operate from a remote area that couldn't support a brick-and-mortar store.

Source: Tom Till, "Forge a Community of Customers," *MyBusiness*, March/April 2000, p. 34.

and the introduction scheduled for October 2001 was delayed by the September 11th terrorist attacks.

ICANN, however, does not register names; this must be done through a domain registration firm. Several domain registrars allow a search of the Internet to see if a proposed name is already taken. InterNic provides an Accredited Registrar Directory that lists ICANN-accredited domain registrars.

http://www.internic.net/regist.html

One U.S.-based registrar is Network Solutions (NSI). Figure 3-2, on page 70, shows the results of an NSI search on the name "longeneckermoorepetty.com." As you can see, at the time this book went to press, the name was available. NSI owns Root Server A, the primary top-level Internet server, which allows Web users to access a Web address anywhere in the world. NSI had the original, exclusive franchise—given by the federal government—to register domain names. Since the exclusive franchise ended in 1999, Root Server A has remained in control of the global distribution of new Web addresses. Occasionally, NSI allows visitors to stand next to Root Server A and pose for pictures.[13]

http://www.netsol.com

Another ICANN-accredited domain name registrar is Namesecure, whose Web page is shown in Figure 3-3, on page 71. Note that the registration costs listed are relatively low.

http://www.namesecure.com

Building a User-Friendly Web Site

First impressions are important, and high-quality Web design gives a small e-commerce business the opportunity to make a good first impression on each visitor.

The technical aspects of developing a Web site are beyond the scope of this chapter. Fortunately, there are many technical specialists available to help design and build a site. Our purpose here is simply to provide some useful tips about Web site design.

FIGURE 3-2

NSI Search on "longeneckermoorepetty.com"

(Note that the "real" Web site for this book can be found at http://longenecker.swcollege.com.)

VeriSign

Please take a business card.

Not just talk.

HOME | FIND A DOMAIN NAME | BUILD YOUR WEB SITE | CHOOSE YOUR WEB OPTIONS | LEARN HOW | MANAGE ACCOUNT RENEW SERVICES

PRIVACY POLICY HELP WHOIS SELL YOUR NAME VIEW ORDER

You are Here: Find a Domain Name -> Search Results

FIND A DOMAIN NAME
Search Results

CONGRATULATIONS!	Price
☑ **longeneckermoorepetty.com** is available	$35.00/year

SEARCH AGAIN | CONTINUE

Other Names You Might Like	Price
☐ longeneckermoorepetty.net	$30.00/year
☐ longeneckermoorepetty.biz	$35.00/year
☐ longeneckermoorepetty.info	$35.00/year
☐ longeneckermoorepetty.tv	$50.00/year
☐ longeneckermoorepetty.org	$25.00/year
☐ longeneckermoorepetty.ws	$35.00/year
☐ longeneckermoorelittle.com	$35.00/year
☐ longeneckermoorelittlest.com	$35.00/year
☐ longeneckermoore-countypetty.com	$35.00/year
☐ longeneckermoorecountypetty.com	$35.00/year
☐ elongeneckermoorepetty.com	$35.00/year

Search Results by Applied Semantics SEARCH AGAIN | CONTINUE

FAQs
- What if I can't find a name that I like on this page?
- What do the different extensions mean?
- What are these 'Other Names' I might like?
- How much does a domain name cost?
- Who has the name that I want?

Back to Top | About Us | Partnerships | Contact Us | Site Map | Disclaimer

Shown in Table 3-3, on page 72, are 10 Web site design tips for e-commerce, excerpted from an article posted on Microsoft's Web site.

http://www.shoebuy.com

Figure 3-4, on page 73, shows the home page of Shoebuy.com, a young entrepreneurial business that sells shoes online. It is a very good example of a user-friendly Web page.

There are many reasons why Web sites fail to retain customers. One of the most frequent problems is slow downloading. Online shoppers are a fickle bunch, and the slightest inconvenience sends them away. If a page takes more than 20 to 30 seconds to load, there's a high chance of abandonment, as Rick Edler discovered. Edler launched a low-tech Web site for his business, Edler Group, at a cost of $285 in 1997. When he later decided he needed something fancier, he hired a Web developer who built a site filled with color graphics and motion—at a cost of $7,000. But it took too long to download. Traffic was below expectations. "So much was happening," Edler says. "You just stared at it like you were watching a commercial. We

http://www.edlergroup.com

FIGURE 3-3 *Web Page of Namesecure*

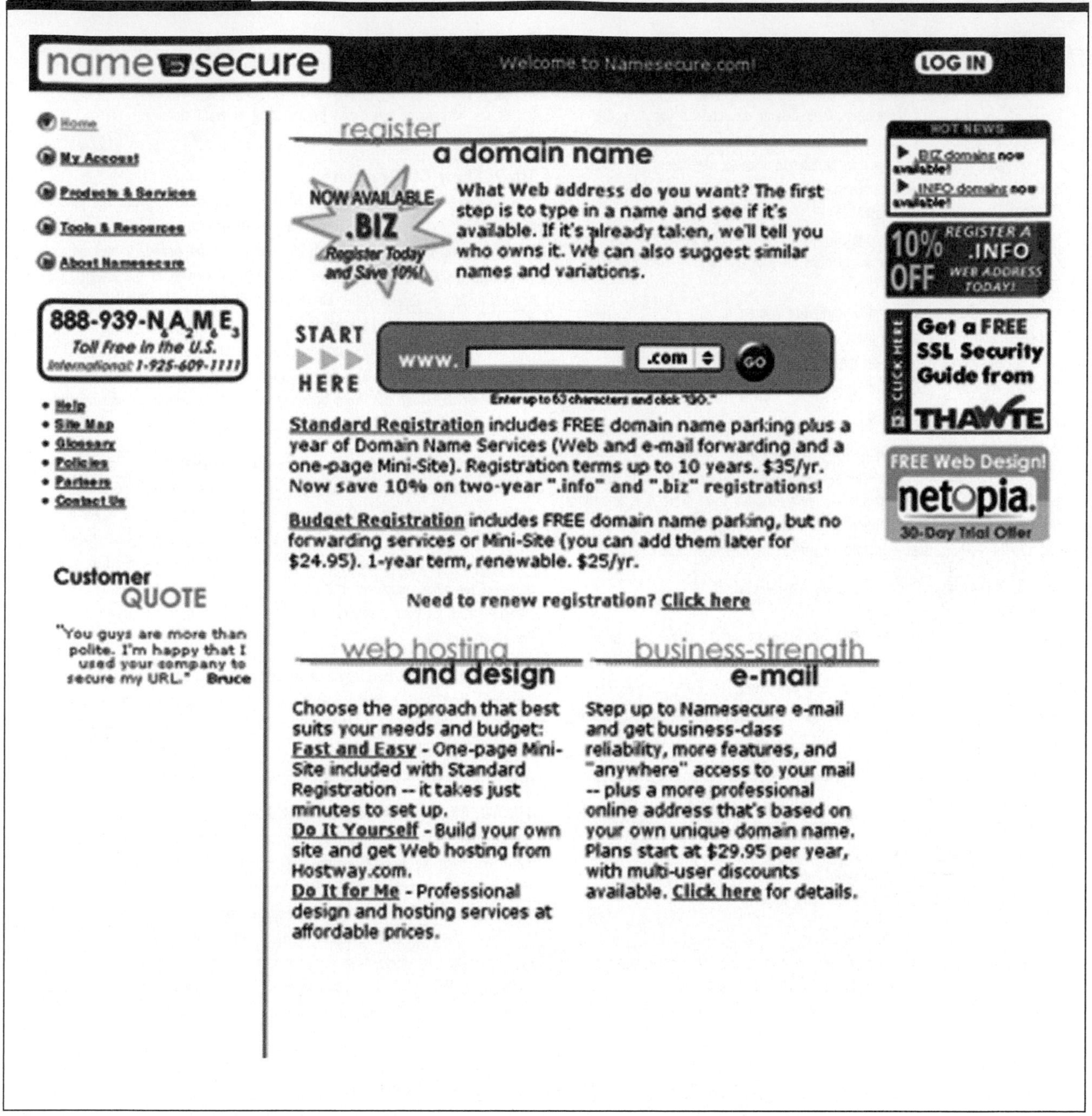

name secure
Welcome to Namesecure.com!
LOG IN

Home
My Account
Products & Services
Tools & Resources
About Namesecure

888-939-NAME
Toll Free in the U.S.
International: 1-925-609-1111

- Help
- Site Map
- Glossary
- Policies
- Partners
- Contact Us

Customer QUOTE

"You guys are more than polite. I'm happy that I used your company to secure my URL." Bruce

register a domain name

NOW AVAILABLE .BIZ Register Today and Save 10%!

What Web address do you want? The first step is to type in a name and see if it's available. If it's already taken, we'll tell you who owns it. We can also suggest similar names and variations.

START HERE www. .com GO

Enter up to 63 characters and click "GO."

Standard Registration includes FREE domain name parking plus a year of Domain Name Services (Web and e-mail forwarding and a one-page Mini-Site). Registration terms up to 10 years. $35/yr. Now save 10% on two-year ".info" and ".biz" registrations!

Budget Registration includes FREE domain name parking, but no forwarding services or Mini-Site (you can add them later for $24.95). 1-year term, renewable. $25/yr.

Need to renew registration? Click here

web hosting and design

Choose the approach that best suits your needs and budget:
Fast and Easy - One-page Mini-Site included with Standard Registration -- it takes just minutes to set up.
Do It Yourself - Build your own site and get Web hosting from Hostway.com.
Do It for Me - Professional design and hosting services at affordable prices.

business-strength e-mail

Step up to Namesecure e-mail and get business-class reliability, more features, and "anywhere" access to your mail -- plus a more professional online address that's based on your own unique domain name. Plans start at $29.95 per year, with multi-user discounts available. Click here for details.

HOT NEWS
BIZ domains now available!
INFO domains now available!

10% OFF REGISTER A .INFO WEB ADDRESS TODAY!

CLICK HERE Get a FREE SSL Security Guide from THAWTE

FREE Web Design! netopia. 30-Day Trial Offer

were scaring people away."[14] The site was finally scrapped and replaced by a new, simpler version.

Remember, Web sites will also fail if they do not satisfy visitors' information needs. Frequently, this is because designers look inward to the business for Web design ideas, rather than outward to customer needs.

TABLE 3-3 *Web Site Design Tips*

Tip 1: Make It Easy to Buy

This tip may seem vague and ambiguous, but it truly is the most important recommendation. Put yourself in your customer's shoes and test your designs. Isolate issues that might block users from making a successful purchase. Ask questions, such as

- How many pages and clicks does it take to make a purchase?
- How much information do users have to fill out initially, versus when they make a second-time purchase?
- Can a quick purchase be made directly from the home page?
- Does the site provide clear instructions on how to store selected items before completing a transaction?
- How well does the site communicate with a user?
- Does the site acknowledge users' actions and provide clear, concise feedback as users progress through the purchasing process?
- Can users collect multiple items before checking out?

Tip 2: Make a Strong First Impression

The e-commerce home page must make a strong first impression. This is where users are grounded to your company and persuaded to start shopping. It is first and foremost important to provide branding for your store. Next, it is important to provide a clear visual definition of your store's categories or departments. This can be accomplished with tabs or within the navigation bar.

Tip 3: Minimize Distractions: Advertising Isn't Always Necessary

You may consider not providing any advertisements on the home page or in other places throughout the purchase process. Remember that the goal of your home page is to encourage shopping and purchasing. You don't want to deter or lose users by having them click on another company's advertisement.

Tip 4: Make It Personal

Looking for a way to build a strong rapport with your shoppers? Provide personalization for the user, after the user registers as a shopper or member. Use this information to provide a personalized greeting to the home page or various department pages. *Welcome, Nadja, enjoy your shopping experience.* Provide a private place that requires a password, where each user can check past orders, order status, wish lists, gift certificates, and so forth.

Tip 5: Avoid Long Instructions

If you need to include long instructions on how to use the site or make a purchase, it is time to redesign! To complete a quick purchase, a user needs minimal-to-no instructions. Most users will not read long instructions, and may turn away in confusion.

Tip 6: Provide Visual Clues to Location

For stores that have multiple departments, it is important to create a sense of varying location. This can be accomplished by changing colors on the navigation bar or the background page, and by providing different titles with text or graphics.

Tip 7: Show Off Products

If at all possible, provide photographs of individual products. Process the photos in three sizes: thumbnail, medium, and large. A thumbnail photo is best used in a list of several products. At the individual product level, provide a medium size image, and the ability to click to view the enlarged version of the product. The larger view is not necessary, but worth considering if your product has details that are not reflected in the medium or thumbnail photograph.

The more details you can provide about the product the better. If you have a long page about the product, be sure to provide the option to purchase or add to your basket or cart from both the top and the bottom of the informational text.

Tip 8: Encourage Spontaneous Purchases

This can be accomplished in various ways. If a product is mentioned on the home page, place product images and details, the sale price, and a direct link to purchase the item. In a news or feature article, include direct links to purchase products discussed within the article. Or on the side column, where advertisements for other companies traditionally would go, create intimate, focused advertisements for your products, with a direct link to purchase the items from the advertisements.

Tip 9: Alternate Background Colors in Long Lists

One good visual trick to make a long table of items easier to read is to alternate a light color background for each row or item. You can see an example of this if you search on an author's name at barnesandnoble.com. The search results return in alternate item background colors of gray and white.

Tip 10: Allow Users to Collect Items

Provide a shopping basket or a place for users to collect items before checking out. Never make the user fill out the lengthy payment, shipping, and other forms more than once in a transaction! At the product level, provide a link to check out and a link to add that product to the shopping cart while continuing to shop.

One item-storage feature that is currently becoming popular is called a wish list. This feature is similar to a shopping cart, but it does not provide purchasing features. Think of it as a place to store items as you are shopping. Perhaps when items in your wish list go on sale, the site can notify you.

Source: Nadja Vol Ochs, "Easy-to-Buy E-Commerce Site Design Tips," http://msdn.microsoft.com/workshop, February 15, 1999.

Promoting the Web Site

How do customers learn about a Web site? You have to tell them—and there are many ways to do this. A dot.com address can be promoted both to existing customers and to prospects by including the URL on existing print promotions,

FIGURE 3-4 *Home page of Shoebuy.com*

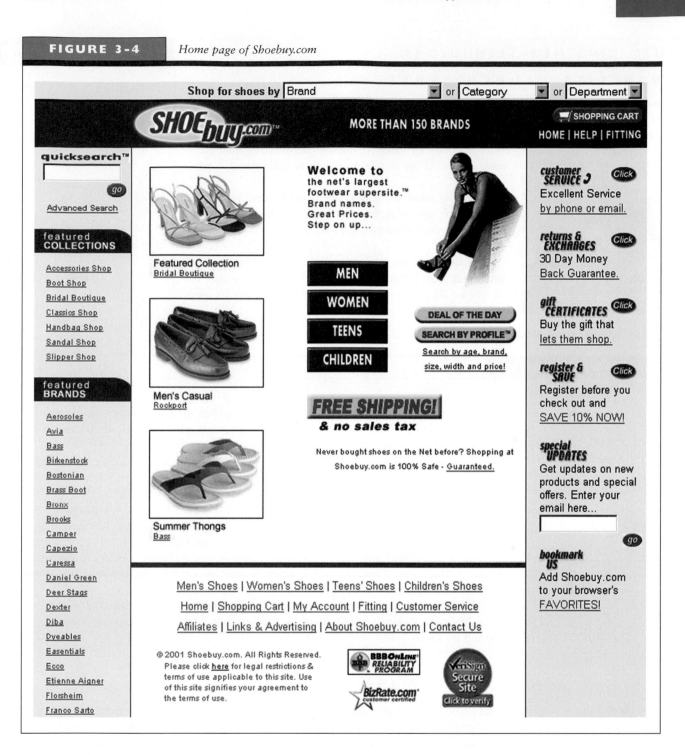

business cards, letterhead, and packaging. Special direct mail and radio campaigns can also be designed for this purpose.

Additionally, a dot.com business can be promoted by placing banner advertisements on other Web sites, where a quick click will send users to the advertised Web

Utilizing New Technology **IN THE TRENCHES**

WEB SITE LAUNCH SPUTTERS

Businesses making the leap to the Web should leave plenty of time for working out problems, advises Dan Caulfield. Caulfield put up his own Web site way back in 1995. However, plans for a new Web page launch for his Chicago-based recruiting business, Hire Quality, Inc., did not go well. "We expected to put our system on the Internet and that people would be able to use it intuitively and quickly. . . . That didn't happen. . . . We almost had to rewrite five years of code to make this work on the Web with multiple users," he says.

Assisted by promotional support on cable TV, Caulfield waited for Web traffic to build. However, visitors to the site couldn't figure out how to use it. Hire Quality's customer service phone representatives were always busy trying to assist clients with the Web site.

The site was eventually improved, but programming costs consumed most of the marketing budget. Caulfield's advice: "Give yourself an extra 30 days before you roll something out. Make sure the site is operational before you even tell anyone you're doing it."

Source: Emily Barker, "Building a Web Site Is Easy," *Inc.*, Vol. 22, No. 2 (February 2000), pp. 50–51.

http://www.hirequality.com

site. The advantage of banner advertisements is that they are viewed by thousands of visitors to other Web sites. Payment for banner advertising is usually based on the number of people who actually click on the banner.

Probably the most direct approach to Web site promotion is making sure that the site is accessed by Internet search engines. Search engines are databases, available on the Internet, that allow users to find Web sites based on keywords included in the site's pages. If a popular search engine does not list a dot.com firm's Web site, many potential visitors will undoubtedly miss it. Registering a site with a search engine is free. However, to get a position at or near the top of a search listing, you may have to pay. Obviously, your Web site should include keywords that someone looking for that particular subject might use. Specific content is also important. For example, including brands with descriptions can help you get better placement.

There are several ways of submitting a Web site to search engines. A description of submission options, adapted from the Internet Marketing Center's Web site, is shown in Table 3-4.

Criminal and Ethical Issues in E-Commerce

Discuss criminal and ethical issues related to e-commerce.

The e-commerce community is young, but it has already demonstrated a vulnerability to crime and questionable business practices. With its low cost of entry and instant access to customers all over the globe, the Internet is a prime venue for criminal activity.

Cybercrime

cybercrime
criminal activity on the Internet

Criminal activity on the Internet has come to be known as **cybercrime.** Cybercrimes having an important impact on e-commerce include hacking, scamming, and viola-

TABLE 3-4 *Methods for Submitting Your Web Site to a Search Engine*

Free Submission Services	There are services such as Postmaster and Submit It that will list your site for free. You enter your information once and then, with a push of a button, it will automatically submit that information to the search engines you choose. The main problem is that you submit the same information to all the search engines, but each one has different requirements and limitations. So what you submit to one search engine to get a high listing may hurt you drastically in another.
Entering Your Site on Each Search Engine Manually (Free)	By far the *best way* to announce your URL for free is to go to each individual search engine separately and submit the information for each Web page you have. This allows you to *maximize your exposure* by completing every field in the submission form to its maximum potential for keywords, descriptions, additions, content, contact information, etc. It also allows you to specifically pick one or multiple categories that would best suit your business, therefore increasing your chances of being seen and attracting visitors to your site.
Paid Submission Services	There are a few different types of paid submission services. Some are very similar to the free services, where it is completely automated and they may charge you a low fee (usually under $75 to submit your information to 100 or more search engines). Other paid submission services manually input information to each search engine as you would yourself, but they input only information that you have provided to them.
Search Engine Submission Software	Generally speaking, most "submission" software is much like the free submission services. So what you submit to one search engine to get a high listing may hurt you in another. However, this is probably *the most economical and efficient way* to get your site listed higher in the search engines because this software helps emphasize important keywords.

Source: Adapted from "Internet Marketing Tips," http://www.marketingtips.com/newsletter, December 1998.

tion of intellectual property rights. Table 3-5 highlights the problems and offers some solutions.

Hacking is a potential problem facing every e-commerce venture. It troubles dot.com businesses in three ways. First, hackers can get control of a site and deface or vandalize it. E-mail, which arrives unrequested, is frequently used by hackers to deliver destructive viruses to a site.

Second, hackers may steal electronic files. This is the cyberspace equivalent of breaking into a traditional brick-and-mortar store and carrying off the contents of the file cabinet. In December of 1999, an Internet music retailer based in Wallingford, Connecticut learned that someone had broken into its computer system and copied files containing customer credit card numbers. The hacker demanded $100,000 in ransom and threatened to publicize the credit card numbers.[15]

Third, some hackers seem to enjoy breaking into a dot.com site just to block customer access. The disruption may be achieved either by bombarding the site with traffic or by redirecting traffic to a competitor's site. The attacks that temporarily crippled CNN.com, Amazon.com, and eBay were of the former type; the office-products retailer Staples suspected that the latter was happening to hits intended for its site. Web sites can guard against hackers with a **firewall,** which is a combination of hardware and software designed to keep unauthorized outsiders from tampering with a computer system.

firewall
a combination of hardware and software designed to keep unauthorized outsiders from tampering with a computer system

Internet scamming is on the rise. "Many consumers shop online and have good experiences . . . but the increases we've seen in both the number of complaints and the amounts of money lost point to the need for more consumer protection and

TABLE 3-5

Some Forms of Cybercrime

	Problem	Legal Solution	Industry Solution
Hacking (illegally breaking into computer systems)	Information can be stolen or damaged.	Use existing laws to pursue hackers.	Use hackers-for-hire and firewall protection.
Scamming (deception to gain others' assets)	Scammers can operate off-shore or outside of a particular country's jurisdiction.	Use existing laws to pursue scammers.	Coordinate efforts among governments. Provide information on scammers and types of fraud.
Violation of intellectual property rights (violation of copyrights, trademarks, trade secrets, patents)	Digital information can be easily copied, reproduced, and sent to others.	Make everything sent online copyright-protected.	Use encryption software to protect valuable copyrighted material, such as music, videos, and books. Use watermarks and other techniques to protect images. Use search systems to locate copyrighted material on Web sites.

Source: Brad Alan Kleindl, *Strategic Electronic Marketing, Managing E-Business* (Cincinnati, OH: South-Western, 2001), p. 286.

http://www.fraud.org

increased education," says Susan Grant, director of Internet Fraud Watch (IFW).[16] An overwhelming 87 percent of the frauds reported to IFW in 1999 were related to online auction sales. Sales of general merchandise represented only 77 percent of the total complaints.

Questionable E-Commerce Business Practices

Several controversial e-commerce practices relate to Internet privacy. The enormous number of data exchanges in e-commerce raises serious questions about personal privacy. Many times, privacy loss involves information of little value to the provider. Nevertheless, there are fears that the Internet can and does go too far.

cookie
a data file that is electronically sent to the customer's computer when other requested materials are downloaded from an Internet Web site

One potential threat to privacy bears a sweet name but a sour taste—cookies. A **cookie** is a data file that is electronically sent to the customer's computer when other requested materials are downloaded from an Internet Web site.

Cookies were developed so that Web sites could recognize return visitors and thereby generate a customized and personalized response. Consider the following hypothetical scenario:

Say a visitor goes to the fictional www.itsyourweather.com. The site asks the computer if it can store a cookie on the user's hard drive. The file in effect says, "This is User #2135."

While there, you, the user, tell the site you live in Omaha, travel to New Zealand and are fascinated by thunderstorms. It notes that User #2135 has these interests.

Next time you visit, it asks your browser if it has a cookie stashed there. "I do indeed," your browser replies and sends it over. "Ah," the site thinks to itself. "User #2135 wants the weather in Omaha and New Zealand plus our latest thunderstorm map."[17]

Customers who object to having cookies on their hard drive can use three methods to control their computer's consumption of cookies:

1. Periodically delete the cookies manually.
2. Set the browser to stop cookies.
3. Install a cookie-manager program (available free on the Web).

Any entrepreneur starting an e-commerce business needs to address privacy issues. The venture's commitment to satisfying consumers' online privacy concerns will create an environment of trust and consumer confidence.

Wonderful opportunities abound in e-commerce. **Moore's Law** says that computing power doubles every 18 months. If this trend continues, the 21st century will bring entirely new industries online. Well-known engineer/entrepreneur Raymond Kurzwel offers some amazing projections for the digital world over the next 20 years. Some highlights from his projections are given in Table 3-6.

Moore's Law
the theory that computing power doubles every 18 months

How will aspiring entrepreneurs use e-commerce to build their businesses? *You hold the answers.* In cyberspace, the concept of "build it and they will come" has created hundreds of dot.com failures. Technology is wonderful but will never substitute for traditional customer service and retention strategies. The appendix to this chapter briefly describes three dot.com failures so that you may learn from their shortcomings.

TABLE 3-6

Some Projections for 2009 and 2019

2009—the digital conversion is nearly complete

- A $1,000 computer will perform a trillion operations per second.
- The majority of text will be entered with continuous speech recognition.
- Most routine business transactions (purchases, travel, reservations) will take place between a human and a virtual personality.
- There will be high-speed wireless access to the Web.
- Translating telephones will be common (speech-to-speech translation).

2019—the network moves to three dimensions

- A $1,000 computer will have roughly the computing power of the human brain.
- Computers will be largely invisible—and embedded almost everywhere.
- Three-dimensional virtual-reality displays—using glasses and contacts—will be used routinely.
- Most learning will come through simulated, software-based teachers.
- The vast majority of transactions will include a simulated person.

Source: Ward Hanson, *Principles of Internet Marketing* (Cincinnati, OH: South-Western, 2000), p. 436.

Looking Back

1 Explain how the Internet developed and how it supports e-commerce activity.

- The Internet enables people to communicate with other connected computer users via electronic mail and real-time conversation.
- The World Wide Web was conceived and initiated at CERN in Switzerland.
- E-commerce is the paperless exchange of business information via the Internet.
- E-commerce is much more than a new way to take customer orders.
- Small firms can be successful online even if they are not first with an e-commerce idea.

2 Understand the benefits of e-commerce to small firms.

- E-commerce offers small firms the opportunity to compete with bigger companies on a more level playing field.
- Internet operations can help small firms with cash flow problems by compressing sales cycles.
- E-commerce enables small firms to build stronger customer relationships.

3 Describe the different business models followed by e-commerce firms.

- A business model describes a group of shared characteristics, behaviors, and goals that a firm follows in a particular business situation.
- A poorly devised business model can be a major factor in business failure.
- Online firms that have other businesses as their principal customers are called business-to-business (B2B) companies.
- An online firm selling primarily to final consumers is called a business-to-consumer (B2C) business.
- Auction sites are online firms that bring buyers and sellers together.
- The three main advantages of online B2C firms are speed of access, speed of transaction, and continuous access to products and services, often referred to as 24/7 e-tailing.
- New versions of the B2B model continue to develop and evolve.
- Transaction sales are the fastest-growing source of revenue for online businesses.
- Revenue-based models emphasize revenue enhancement; expense-based models focus on expense reduction; and growth-based models emphasize customer growth.
- Affiliation involves a formal agreement with the sponsoring firm whereby other Web site owners contract to include on their sites an icon that allows visitors quick access to the site of the sponsoring firm.
- In the early days of the Internet, online sites charged fees for access to online content and/or subscription fees. Other sources of revenue include banner advertising, sales commissions, and sales of products or services.
- Expense reduction is the factor motivating many firms to enter cyberspace. Providing information to customers online can reduce the cost of doing business.
- Firms following the growth-based model are developing a customer base with the hope of cashing in at a later date.
- The role of a Web site can range from merely offering content and information to permitting the buying and selling of products and services online.

4 Identify the initial considerations in launching a dot.com business.

- Contrary to general opinion, plenty of names for dot.com domains remain available.
- Since a domain name gives the small business online identity, it is desirable to select a descriptive and appealing name.
- Once a desired name has been selected, it should be checked for availability and then registered.
- There are several domain registration firms, which allow visitors to search the Internet to see if a proposed name is already taken.
- High-quality Web design gives a small firm the opportunity to make a good first impression on each visitor.
- Slow downloading is a frequent problem with Web sites.
- Web site design should reflect customer needs.
- A dot.com address should be promoted through placement on search engines.

5 Discuss criminal and ethical issues related to e-commerce.

- With its low cost of entry and instant access to customers all over the globe, the Internet is a prime venue for criminal activity.
- Hackers hinder e-commerce through theft, vandalism, and blocking customer access.
- The enormous number of data exchanges in e-commerce raises serious questions about personal privacy.
- Cookies were developed so that Web sites could recognize return visitors and thereby generate a customized and personalized response.

KEY TERMS

Internet, p. 57
World Wide Web (WWW), p. 58
e-commerce, p. 58
brick-and-mortar store, p. 58
Electronic Customer Relationship Marketing (eCRM), p. 60
business model, p. 62
business-to-business (B2B) model, p. 63
business-to-consumer (B2C) model, p. 64
24/7 e-tailing, p. 64
auction sites, p. 65
revenue-based model, p. 65
hits, p. 65
affiliation, p. 65
expense-based model, p. 66
growth-based model, p. 66
content/information-based model, p. 67
transaction-based model, p. 67
cybercrime, p. 74
firewall, p. 75
cookie, p. 76
Moore's Law, p. 77

DISCUSSION QUESTIONS

1. What is the Internet, and what part does it play in e-commerce?
2. Identify and dispel three myths surrounding e-commerce opportunities for small firms.
3. Identify the benefits that small firms gain from e-commerce.
4. Discuss the three different ways of categorizing business models used for e-commerce.
5. Contrast B2B and B2C businesses. Identify some of the reasons final consumers give for not using online shopping.
6. What are some of the different approaches to generating revenue adopted by companies using revenue-based models?
7. Are there dot.com firms currently operating under the content/information-based model? If so, give some examples.
8. Explain how a newly organized dot.com venture would register a name it wanted to use for its business.
9. How can a new e-commerce firm promote its Web site? Give specific examples.
10. What are some of the criminal and ethical issues facing the e-commerce world?

YOU MAKE THE CALL

SITUATION 1

Estate Administrators and Liquidators is based in Sacramento, California and is owned and operated by entrepreneur Sally Wheeler-Valine. Since 1990, the firm has served people seeking to sell the household goods of deceased friends or relatives.

The business auctions items at the site, splitting the proceeds with the family. Any unsold items are taken back to the firm's store and sold, generating a commission based on the selling price.

To accommodate the large volume of merchandise she sells, Wheeler-Valine operates out of a new 13,000-square-foot store. Business revenues climbed for several years, peaking in 1997. However, in 1999, revenues slumped drastically.

Source: Based on a story by Susan Hanson, "Store's Demise Blamed on Web Auctions," *Inc.*, July 2000, p. 41.

Question 1 What impact, if any, do you think the Internet had on Wheeler-Valine's business?

Question 2 In what way(s) could she use e-commerce to grow her business?

Question 3 How much presence on the Web, if any, do you think she should consider?

Question 4 What do you think will happen to this firm if it ignores the Internet?

SITUATION 2

Karen Duke owns and runs Duke Chimney Services in Mechanicsville, Virginia. Her business is selling a wide range of fireplace inserts and related products. The company, which she operates with her husband, employs six people and has revenues of approximately $500,000 a year.

Karen wants to use the Internet in her business but is not exactly sure how to go about it. Most of her business comes from retail customers.

Source: Adapted from Leslie Brokaw, "Better Sales Through Digital Photos," *Inc. Technology*, Vol. 22, No. 13 (2000), p. 28.

Question 1 What kinds of e-commerce strategies would you recommend to Duke for her business?

Question 2 In what way could she use banner advertising in her e-commerce strategy? Be specific.

Question 3 A friend familiar with computer technology has some ideas about incorporating digital photography into Duke's Web site. What do you think he's talking about?

SITUATION 3

A venture capitalist has invested in a company that manufactures picture framing materials in Mississippi. The company's products are sold directly to art publishers and framing shops. Additionally, the firm owns a few retail shops and leases some space in department and hardware stores. Business is slow, and the firm is considering an online store of some sort. The venture capitalist wonders about a new Internet strategy under consideration by the manufacturer.

As part of the planned Internet venture, the firm is considering entering into a partnership with another company that owns an e-commerce catalog of digital images. The digital image firm already has a site on the Web, where visitors can search for an image, enter a credit card number for payment, and then download the image they have selected. The picture frame company is wondering how it can increase its sales of picture framing materials through this partnership.

Source: Based on a story by John Rutledge, "Living with the Net," *Forbes*, Vol. 166, No. 5 (August 21, 2000), p. 103.

Question 1 What are the limitations, if any, of the current business strategy of the digital image company?

Question 2 Do you see any benefits for the picture frame manufacturer in pursuing this partnership? Why or why not?

Question 3 If the partnership has merit, what e-commerce strategy would you suggest? In other words, what form should the partnership take?

EXPERIENTIAL EXERCISES

1. Interview a local small business that you believe might benefit from e-commerce. Prepare a report on the e-commerce strategy being pursued or the reasons this particular business is not involved in e-commerce.
2. Contact the Chamber of Commerce office in your local area and ask what e-commerce assistance it provides to small firms. Report on your findings.
3. Search your local Yellow Pages directory for a Web site designer. Call the designer and ask for a personal interview where you can find out about the services offered. Report on your findings.

EXPLORING THE WEB

1. Compare the following Web sites that offer e-commerce services to companies.
   a. Examine **http://www.cybercash.com** and **http://www.authorize.net**. What service do both sites provide? List the individual services that each company offers.
   b. Examine **http://www.teletech.com** and **http://www.pegasystems.com**. What service do both sites provide? List the individual services that each company offers.
   c. Examine **http://www.everdream.com** and **http://www.centerbeam.com**. What service do both sites provide? List the individual services that each company offers.
   d. Explain which of the previous three categories you would choose to implement first, and why.
2. *Emerging Business* magazine at **http://www.ebmagz.com** offers a series of articles about online services and e-commerce.
   a. Using the Search feature, enter "Promotion" and then read the article entitled "Promote Your Site." List the hints that are different from those in this chapter.
   b. Under the keyword "Promotion," read the article entitled "The Interactive Edge." List the 10 interactive features you can use to engage the customer.
   c. Using the Search feature, enter "charge it" and read the article by that name.
   d. Read one of the other articles and write a paragraph summary.
3. Access a brief history of technology at **http://www.usatoday.com/2000/money/money003.htm**.
   a. When was the Internet (NSFNET) first opened to commercial use?
   b. When did the first graphical browser required for the World Wide Web as we know it come into common use?
   c. What role did Al Gore play in the creation of the Internet?
   d. Compare the date of the first commercial use of the Internet given on this site with that found on UUNET's site at **http://www.uu.net/us/about/facts/timeline**. What is UUNET?

CASE 3

HEADBLADE COMPANY (p. 645)

This case describes how a young entrepreneur built a Web site to sell a new razor designed specifically to shave heads.

Alternative Case for Chapter 3:

Case 20, "Maricopa Ready Mix," p. 693

Appendix 3A
Dot.Coms Become Not.Coms

Three E-Commerce Companies That Didn't Survive

Webvan Rolls to a Stop

"We believe we had a brilliant concept. We were just ahead of our time." So said Webvan spokesman Bud Grebey at last week's announcement that his company had suspended its operations. In fact, Webvan was about 40 years behind its time.

The "pick-pack-ship" model of home delivery was common in the 1950s and 1960s. Dairy and bread companies routinely delivered groceries. But that service eventually declined because it no longer fit consumers' lifestyles, or the new economic realities of distribution. Home delivery was an old business strategy, and migrating it to the Web did not make it futuristic.

Webvan would have us believe that a few years down the road, when bandwidth and Internet access become more prevalent, it would have overcome its problems and become profitable. Yet none of this would change the average \$30–\$35 delivery cost for complex, heterogeneous orders.

The problem wasn't the technology or the service—many of Webvan's customers were very satisfied with its ordering and delivery systems. If you take a survey, many people will say sure, they like the idea of having someone pick, pack, and deliver their groceries. The problem is that few are willing to pay the true costs associated with such a service. For the small group available to accept deliveries and willing to cough up the extra cash, Webvan was great. But such a limited market couldn't generate enough revenues to cover Webvan's cost of doing business.

The downfall of Webvan offers lessons for nearly every type of business. Here are a few of them:

- *Focus on the "commerce," not just the "e."* If you can't master inventory management, sourcing, transportation and distribution, customer attraction and retention, warehousing, and logistics, it doesn't matter how great your Web site is.
- *Don't absorb the cost of functions that consumers are willing to do for free.* After years of availability of phone-in orders and home delivery, a vast majority of consumers have chosen to shop for groceries in a store. They perform the picking and delivery functions at no cost to the retailer. Enter Webvan, which took on these functions at a steep loss to increase trial and acceptance of the service. How could Webvan compete effectively in the long term against stores that get these functions completed for free?
- *Don't offer consumers a new technology unless it solves their problems better than their current solution.* Technology determines only what can be offered

to consumers, but consumers determine which technologies are accepted. Most people migrate to Internet buying only when they are dissatisfied with present solutions. Yet studies show that 75–80 percent of consumers like today's grocery stores. They like the social interaction and the chance to physically examine items before they buy them—especially high-margin items like baked and deli goods and produce. That leaves just 20–25 percent of consumers potentially receptive to online buying and home delivery, begging the question of how many of them will convert to online buying.

- *Create e-tail strategies that match the lifestyle realities of market segments.* Once commonplace, home delivery gave way to large grocery stores because of lifestyle shifts, many triggered by more women working outside of the home. Most consumers who can afford extras like home delivery aren't home during the day and have limited windows of time to accept deliveries. They also consume fewer groceries than other segments, because they dine out more than they eat at home. Webvan appealed mostly to a small segment of the market—high-income households with two or more children, a way to accept deliveries (either a nanny or refrigerated storage box), and a willingness to spend nights shopping on the computer.
- *Don't enter a mature, highly efficient industry with an inefficient strategy.* In the grocery business, the major chains are consolidating into a few extremely efficient giants. Their purchasing power, market coverage, and economies of scale can easily out-muscle miniscule e-tailers. Margins are squeezed so thin by this fierce competition that Webvan's competitors—such as Kroger, Albertsons, Safeway, and Winn-Dixie—average net profits of just 1.08 percent. Opportunities for new firms to enter and transform an industry usually occur when existing firms have high margins, are inefficient, or both.

Webvan's fate was foreseeable to anyone who understood why the home delivery system vanished 30 years ago. However, that doesn't mean that retailers should abandon online business. In fact, it means the opposite. Retailers should embrace the Internet for certain marketing and branding strategies, but never at the peril of ignoring how customers buy and use their products and services.

In the end, consumers will vote with their wallets which solutions best meet their needs and wants. Webvan lost that election, but not without providing valuable lessons about the commerce side of e-commerce.

Source: Roger Blackwell, "Why Webvan Went Bust," Dow-Jones & Co., July 16, 2001. Reprinted with permission of publisher via Copyright Clearance Center.

Furniture.com Collapses

The best-known dot.com we dug into last year was Furniture.com—both in life and in death. Furniture is a notoriously tricky industry. But in January 2000, executives seemed unfazed; they promised Web shoppers 24-hour browsing and six- to eight-week delivery times on everything from table lamps to 10-piece bedroom ensembles.

Convincing customers to buy furniture online was the easy part. The company reported $22 million in net revenues for nine months ending September 2000, more than twice the total 1999 net revenues—and attracted 1 million users a month.

But with the increase in usage came a dramatic jump in customer dissatisfaction. Customer complaints filed with the Better Business Bureau (BBB) in Worcester,

Massachusetts, leaped from 1 in 1999 to 149 in 2000, steep even by dot.com standards, says Barbara Sinnott, president of the Central New England BBB. Most brick-and-mortar companies get three to four complaints a year, tops. The leading complaint: delivery problems, followed by product quality and bill disputes. (Attempts to reach Furniture.com CEO Andrew Brooks were unsuccessful.)

While executives built the Furniture.com brand like nobody's business, they neglected to create the infrastructure to support it. The company failed to factor in the logistics and costs involved in shipping such a bulky commodity cross-country and had no way to track orders.

"Right down to the very last day, they still couldn't make a decision on an information tracking platform," says Ian Nickerson, president of Global Logistics Solutions of Dennis, Massachusetts, one of Furniture.com's regional logistics partners. "We invested a lot of money in technology to track orders so that they could let customers know where their delivery was in the system. But we ended up having to do everything manually."

Furniture.com also created a cancellation policy no furniture company could afford. Contrary to the no-return policy we had reported, customers could cancel orders right until delivery day. With six-week waits turning into six-month delays, a third of all orders were cancelled. Local logistics companies had warehouses of unwanted furniture, according to Nickerson. The result: storage costs that surpassed the already astronomical shipping costs Furniture.com footed for customers.

"They didn't understand the supply chain dynamics well enough, and they didn't understand fundamental operations strategy," says David Pyke, a professor at Dartmouth's Amos Tuck School of Business Administration, who specializes in e-commerce and supply chain management. "Free shipping, free returns, low prices and lots of variety! How can you go wrong? Well, the customer might be happy—if the promises were fulfilled—but the company can't make money like that."

Several rounds of layoffs and $27 million in makeshift funding furnished in June 2000 didn't get Furniture.com any closer to profitability. The online retailer, which launched in January 1998, closed its doors on November 6, 2000 and filed bankruptcy on November 20. Early in 2001 the company hoped to fetch $1.5 million for its domain name and Web platform, says David Madoff of Cohn & Kelakos, the Boston law firm representing Furniture.com. The failed company was also crafting a plan to get furniture stuck in warehouses to customers still waiting for orders.

Source: Stephanie Overby, "Furniture.com Made Too Many Promises It Couldn't Keep," http://www.cio.com, May 1, 2001.

PurpleTie, Inc. Folds

No matter which way you put this one through the spin cycle, the same thing comes out in the wash: When you're growing a business, be patient, know the market, take it slow. If only PurpleTie founder Payam Zamani hadn't let the late-20th-century wave of venture capital money rinse out this good sense.

Zamani, 29, had no experience in the dry cleaning business before founding PurpleTie. Then again, he was no car salesman before founding his first Internet startup, AutoWeb, in 1994. This time his goal was to tidy up the dirty laundry of the antediluvian and disjointed dry-cleaning industry. Big plans included his own dry cleaning processing centers and national expansion of the Pleasanton,

California–based company from its Bay Area base to 25 metropolitan markets in three years.

Although there are few hard numbers on the dry cleaning industry, recently released 1997 U.S. Economic Census figures indicate there were about 30,000 dry cleaners nationwide representing $7 billion in revenue. PurpleTie asserted that there were more like 100,000 shops worth $32 billion. In any case, it's one of the largest industries still dominated by mom-and-pop shops, according to the Silver Spring, Maryland–based International Fabricare Institute (IFI). This was the arena Zamani tried to step into. But he stepped too quickly.

"We had grand visions, and we built too much infrastructure too fast," says David Kallery, PurpleTie's chief operations officer, who spent 25 years at stalwart companies like UPS and Visa before joining the startup. "We should have grown the business organically brick by brick, or as one investor said, route by route. Had we taken that approach, we would've made the $8 million last for several years and built a very successful business."

The Plan

PurpleTie's business plan was this: partner with 5,000- to 10,000-square-foot operations that were already handling work for hotels and large cleaners. "The average dry cleaning business has a half-million dollars in infrastructure. But the facility is used only 6 to 8 hours a day," Zamani said last December. This excess capacity represented a huge opportunity for PurpleTie's consumer business. In exchange for cash, an equity stake in PurpleTie, and a chance to join in a new market, the partners would handle customers' garments to PurpleTie's specifications.

For the consumer, PurpleTie's service had a simple front end. After registering with PurpleTie's Web site, customers created an itemized list of garments to be cleaned and shoes to be shined, then selected one-hour pick-up and next-day delivery windows.

Reminiscent of FedEx's "hub" system, the driver would take the items to a place PurpleTie called its "central sort and data capture center" in Livermore, California. There, systems gathered fabric and brand data and tagged garments with bar codes before whisking the items away to a dry cleaning processing center. Once clean, PurpleTie returned the items to central sort for packaging and routing back to customers. The systems allowed the dry cleaner to track processed garments and create a storehouse of regional consumer habits it hoped to market to apparel makers.

20–20 Hindsight

Founder Zamani, who was unavailable for comment after the March 2 shutdown, used much of the $8 million he'd raised to create the scalable technology and operations necessary for PurpleTie's expansion plans.

PurpleTie used SPOT 2000 dry cleaning software, from Draper, Utah–based Westgate Software, as the center of its back-end technology. Last summer, vice president of technology Markus Zeitler worked closely with Kallery to build PurpleTie's Web site, and install eGain customer service software, Descartes eScheduler mapping software and Descartes RIMMS 3.1 route tracking software. These were all linked to the SPOT 2000 system, housed on PurpleTie's main servers at Exodus Communications in Santa Clara, California. Had PurpleTie expanded to Portland and Seattle during the first half of 2001 as planned, a SPOT 2000 station would

have been installed in each new central sort area and connected back to PurpleTie's main servers.

PurpleTie spent $1 million trying to build its own state-of-the-art 100,000-square-foot dry cleaning facility in Manteca, California, before realizing those plans weren't practical. "We spent an awful lot of time, effort, and money on trying to build that processing center," says Kallery. "The biggest thing that we learned was that there was excess capacity in the market."

When PurpleTie ceased operation, it was only about six months from cash flow breakeven and a year from total breakeven (including corporate overhead). Unfortunately, says Kallery, that $1 million spent on the defunct facility would have been enough to get PurpleTie out of the red. By then the company's initial investors didn't want to put up that additional amount, and Zamani and his team were hard pressed to find another source of funding.

The company tried to cool its burn rate by halving its staff size and trying to collaborate with larger scale dry-cleaning plants. Zamani attempted to paint PurpleTie as a traditional business with a strong e-commerce element. He emphasized its multi-channel approach; the company welcomed telephone and Web orders and planned to open small (500- to 800-square-foot) storefronts in each market.

But it was too late. "One of the keys for [PurpleTie] was selling its services through partner companies, and that proved too muddy a proposition for people to cotton to," says Rob Leather, a San Francisco–based analyst in the digital commerce strategies group at Jupiter Media Metrix. "You have to have a lot clearer results and much clearer value that the investors can see. If you're putting a very risky business model forth that requires consumers to change their behavior, now's not really the time to do that."

And so . . .

PurpleTie was serving 10,000 residential customers and covering 30 percent of the greater San Francisco area in January. On March 9, 2000-customer Clean Sleeves.com acquired the PurpleTie brand and some of its physical assets. "We have big plans, but ours is a self-funded approach and a much more traditional bootstrapping kind of thing," says CleanSleeves.com CEO Kay Madegarian, who cofounded the company in March 1999 and has just six employees. "Our growth curve will be a lot slower."

Madegarian hasn't ruled out the idea of taking her company national, perhaps even under the PurpleTie name. But that won't happen in the near future.

Source: Stephanie Overby, "A Case Study of One Folded Online Dry Cleaner," http://www.cio.com, March 15, 2001.

chapter 4

Global Opportunities

In the Spotlight

Bagels by Bell

People often assume that only large multinational firms have opportunities to conduct international business, but this is not the case. Warren Bell owns Bagels by Bell of Brooklyn, New York, and his product is the fancy of customers on the opposite side of the globe. For years, his core business was selling bagels and other baked goods to East Coast distributors. But then at a trade show in 1998 he met a Japanese distributor who persuaded him to go global. Reengineering a 50-year-old family recipe, Bell baked up a product designed to appeal to Japanese consumers. Unfortunately, the results were less than dazzling.

Bell's early failures taught him an important lesson in international business: Know your overseas customers and adapt to their preferences, regardless of what makes sense in the domestic market. A bagel is a nearly sacred food to New Yorkers; even minor changes like adding raisins are not tolerated. So it was not easy for Bell to accept the idea of folding sweet ingredients into his bagel dough. But his Japanese partner encouraged the redesign, and the results were stunning. Bell's bagels began "flying off shelves in Tokyo and Osaka," raising sales at Bagels by Bell to $1.2 million a year (a 20 percent increase).

"I'm a little guy," says the bagelmaster. "Japan gave us a big kick." In the final analysis, Bell was able to use his unique know-how as a New York bagel maker as a platform for international business, but going global required cultural learning and adaptation along the way.

Source: Jonathan Fahey, "Dough Boy," *Forbes*, Vol. 166, No. 14 (November 27, 2000), p. 270.

Looking Ahead

After studying this chapter, you should be able to

1. *Describe the potential of small firms as global enterprises.*
2. *Identify the basic forces prompting small firms to engage in global expansion.*
3. *Identify and compare strategy options for global businesses.*
4. *Explain the challenges that global enterprises face.*
5. *Recognize the sources of assistance available to support international business efforts.*

The world economy is in transition. National economies were once isolated by trade and investment barriers, differences in language and culture, distinctive business practices, and various government regulations. But these dissimilarities are fading over time as market preferences converge, trade barriers fall, and national economies integrate to form a global economic system. This process is the essence of **globalization.** Though the trend toward convergence has been developing for some time now, the pace is quickening, creating global opportunities that did not exist even a few years ago.

globalization
the expansion of international business, promoted by converging market preferences, falling trade barriers, and the integration of national economies

While the hindrances to global businesses diminish, the commercial potential of markets abroad continues to grow. To track this trend, the Heritage Foundation and *The Wall Street Journal* publish the *Index of Economic Freedom,* an analysis of trade policy, wages and prices, government intervention, and other similar variables in over 150 nations. The *2001 Index of Economic Freedom* reported that "economic freedom continues to grow world-wide, continuing the amazing spread of the past decade."[1] The benefits of economic liberty speak for themselves. The average person in an economically repressed country lives on only $2,800 a year, whereas per capita income in free economies is nearly eight times as great, exceeding $21,000.[2] This positive impact on prosperity translates into increased demand for products and services in international markets, fueling interest in global enterprises.

Small Businesses as Global Enterprises

Describe the potential of small firms as global enterprises.

The potential of global business is clear, but does it extend to small companies? Research has shown that recent startups and even the smallest of businesses are internationalizing at an increasing rate.[3] In fact, some small firms are being launched with cross-border business activities in mind (the "born-global" trend).[4] As global communication systems become more efficient and trade agreements pry open national markets to foreign competition, entrepreneurs are focusing more on international business. Today's sophisticated technologies are expensive to develop and quickly replaced; therefore, it is important to recover R&D costs over a larger market and in less time by taking advantage of international sales. Small firms may decide to go global to expand their opportunities, or they may be forced to enter foreign markets in order to compete with those firms in their industry that have already done so. In any case, the research is clear: *Size does not limit a firm's international activity, and small companies often become global competitors to take advantage of their unique resources.*[5]

Consider Air Excellence International, launched by Bob Williams and Dave Ogborne outside Pittsburgh in 1995. Their firm, which renovates commercial jetliner interiors, is a born-global venture, as the name indicates. Its first customer was a Venezuelan company that contracted for restoration work on a single jetliner. Business gradually expanded as larger airlines contracted for the company's services, and the growth continues. The firm nearly doubled its workforce from 1998 to 1999 (from 26 employees to 50 employees), and the pace continues as more renovation work is scheduled. Demonstrating its commitment to international business, the company has opened a second facility in Ireland to serve anticipated demand from European airlines.[6] Air Excellence International has shown that the global marketplace is not limited to large multinational firms.

The fact that many firms are doing it does not mean that going global is easy for small firms; the challenges small businesses face in international markets are considerable. First, a small business owner must decide whether the company is up to the task. To help entrepreneurs assess the impact of going global on a small business, the U.S. Department of Commerce publishes *A Basic Guide to Exporting*. This handbook outlines important questions entrepreneurs should consider when assessing readiness for the challenges of global business (see Figure 4-1).

http://www.unzco.com/basicguide

Once small business owners decide to expand internationally, it is essential that they study the cultural, political, and economic forces in the foreign markets to figure out how best to adapt the product to local demand or make other adjustments necessary to ensure smooth entry. A practice that is acceptable in one culture may be considered unethical or morally wrong in another. When cultural lines are crossed, even gestures as simple as a "good morning" and a handshake may be misunderstood. The entrepreneur must evaluate the proper use of names and titles and

FIGURE 4-1

Questions to Consider Before Going Global

Management Objectives
- What are the company's reasons for going global?
- How committed is top management to going global?
- How quickly does management expect its international operations to pay off?

Management Experience and Resources
- What in-house international expertise does the firm have (international sales experience, language skills, etc.)?
- Who will be responsible for the company's international operations?
- How much senior management time should be allocated to the company's global efforts?
- What organizational structure is required to ensure success abroad?

Production Capacity
- How is the present capacity being used?
- Will international sales hurt domestic sales?
- What will be the cost of additional production at home and abroad?
- What product designs and packaging options are required for international markets?

Financial Capacity
- How much capital can be committed to international production and marketing?
- How are the initial expenses of going global to be covered?
- What other financial demands might compete with plans to internationalize?
- By what date must the global effort pay for itself?

Source: Adapted from U.S. Department of Commerce, *A Basic Guide to Exporting,* cited in John B. Cullen, *Multinational Management: A Strategic Approach* (Cincinnati, OH: South-Western College Publishing, 1999), p. 193.

be aware of different cultural styles and business practices. The cultural challenges of doing business abroad are great.

Entrepreneurs are likely to make costly mistakes if they fail to study a foreign market carefully. For example, a U.S. mail-order concern offering products to the Japanese didn't realize that the American custom of asking for a credit card number before taking an order would be seen as an insult by customers. This misstep was corrected when a consultant explained that in Japan, where business deals may be secured with a handshake rather than a contract, such an approach is interpreted as indicating a lack of trust. Such insights can go a long way in preventing blunders before they occur.

Differences in types of trading systems and import requirements can also make international trade challenging. A small manufacturer of diagnostic and surgical eye care equipment discovered that a global company must regularly modify its products to meet rigid design specifications, which vary from country to country. For example, before the firm could sell its testing device in Germany, it had to remove an on/off switch on the product's alarm bell. Such adjustments are an unavoidable part of conducting global business.

Trade barriers are falling in some regions of the world, as countries agree to eliminate **tariffs** (taxes charged on imported goods) and trade restrictions. In 1989, Canada and the United States signed the Free Trade Agreement (FTA), which

tariffs
taxes charged on imported goods

IN THE TRENCHES LIVING IN A DIVERSE WORLD

BUSINESS APPROACHES CAN EASILY GET LOST IN THE TRANSLATION

Because of vast differences in cultures and lifestyles, lessons learned in corporate America may not readily transfer to foreign markets. Consider the experience of Anvish Bajaj (see photo) and Suvir Sujan, co-founders of Baazee.com. These e-commerce innovators used eBay Inc. as a model for their Bombay, India–based Internet auction site, but they found that there was a limit to how much their one-year-old enterprise could copy from the San Jose, California online phenomenon. The market in India is so different from that in the United States that Sujan often feels there's no point in even logging onto eBay to check out the latest changes.

What are the differences? There are so many: Credit cards are rare in India. Estimates suggest that as few as 1 in 300 adults connect to the Internet. Shopping trips are considered to be a form of entertainment. Indians associate auctions with bankruptcy liquidations. The country has few brands that Indians trust enough to buy sight unseen.

Baazee.com has these and other obstacles to overcome, and the lessons learned by eBay in the United States will be of limited value as the startup attempts to break into this Eastern market of nearly one billion potential consumers.

Like that of Baazee.com, the success of other Web startups in international markets will depend on the degree to which their founders can determine when to adopt practices from the American experience and when to innovate on their own. The results will speak for themselves, no matter what the language.

Source: Daniel Pearl, "Lost in Translation: U.S. Entrepreneurs Have Learned a Lot About What Does and Doesn't Work, but the Lessons May Not Apply So Easily Abroad," *The Wall Street Journal*, February 12, 2001, p. R12.

http://www.baazee.com

North American Free Trade Agreement (NAFTA) an agreement ensuring free trade between the United States, Canada, and Mexico

European Union (EU) an organization whose purpose is to ensure free trade among member countries

gradually eliminated most tariffs and other trade restrictions between the two countries. This free trade area was extended in 1993, when the United States, Canada, and Mexico established the **North American Free Trade Agreement (NAFTA),** which phases out tariffs over 15 years. These agreements have promoted commerce within North America, just as the formation of the 15-nation **European Union** (EU) in 1993 has facilitated trade among its member countries. Plans for expansion of the EU are already coming together. These agreements and others have eased formal barriers to trade among nations, but cultural, political, and economic differences (discussed later in the chapter) still pose a formidable challenge for small companies.

The Forces Driving Global Businesses

2

Identify the basic forces prompting small firms to engage in global expansion.

At one time, most entrepreneurs in the United States were content to position their startups for the home market and look forward to the day when international sales *might* materialize. With untapped market potential at home and few overseas competitors, many small business owners used this strategy successfully. Today, however, more small businesses are planning from the start to penetrate all available markets, both domestic and foreign.

Given the difficulty of international business, why would any entrepreneur want to get involved? Among the reasons small firms have for going global are some that have motivated international trade for centuries. Marco Polo traveled to China in 1271 to explore the trading of western goods for exotic Oriental silk and spices, which would then be sold in Europe. Clearly, the motivation to take domestic goods to foreign markets and bring foreign goods to domestic markets is as relevant today as it was in 1271. Consider the clothing designer who sells western wear in Tokyo or the independent Oriental rug dealer who scours the markets of Morocco to locate low-cost sources of high-quality Persian carpets.

Complementing these traditional reasons for going global are motivations that once were of little concern to small businesses. One small business international trade expert describes the motivations to go global as follows:

Certainly the overall motivation is increased sales, but that is the simple answer. A more complex analysis opens the door to the real fun—the larger game. Ultimately the goal of global trade is to expand the scope and reach of your company so that the tools and resources available to fight your competition give your company an unbeatable edge—an edge that renews and transforms itself faster than the competition can keep up.[7]

In other words, small firms are looking to do more than simply expand a profitable market when they get involved in international business. No longer insulated from global challengers, they must consider the dynamics of the new competitive environment. The rival on the other side of the street may be a minor threat compared to an online competitor on the other side of the globe!

One way to adjust to these emerging realities is by innovating. In many industries, innovation is essential to competitiveness, and this can give a small company an advantage over its large firm counterparts.[8] Small businesses that invest heavily in research and development often outperform large competitors. But as R&D costs rise, they often cannot be recovered from domestic sales alone. Increasing sales in international markets may be the only viable way to recover the firm's investment.

In some cases, this may require identifying dynamic markets that are beginning to open around the world and locating in or near those markets.

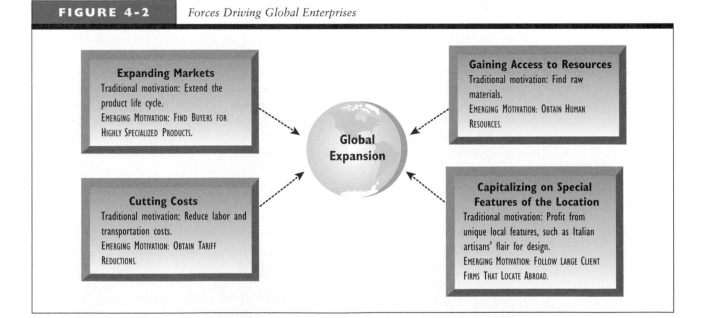

The basic forces behind global expansion can be divided into four general categories (Figure 4-2): expanding markets, gaining access to resources, cutting costs, and capitalizing on special features of the location. Within each category fall some tried and true motivations, as well as some new angles that have emerged with the global economy.

Expanding the Market

More than 95 percent of the world's population lives outside the United States. Thus, globalization greatly increases the size of a firm's potential market.

COUNTRIES TARGETED Because the primary motivation for going global is to develop market opportunities outside the home country, the focus of globalization strategies tends to be those countries with the greatest commercial potential. In the past, these were the developed countries (those with high levels of widely distributed wealth). Today, however, companies are paying greater attention to emerging markets, where income and buying power are growing rapidly. The U.S. Department of Commerce has labeled the largest of these countries as Big Emerging Markets (see Table 4-1).

http://www.ita.doc.gov/bems

Because of their immense populations and potential market demand, countries such as China and India have attracted the greatest attention from international firms. Combined, these two nations account for nearly 40 percent of the world's 6 billion inhabitants, thus providing fertile ground for international expansion. Small companies are among the competitors battling for position in these emerging markets.

Dahlgren & Co. is a 170-employee firm based in Crookston, Minnesota that specializes in the custom processing, roasting, flavoring, and packaging of sunflower seed products. Of the firm's $50 million in sales, 50 percent comes from exports to

FIGURE 4-2 *Forces Driving Global Enterprises*

EMERGING MOTIVATION: OBTAIN HUMAN RESOURCES.

EMERGING MOTIVATION: OBTAIN TARIFF REDUCTIONS.

Traditional motivation: Profit from unique local features, such as Italian artisans' flair for design.

TABLE 4-1

Big Emerging Markets

Country	1999 Population (in millions)	1999 Wealth (GNP per capita)	1998–1999 Economic Growth (%)
Argentina	37	7,600	−4.1
Brazil	168	4,420	−3.2
China	1,250	780	7.2
India	998	450	6.9
Indonesia	207	580	1.9
Mexico	97	4,400	4.1
Poland	39	3,960	3.4
South Africa	42	3,160	.8
South Korea	47	8,490	11.0
Turkey	64	2,900	−6.4
World	**5,975**	**4,890**	**2.7**

Source: World Bank, "Selected World Development Indicators," *World Development Report 2000/2001,* pp. 274–275.

http://www.sunflowerseed.com

more than 30 countries around the world. In an effort to boost Dahlgren's international sales, Tom Miller, vice president of international sales, recently visited China to meet with the president of a snack-food company there. The effort paid off with a $1 million contract. This is a huge deal for a small business, but it only scratches the surface of the potential of a market with a population of more than a billion strong. Dahlgren & Co. recognizes the potential of the Chinese market, which is why its Web site features pages in Chinese as well as in English.[9]

http://www.utstar.com

In 1991, Hong Lu formed Unitech Telecom to sell telecommunications access equipment and services to government-owned phone companies. In its first full year of production, the company had $4 million in equipment sales, almost all of them in China. But Lu was not the first to recognize the country's vast business potential. He quickly learned that telecom giants such as Lucent, Motorola, and Siemens already had a dominating position in the nation's capital, Beijing. "We were nobody—too small for people to pay attention to us," he recalls. Convinced that China had plenty of business potential to tap, Lu turned his attention to the coastal city of Hangzhou. With a population of one million, this urban area offered a sizable customer base, an educated workforce, and less bureaucratic red tape to slow down the fast-moving venture. Since that shift, Lu's firm (now called UTStarcom, Inc.) has done well in China, and the future of the telecommunications industry there looks very bright indeed.[10]

PRODUCTS PROMOTED In the mid-1960s, international business authority Raymond Vernon observed that firms tended to introduce new products in the United States first and then sell them in less-advanced countries later, as demand in the home market declined.[11] In other words, they used international expansion to extend a product's life cycle.

Although this approach is still effective under some circumstances, it has become less viable as customer preferences, income levels, and delivery systems have

become more similar and product life cycles have contracted. Consider the observations of one small business practitioner:

The time lag between U.S. and foreign adoption [has] . . . disappeared. Today it is essential to roll out new products in several countries simultaneously. . . . No longer does the small company have the luxury of using cash flow from domestic sales to support the building of international marketing a few years later. The ever-shortening product cycle virtually dooms such a strategy. Terrific. Now, in addition to getting the product to work, setting up your new team, getting some U.S. customers, and finding money, you now have to worry about selling in six or eight additional countries, most of whom don't even speak English![12]

Products that sell at home are now more likely to be introduced very quickly abroad, with little or no adaptation. The role of television programs, movies, and print media in shaping cultural tastes throughout the world has eased the entry of small businesses into international markets. American interests have long held a starring role in the cultural arena, inspiring widespread purchases of products such as blue jeans and fast food and generating international interest in U.S. sports and celebrities. By informing consumers about the lifestyles of others, globalization is leading the world toward common consumer preferences.

In addition to the trendy products associated with popular culture, another type of product well suited to international markets is the very specialized product. As technology makes possible increasingly sophisticated products, markets are demanding more differentiated products that satisfy their unique needs and interests. Fewer consumers in the home market are likely to be interested in a highly differentiated (and often more expensive) product, so it may become necessary to search for international markets with the same unique demand in order to increase sales enough to recover product development costs. Because small companies often follow focused business strategies (with limited domestic market potential) and aspire to grow rapidly, efforts to exploit the competitive advantage of specialized products across international markets may be even more important to them than to their larger counterparts.[13]

Martin Goodwin and Bob Henry work with a very specialized product in international markets. MSS Global, their Riverside, California company, has progressed from a basement venture to a global enterprise in just a few years. It all started in 1993, when Goodwin ran a supermarket and a few general stores owned by his family. To monitor inventories, price products, and issue purchase orders, he used a dozen separate software programs. In an effort to streamline the process, Goodwin teamed up with Henry, a computer systems specialist, to develop an integrated software package that would handle all of these functions. Goodwin and Henry created Retail, the first Windows-compatible software program for retailers. The product tracks inventory, calculates pricing, gathers customer data, and tracks cashier productivity, so sales trends can be determined with only a few computer keystrokes.

http://www.mssretail.com

The market interest in the United States for this focused product was healthy but limited, leaving MSS Global with scant opportunity to recover development costs. To overcome this constraint, Goodwin and Henry decided to go global. Using strategic partnerships (including an alliance with Microsoft), MSS Global managed to sell nearly 25,000 licenses in 20 countries before the close of the year 2000—amazing growth for a company with only 10 employees! With half of its $2 million in annual revenue coming from international markets, MSS Global can attest to the importance of going global to exploit a competitive advantage.[14]

MAKING THE MOST OF EXPERIENCE No matter which countries are targeted or products promoted, market expansion has the potential to provide benefits beyond the standard per-unit profits on additional items sold. As volume expands, a firm usually can find ways to work smarter or to generate efficiencies. Analysts first observed these **experience curve efficiencies** in the aircraft manufacturing industry. They noticed that each time a manufacturer doubled its total output, the production cost per aircraft dropped by 20 percent. In other words, per-unit costs declined by 20 percent when the firm manufactured four units instead of two, declined again by 20 percent when the firm made eight units instead of four, and so on.

experience curve efficiencies
per-unit savings gained from the repeated production of the same good

learning effects
insights, gained from experience, that lead to improved work performance

economies of scale
efficiencies that result from expansion of production

What can explain this gain in efficiency? Most credit the outcome to learning effects and economies of scale. **Learning effects** occur when the insight an employee gains from experience leads to improved work performance. Learning effects can also take place at the level of the firm if the experiences of individual employees are shared, leading to improved practices and production routines across the organization. These gains from learning are greatest during the startup period and gradually decline over time. Efficiencies from **economies of scale,** on the other hand, continue to rise as the business grows and volume increases, because these savings arise from spreading investment across more units of output and acquiring more specialized (and thus more efficient) plants, equipment, and employees.

Small firms can accelerate the gains from experience curve efficiencies by emphasizing international expansion, assuming that they can manage the growth. Prior to the 1990s, startups were encouraged to consider international expansion only after they had established a solid position in their domestic market. Times have changed. Recent studies have shown that starting with a global presence or globalizing early in a company's life leads to increased performance, especially sales growth. And for high-potential ventures, sales growth is usually considered the most important dimension of performance. The benefits of learning effects and economies of scale are especially apparent in startups based on complex technologies. The possibility of achieving experience curve efficiencies through accelerated globalization of emerging technologies is likely to stimulate the interest of startups and small companies in international business.[15]

Gaining Access to Resources

Just as fortune seekers abandoned their comfortable lives in the eastern United States to flock to California following the discovery of gold at Sutter's Mill in 1848, small firms today leave the United States to gain access to essential raw materials and other factors of production. For example, the oil fields of Kuwait are tended not just by employees of the global oil giants, but also by hundreds of support personnel who work for small companies that have contracted to assist their large clients. These small players choose to locate operations in Kuwait (or Mexico, Saudi Arabia, Venezuela, etc.) for one simple reason: That's where the oil is! The same principle holds for manufacturers that require scarce inputs. For example, an aluminum processor may locate in Jamaica to access required minerals, and a stainless steel smelter may set up production in the Dominican Republic to obtain the ore deposits it needs.

Though small firms have traditionally pursued international ventures to obtain raw materials, increasingly the focus of their search is skilled labor. For example, explosive growth in the software development industry in the United States has led to a shortage of well-trained computer programmers. Since U.S. immigration law restricts the inflow of individuals with these skills from other countries, firms have

had to travel to such countries as India and Russia to obtain the human resources they need. David Birch, a well-known entrepreneurship expert, relates the story of a personal friend who owns a small software development company in Chicago. To hire people to do routine computer programming, he found it necessary to locate his programming operation in Russia.[16] Despite the fact that installation of a telephone can take several months and gangsters sometimes pay visits to demand protection money, the entrepreneur was lured to Russia by the talented human capital, a necessary resource that he found to be in short supply.

Cutting Costs

Sometimes firms go global to reduce the cost of doing business. Among the costs that firms have traditionally reduced by venturing abroad are those for raw materials, labor, and manufacturing overhead.

http://www.kirkhammotorsports.com

Kirkham Motorsports is headquartered in Provo, Utah, where it still builds engines for its high-performance Cobra automobiles. To be cost-competitive, however, the company relocated its labor-intensive preparation of aluminum car bodies to a MiG (Russian fighter jet) factory in Poland.[17] Perhaps Cobra buyers will savor the notion that their lightning-fast cars were constructed in a facility that once produced the jet aircraft that continues to command respect the world over.

Although Kirkham went global to control labor costs, the critical factor is not always labor. For example, transportation costs would likely be the controlling factor for a small business that sells cement products used in construction (concrete columns, bridge girders, formed statuary)—goods that are extremely heavy but do not command a premium price. Since the cost of overseas transportation could exceed the price of the product, international sales would make sense only if the firm were to locate production in-country and near customers.

The advantages of globalization in reducing labor and transportation costs have long been recognized. However, the emerging global economy has brought a new means of lowering costs through relocation.

In recent years, a number of countries have formed regional free trade areas, within which commerce is facilitated by reducing tariffs, simplifying commercial regulations, or even—in the case of the EU—adopting a common currency. These cost-cutting measures can be a powerful inducement to small firms to move into the prescribed area. For example, after the enactment of NAFTA, a number of Japanese firms located manufacturing facilities in Mexico to reap the advantage of reduced tariffs on trade within that region. Recently, NAFTA officials announced that they were accelerating the schedule of tariff reductions, which will provide advantages earlier than expected to firms located within the region.

Capitalizing on Special Features of the Location

Some of the benefits of location are simply the result of unique features of a local environment. For example, Italian artisans have long been well known for their flair for design, and Japanese technicians have shown an ability to harness optical technologies for application in both cameras and copiers. Small companies that depend on a particular strength may find that it makes sense to locate in a region that provides fertile ground for that type of innovation.

Other special benefits of location derive from deliberate government policy. To attract high-tech companies, the government of Dubai, a tiny Arab sheikdom of 800,000 citizens with a land mass about the size of Rhode Island, has stepped up

enforcement of copyright laws, causing software piracy to fall from 99 percent to 40 percent. Coupled with generous tax breaks to firms locating in this Persian Gulf city-state, this initiative has been an undeniable success, snaring more than 200 U.S. companies, including computer hardware manufacturers, software development firms, and other technology providers. Over the last four years, information technology businesses have increased fifteen-fold.[18] Of course, such a deliberate approach can be thwarted by uncontrollable events; the government of Dubai was fortunate to have been operating in a pre–September 11 environment.

Even the appeal of regional free trade areas lies partly in locational features unrelated to cost. As the European countries talked about coming together in the EU, many non-European executives worried that a "Fortress Europe" mentality would arise. That is, they assumed that increased trade among European countries would discourage trade with other nations. In response, many businesses—large and small—located physical facilities in Europe to guarantee future access to that market. In hindsight, they have concluded that the EU has not seriously hindered trade with firms outside of Europe; nonetheless, firms have taken similar measures to ensure market access in other trade areas.

http://www.loranger-mfg.com

Finally, a recent trend among small businesses is to follow large client firms to their new locations. As major corporations locate their operations abroad, their small suppliers may find it necessary to go global along with the client firms to ensure the continuation of important sourcing contracts. The small business owner may have no personal desire to expand internationally, but dependence on a major customer relocating abroad may leave the owner with no alternative. Ford Motor Corporation is convinced that taking its suppliers overseas ensures quality, reduces startup costs, and helps meet local-content restrictions. So when the auto giant decided to open a new plant in Europe, it offered a multi-year contract to Loranger Manufacturing Corporation, a small automobile parts manufacturer based in Warren, Pennsylvania. But there was a catch: The contract required Loranger to locate near the new plant. Since Ford was its primary customer, the small supplier accepted the offer; today, Loranger owns a plant in Hungary, where it employs 150 people and generates nearly $10 million in sales.[19]

Traditional and emerging motivations for small businesses to go global are numerous, but the ultimate incentive is this: If you fail to seize an international market opportunity, someone else will. Under these conditions, the best defense is a good offense. Establishing a position outside of the domestic setting may preempt rivals from exploiting those opportunities and using them against you in the future.

Strategy Options for Global Firms

3

Identify and compare strategy options for global businesses.

Once an entrepreneur has decided to go global, the next step is to plan a strategy that matches the potential of the firm. Throughout most of the 20th century, many small companies were hesitant to step into the world of global trade. Today, such firms are showing signs of "accelerated internationalization." In some industries, even the smallest and newest of firms must globalize just to survive.[20] For most small firms, the first step toward globalization is a decision to export a product to other countries or to import goods from abroad to sell in the domestic market. These initial efforts are often followed by more sophisticated non-export strategies, such as licensing, franchising, forming strategic alliances with international partners, or even locating facilities abroad (see Figure 4-3).

FIGURE 4-3

Strategy Options for Global Enterprises

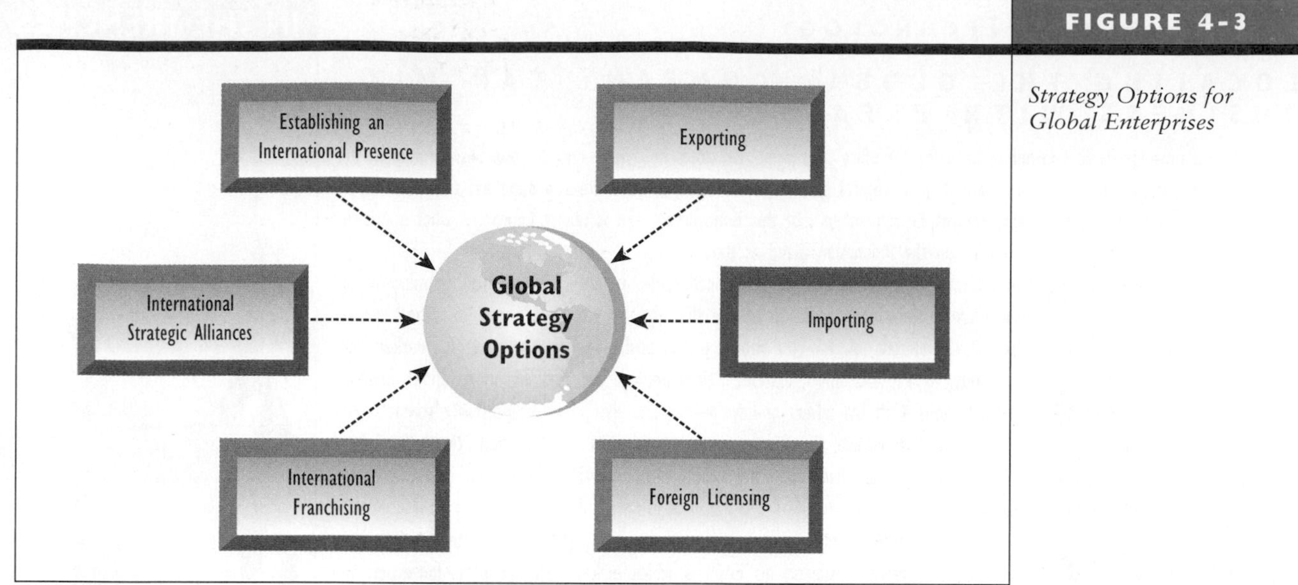

Exporting

exporting
selling products produced in the home country to customers in another country

Exporting involves the sale of products produced in the home country to customers in another country. The U.S. Small Business Administration recently announced that small firms represent approximately 96 percent of American exporters, contributing more than 30 percent of the value of exported goods.[21] In 1998 alone, small businesses in the United States exported $112.2 billion worth of goods and services.[22] Exporting is popular among small businesses because it provides a manageable way of expanding into the international arena:

With increasing global competition, falling barriers to international trade, and improved international communication and information networks, many firms are pressed to compete in international markets. . . . Exporting may offer an effective means for firms to achieve an international position . . . without overextending their capabilities or resources.[23]

Put another way, small export companies can market and distribute their products in other countries without incurring the expense of supporting costly operations in those markets. If the financial benefits from international sales more than offset shipping costs and tariffs, exporting is a favorable option.

trade mission
a trip organized to help small business owners make direct contact with potential buyers abroad

http://www.mooneyfarms.com

One way small companies can look into an export program is to join a **trade mission**—a trip organized to help small businesses meet potential buyers abroad and navigate the cultural and regulatory obstacles of foreign markets. Mary Ellen Mooney took this approach when she joined Baja 2000, a trade mission organized by a consortium of California state trade groups to explore potential markets along Mexico's Baja Peninsula. Mooney is a co-owner of Mooney Farms, a 50-employee family business located in Chico, California that produces sun-dried tomato products. Her three-day visit to Mexico led to a contract to sell $1,200 of product each month to a restaurant in Ensenada—a limited success, but a start nonetheless. She hopes to sell more product south of the border, targeting larger urban centers like Guadalajara, Mexico City, and perhaps even Acapulco. After her trip to Mexico,

UTILIZING NEW TECHNOLOGY

IN THE TRENCHES

LOCATING THE GLOBAL COMPANY CAN MIX BUSINESS WITH PLEASURE

It's 9 A.M. and time for Paolo Conconi to head for the office once again. He closes his eyes—only for one blissful moment—to let his imagination run wild, seeing himself in a tropical paradise, surrounded by palm trees, pristine beaches, and azure-colored ocean waters. Then, when reality returns, he remembers that this is no dream—it is reality. Conconi is what is known as an "extreme telecommuter," and he lives on the Indonesian island of Bali.

When most small business owners think about taking advantage of location, this is not what they have in mind. While some are shaping their plans to ensure that the company has access to critical inputs like raw materials or low-cost labor, prime positioning within strategic markets, or proximity to key customers, extreme telecommuters are thinking more about lifestyle considerations. With the advent of new technologies that make long-distance contact convenient and inexpensive, some entrepreneurs have been cut free from the tether of a physical facility. They live and work where they choose, even if that means moving to Bali.

Conconi grew up in a small town in northern Italy, but in 1992 the then-26-year-old moved to Asia to establish his business, which makes electronic parts for export to Europe. After five years in the busy city life of Hong Kong, he realized that he would rather live elsewhere. His work was portable, so why not relocate? He and his wife now live in Bali, where they have a villa built around a pool, a garden, two servants, and a gardener. Extreme telecommuting presents its share of difficulties, but these are sure to fade away—probably about the time the masseuse comes by the villa to deliver his services. As you can see, location can make all the difference in the world!

Source: Kevin Voigt, "For 'Extreme Telecommuters,' Remote Work Means Really Remote," *The Wall Street Journal,* January 31, 2001, p. B1.

Mooney planned to visit other potential markets, including Venezuela and Canada. Given the advantages of organized tours, other entrepreneurs are dusting off their passports and signing up to participate. As one spokesperson for Baja 2000 observed, "There are more trade missions than ever before, and a growing perception that access to world markets is easier than ever."[24]

In some cases, exporting to international markets may actually promote business in the domestic market, especially when seasonal demand in the home market offsets that from abroad. Very Special Chocolats, a small Canadian producer of specialty chocolates, has turned to global opportunities in Asia so as to use its factory in Azusa, California more efficiently. The firm has $15 million invested in its four production lines in California and employs 100 full-time workers to operate the facility. To manage the spike in demand for chocolates around Christmas, the firm would hire as many as 350 temporary employees for just a few months. Allowing much of its facility to remain idle during the off-season left Very Special Chocolats with a permanent investment that generated product for only part of the year. The excess capacity was becoming a serious financial burden for the small confectioner. To deal with this challenge, the company decided to move into Asian markets, such as Japan, Taiwan, South Korea, and China, where the cycle of holidays is different. Thanks to exports to these countries (representing 15 percent of the firm's total sales), the company is now able to operate its plant full time for nine months out of the year.[25]

The Internet revolution has fueled vigorous growth in export activity. Small firms see the Internet as a powerful tool for increasing their international visibility, allowing them to connect with customers who were previously beyond their reach. Vellus Products Inc. is a luxury pet-products manufacturer based in Columbus, Ohio. President Sharon Doherty realized the benefits of a presence in cyberspace when a dog breeder in Spain contacted her after reading something about Doherty's dog shampoos on the Web. The company's continually expanding Web presence suggests that the strategy is indeed boosting sales. The popularity and prestige of Vellus products are also growing—even the owners of the quarter horses featured in the movie "The Horse Whisperer" use Vellus grooming formulas, a fact that is clearly mentioned on the company's Web site.[26]

http://www.vellus.com

Entertainment Earth is an Internet toy retailer that specializes in action figures. Owners Aaron and Jason Labowitz recently earned a 20 percent profit margin (uncommon in the world of Internet retailing) on annual sales of $1.5 million, and they expect revenues to double within a year. The entrepreneurs target 25- to 35-year-old collectors of action figures who would prefer not to be seen in a toy store. Because the business is Internet-based, they have customers around the world. Jochen Till is a 25-year-old college student in Munich, Germany who loves doing business with the company. This owner of around 300 action figures (mostly characters from "Star Wars" movies) has decided that Entertainment Earth's "service is so good that [he won't] even shop the Web for alternatives." Clearly, Entertainment Earth knows its market, and that market spans the globe.[27]

http://www.entertainmentearth.com

Importing

The flip side of exporting is **importing,** which involves selling goods from abroad in the firm's home market. When a small company finds a product abroad that has market potential at home or identifies a product that would sell at home but cannot find a domestic producer, an import strategy may be the only solution. Rich Birnbaum is the founder of ProWorth, a bare-bones operation in Englewood Cliffs, New Jersey that also employs his brother, as well as several high school students and retirees part-time. Birnbaum sells exquisite Swiss brand-name watches and diamond jewelry through eBay, other online auction services, and the firm's Web site. Birnbaum decided to use eBay because the customer acquisition costs are limited to the cost of a listing (around a dollar per item), which allows him to keep prices low. The venture has been very successful. Launched in January 1999, the company racked up $1 million in sales by year's end, allowing Birnbaum to pay himself a salary of about $100,000 and still break even. And what about the future? The optimistic founder expects sales to increase thirty-fold within a few years—as long as Americans continue to want the fine imports that ProWorth has to offer, that is.[28]

importing
selling goods produced in another country to buyers in the home country

http://www.proworth.com
http://www.ebay.com

Yalanda Lang has an import story with an interesting twist. While shopping in Milan, Italy, Lang watched two women coddling an overpriced bag and decided on the spot that she could design and produce a better product. A new business was born. Lang, an American with European design training, borrowed $50,000 of her parents' personal savings to start a company called INDE (for "independent"). Her plan was to produce high-end women's handbags, positioned to compete with prestige brands like Gucci and Fendi. However, she learned early on that American retail buyers would purchase only low-end handbags from U.S. manufacturers; they look to European producers for prestige products. Lang therefore had no choice but to start her company as an international business. "Strangely enough," she

concluded, "to compete, I need to be in Europe to sell in America." Today, the company has a showroom in Milan, a supporting boutique in Rome, and even a 100-bag deal with a department store in Japan, but imports into the U.S. market have been limited to direct sales generated from a mailing list of 5,000 Neiman Marcus shoppers. Lang continues to produce luxury products in Italy, convinced that her small company will thrive if it can import more of its European-made products into the American market.[29]

Foreign Licensing

foreign licensing
allowing a company in another country to purchase the right to manufacture and sell a company's products in international markets

licensee
the company buying licensing rights

licensor
the company selling licensing rights

royalties
fees paid by the licensee to the licensor for each unit produced under a licensing contract

Exporting is the most popular international strategy among small firms, but it is not the *only* option. Because of limited resources, many small firms are hesitant to go global. One way to deal with this constraint is to follow a licensing strategy. **Foreign licensing** allows a company in another country to purchase the right to manufacture and sell a firm's products in overseas markets. The firm buying these rights is called the **licensee.** The licensee makes payments to the **licensor,** or the firm selling those rights, normally in the form of **royalties**—a fee paid for each unit produced.

International licensing has its drawbacks. For example, the licensee makes all the production and marketing decisions, and the licensor must share returns from sales with the licensee. However, foreign licensing is the least expensive way to go global, since the licensee bears all the cost and risk of setting up a foreign operation.[30]

Recall that MSS Global uses a foreign licensing strategy; it had sold nearly 25,000 licenses in 20 countries by the close of the year 2000. Co-founder Martin Goodwin admits that his 10-person company could never have achieved such rapid expansion on its own: "For us to set up an office and learn that culture and all the tax rules and then to advertise—it's a tremendous headache." Licensing agreements with major computer hardware manufacturers covering the South and Central American markets have paid off. MSS Global may not have a marketing team, a direct sales staff, or even venture capital, but the company makes money every time IBM or NCR sells its product to a foreign retailer. This is the beauty of foreign licensing.[31]

http://www.peacefrogs.com

Small companies tend to think of products when they explore international licensing options, but licensing intangible assets such as proprietary technologies, copyrights, and trademarks may offer even greater potential returns. Just as Disney licenses its famous Mickey Mouse character to manufacturers around the world, a small retailer called Peace Frogs is using licensing to introduce its copyrighted designs in Spain. As Peace Frogs' president, Catesby Jones, explains, "We export our Peace Frogs T-shirts directly to Japan, but in Spain per capita income is lower, competition from domestic producers is stronger, and tariffs are high, so we licensed a Barcelona-based company the rights to manufacture our product."[32] From this agreement Peace Frogs generates additional revenue with almost no added expense.

counterfeit activity
the unauthorized use of intellectual property

Foreign licensing can also be used to protect against **counterfeit activity,** or the unauthorized use of intellectual property. Licensing rights to a firm in a foreign market provides a local champion to ensure that other firms do not use protected assets in an inappropriate way.

International Franchising

international franchising
selling a standard package of products, systems, and management services to a company in another country

International franchising is a variation on the licensing theme. The franchisor offers a standard package of products, systems, and management services to the franchisee, which provides capital, market insight, and hands-on management. Though interna-

IN THE TRENCHES UTILIZING NEW TECHNOLOGY

A MODERN DAY GOLIATH FORMS A PARTNERSHIP WITH A HIGH-TECH DAVID

Will it catch your attention if, the next time you go to a music store to purchase a CD, it comes with a label that scrolls off the titles on that CD and plays a sample of the songs? Before you couldn't get the songs out of your head—now you can't get that label out of your mind!

International Paper Company, the American paper and forest products giant, has entered into a foreign licensing agreement to purchase the right to use technology developed by tiny Power Paper Ltd. to add a bright new twist to packages for everyday products like toys and french fries. Launched in 1997, Power Paper is a small Israeli company with 25 employees and a potent new technology—an ultrathin, flexible battery that can be rolled onto paper like ink. It is hard to imagine ordinary packages sporting moving text and playing music, but Power Paper's breakthrough technology has made battery-powered labels possible—and inexpensive. Moreover, discarding the product poses no threat to the environment.

International Paper knows the world of packaging and does business in more than 50 countries around the globe, but flexible batteries and other such innovations fall far outside of the firm's technological domain. Being nearly 5,000 times the size of Power Paper, though, IP brings tremendous market power to the deal. Recognizing their complementary strengths, IP has agreed to license Power Paper's technology (royalty payments remain secret) and produce more than 500 million "e-packages" by 2003. Power Paper will provide the know-how, and IP will do all of the heavy lifting. This time, it appears that David and Goliath are on the same team.

Source: Queena Sook Kim, "International Paper, Israel's Power Paper Plan Glitzy e-Packages," *The Wall Street Journal,* February 1, 2001, p. A3.

http://www.powerpaper.com

tional franchising was not widely used before the 1970s, today it is the fastest-growing market entry strategy of U.S. firms, with Canada as the dominant market (followed by Japan and the United Kingdom, in that order). This approach is especially popular with U.S. restaurant chains that want to establish a global presence. McDonald's, for example, has raised its famous golden arches in 120 countries around the world. But international franchising is useful to small companies as well. Danny Benususan is the owner of the Blue Note, a jazz club in Manhattan that is now in its second decade of operation. Considered one of the top venues in the world for jazz and other forms of music, this club has attracted the attention of Japanese businesspeople interested in establishing franchises in Tokyo, Osaka, and Fukuoka. Now under the management of Blue Note International, the club has successfully established itself as the world's only franchised jazz club network.[33] The Blue Note has proved that there is more than one way for a small business to globalize.

http://www.mcdonalds.com
http://www.bluenote.net

International Strategic Alliances

international strategic alliance
a combination of the efforts and/or assets of companies in different countries for the sake of pooling resources and sharing the risks of an enterprise

Moving beyond licensing, some small businesses have expanded globally by joining forces with large corporations in cooperative efforts. An **international strategic alliance** allows firms to share risks and pool resources as they enter a new market, matching the local partner's understanding of the target market (culture, legal system, competitive conditions, etc.) with the technology or product knowledge of its

alliance counterpart. One of the advantages of this strategy is that both partners take comfort in knowing that neither is "going it alone."

http://www.bmginc.com
http://www.microsoft.com
http://www.fullarmor.com
http://www.entex.com

Business Marketing Group, Inc. (BMG) is a small firm that specializes in forging strategic alliances between startups and large technology firms. When BMG paired Microsoft with a small company called FullArmor, the startup gained help in designing its software to run on Windows 2000, as well as access to Microsoft-faithful customers at home and abroad. This alliance enabled FullArmor to form a second (but separate) alliance with Entex Information Services to provide services and solutions for Windows 2000. Entex is owned by Siemens, AG, the German engineering powerhouse. Entex/Siemens is one of the top 10 global service providers, so the strategic alliance with Entex has provided FullArmor with indirect access to many international customers—access that FullArmor would not have been able to achieve as an independent enterprise.

Establishing an International Presence

A small business with advanced global aspirations may choose to establish a foreign presence of its own in strategic markets, especially if the firm has already developed an international customer base. Most small companies start by locating a production facility or sales office overseas. As discussed earlier, one avenue pursued by Mary Ellen Mooney in her quest to expand her farming and sun-dried tomatoes business to Mexico and other points south was to join the Baja 2000 trade mission. But Mooney Farms also built its newest plant in Sonora, Mexico, a region known for high-quality fruits and vegetables. By locating its state-of-the-art facility in Sonora, Mooney Farms was able to take advantage of a favorable local climate that allows the company to process tomatoes 10 months out of the year and supply customers with products year round.[34]

Opening an overseas sales office can be a very effective strategy, but small business owners should wait until sales in the local market are great enough to justify the move. An overseas office is costly to establish, staff, manage, and finance; thus, this alternative is beyond the reach of most small companies. Furthermore, the anticipated advantages of overseas offices are sometimes difficult to achieve. Often U.S. firms locate their first international sales office in Canada, but some small companies are finding it profitable to open an office that provides access to the European region (the English-speaking United Kingdom and Ireland are popular locations).

cross-border acquisition
purchase by a business in one country of a company located in another country

greenfield venture
a wholly owned subsidiary formed "from scratch" in another country

Some small firms have grand ambitions that go beyond locating a production facility or sales office overseas. Firms in this category are likely to plan independent operations, such as purchasing a foreign business from another firm through what is known as a **cross-border acquisition** or starting a **greenfield venture** by forming a new wholly owned subsidiary in another country from scratch. In either case, go-it-alone strategies are complex and costly. These options give firms maximum control over their foreign operations and eliminate the need to share any revenues generated; however, they force companies to bear the entire risk of these expensive undertakings. If the subsidiary is a greenfield venture, the firm may have much to learn about running an enterprise in a foreign country, managing host-country nationals, and developing an effective marketing strategy. The commercial potential of a wholly owned international subsidiary may be great, but the challenges of managing it may be even greater. This option is not for the faint of heart.

CHALLENGES TO GLOBAL BUSINESSES

4

Explain the challenges that global enterprises face.

Small businesses face challenges; small *global* businesses face far greater challenges. How well can a small firm do in the global marketplace? The success of enterprising entrepreneurs in international markets proves that small firms can do better than survive—they can thrive! However, success is unlikely without careful preparation. Small business owners must recognize the unique challenges facing global firms and adjust their plans accordingly. Specifically, they need to pay attention to political risks, economic risks, and managerial limitations.

Political Risk

The potential for a country's political forces to negatively affect the performance of business enterprises operating within its borders is defined as **political risk.** Often, this risk is related to the instability of a nation's government, which can create difficulties for outside companies. Potential problems range from threats as trivial as new regulations restricting the content of television advertising to challenges as catastrophic as a government takeover of private assets. Political developments can threaten access to an export market, require a firm to reveal trade secrets, or even demand that work be completed in-country. Figure 4-4 highlights variations in political risk across nations, based on the "Country Risk Rankings" published in *Euromoney* magazine. Countries are color-coded to indicate their riskiness—green

political risk
the potential for political forces in a country to negatively affect the performance of businesses operating within its borders

http://www.euromoney.com

FIGURE 4-4 *"Country Risk Rankings" Map*

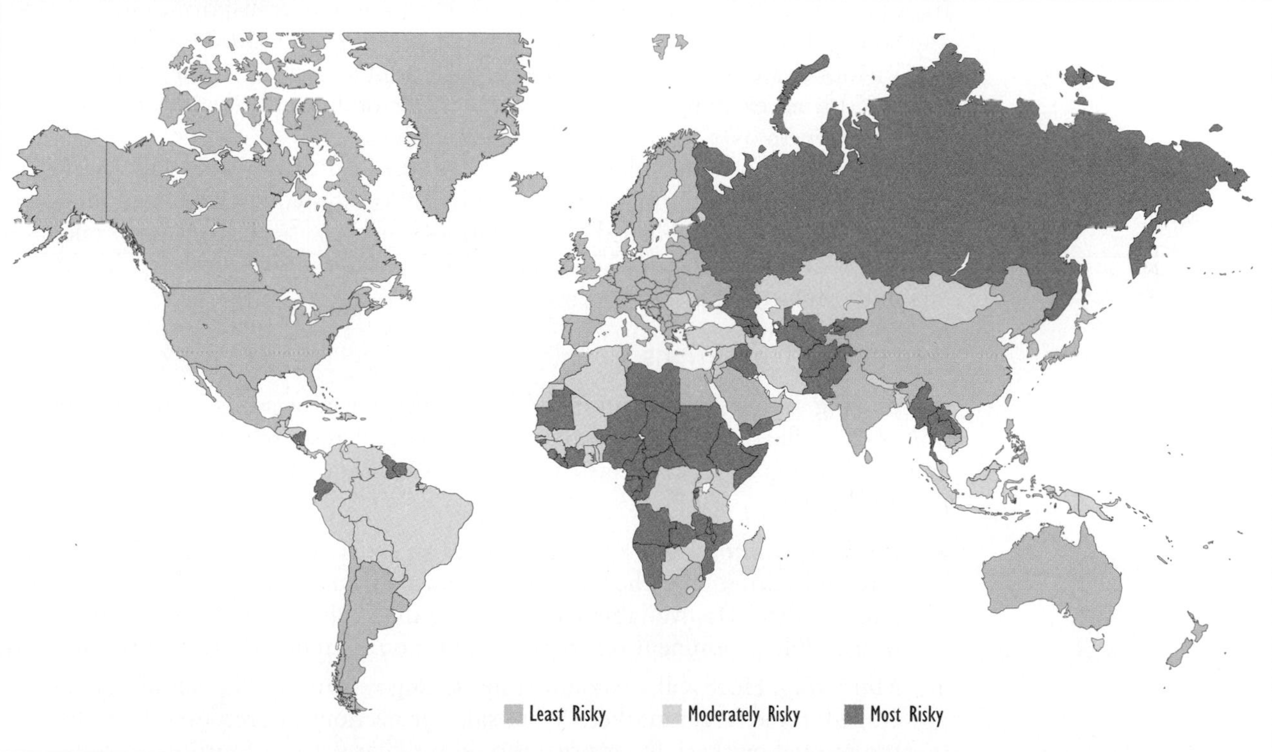

Least Risky
Moderately Risky
Most Risky

represents "go," or safe, countries; yellow, "proceed with caution" countries; and red, "stop and think very carefully" countries. Firms that intend to do business in "red" countries should make appropriate adjustments.

Economic Risk

economic risk
the probability that a government will mismanage its economy and thereby change the business environment in ways that hinder the performance of firms operating there

exchange rates
the value of one country's currency relative to that of another country

Economic risk is the probability that a government will mismanage its economy and change the business environment in ways that hinder the performance of firms operating there. Economic risk and political risk are therefore related. Two of the most serious problems resulting from economic mismanagement are inflation and fluctuations in exchange rates. While a discussion of these factors is beyond the scope of this textbook, it is important to recognize that inflation reduces the value of a country's currency on the foreign exchange market, thereby decreasing the value of cash flows the foreign firm receives from its operations in the local market.

Exchange rates represent the value of one country's currency relative to that of another country—for example, the number of Mexican pesos that can be purchased with one U.S. dollar. Sudden or unexpected changes in these rates can be a serious problem for small international firms, whether the firm exports to that market or has a local presence there.

Mary Ellen Mooney of Mooney Farms has kept an eye on the European market, as well as that of Mexico. She recognized the potential of exporting her sun-dried tomato products to France and came close to striking a deal with a local distributor in 1998, but the contract fell through when the dollar rose sharply against the French franc.[35] To understand her dilemma, suppose the French distributor had been willing to pay 20 francs for a package of sun-dried tomatoes. With an exchange rate of four francs per dollar, Mooney could have converted the 20 francs to $5.00. If $4.50 covered her costs of production, transportation, insurance, and so on, then Mooney would have earned a $.50 profit ($5.00−4.50). But, in reality, Mooney's deal fell through because the dollar *rose* in value relative to the franc. With an exchange rate of five francs per dollar, units selling for 20 francs would be worth only $4.00, a $.50 loss on each sale.

Mooney's experience illustrates how a good deal can quickly fall apart if exchange rates take a turn for the worse. This risk is especially serious for small firms that are just getting established in international markets. Such firms must take measures to protect against currency-related risks, such as stating contracts in U.S. dollars and using currency-hedging strategies.

Managerial Limitations

Conducting business internationally will never be as easy as doing business at home—it is likely to stretch managerial skills and resources to the limit. Global commerce complicates every task and raises difficult questions related to every function of the firm.

- ***Product Planning.*** Will the product/service satisfy customer tastes? Does the foreign location have the employees we need to manufacture the products we plan to offer? Do available workers have the skills required for our operations? Will government restrictions hinder our planned product introductions?
- ***Marketing.*** How will we conduct marketing research? Who should be included in the target market? What sales projections are reasonable in the international market? What price should we charge for our product? How can we deal with counterfeit products manufactured locally?

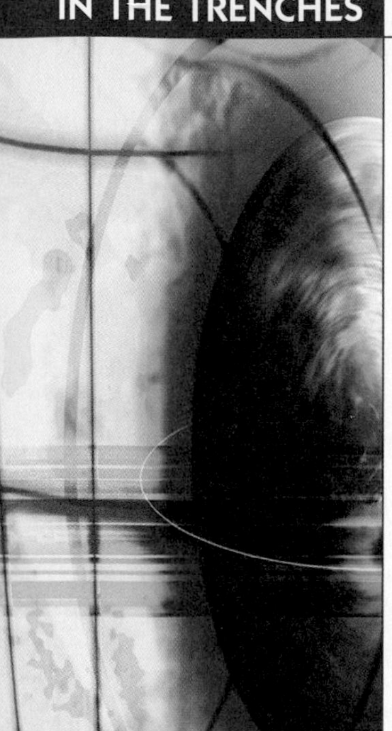

IN THE TRENCHES LIVING IN A DIVERSE WORLD

WHAT HAPPENS WHEN MONEY TALKS IN A DIFFERENT LANGUAGE?

The shift in value of the euro (the new currency of most nations in the European Union) against the dollar has wreaked havoc on small businesses in the United States that sell to customers in Europe. The experience of tiny Hatteras Yachts, Inc. of New Bern, North Carolina illustrates how a change in currency exchange rates can torpedo a deal in no time. Recently, an Italian customer tentatively agreed to buy a 65-foot boat for $2 million. But a decline in the value of the euro raised the dollar-denominated price tag by 10 percent (or $200,000), and the buyer backed out. "He was a little shell-shocked," according to Bryant Phillips, senior vice president of sales and marketing at Hatteras. This lost sale was a serious blow to Hatteras, a company that derives 8 percent of its $150 million in annual sales from Europe.

Large multinational firms have experience dealing with fluctuating currencies. They can hedge their currency exchange risks through forward contracts and foreign-currency options or by maintaining production facilities within the market to which sales are directed. Small firms like Hatteras are more likely to be exposed to the blast of currency storms, since they have fewer tools with which to manage the risks. The winds of currency exchange rates are constantly shifting, and it is important for firms to do what they can to keep from going down with the ship.

Source: Christopher Cooper, "Euro's Drop Is Hardest for the Smallest," *The Wall Street Journal,* October 2, 2000, p. A21.

http://www.hatterasyachts.com

- *Finance.* Can we maintain cash flow for our international operations? How will we manage currency exchange rate fluctuations? Will government policy impact capital transfers? Will local law allow us to repatriate profits from the foreign market? Does the host country government maintain sufficient foreign currency reserves to allow us to take profits out of the country? Will barter or other forms of countertrade be necessary to do business?
- *Management.* Will the management approaches we use at home work in the international setting? How can we identify the people best suited for overseas positions with our company? How much should we pay our local employees? How should we work with labor unions in foreign locations? How can we overcome language, culture, and communication barriers? Can we develop a trusting relationship with foreign employees? What should we do when ethical standards are different in the host nation? Given that the Foreign Corrupt Practices Act prohibits U.S. firms from engaging in certain behaviors, how can we compete when our foreign rivals offer bribes to obtain preferential treatment?
- *Accounting.* What will it take to integrate accounting systems across global operations? How do we account for currency conversions that are constantly changing? Can we harmonize accounting rules that vary from country to country? Does our accounting system capture the information necessary for international trading?

- ***Legal Issues.*** What are the IRS reporting requirements for international firms? How can we be sure that we are paying appropriate taxes in the home and host environments? What is required to comply with local government regulations? Will host country trade restrictions, including tariffs and nontariff barriers, hinder our export program? Do we have patent protections to shield our key technologies?

As you can see, international business decisions are complicated, which explains why so many small firm owners choose to focus solely on their home market. However, the motivations to go global are sound, and others have already proved that it can be done. You can do it, too, if you plan carefully and take advantage of the resources available to help you achieve your global aspirations.

Assistance for Global Enterprises

Recognize the sources of assistance available to support international business efforts.

Help is available to small companies with international interests—you need only open your eyes to find it. Once you decide to enter the global marketplace, you will be amazed at how many resources there are to help you.

Analyzing Markets and Planning Strategy

Among the many activities required to prepare a small firm for the challenges of going global, two are especially fundamental to success abroad: finding international markets that fit the company's unique potentials and putting together a game plan for entry into the markets targeted.

A small business should begin its research of foreign markets and entry strategy options by exhausting secondary sources of information. The U.S. government offers a number of publications on how to locate and exploit global market opportunities. The Small Business Administration's Office of International Trade is responsible for helping small companies expand abroad. The international programs and services of the SBA are delivered through U.S. Export Assistance Centers (USEACs).

http://www.sba.gov/oit
http://www.sba.gov/oit/export/useac.html

One excellent source of information about global marketing is *Opportunities in Exporting,* which is available on the Web site of the SBA Office of International Trade. Also available from the same source is *SBA Guide to Exporting,* which provides an overview of export strategy that is useful for new and experienced exporters. This nuts-and-bolts handbook is designed to guide small firms through the complexities of going global, with chapters focused specifically on identifying markets, choosing an entry strategy, managing transactions, financing trade, arranging transportation, and forming strategic alliances.

Though not focused on small businesses alone, the International Trade Administration of the U.S. Department of Commerce maintains a Web site that supplies helpful insights about international expansion. Publications such as *World Trade* magazine can also be useful, providing timely, in-depth analyses of world trade markets and business issues. Beyond these resources, state and private organizations offer excellent sources of trade information, trade leads, and company databases. One such source, TradePort, offers information online to promote international trade with California-based companies.

http://www.worldtrademag.com
http://www.tradeport.org

Talking with someone who has lived in or even just visited a potential foreign market can be a valuable way to learn about it. For example, conversations with international students at a local university can be very helpful. However, the best way

to study a foreign market is to visit the country personally. A representative of a small firm can do this either as an individual or as a member of an organized group.

Connecting with International Customers

A small company cannot sell abroad unless it connects with customers in targeted international markets. But, have no fear—numerous resources are available to help you connect.

TRADE LEADS Trade leads are essential in identifying potential customers in target markets. Figure 4-5 lists several sources of trade leads. Accessed via the Internet, they provide an inexpensive way to establish vital links with buyers in target markets.

TRADE MISSIONS Joining a trade mission is another excellent way to evaluate a foreign market and link up with overseas customers. As mentioned earlier, a trade mission is a planned visit to a potential foreign market, designed to introduce U.S. firms

FIGURE 4-5 *A Sample of International Trade Leads on the Web*

Bidmix.com	Bidmix.com provides an electronic marketplace for buying and selling worldwide. No membership is required to use the site to search for leads or post new leads. Users can also receive e-mail about new trade leads.
Meetbuyer.com	This site is designed for users all over the world. It features a company directory of members and a product search option. Membership is free.
Online Trade Leads	Onlineleads.com provides trade leads for importers, exporters, and related services. Companies can post, buy, sell, and search entries at no charge.
TradeLeads.com	Use of TradeLeads.com requires a membership. Nonmembers can post leads, but they are unable to read or search for leads.
World Bank FundLine	The World Bank's Private Sector Development Department operates this site to connect potential equity investors with enterprises. Coverage includes countries in Central and Eastern Europe and the former Soviet Union.
World Trade Markets	World Trade Markets allows firms to capture, disseminate, and search Trade Point Trade Leads throughout the world. This database is updated daily by the United Nations, Trade Points, World Trade Markets agents and research staff, and the Internet public.
World Trade Zone	This site fosters international trade. It features a categorized company directory and a searchable listing of trade leads and hosts a mailing list for trade leads.
ASIA: Asian Sources On-Line	Designed for sourcing operations (volume buyers) in Asia, this site can search by country, product, or supplier. It also features other services, such as e-mail alerts, forums, product news, and libraries.
EUROPE: ECeurope.com	This site offers a business-to-business trading bulletin board that helps small- to medium-sized companies access trade leads. A membership is required, but it is free.
Australia: Australia on Display	This site provides trade leads to thousands of Australian companies and their products or services. Users can browse by industry category or keyword.
India: India Trade Board	India Trade Board posts business-to-business messages. Search, buy, and sell options are available.
Ireland: ITW, Business to Business	The Irish Trade Web is a very helpful site for those interested in entering the European market through an agency in Ireland or for companies looking for Irish products to import.

Source: Adapted from the Michigan State University CIBER Web site at http://www.bus.msu.edu/busres/static/trade-leads.htm, August 28, 2001.

to potential foreign buyers and to establish strategic alliances. These missions usually involve groups of five to ten business executives and are designed to maximize international sales. Members of the group typically pay their own expenses and share in the operating costs of the mission. Foreign governments sometimes sponsor trade missions in order to promote business links with U.S. firms.

http://www.sba.gov/oit/info/Guide_to_Exporting

trade intermediary
an agency that distributes a company's products on a contract basis to customers in another country

http://www.americancedar.com

TRADE INTERMEDIARIES Perhaps the easiest way to break into international markets is to use a **trade intermediary**, which is an agency that distributes products to international customers on a contract basis. These agencies tap their established web of contacts, as well as their local cultural and market expertise. In short, an intermediary can manage the entire export end of a business, taking care of everything except filling the orders—and the results can be outstanding. American Cedar, Inc., located in Hot Springs, Arkansas, is a producer of cedar products. With the assistance of a trade intermediary, American Cedar gets 30 percent of its sales from exporting. Company president Julian McKinney reports, "We displayed our products at a trade show, and an export management company found us. They helped alleviate the hassles of exporting directly. Our products are now being distributed throughout the European Community from a distribution point in France."[36] An export management company is only one of the many types of trade intermediaries. Figure 4-6 describes the trade intermediaries that can best provide the assistance small businesses need.

FIGURE 4-6 *Trade Intermediaries Most Suited for Small Businesses*

Export Management Companies	An export management company (EMC) acts as the export department for one or several producers of goods or services. It solicits and transacts business in the names of the producers it represents or in its own name, in exchange for a commission, salary, or retainer plus commission. Some EMCs provide immediate payment for the producer's products by either arranging financing or directly purchasing products for resale. The best EMCs know their products and the markets they serve very well and usually have well-established networks of foreign distributors already in place. This immediate access to foreign markets is one of the principal reasons for using an EMC.
Export Trading Companies	An export trading company (ETC) facilitates the export of U.S. goods and services. Like an EMC, this type of intermediary can either act as the export department for producers or take title to the product and export for its own account. Some ETCs are set up and operated by producers. These can be organized along multiple- or single-industry lines and can also represent producers of competing products.
Export Agents, Merchants, or Remarketers	Export agents, merchants, or remarketers purchase products directly from the manufacturer, packing and marking the products according to their own specifications. They then sell these products overseas in their own names through their contacts and assume all risks for accounts. In transactions with these intermediaries, a firm gives up control over the marketing and promotion of its product. This can hinder future sales abroad if the product is underpriced or incorrectly positioned in the market or if after-sales service is neglected.
Piggyback Marketers	Piggyback marketers are manufacturers or service firms that distribute a second firm's product or service. This is commonly seen when a U.S. company has a contract with an overseas buyer to provide a wide range of products or services.

Source: Adapted from U.S. Department of Commerce, *A Basic Guide to Exporting* (Washington: Department of Commerce and Unz & Co., Inc., 1998-1999), http://www.unzco.com/basicguide/c4.html.

Financing

Arranging financing is perhaps the biggest barrier to international expansion. The more information they have about direct and indirect sources of financing, the more favorably small firms tend to view foreign markets. Sources of this information include private banks and the Small Business Association.

PRIVATE BANKS Commercial banks typically have a loan officer who is responsible for handling foreign transactions. Large banks may have an entire international department. Exporters use banks to issue commercial letters of credit and to perform other financial activities associated with exporting.

A **letter of credit** is an agreement to honor a draft or other demand for payment when specified conditions are met. It helps to assure a seller of prompt payment. A letter of credit may be revocable or irrevocable. An irrevocable letter of credit cannot be changed unless both the buyer and the seller agree to the change. The following steps outline the procedure typically followed when payment is made by an irrevocable letter of credit confirmed by a U.S. bank:

letter of credit
an agreement issued by a bank to honor a draft or other demand for payment when specified conditions are met

1. After exporter and buyer agree on the terms of sale, the buyer arranges for its bank to open a letter of credit. (Delays may be encountered if, for example, the buyer has insufficient funds.)
2. The buyer's bank prepares an irrevocable letter of credit, including all instructions to the seller concerning the shipment.
3. The buyer's bank sends the irrevocable letter of credit to a U.S. bank, requesting confirmation. The exporter may request that a particular U.S. bank be the confirming bank, or the buyer's bank will select one of its U.S. correspondent banks.
4. The U.S. bank prepares a letter of confirmation to forward to the exporter along with the irrevocable letter of credit.
5. The exporter carefully reviews all conditions in the letter of credit. The exporter's freight forwarder is generally contacted to make sure that the shipping date can be met. If the exporter cannot comply with one or more of the conditions, the buyer should be alerted at once.
6. The exporter arranges with the freight forwarder to deliver the goods to the appropriate port or airport.
7. When the goods are loaded, the freight forwarder completes the necessary documents.
8. The exporter (or the freight forwarder) presents to the U.S. bank documents indicating full compliance.
9. The bank reviews the documents. If they are in order, the documents are forwarded to the buyer's bank for review and then transmitted to the buyer.
10. The buyer (or agent) obtains the documents that may be needed to claim the goods.
11. A draft, which may accompany the letter of credit, is paid by the exporter's bank at the time specified; if paid earlier, it may be discounted.

A guarantee from a reputable bank that the exporter will indeed be paid is critical to a small business that has stretched its resources to the limit just to enter the global game and thus cannot afford an uncollected payment. But what if the small business is on the import end of the exchange? How will its interests be protected? The letter of credit provides security for the receiving firm as well, because the

bill of lading
a document indicating that a product has been shipped and the title to that product has been transferred

exporter does not receive payment from the bank until it has released the title, or proof of ownership, of the delivered goods. Once the product has been shipped and the title transferred, the exporter receives a document called a **bill of lading,** which the bank requires before it will pay on the letter of credit. In brief, the letter of credit ensures that the exporter will receive payment only when the goods are delivered in-country, and it also guarantees that the exporter will be paid.

SMALL BUSINESS ADMINISTRATION The Small Business Administration (SBA) serves small U.S. firms primarily through its regional, district, and branch offices. Small businesses that are either already exporting or interested in doing so can receive valuable information from the SBA through conferences and seminars, instructional publications, and export counseling. An extended list of the financial assistance programs offered by the SBA to small firms are posted on the agency's Web site at http://www.sbaonline.sba.gov/oit/txt/export/about.html.

It is clear that a growing number of small firms are choosing to participate in international business. The reasons for this expansion include both time-honored motivations and those emerging in the new competitive landscape. To achieve their global aspirations, most small businesses follow an export strategy; however, this is not the only alternative. Small companies can also implement international strategies that involve licensing, franchising, developing strategic alliances, or establishing a presence in foreign markets. In any case, firms that enter the global arena are certain to run up against serious challenges that purely domestic firms do not have to face. This is the nature of the terrain, but assistance is available in abundance from a number of private and public agencies. With a little help and a lot of hard work, your company can succeed in the global marketplace.

Looking Back

1 Describe the potential of small firms as global enterprises.

- Recent startups and even the smallest of businesses are internationalizing at an increasing rate.
- Small business owners who decide to go global must study the cultural, political, and economic forces in the foreign markets to figure out how best to adapt products and ensure smooth entry.
- Trade barriers are falling in some regions of the world, making it easier for small businesses to go global.

2 Identify the basic forces prompting small firms to engage in global expansion.

- Since more than 95 percent of the world's population lives outside the United States, globalization greatly expands the size of a firm's potential market.
- The 10 Big Emerging Markets are attracting small firms that wish to tap their enormous market potential.
- Small businesses with a highly differentiated product may need an international market in order to increase sales enough to recover product development costs.
- Going global can accelerate gains from experience curve efficiencies (resulting from learning effects and economies of scale), especially for startups based on complex technologies.
- Sometimes small businesses go global to gain access to resources, including raw materials and skilled labor.
- Another reason small firms enter foreign markets is to cut their costs in such areas as labor, transportation, or tariffs.
- Small businesses may want to capitalize on special features of an international location: exploiting the unique features of a local environ-

ment, taking advantage of favorable government policies, establishing a presence within an emerging trade area, or following a large client firm.

3 Identify and compare strategy options for global businesses.

- Exporting is the international strategy most commonly used by small firms. It can be facilitated by using the World Wide Web and joining trade missions that help small businesses make contacts abroad.
- Importing involves selling goods from abroad in the home market. It is a strategy that should be used when products manufactured abroad have market potential at home.
- Non-export strategies include foreign licensing, international franchising, international strategic alliances, and establishing an international presence. They can be more complex than export strategies, but some (especially licensing) are actually the safest options for the small global business.

4 Explain the challenges that global enterprises face.

- Political risk is the potential for a country's political forces to negatively affect the performance of small businesses operating there. Political risk varies greatly across nations.
- Economic risk is the probability that a government will mismanage its economy and change the business environment in ways that hinder the performance of firms operating there (most notably through inflation and unfavorable currency exchange rates).
- Globalization raises numerous concerns related to every function of the firm, thus stretching managerial skills and resources to the limit.

5 Recognize the sources of assistance available to support international business efforts.

- Numerous public and private organizations provide assistance to small businesses in analyzing markets and planning a strategy.
- Small businesses can connect with international customers by reviewing sources of trade leads, joining trade missions, or using the services of trade intermediaries.
- For assistance in financing its entry into a foreign market, a small firm can turn to private banks (which can issue letters of credit) and programs initiated by the Small Business Administration.

KEY TERMS

globalization, p. 89
tariffs, p. 91
North American Free Trade Agreement (NAFTA) p. 92
European Union (EU) p. 92
experience curve efficiencies, p. 96
learning effects, p. 96
economies of scale, p. 96
exporting, p. 99
trade mission, p. 99
importing, p. 101
foreign licensing, p. 102
licensee, p. 102
licensor, p. 102
royalties, p. 102
counterfeit activity, p. 102
international franchising, p. 102
international strategic alliance, p. 103
cross-border acquisition, p. 104
greenfield venture, p. 104
political risk, p. 105
economic risk, p. 106
exchange rates, p. 106
trade intermediary, p. 110
letter of credit, p. 111
bill of lading, p. 112

DISCUSSION QUESTIONS

1. Discuss the importance of a careful cultural analysis to a small firm that wishes to enter an international market.
2. How have trade agreements helped reduce trade barriers? Do you believe these efforts will continue?
3. Do you believe that small firms should engage in international business? Why or why not?
4. Identify the four basic forces driving small businesses to enter the global business arena. Which do you think is the most influential in the globalization of small firms?
5. Give examples of some emerging motivations persuading small business owners to go global. Are any of these motivations likely to remain powerful forces ten years from now? Twenty years from now?

6. Why is exporting the most popular global strategy among small businesses? Do you think this should be the case?
7. What impact has the Internet had on the globalization of small firms? How do you think small companies will use the World Wide Web for business in the future?
8. What are the non-export strategies that small businesses can adapt? In view of the unique needs and capabilities of small firms, what are the advantages and disadvantages of each of these strategies?
9. What are the three main challenges small businesses face when they go global? What strategies can a small company take to deal with each of these challenges?
10. What forms of assistance are available to small global firms? Which is likely to be of greatest benefit to small companies? Why?

You Make the Call

SITUATION 1

Bill Moss and several other small business owners joined a trade mission to China to explore market opportunities there. The group learned that China has a population of 1.3 billion and is the third fastest growing export market for small- and medium-sized U.S. firms. Average annual income in China is approximately $725 per year; typical urban income is about $1,000, with an average high of $3,400 a year in Shanghai. In a given year, the Chinese software market grows by 30 percent and the number of Internet users quadruples. Furthermore, the demand for management consulting services is increasing, especially information technology consulting. Members of the group were surprised by the number of people who had cell phones and regularly surfed the Internet, especially in large urban centers such as Beijing, Shanghai, and Guangzhou. On the downside, they found that counterfeit goods (from clothing and leather goods to software and CDs) were readily available at a fraction of the cost of legitimate merchandise and that local merchants expressed an interest in doing business only with vendors with whom they had established relationships.

Question 1 What types of businesses would prosper in China? Why?

Question 2 What are the challenges and risks associated with doing business in China?

Question 3 What steps should Moss take to address these challenges and risks in order to increase his chance of success in the market?

SITUATION 2

Lynn Cooper owns and operates BFW, Inc. in Lexington, Kentucky, where she produces fiber-optic lights and headgear-mounted video cameras used for medical exams and surgery. She sees exporting as a means of increasing sales, but with just one employee, she wonders how best to handle the additional marketing and distribution exporting would require.

Question 1 What sources of information would be helpful to Cooper?

Question 2 Would you recommend that she consider using an international distributor? If so, what characteristics should she look for in a distributor?

Question 3 Do you think exporting is a feasible alternative for Cooper at this time? Why or why not?

SITUATION 3

Dr. Juldiz Afgazar, a native of the Republic of Kazakhstan, had been invited to spend a semester in the United States as a visiting scholar in entrepreneurial finance. Kazakhstan gained its independence from the former Soviet Union in 1991, and only after that were laws passed allowing citizens to own private businesses. Dr. Afgazar wanted to learn more about the free market economy of the United States to determine whether such a system could be implemented in Kazakhstan.

Prior to this visit to the United States, Dr. Afgazar had not traveled extensively outside her country. Although she enjoyed many aspects of U.S. culture, she was particularly impressed by the seemingly unlimited quantity and variety of goods and foods that were readily available. After a visit to a local restaurant's pizza buffet, she became an avid fan of American-style pizza! Dr. Afgazar found the crisp yeast crust, spicy tomato sauce, melted mozzarella cheese, and assortment of toppings to be a delicious combination. Pizza was an entirely new type of food for her, since it was not available in Kazakhstan. A true entrepreneur, Dr. Afgazar began to wonder if a pizza restaurant could be successful in her country.

Source: Developed by Elisabeth J. Teal of Baylor University, Waco, Texas, and Aigul N. Toxanova of Kokshetau Higher College of Management and Business, Kazakhstan.

Question 1 What obstacles would an entrepreneur have to overcome to establish a pizza restaurant in a country with a developing market-based economy, such as Kazakhstan?

Question 2 Is Dr. Afgazar's idea of developing a pizza restaurant in Kazakhstan ahead of its time? That is, do you think the economy of Kazakhstan is sufficiently developed to support a pizza restaurant?

Question 3 What methods could an entrepreneur use to evaluate the likelihood of success of a pizza restaurant in Kazakhstan?

EXPERIENTIAL EXERCISES

1. Conduct phone interviews with 10 local small business owners to see if they engage in international business. Discuss their reasons for going global or for choosing to do business only domestically.
2. Contact a local banker to discuss the bank's involvement with small firms participating in international business. Report your findings to the class.
3. Review recent issues of *Entrepreneur, Inc.*, or another small business publication, and be prepared to discuss articles related to international business.
4. Find an article about a small business that first expanded internationally using an entry strategy other than exporting. From what you understand of the company's situation, suggest guidelines that could lead a firm to go global with non-export strategies.
5. Consult secondary sources to develop a political/economic risk profile for a given country. Select a small company and explain what it would have to do to manage these risks if it were to enter the market of the country profiled.
6. Speak with the owner of a small international company. Which sources of assistance did that entrepreneur use when launching the global initiative? Which sources did the entrepreneur find most helpful? Which did the entrepreneur find least helpful?

EXPLORING THE WEB

1. Examine the articles on global entrepreneurs at the MSNBC Web site at **http://www.msnbc.com/news/globalentrepreneurs_front.asp**.
   a. In what nations are the headquarters for the various businesses featured here? List the factors that make these locations so attractive to entrepreneurs.
   b. To what nations are products being exported? Explain why these markets were chosen.
   c. What risks are these entrepreneurs facing as a result of their global focus?
2. Access the *Industry Week* article entitled "Global Gold: Small Businesses Capitalize on World Markets" at **http://www.industryweek.com/CurrentArticles/asp/articles.asp?ArticleId=856**.
   a. List the statistics given in the article concerning the importance of small business in U.S. exporting.
   b. Which firm used as an example in the article do you find most impressive? Explain why.
3. The Web site of the Small Business Administration Office of International Trade at **www.sba.gov/oit** provides resources for small businesses wanting to learn more about exporting.
   a. Describe the financial resources that the federal government makes available to small firms wanting to export.
   b. Print the address of the U.S. Export Assistance Center nearest you.
   c. According to the *SBA Guide to Exporting,* why is it important to have an international business plan? What kinds of information should be included?

CASE 4

SUNNY DESIGNS, INC. (p. 647)

This case describes the experiences of an entrepreneur as he attempts to expand his furniture business by establishing a production facility in China.

part 3

Pursuing New Venture Opportunities

chapter 5

Startups and Buyouts

In the Spotlight

Glow Dog, Inc.

Beth Marcus, of Bedford, Massachusetts, and her cockapoo, Luke, were out for a walk one evening when a car almost struck them. "My neighbor came driving around the corner, and we had to leap into the bushes to get out of the way," Marcus recalls. "I wasn't wearing particularly dark clothing, and Luke has a light coat, but this guy didn't see us at all." At the time, Marcus was a consultant for Reflective Technologies, Inc., maker of a reflective fabric called illumiNITE®, which was being targeted to joggers. She decided to start her own firm, Glow Dog®, Inc., to sell light-reflective clothing for pets and their owners.

Glow Dog positioned itself to take advantage of two trends in the United States: a $25 billion market for pet products and a $7.5 billion market for reflective clothing. Through early products such as reflective dog collars and rain slickers, Marcus attracted the attention of Tony Leonardi, president of Petsmart Direct. "We look for something that gives us a competitive edge, and we got that edge with the use of the products we saw from Beth." Recently, Glow Dog had annual sales of $1.2 million, and Marcus sees the company headed toward sales revenues of over $5 million—not a bad outcome from almost getting hit by a car.

Source: Adapted from Mike Hofman, "Hot Startups: A Spot in the Dark," *Inc.,* Vol. 21, No. 10 (July 1999), pp. 38–42.

http://www.glowdog.com

Looking Ahead

After studying this chapter, you should be able to

1. *Identify five factors that determine whether an idea is a good investment opportunity.*
2. *Give three reasons for starting a new business rather than buying an existing firm or acquiring a franchise.*
3. *Distinguish among the different types and sources of startup ideas.*
4. *List some reasons for buying an existing business.*
5. *Summarize three basic approaches for determining a fair value for a business.*
6. *Describe the characteristics of highly successful startups.*

Today's business world is replete with new ideas and efforts by a host of aspiring entrepreneurs to take advantage of opportunities they believe to exist. Rekha Balu explains it well:

As we enter a new millennium, we find ourselves in the Age of the Startup. Everywhere, it seems, people have a new idea that they want to turn into a business, a new business model that they want to turn into a company—or an old company that needs a new idea. If you're not incubating a startup, you're starting an incubator.[1]

Most entrepreneurs have an idea that they want to make happen. And, in many cases, they are making it happen—not only in the United States, but all around the world. During a recent visit to mainland China, we did not have to look far to find startups by individuals trying to capture the business opportunities they saw in developing Chinese markets.

Before looking specifically at the process of starting or buying a company, let's consider how to determine whether an idea for a business actually represents a good opportunity. Most people have some ideas about new products or services that they would like to see made available—but just because something is a good idea does not mean that it is a good opportunity, as you will see.

Identifying and Evaluating Investment Opportunities

Identify five factors that determine whether an idea is a good investment opportunity.

Experience shows that a good idea is not necessarily a good investment opportunity. In fact, when people become infatuated with an idea, they tend to underestimate the difficulty of developing market receptivity to that idea and building a company with which to capture the opportunity. To qualify as a good investment opportunity, a product or service must meet a real need with respect to functionality, quality, durability, and price. Success ultimately depends on convincing consumers of the benefits of the product or service. According to Amar Bhide, a professor at Columbia University, "Startups with products that do not serve clear and important needs cannot expect to be 'discovered' by enough customers to make a difference."[2] Thus, the market ultimately determines whether an idea has potential as an investment opportunity.

There are many other criteria for judging whether a new business idea is a good investment opportunity. Some of the fundamental requirements follow:

- There must be a clearly defined market need for the product or service, and the timing must be right. Even when the concept is good, poor timing can prevent a product or service from constituting a viable investment opportunity. Success requires that the window of opportunity be open and that it remain open long enough for an entrepreneur to exploit the opportunity.
- The proposed business must be able to achieve a durable or sustainable competitive advantage (see Chapter 2). Inability to understand the nature and importance of a competitive advantage has resulted in the failure of many small startups.
- The venture needs to be financially rewarding, and even forgiving, allowing for significant profit and growth potential. The profit margin (profit as a percentage of sales) and return on investment (profit as a percentage of the size of the investment) must be high enough to allow for errors and mistakes and still yield significant economic benefits.
- There must be a good fit between the entrepreneur and the opportunity. In other words, the opportunity must be captured and developed by someone who has the appropriate skills and experience and who has access to the critical resources necessary for the venture's growth.
- There must be no fatal flaw in the venture—that is, no circumstance or development that could in and of itself make the business unsuccessful.

Table 5-1 presents the five evaluation criteria more fully. Above all, beware of being deluded into thinking that an idea is a "natural" and cannot miss. The market can be a harsh disciplinarian for those who have not done their homework. However, for those who succeed in identifying a meaningful opportunity, the rewards can be sizable.

Subsequent to this chapter, we will look at entrepreneurial opportunities that exist in a franchise (Chapter 6) and a family business (Chapter 7). But before directing our attention to these two options, let's consider an even more basic decision that has to be made—whether to start a new business or to buy an existing one. Creating a business from scratch—a **startup**—is the option frequently associated with the term *entrepreneurship*. And there is no question that startups represent a significant opportunity for many entrepreneurs. But entrepreneurs may also realize their dreams by purchasing an existing firm—a **buyout.** We will first look at the startup process and then consider what is involved in buying a business.

startup
creating a new business from scratch

buyout
purchasing an existing business

The Startup: Creating a New Business

2
Give three reasons for starting a new business rather than buying an existing firm or acquiring a franchise.

There are several reasons for starting a business from scratch rather than pursuing other alternatives, such as franchising. They include the following:

1. Developing the commercial market for a recently invented or newly developed product or service
2. Taking advantage of available resources, including an ideal location, recent technological advances in equipment, employees, suppliers, and bankers
3. Avoiding undesirable precedents, policies, procedures, and legal commitments of existing firms

TABLE 5-1 *Evaluation Criteria for a Startup*

Criterion	ATTRACTIVENESS Favorable	Unfavorable
Market Factors		
Need for the product	Well identified	Unfocused
Customers	Reachable; receptive	Unreachable; strong loyalty to competitor's product
Value created by product or service for the customer	Significant	Not significant
Life of product	Longer than time required for customer to recover investment plus profit	Shorter than time required for customer to recover investment
Market structure	Emerging industry; not highly competitive	Mature or declining industry; highly concentrated competition
Market size	Sales of $100 million or more	Unknown or sales of less than $10 million
Market growth rate	Growing by at least 30% annually	Contracting or growing by less than 10% annually
Competitive Advantage		
Cost structure	Low-cost producer	No production cost advantage
Degree of control over		
Prices	Moderate to strong	Nonexistent
Costs	Moderate to strong	Nonexistent
Channels of supply	Moderate to strong	Nonexistent
Barriers to entry:		
Proprietary information or regulatory protection	Have or can develop	Not possible
Response/lead time advantage	Have or can develop	Nonexistent
Legal/contractual advantage	Proprietary or exclusive	Nonexistent
Contacts and networks	Well developed	Limited
Economics		
Return on investment	25% or more; durable	Less than 15%; fragile
Investment requirements	Small to moderate; easily financed	Large; financed with difficulty
Time required to break even or to reach positive cash flows	Under 2 years	More than 3 years
Management Capability	Management team with diverse skills and proven experience	Solo entrepreneur with no related experience
Fatal Flaws	None	One or more

Source: Adapted from Jeffry A. Timmons, *New Venture Creation* (Homewood, IL: Irwin, 1999), pp. 86–87.

Assuming that you have one or more of these reasons for considering a startup, you need to address several basic questions:

- What are the different types of startup ideas you might consider?
- What are some sources for new ideas?
- How can you identify a genuine opportunity that creates value, for both the customer *and* the company's owner(s)?
- How should you refine your idea?
- What might you do to increase your chances that the business will be successful?

Let's examine each of these questions.

Kinds of Startup Ideas

3 *Distinguish among the different types and sources of startup ideas.*

Type A ideas
startup ideas centered around providing customers with an existing product not available in their market

Type B ideas
startup ideas, involving new technology, centered around providing customers with a new product

Type C ideas
startup ideas centered around providing customers with an improved product

http://www.kabloom.com

Figure 5-1 shows the three basic types of ideas that develop into startups: ideas for new markets, new technologies, and new benefits.

Many startups develop from **Type A ideas**—those concerned with providing customers with a product or service that does not exist in their market but already exists somewhere else. Jeremy Kraus's firm, Jeremy's MicroBatch Ice Creams, is an example of a Type A idea. As a college student, Kraus applied the beer industry's microbrew strategy to ice cream, making small quantities and selling the product in limited editions. He went on to develop a relationship with the long-time distributor of Ben & Jerry's ice cream, Dreyer's, which has agreed to market Jeremy's products in the New York area and, eventually, in other geographical markets as well.[3]

Some startups are based on **Type B ideas,** which involve new or relatively new technology. Zalman Silber, for example, raised $6.2 million in 1994 to develop New York Skyride, a simulated helicopter tour of the Big Apple. In 1996, the high-tech appeal of the ride attracted about 19 percent of the 3.4 million tourists who visited the Empire State Building, where the ride is located.[4]

Type C ideas, which represent new and improved ways of performing old functions, account for the largest number of startups. In fact, most new ventures, especially in the service industry, are founded on "me, too" strategies—they differentiate themselves through superior service or cheaper cost. David Hartstein's effort to redefine the floral industry fits into the Type C category. His KaBloom, Ltd. outlets offer more than 200 varieties of fresh-cut flowers, compared with an average of 40 at large supermarkets and 20 at most florists. KaBloom keeps its prices low—about half the industry norm—by buying directly from growers and distributors, as opposed to buying from wholesalers. Its online store charges less than half as much as 1-800-Flowers. KaBloom's physical stores are also better lit and twice as large as many mom-and-pop shops. "A walk in our store is like a walk in a garden," says Hartstein.[5]

Sources of Startup Ideas

Since startups begin with ideas, let's consider some sources of inspiration for new ideas. Several studies have sought to discover where ideas for small business startups originate. Figure 5-2 gives the results of one such study by the National Federation

FIGURE 5-1

Types of Ideas That Develop into Startups

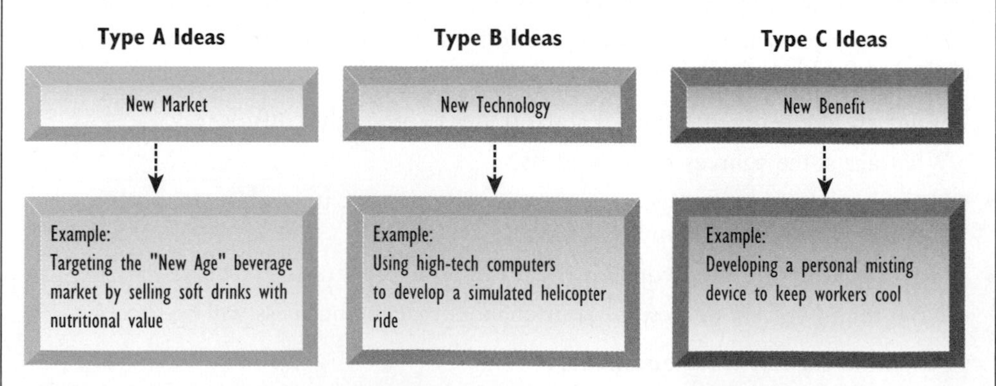

FIGURE 5-2

Sources of Startup Ideas

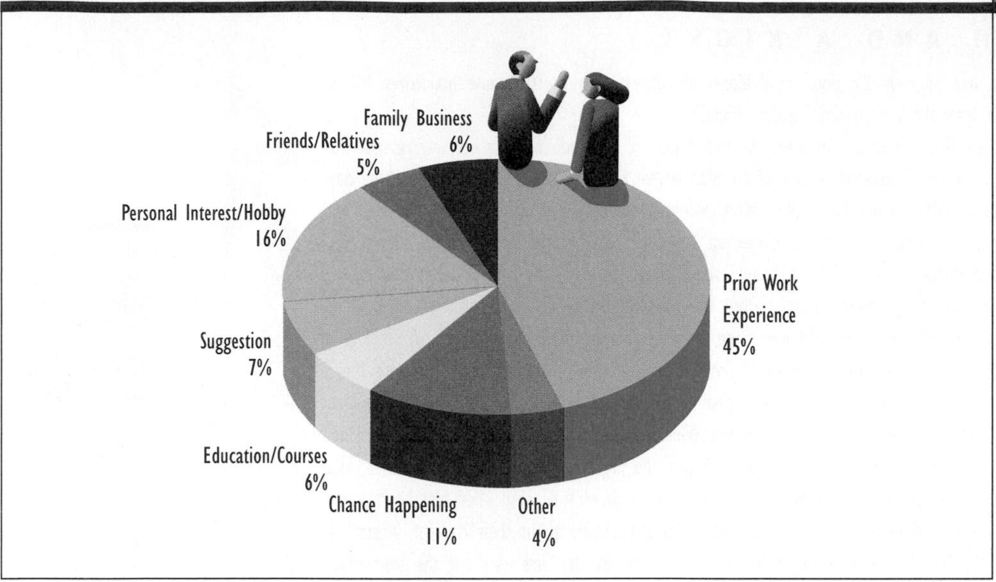

Source: Data developed and provided by the National Federation of Independent Business Foundation and sponsored by the American Express Travel Related Services Company, Inc.

of Independent Business Foundation, which found that "prior work experience" accounts for 45 percent of new ideas. "Personal interest/hobby" represents 16 percent of the total, and "chance happening" accounts for 11 percent. Although a new idea can come from virtually anywhere, we will focus on four possible sources: personal experience, hobbies, accidental discovery, and deliberate search.

PERSONAL EXPERIENCE The primary basis for startup ideas is personal experience, either at work or at home. Knowledge gleaned from a present or recent job often allows a person to see possibilities for modifying an existing product, improving a service, or duplicating a business concept in a different location. Richard Maradik and Jay Graves developed a sophisticated database for the Republican Party in Tennessee to use in its direct-mail fundraising. "We went 10 demographic categories deep into each person," recalls Maradik. "We knew their household income, what kind of car they drove, and what magazines they read." With the blessing of their former employer, Maradik and Graves quit their jobs, deposited $15 in a checking account, and negotiated for some free office space where they put a card table and two chairs. The new business they started was DataMark, a direct-mail database marketing company. The firm eventually grew to 26 employees, with 200 customers and annual sales of $4 million.[6]

http://www.data-mark.com

HOBBIES Sometimes hobbies grow beyond their status as leisure activities to become businesses. For instance, a student who loves skiing might start a ski equipment rental business as a way to make income from an activity that she enjoys. Consider Bill Martin and Greg Wright, who have a passion for the stock market and the Internet. As students at the University of Virginia and Rutgers University, respectively, they created a Web site called Raging Bull, with a message board where

http://ragingbull.lycos.com

ENTREPRENEURSHIP TODAY

THREE WOMEN AND A KIOSK

The business was dreamed up in just one hour by the pool: small kiosks in airports offering 10 minute manicures. It's an idea so simple that it can't miss—at least that's what the founders hope.

The daughter of Cuban immigrants, Vivian Jimenez had spent the better part of a decade working her way up the ladder to become vice president of interactive media services at one of Florida's largest public relations firms. But one June day, somewhere on the road to the Austin airport, Jimenez knew that things would never be the same again. Even though she still held her position at the PR firm, in her heart she was no longer an employee hoping for a better raise, a better job, a better work life. She had become something entirely different. "I am," she declared aloud in the car, "an entrepreneur."

Along with her partners—Karen Janson, a former colleague from the PR firm, and Lorraine Brennan O'Neil, a friend of Janson's—Jimenez had spent the previous months exploring the idea of starting a business. "It was sort of just fun," Jimenez says, recalling the nights and weekends they'd devoted to sketching out a game plan for the business they called 10-Minute Manicure, which they hoped to open in airports. When Jimenez and Janson inquired about attending an airline-industry conference in Austin, the organizer was so taken with their idea that she asked if the women would speak on a panel. It was an offer that both scared and excited them. If the organizer was that enthusiastic about their concept, Janson recalls, they figured they might be onto something. By the time they left the conference, they were sure.

But, for Jimenez, the realization that she could be an entrepreneur was the real revelation of the two-day event. "On our way to the airport afterward, we were rattling off ideas, and I just knew: that's what makes an entrepreneur. Seeing an opportunity and making it happen," she says.

Source: Karen Dillon, "Three Women and a Kiosk," *Inc.*, Vol. 22, No. 1 (January 2000), pp. 60–62.

their friends could chat about stocks. The Web site received only a modest response until Martin and Wright conceived of an "ignored" button, which allows a user to block out messages the user considers worthless or offensive. "We noticed that the biggest problem with message boards was spamming: people being vulgar or just dumb," says Wright. "We wanted people to enjoy what was valuable without worrying about the other stuff." The revised site attracted so many users that @Ventures, a venture-capital firm, invested $2 million in the start-up.[7]

serendipity
the faculty for making desirable discoveries by accident

ACCIDENTAL DISCOVERY Another source of new startup ideas—accidental discovery—involves something called **serendipity**, or the seeming ability to make desirable discoveries by accident. Anyone may stumble across a useful idea in the course of day-to-day living. Take Neil Sater, who had lost his job as a carpenter because of a downturn in residential construction. While at a local greenhouse, he noticed an unusual fountain consisting of "a monolithic slab of slate with water running over it." He thought that a lighter, more portable version might have commercial potential. For $50, he bought the necessary raw materials, and he and his brother-in-law began gluing pieces of slate together. From slate tubes, they designed pieces of furniture, such as side tables. Sater then bartered with a photographer to shoot a portfolio showing the prototypes. Based on the photos, they received orders from several gallery owners. Their break came when their company, Water Wonders, rented a

booth at the International Gift Show in San Francisco. Over five days, they received $50,000 in orders. Water Wonders, which now sells fountains through mail-order houses and at retail chain stores and galleries nationwide, has 60 employees and annual sales of $8 million.[8]

DELIBERATE SEARCH A startup idea may emerge from a prospective entrepreneur's purposeful exploration to find a new idea. Such a deliberate search may be useful because it stimulates a readiness of mind—prospective entrepreneurs who are thinking seriously about new business ideas will be more receptive to new ideas from any source.

Magazines and other periodicals are excellent sources of startup ideas. One way of generating startup ideas is to read about the creativity of other entrepreneurs. For example, many issues of *Inc.* and *Forbes* feature various business opportunities. Visiting the library and even looking through the Yellow Pages in other cities can be productive. Also, traveling to other cities to visit with entrepreneurs in your line of business can be extremely helpful. And, of course, the Internet provides an unlimited amount of information regarding the startup process and even specific opportunities. Table 5-2 lists a few Web sites that could be beneficial for someone starting a business; there are far more sites that could have been mentioned.

Entrepreneurs can evaluate their own capabilities and then look at the new products or services they might be able to produce, or they can first look for needs in the marketplace and then relate those needs to their own capabilities. The latter approach has produced more successful startups, especially in the field of consumer goods and services.

TABLE 5-2

Web Sites Useful When Starting a Business

Online Business Owners Resources	http://www.toolkit.cch.com http://www.amcity.com/extraedge/toolbox http://www.entrepreneurmag.com http://www.morebusiness.com http://www.asbdc.ualr.edu/fod http://www.tradezone.com
Regional Business News/Trends/Opportunities	http://www.amcity.com http://www.djc-or.com/index.cfm http://www.djc.com
Demographic Information/Articles	http://www.americandemographics.com http://www.easidemographics.com/reports
Periodical Search	http://www.newslink.org http://www.ecola.com http://www.all-links.com/newscentral http://www.gebbieinc.com/magurl.htm
Corporate Information	http://www.corporateinformation.com http://www.hoovers.com http://www.thomasregister.com http://www.inil.com/users/dguss/gatpr68.htm http://www.datagalaxy.com http://www.verticalnet.com
Government Information	http://www.lib.lsu.edu/gov/fedgov.html http://www.govcon.com

ENTREPRENEURSHIP TODAY

IN THE TRENCHES

JUST SAY "NO"

Norm Brodsky, an entrepreneur, writer, and frequent advisor to entrepreneurs, observes, "Of all the challenges people face when they decide to start a business, one of the most difficult is learning to just say no" to a poorly conceived idea. He tells the story of one such instance:

We began, as always, by talking about their ideas and goals, and I mentioned to Bob and Tracy that we'd have to do a business plan. . . . So I took them through the process. I had them get in touch with the industry association, do research on the competition, talk with other people in the business—the whole nine yards. I also helped them put together a financial plan, starting with their basic assumptions. How much were they going to pay for a building? What would it cost to get the place ready? How much space would they be able to rent month by month? They began to see in financial terms exactly what it would take for them to make their new venture successful.

They didn't have much luck in finding a site, however. . . . Finally, a real estate agent called them about a place that sounded perfect. It was empty, available, and just the right size. The roof and the parking lot needed to be redone, but the owner had agreed to discount the price of the property by enough to cover the repairs.

They went to view the site and liked what they saw. I did, too, when we all went back together. There was just one little problem: the place was set back off the main road. Oh, well, they said, they "could put up a big sign on the road." Next they discovered that the zoning commission would permit only a small sign on the main road.

Bill Waugh, founder of the restaurant chain Taco Bueno, helped develop the concept of Mexican fast-food restaurants in the 1960s, after he extensively researched the fast-food industry in general and Mexican food in particular. After completing his research, he wanted to acquire a franchise from El Chico, a national chain of Mexican restaurants, but he was turned down as a prospective franchisee. Waugh decided that the research he had done provided a sufficient basis for starting his own Mexican restaurant. Eighty-four restaurants later, he sold his firm to Unigate, Ltd., a company from London, for $32 million. Then, in the late 1980s, Waugh began the research process again, looking for his next venture. This time, he developed a concept for a new fast-food restaurant selling hamburgers, which he named Burger Street. By 2000, as a result of thorough research, he had approximately 25 restaurants in successful operation in the Dallas/Fort Worth, Texas and Tulsa, Oklahoma areas.[9]

A truly creative person can find useful ideas in many different ways. The sources discussed here are only a few of the possibilities. We encourage you to seek and reflect on new venture ideas in whatever circumstances you find yourself.

Refining a Startup Idea

What appears to be a good startup opportunity often requires an extended period of refinement and testing. Although this is particularly true for original inventions, which need developmental work to make them operational, almost any idea for a new business requires careful study and modification before the firm begins operations.

One way to facilitate the needed refinement is to prepare a business plan, which we will discuss in Chapter 8. A business plan helps entrepreneurs think through their ideas and consider all aspects of the proposed business. Outside experts can be asked to review the business plan, and their questions and suggestions used to improve it.

The need to refine ideas is the basis for business plan competitions held around the country, frequently at colleges and universities. The MIT Enterprise Forum at the

Then another issue cropped up. The financial plan included revenues from outdoor storage of boats, equipment, and the like. It turned out, however, that the town wouldn't allow anything to be stored in the open.

The process dragged on for a few weeks, and the information dribbled in. That's what always happens. You don't hear about all the problems at once.

The fourth problem wasn't so little. . . . Asbestos was discovered in the building—the cost of fixing it would be about $250,000.

There comes a point in every deal when you need to lock yourself in a quiet room for an hour and conduct a private review of the facts. . . . So we sat down together and went through the review process. "So what do you think?" Bob asked. "It's your money," I said. "You and Tracy should talk it over and decide." The next day he got back to me. "This is not right for us, is it?" he said. "No, Bob," I said, "I don't think it is."

Bob and Tracy were disappointed. Those decisions are always tough. You naturally tend to focus on what might have been, and so you feel a sense of loss. You don't think about all the aggravation and heartache you're avoiding, and you don't see the new opportunities that lie ahead. But someday you'll look back and realize how right you were to follow your instincts—and just say, "no."

Source: Adapted from Norm Brodsky, "The Road Not Taken," *Inc.*, Vol. 22, No. 3 (March 2000), pp. 43–44.

Massachusetts Institute of Technology is one example. Here, aspiring entrepreneurs present their business plans to a panel of individuals familiar with company startups. The panel generally consists of a venture capitalist, a private investor, a banker, an accountant, and an attorney, among others. These individuals read the business plan and preside at a public forum, where the entrepreneur makes an oral presentation of the plan to an audience of interested individuals. The panel members then, one by one, offer their suggestions for strengthening the proposed venture. Finally, the audience has an opportunity to ask questions and make suggestions. The Enterprise Forum has now spread to major cities across the United States and has been a vehicle for thousands of entrepreneurs seeking a review of their plans by someone with expertise. Whether through the Enterprise Forum or a similar group, an entrepreneur should seize opportunities to have others evaluate the idea being put forth—the earlier in the process this evaluation takes place, the better.

Buying an Existing Business

For would-be entrepreneurs, one alternative to starting from scratch is to buy an established business. The decision to purchase an existing business should be made only after careful consideration of the advantages and disadvantages.

4

List some reasons for buying an existing business.

Reasons for Buying an Existing Business

The reasons for buying an existing business can be condensed into the following three general categories:

1. To reduce some of the uncertainties and unknowns that must be faced in starting a business from the ground up

2. To acquire a business with ongoing operations and established relationships with customers and suppliers
3. To obtain an established business at a price below what it would cost to start a new business

Let's examine each of these reasons in more detail.

REDUCTION OF UNCERTAINTIES A successful business has already demonstrated its ability to attract customers, control costs, and make a profit. Although future operations may be different, the firm's past record shows what it can do under actual market conditions. For example, just the fact that the location must be satisfactory eliminates one major uncertainty. Although traffic counts are useful in assessing the value of a potential location, the acid test comes when a business opens its doors at that location. This test has already been met in the case of an existing firm. The results are available in the form of sales and profit data. Noncompetition agreements are needed, however, to discourage the seller from starting a new company that will compete directly with the one being sold.

ACQUISITION OF ONGOING OPERATIONS AND RELATIONSHIPS The buyer of an existing business typically acquires its personnel, inventories, physical facilities, established banking connections, and ongoing relationships with trade suppliers and customers. Extensive time and effort would be required to build these elements from scratch. Of course, the advantage derived from buying an established firm's assets depends on the nature of the assets. For example, a firm's skilled, experienced employees constitute a valuable asset only if they will continue to work for the new owner. The physical facilities must not be obsolete, and the firm's relationships with banks, suppliers, and customers must be healthy. In any case, new agreements will probably have to be negotiated with current vendors and leaseholders.

A new business owner who fails to carefully consider the nature of the assets may face some unpleasant surprises. Consider the experience of Norman Savage. Shortly after buying a small mortgage company in Fort Wayne, Indiana, Savage learned that the seller had given some employees 20 percent pay increases after the deal was made, effectively buying for himself credit for being a generous boss and leaving the cost of that generosity for Savage to pay. In addition, some of the firm's business licenses were about to expire, and Savage had difficulty locating the necessary documents to renew them. To top it off, one of the office computers needed to be replaced.[10] On the other hand, Thomas J. Cerri encountered no such problems when he bought Mill Valley Lumber Company in Mill Valley, California. He recalls, "When we took over, eight key employees stayed on with us, and it really made all the difference." The sales staff had nearly 100 years of experience among them and "seemed to be friends with everyone in the area." With a well-connected sales staff and other key employees staying on the job, Mill Valley Lumber continued to enjoy a close relationship with its customers despite the invasion of giant competitors like The Home Depot.[11]

A BARGAIN PRICE If the seller is more eager to sell than the buyer is to buy, an existing business may be available at what seems to be a low price. Whether it is actually a good buy, however, must be determined by the prospective new owner. Several factors could make a "bargain price" anything but a bargain. For example, the business may be losing money, the neighborhood it's located in may be deteriorating, or the seller may intend to open another competing business. On the other

IN THE TRENCHES ENTREPRENEURSHIP TODAY

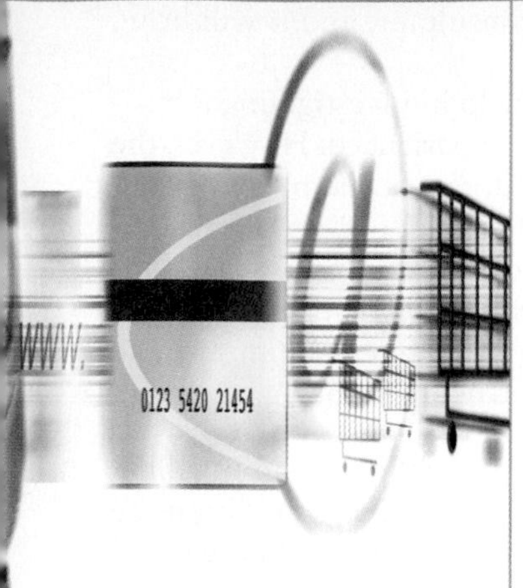

WHEN THE COOKIE CRUMBLES, START OVER AGAIN

After a business failure, many entrepreneurs pick up the pieces and start again. The second time around is often better, as the entrepreneur builds on the lessons learned the first time. Consider entrepreneur Penny McConnell, who successfully started over after her Austin, Texas specialty bakery went through Chapter 7 liquidation.

Penny's Pastries had been operating for almost two years when it landed an account with Southwest Airlines. McConnell had already expanded into a line of prepackaged cookies, but the airline's demand for 500,000 cookies per month stressed the bakery's capacity and eventually led to bankruptcy.

Back in business just months later, McConnell says, "We still want to do big things, but we make sure we get every piece in place first." Her strategy now relies more on her CPA. "We look at numbers, look for trends, and do a lot of tweaking," says McConnell. "Remember, your business has failed; you haven't. Don't get stuck in the negative energy of 'You are a failure.'"

Source: Karen Axelton, "Bouncing Back," *Entrepreneur,* Vol. 28, No. 3 (March 1998), pp. 104–109.

hand, if research indicates that the business indeed is a bargain, purchasing it is likely to turn out to be a wise investment.

Finding a Business to Buy

Sometimes, in the course of day-to-day living and working, a would-be buyer comes across an opportunity to buy an existing business. For example, a sales representative for a manufacturer or a wholesaler may be offered an opportunity to buy a customer's retail business. In other cases, the prospective buyer needs to search for a business to buy.

Sources of leads about businesses available for purchase include suppliers, distributors, trade associations, and even bankers. Realtors—particularly those who specialize in the sale of business firms and business properties—can also provide leads. In addition, there are specialized brokers, called **matchmakers,** who handle all the arrangements for closing a buyout. A large number of matchmakers, such as Certified Business Brokers in Houston, Texas, deal with mergers and acquisitions of small and mid-sized companies in the United States.

matchmakers
specialized brokers who bring together buyers and sellers of businesses

http://www.certifiedbb.com

Investigating and Evaluating Available Businesses

Regardless of the source of the lead, a business opportunity requires careful evaluation—what some call **due diligence.** As a preliminary step, the buyer needs to acquire background information about the business, some of which can be obtained through personal observation or discussion with the seller. Talking with other informed parties, such as suppliers, bankers, employees, and customers of the business, is also important.

due diligence
the exercise of prudence, such as would be expected of a reasonable person, in the careful evaluation of a business opportunity

RELYING ON PROFESSIONALS Although some aspects of due diligence require personal checking, a buyer can also seek the help of outside experts. The two most

valuable sources of outside assistance are accountants and lawyers. It is also wise to seek out others who have acquired a business, in order to learn from their experience. Their perspective will be different from that of a consultant, and it will bring some balance to the counsel received.

The time and money spent on securing professional help in investigating a business can pay big dividends, especially when the buyer is inexperienced. However, the final consequences of a business purchase, good and bad, are borne by the buyer, and thus the prospective buyer should never relinquish the final decision to the experts. For one thing, it is a mistake to assume that professionals' help is either unbiased or infallible, particularly when their fees may be greater if the business is acquired. Prospective buyers should seek advice and counsel, but they must make the final decision themselves, as it is too important to entrust to someone else.

FINDING OUT WHY THE BUSINESS IS FOR SALE The seller's *real* reasons for selling may or may not be the *stated* ones. When a business is for sale, always question the owner's reasons for selling. There is a real possibility that the firm is not doing well or that latent problems exist that will affect its future performance. The buyer must be wary, therefore, of taking the seller's explanations at face value. Here are some of the most common reasons that owners offer their businesses for sale:

- Old age or illness
- Desire to relocate in a different section of the country
- Decision to accept a position with another company
- Unprofitability of the business
- Loss of an exclusive sales franchise
- Maturing of the industry and lack of growth potential

A prospective buyer cannot be certain that the seller-owner will be honest in presenting all the facts about the business, especially concerning financial matters. Too frequently, sellers have "cooked the books" or taken unreported cash out of the business. The only way for the buyer to avoid an unpleasant surprise later is to do his or her best to determine whether the seller is an ethical person.

EXAMINING THE FINANCIAL DATA The first stage in evaluating the financial health of a firm is to review the financial statements and tax returns for the past five years (or for as many years as are available). The first stage helps determine whether the buyer and seller are in the same ballpark. If so, the parties move on to the second stage (discussed in the next section)—valuing the firm.

To determine the history of the business and the direction in which it is moving, the buyer must examine financial data pertaining to the company's operation. If financial statements are available for the past five years, the buyer can use these to get some idea of trends for the business. As an ethical matter, the prospective buyer is obligated to show the financial statements to others only on a need-to-know basis. To do otherwise is a violation of trust and confidentiality.

The buyer should recognize that financial statements may be misleading and may require normalizing to yield a realistic picture of the business. For example, business owners sometimes understate business income in an effort to minimize taxable income. On the other hand, expenses for such entries as employee training and advertising may be reduced to abnormally low levels, in an effort to make the income look good in the hope of selling the business.

FIGURE 5-3

Income Statement as Adjusted by Prospective Buyer

Original Income Statement			Required Adjustments	Adjusted Income Statement	
Estimated sales	$172,000			$172,000	
Cost of goods sold	84,240			84,240	
Gross profit		$87,760			$87,760
Operating expenses:					
Rent	$ 20,000		Rental agreement will expire in six months; rent is expected to increase 20%.	$ 24,000	
Salaries	19,860			19,860	
Telephone	990			990	
Advertising	11,285			11,285	
Utilities	2,580			2,580	
Insurance	1,200		Property is underinsured; adequate coverage will double present cost	2,400	
Professional services	1,200			1,200	
Credit card expense	1,860		Amount of credit card expense is unreasonably large; approximately $1,400 of this amount should be classified as personal expense.	460	
Miscellaneous	1,250	60,225		1,250	64,025
Net income		$27,535			$23,735

Other financial entries that may need adjustment include personal expenses and wage or salary payments. For example, costs related to personal use of business vehicles frequently appear as a business expense. Family members may receive excessive compensation or none at all. All entries must be examined to ensure that they relate to the business and are realistic. Figure 5-3 shows an income statement that has been adjusted by a prospective buyer. Note carefully the buyer's reasons for the adjustments that have been made. Of course, many other adjustments could be made as well.

The buyer should also scrutinize the seller's balance sheet to see whether asset book values are realistic. Property often appreciates in value after it is recorded on the books. In contrast, physical facilities, inventory, and receivables may decline in value, so their actual worth is less than their accounting book value. Although these changes in value are generally not reflected in the accountant's records, they should be considered by the prospective buyer.

Summarize three basic approaches for determining a fair value for a business.

Valuing the Business

Once the initial investigation and evaluation have been completed, the buyer must arrive at a fair value for the firm. Valuing a business is not easy or exact, even in the best of circumstances. Despite the fact that buyers prefer audited financial

ENTREPRENEURSHIP AND ETHICS

IN THE TRENCHES

INVESTIGATING POTENTIAL ASSOCIATES

Cecelia Levine is an entrepreneur who started three maquiladoras in Juarez, Mexico, to manufacture clothing. Beginning in her home in West Texas, Levine has built her business to the point that she is now under contract to produce items for automotive, home furnishings, pet, and clothing industries in the United States. The origin and growth of her business have brought her face to face with a number of ethical issues.

I was a single mother raising three children and trying to make the business go. At a time when things were extremely tight, I received an excellent opportunity. I won a bid to make a clothing item for a large U.S. clothing firm. It would make all the difference in the world in the future of my business.

The president of this large company asked me to come to New York and visit with him so that we could make the arrangements for the design of the plant and start producing the clothing item. I flew to New York at my own expense at a time when I had barely enough money to pay for the tickets. When I went into his office, two copies of the contract were placed on the table. As we went over the contract, I noticed that the price that I was to receive for each item was 25 cents higher than in my proposal. I told him there was a mistake in the price I was to receive for my work and that it was higher than quoted in my bid. I was shocked when he said, "That's right, but I want you to add

statements, many firms operate without them. In valuing such firms, the buyer will have to rely on federal tax returns and state sales tax statements. It may also be helpful to scrutinize invoices and receipts—of both customers and suppliers—as well as the firm's bank statements.

Although numerous techniques are used for valuing a company, they are typically derivations of three basic approaches: (1) asset-based valuation, (2) market-comparable valuation, and (3) cash flow–based valuation. Let's examine each of these approaches in detail.

asset-based valuation approach the determination of the value of a business by estimating the value of its assets

modified book value technique the determination of the value of a business by adjusting book value to reflect differences between the historical cost and the current value of the assets

replacement value technique the determination of the value of a business by estimating the cost of replacing the firm's assets

liquidation value technique the determination of the value of a business by estimating the money available if the firm were to liquidate its assets

ASSET-BASED VALUATION The **asset-based valuation approach** assumes that the value of a firm can be determined by estimating the value of its underlying assets. Three variations of this approach involve estimating (1) a modified book value for the assets, (2) the replacement value of the assets, and (3) the assets' liquidation value. The **modified book value technique** takes the firm's book value, as shown in the balance sheet, and adjusts it to reflect any obvious differences between the historical cost of an asset and its current value. For instance, marketable securities held by the firm may have a market value totally different from their historical book value. The same may be true for real estate. The second asset-based approach, the **replacement value technique,** attempts to determine what it would cost to replace each of the firm's assets. The third method, the **liquidation value technique,** estimates the amount of money that would be received if the firm ended its operations and liquidated the individual assets.

The asset-based valuation approach is not especially effective in helping a prospective buyer decide what to pay for a firm. Historical costs shown on the balance sheet may bear little relationship to the current value of the assets. (The book value of an asset was never intended to measure present value.) Although the three variations adjust for this inherent weakness, they build an estimate of value on a weak foundation. All asset-based techniques fail to recognize the firm as a going

the 25 cents to your price and then take the additional money and open a personal bank account in Mexico in my name."

I can tell you that I could have used the contract. I needed the work, but not under those circumstances. I believe that there are wonderful opportunities in the U.S. and that we don't need to deviate and do things where we won't be able to sleep at night. It is a question of values for me. I stood up and thanked him and walked out of his office.

The firm I am describing is a big company, a name that you see everywhere. I have difficulty believing what happened—that someone would use that type of maneuver. I also know that someone else got the contract, and, as a result, has built a big, big, big plant in Mexico. But I sleep well.

Levine's experience is a good illustration of how the ethical high road is not always the most profitable road. But it also provides an inspiring example of a successful entrepreneur whose integrity is not for sale.

Source: Personal interview with Cecelia Levine.

concern. However, the liquidation value technique does yield an estimate of the value that could be realized if the business were liquidated, which is sometimes good information to have.

MARKET-COMPARABLE VALUATION The **market-comparable valuation approach** relies on financial markets in estimating a firm's value. The simplest version of this method looks only at the actual market prices of firms that are similar to the one being valued and that have been sold recently or are traded publicly on a stock exchange.

market-comparable valuation approach
the determination of the value of a business based on the sale prices of comparable firms

A more sophisticated market-comparable valuation approach assigns firm value based on a multiple of the company's earnings. As a prospective buyer, you might identify recently sold companies having growth prospects and levels of risk comparable to those of the firm you wish to value. For each of these firms, you would calculate the *value-to-earnings ratio,* or **earnings multiple,** as follows:

earnings multiple
ratio determined by dividing a firm's value by its annual earnings; also called *value-to-earnings ratio*

$$\text{Earnings multiple} = \frac{\text{Firm value}}{\text{Annual earnings}}$$

Then, assuming that the prospective company should have the same earnings multiple as similar companies that were recently sold, you would apply the calculated ratio to estimate the prospective company's value.

To get an idea of how the market-comparable valuation approach is used in valuing a firm, assume that you are considering the purchase of the Moore Company, which has annual earnings of $80,000. You are interested in determining a fair value for the company, and you have located three comparable firms that recently sold, on average, for six times their earnings. That is,

$$\text{Earnings multiple} = \frac{\text{Firm value}}{\text{Annual earnings}} = 6$$

Using this information, you estimate the value of the Moore Company as follows:

$$\frac{\text{Moore's value}}{\text{Moore's earnings}} = 6$$

or

$$\text{Moore's value} = 6 \times \text{Moore's earnings}$$

Given Moore's earnings of \$80,000, you can estimate its value to be \$480,000:

$$\begin{aligned}\text{Moore's value} &= 6 \times \$80{,}000 \\ &= \$480{,}000\end{aligned}$$

Thus, it could be argued that \$480,000 is a reasonable price for the Moore Company.

The market-comparable valuation approach is not as easy as it might appear, because finding even one firm that is comparable in every way to the firm being valued is often difficult. Simply finding a firm in the same industry is not enough, although that might provide a rough approximation. The ideal firm is one that is in the same or a similar type of business and has a similar growth rate, financial structure, asset turnover ratio (sales/total assets), and profit margin (profits/sales). Fortunately, considerable information is published about firm purchases. For instance, *Mergerstat,* a financial services publication, publishes the prices of all such sales announced in the public media. Also, many large accounting firms have departments that can provide information about the selling prices of comparable businesses.

http://www.mergerstat.com

Two means of further refining market-comparable valuation are to normalize the prospective company's earnings and to adjust the earnings multiple for factors specific to the business. Normalizing earnings involves adjusting for any unusual items, such as a one-time loss on the sale of real estate or as the consequence of a fire. **Normalized earnings** should include all relevant expenses, such as a fair salary for the owner's time.

normalized earnings
earnings that have been adjusted for unusual items, such as fire damage

The two major factors for which the earnings multiple should be adjusted are the level of risk involved in the business and the expected growth rate of future earnings. The relationships are as follows:

1. The more (less) risky the business, the lower (higher) the appropriate earnings multiple and, as a consequence, the lower (higher) the firm's value.
2. The higher (lower) the projected growth rate in future earnings, the higher (lower) the appropriate earnings multiple and, therefore, the higher (lower) the firm's value.

These relationships are presented graphically in Figure 5-4.

In practice, earnings multiples often are based primarily on conventional wisdom and the experience of the person performing the valuation. For example, some appraisers assign multiples to net income for different types of firms as follows:

Type of Firm	Earnings Multiple
Small, well-established firm, vulnerable to recession	7
Small firm requiring average executive ability but operating in a highly competitive environment	4
Firm that depends on the special, often unusual, skill of one individual or a small group of managers	2

FIGURE 5-4

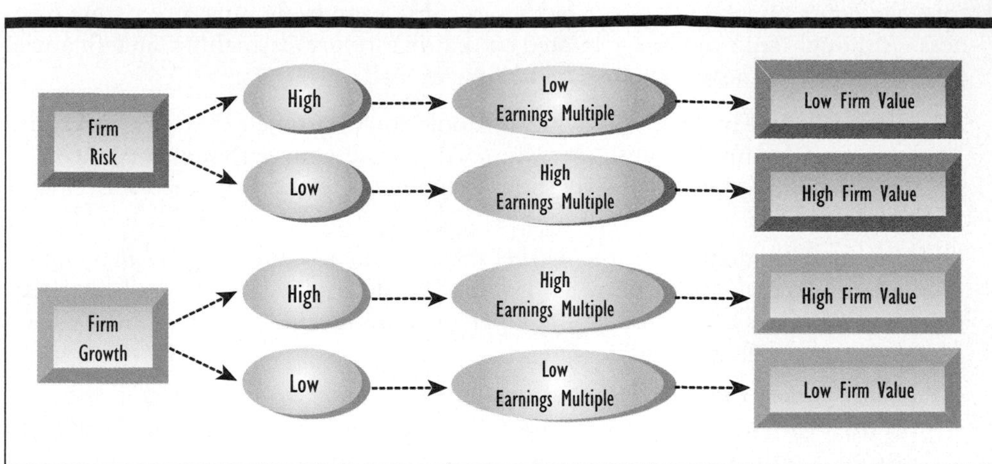

Determinants of a Firm's Earnings Multiple

Representative of the mid-range is a firm that provides gasoline for yachts, which was recently offered for sale at 4.9 times earnings (asking price of \$1.2 million ÷ \$245,000 earnings).[12]

CASH FLOW–BASED VALUATION Although not a popular approach among smaller companies, the **cash flow–based valuation approach,** in which a company is valued based on the amount and timing of its future cash flows, makes a lot of sense. The market-comparable valuation approach, although used more often in practice, presents a conceptual problem. It considers earnings, rather than cash flows, as the item to be valued. From an investor's or owner's perspective, the value of a firm should be based on future cash flows, not reported earnings—especially not reported earnings for just a single year. Valuation is simply too complex a process to be captured by a single earnings figure. For one thing, there are numerous ways of influencing a firm's earnings favorably (even when using generally accepted accounting principles) that have no effect on future cash flows or, even worse, reduce cash flows.

cash flow–based valuation approach
the determination of the value of a business by comparing the expected and required rates of return on the investment

Buying a business is in one sense similar to investing in a savings account in a bank. With a savings account, you are interested in the cash (capital) you need to put into the account and the future cash flows (interest) you will receive. Similarly, when you buy a business, you should be interested in future cash flows received relative to capital invested.

In a cash flow–based valuation, three steps are involved in measuring the value of a firm's future cash flows:

1. Estimate the firm's expected future cash flows.
2. Compute the company's **cost of capital,** which represents the investors' and owners' required rate of return on their investment in the business.
3. Using the firm's cost of capital as the discount rate, calculate the present value of the firm's expected future cash flows, which represents the value of the firm.[13]

cost of capital
investors' and owners' required rate of return on their investment

This approach to valuation is no simple matter and is well beyond the scope of this textbook. However, anyone serious about valuing a business would be well advised to develop a full understanding of the technique or to seek assistance from someone who can help in this regard.

NONQUANTITATIVE FACTORS IN VALUING A BUSINESS In addition to quantitative factors, there are a number of other factors to consider in evaluating an existing business. Although only indirectly related to a firm's future cash flows and financial position, some of these factors should be mentioned.

- ***Competition.*** The prospective buyer should look into the extent, intensity, and location of competing businesses. In particular, the buyer should check to see whether the business in question is gaining or losing in its race with competitors.
- ***Market.*** The adequacy of the market to maintain all competing business units, including the one to be purchased, should be determined. This entails market research, study of census data, and personal, on-the-spot observation at each competitor's place of business.
- ***Future community development.*** Examples of future developments in the community that could have an indirect impact on a business include a change in zoning ordinances already enacted but not yet in effect and a change from a two-way traffic flow to a one-way traffic flow.
- ***Legal commitments.*** Legal commitments may include contingent liabilities, unsettled lawsuits, delinquent tax payments, missed payrolls, overdue rent or installment payments, and mortgages of record against any of the real property acquired.
- ***Union contracts.*** The prospective buyer should determine what type of labor agreement, if any, is in force, as well as the quality of the firm's employee relations.
- ***Buildings.*** The quality of the buildings housing the business should be checked, with particular attention paid to any fire hazards. In addition, the buyer should determine whether there are any restrictions on access to the building.
- ***Product prices.*** The prospective owner should compare the prices of the seller's products with those listed in manufacturers' or wholesalers' catalogs and also with the prices of competing products in the locality. This is necessary to ensure full and fair pricing of goods whose sales are reported on the seller's financial statements.

Negotiating and Closing the Deal

The purchase price of a business is determined by negotiation between buyer and seller. Although the calculated value may not be the price eventually paid for the business, it gives the buyer an estimated value to use when negotiating price. Typically, the buyer tries to purchase the firm for something less than the full estimated value; of course, the seller tries to get more than that value.

In some cases, the buyer may have the option of purchasing the assets only, rather than the business as a whole. When a business is purchased as a total entity, the buyer takes control of the assets but also assumes any outstanding debt, including any hidden or unknown liabilities. Even if the financial records are audited, such debts may not surface. If the buyer instead purchases only the assets, then the seller is responsible for settling any outstanding debts previously incurred. An indemnification clause in the sales contract may serve a similar function, protecting the buyer from liability for unreported debt.

An important part of the negotiation process is the terms of purchase. In many cases, the buyer is unable to pay the full price in cash and must seek extended terms. At the same time, the seller may be concerned about taxes on the profit from the sale. Terms may become more attractive to the buyer and the seller as the amount of the down payment is reduced and/or the length of the repayment period is extended. Like a purchase of real estate, the purchase of a business is closed at a specific time. A title company or an attorney usually handles the closing. Preferably, the closing occurs under the direction of an independent third party. If the seller's attorney is the closing agent, the buyer should exercise caution—a buyer should never go through a closing without the aid of an experienced attorney who represents only the buyer.

A number of important documents are completed during the closing. These include a bill of sale, certifications as to taxing and other governmental regulations, and agreements pertaining to future payments and related guarantees to the seller. The buyer should apply for new federal and state tax identification numbers to avoid being held responsible for past obligations associated with the old numbers.

Increasing the Chances of a Successful Startup

6

Describe the characteristics of highly successful startups.

Anyone who has a dream of owning and operating a small business should do everything possible to enhance the chance of success. Observing successful role models is one way to increase the likelihood of realizing the dream.

A key determinant of success is a firm's sales growth, provided, of course, that the profits and cash flows generated from the sales are adequate. Higher sales enable a firm to cover fixed costs by achieving economies of scale. Although a significant increase in sales can cause financial problems, sales growth is necessary to get beyond mere survival. Growing firms can fail, but the chances for creating economic value—a key barometer of success—and for creating jobs within the community where the business is located are greatly enhanced through growth.

The right beginning is important to a new company's eventual success. Based on a study of 500 companies identified by *Inc.* magazine as the fastest-growing businesses in the United States during the previous five years, Leslie Brokaw has isolated several characteristics common to high-growth firms.

Companies that grow begin differently from the ones that don't in a handful of starkly identifiable ways. The distinguishing traits of a successful startup have to do with the kind of experience and knowledge its founders possess. They have to do with a startup's ability to seek and nurture alliances, whether for financing or product development. And they have to do with the market ambitions a company adopts right at the outset.

Among the observable features Brokaw describes are the following:

- The venture is most often a team effort. A group that brings diversity and balance to the business starts the vast majority of high-growth firms.
- The founders bring meaningful experience to the business. They are not learning the business as they begin the operations.
- The founders of high-growth firms often have started other businesses in the past. Not infrequently, the president had started at least one business before launching her or his most recent venture. However, many of the early startups resulted in failure—only 27 percent of the earlier firms were still in existence.

Living in a Diverse World

AN ENTREPRENEUR IN CHINA

What is it like to start a business in a communist country where there is no tradition of free enterprise and individualism has been punished? The answer to this question is changing quickly with time in some communist countries.

During a visit to Jinan, China, we had the opportunity to meet Zhao Chiang. After graduating from the University of Peking, Zhao had begun working for the Shandong Academy of Social Science as an agricultural economist. Then, in 1992, he heard a speech given by Deng Xia Peng, prime minister of China, in which the prime minister encouraged the Chinese people to start businesses. As a result of that speech, Zhao decided to start his own business—in spite of strong opposition by his father. Zhao's father, age 78, had been a revolutionary leader and, as a long-time Marxist, considered capitalism to be fundamentally evil.

Zhao remembers thinking, "If I do not succeed, I can always go back to the 'bank' [government job]." Zhao believed his success—if it happened—would have to come from his prior experience, which involved organizing engineers and workers on an air conditioning project for the government, and his "social relationships" with government officials. So he decided to start the Jinan Air Conditioning Company.

Zhao soon learned what all entrepreneurs have to learn—that starting a business requires identifying and gaining access to critical resources. In his case, Zhao considered the critical resources to be "ability, good engineers, social relationships, and an alliance with an existing air conditioning company." And his view about profits? "Profitability is the most important thing, which I believe is linked to a good reputation based on the quality of the technology and service."

In the beginning, Zhao had no money to invest. So he "bootstrapped" the business by finding a reputable air conditioning firm with existing contracts. He negotiated a deal with the company to be paid a share of any profits for supervising its jobs. With this money, he started his own company.

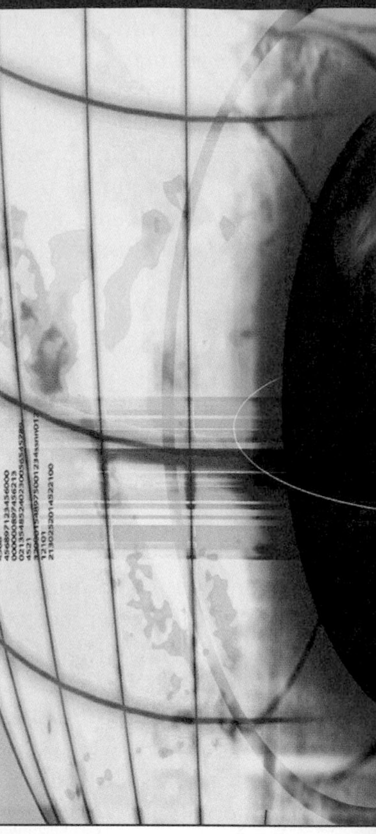

- Most frequently, high-growth firms are in service or manufacturing industries. Almost half of the *Inc. 500* firms are classified as high tech. Twenty-five percent are in manufacturing, compared to 56 percent in services; only 7 percent are in retailing.
- High-growth firms are better financed—but not by much. They begin with more money, but only slightly more.
- The founders of high-growth firms share ownership in the business. They do not keep all the equity; in fact, they frequently own less than half of it. They think it is better to own a part of something large than all of something small.
- High-growth firms do not limit themselves to local markets. The majority of the *Inc. 500* firms receive more than half of their sales from outside their local region. Over one-third of these businesses have sales from overseas customers.

Brokaw concludes with some predictions about the trends of highly successful startups:

We'll find that larger percentages of successful startups will have formed alliances with major companies in their early years. More will be exporting ever greater portions of their output to customers overseas. Today's startups, we'll discover, will

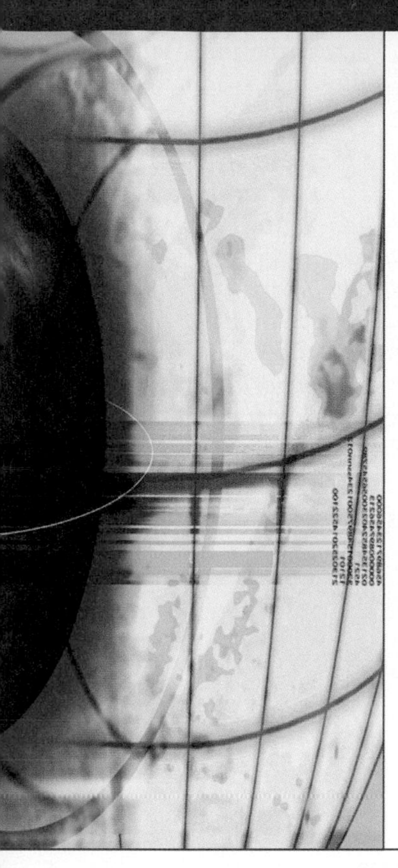

Zhao talks about the importance of having effective communications with your customers. Once, he quoted a very low price for installing some air conditioning units so that he would be below his competition. However, the bid was so low that it would have resulted in a substantial loss. Fortunately, the customer later offered to increase the amount to be paid for the job—an act Zhao believes was a direct result of the effective communications they had with each other.

When Zhao started out, he was successful because he found a niche market in the air conditioning industry that was not being served—selling and installing mid-size units, smaller than the average central air units but larger than the very tiny air conditioners Chinese were using in their homes. At first, he was able to sell and install the units at a profit margin of about 40 percent. However, competition quickly entered the market, which soon resulted in lower margins. Also, one of his former employees started a company to compete with him.

Eventually, York Air Conditioning, a U.S.-based company with a division in Hong Kong, offered Zhao the opportunity to be the exclusive dealer for its products in the Shandong province. York sold a quality product that provided higher profit margins for the dealership. Zhao accepted the offer and became York's only wholesaler and authorized service dealer in his province.

Zhao believes that China will eventually be a land of opportunity for those with experience. In his particular industry, he knows that having a government background is necessary. He also says that honesty and integrity are essential qualities for success.

And what about his father? In the beginning, his father rejected him for becoming a businessperson, even to the point of no longer welcoming his son into his house. But, with time, Zhao says that his father's thinking is changing—as is public opinion in China about those who are starting businesses with the goal of making a profit.

Zhao's experience in starting and building a firm is unique in many ways because of the Chinese culture and political environment. But, it is clear that he has much in common with entrepreneurs in any capitalist country.

Source: Personal interview with Zhao Chiang at his company in Jinan, China, November 4, 2000.

have continued to modify the ways they're set up, whom they become dependent on, and how far-reaching they try to be, all in response to the increasing globalization—and increasing complexity—of the marketplace.[14]

The preceding viewpoint presumes that the goal is to grow—and to grow fast. As was suggested earlier, however, growth has its good side and its bad side. Firms can encounter severe, if not fatal, consequences from growing too fast. DeWayne Eidson, the founder of AvLink (an airplane leasing company), lost sight of that fact during the company's early years and took the firm beyond its capacity to finance growth. The result was company failure and personal bankruptcy for Eidson. In talking about the experience, Eidson, who had previously founded four successful companies, says, "I committed the cardinal sin. I knew not to do it, but just got caught up in trying to grow the company and forgot to watch the cash flows."[15] Thus, a startup must be careful to avoid increasing sales when (1) the cash flows are inadequate to finance the growth and (2) the profits associated with the sales are not sufficient to provide an attractive return on the capital invested—an issue we will discuss more completely in Chapters 8 and 23.

Some entrepreneurs choose not to take advantage of opportunities to grow, preferring to remain small or at least to control the level of growth at what seems to them to be a manageable rate when everything is considered, including personal

priorities. However, an entrepreneur cannot ignore the importance of achieving an adequate level of sales.

The solution is to learn from those who do it well, such as the *Inc. 500* firms described by Brokaw. In conclusion, we offer the following swimming-pool metaphor, from *Inc.* magazine:

More than 7 million U.S. adults are in the shallow end of the start-up pool, trying to develop the skills needed to deal with the deep water. Each is learning the right skills in a different way; all who are successful master the basics. Most of those who become successful find out rather quickly, in less than a year. Others may spend a lot of time—several years—fooling around in the shallow end before they climb out of the pool. But the starting of businesses is a dynamic process, with a constant shifting as new people jump in, others successfully negotiate the deep end, and others climb out of the shallow end. It is also clear that some who leave the pool, whether they're successful or unsuccessful, go back in for another try.[16]

How are your swimming skills?

Looking Back

1 Identify five factors that determine whether an idea is a good investment opportunity.

- There must be a clearly defined market need for the product and/or service, and the timing must be right.
- The firm must have the ability to achieve a durable or sustainable competitive advantage.
- There must be significant profit and growth potential.
- There must be a good fit between the entrepreneur and the opportunity.
- No fatal flaws can exist in the venture.

2 Give three reasons for starting a new business rather than buying an existing firm or acquiring a franchise.

- A new business can feature a recently invented or newly developed product or service.
- A new business can take advantage of an ideal location, recent technological advances in equipment, employees, suppliers, and bankers.
- A new business avoids undesirable precedents, policies, procedures, and legal commitments of existing firms.

3 Distinguish among the different types and sources of startup ideas.

- The different types of startup ideas include ideas for redirecting existing concepts to new markets, technologically derived ideas, and ideas for performing existing functions in a new and improved manner.
- Ideas for new startups come from a variety of sources, including personal experience, hobbies, accidental discovery, and deliberate search.

4 List some reasons for buying an existing business.

- Buying an existing firm can reduce uncertainties.
- In acquiring an existing firm, the entrepreneur can take advantage of its ongoing operations and established relationships.
- It may be available at a bargain price.

5 Summarize three basic approaches for determining a fair value for a business.

- In asset-based valuation, a firm's value is based on the assets it owns.
- In market-comparable valuation, a firm's value is based on the market price of similar companies; in more sophisticated versions, the amount of earnings the business produces is taken into account.

- In cash flow–based valuation, a firm's value is based on the present value of the firm's future cash flows.

6 Describe the characteristics of highly successful startups.

- Most high-growth companies begin through a team effort.
- The founders have related experience.
- The founders have often started other businesses.
- High-growth companies are frequently found in service or manufacturing industries.
- High-growth firms are better financed—but not by much.
- The founders of high-growth companies share ownership in the business.
- High-growth firms do not limit themselves to local markets.

Key Terms

startup, p. 120
buyout, p. 120
Type A ideas, p. 122
Type B ideas, p. 122
Type C ideas, p. 122
serendipity, p. 124
matchmakers, p. 129
due diligence, p. 129
asset-based valuation approach, p. 132
modified book value technique, p. 132
replacement value technique, p. 132
liquidation value technique, p. 132
market-comparable valuation approach, p. 133
earnings multiple, p. 133
normalized earnings, p. 134
cash flow–based valuation approach, p. 135
cost of capital, p. 135

Discussion Questions

1. What is the difference between a good idea and a good opportunity?
2. Why might an entrepreneur prefer to launch an entirely new venture rather than buy an existing firm?
3. Suggest a product or a service not currently available that might lead to a new small business. Would it be a good idea to launch a new business depending solely on that new product or service? Why or why not?
4. Using the categories of ideas given in Figure 5-1, classify a mobile car service that changes oil and filters in parking lots. Can you think of a similar business that might fit in each of the other two categories? Explain.
5. What are possible reasons for buying an existing company versus starting a new business?
6. Suppose that a business available for purchase has shown an average profit of $40,000 for the past five years. During these years, the amount of profit fluctuated between $20,000 and $60,000. The business is in a highly competitive industry, and its purchase requires only a small capital outlay. Thus, the barriers to entry are low. State your assumptions, and then calculate the value that you might use in negotiating the purchase price.
7. Contrast the market-comparable valuation approach with the cash flow–based valuation approach. Which approach is easier to apply? Which is more appropriate?
8. Using the market-comparable valuation approach, value each of the following companies:
   a. Its normalized income is $50,000. The firm requires average executive ability and a comparatively small capital investment. Established goodwill, however, is of distinct importance.
   b. Its normalized income is $80,000. The firm is a small industrial business in a highly competitive industry and requires a relatively small capital outlay. Anyone with a little capital may enter the industry.
   c. Its normalized income is $30,000. The business depends on the special skills of a small group of managers. The business is highly competitive, and the failure rate in the industry is relatively high.
   d. Its normalized income is $60,000. The firm is a personal service business. Little, if any, capital is required. The earnings of the enterprise reflect the owner's skill; the owner is not likely to be able to create an organization that will carry on successfully without him or her.
9. Describe the relationship between a firm's earnings multiple and (a) its level of risk and (b) its prospects for growth.
10. If your goal is to start a business with high-growth potential, how should you structure the firm?

YOU MAKE THE CALL

SITUATION 1

Marty Lane worked for a card company specializing in invitations and announcements. Every day for 25 years, he went to an office, sat at a desk, and took orders over the phone. He hated it. He was bored out of his mind. He didn't know what to do.

So he began skimming the business opportunities section of the Sunday *New York Times.* He wasn't sure what he was looking for. At almost 50 years of age, he had few business skills. Accounting was a foreign language to him. He figured that if he ever bought a business, it would have to be one that didn't require much specialized knowledge—something that would be relatively easy to manage. He considered a franchise, but he found that the good ones were very expensive. Then he came across an Italian-bread route for sale. He thought "How difficult could it be to run a delivery route?" He called the phone number in the ad and spoke with the business broker who was handling the sale.

It turned out that the route was in Queens, not far from where Lane and his wife, Annabelle, lived. It was a one-person operation. The individual who owned it had had the route for 20 years and took home about $65,000 a year. He wanted $200,000 for the business, but he was willing to help finance the deal. If Lane would put $60,000 down, he could pay the balance over five years at 10 percent interest, or about $35,000 a year. That would leave Lane with an annual income of $30,000 until the debt was paid. Combined with Annabelle's salary, it would be enough to make ends meet. If he worked hard, moreover, he could expect his sales, and his income, to grow by 10 to 15 percent a year.

It seemed perfect. Lane went to meet with the owner and returned sounding even more enthusiastic. "This is a can't-miss deal," he told his wife. "The guy has signed contracts with all the places he delivers to, and none of them is more than 25 miles from here. I could do the entire route in seven hours."

However, Annabelle wasn't buying. "You're not quitting your job until you talk to an expert," she said. Lane agreed to meet with a broker.

On the date of the meeting, Lane brought all his paperwork along. He laid out the terms of the deal in great detail. "What do you think?" he asked.

The broker said "Tell me something, Marty. Do you like this business?"

He shrugged. "I can't really say. I haven't tried it yet."

"What's involved in it besides picking up the bread and delivering it to the stores?"

"I'm not sure," he said. "Whatever it is, it can't be that complicated."

"What happens if the truck breaks down?"

"I don't know," he said. "I guess I'll just work it out."

After asking Lane a series of questions along those lines, the broker finally said, "Listen, Marty. You want to know if this deal makes sense from a financial standpoint. That's easy to check. The guy has an income tax return, and his sales are verifiable. This isn't a cash business, after all. He sells to delis and supermarkets. They pay by check. We can go over his expense figures and make sure they're realistic, but my guess is that the deal is OK. If you're asking me whether I could negotiate him down a little, the answer is probably yes."

Lane turned to his wife: "See, I told you he'd approve."

The broker said, "I didn't approve anything. Only you can do that, and you're not ready to."

"What do you mean?" he asked.

"You haven't done your homework," the broker said. "You don't know what you're actually going to do in this business, and you don't know if you'll be happy doing it."

"How am I going to find that out?" Lane asked.

Question 1 How would you suggest that Lane find out if he would be happy in this business?

Question 2 Which valuation methods could Lane use to value the business?

Question 3 Is Lane relying too much on nonquantitative factors?

SITUATION 2

Four years after starting their business, Bill and Janet Brown began to have thoughts of selling out. Their business, Bucket-to-Go, had been extremely successful, as indicated by an average 50 percent increase in revenue in each of its years in existence. Bucket-to-Go began when Bill turned his hobby of making wooden buckets into a full-time business. The buckets were marketed nationwide in gift shops and garden centers.

Sam Kline learned of the buyout opportunity after contacting a business broker. Kline wanted to retire from corporate life and thought this business would be an excellent opportunity.

Question 1 Which valuation technique do you think Kline should use to value the business? Why?

Question 2 What accounting information should Kline consider? What adjustments might be required?

Question 3 What qualitative information should Kline evaluate?

SITUATION 3

Josh, a young man in his early thirties, is thinking about purchasing a small packager of herbal lotions, which sells through independent sales representatives to specialty stores and chains. The current owner has been running the company out of her home. She has owned the business for three years and has done fairly well, or so it appears from her financial statements. She's pregnant and wants to sell the business for $250,000.

Although the firm is relatively new, it is already generating relatively good profits. In the past year, the pre-tax profits were $40,000 on sales of $201,000. Josh thinks that he can grow these profits and build a substantial business of his own—something he has dreamed about doing for years.

Josh has received a confidentiality agreement. He is to meet with the owner in the morning to sign the agreement and put down $100,000 as earnest money, 60 percent of which is not refundable if the deal is not closed.

Source: This situation is taken from Norm Brodsky, "Caveat Emptor," *Inc.*, Vol. 20, No. 11 (August 1998), pp. 31–32.

Question 1 What do you think about the asking price relative to the earnings? What additional information might you want to have regarding the firm's earnings?

Question 2 Should Josh accept the term stating that 60 percent of the down payment is nonrefundable? How might he revise this term?

Question 3 What other information should Josh request as part of his due diligence before buying the business?

EXPERIENTIAL EXERCISES

1. Look through some small business periodicals in your school's library for profiles of five or six new startups. Report to the class, describing the sources of the startup ideas.
2. Consult the Yellow Pages of your local telephone directory to locate the name of a business broker. Interview the broker and report to the class on how she or he values businesses.
3. Select a startup you are familiar with and then evaluate the extent to which you are qualified to operate that startup, writing a description of your experiential and educational background.
4. Consult your local newspaper's new business listings and then contact one of the firms to arrange a personal interview. Report to the class on how the idea for the new business originated. Classify the type of idea according to the categories in Figure 5-1.

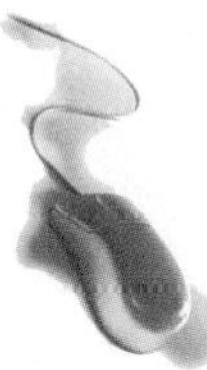

EXPLORING THE WEB

1. At **http://www.businessknowhow.com**, you'll find a helpful department called Starting a Business.
   a. Access the Getting Started message board. List some of the types of businesses people are asking about.
   b. Access 12 Ways to Start a Business. List the 12 steps to take in order to expand your ideas for a new business. For three of the examples given, explain whether they are Type A, B, or C ideas.
   c. Follow the link to the Business Planning Worksheet, and print the worksheet. Decide which questions are relevant to deciding whether to start a particular business.
   d. Read the article "200 Ways to Start Your Own Business." Read the list of business ideas, and list the five areas in which you would be most likely to start a business.
2. Money*Soft* offers software to help entrepreneurs buy an existing business. Access its Web site at **http://www.moneysoft.com**, and then click Buy-Out Plan.
   a. What does the software do?
   b. How much does the software cost?
   c. Why is the "no spreadsheet required" feature so important? Would you find it of benefit in evaluating a buyout?

CASE 5

STITCH CRAFT (p. 649)

This case describes an opportunity to take over a small business.

Alternative Cases for Chapter 5:

Case 1, "Steve's Olympic Tees," p. 637
Case 6, "Universal Business Brokers," p. 652
Case 12, "Stegmart," p. 672
Case 13, "Calvert Toyota," p. 674
Case 16, "EBC Computers Inc.," p. 683

chapter 6

Franchising Opportunities

In the VIDEO Spotlight

FastSigns

In this episode of "Small Business School," the series on PBS stations, you will meet Gary Salomon, the founder of FastSigns. In 1985, when Gary saw how a computer could be used to make high-quality signs in hours instead of days, he jumped at the opportunity to build a business offering this service internationally. Today his company, FastSigns, is America's leading sign company, with over 400 worldwide locations.

Gary wrote his first business plan on a napkin. Then, with $40,000 he and two partners got from a small bank loan and personal funds, they set up the first store. They ran the store themselves long enough to prove their theory that the idea could be duplicated and that the franchise owners they would recruit could make a good living.

You might think that Gary would try to sell his franchises to people who already knew something about the sign business, but that was never his strategy. He has always recruited professional managers, sales people, and marketers. That way he doesn't have to listen to people say, "That's not how we did it in my old sign company." The day I was in Dallas and observed a franchise training session, I met a former banker who had decided to join FastSigns because he had seen the profits enjoyed by other owners.

"We never tried to sell a franchise to someone that had been in the sign business before."

—Gary Salomon

I learned from Gary that you do not have to invent a product to own it. When he first saw the technology he is using today, he struck a deal with the inventor. He learned how to use the technology, and, with vision and sweat equity, he dominates the marketplace. As you

Go to page 732 for More! on FastSigns.

will observe, he is soft-spoken and listens intently. Entrepreneurs cannot be stereotyped. The only common quality they all possess is courage. ◆

—*Hattie Bryant, Producer, "Small Business School," The Series on PBS Stations, Worldnet, and the Web, http://smallbusinessschool.org*

Looking Ahead

After studying this chapter, you should be able to

1. *Explain franchising terms and the structure of the industry.*
2. *Identify the major pros and cons of franchising.*
3. *Describe the process for evaluating a franchise opportunity.*
4. *Discuss certain legal considerations in franchising.*

Chapter 5 examined how entrepreneurs can enter the business world by buying an existing business or starting from scratch. This chapter examines another option—franchising.

Franchising is not a new concept. In fact, it has existed in the United States for a long time. One of the first franchise arrangements was a nineteenth-century distribution relationship between Singer Sewing Machine Company and its dealers. Post–World War II franchise growth occurred as the franchising principle was espoused by such businesses as motels, variety shops, drugstores, and employment agencies. The boom in franchise growth in the 1960s and 1970s featured the franchising of fast-food outlets.

Franchising growth continued in the 1990s, with a major emphasis on global franchising. Now, in the new millennium, franchising occurs in every imaginable product and service category. Franchising will, no doubt, continue to help thousands of entrepreneurs realize their business ownership dreams each year.

The Terminology and Structure of Franchising

Explain franchising terms and the structure of the industry.

franchising
a marketing system involving a legal agreement, whereby the franchisee conducts business according to terms specified by the franchisor

franchisee
an entrepreneur whose power is limited by a contractual relationship with a franchisor

The term *franchising* was derived from a French word meaning "freedom" or "exemption from duties." In business, franchising describes a unique type of business option that offers entrepreneurs the possibility of reducing the overall risk associated with buying an independent business or starting a business from scratch. The franchise arrangement allows new business operators to benefit from the accumulated business experience of all members of the franchise system.

Franchising Terms

In this book, we use a broad definition of franchising to encompass the term's diversity: **Franchising** is a marketing system revolving around a two-party legal agreement whereby one party (the **franchisee**) is granted the privilege to sell a product or service and conduct business as an individual owner but is required to operate

franchisor
the party in a franchise contract that specifies the methods to be followed and the terms to be met by the other party

franchise contract
the legal agreement between franchisor and franchisee

franchise
the privileges conveyed in a franchise contract

product and trade name franchising
a franchise agreement granting the right to use a widely recognized product or name

business format franchising
a franchise arrangement whereby the franchisee obtains an entire marketing system and ongoing management guidance from the franchisor

master licensee
an independent firm or individual acting as a sales agent with the responsibility for finding new franchisees within a specified territory

multiple-unit ownership
holding by a single franchisee of more than one franchise from the same company

area developers
individuals or firms that obtain the legal right to open several franchised outlets in a given area

piggyback franchising
the operation of a retail franchise within the physical facilities of a host store

http://www.franchise.org

according to methods and terms specified by the other party (the **franchisor**). For example, McDonald's Corporation (the franchisor) franchises quick-service, fast-food outlets to local owners (franchisees).

The potential value of any franchising arrangement is defined by the rights contained in a legal agreement known as the **franchise contract;** the rights it conveys are called the **franchise.** The extent and importance of these rights may be quite varied. When the main benefit the franchisee receives is the privilege of using a widely recognized product name, the arrangement between the franchisor (supplier) and the franchisee (buyer) is called **product and trade name franchising.** Automobile tire outlets carrying the Goodyear brand name and soft drink bottlers distributing Dr Pepper are both engaged in this type of franchising.

Alternatively, entrepreneurs who receive an entire marketing and management system are participating in a broader type of arrangement referred to as **business format franchising.** Fast-food outlets (e.g., Burger King), hotels and motels (e.g., Holiday Inn), and business services (e.g., Mail Boxes Etc.) typically engage in this type of franchising. The volume of sales and the number of franchise units associated with business format franchising have increased steadily over the years.

A **master licensee** is a firm or individual having a continuing contractual relationship with a franchisor to sell its franchises. This independent company or businessperson is a type of middleman or sales agent. Master licensees are responsible for finding new franchisees within a specified territory. Sometimes they even provide support services such as training and warehousing, which are more traditionally provided by the franchisor. Also gaining widespread usage is **multiple-unit ownership,** in which a single franchisee owns more than one unit of the franchised business. Some of these franchisees are **area developers**—individuals or firms that obtain the legal right to open several outlets in a given area.

Piggyback franchising refers to the operation of a retail franchise within the physical facilities of a host store. Examples of piggyback franchising include a cookie franchise doing business inside an Arby's fast-food outlet and a car-phone franchise operating within an automobile dealership. This form of franchising benefits both parties. The host store is able to add a new product line, and the franchisee obtains a location near prospective customers.

The Structure of the Franchising Industry

Franchisors and franchisees are the two main parties in the franchise industry. A franchisor may be a manufacturer or any other channel member who has an attractive business concept worthy of duplication. As shown in Figure 6-1, a franchise can be sold by the franchisor directly to individual franchisees or marketed through master licensees or area developers. Most franchisors also own one or more outlets that are not franchised. These outlets are referred to as company-owned stores.

In addition to these parties, the franchising industry contains other important groups. These groups, called *facilitators,* include industry associations, governmental agencies, and private businesses.

The International Franchise Association (IFA), for example, is an industry association that serves franchise members by attempting to safeguard and enhance the business and regulatory environment of the industry. It has over 30,000 members—franchisors, franchisees, and suppliers—that operate in more than 100 countries.

IN THE TRENCHES ENTREPRENEURSHIP TODAY

THE NEW BREED

Today's prototype franchisee differs from those 10 or 20 years ago. Representative of the new breed is Steven Siegel, who went from practicing law to being a partner in Watermark Donut Company in South Boston, Massachusetts—owner of 39 Dunkin' Donuts franchises. "I'm an old franchisor attorney, which has really helped over the years because I understand how franchisors think," he says. "I have a better understanding of the whole process and how it works."

Siegel's involvement in franchising began in the early 1980s. After spearheading a venture-capital deal, he attended Dunkin' Donuts University in preparation for opening five stores in England. After a year of operating these units, he returned to the Boston area and, shortly afterward, convinced his three law partners to join together to form Watermark Donut Company. His experiences in England, coupled with his idea to use a central kitchen to cook the doughnuts in South Boston, have contributed to Watermark's success.

Several of Siegel's operational practices have been embraced by Dunkin' Donuts. "He and his group have been very helpful in refining large-scale donut production in a central facility," says Larry Hartman, senior vice president for Allied Domecq Retailing USA, which operates Dunkin' Donuts. "He has done it successfully, he and his group have shared their experiences and have been beneficiaries with the additional work we've done."

Siegel is also active in the International Franchising Association (IFA). In 2002, he is scheduled to become the first franchisee to be president of that group.

Source: From material from *Nation's Restaurant News*, http://www.nrn.com; and adapted from Dale D. Buss, "New Dynamics for a New Era," *Nation's Business*, Vol. 87, No. 6 (June 1999), p. 45.

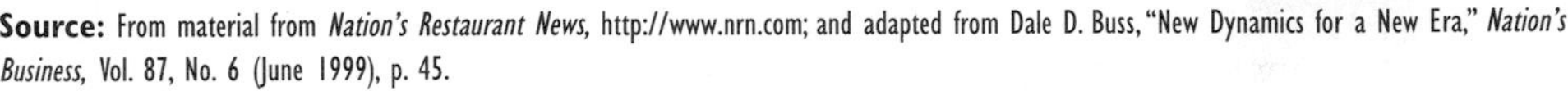

FIGURE 6-1 *The Structure of Franchising*

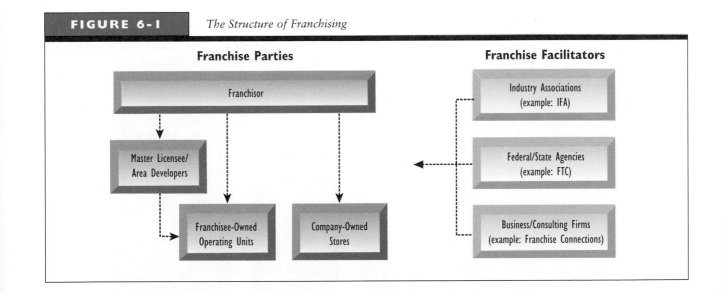

Franchise Parties

Franchisor

Master Licensee/ Area Developers

Franchisee-Owned Operating Units

Company-Owned Stores

Franchise Facilitators

Industry Associations (example: IFA)

Federal/State Agencies (example: FTC)

Business/Consulting Firms (example: Franchise Connections)

Nevertheless, the IFA is highly selective, and not all companies applying for membership are accepted. Referring to itself as "The Voice of Franchising," the IFA sponsors legal and government affairs symposiums, franchise management workshops, seminars on franchisor/franchisee relations, and trade shows. The IFA also champions the causes of minority business groups. For example, the Women's Franchise Committee (WFC), formed in 1996, represents women in the franchising industry. The WFC provides leadership conferences, mentoring programs, a network of professionals, and other services to women franchisees.

http://www.ftc.gov

Numerous federal and state agencies are involved in the franchise industry. Agencies such as the Federal Trade Commission (FTC) provide information on franchise opportunities and enforce franchising laws and regulations. Presale franchise disclosure practices are subject to special scrutiny by these agencies.

http://www.franchiseconnections.com
http://www.thefranchisecompany.com

A third category of facilitators includes private businesses providing franchise information and consulting services to franchisors and franchisees. For example, Franchise Connections and The Franchise Company are two businesses that assist with franchising evaluation and offer development services.

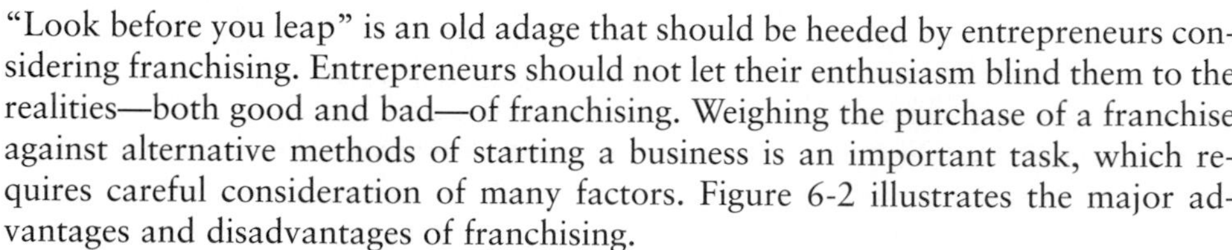

The Pros and Cons of Franchising

2 *Identify the major pros and cons of franchising.*

"Look before you leap" is an old adage that should be heeded by entrepreneurs considering franchising. Entrepreneurs should not let their enthusiasm blind them to the realities—both good and bad—of franchising. Weighing the purchase of a franchise against alternative methods of starting a business is an important task, which requires careful consideration of many factors. Figure 6-2 illustrates the major advantages and disadvantages of franchising.

Given the different personal goals and circumstances of different individuals, franchising will not be the ideal choice for all prospective entrepreneurs. However, many people find a franchise to be the best alternative. When you are evaluating future entrepreneurial opportunities, carefully weigh the pros and cons of franchising presented in this chapter.

Advantages of Franchising

Buying a franchise can be attractive for a variety of reasons. The greatest overall advantage by far is its probability of success. Business data on failures of franchises are

FIGURE 6-2

Major Pluses and Minuses in the Franchising Calculation

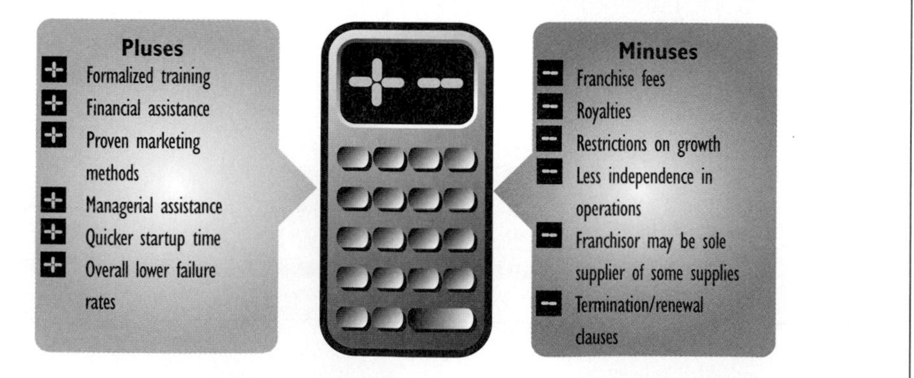

difficult to find and evaluate. Nevertheless, the success rate for franchises seems to be much higher than that for nonfranchised businesses. One explanation for the lower failure rate is that most franchisors are highly selective when granting franchises. Many potential franchisees who qualify financially are still rejected.

There are three additional, and more specific, reasons why a franchise opportunity is appealing. A franchise is typically attractive because it offers (1) training, (2) financial assistance, and (3) operating benefits. Naturally, all franchises are not equally strong in all these aspects. For example, McDonald's offers excellent training but no financing.

TRAINING The training received from franchisors is invaluable to many small entrepreneurs because it alleviates weaknesses in their managerial skills. Training by the franchisor often begins with an initial period of a few days or a few weeks at a central training school or at another established location and then continues at a franchise site.

The training by Kwik Kopy Printing, a successful business services franchisor, is very extensive, covering the technical aspects of running a printing business as well as the standard topics of accounting, computers, and leadership. Its training facility, located in picturesque Northwest Forest, a few miles from Houston, Texas, looks like an amusement park, with a full-size replica of the Alamo. However, franchise trainees quickly realize that the three-week training program is very demanding. Classes start at 7:00 A.M. and conclude at 6:00 P.M., Monday through Friday, and they continue for a half-day on Saturday.

http://www.kwikkopy.com

Another very famous franchisor, McDonald's, is widely recognized for its off-site franchisee training effort at Hamburger University. Subway is also a strong believer in initial training for prospective franchisees. Consider this recent description of Subway's training philosophy:

http://www.mcdonalds.com
http://www.subway.com

People who see lunchmeat in their futures have to first prove they were paying attention in grade school. All would-be franchisees are given a test of basic math skills and English language ability, according to Subway's director of training, Alexander Dembski. "If you can't pass that test, you won't become a franchisee. We were getting in people who were sometimes very nice people, but did not have the ability to communicate with customers or employees, or did not have the basic math ability to understand how to analyze their business. We do them no favor letting them come in. We hurt ourselves, and we hurt them."

Once past that hurdle, the new franchisee gets into former high school history teacher Dembski's classroom at Subway headquarters in Milford, Conn. Dembski runs a two-week, 55-hour program and then sends students to Subway stores near headquarters for an additional 34 hours of on-the-job training.

The new franchisees spend an entire Saturday, usually the busiest lunch day of the week, helping out at a local store. "That full day in-store just made the loose ends come together for them," Dembski says. By the second week, the new sandwich makers run a shop by themselves.

There is a final exam at Subway, and about 10 percent of new franchisees flunk. They get to retake courses they may need or get one-on-one instruction if necessary. But until they pass, they can't own a Subway sandwich shop.[1]

Naturally, both the nature of a product and the type of business affect the amount and type of training needed by the franchisee. In most cases, training constitutes an

important advantage of the franchising system, as it permits individuals who have had little training or education to start and succeed in businesses of their own.

Initial training is ordinarily supplemented with subsequent training and guidance. This may involve refresher courses and/or visits by a company representative to the franchisee's location from time to time. The franchisee may also receive manuals and other printed materials that provide guidance in operating the business. Although the franchisor normally places considerable emphasis on observing strict controls, much of the continuing training goes far beyond the application of controls. In particular cases, however, it may be difficult to distinguish between guidance and control.

Although many franchising systems have developed excellent training programs, be aware that this is by no means universal. Some unscrupulous promoters falsely promise extensive training and then leave the entrepreneur to run his or her own business with little or no guidance.

FINANCIAL ASSISTANCE The costs of starting an independent business are often high, and the typical entrepreneur's sources of capital are quite limited. The entrepreneur's standing as a prospective borrower is weakest at this time. By teaming up with a franchising organization, the aspiring franchisee may enhance her or his likelihood of obtaining financial assistance.

BUILDING CUSTOMER LOYALTY

IN THE TRENCHES

STICK MAN UNIVERSITY

It's back to school again. Doesn't it ever end? Not for entrepreneurs choosing franchising. They need good franchise training. However, the training facilities available to a franchisee are different from the traditional college classroom. For example, at Stick Man University® in Lansing, Michigan, you may be staring at a cutaway of a moving truck wondering what item is packed where.

Stick Man University—the name is based on the company logo of two stick figures—provides a 10-day training program for new franchisees of Two Men and a Truck®, an Okemus, Michigan–based franchise of local moving companies that was founded in 1985 by Mary Ellen Sheets. Today, Two Men and a Truck has 94 franchises with 105 locations in 23 states.

At Stick Man University, the curriculum consists of packing and moving techniques, including the finer points of bubble-wrapping. Attendees get hands-on experience in stacking furniture and learn to "pack boxes in a way that keeps Grandma's glass vase intact from one end of town to the next."

There is also heavy emphasis on the business of running a business, including the importance of customer service. "One of the most important parts of customer service is doing what you say you're going to do when you say you're going to do it," says Sally Degnan, the university's training director.

Graduates of Stick Man University get a t-shirt, showing a picture of a moving truck with a tassel on the side, and a certificate. More importantly, they get the training they need to make their franchise successful.

Source: Richard Landesberg, "A New Career for You Might Start at Franchise U.," *Success Magazine*, http://www.successmagazine.com, July-August 2000.

http://www.twomen.com

If the franchising organization considers the applicant to be a suitable prospect with a high probability of success, it frequently extends a helping hand financially. For example, the franchisee is seldom required to pay the complete cost of establishing the business. In addition, the beginning franchisee is normally given a payment schedule that can be met through successful operation. Also, the franchisor may permit the franchisee to delay payments for products or supplies obtained from the parent organization, thus increasing the franchisee's working capital.

Association with a well-established franchisor may also improve a new franchisee's credit standing with a bank. The reputation of the franchising organization and the managerial and financial controls that it provides serve to recommend the new franchisee to a banker. Also, the franchisor will frequently cosign a note with a local bank, thus guaranteeing the franchisee's loan.

The U.S. Small Business Administration (SBA) has introduced the Franchise Registry, which greatly expedites loan processing for small business franchisees. The Registry "enables lenders and SBA local offices to verify a franchise system's lending eligibility through the Internet. This reduces red tape, time, and cost for all concerned."[2] Listing on this registry means that the SBA has found that the particular franchise agreement does not impose unacceptable control provisions on the franchisee. Therefore, loan applications for registered franchises can be reviewed and processed more quickly.

OPERATING BENEFITS Most franchised products and services are widely known and accepted. For example, consumers will readily buy Baskin-Robbins ice cream or use PIP Printing services because they are aware of the reputation these businesses have. Travelers will recognize a restaurant or a motel because of its name or type of roof or some other feature such as the "Golden Arches" of McDonald's. They may turn into a Denny's restaurant or a Holiday Inn because of their previous experiences with the chain and their knowledge that they can depend on the food and service these outlets provide. Thus, franchising offers both a proven line of business and product/service identification.

An entrepreneur who enters into a franchising agreement acquires the right to use the franchisor's nationally advertised trademark or brand name. This serves to identify the local enterprise with the widely recognized product or service. Of course, the value of product identification depends on the type of product or service and the extent to which it has been promoted. In any case, the franchisor must maintain the value of its name by continued advertising and promotion.

In addition to a proven line of business and readily identifiable products or services, franchisors offer well-developed and thoroughly tested methods of marketing and management. The operating manuals and procedures supplied to franchisees enable them to operate more efficiently from the start. This is one reason why franchisors insist on the observance of quality methods of operation and performance. If a franchise were allowed to operate at a substandard level, it could easily destroy customers' confidence in the entire system.

The existence of proven products and methods, however, does not guarantee that a franchise will succeed. For example, a location that the franchisor's marketing research shows to be satisfactory may turn out to be inferior. Or the franchisee may lack ambition or perseverance. But the fact that a franchisor has a record of successful operation proves that the system can work and has worked elsewhere.

ENTREPRENEURSHIP TODAY

IN THE TRENCHES

NOW AUDITIONING

Dave Siemienski and Howard Davidson operate a Cold Stone Creamery franchise in Glendale, California. Their store is one of more than 125 Cold Stone Creamery stores operating in 24 states, delivering premium ice cream and yogurt blended on an ice-cold stone. This particular franchise offers one other commodity—entertainment. Employees are known for their extroverted personalities and ability to sing for customers.

Dave and Howard were finding it difficult to deliver this entertainment because their franchise had too many positions and not enough employees. "It was a constant battle," says Dave. They couldn't hire just anybody for the Creamery crew because they needed to recruit special people who could add to the unique atmosphere of Cold Stone Creamery.

Their recruiting began with a sign in the store window that read "Now Auditioning!" From there, the idea took off. Dave and Howie did the standard preliminary screening of applicants and then asked them to sing and entertain. "It was the first time anyone even asked me to do something crazy like sing to get a job," said one crew member.

But this approach has worked. Auditions now take place in the local school gym with music students and theater students standing in line for a chance to work at the Cold Stone Creamery. In fact, the president of Cold Stone Creamery has shared the Glendale recruitment strategy with all its franchisees, with encouragement to follow Dave and Howie's lead and post their own "Now Auditioning" signs instead of the old "Now Hiring" signs.

Source: Kathy Heasley, "Casting Call: Cold Stone Creamery Is Hottest Gig in Town," *Franchising World* (July-August 2000), pp. 16–17.

http://www.coldstonecreamery.com

Limitations of Franchising

Franchising is like a coin—it has two sides. We have presented the positive side of franchising, but it is important that you also learn about its negative side. Three shortcomings, in particular, permeate the franchise form of business: (1) the costs associated with the franchise, (2) the operating restrictions that can be a part of the franchise agreement, and (3) the loss of entrepreneurial independence.

FRANCHISE COSTS Generally speaking, higher costs characterize the better known and more successful franchises. Franchise costs have several components, all of which need to be recognized and considered.

1. ***Initial franchise fee.*** The total cost of a franchise begins with an initial franchise fee, which may range from several hundred to several thousand dollars. The initial fee for a Smoothie King is $20,000; McDonald's initial fee is $45,000.
2. ***Investment costs.*** Significant costs may be involved in renting or building an outlet and stocking it with inventory and other equipment. Also, certain insurance premiums, legal fees, and other startup expenses must be paid. It is often recommended that funds be available to cover personal expenses and emergencies for at least six months. A reputable franchisor will always provide a detailed estimate of investment costs; Table 6-1 shows the information provided by McAlister's Deli, a franchised restaurant. Curves for Women, a women's workout facility, requires that a prospective franchisee have a minimum of $14,900 in startup cash. The total startup cash investment for a KFC restaurant exceeds $1,000,000.

TABLE 6-1

Investment Costs for a McAlister's Deli Franchise

Type of Cost	Existing Location (Strip Center)	New Construction
Initial franchise fee	$15,000–$30,000	$15,000–$30,000
Rent	$8,000–$12,000	NA
Leasehold improvements	$75,000–$175,000	NA
Land	NA	$200,000–$400,000
Construction	NA	$375,000–$450,000
Furniture, fixtures & equipment	$0–$180,000	$0–$180,000
POS system	$0–$30,000	$0–$30,000
Initial inventory	$8,000–$15,000	$8,000–$15,000
Insurance	$2,000–$8,000	$2,000–$8,000
Training	$10,000–$20,000	$10,000–$20,000
Grand opening advertising	$4,000	$4,000
Signage	$10,000–$30,000	$10,000–$30,000
Additional funds	$15,000–$30,000	$15,000–$30,000
Total	**$147,000–$534,000**	**$639,000–$1,197,000**

Source: From material from http://www.mcalistersdeli.com/investment.html.

3. ***Royalty payments.*** A common practice is for the franchisor to receive continuing royalty payments, based on a percentage of the franchisee's gross income. McAlister's Deli, for example, charges a 5 percent royalty fee. McDonald's currently charges a "service fee" of 4 percent of monthly sales plus the greater of (a) a monthly base rent or (b) a percentage rent that represents at least 8.5 percent of monthly sales.
4. ***Advertising costs.*** Many franchisors require that franchisees contribute to an advertising fund to promote the franchise. These fees are generally 1 to 2 percent of sales.

If entrepreneurs could generate the same level of sales by setting up an independent business, they would save the franchise fee and some of the other costs. However, if the franchisor provides the benefits previously described, the money franchisees pay for their relationship with the franchisor may prove to be a very good investment.

RESTRICTIONS ON BUSINESS OPERATIONS Franchisors, understandably concerned about the image of their businesses, make every effort to control how franchisees conduct certain aspects of the franchise business. Thus, the franchisee is restricted in her or his ability to use personal business judgment. The following types of control are frequently exercised by a franchisor:

- Restricting sales territories
- Requiring site approval for the retail outlet and imposing requirements regarding outlet appearance
- Restricting goods and services offered for sale
- Restricting advertising and hours of operation

LOSS OF INDEPENDENCE Frequently, individuals leave salaried employment for entrepreneurship because they dislike working under the direct supervision and control of others. Upon entering into a franchise relationship, such individuals may find that a different pattern of supervision has taken over. The franchisee surrenders a considerable amount of independence in signing a franchise agreement.

Even though the franchisor's influence on business operations may be helpful in ensuring success, the level of control exerted may be unpleasant to an entrepreneur who cherishes independence. In addition, some franchise contracts go to extremes, covering unimportant details or specifying practices that are more helpful to others in the chain than to the local operation. For example, a food franchise may be prevented from selling a nonapproved product in a local market.

Also, entrepreneurs should recognize that they can lose the right to a franchise if they do not abide by performance standards or fail to pay royalties. Additionally, there is no guarantee that a franchise will be renewed beyond the contracted time, which is typically 15 to 20 years.

Evaluating Franchise Opportunities

Describe the process for evaluating a franchise opportunity.

After making the initial decision to pursue a franchise opportunity, the prospective franchisee must determine a franchise candidate and investigate it completely. As we discuss the investigation process, we will use examples featuring Curves for Women, the women's fitness franchise.

Selecting a Franchise

With the growth of franchising over the years, the task of initially selecting an appropriate franchise has become much easier. Personal observation frequently sparks interest, or awareness may begin with exposure to an advertisement in a newspaper or magazine or on the Internet. The headlines of these advertisements usually appeal to the financial and personal rewards sought by the entrepreneur. *The Wall Street Journal, Entrepreneur,* and *Inc.* are examples of publications that include advertisements of franchisors.

Investigating the Potential Franchise

The nature of the commitment required in franchising justifies careful investigation. Launching a franchised business typically involves a substantial financial investment, usually many thousands of dollars. Furthermore, the business relationship is one that may be expected to continue over a period of years.

The evaluation process is a two-way effort. The franchisor wishes to investigate the franchisee, and the franchisee obviously wishes to evaluate the franchisor and the type of opportunity being offered. Time is required for this kind of analysis. You should be skeptical of a franchisor who pressures you to sign a contract without time for proper investigation.

What should be the prospective entrepreneur's first step in evaluating a franchising opportunity? What sources of information are available? Do government agencies provide information on franchising? Basically, three sources of information should be tapped: (1) independent, third-party sources, (2) the franchisors themselves, and (3) existing and previous franchisees.

INDEPENDENT, THIRD-PARTY SOURCES OF INFORMATION State and federal agencies are valuable sources of franchising information. Since most states require registration of franchises, a prospective franchisee should not overlook state offices as a source of assistance. The Federal Trade Commission publishes the *Franchise Opportunities Handbook,* which is a useful directory of hundreds of franchisors. Also, a comprehensive listing of franchisors can be found in the *Franchise Opportunities Guide,* which is published by the International Franchise Association (IFA). Figure 6-3 on page 156 displays selected listings from this guide. (Note the entry for Curves for Women.) Similar information is available on the IFA Web site.

http://www.franchise.org

Business publications are also excellent sources of franchisor ratings. *Entrepreneur, Inc.*, and *The Wall Street Journal,* to name a few, can be found in most libraries, and all have Web sites with archives. *Entrepreneur's Be Your Own Boss* magazine for February 2000, for example, contained a profile of the "Top 50 New Franchises" (see Figure 6-4 on page 157). A number of factors were weighed to arrive at the rankings, the most important being financial strength and the franchising system's growth rate and size. Other considerations included litigation history and whether the company provides financing. Notice that Curves for Women topped the list!

http://www.entrepreneurmag.com
http://www.inc.com
http://www.startup.wsj.com

A search of the Web uncovered several articles describing the Curves for Women franchise. Frequently, such articles provide information not available from the franchisor or from government agencies. They often give an extensive profile of franchise problems and strategy changes within a company. Third-party coverage helps in evaluating the credibility of information provided directly by the franchisor. The Internet search also revealed that Curves for Women is listed in the Small Business Administration's (SBA's) new Franchise Registry, discussed earlier in this chapter.

In recent years, franchise consultants have appeared in the marketplace to assist individuals seeking franchise opportunities. Some consulting firms, such as FranCorp, present seminars on choosing the right franchise. Of course, the prospective franchisee needs to be careful to select a reputable consultant. Since franchise consultants are not necessarily attorneys, an experienced franchise attorney should evaluate all legal documents.

THE FRANCHISOR AS A SOURCE OF INFORMATION Obviously, the franchisor being evaluated is a primary source of information. However, information provided by a franchisor must be viewed in light of its purpose—to promote the franchise.

One way to obtain information about a franchisor is to correspond directly with the franchisor. After finding the Internet address for Curves for Women in the list shown in Figure 6-4, we accessed its home page to learn more about the franchise (see Figure 6-5 on page 158). Within a few days of requesting information, we received a packet containing an attractive brochure describing the franchise, a Uniform Franchise Offering Circular (discussed on page 162), and a videotape. The brochure included such information as startup costs and franchisees' testimonials.

http://www.curvesforwomen.com

It is important for potential franchisees to remember that many of the financial figures provided in the franchisor's information packet are only estimates. While profit claims are becoming more common, reputable franchisors are careful not to misrepresent what a franchisee can expect to attain in terms of sales, gross income, and profits. The importance of earnings to a prospective franchisee makes the subject of profit claims a particularly sensitive one.

FIGURE 6-3 *Franchise Profiles from the Franchise Opportunities Guide*

CURVES FOR WOMEN
Curves International
(800) 848-1096
(254) 399-9285
(254) 399-9731
400 Schroeder Drive, Waco, TX 76710-7807
E-Mail: curvesadm@aol.com
Internet: http://www.curvesforwomen.com
Full Member

TYPE OF BUSINESS: Thirty minute fitness and weight loss center for women

HISTORY: 746 franchised units; in business since 1995; franchising since 1995

CASH INVESTMENT: $14,900–$19,900 startup cash; $20,425–$30,850 total investment required.
$6,900 down payment; balance $13,000; 15% over 30 months.

TRAINING/SUPPORT: Initial five day training session, company representative assists at opening, regional meetings, annual convention, monthly advertising and promotional packet, and toll free number.

CONTACT: Gary A. Findley, President/COO;
Kevin D. Ayers, Legal Counsel

MCDONALD'S CORPORATION
(630) 623-5550
(630) 623-3057 FAX
Campus Office Building, Oak Brook, IL 60521
Internet: http://www.mcdonalds.com
Full Member

TYPE OF BUSINESS: Quick service restaurant.

HISTORY: 18,361 franchised units; 5,262 company-owned units; in business since 1955; franchising since 1955.

CASH INVESTMENT: $408,600–$647,000 total investment required. McDonald's does not provide financing.

TRAINING/SUPPORT: Addresses all aspects of operating a McDonald's restaurant. Most training takes place in a McDonald's restaurant. Also, includes classroom training and seminars. McDonald's pays the cost of training materials. Must complete before considered for a franchise.

QUALIFICATIONS: Entrepreneurial spirit, ability to manage finances; motivate and train people; willingness to complete a comprehensive training program and devote full time and best efforts to operating the restaurant; financial qualifications.

CONTACT: Bob Villa, Franchise Coordinator

POSTNET INTERNATIONAL FRANCHISE CORPORATION
(800) 841-7171
(702) 792-7100
(702) 792-7115 FAX
181N Arroyo Grande Blvd., Building A, Suite 100, Henderson, NV 89014
E-Mail: info@postnet.net
Internet: http://www.postnet.net
Full Member

TYPE OF BUSINESS: PostNet provides a full range of mailbox rentals & services, full-service digital copy/print center as well as FedEx, UPS, & DHL shipping services.

HISTORY: 650 franchised units; in business since 1985; franchising since 1993.

CASH INVESTMENT: $35,000–$40,000 startup cash; $90,00–$125,000 total investment required. No direct financing available, but have third party sources for SBA and operating leases.

TRAINING/SUPPORT: Up to one week of classroom training at Corp office & one week at your location. Will cover center set-up, operations, advertising, marketing, etc.

QUALIFICATIONS: Individuals with a minimum net worth of $150,000 and available cash of $35,000. Should enjoy working with public & have entrepreneurial nature.

CONTACT: Brian Spindel, Executive VP, COO

COLD STONE CREAMERY, INC.
(480) 348-1704
(480) 348-1718 FAX
16101 North 82nd Street, Scottsdale, AZ 85260
Internet: http://www.coldstonecreamery.com
Full Member

TYPE OF BUSINESS: People, Product, Concept. Our team is made up of seasoned professionals who deliver a proven system for providing the world's best ice cream experience. Making our franchisees successful is our number one priority. Ice cream & waffle cones are made fresh daily right in the stores. Fresh-baked brownies & brand name mix-ins make every dessert pure delight. Operationally, we are unmatched, & are the nation's fastest growing franchisor of creameries.

HISTORY: 60 franchised units; 3 company-owned units; in business since 1988; franchising since 1995.

CASH INVESTMENT: $183,000–$269,500 total investment required.

TRAINING/SUPPORT: We provide a 10-day intensive training program for all new franchisees & crew at our Creamery Hdqts. Training consists of classroom, in-store operations from start to finish, advertising & marketing. Ongoing support.

QUALIFICATIONS: Cold Stone Creamery is looking for energetic, enthusiastic people with a positive attitude that are looking to create their own happiness!

CONTACT: Sheldon Harris, Vice President of Development; Steve Burk, Director of Development

FIGURE 6-4 *The Nation's Top 50 New Franchises*

Franchise	Phone Web site or e-mail address	Description	Franchising since	Total costs	No. of units
1. Curves for Women	(800) 848-1095/(254) 399-9285 www.curvesforwomen.com	Women's fitness & weight-loss centers	1995	$20.6K–31.1K	708
2. Ace America's Cash Express	(888) 713-3338 www.acecashexpress.com	Check cashing & related financial services	1996	$77.5K–186.1K	916
3. Home Instead Senior Care	(888) 484-5759/(402) 498-4466 www.homeinstead.com	Non-medical senior care services	1995	$23.1K–29.8K	198
4. Cash Converters Int'l. Franchise Group	(888) 910-2274/(847) 330-1122 www.cashconverters.com	Pre-owned merchandise stores	1996	$253K–470K	547
5. The Mad Science Group	(800) 586-5231 www.madscience.org	Science activities for children	1995	$60K–70K	107
6. Mister Money–USA Inc.	(800) 827-7296/(970) 493-0574 www.mistermoney.com	Pawn shops	1995	$64K–200K	39
7. House Doctors	(800) 319-3359 www.housedoctors.com	Handyman services/home repairs	1995	$18.5K–38.6K	143
8. Atlanta Bread Co.	(770) 432-0933 www.atlantabread.com	Bakery/cafe	1995	$362K–584K	79
9. Bennigan's Grill & Tavern	(800) 543-9670 www.mrg.net	Casual-theme restaurant	1995	$1.1M–2.2M	238
10. Wetzel's Pretzels	(626) 432-6900	Hand-rolled soft pretzels	1996	$111K–180K	84
11. Sport Clips	(800) 872-4247 www.sportclips.com	Sports-themed hair salons for men & boys	1995	$98K–166.5K	27
12. Dealer Specialties Int'l. Inc.	(800) 647-8425 www.getauto.com	Used-car window stickers	1996	$10.2K–35.4K	172
13. Tilden For Brakes Car Care Centers	(800) 845-3367 www.tildencarcare.com	Full-service automotive repair	1996	$131.5K–171.2K	55
14. MilliCare Environmental Services	(888) 886-2273 www.millicare.com	Commercial carpet maintenance	1996	$77K–166.9K	74
15. Talking Book World	(800) 403-2933/(248) 945-9999 www.talkingbookworld.com	Audiobook rentals & sales	1995	$150K–225K	37
16. Colter's Bar-B-Q	(214) 987-5910 www.coltersbbq.com	Barbecue restaurant	1995	$150K–650K	18
17. Hayes Handpiece Franchises Inc.	(760) 602-0521 www.hayeshandpiece.com	Dental handpiece repairs	1995	$21.5K–23K	49

Source: By permission of *Entrepreneur* magazine, 2445 McCabe Way, Irvine, California 92614. For subscription information call 1-800-421-6229. #8788 Reprinted by Reprint Management Services, (717) 399-1900, http://www.rmsreprints.com—sales@rmsreprints.com.

FIGURE 6-5

Home Page of Curves for Women

disclosure document
a detailed statement provided to a prospective franchisee, containing such information as the franchisor's finances, experience, size, and involvement in litigation

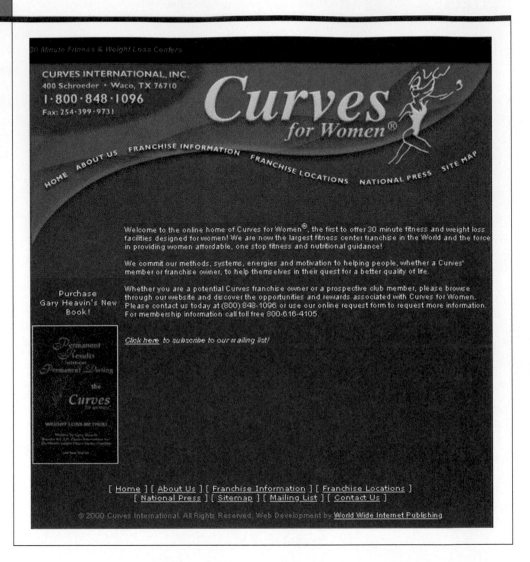

After an entrepreneur has expressed further interest in a franchise by completing the application form and the franchisor has tentatively qualified the potential franchisee, a meeting is usually arranged to discuss the disclosure document. A **disclosure document** is a detailed statement of such information as the franchisor's finances, experience, size, and involvement in litigation. The document must inform potential franchisees of any restrictions, costs, and provisions for renewal or cancellation of the franchise. Important considerations related to this document are examined more fully later in this chapter.

EXISTING AND PREVIOUS FRANCHISEES AS SOURCES OF INFORMATION There may be no better source of franchise facts than existing franchisees. Sometimes, however, the location of other franchisees precludes a visit to their business site. In that case, a simple telephone call can provide you with the viewpoint of a person in the position you are considering. If possible, also talk with franchisees who have left the business; they can offer valuable input about their decision to give up the franchise.

Finding Global Franchising Opportunities

A great opportunity continues to exist for small business firms in the United States to franchise internationally. Traditionally, U.S. franchisors did most of their international franchising in Canada because of that country's proximity and language similarity. This, however, has changed. A combination of events, including the structuring of the European Economic Community, the collapse of the Soviet Union, and the passage of the North American Free Trade Agreement, have opened other foreign markets to U.S. franchisors.[3]

Although the appeal of foreign markets is substantial, the task of franchising abroad is not easy. One franchisor's manager of international development expressed the challenge this way:

In order to successfully franchise overseas, the franchisor must have a sound and successful home base that is sufficiently profitable. The financial position of the franchisor must be secure and [the franchisor] must have resources which are surplus to—or can be exclusively diverted from—[its] domestic requirements. [The franchisor] must also have the personnel available to devote solely to international operations, and above all . . . must be patient. On the whole, the development of international markets will always take longer and make greater demands on the resources of the franchisor than first anticipated.[4]

Several sources of international franchising information are available for entrepreneurs. Many U.S. government publications are helpful, as is the information on several Web sites such as that of *The International Herald-Tribune*. Also, individual foreign countries may host Web sites that contain useful information about franchising opportunities in that country; the British Franchising Association's site is one example.

http://www.franchiseintl.com
http://www.british-franchise.org

Franchising from the Franchisor's Perspective

Let's briefly consider the franchising option from the perspective of a potential franchisor. Why would an entrepreneur wish to become a franchisor rather than operate only company-owned outlets? At least three general benefits can be identified:

1. ***Reduction of capital requirements.*** Franchising allows a firm to expand without diluting capital. Through fee and royalty arrangements, the firm involved in franchising in effect borrows capital from franchisees for channel development and thus has lower capital requirements than does a wholly owned chain.
2. ***Increase in management motivation.*** Franchisees, as owners, are more highly motivated than are salaried employees because of profit incentives and their vested interest in the business. Since franchising is decentralized, the franchisor is also less susceptible to labor-organizing efforts than are more centralized organizations.
3. ***Speed of expansion.*** Franchising lets a business enter more markets more quickly than it could using only its own resources.

There are also distinct drawbacks associated with franchising from the franchisor's perspective. At least three drawbacks can be isolated:

1. ***Reduction in control.*** A franchisor's control over the business is reduced because franchisees are not employees. This is a major concern for most franchisors.
2. ***Sharing of profits.*** Only part of the profit belongs to the franchisor.

3. ***Increase in operational support costs.*** The costs associated with such areas as accounting and legal services are generally higher for franchises than for more centralized organizations.

In addition to the large, high-profile franchisors, such as McDonald's, there are many less known but also successful franchises. Have you heard of Snap-on-Tools, with its 4,000-plus franchises, or CleanNet USA, with over 2,000 franchised outlets? Snap-on-Tools has been in business since 1920, and CleanNet has been franchising since 1988.

Legal Considerations in Franchising

4 *Discuss certain legal considerations in franchising.*

An entrepreneur who is interested in franchising must give careful consideration to legal issues. Of particular importance to prospective franchisees are the franchise contract and franchise disclosure requirements.

The Franchising Contract

The basic features of the relationship between the franchisor and the franchisee are embodied in the franchise contract. This contract is typically a complex document,

Utilizing New Technology — **In the Trenches**

THE WEB BRINGS FRANCHISEES TOGETHER

New technology can benefit a franchisor-franchisee relationship, if it is used properly and creatively. For example, the owners of PostNet International Franchise Corporation have embraced Internet technology with a Web site that helps franchisees help themselves.

Entrepreneurs Steven Greenbaum and Brian Spindel run PostNet. Over 700 franchisees in 25 countries provide PostNet postal and business service centers. Prior to the Internet, PostNet's home office in Henderson, Nevada would process and answer franchisee questions using its 30-plus person staff. But this has changed. In 1997, PostNet launched the Franchisee Web as a new Web site feature. "The Franchise Web message boards give users a chance to solve problems, celebrate triumphs, and sometimes just vent. More than 90 percent of the franchisees regularly visit the message boards," says Executive Vice President Brian Spindel.

The Web site also links franchisees to approved vendors, contains archived newsletters, and allows franchisees to download marketing materials by using a password-protected feature. Franchisees can also upload customer databases to a central server. PostNet can then handle direct mail campaigns for the franchisee. These efforts appear to pay off. In just a few years, Greenbaum says, "our annual increase in same-store sales has been in excess of 20 percent, and we think that's a direct result of [the franchisee's] ability to learn and share."

Spindel believes the Web site has also paid off in increased franchisee communication and involvement. In fact, PostNet's Web site won first place in the "Community" category of *Inc.*'s Web Awards 2000.

Source: From material from http://www.postnet.net; and Mary Kwak, "Posted Notes," *Inc. Technology,* Vol. 22, No. 17 (November 14, 2000), p. 83.

http://www.postnet.net

running to many pages. Because of its importance as the legal basis for the franchised business, the franchise contract should never be signed by the franchisee without legal counsel. In fact, reputable franchisors insist that the franchisee have legal counsel before signing the agreement. An attorney may anticipate trouble spots and note any objectionable features of the contract.

In addition to consulting an attorney, a prospective franchisee should use as many other sources of help as practical. In particular, he or she should discuss the franchise proposal with a banker, going over it in as much detail as possible. The prospective franchisee should also obtain the services of a professional accounting firm in examining the franchisor's statements of projected sales, operating expenses, and net income. An accountant can help in evaluating the quality of these estimates and in identifying projections that may be unlikely to be realized.

One of the most important features of the franchise contract is the provision relating to termination and transfer of the franchise. Some franchisors have been accused of devising agreements that permit arbitrary cancellation. Of course, it is reasonable for the franchisor to have legal protection in the event that a franchisee fails to obtain a satisfactory level of operation or to maintain satisfactory quality standards. However, the prospective franchisee should be wary of contract provisions that contain overly strict cancellation policies. Similarly, the rights of the franchisee to sell the business to a third party should be clearly stipulated. A franchisor who can restrict the sale of the business to a third party could potentially assume ownership of the business at an unreasonably low price. The right of the franchisee to renew the contract after the business has been built up to a successful operating level should also be clearly stated in the contract.

Franchise Disclosure Requirements

The offer and sale of a franchise are regulated by both state and federal laws. At the federal level, the minimum disclosure standards are specified by Rule 436 of the Federal Trade Commission. The Rule, formally entitled "Disclosure Requirements and Prohibitions Concerning Franchising and Business Opportunity Ventures," went into effect in October of 1979. An overview of the Rule, the full text of which is shown on the Federal Trade Commission's Web site, follows:

http://www.ftc.gov

A. *Basic Requirement: Franchisors must furnish potential franchisees with written disclosures providing important information about the franchisor, the franchised business and the franchise relationship, and give them at least ten business days to review it before investing.*
B. *Disclosure Option: Franchisors may make the required disclosures by following either the Rule's disclosure format or the Uniform Franchise Offering Circular Guidelines prepared by state franchise law officials.*
C. *Coverage: The Rule primarily covers business-format franchises, product franchises, and vending machine or display rack business opportunity ventures.*
D. *No Filing: The Rule requires disclosure only. Unlike state disclosure laws, no registration, filing, review or approval of any disclosures, advertising or agreements by the FTC is required.*
E. *Remedies: The Rule is a trade regulation rule with the full force and effect of federal law. The courts have held it may only be enforced by the FTC, not private parties. The FTC may seek injunctions, civil penalties and consumer redress for violations.*

F. *Purpose: The Rule is designed to enable potential franchisees to protect themselves before investing by providing them with information essential to an assessment of the potential risks and benefits, to meaningful comparisons with other investments, and to further investigation of the franchise opportunity.*[5]

The Small Business Franchise Act of 1999 (H.R. 3308) was introduced in the 106th Congress but has not yet been passed. If it becomes law, additional minimum standards of fair conduct in franchise sales and franchise business relationships will be established.

In addition, 15 states have presale disclosure requirements that affect the offer and sale of a franchise. Addresses of the state offices administering franchise disclosure laws can be found on the Federal Trade Commission's Web page at http://www.ftc.gov/bcp/franchise/netdiscl.htm.

Uniform Franchise Offering Circular (UFOC) a document accepted by the Federal Trade Commission as satisfying its franchise disclosure requirements

http://www.nasaa.org

A document called the **Uniform Franchise Offering Circular** (UFOC) provides the accepted format for satisfying the franchise disclosure requirements of the FTC (see Figure 6-6). The original UFOC format was amended in April 1993 by its creator, the North American Securities Administrators Association (NASAA). Effective January 1, 1996, all franchisors using the UFOC disclosure format were obliged to abide by the new amendments.

The UFOC disclosure must include information on a variety of items, including litigation and bankruptcy history, investment requirements, and conditions that would affect renewal, termination, or sale of the franchise. Most franchise experts recommend that a franchisee attorney and an accountant review the document.

A Final Note

Every industry has its share of shady operations, and franchising is no exception. Unscrupulous fast-buck artists offer a wide variety of fraudulent schemes to attract unsuspecting investors. The franchisor in such cases is interested merely in obtaining the capital investment of the franchisee and not in nurturing a relationship.

The possibility of fraudulent schemes requires alertness on the part of prospective franchisees. Only careful investigation of the company and the product can distinguish between fraudulent operators and legitimate franchising opportunities.

FIGURE 6-6

Items Covered in the Uniform Franchise Offering Circular (UFOC)

1. The franchisor, its predecessors and affiliates
2. Business experience
3. Litigation
4. Bankruptcy
5. Initial franchise fee
6. Other fees
7. Initial investment
8. Restrictions on sources of products and services
9. Franchisee's obligations
10. Financing
11. Franchisor's obligations
12. Territory
13. Trademarks
14. Patents, copyrights, and proprietary information
15. Obligation to participate in the actual operation of the franchise
16. Restrictions on what the franchisee may sell
17. Renewal, termination, transfer, and dispute resolution
18. Public figures
19. Earnings claims
20. List of outlets
21. Financial statements
22. Contracts
23. Receipt

Source: Excerpted from NASAA materials.

In conclusion, we want to emphasize that franchising has made business ownership possible for many individuals who were unable to enter business in other ways and who otherwise would never have escaped salaried employment. In this way, franchising has contributed to the success of many entrepreneurs.

LOOKING BACK

1 Explain franchising terms and the structure of the industry.

- Franchising is a formalized arrangement that describes a certain way of operating a small business.
- The main parties in the franchising system are the franchisor and the franchisee.
- The potential value of any franchising arrangement is determined by the rights contained in the franchise contract.
- Product and trade name franchising and business format franchising are the two types of franchising.
- Contracting with master licensees, multiple-unit ownership—sometimes by area developers—and piggyback franchising are special approaches to franchising.
- Facilitating groups include industry associations, governmental agencies, and private businesses.

2 Identify the major pros and cons of franchising.

- The overall attraction of franchising is its high rate of success.
- A franchise may be favored over other alternatives because it offers training, financial assistance, and operating benefits.
- The major limitations of franchising are its costs, restrictions on business operations, and loss of entrepreneurial independence.

3 Discuss the process for evaluating a franchise opportunity.

- The substantial investment required by most franchisors justifies careful investigation by a potential franchisee.
- Independent third parties, such as state and federal government agencies and the International Franchise Association, can be valuable sources of franchise information.
- The most logical source of the greatest amount of information about a franchise is the franchisor.
- Existing and previous franchisees are good sources of information for evaluating a franchise.
- The major benefits of becoming a franchisor are reduction of capital requirements, increase in management motivation, and speed of expansion.
- The major drawbacks to franchising are reduction in control, sharing profits, and increase in operational support costs.

4 Discuss certain legal considerations in franchising.

- A franchise contract is a complex document and should be evaluated by a franchise attorney.
- An important feature of the franchise contract is the provision relating to termination and transfer of the franchise.
- Franchise disclosure requirements are specified by FTC Rule 436.
- A revised Uniform Franchise Offering Circular (UFOC) has been approved by the FTC.
- Prospective franchisees should be alert to possible franchising frauds.

KEY TERMS

franchising, p. 145
franchisee, p. 145
franchisor, p. 146
franchise contract, p. 146
franchise, p. 146
product and trade name franchising, p. 146
business format franchising, p. 146
master licensee, p. 146
multiple-unit ownership, p. 146
area developers, p. 146
piggyback franchising, p. 146
disclosure document, p. 158
Uniform Franchise Offering Circular (UFOC), p. 162

DISCUSSION QUESTIONS

1. What makes franchising different from other forms of business? Be specific.
2. What is the difference between product and trade name franchising and business format franchising? Which one accounts for the majority of franchising activity?
3. Identify and describe the parties in the franchising system.
4. Discuss the advantages and limitations of franchising from the viewpoints of the potential franchisee and the potential franchisor.
5. Should franchise information provided by a franchisor be discounted? Why or why not?
6. Do you believe the government-required disclosure document is useful for franchise evaluation? Defend your position.
7. Evaluate loss of control as a disadvantage of franchising from the franchisor's perspective.
8. What types of restrictions on franchisee independence might be included in a typical franchise contract?
9. What problems might arise when a potential franchisee, in the process of evaluating a franchise, attempts to consult previous franchisees?
10. What types of franchise information could you expect to obtain from business periodicals that you could not secure from the franchisor?

YOU MAKE THE CALL

SITUATION 1

In northern Illinois, a 67-year-old retired nurse named Seattle Sutton operates a $6 million-a-year meal delivery business. Her customers include office employees, construction workers, and shut-ins. Her centrally located, state-of-the-art kitchen, which is the size of a basketball court, allows her staff to serve almost 3,000 customers in and around Chicago. She promotes the business in 30-second television commercials in which she appears in a white lab coat and speaks in a cheery North Dakota accent.

Sutton started Seattle Sutton's Healthy Eating in 1985. She had often entertained the thought of franchising and finally, in 1998, took the plunge. She filed the necessary state registration forms, hired some franchising experts, and began looking for franchisee candidates to duplicate her business elsewhere.

Source: Dan Morse, "Turning Your Business into a Franchise Can Pay Off," *The Wall Street Journal Interactive Edition,* http://www.startup.wsj.com/franchising, June 7, 2001.

Question 1 What different sources of franchise information would you recommend to someone interested in buying this franchise?

Question 2 What kinds of training could a franchisor like Sutton offer to prospective franchisees?

Question 3 What do you believe would be the major obstacles, if any, to selling this franchise?

SITUATION 2

Hard times in the agricultural commodities market led broker Zane Stites to consider leaving his independent business and looking for new opportunities. This time around, Stites was committed to going into business with his wife, Susan, and their teenage son and daughter. His goal was to keep the family close and reduce the stress in their lives. In his previous job as a broker, Stites would leave home early and return late, with little time for his wife or children.

Before making a decision about leaving his job, Stites looked at several franchise opportunities. One possibility that he and Susan were seriously considering was a custom framing franchise that had been in existence for over 10 years and had almost 100 stores nationwide. However, the Stites were concerned about their lack of experience in this area and also about how long it would take to get the business going.

Question 1 How important should their lack of prior experience be to the Stites's decision?

Question 2 What other characteristics of the franchise should they investigate? What sources would you recommend for this information?

Question 3 Can they reasonably expect to change their lifestyle as owners of a franchise? Explain.

SITUATION 3

Judy Patterson, Connie Post, and Kriste Burnside were all friends, working together in the accounting department of a local manufacturing business in Waco, Texas. They enjoyed working out at a local exercise facility during their lunch hour.

One day, they learned that the owner of the gym was planning to move to Arizona and needed to sell the business. "We kind of hoped the owners of the company we worked for would buy it so we'd have free memberships," said Patterson. But that didn't happen, so the three friends formed a corporation to consider the purchase of the franchise.

Source: Mike Copeland, "Trio on Learning Curve," *The Waco Tribune-Herald,* April 30, 2000, p. 4B.

Question 1 What sources of information about this franchise would you recommend that the friends consider?

Question 2 Is their work-out experience sufficient to prepare them for ownership of this franchise?

Question 3 Would the three friends be making a wise decision if they decided to buy this franchise? Why or why not?

Experiential Exercises

1. Interview a local owner-manager of a widely recognized retail franchise such as McDonald's. Ask him or her to explain the process of obtaining the franchise and what he or she considers to be the advantages of franchising over starting a business from scratch.
2. Find a franchise advertisement in a recent issue of a business magazine. Research the franchise, and report back to class with your findings.
3. As a class, consider the potential for locating a hypothetical new fast-food restaurant next to your campus. (Be as specific about the assumed location as you can.) Divide into two groups, one that supports buying a franchised operation and one that favors starting an independent nonfranchised business. Plan a debate on the merits of each operation for the next class meeting.

Exploring the Web

1. To answer the following questions, access **http://www.betheboss.com**.
   a. Follow the link labeled Franchising—An Interactive Self-Test. Take the test to determine whether you would be a good candidate for franchising.
   b. Examine the costs of franchising from the franchisee's perspective. According to material on the site, what percentage of franchisees are happy with their decision?
   c. Under Make a Decision, what method is suggested for weighing the pros and cons of franchising?
2. Access the Web site of the franchisor of your choice (for example, McDonald's at **http://www.mcdonalds.com/corporate/franchise/index.html**).
   a. What information is given regarding the required investment and qualifications for potential franchisees?
   b. Order a brochure or additional information on franchise opportunities.
   c. State whether any global opportunities exist and, if so, where they are.
3. The Franchise Handbook On-line at **http://www.franchise1.com** touts itself as *the* comprehensive directory of franchises.
   a. Under Featured Franchises, choose one of the categories and view the results. What percentage of the firms listed are companies with which you are already familiar?
   b. Follow the link to Articles. Read one of the articles and briefly summarize the advice given on franchising.
   c. When and where is the next franchise show near you?

Case 6

UNIVERSAL BUSINESS BROKERS (p. 652)

This case describes an entrepreneurial firm's intensification of franchising efforts.

Alternative Cases for Chapter 6:
Case 8, "Robinson Associates, Inc.," p. 658

chapter 7

The Family Business

In the Spotlight

Frieda's, Inc.

A difficult challenge for most family businesses is the transfer of leadership and ownership from one generation to another. Frieda Caplan, founder of a specialty produce business in southern California, faced that challenge as she neared retirement.

After graduating from college, Caplan worked for an aunt and uncle who ran a wholesale produce stand and who soon encouraged her to start her own business. In her new business, founded in 1962, she took the fuzzy Chinese gooseberry and introduced it to the American market as the kiwi fruit. By 1986, Frieda's, Inc. was an industry leader, and Caplan decided to turn it over to her two daughters, who worked in the business. This transfer required decisions regarding both leadership and ownership.

The first step in establishing clear-cut leadership was taken by naming Karen, the older daughter, as president and her younger sister, Jackie, as vice president. Ownership was similarly split, with 55 percent to Karen and 45 percent to Jackie.

Transfer of ownership was structured carefully to minimize estate taxes. Frieda and her husband used their one-time estate tax exemption to give $1.2 million worth of the company to their daughters, and they financed the balance with a 10-year, low-interest loan.

The owners effected a successful transition by avoiding dangerous pitfalls in both leadership and ownership areas. In the intervening 14

http://www.friedas.com

years, the business has grown to about $35 million in sales, nearly four times the sales volume when the daughters took over. Karen and Jackie each have two young children, so they will eventually face the question of transferring the business to a third generation. ◆

Source: Jim Hopkins, "Family Firms Confront Calamities of Transfer," *USA Today*, August 29, 2000, pp. 1B–2B.

Looking Ahead

After studying this chapter, you should be able to

1. *Discuss the factors that make a family business unique.*
2. *Explain the cultural context of a family business.*
3. *Outline the complex roles and relationships involved in a family business.*
4. *Identify management practices that enable a family business to function effectively.*
5. *Describe the process of managerial succession in a family business.*

In the two previous chapters, we looked at startups, buyouts, and franchises as routes to entrepreneurship. For some, there is also a fourth type of opportunity, that of joining a family business started by parents, grandparents, or other relatives. Some young people, indeed, have been steered toward such a career since infancy. For others, a position in the family firm is merely one possibility among many career options to be considered during or after their college years. In any case, a family business offers another doorway to entrepreneurship for those whose families are involved in their own businesses. Ideally, the decision to join the family firm should be based on an understanding of the dynamics of such a business. This chapter examines the distinctive features that characterize the entrepreneurial alternative known as the family business.

The Family Business: A Unique Institution

A family firm differs from other types of small businesses in many ways. Its decision making, for example, involves a mixture of family and business values. This section discusses some characteristics of this unique institution.

Discuss the factors that make a family business unique.

What Is a Family Business?

A **family business** is a company in which two or more members of the same family share ownership or work together in its operation. The nature and extent of that involvement vary. In some firms, some family members work part-time. In a small restaurant, for example, one spouse may serve as host and manager, the other may keep the books, and the children may work in the kitchen or as servers.

family business
a company in which two or more members of the same family share ownership or work together in its operation

A firm is also recognized as a family business if it passes from one generation to another. For example, Thompson's Plumbing Supply is now headed by Bill

Thompson, Jr., son of the founder, who is deceased. Bill Thompson III has started to work on the sales floor, after serving in the stockroom during his high school years. He is the heir apparent, who will someday replace his father. People in the community think of Thompson's Plumbing Supply as a family business.

Most family businesses are small. However, family considerations may continue to be important even when such businesses become large corporations. In companies such as Wal-Mart, Levi Strauss, Ford Motor Company, and Marriott Corporation, the founding family is still involved, to some extent, in the ownership and operation of the business.

Family and Business Overlap

Any family business is composed of both a family and a business. Although the family and the business are separate institutions—each with its own members, goals, and values—they overlap in the family firm. For many people, these two overlapping institutions are the most important areas of their lives.

Families and businesses exist for fundamentally different reasons. The family's primary function is the care and nurturing of family members, while the business is concerned with the production and distribution of goods and/or services. The family's goals are the fullest possible development of each member, regardless of limitations in ability, and the provision of equal opportunities and rewards for each member; the business's goals are profitability and survival.

Individuals involved, directly or indirectly, in a family business have interests and perspectives that differ according to their particular situations. The model in Figure 7-1 shows the ways in which individuals may be involved—as members of the family, employees of the business, owners of the business, and various combi-

FIGURE 7-1

The Three-Circle Model of Family Business

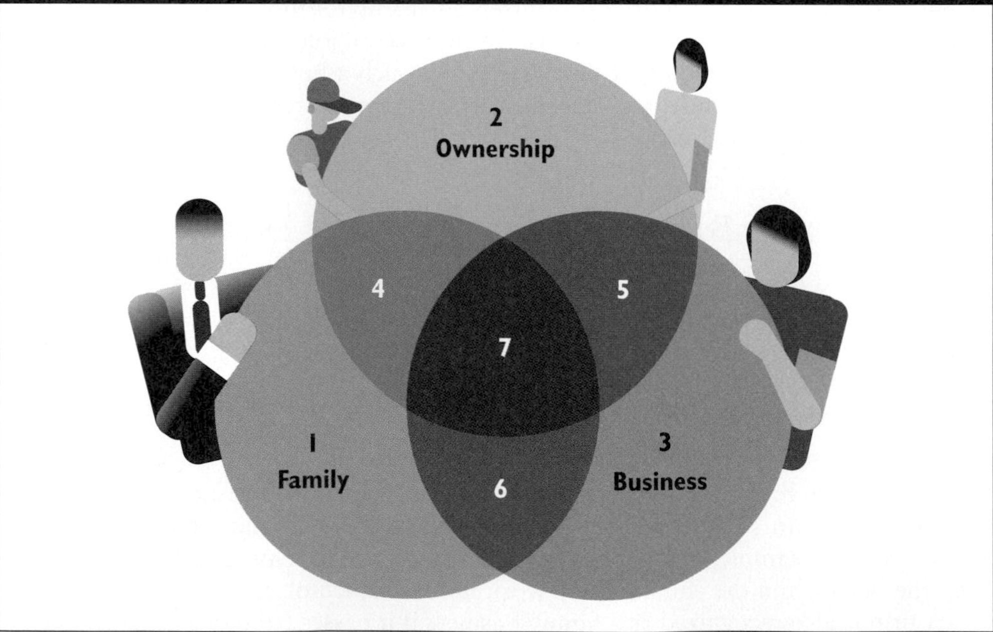

Source: Three-Circle Model developed by Renato Tagiuri and John A. Davis. Found in "Bivalent Attributes of the Family Firm." 1982. Working paper, Harvard Business School, Cambridge, MA. Reprinted 1996, *Family Business Review*, Vol. IX, No. 2, pp. 199–208.

IN THE TRENCHES ENTREPRENEURSHIP AND ETHICS

BALANCING FAMILY AND ENTREPRENEURIAL INTERESTS

A parent's business career and family interests often conflict. In entrepreneurial families, the competition between business and family can become severe.

When Heather Blease started Envisionet (to provide tech support and customer service for clients' Web sites) in Brunswick, Maine, she still found time for her sons. She attended their sporting events and volunteered at kindergarten. Then the business grew.

With 1,000 employees and $12 million in revenues, it became more difficult to squeeze out family time. The business seemed to dominate her life. Blease tried to reserve evenings and weekends for her kids, but it was still a struggle. At times, she heard the plaintive query of her seven-year-old son—a cry that haunts many parents: "Mommy, do you love your company more than me?" Of course, Blease, like every other entrepreneur, wished that question had never had to be asked. (Envisionet was later sold to Microdyne Outsourcing.)

Source: Meg Lundstrom, "Mommy, Do You Love Your Company More Than Me?" *Business Week,* No. 3660 (December 20, 1999), p. 175.

nations of these. A family member working in the firm but having no ownership interest (sector 6) might favor more generous employment and advancement opportunities for family members than, say, a family member who owns part of the business but works elsewhere (sector 4) or an employee with neither family nor ownership interest (sector 3).

Differing interests can complicate the management process by creating tension and sometimes leading to conflict. Relationships among family members in a business are more sensitive than relationships among unrelated employees. For example, disciplining an employee who consistently arrives late is much more problematic if he or she is also a family member. Or, consider a performance review session between a parent-boss and a child-subordinate. Even with nonfamily employees, performance reviews can be potential minefields. The existence of a family relationship adds emotional overtones that vastly complicate the review process.

Competition Between Business and Family

Which comes first, the family or the business? In theory, at least, most people opt for the family. Few business owners would knowingly allow the business to destroy their family. In practice, however, the resolution of such tensions becomes difficult. For example, despite being motivated by a sense of family responsibility, a parent may nevertheless become so absorbed in the business that he or she spends insufficient time with the children.

Many families are accustomed to making minor sacrifices for the good of the business. In many family businesses, for example, the long hours needed in the business sometimes mean missing dinner with the family or skipping a Little League game. Families usually tolerate some inconveniences and disruptions to family life. Occasionally, however, the clash of business interests and family interests is so

persistent or so severe that entrepreneurs must decide which comes first. Even when the stakes are high, some choose business over family. Others declare that their highest loyalty belongs to the family but deny it with their behavior.

A magazine article arguing that trying to balance work and family is futile drew sharply different reactions from two respondents:[1]

> Favoring Work: *"I know many women who have had to make that tough choice more than once. It's not easy. But . . . given the choice, I realize I would still leap at the chance to build something great, namely, a business."*
>
> Favoring Family: *"I'm a man whose 'terra firma' is his faith and his family, not his business . . .; whose concept of building something great includes the character of his kids and the strength of his marriage . . .; and who, despite the pressures involved in starting a business, still considers work to be a means to an end, not an end in itself. . . . I could write more, but I've got to prepare for tonight's baseball practice: 13 sixth-grade boys are counting on their coach actually being there."*

If the business is to survive, its interests cannot be unduly compromised to satisfy family wishes. To grow, family firms must recognize the need for professional management and the fact that family interests must sometimes be secondary. An example is found in the experience of Ingvar Kamprad, founder of Ikea, a large family business in Sweden.

http://www.ikea.com

Kamprad started Ikea to sell good furniture at reasonable prices to middle-class families. The business has grown into the world's biggest furniture retailer, with stores in 29 countries, but it is still a family business. Although Kamprad's personal fortune is estimated at $3 billion, he retains a simple lifestyle, traveling tourist-class, carrying his own bags, and wearing open-necked denim shirts. One of Kamprad's three sons—Peter, 36; Jonas, 33; and Matthias, 31—would seem the logical choice to succeed him, as each has worked for Ikea. But Kamprad is not one to de-emphasize the abilities needed to lead a business of this type, a business that has grown immensely during its brief existence. "I admire my three sons. They're very clever," says Kamprad, adding candidly, "but I don't think any of them is capable of running the company, at least not yet."[2]

The underlying idea is that family members can contribute to the success of a family business but that membership in the family does not automatically endow them with abilities needed in key positions. The health and survival of a family business require proper attention to both business and family interests, as well as a proper balancing of those interests. Otherwise, in the long run at least, results will be unsatisfactory for both. Decisions on the advancement of individual family members should be made carefully, based on leadership ability and in consultation with the firm's board of directors and/or other knowledgeable outside observers. Such decisions, furthermore, should be made in advance (and revised if necessary) rather than postponed until an emergency requires the hurried appointment of a new manager.

Advantages of a Family Business

Problems associated with family businesses can easily blind young people to the advantages that can be derived from participating in the business. The many benefits

associated with family involvement should be recognized and put to use in recruiting younger members to work in the family firm.

A primary benefit derives from the strength of family relationships. Family members have a unique motivation because the firm is a family firm. Business success is also family success. Studies have shown, for example, that family CEOs possess greater internal motivation than do nonfamily CEOs and have less need to receive additional incentives through compensation.[3] CEOs, and other family members as well, are drawn to the business because of family ties, and they tend to stick with the business through thick and thin. A downturn in business fortunes might cause nonfamily employees to seek greener pastures elsewhere. A son or daughter, however, may be reluctant to leave. The family name, the family welfare, and possibly the family fortune are at stake. In addition, a person's reputation in the family and in the business community may hinge on whether she or he can continue the business that Mom or Grandfather built.

Family members may also sacrifice income to keep a business going. Rather than draw large salaries or high dividends, they are likely to permit resources to remain in the business in order to meet current needs. Many families have postponed the purchase of a new car or new furniture long enough to let a business get started or to get through a period of financial stress.

Some family businesses use the family theme in advertising, to distinguish themselves from their competitors. Such advertising campaigns often attempt to convey the fact that family-owned firms have a strong commitment to the business, high ethical standards, and a personal commitment to serving their customers and the local community.

A Texas funeral home, founded in 1925, strongly emphasizes the family theme in its advertising. Here is a statement from its advertising letter:

Now, for the past 11 years the Funeral Home has been under the direction of Hatch Bailey, great-grandson and grandson of the founders. Yes, this absolutely is a family serving families.

Does it matter that Wilkirson-Hatch-Bailey is Waco's Family-Owned Funeral Home? We think it makes all the difference in the world.[4]

http://www.wilkirsonhatchbailey.com

The letter then details the local roots, commitments, and longevity of this family and this business. It is signed, appropriately, by Hatch Bailey, Roberta Hatch Bailey, A. W. (Bill) Bailey, Jr., Wes Wilkirson Bailey, and Roy Bailey.

Other features of family involvement in a firm can also contribute to superior business performance. Peter Davis, director of the Wharton Applied Research Center at the Wharton School in Philadelphia, suggests these three additional features:[5]

1. ***Preserving the humanity of the workplace.*** A family business can easily demonstrate higher levels of concern for individuals than are found in the typical corporation.
2. ***Focusing on the long run.*** Family managers can take the long-run view more easily than can corporate managers who are being judged on year-to-year results.
3. ***Emphasizing quality.*** Because they have a stake in preserving the reputation of the family, family members are likely to maintain a tradition of providing quality and value to the consumer.

All five advantages are shown graphically in Figure 7-2 on page 172.

FIGURE 7-2

Advantages of a Family Business

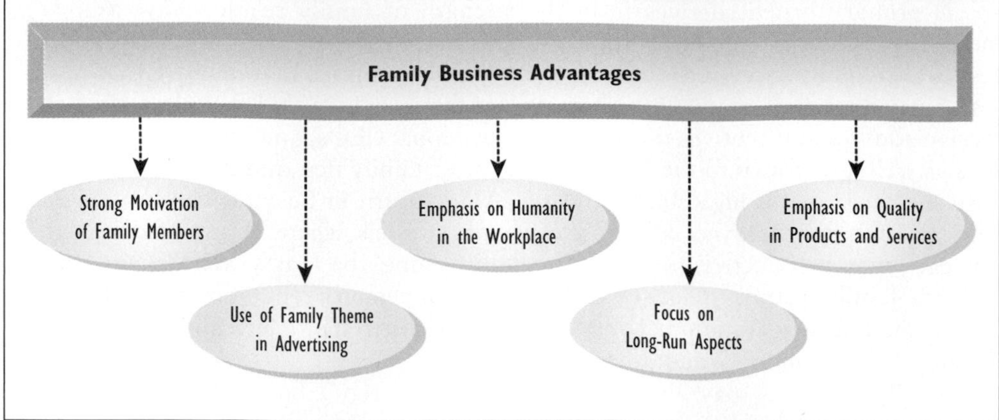

The Culture of a Family Business

2 *Explain the cultural context of a family business.*

organizational culture patterns of behaviors and beliefs that characterize a particular firm

Like other organizations, family firms develop certain ways of doing things and certain priorities that are unique to each particular firm. These special patterns of behaviors and beliefs comprise the firm's **organizational culture.** As new employees and family members enter the business, they pick up these special viewpoints and ways of operating.

The Founder's Imprint on the Culture

The distinctive values that motivate and guide an entrepreneur in the founding of a firm may help create a competitive advantage for the new firm. For example, the founder may cater to customer needs in a special way and make customer service a guiding principle for the firm. The new firm may go far beyond normal industry practices in making sure customers are satisfied, even if it means working overtime or making a delivery on Saturday. Those who work in such an enterprise quickly learn that customers must always be handled with very special care.

In a family business, the founder's core values may become part of both the business culture and the family code—"the things we believe as a family." John Robben, the second-generation CEO of RobToy, Inc., describes the legacy of his father, who founded the firm:

But he left us much more than his confidence and his willingness to take a chance. My father never lied; nor did he ever cheat anyone or take a dollar he didn't honestly earn. He passed these values on, first to me and then, through me, to his grandchildren. It's funny how that worked. He never talked about these things, he just did them.[6]

Robben's last sentence illustrates the way in which cultural values are transmitted. Family members and others in the firm learn what's important and absorb the traditions of the firm simply by functioning as part of the organization.

Ivan Lansberg has discussed a darker possibility—that of a founder's negative imprint on the organizational culture.[7] Successful business founders may develop an unhealthy *narcissism,* or exaggerated sense of self-importance. Such individuals occasionally develop a craving for attention, a fixation with success and public recog-

nition, and a lack of empathy for others. Unfortunately, these attitudes can harm the business by creating a general feeling of superiority and a sense of complacency. While contributions of founders deserve proper acknowledgment, such extremes must be avoided.

Cultural Patterns

The culture of a particular firm includes numerous distinctive beliefs and behaviors. Close examination of those beliefs and behaviors will reveal various cultural patterns that help explain the way in which the firm functions.

W. Gibb Dyer, Jr., a professor at Brigham Young University, has identified a set of cultural patterns that apply to three facets of family firms: the actual business, the family, and the governance (board of directors) of the business.[8] As illustrated in Figure 7-3, the business pattern, the family pattern, and the governance pattern form an overall **cultural configuration** that constitutes a family firm's total culture.

cultural configuration the total culture of a family firm, consisting of the firm's business, family, and governance patterns

An example of a business pattern is a firm's system of beliefs and behaviors concerning the importance of quality. Members of an organization tend to adopt a common viewpoint concerning the extent to which effort, or even sacrifice, should be devoted to customer service and product quality. When the leader of a firm consistently demonstrates a commitment to serving customers, he or she encourages others to appreciate the same values. Through decisions and practices that place a high priority on customer service, therefore, the leader of a family business can build a business pattern based on a strong commitment to producing high-quality goods and services.

In the early stages of a family business, according to Dyer, a common cultural configuration consists of a paternalistic business pattern, a patriarchal family pattern, and a rubber-stamp board of directors (governance pattern). This simply means that family relationships are more important than professional skills, that the founder is the undisputed head of the clan, and that the board automatically supports the founder's decisions.

FIGURE 7-3

Cultural Configuration of a Family Firm

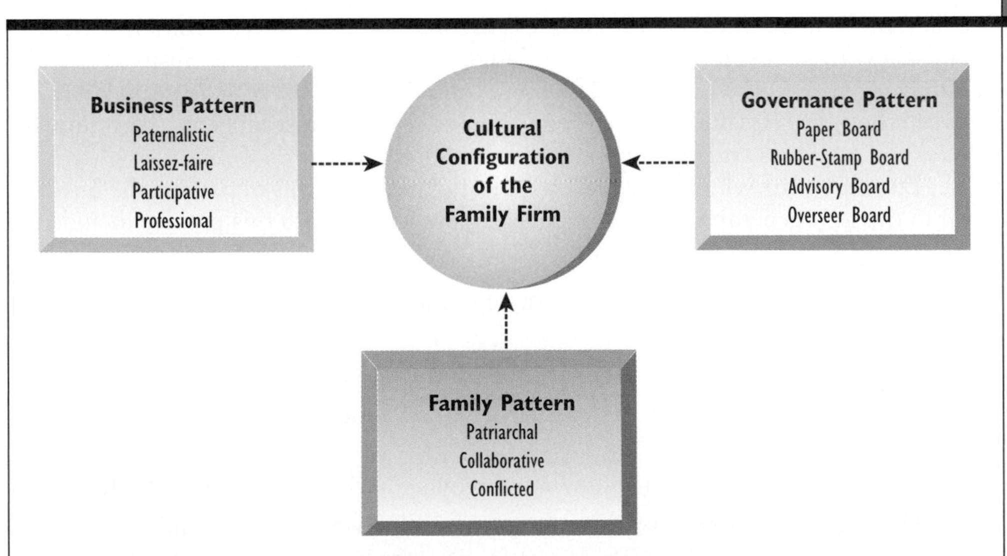

Source: Adapted from W. Gibb Dyer, Jr., *Cultural Change in Family Firms* (San Francisco: Jossey-Bass, 1986), p. 22.

Culture and Leadership Succession

The process of passing the leadership of a family firm from one generation to another is complicated by, and interwoven with, changes in the family business pattern. To appreciate this point, think about the paternalistic/patriarchal cultural configuration, which is quite common in the early days of a family business. Changing conditions may render that cultural configuration ineffective. As a family business grows, it requires a greater measure of professional expertise. Thus, the firm may be pressured to break from the paternalistic mold, which gives first priority to family authority and less attention to professional abilities. Likewise, the aging of the founder and the maturation of the founder's children tend to weaken the patriarchal family culture with its one dominant source of authority—a parent who "always knows best."

Succession may occur, therefore, against the backdrop of a changing organizational culture. Or the change in leadership itself may play a role in introducing or bringing about a break with traditional methods of operation. To some extent, the successor may act as a change agent. For example, a son or daughter with a business degree may replace dated managerial practices with a more up-to-date professional approach.

As you can see, growth of the business and changes in leadership over time will make some cultural change necessary. However, certain values are timeless and should never be changed—the commitment to honesty, for example. While some traditions may embody inefficient business practices and require change, others are basic to the competitive strength and integrity of the firm.

Family Roles and Relationships

Outline the complex roles and relationships involved in a family business.

The overlapping of two institutions—a family and a business—makes the family firm incredibly difficult to manage. This section examines a few of the many possible family roles and relationships that contribute to this managerial complexity.

Mom or Dad, the Founder

A common figure in family businesses is the man or woman who founded the firm and plans to pass it on to a son or a daughter. In most cases, the business and the family have grown simultaneously. Some founders achieve a delicate balance between their business and family responsibilities. Others must diligently plan time for weekend activities and vacations with the children.

Entrepreneurs who have children typically think in terms of passing the business on to the next generation. Parental concerns associated with this process include the following:

- Does my child possess the temperament and ability necessary for business leadership?
- How can I, the founder, motivate my child to take an interest in the business?
- What type of education and experience will be most helpful in preparing my child for leadership?
- What timetable should I follow in employing and promoting my child?
- How can I avoid favoritism in managing and developing my child?
- How can I prevent the business relationship from damaging or destroying the parent–child relationship?

Of all the relationships in a family business, the parent–child relationship has been recognized for generations as the most troublesome. In recent years, the problems inherent in the parent–child relationship have been addressed by counselors, seminars, and numerous books. In spite of this extensive attention, however, the parent–child relationship continues to perplex numerous families involved in family businesses.

Husband–Wife Teams

Some family businesses are owned and managed by husband–wife teams. Their roles vary depending on their backgrounds and expertise. In some cases, the husband serves as general manager and the wife runs the office. In others, the wife functions as operations manager and the husband keeps the books. Whatever the arrangement, both individuals are an integral part of the business.

A potential advantage of the husband–wife team is the opportunity it affords a couple to share more of their lives. For some couples, however, the potential benefits become eclipsed by problems related to the business. Differences of opinion about business matters may carry over into family life. And the energy of both parties may be so dissipated by their work in a struggling company that little zest remains for a strong family life.

Many couples have developed coping patterns that involve both partners in raising the children. Doug and Kimberly Rath, for example, are an entrepreneurial couple who founded Talent Plus, a human resources firm in Lincoln, Nebraska.[9] When Kim was traveling on business, Doug faxed her their daughter's grades; after her son scored eight goals in one soccer game, Doug handed the boy his cellular phone as he walked off the field so that he could share the moment with Mom.

http://www.talentplus.com

Sons and Daughters

Should sons and daughters be groomed for the family business, or should they pursue careers of their own choosing? In the entrepreneurial family, the natural tendency is to think in terms of a family business career and to push a child, either openly or subtly, in that direction. Little thought may be given to the basic issues involved, which include the child's talent, aptitude, and temperament. The child may be a chip off the old block but may also be an individual with different talents and aspirations. He or she may prefer music or medicine to the world of business and may fit the business mold very poorly. It is also possible that the abilities of the son or daughter may simply be insufficient for a leadership role. Or, a child's talents may be underestimated by parents simply because there has been little opportunity for the child to develop or demonstrate those talents.

Another issue is personal freedom. Today's society values the right of the individual to choose his or her own career and way of life. If this value is embraced by a son or daughter, that child must be granted the freedom to select a career of his or her own choosing.

A son or daughter may feel a need to go outside the family business, for a time at least, to prove that "I can make it on my own." To build self-esteem, he or she may wish to operate independently of the family. Entering the family business immediately after graduation may seem stifling, as the child continues to "feel like a little kid with Dad telling me what to do."

If the family business is profitable, it does provide rewards. A son or daughter may be well advised to give serious consideration to accepting such an opportunity.

If the business relationship is to be satisfactory, however, family pressure must be minimized. Both parties must recognize the choice as a business decision as well as a family decision—and as a decision that may be reversed.

Sibling Cooperation, Sibling Rivalry

In families with a number of children, two or more may become involved in the family business. This depends, of course, on the interests of the individual children. In some cases, parents feel fortunate if even one child elects to stay with the family firm. Nevertheless, it is not unusual for several siblings to take positions within the firm. Even those who do not work in the business may be more than casual observers on the sidelines because of their stake as heirs or partial owners.

At best, siblings work as a smoothly functioning team, each contributing services according to his or her respective abilities. Just as some families experience excellent cooperation and unity in their family relationships, some family businesses benefit from effective collaboration among brothers and sisters.

http://www.peterpan-bus.com

However, just as there are sometimes squabbles within a family, there can also be sibling rivalry within a family business. Business issues tend to generate competition, and this affects family, as well as nonfamily, members. Siblings, for example, may disagree about business policy or about their respective roles in the business. Rivalry quickly became a problem among the three siblings involved in Peter Pan Bus Lines in Springfield, Massachusetts.[10] As Paul and Mary (pictured) tried to work with Peter Jr. at the bus line's corporate headquarters, the three third-generation family members began undercutting each other. The tension between Peter Jr. and Paul was particularly intense, and lower-level employees, when asked in employee surveys about company problems, put "company squabbles" at the top of the list. Eventually, the father split the ownership of the bus line and certain real estate holdings in such a way that the siblings could operate more independently of each other. The new arrangement did not bring the children closer to each other but did eliminate a lot of friction.

In-Laws In and Out of the Business

As sons and daughters marry, daughters-in-law and sons-in-law become significant actors in the family business drama. Some in-laws become directly involved by accepting positions in the family firm. If a son or daughter is also employed in the firm, rivalry and conflict may develop. For example, family members may disagree about how rewards for performance should compare for an in-law and a son or daughter.

For a time, effective collaboration may be achieved by assigning family members to different branches or roles within the company. Eventually, competition for top leadership will force decisions that distinguish among children and in-laws em-

IN THE TRENCHES ENTREPRENEURSHIP TODAY

A MIXTURE OF FAMILY MEMBERS

Widely varying combinations of family members are found in family firms. Together, Susan and David Hurst founded The Market at North Shore, a gourmet food and catering shop in Atlantic Beach, Florida.

Thus, the business started with wife and husband entrepreneurs. Then they added Susan's mother, 64, who makes desserts, and David's mother, 62, who is the office manager. In some firms, such a mixture of family members could prove explosive and detrimental to the business. In this case, the combination works well and makes for a healthy business.

"Customers are amazed I can work with my husband, my mother and my mother-in-law and that we all still love each other," says Susan. "They took care of us for so many years, it's time to take care of them."

Source: Stephanie Armour, "More Kids Putting Parents on Payroll," *USA Today,* April 29, 1998, p. 1B.

ployed in the business. Being fair and retaining family loyalty become more difficult as the number of family employees increases.

Sons, daughters, sons-in-law, and daughters-in-law who are on the sidelines are also participants with an important stake in the business. For example, if a daughter is married to someone on the family payroll, she will see a decision by a parent affecting her husband as both a family decision and a business decision. Giving the nod to a son-in-law thus becomes more than merely promoting another employee in a business.

The Entrepreneur's Spouse

One of the most critical roles in the family business drama is that of the entrepreneur's spouse. Traditionally, this role has been fulfilled by the male entrepreneur's wife and the mother of his children. However, more women are becoming entrepreneurs, and many husbands have now assumed the role of entrepreneur's spouse.

In order for the spouse to play a supporting role in the entrepreneur's career, there must be communication between the spouse and the entrepreneur and the spouse must be a good listener. The spouse needs to hear what's going on in the business; otherwise, she or he feels detached and must compete for attention. The spouse can offer understanding and act as a sounding board for the entrepreneur only if they communicate on matters of obvious importance to them both individually and as a family.

It is easy for the spouse to function as worrier for the family business. This is particularly true if there is insufficient communication about business matters. One spouse expressed her feelings in the following way:

I've told my husband that I have an active imagination—very active. If he doesn't tell me what's going on in the business, well, then I'm going to imagine what's going on and blow it all out of proportion. When things are looking dark, I'd rather know the worst than know nothing.[11]

As parent, the spouse helps prepare the children for possible careers in the family business. The spouse may also serve as mediator in business relationships

between the entrepreneur and the children. One wife's comments to her husband, John, and son Terry illustrate the nature of this function:

- "John, don't you think that Terry may have worked long enough as a stock-person in the warehouse?"
- "Terry, your father is going to be very disappointed if you don't come back to the business after your graduation."
- "John, do you really think it is fair to move Stanley into that new office? After all, Terry is older and has been working a year longer."
- "Terry, what did you say to your father today that upset him?"

Ideally, the entrepreneur and his or her spouse form a team committed to the success of both the family and the family business. Such teamwork does not occur automatically—it requires a collaborative effort by both parties to the marriage.

Professional Management of the Family Firm

4

Identify management practices that enable a family business to function effectively.

The complexity of relationships in family firms requires enlightened management. To a considerable extent, this just means good professional management. However, certain techniques are particularly useful in dealing with the problems inherent in the family firm.

The Need for Good Management

Good management is necessary for the success of any business, and the family firm is no exception. Significant deviations for family reasons from what might be called good management practices, therefore, only serve to weaken the firm. Such a course of action runs counter to the interests of both the firm and the family.

A number of "best practices" have been proposed by John L. Ward, a noted specialist in family business and a distinguished professor at Loyola University Chicago.[12] Some of these practices are as follows:

1. Stimulate new thinking and fresh strategic insights.
2. Attract and retain excellent nonfamily managers.
3. Create a flexible, innovative organization.
4. Create and conserve capital.
5. Prepare successors for leadership.
6. Exploit the unique advantages of family ownership.

The family firm is a business—a competitive business. Observing these and other practices of good management will help the business thrive and permit the family to function as a family. Disregarding them will pose a threat to the business and impose strains on family relationships.

Nonfamily Employees in a Family Firm

Those employees who are not family members are still affected by family considerations. In some cases, their opportunities for promotion are lessened by the presence of family members who seem to have the inside track. Few parents will promote an outsider over a competent daughter or son who is being groomed for future leader-

ship. The potential for advancement of nonfamily employees, therefore, may be limited, and they may experience a sense of unfairness and frustration.

Consider the case of a young business executive who worked for a family business that operated a chain of restaurants. When hired, he had negotiated a contract that gave him a specified percentage of the business based on performance. Under this arrangement, he was doing extremely well financially—until the owner called on him to say "I am here to buy you out." When the young man asked why, the owner replied, "You are doing too well, and your last name is not the same as mine!"

The extent of limitations on nonfamily employees depends on the number of family members active in the business and the number of managerial or professional positions in the business to which nonfamily employees might aspire. It also depends on the extent to which the owner demands competence in management and maintains an atmosphere of fairness in supervision. To avoid future problems, the owner should make clear, when hiring nonfamily employees, the extent of opportunities available and identify the positions, if any, that are reserved for family members.

Those outside the family may also be caught in the crossfire between family members who are competing with each other. It is difficult for outsiders to maintain strict neutrality in family feuds. If a nonfamily employee is perceived as siding with one of those involved in the feud, he or she may lose the support of other family members. Hard-working employees often feel that they deserve hazard pay for working in a firm plagued by family conflict.

Family Retreats

Some families hold retreats in order to review family business concerns. A **family retreat** is a meeting of family members, usually at a remote location, to discuss family business matters. An attempt is made to create an informal atmosphere. Nancy Upton, founder of the Institute for Family Business at Baylor University, has conducted many family retreats. She describes the general purpose and format of such retreats as follows:

family retreat
a gathering of family members, usually at a remote location, to discuss family business matters

The purpose of the retreat is to provide a forum for introspection, problem solving and policy making. For some participants this will be their first opportunity to talk about their concerns in a nonconfrontational atmosphere. It is also a time to celebrate the family and enhance its inner strength.

A retreat usually lasts two days and is held far enough away so you won't be disturbed or tempted to go to the office. Every member of the family, including in-laws, should be invited.[13]

The prospect of sitting down together to discuss family business matters may seem threatening to some family members. As a result, some families avoid extensive communication, fearing that it will stir up trouble. They assume that making decisions quietly or secretly will preserve harmony. Unfortunately, such an approach often conceals serious differences that become increasingly troublesome. Family retreats are designed to open lines of communication and to bring about understanding and agreement on family business issues.

Initiating discussion can be difficult, so family leaders often invite an outside expert or facilitator to lead early sessions. The facilitator can help develop an agenda and establish ground rules for discussion. While chairing early sessions, the moderator can establish a positive tone that emphasizes family achievements and encourages rational consideration of sensitive issues. If family members can develop an

atmosphere of neutrality, however, they may be able to chair the sessions without using an outsider.

Families that hold retreats often speak of the joy of sharing family values and stories of past family experiences. Thus, retreats can strengthen the family as well as the business.

Family Councils

family council
an organized group of family members who gather periodically to discuss family-related business issues

A family retreat could pave the way for creation of a family council, in which family members meet to discuss values, policies, and direction for the future. A **family council** functions as the organizational and strategic planning arm of a family. It provides a forum for the ongoing process of listening to the ideas of all members and discovering what they believe in and want from the business. A family council formalizes the participation of the family in the business to a greater extent than does the family retreat. It can also be a focal point for planning the future of individual family members, the family as a whole, and the business, as well as how each relates to the other.

A council should be a formal organization that holds regular meetings, keeps minutes, and makes suggestions to the firm's board of directors. Experts recommend that it be open to all interested family members and spouses of all generations. During the first several meetings, an acceptable mission statement is usually generated, as well as a family creed.

Family businesses that have such councils find them useful for developing family harmony. The meetings are often fun and informative and may include speakers who discuss items of interest. Time is often set aside for sharing achievements, milestones, and family history. The younger generation is encouraged to participate because much of the process is designed to increase their understanding of family traditions and business interests and to prepare them for working effectively in the business.

As with family retreats, an outside facilitator may be useful in getting a council organized and helping with initial meetings. Subsequently, the organization and leadership of meetings can rotate among family members.

The Process of Leadership Succession

Describe the process of managerial succession in a family business.

The task of preparing family members for careers and, ultimately, leadership within the business is difficult and sometimes frustrating. Professional and managerial requirements tend to become intertwined with family feelings and interests. This section looks at the career development and leadership transfer processes and some of the difficulties associated with them.

Available Family Talent

A stream can rise no higher than its source, and the family firm can be no more brilliant than its leader. The business is dependent, therefore, on the quality of leadership talent provided. If the available talent is not sufficient, the owner must bring in outside leadership or supplement family talent to avoid a decline under the leadership of second- or third-generation family members.

The question of competency is both a critical and a delicate issue. With experience, individuals can improve their abilities; younger people should not be judged

too harshly too early. Furthermore, potential successors may be held back by the reluctance of a parent-owner to delegate realistically to them.

A family firm need not accept the existing level of family talent as an unchangeable given. Instead, the business may offer various types of developmental programs to teach younger family members and thereby improve their skills. Some businesses, for example, include mentoring as a part of such programs.[14] **Mentoring** is the process by which a senior person in the firm guides and supports the work, progress, and professional relationships of a new or less-experienced employee.

mentoring
guiding and supporting the work and development of a new or less-experienced organization member

Perhaps the fairest and most practical approach is to recognize the right of family members to prove themselves. A period of development and testing may occur either in the family business or, preferably, in another organization. If children show themselves to be capable, they earn the right to increased leadership responsibility. If potential successors are found, through a process of fair assessment, to have inadequate leadership abilities, preservation of the family business and the welfare of family members demand that they be passed over for promotion. The appointment of competent outsiders to these jobs, if necessary, increases the value of the firm for all family members who have an ownership interest in it.

Stages in the Process of Succession

Sons or daughters do not typically assume leadership of a family firm at a particular moment in time. Instead, a long, drawn-out process of preparation and transition is customary—a process that extends over years and often decades. Figure 7-4 on page 182 portrays this process as a series of **stages in succession.**[15]

stages in succession
phases in the process of transferring leadership from parent to child in a family business

PREBUSINESS STAGE In Stage I, a potential successor becomes acquainted with the business as a part of growing up. The young child accompanies a parent to the office, store, or warehouse or plays with equipment related to the business. There is no formal planning for the child's preparation for entering the business in this early stage. It simply forms a foundation for the more deliberate stages of the process that occur in later years.

INTRODUCTORY STAGE Stage II also includes experiences that occur before the successor is old enough to begin part-time work in the family business. It differs from Stage I in that family members deliberately introduce the child to certain people associated directly or indirectly with the firm and to other aspects of the business. In an industrial equipment dealership, for example, a parent might let the child ride on a bulldozer, explain the difference between a front loader and a backhoe, or introduce the child to the firm's banker.

INTRODUCTORY FUNCTIONAL STAGE In Stage III, the son or daughter begins to function as a part-time employee, often during vacations or after school. At this stage, the son or daughter develops an acquaintance with some of the key individuals employed in the firm. Such work often begins in the warehouse, office, or production department and may involve assignments in various functional areas as time goes on. The introductory functional stage includes the child's formal education as well as experience gained in other organizations.

FUNCTIONAL STAGE Stage IV begins when the potential successor enters full-time employment, typically following the completion of his or her formal education.

FIGURE 7-4

A Model of Succession in a Family Business

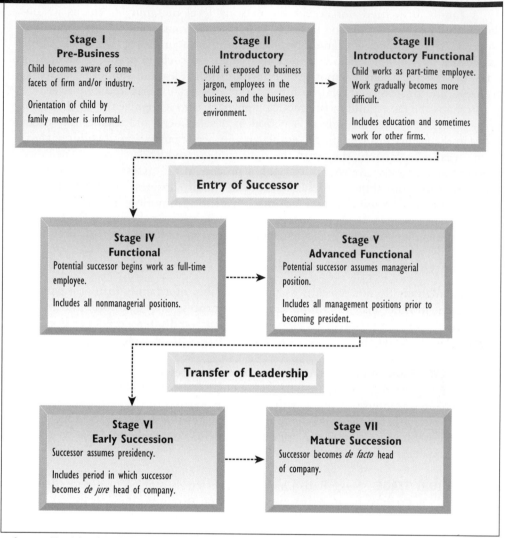

Source: Adapted from Justin G. Longenecker and John E. Schoen, "Management Succession in the Family Business," *Journal of Small Business Management,* Vol. 16 (July 1978), pp. 1–6.

Prior to moving into a management position, the son or daughter may work as an accountant, a salesperson, or an inventory clerk, possibly gaining experience in a number of such positions.

ADVANCED FUNCTIONAL STAGE As the potential successor assumes supervisory duties, he or she enters the advanced functional stage, or Stage V. The management positions at this stage involve directing the work of others but not managing the entire firm.

EARLY SUCCESSION STAGE In Stage VI, the son or daughter is named president or general manager of the business. As *de jure* head of the business, he or she presumably exercises overall direction, but a parent is still in the background. The leader-

IN THE TRENCHES UTILIZING NEW TECHNOLOGY

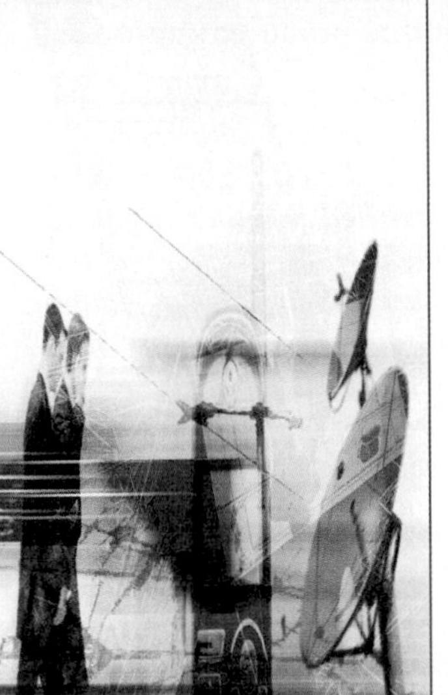

NEW GENERATION AND NEW TECHNOLOGY

Family businesses may become mired in the past and fail to keep up with changing technology and emerging markets. At times, a leadership change from one generation to another can rescue a business from such a fate by drawing on the expertise of younger family members.

In 1983, Tom Jennison opened Jennison Manufacturing Corporation, a gritty, small tool-and-die operation in Carnegie, Pennsylvania, a faded steel town. Two of its basic, simple products were parts for gas masks and injection molds for making toilet mechanisms.

As Tom began to computerize the business in 1988, he ran into major problems and called on son Mike, a junior at Penn State University. Mike came home to help his father get the system working smoothly.

With a finance degree, excellent computer skills, and the ambition to develop a high-tech product, Mike joined the firm after graduation. He began developing a home-wiring control box—a device that would serve as a command center for things like home computer networks, stereo systems, telephone lines, and cable TV. Even though Tom didn't understand the product, he invested $200,000 in seed capital and later helped raise $1 million in expansion capital.

Tom and Mike are building a new facility and expect to employ 120 people in producing the new product. The rest of the business will continue to employ about 60 people. In this case, the process of transferring leadership to a second generation involves not only training a potential successor but also moving the business into new areas of technology and new markets.

Source: Timothy Aeppel, "A Father and Son Meld New Economy and Old, and the Business Flows," *The Wall Street Journal,* May 24, 2000, pp. A1, A16.

ship role does not transfer as easily or absolutely as the leadership title does. The successor has not necessarily mastered the complexities of the role, and the predecessor may be reluctant to give up all decision making.

MATURE SUCCESSION STAGE Stage VII is reached when the transition process is complete. The successor is leader in fact as well as in name. In some cases, this does not occur until the predecessor dies. In the best case scenario, Stage VII begins two or three years after the successor assumes the leadership title.

Reluctant Parents and Ambitious Children

When the founder of a business is preparing her or his child to take over the firm, the founder's attachment to the business must not be underestimated. Not only is a father, for example, tied to the firm financially—it is probably his primary, if not his only, major investment—but he is also tied to it emotionally. The business is his "baby," and he is understandably reluctant to entrust its future to one whom he sees as immature and unproven. Unfortunately, parents often have a way of seeing their children as immature long after their years of adolescence.

The child may be ambitious, well educated, and insightful regarding the business. His or her tendency to push ahead—to try something new—often conflicts

with the father's caution. As a result, the child may see the father as excessively conservative, stubborn, and unwilling to change.

A study examined 18 family-owned businesses in which daughters worked as managers with their fathers. Interviews with family members produced this overall picture of the daughters' positions:

In 90 percent of the cases, the daughters reported having to contend with carryover, conflict, and ambiguity in their business roles in the firm and as daughters. While the majority of the women interviewed had previously worked in other organizations and had developed their identities as businesswomen, they discovered that when they joined the family business they were torn between their roles as daughter and their business roles. They found their relationships with the boss transformed, since the boss was not only the boss, but the father as well. These daughters reported that they often found themselves reduced to the role of "daddy's little girl" (and, in a few cases, "mommy's little girl"), in spite of their best intentions.[16]

At the root of many such difficulties is a lack of understanding between parent and child. They work together without a map showing where they are going. Children in the business, and also their spouses, may have expectations about progress that, in terms of the founder's thinking, are totally unrealistic. The successor tends to sense such problems much more acutely than does his or her parent. But many of the problems could be avoided if a full discussion of the development process took place early in the process.

Transfer of Ownership

transfer of ownership distribution of ownership of the family business to the next generation

A final and often complex step in the traditional succession process in the family firm is the **transfer of ownership.** Recall the opening spotlight of this chapter, which described the transfer of both leadership and ownership by a founding entrepreneur to her two daughters. Questions of inheritance affect not only the leadership successor but also other family members having no involvement in the business. In distributing their estate, parent-owners typically wish to treat all their children fairly, both those involved in the business and those on the outside.

One of the most difficult decisions is determining the future ownership of the business. If there are several children, for example, should they all receive equal shares? On the surface, this seems to be the fairest approach. However, such an arrangement may play havoc with the future functioning of the business. Suppose that each of five children receives a 20 percent ownership share, even though only one of them is active in the business. The child active in the business—the leadership successor—becomes a minority stockholder completely at the mercy of relatives on the outside.

A parent might attempt to resolve such a dilemma by changing the ownership structure of the firm. Those children active in the firm's management, for example, might be given common (voting) stock and others given preferred (nonvoting) stock. However, this is still troublesome because of the relative weaknesses of various ownership securities.

Tax considerations are relevant, of course, and they tend to favor gradual transfer of ownership to all heirs. As noted, however, transfer of equal ownership shares to all heirs may be inconsistent with the future efficient operation of the business.

Furthermore, tax advantages should not be allowed to blind one to possible adverse effects on management.

Ideally, the founder has been able to arrange his or her personal holdings to create wealth outside the business as well as within it. In that case, he or she may bequeath comparable shares to all heirs while allowing business control to remain with the child or children active in the business. Planning and discussing the transfer of ownership is not easy, but such action is recommended. Over a period of time, the owner must reflect seriously on family talents and interests as they relate to the future of the firm. The plan for transfer of ownership can then be firmed up and modified as necessary when it is discussed with the children or other potential heirs. In discussing exit strategies in Chapter 14, we explain a variety of possible financial arrangements in the transfer of ownership.

LOOKING BACK

1 Discuss the factors that make a family business unique.

- Family members have a special involvement in a family business.
- Business interests (production and profitability) overlap family interests (care and nurturing) in a family business.
- Entrepreneurs face difficult choices in reconciling the competing demands of business and family.
- The advantages of a family business include the strong commitment of family members to the success of the firm, the use of a family theme in advertising, an emphasis on humanity in the workplace, a focus on long-term goals, and an emphasis on product/service quality.

2 Explain the cultural context of a family business.

- Special patterns of beliefs and behaviors constitute the organizational culture of a family business.
- The founder often leaves a deep imprint on the culture of a family firm.
- The cultural configuration is formed by the business pattern, family pattern, and governance (or board-of-directors) pattern.
- Changes in culture often occur as leadership passes from one generation to the next.

3 Outline the complex family roles and relationships involved in a family business.

- A primary and sensitive relationship is that between founder and son or daughter.
- Some couples in business together find their marriage relationship strengthened, while others find it weakened.
- Sons, daughters, in-laws, and other relatives may either enjoy cooperation or engage in family quarrels as they work together in a family business.
- In-laws play a crucial role in the family business, either as direct participants or as sideline observers.
- The role of the founder's spouse is especially important, as he or she often serves as a mediator in family disputes and helps prepare the children for possible careers in the family business.

4 Identify management practices that enable a family business to function effectively.

- Good management practices are as important as good family relationships in the successful functioning of a family business.
- Family members should be treated fairly and consistently, in accordance with their abilities and performance.
- Motivation of nonfamily employees can be enhanced by open communication and fairness.
- Family retreats bring all family members together to discuss business and family matters.
- Family councils provide a formal framework for the family's ongoing discussion of family and business issues.

5 Describe the process of managerial succession in a family business.

- The quality of leadership talent available in the family determines the extent to which outside managers are needed.
- Succession is a long-term process starting early in the successor's life.

- The succession process begins with the prebusiness stage and includes part-time jobs and full-time managerial work.
- Tension often arises between the founder and the potential successor as the latter gains experience.
- Transfer of ownership involves issues of fairness, taxes, and managerial control.
- Planning and discussing the transfer of ownership is sometimes difficult but usually desirable.

Key Terms

family business, p. 167
organizational culture, p. 172
cultural configuration, p. 173
family retreat, p. 179
family council, p. 180
mentoring, p. 181
stages in succession, p. 181
transfer of ownership, p. 184

Discussion Questions

1. How are family businesses and other types of small businesses similar or different? Explain what makes a business a family business.
2. Suppose that you, as founder of a business, have a vacant sales manager position. You realize that sales may suffer somewhat if you promote your son from sales representative to sales manager. However, you would like to see your son make some progress and earn a higher salary to support his wife and young daughter. How would you go about making this decision? Would you promote your son?
3. What benefits result from family involvement in a business?
4. Why does a first-generation family business tend to have a paternalistic business pattern and a patriarchal family pattern?
5. As a recent graduate in business administration, you are headed for a job in the family business. As a result of your education, you have become aware of some outdated business practices in the family firm. In spite of them, the business is showing a good return on investment. Should you rock the boat? How should you proceed in correcting what you see as obsolete traditions?
6. Describe a founder–son or founder–daughter relationship in a family business with which you are familiar. What strengths or weaknesses are evident in that business relationship?
7. Should a son or daughter feel an obligation to carry on a family business? What is the source of such a feeling?
8. Assume that you are an ambitious, nonfamily manager in a family firm and that one of your peers is the son or daughter of the founder. What, if anything, would keep you interested in pursuing a career with this company?
9. Identify and describe the stages outlined in the model of succession shown in Figure 7-4.
10. In making decisions about transferring ownership of a family business from one generation to another, how much emphasis should be placed on estate tax laws and other concerns that go beyond the family? Why?

YOU MAKE THE CALL

SITUATION 1

The three Dorsett brothers are barely speaking to each other. "Phone for you" is about all they have to say.

It hasn't always been like this. For more than 30 years, Tom, Harry, and Bob Dorsett have run the successful manufacturing business founded by their father. For most of that time, they have gotten along rather well. They've had their differences and arguments, but important decisions were thrashed out until a consensus was reached.

Each brother has two children in the business. Tom's oldest son manages the plant, Harry's oldest daughter keeps the books, and Bob's oldest son is an outside salesman. The younger children are learning the ropes in lower-level positions. The problem? Compensation. Each brother feels that his own children are underpaid and that some of his nieces and nephews are overpaid. After violent arguments, the Dorsett brothers just quit talking while each continues to smolder.

The six younger-generation cousins are still on speaking terms, however. Despite the differences that exist among them, they manage to get along with one another. They range in age from 41 down to 25.

The business is in a slump but not yet in danger. Because the brothers aren't talking, important business decisions are being postponed.

The family is stuck. What can be done?

Source: "Anger over Money Silences Brothers," *Nation's Business*, Vol. 78, No. 10 (October 1990), p. 62.

Question 1 Why do you think the cousins get along better than their fathers do?

Question 2 How might this conflict over compensation be resolved?

SITUATION 2

Harrison Stevens, second-generation president of a family-owned heating and air conditioning business, was concerned about his 19-year-old son, Barry, who worked as a full-time employee in the firm. Although Barry had made it through high school, he had not distinguished himself as a student or shown interest in further education. He was somewhat indifferent in his attitude toward his work, although he did reasonably—or at least minimally—satisfactory work. His father saw Barry as immature and more interested in riding motorcycles than in building a business.

Stevens wanted to provide his son with an opportunity for personal development. As he saw it, the process should begin with learning to work hard. If Barry liked the work and showed promise, he might eventually be groomed to take over the business. His father also held a faint hope that hard work might eventually inspire him to get a college education.

In trying to achieve these goals, Stevens sensed two problems. The first problem was that Barry obviously lacked proper motivation. The second problem related to his supervision. Supervisors seemed reluctant to be exacting in their demands on Barry. Possibly because they feared antagonizing the boss by being too hard on his son, they allowed Barry to get by with marginal performance.

Question 1 In view of Barry's shortcomings, should Harrison Stevens seriously consider him as a potential successor?

Question 2 How could Barry be motivated? Can Stevens do anything more to improve the situation, or does the responsibility lie with Barry?

Question 3 How could the quality of Barry's supervision be improved to make his work experience more productive?

SITUATION 3

Rob, 37, and Julie, 36, are siblings in their family's $15 million medical products firm. Both are capable leaders and have experienced success in their respective areas of responsibility. Compared to Julie, Rob is more introverted, a more thorough planner, and much better on detail and follow through. In contrast, Julie is more creative, more extroverted, and stronger in interpersonal skills. Since childhood, they have been rather competitive in their relationships. Their 62-year-old father is contemplating retirement and considering the possibility of co-leadership, with each child eventually holding a 50-percent ownership interest.

Question 1 If you were to choose one leader for the firm, based on the brief description above, which sibling would you recommend? Why?

Question 2 What are the strengths and/or weaknesses of the co-leadership idea? Would you favor it or reject it?

Question 3 As the father, how could you secure practical advice to help you in this decision?

Experiential Exercises

1. Interview a college student who has grown up in a family business about the ways he or she has been trained or educated, both formally and informally, for entry into the business. Prepare a brief report, relating your findings to the stages in succession shown in Figure 7-4.
2. Interview another college student who has grown up in a family business about parental attitudes toward his or her possible entry into the business. Submit a one-page report describing the extent of pressure on the student to enter the family business and the direct or indirect ways in which family expectations have been communicated.
3. Identify a family business and prepare a brief report on its history, including its founding, family involvement, and any leadership changes that have occurred.
4. Read and report on a biography or history book pertaining to a family in business or a family business.

Exploring the Web

1. *Family Business* magazine, which can be found at **http://www.familybusinessmagazine.com**, addresses issues and concerns affecting owners and managers of family companies.
   a. Access the link to FBs in the News. As you look through the list, note the proportion of the businesses that are small businesses. What large companies are you surprised to find are family businesses?
   b. From the main page, access Tools and Tests, and follow the link to take the quiz "Are you a FAMILY business or a family BUSINESS?" Even if you are not part of a family business, take the quiz to find out what your preferences are. Report the results.
   c. Follow the links to the Forum, and list the topics of discussion. Which topic has the most postings?
   d. Read the case study at the bottom of the Forum page. Answer the questions and send the answers by e-mail to your instructor (only registered users may post messages on the Forum).
2. Access the Web site of Family Firm Institute (FFI) at **http://www.ffi.org**.
   a. Follow the link to Facts and Figures. Compare the statistics on the relative importance of family businesses in the United States and the United Kingdom. Which nation's economy feels the greatest impact from family businesses?
   b. What is the main publication of FFI? How often is it published?
   c. What benefits will you receive if you become a member of FFI?

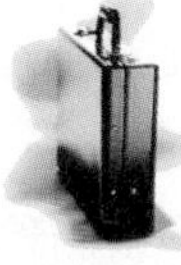

Case 7

THE BROWN FAMILY BUSINESS (p. 656)

This case presents the philosophy, criteria, and procedures adopted by one family to regulate work opportunities for family members in the family business.

Alternative Cases for Chapter 7:

Case 18, "Central Engineering," p. 688
Case 19, "Gibson Mortuary," p. 691
Case 21, "AFCO," p. 695

part

4

The New Venture Business Plan

chapter

8

The Role of the Business Plan

In the Spotlight

Application Technologies

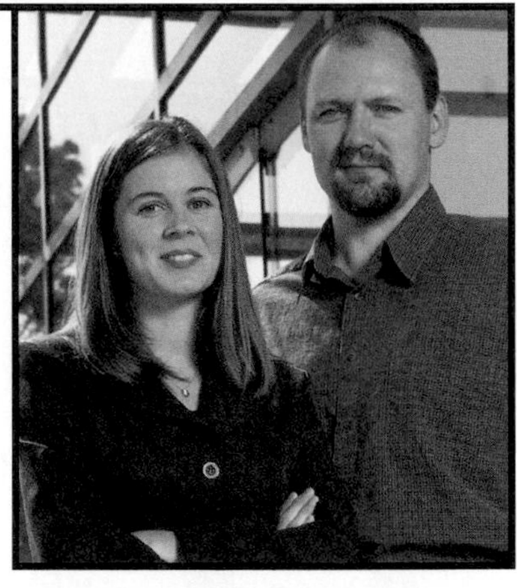

On a warm evening in June, Johann and Emmarance Verheem took a walk on the beach in the San Diego suburb of Del Mar. They conversed in their native Afrikaans, trying to decide whether Johann should leave his job at Guthy-Renker and start his own company.

The idea of risking his livelihood for a startup play made them quite apprehensive. On the other hand, if he didn't take the plunge now, when would he? Alex De Noble, director of academic programs at San Diego State University's Entrepreneurial Management Center and Verheem's favorite management professor, had called and urged Verheem to make up his mind.

The next morning, Verheem gave De Noble the news. He was going for it. De Noble was ecstatic. "All right!" he cheered.

Verheem's venture, Application Technologies (AT), is a real "not-com"—the company develops and licenses new packaging products. In the beginning, however, the focus was to be on a simple concept called an Appli-K pouch, which Verheem had developed more than a year earlier, as part of his M.B.A. studies.

In his job at Guthy-Renker, Verheem had scouted for products that would sell well on television. That meant meeting inventors with all kinds of crazy ideas. One such inventor was Kurt Koptis. In July 1998, Koptis called Verheem and said, "I have a really cool product." After their discussion, Verheem told Koptis he would develop the concept as a project for a business plan class he was taking in the fall—a class taught by De Noble. That way, they could do some research on

the market potential and get good advice from other students and professors.

The grade for the class was based on teamwork, and Verheem already knew the person he wanted to work with—Natasha King. Verheem and King, both excellent students accustomed to earning straight A's, pulled an all-nighter and finished their business plan. De Noble gave it a B–. It was the lowest grade either student had ever received. Of course, now that De Noble is a board member of and an equity participant in AT, King won't let him live it down. "I'll never forget it," she says.

Apparently, neither will De Noble. "I'm going to go down like the professor who gave Fred Smith a C," he says, recalling the infamously bad reception that Smith's plan for FedEx got in business school. Still, he defends his decision. "The grade was for the plan itself, not for the business," he says. "The plan did not articulate the vision well. It needed work."

De Noble loved the vision, if not the plan, and he proved it. He chose Verheem and King to present the plan in one student business plan competition after another. Verheem and King kept shifting their model according to input they got from venture capitalists and other experts who served as contest judges. In the end, though, they returned to their original concept. "The B-minus plan," says King, now marketing manager for AT. "It's back." ◆

Source: Adapted from Michael Warshaw, "The Start-Up Diaries: Plan B-Minus," *Inc.*, Vol. 22, No. 1 (January 2000), pp. 56–58.

LOOKING AHEAD

After studying this chapter, you should be able to

1. *Answer the question "What is a business plan?"*
2. *Explain the need for a business plan from the perspectives of both internal and external users.*
3. *Describe what determines how much planning an entrepreneur and a management team are likely to do.*
4. *List practical suggestions to follow in writing a business plan and outline the key sections of a business plan.*
5. *Identify available sources of assistance in preparing a business plan.*

Think back to the last term paper you wrote. Did you experience the frustration of not knowing what to write about and difficulty in getting started? The all-too-frequent result of such frustration and difficulty is procrastination. Many times, students begin the writing process only when they are faced with an impending deadline.

In some ways, preparing a business plan is similar to writing a term paper. Getting started may be agonizing, and you may find it difficult to decide what to say, especially if you lack experience and aren't sure what issues need to be addressed. Even when you know the issues, you may have difficulty expressing your goals and the strategies you plan to use for achieving those goals. But just as you learn from writing a term paper, you increase your understanding of a business opportunity as

you write your business plan. Carried out correctly, the process of preparing the plan will clarify what you want to accomplish in a new business and, equally important, what factors might determine your success or failure in the venture.

If you have felt pride on completing a term paper, you will feel exhilaration after writing an effective business plan, in anticipation of what may prove to be the most exciting—and possibly terrifying—experience of your professional career. The business plan—its preparation, content, and organization—will serve as the thread that weaves a common purpose through Chapters 8–14.

What Is a Business Plan?

Answer the question "What is a business plan?"

business plan
a document that sets out the basic idea underlying a business and related startup considerations

A **business plan** is a written document that sets out the basic idea underlying a business and related startup considerations. For the entrepreneur starting a new venture, a business plan has four basic objectives. First, it identifies the nature and the context of the business opportunity—why does such an opportunity exist? Second, it presents the approach the entrepreneur plans to take to exploit the opportunity. Third, it identifies the factors that will most likely determine whether the venture will be successful. Finally, it serves as a tool for raising financial capital.

A business plan can be viewed as an entrepreneur's game plan; it crystallizes the dreams and hopes that motivated the entrepreneur to attempt to start the business. The business plan should lay out your basic idea for the venture, describe where you are now, indicate where you want to go, and outline how you propose to get there. Above all, your business plan should explain the key variables for success or failure, thereby helping you prepare for different situations that may occur by thinking about what could go right and what could go wrong. In fact, this is a business plan's most important function. While your business plan will represent your vision and goals for the firm, it will rarely reflect what actually happens. Within the context of a startup, there are just too many unexpected factors that can affect the final outcome. Thus, a business plan is in large part an opportunity for an entrepreneur and a management team to think about the key drivers of a venture's success or failure.

As the entrepreneur's blueprint for creating a new venture, the business plan is, in essence, a bridge between an idea and reality. Without first mentally visualizing the desired end result, the entrepreneur is not likely to see the venture become a physical reality. For anything that is built—a house or a business—there is always a need for a written plan. The role of the business plan is to provide a clear visualization of what the entrepreneur intends to do.

The focus in this book is on business plans that propose the launching of a new business. In such plans, the entrepreneur makes projections about the marketing, operational, and financial aspects of the proposed business for the first three to five years. However, a business plan may also address a major expansion of an existing firm. For example, an entrepreneur who has started a small local business may propose opening additional branches or extending the business's success in other ways. Or, a business plan may be a response to some change in the external environment (such as the government, demographics, or industry) that presents new opportunities. Therefore, writing a business plan should be thought of as an ongoing process and not as the means to an end product. This last point is very important and deserves to be repeated: *Writing a business plan is primarily an ongoing process and only secondarily the means to an end product or outcome.*

The Need for a Business Plan

Explain the need for a business plan from the perspectives of both internal and external users.

Most entrepreneurs are results-oriented, and for good reason. A "can do" attitude is essential in starting a new business. Without it, entrepreneurs run the risk of becoming paralyzed by inaction or, worse, by overanalysis. Getting the business operational should be a high priority. However, the entrepreneur who rules out planning, based on the rationale that it is a waste of time, could be making a big mistake. The solution is not to avoid planning, but to engage in *effective* planning, which requires an understanding of the critical issues related to the business. As Jack Stack, an advisor to small companies, says, "To build a great company, you need an operating model that you constantly refine and improve. By model, I mean a complete set of systems, a methodology that defines the way you run every aspect of your business."[1] Developing such a model is the essence of a business plan.

Users of a Business Plan

A business plan has two primary functions: (1) to provide a clearly articulated statement of goals and strategies for internal use and (2) to serve as a selling document to be shared with outsiders. Figure 8-1 provides an overview of those who might have an interest in a business plan for a new venture. One main group of users consists of outsiders who are critical to the firm's success: customers, suppliers, and investors. The other major group is the internal users of the business plan: the new firm's management and its employees. Let's consider the internal users first.

INTERNAL USERS OF THE BUSINESS PLAN Any activity begun without adequate preparation tends to be haphazard. This is particularly true of such a complex process as initiating a new business. Although planning is a mental process, it must go beyond the realm of speculation. Thinking about a proposed new business must become more rigorous as rough ideas crystallize and are quantified. A written plan is essential to ensure systematic coverage of the important factors to be considered in starting a new business. By identifying the variables that can affect the success or failure of the business, the business plan becomes a model that helps the entrepreneur and any employees focus on important issues and activities for the new venture.

FIGURE 8-1

Users of New Venture Business Plans

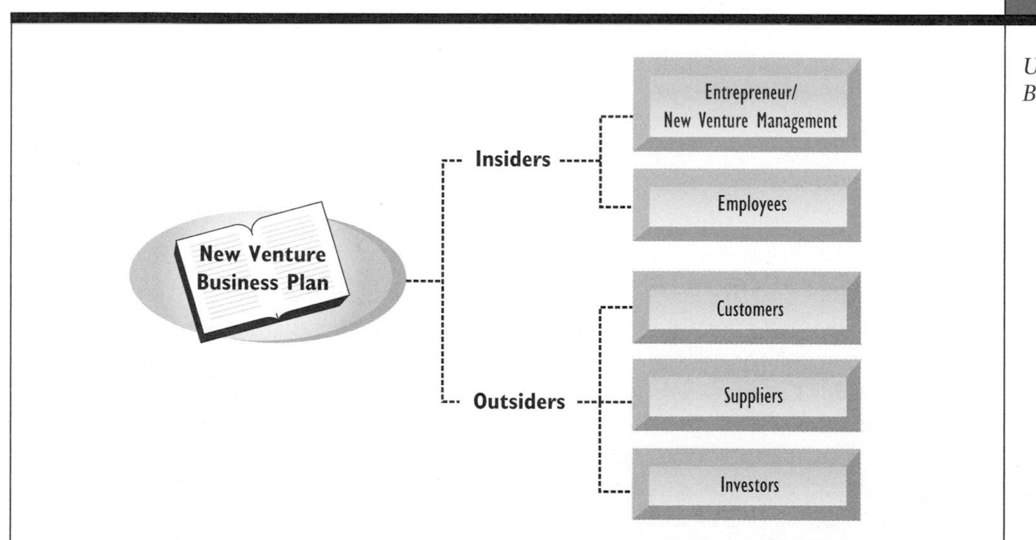

Preparing a formal written plan imposes needed discipline on the entrepreneur and the management team. In order to prepare a written statement about marketing strategy, for example, the entrepreneur and the team must perform some type of market research. Likewise, a study of financial needs requires a review of projected sales and expenditures, month by month. Otherwise, even a good opportunity is likely to fail because of negative cash flows. In short, business plan preparation forces an entrepreneur to exercise greater discipline during the startup process.

Finally, a business plan can be effective in selling the new venture to those within the company. It provides a structure for communicating the entrepreneur's mission to current—and prospective—employees of the firm.

Remember, though, that the business plan, no matter how essential, is not the business. A good plan does not guarantee a good business. Building a good business involves much more.

THE BUSINESS PLAN AND OUTSIDERS Outsiders can face significant risk in doing business with a startup. As noted by Amar Bhide,

Some entrepreneurs may have an innate capability to outperform their rivals, acquire managerial skills, and thus build a flourishing business. But it is difficult for customers (and others) to identify founders with these innate capabilities.[2]

By enhancing the firm's credibility, the business plan can serve as an effective selling tool with prospective customers and suppliers, as well as investors. Suppliers, for example, extend trade credit, which is often an important part of a new firm's financial plan. A well-prepared business plan may be helpful in gaining a supplier's trust and securing favorable credit terms. Occasionally, a business plan can improve sales prospects. For example, by convincing prospective customers of a firm's potential for longevity, the plan may reassure those customers that the new firm is likely to be around to service a product or to continue as a procurement source.

Almost anyone starting a business faces the task of raising financial resources to supplement personal savings. Unless an entrepreneur has a rich relative or friend who will supply funds, he or she may have to appeal to bankers, individual investors, or venture capitalists. The business plan serves as the entrepreneur's calling card when he or she is approaching these sources of financing.

Both investors and lenders use the business plan to better understand the new venture, the type of product or service it offers, the nature of the market, and the qualifications of the entrepreneur and the management team. A venture capital firm or other sophisticated investors would not consider investing in a new business before reviewing a properly prepared business plan. And the plan can be extremely helpful in establishing a good relationship for a new firm with a commercial bank.

The significance of the business plan in dealing with outsiders is aptly expressed by Mark Stevens:

If you are inclined to view the business plan as just another piece of useless paperwork, it's time for an attitude change. When you are starting out, investors will justifiably want to know a lot about you and your qualifications for running a business and will want to see a step-by-step plan for how you intend to make it a success. If you are already running a business and plan to expand or diversify, investors and lenders will want to know a good deal about the company's current status, where it is headed and how you intend to get it there. You must provide them with a plan that makes all of this clear.[3]

The business plan is not, however, a legal document for actually raising the needed capital. When it comes time to solicit investors, a **prospectus**, or offering memorandum, must be used. This document contains all the information necessary to satisfy federal and state requirements for warning potential investors about the possible risks of the investment. But the prospectus alone is not an effective marketing document with which to sell a concept. An entrepreneur must first use the business plan to create interest in the startup and then follow up with a formal offering memorandum to those investors who seem genuinely interested.

prospectus
a marketing document used to solicit investors' monies

The Investor's Perspective

If you intend to use a business plan to raise capital, it is important to understand the investor's basic perspective. You must see the world as the investor sees it—that is, you must think as the investor thinks. For most entrepreneurs, this is more easily said than done, as an entrepreneur generally perceives a new venture very differently than an investor does. The entrepreneur characteristically focuses on the positive potential of the startup—what will happen if everything goes right. The prospective investor, on the other hand, plays the role of the skeptic, thinking more about what could go wrong. One investor in small firms, Daniel Lubin, admits, "The first thing I look for is a lie or bad information—a reason to throw it out."[4] Like most investors, Lubin receives a large number of business plans and gives most of them the attention the average person gives to junk mail. An entrepreneur's failure not only to understand but also to appreciate this difference in perspectives almost certainly ensures rejection by an investor. As noted by William Sahlman at the Harvard Business School,

What's wrong with most business plans? The answer is relatively straightforward. Most waste too much ink on numbers and devote too little to the information that really matters to intelligent investors. As every seasoned investor knows, financial projections for a new company—especially detailed, month-by-month projections that stretch out for more than a year—are an act of imagination.

An entrepreneurial venture faces far too many unknowns to predict revenues, let alone profits. Moreover, few if any entrepreneurs correctly anticipate how much capital and time will be required to accomplish their objectives. Typically, they are wildly optimistic, padding their projections. Investors know about the padding effect and therefore discount the figures in business plans. These maneuvers create a vicious circle of inaccuracy that benefits no one.

Don't misunderstand me: Business plans should include some numbers. But those numbers should appear mainly in the form of a business model that shows the entrepreneurial team has thought about failure. . . . The model should also address the break-even issue: At what level of sales does the business begin to make a profit? And even more important, when does cash flow turn positive? Without a doubt, these questions deserve a few pages in any business plan.[5]

At the most basic level, a prospective investor has a single goal: to maximize potential return on an investment through the cash flows that will be received, while minimizing risk exposure. Even venture capitalists, who are thought to be great risk takers, want to minimize their risk. Like any informed investor, they will look for ways to shift risk to the entrepreneur.

Given the fundamental differences in perspective between the investor and the entrepreneur, the important question becomes "How do I write a business plan that

will capture a prospective investor's interest?" There is no easy answer, but two things are certain: (1) Investors have a short attention span, and (2) certain features appeal to investors, while others are distinctly unappealing.

THE INVESTOR'S SHORT ATTENTION SPAN Kenneth Blanchard and Spencer Johnson wrote a popular book about being a one-minute manager—a manager who practices principles that can be applied quickly but produce large results.[6] Investors in startup and early-stage companies are, in a sense, one-minute investors. Because they receive many business plans, they cannot read them in any detailed fashion. Tim Smith, an officer of the Capital Southwest Corporation, a Dallas-based venture capital firm, observed, "We receive some 300 or more plans per year but invest only in three or four firms in any given year. Thus, we simply do not have the luxury to analyze each opportunity thoroughly."[7]

The speed with which business plans are initially reviewed requires that they be designed to communicate effectively and quickly to prospective investors. They must not sacrifice thoroughness, however, or substitute a few snappy phrases for basic factual information. After all, someone will eventually read the plan carefully. To get that careful reading though, the plan must first gain the interest of the investor; and it must be formulated with that purpose in mind. While many factors may stimulate interest, some basic elements of a business plan that tend to attract or repel prospective investors deserve consideration.

BUSINESS PLAN FEATURES THAT ATTRACT OR REPEL INVESTORS In order to raise capital from outside investors, the business plan must be the "right" plan—that is, it must speak the investors' language. You must know what is important and what is not important to investors and how to present your idea or concept in a way that is meaningful to them. Otherwise, you will immediately lose credibility—and a potential source of financing.

http://web.mit.edu/entforum/www

Based on their experience with the MIT Enterprise Forum, Stanley R. Rich and David E. Gumpert identified characteristics of a business plan that enhance the probability of receiving funding from an investor. (The MIT Enterprise Forum sponsors sessions across the United States in which prospective entrepreneurs present business plans to panels of venture capitalists, bankers, marketing specialists, and other experts.) Figure 8-2 lists some of those features. For instance, to be effective, the plan cannot be extremely long or encyclopedic in detail. It should seldom exceed 40 pages in length, as investors generally will look at brief reports and avoid those that take too long to read. Also, the overall appearance of the report should be attractive, and the report should be well organized, with numbered pages and a table of contents.

Investors are also more *market-oriented* than *product-oriented,* realizing that most patented inventions never earn a dime for the inventors. The essence of the entrepreneurial process is to identify new products, but only if they meet an identifiable customer need. Thus, it is essential for the entrepreneur to appreciate investors' market orientation and, more importantly, to join investors in their concern about market prospects.

Additional features that interest investors include the following:

- Evidence of customer acceptance of the venture's product or service
- An appreciation of investors' needs, through recognition of their particular financial goals, as evidenced in their required rates of return

FIGURE 8-2

Features of a Successful Business Plan

- It must be arranged appropriately, with an executive summary, a table of contents, and chapters in the right order.
- It must be the right length and have the right appearance—not too long and not too short, not too fancy and not too plain.
- It must give a sense of what the founders and the company expect to accomplish three to seven years into the future.
- It must explain in quantitative and qualitative terms the benefits to the user of the company's products or services.
- It must present hard evidence of the marketability of the products or services.
- It must justify financially the means chosen to sell the products or services.
- It must explain and justify the level of product development which has been achieved and describe in appropriate detail the manufacturing process and associated costs.
- It must portray the partners as a team of experienced managers with complementary business skills.
- It must suggest as high an overall "rating" as possible of the venture's product development and team sophistication.
- It must contain believable financial projections, with the key data explained and documented.
- It must show how investors can cash out in three to seven years, with appropriate capital appreciation.
- It must be presented to the most potentially receptive financiers possible to avoid wasting precious time as company funds dwindle.
- It must be easily and concisely explainable in a well-orchestrated oral presentation.

Source: "Plans That Succeed," pp. 126–127 from *Business Plans That Win $$$: Lessons from the MIT Enterprise Forum* by Stanley R. Rich and David E. Gumpert. Reprinted by permission of Sterling Lord Literistic, Inc. Copyright © 1985 by Stanley R. Rich and David E. Gumpert.

- Evidence of focus, through concentration on a limited number of products or services
- Proprietary position, as represented by patents, copyrights, and trademarks[8]

On the other hand, the following are some features that create unfavorable re actions among prospective investors:

- Infatuation with the product or service rather than familiarity with and awareness of marketplace needs
- Financial projections at odds with accepted industry norms
- Unrealistic growth projections
- Need for custom or applications engineering, which makes substantial growth difficult[9]

Finally, as noted earlier, investors are quickly disillusioned by plans that contain page after page of detailed computer-generated financial projections, suggesting—intentionally or unintentionally—that the entrepreneur can predict with great accuracy what will happen. The experienced investor knows differently.

How Much Business Planning Is Needed?

Describe what determines how much planning an entrepreneur and a management team are likely to do.

To this point, we have presented the process of writing a business plan in either/or terms—either you do it or you don't. We have done so in an effort to make a case for writing a plan, to persuade you that a plan is important both as a guide for future action and as a selling document.

In reality, it is a matter of degree. Even if you are convinced of the necessity of having a business plan, you must still decide on the level of effort you are willing to give to preparing the plan. A plan can be written on the back of an envelope, it can

ENTREPRENEURSHIP AND ETHICS

IN THE TRENCHES

IS HONESTY THE BEST POLICY IN THE INTERNET ECONOMY?

When presenting your goals and plans for a new company, how careful should you be not to overstate what you honestly believe will be achievable? In other words, how important is integrity? We realize that it is not important in all firms—but it should be.

What's the road to success for a startup? For many companies, it's whatever road leads them to the most business in the least amount of time. The Internet economy worships at the altar of fast action, fast growth, and fast results. Plenty of companies (and the people who lead them) are prepared to cut a few ethical corners in order to move faster: not gross violations, such as accounting manipulations or outright fraud, but day-to-day dilemmas—leadership moments in which you do either the right thing or the expedient thing. Are you aboveboard with investors when you know that the next quarter may be disappointing? Will you say anything to recruit a great job candidate, or are you honest about the risks involved in an assignment?

There's a widespread feeling among entrepreneurs and venture capitalists that if a new company doesn't display a bit of bluster and outright exaggeration in its launch phase, it won't be taken seriously—and it won't get a chance to change the world. What fun is starting a company if you can't be a little devious?

be filled with intricate details, or it can fall anywhere you choose along the continuum between these extremes.

In making a decision regarding the extent of planning, an entrepreneur must deal with tradeoffs. Preparing a business plan requires both time and money, two resources that are always in limited supply. Other considerations come into play as well:

- ***Management style and ability.*** The extent of planning depends, in part, on the ability of the entrepreneur to grasp multiple and interrelated dimensions of the business, to keep all necessary information in his or her head, and to retrieve it in an orderly fashion. It also depends on the lead entrepreneur's management style. These are practical matters that affect the *actual* amount of planning, but they may not lead to the *ideal* amount of planning.
- ***Preferences of the management team.*** The amount of planning also depends on the management team's personal preferences. Some management teams want to participate in the planning process; others do not. Lack of interest on the part of management is likely to lead to insufficient planning.
- ***Complexity of the business.*** The level of complexity of a business affects how much planning is appropriate.
- ***Competitive environment.*** If the firm will be operating in a highly competitive environment, where it must be scrupulously managed in order to survive, a significant amount of planning will be needed.
- ***Level of uncertainty.*** Ideally, ventures facing a volatile, rapidly changing environment would prepare for all eventualities through extensive planning. In reality, however, entrepreneurs are more inclined to plan when there is less uncertainty because they can better anticipate future events—which is the opposite of what they should be thinking.[10]

Some of the clearest thinking about integrity in the Internet economy comes from Darlene Mann, a general partner at Onset Ventures, in Menlo Park, California. Her firm has bankrolled dozens of startups, and she has worked inside numerous high-tech companies. If executives want "integrity" to be more than just a buzzword in a mission statement, she says, they need to think hard about three issues: the growth goals that they promise to customers and investors, the career opportunities that they promise to employees, and the tone that they strike in day-to-day negotiations with business partners. In some cases, Mann acknowledges, keeping one's word carries extra shorter costs. But wiggling away from the truth can be disastrously expensive in the long run.

The point, says Mann, isn't that startups need to let go of their ambitious dreams. But they do need to ensure that promises made to the outside world are believable to their own people. Otherwise, they will be built on a foundation of cynicism and distrust.

Source: George Anders, Honesty Is the Best Policy—Trust Us," *Fast Company*, Vol. 37 (August 2000), p. 262.

So the issue goes beyond the question "Do I plan?" It includes the decision as to *how much* to plan, which, in turn, involves difficult tradeoffs. In his study of *Inc. 500* companies (firms identified by *Inc.* magazine as the fastest growing firms in the United States), Amar Bhide concludes that a lack of planning may even make sense with some companies:

Capital-constrained entrepreneurs cannot afford to do much prior analysis and research. The limited profit potential and high uncertainty of the opportunity they usually pursue also make the benefits low compared to the costs.[11]

So, the attention given to planning should vary with the situation. Rather than conclude that planning is unnecessary or will not be beneficial, however, an entrepreneur starting a new business simply needs to use good judgment about the nature and the amount of the planning.

Preparing a Business Plan

Two issues are of primary concern in preparing a business plan: (1) the basic format and effectiveness of the written presentation and (2) the content of the plan.

List practical suggestions to follow in writing a business plan and outline the key sections of a business plan.

Formatting and Writing a Business Plan

The quality of a completed business plan ultimately depends on the quality of the underlying business concept. As already noted, the plan is not the business. A poorly conceived new venture idea cannot be rescued by good writing. A good concept may be destroyed, however, by writing that fails to effectively communicate.

Clear writing gives credibility to the ideas presented in a business plan. Factual support must be supplied for any claims or promises made. When promising to

provide superior service or explaining the attractiveness of the market, for example, the entrepreneur must include strong supporting evidence. In short, the plan must be believable.

Skill in written communication is necessary to present the business concept in an accurate, comprehensible, and enthusiastic way. Although it is beyond the scope of this book to discuss general writing principles, the public accounting firm Arthur Andersen and Company, in its booklet *An Entrepreneur's Guide to Developing a Business Plan,* offers the following practical suggestions specifically related to writing a business plan:

- Provide a table of contents and individual section tabs for easy reference.
- Use a typewritten 8½- × 11-inch format and photocopy the plan to minimize costs.
- Package the plan in a loose-leaf binder to facilitate future revisions.
- To add interest and aid readers' comprehension, use charts, graphs, diagrams, tabular summaries, maps, and other visual aids.
- To ensure that the business plan is treated in a confidential manner, indicate on the cover and again on the title page of the plan that all information is proprietary and confidential. Number each copy of the plan and account for each outstanding copy by requiring each recipient of the plan to acknowledge receipt in writing.
- If your startup is of a particularly sensitive nature because it is based on advanced technology, consider whether you should divulge certain information—details of a technological design, for example, or the highly sensitive specifics of a marketing strategy—even to a prospective investor. You might want to develop an in-depth plan for internal purposes and then use appropriate extracts from it to put together a document that effectively supports your funding proposal.
- As you complete major sections of the plan, ask carefully chosen third parties who have themselves raised capital successfully—including accountants, lawyers, and other entrepreneurs—to give their perspectives on the quality, clarity, reasonableness, and thoroughness of the plan. Once the business plan is in close-to-final form, ask these independent reviewers for final comments before you reproduce and distribute the plan.[12]

Deciding on the Content of a Business Plan

Four interdependent factors should be given thorough consideration in deciding on the content of a business plan for a startup company:

- ***The people.*** A description of the men and women starting and running the venture, as well as any outside parties, such as lawyers, accountants, and suppliers, providing key services or important resources.
- ***The opportunity.*** A profile of the business itself—what it will sell and to whom, how much and how rapidly it can grow, what its financial outlook is, who and what may stand in the way of its success.
- ***The context.*** The big picture—the regulatory environment, interest rates, demographic trends, inflation, and other factors that inevitably change but cannot be controlled by the entrepreneur.

- ***Risk and reward.*** An assessment of everything that can go wrong or right, with a discussion of how the entrepreneurial team can respond to the various challenges.[13]

Keep these general factors in mind as you compose the specific content of your business plan.

Although the business plan for each new venture is unique and no single format or formula can guarantee success, there are guidelines a prospective entrepreneur can follow in preparing a plan. Most business plans exhibit considerable similarity in basic content.

Figure 8-3 summarizes the major sections common to most business plans, providing a bird's-eye view of the overall content. We will now briefly consider each of

FIGURE 8-3

Abbreviated Business Plan Outline

Title Page: Provides names, addresses, and fax and phone numbers of the venture and its owners and management personnel; date prepared; copy number; and contact person.

Table of Contents: Provides page numbers for the key sections of the business plan.

Executive Summary: Provides a one- to three-page overview of the total business plan. Written after the other sections are completed, it highlights their significant points and, ideally, creates enough excitement to motivate the reader to continue reading.

Vision and Mission Statement: Concisely describes the intended strategy and business philosophy for making the vision happen.

Company Overview: Explains the type of company, such as manufacturing, retail, or service; provides background information on the company if it already exists; describes the proposed form of organization—sole proprietorship, partnership, or corporation. This section should be organized as follows: company name and location, company objectives, nature and primary product or service of the business, current status (startup, buyout, or expansion) and history (if applicable), and legal form of organization.

Products and/or Services Plan: Describes the product and/or service and points out any unique features; explains why people will buy the product or service. This section should offer the following descriptions: products and/or services; features of the product or service providing a competitive advantage; available legal protection—patents, copyrights, trademarks; and dangers of technical or style obsolescence.

Marketing Plan: Shows who the firm's customers will be and what type of competition it will face; outlines the marketing strategy and specifies the firm's competitive edge. This section should offer the following descriptions: analysis of target market and profile of target customer; methods of identifying and attracting customers; selling approach, type of sales force, and distribution channels; types of sales promotions and advertising; and credit and pricing policies.

Management Plan: Identifies the key players—active investors, management team, and directors—citing the experience and competence they possess. This section should offer the following descriptions: management team, outside investors and/or directors and their qualifications, outside resource people and their qualifications, and plans for recruiting and training employees.

Operating Plan: Explains the type of manufacturing or operating system to be used; describes the facilities, labor, raw materials, and product processing requirements. This section should offer the following descriptions: operating or manufacturing methods, operating facilities (location, space, and equipment), quality-control methods, procedures to control inventory and operations, sources of supply, and purchasing procedures.

Financial Plan: Specifies financial needs and contemplated sources of financing; presents projections of revenues, costs, and profits. This section should offer the following descriptions: historical financial statements for the last three to five years or as available; pro forma financial statements for three to five years, including income statements, balance sheets, cash flow statements, and cash budgets (monthly for first year and quarterly for second year); break-even analysis of profits and cash flows; and planned sources of financing.

Appendix of Supporting Documents: Provides materials supplementary to the plan. This section should offer the following descriptions: management team biographies, any other important data that support the information in the business plan, and the firm's ethics code.

these sections. Chapters 9 through 14 look at the individual sections of the business plan in more detail.

TITLE PAGE The title page is the first page of the business plan and should contain the following information:

- Company name, address, phone number, fax number, and Web address
- Company logo, if available
- Names, titles, addresses, and phone numbers of the owners and key executives
- Date on which the business plan was issued
- Number of the copy (to help keep track of how many copies are outstanding)
- Name of the preparer, if other than the owners and key executives

TABLE OF CONTENTS The table of contents provides a sequential listing of the sections of the plan, with page numbers.

executive summary
a section of the business plan that conveys a clear and concise overall picture of the proposed venture

EXECUTIVE SUMMARY The **executive summary** is crucial for getting the attention of the one-minute investor. It must convey a clear and concise picture of the proposed venture and, at the same time, create a sense of excitement regarding its prospects. This means that it must be written—and, if necessary, rewritten—to achieve clarity and create interest. Even though the executive summary comes at the beginning of the business plan, it provides an overview of the whole plan and should be written last. Depending on the situation and the preference of the entrepreneur, the executive summary may be in the form of a synopsis or a narrative.

Synopsis. The synopsis is the more straightforward of the two summary formats. A synopsis briefly covers all aspects of the business plan, giving each topic relatively equal treatment. It simply relates, in abbreviated fashion, the conclusions of each section of the completed business plan. Although it is relatively easy to prepare, the synopsis can be rather dry reading for the prospective investor.

Narrative. Because the narrative tells the reader a story, it can convey greater excitement than the synopsis. However, composing an effective narrative requires a gifted writer who can communicate the necessary information and engender enthusiasm without crossing the line into hyperbole. A narrative is more appropriate for businesses that are breaking new ground, with either a new product, a new market, or new operational techniques. It is also a better format for businesses that have one dominant advantage, such as holding an important patent or being run by a well-known entrepreneur. Finally, the narrative works well for companies with interesting or impressive backgrounds or histories.[14]

A sample executive summary from the business plan of a direct mail outlet is shown in Figure 8-4 on pages 204 and 205. Would you consider the example to be a synopsis- or narrative-style executive summary?

mission statement
a concise written description of a firm's philosophy

VISION AND MISSION STATEMENT The firm's **mission statement** concisely describes, in writing, the intended strategy and business philosophy for making the entrepreneur's vision a reality. In a few sentences, it should convey how combined efforts in all areas of the business will move it toward its goal. In addition, it should distin-

guish the firm from all others. Mission statements can and do vary in length, content, format, and specificity. However, it is essential that a mission statement remain simple, believable, and achievable.

COMPANY OVERVIEW The main body of the business plan begins with a brief description of the firm. If the firm is already in existence, its history is included. This section informs the reader of the type of business being proposed, the firm's objectives, where the firm is located, and whether it will serve a local or international market. In many cases, legal issues—especially those concerning the firm's form of organization—are addressed in this section of the plan. (Legal issues regarding the form of organization are discussed in Chapter 10.) In writing this section, the entrepreneur should answer the following questions:

- When and where was this business started?
- What changes have been made in structure and/or ownership?
- In what stage of development is the firm—for example, seed stage or full product line?
- What has been achieved to date?
- What is the firm's distinctive competence?
- What are the basic nature and activity of the business?
- What is its primary product or service?
- What customers will be served?
- What are the firm's objectives?
- What is the firm's form of organization—sole proprietorship, partnership, or corporation?
- What are the current and projected economic states of the industry?
- Does the firm intend to become a publicly traded company or an acquisition candidate?

PRODUCTS AND/OR SERVICES PLAN As its title reveals, the **products and/or services plan** discusses those products and/or services to be offered to the firm's customers. If a new or unique physical product is to be offered and a working model or prototype is available, a photograph of it should be included in this section of the business plan. Investors will naturally show the greatest interest in products that have been developed, tested, and found to be functional. Any innovative features should be identified and any patent protection explained. Although, in many instances, the product or service may be similar to those offered by competitors—electrical contracting, for example—any special features should be clearly identified. (Chapters 15 discusses this topic more fully.)

products and/or services plan
a section of the business plan that describes the product and/or service to be provided and explains its merits

MARKETING PLAN As stated earlier, prospective investors and lenders attach a high priority to market considerations. They do not want to invest in a product that is well engineered but unwanted by customers. The **marketing plan,** therefore, must identify user benefits and the type of market that exists. Depending on the type of product or service being offered, the marketing plan may be able not only to identify but also to quantify the financial benefit to the user—for example, by showing how quickly a user can recover the cost of the product or service through savings in

marketing plan
a section of the business plan that describes the user benefits of the product or service and the type of market that exists

FIGURE 8-4

An Example of an Executive Summary for a Direct Mail Outlet

The following Executive Summary information is qualified in its entirety by the more detailed information appearing elsewhere in this business plan. The document is confidential and can be substantiated by many years of ongoing work, extensive research, and the experience of the Post Direct team of marketing experts.

Contacts:	John Kingham, President
	Benjamin Miller, Vice President/Secretary
Address:	52½ Burr Rd.
	Silver Spring, MD 20907
Telephone:	(301) 555-3492
Fax:	(301) 555-3494

Vision and Mission Statement

Post Direct plans to be a chain of direct mail outlets specializing in the highest-quality, four-color postcard cooperative and solo direct mail in the nation. Post Direct is a high-quality production operation, demographically targeted to the best and most affluent of upscale markets. In other words, Post Direct is the Tiffany of direct mail. The outlets are targeted to be located in major metropolitan areas.

Company Overview

The Company evolved out of Kingham and Associates Advertising, Inc., a full-service advertising agency, which is owned by John Kingham. Mr. Kingham is also president of that corporation. Kingham founded the original Post Direct outlet in May 1994. He was assisted in The Company's development by Benjamin Miller, who joined the firm in September of 1994. Their first issue was published in November 1994. Additional issues were published in March 1995, May 1995, September 1995, November 1995, March 1996, May 1996, September 1996, December 1996, and April 1997. Post Direct was incorporated on September 3, 1995. The chain now consists of one corporate outlet in Silver Spring, Maryland, which serves the Washington metropolitan market. Locations for the Post Direct outlets are planned in prime metropolitan areas to attract upscale customers and generate high sales. Demographics include 30- to 64-year-old adults with household incomes of $75,000 and up.

John Kingham and Benjamin Miller have perfected Post Direct to the point that it has become one of the best direct mail companies in the Washington metropolitan marketing area. Easily manageable and profitable, this particular business appeals directly to the now displaced business and professional persons who want to be in business for themselves but not by themselves. It continues to capitalize on the ever-growing demand for quality and effective direct mail opportunities, knowledgeable service, and competitive prices. The Company will market its products through a network of approximately 25 outlets.

Products and/or Services Plan

The Company has developed a concept of truly excellent quality direct mail pieces at competitive prices. Post Direct has gained a reputation for originality and good service that has resulted in high customer loyalty. What makes The Company unique is its ability to offer marketing for cooperative and solo direct mail.

operating costs. Of course, benefits may also take such forms as savings in time or improvements in attractiveness, safety, or health.

The marketing plan should document customer interest by showing that a market exists and that customers are ready to buy the product or service. This market analysis must be detailed enough to provide a reasonable estimate of demand. An estimate of demand must be analytically sound and based on more than assumptions if it is to be accepted as credible by prospective investors. (Note that some business plans include a market analysis section as a precursor to the marketing plan section.)

FIGURE 8-4

(Continued)

Marketing Plan

Post Direct will use the franchising method of marketing to attract prospective franchisees and to duplicate the Post Direct system nationwide. The franchise is competitively priced, easy to operate, and profitable. For this reason, prospective franchisees, who have longed to be in business for themselves but not by themselves, will be attracted to the concept.

Although attractive to America's advertising specialists, Post Direct outlets are also an excellent investment for the sophisticated businessperson. Such people have the business acumen to recognize that franchising has matured and that it is attracting investors interested in building a successful track record. With Post Direct, an individual can achieve his or her dreams of creating a successful business by working smarter with less overhead and greater profits. According to various trade articles, the market potential for direct mail marketing is excellent. It is growing at the rate of 35 to 40 percent each year, according to the Direct Marketing Association.

Financial Plan

The Company is self-financed and is providing the required investment for its franchising development.

Startup investment for corporate Post Direct outlets will range from $21,000 to $27,000, depending upon location. Franchised outlets will include these same startup costs plus a modest franchise fee ranging from $20,000 to $75,000, depending upon the marketing areas being considered.

The costs for developing the corporate and franchise expansion are projected to run from $250,000 the first year to over $500,000 the third year. One of the additional corporate outlets will serve the Alexandria, Virginia market, and the other will serve the southern Georgia market. Development funds will be used for normal developmental and administrative expenses including those for legal fees, franchise sales, and training and operations manuals.

The key to marketing direct mail is name recognition. For this reason, it is recommended that Post Direct continue to develop its own marketing, design, promotion, and advertising techniques. This requires a considerable investment of capital for advertising and promotion purposes. Years of experience in advertising, radio, and direct mail management, along with designing instincts, copy expertise, and marketing abilities, make this the perfect time to exploit the Post Direct concept.

The future expansion of Post Direct will be controlled, yet speedy. Money will be needed for marketing and promotional needs. In moving into new market areas, The Company will be highly selective of its franchisees in order to effectively develop the key marketing areas that fit the company's growth criteria.

Through forecasting, we project that The Company's net income, before taxes, from franchised and corporate outlets will be as follows:

Fiscal 2000 $460,000
Fiscal 2001 $698,000

The Company's royalty income from franchisees alone (at 10%) will be

2001 $ 670,000
2002 $1,230,000
2003 $1,707,500

When all 25 franchisees operate for a full year, royalties will amount to $2,000,000 per year.

Source: Adapted from Angela Shupe, *Business Plans Handbook* (Detroit: Gale Research, 1997), pp. 148–150.

The marketing plan must also examine the competition and describe elements of the proposed marketing strategy—for example, by specifying the type of sales force and the methods of promotion and advertising that will be used. (Chapter 9 provides in-depth coverage of the marketing plan.)

MANAGEMENT PLAN Prospective investors look for well-managed companies. Of all the factors they consider, the quality of the management team is paramount; it is even more important than the nature of the product or service. Investors frequently

say that they would rather have an "A" management team and a "B" product or service than a "B" team and an "A" product. Unfortunately, an entrepreneur's ability to conceive an idea for a new venture is no guarantee of her or his managerial ability. The **management plan,** therefore, must detail the proposed firm's organizational structure and the backgrounds of those who will fill its key positions.

management plan
a section of the business plan that describes a new firm's organizational structure and the backgrounds of its key players

Ideally, investors desire a well-balanced management team—one that includes financial and marketing expertise as well as production experience and innovative talent. Managerial experience in related enterprises and in other startup situations is particularly valuable in the eyes of prospective investors. (The factors involved in preparing the management plan are discussed in detail in Chapter 10.)

operating plan
a section of the business plan that offers information on how a product will be produced or a service provided, including descriptions of the new firm's facilities, labor, raw materials, and processing requirements

OPERATING PLAN The **operating plan** offers information on how the product will be produced or the service provided; its importance varies from venture to venture. This plan discusses such items as location and facilities: how much space the business will need and what type of equipment it will require. (These aspects of the operating plan are discussed at length in Chapter 11.) The operating plan should also explain the firm's proposed approach to assuring quality, controlling inventory, and using subcontractors or obtaining raw materials. (These aspects are discussed in detail in Chapter 20.)

financial plan
a section of the business plan that provides an account of the new firm's financial needs and sources of financing and a projection of its revenues, costs, and profits

pro forma statements
projections of a firm's financial condition

FINANCIAL PLAN Financial analysis constitutes another crucial piece of the business plan; it is contained in the **financial plan** section of the business plan. **Pro forma statements,** which are projections of the company's financial statements, are presented for up to five years. The forecasts include balance sheets, income statements, and statements of cash flows on an annual basis for three to five years, as well as cash budgets on a monthly basis for the first year and on a quarterly basis for the second and third years. It is vital that the financial projections be supported by well-substantiated assumptions and explanations of how the figures have been determined.

While all the financial statements are important, statements of cash flows deserve special attention, because a business can be profitable but fail to produce positive cash flows. A statement of cash flows identifies the sources of cash—how much will be raised from investors and how much will be generated from operations. It also shows how much money will be devoted to investments in such areas as inventories and equipment. The statement of cash flows should clearly indicate how much cash is needed from prospective investors and for what purpose.

Since experience tells them that the eventual return on their investment will depend largely on their ability to cash out, most investors want to invest in a privately held company for only a limited period and want to be told how and when they may expect to cash out of the investment. Therefore, the plan should outline the mechanism available to investors for exiting the firm. (The preparation of pro forma statements and the process of raising the needed capital are discussed in Chapters 12 and 13. Chapter 14 presents the possible ways for an investor—and the entrepreneur—to cash out, or exit, the business investment.)

APPENDIX OF SUPPORTING DOCUMENTS The appendix should contain various supplementary supporting materials and attachments to expand the reader's understanding of the plan. These supporting documents include any items referenced in the text of the business plan, such as the résumés of the key investors and owners/managers; photographs of products, facilities, and buildings; professional references; marketing research studies; pertinent published research; and signed contracts of sale.

The fact that it appears at the end of the plan does not mean that the appendix is of secondary importance. First, the reader needs to understand the assumptions underlying the premises set forth in the plan. Also, nothing is more important to a prospective investor than the qualifications of the management team. Thus, the presentation of the management team's résumés is no small matter, and each résumé should be carefully prepared.

Resources for Business Plan Preparation

Identify available sources of assistance in preparing a business plan.

We have just provided an overview of the business plan. A multitude of books and computer software packages are now available to guide you step by step through the preparation of a business plan. (A listing of some helpful books, Web sites, and computer software packages appears at the end of this chapter.) Such resources can be invaluable in the preparation of a business plan. In general, however, you should resist the temptation to adapt an existing business plan for your own use. Changing the numbers and some of the verbiage of another firm's business plan is simply not effective.

Computer-Aided Business Planning

Templates are available on the accompanying CD-ROM to assist you in preparing a simplified business plan. For additional information on business plans, visit the Web page at http://longenecker.swcollege.com.

A computer facilitates preparation of a business plan. Its word-processing capabilities, for example, can speed up the writing of narrative sections of the report, such as the description of the product and the review of key management personnel. Working from the original word-processing file in which the narrative was composed, the entrepreneur can correct and refine a series of drafts and then print out the final plan in the form in which it will be presented to investors or others.

The computer is even more helpful for preparing the financial statements needed in the plan. Since the various numbers in a financial plan are interwoven in many ways, a change in one item—such as sales volume, interest rate, or cost of goods sold—will cause a ripple effect throughout the entire plan. A long, tedious set of calculations is required if the entrepreneur wishes to check out various assumptions by hand. With a computer spreadsheet, an entrepreneur can accomplish this task easily, experimenting with best-case and worst-case scenarios and quickly ascertaining their effects on the firm's balance sheet, operating profits, and cash flows.

There are a number of business plan software packages whose basic objective is to help an entrepreneur think through the important issues in beginning a new company and organize his or her thoughts to create an effective presentation. However, these software packages are not capable of producing a unique plan and thus may limit an entrepreneur's creativity and flexibility. Remember, there is no simple procedure for writing a business plan—no "formula for success"—despite what software advertisements may claim. If you recognize their limitations, however, you can use business plan software packages to facilitate the process.

Throughout this part of the book (Part 4, "The New Venture Business Plan"), each chapter ends with a special set of exercises to take you through the process of writing a business plan. Appearing in Chapters 8–14, the exercises essentially consist of questions to be thoughtfully considered and answered. These exercise sets are entitled "The Business Plan: Laying the Foundation" because they deal with issues that are important to starting a new venture and provide guidelines for preparing different sections of a business plan.

UTILIZING NEW TECHNOLOGY

IN THE TRENCHES

GETTING HELP WITH THE BUSINESS PLAN

Gearing up to start a new business can be fun and invigorating. But actually writing a business plan can cause the most eager entrepreneur to succumb to prolonged fits of snoring. And that's a real problem because, without a good business plan, you won't actually get to run the business—at least not for long.

Palo Alto Software has developed a Web site, designed to help you tackle just one small part of your business plan at a time. Bplans.com asks a few general questions about your prospective business. Then it points you toward business plans, archived online, for companies that are at least somewhat similar to yours. You can jump right in from there, downloading sample plans. Just don't use them as a crutch to avoid the sort of hard thinking that writing a business plan should prompt.

After reviewing a few sample plans, you may decide to try out the "Mini Business Planner," which offers guidance in writing one small chunk at a time. If you follow the template, your plan will be quite repetitious—but at least you won't leave anything out. The site provides online calculators to figure out startup costs and how long it will take to break even. Your plan-in-progress is stored on the Bplans.com site, and you can have it e-mailed to you at any time.

Bplans.com encourages users to submit questions online, which one of the site's small business consultants will take a swing at answering. Note that a very general question will get a very general answer—one that may not go into the sort of detail you need. Case in point: One business owner was having trouble financing his company's growth because suppliers were demanding quick payment while customers dragged their feet. The consultant gave some tips for getting money out of clients but didn't mention *factoring*—the practice of selling receivables at a slight discount in exchange for money up front.

Bplans.com lacks a good overview of the whole business plan process. Before you start writing, it would be helpful to know, for example, that investors will likely read the executive summary and management bios before anything else. If those sections don't sparkle, the rest of your plan probably won't get a second look. Similarly, you should know that skimping on the competition section of your plan—or, worse, declaring that you have no competition at all—will immediately ruin your credibility. For those sort of tips, head over to SOYOUWANNA.COM and find "So You Wanna Write a Business Plan." Read the whole thing, get inspired, and pull out those financial projections. Then head over to Bplans.com, and start writing.

Source: Adapted from Kimberly Weisul, "The Write Stuff for Your Business Plan," BusinessWeek online, http://www.businessweek.com, November 20, 2000.

http://www.bplans.com

Professional Assistance in Business Planning

As already discussed, company founders are most notably doers—and evidence suggests that they had better be, if the venture is to be successful. Furthermore, most entrepreneurs lack the breadth of experience and know-how, as well as the inclination, needed for planning.

An entrepreneur who is not able to answer the tough questions about the business may need a business planning advisor—someone accustomed to working with small companies, startups, and owners who lack financial management experience. Such advisors include the following:

- Attorneys, who can make sure that the company has the necessary patent protection, review contracts, consult on liability and environmental concerns, and advise on the best form of organization.
- Marketing specialists, who can perform market analyses and evaluate market acceptance of a new product.
- Engineering and production experts, who can perform product development, determine technical feasibility of products, and assist in plant layout and production planning.

- Accounting firms, which can guide the development of the written plan, assist in making financial projections, and advise on establishing a system of financial control.
- Incubator organizations, which offer space for fledgling companies and can advise on structuring new businesses. (Incubators are discussed in detail in Chapters 11 and 18.)
- Small business development corporations (SBDCs) and regional and local economic development offices, which can offer general assistance.

An investment banker or financial intermediary can draw up a business plan as part of a firm's overall fundraising efforts. However, as explained by Jill Andresky Fraser, "His strategy will cost you—you may pay an hourly fee as well as a contingency percentage based on the amount raised or even an equity stake. However, a well-chosen intermediary will have contacts you lack, and may even help you reformulate your business plan entirely."[15] For someone not able to afford such fees, two good sources of assistance are the Small Business Administration (SBA) and the Service Corps of Retired Executives (SCORE). Both organizations have programs to introduce business owners to volunteer experts who will advise them.

Securing help in business plan preparation does not relieve the entrepreneur of responsibility for being the primary planner; her or his basic ideas are essential to producing a plan that is realistic and believable. Furthermore, the plan will eventually have to be interpreted and defended to outsiders. To effectively present it, the entrepreneur must be completely familiar with the plan.

Now that this chapter has made you more aware of the importance and fundamentals of the business plan, the chapters that follow will examine more closely each of the plan's components.

LOOKING BACK

1 Answer the question "What is a business plan?"

- A business plan identifies the nature and context of the business opportunity and describes why the opportunity exists.
- A business plan presents the approach the entrepreneur will take to exploit the opportunity.

2 Explain the need for a business plan from the perspectives of both internal and external users.

- The business plan provides a clearly articulated statement of the firm's goals and strategies, helping the entrepreneur focus on important issues.
- The business plan helps identify the important variables that will determine the success or failure of the firm.
- The business plan is used as a selling document to outsiders.
- The business plan tells a prospective investor how the business will help achieve the investor's personal goal—to maximize potential return on investment through cash flows received from the investment, while minimizing personal risk exposure.
- The business plan shows an investor how he or she can cash out of the investment with appropriate capital appreciation.

3 Describe what determines how much planning an entrepreneur and a management team are likely to do.

- The allocation of time and money, two scarce resources, affects how much planning will be done.

- Other factors that affect the extent of planning include (1) the entrepreneur's management style and ability, (2) management team preferences, (3) the complexity of the business, (4) the competitive environment, and (5) the level of uncertainty in the environment.

4 List practical suggestions to follow in writing a business plan, and outline the key sections of a business plan.

- To maximize the effectiveness of a business plan, you should (1) provide a table of contents and section tabs for easy reference, (2) package the plan in a loose-leaf binder to facilitate revisions, (3) use charts, graphs, diagrams, tabular summaries, and other visual aids to create interest and make the presentation easy to follow, (4) consider withholding highly sensitive specifics, and (5) ask carefully chosen third parties to give their assessment of the quality of the plan.
- Key sections of a business plan are the (1) title page, (2) table of contents, (3) executive summary, (4) vision and mission statement, (5) company overview, (6) products and/or services plan, (7) marketing plan, (8) management plan, (9) operating plan, (10) financial plan, and (11) appendix of supporting documents.

5 Identify available sources of assistance in preparing a business plan.

- A variety of books and computer software packages are available to assist in the preparation of a business plan.
- Professionals with planning expertise, such as attorneys, accountants, and other entrepreneurs, can provide useful suggestions and assistance in the preparation of a business plan.

Key Terms

business plan, p. 192
prospectus, p. 195
executive summary, p. 202
mission statement, p. 202
products and/or services plan, p. 203
marketing plan, p. 203
management plan, p. 206
operating plan, p. 206
financial plan, p. 206
pro forma statements, p. 206

Discussion Questions

1. What benefits are associated with the preparation of a written business plan for a new venture? Who uses such a plan?
2. Why do entrepreneurs tend to neglect initial planning? Why would you personally be tempted to neglect it?
3. In what way might a business plan be helpful in recruiting key management personnel?
4. How might an entrepreneur's perspective differ from an investor's in terms of the business plan?
5. Would an intelligent investor really make a decision based on a one-minute review of a business plan? Discuss.
6. Investors are said to be more market-oriented than product-oriented. What does this mean? What is the logic behind this orientation?
7. Why is a shorter business plan better than a longer one, especially since a more lengthy plan could include more supporting data?
8. What advantages are realized by using a computer in preparing the narrative sections of a business plan? In preparing the financial plan?
9. How might you quantify the user benefits for a new type of production tool?
10. If the income statement of a financial plan shows that the business will be profitable, why is there a need for a statement of cash flows?

YOU MAKE THE CALL

SITUATION 1

Michael Richcreek is the owner of Rolling Wheels Mobile Home Repair, in Swayzee, Indiana, a mobile-home maintenance and repair business he operates on a part-time basis. Richcreek is now trying to acquire financing to buy a mobile-home park with an asking price of $1.2 million; he has approximately $40,000 in cash to invest. He realizes that he would need to prepare a business plan to sell the concept to a prospective investor. But he also recognizes that he does not have the knowledge or expertise to write a business plan, financial plan, or any of the other plans required to secure the funds needed for this venture.

Source: Adapted from Jill Andresky Fraser, "Who Can Help Out with a Business Plan?" *Inc.*, Vol. 21, No. 8 (June 1999), pp. 115–117.

Question 1 Given Richcreek's seeming inability to write a business plan, do you think that a computer software package could help him? Why, or why not?

Question 2 What are some questions that Richcreek should try to answer before writing a business plan?

Question 3 Given the situation, where should Richcreek go to get help in preparing a business plan? Where should he *not* go for assistance?

SITUATION 2

A young journalist is contemplating launching a new magazine that will feature wildlife, plant life, and the beauty of nature around the world. The prospective entrepreneur intends each issue to contain several feature articles—for example, the dangers and benefits of forest fires, features of Rocky Mountain National Park, wildflowers found at high altitudes, and the danger of acid rain. The magazine will make extensive use of color photographs, and its articles will be technically accurate and interestingly written. Unlike *National Geographic*, the proposed publication will avoid articles dealing with the general culture and confine itself to topics closely related to the natural world. Suppose you are a venture capitalist examining a business plan prepared by this journalist.

Question 1 What are the most urgent questions you would want the marketing plan to answer?

Question 2 What details would you look for in the management plan?

Question 3 Do you think this entrepreneur would need to raise closer to $1 million or $10 million in startup capital? Why?

Question 4 At first glance, are you inclined to accept or reject the proposal? Why?

SITUATION 3

Ed Jones and John Rose decided to start a new business to manufacture noncarbonated soft drinks. They believed that their location in East Texas, close to high-quality water, would give them a competitive edge. Although Jones and Rose had never worked together, Jones had 17 years of experience in the soft drink industry. Rose had recently sold his own firm and had funds to help finance the venture; however, the partners needed to raise additional money from outside investors. Both men were excited about the opportunity and spent almost 18 months developing their business plan. The first paragraph of their executive summary reflected their excitement:

The "New Age" beverage market is the result of a spectacular boom in demand for drinks with nutritional value from environmentally safe ingredients and waters that come from deep, clear springs free of chemicals and pollutants. Argon Beverage Corporation will produce and market a full line of sparkling fruit drinks, flavored waters, and sports drinks that are of the highest quality and purity. These drinks have the same delicious taste appeal as soft drinks while using the most healthful fruit juices, natural sugars, and the purest spring water, the hallmark of the "New Age" drink market.

With the help of a well-developed plan, the two men were successful in raising the necessary capital to begin their business. They leased facilities and started production. However, after almost two years, the plan's goals were not being met. There were cost overruns, and profits were not nearly up to expectations.

Question 1 What problems might have contributed to the firm's poor performance?

Question 2 Although several problems were encountered in implementing the business plan, the primary reason for the low profits turned out to be embezzlement. Jones was diverting company resources for personal use, even taking some of the construction material purchased by the company and using it to build his own house. What could Rose have done to avoid this situation? What are his options after the fact?

Experiential Exercises

1. Suppose that you want to start a business to produce and sell a product designed to hold down a tablecloth on a picnic table so that the wind will not blow it off. Prepare a one-page outline of the marketing plan for this product. Be as specific and comprehensive as possible.
2. A former chef wants to start a business to supply temporary kitchen help (such as chefs, sauce cooks, bakers, and meat cutters) to restaurants in need of staff during busy periods. Prepare a one-page report explaining which section or sections of the business plan would be most crucial to this new business and why.
3. Suppose that you wish to start a tutoring service for college students in elementary accounting courses. List the benefits you would realize from preparing a written business plan.
4. Interview a person who has started a business within the past five years. Prepare a report describing the extent to which the entrepreneur engaged in preliminary planning and his or her views about the value of business plans.

Exploring the Web

1. Access the Writing a Business Plan link at **http://www.inc.com**.
   a. Follow the link to Build a Strong Business Plan: Section by Section. Print the outline for a complete business plan.
   b. What advice is offered about the executive summary?
   c. Inc.com offers a wealth of information on business plans. Read an article, and write a one-paragraph summary.
2. Access **http://www.startup.com** to answer the following questions.
   a. What is the main service this company performs to aid startup businesses in getting off the ground so quickly?
   b. Print the ethical requirements (found under About Us and Policies) for entrepreneurs wishing to use this service. How important is it to abide by these ethical principles?
   c. Would an entrepreneur need to submit a business plan when contacting Startup.com?

Case 8

ROBINSON ASSOCIATES, INC. (p. 658)

This case presents a business plan for a proposed management consulting firm.

The Business Plan

Laying the Foundation

The chapters in Part 4, "The New Venture Business Plan," deal with issues that are important in starting a new venture. This chapter presented an overview of the business plan and its preparation. Chapters 9 through 14 focus on major segments of the business plan, such as the management plan, the marketing plan, and the financial plan. After you have carefully studied these chapters, you will have the knowledge you need to prepare a business plan.

Recognizing that applying what you study facilitates learning, we have included, at the end of each chapter in Part 4, a list of important questions that need to be addressed in preparing a particular segment of a business plan. In this chapter, we also include lists of books, Web sites, and software packages useful for preparing business plans.

BOOKS ON PREPARING BUSINESS PLANS

The following supplement to this textbook offers an in-depth discussion of the preparation of business plans and includes sample plans:

Longenecker, Justin G., Carlos W. Moore, and J. William Petty. *Preparing the Business Plan.* Cincinnati: South-Western, 2002.

Other helpful references include the following:

Abrams, Rhonda M. *The Successful Business Plan: Secrets and Strategies,* 3rd ed. Grants Pass, OR: Oasis Press, 2000.

Arkebauer, James B. *McGraw-Hill Guide to Writing a High-Impact Business Plan: A Proven Blueprint for First-Time Entrepreneurs.* New York: McGraw Hill, 1994.

Arthur Andersen and Company. *An Entrepreneur's Guide to Developing a Business Plan.* Chicago: Author, 1990.

Bangs, David H., Jr. *The Business Planning Guide: Creating a Plan for Success in Your Own Business,* 8th ed. Dover, NH: Upstart Publishing, 1998.

Deloitte & Touche, LLP. *Writing an Effective Business Plan.* New York: Author, 1998.

Eglash, Joanne. *How to Write a .Com Business Plan: The Internet Entrepreneur's Guide to Everything You Need to Know About Business Plans and Financing Options.* New York: McGraw-Hill, 2000.

Gumpert, David E. *How to Really Create a Successful Business Plan,* 3rd ed. Boulder, CO: Inc. Business, 1996.

Henricks, Mark. *Business Plans Made Easy.* Newburgh, NY: Entrepreneur Media, Inc., 1999.

Horan, Jim T. *The One Page Business Plan: Start with a Vision, Build a Company.* El Sobrante, CA: One Page Business Plan Company, 1998.

McKeever, Mike P. *How to Write a Business Plan,* 5th ed. Nolo.com, November 1999.

Patsula, Peter, J. *Successful Business Planning in 30 Days: A Step-by-Step Guide for Writing a Business Plan and Starting Your Own Business.* Mansfield, OH: Patsula Media, 2000.

Pinson, Linda, and Jerry Jinnett. *Anatomy of a Business Plan,* 4th ed. Chicago: Enterprise/Dearborn, 1999.

Purdy, Warren G. *The Guide to Retail Business Planning: The Complete Handbook for Creating a Winning Plan for Any Retail Business.* Florence, KY: Thomson Learning, 1998.

Rich, Stanley R., and David E. Gumpert. *Business Plans That Win $$$: Lessons from the MIT Enterprise Forum.* New York: HarperCollins, 1987.

Ross, L. Manning. *Businessplan.Com: How to Write an Ecommerce Business Plan,* 2nd ed. Central Point, OR: The Oasis Press, 2000.

Siegel, Eric, Brian Ford, and Jay Bornstein. *The Ernst & Young Business Plan Guide.* New York: John Wiley & Sons, 1993.

Tiffany, Paul, and Steven Peterson. *Creating Business Plans for Dummies.* Foster City, CA: IDG Books Worldwide, 1997.

Touche Ross & Co. *The Business Plan: A Touche Ross Guide to Writing an Effective Business Plan.* Los Angeles: Author, 1997.

Williams, Edward E. *Business Planning: 25 Keys to a Sound Business Plan.* (The New York Times Pocket MBA Series). New York: *New York Times,* 1999.

WEB SITES ON PREPARING BUSINESS PLANS

The following Web sites can be extremely helpful in preparing a business plan.

American Express:
http://home3.americanexpress.com/smallbusiness/resources/starting/biz_plan

BizPlanit:
http://www.bizplanit.com

CCH Business Owner's Toolkit:
http://www.toolkit.cch.com

Palo Alto Software, Inc., Bplans.com:
http://www.bplans.com

Service Corps of Retired Executives (SCORE):
http://www.score.org

Small Business Administration, Business Plan Outline:
http://www.sba.gov/starting/indexbusplans.html

SOFTWARE ON PREPARING BUSINESS PLANS

The following two software packages provide good examples of the types of computerized assistance available for preparing business plans:

BIZPLAN*Builder,* available at **http://www.jian.com**

Business Plan Pro, available at **http://www.palo-alto.com**

COMPANY DESCRIPTION QUESTIONS

Now that you have learned the main concepts of business plan preparation, you can begin the process of creating a business plan by writing a general company description. In thinking about the key issues in starting a new business, respond to the following questions:

1. When and where is the business to start?
2. What is the history of the company?
3. What changes have been made in structure or ownership?
4. In what stage of development is the company?
5. What has been achieved to date?
6. What is the company's distinctive competence?
7. What are the basic nature and activity of the business?
8. What is its primary product or service?
9. What customers will be served?
10. What is the company's mission statement?
11. What are the company's objectives?
12. What is the company's form of organization?
13. What are the current and projected economic states of the industry?
14. Does the company intend to become a publicly traded company or an acquisition candidate?

chapter 9

Developing the Marketing Plan

In the Spotlight

BBH Exhibits, Inc.

Finding a market and then developing a marketing plan to meet customer needs are essential steps in developing a successful business venture. Consider BBH Exhibits, Inc. and the marketing strategy of its founder, president, and CEO, Stacy F. King. Her company, based in San Antonio, Texas, was started in 1992 and after nine years is already a premier provider of traveling museum exhibits. How did her firm become so successful so quickly? She had a marketing plan.

After college and a brief stay at Neiman Marcus in Dallas, Texas, where King was the youngest buyer in the store's history, she left to pursue her entrepreneurial dream. King believed that there was a market for educational exhibits providing high-quality, multisensory experiences and that she could meet those needs. Her plan was to quickly grab hold of the exhibits market—and she did, beginning with her first brainchild exhibit, Backyard Monsters.

King promotes her exhibits to corporate sponsors, such as Ford, IBM, and Hertz, who pay for some of the up-front development costs associated with producing the museum exhibits. In return, the companies receive name recognition and positive goodwill. Her firm reports that over 60 million people have already enjoyed a BBH exhibit, providing the company with annual revenues of over $5 million.

Referring to King and BBH, Carol Valenta, a vice president at the St. Louis Science Center, says, "We've tried to create traveling exhibits on our own but haven't come up to their level." Clearly, King controls a niche market by meeting the needs of its customers. ◆

Source: From material from http://www.bbhinc.net; and Kerry A. Dolan, "From Couture to Critters," *Forbes,* Vol. 167, No. 2 (January 22, 2001), pp. 116–117.

http://www.bbhinc.net

LOOKING AHEAD

After studying this chapter, you should be able to

1. *Describe small business marketing.*
2. *Discuss the nature of the marketing research process.*
3. *Define market segmentation and its related strategies.*
4. *Explain the different methods of forecasting sales.*
5. *Identify the components of a formal marketing plan.*

As important as they are, neither a good organizational plan nor a sound financial strategy can substitute for a well-developed marketing plan. Therefore, the best new venture business plans discuss marketing strategy, in an effort to convince potential investors of the likelihood of success.

Unfortunately, some entrepreneurs ignore marketing in the early stages of planning their new ventures. They concentrate on the cart and neglect the horse—emphasizing the idea behind the product or service while overlooking the marketing activities that will carry the idea to customers. Consider the following conversation between a first-time entrepreneur and a marketing consultant:

Marketing Consultant: May I see your marketing plan?
Entrepreneur: You could if I had one, but I don't. It's a great concept, and I just know people will want to buy it.
Marketing Consultant: How do you know that these people will be so eager to buy? Is this what your consumer research indicates?
Entrepreneur: I don't have any research . . . but my friends tell me it's a fantastic idea that will sell like hotcakes.

Such optimism is commendable, but becoming infatuated with an idea can have devastating consequences. An entrepreneur needs to understand marketing activities and how they can be used to identify a market, ascertain market potential, and then transfer the idea into a product or service for potential customers.

This chapter describes small business marketing, paying special attention to the role of marketing research, market segmentation, and forecasting in developing information for the marketing plan but also identifying other marketing activities needed to transform the entrepreneur's idea into a marketable product or service. Each of these activities should be described in the marketing plan component of the overall business plan. (Additional discussions of marketing activities are found in Chapters 15 through 17.)

WHAT IS SMALL BUSINESS MARKETING?

Describe small business marketing.

Marketing means different things to different people. Some entrepreneurs view marketing as simply selling a product or service. Others view marketing as those activities directing the flow of goods and services from producer to consumer or user. In reality, small business marketing is much broader. It consists of many activities, some of which occur even before a product is produced and ready for distribution and sale.

small business marketing
business activities that identify a target market, determine that market's potential, and prepare, communicate, and deliver a bundle of satisfaction to that market

market analysis
an evaluation process that encompasses market segmentation, marketing research, and sales forecasting

marketing mix
the combination of product, pricing, promotion, and distribution activities

We offer a comprehensive definition of small business marketing in order to portray its true scope. **Small business marketing** consists of those business activities that relate directly to (1) identifying a target market, (2) determining target market potential, and (3) preparing, communicating, and delivering a bundle of satisfaction to the target market.

This definition identifies several marketing activities essential to every small business (see Figure 9-1). Marketing research, market segmentation, and sales forecasting are the key tools that comprise **market analysis.** Product, pricing, promotion, and distribution activities combine to form the **marketing mix.**

Marketing Philosophies Make a Difference

Just as an individual's personal philosophy about life influences the strategy that person uses to achieve personal goals, a firm's marketing philosophy determines how strategic marketing activities are used to achieve business goals. Three different marketing perspectives that permeate small businesses are the production-oriented, sales-oriented, and consumer-oriented philosophies.

A *production-oriented philosophy* emphasizes the product as the single most important part of the business. The firm concentrates resources on developing the product or service in the most efficient manner, even if promotion, distribution, and other marketing activities are slighted. On the other hand, a *sales-oriented philosophy* deemphasizes production efficiencies and customer preferences in favor of a focus on sales. Achieving sales goals becomes the firm's highest priority. Finally, a firm adopting a *consumer-oriented philosophy* believes everything, including production and sales, centers around the consumer and his or her needs. The result: All marketing efforts begin and end with the consumer.

A Consumer Orientation—The Right Choice

Over the years, both large and small businesses have gradually shifted their marketing emphasis from production to sales and, more recently, to consumers. *We strongly recommend that all new businesses begin with a consumer orientation, as*

FIGURE 9-1

Small Business Marketing Activities

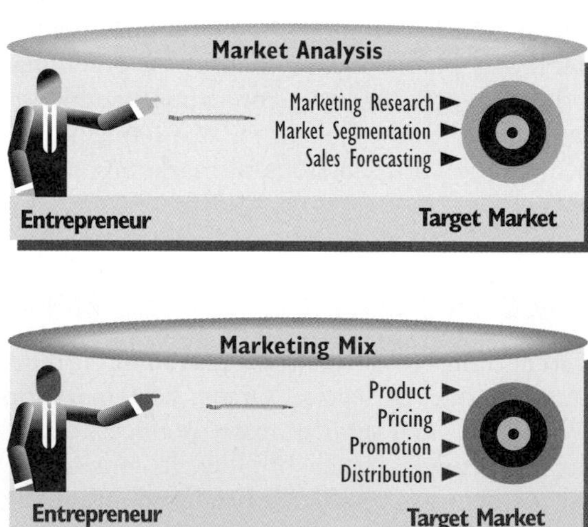

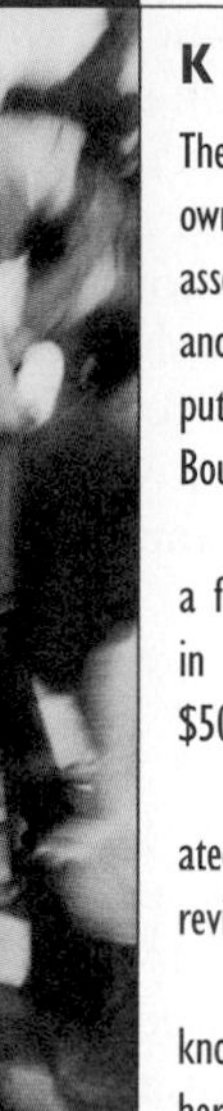

IN THE TRENCHES

Building Customer Loyalty

KEEP THE KIDS HAPPY

The consumer-oriented strategy of entrepreneur Maxine Clark is quite clear: Keep the kids happy by letting them build their own toys. She is the founder of Build-A-Bear Workshops, retail stores where children can assemble their own teddy bears. In the stores, kids choose the unstuffed animal they want and, with the help of an employee, fill their animal with white fluff. Then, using a computer, the children name their animal—and, of course, they buy outfits from the "Bear Boutique" before leaving the store.

Clark's idea was inspired by visits to toy factories and researched with the help of a friend's daughter, Katie. Clark opened her first store in St. Louis in 1997, with $750,000 in personal savings. Four years later, she has 53 stores, with annual revenues of over $50 million.

Having listened to Katie's opinion before starting her business, Clark has now created a Cub Advisory Board made up of 20 St. Louis–area children, ages 6–15. The board reviews programs and new ideas and communicates with Clark regularly via mail or e-mail.

Clark frequently leaves the company headquarters to work in one of the stores. She knows it is important to stay in close contact with her young customers if she is to achieve her goal—customer satisfaction.

Source: From material from http://www.buildabear.com; Sharon Nelton, "Building an Empire One Smile at a Time," *Success*, http://www.successmag.com, December 1, 2000; and Tom Post, "Yes, There Is a Pulse," *Forbes*, Vol. 164, No. 1 (July 5, 1999), p. 105.

http://www.buildabear.com

this philosophy is most consistent with long-term success. Remember, customer satisfaction is not a means to achieving a certain goal—it is the goal!

Why have some small firms failed to adopt a consumer orientation when the benefits seem so obvious? The answer lies in three key factors. First, the state of competition always affects a firm's marketing orientation. If there is little or no competition and if demand exceeds supply, a firm is tempted to emphasize only production. This is usually a short-term situation, however, and one that often leads to disaster.

Second, many small business managers have strong production skills but are weak in marketing ability. Naturally, these managers will attend primarily to production considerations.

Third, some managers are simply too focused on the present. They expect the firm's marketing efforts to reap immediate dividends and, consequently, favor a sales-oriented philosophy. However, putting too much emphasis on selling merchandise often creates customer dissatisfaction, especially if high-pressure selling is used with little regard for customers' needs.

Both the production- and the sales-oriented philosophies may generate short-run success. However, a consumer orientation not only recognizes production efficiency goals and professional selling but also adds concern for customer satisfaction. In effect, a firm that adopts a consumer orientation incorporates the best of each marketing philosophy. Chapter 15 further examines the importance of a customer satisfaction strategy.

Marketing Research for the New Venture

Entrepreneurs can develop marketing plans for their new ventures based on intuition alone, or they can supplement their judgment with sound market information. *In every case, it is advisable to put entrepreneurial excitement on hold until marketing research facts have been collected and evaluated.* A marketing plan based on research will undoubtedly be stronger than a plan without such a foundation.

As important as marketing research is, however, it should never be used to suppress entrepreneurial enthusiasm and a hands-on feel for the market. It should be viewed as a supplement to, not a replacement for, intuitive judgment and a sense of cautious experimentation in launching new products and services.

The Nature of Marketing Research

2

Discuss the nature of the marketing research process.

marketing research
the gathering, processing, reporting, and interpreting of market information

Marketing research may be defined as the gathering, processing, reporting, and interpreting of marketing information. A small business typically conducts less marketing research than does a big business, partly because of the expense involved but also because of lack of understanding of the basic research process. Our discussion of marketing research focuses on the more widely used practical techniques that small business firms can employ as they analyze potential target markets and make other marketing decisions.

Although an entrepreneur can conduct marketing research without the assistance of an expert, the cost of hiring such an expert is often money well spent, as the expert's advice may help increase revenues or cut costs. The prices for research services reflect the fact that marketing researchers are trained, experienced professionals. For example, focus groups run from $3,000 to $10,000 each, and a telephone survey may range anywhere from $5,000 to $25,000 or more, depending on the number of interviews and the length of the questionnaire. However, companies such as SurveySite, Inc. are now reducing overall research costs by taking advantage of the Internet to offer Web-based surveys and online focus groups.

http://www.surveysite.com

An entrepreneur should always compare the expected costs of marketing research with the expected benefits before committing to research. Although such analysis is never exact, it will help the entrepreneur decide what research should be conducted. Because the large costs associated with marketing research represent a substantial investment for most small businesses, owners should ask themselves the following questions before contacting a research firm:

- Is the research really necessary?
- Will the data obtained justify the expense?
- Can I do the research myself?

Steps in the Marketing Research Process

The typical steps in the marketing research process are (1) identifying the informational need, (2) searching for secondary data, (3) collecting primary data, and (4) interpreting the data gathered.

IDENTIFYING THE INFORMATIONAL NEED The first step in marketing research is to identify and define the informational need. Although this step seems almost too obvious to mention, the fact is that entrepreneurs sometimes commission surveys without pinpointing the specific information most relevant to their venture. A broad

statement such as "Our need is to know if the venture will be successful" is obviously not helpful in guiding the research process, but even a more specific goal may be misdirected. For example, an entrepreneur contemplating a location for a restaurant may decide to conduct a survey to ascertain customer menu preferences and reasons for eating out when, in fact, the more relevant information would be how often residents of the target area eat out and how far they are willing to drive to eat in a restaurant.

When an entrepreneur defines the venture's informational need correctly, research can be designed to concentrate on that specific need. Later in this chapter, you will see a survey questionnaire developed for a car-wash owner who wanted to ascertain customer satisfaction. The informational need that the entrepreneur identified was clear: Determine the level of customers' satisfaction with the car-cleaning experience.

SEARCHING FOR SECONDARY DATA Information that has already been compiled is known as **secondary data.** Generally, gathering secondary data is less expensive than gathering new, or primary, data. Therefore, after defining informational needs, entrepreneurs should exhaust available sources of secondary data before going further into the research process. It may be possible to base much of the marketing plan for the new venture solely on secondary data. "It's a myth that only the big guys have the wherewithal to do market research," says Mary Beth Campau, assistant vice president for reference services at Dun & Bradstreet Information Services. "There is a wealth of timely information from a variety of sources available in public and university libraries throughout the United States. Just ask the librarians, and they'll be happy to point you in the right direction."[1]

secondary data
market information that has been previously compiled

http://www.dnb.com

Another helpful source of secondary data for the small firm is the Small Business Administration (SBA). This agency publishes extensive bibliographies in many decision areas, including marketing research. Software programs and hundreds of Web sites (many offering free information) can also help an entrepreneur research customers.

http://www.sba.gov

Unfortunately, several problems accompany the use of secondary data. One problem is that such data may be outdated. Another problem is that the units of measure in the secondary data may not fit the current problem. For example, a firm's market might consist of individuals with incomes between $20,000 and $25,000, while secondary data show the number of individuals with incomes between $15,000 and $50,000.

Finally, the question of credibility is always present. Some sources of secondary data are less trustworthy than others. Mere publication of data does not in itself make the data valid and reliable. It is advisable to compare several different sources to see if they are reporting similar data. Professional research specialists can also help assess the credibility of secondary sources.

COLLECTING PRIMARY DATA If the secondary data are insufficient, a search for new information, or **primary data,** is the next step. The techniques used in accumulating primary data are often classified as observational methods and questioning methods. Observational methods avoid interpersonal contact between respondents and the researcher, while questioning methods involve some type of interaction with respondents.

primary data
new market information that is gathered by the firm conducting the research

Observational Methods Observation is probably the oldest form of research in existence. Indeed, learning by observing is quite common. Thus, it is hardly surprising that observation can provide useful information for small businesses. An excellent

UTILIZING NEW TECHNOLOGY

IN THE TRENCHES

WEB CUSTOMERS VOICE OPINIONS

Dale Bathum's idea for a nontraditional golf shoe has taken his firm, Bite Footwear, from a startup in 1996 to a successful manufacturer with over $4 million in sales in the first half of 2001. With its 35-year-old entrepreneur at the helm, the Preston, Washington company now sells sporting shoes and apparel to over 2,000 retail customers worldwide.

Bathum has always gathered research information prior to introducing new products. As an example, he cites a proposed design for a shoe named Reverse Pivot, which Bite hoped would be a smash hit. Before committing to its introduction, the firm posted a photo of and information about the shoe on its Web site and e-mailed 50 loyal customers for comments regarding the shoe's style and price. Although many golfers liked the Reverse Pivot style, most retail buyers didn't and were hesitant to say that they would order the shoe—so the design was scrapped.

Later, in 1998, while developing a design for the bowling-shoe market, Bite again displayed prototypes online to gather buyer feedback. "Before the Web, we flew in key buyers from all over the country to see the line," says Bathum. "That was super-expensive."

After receiving buyers' e-mail responses to prototypes, company representatives always telephone respondents. "You have a reason to call them up, other than trying to sell them something," Bathum says. "Plus, they feel as if they are a part of the process."

This entrepreneur understands how to use the Web as both a marketing channel and a research tool.

Source: From material from http://www.bitefootwear.com, July 31, 2001; and Anne Marie Borrego, "Will They Bite?" http://www.inc.com, November 15, 1999.

http://www.bitefootwear.com

http://www.sudburysoup.com

method of observational research has been devised by Jean Sullivan, who experiments with new soup ideas for her Sudbury Soup Company, located in Concord, Massachusetts. She arranges tastings in most of the supermarkets where her soups are sold and closely observes shoppers' reactions to the samples she cooks for them.[2]

Observational methods can be economical. Furthermore, they avoid the potential bias that can result from a respondent's contact with an interviewer during questioning. Observation—for example, counting customers going into a store—can be conducted by a person or by mechanical devices, such as hidden video cameras. The cost of mechanical observation devices is rapidly declining, bringing them within the budget of many small businesses. When Scott Semel and Reed Chase wanted to learn more about their competitors and customers after buying a candy-importing company, Cody-Kramer Imports, in Blauvolt, New York, what did they do? They attended several major industry trade shows and checked out competitors' booths. They also wandered the aisles of candy retailers, observing whatever they could about candy-buying customers.[3]

Questioning Methods Surveys and experimentation are both questioning methods that involve contact with respondents. Surveys can be conducted by mail, telephone, or personal interview. Mail surveys are often used when target respondents are

widely dispersed; however, they usually yield low response rates. Telephone surveys and personal interview surveys achieve higher response rates. However, personal interview surveys are expensive. Moreover, individuals are often reluctant to grant personal interviews because they suspect that a sales pitch is forthcoming. Some marketing researchers, such as NetReflector InstantSurvey, offer firms a new way to survey customers—through an online questionnaire. However, Internet surveying is so new that credible data are lacking on response rates. Some Web sites claim that online surveys have better response rates than do paper surveys.

http://www.netreflector.com

A questionnaire is the basic instrument guiding the researcher and the respondent when a survey is being taken. A questionnaire should be developed carefully and pre-tested before it is used in the market. Several considerations should be kept in mind in designing and testing a questionnaire:

- Ask questions that relate to the issue under consideration. An interesting question may not be relevant. A good test of relevance is to assume an answer to each question and then ask yourself how you would use that information.
- Select the form of question that is most appropriate for the subject and the conditions of the survey. Open-ended and multiple-choice questions are two popular forms.
- Carefully consider the order of the questions. Asking questions in the wrong sequence can produce biased answers to later questions.
- Ask the more sensitive questions near the end of the questionnaire. Age and income, for example, are usually sensitive topics.
- Carefully select the words in each question. They should be as simple, clear, and objective as possible.
- Pre-test the questionnaire by administering it to a small sample of respondents who are representative of the group to be surveyed.

Figure 9-2 shows a questionnaire developed for a car-wash owner. This survey instrument illustrates how the above considerations can be incorporated into a questionnaire. Note the use of both multiple-choice and open-ended questions. Responses to the open-ended questions were particularly useful to this firm.

INTERPRETING THE DATA GATHERED After the necessary data have been gathered, they must be transformed into usable information. Without interpretation, large quantities of data are only facts. Methods of summarizing and simplifying information for users include tables, charts, and other graphics. Descriptive statistics such as the mean, mode, and median are most helpful during this step in the research procedure. Inexpensive personal computer software is now available to perform statistical calculations and generate report-quality graphics.

It should be re-emphasized that formal marketing research is not always necessary in launching a new venture. Bill Madway, founder and president of Madway Business Research, Inc. in Malvern, Pennsylvania, says, "Sometimes, you cannot answer a question with research . . . you just have to test it. Then the question is whether you can afford to test something that might not work. If there's very little risk involved or you can test it on a very small scale, you might decide to jump in. But the bigger the risk, the more valuable advance information becomes."[4]

FIGURE 9-2

Small Business Survey Questionnaire

PLEASE—WE NEED YOUR HELP!

You're The Boss. ***All of us here at Genie Car Wash have just one purpose . . . TO PLEASE YOU!***

Date ____________________ Time ____________________ of Visit

How are we doing?

	Yes	No		
1. Personnel—courteous and helpful?				
Service writer	☐	☐		
Vacuum attendants	☐	☐		
Cashier	☐	☐		
Final finish & inspection	☐	☐		
Management	☐	☐		
2. Do you feel the time it took to wash your car was . . .				
Right amount of time	☐			
Too much time	☐			
Not enough time	☐			
	Excel	**Good**	**Avg**	**Poor**
3. How do you judge the appearance of the personnel?	☐	☐	☐	☐
4. Please rate the quality of workmanship on the interior of your car.				
Inside vacuum	☐	☐	☐	☐
Dashboard	☐	☐	☐	☐
Doorjambs	☐	☐	☐	☐
Ash trays	☐	☐	☐	☐
Windows	☐	☐	☐	☐
Console	☐	☐	☐	☐
5. Please rate the quality of workmanship on the exterior of your car.				
Tires and wheels	☐	☐	☐	☐
Bumpers and chrome	☐	☐	☐	☐
Body of car	☐	☐	☐	☐
Grill	☐	☐	☐	☐
6. Please rate the overall appearance of our facility.				
Outside building & grounds	☐	☐	☐	☐
Inside building	☐	☐	☐	☐
Rest rooms	☐	☐	☐	☐
7. Please rate your overall impression of the experience you had while at Genie Car Wash.	☐	☐	☐	☐

It is important that we clean your car to your satisfaction. Additional comments will be appreciated.

____

____

____

OPTIONAL

Your Name ____________________

Address ____________________

City ____________________ State __________ Zip __________

Thank you!

Understanding Potential Target Markets

The term *market* means different things to different people. It may refer to a physical location where buying and selling take place ("They went to the market"), or it may be used to describe selling efforts ("We must market this product aggressively"). Still another meaning is the one we emphasize in this chapter: A **market** is a group of customers or potential customers who have purchasing power and unsatisfied needs. Note carefully the three ingredients in this definition of a market.

market
a group of customers or potential customers who have purchasing power and unsatisfied needs

First, a market must have buying units, or *customers*. These units may be individuals or business entities. Thus, a market is more than a geographic area; it must contain potential customers.

Second, a market must contain buying units with *unsatisfied needs*. Consumers, for instance, will not buy unless they are motivated to do so—and motivation can occur only when a customer recognizes his or her unsatisfied needs. It would be extremely difficult, for example, to sell luxury urban apartments to desert nomads!

Third, customers in a market must have *purchasing power*. Assessing the level of purchasing power in a potential market is very important. Customers who have unsatisfied needs but who lack money and/or credit do not constitute a viable market because they have nothing to offer in exchange for a product or service. In such a situation, no transactions can occur.

In light of our definition of a market, determining market potential is the process of locating and investigating buying units that have both purchasing power and needs that can be satisfied with the product or service that is being offered.

Market Segmentation and Its Variables

Define market segmentation and its related strategies.

In Chapter 2, cost-advantage and marketing-advantage strategies were applied to marketplaces that were relatively homogeneous, or uniform, in nature. These strategies can also be used to focus on a limited market within an industry. In his book *Competitive Advantage*, Michael Porter refers to this type of competitive strategy—in which cost and marketing advantages are achieved within narrow market segments—as a *focus strategy*.[5]

A focus strategy depends on market segmentation and arises from stiff competition. Formally defined, **market segmentation** is the process of dividing the total market for a product or service into groups with similar needs, such that each group is likely to respond favorably to a specific marketing strategy. Developments in the cell phone industry provide a good example of real-world market segmentation. Initially, cell phone service providers aimed at a very broad market and practiced very little market segmentation. But as competition developed, they began to focus on market segments, such as small businesses, families, younger customers, and firms demanding Internet connections for their traveling employees.

market segmentation
the division of a market into several smaller groups with similar needs

In order to divide the total market into appropriate segments, an entrepreneur must consider **segmentation variables,** which are parameters that identify the particular dimensions that distinguish one form of market behavior from another. Two broad sets of segmentation variables that represent major dimensions of a market are benefit variables and demographic variables.

segmentation variables
the parameters used to distinguish one form of market behavior from another

benefit variables
specific characteristics that distinguish market segments according to the benefits sought by customers

BENEFIT VARIABLES The definition of a market highlights the unsatisfied needs of customers. **Benefit variables** are related to customer needs since they are used to identify segments of a market based on the benefits sought by customers. For

example, the toothpaste market has several benefit segments. The principal benefit to parents might be cavity prevention for their young children, while the principal benefit to teenagers might be fresh breath. Toothpaste is the product in both cases, but it has two different market segments.

DEMOGRAPHIC VARIABLES Benefit variables alone are insufficient for market analysis; it is impossible to implement forecasting and marketing strategy without defining the market further. Therefore, small businesses commonly use demographic variables as part of market segmentation. Typical demographic variables are age, marital status, sex, occupation, and income. Recall the definition of a market—customers with purchasing power and unsatisfied needs. **Demographic variables** refer to certain characteristics that describe customers and their purchasing power.

demographic variables
specific characteristics that describe customers and their purchasing power

Types of Market Segmentation Strategies

There are several types of market segmentation strategies. The three types discussed here are the unsegmented approach, the multisegmentation approach, and the single-segmentation approach. These strategies can best be illustrated by using an example—a hypothetical small firm called the Community Writing Company.

THE UNSEGMENTED STRATEGY When a business defines the total market as its target, it is following an **unsegmented strategy** (also known as **mass marketing**). This strategy can sometimes be successful, but it assumes that all customers desire the same basic benefit from the product or service. This may hold true for water but certainly does not hold true for shoes, which satisfy numerous needs through many styles, prices, colors, and sizes. With an unsegmented strategy, a firm develops a single marketing mix—one combination of product, price, promotion, and distribution. Its competitive advantage must be derived from either a cost or a marketing advantage. The unsegmented strategy of the Community Writing Company is shown in Figure 9-3. The Community Writing Company's product is a lead pencil that is sold at the single unit price of $0.79 and is promoted through one medium and an extensive distribution plan. Even with an unsegmented strategy, some segmenting must occur. Note in Figure 9-3 that the market does not include everyone in the universe—just those who might use writing instruments.

unsegmented strategy (mass marketing)
a strategy that defines the total market as the target market

THE MULTISEGMENTATION STRATEGY With a view of the market that recognizes individual segments with different preferences, a firm is in a better position to tailor marketing mixes to various segments. If a firm determines that two or more market segments have the potential to be profitable and then develops a unique marketing mix for each segment, it is following a **multisegmentation strategy.**

multisegmentation strategy
a strategy that recognizes different preferences of individual market segments and develops a unique marketing mix for each

Let's assume that the Community Writing Company has recognized three separate market segments: students, professors, and executives. Following the multisegmentation approach, the company develops a competitive advantage with three marketing mixes, based on differences in pricing, promotion, distribution, or the product itself, as shown in Figure 9-4 on page 228. Marketing Mix 1 consists of selling felt-tip pens to students through bookstores at the lower-than-normal price of $0.49 and supporting this effort with a promotional campaign in campus newspapers. With Marketing Mix 2, the company markets the same pen to universities for use by professors. Professional magazines are the promotional medium used in this

FIGURE 9-3

An Unsegmented Market Strategy

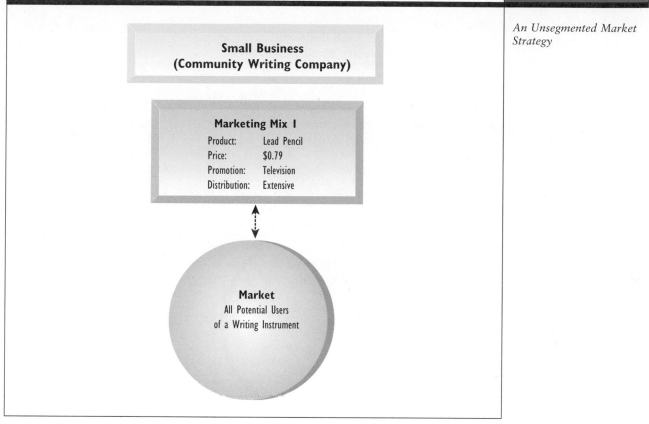

mix, distribution is direct from the factory, and the product price is $1.00. Finally, Marketing Mix 3, which is aimed at corporate executives, consists of selling a gold fountain pen, priced at $50.00, only in exclusive department stores and promoting it by personal selling. Note the distinct differences in these three marketing mixes. Small businesses tend to resist the use of the multisegmentation strategy because of the risk of spreading resources too thinly among several marketing efforts.

THE SINGLE-SEGMENTATION STRATEGY When a firm recognizes that several distinct market segments exist but chooses to concentrate on reaching only one segment, it is following a **single-segmentation strategy.** The segment selected is the one that seems to offer the greatest profitability. Once again, a competitive advantage is achieved through a cost- or marketing-advantage strategy. In Figure 9-5 on page 229, the Community Writing Company decides to pursue a single-segmentation approach and selects the student market segment.

single-segmentation strategy
a strategy that recognizes the existence of several distinct market segments but focuses on only the most profitable segment

The single-segmentation approach is probably the wisest strategy for small businesses to use during initial marketing efforts. It allows a small firm to specialize and make better use of its limited resources. Then, once its reputation has been built, the firm will find it easier to enter new markets.

FIGURE 9-4 *A Multisegmentation Market Strategy*

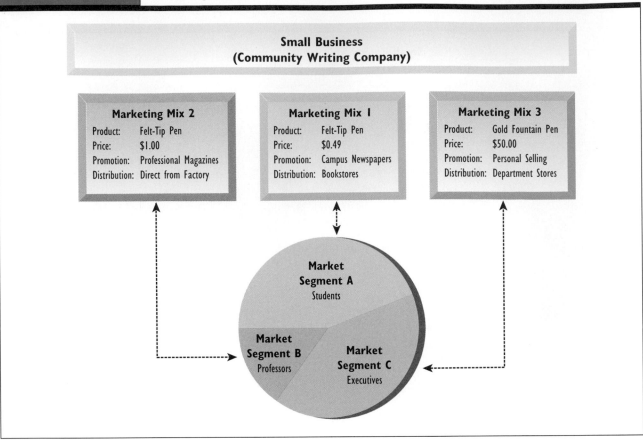

Estimating Market Potential

A small business can be successful only if an adequate market exists for its product or service. The sales forecast is the typical indicator of market adequacy. Forecasting is particularly important prior to starting a business. An entrepreneur who enters the marketplace without it is much like a high diver who leaves the board without checking the depth of the water. Many types of information from numerous sources are required to determine market potential. This section examines market components and the forecasting process.

Explain the different methods of forecasting sales.

sales forecast
a prediction of how much of a product or service will be purchased within a market during a specified time period

The Sales Forecast

Formally defined, a **sales forecast** estimates how much of a product or service can be sold within a given market in a defined time period. The forecast can be stated in terms of dollars and/or units.

Because a sales forecast revolves around a specific target market, the market should be defined as precisely as possible. The market description forms the forecasting boundary. If the market for electric razors is described as "men," the sales forecast will be extremely large. A more precise definition, such as "men between

FIGURE 9-5

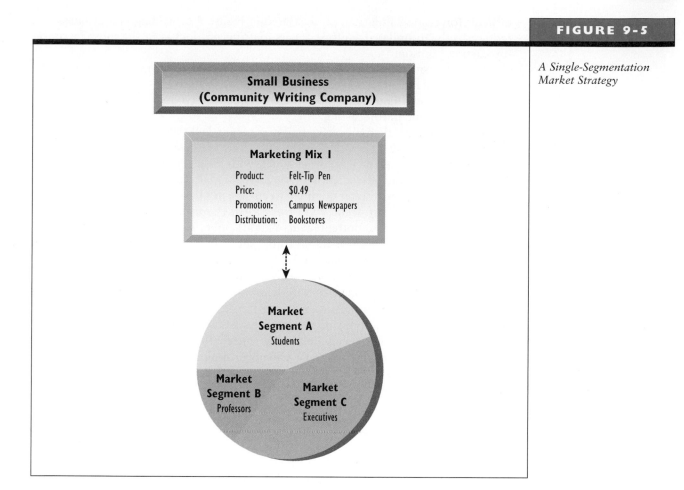

A Single-Segmentation Market Strategy

the ages of 15 and 25 who are dissatisfied with nonelectric shavers," will result in a smaller but possibly more useful forecast.

It is also important to note that a sales forecast implies a specified time period. One sales forecast may cover a year or less, while another may extend over several years. Both short-term and long-term forecasts are needed in a well-constructed business plan.

A sales forecast is an essential component of the business plan because it is critical to assessing the feasibility of a new venture. If the market is insufficient, the business is destined for failure. A sales forecast is also useful in other areas of business planning. Production schedules, inventory policies, and personnel decisions all start with a sales forecast. Obviously, a forecast can never be perfect; entrepreneurs should remember that a forecast can be wrong in either direction—underestimating potential sales or overestimating potential sales.

Limitations to Forecasting

For a number of practical reasons, forecasting is used less frequently by small firms than by large firms. First, for any new business, forecasting circumstances are unique. Entrepreneurial inexperience, coupled with a new idea, represents the most

difficult forecasting situation, as illustrated in Figure 9-6. An ongoing business that requires only an updated forecast for its existing product is in the most favorable forecasting position.

Second, a small business manager may be unfamiliar with methods of quantitative analysis. While not all forecasting must be quantitatively oriented—qualitative forecasting is helpful and may be sufficient—quantitative methods have repeatedly proven their value in forecasting.

Third, the typical small business entrepreneur lacks familiarity with the forecasting process and/or personnel with such skills. To overcome these deficiencies, some small firms attempt to keep in touch with industry trends through contacts with appropriate trade associations. The professional members of a trade association staff are frequently better qualified to engage in sales forecasting. Most libraries have a copy of *National Trade and Professional Associations of the United States,* which lists these groups. Entrepreneurs can also obtain current information about business trends by regularly reading trade publications and economic newsletters such as the *Kiplinger Washington Letter, Business Week,* and *The Wall Street Journal.* Government publications, such as the *Survey of Current Business,* the *Federal Reserve Bulletin,* and *Monthly Labor Review,* are also of interest in a general way. Subscribing to professional forecasting services is a way to obtain forecasts of general business conditions or specific forecasts for given industries.

Despite the difficulties, a small business entrepreneur should not slight the forecasting task. Instead, he or she should remember how important the sales outlook in the business plan is to obtaining financing. The statement "We can sell as many as we can produce" does not satisfy the information requirements of potential investors.

FIGURE 9-6

Dimensions of Forecasting Difficulty

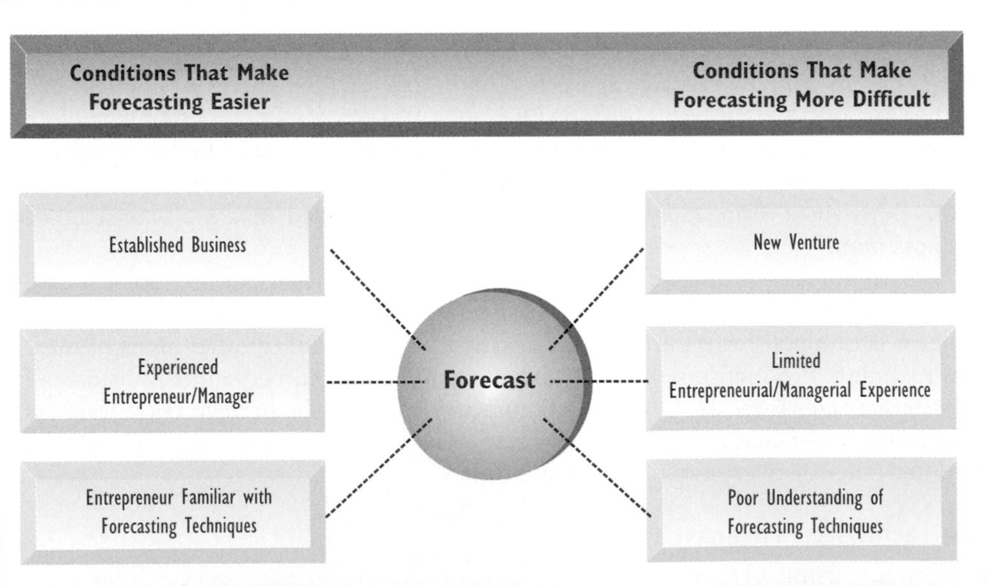

The Forecasting Process

Estimating market demand with a sales forecast is a multistep process. Typically, the sales forecast is a composite of several individual forecasts, so the process involves merging these individual forecasts properly.

The forecasting process can be characterized by two important dimensions: (1) the point at which the process is started and (2) the nature of the predicting variable. Depending on the starting point, the process may be designated as a *breakdown process* or a *buildup process*. The nature of the predicting variable determines whether the forecasting is direct or indirect.

THE STARTING POINT In the **breakdown process,** sometimes called the **chain-ratio method,** the forecaster begins with a variable that has a very large scope and systematically works down to the sales forecast. This method is frequently used for consumer products forecasting. The initial variable might be a population figure for the targeted market. Through the use of percentages, an appropriate link is built to generate the sales forecast. For example, consider the market segment identified in the hypothetical Community Writing Company. Assume that the target market is older students (25 years of age or over), seeking convenience and erasability in their writing instrument. Assume further that the initial geographic target is the state of Idaho. Table 9-1 outlines the breakdown process. The more links in the forecasting chain, the greater the potential for error.

breakdown process (chain-ratio method)
a forecasting method that begins with a macro-level variable and works down to the sales forecast

In contrast to the breakdown process, the **buildup process** calls for identifying all potential buyers in a target market's submarkets and then adding up the estimated demand. For example, a local dry-cleaning firm forecasting demand for cleaning high school letter jackets might estimate its market share within each area

buildup process
a forecasting method in which all potential buyers in the various submarkets are identified and then the estimated demand is added up

TABLE 9-1

Sales Forecasting with the Breakdown Method

Linking Variable	Source	Estimating Value	Market Potential*
1. Idaho state population	U.S. census of population		1,000,000
2. State population in target age category	*Sales & Marketing Management Survey of Buying Power*	12%	120,000
3. Target age enrolled in colleges and universities	Idaho Department of Education	30%	36,000
4. Target age college students preferring convenience over price	Student survey in a marketing research class	50%	18,000
5. Convenience-oriented students likely to purchase new felt-tip pen within next month	Personal telephone interview by entrepreneur	75%	13,500
6. People who say they are likely to purchase who actually buy	Article in *Journal of Consumer Research*	35%	4,725
7. Average number of pens bought per year	Personal experience of entrepreneur	4	18,900 ↑ SALES FORECAST FOR IDAHO

*Figures in this column, for variables 2–7, are derived by multiplying the percentage or number in the Estimating Value column times the amount on the previous line of the Market Potential column.

school as 20 percent. Then, by determining the number of high school students obtaining a letter jacket in each school—perhaps from school yearbooks—an analyst could estimate the total demand.

The buildup process is especially helpful for industrial goods forecasting. To estimate potential, forecasters often use data from the census of manufacturers by the U.S. Department of Commerce. The information can be broken down according to the North American Industry Classification System (NAICS), which classifies businesses by type of industry. Once the code for a group of potential industrial customers has been identified, the forecaster can obtain information on the number of establishments and their geographic location, number of employees, and annual sales. A sales forecast can be constructed by summing this information for several relevant codes.

http://www.naics.com

direct forecasting
a forecasting method in which sales is the predicting variable

indirect forecasting
a forecasting method in which variables are related to sales to project future sales

THE PREDICTING VARIABLE In **direct forecasting,** which is the simplest form of forecasting, sales is the forecasted variable. Many times, however, sales cannot be predicted directly and other variables must be used. **Indirect forecasting** takes place when surrogate variables are used to project the sales forecast. For example, if a firm lacks information about industry sales of baby cribs but has data on births, the strong correlation between the two variables allows planners to use the figures for births to help forecast industry sales for baby cribs.

The Formal Marketing Plan

5
Identify the components of a formal marketing plan.

After the market analysis is completed, the entrepreneur is ready to write the formal marketing plan. Each business venture is different, and, therefore, each marketing plan will be unique. An entrepreneur should not feel that he or she must develop a cloned version of a plan created by someone else. The marketing plan should include sections on market analysis, the competition, and marketing strategy. This section describes these major elements of the formal marketing plan. A more detailed discussion of marketing activities and strategies for both new and ongoing small businesses is provided in Chapters 15 through 17.

Market Analysis

customer profile
a description of potential customers in a target market

In the market analysis section of the marketing plan, the entrepreneur should describe the customers in the target market. This description of potential customers is commonly called a **customer profile.** Marketing research information, compiled from both secondary and primary data, can be used to construct this profile. A detailed discussion of the major benefits to customers provided by the new product or service should be included. Obviously, these benefits must be reasonable and consistent with statements in the "Products and/or Services" section of the business plan.

If an entrepreneur envisions several target markets, each segment must have a corresponding customer profile. Likewise, different target markets may necessitate an equal number of related marketing strategies.

Another major element of market analysis is the actual sales forecast. It is usually desirable to include several sales forecasts covering the three sales scenarios "most likely," "pessimistic," and "optimistic." These scenarios provide investors and the entrepreneur with different forecasts on which to base their evaluations.

As we pointed out earlier in this chapter, forecasting sales for a new venture is extremely difficult. While it may be necessary to make assumptions during fore-

IN THE TRENCHES | ENTREPRENEURSHIP TODAY

KNOW YOUR COMPETITORS

Frequently, entrepreneurs ignore the competition until their own ventures are under way, when it may be too late. A better strategy is to evaluate competitors before beginning a business.

This is the strategy entrepreneur Amy Ratekin followed before launching Little Elf, an event décor and gift service, in 1996. "I wanted to learn from the best," she says. "By discovering what other businesses in the industry do, finding out what works in other parts of the country and even other parts of the world, and using the ideas in my business, I have become very successful."

For example, before opening her business, Ratekin visited two local balloon companies and learned how they assembled their baskets and bouquets. Her husband then reproduced some of the ideas in their own shop design. Studying the competition also helped her learn that many existing businesses were not educating customers about how this type of service could be used. She says, "People don't know what's available. By teaching them, you increase your business."

Her home-based business operates in West Des Moines, Iowa, with 4 family members as part-time employees and 16 others as "per-needed" employees who help prepare event decorations and balloon sculptures for corporations and special events.

Source: Personal communication with Amy Ratekin, July 31, 2001; and Jacqueline Lynn, "Know the Enemy," *Entrepreneur,* http://www.entrepreneur.com, December 1999.

casting, they should be minimized. The forecasting method should be described and supported by empirical data wherever feasible.

The Competition

Frequently, entrepreneurs ignore the reality of competition for their new ventures, believing that the marketplace contains no close substitutes or that their success will not attract other entrepreneurs. This is simply not realistic.

Existing competitors should be studied carefully, and their key management personnel profiled. A brief discussion of competitors' overall strengths and weaknesses should be a part of this section of the plan. Also, related products currently being marketed or tested by competitors should be noted. An assessment should be made of the likelihood that any of these firms will enter the entrepreneur's target market.

Many competitors can be monitored by visiting their Web sites. Ann Blakeley, president of Orlando, Florida–based Earth Resources Corporation, a hazardous materials technology firm, uses search engines like AltaVista to check out her competitors. "I check every couple of months just to make sure nothing has changed," Blakeley says. "If any competitors have new products, odds are they'll put it on their Web pages."[6]

Marketing Strategy

A well-prepared market analysis and a discussion of the competition are important to the formal marketing plan. But the information on marketing strategy forms the most detailed section of the marketing plan and, in many respects, is subject to the closest scrutiny from potential investors. Such strategy plots the course of marketing actions that will give life to the entrepreneur's vision.

Four areas of marketing strategy should be addressed in the plan: (1) product development activities that will transform the basic product or service idea into a total product or service offering, (2) promotion activities that will communicate the necessary information to target markets, (3) distribution activities regarding the delivery of the product to customers, and (4) pricing activities that will set an acceptable exchange value on the total product or service.

Obviously, the nature of a new venture has a direct bearing on the emphasis given to each of these areas. For example, a service business will not have the same distribution problems as a product business, and the promotional challenges facing a new retail store will be quite different from those faced by a new manufacturer. Despite these differences, we can offer a generalized format for presenting marketing strategy in a business plan.

THE TOTAL PRODUCT AND/OR SERVICE Within this section of the marketing plan, the entrepreneur includes the name of the product or service and why it was selected. Any legal protection that has been obtained for the name should be described. It is also important to explain the logic behind the name selection. An entrepreneur's family name, if used for certain products or services, may make a positive contribution to sales. In other situations, a descriptive name that suggests a benefit of the product may be more desirable. Whatever the logic behind the choice of name, the selection should be defended.

Other components of the total product, such as the package, should be presented via drawings. Sometimes, it may be desirable to use professional packaging consultants to develop these drawings. Customer service plans such as warranties and repair policies need to be discussed here. These elements of the marketing strategy should be tied directly to customer satisfaction. (Consumer satisfaction and product or service strategy are discussed in more depth in Chapter 15.)

THE DISTRIBUTION PLAN Quite often, new ventures will use established intermediaries as their channels of distribution. This distribution strategy expedites the process and reduces the necessary investment. How those intermediaries will be persuaded to carry the new product should be explained in the distribution plan. Any intention the new business may have to license its product or service should also be covered in this section.

Some new retail ventures require fixed locations; others need mobile stores. The layouts and configurations of retail outlets should be explained here.

When a new firm's method of product delivery is exporting, the distribution plan must discuss the relevant laws and regulations governing that activity. Knowledge of exchange rates and distribution options must be reflected in the material included in this section. (Distribution concepts are explained in detail in Chapter 15.)

THE PRICING PLAN At the very minimum, the price of a product or service must cover the costs of bringing it to customers. Therefore, the pricing plan must include a schedule of both production and marketing costs. Break-even computations

should be included for alternative prices. Naturally, forecasting methods used for analysis in this section should be consistent with those used in preparing the market analysis section. However, setting a price based exclusively on break-even analysis is not advisable, as it ignores other aspects of pricing. If the entrepreneur has found a truly unique niche, she or he may be able to charge a premium price—at least for the initial operating period.

The closest competitor should be studied to learn what that firm is charging. To break into a market, the price of the new product or service will usually have to come within a reasonable range of the competition's. (Chapter 16 examines break-even analysis and pricing strategy in more depth.)

THE PROMOTIONAL PLAN The promotional plan should describe the entrepreneur's approach to creating customer awareness of the product or service and motivating customers to buy. Among the many promotional options available to the entrepreneur are personal selling and advertising.

If personal selling is appropriate, the plan should outline how many salespeople will be employed and how they will be compensated. The proposed system for training the sales force should be mentioned. If advertising is to be used, a list of the specific media should be included and advertising themes should be described. Often, it is advisable to seek the services of a small advertising agency. In this case, the name and credentials of the agency should be provided. A brief mention of successful campaigns supervised by the agency can add to the appeal of this section of the marketing plan. (Personal selling and advertising are discussed more extensively in Chapter 17.)

LOOKING BACK

1 Describe small business marketing.

- Small business marketing consists of numerous activities, including market analysis and determining the marketing mix.
- Three distinct marketing philosophies are the production-, sales-, and consumer-oriented philosophies.
- A small business should adopt a consumer orientation to marketing, as that philosophy is most consistent with long-term success.

2 Discuss the nature of the marketing research process.

- Marketing research is the gathering, processing, reporting, and interpreting of marketing information.
- The cost of marketing research should be evaluated against its benefits.
- The steps in marketing research are identifying the informational need, searching for secondary and primary data, and interpreting the data gathered.

3 Define market segmentation and its related strategies.

- A market is a group of customers or potential customers who have purchasing power and unsatisfied needs.
- A focus strategy relies on market segmentation, which is the process of dividing the total market for a product or service into groups, each of which is likely to respond favorably to a specific marketing strategy.
- Three types of market segmentation strategies are (1) the unsegmented approach, (2) the multisegmentation approach, and (3) the single-segmentation approach.

4 Explain the different methods of forecasting sales.

- A sales forecast is an estimation of how much of a product or service will be purchased within a market during a defined time period.
- The forecasting process may be either a breakdown or a buildup process and may be either direct or indirect, depending on the predicting variable.

5 Identify the components of a formal marketing plan.

- The marketing plan should include sections on market analysis, the competition, and marketing strategy.
- The market analysis should include a customer profile.
- Four areas of marketing strategy that should be discussed in the marketing plan are decisions affecting the total product or service, pricing decisions, promotional decisions, and distribution decisions.

Key Terms

small business marketing, p. 218
market analysis, p. 218
marketing mix, p. 218
marketing research, p. 220
secondary data, p. 221
primary data, p. 221
market, p. 225
market segmentation, p. 225
segmentation variables, p. 225
benefit variables, p. 225
demographic variables, p. 226
unsegmented strategy (mass marketing), p. 226
multisegmentation strategy, p. 226
single-segmentation strategy, p. 227
sales forecast, p. 228
breakdown process (chain-ratio method), p. 231
buildup process, p. 231
direct forecasting, p. 232
indirect forecasting, p. 232
customer profile, p. 232

Discussion Questions

1. What is the scope of small business marketing? Has it always been as broad as it is now? Why or why not?
2. How do the three marketing philosophies differ? Select a product and discuss marketing tactics that could be used to implement each philosophy.
3. What are the obstacles to adopting a consumer orientation in a small firm?
4. What are the steps in the marketing research process?
5. What are the major considerations in designing a questionnaire?
6. Briefly explain the three components of the definition of a market, as presented in this chapter.
7. What types of variables are used for market segmentation? Would a small firm use the same variables as a large business? Why or why not?
8. Explain the difference between a multisegmentation strategy and a single-segmentation strategy. Which one is more likely to be appealing to a small firm? Why?
9. Explain why forecasting is used more widely by large firms than by small ones.
10. Briefly describe each of the components of a formal marketing plan.

You Make the Call

SITUATION 1

In 1991, brothers Josh and Seth Frey were driving an ice cream truck. After buying a former postal vehicle and converting it into a dessert-mobile, they operated it between semesters at the University of Wisconsin at Madison. Seth, a senior, planned to join the corporate world after graduating, but Josh was enjoying being his own boss. The Hebrew and history major felt he had finally figured out his future. Still, he didn't want to be the neighborhood ice cream guy for the rest of his life.

What else could he sell? Care packages. Josh was impressed that a few dorms at his university offered care packages for parents to send to their kids. How could Josh improve on the product? The care packages should be offered campus-wide, he thought.

Source: Geoff Williams, "Staying Power," *Entrepreneur,* Vol. 26, No. 6 (June 1998), p. 154.

Question 1 What type of research could Josh use to estimate demand for the care packages?

Question 2 How could he develop a sales forecast for his product?

Question 3 Would the Internet be helpful to his marketing plan?

SITUATION 2

Alibek Iskakov has opened a small café named Oasis in Kokshetau, a city in Kazakhstan. In order to get primary data on the market for his café, he conducted a survey of 100 people—45 men and 55 women. Forty-eight respondents were between 18 and 24 years old, 38 were between 25 and 50 years old, and 14 were over 50 years old. The survey asked the following questions:

1. How often do you visit restaurants?
2. What is your favorite restaurant in Kokshetau? Why?
3. What is the most important factor for you in choosing a restaurant?
4. Would a small, neat café with traditional food appeal to you?
   a. (If no) Why not?
   b. (If yes) When would you patronize it?
5. How much are you willing to pay for dinner?

Question 1 What are the strengths and weaknesses of the sample used in this survey?

Question 2 Evaluate the questions used in the survey.

SITUATION 3

Mary Wilson is a 31-year-old wife and mother who wants to start her own company. She has no previous business experience but has an idea for marketing an animal-grooming service, with an approach similar to that used for pizza delivery. When a customer calls, she will arrive in a van in less than 30 minutes and will provide the grooming service. Many of her friends think the idea has promise but dismiss her efforts to seriously discuss the venture. However, Wilson is not discouraged; she plans to purchase the van and the necessary grooming equipment.

Question 1 What target market or markets can you identify for Wilson? How could she forecast sales for her service in each market?

Question 2 What advantage does her business have over existing grooming businesses?

Question 3 What business name and promotional strategy would you suggest that Wilson use?

Experiential Exercises

1. Interview a local small business manager about what he or she believes is the marketing philosophy followed by the business.
2. Assume you are planning to market a new facial tissue. Write a detailed customer profile, and explain how you would develop the sales forecast for this product.
3. Interview a local small business owner to determine the type of marketing research, if any, he or she has used.
4. Visit a local small retailer and observe its marketing efforts—salesperson style, store atmosphere, and warranty policies, for example. Report your observations to the class, and make recommendations for improving these efforts to increase customer satisfaction.

Exploring the Web

1. The Canada/British Columbia Business Service Centre (**http://www.sb.gov.bc.ca**) has excellent resources specifically for small businesses. Follow the Online Small Business Workshop link, and then choose Sales Forecasting.
   a. List and briefly explain the four steps in creating a sales forecast for a new business.
   b. What forms the basis for forecasting sales for an existing business? How does one determine what percentage of growth to assume?
   c. In the business plan, should the sales forecast be shown with monthly, quarterly, or annual figures?
2. To answer the following questions, access the NetReflector site at **http://www.netreflector.com**.
   a. Read About Us to find out what type of company NetReflector is.
   b. View the Flash tour of InstantSurvey. What other features are included in the service when you use InstantSurvey?
   c. Take one of the sample surveys created by InstantSurvey. Write a paragraph explaining what you thought of the experience and whether you think others would complete the survey.
   d. Check the Frequently Asked Questions about InstantSurvey. How effective is it, compared to printed surveys? What are the drawbacks of using InstantSurvey?
3. Access the Small Business Administration's Web site at **http://www.sba.gov**, and choose Women's Online Business Center. Under Business Basics, select Marketing.
   a. Follow the link to Purpose of the Marketing Plan. According to the article, what time frame should be included in the plan? How often should the plan be updated?
   b. Click Marketing Plan Components, a Quick Review. List the eight components of the marketing plan.
   c. View the Creative Cuisine sample marketing plan. What is the source of the information on current market size?
   d. View the Competitive Analysis. Which competitor seems to be the strongest? the weakest?

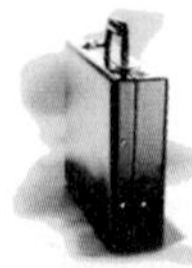

Case 9

SCRUBADUB AUTO WASH (p. 662)

This case features a company that realized the importance of a marketing plan.

Alternative Cases for Chapter 9:

Case 1, "Steve's Olympic Tees," p. 637
Case 6, "Universal Business Brokers," p. 652
Case 15, "Professional Sports Authenticator," p. 681
Case 17, "Flower Girl," p. 686

The Business Plan

Laying the Foundation

As part of laying the foundation for your own business plan, respond to the following questions regarding marketing research, sales forecasting, and the marketing plan.

MARKETING RESEARCH QUESTIONS

1. What types of research should be conducted to collect the information you need?
2. How much will this research cost?
3. What sources of secondary data will address your informational needs?
4. What sources of relevant data are available in your local library?
5. What sources of outside professional assistance would you consider using to help with marketing research?

MARKET SEGMENTATION QUESTIONS

1. Will you focus on a limited market within the industry?
2. What segmentation variables will you use to define your target market?
3. If you determine that several distinct market segments exist, will you concentrate on just one segment?

FORECASTING QUESTIONS

1. How do you plan to forecast sales for your product or service?
2. What sources of forecasting assistance have you consulted?
3. What sales forecasting techniques are most appropriate to your needs?
4. What is the sales forecast for your product or service?

MARKETING PLAN QUESTIONS

1. What is the customer profile for your product or service?
2. How will you identify prospective customers?
3. What geographical area will you serve?
4. What are the distinguishing characteristics of your product or service?
5. What steps have already been taken to develop your product or service?
6. What do you plan to name your product or service?
7. Will there be a warranty?
8. How will you set the price for your product or service?
9. What type of distribution plan will you use?
10. Will you export to other countries?
11. What type of selling effort will you use?
12. What special selling skills will be required?
13. What types of advertising and sales promotion will you use?

chapter 10

MANAGEMENT TEAMS, ORGANIZATIONAL FORMS, AND STRATEGIC ALLIANCES

In the VIDEO Spotlight

Sundance Catalog

In this episode of "Small Business School," the series on PBS stations, you will meet Harry Rosenthal. When Robert Redford made the decision to create a catalog company to sell the products carried in his resort gift shop located near Provo, Utah, he knew that he didn't know where to begin. Research led him to Harry, an attorney-turned-entrepreneur who had launched and run a profitable catalog called Right Start. Harry sold out of Right Start, which is still thriving today, to take on the challenge of another startup.

Robert Redford was smart to hire a person with experience to deploy the Sundance catalog. Redford brought to the table the Sundance Resort and Sundance Film Festival brand that he had been building since the late 60s. Guests at the resort would purchase items in the gift shop, then get home and want items sent to friends. Calls to the gift shop provided the motivation for the enterprise; the fact that customers drove the entire idea is why I think the business succeeds today. Besides, the Sundance operation needed cash to preserve its land and do its charity work.

I was fascinated by the product selection meeting you will see and the attention to detail taken to ensure that the technology is powerful enough to support a growing business. And I was surprised to hear Harry say candidly that having a celebrity spokesperson is not all a bed of roses. I know that viewing the entire program will give you terrific insight into a well-conceived and well-run small business. ◆

—Hattie Bryant, Producer, "Small Business School," The Series on PBS Stations, Worldnet, and the Web, http://smallbusinessschool.org

"We always try to deliver such high quality that when it shows up at the customer's door, it's always at least a little better than they even thought it was going to be."

—Harry Rosenthal

Go to page 734 for More! on Sundance Catalog.

LOOKING AHEAD

After studying this chapter, you should be able to

1 *Describe the characteristics and value of a strong management team.*

2 *Explain the common legal forms of organization used by small businesses.*

3 *Identify factors to consider in choosing among the primary legal forms of organization.*

4 *Describe the unique features and restrictions of specialized organizational forms such as limited partnerships, S corporations, and limited liability companies.*

5 *Explain the nature of strategic alliances and their uses in small businesses.*

6 *Describe the effective use of boards of directors and advisory councils.*

7 *Explain how different forms of organization are taxed by the federal government.*

If two heads are better than one, then every small company can benefit from having a management team. In all but the simplest businesses, the entrepreneur's personal talents must be supplemented with the experience and abilities of other individuals. The prospects for any venture are most promising when a firm's leadership is composed of competent, resourceful, and tenacious individuals. It is important, therefore, that an entrepreneur identify and attract a strong management team. A business plan that provides for strong leadership is appealing to both potential investors and prospective managerial personnel.

In addition to assembling a well-balanced leadership group, an entrepreneur must select an ownership structure—that is, a legal form of organization. The direction of the business will be strongly affected by the entrepreneur's choice of a proprietorship, a partnership, a corporation, or one of various other forms.

This chapter focuses on the composition of the management team and the legal structure of a new business. Decisions in this area are crucial, because even brilliant ideas can be doomed by faulty management.

THE MANAGEMENT TEAM

Describe the characteristics and value of a strong management team.

If a firm is extremely small, the founder will probably be the key manager and perhaps the only manager. In most firms, however, others share leadership roles with the owner or owners. The concept of a management team, therefore, is relevant to small business. In general, the **management team** includes both managers and other professionals or key persons who help give a new firm its general direction.

management team managers and other key persons who give a company its general direction

The Characteristics of a Strong Management Team

Strong management can make the best of a good business idea by securing the resources needed to make it work. Of course, even a highly competent management team cannot rescue a firm that is based on a weak business concept or that lacks adequate resources. The importance of strong management to startups is evident in the attitudes of prospective investors, who consider the quality of a new venture's management to be the single most important factor in decisions to invest or not to invest. One entrepreneurship expert sums up popular opinion this way:

If there is one issue on which the majority of theorists and practitioners agree, it is that a high-quality management team is a key ingredient in the success of many high-growth ventures . . . and most of the reasons for failure may be traced to specific flaws in the venture team.[1]

A management team brings greater strength to a venture than does an individual entrepreneur. One reason is that a team can provide a diversity of talent to meet various staffing needs. This is particularly important for high-tech startups. In addition, a team can provide greater assurance of continuity, since the departure of one member of a team is less devastating to a business than the departure of a sole entrepreneur.

Building a Management Team

The management team generally consists of individuals with supervisory responsibilities, as well as nonsupervisory personnel who play key roles in the business. For example, members of the management team might include a financial manager who supervises a small office staff and an individual who directs the startup's marketing effort.

The competence required in a management team depends on the type of business and the nature of its operations. For example, a software development firm and a restaurant call for drastically different types of business experience. Whatever the business, a small firm needs managers with an appropriate combination of educational background and experience. In evaluating the qualifications of an applicant for a key position, an entrepreneur needs to know whether she or he has experience in a related type of business, as a manager, or as an entrepreneur.

Not all members of a management team need competence in all areas—the key is balance. If one member has expertise in finance, another should have an adequate marketing background. And there should be someone who can supervise employees effectively.

Even when entrepreneurs recognize the need for team members with varying expertise, they frequently seek to replicate their own personalities and management styles. While personal compatibility and the cooperation of team members are necessary for effective collaboration, a healthy situation exists when the qualifications of team members are diverse. Dr. Stephen R. Covey, a management consultant, puts it this way:

In my opinion, the No. 1 mistake that most entrepreneurs make is that they never know how to develop a complementary team. They're always kind of cloning themselves, that is, trying to turn their employees into duplicates of themselves. . . . You have to empower other people and build on their strengths to make your own weaknesses irrelevant.[2]

Planning the company's leadership, then, should produce a management team that is able to give competent direction to the new firm. The team should be balanced in terms of covering the various functional areas and offering the right combination of education and experience. It may comprise both insiders and outside specialists.

In addition to selecting members of the management team, an entrepreneur must design an internal management structure that defines relationships among all members of the organization. Relationships among the various positions—such as advertising manager, marketing director, financial officer, and human resources manager—need to be understood. Although these relationships need not be worked

out in great detail, planning should be sufficient to ensure orderly operations and avoid an overlapping of responsibilities that invites conflict (as discussed in Chapter 18).

The management plan should be drafted in a way that provides for business growth. Any unfilled positions should be specified, and job descriptions should spell out the duties of and necessary qualifications for such positions. Methods for selecting key employees should also be explained. When the business is organized as a partnership, the partners need to think about the possible breakup of the partnership—ownership shares should be carefully considered and specified in the plan. Similarly, compensation arrangements, including bonus or other incentive plans for key organization members, call for detailed planning.

Outside Professional Support

The managerial and professional talent of an internal management team for a new venture—that is, the full-time personnel—can be supplemented by drawing on outside assistance. For example, a small firm may shore up weak areas by developing working relationships with such external professional organizations as a commercial bank, a law firm, and a certified public accounting firm. To some extent, reliance on outside advisors can compensate for insufficient internal staffing. A number of outside sources of managerial assistance are identified and discussed in Chapter 18.

An active board of directors can also provide counsel and guidance to the management team. Directors may be appointed on the basis of their business experience, technical expertise, or financial investment in the company. Selection of and compensation for directors are discussed later in this chapter.

Legal Forms of Organization

In launching a new business, an entrepreneur must choose a form of legal organization. The most common options are sole proprietorship, partnership, and the C corporation. More specialized forms of organization exist, but the vast number of small businesses find one of these common forms suitable for their needs. Therefore, our discussion focuses primarily on these options, although explanations are also given of three specialized forms. Figure 10-1 shows the various forms of organization.

Explain the common legal forms of organization used by small businesses.

The Sole Proprietorship Option

A **sole proprietorship,** the most rudimentary business form, is a company owned by one person. An individual proprietor has title to all business assets and is subject to the claims of creditors. He or she receives all of the firm's profits but must also assume all losses, bear all risks, and pay all debts. Forming a sole proprietorship is the simplest and cheapest way to start operation and is usually most appropriate for a new small business.

sole proprietorship
a business owned by one person

In a sole proprietorship, an owner is free from interference by partners, shareholders, and directors. However, a sole proprietorship lacks some of the advantages of other legal forms. For example, there are no limits on the owner's personal liability—that is, the owner of the business has **unlimited liability** and thus his or her personal assets can be taken by creditors if the business fails. For this reason, the sole proprietorship form is a practical choice for only very small businesses. In

unlimited liability
liability on the part of an owner that extends beyond the owner's investment in the business

FIGURE 10-1

Forms of Legal Organization for Small Businesses

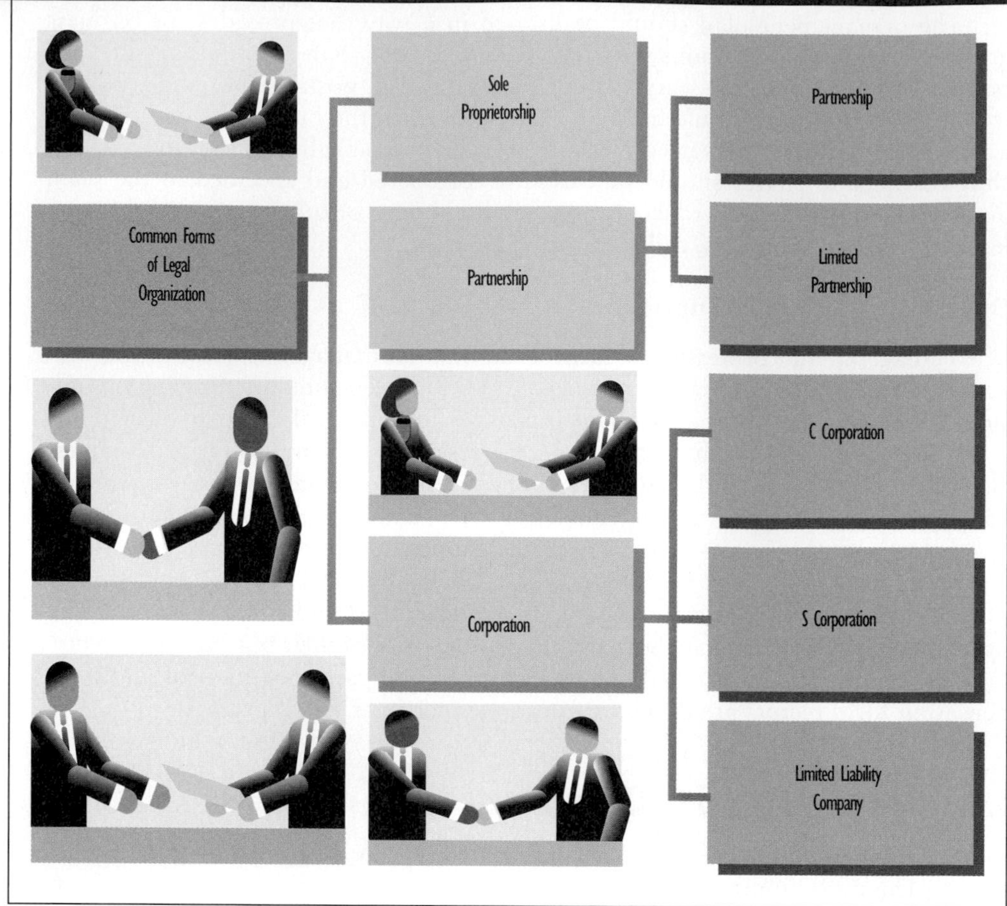

addition, sole proprietors are not employees and cannot receive the advantage of many tax-free fringe benefits such as insurance and hospitalization plans, which are customarily provided by corporations for their employees.

The death of the owner terminates the legal existence of a sole proprietorship. Thus, the possibility of the owner's death may cloud relationships between a business and its creditors and employees. It is important that the owner have a will, because the assets of the business minus its liabilities will belong to her or his heirs. In a will, a sole proprietor can give an executor the power to run the business for the heirs until they can take it over or it can be sold.

Another contingency that must be provided for is the possible incapacity of the sole proprietor. If she or he were badly hurt in an accident and unconscious for an extended period, the business could be ruined. A sole proprietor can guard against this contingency by giving a competent person a legal power of attorney to carry on in such circumstances.

In some cases, the sole proprietorship option is virtually ruled out by circumstances. For example, if the nature of a business involves a high exposure to legal risks, as in the case of a manufacturer of a potentially hazardous product, a legal form that provides greater protection against personal liability will be required.

The Partnership Option

A **partnership** is a legal entity formed by two or more co-owners to operate a business for profit. Because of a partnership's voluntary nature, owners can set it up quickly, avoiding many of the legal requirements involved in creating a corporation. A partnership pools the managerial talents and capital of those joining together as business partners. As in a sole proprietorship, however, the owners share unlimited liability.

partnership
a legal entity formed by two or more co-owners to carry on a business for profit

QUALIFICATIONS OF PARTNERS Any person capable of contracting may legally become a business partner. Individuals may become partners without contributing capital or having a claim to assets at the time of dissolution; such persons are partners only in regard to management and profits. The formation of a partnership, however, involves consideration not only of legal issues but also of personal and managerial factors. A strong partnership requires partners who are honest, healthy, capable, and compatible.

Operating a business as a partnership has benefits, but it is also fraught with problems. When *Inc.* magazine surveyed individuals about their opinions regarding the partnership form of ownership, almost 60 percent of the respondents considered a partnership to be a "bad way to run a business."[3] The respondents were also asked to identify what they believed to be good and bad qualities associated with the partnership form (see Figure 10-2). The benefits of partnerships included the ability to share the workload and the emotional and financial burdens of the enterprise and to buy management talent that would break the budget if hired directly. Respondents also recognized that partners can add companionship to life in a small business.

On the downside, 60 percent believed the personal conflicts common in partnerships more than offset the benefits, and almost as many said that partners never live up to each other's expectations. More than 50 percent were concerned that partnerships could weaken leadership, and some recognized that they dilute equity and tend to complicate decision making. Interestingly, few of the perceived pros or cons are directly associated with financial matters. Those disliking partnerships focused on the deterioration of the relationship. Many spoke of a partner's dishonesty, at worst, and differing priorities, at best. However, some of the respondents who considered a partnership a bad way to run a business did note some redeeming qualities. Similarly, advocates of the partnership form noted some inherently bad qualities. Thus, the issue is not black and white. The important point of these findings is that a partnership should be formed only if it is clearly the best option when all matters are considered.

Individuals contemplating forming a partnership should discuss the following questions. The objective of these questions is to clarify expectations before an agreement between partners is finalized.

- ***What is our business concept?*** This is a broad topic, and sometimes it helps to ask a third party to listen in, just to see if the partners are on each other's wavelength. First, the partners need to decide who will make the widgets and who will sell them. Then they need to talk about growth. Are they building the company to sell it, or are they after long-term growth? It's also important to discuss exactly how the business will be run. Do they want participative management, or will employees simply hunker down at machines and churn out parts? "If one guy is a fist-pounder with a 'do-it-as-I-say' mentality, and the other believes that people ought to feel good about their jobs, that

FIGURE 10-2

The Advantages and Disadvantages of Partnerships

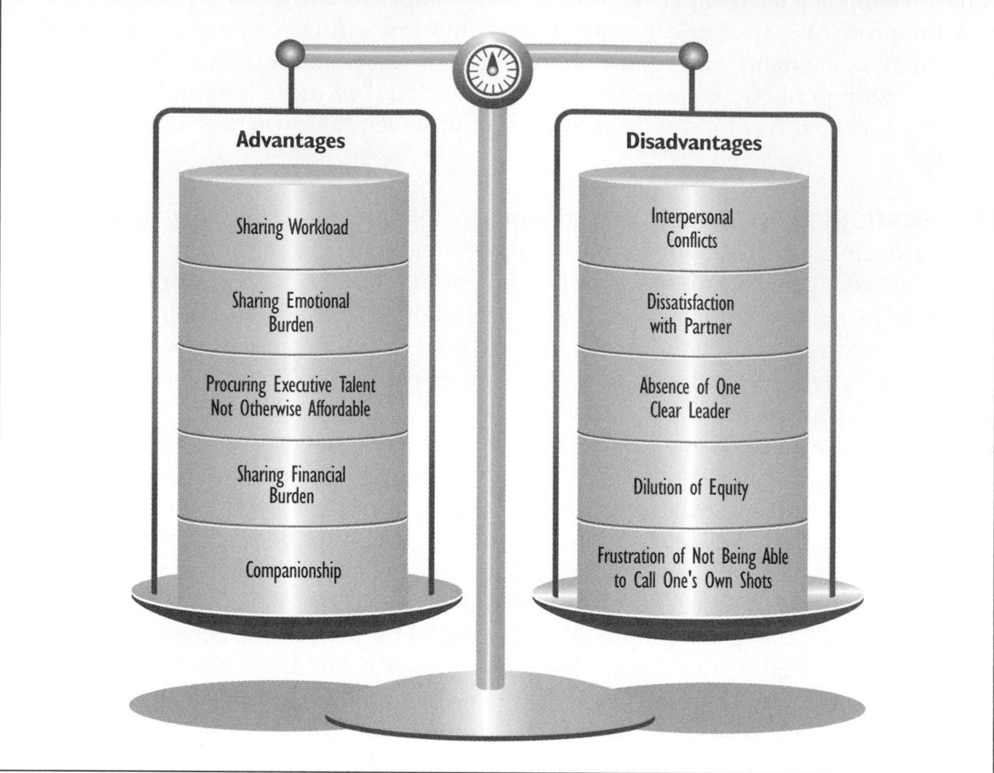

probably represents an irreconcilable difference," says Sam Lane, a consultant who works with partners.

- ***How are we going to structure ownership?*** It sounds great for two people to scratch out 50-50 on a cocktail napkin and leave it at that. But, in practice, splitting the company down the middle leaves both partners with equal control, which can paralyze the business. If neither is willing to settle for 49 percent, then the partners should build some arbitration into the partnership agreement.
- ***Why do we need each other?*** "I thought it would be much less scary with two of us," says Arthur Eisenberg, explaining his rationale for teaming up with his partner. That may be so, but bringing on a partner means sharing responsibility and authority. "If you are taking on a partner because you are afraid of going it alone, find some other way to handle the anxiety," advises Mardy Grothe, a psychologist.
- ***How do our lifestyles differ?*** The fact that one partner is single and the other has a family, for example, can affect more than just the time each puts in. It may mean that one partner needs to pull more money out of the business. Or it may affect a partner's willingness to take risks with the company. "All of this stuff needs to get talked out," says Peter Wylie, a psychologist. "The implications are profound."[4]

As already suggested, failure to clarify expectations is a frequent deterrent to building an effective working relationship.

RIGHTS AND DUTIES OF PARTNERS Partners' rights and duties should be stated explicitly in writing in a **partnership agreement.** This document should be drawn up before the firm begins operating and, at the very least, should cover the following items:

partnership agreement
a document that states explicitly the rights and duties of partners

1. Date of formation of the partnership
2. Names and addresses of partners
3. Statement of fact of partnership
4. Statement of business purpose(s)
5. Duration of the business
6. Name and location of the business
7. Amount invested by each partner
8. Sharing ratio for profits and losses
9. Partners' rights, if any, regarding withdrawal of funds for personal use
10. Provision for accounting records and their accessibility to partners
11. Specific duties of each partner
12. Provision for dissolution and sharing of the net assets
13. Restriction of partners from assuming special obligations, such as endorsing a note for another person
14. Provision for protection of surviving partners, decedent's estate, and so forth in the event of a partner's death

Unless the articles specify otherwise, a partner is generally recognized as having certain implicit rights. For example, partners share profits or losses equally, unless they have agreed to a different ratio.

In a partnership, each partner has **agency power,** which means that a business decision by one partner can bind all members of the firm. Good faith, together with reasonable care in the exercise of managerial duties, is required of all partners in a business. Since the partnership relationship is fiduciary in character, a partner cannot compete in another business and remain a partner. Nor can a partner use business information solely for personal gain.

agency power
the ability of any one partner to legally bind the other partners

HELP FOR AILING PARTNERSHIPS All partnerships experience stress, and many do not survive the challenge. According to Dr. David Gage, a psychologist who runs Business Mediation Associates in Washington, D.C., the "divorce" rate of business partnerships is higher than that of marriages. Typically, problems stem from turf battles over control. If the individual duties of the partners are unclear or if one party does not accept the role of the other, conflict is almost assured. Gage says this is especially common in family partnerships.

http://www.business-mediation.com

A classic example is the case where the son is named president and dad is named vice president. Regardless of the titles, dad still expects to have the last say in everything.[5]

Complications can arise even if partners have been careful to match their expectations at the start of the partnership and the business arrangement has been formalized through a partnership agreement. When problems emerge and trust begins to break down, partners should move quickly to try to resolve underlying issues. If they cannot do so, they should consider hiring a business mediator. Working with a business mediator can be expensive (sometimes exceeding $500 an hour), but the dissolution of the partnership is likely to be far more financially damaging.[6]

TERMINATION OF A PARTNERSHIP Death, incapacity, or withdrawal of any one of the partners ends a partnership and necessitates liquidation or reorganization of the

Entrepreneurship and Ethics

IN THE TRENCHES

BREAKING UP IS NOT SO HARD TO DO

Ethical issues have derailed many high-potential partnerships. In November of 1996, Ed Harris invited a friend to join him in a startup, with the ownership split 50-50. They officially launched the business in February of 1997. In less than one year, the California-based venture's sales expanded from around $1,000 to $56,000 per month. As the business developed, so did the personal relationship between the partners. As Harris recalls, "In all aspects of business and personal interaction, ours was a relationship that was built on mutual trust and understanding."

In December of 1997, the founders decided to value the company so that they could issue stock to employees. It was at this point that things began to break down. Given the opportunity to change things, Harris's partner came up with a plan that would transform the 50-50 partnership into a 70-30 enterprise, favoring him. All attempts to negotiate a reasonable outcome were unsuccessful, so Harris filed for dissolution of the business in February of 1998.

Reflecting on this failed partnership, Harris says, "As with any relationship, marriage or business, trust is everything. Look deep into a person's soul, get to know him or her well, and examine qualities you like and dislike before you enter into a long-term relationship. Also, it never hurts to have an attorney on your side."

Source: Ed Harris, "Why My Startup Failed," *Forbes ASAP,* February 22, 1999, p. 18.

business. While liquidation often results in substantial losses to all partners, it may be legally necessary, because a partnership represents a close personal relationship of the parties that cannot be maintained against the desire of any one of them.

This disadvantage may be partially overcome at the time a partnership is formed by stipulating in the articles that surviving partners can continue the business after buying the decedent's interest. This option can be facilitated by having each partner carry life insurance that names the other partners as beneficiaries.

The C Corporation Option

corporation
a business organization that exists as a legal entity and provides limited liability to its owners

C corporation
an ordinary corporation, taxed by the federal government as a separate legal entity

legal entity
a business organization that is recognized by the law as having a separate legal existence

In 1819, Chief Justice John Marshall of the United States Supreme Court defined a **corporation** as "an artificial being, invisible, intangible, and existing only in contemplation of the law." The ordinary corporation is often called a **C corporation** to distinguish it from more specialized forms. With these words, the Supreme Court recognized the corporation as a **legal entity,** meaning that a corporation can sue and be sued, hold and sell property, and engage in business operations that are stipulated in the corporate charter. The corporation discussed in this section is the C corporation.

A corporation is chartered under state laws. The length of its life is independent of its owners' (stockholders') lives. The corporation, and not its owners, is liable for the debts of the business. The directors and officers serve as agents to bind the corporation.

THE CORPORATE CHARTER To form a corporation, one or more persons must apply to the secretary of state (at the state level) for permission to incorporate. After preliminary steps—including payment of an incorporation fee—have been completed, the written application (which should be prepared by an attorney) is approved by the secretary of state and becomes the corporation's charter. In some states, documents showing that the corporation exists are called *articles of incorporation* or *certificates of incorporation*. A **corporate charter** typically provides the following information:

corporate charter
a document that establishes a corporation's existence

1. Name of the company
2. Formal statement of the company's formation
3. Purposes and powers—that is, type of business
4. Location of principal office in the state of incorporation
5. Duration (perpetual existence, 50-year life and renewable charter, or other)
6. Classes and preferences of classes of stock
7. Number and par (or stated) value of shares of each class of stock authorized
8. Voting privileges for each class of stock
9. Names and addresses of incorporators and first year's directors
10. Names and addresses of and amounts subscribed by each subscriber to capital stock
11. Statement of limited liability of stockholders (if required specifically by state law)
12. Statement of alterations of directors' powers, if any, from the general corporation law of the state

A corporation's charter should be brief, in accord with state law, and broad in the statement of the firm's powers. Details should be left to the bylaws.

RIGHTS AND STATUS OF STOCKHOLDERS Ownership in a corporation is evidenced by **stock certificates**, each of which stipulates the number of shares owned by a stockholder. An ownership interest does not confer a legal right to act for the firm or to share in its management. It does, however, provide the stockholder with the right to receive dividends in proportion to stockholdings—but only when the dividends are properly declared by the firm. Ownership of stock typically carries a **pre-emptive right,** or the right to buy new shares, in proportion to the number of shares already owned, before new stock is offered for public sale.

stock certificate
a document specifying the number of shares owned by a stockholder

pre-emptive right
the right of stockholders to buy new shares of stock before they are offered to the public

The legal status of stockholders is fundamental, of course, but it may be overemphasized. In many small corporations, the owners typically serve both as directors and as managing officers. The person who owns most or all of the stock can control a business as effectively as if it were a sole proprietorship. Thus, this form of organization works well for individual- and family-owned businesses, where maintaining control of the firm is important.

Major stockholders must be concerned about their working relationships, as well as their legal relationships, with other owners who are active in the business. Cooperation among all owners and managers of a new corporation is necessary for its success. Specifying legal technicalities is important, but it provides an inadequate basis for successful collaboration. Owners and the members of the management team need to clarify their expectations of each other's roles as best they can. Failure to have clear expectations about working relationships can cause one or more persons to feel that others serving as managers or co-owners are not honoring their word.

LIMITED LIABILITY OF STOCKHOLDERS For most stockholders, their limited liability is a major advantage of the corporate form of organization. Their financial liability

is limited to the amount of money they invest in the business. Creditors cannot require them to sell personal assets to pay corporation debts. However, small corporations are often in a somewhat shaky financial condition during their early years of operation. As a result, a bank that makes a loan to a small firm may insist that the owners assume personal liability for the firm's debts by signing the promissory notes not only as representatives of the firm but personally as well. If the corporation is unable to repay the loan, the banker can then look to the owners' personal assets to recover the amount of the loan. In this case, the corporate advantage of limited liability is lost.

Why would owners agree to personally guarantee a firm's debt? Simply put, they may have no choice if they want the money. Most bankers are not willing to loan money to an entrepreneur who is not prepared to put his or her own personal assets at risk.

The courts may also override the concept of limited liability for shareholders and hold them personally liable in certain unusual cases—for example, if personal and corporate funds have been mixed together or if the corporation was formed to try to evade an existing obligation.

DEATH OR WITHDRAWAL OF STOCKHOLDERS Unlike a partnership interest, ownership in a corporation is readily transferable. Exchange of shares of stock is sufficient to convey an ownership interest to a different individual.

Stock of large corporations is exchanged constantly without noticeable effect on the operation of the business. For a small firm, however, a change of owners, though legally similar, can involve numerous complications. For example, finding a buyer for the stock of a small firm may prove difficult. Also, a minority stockholder in a small firm is vulnerable. If two of three equal shareholders in a small business sold their stock to an outsider, the remaining shareholder would then be at the mercy of that outsider. The minority stockholder might be removed from any managerial post he or she happened to hold or be legally ousted from the board of directors and no longer have a voice in the management of the business.

The death of a majority stockholder can have unfortunate repercussions in a small firm. An heir, the executor, or a purchaser of the stock might well insist on direct control, with possible adverse effects for other stockholders. To prevent problems of this nature, legal arrangements should be made at the outset to provide for management continuity by surviving stockholders and fair treatment of a stockholder's heirs. As in the case of a partnership, mutual insurance can ensure the ability to buy out a deceased stockholder's interest. This arrangement would require an option for the corporation or surviving stockholders to (1) purchase the decedent's stock before it is offered to outsiders and (2) specify the method for determining the stock's price per share. A similar arrangement might be made to protect remaining stockholders in case one of the owners wished to retire from the business at any time.

Identify factors to consider in choosing among the primary legal forms of organization.

Choosing an Organizational Form

Choosing a legal form for a new business deserves careful attention because of the various, sometimes conflicting features of each organizational option. Depending on the particular circumstances of a specific business, the tax advantages of one form, for example, may offset the limited-liability advantages of another form. Some

tradeoffs may be necessary. Ideally, an experienced attorney should be consulted for aid in selecting the most appropriate form of organization.

Table 10-1 summarizes the main considerations in selecting one of the three primary forms of ownership. A brief description of each factor follows.

- *Initial organizational requirements and costs.* Organizational requirements and costs increase as the formality of the organization increases. That is, a sole proprietorship is typically less complex and less expensive to form than a partnership, and a partnership is less complex and less expensive to form than a corporation. In view of the relatively modest costs, however, this consideration is of minimal importance in the long term.
- *Liability of owners.* A sole proprietorship and a partnership have the inherent disadvantage of unlimited liability for the owners. With these forms of organization, there is no distinction between the firm's assets and the owners' personal assets. Creditors lending money to the business can require the owners to sell personal assets if the firm is financially unable to repay its loans. In contrast, the corporate form limits the owners' liability to their investment in the business. If a corporation is small, however, its owners are often required to guarantee a loan personally.
- *Continuity of business.* A sole proprietorship is immediately dissolved on the owner's death. Likewise, a partnership is terminated on the death or withdrawal of a partner, unless the partnership agreement states otherwise. A corporation, on the other hand, offers continuity. The status of an individual investor does not affect the corporation's existence.
- *Transferability of ownership.* Ownership is transferred most easily in the corporation. The ability to transfer ownership, however, is intrinsically neither good nor bad. Its desirability depends largely on the owners' preferences. In certain businesses, owners may want the option of evaluating any prospective new investors. In other circumstances, unrestricted transferability may be preferred.
- *Management control.* A sole proprietor has absolute control of the firm. Control within a partnership is normally based on the majority vote—an increase in the number of partners reduces each partner's voice in management. Within a corporation, control has two dimensions: (1) the formal control vested in the stockholders who own the majority of the voting common shares and (2) the functional control exercised by the corporate officers in conducting daily operations. In a small corporation, these two forms of control usually rest in the same individuals.
- *Attractiveness for raising capital.* A corporation has a distinct advantage when raising new equity capital, due to the ease of transferring ownership through the sale of common shares and the flexibility in distributing the shares. In contrast, the unlimited liability of a sole proprietorship and a partnership discourages new investors.
- *Income taxes.* Income taxes frequently have a major effect on an owner's selection of a form of organization. In the last section of this chapter, we look more closely at federal tax laws as they relate to choosing a form of organization.

Some entrepreneurship experts insist that the two default forms of business—sole proprietorship and partnership—should *never* be adopted. While these forms

TABLE 10-1

Comparison of Legal Forms of Organization

Form of Organization	Initial Organizational Requirements and Costs	Liability of Owners	Continuity of Business
Sole proprietorship	Minimum requirements; generally no registration or filing fee	Unlimited liability	Dissolved upon proprietor's death
Partnership	Minimum requirements; generally no registration or filing fee; written partnership agreement not legally required but strongly suggested	Unlimited liability	Unless partnership agreement specifies differently, dissolved upon withdrawal or death of partner
C Corporation	Most expensive and greatest requirements; filing fees; compliance with state regulations for corporations	Liability limited to investment in company	Continuity of business unaffected by shareholder withdrawal or death
Form of organization preferred	Proprietorship or partnership	C Corporation	C Corporation

clearly have drawbacks, they are workable. A recent report by the IRS shows that nearly three-fourths of all new businesses are formed as sole proprietorships; 8 percent are set up as partnerships, and 20 percent are established as corporations.[7]

Greg Maciolek's experience illustrates the factors many small business owners consider when they select a form of organization. In 1993, Maciolek started Discount Flags & Poles to sell flags at flea markets in Knoxville, Tennessee. Because he anticipated that this company would always be a small sideline business with no permanent location, he opted for the simplest form—a sole proprietorship. Later, when Maciolek started a management consulting firm called Integrated Management Resources (IMR), which required greater startup assets and would be exposed to considerable liability risk, he chose to organize it as a corporation.[8]

http://www.integratedmanagementresources.com

Describe the unique features and restrictions of specialized organizational forms such as limited partnerships, S corporations, and limited liability companies.

Specialized Forms of Organization

The majority of new and small businesses use one of the three major organizational forms just described—the sole proprietorship, partnership, or C corporation. However, other specialized types of organizations are frequently used by small firms. Three of these specialized forms deserve mention: the limited partnership, the S corporation, and the limited liability company.

limited partnership
a partnership with at least one general partner and one or more limited partners

THE LIMITED PARTNERSHIP A small business sometimes finds it desirable to use a special form of partnership called the **limited partnership.** This form consists of at least one general partner and one or more limited partners. The **general partner** remains personally liable for the debts of the business; **limited partners** have limited personal liability as long as they do not take an active role in the management of the

Transferability of Ownership	Management Control	Attractiveness for Raising Capital	Income Taxes
May transfer ownership in company name and assets	Absolute management freedom	Limited to proprietor's personal capital	Income from the business is taxed as personal income to the proprietor
Requires the consent of all partners	Majority vote of partners required for control	Limited to partners' ability and desire to contribute capital	Income from the business is taxed as personal income to the partners
Easily transferred by transferring shares of stock	Shareholders have final control, but usually board of directors controls company policies	Usually the most attractive form for raising capital	The C corporation is taxed on its income and the stockholder is taxed if and when dividends are received
Depends on the circumstances	Depends on the circumstances	C Corporation	Depends on the circumstances

partnership. In other words, limited partners risk only the capital they invest in the business. An individual with substantial personal assets can, therefore, invest money in a limited partnership without exposing his or her personal estate to liability claims that might arise through activities of the business. If a limited partner becomes active in management, however, his or her limited liability is lost. To form a limited partnership, partners must file a certificate of limited partnership with the proper state office, as state law governs this form of organization.

general partner
a partner in a limited partnership who has unlimited personal liability

limited partner
a partner in a limited partnership who is not active in its management and has limited personal liability

S corporation (Subchapter S corporation)
a type of corporation that is taxed by the federal government as a partnership

THE S CORPORATION The designation **S corporation**, or **Subchapter S corporation**, is derived from Subchapter S of the Internal Revenue Code, which permits a business to retain the limited-liability feature of a C corporation while being taxed as a partnership. To obtain S corporation status, a corporation must meet certain eligibility requirements.

- No more than 75 stockholders are allowed. (Husband and wife count as a single stockholder.)
- All stockholders must be individuals or certain qualifying estates and trusts. (The rules have been modified in recent years to allow more types of trusts to hold Subchapter S stock.)
- Only one class of stock can be outstanding.
- The corporation must be a domestic one.
- Fiscally, the corporation must operate on a calendar year basis.
- No nonresident alien stockholders are permitted.

A restriction preventing S corporations from owning other corporations, including C corporations, has recently been removed, resulting in tax advantages for some small firms. Whereas in the past different businesses had to be legally separate, the new rules permit individual subsidiaries to consolidate under one S corporation and submit one tax return.[9]

Once a corporation attains S status, it stops paying corporate income taxes and instead passes taxable income or losses on to the stockholders. This allows stockholders to receive dividends from the corporation without double taxation on the corporation's profit (once as a corporate tax and again as a personal tax). A competent tax attorney should be consulted before S status is elected, as tax law changes have considerable effect on the S corporation arrangement.

limited liability company
a corporation in which stockholders have limited liability but pay personal income taxes on business profits

THE LIMITED LIABILITY COMPANY The **limited liability company**, a relatively new form of organization, is now available in most states. This form differs from the C corporation in that it avoids double taxation. In other words, the limited liability company does not pay tax on corporate income but simply passes the income on to owners, who pay taxes on it as part of their personal income taxes.

The major advantage of the limited liability company over the partnership form is the limited liability that it affords. While general partners are exposed to personal liability, owners in a limited liability company are, as the name implies, protected with respect to their personal assets.

The limited liability company is less flexible than the C corporation. Some state statutes specify that the company must dissolve after 30 or 40 years. Also, ownership interests in a limited liability company are less freely transferable than those of a C corporation. Furthermore, for the reasons stated, the limited liability company will be considered inferior to the C corporation if the business wishes to go public at a later time.

Changing Ownership Structures

Depending on the company's goals and other business concerns, many small business owners could improve their financial results by changing the ownership structure of their business. The following factors may influence a firm's decision.[10]

- In order to obtain capital from venture capitalists or a public stock offering, a company must be set up as a C corporation.
- A stock option plan for employees is most easily established in a C corporation (or in an S corporation if the number of covered employees, plus the number of previous shareholders, does not exceed the 75-owner limit).
- Switching from a C corporation to an S corporation boosts owners' income by eliminating the impact of double taxation.
- If a firm is losing money, changing to an S corporation permits more favorable tax treatment for most losses.
- Owners can reduce the after-tax cost of adding fringe benefit programs by adopting an S corporation structure (though these costs may be offset by losses from double taxation).

STRATEGIC ALLIANCES

Explain the nature of strategic alliances and their uses in small businesses.

strategic alliance
an organizational relationship that links two or more independent business entities in a common endeavor

A **strategic alliance** is an organizational relationship that links two or more independent business entities in some common endeavor. Although it involves a form of partnering and cooperation between businesses, technically a strategic alliance is not a legal form of organization, as it doesn't affect the independent legal status of the participating business partners. It is a way in which firms can improve their individual effectiveness by sharing certain resources.

According to Gene Slowinski, a strategic alliance expert, "Strategic alliances are definitely becoming crucial in building businesses of all kinds and at an earlier stage than ever before. . . . They can significantly decrease cycle time for startups by allowing them to access someone else's worldclass resources."[11] Since a competitive advantage often goes to the entrepreneur who is quick to exploit it, many small business owners see strategic alliances as an essential part of their plan for growth. Such alliances represent one way to cope with the rapid pace of change in today's business environment. (See Chapter 4 for a discussion of strategic alliances as a strategy option for global enterprises.)

Strategic Alliances with Large Companies

Large corporations create strategic alliances not only with other large corporations but also with small businesses. Typically, these alliances are formed to join the complementary skills and expertise of two firms, in order to promote the competitive edge of both parties. Large manufacturers, for example, sometimes team up with innovative small manufacturers in product development efforts. The financial resources of the large company and the creativity of the small company can be combined to the benefit of both businesses. Also, giant retailers form alliances with smaller suppliers so as to work hand in hand to achieve specific quality requirements and meet demanding delivery schedules.

Combining the speed, flexibility, and creative energy of a small business with the infrastructure of a large corporation can be a winning strategy. Consider the case of A.L.I. Technologies, Inc. (ALI), a Canadian digital-imaging firm. In 1997, with potent technology but only 40 employees, ALI formed a strategic alliance with IBM to develop large-scale medical image storage systems for regional hospital networks. On its own, ALI did not have the financial strength, expertise, and reputation to achieve its global ambitions; it needed IBM's deep pockets and connections to provide a bridge to new markets. As the ALI/IBM alliance illustrates, a well-designed strategic alliance can create synergies that generate new business opportunities for both partners.[12]

http://www.alitech.com
http://www.ibm.com

Strategic Alliances with Small Companies

Small businesses can also form strategic alliances with other small firms in ways that enhance mutual competitive strength. Here's a specific example of one such situation. Alan Wolan, a postcard entrepreneur in New York City, sold advertising on postcards that were given away in bars, restaurants, health clubs, and retail stores.[13] Restaurateurs and others were happy to carry the free cards, which helped create goodwill that could turn into repeat business.

Wolan believed the business held great promise, but he lacked money and found that competitors in other areas were in a similar position. All of them shared a sense

LIVING IN A DIVERSE WORLD

IN THE TRENCHES

STRATEGIC ALLIANCES ON THE CHEAP

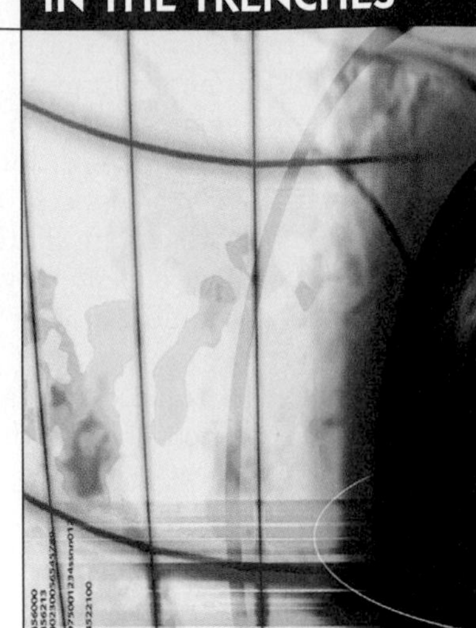

There is no question that we live in a diverse world. But while most people think about diversity in terms of age, sex, culture, and race, entrepreneurs are often more focused on the diversity of the business terrain. How can an entrepreneur best launch a company with many diverse business needs? If the new venture is flush with capital, the answer is simply to buy whatever is needed. But starting a business on a shoestring requires creativity.

When Steve and Andy Grundy launched Spun.com, a Chicago-based CD-exchange Internet venture, they were cash poor but innovation rich. Their very limited amount of startup capital required them to come up with creative solutions to diverse business challenges. Keeping inventory and employees to a minimum, they focused on forming plenty of smart strategic alliances.

In the company's first year of operation, the Grundys procured about $2.5 million worth of assistance from a variety of professionals—designers, writers, programmers,

http://www.spun.com

of urgency as they watched the progress of a large and better financed competitor, Max Racks, which seemed poised to conquer the market in metropolitan areas.

http://www.gocard.com

In the summer of 1995, Wolan's Five Fingers Inc. and two other firms in Los Angeles and Chicago started a network, later named GoCard, designed to enable them to sell national distribution to big accounts such as the Gap, Tanqueray, and Hanes. The group soon expanded to include 7 firms in 14 cities. They buy supplies together and share knowledge but otherwise remain autonomous. Although the future strength of this strategic alliance is uncertain, its benefits have been sufficient to bond the alliance members.

Strategic alliances hold great promise for small entrepreneurial businesses. By combining resources with other carefully selected firms, small firms can increase their competitive strength and reach goals that would otherwise be too costly or too difficult for them to accomplish on their own.

Making a Match

Although an appropriate strategic alliance may be essential to business growth, finding a suitable partner can be challenging. Many small business owners have given up in frustration after months—even years—of trying to establish such connections.

Launched in 1999, Staffcentrix is an Internet outsourcing company based in Woodstock, Connecticut. Despite having only $10,000 in first-year sales, the company was able to form alliances with Microsoft, the United Nations, and Waterside Productions. How did co-founders Christine Durst and Michael Haaren pull it off? First, they identified potential e-mail contacts by scouring the Web sites of prospective partners and taking note of anyone associated with any projects parallel to Staffcentrix's interests. Using this information, they created a "contact profile," which detailed each contact's personal involvement with these projects. Then Durst and Haaren sent personal e-mail messages to these contacts, promoting an alliance with Staffcentrix. Within months, the company was up and running with big-name partners.[14]

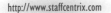

http://www.staffcentrix.com

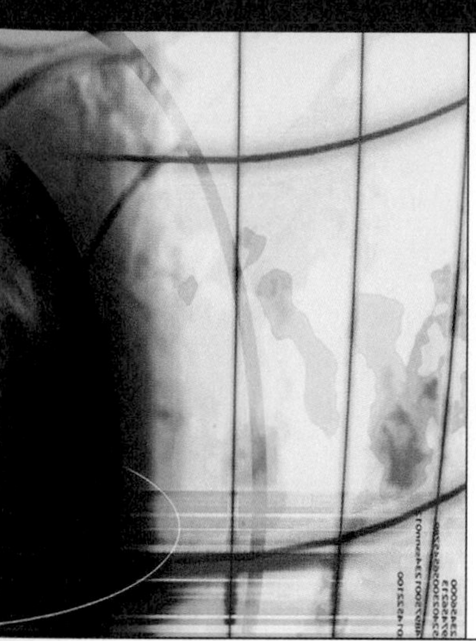

lawyers, accountants, etc.—by trading their own expertise or offering small equity stakes in exchange for services rendered. They obtained access to millions of dollars in inventory by striking an agreement with Alliance Entertainment Corporation, a wholesaler of digital products. The agreement allows Spun.com to reduce carrying costs by ordering products from Alliance only after they have been sold through Spun. Spun.com pays $1,500 per week to All Music Guide to provide its customers with access to album reviews, artwork, and musician biographies. This content would have cost up to $20 million to amass. Rather than paying nearly $500,000 for a five-year lease on processing and office facilities, Spun.com contracted with a firm called Available Business Group to provide warehouse space and logistic support at an annual cost of $5,000. Though competitors typically spend around $70 to acquire an online music customer, Spun.com has reduced these costs to $20 per buyer by forming creative linkages with other music-related sites such as Cyberradio2000.com and AMFM Media Networks.

Spun.com sold 16,200 CDs in its first three months of operation, producing $150,000 in revenue—not bad for a company with a nearly cashless business plan. Starting with limited capital and giving up only 25 percent of the firm's equity to investors, the Grundy brothers were able to establish a thriving business. Their success resulted from a number of creative strategic alliances that allowed them to save nearly $40 million in startup costs.

Source: Joanne Gordon, "Cheap Tricks," *Forbes*, Vol. 165, No. 4 (February 21, 2000), p. 116.

To help them make essential linkages, especially with large corporations, many entrepreneurs consult strategic alliance matchmakers. These brokers provide two basic services. First, they maintain a wealth of contacts with decision makers at corporations that have the resources small companies need to fill in the gaps in their operations. Second, they help entrepreneurs fine-tune their alliance proposals to ensure that corporate insiders take them seriously.

Mick Dusche, a product manager at Microsoft, estimates that he receives hundreds of partnership requests every month. "To get my time or my developers' time," Dusche explains, "they need to show us an articulate, crisp business plan about why we should be willing to invest our resources."[15]

Creating and Maintaining Successful Strategic Alliances

Strategic alliances are neither easy to set up nor simple to maintain. Many alliances encounter trouble along the way, and a number of them fail altogether. In fact, recent research indicates that two-thirds of all alliances run into serious problems within two years of their creation, and 70 percent of them do not survive.[16] Fortunately, when setting up alliances, entrepreneurs can take steps to improve their chances of success:

- Establish a healthy network of contacts. These people can lead you to still other contacts, and eventually to the one you need. Industry analysts, executive recruiters, public relations agencies, business reporters, and even the government can provide important leads.
- Identify and contact individuals within a firm who are likely to return your call. "Dialing high" (calling contacts at the vice presidential level or higher) works in small- or medium-sized firms, but in large firms you may need to call managers or other mid-level employees to get a response.
- Outline the partner's potential financial benefits from the alliance. If possible, show that your firm can deliver value to the alliance across several fronts.

UTILIZING NEW TECHNOLOGY

IN THE TRENCHES

A MATCH MADE IN WASHINGTON

Small firms may recognize the value of forming a strategic alliance with a large partner but not know how to establish such a relationship. In these cases, a firm specializing in strategic partnership matchmaking may be able to help.

Shortly after Richard Farrell founded FullArmor Corporation, a 12-person software development startup based in Boston, he ran up against this very challenge. FullArmor offers an innovative product that allows firms to be selective about which software applications their employees can access. Farrell found that potential customers were hesitant to buy the product because he could not assure them that his technology would be compatible with future releases of Microsoft's Windows operating system (which nearly all of the client firms use). It became clear that the startup was unlikely to thrive without inside technical information from Microsoft. And a Microsoft insider made it clear that Farrell would need help if he wanted to make crucial business connections within the firm.

Enter Sarah Gerdes, CEO of Business Marketing Group (BMG), a small firm specializing in matchmaking for small companies that want to join

http://www.fullarmor.com

- Learn to speak and understand the "language" of your partner. You will not pick up on subtle messages in conversations with partners unless you know how they communicate, and this can eventually make or break the alliance.

Although some strategic alliances fail as a result of insurmountable difficulties, sound planning and execution can prevent unnecessary failures. A few of the more common problems alliances face are presented below, along with a strategy for addressing each one.

- ***Contacts within the partner firm may be lost.*** To protect the alliance, establish relationships with other decision makers who can keep the connection going.
- ***The partner firm may change its strategy.*** To improve the alliance's chance of success, learn all you can about the partner and try to determine whether its current strategy is likely to change in the near future.
- ***Intellectual property transfers may spoil the relationship.*** Since it is impossible to prevent partnering firms from learning from one another, be sure you understand your rights with respect to use of the other firm's intellectual property within and outside the partnership.

THE BOARD OF DIRECTORS

6 *Describe the effective use of boards of directors and advisory councils.*

A common stockholder ordinarily casts one vote per share in stockholders' meetings. Thus, the stockholder indirectly participates in management by helping elect the directors. The **board of directors** is the governing body for corporate activity. It elects the firm's officers, who manage the enterprise with the help of management specialists. The directors also set or approve management policies, consider reports on operating results from the officers, and declare dividends (if any).

forces with large firms, especially Microsoft. Gerdes has a knack for getting the inside scoop on the inner workings of Microsoft. In fact, some say that she knows more about the firm's strategic direction than some Microsoft employees. Tapping her numerous contacts in Microsoft and relying on her wealth of insight about the firm, Gerdes was able to introduce FullArmor to the individuals who could put the startup on the software map. The effort was worth the trouble, and the strategic alliance continues to thrive.

BMG is only one of a growing number of matchmakers that specialize in helping small businesses form strategic alliances with large corporate partners. However, BMG's services don't come cheap. Recognizing the value of her assistance, many small startups have been more than happy to pay Gerdes $6,500 merely to help them create a relationship with a target company. Having her shepherd the relationship from beginning to end can cost $75,000 or more, plus 1.5 percent to 3 percent of any licensing and acquisition deals. About one-third of Gerdes's clients pay for her services with an equity position in their firms. As one investment banker observed, "It's a win-win—she builds a thriving business if her clients do."

Source: Christopher Caggiano, "Hotlinks," *Inc.*, Vol. 21, No. 14 (October 1999), pp. 72–81.

The Growing Need for a Board of Directors

board of directors
the governing body of a corporation, elected by the stockholders

All too often, the majority stockholder in a small corporation (the entrepreneur) appoints a board of directors only to fulfill a legal requirement. Such owners make little or no use of directors in managing their companies. In fact, the entrepreneur may actively resist efforts of these directors to provide managerial assistance. When appointing a board of directors, such an entrepreneur tends to select personal friends, relatives, or businesspersons who are too busy to analyze the firm's circumstances and are not inclined to argue. Board meetings may be mere formalities to satisfy legal requirements. Some entrepreneurs, however, have found an active board to be both practical and beneficial.

The use of boards of directors is becoming increasingly attractive for a number of reasons. The growing complexity of small businesses—resulting from globalization and technological developments, for example—makes the expertise of well-chosen directors especially valuable. In a family business, outsiders can play a unique role in helping evaluate family talent and mediate differences among family members.

The Use of Outside Directors by Small Companies

Objectivity is a particularly valuable contribution of outside directors. They can look at issues more dispassionately than can insiders who are involved in daily decision making. Outside directors, for example, are freer to evaluate and to question a firm's ethical standards. Some operating executives, without the scrutiny of outside directors, may rationalize unethical or illegal behavior as being in the best interest of the company.

In a family business, an outside board can help mediate and resolve issues related to leadership succession, in addition to providing more general direction. As outsiders, they bring to the business a measure of detachment from potentially explosive emotional differences.

ENTREPRENEURSHIP AND ETHICS

IN THE TRENCHES

INSIDE DIRECTORS MIND THEIR OWN BUSINESS

Many startups pack their boards of directors with insiders so that they can make decisions quickly. For example, the board of Razorfish, an Internet consulting firm, has eight members, five of whom are insiders. Chairman and CEO Jeff Dachis defends the practice, claiming that insiders make better decisions for the firm because they have a greater stake in the firm's future. While there is obviously truth in this statement, questions of effective, ethical corporate governance arise. Specifically, is a board dominated by insiders likely to make unethical decisions?

SportsLine.com operates the CBS SportsLine Web site. By mid-1998, when the firm was struggling, its share price took a quick drop, from a high near $40 to less than half that price. SportsLine's board of nine members (including CEO Mike Levy and six individuals who have business dealings with the company) had granted stock options to directors and officers of the firm some three months earlier, but these could be exercised only if the stock price was above the strike price of $29.50. Since the stock price was already at less than $20, the options were useless. So, in September of 1998, the board decided to reprice the options from $29.50 to just over $14, yielding a windfall of $3.5 million to managers and directors. Levy, whose options were not repriced, maintains that the practice was necessary to keep management from leaving the firm, but ethical questions remain. The practice of stacking the board with insiders, despite its advantages, clearly leaves room for inappropriate actions.

Source: Peter Elkind, "The New Role of Directors," *Fortune,* Vol. 141, No. 6 (March 20, 2000), pp. 116–117.

http://www.razorfish.com

Contributions of Directors

A properly assembled board of directors can bring supplementary knowledge and broad experience to corporate management. By virtue of their backgrounds, directors can fill gaps in the experience of a management team. The board should meet regularly to provide maximum assistance to the chief executive. In board meetings, ideas should be debated, strategies determined, and the pros and cons of policies explored. In this way, the chief executive is assisted by the experience of all the board members. Their combined knowledge makes possible more intelligent decisions on issues crucial to the firm.

By utilizing the experience of a board of directors, the chief executive of a small corporation is in no way abdicating active control of its operations. Instead, by consulting with and seeking the advice of the board's members, he or she is simply drawing on a larger pool of business knowledge. A group will typically make better decisions than will a single individual working in isolation.

An active board of directors serves management in several important ways: by reviewing major policy decisions, by advising on external business conditions and on proper reaction to the business cycle, and by providing informal advice from time to time on specific problems that arise. With a strong board, a small firm may gain greater credibility with the public, as well as with the business and financial community.

Selection of Directors

Many resources are available to an entrepreneur who is attempting to assemble a cooperative and experienced group of directors. The firm's attorney, banker, accountant, other business executives, and local management consultants might all be considered as potential directors, but such individuals lack the independence needed to critically review an entrepreneur's plans. Also, the owner is already paying for their expertise. For this reason, the owner needs to consider the value of an outside board—one with members whose income does not depend on the firm.

Although the following excerpt refers specifically to a family business, it expresses the importance to any firm of selecting a truly independent group of board members:

Probably the strongest argument for adding outsiders to the family business board is to make qualified and objective confidants available to the chief executive. Too many family business directors seek to tell the CEO what he wants to hear. This is understandable if the directors are other family members, employees, or outsiders who depend on the family for income.[17]

The nature and needs of a business will help determine the qualifications required in its directors. For example, a firm that faces a marketing problem may benefit greatly from the counsel of a board member with a marketing background. Business prominence in the community is not essential, although it may help give the company credibility and enable it to attract other well-qualified directors.

After deciding on the qualifications to look for, a business owner must seek suitable candidates as board members. Suggestions may be obtained from the firm's accountant, attorney, banker, and other associates in the business community. Owners or managers of other, noncompeting small companies, as well as second- and third-level executives in large companies, are often willing to accept such positions. Before offering candidates positions on the board, however, a business owner would be wise to do some discreet background checking.

Compensation of Directors

The compensation paid to board members varies greatly, and some small firms pay no fees at all. It is not unusual, though, for a small firm to pay a director from $200 to $300 monthly or $1,000 or more for each of four quarterly meetings. However, the board is less likely to be limited to local talent if the company is willing to pay members' travel expenses when they attend meetings. Some small businesses also offer board members stock-option packages, depending on industry practice and plans for growth. For example, stock options often play a critical role in attracting talent to fast-growth Internet companies.[18]

The relatively modest compensation offered for the services of well-qualified directors suggests that financial compensation is not their primary motivation for serving on a board. Reasonable compensation is appropriate, however, if directors are making important contributions to the firm's operations.

An Alternative: An Advisory Council

In recent years, increased attention has been directed to the legal responsibilities of directors. Because outside directors may be held responsible for illegal company actions, even though they are not directly involved in wrongdoing, some individuals are

Entrepreneurship and Ethics — **IN THE TRENCHES**

LOCATION IS NINE-TENTHS OF THE LAW

When it comes to reducing a company's income tax burden, some strategies are ethically sound whereas others clearly are not. Still other strategies are questionable, at best.

It is perfectly legal for a U.S. firm to form what is called a foreign sales corporation (FSC), which permits the company to cut its income tax rate on all profits earned from exports. The company need only be organized as a C corporation, and the products sold must have at least 50 percent U.S. content. This approach is gaining in popularity as more companies turn to international markets to fuel sales growth.

In contrast, it is not ethical for a company to reduce its tax liabilities by shifting earnings from high-tax countries to low-tax locations simply by raising or lowering the prices it charges itself for goods it imports from its own overseas subsidiary (a practice known as *transfer price manipulation*). This practice is specifically excluded by U.S. law.

advisory council
a group that functions like a board of directors but acts only in an advisory capacity

reluctant to accept directorships. Thus, some small companies use an **advisory council** as an alternative to a board of directors. Qualified outsiders are asked to serve on a council as advisors to the company. This group then functions in much the same way as a board of directors does, except that its actions are only advisory in nature.

The following account describes the potential value of an advisory council:

A seven-year-old diversified manufacturing company incurred its first deficit, which the owner-manager deemed an exception that further growth would rectify. Council members noted, however, that many distant operations were out of control and apparently unprofitable. They persuaded the owner to shrink his business by more than one-half. Almost immediately, the business began generating profits. From its reduced scale, growth resumed—this time soundly planned, financed, and controlled.[19]

The legal liability of members of an advisory council is not completely clear.[20] However, a clear separation of the council from the board of directors is thought to lighten, if not eliminate, the personal liability of its members. Since it is advisory in nature, the council also may pose less of a threat to the owner and possibly work more cooperatively than a conventional board.

U.S. Income Taxes and Organizational Form

7
Explain how different forms of organization are taxed by the federal government.

To help you understand the federal income tax system, we must answer the twofold question "Who is responsible for paying taxes, and how is tax liability ascertained?" The following sections discuss how taxes are determined for the major forms of organization and the tax savings associated with Section 1244 stock.

While FSCs are beneficial and legal and transfer price manipulation is clearly against the law, other tax avoidance strategies are more difficult to evaluate. The expansion of Internet-based enterprises has widened this ethical grey zone. For example, increasing numbers of dot.coms are locating in tax havens in the Caribbean and elsewhere. Playcentric.com has only 10 employees, but it has plans to undercut Amazon.com's prices on music and video sales by 45 percent and still make a profit. To do this, Playcentric plans to slash the firm's corporate income tax expenses by locating its computer servers in Bermuda, placing its operating unit in Barbados, and establishing distribution through a big record-store chain in Toronto, Canada—all well-known tax havens.

Other companies have chosen their locations for similar reasons. The tiny publisher ISI Publications Ltd. sells hard-to-find business books on BOOKSonBIZ.com in Bermuda. The U.S. online stockbroker E*TRADE Group, Inc. has set up international trading operations in Bermuda. The successful Ships-for-sale.com, offering Soviet-era submarines and other seagoing vessels, operates out of Cyprus. Are these operations legal? The Internal Revenue Service is not so sure. But given the ambiguity of offshore tax codes, e-commerce companies are certain they will earn millions of dollars before authorities can sort things out.

Source: Michael Allen, "As Dot-Coms Go Bust in U.S., Bermuda Hosts an Odd Little Boomlet," *The Wall Street Journal,* January 8, 2001, p. A1; and Joan Szabo, "A Business on Paper," *Entrepreneur,* Vol. 28, No. 2 (February 2000), p. 68.

How Businesses Are Taxed

The three major forms of organization are taxed in different ways.

SOLE PROPRIETORSHIP Self-employed individuals who operate a business as a sole proprietorship report income from the business on their individual federal income tax returns. They are then taxed at the rates set by law for individuals. For tax year 2001, the tax rates for a married couple reporting their income jointly were as follows:

Range of Taxable Income	Tax Rate
$0–$45,200	15.0%
$45,201–$109,250	27.5%
$109,251–$166,500	30.5%
$166,501–$297,350	35.5%
Over $297,350	39.1%

As an example, assume that a sole proprietor, who is married and files a joint return with her spouse, has taxable income of $150,000 from a business. The taxes owed on this income would be $36,822.50, computed as follows:

	Income	× Tax Rate	= Taxes
First	$ 45,200	15%	$ 6,780.00
Next	$ 64,050	27.5%	$17,613.75
Next	$ 40,750	30.5%	$12,428.75
Total	$150,000		$36,822.50

PARTNERSHIP A partnership reports the income it earns to the Internal Revenue Service, but the partnership itself does not pay any taxes. The income is allocated to the partners according to their agreement. The partners each report their own shares of the partnership income on their personal tax returns and pay any taxes owed.

C CORPORATION The corporation, as a separate legal entity, reports its income and pays any taxes related to these profits. The owners (stockholders) of the corporation need only report on their personal tax returns any amounts paid to them by the corporation in the form of dividends. For tax year 2001, the corporate tax rates were as follows:

Range of Taxable Income	Tax Rate
$0–$50,000	15%
$50,001–$75,000	25%
$75,001–$100,000	34%
$100,001–$335,000	39%
$335,001–$10,000,000	34%
$10,000,001–$15,000,000	35%
$15,000,001–$18,333,333	38%
Over $18,333,333	35%

Thus, the tax liability of the K&C Corporation, which had $150,000 in taxable income, would be $41,750, calculated as follows:

	Income	× Tax Rate	= Taxes
First	$ 50,000	15%	$ 7,500
Next	$ 25,000	25%	$ 6,250
Next	$ 25,000	34%	$ 8,500
Remaining	$ 50,000	39%	$19,500
Total	$150,000		$41,750

If the K&C Corporation paid a dividend to its owners in the amount of $40,000, the owners would need to report this dividend income when computing their personal income taxes. Thus, the $40,000 would be taxed twice, first as part of the corporation's income and then as part of the owners' personal income. However, this double taxation could be avoided if the firm were an S corporation.

Section 1244 Stock

ordinary income income earned in the ordinary course of business, including any salary

capital gains and losses gains and losses incurred from sales of property that are not a part of the firm's regular business operations

Section 1244 stock stock that offers some tax benefit to the stockholder in the case of corporate failure

For tax purposes, **ordinary income** is income earned in the everyday course of business. Salary is considered ordinary income. **Capital gains and losses** are financial gains and losses incurred from the sale of property that is not a part of a firm's regular business operations, such as gains or losses from the sale of common stock.

Typically, capital losses may be deducted only from capital gains, not from ordinary income. However, holding stock issued pursuant to Section 1244 of the Internal Revenue Code—**Section 1244 stock**—somewhat protects the stockholder in case of corporate failure. If such stock becomes worthless, the loss (up to $100,000 on a joint tax return) may be treated as an *ordinary* tax-deductible loss. Thus, when initially organizing a corporation, an owner would do well to consider issuing Section 1244 stock. Then, in the case of business failure, the owner could realize a tax savings that would not be allowed with regular stock.

Looking Back

1 Describe the characteristics and value of a strong management team.

- A strong management team nurtures a business idea and helps provide the necessary resources to make it succeed.
- The skills of management team members should complement each other, forming an optimal combination of education and experience.
- An entrepreneur should create a management structure that defines relationships among employees.
- A small firm can enhance its management by drawing on the expertise of outside professional groups.

2 Explain the common legal forms of organization used by small businesses.

- The most common legal forms of organization used by small businesses are the sole proprietorship, the partnership, and the C corporation.
- In a sole proprietorship, the owner receives all profits and bears all losses. The principal disadvantage of this form is the owner's unlimited liability.
- In a partnership, which should be established on the basis of a written partnership agreement, success depends on the partners' ability to build an effective working relationship.
- Corporations are particularly attractive because of their limited-liability feature. The fact that ownership is easily transferable makes them well suited for combining the capital of numerous owners.

3 Identify factors to consider in choosing among the primary legal forms of organization.

- The key factors in the choice among different legal forms of organization are organizational requirements and costs, liability of the owners, continuity of the business, transferability of ownership, management control, attractiveness for raising capital, and income taxes.
- Nearly three-fourths of all small businesses are organized as sole proprietorships, 8 percent are set up as partnerships, and 20 percent are formed as corporations.

4 Describe the unique features and restrictions of specialized organizational forms such as limited partnerships, S corporations, and limited liability companies.

- In a limited partnership, general partners have unlimited liability, while limited partners have only limited liability as long as they are not active in the firm's management.
- S corporations, also called Subchapter S corporations, enjoy a special tax status that permits them to avoid the corporate tax but requires individual stockholders to pay personal taxes on their proportionate shares of the business profits.
- In limited liability companies, individual owners have the advantage of limited liability but pay only personal income taxes on the firm's earnings.

5 Explain the nature of strategic alliances and their uses in small business.

- Strategic alliances allow business firms to combine their resources without compromising their independent legal status.
- Strategic alliances may be formed by two or more independent businesses to achieve some common purpose. For example, a large corporation and a small business or two or more small businesses may collaborate on a joint project.
- Strategic alliance matchmakers can help small businesses find suitable alliance partners.
- Entrepreneurs can improve their chances of creating and maintaining a successful alliance by establishing productive connections, identifying the best person to contact, confirming the long-term benefits of the alliance, and learning to speak the partner's "language."

6 Describe the effective use of boards of directors and advisory councils.

- Boards of directors can assist small corporations by offering counsel and assistance to their chief executives.
- To be most effective, members of the board should be properly qualified, independent outsiders.
- One alternative to an active board of directors is an advisory council, whose members are not personally liable for the company's actions.

7 Explain how different forms of organization are taxed by the federal government.

- Self-employed individuals who operate businesses as sole proprietorships report income from the businesses on their individual tax returns.
- A partnership reports the income it earns to the Internal Revenue Service, but the partnership itself does not pay income taxes. The income is allocated to the owners according to their partnership agreement.
- A corporation reports its income and pays any taxes due on this corporate income. Individual stockholders must also pay personal income taxes on dividends paid to them by a corporation.

KEY TERMS

management team, p. 241
sole proprietorship, p. 243
unlimited liability, p. 243
partnership, p. 245
partnership agreement, p. 247
agency power, p. 247
corporation, p. 248
C corporation, p. 248
legal entity, p. 248
corporate charter, p. 249
stock certificate, p. 249
pre-emptive right, p. 249
limited partnership, p. 252
general partner, p. 253
limited partner, p. 253
S corporation (Subchapter S corporation), p. 253
limited liability company, p. 254
strategic alliance, p. 255
board of directors, p. 259
advisory council, p. 262
ordinary income, p. 264
capital gains and losses, p. 264
Section 1244 stock, p. 264

DISCUSSION QUESTIONS

1. Why would investors tend to favor a new business led by a management team over one headed by a lone entrepreneur? Is this preference justified?
2. Discuss the merits of the three major legal forms of organization.
3. Does the concept of limited liability apply to a sole proprietorship? Why or why not?
4. Suppose a partnership is set up and operated without a formal partnership agreement. What problems might arise? Explain.
5. Evaluate the three major forms of organization in terms of management control by the owner and sharing of the firm's profits.
6. What is an S corporation, and what is its principal advantage?
7. Why are strategic alliances important for many small businesses? What steps can an entrepreneur take to create strategic alliances and to prevent their failure?
8. How might a board of directors be of value to management in a small corporation? What qualifications are essential for a director? Is ownership of stock in the firm a prerequisite for being a director?
9. What may account for the failure of most small corporations to use boards of directors as more than rubber stamps?
10. How do advisory councils differ from boards of directors? Which would you recommend to a small company owner? Why?

YOU MAKE THE CALL

SITUATION 1

Ted Green and Mark Stroder became close friends as 16-year-olds when both worked part-time for Green's dad in his automotive parts store. After high school, Green went to college, while Stroder joined the National Guard Reserve and devoted his weekends to auto racing. Green continued his association with the automotive parts store by buying and managing two of his father's stores.

In 1995, Green conceived the idea of starting a new business that would rebuild automobile starters, and he asked Stroder to be his partner in the venture. Originally, Stroder was somewhat concerned about working with Green because their personalities are so different. Green has been described as outgoing and enthusiastic, while Stroder is reserved and skeptical. However, Stroder is now out of work, and so he has agreed to the offer. They will set up a small shop behind one of Green's automotive parts stores. Stroder will do all the work; Green will supply the cash.

The "partners" have agreed to name the business STARTOVER, and now they need to decide on a legal form of organization.

Question 1 How relevant are the individual personalities to the success of this entrepreneurial team? Do you think Green and Stroder have a chance to survive their "partnership"? Why or why not?

Question 2 Do you consider it an advantage or a disadvantage that the members of this team are the same age?

Question 3 Which legal form of organization would you propose for STARTOVER? Why?

Question 4 If Stroder and Green decided to incorporate, would STARTOVER qualify as an S corporation? If so, would you recommend this option? Why or why not?

SITUATION 2

Matthew Freeman started a business in 1993 to provide corporate training in project management. He initially organized his business as a sole proprietorship. Until 1999, he did most of his work on a contract basis for Corporation Education Services (CES). Under the terms of his contract, Freeman was responsible for teaching 3- to 5-day courses to corporate clients—primarily Fortune 1000 companies. He was compensated according to a negotiated daily rate, and expenses incurred during a course (hotels, meals, transportation, etc.) were reimbursed by CES. Although some expenses were not reimbursed by CES (such as those for computers and office supplies), Freeman's expenses usually amounted to less than 1 percent of his revenues.

In 1999, Freeman increasingly found himself working directly with corporate clients rather than contracting with CES. Over the years, he had considered incorporating, but had assumed the costs and inconveniences of this option would outweigh the benefits. However, some of his new clients said that they would prefer to contract with a corporation rather than with an individual. And, Freeman sometimes wondered about potential liability problems. On the one hand, he didn't have the same liability issues as some other businesses—he worked out of his home, clients never visited his home office, all courses were conducted in hotels or corporate facilities, and his business involved only services. But he wasn't sure what would happen if a client were dissatisfied with the content and outcomes of his instruction. Finally, he wondered whether there would be tax advantages to incorporating.

Question 1 What are the advantages and disadvantages of running the business as a sole proprietorship? As a C corporation?

Question 2 If Freeman decided to incorporate his business, which types of corporations could he form? Which type would you recommend? Why?

SITUATION 3

For years, a small distributor of welding materials had followed the practice of most small firms, treating the board of directors as merely a legal necessity. Composed of two co-owners and a retired steel company executive, the board was not a working board. But the company, run informally with traditional management methods, was profitable.

After attending a seminar, the majority owner decided that a board might be useful for more than legal or cosmetic purposes. Thus, he invited two outsiders—both division heads of larger corporations—to join the board. This brought the membership of the board to five. The majority owner believed the new members would be helpful in opening up the business to new ideas.

Question 1 Can two outside members on a board of five make any real difference in the way the board operates?

Question 2 Evaluate the owner's choices for board members.

Question 3 What will determine the usefulness or effectiveness of this board? Do you predict that it will be useful? Why or why not?

Experiential Exercises

1. Prepare a one-page résumé of your personal qualifications to launch a term-paper-typing business at your college or university. Then write a critique that might be prepared by an investor, evaluating your strengths and weaknesses as shown on the résumé.
2. Interview an attorney whose clients include small businesses. Inquire about the legal considerations involved in choosing the form of organization for a new business. Report your findings to the class.
3. Interview the partners of a local business. Inquire about the factors they considered when drawing up their partnership agreement. Report your findings to the class.
4. Discuss with a corporate director, attorney, banker, or business owner the contributions of directors to small firms. Prepare a brief report on your findings. If you discover a particularly well-informed individual, suggest that person to your instructor as a possible speaker.

Exploring the Web

1. To answer the following questions, access **http://www.Quicken.com**, the Web site sponsored by the company that produced the popular financial software. Click the Small Business tab, and then choose Start a Business.
   a. Approximately how much does it cost to use the incorporation service offered here? How much are your state's filing fees to incorporate, set up an LLC, or create a nonprofit entity?
   b. According to this site, what are the three main reasons a small business would choose to incorporate rather than form an LLC?
   c. What five benefits are gained by a company that elects to become an S corporation?
2. Compare three of the following articles and then answer the questions below.
   "Small Businesses Seek Directors," at **http://phoenix.bcentral.com/phoenix/stories/1998/01/26/smallb1.html**
   "Who Should Be on Your Board of Directors?" at **http://www.jsonline.com/bym/biz2biz/feb00/bwho021800.asp**
   "Boards of Directors: 10 Common Mistakes," at **http://www.business-survival.com/articles/startrun/Assembleboard.html**
   a. Do small startups typically have or not have a board of directors? How common are advisory boards?
   b. What mistakes do entrepreneurs make in choosing members of their company's board of directors?
3. Access The Small Business Advocate site at **http://www.smallbusinessadvocate.com**, and search the Archives for "strategic alliance."
   a. In the May 4, 1999 interview, what example is presented of something that a small business should not overlook when establishing a strategic alliance?
   b. The interviews conducted on June 16 and July 1, 1999 deal with creating strategic alliances for what business purposes?
   c. Examine the Web site. Explain what The Small Business Advocate is and what other resources are available on the site.

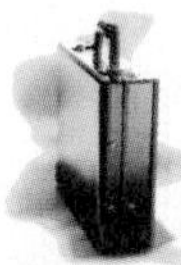

Case 10

CORRTECH SYSTEMS, INC. (p. 666)

This case deals with the formation of strategic alliances between small technology companies and a large computer firm.

Alternative Case for Chapter 10:
Case 18, "Central Engineering," p. 688

The Business Plan

LAYING THE FOUNDATION

As part of laying the foundation to prepare your own business plan, respond to the following questions regarding your management team and legal form of organization.

MANAGEMENT PLAN QUESTIONS

1. Who are the members of your management team? What are the skills, education, and experience of each member?
2. What other key managers do you plan to recruit?
3. Who are the active investors and the directors of the company? What are their qualifications?
4. Do you plan to use consultants? If so, please describe their qualifications.
5. What are your plans for future employee recruitment?
6. What are the compensation and benefit plans for the board members, managers, and employees?
7. What style of management will be used? What is the decision-making process in the company? What mechanisms are in place for effective communications between managers and employees? If possible, present a simple organization chart.
8. How will personnel be motivated? How will creativity be encouraged? How will commitment and loyalty be developed?
9. What are the employee retention and training programs? Who is responsible for job descriptions and employee evaluations?

LEGAL PLAN QUESTIONS

1. Will the business function as a sole proprietorship, partnership, or corporation? If a corporation, will it be a C corporation, an S corporation, or a limited liability company?
2. What are the liability implications of the legal form of organization chosen?
3. What are the tax advantages and disadvantages of this form of organization?
4. Where will the corporation be chartered?
5. If a corporation, when will it be incorporated?
6. What attorney or legal firm has been selected to represent the firm? What type of relationship exists with the firm's attorney or law firm?
7. What legal issues are presently or potentially significant?
8. What licenses and/or permits may be required?
9. What strategic alliances are in place, and what do you plan to establish in the future? What are the forms and nature of these alliances? What are the responsibilities of and benefits to the parties involved? What are the exit strategies?

chapter 11

SELECTING A LOCATION AND PLANNING THE FACILITIES

In the Spotlight

FitnessLink

Entrepreneurs frequently embark on home-based businesses out of family considerations. This was the motivation for Shannon Entin, who believed that she and her husband wouldn't have enough time to devote to children because both were working outside the home. He was a full-time researcher for Bloomberg Financial Markets, and she was a part-time fitness instructor. Thinking that staying at home would provide more time to start a family, Entin decided to create a home-based, online fitness magazine.

She began by spending $1,000 on upgrading her computer and purchasing desktop publishing software and a book on HTML, the programming language used to publish on the Web. Once she was satisfied with the Web site she had designed, Entin found an Internet service provider to maintain the site—she was now ready to launch FitnessLink.

Several advertisers quickly lined up to post their banner ads on the site. As FitnessLink's pages grew in number, Entin's heavy workload led to 90-hour weeks, and her goal of starting a family was postponed. Finally, she hired a second designer and began outsourcing jobs to more than a dozen freelancers, who now produce content for the magazine.

Entin's business hours have been greatly reduced, and she is able to spend more time with her son, Logan, born in 1998. The home-based venture is an unqualified success; in 2000, FitnessLink made $156,000 in profit. ◆

Source: From material from http://www.fitnesslink.com; and Amanda Walmac, "Making Money @ Home," *Family Money,* Vol. 4, No. 6 (November–December 2000), p. 43.

http://www.fitnesslink.com

LOOKING AHEAD

After studying this chapter, you should be able to

1. *Identify the factors affecting choice of a business location.*
2. *Describe the attraction and challenges of a home-based business.*
3. *Explain how efficiency can be achieved in the layout of a physical facility.*
4. *Understand the equipment needs of small firms.*

A business idea begins to take shape as an entrepreneur formulates a business plan. The idea becomes more tangible as the entrepreneur selects the resources needed to implement the plan, including the business site and any necessary facilities and equipment. For some entrepreneurial ventures, these resources may be limited to a briefcase, cell phone, desk space at home, and a site on the Internet; for others, they may include a new building. Regardless of the specific resources needed, every sound location decision is founded on certain basic principles.

This chapter addresses some of the major factors involved in choosing a business location and designing the physical facilities. A discussion of how these key factors support selection of the proposed location should be included in the business plan. The extent of this discussion will vary from plan to plan because of the wide variation in the nature of new business ventures.

THE LOCATION DECISION

For many entrepreneurs, choosing a location for a small business is a one-time decision—made only when the business is first established or purchased. However, an entrepreneur must occasionally consider relocating the business to reduce operating costs, get closer to customers, or gain other advantages. Also, as a business grows, it is sometimes desirable to expand operations to other locations.[1]

Identify the factors affecting choice of a business location.

The Importance of the Location Decision

The importance of the location decision is underscored by the costs and impracticality of pulling up stakes and moving an established business. Also, if the choice of site is particularly poor, the business may never be able to get off the ground, even with adequate financing and superior managerial ability. This effect is so clearly recognized by national chains that they spend thousands of dollars investigating sites before establishing new stores. As noted in Chapter 6, one of the reasons franchising is so attractive is that franchisors typically assist an entrepreneur in site selection.

The choice of a good location is much more vital to some businesses than to others. For example, the site chosen for a dress shop can make or break the business because it must be convenient for customers. In contrast, the physical location of the office of a painting contractor is of less importance, since customers do not need frequent access to the facility. Even painting contractors, however, may suffer if their business site is poorly chosen. For example, some communities are more willing or able than others to invest resources to keep property in good condition, thereby providing greater opportunities for painting jobs.

Key Factors in Selecting a Good Location

Five key factors, shown in Figure 11-1, guide the location process: customer accessibility, environmental business conditions, resource availability, personal preference, and site availability and costs. In a particular situation, one factor may carry more weight than others, but each always has an influence on the final location decision.

CUSTOMER ACCESSIBILITY The foremost consideration in selecting a location should be customer accessibility. Retail outlets and service firms are typical examples of businesses that must be located so as to make access convenient for target customers. Rarely will customers be willing to regularly travel long distances to shop. Consider Glenn Campbell and Scott Molander's idea to sell hats in high traffic areas. Each store location in shopping malls and airports offers a vast assortment of officially licensed baseball-style hats. The first store was opened in 1995, and in five years, the company grew to 157 stores.[2]

Many products, such as snack foods and gasoline, are convenience goods, which require a retail location close to target customers; otherwise, consumers will substitute competitive brands. Services such as tire repair and hair styling are also classified as convenience items and require a location accessible to customers.

Customer accessibility is vital in industries in which the cost of shipping the finished product is high relative to the product's value. For example, packaged ice and soft drinks must be produced near consuming markets, because transporting these products can be an expensive process.

Convenient access for customers is one reason small businesses have successfully created such a strong presence on the Internet. With the appropriate computer connection, customers can access a small business's home page from anywhere in the world.

FIGURE 11-1

Five Key Factors in Determining a Good Business Location

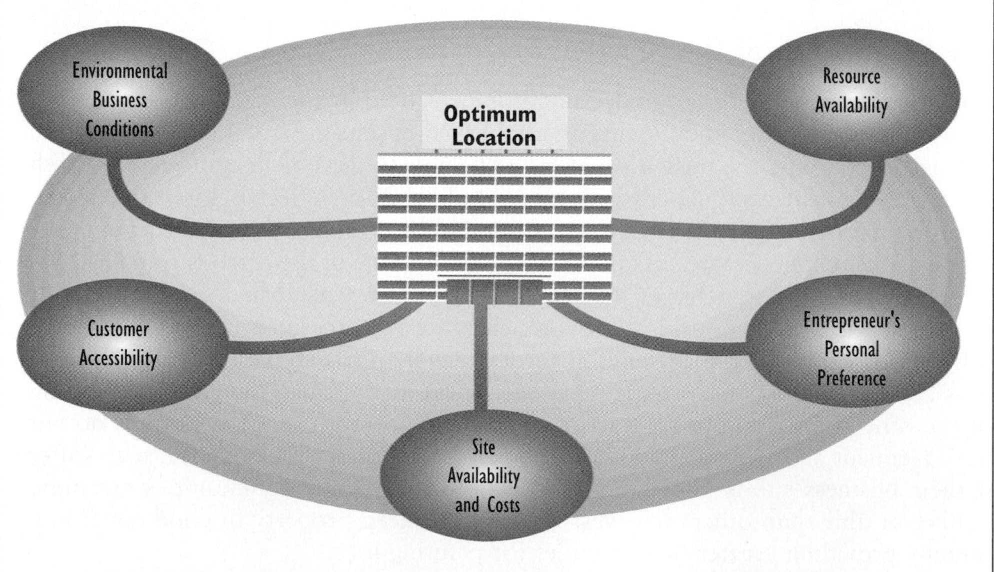

Locating close to niche market customers often dictates a site that otherwise would be less than desirable. For example, a small apparel retail store, Transfer Clothing Inc., is located underground in a subway station of New York City, and the Cavern Supply Company, a cafeteria, is located 750 feet straight down in Carlsbad Caverns National Park. Transfer Clothing is one of 165 merchants peddling magazines, food, clothing, and haircuts in New York's subway stations. Cavern Supply contends daily with 80 percent humidity and bats.[3] Neither business occupies an attractive site. However, they both recognize the need to be accessible to potential customers.

ENVIRONMENTAL BUSINESS CONDITIONS A small business is affected in a number of ways by the environment within which it operates. Environmental conditions can hinder or promote success. For example, weather is an important environmental factor influencing the demand for products such as air conditioners and outdoor swimming pools. Competition, legal requirements, and the tax structure are a few of the many other critical environmental factors.

Every entrepreneur seeks profits; therefore, all factors affecting the financial picture are of great concern. State and local governments can help or hinder a new business by forgiving or levying taxes. Considerable variation exists across the United States in state corporate income taxes, with only a few states having no such tax. One state with an advantageous tax policy is Wyoming. Its Web site proudly states, "The state of Wyoming does not levy a personal or corporate income tax. There is no current legislation in the works to create an income tax."[4] Obviously, the best time to evaluate environmental conditions is prior to making a location commitment.

Many states offer location incentives. One strategy is to establish **enterprise zones** in order to bring jobs to economically deprived areas. Sponsored by local city/county governments, these zones lure businesses by offering regulatory and tax relief. In exchange for locating or expanding in these areas, eligible business firms receive total exemption from the property taxes normally assessed on a new plant and equipment for three to five years. As of January 2001, Oregon had 44 enterprise zones.[5]

enterprise zones
state-designated areas that are established to bring jobs to economically deprived regions through regulatory and tax incentives

Enterprise zones are not a cure-all. Locating in an enterprise zone will not solve problems created by poor management or make up for an ill-conceived idea. However, enterprise zones can be used as a catalyst to help jump-start a small firm.

The federal government also provides a variety of programs to assist small firms. One program, introduced by the Clinton administration in 1994, is the **Empowerment Zone/Enterprise Communities** (EZ/EC) initiative. This 10-year plan makes funds available through social service block grants and tax breaks. Employers in an EZ are eligible for wage tax credits, worth $3,000 for every employee who lives within the zone boundaries. EZ businesses are also eligible for increased tax expensing for equipment purchases.[6]

Empowerment Zone/Enterprise Communities (EZ/EC)
a program of the federal government that provides financial support to local communities for the purpose of economic advancement

While most efforts of state and city governments are designed to support startups, some cities have regulations that restrict new business operations under certain circumstances. For example, in San Antonio, Texas, repairing or upholstering furniture in the home is prohibited. Detroit, Michigan doesn't permit vendors to sell any hot food except hot dogs and sausages. And, in San Diego, California, shoeshiners are banned from public areas.[7]

RESOURCE AVAILABILITY The availability of resources associated with producing a product and operating a business should also be considered in selecting a location. Raw materials, labor supply, and transportation are some of the factors that have a

ENTREPRENEURSHIP TODAY

IN THE TRENCHES

HITTING PAYDIRT

Sometimes a location is so suitable to a particular business that the key resources available determine the nature of the startup. Consider, for example, the decision of Barbara Bradshaw, founder of Eastex Farms near Rusk, Texas.

When Bradshaw remarried 15 years ago, she left her Houston, Texas employment agency and moved to the farm of her new husband, who was a fruit and vegetable grower. "My husband was growing fruit and couldn't sell it all," she recalls. "Well, I'm a little Greek, a little Lebanese, so I've cooked all my life. I started looking at the feasibility of putting old-fashioned pickled products in a jar." Why not take advantage of the rich, red soils of East Texas and locate a gourmet food business on the family farm, which already produced the required ingredients?

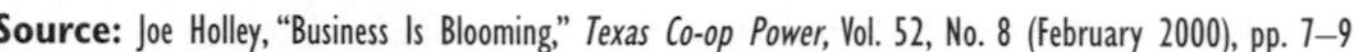

So Bradshaw took some courses at a nearby college, obtained the required state and federal licenses, and began producing an innovative product line, recently renamed Gourmet Gardens. Over 50 different fruits and vegetables are put up in old-fashioned Mason jars. Her peach cobbler, relishes, and "sweet fire" salsas are now sold in every state.

Her mom-and-pop operation employs her daughter, Kara, and her son, Howard, who recently moved from Dallas to become general manager. "Every year," says Bradshaw, "we've doubled our sales, except one year when we tripled."

By locating her business on the family farm, Bradshaw has benefited from the involvement of family members and has also reaped the benefits of a critical production resource—the land.

Source: Joe Holley, "Business Is Blooming," *Texas Co-op Power*, Vol. 52, No. 8 (February 2000), pp. 7–9

http://www.tx-marketeers.com/Eastexfarms

bearing on location. Nearness to raw materials and suitability of labor supply are particularly critical considerations in the location of a manufacturing business.

Nearness to Raw Materials. If required raw materials are not abundantly available in all areas, a region in which these materials abound offers special locational advantages. For a business dependent on bulky or heavy raw materials that lose much of their bulk or weight in the manufacturing process, proximity to these materials is a powerful force driving the location decision. A sawmill is an example of a business that must stay close to its raw materials in order to operate economically.

However, a firm can be *too* dependent on one source of raw material. Such was the case for Alaska Forest Creations, a 10-employee, wooden-bowl manufacturing business. When Mike Ronchetti moved his business from Anchorage to the Jongass National Forest in southeastern Alaska, his strategy was to be closer to what seemed to be a limitless supply of wood. Bad economic times, however, caused several sawmills to close and the remaining mills couldn't fill his orders. The result: Ronchetti was forced to close his business.[8]

Suitability of Labor Supply. A manufacturer's labor requirements depend on the nature of its production process. Available supply of labor, wage rates, labor productivity, and a history of peaceful industrial relations are all particularly important considerations for labor-intensive firms. In some cases, the need for semiskilled or unskilled labor justifies locating in an area with surplus labor. In other cases, firms find it desirable to seek a pool of highly skilled labor.

Availability of Transportation. Access to good transportation is important to almost all firms. For example, good highways and bus systems provide customers with convenient access to retail stores. For small manufacturers, quality transportation is especially vital. They must carefully evaluate all the trucking routes that support their logistic needs, considering the costs of both transporting supplies to the manufacturing location and shipping the finished product to customers. It is critical that they know whether these costs will allow their product to be competitively priced.

PERSONAL PREFERENCE OF THE ENTREPRENEUR As a practical matter, many entrepreneurs tend to discount customer accessibility, environmental business conditions, and resource availability and consider only their home community. The possibility of locating elsewhere never enters their minds. Just because an individual has always lived in a particular town, however, does not automatically make the town a satisfactory business location!

On the other hand, locating a business in one's home community is not necessarily illogical. In fact, there are certain advantages. From a personal standpoint, the entrepreneur generally appreciates and feels comfortable with the atmosphere of the home community, whether it is a small town or a large city. From a practical business standpoint, the entrepreneur can more easily establish credit. Hometown bankers can be dealt with more confidently, and other businesspersons may be of great service in helping evaluate a given opportunity. If potential customers are local residents, the prospective entrepreneur probably has a better idea of their tastes and preferences than an outsider would have. Relatives and friends may be the entrepreneur's first customers and may help advertise his or her products or services.

Personal preference does not always dictate a local site. Sometimes the choice is a location offering unique lifestyle advantages. Entrepreneur Pete Nelson has a home office 10 feet off the ground, in a stand of 70-year-old Douglas firs in Fall City, Washington, where he operates TreeHouse Workshop, a general contracting business. Nelson and his wife, Judy, enjoy the outdoor location of their home-based business, where they are "face-to-beak with woodpeckers and wrens" on the other side of their office window.[9] Personal preference, however, should not be allowed to take priority over obvious location weaknesses.

SITE AVAILABILITY AND COSTS Once an entrepreneur has settled on a certain area of the country, a specific site must still be chosen. The availability of potential sites and the costs associated with obtaining them must be investigated.

Site Availability. An entrepreneur, evaluating a site for his new business, is said to have exclaimed, "It must be a good site—I know of four businesses that have been there in the last two years!" Fortunately, such a misguided approach to site evaluation is not typical of entrepreneurs, many of whom recognize the value of seeking professional assistance in determining site availability and appropriateness. Local realtors are one good source.

If an entrepreneur's top choices are unavailable, other options must be considered. One choice is shared facilities. In recent years, business incubators have sprung up in all areas of the country. A **business incubator** is a facility that rents space to new businesses or to people wishing to start businesses. Incubators are often located in recycled buildings, such as abandoned warehouses or schools. They serve fledgling businesses by making space available, offering management advice, and providing clerical assistance, all of which help lower operating costs. An incubator

business incubator
a facility that provides shared space, services, and management assistance to new businesses

tenant can be fully operational the day after moving in, without buying phones, renting a copier, or hiring office employees.

The purpose of business incubators is to see new businesses hatch, grow, and leave the incubator. Most incubators—though not all—have some type of government or university sponsorship and are motivated by a desire to stimulate economic development. Although the building space provided by incubators is significant, their greatest contribution is the business expertise and management assistance they provide. (Further discussion of incubators can be found in Chapter 18.)

Site Costs Ultimately, the site selection process must depend on evaluation of relevant costs. Unfortunately, an entrepreneur is frequently unable to afford the "best" site. The costs involved in building on a new site may be prohibitive, or the purchase price of an existing structure may exceed the entrepreneur's budget.

Assuming that a suitable building is available, the entrepreneur must decide whether to lease or buy. Although ownership confers greater freedom in the modification and use of a building, the advantages of leasing usually outweigh these benefits. We recommend that most new firms lease for two reasons:

1. A large cash outlay is avoided. This is important for a new small firm, which typically lacks adequate financial resources.
2. Risk is reduced by avoiding substantial investment and by postponing commitments for space until the success of the business is assured and the nature of building requirements is better known.

When entering into a leasing agreement, the entrepreneur should check the landlord's insurance policies to be sure there is proper coverage for various types of risks. If not, the leasee should seek coverage under his or her own policy. It is important to have the terms of the leasing agreement reviewed by an attorney. Sometimes, an attorney can arrange for special clauses to be added to a lease, such as an escape clause that allows the leasee to exit the agreement under certain conditions. And an attorney can ensure that an entrepreneur will not be unduly exposed to liability for damages caused by the gross negligence of others. Consider the experience of one firm that wished to rent 300 square feet of storage space in a large complex of offices and shops. On the sixth page of the landlord's standard lease, the firm's lawyer found language that could have made the firm responsible for the entire 30,000-square-foot complex if it burned down, regardless of blame!

The high cost of commercial sites, whether leased or purchased, is one reason many entrepreneurs consider locating a business in the home. Let's now turn our attention to home-based businesses.

Home-Based Businesses

2

Describe the attraction and challenges of a home-based business.

home-based business
a business that maintains its primary facility in the residence of its owner

Rather than lease or buy a commercial site, increasing numbers of entrepreneurs are electing to use their basement, garage, or spare room for their business operation, creating a **home-based business.** The American Association of Home-Based Businesses estimated that in 2001 there were over 24 million home-based businesses in the United States.[10] Historically, businesses operated out of homes fit the following description:

Home, to corporate America, has traditionally been a business backwater, the domain of piano teachers, part-timers, and multilevel-marketing schemers—a location that has been demeaned by all those Earn Money at Home classified ads.[11]

In the past, a home location for a business was regarded as second-rate. "Ten years ago, if you were working out of your home, it was like you had some sort of disease," says Don Vlaek, a former employee at a pizza business who now works from his home as a consultant. But times have changed, and home-based entrepreneurs no longer feel embarrassed about their location. The home office, once simply a stage in the growth of many businesses, is a viable permanent option for some. At present, many entrepreneurs have no plans to ever move out of the home.

http://www.aahbb.org

The Attraction of Home-Based Businesses

Why do many entrepreneurs find operating a business at home so attractive? Although motivations vary (see Figure 11-2), the main attraction of a home-based business relates to financial and family lifestyle considerations.

FINANCIAL CONSIDERATIONS Like most business ventures, a home-based business has an important goal—earning money—and locating at home helps increase profits by reducing costs. This was the motivation for Geri Loendorf from Fullerton, California, who started an online jewelry auction business named GEMdesign. To supplement the family income, she creates bejeweled stickpins and hatpins, which she sells on her Web site. Bidding starts at about $5.00 for an average pin.[12]

http://www.gemdesign.bigstep.com

The cost of a "real office" prompted Mike Ball to operate his ad agency in a former boathouse/garage that overlooks Whitmore Lake, near Ann Arbor, Michigan. Ball started working at home in 1991, intending to relocate to a commercial site.

But when the time came, he asked himself, why assume the monthly overhead of rent on a 2,000-square-foot office, which he would have to fill with a secretary/office manager, a production assistant, an art director, and perhaps an account executive—employees he'd have to pink-slip should business fluctuate? . . . Ball decided to stay the course, sailing on with his virtual company and sub-contracting work out to other home-based entrepreneurs. He communicates with them, and with his clients by fax, E-mail, and a corporate Web site.[13]

FIGURE 11-2

Entrepreneurs' Reasons for Operating a Home-Based Business

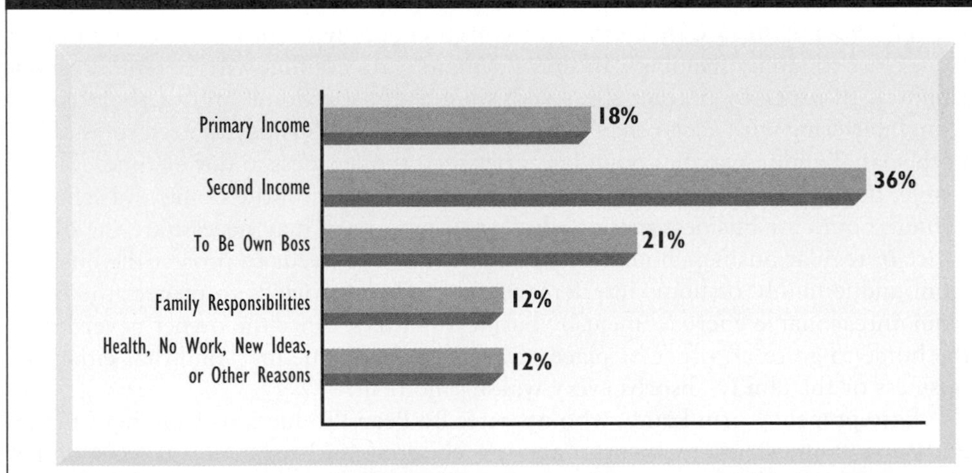

Source: Based on "Home-Based Business: The Hidden Economy," *The Small Business Advocate,* Vol. 19, No. 2 (Spring 2000), p. 6.

FAMILY LIFESTYLE CONSIDERATIONS Many young entrepreneurs remain in a family business because of close family ties. Similarly, entrepreneurs who locate business operations in the home are frequently motivated by the desire to spend more time with family members. Consider the following examples:

Nine years of hard work at two Chicago ad agencies had earned Barbara Casey an account executive title and a comfortable $50,000 salary. But after giving birth to her first child five years ago, Casey decided to cut back to a four-day week. Her boss objected, so Casey walked out and started a small ad shop in her Naperville, Illinois home. When her business outgrew the guest bedroom, she and her husband bought a bigger house.[14]

Greg Wilcox, who runs a home-based business in Edina, Minnesota, with his partner, Dyke Williams, had to contend with a child who was sleepless in Minneapolis. . . . "The original idea was that we both wanted to have an active role in raising our kids," explains Wilcox. "We had fathers who ran their own businesses. Typically, they worked 80 hours a week, and we saw them very little. We didn't want that to happen to us. On the other hand, Victoria [Greg's wife] didn't want to give up being a nurse. We felt the need to have one parent home with the kids because we didn't want to do day care!"[15]

Still another example comes from Prince Dailey, owner of Prince Upholstery, a home-based business in Stratford, Connecticut.

I did most work at night after their [the children's] bedtime. This let me spend a few hours with the kids and still work uninterrupted. Later, I involved the kids. I gave them screwdrivers to help take apart chairs or scissors and needles to cut and sew fabric. They felt they were helping, and it gave me peace of mind.[16]

Challenges of Operating a Business at Home

Just as most businesses located at commercial sites have their problems, home-based businesses face special challenges attributable to their location. We will look briefly at three of these challenges—family and business conflicts, business image, and legal considerations.

FAMILY AND BUSINESS CONFLICTS For entrepreneurs who locate at home in order to be close to family members, business demands can conflict with parental responsibilities. In order to prevent the responsibilities of the home and of the business from interfering with each other, owners of home-based businesses need to establish both spatial and nonspatial boundaries between the business and the home. For example, the owner should set aside specific business space in the home and schedule definite hours for business matters. In fact, clients' calls may necessitate the observance of regular business hours. And just as the owner needs to protect the business from undue family or home interference, he or she also needs to protect the home from unreasonable encroachment by business matters. Since the owner never leaves the home to go to an office or place of business, he or she may find that either the business or the family absorbs every waking moment.

http://www.bopeepproductions.com

Entrepreneur Karin Lamb, who operates Bo Peep Productions from her Eureka, Montana home, tries to incorporate her children into as many aspects of her videotape-for-toddlers business as possible. But she recognizes the need for limits. She expresses her philosophy in the following way:

IN THE TRENCHES

BUILDING CUSTOMER LOYALTY

MOVING OUT

The home location environment is a mistake for some types of businesses. Just ask Ed Storey, owner of Essex Builders Group in Winter Park, Florida.

In 1991, Storey and his wife founded their company in their home. The idea of a home-based business seemed great to them because their big house would make it possible to work night and day, if needed. Before launching, Storey spent about a month arranging for insurance, checking out zoning regulations, obtaining necessary supplies and equipment, and installing separate lines for the office phone and fax.

The first few days were okay, but then, as Storey puts it, "It became clear to me very quickly that there were a lot of distractions in the house. At that time, I had two sons at home. On top of that, the phone was always ringing, what with solicitations and personal calls. We had a house cleaner once a week. There were always interruptions."

Storey was also concerned that being based at home wasn't giving his startup business the image of stability he wanted. "When you need to meet with clients, saying that you're operating out of your house doesn't work," he says.

After two weeks, Essex Builders moved into a corporate suite. Now, the distractions are gone, and the company's proximity to other businesses has proven most beneficial.

It was reported that the Essex Builders Group had booked $55 million of new multifamily building in Winter Park, Florida for 2001! "I have no doubt that we could not have grown the way we did during the past eight years if we had stayed at home," says Storey.

Source: Adapted from material from http://www.globest.com; and Jill Andresky Fraser, "Home Grown," *Inc.*, Vol. 21, No. 18 (December 1999), p. 106.

I've always been fairly flexible and relaxed, not one to adhere to a specific schedule. When my children were younger, I would see what was going on with them, then develop my schedule around that. As they've grown older, and since I'm home-schooling them, there are times when I can set them at a task and set myself at a task. . . . With older youngsters . . . it's important to teach them to respect certain limits. Their critical limit is a closed office door. They know that means "Don't disturb me unless it's an emergency."[17]

Business and family conflicts can take a personal toll on the family. Juggling the needs of business clients and family members can be so stressful that the home business has to relocate.

BUSINESS IMAGE Maintaining an image of professionalism when working at home is a major challenge to home-based entrepreneurs. Allowing young children to answer the telephone, for example, may dispel a professional image. Likewise, a baby crying or a dog barking in the background during a phone call can be distracting to a client.

If clients or salespeople visit the home-based business, it is critical that a professional office area be maintained. Space limitations sometimes make this difficult. Such was the experience of Scott Walker, owner of a family-owned firm that manufactures the novelty party game Walla Balla. His office is located in the basement of his home. Walker recalls the day when a salesperson came to the office: "She came into the house and down the dark stairs to our dimly lit basement office. Throughout the entire meeting, I could tell she was uncomfortable about her surroundings."[18]

zoning ordinances
local laws regulating land use

LEGAL CONSIDERATIONS Some local laws pose a problem for home-based businesses. **Zoning ordinances,** for example, regulate the types of enterprises permitted in various geographical areas. Some cities outlaw any type of home-based business within city limits.

David Hanania, founder and president of Home Business Institute, based in White Plains, New York, points out that many zoning laws, dating as far back as the 1930s, have never been updated. The intent of such laws is to protect a neighborhood's residential quality by preventing commercial signs and parking problems. Unfortunately, some entrepreneurs unwittingly run up against these zoning laws.

There are also tax issues related to a home-based business. Generally, a separate space must be clearly devoted to business activities in order for the entrepreneur to claim a tax deduction. A certified public accountant can be helpful in explaining these tax regulations.

Insurance considerations may also affect a home-based business. An entrepreneur's homeowner's policy is not likely to cover business activities, liabilities, and equipment.

Technology and Home-Based Businesses

Advancements in business-application technology are a major catalyst in the rapid growth of home-based businesses. Personal computers, fax machines, voice mail, and e-mail are among the technological tools that help the home-based business compete effectively with commercial-site businesses. Such technology makes it possible to open many types of businesses almost anywhere.

One important technological tool available to home-based businesses is the World Wide Web. Millions of small firms—many of them based at home—are using the Web to sell products and services. (Recall the discussion of e-commerce in Chapter 3.) Virtually every product sold in traditional retail outlets is now sold over the Internet.

More recently, new technology has allowed long-distance calls to be placed over the Internet through special computer software. Once a Web phone is set up, dialing a call is much like surfing the Web. Candie Yoder, owner of ImageStream Internet Solutions in Plymouth, Indiana, has cut her company's long-distance phone bill in half by using the new technology. She says, "I thought about using e-mail more, but people prefer a human voice. So, I decided to see if a Web phone could save us money. It did."[19]

http://www.imagestream-is.com

Banking via the Web also supports home-based businesses. Electronic banking is expanding each year, as customers come to expect more convenience and time-saving services from financial institutions.

Designing the Physical Facilities

Explain how efficiency can be achieved in the layout of a physical facility.

A business plan should describe the physical space in which the business will be housed. Although the plan may call for a new building or an existing structure, ordinarily a new business occupies an existing building, with minor or major remodeling. Therefore, the following discussion will focus on designs for existing facilities.

Functional Requirements

When specifying building requirements, the entrepreneur must avoid committing to a space that is too large or too luxurious. At the same time, the space should not be too small or too austere for efficient operation. Buildings do not produce profits di-

rectly; they merely house the operations and personnel that do so. Therefore, the ideal building is practical, not pretentious.

The general suitability of a building for a given type of business operation depends on the functional requirements of the business. For example, a restaurant should ideally be on one level. Other important factors are the age and condition of the building, fire hazards, heating and air conditioning, lighting and restroom facilities, and entrances and exits. Obviously, these factors are weighted differently for a factory operation than for a wholesale or retail operation. But in any case, the comfort, convenience, and safety of the business's employees and customers must not be overlooked.

Building Layout

Achieving a good layout involves arranging physical facilities so that they contribute to efficient business operations. We will take a brief look at general layout problems common to manufacturers (whose primary concern is production) and retailers (whose primary concern is customer traffic).

FACTORY LAYOUT Factory layout presents a three-dimensional space problem. Overhead space may be utilized for power conduits, pipelines for exhaust systems, and the like. In addition, proper design of storage areas and handling systems makes use of space near the ceiling. Space must also be allowed for the unobstructed movement of products from one location to another.

The ideal setup for a manufacturing process is to have a straight-line, forward movement of materials from receiving room to shipping room. If this ideal cannot be realized for a given process, backtracking, sidetracking, and long hauls of materials should at least be minimized, to reduce production delays.

Two contrasting types of layouts are used in industrial firms. A **process layout** groups similar machines together. Drill presses, for example, are separated from lathes in a machine shop using a process layout. The alternative, a **product layout,** arranges special-purpose equipment along a production line in the sequence in which it is used in processing. The product is moved progressively from one work station to the next, and the machines are located at the stations where they are needed for the various stages of production.

process layout
a factory design that groups similar machines together

product layout
a factory design that arranges machines according to their roles in the production process

RETAIL STORE LAYOUT The objectives for retail store layout include displaying merchandise so as to maximize sales and customer service. Convenient and attractive surroundings contribute to a customer's continued patronage. Color, music, and even aroma are all important layout factors for a retail business. Another objective is protecting a store's equipment and merchandise. Finally, an efficient layout lowers operating costs. In order to achieve all these objectives, the flow of customer traffic must be anticipated and planned.

The grid pattern and the free-flow pattern are the two most widely used layouts. A **grid pattern** is the plain block layout typical of supermarkets and hardware stores. It provides maximum merchandise exposure and simplifies security and cleaning. A **free-flow pattern** makes less efficient use of space but has greater visual appeal and allows customers to move in any direction at their own speed. Free-flow patterns result in curving aisles and greater flexibility in merchandise presentation.

grid pattern
a block-like retail store layout that provides for good merchandise exposure and simplifies security and cleaning

free-flow pattern
a flexible retail store layout that is visually appealing and gives customers freedom of movement

Building Customer Loyalty

IN THE TRENCHES

DESIGNING THE FACILITIES

Displaying merchandise more effectively can help maximize sales and customer service in the retail clothing business. That's why Sally Odegaard asked consultant Marka Sims-Palmer to help her redesign the layout of her 18-year-old Waco, Texas women's fashion shop, named Olga's. "You can always do better, and I hope to get more perfect every day," says Odegaard.

Each year Sims-Palmer selects two shops nationwide for a makeover. The consultant says that the stores she works with show an average increase in sales of 25 to 40 percent after she leaves.

Sims-Palmer suggests having a sitting area for men who don't want to stand while spouses are shopping. She also recommends that Olga's leave more space between clothing racks because, she says, "Women have been known to bolt from stores when someone brushes against their backsides." She thinks Olga's needs "themes" for its changing rooms, as well as later closing times to accommodate "baby boomer" schedules. And Sims-Palmer wants Odegaard to encourage staffers to leave the check-out stand to greet customers with a friendly "hello."

This consultant is helping a small business owner better understand the role of store design and employee training in making the retail shopping experience more fun for the customer. And the owner realizes that enhancing the shopping experience will in turn make the business more rewarding for her.

Source: Mike Copeland, "Getting Feel for Success," *Waco Tribune-Herald,* October 1, 1999, p. 12A.

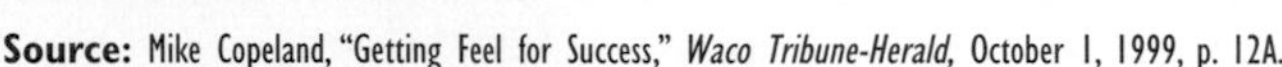

self-service layout
a type of retail store design that gives customers direct access to merchandise

Most retailers, especially food merchandisers, use a **self-service layout,** which permits customers direct access to the merchandise. Not only does self-service reduce selling expenses; it also permits shoppers to examine the goods before buying.

Some types of merchandise—for example, magazines and candy—are often purchased on an impulse basis. Impulse goods should be placed where customers can see them easily; some are typically displayed near the cash register. Products that customers need and for which they specifically come to the store may be placed in less conspicuous spots. Bread and milk, for example, are located at the back of a food store, with the idea that customers will buy other items as they walk down the aisles.

Various areas of a retail store differ markedly in sales value. Certainly, the best space should be given to departments or merchandise producing the greatest sales and profits. Customers typically turn to the right on entering a store, and so the right front space is considered the most valuable. The second most valuable retail areas are the center front and right middle spaces. Department stores often place high-margin giftware, cosmetics, and jewelry in these areas. The third most valuable areas are the left front and center middle spaces; the left middle space is fourth in importance. Since the back areas are the least important as far as retail space value is concerned, service facilities and the general office are typically found in the rear of a store. Finally, the first floor has greater space value than a higher floor in a multi-story building.

EQUIPPING THE PHYSICAL FACILITIES

The final step in arranging for physical facilities is the purchase or lease of equipment and tools. The types of equipment and tools required obviously depend on the nature of the business. Even within the three areas discussed here—manufacturing, retailing, and office equipment—there is great variation in the need for tools and equipment.

4 *Understand the equipment needs of small firms.*

Manufacturing Equipment

Machines used in a factory may be either general purpose or special purpose.

general-purpose equipment
machines that serve many functions in the production process

GENERAL-PURPOSE EQUIPMENT **General-purpose equipment** requires a minimum investment and is easily adapted to varied types of operations. Small machine shops and cabinet shops, for example, utilize this type of equipment. General-purpose equipment for metalworking includes lathes, drill presses, and milling machines. In a woodworking plant, general-purpose machines include ripsaws, planing mills, and lathes. In each case, jigs, fixtures, and other tooling items set up on the basic machinery can be changed so that two or more shop operations can be accomplished using the same piece of equipment. General-purpose equipment contributes important flexibility in industries in which products are so new that the technology is not yet well developed or there are frequent design changes.

special-purpose equipment
machines designed to serve specialized functions in the production process

SPECIAL-PURPOSE EQUIPMENT **Special-purpose equipment** can reduce costs in industries in which the technology is fully established and capacity operation is more or less ensured by high sales volume. Bottling machines and automobile assembly-line machinery are examples of special-purpose equipment used in factories. A milking machine in a dairy is an example of special-purpose equipment used by small firms. A small firm cannot, however, use special-purpose equipment economically unless it makes a standardized product on a fairly large scale. Using special-purpose machines with specialized tooling results in greater output per machine-hour of operation. The labor cost per unit of product is, therefore, lower. However, the initial cost of such equipment is much higher, and it has little or no resale value because of its highly specialized function.

Retail Store Equipment

Small retailers need merchandise display racks or counters, storage racks, shelving, mirrors, seats for customers, customer pushcarts, cash registers, and other items to facilitate selling. Such equipment may be costly, but it is usually less expensive than that necessary for a factory operation.

If a store is intended to serve a high-income market, its fixtures should display the elegance and style expected by such customers. For example, polished mahogany showcases with bronze fittings lend a richness to the atmosphere. Indirect lighting, thick rugs, and big easy chairs also contribute to an air of luxury. In contrast, a store that caters to lower-income customers should concentrate on simplicity, as luxurious fixtures create an atmosphere inconsistent with low prices.

Office Equipment

The business plan should list the major pieces of equipment needed to furnish a business office. Careful selection of equipment helps a business operate efficiently.

Also, by identifying major equipment needs in this section of the business plan, the entrepreneur can ensure that the financial section of the plan includes funds for their purchase.

Obviously, every business office needs furniture, storage cabinets, and other such items. The more challenging task is selecting office equipment—computers, fax machines, copiers, printers, and telephone systems—that reflects the latest advances in technology applicable to a particular business.

COMPUTERS Today, it is difficult to imagine a business without a computer, as computer prices are currently at levels affordable by almost any small business. Computers, office management software, and related technology, such as e-mail and the Internet, have changed the face of office operations. The importance of the Internet to small business was discussed in Chapter 3.

FAX MACHINES Fax machines allow the transmission of hard copy via telephone lines. They are widely used in all types of businesses, large and small. Recent developments in fax technology have improved both print quality and speed.

COPIERS AND PRINTERS Machines that combine copying and printing are now available for the office. For computers, laser printers are currently the choice of the overwhelming majority of businesses. The major considerations in selecting a printer are print speed, document handling features, resolution, number of users that can be served, ability to do double-sided printing, built-in fonts, memory, and graphics capabilities.

TELEPHONE SYSTEMS There are many factors to consider in buying a phone system—existing wiring in the building (particularly in a home), any necessary interfacing with computers, and expected volume of calls. Voice mail technology, such as interactive voice response (IVR), is usually desirable for the small firm. IVR offers callers a menu of options that they can choose by pressing phone buttons.

Voice mail and IVR systems need to be selected carefully. Some customers do not like voice mail systems and feel frustrated when they are unable to speak to a person.

Building Image

All new ventures, whether they are retailers, wholesalers, manufacturers, or service businesses, should be concerned with projecting the appropriate image to customers and the public at large. The appearance of the workplace should create a favorable impression about the quality of a firm's product or service and, generally, about the way the business is operated.

Before making design changes, a business should think about the image it wants to convey, according to interior designer Sandy Lucas of the Bryan Design Associates, in Houston, Texas. Spring Engineers, Inc., a 50-employee business in Dallas, Texas that makes springs for tools and other applications, hired Lucas to design a new facility. "We have a lot of vendors and suppliers coming to visit, and we often bring customers for tours of the machine shop," says president Kevin Grace. "It's very important that we make an impression that although we're a small business, we're a substantial one."[20] For a small firm of this type, it is important to use the physical facilities to convey the image of a stable, professional company.

LOOKING BACK

1 Identify the factors affecting choice of a business location.

- Customer accessibility is a key factor in the location decision of retail and service businesses.
- Climate, competition, legal requirements, and the tax structure are types of environmental factors affecting the location decision.
- Availability of resources such as raw materials, labor supply, and transportation is important to location decisions.
- The entrepreneur's personal preference is a practical consideration in selecting a location.
- An appropriate site must be available and within the entrepreneur's budget.

2 Describe the attraction and challenges of a home-based business.

- Home-based businesses are started to both make money and incorporate family lifestyle considerations.
- Operating a business at home can create conflicts with family members and pose business image and legal challenges.
- Technology has helped entrepreneurs start home-based businesses.

3 Explain how efficiency can be achieved in the layout of a physical facility.

- Leasing space doesn't require a large cash outlay, but buying increases freedom in modifying and using space.
- Good layout emphasizes productivity for manufacturers and customer accessibility for retailers.

4 Understand the equipment needs of small firms.

- Most small manufacturing firms must use general-purpose equipment, although some can use special-purpose equipment for standardized operations.
- Small retailers must have merchandise display racks and counters, mirrors, and other equipment that facilitate selling.
- Display counters and other retailing equipment should create an atmosphere appropriate for customers in the retailer's target market.
- Small business offices can be equipped with the latest technological devices.

KEY TERMS

enterprise zones, p. 273
Empowerment Zone/Enterprise Communities (EZ/EC), p. 273
business incubator, p. 275
home-based business, p. 276
zoning ordinances, p. 280
process layout, p. 281
product layout, p. 281
grid pattern, p. 281
free-flow pattern, p. 281
self-service layout, p. 282
general-purpose equipment, p. 283
special-purpose equipment, p. 283

Discussion Questions

1. What are the key attributes of a good business location? Which of these would probably be most important for a retail location? Why?
2. What is the special appeal of an enterprise zone to an entrepreneur seeking the best site for his or her business?
3. Which resource factors might be most vital to a new manufacturing venture that produces residential home furniture? Why?
4. Is the hometown of the business owner likely to be a good location? Is it logical for an owner to allow personal preferences to influence a decision about business location? Explain your answers.
5. Under what conditions would it be most appropriate for a new firm to buy rather than rent a building for the business?
6. What factors should an entrepreneur evaluate when considering a home-based business? Be specific.
7. In a home-based business, there is typically some competition, if not conflict, between the interests of the home and those of the business. What factors determine whether the risk is greater for the home or the business?
8. What legal issues should one consider before starting a home-based business?
9. When should a small manufacturer utilize (a) a process layout and (b) a product layout? Explain.
10. Discuss the conditions under which a new small manufacturer should buy (a) general-purpose equipment and (b) special-purpose equipment.

You Make the Call

SITUATION 1

A husband and wife operate small department stores in two midwestern towns with populations of about 2,000 each. Their clientele consists of the primarily blue-collar and rural populations of those two areas. After several years of successful operation, they have decided to open a third store in a town of 5,000 people. Most of the businesses in this larger town are located along a six-block strip—an area commonly referred to as "downtown." One attractive site for the store is in the middle of the business district, but the rental fee for that location is very high. Another available building, vacated several years earlier by Montgomery Ward, is located on a block at one end of the business district. Other businesses on the same block include a television and appliance store and some service businesses. Two clothing stores are located in the next block—closer to the center of town. The rent for the former Montgomery Ward store is much more reasonable than that for the downtown site, a three-year lease is possible, and a local bank is willing to loan sufficient funds to accomplish the necessary remodeling.

Question 1 Does the location in the middle of the business district seem to be substantially better than the other site?

Question 2 How might these owners evaluate the relative attractiveness of the two sites?

Question 3 To what extent would the department store benefit from having the service businesses and the television and appliance business in the same block?

Question 4 What other market or demographic factors, if any, should the owners consider before opening a store in this town?

SITUATION 2

A business incubator rents space to a number of small firms that are just beginning operations or are fairly new. In addition to supplying space, the incubator provides a receptionist, computer, conference room, fax machine, and copy machine. It also offers management counseling and assists new businesses in getting reduced advertising rates and reduced legal fees. One client of the incubator is a jewelry repair, cleaning, and remounting service that does work on a contract basis for pawn shops and jewelry stores. Another is a home health-care company that employs a staff of nurses to visit the homes of elderly people who need daily care but who cannot afford or are not yet ready to go to a nursing home.

Question 1 Evaluate each of the services offered by the incubator in terms of its usefulness to these two businesses. Which of the two businesses seems to be a better fit for the incubator? Why?

Question 2 If rental costs for incubator space were similar to rental costs for space outside the incubator, would the benefits of the services offered seem to favor location in the incubator? Why or why not?

SITUATION 3

Entrepreneur Karen Moore wants to start a catering and decorating business to bring in money to help support her two young children. Moore is a single parent; she works in the banking industry but has always had the desire to start a business. She enjoys decorating for friends' parties and is frequently told, "You should do this professionally. You have such good taste, and you are so nice to people."

Moore has decided to take this advice but is unsure whether she should locate in a commercial site or in her home, which is in rural central Texas. She is leaning toward locating at home because she wants more time with her children. However, she is concerned that the home-based location is too far away from the city, where most of her potential customers live.

Initially, her services would include planning for wedding receptions and other special events, designing flower arrangements, decorating the sites, and even cooking and serving meals.

Question 1 What do you see as potential problems with locating Moore's new business at home?

Question 2 What do you see as the major benefits for Moore of a home-based business?

Question 3 How could Moore use technology to help her operate a home-based business?

EXPERIENTIAL EXERCISES

1. Search for articles in business periodicals that provide rankings of states or cities as business sites. Report on your findings.
2. Identify and evaluate a local site that is now vacant because of a business closure. Point out the strengths and weaknesses of that location for the former business, and comment on the part location may have played in the closure.
3. Interview a small business owner concerning the strengths and weaknesses of that business's location. Prepare a brief report summarizing your findings.
4. Visit three local retail stores and observe the differences in their layouts and flow of customer traffic. Prepare a report describing the various patterns used and explaining the advantages of what you consider to be the best pattern.

Exploring the Web

1. The Arizona Chamber of Commerce offers a Guide to Establishing and Operating a Business online at **http://www.abgnews.com/bizbook/smbizmain.html**. Follow the link to Preliminary Planning.
   a. Choose Selecting a Business Location. List the tips given here that have not already been discussed in the textbook.
   b. Choose the link to Home Based Business. What are the four considerations, besides zoning regulations, that help determine whether a business should be located in the home?
   c. Assume that you are thinking of establishing a business within Maricopa County, Arizona. Choose the link for Demographics, and determine whether or not the population is growing in that area.
   d. Follow the Financial Assistance link. What benefits does Arizona offer to companies that are established in enterprise zones?
2. To answer the following questions, access **http://www.Onvia.com**, choose Business Tools, and follow the Starting Your Business link.
   a. Check How to Buy Office Equipment and Furniture. List three ways to obtain office equipment.
   b. Read How to Build a Home Office. List the tips for locating an office within the home, and what equipment is recommended for day-to-day work.
   c. Choose one of the other How To topics related to location and planning facilities. Write a brief summary of the tips found there.
3. Go to **http://www.siteselection.com** to answer the following questions.
   a. Follow a link for one of the regional reviews. Describe the features of the region as well as the types of industry that are currently locating there.
   b. Follow the link to Area Demographics. Choose a state or metropolitan index, and view the data. Explain whether you think this is a good location for a new retail store selling baby equipment and furnishings.
   c. Read one of the articles on the main page, such as Blockbuster of the Week. What company is featured, and why did it choose its particular location?

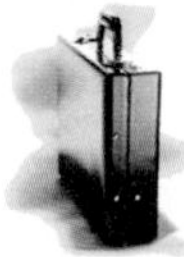

Case 11

LOGAN BEACH (p. 669)

This case follows the owner of a new restaurant during the first few days after its opening and presents some lessons learned the hard way.

Alternative Cases for Chapter 11:

Case 1, "Steve's Olympic Tees," p. 637

Case 2, "The Fantastic Catalog Company," p. 641

The Business Plan

Laying the Foundation

As part of laying the foundation for preparing your own business plan, respond to the following questions regarding location and physical facilities.

LOCATION QUESTIONS

1. How important are your personal reasons for choosing a location?
2. What environmental factors will influence your location decision?
3. What resources are most critical to your location decision?
4. How important is customer accessibility to your location decision?
5. How will the formal site evaluation be conducted?
6. What laws and tax policies of state and local governments have been considered?
7. What is the cost of the proposed site?
8. Will a home-based business be a possibility?
9. What are the advantages and disadvantages of a home-based business?
10. Is an enterprise zone available in the area where you want to locate?

PHYSICAL FACILITY QUESTIONS

1. What are the major considerations in choosing between a new and an existing building?
2. What is the possibility of leasing a building or equipment?
3. How feasible is it to locate in a business incubator?
4. What is the major objective of your building layout?
5. What types of equipment do you need for your business?

chapter 12

Projecting Financial Requirements

In the Spotlight

Hi-Shear Technology

In 1999, cash flow was becoming a problem for Hi-Shear Technology, a $20-million aerospace subcontractor in Torrance, California. Federal funding for military and space programs was declining, and customers had begun delaying orders. To solve this problem, the company needed financial information about its own operations.

The firm's CEO, Linda Nespole, devised a cost-control blueprint to quickly bolster Hi-Shear's profits and cash flows. She began charting the firm's expenses and acting on her findings. The result: significant savings and, most importantly, improved cash flows.

Though it took a cash crunch to initiate the cost-cutting procedures, the effectiveness of the measures made saving money a priority for Hi-Shear's 125 employees. The maintenance staff now tracks meter readings daily. Administrators review utility bills quarterly, and Nespole comparison-shops for all insurance policies annually, even calling human resources directors at other companies to ask about their providers. Janitors shut down air conditioners at night and have stopped heating such areas as storage.

Although many businesses today search for outside consultants, such as utility or telecommunications auditors, to help control costs, Nespole has found that the time is better spent evaluating current service providers. "It's very easy," she says. "You just have to make the time."

http://www.hstc.com

Nespole's successful efforts at reducing expenses demonstrate the value of understanding a company's financial information and taking action based on the implications of the numbers. ◆

Source: Adapted from Ilan Mochari, "A Simple Little System," *Inc.*, Vol. 21, No. 13 (October 1999), p. 87.

LOOKING AHEAD

After studying this chapter, you should be able to

1. *Describe the purpose and content of the income statement and the balance sheet.*
2. *Compute a firm's cash flows.*
3. *Forecast a new venture's profitability.*
4. *Estimate the assets needed and the financing required for a new venture.*

A good idea may or may not be a good investment opportunity. To represent a good investment opportunity, a product or service must both create a competitive advantage and meet a definite customer need. Whether an investment opportunity exists depends on (1) the level of profitability that can be achieved and (2) the size of the investment required to capture the opportunity. Therefore, projections of a venture's profits and its asset and financing requirements are essential in determining whether the venture is economically feasible. In order to make the necessary financial projections, an entrepreneur must first have a complete understanding of financial statements.

UNDERSTANDING FINANCIAL STATEMENTS

Describe the purpose and content of the income statement and the balance sheet.

Financial statements, also called **accounting statements**, provide important information about a firm's performance and financial resources. The two key financial statements are the income statement and the balance sheet. Understanding the purpose and content of each of these financial statements is essential if an entrepreneur is to determine the startup's financial requirements and assess the financial implications of a business plan.

financial statements (accounting statements) reports of a firm's financial performance and resources, including an income statement and a balance sheet

The Income Statement

income statement (profit and loss statement) a financial report showing the profit or loss from a firm's operations over a given period of time

An **income statement**, or **profit and loss statement**, indicates the amount of profits generated by a firm over a given time period, often a year. In its most basic form, the income statement may be represented by the following equation:

$$\text{Sales revenue} - \text{Expenses} = \text{Profits}$$

Thus, the income statement answers the question "How profitable is the business?" In providing the answer, the statement reports financial information related to five broad areas of business activity:

1. Sales revenue derived from selling the company's product or service

2. Costs of producing or acquiring the goods or services to be sold
3. Operating expenses, which include marketing and selling expenses, general and administrative expenses, and depreciation expense
4. Financing costs of doing business—specifically, the interest paid to the firm's creditors
5. Tax payments

cost of goods sold the cost of producing or acquiring goods or services to be sold by a firm

gross profit sales less the cost of goods sold

operating expenses costs related to marketing and distributing a firm's product or service, general administrative expenses, and depreciation expense

operating income earnings before interest and taxes are paid

financing costs the amount of interest owed to lenders on borrowed money

As Figure 12-1 shows, the income statement begins with sales revenue, from which is subtracted the **cost of goods sold,** or the cost of producing or acquiring the product or service, to yield the firm's **gross profit.** Next, **operating expenses,** consisting of marketing and selling expenses, administrative expenses, and depreciation expense, are deducted, to determine **operating income** (also called, *earnings before interest and taxes*). To this point, the firm's income has been affected only by the activities involved in (1) producing or acquiring the goods or service, (2) selling and marketing expenses, and (3) general adminstrative expenses, all of which result from a firm's *operating* activities—as opposed to its *financing* activities. Note that no interest expense has been subtracted to this point.

Earnings before taxes are found by deducting from the firm's operating income its **financing costs**—the firm's interest expense on its debt. Next, the firm's income taxes are calculated, based on its earnings before taxes and the applicable tax rate for the amount of income reported. For instance, if a firm had earnings before taxes of $100,000 and its tax rate was 28 percent, then it would owe $28,000 in taxes (0.28 × $100,000 = $28,000). (When small firms sell their products or services on a cash-only basis, some business owners are tempted *not* to report all income for tax purposes. Such an action is neither legal nor ethical.)

FIGURE 12-1 *The Income Statement: An Overview*

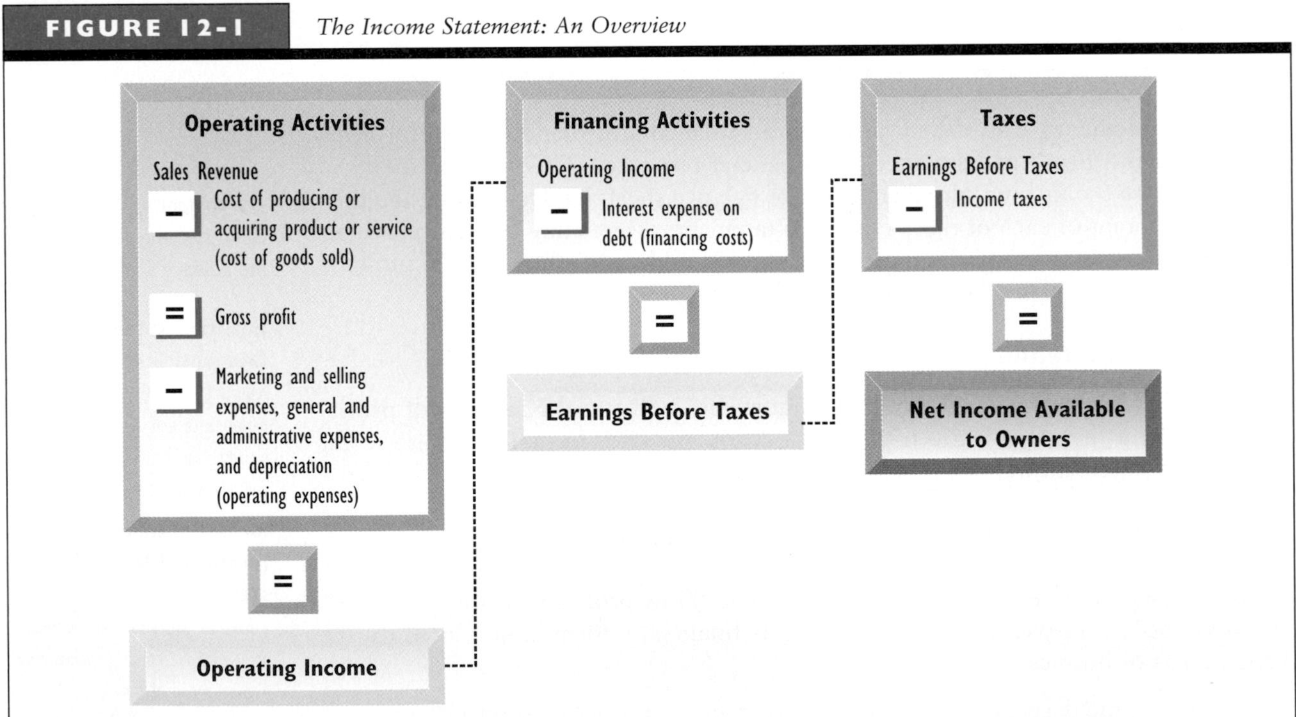

net income available to owners (net income) income that may be distributed to the owners or reinvested in the company

The resulting figure is the **net income available to owners** (frequently called **net income**), which represents income that may be reinvested in the firm or distributed to its owners—provided, of course, cash is available to do so. As you will come to understand, *a positive net income on an income statement does not necessarily mean that a firm has generated positive cash flows.*

Figure 12-2 shows the 2002 income statement for Bates & Associates, an equipment leasing company. The company had sales of $850,000 for the 12-month period ending December 31, 2002. The cost of goods sold was $550,000, resulting in a gross profit of $300,000. The company had $200,000 in operating expenses, which included marketing expenses, general and administrative expenses, and depreciation. After total operating expenses were subtracted, the company's operating income (earnings before interest and taxes) amounted to $100,000. To this point, we have calculated profits based only on expenses related to the firm's operating activities. We have thus far excluded interest expense, which is the result of the firm's financing decisions—something we will consider later in this chapter. Thus, the figure for operating income represents the income that Bates & Associates would generate if it were an all-equity company—that is, a business without any debt. The figure for operating income is important to the owners because it best measures a company's profitability on its asset investment, before any money is distributed to investors and creditors. Thus, it measures the economic attractiveness of a business opportunity.

Bates & Associates' interest expense of $20,000 (the expense it incurred by using debt financing) is then deducted, to arrive at the company's earnings (profits) before taxes of $80,000. If we assume a 25 percent tax rate, the company will incur $20,000 in income taxes, leaving a net income of $60,000. The net income of $60,000 represents the "bottom line" of the income statement. This amount is the profit that was earned for the firm's owners on their investment. However, as shown at the bottom of Figure 12-2, dividends in the amount of $15,000 were paid to Bates's owners; the remaining $45,000 ($60,000 net income less $15,000 in dividends) was retained by the firm and will appear as an increase in retained earnings on the balance sheet.

FIGURE 12-2

Income Statement for Bates & Associates Leasing Company for the Year Ending December 31, 2002

Sales revenue		$850,000
Cost of goods sold		550,000
Gross profit on sales		$300,000
Operating expenses:		
Marketing expenses	$90,000	
General and administrative expenses	80,000	
Depreciation	30,000	
Total operating expenses		$200,000
Operating income		$100,000
Interest expense		20,000
Earnings before taxes		$ 80,000
Income tax (25%)		20,000
Net income		$ 60,000
Dividends paid		15,000
Change in retained earnings		$ 45,000

ENTREPRENEURSHIP TODAY

KNOW WHAT YOU DON'T KNOW

Far too often, entrepreneurs fail to take seriously the need for good accounting information, either for internal decision making or for external needs, like raising capital. It was an awkward moment when Joe Theisen discovered that he needed help managing his company's finances; he was at a meeting with his banker, asking for more money.

In search of a $300,000 increase in his line of credit, Theisen, president of Cambria Environmental Technology, located in Oakland, California, watched his banker hone in on the company's accounts receivable aging, which didn't match up with its monthly financial statements. He remembers that the banker suggested only two possible explanations for the discrepancy: "We were either crooks or were boobs, and I tried desperately to convince them of the latter," says Theisen. Shortly thereafter, he and his partner hired a controller, who helped Theisen identify and correct problems he hadn't even realized the company had. The controller "opened Pandora's box and then cleaned it out," says Theisen.

Source: "We'd Rather Be Idiots," *Inc. 500,* Vol. 21, No. 15 (1999), p. 145.

The Balance Sheet

balance sheet
a financial report showing a firm's assets, liabilities, and owners' equity at a specific point in time

While an income statement reports the financial results of business operations over a period of time, a **balance sheet** provides a snapshot of a business's financial position at a *specific point in time.* Thus, a balance sheet captures the cumulative effects of all earlier financial decisions. At a given point in time, the balance sheet shows the assets a firm owns, the liabilities (or debt) outstanding or owed, and the amount the owners have invested in the business (their equity). In its simplest form, a balance sheet follows this formula:

$$\text{Total assets} = \text{Outstanding debt} + \text{Owners' equity}$$

Figure 12-3 illustrates the elements in a balance sheet of a typical small firm. Each of the three main components of the balance sheet—assets, debt capital, and owners' equity—is discussed in the following sections.

Assets

A company's assets, shown on the left side of Figure 12-3, fall into three categories: (1) current assets, (2) fixed assets, and (3) other assets.

current assets (gross working capital)
assets that can be converted into cash within a company's operating cycle

Current assets, or **gross working capital,** comprise those assets that are relatively liquid; that is, they can be converted into cash within the firm's normal operating cycle. Current assets primarily include cash, accounts receivable, and inventories. Ineffective management of current assets is a prime cause of financial problems in small companies. (We will discuss this issue more thoroughly in Chapter 23.)

- *Cash.* Every firm must have cash for current business operations. A reservoir of cash is also needed to compensate for the uncertainty of the cash flows into a business (cash receipts) and out of a business (cash expenditures). Thus, the size of a firm's cash reservoir is determined not only by the volume of sales, but also by the predictability of cash receipts and cash payments.

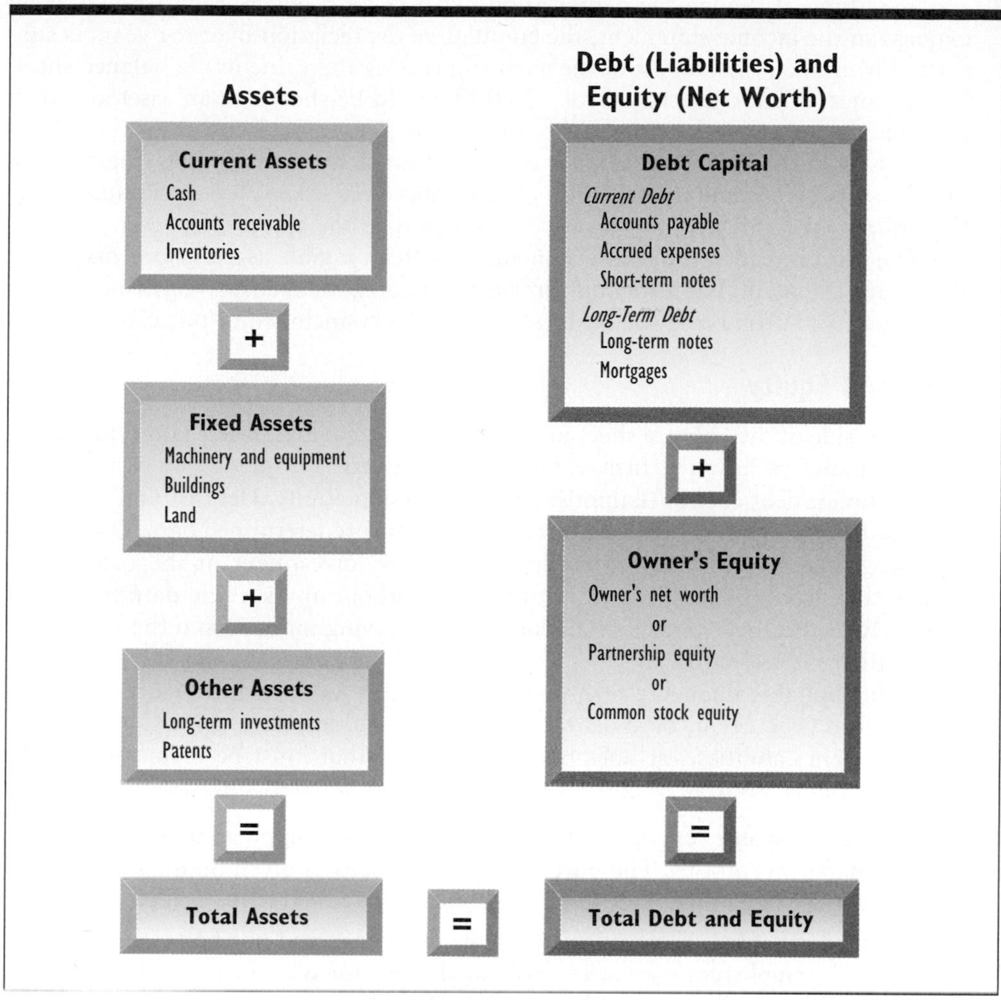

FIGURE 12-3

The Balance Sheet: An Overview

Assets		Debt (Liabilities) and Equity (Net Worth)
Current Assets Cash Accounts receivable Inventories + **Fixed Assets** Machinery and equipment Buildings Land + **Other Assets** Long-term investments Patents =		**Debt Capital** *Current Debt* Accounts payable Accrued expenses Short-term notes *Long-Term Debt* Long-term notes Mortgages + **Owner's Equity** Owner's net worth or Partnership equity or Common stock equity =
Total Assets	=	**Total Debt and Equity**

- *Accounts receivable.* The firm's **accounts receivable** consist of payments due from its customers from previous credit sales. Accounts receivable can become a significant asset for firms that sell on a credit basis.
- *Inventories.* The raw materials and products held by the firm for eventual sale constitute the **inventory.** Although their relative importance differs from one type of business to another, inventories often account for a major part of a firm's working capital. Seasonality of sales and production levels affect the size of inventories. Retail stores, for example, may find it desirable to carry a larger-than-normal inventory during the pre-Christmas season.

accounts receivable
the amount of credit extended to customers that is currently outstanding

inventory
a firm's raw materials and products held in anticipation of eventual sale

Fixed assets are the more permanent assets in a business. They might include machinery and equipment, buildings, and land. Some businesses are more capital-intensive than others—for example, a motel is more capital-intensive than a gift store—and, therefore, have more fixed assets.

fixed assets
relatively permanent assets intended for use in the business, such as plant and equipment

depreciable assets
assets whose value declines, or depreciates, over time

net fixed assets
gross fixed assets less accumulated depreciation

gross fixed assets
original cost of depreciable assets before any depreciation expense has been taken

accumulated depreciation
total depreciation expense taken over the assets' life

other assets
assets other than current assets and fixed assets, such as patents, copyrights, and goodwill

debt capital
business financing provided by creditors

current debt (short-term liabilities)
borrowed money that must be repaid within 12 months

accounts payable (trade credit)
outstanding credit payable to suppliers

accrued expenses
short-term liabilities that have been incurred but not paid

short-term notes
cash amounts borrowed from a bank or other lending sources that must be repaid within a short period of time

long-term debt
loans from banks or other sources with repayment terms of more than 12 months

mortgage
a long-term loan from a creditor for which real estate is pledged as collateral

owners' equity
owners' investments in a company, plus profits retained in the firm

Most fixed assets are also **depreciable assets,** as their value declines or depreciates over time. Although the depreciation expense for a given year is shown as an expense in the income statement, the cumulative depreciation over the years is subtracted from the original cost of the asset to produce the value in the balance sheet. For instance, a truck purchased for $20,000 would be shown as an asset and then its value decreased over its useful life of four or five years. Thus, the value of **net fixed assets** in the balance sheet is the value of **gross fixed assets** (the original cost of the assets before any depreciation expense has been taken) less **accumulated depreciation** (the total depreciation expense taken over the assets' life).

The third category, **other assets,** includes such intangible assets as patents, copyrights, and goodwill. For a startup company, organizational costs—costs incurred in organizing and promoting the business—may also be included in this category.

Debt and Equity

The right side of the balance sheet in Figure 12-3, Debt (Liabilities) and Equity (Net Worth), indicates how the firm is financing its assets. Financing comes from two main sources: debt capital (liabilities) and ownership equity. Debt capital is money that has been borrowed and must be repaid at some predetermined date. Ownership equity, on the other hand, represents the owners' investment in the company—money they have personally put into the firm without any specific date for repayment. Owners recover their investment by withdrawing money from the firm or by selling their interest in it.

Debt capital is financing provided by a creditor. As shown in Figure 12-3, it is divided into (1) current, or short-term, debt and (2) long-term debt. **Current debt,** or **short-term liabilities,** includes borrowed money that must be repaid within the next 12 months. Sources of current debt may be classified as follows:

- **Accounts payable** represents the credit extended by suppliers to a firm when it purchases inventories. The purchasing firm usually is given 30 or 60 days to pay for the inventory. This form of credit is also called **trade credit.**
- **Accrued expenses** are expenses that have been incurred but not yet paid. For example, employees may have performed work for which they will not be paid until the following week or month. Accrued expenses include accrued taxes, which are owed but have not been paid.
- **Short-term notes** represent cash amounts borrowed from a bank or other lending source for a short period of time, such as 90 days. Short-term notes are a primary source of financing for most small businesses, as these businesses have access to fewer sources of long-term capital than do their larger counterparts.

Long-term debt includes loans from banks or other sources that lend money for longer than 12 months. When a firm borrows money for 5 years to buy equipment, it signs an agreement—a long-term note—promising to repay the money in 5 years. When a firm borrows money for 30 years to purchase real estate, such as a warehouse or office building, the real estate usually stands as collateral for the long-term loan, which is called a **mortgage.** If the borrower is unable to repay the loan, the lender can take the real estate in settlement.

Owners' equity is money that the owners invest in a business. Note that they are only *residual owners* of the business; that is, creditors must be paid before the

owners can retrieve any of their equity capital out of the business's income. Likewise, if the company is liquidated, creditors are always paid before the owners are paid.

The amount of ownership equity in a business is equal to (1) the total amount of the owners' investments in the business and (2) the cumulative profits (net of any losses) since the firm's beginning less any cash withdrawals by the owners. The second item (profits less withdrawals) is frequently called **retained earnings**—because these earnings have been reinvested in the business instead of being distributed to the owners. Thus, the basic formula for owners' equity capital is as follows:

retained earnings
profits less withdrawals (dividends)

$$\text{Owners' equity} = \text{Owners' investment} + \underbrace{\text{Cumulative profits} - \text{Owners' cumulative cash withdrawals}}$$

or

$$\text{Owners' equity} = \text{Owners' investment} + \text{Earnings retained within the business}$$

Figure 12-4 on page 298 presents balance sheets for Bates & Associates Leasing Company for December 31, 2001 and December 31, 2002, along with the change for each category. By referring to the columns representing the two balance sheets, you can see the financial position of the firm at the beginning *and* at the end of 2002.

The 2001 and 2002 balance sheets for Bates & Associates show that the firm began 2002 (ended 2001) with $800,000 in total assets and ended 2002 with total assets of $920,000. We can also see how much has been invested in current assets (cash, accounts receivable, and inventories) and in fixed assets. Finally, we can observe how much debt and equity was used to finance the assets. For instance, debt represents approximately 30 percent of the financing and equity about 70 percent. That is, the firm's assets were financed 30 percent by debt and 70 percent by equity. About half of the equity came from investments made by the owners (common stock), and the other half came from reinvesting profits in the business (retained earnings). Referring back to the income statement in Figure 12-2, note that the $45,000 increase in retained earnings, shown in the Changes column in Figure 12-4, equals the firm's net income for the year less the dividends paid to the owners.

In summary, financing for a new business derives from two sources: debt capital and ownership equity. Debt capital is money borrowed from financial institutions, suppliers, and other lenders. Owners' equity represents the owners' investment directly in the company, either through funds invested in the firm or through profits retained in the business.

To conclude, let's consider how the income statement and the balance sheet complement each other. Because the balance sheet is a snapshot of a firm's financial condition at a point in time and the income statement reports results over a given time period, both are required for a complete picture of a firm's financial position. Figure 12-5 on page 299 shows how the income statement and the balance sheet fit together. To understand how a firm performed during 2002, you must know the firm's financial position at the beginning of the year (balance sheet on December 31, 2001), its financial performance during the year (income statement for 2002), and its financial position at the end of the year (balance sheet on December 31, 2002).

FIGURE 12-4

Balance Sheets for Bates & Associates Leasing Company for December 31, 2001 and 2002

	2001	2002	Changes
Assets			
Current assets			
Cash	$ 45,000	$ 50,000	$ 5,000
Accounts receivable	75,000	80,000	5,000
Inventories	180,000	220,000	40,000
Total current assets	$300,000	$350,000	$ 50,000
Fixed assets:			
Gross plant and equipment	$790,000	$890,000	$100,000
Accumulated depreciation	(360,000)	(390,000)	(30,000)
Net plant and equipment	$430,000	$500,000	$ 70,000
Land	70,000	70,000	0
Total fixed assets	$500,000	$570,000	$ 70,000
TOTAL ASSETS	$800,000	$920,000	$120,000
Debt (Liabilities) and Equity			
Current liabilities:			
Accounts payable and accruals	$ 15,000	$ 20,000	$ 5,000
Short-term notes	60,000	80,000	20,000
Total current liabilities	$ 75,000	$100,000	$ 25,000
Long-term notes	150,000	200,000	50,000
Total liabilities	$225,000	$300,000	$ 75,000
Common stock	$300,000	$300,000	$ 0
Retained earnings	275,000	320,000	45,000
Total stockholders' equity	$575,000	$620,000	$ 45,000
TOTAL DEBT AND EQUITY	$800,000	$920,000	$120,000

DETERMINING CASH FLOWS

2 *Compute a firm's cash flows.*

"Cash flow problems" are a frequently expressed concern of small business owners. Even a successful company may encounter problems with cash flows. For this reason, understanding cash flows is extremely important and warrants the time it takes to learn how to compute and interpret them.

An entrepreneur recently told us how intimidated she felt when her accountant presented the firm's monthly financial reports and how difficult she found it to understand cash flows. Our advice was to get a new accountant—one who would explain the statements carefully—and also to spend the time necessary to gain a solid understanding of the financial statements and the firm's cash flows.

accrual-basis accounting a method of accounting that matches revenues when they are earned against the expenses associated with those revenues, no matter when they are paid

It's important to note that the profits shown on a company's income statement are not the same as its cash flows, although both are measures of a firm's performance. Many entrepreneurs have been deceived by a good-looking income statement, only to discover that their companies are running out of cash. Effectively managing cash flows is essential. To do so, the small business owner must understand the sources and uses of the firm's cash.

First, it is necessary to realize that an income statement is not a measure of information about cash flows because it is calculated on an *accrual* basis rather than a *cash* basis. In **accrual-basis accounting,** income is recorded when it is earned—

FIGURE 12-5

The Fit of the Income Statement and Balance Sheet

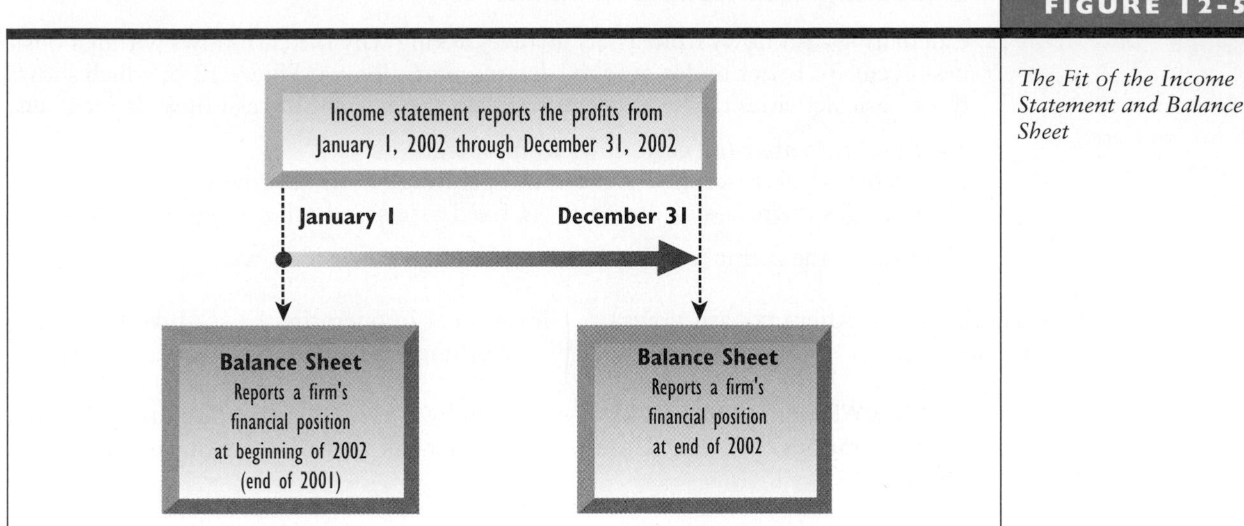

whether or not the income has been received in cash—and expenses are recorded when they are incurred—even if money has not actually been paid out. Because sales reported in an income statement include both cash sales and credit sales, the total sales volume for a year does not correspond *exactly* to the actual cash collected. Similarly, some inventory purchases are financed by credit, so inventory purchases do not exactly equal cash expended. Also, as noted earlier, the accrual system of accounting does not record as an expense in the income statement the purchase price of equipment that will last for more than a year. Instead, the total amount is recorded as an asset, and the cost is depreciated over the useful life of the item. Recording an annual **depreciation expense**, the accountant's measure of the costs associated with using an asset that benefits the firm's operations over more than one year, is a way to match the cost of an asset with the sales generated from its use; consequently, it is *not* a cash flow. In **cash-basis accounting**, on the other hand, income is reported when cash is received, and expenses are recorded when they are paid.

depreciation expense
costs related to a fixed asset, such as a building or equipment, distributed over its useful life

cash-basis accounting
a method of accounting that reports transactions only when cash is received or a payment is made

In computing cash flows, we distinguish between cash flows that occur from operating the business, which we call *cash flows from assets,* and cash flows received from or paid to lenders and investors, which we call *cash flows from financing*. Cash flows from assets are generated without external financing, such as obtaining a bank loan or issuing new stock to investors. Thus, cash flows from assets indicate whether the business itself can finance its growth—whether the firm can support **sustainable growth.** Positive cash flows from assets allow the company to distribute any remaining cash to the firm's lenders and investors. However, negative cash flows from assets require the company to rely on outside investors to cover expenses.

sustainable growth
growth that can be financed from cash flows generated from operating the business

Negative cash flow is not necessarily bad; in fact, it may be good if the firm is making investments that will produce large profits in the future. But it is critical that the owner of a small business understand *why* cash flows from assets are negative. So, let's consider in more detail these two measures of cash flows—cash flows from assets and cash flows from financing.

Computing Cash Flows from Assets

cash flows from assets
after-tax cash flows generated from operations less the firm's investments in assets

Calculating cash flows from assets involves asking why the cash flows within a business occur. To better understand the determinants, look at Figure 12-6, which shows three basic activities that increase or decrease the amount of **cash flows from assets:**

1. The firm's after-tax cash flows from operations
2. Changes (increases or decreases) in operating working capital
3. Changes (increases or decreases) in fixed assets and other long-term assets.

Specifically, the formula for cash flows from assets is as follows:

$$\begin{matrix}\text{Cash flows} \\ \text{from assets}\end{matrix} = \begin{pmatrix}\text{After-tax cash flows} \\ \text{from operations}\end{pmatrix} - \begin{pmatrix}\text{Investment in operating} \\ \text{working capital}\end{pmatrix} - \begin{pmatrix}\text{Investment in} \\ \text{long-term assets}\end{pmatrix}$$

after-tax cash flows from operations
cash flows generated from operating a business, calculated by adding back to net income depreciation expense and interest expense

CASH FLOWS FROM OPERATIONS Let's begin by considering the after-tax cash flows from operations. We calculate the firm's **after-tax cash flows from operations** as follows:

$$\begin{matrix}\text{After-tax cash flows} \\ \text{from operations}\end{matrix} = \text{Net income} + \begin{matrix}\text{Depreciation} \\ \text{expense}\end{matrix} + \begin{matrix}\text{Interest} \\ \text{expense}\end{matrix}$$

In this equation, depreciation expense is added back to income because it is not a cash expense (even though it appears in the income statement). Interest expense is also added back, as it will be accounted for in the calculation of cash flows from financing. Cash flows from operations can be either positive or negative. If it is positive, it adds to the cash flows from assets; if it is negative, it reduces the cash flows from assets.

As an illustration of this computation, let's look again at Bates & Associates' income statement in Figure 12-2. We can compute the firm's after-tax cash flows from operations as follows:

Net income	$ 60,000
Plus depreciation	30,000
Plus interest expense	20,000
After-tax cash flows from operations	$110,000

FIGURE 12-6

Computing Cash Flows from Assets

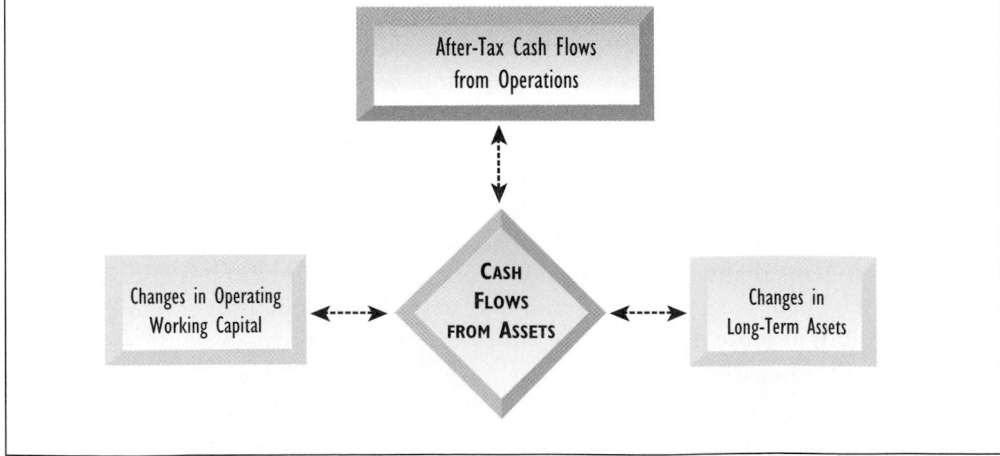

By taking Bates's income and adding back (1) the non-cash expense of depreciation and (2) the interest expense, which is a *financing* cash flow to be recognized later, we see that the firm has a positive cash flow from operations of $110,000. But to this point, we have recognized only the cash flows associated with the income statement. Now we will consider cash flow items associated with the firm's investments—that is, the money it puts into working capital and long-term assets.

CHANGES IN OPERATING WORKING CAPITAL As shown in Figure 12-6, cash flows from assets are affected by the change in the firm's operating working capital. A firm's **operating working capital** is the money that has been invested in the company's current assets (such as cash, accounts receivable, and inventories) less accounts payable and accruals (the two sources of credit arising from the normal day-to-day operating activities of buying and selling the firm's goods):

operating working capital
money invested in current assets less accounts payable and accruals

$$\text{Operating working capital} = \text{Current assets} - \text{Accounts payable and accruals}$$

It is essential to understand that *if a firm increases its working capital, it is using cash and so the amount of cash available to the firm decreases—that is, cash flows from assets are decreased when a firm invests in working capital. If working capital is decreased, however, the amount of cash available increases—that is, cash flows from assets are increased when less money is tied up in working capital.* These relationships prescribe how cash flows move through a company.

Increase in operating working capital	→	Decrease in cash flows from assets
Decrease in operating working capital	→	Increase in cash flows from assets

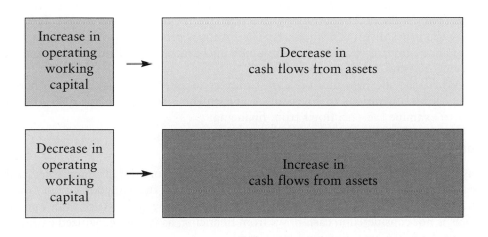

For Bates & Associates, operating working capital increased by $45,000 in 2002. The increase is calculated as follows from the change in working capital shown in the firm's balance sheets (see Figure 12-4):

	2001	2002	Changes
Current assets	$300,000	$350,000	$50,000
Accounts payable and accruals	15,000	20,000	5,000
Operating working capital	$285,000	$330,000	$45,000

The $45,000 increase in working capital means that Bates & Associates used some of its cash to invest in working capital—resulting in a decrease in cash flows from assets.

CHANGES IN LONG-TERM ASSETS A firm's cash flows from assets are also affected by its investment in long-term assets. As one would expect, a *decrease* in long-term assets means that the firm has sold assets and thus increased its cash flows. But an *increase* in long-term assets—investing money in long-term assets—causes cash flows to go down.

In our example, Bates & Associates increased its investment in fixed assets (long-term assets) by $100,000. As indicated in the balance sheets in Figure 12-4, gross plant and equipment increased by $100,000, while land remained unchanged. (Note that in the computation of change we used *gross* plant and equipment rather than *net* plant and equipment. Net plant and equipment is affected by the amount of depreciation that has been taken on the assets, which has nothing to do with cash flows.)

In summary, cash flows from assets are driven by a firm's cash flows from day-to-day operations and its investments, both in working capital and in long-term assets. For Bates & Associates, the net result is a negative cash flow of $35,000, calculated as follows:

After-tax cash flows from operations	$110,000
Less increase in operating working capital	45,000
Less increase in long-term assets	100,000
Cash flows from assets	($ 35,000)

So even though it was profitable, Bates & Associates still experienced negative cash flows from its assets. The cash flows generated from operations were more than offset by the firm's investment in assets. The firm was growing too fast for growth to be financed from operations, which is not uncharacteristic of businesses that are growing quickly.

Where did the firm find the cash to invest in assets when it did not generate enough from operations to cover all its investments? To answer this question, we have to examine the cash flows from financing.

Computing Cash Flows from Financing

cash flows from financing
cash flows generated by payments made to or received by a firm's investors or creditors

Cash flows that investors either provide to or receive from the firm are called **cash flows from financing.** Investors include both lenders and the company's equity owners. It is important to note that the financing provided by accounts payable and accruals is not considered in cash flows from financing, as it was recognized earlier as part of the firm's operating working capital.

Cash flows to and from investors are shown in Figure 12-7. As you can see, cash inflows to the firm from investors come from either (1) an increase in the firm's debt (when the firm borrows more money) or (2) an increase in equity (when the firm issues new stock to investors). On the other hand, cash outflows from the firm to investors include (1) interest paid by the firm to lenders plus dividends paid by the firm to the owners, (2) a decrease in the firm's debt as a result of the firm repaying a loan, and (3) a decrease in equity as a consequence of repurchasing an owner's stock.

For 2002, Bates & Associates had positive cash flows of $35,000 from financing, determined as follows:

FIGURE 12-7

Cash Flows from Financing

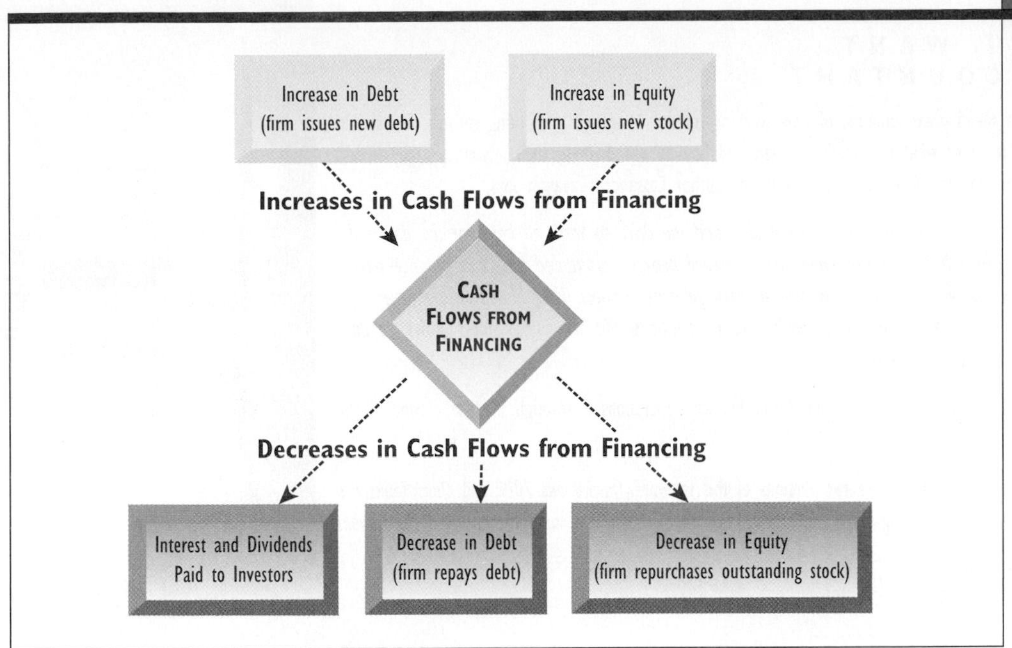

Interest paid to lenders	$(20,000)
Dividends paid to owners	(15,000)
Increase in loans to the firm (increase in interest-bearing debt)	70,000
Change in outstanding stock	0
Cash flows from financing	$ 35,000

Thus, Bates & Associates' investors received $35,000 ($20,000 + $15,000) in interest and dividends but loaned $70,000 to the business, which resulted in a positive overall cash flow of $35,000 to the firm. It is not a coincidence that Bates & Associates' cash flows from financing exactly equal the shortfall indicated when we computed its cash flows from assets; the two will always be equal. If positive, cash flows from assets will be the amount distributed to the investors; if negative, they will be the amount that investors must provide.

The computations and implications of a firm's cash flows have been explained here in greater detail than in most other textbooks devoted to small business management. This is because we believe strongly that an entrepreneur who does not understand how decisions impact cash flows is almost surely destined to fail. If a firm runs out of cash, "the game is over."

FINANCIAL FORECASTING

3

Forecast a new venture's profitability.

Using the basic financial information discussed so far in this chapter, an owner-manager can develop **pro forma financial statements,** or projected financial statements. The importance of solid financial forecasting is described quite aptly by Linda Elkins, an advisor for smaller firms:

ENTREPRENEURSHIP TODAY

IN THE TRENCHES

SO YOU DON'T WANT TO BE AN ACCOUNTANT

Few entrepreneurs have the desire to spend great amounts of time working on the company's accounting records, nor should they. While all business owners need to know what the numbers mean and how to use them to their advantage, they should not be spending a lot of time determining the firm's financial results. As author Cassandra Cavanah says,

Running a successful business requires a lot more than just a good idea and the drive to work all hours of the day and night. You also need to be able to read a balance sheet, know the difference between profit and loss, and produce payroll checks and invoices—in other words, you have to know how to manage your business. Most entrepreneurs have struggled through paper accounting methods and different spreadsheet-based solutions. But, as your business grows, so does your need to stay on top of all its critical leverage points.

A popular way for small business owners to oversee their firm's financial operations is through the use of one of the following accounting software packages:

- QuickBooks (http://www.quickbooks.com). There are two versions of this software, *QuickBooks 2000* and *QuickBooks Pro 2000.* In addition to all the standard accounting functions found in *QuickBooks 2000,* the more sophisticated *QuickBooks*

pro forma financial statements
statements that project a firm's financial performance and condition

Clearly, financial projections are not just a management frill. They are at the heart of managing well. Informed business decisions are dependent on cost estimates and other projections that enable a business owner to see his or her company in its entirety. Whether a company is a start-up or an ongoing business, financial projections are key to successful management. They provide an important test of feasibility for new firms and give existing businesses a chance to spot problems and make corrections before it's too late.[1]

The purpose of pro forma financial statements is to answer three questions:

1. How profitable can the firm expect to be, given the projected sales levels and the expected sales–expense relationships?
2. How much and what type of financing (debt or equity) will be used?
3. Will the firm have adequate cash flows? If so, how will they be used; if not, where will the additional cash come from?

Without the answers to these questions, the search for specific sources of financing will probably meet with failure—not because the concept of the venture is flawed, but because accurate forecasting is essential to the success of any new business. Michael P. Ferron, an accountant in Rochester, New York, cites an example of a small builder who failed to forecast accurately:

One of our clients was a small builder, a one-man operation with subcontractors doing the work. He had three or four houses going up at one time and didn't project his cash flow. He figured with draws and closings on his houses he could always keep current, but there was a dry period between closings, and his creditors forced him to file for bankruptcy. This could easily have been avoided by projecting accurately to begin with.[2]

In the remainder of this chapter, you will find the information necessary to answer questions 1 and 2, regarding profitability and financing requirements. Once you have

Pro provides such features as job costing, employee-time billing, customizable job bidding, and partial-progress invoicing. Both versions include online payroll services that calculate earnings, deductions, and federal and state taxes.

- Peachtree (http://www.peachtree.com). Similar to QuickBooks, Peachtree offers accounting software that takes full advantage of the Internet. Peachtree Today offers hyperlinks within the program to common actions and tutorials, as well as news and information available online. The My Business page gives users an overview of such topics as receivables, payables, budget issues, and cash balances.
- Oracle Small Business (http://www.oraclesmallbusiness.com). The basic version of *Oracle Small Business Suite* can be accessed on the Internet for free; an enhanced version is available for a monthly fee. However, its capabilities are more limited than those of QuickBooks and Peachtree programs.

These accounting packages can meet the needs of small companies, but the entrepreneur may find them to be inadequate as the firm grows larger and its needs for more complex accounting functions increase.

Source: Adapted from Cassandra Cavanah, "Cyber CPAs," *Entrepreneur,* Vol. 28, No. 10 (October 2000), pp. 71–73.

answered the first two questions, you can then compute a firm's cash flows, as described earlier in this chapter, or develop a cash budget, as explained in Chapter 23.

Forecasting Profitability

Profits reward an owner for investing in a company and constitute a primary source of financing for future growth. However, as we have already noted, a profitable company does not necessarily have positive cash flows. For example, Bates & Associates had $60,000 in net income, but the firm's cash flows from assets were a negative $35,000. Even so, profits can help finance a firm's growth, and therefore an entrepreneur must understand the factors that drive profits. A firm's net income is dependent on four variables:

1. ***Amount of sales.*** The dollar amount of sales equals the price of the product or service times the number of units sold or the amount of service rendered. Most projections regarding a firm's financial future are driven directly by assumptions about future sales. (See Chapter 9 for further discussion about sales forecasting.)
2. ***Cost of goods sold and operating expenses.*** This variable includes (a) the cost of goods sold, (b) expenses related to marketing and distributing the product, (c) general and administrative expenses, and (d) depreciation expenses. As far as possible, these expenses should be classified as either *fixed* operating expenses (those that do not vary with a change in sales volume) or *variable* operating expenses (those that change proportionally with sales).
3. ***Interest expense.*** An entrepreneur who borrows money agrees to pay interest on the loan principal. For example, a loan of $25,000 for a full year at a 12 percent interest rate results in an interest expense of $3,000 for the year (0.12 × $25,000).
4. ***Taxes.*** A firm's income taxes are figured as a percentage of taxable income. Income tax rates increase as the amount of income increases, as discussed in Chapter 10.

Let's consider a hypothetical example that demonstrates how to estimate a new venture's profits. Assume that Krista Lynn is planning to start a new business called Cameron Products, Inc., which will make stair parts for luxury homes. A newly developed lathe will allow the firm to be responsive to varying design specifications in a very economical manner. Based on a study of potential market demand and expected costs-to-sales relationships, Lynn has made the following estimates for the first two years of operations:

1. ***Amount of sales.*** Cameron expects to sell its product for \$125 per unit, with total sales for the first year projected at 2,000 units, or \$125 × 2,000 = \$250,000, and total sales for the second year projected at 3,200 units, or \$125 × 3,200 = \$400,000.
2. ***Cost of goods sold and operating expenses.*** Fixed cost of goods sold (such as production costs, employee salaries, and equipment depreciation) is expected to amount to \$100,000 per year, while fixed operating expenses (marketing expenses and administrative expenses) are estimated at \$50,000 per year. The variable costs of producing the stair parts will be around 20 percent of dollar sales, and the variable operating expenses will be approximately 30 percent of dollar sales. In other words, at a selling price of \$125 per unit, the combined variable costs per unit, both for producing the stair parts and for marketing them, will be 50 percent of the sales price (0.20 + 0.30) × \$125 = \$62.50.
3. ***Interest expense.*** The bank has agreed to loan the firm \$100,000 at an interest rate of 12 percent.
4. ***Taxes.*** It is assumed that the income tax rate will be 25 percent; that is, taxes will be 25 percent of earnings before taxes (taxable income).

Given the above estimates, we can forecast Cameron's net income, as shown in the pro forma statements in Figure 12-8. We first enter our assumptions on an Excel spreadsheet (rows 6–15 in Figure 12-8). In the respective cells, we then enter the appropriate equations for calculating the projected numbers. These equations are provided in columns D and E of Figure 12-8.

Projecting the firm's income involves the following steps:

Step 1. Begin with the assumed sales projections.

Step 2. Compute the firm's total cost of goods sold by adding the fixed cost of goods sold to the variable cost of goods sold for the projected level of sales. Subtract these costs from sales to get the firm's gross profits.

Step 3. Compute total operating expenses by adding fixed operating expenses to the variable operating expenses for the projected level of sales. Subtract these expenses from gross profits to determine operating profits.

Step 4. Calculate the interest expense for each year by multiplying interest rate times the amount of debt outstanding, and deduct the result from operating profits to determine earnings before taxes.

Step 5. Calculate estimated income taxes by multiplying the assumed 25 percent income tax rate times the earnings before taxes, and then subtract the estimated taxes from earnings before taxes to compute net income. Note that taxes are zero for the first year because of the \$37,000 loss. Typically, when a firm has a loss from its operations, it owes no taxes for that year, and tax laws allow it to apply the loss against income in following years. For simplicity, however, we will assume that the loss in the first year cannot be carried forward to the second year.

FIGURE 12-8 *Pro Forma Income Statements for Cameron Products, Inc.*

	A	B	C	D	E
1					
2	Cameron Products, Inc.				
3	Pro Forma Income Statements				
4					
5	ASSUMPTIONS				
6	Year 1 projected unit of sales	2,000			
7	Year 2 projected unit of sales	3,200			
8	Selling price	$ 125.00			
9	Fixed cost of goods sold	$100,000			
10	Fixed operating expenses	$ 50,000			
11	Variable cost of goods sold	20%			
12	Variable operating expenses	30%		Equations based on assumptions	
13	Income tax rate	25%			
14	Amount of debt	$100,000			
15	Interest rate	12%			
16					
17	PRO FORMA INCOME STATEMENTS				
18				Equations for	
19		Year 1	Year 2	Year 1	Year 2
20	Sales	$250,000	$400,000	=B6*B8	=B7*B8
21	Cost of goods sold				
22	Fixed cost of goods sold	$100,000	$100,000	=B9	=B9
23	Variable cost of goods sold (20% of sales)	50,000	80,000	=B11*B20	=B11*C20
24	Total cost of goods sold	$150,000	$180,000	=B22+B23	=C22+C23
25	Gross profits	$100,000	$220,000	=B20–B24	=C20–C24
26	Operating expenses				
27	Fixed operating expenses	$ 50,000	$ 50,000	=B10	=B10
28	Variable operating expenses (30% of sales)	75,000	120,000	=B12*B20	=B12*C20
29	Total operating expenses	$125,000	$170,000	=B27+B28	=C27+C28
30	Operating profits	$ (25,000)	$ 50,000	=B25–B29	=C25–C29
31	Interest expense (interest rate 12%)	12,000	12,000	=B14*B15	=B14*B15
32	Earnings before taxes	$ (37,000)	$ 38,000	=B30–B31	=C30–C31
33	Taxes (25% of earnings before taxes)	0	9,500	=0	=B13*C32
34	Net income	$ (37,000)	$ 28,500	=B32–B33	=C32–C33

The computations in Figure 12-8 indicate that Cameron will have a $37,000 loss in its first year, followed by a positive net income of $28,500 in its second year. A startup typically experiences losses for a period of time, frequently as long as two or three years.[3] In a real-world situation, an entrepreneur should project the profits of a new company three to five years into the future, as opposed to the two-year projection shown for Cameron.

Forecasting Assets and Financing Requirements

4

Estimate the assets needed and the financing required for a new venture.

Let's now shift our attention from forecasting profits to estimating financial requirements. The specific needs of a proposed venture govern the nature of its initial financial requirements. If the firm is a food store, financial planning must provide for the building, cash registers, shopping carts, shelving, inventory, office equipment, and other items required for this type of operation. An analysis of capital requirements for this or any other type of business should also consider (1) the investments needed and expenses incurred to start the company and allow it to grow and (2) the owners' personal expenses, especially if other income is not available for living purposes. The uncertainties surrounding an entirely new venture make estimating financial requirements difficult. Even for an established business, forecasts are never exact. Nevertheless, when seeking initial capital, an entrepreneur must be ready to answer the questions "How much financing is needed?" and "For what purpose?"

The amount of capital needed by new businesses for investments and expenses varies considerably. High-technology businesses—such as computer manufacturers, designers of semiconductor chips, and gene-splicing companies—often require millions of dollars in initial financing. Most service businesses, on the other hand, require less initial capital. An entrepreneur may use a double-barreled approach to estimating asset requirements by (1) using industry standard ratios to estimate dollar amounts and (2) cross-checking those dollar amounts through break-even analysis and empirical investigation. Robert Morris Associates, Dun & Bradstreet, banks, trade associations, and similar organizations compile industry standard ratios for numerous types of businesses. If standard ratios cannot be located, then common sense and educated guesswork must be used to estimate asset requirements.

Whether or not the owner's personal living expenses during the initial period of operation are part of the business's capitalization, they must be considered in the financial plan. Inadequate provision for personal expenses will inevitably lead to a diversion of business assets and a departure from the plan. Therefore, failure to incorporate these expenses into the financial plan as a cash outflow raises a red flag to any prospective investor.

The key to effectively forecasting financing requirements is first understanding the relationship between a firm's projected sales and its assets. A firm's sales are the primary force driving future asset needs. Figure 12-9 depicts this relationship, which can be expressed as follows:

The greater a firm's sales, the greater the asset requirements will be and, in turn, the greater the need for financing.

DETERMINING ASSET REQUIREMENTS Since asset needs tend to increase as sales increase, a firm's asset requirements are often estimated as a percentage of sales. Therefore, if future sales have been projected, a ratio of assets to sales can be used to estimate asset requirements. Suppose, for example, that a firm's sales are expected to be $1 million. If assets in the firm's particular industry tend to run about 50 percent of sales, the firm's asset requirements would be estimated to be $0.50 \times \$1{,}000{,}000 = \$500{,}000$.

Although the assets-to-sales relationship varies over time and with individual firms, it tends to be relatively constant within an industry. For example, assets as a

IN THE TRENCHES

ENTREPRENEURSHIP TODAY

THINK ABOUT PERSONAL FINANCES TOO

The great irony for many entrepreneurs is that building value in their companies requires such sacrifices that their personal finances suffer. Loren Comitor's story describes the dilemma experienced by many entrepreneurs.

Before starting his own business 22 years ago, Comitor was earning the kind of salary and benefits most people only dream about. He says, "Overnight, I went from a very comfortable corporate blanket to a parachute jump of survival. And the question was, would I manage to get the chute open in time?" Today, Comitor's advertising business, CCM&A, in Northbrook, Illinois, supports a comfortable life for his family of four. But the sacrifices Comitor made while launching his company took their toll on his personal finances: "I haven't even begun saving for my kids' college education. I'm living well, but sometimes it doesn't seem like much to show for all those years of work building my own business."

Roy Ballentine, a financial advisor, offers this advice: "It's in an entrepreneur's best interest to diversify personal assets outside the company when possible. Every year, I've watched one or two business owners go from having an enormous personal net worth—all tied up in their companies—to losing almost everything, because their businesses hit a glitch and creditors were able to seize almost everything."

Ballentine's advice is sound, but difficult—if not impossible—to follow when trying to get a new company up and running. But, at some point, an entrepreneur must take the time to consider his or her personal financial situation.

Source: "Are You Financially Fit," Inc. Online, 1998.

percentage of sales average 20 percent for grocery stores, compared to 65 percent for oil and gas companies.

This method of estimating asset requirements is called the **percentage-of-sales technique.** It can also be used to project figures for individual assets, such as accounts receivable and inventories.

percentage-of-sales technique
a method of forecasting asset investments and financing requirements

As an illustration of the use of the percentage-of-sales technique for forecasting purposes, let's consider the following example. Katie Dalton is planning to start a new business, Trailer Craft, Inc., to produce small trailers to be pulled behind motorcycles. After studying a similar company in a different state, she believes the business could generate sales of approximately $250,000 in its first year and have significant growth potential in following years. Based on her investigation of the

FIGURE 12-9

Assets-to-Sales-Financing Relationships

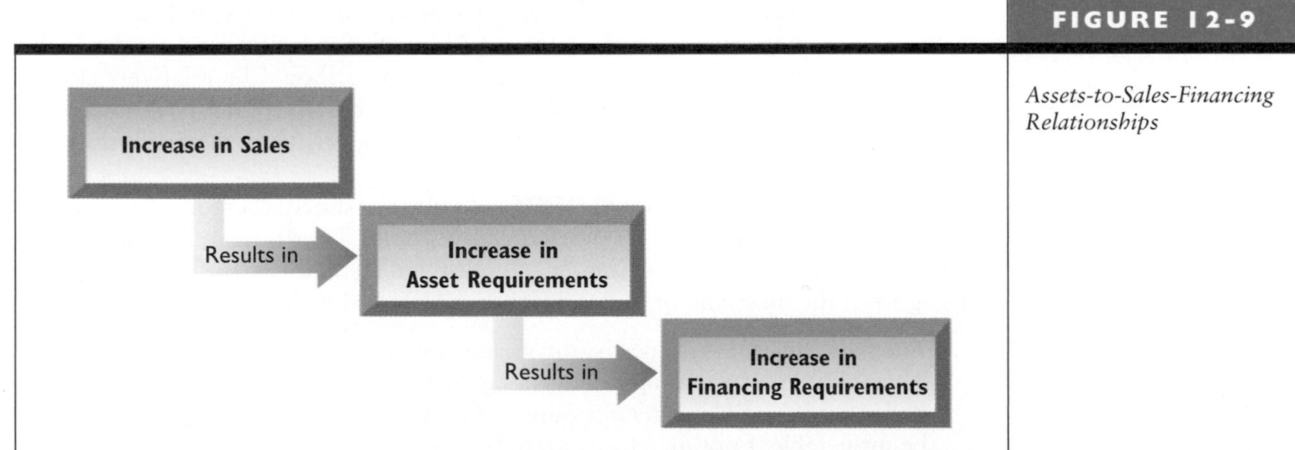

ENTREPRENEURSHIP TODAY

IN THE TRENCHES

FAILURE TO FORECAST CAN SPELL DISASTER

Failure to master the basics of financial projections can sink a business in short order. John Reith, vice president of NationsBank in Prince Frederick, Maryland, recalls the experience of a successful electrical contractor who leaped at an opportunity to expand into mechanical contracting—plumbing, piping, and duct work. The firm won bids for mechanical contracts without first doing adequate research on its own prospective costs.

Only much later did the company discover that its costs for materials, labor, and fees were much higher than it had expected. Because the firm had no projections to use for comparison, the problem wasn't discovered until over a year after the firm had bid on the project. Reith says, "They were a seat-of-the-pants business with no formal accounting control to see on an interim basis how they were doing. They knew things were getting tight, but they didn't know why."

The company's accountant spotted the problem while preparing the firm's tax return. Total revenues had jumped remarkably, but profit margins had grown thinner and thinner. With the accountant's help, the owner discovered that the electrical-contracting part of the business was doing well, but the mechanical-contracting sector was draining the business dry.

"But it was too late," says Reith. "Eventually the business had to close. Had they done their projections to begin with, they would have seen what was happening."

Source: Linda Elkins, "Real Numbers Don't Deceive," *Nation's Business*, Vol. 85, No. 3 (March 1997), pp. 51–52.

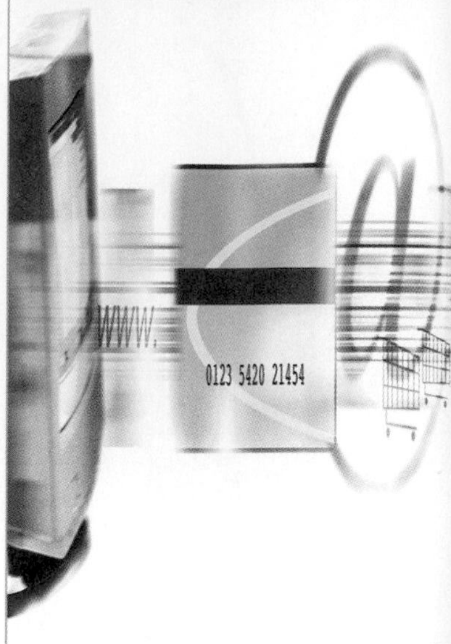

opportunity, Dalton estimated the firm's current asset (cash, accounts receivable, and inventories) requirements as a percentage of sales.

Assets	Percentage of Sales
Cash	5%
Accounts receivable	10%
Inventories	25%

Dalton also found a building suitable for a manufacturing facility for $50,000. Given anticipated sales of $250,000 and the assets-to-sales relationships shown, she was able to forecast the asset requirements for Trailer Craft. The projected figures are shown in Figure 12-10.

Thus, Dalton expects to need $150,000 in assets, some immediately and the rest in short order in the first year of operation. Although the figures used to obtain this estimate are only rough approximations, the estimate should be relatively close if Dalton has identified the assets-to-sales relationships correctly and if sales materialize as expected. Let's now consider the corresponding financing requirements.

DETERMINING FINANCING REQUIREMENTS As already stated, there must be a corresponding dollar of financing for every dollar of assets. To effectively forecast a company's financing needs, an entrepreneur must understand certain basic principles that govern the financing of firms, which can be stated as follows:

1. The more assets a firm needs, the greater the firm's financial requirements. Thus, a firm experiencing rapid sales growth has greater asset requirements and, consequently, greater pressure to find financing—and that pressure can be intolerable if not managed carefully.

FIGURE 12-10

Asset Requirements for Trailer Craft, Inc.

	A	B	C
1			
2	ASSUMPTIONS		
3	Sales	$250,000	
4	Cash/sales	5%	Equations based on assumptions
5	Accounts receivable/sales	10%	
6	Inventories/sales	25%	
7			
8	Cash	$ 12,500	=B3*B4
9	Accounts receivable	25,000	=B3*B5
10	Inventories	62,500	=B3*B6
11	Total current assets	$100,000	=B8+B9+B10
12	Fixed assets	50,000	Given
13	Total assets	$150,000	=B11+B12
14			
15			

2. A firm should finance its growth in such a way as to maintain proper liquidity. **Liquidity** measures the degree to which a firm has current assets available to meet maturing short-term debt. The need for adequate liquidity in small firms deserves special emphasis. A common weakness in small business financing is a disproportionately small investment in liquid assets. Too much money is tied up in assets that are difficult to convert to cash, and the business must depend on daily receipts to meet daily obligations. A slump in sales or an unexpected major expense may force the firm into bankruptcy. A conventional measurement of liquidity is the **current ratio,** which compares a firm's current assets (mainly cash, accounts receivable, and inventories) to its current liabilities (such as accounts payable and short-term debt). The current ratio is calculated as follows:

liquidity
the degree to which a firm has working capital available to meet maturing debt obligations

current ratio
a measure of a company's relative liquidity, determined by dividing current assets by current liabilities

$$\frac{\text{Current assets}}{\text{Current liabilities}} = \text{Current ratio}$$

To ensure payment of short-term debts as they come due, an entrepreneur might maintain a current ratio of at least 2—that is, have current assets equal to twice current liabilities. (Chapter 22 provides an in-depth discussion of liquidity and the use of the current ratio.)

3. The amount of total debt that can be used in financing a business is limited by the amount of funds provided by the owners. A bank will not provide all the financing for a firm; owners must put some of their own money into the venture. Thus, a business plan may specify that at least half of the firm's financing will come from the owners and the rest will come from debt. In other words, management should limit the firm's **debt ratio,** which expresses debt as a percentage of total assets (that is, total debt divided by total assets). (See Chapter 22 for further discussion of the debt ratio.)

debt ratio
a measure of the fraction of a firm's assets that are financed by debt, determined by dividing total debt by total assets

Entrepreneurship and Ethics

IN THE TRENCHES

ALWAYS A PAYROLL TO MEET

When faced with a cash flow crisis, a fast-growing business may encounter ethical issues. The following story, as told and commented on by Jeffrey Seglin, an associate editor at *Inc.* magazine, illustrates the point.

The CEO of a fast-growing software company was three weeks away from facing a payroll he knew he wouldn't be able to meet. Then a check for $94,000 showed up on his desk. That amount, as he was instantly aware, was more than enough to cover a full payroll period, relieving him of an oppressive burden and ensuring that his six-year-old company would stay intact—until the next payroll came due, anyway.

If there were compelling reasons not to use the money for payroll—and there were—the CEO chose to overlook them. It's understandable. Every fast-growing business, no matter how successful, struggles with cash flow problems. But cash flow is not only a management issue of whom to pay what and how much to pay when. It's also fraught with ethical implications—or it should be. Managing payroll, after all, also means making judgments about how other companies ought to be treated. Sure, you can slow down accounts payable, but aren't your suppliers as agonized about cash flow as you are? And while it may make for a sound management decision to spend money expanding operations—rather than pay vendors whose invoices are caked with dust—is it an honest way to deal with others?

But who has the time to spend fretting about right and wrong when what's at stake is a matter of life and death? Not the CEO of the software company who found himself in this position—even though the order had come from a customer looking for a customized version of software that the CEO knew his firm couldn't possibly deliver.

spontaneous financing
short-term debts, such as accounts payable, that automatically increase in proportion to a firm's sales

4. Some types of short-term debt rise spontaneously, or automatically, as a firm grows. Such **spontaneous financing** increases as a natural consequence of an increase in the firm's sales. For instance, a rise in sales requires more inventories, causing accounts payable to increase when a firm purchases inventory on credit. If sales increase by $1, accounts payable might increase by $.15 or, in other words, 15 percent of sales. This type of financing, which includes accounts payable and accrued operating expenses such as accrued wages, is significant for most smaller companies.

external equity
capital that comes from the owners' investment in a firm

profit retention
the reinvestment of profits in a firm

internal equity
capital that comes from retaining profits within a firm

5. There are two sources of equity capital: external and internal. Initially, the equity in a company comes from the investment the owners make in the firm. These funds represent **external equity.** Once the company is in operation, additional equity may come from **profit retention,** as profits are retained within the company rather than distributed to the owners. These funds are called **internal equity.** For the typical small firm, internal equity is the primary source of capital for financing growth. (Be careful not to think of retained profits as a big cash resource. As already noted, a firm may have significant earnings but no cash to reinvest. This problem will be discussed further in Chapters 22 and 23.)

In summary,

$$\text{Total asset requirements} = \text{Total sources of financing} = \text{Spontaneous financing} + \text{Profits retained within the business} + \text{External sources of financing}$$

This equation captures the essence of forecasting financial requirements. The entrepreneur who thoroughly understands these relationships should be able to accurately forecast his or her firm's financial requirements.

So what was he to do? He asked his top management team for advice. His chief financial officer, concerned about cash flow, wanted to cash the check. The vice president of sales, whose compensation was tied to revenues, expressed a similar sentiment. But the vice president of client services thought it was a bad idea to alienate a big customer. Not surprisingly, the CEO's top managers' responses reflected their own self-interest. But nobody talked about whether misleading the customer was the ethical thing, the right thing to do.

For the next three weeks, the CEO and his key managers aggressively went after every receivable and slowed down every payable. By the end of the second week, it became clear that the efforts were paying off. The company had brought in enough money to cover payroll. "Exactly at the point where I knew we had managed through our cash flow crisis and where we really knew what we were getting into," he says, "I went to the customer and returned the check, telling them that I couldn't fulfill that commitment."

What would you have done in this situation? In making your decision, remember that how you address such issues can have broader implications than you may realize. Ultimately, bad ethics can cause bad business practices to be considered acceptable behavior.

Source: Jeffrey L. Seglin, "Always a Payroll to Meet," *Inc.*, Vol. 20, No. 1 (January 1998), p. 31.

Recall that for Trailer Craft, Inc., prospective owner Katie Dalton projected initial asset requirements of $150,000 on the basis of $250,000 in sales (see Figure 12-10). Given the following set of assumptions, we can estimate the sources of financing for these asset requirements:

1. Dalton has negotiated with a supplier to receive 30 days' credit on inventory purchases, which means that accounts payable will average about 8 percent of sales (30 days ÷ 365 days in a year = 8.2%).
2. Accruals (unpaid taxes and unpaid wages, for example) should run approximately 4 percent of annual sales.
3. Dalton plans to invest $70,000 of her personal savings to provide the needed equity for the business.
4. The bank has agreed to provide a short-term line of credit of $20,000 to Trailer Craft, which means that the firm can borrow up to $20,000 as the need arises. When the firm has excess cash, it may choose to pay down the line of credit. During the spring and summer, when business is particularly brisk, Trailer Craft may need to borrow the entire $20,000 to buy inventory and extend credit to customers. However, during the winter months, a slack time, less cash will be needed, and the loan balance could possibly be reduced.
5. The bank has also agreed to help finance the purchase of a building for manufacturing and warehousing the firm's product. Of the $50,000 needed, the bank will lend the firm $35,000, with the building serving as collateral for the loan.
6. As part of the loan agreement, the bank has imposed two restrictions: (1) The firm's current ratio (current assets divided by current liabilities) must stay at 1.75 or above, and (2) no more than 60 percent of the firm's financing may come from debt, either short term or long term (that is, total debt should be no more than 60 percent of total assets). Failure to comply with either of these conditions will cause the bank loans to come due immediately.

With this information, we can estimate the initial sources of financing for Trailer Craft as follows:

- Accounts payable: 0.08 × \$250,000 in sales = \$20,000
- Accruals: 0.04 × \$250,000 in sales = \$10,000
- Credit line: \$15,000 of the \$20,000 line of credit will be needed to satisfy the firm's financing needs (\$15,000 will make the total debt and equity equal to the \$150,000 of assets.)
- Long-term debt: the bank loan of \$35,000 for the purchase of real estate
- Equity: \$70,000 invested by Dalton

Based on the above assumptions, the balance sheet at the end of the first year, along with the computations, would appear as shown in Figure 12-11.

Two comments should be made about the projected balance sheet in Figure 12-11. First, uses must always equal sources. Therefore, assets must equal debt plus equity. For Trailer Craft, beginning asset requirements were estimated to be \$150,000; thus, debt and equity must also total \$150,000. Only \$15,000 of the \$20,000 credit line is needed to bring the total debt and equity to \$150,000. Second, if all goes as planned,

FIGURE 12-11

Projected Beginning Balance Sheet for Trailer Craft, Inc.

	A	B	C
1			
2	ASSUMPTIONS		
3	Sales	\$250,000	
4	Cash/sales	5%	
5	Accounts receivable/sales	10%	
6	Inventories/sales	25%	Equations based on assumptions
7	Accounts payable/sales	8%	
8	Accruals/sales	4%	
9			
10			
11	Cash	\$ 12,500	=B3*B4
12	Accounts receivable	25,000	=B3*B5
13	Inventories	62,500	=B3*B6
14	Total current assets	\$100,000	=B11+B12+B13
15	Fixed assets	50,000	Given
16	Total assets	\$150,000	=B14+B15
17			
18	Debt		
19	Accounts payable	\$ 20,000	=B3*B7
20	Accruals	10,000	=B3*B8
21	Credit line	15,000	(needed from line of credit)
22	Total current liabilities	\$ 45,000	=B19+B20+B21
23	Long-term debt	35,000	(real estate loan)
24	Total debt	\$ 80,000	=B22+B23
25	Equity	\$ 70,000	(owner's investment)
26	Total debt and equity	\$150,000	=B24+B25

Trailer Craft will be able to satisfy the bank's loan restrictions in terms of both the current ratio and the debt ratio. From the balance sheet, these ratios can be computed as follows:

$$\text{Current ratio} = \frac{\text{Current assets}}{\text{Current liabilities}} = \frac{\$100{,}000}{\$45{,}000} = 2.22$$

and

$$\text{Debt ratio} = \frac{\text{Total debt}}{\text{Total assets}} = \frac{\$80{,}000}{\$150{,}000} = 0.533\text{, or } 53.3\%$$

The current ratio is 2.22, which is above the bank's requirement of at least 1.75. And total debt is 53.3 percent of total assets, which is below the 60 percent maximum limit imposed by the bank. Both outcomes fall within the bank's restrictions.

Note that the forecasting process requires an entrepreneur to exercise subjective judgment in making predictions. The overall approach to forecasting is straightforward—entrepreneurs make assumptions and, based on these assumptions, determine financing requirements. But entrepreneurs may be tempted to overstate their expectations in order to acquire the necessary financing. Here are some practical suggestions about making financial forecasts:[4]

1. Businesspeople are frequently too optimistic in making their sales projections. Don't stretch to reach your numbers; be factual and conservative.
2. Beware of the "hockeystick" problem, where actual sales numbers are flat or rising slightly, like the blade of a hockey stick, but sales projections soar upward like a hockey stick's handle. Such projections are always suspect, and only the most astonishing changes in a business or market can justify a sudden, rocket-like performance.
3. Build projections quantitatively from clear assumptions about your marketing and pricing plans. Don't be vague, and don't guess. Spell out the kinds of marketing you plan to do; for example, state how many customers you expect to attract and calculate a projected average sale per customer.
4. Be certain to document the reasoning behind each projection in a written list of assumptions. Without such a list, no one reading your numbers will be able to make sense of them. Also, only by looking at your assumptions will you be able to understand the differences when you compare your projections with actual results.
5. When projecting sales and expenses, use industry-specific comparative data to guide your calculations. One good source of such data is the *Annual Statement Studies,* published by Robert Morris Associates, a Philadelphia-based national association of bank loan officers. Each year, the association compiles average financial statements for companies of various sizes in many different industries.
6. Projections are immediately suspect if profit margins (profits ÷ sales) or expenses are significantly higher or lower than the average figures reported by firms in the industry with similar revenues and numbers of employees. In general, a new business cannot expect to exceed the industry average in sales or profit margins.
7. After you have prepared pro forma financial statements, check them against actual results at least once a month, and modify your projections as needed. No other tools will help you become a better manager faster.

http://www.rmahq.org

Not delivering on promises is likely to place entrepreneurs in situations where they are unable to honor future financial commitments. It is better not to have received financing than to take the money and not repay it as promised. And intentionally overstating expectations to gain access to financing is unethical. The information in this chapter on financial planning for a new company will serve as a foundation for an examination of the entrepreneur's search for financing, which is examined in Chapter 13.

LOOKING BACK

1 Describe the purpose and content of the income statement and the balance sheet.

- An income statement presents the financial results of a firm's operations over a given time period in selling the product or service, in producing or acquiring the goods or services, in running the firm, in financing the firm, and in paying taxes.
- A balance sheet provides a snapshot of a firm's financial position at a specific point in time, showing the amount of assets the firm owns, the amount of outstanding debt, and the amount of owners' equity.

2 Compute a firm's cash flows.

- The income statement will not measure a firm's cash flows, as it is calculated on an accrual basis rather than on a cash basis.
- Measuring cash flows from assets involves calculating a firm's after-tax cash flows from operations and then subtracting investments in operating working capital and investments in fixed and other long-term assets.
- The cash flows from financing are equal to the change in the amount of debt (interest-bearing debt only) and equity outstanding less the interest and dividends paid to the firm's investors.

3 Forecast a new venture's profitability.

- The purpose of pro forma financial statements is to determine (1) future profitability based on projected sales levels, (2) how much and what type of financing will be used, and (3) whether the firm will have adequate cash flows.
- A firm's net income is dependent on (1) amount of sales, (2) cost of goods sold and operating expenses, (3) interest expense, and (4) taxes.
- Estimates of fixed operating expenses and variable operating expenses based on the projected level of sales are deducted from gross sales profits to obtain a forecasted operating profit.

4 Estimate the assets needed and the financing required for a new venture.

- Funding for a new venture should cover its asset requirements and also the personal living expenses of the owner.
- A direct relationship exists between sales growth and asset needs; as sales increase, more assets are required. And, for every dollar of assets needed, there must be a corresponding dollar of financing.
- The two basic types of capital used in financing a company are debt financing and ownership equity.

KEY TERMS

financial statements (accounting statements), p. 291
income statement (profit and loss statement), p. 291
cost of goods sold, p. 292
gross profit, p. 292
operating expenses, p. 292
operating income, p. 292
financing costs, p. 292
net income available to owners (net income), p. 293
balance sheet, p. 294
current assets (gross working capital), p. 294
accounts receivable, p. 295
inventory, p. 295
fixed assets, p. 295
depreciable assets, p. 296
net fixed assets, p. 296
gross fixed assets, p. 296
accumulated depreciation, p. 296
other assets, p. 296
debt capital, p. 296
current debt (short-term liabilities), p. 296
accounts payable (trade credit), p. 296
accrued expenses, p. 296
short-term notes, p. 296
long-term debt, p. 296
mortgage, p. 296

owners' equity, p. 296
retained earnings, p. 297
accrual-basis accounting, p. 298
depreciation expense, p. 299
cash-basis accounting, p. 299
sustainable growth, p. 299
cash flows from assets, p. 300
after-tax cash flows from operations, p. 300
operating working capital, p. 301
cash flows from financing, p. 302
pro forma financial statements, p. 304
percentage-of-sales technique, p. 309
liquidity, p. 311
current ratio, p. 311
debt ratio, p. 311
spontaneous financing, p. 312
external equity, p. 312
profit retention, p. 312
internal equity, p. 312

DISCUSSION QUESTIONS

1. What is the relationship between an income statement and a balance sheet?
2. Explain the purposes of the income statement and balance sheet.
3. Distinguish among (a) gross profit, (b) operating income (earnings before interest and taxes), and (c) net income available to owners.
4. Why aren't a firm's cash flows equal to its profit?
5. What determines a company's profitability?
6. Describe the process for estimating the amount of assets required for a new venture.
7. Suppose that a retailer's estimated sales are $900,000 and the normal sales-to-inventory ratio, or inventory turnover, for the industry is 6. What dollar amount should be planned on for inventory for the new business?
8. Distinguish between owners' equity capital and debt capital.
9. Distinguish between cash flows from assets and cash flows from financing.
10. How are a startup's financial requirements estimated?

YOU MAKE THE CALL

SITUATION 1

At the beginning of 2002, J. T. Rose purchased a small business, the Hargrove Company, whose income statement and balance sheets are shown below.

Income Statement for Hargrove Company for 2002

Sales revenue		$175,000
Cost of goods sold		105,000
Gross profit		$ 70,000
Operating expenses:		
Depreciation	$ 5,000	
Administrative expenses	20,000	
Selling expenses	26,000	
Total operating expenses		$ 51,000
Operating income		$ 19,000
Interest expense		3,000
Earnings before taxes		$ 16,000
Taxes		8,000
Net income		$ 8,000

Balance Sheets for Hargrove Company for 2001 and 2002

	2001	2002
Assets		
Current assets:		
Cash	$ 8,000	$ 10,000
Accounts receivable	15,000	20,000
Inventories	22,000	25,000
Total current assets	$45,000	$ 55,000
Fixed assets:		
Gross fixed assets	$50,000	$ 55,000
Accumulated depreciation	15,000	20,000
Total fixed assets	$35,000	$ 35,000
Other assets	12,000	10,000
TOTAL ASSETS	$92,000	$100,000
Debt (Liabilities) and Equity		
Current debt:		
Accounts payable	$10,000	$ 12,000
Accruals	7,000	8,000
Short-term notes	5,000	5,000
Total current debt	$22,000	$ 25,000
Long-term debt	15,000	15,000
Total debt	$37,000	$ 40,000
Equity	$55,000	$ 60,000
TOTAL DEBT AND EQUITY	$92,000	$100,000

The firm has been profitable, but Rose has been disappointed by the lack of cash flows. He had hoped to have about $10,000 a year available for personal living expenses. However, there never seems to be much cash available for purposes other than business needs. Rose has asked you to examine the financial statements and explain why, although they show a profit, he does not have any discretionary cash for personal needs. He observed, "I thought that I could take the profits and add depreciation to find out how much cash I was generating. However, that doesn't seem to be the case. What's happening?"

Question 1 Given the information provided by the financial statements, what would you tell Rose? (As part of your answer, calculate the firm's cash flows.)

Question 2 How would you describe the primary sources and uses of cash for the Hargrove Company?

SITUATION 2

The Donahoo Furniture Sales Company was formed on December 31, 2001, with $1,000,000 in equity plus $500,000 in long-term debt. On January 1, 2002, all of the firm's capital was held in cash. The following transactions occurred during January 2002.

- January 2: Donahoo purchased $1,000,000 worth of furniture for resale. It paid $500,000 in cash and financed the balance using trade credit that required payment in 60 days.
- January 3: Donahoo sold $250,000 worth of furniture that it had paid $200,000 to acquire. The entire sale was on credit terms of net 90 days.
- January 15: Donahoo purchased more furniture for $200,000. This time, it used trade credit for the entire amount of the purchase, with credit terms of net 60 days.
- January 31: Donahoo sold $500,000 worth of furniture, for which it had paid $400,000. The furniture was sold for 10 percent cash down, with the remainder payable in 90 days. In addition, the firm paid a cash dividend of $100,000 to its stockholders and paid off $250,000 of its long-term debt.

Question 1 What did Donahoo's balance sheet look like at the outset of the firm's life?

Question 2 What did the firm's balance sheet look like after each transaction?

Question 3 Ignoring taxes, determine how much income Donahoo earned during January. Prepare an income statement for the month. Recognize an interest expense of 1 percent for the month (12 percent annually) on the $500,000 long-term debt, which has not been paid but is owed.

Question 4 What was Donahoo's cash flow for the month of January?

SITUATION 3

Trailer Craft, Inc., used as an example in this chapter, is an actual firm (although some of the facts were changed to maintain confidentiality). Stuart Hall bought the firm from its founding owners and is moving its operations to his hometown. Although he estimated the firm's asset needs and financing requirements, he has no certainty that these projections will be realized. The figures merely represent the most likely case. Hall also made some projections that he considers to be the worst-case and best-case sales and profit figures. If things do not go well, the firm might have sales of only $150,000 in its first year, resulting in net income of 10 percent on each sales dollar. However, if the potential of the business is realized, Hall believes that sales could be as high as $400,000, with net income representing 15 percent of sales. If he needs any additional financing beyond the existing line of credit, he could conceivably borrow another $5,000 in short-term debt from the bank by pledging some personal investments. Any additional financing would need to come from Hall himself, thereby increasing his equity stake in the business.

Source: Personal conversation with Stuart Hall. (Numbers are hypothetical.)

Question If all of Trailer Craft's other relationships hold, how will Hall's worst-case and best-case projections affect the balance sheet? Rework the balance sheet, and then compare your results with the original projected balance sheet shown in Figure 12-11.

EXPERIENTIAL EXERCISES

1. Interview an owner of a small firm about the financial statements she or he uses. Ask the owner how important financial data are to her or his decision making.
2. Acquire a small firm's financial statements. Review the statements and describe the firm's financial position. Find out if the owner agrees with your conclusions.
3. Dun & Bradstreet and Robert Morris Associates compile financial information about many companies. They provide, among other information, income statements and balance sheets for an average firm in an industry. In the library, look up financial information on two industries of your choice, and compute the following data for each industry:
   a. The percentages of assets in (1) current assets and (2) fixed assets (plant and equipment)
   b. The percentages of financing from (1) spontaneous financing and (2) internal equity
   c. The cost of goods sold and the operating expenses as percentages of sales
   d. The total assets as a percentage of sales

Given your findings, how would you summarize the differences between the two industries?

4. Obtain the business plan of a firm that is 3 to 5 years old. Compare the techniques used in the plan to forecast the firm's profits and financing requirements with those presented in this chapter. If actual data are available, compare the financial forecasts with the eventual outcome. What accounts for the differences?

EXPLORING THE WEB

1. Lycos offers templates to help small business owners set up their financial statements. Access **http://www.lycos.com**, choose Small Business, and then Tools under Finance.
   a. Download the balance sheet template, which is an Excel template. Enter data in the balance sheet and save it for future use.
   b. Repeat the process to download the income statement template.
   c. Also download the template for a daily cash sheet (this topic is discussed in Chapter 23).
2. The Entrepreneurial Edge offers additional information on financial statements. Go to **http://www.lowe.org** and choose Business Builder for Money. Then click Financial Statements.
   a. Under How to Create a Budget, what are two types of budgets, and what is each used for?
   b. Read the article about profit–loss (income) statements. Give two reasons for preparing an income statement.
   c. Read about how to prepare and analyze a balance sheet. When should the owner of a new business prepare a balance sheet?

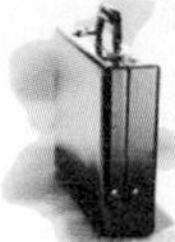

CASE 12

STEGMART (p. 672)

This case provides the data necessary to prepare pro forma financial statements for a small startup company.

Alternative Cases for Chapter 12:
Case 5, "Stitch Craft," p. 649
Case 8, "Robinson Associates, Inc.," p. 658
Case 22, "Artho, Inc.," p. 697

The Business Plan

LAYING THE FOUNDATION

As part of laying the foundation to prepare your own business plan, you will need to develop the following:

1. Historical financial statements (if applicable) and five years of pro forma financial statements, including balance sheets, income statements, and statements of cash flows.
2. Monthly cash budgets for the first year and quarterly cash budgets for the second year. (See Chapter 23 for an explanation of cash budgets.)
3. Profit and cash flow break-even analysis. (See Chapter 16 for an explanation of break-even analysis.)
4. Financial resources required now and in the future, with details on the intended use of funds being requested.
5. Underlying assumptions for all pro forma statements.
6. Current and planned investments by the owners and other investors.

chapter 13

Finding Sources of Financing

In the VIDEO Spotlight

We'll Show You the Money

In this episode of "Small Business School," the series on PBS stations, you will meet businesspeople who have used many different techniques to raise money to start and grow companies. Traditionally, small business owners borrow money from family and friends or use their savings to start a business. And, to grow, they tend to use retained earnings, because they are conservative and don't want to pay interest on money. I have made my company work this way since 1979, and most of the people featured in this series have used this strategy as well.

However, many business owners find that their ideas are much bigger than their pocketbook, and they have to go after OPM (other people's money). Andy Wilson, founder of Boston Duck Tours, tells how he was completely out of cash and still needed over $1 million to get his company out of his head and onto the road. He found a venture capitalist who raised the money. Even though Wilson's business is a popular attraction in Boston, this episode illustrates that it can take years to pay back borrowed money and realize some personal wealth.

Andy Murstein, Bill Hagstrom, and Bob Simpson relate how they went to Wall Street for the money they needed, and Anne Beiler tells about her angel investor. Fred Hoar, a founder of a group in Silicon Valley called The Band of Angels, explains why this group has been so important to the creation of value and the making of many millionaires.

We're looking for demand-driven products.

—Vince Occhipinti,
Venture Capitalist

In this episode, you'll also hear from the founders of Jagged Edge Mountain Gear, who found a good banker who consolidated their bad

Go to page 736 for More! on Financing.

debt and filed the necessary paperwork to secure backing from the Small Business Adminstration. If a person is determined to own a business, I am convinced that he or she can find the money—especially in the United States. ◆

—*Hattie Bryant, Producer, "Small Business School," The Series on PBS Stations, Worldnet, and the Web, http://smallbusinessschool.org*

LOOKING AHEAD

After studying this chapter, you should be able to

1. *Describe how the nature of a firm affects its financing sources.*
2. *Evaluate the choice between debt financing and equity financing.*
3. *Describe various sources of financing available to small firms.*

Chapter 12 addressed two questions:

- *How much* financing is needed?
- *What types* of financing are available?

Three basic types of financing were identified:

1. *Profit retention,* which involves avoiding cash withdrawals, such as dividends to the owners. Instead, the cash is used to finance growth.
2. *Spontaneous financing,* which arises automatically with increases in sales. For instance, as a firm's sales grow, it must purchase more inventories and the supplier extends more credit. The increase in accounts payable is simply part of the normal operating cycle and occurs as part of day-to-day operations.
3. *External financing,* which comes from outside investors. Creditors (such as bankers), additional equity investors (such as common stockholders), or sole proprietors may provide this type of financing.

This chapter discusses sources of spontaneous and external financing for small firms. But first we must consider *how* a company should be financed. An understanding of this core issue is critical to identifying appropriate sources of financing.

THE NATURE OF A FIRM AND ITS FINANCING SOURCES

Describe how the nature of a firm affects its financing sources.

Four basic factors determine how a firm is financed: (1) the firm's economic potential, (2) the maturity of the company, (3) the nature of its assets, and (4) the personal preferences of the owners with respect to the tradeoffs between debt and equity.

Economic Value Potential

A firm with potential for high growth and large profits has many more possible sources of financing than does a firm that provides a good lifestyle for the owner but little in the way of attractive returns. Only those firms providing rates of returns that exceed the investor's required rate of return create value for the investor. In fact, most investors in startup companies limit their investing to firms that offer potentially high

returns within a five- to ten-year period. Clearly, a company that provides a comfortable lifestyle for its owner but does not create sufficient profits to attract outside investors will have more limited sources of financing.

Company Maturity

The age of a company has a direct bearing on the types of available financing. In the early years of a business, most entrepreneurs "bootstrap" their financing—that is, they depend on their own initiative to come up with the necessary capital. Only after the business has an established track record will most bankers and other financial institutions be interested in providing capital. Even venture capitalists restrict their investments in startup companies. Many believe that the additional risk associated with a startup is too great relative to the returns they can expect to receive. On average, about three-fourths of a venture capitalist's investments are in later-stage businesses; only a few venture capitalists focus heavily on startups. Similarly, bankers dislike making loans to a company that has no history. They demand evidence that the business will be able to repay a loan—and that evidence usually must be based on what the firm has done in the past and not what the owner says it will achieve in the future. So, a firm's life-cycle position is a critical factor in raising capital.

Types of Assets

There are two kinds of assets a bank looks at when it comes to financing a company: tangible and intangible. Tangible assets, which can be seen and touched, include inventories, equipment, and buildings. The cost of these assets appears on the firm's balance sheet, which the banker receives along with the firm's financial statements. Tangible assets serve as great collateral when a firm is requesting a bank loan. On the other hand, intangible assets, such as goodwill, research and development, and even the quality of a firm's employees, have little value as collateral. As a result, companies with substantial tangible assets have a much easier time borrowing money than do companies whose assets take the form of computer software or research and development.

Owner Preferences for Debt or Equity

The owner of a company faces the question "Should I finance with debt or equity or some mix of the two?" The answer depends, in part, on his or her personal preference. The ultimate choice between debt and equity involves certain tradeoffs, which will be explained in the following section.

Debt or Equity Financing?

2
Evaluate the choice between debt financing and equity financing.

The choice between debt and equity financing must be made early in a firm's life cycle because the decision may make the difference between financial success and failure. Furthermore, most providers of capital specialize in *either* debt or equity financing. To make an informed decision, a small business owner needs to recognize and understand the tradeoffs between debt and equity with regard to (1) potential profitability, (2) financial risk, and (3) voting control. The relationships, which are presented graphically in Figure 13-1, are as follows:

1. Borrowing money, rather than investing more ownership capital (equity) in the business, increases the *potential* for higher rates of return on the owners' investment. But at the same time, increased debt exposes the owners to greater financial risk, including the likelihood of losses and difficulty in repaying the lender.

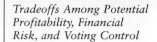

FIGURE 13-1

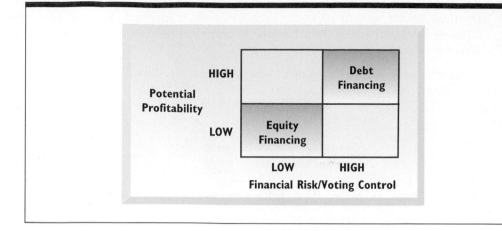

Tradeoffs Among Potential Profitability, Financial Risk, and Voting Control

Potential Profitability		LOW	HIGH
	HIGH		Debt Financing
	LOW	Equity Financing	

Financial Risk/Voting Control

Borrowing also allows the owners to retain voting control of the company and to avoid investing more money or sharing ownership with other investors.

2. If owners choose to invest more equity in a business or to find other equity investors (rather than increase debt), they limit their potential rate of return, but they also lower the firm's financial risk. If the increase in equity comes from new investors, the owners must share control of the firm with them.

Let's consider each of the above tradeoffs in turn.

Potential Profitability

To see how the choice between debt and equity affects potential profitability, consider the Levine Company, a new firm that's still in the process of raising needed capital.

- The owners have already invested $100,000 of their own money in the new business. To complete the financing, they need another $100,000.
- The owners have identified investors who would provide $100,000 for a 30 percent share of the firm's outstanding stock. Note that even though the new investors would be contributing half the money used to finance the firm ($100,000 from the owners, and $100,000 from the new investors), they would not receive half the stock. They recognize the value of the founders' "sweat equity"—that is, the time and effort they have contributed in starting the business.
- If Levine borrowed the money, the interest rate on the debt would be 10 percent, so the interest expense each year would be $10,000 (0.10 × $100,000).
- The firm's operating income (earnings before interest and taxes) is expected to be $28,000, determined as follows:

Sales revenue		$150,000
Cost of goods sold		80,000
Gross profit		$ 70,000
Operating expenses:		
General and administrative expenses	$20,000	
Marketing expenses	22,000	
Total operating expenses		$ 42,000
Operating income (earnings before interest and taxes)		$ 28,000

- The firm's total assets are projected to be $200,000.
- Based on the projected operating income of $28,000 and assets of $200,000, the firm expects to earn $0.14 for each $1 of assets invested ($28,000 income ÷ $200,000 assets). In other words, there will be a 14 percent rate of return on the firm's assets.

If the firm issues stock, its balance sheet will read as follows:

Total assets	$200,000
Debt	$ 0
Equity	200,000
Total debt and equity	$200,000

But if the firm borrows money, the balance sheet will appear as follows:

Total assets	$200,000
Debt (10% interest rate)	$100,000
Equity	100,000
Total debt and equity	$200,000

If we assume no taxes (just to keep things simple), we can use the above information to project the firm's net income under the two financing plans:

	Equity	Debt	
Operating income	$28,000	$28,000	
Interest expense	0	10,000	(0.10 × $100,000)
Net income	$28,000	$18,000	

As the income statement reveals, net income is greater if the firm finances with equity rather than with debt (because there is no interest expense when one finances with equity). However, the owners' rate of return on investment, or *return on equity,* is more important than the firm's net income (operating income less interest expense). The owners' equity (or investment) equals the total assets less the debt financing. Thus, the owners' return on equity can be computed as follows:

$$\text{Owners' return on equity} = \frac{\text{Net income}}{\text{Owners' equity investment}}$$

So when the firm uses equity financing, the owners' return on equity is 14 percent, computed as follows:

$$\text{Owners' return on equity} = \frac{\text{Net income}}{\text{Owners' equity investment}}$$

$$= \frac{\$28,000}{\$200,000} = 0.14, \text{ or } 14\%$$

But if the additional financing comes from debt, with interest expense of $10,000 and equity investment of only $100,000, then the rate of return on equity is 18 percent. It is calculated as follows:

$$\text{Owners' return on equity} = \frac{\text{Net income}}{\text{Owners' equity investment}}$$

$$= \frac{\$18{,}000}{\$100{,}000} = 0.18, \text{ or } 18\%$$

Thus, the owners' return on equity is higher if debt is used. By using only personal funds, the owners will earn \$0.14 for every \$1 invested; by using debt, however, they will earn \$0.18 for every \$1 invested. So, in terms of a rate of return on their investment, the owners do better by borrowing money at a 10 percent interest rate than by issuing stock to new owners, who will share in the profits. That makes sense, because the firm is earning 14 percent on its assets but only paying creditors at a 10 percent rate. The owners benefit from the difference. These relationships are shown in Figure 13-2.

As a general rule, as long as a firm's rate of return on its assets (operating income ÷ total assets) is greater than the cost of the debt (interest rate), the owners' return on equity will increase as the firm uses more debt. Levine hopes to earn 14 percent on its assets but pay only 10 percent in interest for the debt financing. Using debt, therefore, increases the owners' opportunity to enhance the rate of return on their investment.

FIGURE 13-2

Debt Versus Equity at the Levine Company

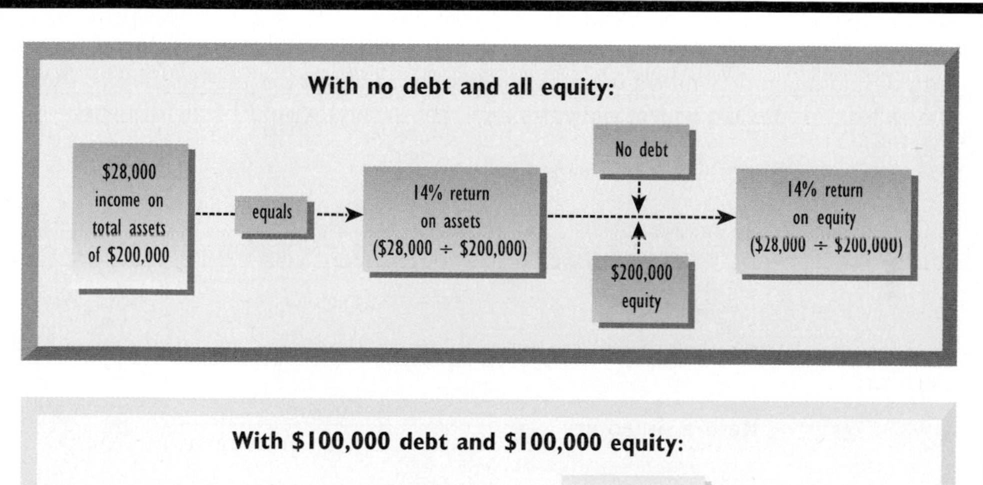

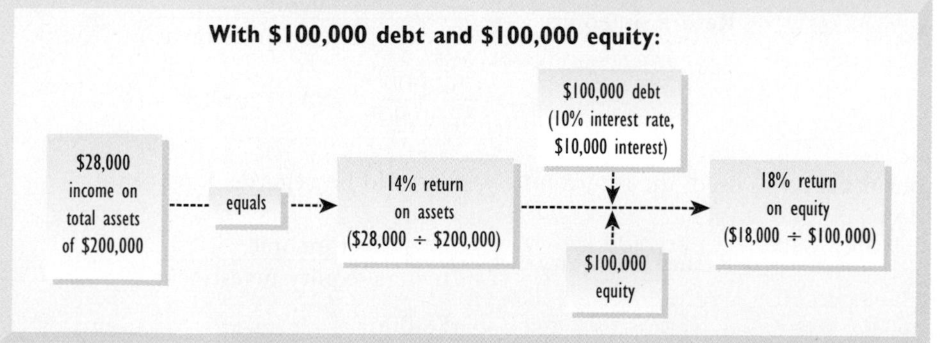

Financial Risk

If debt is so beneficial in terms of producing a higher rate of return for the owners, why wouldn't Levine's owners use as much debt as possible—even 100 percent debt—if they could? Then the rate of return on the owners' investment would be even higher. For example, if the Levine Company financed its entire need for capital—$200,000—with 90 percent debt and 10 percent equity—$180,000 in debt and $20,000 in equity—the firm's net income would be $10,000, computed as follows:

Operating income	$28,000	
Interest expense	18,000	(0.10 × $180,000)
Net income	$10,000	

While the firm's net income has been reduced to $10,000, the owners now have to invest only $20,000—a big reduction. And the return on equity is now a whopping 50 percent ($10,000 net income ÷ $20,000 owners' investment).

That's the good news. The bad news: *Debt is risky.* If the firm fails to earn profits, creditors will still insist on their interest payments. Debt demands its pound of flesh from the owners regardless of the firm's performance. In an extreme case, creditors can force a firm into bankruptcy if it fails to honor its financial obligations.

Equity, on the other hand, is less demanding. If a firm does not reach its goal for profits, an equity investor must accept the disappointing results and hope for better results next year. Equity investors cannot demand more than what is earned.

Another way to view the negative side of debt is to contemplate what happens to the return on equity if a business has a bad year. Let's consider what would happen if the Levine Company experienced poor results. Instead of earning 14 percent on its assets as hoped, or $28,000 in operating profits, suppose the firm made a mere $2,000, or only 1 percent on its assets of $200,000. The owners' return on equity would again depend on whether the firm used debt or equity to finance the second $100,000 investment in the company. The results would be as follows:

	Equity	Debt	
Operating income	$2,000	$ 2,000	
Interest expense	0	10,000	(0.10 × $100,000)
Net income	$2,000	($ 8,000)	

If the added financing came in the form of equity, the return on equity would be 1 percent:

$$\text{Return on equity} = \frac{\text{Net income}}{\text{Owners' equity investment}}$$

$$= \frac{\$2{,}000}{\$200{,}000} = 0.01, \text{ or } 1\%$$

But if debt was used, the return on equity would be negative 8 percent:

$$\text{Return on equity} = \frac{\text{Net income}}{\text{Owners' equity investment}}$$

$$= \frac{-\$8{,}000}{\$100{,}000} = -0.08, \text{ or } -8\%$$

IN THE TRENCHES ENTREPRENEURSHIP TODAY

DEBT VERSUS EQUITY

How a company raises expansion capital can have a profound effect on its owner. A look behind the scenes at two entrepreneurs who made it through the financing process highlights differences between debt and equity financing.

Entrepreneur Jane Witheridge borrowed the money to purchase and expand her small business, Garden-ville, a firm that sells mulches, composts, and fertilizers. Witheridge paid $500,000 in cash, with the seller holding a note for the remainder of the sales price. "I was able to pull in a favor from a friend, who got me a second mortgage on my house for the upfront payment," she remembers. She then borrowed the money from a bank to pay off the company's debt.

With the large amount of debt owed, Witheridge and her team feverishly went to work. To generate cash flows, they streamlined product lines, ended unprofitable contracts, and trained sales people to focus on products that added to the bottom line. Witheridge explains, "I thought I'd have the time to do all this once the capital was there. But we had to hit the ground running. We had no margin for error."

Three years later, Witheridge observes, "I may own equity, but I'm still paying off the previous owner. Even now, we are constrained. But I have the confidence now we can make it on our own. . . . I often wonder what we could have done if we'd raised equity financing. I'm sure we wouldn't have found our way to the efficiencies as quickly."

A second entrepreneur, Farhad Mohit, opted instead to sell ownership of his BizRate.com to venture capital investors. Mohit had several firms vying for the opportunity to fund his company. He received $4.5 million from two of them. "Suddenly, it became serious," Mohit says. "I had real pressure, because with the money, I had to make something happen. I had guys in suits asking for budgets for putting the capital to work." But raising the equity capital paid off. When the firm got financing, there were only six employees; 18 months later, there were almost 100.

Who made the better choice—Witheridge, who raised debt capital, or Mohit, who chose equity capital? There is no right or wrong answer when it comes to choosing between debt and equity. While the answer depends in part on the situation, it also depends on the owners' personal preferences.

Source: Adapted from Cynthia Harrington, "Hold 'Em," *Entrepreneur*, Vol. 28, No. 7 (July 2000), pp. 78 83.

http://www.garden-ville.com

In this case, the owners would be better off if they financed solely with equity. Thus, debt is a two-edged sword; it cuts both ways. If debt financing is used and things go well, they will go *very* well for the owners—but if things go badly, they will go *very* badly. In short, debt financing makes doing business more risky.

Voting Control

The third issue in choosing between debt and equity is the degree of control retained by owners. Most owners of small firms resist giving up control to outsiders.

For the Levine Company, raising new capital through equity financing means giving up 30 percent of the firm's ownership, with the original owners still controlling 70 percent of the stock. However, many small firm owners are reluctant to give away any of the company's ownership. They do not want to be accountable in any way to minority owners, much less take a chance of eventually losing control of the business.

Given this aversion to losing control, many small business owners choose to finance with debt rather than with equity. They realize that debt increases risk, but it also permits them to retain full ownership of the firm.

With an understanding of the basic tradeoffs to be considered when choosing between debt and equity, we can now look at specific sources of financing. Where do small business owners go to find the money to finance their companies?

SOURCES OF FINANCING

3

Describe various sources of financing available to small firms.

When initially financing a small business, an entrepreneur will often first use personal savings and then attempt to gain access to the savings of family and friends. Only if these sources are inadequate will the entrepreneur turn to more formal channels of financing, such as banks and outside investors.

Major sources of debt financing are individual investors (often friends and family), business suppliers, asset-based lenders, commercial banks, government-sponsored programs, and community-based financial institutions. And the primary sources of equity financing are personal savings, friends and family, private investors in the community, large corporations, venture capitalists, and the sale of stock in public equity markets (going public).

To gain insight into how startups are financed, consider the responses given by owners of the *Inc. 500* firms—the 500 fastest growing privately held firms in the United States—when they were asked about the financing sources they used to start up their firms:[1]

Personal savings	79%	Bank loans	7%
Family members	16%	Private investors	5%
Partners	14%	Mortgaged property	4%
Personal charge cards	10%	Venture capital	3%
Friends	7%	Other	8%

Figure 13-3 gives an overview of the sources of financing of smaller companies. Keep in mind that the use of these and other sources of funds is not limited to a startup's initial financing. Such sources may also be used to finance a firm's day-to-day operations and business expansions.

FIGURE 13-3

Sources of Funds

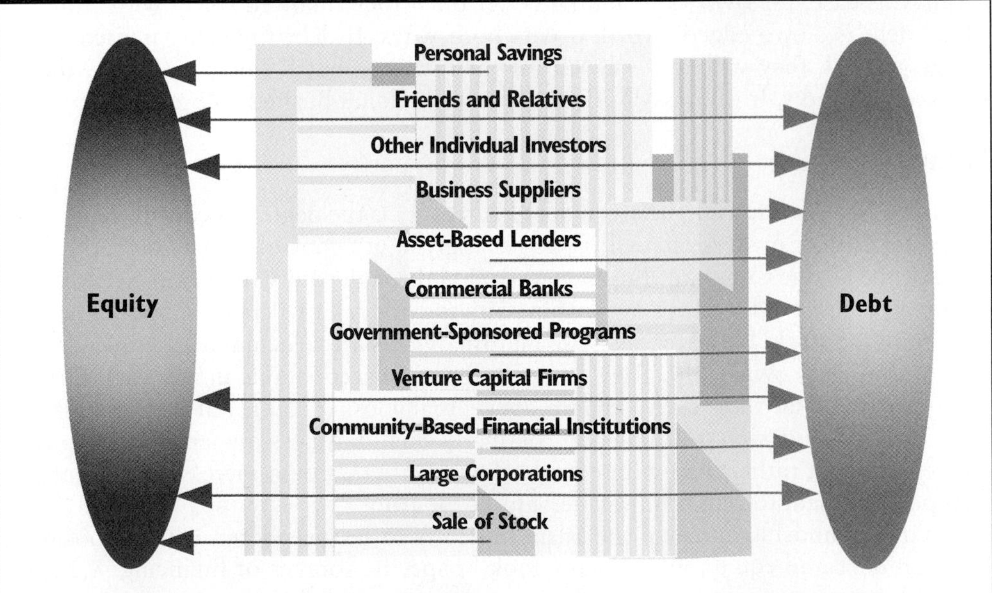

Individual Investors

The search for financial support usually begins close to home. The aspiring entrepreneur frequently has three sources of early financing: (1) personal savings, (2) friends and relatives, and (3) other individual investors.

PERSONAL SAVINGS It is imperative for an entrepreneur to have some personal assets in the business, and these typically come from personal savings. Indeed, personal savings is the source of equity financing most frequently used in starting a new business. With few exceptions, the entrepreneur must provide an equity base. A new business needs equity to allow for a margin of error. In its first few years, a firm can ill afford large fixed outlays for debt repayment. Also, a banker—or anyone else for that matter—is unlikely to loan a venture money if the entrepreneur does not have his or her own money at risk.

A problem for many people who want to start a business is a lack of sufficient personal savings for this purpose. It can be very discouraging when the banker asks, "How much will you be investing in the business?" or "What do you have for collateral to secure the bank loan you want?" There is no easy solution to this problem, which is faced by an untold number of entrepreneurs. Nonetheless, many individuals who lacked personal savings for a startup have found a way to accomplish their goal of owning their own company. In most cases, it required creativity and some risk taking—as well as finding a partner who could provide the financing or friends and relatives who were willing to help.

FRIENDS AND RELATIVES At times, loans from friends or relatives may be the only available source of new financing. Such loans can often be obtained quickly, as this type of financing is based more on personal relationships than on financial analysis. However, friends and relatives who provide business loans sometimes feel that they have the right to offer suggestions concerning the management of the business. Also, hard business times may strain the bonds of friendship. But if relatives and friends are the only available source of financing, the entrepreneur has no alternative. To minimize the chance of damaging important personal relationships, however, the entrepreneur should plan for repayment of such loans as soon as possible. In addition, any agreements made should be put in writing, as memories tend to become fuzzy over time. It's best to clarify expectations up front rather than be disappointed or angry later.

We know of an entrepreneur who borrowed money from a friend to start a restaurant. At least, the entrepreneur thought it was a loan. The friend thought he was making an equity investment—which meant that he would share the gains and losses along with the entrepreneur. The restaurant was a failure and soon closed. Later, when the entrepreneur was able, he tried to repay the friend. The friend argued, "You don't owe me any money. I was not loaning you the money; I was investing in the business with you. So you owe me nothing." The entrepreneur insisted that he should repay the friend. The two friends went on to start another business, which was a great success. Of course, stories about friends loaning money to friends rarely end so well. Thus, it is important to clarify expectations and do whatever it takes to honor your commitments.

OTHER INDIVIDUAL INVESTORS A large number of private individuals invest in others' entrepreneurial ventures. They are primarily people with moderate to significant business experience and may on rare occasions be affluent professionals, such as lawyers and physicians. This type of financing has come to be known as **informal venture capital** because no established marketplace exists in which these individuals

informal venture capital funds provided by wealthy private individuals (business angels) to high-risk ventures

Utilizing a New Technology

IN THE TRENCHES

INVESTING ONLINE

Wayne Marshall, 57, had always invested in blue-chip growth stocks. But when he retired from his job as a marketing manager for DuPont, he took up investing as a hobby and found himself wanting riskier investment opportunities—so Marshall went online to invest in new business ventures. At a Web site called OffRoad Capital, Marshall invested $25,000 to buy shares in PlexusNet Broadcasting, an Internet firm that produces online conferences and exhibitions. Using OffRoad to obtain equity financing, PlexusNet raised $4.5 million.

Prior to making an investment, potential investors can view financial information about a new venture at OffRoad's Web site, as well as ask company executives questions during a Webcast. In its first year, OffRoad signed up approximately 5,000 individuals and raised $42 million for seven companies. OffRoad also forged alliances with Charles Schwab and with Robertson Stephens, a San Francisco investment bank.

Source: Susan Scherreik, "Being a Venture Capitalist Is Getting Easier," Business Week Online, http://www.businessweek.com, May 22, 2000.

http://www.offroadcapital.com

regularly invest. Somewhat appropriately, these investors have acquired the label *business angels*. They represent the oldest and largest segment of the U.S. venture capital industry, which consists of more than three million individuals, typically with an average net worth in excess of $1 million (excluding personal residences). The majority of these individuals are self-made millionaires, who have substantial business and entrepreneurial experience.[2] A few of the better recognized business angels are Ken Oshman, founder of Rolm Corporation; Paul Allen, co-founder of Microsoft Corporation; and Warren Musser, founder of Safeguard Scientifics. These three individuals alone have helped finance a large group of new companies. But even more important are the numerous private investors across the country who, without fanfare, invest in thousands of new companies each year.

The total amount invested by business angels is not known with any certainty. Estimates of the size of this informal venture capital market vary considerably, but conservative estimates suggest that about 400,000 angels invest approximately $30 to $40 billion every year in over 50,000 ventures.[3] They generally make investments that are relatively small—over 80 percent of business angels invest in startup firms with fewer than 20 employees. They invest locally, usually no more than 50 miles from their homes. And they invest in a wide variety of business sectors, although they are increasingly moving toward larger deals and technology-based industries.[4]

The traditional path to informal investors is through contacts with business associates, accountants, and lawyers. Other entrepreneurs are also a primary source of help in identifying prospective informal or private investors. The recent proliferation of formal angel networks and angel alliances has pushed the number of such groups to over 150.[5] In forums across the country, entrepreneurs make presentations to groups of private investors gathered to hear about new ventures. For example, the Technology Capital Network at MIT, based in Boston, receives proposals from potential investors and entrepreneurs and, for a fee, attempts to find a match. Such networks can greatly increase the odds of finding an investor.

http://www.tcnmit.org

In addition to providing needed money, private investors frequently contribute know-how to a business. Many of these individuals invest in the type of business in which they have had experience, and they can be very demanding. Thus, the entrepreneur must be careful in structuring the terms of the investors' involvement.

IN THE TRENCHES ENTREPRENEURSHIP TODAY

SOME PREFER ANGELS

In 1993, Mark Torrance began StockMaster.com Inc. At the time, he was a graduate student and had no idea the firm would blossom into a viable business. At first, his only goal was to find a way to chart his own portfolio. By the summer of 1996, however, things had changed. Torrance was running the company out of his condo in Quincy, Massachusetts, and he had moved StockMaster to an Internet service provider's server. His wife, Leslie, had borrowed $30,000 on her credit card to be used as capital in the business. Torrance was a tech-savvy dot.com Internet founder without startup funding.

By the end of 1997, StockMaster had turned a profit on $1 million in revenues, which came from its advertisers and from designing and producing content for investor-relations Web pages. By that time Torrance had moved the company to Silicon Valley. But by the end of 1998, StockMaster still had raised no seed money—even though the firm was profitable. Torrance's discouragement was mounting. "We had 12 employees, and I was stretched completely thin," he says.

Torrance knew he needed capital, but like many other small business owners, he was unclear about how to get it. He couldn't afford to use an investment bank, and he didn't want to lose his focus on the day-to-day operations. So, he turned to his new chief financial officer, Jim Drury, for a solution. Over the next two months, Drury developed a game plan to begin networking and studying how other companies had raised capital. His strategy ended up paying big dividends for StockMaster.

When Drury set out to raise money, StockMaster, with five years of bootstrapping, looked a lot more like a conventional brick-and-mortar small business than it did a cash-infused Internet startup. And like many other dot.com owners, Torrance wasn't overjoyed about his financing possibilities, despite all he'd heard about an abundance of capital. He'd had some venture capitalists express interest, but "I thought their offers would be more like buyouts. VCs might say, 'Give up two-thirds. We'll grow it for you,'" he says.

Torrance had come too far to relinquish so much. So Drury decided that StockMaster should target angel investors rather than venture capitalists. The decision was consistent with Torrance's company goals, in terms of both maintaining control and maximizing cash-outs through an initial public offering. Torrance's main objective was to avoid surrendering a big share of equity. "It's my first company, and I value highly how much wealth I'm building," he explained.

Source: Ilan Mochari, "The Do-It-Yourself Angel Round," *Inc.,* Vol. 22, No. 5 (April 2000), p. 123.

http://www.stockmaster.com

Business Suppliers and Asset-Based Lenders

Companies that have business dealings with a new firm are also possible sources of funds for financing inventories and equipment. Both wholesalers and equipment manufacturers/suppliers can provide trade credit (accounts payable) or equipment loans and leases.

ACCOUNTS PAYABLE (TRADE CREDIT) Credit extended by suppliers is very important to a startup. In fact, trade (or mercantile) credit is the source of short-term funds most widely used by small firms. **Accounts payable (trade credit)** is of short duration—30 days is the customary credit period. Most commonly, this type of credit involves an unsecured, open-book account. The supplier (seller) sends merchandise to the purchasing firm; the buyer then sets up an account payable for the amount of the purchase.

accounts payable (trade credit)
financing provided by a supplier of inventory to a given company

The amount of trade credit available to a new company depends on the type of business and the supplier's confidence in the firm. For example, wholesale distributors of sunglasses—a very seasonal product line—often provide trade credit to retailers by granting extended payment terms on sales made at the start of a season.

The sunglass retailers, in turn, sell to their customers during the season and make the bulk of their payments to the wholesalers after they have sold and collected the cash for the sunglasses. Thus, the retailer obtains cash from sales before paying the supplier. More often, however, a firm has to pay its suppliers prior to receiving cash from its customers. In fact, this can be a serious problem for many small firms, particularly those that sell to large companies. This issue will be addressed in a discussion of asset management in Chapter 23.

equipment loan
an installment loan from a seller of machinery used by a business

EQUIPMENT LOANS AND LEASES Some small businesses, such as restaurants, use equipment that is purchased on an installment basis through an **equipment loan.** A down payment of 25 to 35 percent is usually required, and the contract period normally runs from three to five years. The equipment manufacturer or supplier typically extends credit on the basis of a conditional sales contract (or mortgage) on the equipment. During the loan period, the equipment cannot serve as collateral for another loan.

Instead of borrowing money from suppliers to purchase equipment, an increasing number of small businesses are beginning to lease equipment, especially computers, photocopiers, and fax machines. Leases typically run for 36 to 60 months and cover 100 percent of the cost of the asset being leased, with a fixed rate of interest included in the lease payments. However, manufacturers of computers and industrial machinery, working hand in hand with banks or financing companies, are generally receptive to tailoring lease packages to the particular needs of customers.

It has been estimated that 80 percent of all firms lease some or all of their business equipment. Three reasons are commonly given for the increasing popularity of leasing: (1) the firm's cash remains free for other purposes, (2) lines of credit (a form of bank loan discussed later in this chapter) can be used for other purposes, and (3) leasing provides a hedge against equipment obsolescence.

While leasing is certainly an option to be considered for financing the acquisition of needed equipment, an entrepreneur should not simply assume that leasing is always the right decision. Only by carefully comparing the interest charged on a loan to the cost of a lease, the tax consequences of leasing versus borrowing, and the significance of the obsolescence factor can an owner make a good choice. Also, the owner must be careful about contracting for so much equipment that it becomes difficult to meet installment or lease payments.

asset-based loan
a line of credit secured by working-capital assets

ASSET-BASED LENDING As its name implies, an **asset-based loan** is a line of credit secured primarily by assets such as receivables, inventory, or both. The lender cushions its risk by advancing only a percentage of the value of a firm's assets—generally, 65 to 85 percent against receivables and up to 55 percent against inventory. However, assets such as equipment (if not leased) and real estate can also be used. Asset-based lending is a viable option for young, growing businesses caught in a cash flow bind.

factoring
obtaining cash by selling accounts receivable to another firm

Of the several categories of asset-based loans, the most frequently used is factoring. **Factoring** is an option that makes cash available to a business before accounts receivable payments are received from customers. Under this option, a factor (often owned by a bank holding company) purchases the accounts receivable, advancing to the business from 70 to 90 percent of the amount of an invoice. The factor, however, has the option of refusing to advance cash on any invoice considered questionable. The factor charges a servicing fee, usually 2 percent of the value of the receivables, and an interest charge on the money advanced prior to collection of the receivables. The interest charge may range from 2 to 3 percent above the prime rate. For example, Lori Bonn Gallagher, founder of Lori Bonn Design, Inc., relied on fac-

http://www.loribonn.com

IN THE TRENCHES ENTREPRENEURSHIP TODAY

HEALTH ANGELS AND STARTUPS

When Alan Solomont sold his Newton, Massachusetts health-care company for $100 million, he gathered some friends, most of them fellow health-care executives, and formed AngelHealthcare to make investments in emerging medical companies.

The group has studied 100 business plans and invested nearly $3 million in six startups. It is too early to know whether any of the new ventures will be winners, but Solomont has seen enough to convince himself of one thing: There is a role for a group like his, even in a world awash with investment dollars. "Venture capitalists won't go in as early as we will," said Solomont. The group invests in early-stage companies that have raised money from friends and family and are looking for money to get to the next stage.

When the group first started, it heard a lot of business plan presentations from aspiring e-health firms, but it passed on all of them. The prices were too high, and the business models didn't make any sense.

To date, they have invested in a blend of medical software, medical financial services, medical devices, and medical ideas that don't fit into any obvious categories. For example, Functional Foods, a nutrition firm, has two products—one for diabetes, the other for weight loss—that will be sold at pharmacies. Bob Jones, chief executive of Functional Foods, says the investors brought more than money to the table. "These are all people who made their money in health care," he said. "It is nice to tap them, not only for their wallets, but for the experience base they have."

Source: Steven Syre and Charles Stein, "There's a Place for Angels of Health," *The Boston Globe,* December 8, 2000, pp. D1–D2.

toring to finance part of the operations of her new firm. By factoring, she received the cash from sales much earlier than if she had waited to collect the amount from the customer. She needed the money to buy new inventory to sell to other customers. However, as her firm became more established, she was able to acquire a bank loan, which was cheaper than factoring receivables.[6]

Commercial Banks

Commercial banks are the primary providers of debt capital to small companies. However, banks tend to limit their lending to providing for the working-capital needs of *established* firms. Quite simply, they want firms with proven track records, and preferably plenty of collateral in the form of hard assets. Bankers are especially reluctant to loan money to finance losses, R&D expenses, marketing campaigns, and other "soft" assets. Such expenditures will need to be financed by equity sources. Nevertheless, it is wise to cultivate a banker earlier rather than later, and well in advance of making a loan request.

TYPES OF BANK LOANS Bankers primarily make business loans in one of three forms: lines of credit, term loans, and mortgages.

Lines of Credit A **line of credit** is an informal agreement or understanding between the borrower and the bank as to the maximum amount of credit the bank will provide the borrower at any one time. Under this type of agreement, the bank has no legal obligation to provide the stated capital. (A similar arrangement that does legally commit the bank is a **revolving credit agreement.**) The entrepreneur should arrange for a line of credit in advance of actual need because banks extend credit only in situations about which they are well informed. Attempts to obtain a loan on a spur-of-the-moment basis are generally ineffective.

line of credit
an informal agreement between a borrower and a bank as to the maximum amount of funds the bank will provide at any one time

revolving credit agreement
a legal commitment by a bank to lend up to a maximum amount

term loan
money loaned for a five- to ten-year term, corresponding to the length of time the investment will bring in profits

Term Loans Under certain circumstances, banks will loan money on a five- to ten-year term. Such **term loans** are generally used to finance equipment with a useful life corresponding to the loan's term. Since the economic benefits of investing in such equipment extend beyond a single year, banks can be persuaded to lend on terms that more closely match the cash flows to be received from the investment. For example, if equipment has a useful life of seven years, it might be possible to repay the money needed to purchase the equipment over, say, five years. It would be a mistake for a firm to borrow money for a short term, such as six months, when the money is to be used to buy equipment that is expected to last for seven years. *Failure to match the loan's payment terms with the expected cash inflows from the investment is a frequent cause of financial problems for small firms.* The importance of synchronizing cash inflows with cash outflows when structuring the terms of a loan cannot be overemphasized.

chattel mortgage
a loan for which items of inventory or other moveable property serve as collateral

real estate mortgage
a long-term loan with real property held as collateral

Mortgages Mortgages, which represent a long-term source of debt capital, are of two types: chattel mortgages and real estate mortgages. A **chattel mortgage** is a loan for which certain items of inventory or other movable property serve as collateral. The borrower retains title to the inventory but cannot sell it without the banker's consent. A **real estate mortgage** is a loan for which real property, such as land or a building, provides the collateral. Typically, these mortgages extend over 25 or 30 years.

UNDERSTANDING A BANKER'S PERSPECTIVE To be effective in acquiring a loan, an entrepreneur needs to understand a banker's perspective about making loans. All bankers have two fundamental concerns when they make a loan: (1) how much income the loan will provide the bank, either in interest income or in other forms of income such as fees, and (2) the likelihood that the borrower will default on the loan. A banker is not interested in taking large amounts of risk and will, therefore, design loan agreements so as to reduce the risk to the bank.

In making a loan decision, a banker looks at the proverbial "five C's of credit": (1) the borrower's *character,* (2) the borrower's *capacity* to repay the loan, (3) the *capital* being invested in the venture by the borrower, (4) the *conditions* of the industry and economy, and (5) the *collateral* available to secure the loan.

It is imperative that the borrower's character be above reproach. A bad credit record or any indication of unethical behavior will make getting a loan extremely difficult. The borrower's capacity is measured by the banker's confidence in the firm's ability to generate the cash flows necessary to repay the loan. In the banker's mind, the firm's cash flows represent the primary source for repaying the loan. To evaluate capital, the banker looks at the equity investment of the owners in the business—the more equity, the better. Although they are completely outside the control of the entrepreneur, the current economic conditions may be a big factor in the receptivity of bankers to loan requests. In the late 1980s and early 1990s, many banks essentially quit making loans to small businesses, as a result of a financial crisis that had developed among banks and savings and loan institutions. Federal regulators discouraged loans to the point that the top priority of many banks was to avoid making a bad loan. Numerous small companies with unblemished records had their loans canceled, through no fault of their own. Finally, collateral is of key importance to bankers as a secondary source for repaying the loan in case the firm's cash flows are insufficient.

Obtaining a bank loan requires cultivation of a banker and personal selling. Although a banker's review of a loan request certainly includes analysis of economic and financial considerations, this analysis is best complemented by a personal relationship between banker and entrepreneur. This is not to say that a banker would

allow personal feelings to override the facts provided by a careful loan analysis. But, after all, a banker's decision as to whether to make a loan is driven in part by the banker's confidence in the entrepreneur as a person and a professional. Intuition and subjective opinion based on past experience often play a role here.

When seeking a loan, an entrepreneur will be required to provide certain information in support of the loan request. Failure to provide such information in an effective manner will almost certainly result in rejection by the banker. Thus, the goal is not merely to present the needed information, but to make an *effective* presentation. Providing inaccurate information or not being able to justify assumptions made in forecasting financial results is sure to make the banker question the entrepreneur's business acumen. An entrepreneur is likely to have to answer the following key questions before a loan will be made:

- What are the strengths and qualities of the management team?
- How has the firm performed financially?
- How much money is needed?
- What is the venture going to do with the money?
- When is the money needed?
- When and how will the money be paid back?
- Does the borrower have qualified support people, such as a good public accountant and attorney?

A well-prepared written presentation—something like a shortened version of a business plan—is helpful, if not necessary. Capturing the firm's history and future in writing suggests that the entrepreneur has given thought to where the firm has been and is going. As part of this presentation, a banker expects a prospective borrower to provide the following detailed financial information:

- Three years of the firm's historical financial statements, if available, including balance sheets, income statements, and cash flow statements
- The firm's pro forma financial statements (balance sheets, income statements, and cash flow statements), in which the timing and amounts of the debt repayment are included as part of the forecasts
- Personal financial statements, showing the borrower's personal net worth (net worth = assets − debt) and estimated annual income

Note that a banker will not make a loan without knowing the personal financial strength of the borrower. After all, in the world of small business, the owner *is* the business.

SELECTING A BANKER The wide variety of services provided by banks makes choosing a bank a critical decision. For a typical small firm, the provision of checking-account facilities and the extension of short-term (and possibly long-term) loans are the two most important services of a bank. Normally, loans are negotiated with the same bank in which the firm maintains its checking account. In addition, the firm may use the bank's safety deposit vault or its services in collecting notes or securing credit information. An experienced banker can also provide management advice, particularly in financial matters, to a new entrepreneur.

The location factor limits the range of possible choices of banks. For convenience in making deposits and conferring about loans and other matters, a bank should be located in the same general vicinity as the firm. All banks are interested

in their home communities and, therefore, tend to be sympathetic to the needs of local business firms. Except in very small communities, two or more local banks are usually available, thus permitting some freedom of choice.

Banks' lending policies are not uniform. Some bankers are extremely conservative, while others are more willing to accept some risks. If a small firm's loan application is neither obviously strong nor patently weak, its prospects for approval depend heavily on the bank's approach to small business accounts. Differences in willingness to lend have been clearly established by research studies, as well as by the practical experience of many business borrowers.

NEGOTIATING THE LOAN In negotiating a bank loan, the owner must consider the terms that will accompany the loan. Four terms are particularly important: (1) the interest rate, (2) the loan maturity date, (3) the repayment schedule, and (4) the loan covenants.

prime rate
the interest rate charged by a commercial bank on loans to its most creditworthy customers

LIBOR (London InterBank Offered Rate)
the interest rate charged by London banks on loans to other London banks

Interest Rate The interest rate charged by banks is usually stated in terms of either the prime rate or the LIBOR. The **prime rate** is the rate of interest charged by banks on loans to their most creditworthy customers. The **LIBOR (London InterBank Offered Rate)** is the interest rate that London-based banks charge other banks in London, which is considerably lower than the prime rate. This rate is published each day in *The Wall Street Journal.*

If a banker quotes a rate of "prime plus three" and the prime rate is 8 percent, the interest rate for the loan will be 11 percent. If, alternatively, the bank is willing to loan at "LIBOR plus four" when the LIBOR is at 6 percent, then the loan rate will be 10 percent. Typically, the interest will be less if the loan rate is tied to the LIBOR than if it is based on the prime rate. The use of the LIBOR as a base rate for determining the interest rate for a business loan developed in the late 1990s, as banks began competing more aggressively for loans.

The interest rate can be a floating rate that varies over the loan's life—that is, as the prime rate or LIBOR changes, the interest rate on the loan changes—or it can be fixed for the duration of the loan. Although a small firm should always seek a competitive interest rate, concern about the interest rate should not override consideration of the loan's maturity date, its repayment schedule, and any loan covenants.

Loan Maturity Date As already noted, a loan's term should coincide with the use of the money—short-term needs require short-term financing, while long-term needs demand long-term financing. For example, since a line of credit is intended only to help a firm with its short-term needs, it is generally limited to one year. Some banks require that a firm "clean up" a line of credit one month each year. Because such a loan can be outstanding for only 11 months, the borrower can use the money to finance seasonal needs but cannot use it to provide permanent increases in working capital, such as accounts receivable and inventories.

Repayment Schedule With a term loan, the schedule for repayment is generally arranged in one of two ways. The loan can be repaid in (1) *equal* monthly or annual payments that cover both interest on the remaining balance and payment on the principal or (2) *decreasing* monthly or annual payments that cover both equal payments on the principal and interest on the remaining balance.

For example, assume that a firm is negotiating a $250,000 term loan, at an interest rate of 10 percent, to be repaid in five equal annual payments. Entering into a financial calculator (or a computer spreadsheet) the values

PV = −250,000 (present value)
N = 5 (number of payments)
I/YR = 10 (interest rate per year)
FV = 0 (future value in 5 years)

we find that the equal annual payment (the PMT key on the calculator) is $65,949.37.

If, on the other hand, we calculate payments so that each yearly payment represents repayment of one-fifth of the principal plus the amount of interest owed on the remaining principal, the annual payments will be different each year. The annual payments are calculated as follows:

End of Year	Loan Balance[a]	Payment on Principal[b]	Interest Payment[c]	Total Annual Payment[d]
	$250,000			
1	200,000	$50,000	$25,000	$75,000
2	150,000	50,000	20,000	70,000
3	100,000	50,000	15,000	65,000
4	50,000	50,000	10,000	60,000
5	0	50,000	5,000	55,000

[a]Loan balance = prior loan balance − $50,000 annual payment on principal
[b]Payment on principal = $250,000 ÷ 5 years
[c]Interest payment = 10% × remaining loan balance as of the beginning of the year (end of prior year)
[d]Total annual payment = payment on principal + interest payment

Now the payment in the first year is $75,000, consisting of a $50,000 payment on principal ($250,000 ÷ 5 years) and a $25,000 interest payment (10% × $250,000). The amount of the annual payment declines each year as the principal balance is paid down, decreasing interest expense. Note that in the early years the total annual payments under this repayment schedule are higher than the equal annual payments under the previous schedule ($65,949), but in later years they are lower.

The important thing for an entrepreneur is to know which repayment plan the banker expects to use. When Mike Calvert purchased a Toyota dealership in Houston, Texas, he found it necessary to borrow most of the purchase price from a bank. Until he arrived at the bank to sign the note, he thought that all the loan terms had been finalized. He was surprised to see that the monthly payments on the note were significantly more than he had expected. The reason: Calvert had calculated the loan payment by assuming equal monthly payments of about $51,000 per month. The bank, on the other hand, was requiring repayment based on equal principal payments plus interest. As a consequence, monthly payments at the outset were to be $66,000, or $15,000 more than Calvert had expected. At the time, he was shocked and somewhat worried about having to meet such a large monthly payment. Today, however, Calvert is thankful that he accepted the bank's repayment schedule, because he appreciates the current lower payments.

Loan Covenants In addition to setting the interest rate and specifying when and how the loan is to be repaid, a bank normally imposes other restrictions on the borrower. **Loan covenants** restrict borrowers from certain activities that might lessen their ability to repay the loan. Following are some types of loan covenants a borrower might encounter:

loan covenants
bank-imposed restrictions on a borrower that enhance the chances of timely repayment

1. A bank will usually require that the business provide financial statements on a monthly basis or, at the very least, quarterly.

2. As a way to restrict a firm's management from siphoning cash out of the business, the bank may limit managers' salaries. It also may not allow any personal loans from the business to the owners.
3. A bank may put limits on various financial ratios to make certain that a firm can handle its loan payments. For example, to ensure sufficient liquidity, the bank may require that the firm's current assets be at least twice its current liabilities (that is, current assets ÷ current liabilities must be equal to or greater than 2). Or the bank might limit the amount of debt the firm can borrow in the future, as measured by the ratio of total debt to the firm's total assets (total debt ÷ total assets).[7]
4. The borrower will normally be required to personally guarantee the firm's loan. A banker wants the right to look at both the firm's assets and the owner's personal assets before making a loan. If a business is structured as a corporation, the owner and the corporation are separate legal entities and the owner can escape personal liability for the firm's debts—that is, the owner has **limited liability.** However, most banks are not willing to lend money to any small business without the owner's personal guarantee as well.

limited liability
the restriction of an owner's legal financial responsibilities to the amount invested in the business

When Bill Bailey, owner of Cherokee Communications, a pay-phone company located in Jacksonville, Texas, borrowed money, the loan was made on certain conditions—conditions that were intended to protect the banker. If Cherokee violated these loan covenants, the loan would become due immediately—or Bailey would have to get the banker's blessing to continue operations without repaying the loan at the time. Some of the loan covenants were as follows:[8]

- Bailey, as the owner, was required to personally guarantee the loan.
- The firm had to provide monthly financial statements to the bank within 30 days of the month's end.
- There were to be no dividend payments to the owners.
- Bailey could not change the fundamental nature of the business.
- Without prior agreement, there could be no additional liens on equipment by other lenders.
- Debt could not exceed a certain amount, nor could it be greater than a certain percentage of the firm's total assets.
- Without prior approval, no assets could be sold and no acquisitions or mergers with other firms could take place.
- The proceeds of the loan could not be used for any other purpose than that designated by the bank.
- There was a limit on the amount of capital expenditures the firm could make.
- Executive compensation could not exceed a certain amount.
- The firm's net worth could not fall below a certain amount.

Regarding loan covenants, Jill Andresky Fraser, finance editor for *Inc.* magazine, offers this advice:[9]

1. Ask to see a sample list of the covenants before the closing date so that you can avoid a situation in which desperation for funds—or a lack of careful analysis—persuades you to simply sign anything. Make certain that you can live with the bank's terms about the consequences of being out of compliance.
2. To see if you could have complied with all loan covenants, especially key ratios, if your loan had been in place during the most recent one-, two-, and three-year periods, analyze your company's past performance over these periods.

IN THE TRENCHES ENTREPRENEURSHIP TODAY

FINANCING IN AN UNFRIENDLY ENVIRONMENT

In the latter part of 2000, financing startups became increasingly difficult. The huge declines in the values of many high-tech firms, as well as the demise of many Internet companies, meant that some traditional sources of financing were no longer available.

Parul Thakore, 25, launched a high-tech startup in October 2001—the same month that the Nasdaq dropped more than 15 percent and 35 dot.com companies called it quits. Thakore, a recent business school graduate, was the only MBA in her class brave enough to immediately start a company in the softening economy. Friends and family thought she was slightly nuts.

Thakore had no illusions about making millions. She and her co-founder took $250,000 from their savings to start CypherWire, a wireless consulting and development firm. She knew money would be hard to come by, so she located her company in Buffalo, New York instead of a more expensive city. A slate of recent closures in Buffalo enabled her to lease a sparsely furnished office at a bargain price. It also allowed her to quickly hire five employees. "We're learning from others' lessons," Thakore says.

She has no immediate plans to expand and is keeping costs low. Although $250,000 in seed money is paltry compared with the millions of dollars many startups received from venture capitalists in recent years, experts say Thakore is lucky to have had other sources of capital.

Source: Michelle Kesler, "Start-Ups Brave Hostile Environment," *USA Today,* May 22, 2001, p. 3B.

http://www.cypherwire.com

3. If results indicate possible future problems, schedule a visit with your banker and suggest more realistic covenants.

Government-Sponsored Programs and Agencies

Several government programs provide financing to small businesses. Over the past decade, federal and state governments have allocated increasing amounts of money to financing new businesses. Local governments have likewise increased their involvement in providing financial support to startups in their areas. Though funds are available, they are not always easy to acquire. Time and patience on the part of the entrepreneur are required. Let's take a look at some of the more familiar government loan programs.

FEDERAL ASSISTANCE The federal government has a long history of helping new businesses get started, primarily through the programs and agencies of the Small Business Administration.

Small Business Administration (SBA) Loans There are two basic types of Small Business Administration (SBA) loans: guaranty loans and direct loans. **Guaranty loans** are made by private lenders, usually commercial banks, and may be for as much as $750,000. For loans not exceeding $155,000, the SBA guarantees 90 percent. For loans exceeding $155,000, the guaranty percentage is 85 percent. To obtain a guaranty loan, a small business must submit a loan application to a lender—such as a bank. After an initial review, the lender forwards the application to the SBA. Once the loan has been approved by the SBA, the lender disburses the funds. A **direct loan** is available only if a small business has been unable to obtain a guaranty loan. This type of loan is usually limited to a maximum of $150,000.

guaranty loan
money provided by a private lender, with the Small Business Administration guaranteeing repayment

direct loan
money provided directly by the Small Business Administration

http://www.sba.gov/financing

small business investment companies (SBICs)
privately owned banks, regulated by the Small Business Administration, that supply capital to small businesses

Small Business Investment Companies (SBICs) In 1958, Congress passed the Small Business Investment Act. This act established privately owned capital banks, or **small business investment companies (SBICs),** whose purpose is to provide long-term loans and/or equity capital to small businesses. SBICs are licensed and regulated by the SBA. They may obtain a substantial part of their capital from the SBA at attractive rates of interest.

Although SBICs may either lend funds or supply equity funds, the Small Business Investment Act places a strong emphasis on equity financing. An SBIC that provides equity financing does so either by directly purchasing a small firm's stock or, more commonly, by purchasing a firm's debt that may be converted into stock at the option of the SBIC.

Small Business Innovative Research (SBIR) program
a government program that helps finance companies that plan to transform laboratory research into marketable products

Small Business Innovative Research (SBIR) Program In 1993, The U.S. Congress created the **Small Business Innovative Research (SBIR) program** to help finance small firms that plan to transform laboratory research into marketable products. Eligibility for the program is based less on the potential profitability of a venture than on the likelihood that the firm will provide a product of interest to a particular federal agency.

STATE AND LOCAL GOVERNMENT ASSISTANCE State and local governments are becoming increasingly active in financing new businesses. The nature of the financing varies, but each program is generally geared to augment other sources of funding.

California was one of the first states to create a business and industrial development corporation to lend money to new businesses. Minnesota provided $50 million to create Minnesota Technology, a source of financing for new technology companies located in the state. Massachusetts, Pennsylvania, and Maryland are among the states that have designated funding for local startups. Maryland, in cooperation with three public-employee pension funds (mutual funds that invest the retirement savings of state employees), has committed money to a venture trust to finance smaller companies.

http://www.ci.des-moines.ia.us

Some large cities also provide funds for new business ventures. For example, Des Moines, Iowa has established a Golden Circle Loan Guarantee Fund to guarantee bank loans of up to $250,000 to small companies.

Other Sources of Financing

The sources of financing that have been described thus far represent the primary avenues for obtaining money for small firms. The remaining sources are generally of less importance but should not be ignored by an entrepreneur in search of financing.

venture capitalist
an investor or investment group that commits money to new business ventures

VENTURE CAPITAL FIRMS Technically speaking, anyone investing in a new business venture is a **venture capitalist.** However, the term *venture capitalist* usually refers to a corporation or partnership that operates as an investment group. Most often, the investment takes the form of convertible debt or convertible preferred stock. In this way, venture capitalists ensure themselves senior claim over the owners and other equity investors in the event the firm is liquidated, but they can also convert to stock and participate in the increased value of the business if it is successful. These investors generally try to limit the length of their investment to between five and seven years, though it is frequently closer to ten years before they are able to cash out.

At the beginning of the 1990s, U.S. venture capitalists were investing less than $10 billion annually. By 2000, however, a record $103 billion had been invested, far exceeding the prior record in 1999 of $59 billion. As 2001 unfolded, it appeared that the investment level would be closer to the 1999 figure.

Most venture capitalists focus on investments in high-tech firms, particularly those located in areas like Silicon Valley and Route 128 in Boston. Investments by type of industry are displayed in Table 13-1, which clearly shows that a large number of the investments in 2000 were in Internet companies. This trend continued into 2001, even though the news regularly reported the demise of Internet firms. Obviously, the high values assigned to Internet companies had fallen sharply, but the number and dollar amount of total investments were not falling precipitously, as many had expected. Jesse Reyes, vice president of Venture Economics, observed:

While it is true that VCs are no longer backing every Internet idea out there, they are continuing to invest in the future the Internet promises. However, they are doing this through selective investments rather than playing the speculative investment game that was so prevalent in the past couple of years. . . . VCs continue to invest in technology and other high-growth potential industries, albeit at a slower pace.[10]

Although venture capital as a source of financing receives significant coverage in the business media, few small companies ever receive this kind of funding. Fewer than 1 percent of the business plans received by any venture capitalist are eventually funded—not exactly an encouraging statistic. Failure to receive funding from a venture capitalist, however, does not indicate that the business plan is not a good one. Often, the venture is simply not a good fit for the investor. So before trying to compete for venture capital financing, an entrepreneur should assess whether the firm and the management team provide a good fit for that venture capitalist.

COMMUNITY-BASED FINANCIAL INSTITUTIONS Community-based financial institutions are lenders that serve low-income communities and receive funds from federal, state, and private sources. They are increasingly becoming a source of financing for small companies that otherwise would have little or no access to startup funding. Typically, community-based lenders provide capital to businesses that don't have the potential for spectacular growth demanded by venture capitalists, but that do have the potential to make modest profits, serve the community, and create jobs. An example of a community-based financial institution is the Delaware Valley Reinvestment Fund, which provides financing for small companies in Philadelphia's inner-city area.

community-based financial institution
a lender that provides financing to small businesses in low-income communities for the purpose of encouraging economic development

http://www.efgp.org

TABLE 13-1

Investments of Venture Capitalists by Industry

Industry	No. of Companies	Average Investment per Company (in millions of dollars)	Total Invested (in millions of dollars)	Percentage of Total
Internet Specific[a]	394	$10.39	$4,093.50	34.9%
Computer Software & Services	217	10.12	2,196.86	18.7
Communications & Media	122	14.47	1,765.50	15.1
Semiconductors/Electronics	76	18.01	1,368.79	11.7
Medical/Health	84	10.06	845.21	7.2
Biotechnology	53	9.87	523.25	4.5
Other Products	54	6.92	373.85	3.2
Computer Hardware	34	9.67	328.93	2.8
Industrial/Energy	17	7.8	132.61	1.1
Consumer Related	21	4.74	99.60	0.9

[a]Internet Specific includes only companies that would not exist without the Internet and do not fit into any other industry sector category.

Source: Venture Economics/National Venture Capital Association, "Venture Capital Investment Activity Returns to 1999 Levels," May 2, 2001 news release.

LARGE CORPORATIONS Large corporations on occasion make funds available for investment in smaller firms when it is in their self-interest to maintain a close relationship with such a firm. Larger firms are now becoming even more involved in providing financing and technical assistance to smaller businesses. For one thing, as larger corporations have downsized their operations, it has become more important to their bottom line that their suppliers—frequently smaller firms—stay healthy.

http://www.fizzion.com

An example of a large corporation investing in smaller firms is Coca-Cola, which in early 2001 invested $250,000 in eight startups. The purpose of the investments was to develop technologies that would benefit operations, such as bottling and distribution. Coca-Cola also hopes to profit when the companies go public. The program—a wholly owned subsidiary called Fizzion—is part of a push to make Coca-Cola more innovative. By involving employees in startups, the company can give managers "a real sense for what it's like to move against deadlines of time and money," says Fizzion CEO Chris Lowe. Although large companies also face those issues, they're "not of the same character or ilk" as in a startup, Lowe says.[11]

STOCK SALES Another way to obtain capital is by selling stock to outside individual investors through either private placement or public sale. Finding outside stockholders can be difficult when a new firm is not known and has no ready market for its securities, however. In most cases, a business must have a history of profitability before its stock can be sold successfully.

Whether it is best to raise outside equity financing depends on the firm's long-range prospects. If there is opportunity for substantial expansion on a continuing basis and if other sources are inadequate, the owner may logically decide to bring in other owners. Owning part of a larger business may be more profitable than owning all of a smaller business.

private placement
the sale of a firm's capital stock to selected individuals

Private Placement One way to sell common stock is through **private placement,** in which the firm's stock is sold to selected individuals—usually the firm's employees, the owner's acquaintances, members of the local community, customers, and suppliers. When a stock sale is restricted to private placement, an entrepreneur can avoid many requirements of the securities laws.

initial public offering (IPO)
the issuance of stock that is to be traded in public financial markets

http://www.sec.gov

Public Sale When small firms—typically, *larger* small firms—make their stock available to the general public, this is called going public, or making an **initial public offering (IPO).** The reason often cited for a public sale is the need for additional working capital.

In undertaking a public sale of its stock, a small firm subjects itself to greater governmental regulation. Not only are there state regulations pertaining to the public sale of securities, but the federal Securities and Exchange Commission (SEC) also oversees such offerings. And this oversight does not end when the stock has been issued. The firm is required to report its financial results quarterly in 10Q reports and annually in 10K reports. The SEC carefully scrutinizes these reports before they can be made available to the public. At times, SEC requirements can be very burdensome.

Common stock may also be sold to underwriters, which guarantee the sale of securities. Compensation and fees paid to underwriters typically make the sale of securities in this manner expensive. Fees may range from 10 to 30 percent of the sale, with 18 to 25 percent being typical. Options and other fees may cause the actual costs to run even higher. The reason for the high costs is, of course, the elements of uncertainty and risk associated with public offerings of the stock of small, relatively unknown firms.

Looking Back

1 Describe how the nature of a firm affects it financing sources.

- There are four basic factors that determine *how* a firm is financed: (1) the firm's economic potential, (2) the maturity of the company, (3) the nature of the firm's assets, and (4) the personal preference of the owners as they consider the tradeoffs between debt and equity.
- An entrepreneurial firm that has high growth potential has many more possible sources of financing than does a firm that provides a good lifestyle for the owner but nothing in the way of attractive returns to investors.
- The age and maturity of a company has a direct bearing on the types of financing that are available.
- The types of assets held by the business really matter when it comes to financing.

2 Evaluate the choice between debt financing and equity financing.

- Choosing between debt and equity financing involves tradeoffs with regard to potential profitability, financial risk, and voting control.
- Borrowing money rather than issuing common stock (owners' equity) creates the potential for higher rates of return to the owners and allows the owners to retain voting control of the company, but it also exposes the owners to greater financial risk.
- Issuing common stock rather than borrowing money results in lower potential rates of return to the owners and the loss of some voting control, but it does reduce their financial risk.

3 Describe various sources of financing available to small firms.

- Three sources of early financing for an entrepreneur are personal savings, friends and relatives, and other individual investors.
- Business suppliers, a major source of financing for the small firm, can offer trade credit (accounts payable) and equipment loans and leases.
- Asset-based lending is financing secured by working-capital assets, such as accounts receivable and inventory.
- Commercial banks are the primary providers of debt financing to small companies, offering lines of credit, term loans, and mortgages.
- Government-sponsored programs and agencies at the federal, state, and local levels provide financing to small businesses.
- Community-based financial institutions, large corporations, venture capitalists, and stock sales represent other sources of financing for the small firm.

Key Terms

informal venture capital, p. 329
accounts payable (trade credit), p. 331
equipment loan, p. 332
asset-based loan, p. 332
factoring, p. 332
line of credit, p. 333
revolving credit agreement, p. 333
term loan, p. 334
chattel mortgage, p. 334
real estate mortgage, p. 334
prime rate, p. 336
LIBOR (London InterBank Offered Rate), p. 336
loan covenants, p. 337
limited liability, p. 338
guaranty loan, p. 339
direct loan, p. 339
small business investment companies (SBICs), p. 340
Small Business Innovative Research (SBIR) program, p. 340
venture capitalist, p. 340
community-based financial institution, p. 341
private placement, p. 342
initial public offering (IPO), p. 342

Discussion Questions

1. How does the nature of a business affect its sources of financing?
2. Explain the three tradeoffs that guide the choice between debt financing and equity financing.
3. Assume that you are starting a business for the first time. What do you believe are the greatest personal obstacles to obtaining funds for the new venture? Why?

4. If you were starting a new business, where would you start looking for capital?
5. Explain how trade credit and equipment loans can provide initial capital funding.
6. a. Describe the different types of loans made by a commercial bank.
   b. What does a banker need to know in order to decide whether to make a loan?
7. a. What are the usual forms of venture capital investments?
   b. Why is venture capital an inappropriate type of financing for most small firms?
8. In what ways does the federal government help with initial financing for small businesses?
9. How is the Internet being used to raise capital?
10. What advice would you give an entrepreneur who is trying to finance a startup?

YOU MAKE THE CALL

SITUATION 1

David Bernstein needs help financing his Lodi, New Jersey–based Access Direct Inc., a six-year-old, $3.5 million company. "We're ready to get to the next level," says Bernstein. "But we're not sure which way to go." Access Direct spruces up and then sells used computer equipment for corporations; it is looking for up to $2 million in order to expand. "Venture capitalists, individual investors, or banks," says Bernstein, who owns the company with four partners, "we've thought about them all."

Question 1 What is your impression of Bernstein's perspective on raising capital to "get to the next level"?

Question 2 What advice would you offer Bernstein as to both appropriate and inappropriate sources of financing in his situation?

SITUATION 2

Carter Dalton is well on his way to starting a new venture—Max, Inc. He has projected a need for $350,000 in initial capital. He plans to invest $150,000 himself and either borrow the additional $200,000 or find a partner who will buy stock in the company. If Dalton borrows the money, the interest rate will be 12 percent. If, on the other hand, another equity investor is found, he expects to have to give up 60 percent of the company's stock. Stegemoller has forecasted earnings of about 18 percent in operating income on the firm's total assets.

Question 1 Compare the two financing options in terms of projected return on the owner's equity investment. Ignore any effect from income taxes.

Question 2 What if Dalton is wrong and the company earns only 5 percent in operating income on total assets?

Question 3 What must Dalton consider in choosing a source of financing?

SITUATION 3

James Ridings's firm, Craftmade International, Inc., sells ceiling fans. Originally, Ridings was a sales representative for a company that sold plumbing supplies. When the company added ceiling fans to its line, Ridings developed a number of customers who bought the fans. Some time later, when the firm eliminated the ceiling fans, Ridings had customers and nothing to sell them. Consequently, he became partners with James Ivins, a sales representative for a firm that imported ceiling fans. They scraped together $30,000 and bought 800 fans from Taiwan, which were quickly sold. Encouraged, Ridings raised $45,000 to buy more fans. Again, they sold quickly. By the end of the first year, Ridings and Ivins had put together a sales force of 15 people and were selling 3,000 fans per month. By the second year, the two men had started designing their own high-quality and high-profit-margin fans. Sales had grown to $10 million, and the firm was profitable. However, while the firm's sales were increasing at 50 percent per year, a problem developed: The firm ran into cash problems. At one critical point, Ridings had to persuade a supplier to accept stock in lieu of payment on a $224,000 order. Another time, Ridings and Ivins had to approach 16 bankers within a matter of a few days before finding someone who would loan them $100,000 to pay their bills.

Question 1 Craftmade International, Inc. is a successful firm when it comes to growing, but what are its owners overlooking?

Question 2 What steps would you suggest to Ridings and Ivins to solve their problems?

EXPERIENTIAL EXERCISES

1. Interview a local small business owner to determine how funds were obtained to start the business. Be sure you phrase questions so that they are not overly personal, and do not ask for specific dollar amounts. Write a brief report on your findings.
2. Interview a local banker about lending policies for small business loans. Ask the banker to comment on the importance of a business plan to the bank's decision to loan money to a small business. Write a brief report on your findings.

3. Review recent issues of *Entrepreneur* or *Inc.* magazine, and report to the class on the financing arrangements of firms featured in these magazines.
4. Interview a stockbroker or investment analyst on his or her views regarding the sale of common stock by a small business. Write a brief report on your findings.

EXPLORING THE WEB

1. Access the Small Business Administration site at **http://www.sba.gov**, and then follow the link to Financing Your Business.
   a. Read about the 7A Loan Guarantee. Who actually provides the financing? What does the SBA do? What types of businesses are not eligible for financing through the SBA? How much money can be borrowed under this program? What is the term length of a loan for working capital? for real estate purchases?
   b. Read about the SBA LowDoc. What are the main differences between this loan and the 7A?
   c. Follow the link to CDC 504 Loans. What items are financed under this program?
   d. Access the information about Microloans. What are the maximum amount and term (number of years) for this type of loan?
2. Access the Web site of a local bank.
   a. What banking services are offered to businesses?
   b. What types of commercial loans are offered? Search specifically for lines of credit.
   c. List the name and telephone number of a commercial loan officer.
   d. Compare the resources of two very large banks, such as Wells Fargo and Bank of America. What financial resources are available for small businesses?

CASE 13

CALVERT TOYOTA (p. 674)

This case presents possible financing arrangements for a new venture.

Alternative Cases for Chapter 13:

Case 8, "Robinson Associates, Inc.," p. 658
Case 22, "Artho, Inc.," p. 697

The Business Plan

LAYING THE FOUNDATION

As part of laying the foundation for your own business plan, respond to the following questions regarding the financing of your venture:

1. What is the total financing required to start up the business?
2. How much money do you plan to invest in the venture? What is the source of this money?
3. Will you need financing beyond what you personally plan to invest?
4. If additional financing is needed for the startup, how will you raise it? How will the financing be structured—debt or equity? What will the terms be for the investors?
5. Based on your pro forma financial statements, will there be a need for future financing within the first five years of the firm's life? If so, where will it come from?
6. How and when will you arrange for investors to cash out of their investment?

chapter 14

Exit Strategies

In the Spotlight

IRIS

Exiting, or *harvesting*, a company is not as easy as you might think. Even if you can get a lot of money for the business, you have to consider many other factors, not the least of which is how your self-identity will change.

When four friends—Maggie Etheridge, Eddie Ureno, Dan Woolley, and Greg Robertson—started IRIS to provide a computerized multiple listing service for realtors, they agreed on one thing: They wanted to sell the company, and the sooner the better. Eight years, 50 employees, and four attempts later, they finally succeeded. But even so, the co-owners suffered some post-sale blues as they considered their futures together—and apart. After the sale, they continued to work for the company, but things were certainly not the same.

Greg had a hard time explaining his initial reticence about selling the company, except to say, "I like being Greg Robertson, software-company owner." After a three-year contract with the buying firm was to end, he planned on starting another company in a different industry. Dan was also looking for another business to start. Maggie thought she would go into business with her mother, probably in real estate. In contrast, Eddie planned to

sail off into the sunset—literally. He had his eye on a 42-foot cruiser. "I'm serious about sailing, and I think I could do it for a long time," he says. ◆

Source: Adapted from Susan Greco, "The Long Good-bye," *Inc. 500*, Vol. 22, No. 15 (October 17, 2000), pp. 88–94.

Looking Ahead

After studying this chapter, you should be able to

1. *Explain the importance of having an exit strategy.*
2. *Describe the options available for exiting.*
3. *Explain how to value a firm being sold and how to decide on the method of payment.*
4. *Provide advice on developing an effective exit strategy.*

In the previous chapters, we have talked about recognizing business opportunities and developing strategies for capturing these opportunities. Such activities represent the cornerstone for everything a company does. But that's not the end of the story. Experience suggests that an entrepreneur developing a company strategy should think about more than just starting (founding or acquiring) and growing a business; the entrepreneurial process is not complete until the owners and any other investors have exited the venture and captured much of the value created by the business. This final, but extremely important, phase can be enhanced through an effective exit strategy.

The Importance of the Exit

1 *Explain the importance of having an exit strategy.*

exiting (harvesting) the process used by entrepreneurs and investors to reap the value of a business when they get out of it

Exiting—or **harvesting**, as it frequently called—is the method entrepreneurs and investors use to get out of a business and, ideally, reap the value of their investment in the firm. Many entrepreneurs successfully grow their businesses but fail to develop effective exit strategies. As a result, they are unable to capture the full value of the business that they have worked so hard to create.

During the past decade, an unprecedented number of opportunities have occurred for entrepreneurs to sell their firms. In the last few years, investors have been actively buying groups of firms in the same industry and then consolidating them into a single, larger company. According to a national survey conducted by Arthur Andersen and Mass Mutual, 48 percent of family-owned companies will change hands between 1997 and 2003.[1] Many entrepreneurs who founded companies in the 1950s and 1960s are—or soon will be—engaged in an exit strategy. They will be transferring ownership either to the next generation of family members or to other individuals and investors who have an interest in the business. Most entrepreneurs do not like to think about the exit, even though few events in the life of an entrepreneur, and of the firm itself, are more significant. Consequently, the decision to exit is frequently the result of an unexpected event, possibly a crisis, rather than a well-conceived strategy.

An entrepreneur needs to understand that exiting, or harvesting, encompasses more than merely selling and leaving a business; it involves capturing value (cash flows), reducing risk, and creating future options. In addition, for the entrepreneur, there are personal and nonfinancial considerations. An owner may receive a lot of money for the firm but still be disappointed with the decision to exit the business if he or she is not prepared for a change in lifestyle. Thus, carefully designing an

ENTREPRENEURSHIP TODAY

IN THE TRENCHES

WHAT'S YOUR EXIT STRATEGY?

The need to develop an exit, or harvest, strategy is not a notion that is readily accepted by most entrepreneurs. The initial reaction of Jennifer Lawton, cofounder and CEO of Net Daemons Associates, a computer-networking and consulting firm, illustrates the mind-set of many entrepreneurs on the subject of exiting. Fortunately, she finally came to see the importance of anticipating the exit.

When I became an entrepreneur, I was naive about exit strategies. "Exit strategy?" I said the first time the question was asked of me. "You want to know what my exit strategy is?" I couldn't understand why, in the frenzy of creating a business, I had to think about an exit. Now, five years later, I know that an exit strategy is far less an expectation of an exit and much more a begging of the critical question, How high is your highest bar?

While still objecting to the phrase itself, I now believe that having an exit strategy is vital to the success of both a company and its leader. I spent my first two years in business not knowing that I needed one, the next year overcoming my objections to the images the phrase conjured up, and the fourth year dedicating my time to the creation, development, and refinement of an exit strategy.

I began to consider the exit strategy question as an opportunity to educate myself about what was truly being asked. I began to see my exit strategy less as a termination and more as a logical part of the goals I had set for both my company

intentional exit strategy is as essential to an entrepreneur's personal success as it is to his or her financial success.

The exit is vitally important to a firm's investors as well. Investors who provide high-risk capital—particularly venture capitalists—generally insist on a well-thought-out exit strategy. Investors realize that it is easy to put money into a business, but difficult to get it out. As a result, a firm's appeal to investors is driven by the availability of exit options. If investors are not convinced that opportunities will exist for exiting the investment, there will be no investment.

METHODS OF EXITING A BUSINESS

2 *Describe the options available for exiting.*

The four basic ways to exit an investment in a privately owned company are (1) selling the firm, (2) releasing the firm's cash flows to its owners, (3) offering stock to the public through an initial public offering (IPO), and (4) issuing a private placement of the stock. These options are shown graphically in Figure 14-1.

Selling the Firm

As in any exit strategy, the financial issues arising from the sale of a firm include how to value the firm and how to structure the sale. Most frequently, an entrepreneur's motivation for selling a company relates to estate planning and the opportunity to diversify her or his portfolio of investments.

Sale transactions can, for all practical purposes, be reduced to three types, based on the motives of the buyers: strategic acquisitions, financial acquisitions, and employee acquisitions. A strategic buyer is interested in synergies that can be gained from the acquisition, a financial buyer is more often interested in the firm as a stand-alone business, and an employee buyer is primarily interested in preserving employment. Let's consider each type of transaction in more detail.

and myself. While I may, at some point in my tenure as CEO, actually "exit," I may also pursue an acquisition, take the company public, merge with another concern, methodically increase sales to the next level, or shoot for rapid 200% growth.

In achieving any of these goals, I will have, in fact, "exited." My company will have moved from one phase to the next, its exit from one level becoming its entrance to the next. In other words, there isn't much to fear about the concept, because an exit strategy can—and must—change, as the business and its goals change. Your exit strategy is, therefore, no more frightening than the goal you're working toward, the highest you'll raise your bar.

Conversely, there is plenty to fear about continuing to work in entrepreneurial nirvana with no consideration of its end or change: The reality is that unless you define that end or change, your business may change in a way that wasn't in your plan.

Write your exit strategy down. Have a road map with a start and a finish. Know how to answer the "What is your exit strategy?" question, but also know that you're really answering the "What are your vision and goal?" question. And realize that, through identifying your exit strategy, you have a chance to preserve and control your own entrepreneurial nirvana.

Source: Jennifer Lawton, "Exit Strategies: What's Yours?," http://www.entreworld.org, September 1, 1997.

STRATEGIC ACQUISITIONS From a seller's perspective, the key point in a **strategic acquisition** is that the value buyers place on the business depends on the synergies they think they can create by combining the acquired firm with complementary businesses. Since the value of a business to a buyer is derived from both its stand-alone characteristics and its synergies, strategic buyers often will pay a higher price than will financial buyers, who value the business only as a stand-alone entity. Thus, in strategic acquisitions, the critical issue is the degree of strategic fit between the firm to be exited and a potential buyer. If the potential buyer is a current rival and if the acquisition would provide long-term, sustainable competitive advantages (such as lower cost of production or superior product quality), the buyer may be willing to pay a premium for the firm.

strategic acquisition
a purchase in which the value of the business is based on both the firm's stand-alone characteristics and the synergies that the buyer thinks can be created

FIGURE 14-1

Methods for Exiting a Business

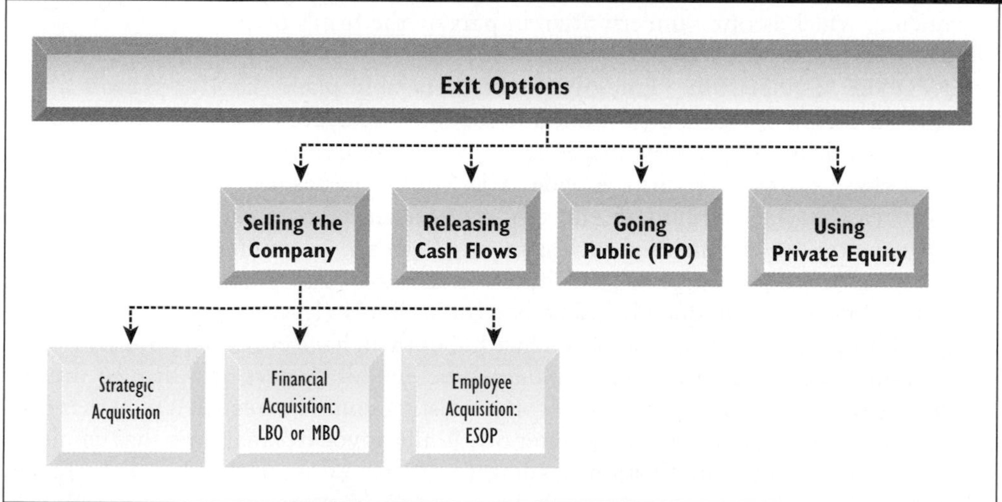

financial acquisition
a purchase in which the value of the business is based on the stand-alone cash-generating potential of the firm being acquired

FINANCIAL ACQUISITIONS Unlike strategic buyers, buyers in **financial acquisitions** look primarily to a firm's stand-alone cash-generating potential as its source of value. Often, the value a financial buyer hopes to tap relates to stimulating future sales growth, reducing costs, or both. This fact has an important implication for the owner of the firm being purchased. The buyer often will make changes in the firm's operations that translate into greater pressures on the firm's personnel, resulting in layoffs that the current owner might find objectionable. As a result, financial acquisitions are not popular among many small business owners.

leveraged buyout (LBO)
a purchase heavily financed with debt, where the potential cash flow of the target company is expected to be sufficient to meet debt repayments

bust-up LBO
a leveraged buyout involving the purchase of a company with the intent of selling off its assets

build-up LBO
a leveraged buyout involving the purchase of a group of similar companies with the intent of making the firms into one larger company

During the 1980s, the **leveraged buyout** (LBO), a financial acquisition involving a very high level of debt financing, became synonymous with the **bust-up LBO,** in which the new owners pay the debt down rapidly by selling off the acquired firm's assets. Frequently, acquisitions were financed with $9 in debt for every $1 in equity—thus the name *leveraged* buyout.

In the 1990s, however, the bust-up LBO was replaced by the build-up LBO. As the name suggests, the **build-up LBO** involves constructing, out of a group of smaller firms, a larger enterprise that might eventually be taken public via an initial public offering (IPO). Large private investors have successfully refined the build-up LBO and tapped public capital markets at unprecedented levels.

The process begins with the acquisition of a company, which then acquires a number of smaller businesses that in some way complement it. These subsequent acquisitions may expand capacity in related or new businesses. The newly formed combination is operated privately for five to seven years in order to establish a successful track record and then is taken public. These acquisitions continue to rely on heavy debt financing, but to a lesser extent than in the 1980s. Typically, there might be $7 in debt for every $1 in equity.

management buyout (MBO)
a leveraged buyout in which the firm's top managers become significant shareholders in the acquired firm

Build-up LBOs have occurred in a number of industries where smaller companies frequently operate, such as funeral services and automobile dealerships. Such LBOs frequently include the firm's top management as significant shareholders in the acquired firm—in which case the arrangement is referred to as a **management buyout** (**MBO**). There is evidence that MBOs can contribute significantly to a firm's operating performance by increasing management's focus and intensity.[2] In view of this evidence, an MBO is a potentially viable means of transferring firm ownership for both large and small businesses. In many entrepreneurial businesses, managers have a strong incentive to become owners, but they often lack the financial capacity to acquire the firm. An MBO can solve this problem through the use of debt financing, which is often underwritten in part by the firm's owner.

employee stock ownership plan (ESOP)
a method by which a firm is sold either in part or in total to its employees

EMPLOYEE ACQUISITIONS **Employee stock ownership plans** (ESOPs) provide a way for a business's founder to cash out and for the employees to acquire an ownership interest in their company. In an ESOP, employees' retirement contributions are used to purchase shares in the firm. A wide variety of businesses have used these plans for many reasons. As a method of selling an entrepreneurial company, though, an ESOP is frequently the exit method of last resort. Even so, 12 million participating employees in more than 10,000 firms have formed ESOPs to purchase large blocks of outstanding stock, frequently using borrowed funds (leveraged ESOPs). Most of these businesses are small, and only a handful of them have ever been publicly traded.

Employee ownership is not a panacea. Selling all or part of a firm to the employees works only when the sale resolves existing conflicts in such a way that both the owner and the employees are better off. While advocates maintain that employee ownership improves motivation, leading to greater effort and reduced waste, the

IN THE TRENCHES ENTREPRENEURSHIP TODAY

A CLOSE LOOK AT AN LBO

Robert Hall, the former owner of Visador Corporation, sold his firm to a financial buyer, who financed the purchase as a leveraged buyout (LBO). A look at the company's financial structure before and after the sale provides a good picture of an LBO.

	Before the Sale	After the Sale
Current liabilities	$ 3,433,532	$11,018,041
Long-term liabilities	1,350,000	47,720,878
Deferred income taxes	569,736	1,742,165
Total liabilities	$ 5,353,268	$60,481,084
Equity	12,948,456	6,789,340
Total liabilities and equity	$18,301,724	$67,270,424

There is quite a difference between Visador Corporation's before-sale and after-sale balance sheet in two respects. First, the total debt and equity increased from $18.3 million to $67.3 million. This increase was the result of changing the amounts on the balance sheet from the historical accounting numbers to numbers that reflect the firm's current value to the buyer. In other words, the founders of Visador had invested $18 million in the firm over its life up to the point of the acquisition. However, the buyer believed the business was worth $67 million.

The second change relates the firm's heavy use of debt. Before the sale, there was $0.41 in debt per $1 in equity; after the sale, there was $8.91 in debt for every $1 in equity. This large increase in debt required the new management to change the way in which the firm operated. The goal was no longer to make a profit; instead, the focus was on generating sufficient cash flows to service the debt. This goal was accomplished through significant reductions in the number of employees and elimination of any activities that did not contribute to the cash flow objectives. These changes were very disappointing to Hall, who had many close friends among those who eventually lost their jobs.

Source: Personal interview with Robert Hall, former CEO of Visador Corporation, 1998.

value of any greater employee effort resulting from improved motivation will vary significantly from firm to firm.

Releasing the Firm's Cash Flows

The second exit strategy involves the orderly withdrawal of the owners' investment in the form of the firm's cash flows. The withdrawal process could be immediate if the owners simply sold off the assets of the firm and ceased business operations. However, for a value-creating firm—one that earns attractive rates of return for its investors—this does not make economic sense. The mere fact that a firm is earning high rates of return on the firm's assets indicates that the business is worth more as a going concern than a dead one. Thus, shutting down the company is not an economically rational option. Instead, the owners might simply stop growing the business; by doing so, they increase the cash flows that can be returned to the investors.

In a firm's early years, all its cash flow is usually devoted to growing the business. Thus, the firm's cash flow during this period is zero—or, more likely, negative—requiring its owners to seek outside cash to finance future growth. As the firm matures and opportunities to grow the business decline, sizable cash flows frequently become available to its owners. Rather than reinvest all the cash flows in the firm, the owners can

begin to withdraw the cash, thus exiting their investment. If they decide to do so, only the amount of cash necessary to maintain current markets is retained and reinvested; there is little, if any, effort to grow the present markets or expand into new markets.

Exiting by withdrawing a firm's cash from the business has two important advantages: The owners can retain control of the firm while they harvest their investment, and they do not have to seek out a buyer or incur the expenses associated with consummating a sale. There are disadvantages, however. Reducing reinvestment when the firm faces valuable growth opportunities results in lost value creation and could leave a firm unable to sustain its competitive advantage. The end result may be an unintended reduction in harvestable value below the potential value of the firm as a long-term going concern. Also, there may be tax disadvantages to an orderly liquidation, compared with other exit methods. For example, if a firm simply distributes the cash flows as dividends, the income may be taxed both as corporate income and as personal dividend income to the stockholders. (Of course, this would not be a problem for a sole proprietorship, partnership, limited liability company, or S corporation.)

Finally, for the entrepreneur who is simply tired of day-to-day operations, siphoning off the cash flows over time may require too much patience. Unless other people in the firm are qualified to manage it, this strategy may be destined to fail.

Going Public

The third method of exiting is going public. Many entrepreneurs consider the prospect of an initial public offering (IPO) as the "holy grail" of their career, as firms involved in an IPO are generally star performers. However, most entrepreneurs do not really understand the IPO process, especially when it comes to (1) how going public relates to the exit and (2) the actual process by which a firm goes public.

initial public offering (IPO)
the first sale of shares of a company's stock to the public

THE IPO AS AN EXIT STRATEGY An **initial public offering (IPO)** is used primarily as a way to raise additional equity capital to finance company growth, and only secondarily as a way to harvest the owner's investment. Lisa D. Stein, vice president of Salomon Smith Barney, offered the following reasons for going public:[3]

- To raise capital to repay outstanding debt
- To support future growth
- To fund future acquisitions
- To create a liquid market for the company's stock
- To broaden the company's shareholder base
- To create ongoing interest in the company and its continued development

Similar conclusions were reached in a study in which the CEOs of firms that had gone public were asked to indicate the level of importance of 17 different possible motivations. The following motivations received the highest percentage of "very important" ratings:[4]

Raise capital for growth	85%
Raise capital to increase working capital	65%
Facilitate acquiring another firm	40%
Establish a market value for the firm	35%
Enhance the firm's ability to raise capital	35%

The CEOs clearly consider financing future growth to be the primary objective of going public.

Having publicly traded stock can be beneficial to owners in that a public market provides a ready market for selling stock and facilitates the eventual exit of their investment. In fact, there is evidence that IPOs eventually lead to an exit. While *startup* and *high-growth* firms tend to go public in order to finance expansion, *established* companies go public in order to liquidate the shareholdings of owners. It has been shown that the median percentage of ownership by a firm's officers and directors declines from 68 percent to 18 percent in the 10 years following an IPO.[5] Thus, although an IPO is not primarily an exit mechanism, going public does provide the owners with increased liquidity—which facilitates their eventual exit.

THE IPO PROCESS The basic steps in the IPO process are as follows:[6]

Step 1. The firm's owners decide to go public.

Step 2. If not already completed, an audit of the last three years of financial statements is conducted.

Step 3. An investment banker is selected to guide management in the IPO process.

Step 4. An S-1 Registration Statement is filed with the SEC. (The Registration Statement is subject to an SEC review period of approximately 30 to 35 days.)

Step 5. Management responds to suggested comments by the SEC and issues a Red Herring/Prospectus, describing the firm and the offering.

Step 6. The firm spends the next 10 to 15 days "on the road," explaining its attributes to potential investors.

Step 7. On the day before the offering is released to the public, the actual offering price is decided upon. Based on the demand for the offering, the shares will be priced to create active trading of the stock.

Step 8. Months of work come to fruition in a single event—offering the stock to the public and seeing how it is received.

The IPO process may be one of the most exhilarating—but frustrating and exhausting—experiences of an entrepreneur's life. Owner-managers frequently discover that they do not like being exposed to the variability of public capital markets and to the prying questions of public-market investors. In a survey of the *Inc.* 100 companies, CEOs who had participated in public offerings indicated that they had spent, on average, 33 hours per week for four and a half months on the offering.[7] To many, the cost of the IPO process seemed exorbitant. They found themselves being misunderstood and having little influence on the decisions being made, and they were frequently disillusioned with investment bankers and the entire process. At some point, they wondered where they had lost control of the process—a feeling shared by many entrepreneurs involved in a public offering.

To understand an IPO, you must consider the shift in power that occurs during the process. When the chain of events begins, the firm's managers are in control. They dictate whether or not to go public and who the investment banker will be. After the prospectus has been prepared and the road show is under way, however, the firm's managers, including the entrepreneur, are no longer the primary decision makers. The investment banker is now in control. Finally, the marketplace, in concert with the investment banker, begins to take over. Ultimately, it is the market that dictates the final outcome.

In addition to the issue of control, it is important that the entrepreneur understand the investment banker's motivations in the IPO process. Who is the investment banker's primary customer? Clearly, the issuing firm is compensating the underwriter for its services through the fees paid and participation in the offering. But helping a firm with an IPO is usually not as profitable for the investment banker as are other activities, such as involvement in corporate acquisitions. The investment banker is also selling the securities to its customers on the other side of the trade. These are the people who will continue to do business with the investment banker in the future. Thus, the investment banker is somewhat conflicted as to who is the "customer."

Using Private Equity

The fourth method of exiting is the use of private equity. With an IPO, a portion of the firm's equity is sold in *public* equity markets. There is, however, an alternative form of equity, in which *private* equity capital is infused to help a family-controlled firm transfer ownership from one generation to the next and eventually to outside investors, while at the same time providing growth capital. **Private equity** is money provided by venture capitalists or private investors. The private investors may be individuals or small groups of individuals who act together to invest in companies.

private equity
money provided by venture capitalists or private investors

Trying to meet the owners' need for cash and the firm's need for growth capital while retaining control is perhaps the most difficult task facing family firms. The difficulty is compounded when the family is attempting to transfer ownership and leadership to the next generation. The situation can be further complicated by the capital and liquidity needs of estate planning and the fact that most family business owners hold their primary assets within the business.

In the transfer of ownership within a family-owned firm, tradeoffs among three factors are of primary importance: (1) liquidity for exiting family members, (2) continued financing for company growth, and (3) maintenance of family control of the firm. In a survey of entrepreneurs who had transferred or were planning to transfer ownership of their businesses, 85 percent of the respondents stated that maintaining control of the firm was "very important."[8] About 45 percent also considered providing capital for the firm's future growth and meeting the personal liquidity needs of family members "very important." When asked how the transfer had been or would be financed, the entrepreneurs responded as follows:

Gift	38%
Seller financing	24%
Acquirer's personal financing	14%
Third-party financing	12%
Other	12%

This sample indicates that family-owned firms use a limited number of alternatives to finance a transition. In many cases, the owners exiting the firm apparently had sufficient personal liquidity that they did not require external financing. Others financed the transition from the firm's operating cash flows, but only by limiting the firm's growth opportunities. The primary source for those who sought third-party financing was a banker.

Firm Valuation and the Exit

As a firm moves toward the harvest, two questions regarding value are of primary importance: the actual value and the method of payment.

Explain how to value a firm being sold and how to decide on the method of payment.

The Actual Value

Owners can harvest only what they have created. Value is created when a firm's return on invested capital is greater than the investors' **opportunity cost of funds,** which is the rate of return that could be earned on an investment of similar risk. Growing a venture to the point of diminishing returns and then selling it to others who can carry it to the next level is a proven way to create value. How this incremental value is shared between the old and the new owners depends largely on the relative strengths of each party in the negotiations—that is, who wants the deal the most or who has the best negotiating skills.

opportunity cost of funds
the rate of return that could be earned on another investment of similar risk

While valuing a company may be necessary on several occasions during the life of the business, it is never more important than at the time of the exit. More often than not, buyers and sellers base the harvest value of a firm on the observed market value of a comparable company relative to its earnings. Such a **market comparable valuation** can be based on the market price of a publicly traded security or an actual transaction involving the sale of a comparable company.

market comparable valuation
basing the value of a privately held company on the value of a similar or comparable publicly traded company

In valuing a business based on its earnings, we may use net income, operating income, or **earnings before interest, taxes, depreciation, and amortization** (EBITDA). In most cases, however, EBITDA is used for estimating the value of a privately held company. For instance, a buyer might try to acquire a business's equity for about five times EBITDA less the outstanding debt—but the price could reflect substantially higher or lower valuation multiples, depending on how badly the buyer wants the business.

earnings before interest, taxes, depreciation, and amortization (EBITDA)
a company's earnings before subtraction of interest expense, taxes, and noncash expenses, such as depreciation and amortization

Typically, a **valuation multiple** is based on the experience and judgment of the person doing the valuation. In determining the multiple, the assessor makes implicit assumptions about the firm's riskiness and its expected future growth in earnings. The greater the firm's risk, the lower the multiple should be; the greater the expected growth in earnings, the higher the multiple should be. Valuation multiples will also vary with competitive conditions. For example, in the early 1990s, firms were selling for four to five times EBITDA. In the late 1990s and early 2000s, the multiples were six to seven times EBITDA.

valuation multiple
a multiple of a firm's earnings, used to value the company

The experience of Visador Corporation (In the Trenches, page 351) served as an example of a leveraged buyout transaction. The original offer that Robert Hall, the owner, received for his firm was based on a multiple of EBITDA. The letter he received from the buyer contained the following calculations to support the offer being made (numbers have been rounded):

Net income	$ 4,675,000
Income taxes	3,175,000
Interest expense	115,000
Depreciation and amortization	1,175,000
Earnings before interest, taxes, depreciation, and amortization (EBITDA)	$ 9,140,000
Valuation multiple	× 5
Firm value	$45,700,000
Long-term debt	1,350,000
Equity value	$44,350,000

chapter 15

Customer Service, Product, and Distribution Strategies

In the VIDEO Spotlight

NoUVIR Research

"We are about saving the world's art."
—Ruth Ellen Miller

In this episode of "Small Business School," the series on PBS stations, you will meet Ruth Ellen and Jack Miller, founders of NoUVIR Research. NoUVIR stands for "No UltraViolet, no InfraRed." The company builds fiber-optic lighting systems that illuminate many of the world's most valuable objects.

In 2000, Ruth Ellen was named Small Business Person of the Year by the state of Delaware because she is making a huge impact on the way people view art. With nine employees, she and her father are shipping their product to places like the Baseball Hall of Fame and the Smithsonian. Their invention, the cold nose projector, is used to light the original copy of the Constitution and the Declaration of Independence because fiber-optic lighting uses no damage-causing rays.

To win new customers, the Millers conduct full-day seminars at museums that are good prospects for their systems. In addition, they mail catalogs and flyers to a targeted list. Their Web site has proven to be a marketing time-saver, as it clearly explains in a fun way why NoUVIR's products should be considered.

Their strategy from day one was to invent a way to allow museum goers to see art in optimum lighting and at the same time not destroy the precious objects. NoUVIR targets the museum market because most large manufacturers don't take the time to develop products for what they consider to be a limited marketplace. With over 100 patents between them, Ruth Ellen and Jack are respected scientists who spent three years in the development of their first projec-

Go to page 738 for More! on NoUVIR Research.

tor; now their company is growing faster than they ever imagined. I loved watching the two of them "ping-pong" ideas, which is how they describe their creative process. ◆

—*Hattie Bryant, Producer, "Small Business School," The Series on PBS Stations, Worldnet, and the Web, http://smallbusinessschool.org*

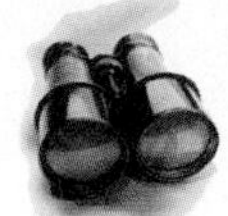

LOOKING AHEAD

After studying this chapter, you should be able to

1. *Explain how customer satisfaction influences customer loyalty.*
2. *Identify the key characteristics of consumer behavior.*
3. *Explain product strategy and related concepts.*
4. *Describe the components of a firm's total product offering.*
5. *Describe the legal environment affecting product decisions.*
6. *Explain the role of distribution in marketing.*
7. *Describe the major considerations in structuring a distribution system.*

Chapter 9 introduced the components of a comprehensive marketing plan for a new venture—product and/or service strategy, distribution strategy, pricing strategy and promotional strategy. Part 5 of this book, comprising Chapters 15, 16, and 17, examines these components more fully. The marketing ideas presented in these chapters should be useful for both new and existing small businesses.

This chapter begins with a discussion of customer service and the related concept of consumer behavior. Next, product strategies used by small firms are examined and finally, the role and structure of a distribution system are considered.

CUSTOMER SATISFACTION: THE KEY TO CUSTOMER LOYALTY

To be successful in the long run, small firms must develop and maintain loyal customers, as it costs far more to replace a customer than to keep one. Three basic beliefs form the foundation of our discussion of customer loyalty:

1

Explain how customer satisfaction influences customer loyalty.

1. Superior customer service creates customer satisfaction.
2. Customer satisfaction produces customer loyalty.
3. Small firms possess great potential for providing superior customer service.

As these beliefs suggest, failure to emphasize customer service jeopardizes the attainment of customer satisfaction and customer loyalty. Figure 15-1 on page 370 depicts this relationship.

Components of Customer Satisfaction

A number of factors under a firm's control contribute to customer satisfaction. One classic article discussing satisfied customers identifies the following four key elements:[1]

1. The most basic benefits of the product or service—the elements that customers expect all competitors to deliver

FIGURE 15-1

Relationship of Customer Service to Customer Loyalty

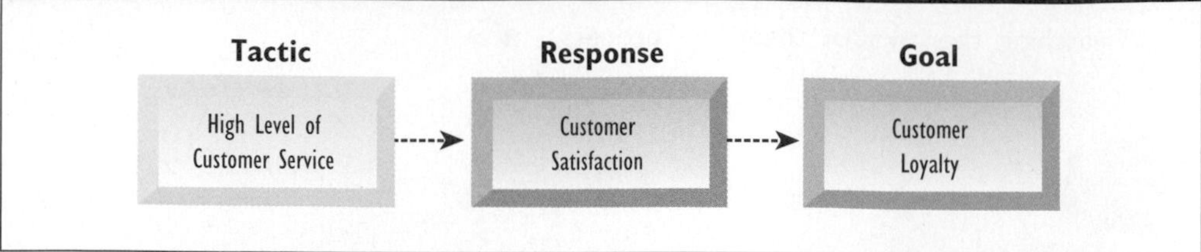

2. General support services, such as customer assistance
3. A recovery process for counteracting bad experiences
4. Extraordinary services that excel in meeting customers' preferences and make the product or service seem customized

Extraordinary service is the ingredient that small firms are in a unique position to offer. Relationship marketing proponent Patrick Daly, who oversees a customer relations program for a company in Redwood City, California, suggests the following ways to develop extraordinary services:[2]

- *Naming names.* In today's detached, "just give me your account number" world, nothing is more well received than individual, personalized attention. Even though you may already be courteous and friendly to customers, greeting them by name is valued 10 times more on the "worthy of loyalty" scale.
- *Custom care.* Customers pretty much know what they do and don't want from your company. If you remember what they want on an individual basis—even if it's something as simple as knowing a dry cleaning customer likes light starch in his collars—then you have mastered one of the key elements of a strong loyalty program.
- *Keeping in touch.* You can't communicate enough on a me-to-you basis with your customers. And don't just connect to make a pitch. Clip out a newspaper or magazine article that pertains to a customer's business and send it to him or her with a note saying "FYI—thought you'd be interested." When customers know that you're taking time to think about them, they don't forget it.
- *"Boo-boo research."* Part of any customer loyalty program is taking the time to reach out to lost customers to learn why they went elsewhere. In many cases, just contacting them and showing them that you really care about getting their business will win them back—along with their contribution to your profits.

The Customer Service Commitment

Providing exceptional customer service can give small firms a competitive edge, regardless of the nature of the business. Small firms must realize that offering top-notch customer service is something they can do better than a large firm.

One report on the state of customer service across the country did not have good news: There is a customer service problem among retail businesses. Here are a few reported examples of sources of customer irritation:[3]

- You call a department store's customer-service line. A recording tells you "Your call is important to us. . . . " Then comes the elevator music. Five minutes later, you're still waiting.

IN THE TRENCHES Building Customer Loyalty

SERVICE SELLS

Service sells. It also creates customer loyalty, even in e-commerce firms. Just ask Patricia Gallup and David Hall, who started a business to sell computers and related products in 1982. After experiencing difficulties in buying a computer for Hall's family business, they recognized that there was a niche for a firm that would serve as an intermediary for people unfamiliar with technology. Shortly thereafter, they launched PC Connection using $8,000 in combined savings.

Gallup and Hall created a business culture deeply rooted in providing exemplary service as a way to build long-term customer relationships. And it works well. In 2000, PC Connection received *PC World* magazine's "PC World Class Award" as the best online computer store. CEO Gallup describes the company's goals and service strategy as follows:

We always aimed at being a one-stop-shopping situation. We didn't want customers to have to go elsewhere. More important, we wanted to offer the best customer service in the industry. One of the first things we did was to develop a technical-support group that could supply information to people before, during, and after the sale. The advice was free, and people could call in even if they hadn't purchased the product from us.

Gallup believes that a high level of customer service and a passion for knowing their customers create loyal customers who won't shop elsewhere. Since 1995, PC Connection has grown at a compound annual rate of nearly 40 percent. Service really does sell.

Source: From material from http://www.pcconnection.com, June 1, 2001.

http://www.pcconnection.com

- [A shopper] entered a . . . shoe store in Washington, D.C.; he knew what he wanted—a pair of brown loafers. There were two salesmen, one waiting on a customer, the other looking out the window. The window-gazer neither greeted [the shopper] nor offered help.
- There are long lines and there's one person at the cash register, and the cashier calls for help and nobody comes.

What is the special significance of these customer problems to small businesses? It is that small firms are *potentially* in a much better position to achieve customer satisfaction than are big businesses. Why? Because each of the problems just identified is solvable by simply giving customers more attention and respect. And managing respect is easier for a small firm, because it has fewer employees and can vest in each employee the authority to act in customers' best interests. In contrast, a large business often assigns that responsibility to a single manager, who does not have daily contact with customers.

Consider the success that one firm had after developing customer service tactics. Sewell Village Cadillac, a car dealership in Dallas, Texas, is famous for customer service. Its owner, Carl Sewell, began the service journey in 1967 when Sewell Village was in third place among three Dallas Cadillac dealers. He realized that most people didn't like doing business with car dealers. Therefore, he simply began asking customers what they didn't like about car dealers. Three major areas of dissatisfaction were identified—service hours, being without a car during service, and poor or incorrect repairs. By responding to these concerns, Sewell Village Cadillac increased its customer satisfaction image.

http://www.sewell.com

Many types of customer service cost very little, but superior levels of customer service do not come cheaply. There are definite costs associated with superior service before, during, and after a sale. These costs can be reflected in a product's or service's

price, or they can sometimes be scheduled separately, based on the amount of service requested. Most customers are willing to pay for good service.

Evaluating Customer Service

The way customer service problems are most commonly recognized is through customer complaints. Every firm strives to eliminate customer complaints. When they occur, however, they should be analyzed carefully to uncover possible weaknesses in customer service.

Managers can also learn about customer service problems through personal observation and other observation techniques. By talking directly to customers or by playing the customer's role anonymously—for example, by making a telephone call to one's own business—a manager can evaluate service. Some restaurants and motels invite feedback on customer service by providing comment cards to customers. Whatever method is used, evaluating customer service is essential for any business.

UNDERSTANDING THE CUSTOMER

2
Identify the key characteristics of consumer behavior.

Customer satisfaction results from a customer's interaction with the firm. Therefore, better understanding of consumers should lead to higher levels of customer satisfaction and loyalty. The concepts of consumer behavior presented here can help an entrepreneur better understand customers, who must be seen first and foremost as human beings. Also helpful to some entrepreneurs are consumer behavior courses, often offered at local colleges. Figure 15-2 presents a model of consumer behavior structured around three interrelated aspects: the decision-making process, psychological influences, and sociological influences.

Stages in Consumer Decision Making

The model of consumer behavior in Figure 15-2 views consumers as problem solvers. According to this model, consumer decision making comprises four stages:

FIGURE 15-2

Simplified Model of Consumer Behavior

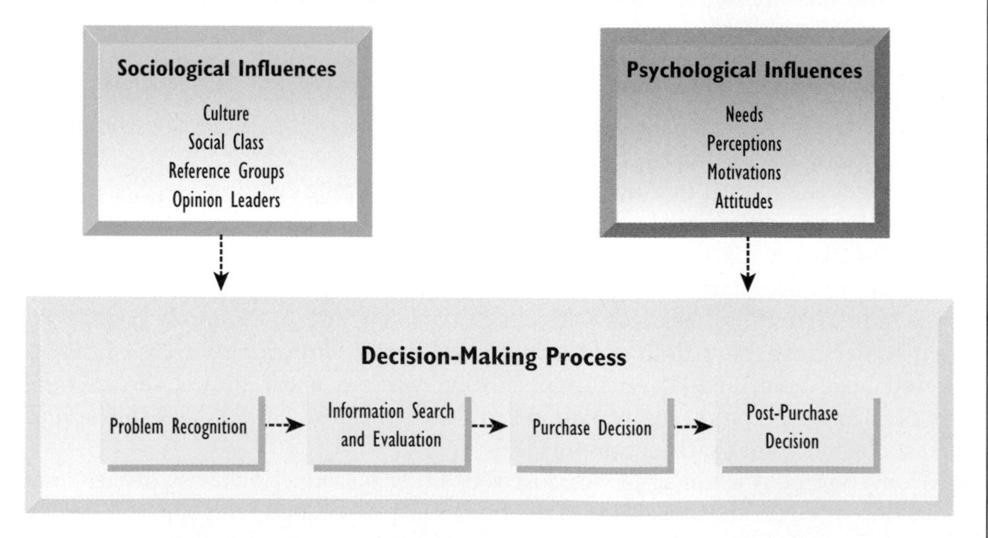

Stage 1. Problem recognition
Stage 2. Information search and evaluation
Stage 3. Purchase decision
Stage 4. Post-purchase evaluation

Let's use this widely accepted theory to examine consumer decision making among small business customers.

STAGE 1: PROBLEM RECOGNITION Problem recognition occurs when a consumer realizes that her or his current state of affairs differs significantly from some ideal state. Some problems are routine conditions of depletion, such as a lack of food when lunchtime arrives. Other problems arise less frequently and may evolve slowly. A decision to replace the family dining table, for example, may take years to develop.

A consumer must recognize a problem before purchase behavior can begin. Thus, the problem recognition stage cannot be avoided. Many small firms develop their product strategy as if consumers were in later stages of the decision-making process, when in reality consumers have not yet recognized a problem!

Many factors influence consumers' recognition of a problem—either by changing the actual state of affairs or by affecting the desired state. Here are a few examples:

- Change in financial status (a job promotion with a salary increase)
- Change in household characteristics (the birth of a baby)
- Normal depletion (using up the last tube of toothpaste)
- Product or service performance (breakdown of the VCR)
- Past decisions (poor repair service on car)
- Availability of products (introduction of a new product)

An entrepreneur must understand the problem recognition stage in order to decide on the appropriate marketing strategy to use. In some situations, a small business owner needs to *influence* problem recognition. In other situations, she or he may simply be able to *react* to problem recognition by consumers.

STAGE 2: INFORMATION SEARCH AND EVALUATION The second stage in consumer decision making involves consumers' collection and evaluation of appropriate information from both internal and external sources. The consumer's principal objective is to establish **evaluative criteria**—the features or characteristics of the product or service that the consumer will use to compare brands.

evaluative criteria
the features of a product or service that customers use to compare brands

evoked set
a group of brands that a customer is both aware of and willing to consider as a solution to a purchase problem

Small business owners should understand which evaluative criteria consumers use to formulate their evoked set. An **evoked set** is a group of brands that a consumer is both aware of and willing to consider as a solution to a purchase problem. Thus, the initial challenge for a new firm is to gain *market awareness* for its product or service. Only then will the brand have the opportunity to become part of consumers' evoked sets.

STAGE 3: PURCHASE DECISION Once consumers have evaluated brands in their evoked set and made their choice, they must still decide how and where to make the purchase. A substantial volume of retail sales now comes from nonstore settings such as catalogs, TV shopping channels, and the Internet. These outlets have created

a complex and challenging environment in which to develop marketing strategy. Consumers attribute many different advantages and disadvantages to various shopping outlets, making it difficult for the small firm to devise a single correct strategy. Sometimes, however, simple recognition of the factors can be helpful.

Of course, not every purchase decision is planned prior to entering a store or looking at a mail-order catalog. Studies show that most types of purchases from traditional retail outlets are not intended prior to the customers' entering the store. This fact places tremendous importance on such features as store layout, sales personnel, and point-of-purchase displays.

STAGE 4: POST-PURCHASE EVALUATION The consumer decision-making process does not end with a purchase. Small firms that desire repeat purchases from customers (and they all should) need to understand post-purchase behavior. Figure 15-3 illustrates several consumer activities that occur during post-purchase evaluation. Two of these activities—post-purchase dissonance and consumer complaints—are directly related to customer satisfaction.

cognitive dissonance
the anxiety that occurs when a customer has second thoughts immediately following a purchase

Post-purchase dissonance is a type of **cognitive dissonance,** a tension that occurs immediately following a purchase decision when consumers have second thoughts as to the wisdom of their purchase. This anxiety is obviously uncomfortable for consumers and can negatively influence product evaluation and customer satisfaction. Small firms need to find effective ways to manage cognitive dissonance among their customers.

What do these consumers do when they are displeased? As Figure 15-4 shows, consumers have several options for dealing with their dissatisfaction, and most of these options threaten repeat sales. Only one—a private inquiry to the offending business—is desirable to the business. The odds are not encouraging. Once again, they indicate the importance of quality customer service—both before and after a sale.

FIGURE 15-3 *Post-Purchase Activities of Consumers*

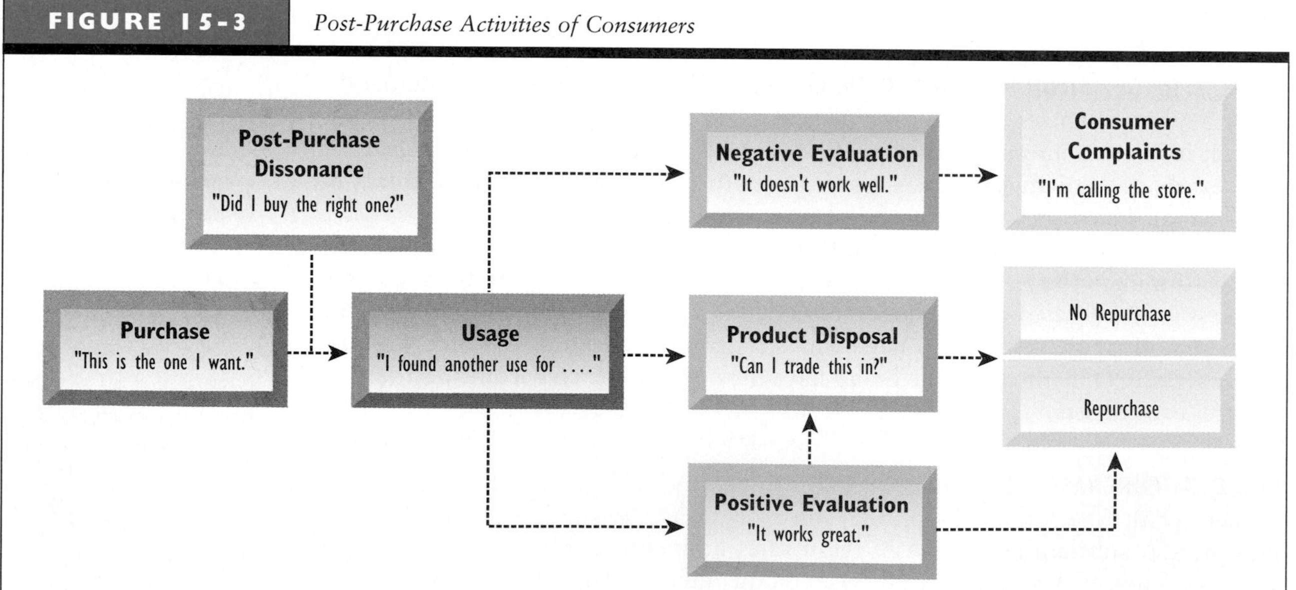

FIGURE 15-4

Consumer Options for Dealing with Product or Service Dissatisfaction

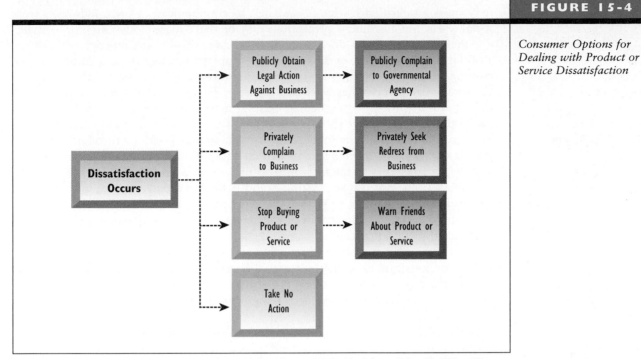

Source: Adapted from Del I. Hawkins, Roger J. Best, and Kenneth A. Coney, *Consumer Behavior,* 8th ed. (Boston: McGraw Hill, 2001), p. 642.

Psychological Influences

The next major component of the consumer behavior model, as presented in Figure 15-2, is psychological influences. The four psychological influences that have the greatest relevance to small businesses are needs, perceptions, motivations, and attitudes.

needs
the starting point for all behavior

NEEDS **Needs** are often described as the starting point for all behavior. Without needs, there would be no behavior. Although consumer needs are innumerable, they can be identified as falling into four categories—physiological, social, psychological, and spiritual.

Consumers' needs are never completely satisfied, thereby ensuring the continued existence of business. One of the more complex characteristics of needs is the way in which they function together in generating behavior. In other words, various needs operate simultaneously, making it difficult to determine which need is being satisfied by a specific product or service. Nevertheless, careful assessment of the needs-behavior connection can be very helpful in developing marketing strategy. Different purchases of the same product satisfy different needs. For example, consumers purchase food products in supermarkets to satisfy physiological needs. But they also purchase food in status restaurants to satisfy their social and/or psychological needs. Also, certain foods are demanded by specific market segments to satisfy those consumers' religious, or spiritual, needs. A needs-based strategy would result in a different marketing approach in each of these situations.

perception
the individual processes that give meaning to the stimuli confronting consumers

PERCEPTIONS A second psychological factor, **perception,** encompasses those individual processes that ultimately give meaning to the stimuli confronting consumers. When this meaning is severely distorted or entirely blocked, consumer perception can

cloud a small firm's marketing effort and make it ineffective. For example a retailer may mark its fashion clothing "on sale" to communicate a price reduction from usual levels, but customers' perceptions may be that "these clothes are out of style."

Perception is a two-sided coin. It depends on the characteristics of both the stimulus and the perceiver. Consumers attempt to manage huge quantities of incoming stimuli through **perceptual categorization,** a process by which things that are similar are perceived as belonging together. Therefore, if a small business wishes to position its product alongside an existing brand and have it accepted as comparable, the marketing mix should reflect an awareness of perceptual categorization. Similar quality can be communicated through similar prices or through a package design with a color scheme similar to that of an existing brand. These techniques will help a consumer fit the new product into the desired product category.

perceptual categorization
the process of grouping similar things so as to manage huge quantities of incoming stimuli

Small firms that use an existing brand name for a new product are relying on perceptual categorization to pre-sell the new product. If, on the other hand, the new product is generically different or of a different quality, a unique brand name should be selected to avoid perceptual categorization by the consumer.

If a consumer has strong brand loyalty to a product, it is difficult for other brands to penetrate his or her perceptual barriers. That individual is likely to have distorted images of competing brands because of a pre-existing attitude. Consumers' perceptions thus present a unique communication challenge.

MOTIVATIONS Unsatisfied needs create tension within an individual. When this tension reaches a certain level, the individual becomes uncomfortable and is motivated to reduce the tension.

Everyone is familiar with hunger pains, which are manifestations of the tension created by an unsatisfied physiological need. What directs a person to obtain food so that the hunger pains can be relieved? The answer is motivation. **Motivations** are goal-directed forces that organize and give direction to tension caused by unsatisfied needs. Marketers cannot create needs, but they can offer unique motivations to consumers. If an acceptable reason for purchasing a product or service is provided, it will probably be internalized by the consumer as a motivating force. The key for the marketer is to determine which motivations the consumer will perceive as acceptable in a given situation. The answer is found through an analysis of other consumer behavior variables.

motivations
forces that organize and give direction to the tension caused by unsatisfied needs

Like physiological needs, the other three classes of needs—social, psychological, and spiritual—can be similarly connected to behavior through motivations. For example, when incomplete satisfaction of a person's social needs is creating tension, a firm may show how its product can fulfill those social needs by providing acceptable motivations to that person. A campus clothing store might promote styles that communicate that the college student wearing those clothes has obtained membership in a group such as a fraternity or sorority.

Understanding motivations is not easy. Several motivations may be present in any situation, and they are often subconscious. However, they must be investigated in order for the marketing effort to be successful.

ATTITUDES Like the other psychological variables, attitudes cannot be observed, but everyone has them. Do attitudes imply knowledge? Do they imply feelings of good or bad, favorable or unfavorable? Does an attitude have a direct impact on behavior? The answer to each of these questions is a resounding yes. An **attitude** is an enduring opinion, based on a combination of knowledge, feeling, and behavioral tendency.

attitude
an enduring opinion based on knowledge, feeling, and behavioral tendency

An attitude may act as an obstacle or a catalyst in bringing a customer to a product. For example, consumers with the belief that a local, family-run grocery store has higher prices than a national supermarket chain may avoid the local store. Armed with an understanding of the structure of a particular attitude, a marketer can approach the consumer more intelligently.

Sociological Influences

Sociological influences as shown in Figure 15-2, comprise the last component of the consumer behavior model. Among these influences are culture, social class, reference groups, and opinion leaders. Note that each of these sociological influences represents a different degree of group aggregation: Culture involves large masses of people, social classes and reference groups are smaller groups of people, and opinion leaders are single individuals who exert influence.

CULTURE In marketing, **culture** refers to the behavioral patterns and values that characterize a group of customers in a target market. These patterns and beliefs have a tremendous impact on the purchase and use of products. Marketing managers often overlook the cultural variable because its influences are so neatly embedded within the society. Culture is somewhat like air. You do not think about its function until you are in water over your head! International marketers who have experienced more than one culture can readily attest to the reality of cultural influence.

culture
behavioral patterns and values that characterize a group of consumers in a target market

The prescriptive nature of culture should concern the entrepreneur. Cultural norms create a range of product-related acceptable behaviors that influence what consumers buy. However, because culture does change by adapting slowly to new situations, what works well as a marketing strategy today may not work a few years from now.

An investigation of culture within a narrower boundary—defined by age, religious preference, ethnic orientation, or geographical location—is called *subcultural analysis*. Here, too, unique patterns of behavior and social relationships must concern the marketing manager. For example, the needs and motivations of the youth subculture are far different from those of the senior citizen subculture, and certain food preferences are unique to particular ethnic cultures. Small business managers who familiarize themselves with cultures and subcultures are able to create better marketing mixes.

SOCIAL CLASS Another sociological factor affecting consumer behavior is social class. **Social classes** are divisions within a society having different levels of social prestige. The social class system has important implications for marketing. Different lifestyles correlate with different levels of social prestige, and certain products often become symbols of a type of lifestyle.

social classes
divisions within a society having different levels of social prestige

For some products such as packaged goods, social class analysis will probably not be very useful. For others such as home furnishings, such analysis may help explain variations in shopping and communication patterns.

Unlike a caste system, a social class system provides for upward mobility. The social status of parents does not permanently fix the social class of their child. Occupation is probably the single most important determinant of social class. Other determinants used in social class research include possessions, source of income, and education.

REFERENCE GROUPS Technically, social class could be considered a reference group. However, marketers are generally more concerned with small groups such as families, work groups, neighborhood groups, or recreational groups. **Reference groups** are those smaller groups that an individual allows to influence his or her behavior.

reference groups
groups that an individual allows to influence his or her behavior

The existence of group influence is well established. The challenge to the marketer is to understand why this influence occurs and how it can be used to promote the sale of a product. Individuals tend to accept group influence because of the benefits they perceive as resulting from it. These perceived benefits give the influencers various kinds of power. Five widely recognized forms of power, all of which are available to the marketer, are reward, coercive, referent, expert, and legitimate power.

Reward power and coercive power relate to a group's ability to give and to withhold rewards. Rewards may be material or psychological. Recognition and praise are typical psychological rewards. A Tupperware party is a good example of a marketing technique that takes advantage of reward power and coercive power. The ever-present possibility of pleasing or displeasing the hostess-friend tends to encourage the guest to buy.

Referent power and expert power involve neither rewards nor punishments. They exist because an individual attaches great importance to being like the group or perceives the group as being knowledgeable. Referent power influences consumers to conform to a group's behavior and to choose products selected by the group's members. Children will often be affected by referent power, so marketers can create a desire for products by using cleverly designed advertisements or packages.

Legitimate power involves the sanctioning of what an individual ought to do. We are most familiar with legitimate power at the cultural level, where it is evident in the prescriptive nature of culture, but it can also be used in smaller groups.

OPINION LEADERS According to widely accepted communication principles, consumers receive a significant amount of information through individuals called **opinion leaders,** who are group members playing a key communications role.

opinion leader
a group leader who plays a key communications role

Generally speaking, opinion leaders are knowledgeable, visible, and exposed to the mass media. A small business firm can enhance its own image by identifying with such leaders. For example, a farm-supply dealer may promote its products in an agricultural community by holding demonstrations of these products on the farms of outstanding local farmers, who are the community's opinion leaders. Similarly, department stores may use attractive students as models when showing campus fashions.

PRODUCT STRATEGY

3
Explain product strategy and related concepts.

Although the word *product* can be used to describe both goods and services, the marketing strategies are not the same. Tangibility, amount of time separating production and consumption, standardization, and perishability define a number of differences between the two types of strategies; a pencil cannot be marketed in the same way as a haircut. The major implication of this distinction is that services present unique challenges for strategy development.

Having acknowledged that the marketing of services gives rise to many additional concerns, we will limit our discussion here to general issues of overall product strategy. Therefore, from this point on, a **product** will be considered to include the total bundle of satisfaction offered to customers in an exchange transaction—whether it be a service, a good, or a combination of the two. In addition to the

product
a total bundle of satisfaction—a service, a good, or both—offered to consumers in an exchange transaction

physical product or core service, a product also includes complementary components, such as packaging or a warranty. Of course, the physical product or core service is usually the most important element in the total bundle of satisfaction. But sometimes that main element is perceived by customers to be similar for all products. In that case, complementary components become the most important features of the product. For example, a particular brand of cake mix may be preferred by consumers not because it is a better mix, but because of the unique toll-free telephone number on the package that can be called for baking hints. Or a certain dry cleaner may be chosen over others because it treats customers with respect, not because it cleans clothes exceptionally well.

Product strategy describes the manner in which the product component of the marketing mix is used to achieve the objectives of a firm. A **product item** is the lowest common denominator in a product mix. It is the individual item, such as one brand of bar soap. A **product line** is the sum of the related individual product items. The relationship is usually defined generically. Two brands of bar soap are two product items in one product line. A **product mix** is the collection of product lines within a firm's ownership and control. A firm's product mix might consist of a line of bar soaps and a line of shoe polishes. **Product mix consistency** refers to the closeness, or similarity, of the product lines. The more items in a product line, the more depth it has. The more product lines in a product mix, the greater the breadth of the product mix.

product strategy
the way the product component of the marketing mix is used to achieve a firm's objectives

product item
the lowest common denominator in the product mix—the individual item

product line
the sum of related individual product items

product mix
a firm's total product lines

product mix consistency
the similarity of product lines in a product mix

Although a company's product strategy will determine the nature of the items it includes in its product mix, all new products go through some kind of development process. Thus, it is useful to look at the basic phases in the product development process.

The Product Development Process

A major responsibility of the entrepreneur is to find, evaluate, and introduce new products. This responsibility requires that the entrepreneur establish a process for developing new products. In big business, committees or entire departments are created for that purpose. Even for small firms, however, new product development needs to be a formalized process.

Entrepreneurs tend to treat new product development as a mountainous task—and it usually is. Many find that the following four-stage, structured approach is the best way to tackle product development.

IDEA ACCUMULATION The first stage of the product development process—idea accumulation—involves increasing the pool of ideas under consideration. New products start with ideas, and these ideas have varied origins. The many possible sources include the following:

- Sales, engineering, or other personnel within the firm
- Government-owned patents, which are generally available on a royalty-free basis
- Privately owned patents listed by the U.S. Patent Office
- Other small companies that may be available for acquisition or merger
- Competitors' products and advertising
- Requests and suggestions from customers

BUSINESS ANALYSIS Business analysis is the second stage in the product development process. Every new product idea must be carefully studied in relation to several financial considerations. Costs and revenues are estimated and analyzed with techniques such as break-even analysis. Any idea failing to show that it can be profitable is discarded during the business analysis stage. Four key factors need to be considered in conducting a business analysis:

1. ***Product's relationship to the existing product line.*** Some firms intentionally add very different products to their product mix. However, in most cases, any product item or product line added should be consistent with—or somehow related to—the existing product mix. For example, a new product may be designed to fill a gap in a firm's product line or in the price range of the products it currently sells. If the product is completely new, it should have at least a family relationship to existing products. Otherwise, the new product may call for drastic and costly changes in manufacturing methods, distribution channels, type of promotion, and/or manner of personal selling.
2. ***Cost of development and introduction.*** One problem in adding new products is the cost of their development and introduction. Considerable capital outlays may be necessary, including expenditures for design and development, market research to establish sales potential and volume potential, advertising and sales promotion, patents, and additional equipment. One to three years may pass before profits are realized on the sale of a new product.
3. ***Available personnel and facilities.*** Obviously, having adequate skilled personnel and production equipment is preferable to having to add employees and buy equipment. Thus, introducing new products is typically more appealing if the personnel and the required equipment are already available.
4. ***Competition and market acceptance.*** Still another factor to be considered in a business analysis is the potential competition facing a proposed product in its target market. Competition must not be too severe. Some studies, for example, suggest that new products can be introduced successfully only if 5 percent of the total market can be secured. The ideal solution, of course, is to offer a product that is sufficiently different from existing products or that is in a cost and price bracket where it avoids direct competition.

TOTAL PRODUCT DEVELOPMENT The next stage of product development—total product development—entails planning for branding, packaging, and other supporting efforts such as pricing and promotion. An actual prototype may be needed at this stage. After these components are considered, many new product ideas are discarded.

PRODUCT TESTING The last step in the product development process is product testing. Through testing, the physical product should be proven acceptable. While the product can be evaluated in a laboratory setting, a limited test of market reaction to it should also be conducted. Consider the modest test marketing done by Millie Thomas, president of RGT Enterprises, Inc., in Fort Collins, Colorado, who wanted to develop a new children's toothbrush but had little money for market testing. She took a clay prototype of her triangular-stemmed toothbrush to pediatric dentists and day-care centers to get parents' reactions to the new design. There was a very positive response, so after a few design refinements, she began production. Her products are now sold in stores nationwide.[4]

Product Strategy Options

Failure to clearly understand product strategy options will lead to ineffectiveness and conflict in the marketing effort. The major product strategy alternatives of a small business can be condensed into six categories, based on the nature of the firm's product offering and the number of target markets:

1. One product/one market
2. One product/multiple markets
3. Modified product/one market
4. Modified product/multiple markets
5. Multiple products/one market
6. Multiple products/multiple markets

Each alternative represents a distinct strategy, although two or more of these strategies can be pursued concurrently. A small firm, however, will usually pursue the alternatives in the order listed. Also, keep in mind that once any product strategy has been implemented, sales can be increased through certain additional growth tactics. For example, within any market, a small firm can try to increase sales of an existing product by doing any or all of the following:

- Convincing *nonusers* in the targeted market to become customers
- Persuading current customers to *use more* of the product
- Alerting current customers to *new uses* for the product

When small firms add products to their product mix, they generally select related products. But there are, of course, strategies that involve unrelated products. For example, a local dealer selling Italian sewing machines might add a line of microwave ovens, a generically unrelated product. A product strategy that includes a new product quite different from existing products can be very risky. However, this strategy is occasionally used by small businesses, especially when the new product fits existing distribution and sales systems or requires similar marketing knowledge.

Adding a new, unrelated product to the product mix to target a new market is an even higher risk strategy, as a business is attempting to market an unfamiliar product in an unfamiliar market. One electrical equipment service business recently added a private employment agency. If successful, this product strategy could provide a hedge against volatile shifts in market demand. A business that sells both snowshoes and suntan lotion expects that demand will be high in one market or the other at all times.

Building the Total Product Offering

A major responsibility of marketing is to transform a basic product into a total product offering. Even when an idea for a unique new pen has been developed into physical reality in the form of the basic product, it is still not ready for the marketplace. The total product offering must be more than the materials molded into the shape of the new pen. To be marketable, the basic product must be named, have a package, perhaps have a warranty, and be supported by other product components. Let's now examine a few of the components of a total product offering.

4

Describe the components of a firm's total product offering.

ENTREPRENEURSHIP TODAY

MARKETING MAZE

Many service businesses remain profitable by offering only a single product or service to one market. This is the strategy used by The MAiZE since its inception in 1996. Its mission—"to provide an enjoyable and educational source of good farmin' fun to communities around the country"—has involved one primary service.

The story began when Brett Herbst, a Brigham Young University agribusiness graduate, launched his first corn maze in American Fork, Utah. A field of corn (maize) was plowed into a network of twists and turns to form a huge maze. Visitors were then charged a fee to challenge the maze. After drawing 18,000 people to his maze in three weeks, Herbst recognized an opportunity to help farmers create and promote their own mazes—and to collect a fee of $1,500 plus 6 percent of revenues.

Bob Schmidt, of Greenback, Tennessee, is one of the company's clients. In September and October, 1999, Schmidt's maze welcomed more than 27,000 visitors, at an average ticket price of $4. And Schmidt still gets to harvest the corn after the maze season ends.

In just five years, Herbst has grown his business into the world's largest cornfield maze company with more than 100 mazes. The MAiZE has carved out a strong market niche with a single basic service.

Source: From material from http://www.cornfieldmaize.com, May 29, 2001; and personal conversation with Kamille Thorne, public relations director of The MAiZE.

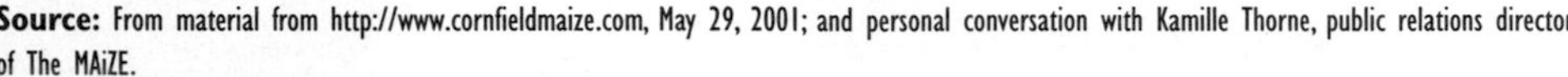

Branding

brand
a verbal and/or symbolic means of identifying a product

An essential element of a total product offering is a brand. A **brand** is a means of identifying the product—verbally and/or symbolically. The name Xerox is a brand, as are the golden arches of McDonald's. Since a product's brand name is so important to the image of the business and its products, considerable attention should be given to the selection of a name.

In general, five rules apply in naming a product:

1. ***Select a name that is easy to pronounce and remember.*** You want customers to remember your product. Help them do so with a name that can be spoken easily—for example, TWO MEN & A TRUCK (a moving service) or Water Water Everywhere (a lawn irrigation business). Before choosing to use your own name to identify a product, evaluate it carefully to ensure its acceptability. Dave Thomas, the founder of a major fast-food chain, successfully used his daughter's name for his company, Wendy's.
2. ***Choose a descriptive name.*** A name that is suggestive of the major benefit of the product can be extremely helpful. As a name for a sign shop, Sign Language correctly suggests a desirable benefit. Blind Doctor is a creative name for a window blind repair business. However, Rocky Road would be a poor name for a business selling mattresses!
3. ***Use a name that can have legal protection.*** Be careful to select a name that can be defended successfully. Do not risk litigation by copying someone else's brand name. A new soft drink named Professor Pepper would likely be contested by the Dr Pepper company.

4. ***Select a name with promotional possibilities.*** Exceedingly long names are not, for example, compatible with good copy design on billboards, where space is at a premium. A competitor of the McDonald's hamburger chain is called Wuv's, a name that will easily fit on any billboard.
5. ***Select a name that can be used on several product lines of a similar nature.*** Customer goodwill is often lost when a name doesn't fit a new line. The name Just Brakes is excellent for an auto service shop that repairs brakes—unless the shop later plans to expand into muffler repair.

Trademark and **service mark** are legal terms indicating the exclusive right to use a brand. Once an entrepreneur has found a name or symbol that is unique, easy to remember, and related to the product or service, an attorney who specializes in trademarks and service marks should be hired to run a name or symbol search and then to register the trade name or symbol.

trademark
an identifying feature used to distinguish a manufacturer's product

service mark
a legal term indicating the exclusive right to use a brand to identify a service

Packaging

Packaging is another important part of the total product offering. In addition to protecting the basic product, packaging is a significant tool for increasing the value of the total product.

Consider for a moment some of the products you purchase. How many do you buy mainly because of a preference for package design and/or color? Innovative packaging is frequently the deciding factor for consumers. If a product is otherwise very similar to competitive products, its package may create the distinctive impression that makes the sale. For example, biodegradable packaging materials may distinguish a product from its competition. The original L'eggs packaging design is an example of creative packaging that sells well.

Labeling

Another part of the total product is its label. Labeling serves several important purposes for manufacturers, who apply most labels. One of its purposes is to show the brand, particularly when branding the basic product would be undesirable. For example, a furniture brand is typically shown on a label and not on the basic product. On some products, brand visibility is highly desirable; Calvin Klein jeans would probably not sell as well with the name label only inside the jeans.

A label is also an important informative tool for consumers. It often includes information on product care and use and may even provide information on how to dispose of the product.

Laws concerning labeling requirements should be reviewed carefully. Be innovative in your labeling information, and consider including information that goes beyond the specified minimum legal requirements.

Warranties

A **warranty** is simply a promise, written or unwritten, that a product will do certain things or meet certain standards. All sellers make an implied warranty that the seller's title to the product is good. A merchant seller, who deals in goods of a particular kind, makes the additional implied warranty that those goods are fit for the ordinary purposes for which they are sold. A written warranty on a product is not always necessary. In fact, many firms operate without written warranties, as they are concerned that a written warranty will only serve to confuse customers or make them suspicious.

warranty
a promise that a product will perform at a certain level or meet certain standards

Warranties are important for products that are innovative, relatively expensive, purchased infrequently, relatively complex to repair, and positioned as high-quality goods. A business should consider the following factors in rating the merits of a proposed warranty policy:

- Cost
- Service capability
- Competitive practices
- Customer perceptions
- Legal implications

Product Strategy Within the Legal Environment

5

Describe the legal environment affecting product decisions.

To this point, our focus has been on customer loyalty, consumer behavior, and product strategy, with the ultimate goal of building the total product offering. Decisions about these factors are always made within the guidelines and constraints of the legal environment of the marketplace. Let's now examine a select few of these laws, by means of which the government protects both the rights of consumers and the intangible assets of firms.

Consumer Protection

Federal regulations on such subjects as labeling and product safety have important implications for product strategy.

LABELING The Nutrition Labeling and Education Act of 1990 requires that every food product covered by the law have a standard nutrition label, listing the amounts of calories, fat, salt, and nutrients. The law also addresses the accuracy of advertising claims such as "low salt" and "fiber prevents cancer." Some experts estimate the labeling costs at thousands of dollars per product.

http://www.cpsc.gov

PRODUCT SAFETY To protect the public against unreasonable risk of injury, the federal government enacted the Consumer Product Safety Act of 1972. This act created the Consumer Product Safety Commission to set safety standards for toys and other consumer products and to ban goods that are exceptionally hazardous.

Protection of Intangible Assets

Figure 15-5 shows the four primary means firms can use to protect their intangible assets. These are trademarks, patents, copyrights, and trade dress.

TRADEMARK PROTECTION Protecting a trademark is important to a manufacturer or merchant. In some cases, a color or scent can be part of a trademark. Small manufacturers, in particular, often find it desirable to feature an identifying trademark in advertising.

Since names that refer to products are often registered trademarks, potential names should be investigated carefully to ensure that they are not already in use. Given the complexity of this task, many entrepreneurs seek the advice of attorneys experienced in trademark search and registration.

FIGURE 15-5

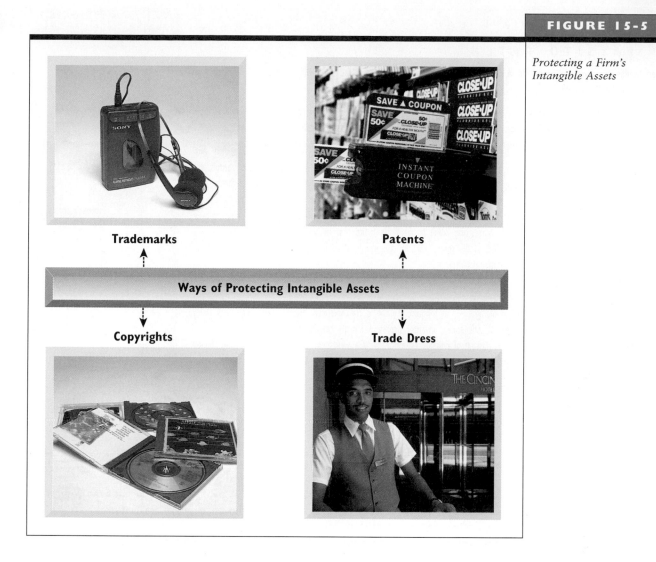

Protecting a Firm's Intangible Assets

Trademarks

Patents

Ways of Protecting Intangible Assets

Copyrights

Trade Dress

An entrepreneur may conduct the trademark search personally, however, by using the Trademark Search Library of the U.S. Patent and Trademark Office (PTO) in Arlington, Virginia. A trademark search can also be made on the Internet by going to http://www.uspto.gov.

http://www.uspto.gov

Common law recognizes a property right in the ownership of trademarks. However, reliance on common-law rights is not always adequate. For example, Microsoft Corporation, the major supplier of personal computer software, claimed it had common-law rights to the trademark *Windows* because of the enormous industry recognition of the product. Nevertheless, when Microsoft filed a trademark application in 1990 seeking to gain exclusive rights to the name *Windows,* the U.S. Patent and Trademark Office rejected the bid, claiming that the word was a generic term and, therefore, in the public domain.

ENTREPRENEURSHIP TODAY

IN THE TRENCHES

IT PAYS TO PATENT

Listen to this description of patent No. 4,591,071 appearing on the U.S. Patent Trademark Office database, a computerized record of official U.S. patents:

A toy squirt gun that shoots a continuous high velocity stream of water. The squirt gun is configured as a structure facilitating partial filling with water leaving a void for compressed air. The squirt gun includes a nozzle for ejecting water at high velocity, a pressurization pump for compressing air into the gun to pressurize water contained therein, and a trigger. . . .

Translation: It's a water gun, called Super Soaker. Its inventor is Lonnie Johnson, who was granted a patent on May 27, 1986. A patent gives the inventor the right to keep others from duplicating the product but doesn't guarantee success. After getting the Super Soaker patent, Johnson believed he would be hearing "from people wanting my invention. And, of course, that didn't happen." He found that he needed around $200,000 to produce 1,000 of the squirt guns. An alternative, of course, was to license the patent to an existing manufacturer.

Eventually, Johnson chose the licensing arrangement; his company, Johnson Research & Development, now earns a percentage of all sales. The Super Soaker is 1 of more than 50 patents granted to Johnson. "Lonnie is the American success story," says Dick Apley, director of independent inventor programs for the U.S. Patent Office.

To date, total revenue estimates for the squirt gun range as high as $400 million! And Johnson's key to a share of that revenue hinges on his ownership of the patent.

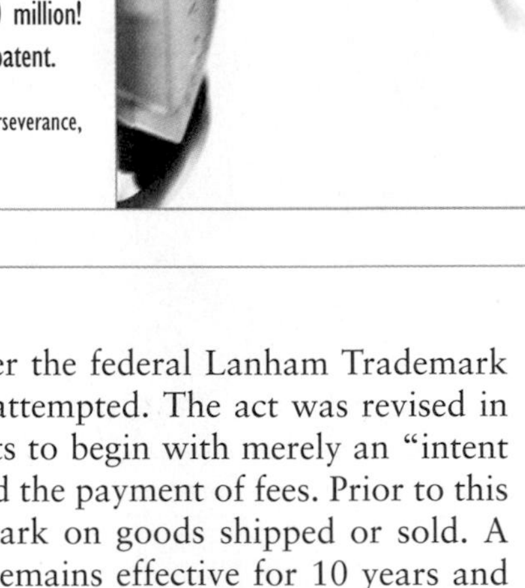

Source: Timothy Roche, "Soaking in Success," *Time,* Vol. 156, No. 23 (December 4, 2000); and Jim Hopkins, "Getting Patent Takes Pain, Perseverance, Planning," *USA Today,* April 11, 2001, p. 9B.

http://www.supersoaker.com

Registration of trademarks is permitted under the federal Lanham Trademark Act, making protection easier if infringement is attempted. The act was revised in November 1989 and now allows trademark rights to begin with merely an "intent to use," along with the filing of an application and the payment of fees. Prior to this revision, a firm had to have already used the mark on goods shipped or sold. A trademark registered after November 16, 1989 remains effective for 10 years and may be renewed for additional 10-year periods. Application for such registration can be made to the U.S. Patent and Trademark Office over the Internet.

A small business must use a trademark properly in order to protect it. Two rules can help. The first rule is to make every effort to see that the trade name is not carelessly used in place of the generic name. For example, the Xerox company never wants people to say that they are "xeroxing" something when they are using one of its competitors' copiers. The second rule is to inform the public that the trademark is a trademark by labeling it with the symbol ™. If the trademark is registered, the symbol ® or the phrase "Registered in the U.S. Patent and Trademark Office" should be used.

patent
the registered, exclusive right of an inventor to make, use, or sell an invention

utility patent
registered protection for a new process or a product's function

design patent
registered protection for the appearance of a product and its inseparable parts

PATENT PROTECTION A **patent** is the registered, exclusive right of an inventor to make, use, or sell an invention. The two primary types of patents are utility patents and design patents. A **utility patent** covers a new process or protects the function of a product. A **design patent** covers the appearance of a product and everything that

is an inseparable part of the product. Utility patents are granted for a period of 20 years, while design patents are effective for 14 years. Patent law also provides for **plant patents,** which cover any distinct and new variety of plants.

plant patent
registered protection for any distinct and new variety of plant

Items that may be patented include machines and products, improvements on machines and products, and original designs. Some small manufacturers have patented items that constitute the major part of their product line. Indeed, some businesses such as Polaroid and IBM can trace their origins to a patented invention. Small business owners preparing a patent application often retain a patent attorney to act for them. A patent search can be conducted on the Internet.

Lawsuits concerning patent infringements are costly and should be avoided, if possible. Coming up with the money and legal talent to enforce this legal right is one of the major problems associated with patent protection in small businesses. Monetary damages and injunctions are available, however, if an infringement can be proved.

COPYRIGHTS A **copyright** is the exclusive right of a creator (author, composer, designer, or artist) to reproduce, publish, perform, display, or sell work that is the product of that person's intelligence and skill. Works created on or after January 1, 1978 receive copyright protection for the duration of the creator's life plus 50 years. A "work made for hire" is protected for 100 years from its creation or 75 years from publication, whichever is shorter. Copyrights are registered in the Copyright Office of the Library of Congress.

copyright
the exclusive right of a creator to reproduce, publish, perform, display, or sell his or her own works

http://www.loc.gov

Under the Copyright Act of 1976, copyrightable works are automatically protected from the moment of their creation. However, any work distributed to the public should contain a copyright notice. This notice consists of three elements (which can be found on the copyright page of this textbook):

1. The symbol ©
2. The year the work was published
3. The copyright owner's name

The law provides that copyrighted work cannot be reproduced by another person or persons without authorization. Even photocopying of such work is prohibited, although an individual may copy a limited amount of material for such purposes as research, criticism, comment, and scholarship. A copyright holder can sue a violator for damages.

TRADE DRESS A small business may also possess a valuable intangible asset called trade dress. **Trade dress** describes those elements of a firm's distinctive operating image not specifically protected under a trademark, patent, or copyright. Trade dress is the "look" that a firm creates to establish its marketing advantage. For example, if the employees of a pizza retailer dress as prison guards and prisoners, a "jailhouse" image could become uniquely associated with this business and, over time, become its trade dress. One court has defined trade dress as "the total image of a product, including features such as size, shape, color or color combinations, texture, graphics, or even particular sales techniques."[5] Although there are currently no statutes covering trade dress, the courts are beginning to recognize the value of this asset.

trade dress
elements of a firm's distinctive image not protected by a trademark, patent, or copyright

The Role of Distribution Activities in Marketing

6 *Explain the role of distribution in marketing.*

distribution
physically moving products and establishing intermediary relationships to support such movement

physical distribution (logistics)
the activities of distribution involved in the physical relocation of products

channel of distribution
the system of relationships established to guide the movement of a product

Entrepreneurs often regard distribution as the least glamorous marketing activity. Nevertheless, an effective distribution system is just as important as a unique package, a clever name, or a creative promotional campaign. Thus, a small business manager should understand the basic principles of distribution, which apply to both domestic and international distribution activities.

In marketing, **distribution** encompasses both the physical movement of products and the establishment of intermediary (middleman) relationships to achieve product movement. The activities involved in physically moving a product are called **physical distribution, or logistics;** the system of relationships established to guide the movement of a product is called the **channel of distribution.**

Distribution is essential for both tangible and intangible goods. Since distribution activities are more visible for tangible goods (products), our discussion will focus on products. Most intangible goods (services) are delivered directly to the user. An income tax preparer and a barber, for example, serve clients directly. However, marketing a person's labor can involve channel intermediaries. An employment agency, for example, provides an employer with temporary personnel.

Functions of Intermediaries

Intermediaries can often perform marketing functions better than the producer or the user of a product. A producer can perform its own distribution functions—including delivery—if the geographic area of the market is small, customers' needs are specialized, and risk levels are low, as they might be for a producer of doughnuts. However, intermediaries generally provide more efficient means of distribution if customers are widely dispersed or if special packaging and storage are needed. Many types of small firms, such as retail stores, function as intermediaries.

merchant middlemen
intermediaries that take title to the goods they distribute

agents/brokers
intermediaries that do not take title to the goods they distribute

Some intermediaries, called **merchant middlemen,** take title to the goods they distribute, thereby helping a small firm to share or totally shift business risk. Other intermediaries, such as **agents** and **brokers,** do not take title to the goods and, therefore, assume less of the market risk than do merchant middlemen.

Channels of Distribution

direct channel
a distribution system without intermediaries

indirect channel
a distribution system with one or more intermediaries

A channel of distribution can be either direct or indirect. In a **direct channel** of distribution, there are no intermediaries—the product goes directly from producer to user. An **indirect channel** of distribution has one or more intermediaries between producer and user.

dual distribution
a distribution system that involves more than one channel

Figure 15-6 depicts the various options available for structuring a channel of distribution. E-commerce (online merchandising) and mail-order marketing are direct channel systems for distributing consumer goods. Amazon.com is an example of an online merchandiser that uses a direct channel to final consumers. The systems shown on the right-hand side of Figure 15-6 are indirect channels involving one, two, or three levels of intermediaries. As a final consumer, you are naturally familiar with retailers. Industrial purchasers are equally familiar with industrial distributors. Channels with two or three stages of intermediaries are probably the ones most typically used by small firms with geographically large markets. It is important to note that a small firm may use more than one channel of distribution—a practice called **dual distribution.**

FIGURE 15-6 *Alternative Channels of Distribution*

Direct Channel

Indirect Channels

Retailer Channel

Wholesaler Channel

Agent/Broker Channel

Producer → Consumers or Industrial User

Producer → Retailers or Industrial Distributor → Consumers or Industrial User

Producer → Wholesalers → Retailers or Industrial Distributor → Consumers or Industrial User

Producer → Agents or Brokers → Wholesalers → Retailers or Industrial Distributor → Consumers or Industrial User

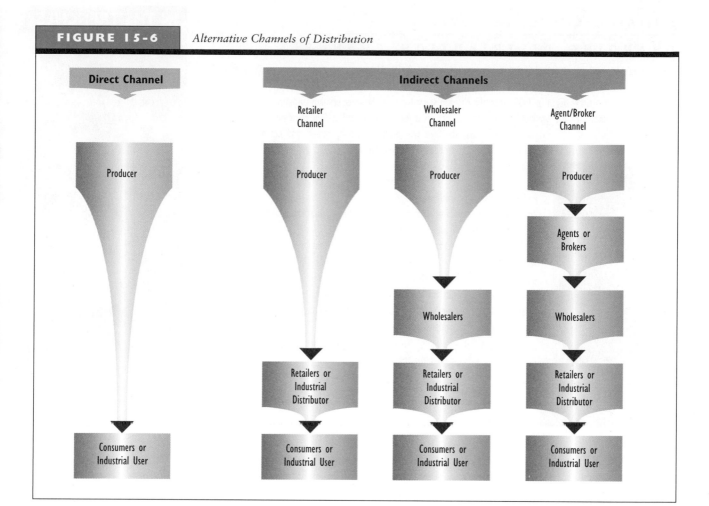

Firms that successfully employ a single distribution channel may switch to dual distribution if they determine that an additional channel will improve overall profitability. For example, the Boston Book Company, in business since 1979, occupies a shop in the downtown area of Boston, Massachusetts but also maintains a Web site where books can be purchased online.

http://www.rarebook.com

Structuring a Distribution Channel

A logical starting point in structuring a distribution system is to observe systems used by competing businesses. Such analysis should reveal some practical alternatives. However, a small firm should also consider three important factors—costs, coverage, and control.

Describe the major considerations in structuring a distribution system.

Considerations in Building a Channel of Distribution

The three main considerations in building a channel of distribution are costs, coverage, and control.

Building Customer Loyalty

CHANGING DISTRIBUTION CHANNELS

Based in Fair Lawn, New Jersey, Private Label was founded in 1995 by David and Nira Naor and Jim and Ornit Michael. By thinking creatively, these entrepreneurs managed to bypass traditional distribution channels.

The business actually began in 1992, when the Michaels started a home business, printing customers' names on the outside of marking pens. They also produced another type of pen used for correcting "red eye" in photographs. These pens were sold to distributors, who then sold them to specialty camera and photo shops. With this indirect channel of distribution, however, the business was earning only a few cents on each pen.

Then the Michaels hit on a new approach. They decided to dress up the pens in packaging aimed at consumers and sell them directly to retailers such as CVS and Walgreens. They would make more money, even though the pens would sell for less than half what they cost in the photo stores.

The decision to change to a direct channel distribution strategy was based on research by Jim Michael, who found that many large retailers were requesting items of this kind. Private Label's strategy change was justified by the response of drugstore chain merchandise managers, who had received samples. A Walgreens buyer, for example, placed an order for 60,000 red-eye pens from a cellular phone in his car. The Eckerd drug chain sent an order by fax without advance notice.

Private Label is currently expanding into other markets, with creative products such as surgical markers, fabric pens, and food markers.

Source: Jim Hopkins, "Couples Make Their Mark in Pen Business," *USA Today,* June 12, 2000, p. 4B.

COSTS The absence of intermediaries does not make a direct channel inherently less expensive than an indirect channel. The least expensive channel may be indirect. For example, a firm producing handmade dolls need not purchase trucks and warehouses to distribute its product directly to customers but can instead rely on established intermediaries that own such facilities. Small firms should look at distribution costs as an investment—spending money in order to make money. They should ask themselves whether the money they "invest" in intermediaries (by selling the product to them at a reduced price) would still get the job done if they used direct distribution.

COVERAGE Small firms can often use indirect channels of distribution to increase market coverage. Suppose a small manufacturer's internal sales force can make 10 contacts a week with final users of the firm's product. Creating an indirect channel with 10 industrial distributors, each making 10 contacts a week, could expose the product to 100 final users a week.

CONTROL A direct channel of distribution is sometimes preferable because it provides more control. Intermediaries may not market a product as desired. A small firm must carefully select intermediaries that provide the desired support.

Control is the main reason Robin Rose, of Robin Rose Ice Cream in Venice, California, distributes her products directly to customers. The reputation of Robin Rose ice cream depends on its freshness and quality; therefore, she has purposely remained small in order to control both the production and the distribution of her ice cream.[6]

Determining the Scope of Physical Distribution

In addition to the intermediary relationships that make up a channel, there must also be a system of physical distribution. The main component of physical distribution is transportation. Additional components are storage, materials handling, delivery terms, and inventory management. The following sections briefly examine all of these topics except inventory management, which is discussed in Chapter 20.

TRANSPORTATION The major decision regarding the physical transportation of a product is which mode to use. Available modes of transportation are traditionally classified as airplanes, trucks, railroads, pipelines, and waterways. Each mode has unique advantages and disadvantages. The choice of a specific mode of transportation is based on several criteria: relative cost, transit time, reliability, capability, accessibility, and traceability.

Transportation intermediaries are legally classified as common carriers, contract carriers, and private carriers. **Common carriers,** which are available for hire to the general public, and **contract carriers,** which engage in individual contracts with shippers, are subject to regulation by federal and/or state agencies. Lines of transport owned by the shippers are called **private carriers.**

common carriers
transportation intermediaries available for hire to the general public

contract carriers
transportation intermediaries that contract with individual shippers

private carriers
lines of transport owned by the shippers

STORAGE Lack of space is a common problem for small businesses. When a channel system uses merchant middlemen or wholesalers, title to the goods is transferred, as is responsibility for the storage function. On other occasions, the small business must plan for its own warehousing. If a firm is too small to own a private warehouse, it can rent space in public warehouses. If storage requirements are simple and do not involve much special handling equipment, a public warehouse can provide economical storage.

MATERIALS HANDLING A damaged product in the right place at the right time is worth little. Therefore, a physical distribution system must arrange for suitable materials-handling methods and equipment. Forklifts, as well as special containers and packaging, are part of a materials-handling system.

DELIVERY TERMS A small but important part of a physical distribution system is the delivery terms, specifying which party is responsible for several aspects of the distribution:

- Paying the freight costs
- Selecting the carriers
- Bearing the risk of damage in transit
- Selecting the modes of transport

The simplest delivery term and the one most advantageous to a small business as seller is F.O.B. (free on board) origin, freight collect. This shifts all the responsibility

for freight costs to the buyer. Title to the goods and risk of loss also pass to the buyer at the time the goods are shipped.

LOGISTICS COMPANIES Logistics companies specialize in transportation and distribution services, providing trucking, packaging, and warehousing services for small- and medium-size companies with limited in-house staffing. Many small businesses believe that using these third-party logistics firms is more cost-effective than carrying out the same functions in-house. For example, Premier Inc. of Greenwich, Connecticut uses a firm named APL Logistics to handle the packaging and shipping of its health and beauty-aid products. Products produced in plants around the country go to the APL warehouse in Dallas, Texas and are then shipped to distribution outlets nationwide.

http://www.apllogistics.com

LOOKING BACK

1 Explain how customer satisfaction influences customer loyalty.

- Customer satisfaction can provide a competitive edge for small firms.
- Small firms can provide extraordinary service that makes their product or service seem customized.
- Technology, such as voice mail systems, must be managed well so that personal interaction with customers is maintained.
- Managers can learn about customer service problems through techniques such as personal observation and surveys.

2 Identify the key characteristics of consumer behavior.

- It is helpful to view consumers as problem solvers who are going through several stages, from problem recognition to post-purchase behavior.
- Psychological influences affecting consumer behavior include needs, perceptions, motivations, and attitudes.
- Sociological influences affecting consumer behavior encompass culture, social class, reference groups, and opinion leaders.

3 Explain product strategy and related concepts.

- Product strategy describes how a product is used to achieve a firm's goals.
- The product life cycle is a valuable tool for managing the product mix.
- The stages of new product development are idea accumulation, business analysis, total product development, and product testing.

4 Describe the components of a firm's total product offering.

- The name is a critical component of a product; it should be easy to pronounce and remember, descriptive, eligible for legal protection, full of promotional possibilities, and suitable for use on several products.
- Packaging is a significant tool for increasing total product value.
- A label is an important informative tool, providing instructions on product use, care, and disposal.
- A warranty can be valuable for achieving customer satisfaction.

5 Describe the legal environment affecting product decisions.

- Federal legislation regarding labeling and product safety was designed to protect consumers.
- The legal system provides protection for a firm's intangible assets through trademarks, patents, copyrights, and trade dress.

6 Explain the role of distribution in marketing.

- Distribution encompasses both the physical movement of products and the establishment of relationships to guide the movement of products from producer to user.
- A distribution channel can be either direct or indirect. Some firms successfully employ more than one channel of distribution.

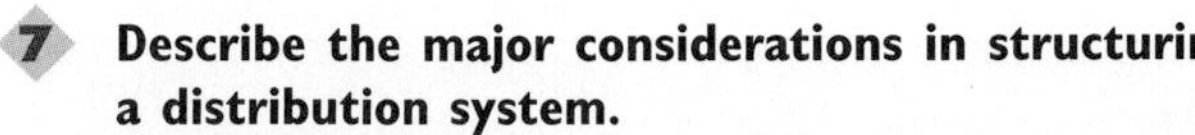

7 Describe the major considerations in structuring a distribution system.

- Costs, coverage, and control are the three main considerations in building a channel of distribution.
- Transportation, storage, materials handling, delivery terms, and inventory management are the main components of a physical distribution system.

Key Terms

evaluative criteria, p. 373
evoked set, p. 373
cognitive dissonance, p. 374
needs, p. 375
perception, p. 375
perceptual categorization, p. 376
motivations, p. 376
attitude, p. 376
culture, p. 377
social classes, p. 377
reference groups, p. 378
opinion leader, p. 378
product, p. 378
product strategy, p. 379
product item, p. 379
product line, p. 379
product mix, p. 379
product mix consistency, p. 379
brand, p. 382
trademark, p. 383
service mark, p. 383
warranty, p. 383
patent, p. 386
utility patent, p. 386
design patent, p. 386
plant patent, p. 387
copyright, p. 387
trade dress, p. 387
distribution, p. 388
physical distribution (logistics), p. 388
channel of distribution, p. 388
merchant middlemen, p. 388
agents/brokers, p. 388
direct channel, p. 388
indirect channel, p. 388
dual distribution, p. 388
common carriers, p. 391
contract carriers, p. 391
private carriers, p. 391

Discussion Questions

1. Discuss the role of quality customer service in the creation of a competitive advantage.
2. Why may a small firm be in a better situation than a large firm to offer exceptional customer service?
3. Think of a recent experience you had with exceptionally good or exceptionally poor customer service. What do you think made the service exceptional?
4. Briefly describe the four stages of the consumer decision-making process. Why is the first stage so vital to consumer behavior?
5. List the four psychological and the four sociological influences discussed in this chapter. What is their relevance to consumer behavior?
6. Identify and briefly describe the three ways to increase sales of an existing product once a product strategy has been implemented.
7. Select two product names, and then evaluate each with respect to the five rules for naming a product.
8. Explain how registration of a small firm's trademark would be helpful in protecting its brand.
9. Why do small firms need to consider indirect channels of distribution for their products? Why involve intermediaries in distribution at all?
10. Discuss the major considerations in structuring a channel of distribution.

You Make the Call

SITUATION 1

Paul Layer, 43, is the owner of Aspen Funeral Alternatives in Albuquerque, New Mexico. Aspen is located in a converted restaurant with fluorescent lights, and its chapel has chairs, not pews. "It looks more like your insurance company or local business office rather than a funeral home," Layer says.

Aspen has adopted a strategy of discounted prices for funeral products and services. Its Web site (http://www.aspenfuneral.com) promotes low-cost alternatives with no fancy facilities, no limousines, and no hearses. A general price list, covering Aspen's professional services, use of its facilities, and caskets, is posted on the site.

Source: Lorrie Grant, "Funeral Stores Sell Inevitable in Style," *USA Today,* May 30, 2001, p. 3B.

Question 1 What psychological influences might impact customers' choice of this funeral home?

Question 2 What sociological influences might affect a customer's decision to use Aspen's services?

Question 3 Relate the stages of consumer decision making to a person's decision to use a particular funeral home. What could Aspen do to improve customer satisfaction?

SITUATION 2

John Kowalski, of Aliquippa, Pennsylvania, is the man behind the Load Hog, a device that enables pickup truck beds to function like dump trucks. The Load Hog evolved from a product originally introduced by an Australian importer back in 1992. After years of product development by Kowalski, at a price tag of $350,000, the Load Hog exhibits virtually no trace of the Australian product.

John and his wife, Carol, have promoted the Load Hog to truck dealers as an after-market product. They have exhibited at outdoor-vehicle and specialty-equipment shows and have sold around 400 of the units by mail order. More recently, they have launched a Web site (http://www.loadhog.com).

Source Leigh Buchanan, "Pickup Artist," *Inc.,* Vol. 23, No. 8 (June 2001), pp. 68–73.

Question 1 Do you think there may be other channels of distribution that Kowalski might use? If so, what are they?

Question 2 What other related products might be added to the product mix?

Question 3 What do you think about the choice of the name for the device?

SITUATION 3

Kim Hodges operates a 3-year-old furniture company named Metallika in Waco, Texas. Does the name sound familiar? According to a lawyer for the heavy-metal rock band Metallica, it sounds too familiar. In a letter to Hodges, the lawyer wrote, "Specifically, we need you to change the name of your business to a name that does not include the terms Metallika, Metalika, Metallica, Metalica, or any name, term, logo, domain name or vanity telephone number similar thereto."

The lawyer said if Hodges chooses not to change the name of his company, they might sue for damages, company profits, and attorneys' fees.

Source: Mike Copeland, "Metallika Rocked by Metallica," *Waco Tribune Herald,* December 9, 2000, p. 1A.

Question 1 What course of action would you recommend to Hodges?

Question 2 What can Hodges say in defense of the name he chose for his furniture business?

Experiential Exercises

1. For several days, make notes on your own shopping experiences. Summarize what you consider to be the best customer service you receive.
2. Ask some owners of small firms in your area to describe their new product development processes. Report your findings to the class.
3. Visit a local retail store and observe brand names, package designs, labels, and warranties. Choose good and bad examples of each, and report back to the class.
4. Consider your most recent meaningful purchase. Compare the decision-making process you used to the four stages of decision making presented in this chapter. Report your conclusions.
5. Interview two different types of local retail merchants (for example, a boutique owner and a manager of a franchise) to determine how the merchandise in their stores was distributed to them. Contrast the channels of distribution used, and write a brief report on your findings.

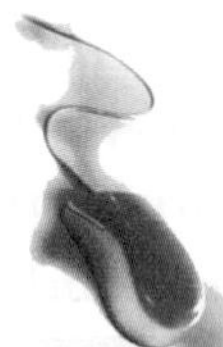

EXPLORING THE WEB

1. Access the U.S. Trademark Electronic Search System at **http://www.uspto.gov**.
   a. Invent a trade name, and search to see whether it is already registered. Keep trying until you find one that is in the database. Print the list of results.
   b. Follow the link to one of the "live" products. Print the trademark registration information.
   c. Use a search engine to search for the trade name. Did you turn up the same company or product?
2. Access the Lowe Foundation's Entrepreneurial Edge online at **http://www.lowe.org**. Under Business Builders, click Customers, and then follow the link to Customer Satisfaction.
   a. List some statistics about the effects of improving customer satisfaction.
   b. What five mistakes might a company make once it has gotten customer feedback?
   c. What sources of information can be used to get customer satisfaction data?
   d. List the steps in creating a valuable survey.
   e. Report on some ways to save money in the process of getting customer feedback.
3. Maintaining customer loyalty is important to every business. Merchant's Advantage offers a way to enhance customer relationships at **http://www.merchantsadvantage.com/loyalty.cfm**.
   a. What method does it offer? What is included?
   b. Read the article from *BrandWeek* entitled "Retailers' Invisible Customers Are Crying Out for Recognition." You can access the article at **http://www.findarticles.com/cf_dls/m0BDW/15_41/61969885/p1/article.jhtml**. Describe the mistakes made by certain stores.
   c. What store successfully meets customers' needs? Explain what that store does right.

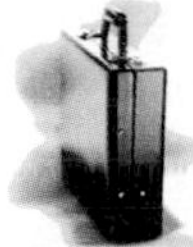

CASE 15

PROFESSIONAL SPORTS AUTHENTICATOR (p. 681)

This case describes how an entrepreneur developed customer loyalty to his firm.

Alternative Cases for Chapter 15:

Case 3, "HeadBlade Company," p. 645
Case 17, "Flower Girl," p. 686

The price per unit is only $0.20 lower in Situation B than in Situation A. However, the total difference in revenue is $50,000! Clearly, a small business can lose significant revenues if a price is set too low.

Pricing is also important because it indirectly affects sales quantity. In the above example, quantity sold was assumed to be independent of price—and it very well may be for a change in price from $3.00 to $2.80. However, a larger decrease or increase might substantially affect the quantity sold. Pricing, therefore, has a dual influence on total sales revenue. It is important *directly* as part of the gross revenue equation and *indirectly* through its impact on demand.

Before beginning a more detailed analysis of pricing, we should note that services are generally more difficult to price than products because of their intangible nature. However, the impact of price on revenue and profits is the same. Because estimating the cost of providing a service and the demand for that service can be problematic, our discussions will focus on product pricing.

Cost Determination for Pricing

total cost
the sum of cost of goods sold, selling expenses, and overhead costs

For a business to be successful, its pricing must cover total cost plus some profit margin. Pricing, therefore, must be based on an understanding of the basic behavior of costs. As illustrated in Figure 16-1, **total cost** includes three components. The first is the cost of goods offered for sale. An appliance retailer, for example, must include in the selling price the cost of the appliance and related freight charges. The second component is the selling cost, which includes the direct cost of the salesperson's time (salary plus commissions), as well as the cost of other selling activities such as advertising and sales promotion. The third component is the overhead cost applicable to the given product. Included in this cost are warehouse storage, office supplies, utilities, taxes, and salaries. *All* of these cost classifications must be incorporated into the pricing process.

total variable costs
costs that vary with the quantity produced or sold

total fixed costs
costs that remain constant as the quantity produced or sold varies

Costs behave differently as the quantity produced or sold increases or decreases. **Total variable costs** are those that increase in total as the quantity of product increases. Material costs and sales commissions are typical variable costs incurred as a product is made and sold. **Total fixed costs** are those that remain constant at different levels of quantity sold. For example, advertising campaign expenditures, factory equipment costs, and salaries of office personnel are fixed costs.

FIGURE 16-1

The Three Components of Total Cost in Determining Price

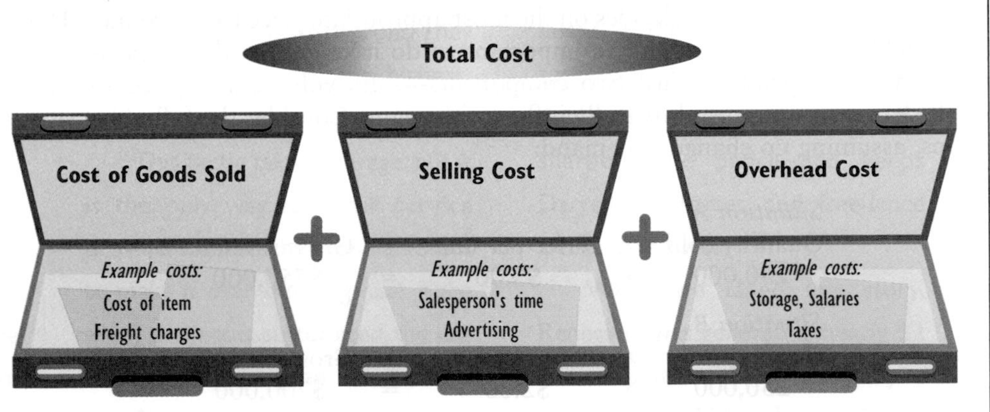

FIGURE 16-2

Cost Structure of a Hypothetical Firm, 2001

Sales revenue (25,000 units @ $8)		$200,000
Total costs:		
Fixed costs	$75,000	
Variable costs ($2 per unit)	50,000	
		125,000
Gross margin		$ 75,000

Average cost $= \frac{\$125,000}{25,000} = \$5$

An understanding of the behavior of different kinds of costs can help a seller minimize pricing mistakes. Although fixed and variable costs do not behave in the same way, small businesses often treat them identically. An approach called average pricing exemplifies this dangerous practice. With **average pricing,** you divide the total cost (fixed costs plus variable costs) over a previous period by the quantity sold in that period to arrive at an average cost, which is then used to set the current price. For example, consider the cost structure of a firm selling 25,000 units of a product in 2001 at a sales price of $8.00 each (see Figure 16-2). The average unit cost at the 2001 sales volume of 25,000 units is $5.00 (that is, $125,000 ÷ 25,000). The $3.00 markup provides a profit at this sales volume (25,000 × $3 = $75,000).

average pricing
an approach in which total cost for a given period is divided by quantity sold in that period to set a price

However, consider the impact on profit if sales in 2002 reach only 10,000 units and the selling price has been set at the same $3.00 markup, based on the average cost in 2001 (see Figure 16-3). At the lower sales volume (10,000 units), the average unit cost increases to $9.50 (that is, $95,000 ÷ 10,000). This increase is, of course, attributable to the need to spread the constant fixed cost over fewer units. *Average pricing overlooks the reality of higher average costs at lower sales levels.*

On rare occasions, pricing at less than total cost can be used as a special short-term strategy. Suppose some fixed costs are ongoing even if part of the production facility is temporarily idle. In this situation, pricing should cover all marginal or incremental costs—that is, those costs incurred specifically to get additional business. In the long run, however, all costs must be covered.

FIGURE 16-3

Cost Structure of a Hypothetical Firm, 2002

Sales revenue (10,000 units @ $8)		$80,000
Total costs:		
Fixed costs	$75,000	
Variable costs ($2 per unit)	20,000	
		95,000
Gross margin		($15,000)

Average cost $= \frac{\$95,000}{10,000} = \$9.50$

How Customer Demand Affects Pricing

Cost analysis can identify a level below which a price should not be set for normal purposes: a minimum price. However, it does not show how much the actual price might exceed that minimum figure and still be acceptable to customers. Demand factors must be considered before this determination can be made.

elasticity of demand the degree to which a change in price affects the quantity demanded

elastic demand demand that changes significantly when there is a change in the price of the product

inelastic demand demand that does not change significantly when there is a change in the price of the product

THE ELASTICITY OF DEMAND Customer demand for a product is often sensitive to the price level. *Elasticity* is the term used to describe this sensitivity, and the effect of a change in price on the quantity demanded is called **elasticity of demand.** A product is said to have **elastic demand** if an increase in its price *lowers* total revenue or a decrease in its price *raises* total revenue. A product is said to have **inelastic demand** if an increase in its price *raises* total revenue or a decrease in its price *lowers* total revenue.

In some markets, the demand for products is very elastic. With a lower price, the amount purchased increases sharply, thus providing higher revenue. For example, in the personal computer industry, a decrease in price will frequently produce a more than proportionate increase in quantity sold, resulting in higher total revenues. For products such as salt, however, the demand is highly inelastic. Regardless of price, the quantity purchased will not change significantly, because consumers use a fixed amount of salt.

The concept of elasticity of demand is important because the degree of elasticity sets limits on or provides opportunities for higher pricing. A small firm should seek to distinguish its product or service in such a way that small price increases will incur little resistance from customers and thereby yield increasing total revenue.

PRICING AND A FIRM'S COMPETITIVE ADVANTAGE Several factors affect the attractiveness of a product or service to customers. One factor is the firm's competitive advantage. If consumers perceive the product or service as an important solution to their unsatisfied needs, they will demand more.

Only in rare cases are identical products and services offered by competing firms. In most cases, products differ in some way. Even if products are physically similar, the accompanying services typically differ. Speed of service, credit terms offered, delivery arrangements, personal attention from a salesperson, and warranties are but a few of the factors that serve to distinguish one product from another. A unique combination of goods and services may well justify a higher price.

prestige pricing setting a high price to convey an image of high quality or uniqueness

A pricing tactic that reflects competitive advantage is **prestige pricing**—setting a high price to convey an image of high quality or uniqueness. Its influence varies from market to market and product to product. Because higher income markets are less sensitive to price variations than lower income ones, prestige pricing typically works better in high income markets. Products sold in markets with low levels of product knowledge are good candidates for prestige pricing.

When customers have low product knowledge, they often use price as a surrogate indicator of quality. For example, a company selling windshield-washer fluid found that the product cost pennies to manufacture and, therefore, was profitable even when sold at a very low price. However, the firm recognized an opportunity and raised its price repeatedly, making prestige pricing extremely profitable. Another example is found in the testimony of Chris J. Ketron, owner of Gallery House Furniture in Bristol, Virginia:

We . . . were bringing in around $30,000 monthly in revenues—a tiny amount next to the megadollars in my area. I thought that lowering my prices would enable me

IN THE TRENCHES ENTREPRENEURSHIP TODAY

RAISING PRICES

Once a firm sets a price, increasing it without creating a negative customer reaction can be difficult. Nevertheless, it is frequently necessary to raise prices, and customers will be more understanding if the increase is introduced correctly.

Eric Schechter, founder and president of Great American Merchandise and Events (GAME) of Scottsdale, Arizona, was concerned about client reaction when he initiated a price increase for the firm's services in 1999. GAME manages events and fund-raisers for nonprofit and corporate clients. One of its most popular promotions is a "duck race," in which participants sponsor plastic ducks in a river race. The company stages its Derby Duck Races® in more than 100 U.S. cities and 7 other countries.

When the company decided to raise its price, it was "up front" about the change, discussing it first in a letter mailed to all clients. Schechter felt that the new price would be better accepted if he could demonstrate a related increase in product value. Therefore, a longstanding separate fee for promotional materials was eliminated, and services were enhanced to expand the overall value of GAME's programs.

The results were great! While a few customers were lost, Schechter estimates that the net effect on the bottom line was a yearly increase of $200,000. Notable clients of this 25-employee firm include Toys "R" Us, Boys and Girls Clubs of America, and Goodwill Industries.

Source: From material from http://www.duckrace.com/company/index.cfm; and Karen M. Kroll, "Pricing Right," *Independent Business*, Vol. 10, No. 4 (July-August 1999), pp. 26–27.

http://www.duckrace.com

to compete better. What I found out was that my price cutting provoked a 'must be something wrong with it' attitude among my customers. I ditched the lower prices and started to display higher-end merchandise. . . . I'm now doing . . . more in sales . . . and I'm selling fewer pieces to get it.[1]

APPLYING A PRICING SYSTEM

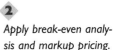

Apply break-even analysis and markup pricing.

A typical entrepreneur is unprepared to evaluate a feasible pricing system until he or she understands potential costs, revenue, product demand, and distribution channels for the venture. To better comprehend these factors and to determine the acceptability of various prices, the entrepreneur can use break-even analysis. An understanding of markup pricing is also valuable, as it provides the entrepreneur with an awareness of pricing practices of intermediaries—wholesalers and retailers.

Break-Even Analysis

Break-even analysis involves comparing alternative cost and revenue estimates in order to determine the acceptability of each price. A comprehensive break-even analysis has two phases: (1) examining revenue–cost relationships and (2) incorporating actual sales forecasts into the analysis. Break-even analysis is typically presented by means of formulas or graphs; this discussion uses a graphic presentation.

EXAMINING COST AND REVENUE RELATIONSHIPS The objective of the first phase of break-even analysis is to determine the quantity at which the product, at an assumed price, will generate enough revenue to start earning a profit. Figure 16-4(a) presents a simple break-even chart reflecting this comparison. Total fixed costs are represented by a horizontal section at the bottom of the graph, indicating that they do not change with the volume of production. The section for total variable costs is a triangle that slants upward, depicting the direct relationship of total variable costs to output. The entire area below the upward-slanting total cost line represents the combination of fixed and variable costs. The distance between the sales and total cost lines gives the profit or loss position of the company at any level of sales. The point of intersection of these two lines is called the **break-even point,** because sales revenue equals total cost at this sales volume.

break-even point
sales volume at which total sales revenue equals total costs

To evaluate other break-even points, additional sales lines for other prices can be plotted on the chart. On the flexible break-even chart shown in Figure 16-4(b), the higher price of $18 yields a more steeply sloped sales line, resulting in an earlier break-even point. Similarly, the lower price of $7 produces a flatter revenue line, delaying the break-even point. Additional sales lines could be plotted to evaluate other proposed prices.

Because it shows the profit area growing larger and larger to the right, the break-even chart implies that quantity sold can increase continually. This assumption is unrealistic and should be clarified by modifying the break-even analysis with demand information.

FIGURE 16-4 *Break-Even Graphs for Pricing*

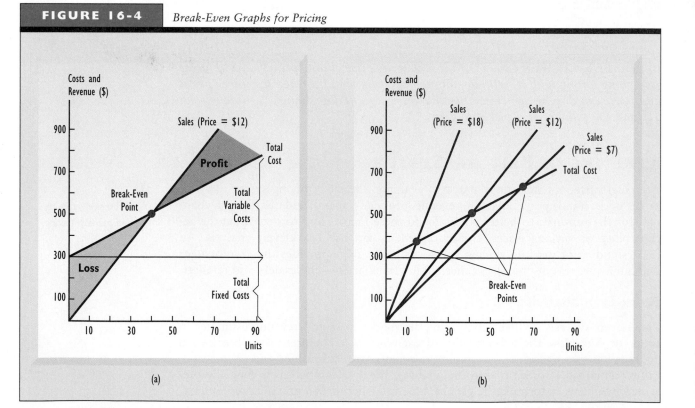

INCORPORATING SALES FORECASTS The indirect impact of price on quantity sold complicates pricing decisions. Demand for a product typically decreases as price increases. However, in certain cases, price may influence demand in the opposite direction, resulting in increased demand for a product at higher prices. Therefore, estimated demand for a product at various prices, as determined through marketing research, should be incorporated into the break-even analysis.

An adjusted break-even chart that incorporates estimated demand is developed by using the initial break-even data and adding a demand curve. A schedule showing the estimated number of units demanded and total revenue at three prices is shown in Figure 16-5, along with a break-even chart on which a demand curve is plotted from these data. This graph allows a more realistic profit area to be identified. The break-even point in Figure 16-5 for a unit price of $18 corresponds to a quantity sold that appears impossible to reach at the assumed price (the break-even point does not fall within the sales curve), leaving $7 and $12 as feasible prices. Clearly, the preferred price is $12. The potential for profit at this price is indicated by the shaded area in the graph.

Markup Pricing

Up to this point, we have made no distinction between pricing by manufacturers and pricing by intermediaries such as wholesalers and retailers, since break-even concepts apply to all small businesses, regardless of their position in the distribution channel. Now, however, we briefly present some of the pricing formulas used by

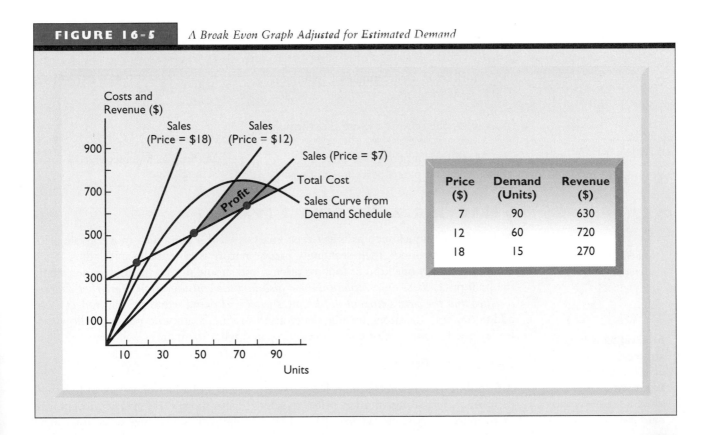

FIGURE 16-5 *A Break-Even Graph Adjusted for Estimated Demand*

Price ($)	Demand (Units)	Revenue ($)
7	90	630
12	60	720
18	15	270

markup pricing
applying a percentage to a product's cost to obtain its selling price

wholesalers and retailers. In the retailing industry, where businesses often carry many different products, **markup pricing** has emerged as a manageable pricing system. With this cost-plus approach to pricing, retailers are able to price hundreds of products much more quickly than they could using individual break-even analyses. In calculating the selling price for a particular item, a retailer adds a markup percentage (sometimes referred to as a markup rate) to cover the following:

- Operating expenses
- Subsequent price reductions—for example, markdowns and employee discounts
- Desired profit

It is important to have a clear understanding of markup pricing computations. Markups may be expressed as a percentage of either the *selling price* or the *cost*. For example, if an item costs $6 and sells for $10, the markup of $4 represents a 40 percent markup on the selling price [$4 (markup) ÷ $10 (selling price) × 100] or 66⅔ percent of the cost [$4 (markup) ÷ $6 (cost) × 100]. Two simple formulas are commonly used for markup calculations:

$$\frac{\text{Markup}}{\text{Selling price}} \times 100 = \text{Markup expressed as a percentage of selling price}$$

or

$$\frac{\text{Markup}}{\text{Cost}} \times 100 = \text{Markup expressed as a percentage of cost}$$

To convert markup as a percentage of selling price to markup as a percentage of cost, use the following formula:

$$\frac{\text{Markup as a percentage of selling price}}{100\% - \text{Markup as a percentage of selling price}} \times 100 = \text{Markup as a percentage of cost}$$

To convert the other way, use this formula:

$$\frac{\text{Markup as a percentage of cost}}{100\% + \text{Markup as a percentage of cost}} \times 100 = \text{Markup as a percentage of selling price}$$

Selecting a Pricing Strategy

3
Identify specific pricing strategies.

Although techniques such as break-even analysis yield a good idea of a feasible price for a specific product, their seemingly precise nature is potentially misleading. Such analyses are only one kind of tool for pricing and should not by themselves determine the final price. *Price determination must also include consideration of market characteristics and the firm's current marketing strategy.*[2] Pricing strategies that reflect these additional considerations include penetration pricing, skimming pricing, follow-the-leader pricing, variable pricing, price lining, and what the market will bear.

penetration pricing strategy
setting lower than normal prices to hasten market acceptance of a product or service or to increase market share

Penetration Pricing

A firm that uses a **penetration pricing strategy** prices a product or service at less than its normal, long-range market price in order to gain more rapid market acceptance or to increase existing market share. This strategy can sometimes discourage new

IN THE TRENCHES

Building Customer Loyalty

SELLING YOUR PRICE

Basing the price of a product or service solely on cost is less than ideal. The price should also reflect the total value and benefits received by customers. In addition, a small firm needs to communicate to customers the value represented by the price—and this can require a bit of salesmanship.

Consider the approach of E. Kelly Hanson, founder and president of Sun Tzu Security, Ltd., based in Milwaukee, Wisconsin. This 8-person information security firm was one of the first providers in the nation to offer turnkey information security solutions.

Upon hearing that a prospective client was going to use a larger competitor who had submitted a lower-priced bid, Hanson was greatly disturbed. "I really got a bee in my bonnet," she says. She immediately contacted the prospect to explain the value of her firm's service.

Hanson said that while the prospect's firm was small, it would receive a high level of attention and service from Sun Tzu. She gave the prospect the name of two of Sun Tzu's clients, also small businesses, who had come from the larger firm after finding that their needs often were ignored. "They hadn't asked how they would be treated by the other firm," says Hanson. "The other shop often used small projects just to fill in the gaps."

After listening to Hanson's sales pitch, the client signed on with Sun Tzu and has remained a loyal customer.

Source: From material from http://www.suntzu.net; and Karen M. Kroll, "Pricing Right," *Independent Business*, Vol. 10, No. 4 (July-August 1999), p. 30.

http://www.suntzu.net

competitors from entering a market niche if they mistakenly view the penetration price as a long-range price. Obviously, a firm that uses this strategy sacrifices some profit margin to achieve market penetration.

Skimming Pricing

A **skimming price strategy** sets prices for products or services at high levels for a limited period of time before reducing prices to lower, more competitive levels. This strategy assumes that certain customers will pay a higher price because they view a product or service as a prestige item. Use of a skimming price is most practical when there is little threat of short-term competition or when startup costs must be recovered rapidly.

skimming price strategy
setting very high prices for a limited period before reducing them to more competitive levels

Follow-the-Leader Pricing

A **follow-the-leader pricing strategy** uses a particular competitor as a model in setting a price for a product or service. The probable reaction of competitors is a critical factor in determining whether to cut prices below a prevailing level. A small business in competition with larger firms is seldom in a position to consider itself the price leader. If competitors view a small firm's pricing as relatively unimportant, they may permit a price differential to exist. On the other hand, some competitors may view a smaller price-cutter as a direct threat and counter with reductions of

follow-the-leader pricing strategy
using a particular competitor as a model in setting prices

their own. In such a case, the use of a follow-the-leader pricing strategy accomplishes very little.

Variable Pricing

variable pricing strategy setting more than one price for a good or service in order to offer price concessions to certain customers

dynamic pricing strategy charging more than the standard price when the customer's profile suggests that the higher price will be accepted

Some businesses use a **variable pricing strategy** to offer price concessions to certain customers, even though they may advertise a uniform price. Lower prices are offered for various reasons, including a customer's knowledge and bargaining strength. In some fields of business, therefore, firms make two-part pricing decisions: They set a standard list price but offer a range of price concessions to particular buyers.

Sellers using a type of variable pricing called **dynamic pricing** charge *more* than the standard price after gauging a customer's financial means and desire for the product. The information-gathering capability of the Internet has allowed such retailers as Amazon.com to use dynamic pricing. Consider a recent account of Amazon.com's pricing strategy:

The Internet was supposed to empower consumers, letting them compare deals with the click of a mouse. But it is also supplying retailers with information about their customers that they never had before, along with the technology to use all this accumulated data. While prices have always varied by geography, local competition and whim, retailers were never able to effectively target individuals until the Web.

"Dynamic pricing is the new reality, and it's going to be used by more and more retailers," said Vernon Keenan, a San Francisco Internet consultant. "In the future, what you pay will be determined by where you live and who you are. It's unfair, but that doesn't mean it's not going to happen."

With its detailed records on the buying habits of 23 million consumers, Amazon is perfectly situated to employ dynamic pricing on a massive scale. But its trial ran into a snag early this month when the regulars discussing DVDs at the Web site DVDTalk.com noticed something odd.

One man recounted how he ordered the DVD of Julie Taymor's "Titus," paying \$24.49. The next week he went back to Amazon and saw that the price had jumped to \$26.24. As an experiment, he stripped his computer of the electronic tags that identified him to Amazon as a regular customer. Then the price fell to \$22.74.[3]

Price Lining

price lining strategy setting a range of several distinct merchandise price levels

A **price lining strategy** establishes distinct price categories at which similar items of retail merchandise are offered for sale. For example, men's suits (of differing quality) might be sold at \$250, \$450, and \$800. The inventory level of the different lines depends on the income levels and buying desires of a store's customers. A price lining strategy has the advantage of simplifying the selection process for the customer and reducing the necessary minimum inventory.

What the Market Will Bear

The strategy of pricing on the basis of what the market will bear can be used only when the seller has little or no competition. Obviously, this strategy will work only for nonstandardized products. For example, a food store might offer egg roll wrappers that its competitors do not carry. Busy consumers who want to fix egg rolls but

IN THE TRENCHES **BUILDING CUSTOMER LOYALTY**

VALUE PRICING

Entrepreneurs sometimes price their products and services too low, creating customer expectations that are difficult to escape. Consider what happened to Synergy Investment, a Framingham, Massachusetts firm founded by Daniel Gould. Synergy provides turnkey implementation of personalized energy-efficient solutions for lighting and building systems.

In 1994, this startup created a niche with few competitors. However, a low pricing strategy kept Gould hustling, offering his customers what he calls "the Wal-Mart attitude—give them rock-bottom prices all the time." Using this strategy, Gould found that he didn't have much to show for all his work. "Basically, I was giving it away," he says.

With more experience came recognition of the true value of his service. Gould realized, "I could've charged more, and people wouldn't have blinked."

Gould has continually raised his prices over the past few years but remains a low-cost provider. "When I started the business, I was happy just to draw a salary," he says. "It's been a slow awakening to what is necessary to charge to be slightly profitable by the end of the year."

Synergy has performed lighting service for clients such as Macy's; Wendy's; Bed, Bath and Beyond; and Nine West. The firm was ranked number 219 on the *Inc. 2000* list of the 500 fastest-growing companies in America.

Source: From material from http://www.synergyinv.com; and Rifka Rasenwein, "If Only . . . ," *Inc. 2000,* Vol 22, No. 15 (October 17, 2000), p. 104.

http://www.synergyinv.com

have neither the time nor the knowledge to prepare the wrappers themselves will buy them at any reasonable price.

A Final Note on Price Strategies

In some situations, local, state, and federal laws must be considered in setting prices. For example, the Sherman Antitrust Act generally prohibits price fixing. Most federal pricing legislation is intended to benefit small firms as well as consumers by keeping large businesses from conspiring to set prices that stifle competition.

When a small business markets a line of products, some of which may compete with each other, pricing decisions must take into account the effects of a single product price on the rest of the line. For example, the introduction of a cheese-flavored chip will likely affect sales of an existing naturally flavored chip. Pricing can become extremely complex in these situations.

Continually adjusting a price to meet changing marketing conditions can be both costly to the seller and confusing to buyers. An alternative approach is to use a system of discounting designed to reflect a variety of needs. For example, a seller may offer a trade discount to a particular buyer (such as a wholesaler) because that buyer performs a certain marketing function for the seller (such as distribution). The stated, or list, price is unchanged, but the seller offers a lower actual price by means of a discount.

Small firms should not treat pricing mistakes as uncorrectable decisions. Remember that pricing is not an exact science. *If the initial price appears to be off target, just make any necessary adjustments and keep on selling!*

Offering Credit

4

Explain the benefits of credit, factors that affect credit extension, and types of credit.

In a credit sale, the seller conveys goods or services to the buyer in return for the buyer's promise to pay later. The major reason for granting credit is to make sales; credit encourages decisions to buy by providing an incentive for customers to buy now and pay later. Most firms offering credit actively promote this option to potential customers. An added bonus to the seller is credit records containing information that can be used for sales promotion, such as direct-mail appeals to customers.

Benefits of Credit

If credit buying and selling did not benefit both parties in a transaction, their use would cease. Borrowers obviously enjoy the availability of credit, and small firms, in particular, benefit from the extension of credit by other lenders. Credit provides small firms with working capital, often allowing marginal businesses to continue operations. Additional benefits of credit to borrowers are as follows:

- The ability to satisfy immediate needs and pay for them later
- Better records of purchases on credit billing statements
- Better service and greater convenience when exchanging purchased items
- Establishment of a credit history

Traditional short-term creditors include suppliers and local banks. Lenders extend credit to customers in order to facilitate increased sales volume and also to earn money on unpaid balances. Lenders expect the increased revenue to more than offset the costs of extending credit, so profits will increase. Other benefits of credit to sellers are as follows:

- Closer association with customers because of implied trust
- Easier selling through telephone- and mail-order systems and over the Internet
- Smoother sales peaks and valleys, since purchasing power is always available
- Easy access to a tool with which to stay competitive

Factors That Affect Selling on Credit

An entrepreneur must decide whether to sell on credit or for cash only. In many cases, credit selling cannot be avoided, as it is standard trade practice in many types of business. It is important to note that credit-selling competitors will almost always outsell a cash-only firm.

Although a seller always hopes to increase profits by allowing credit sales, it is not a risk-free practice. Small firms frequently shift or at least share credit risk by accepting credit cards carried by customers rather than offering their own credit. For example, the operator of a Texaco gasoline station may accept Texaco credit cards or other major credit cards, thereby avoiding credit management. The business will pay a fee to the credit card company, but that cost may be less than the expense of managing its own independent credit system, including bad debts. A retailer following this strategy must obtain merchant status with individual credit card companies. This is not an automatic process and can be problematic, particularly for home-based businesses.

IN THE TRENCHES ENTREPRENEURSHIP TODAY

GIVE ME CREDIT

NetForce Technologies was founded in 1993 in Austin, Texas by Tommy Wald. The firm was one of the first independent computer network consulting firms in the area. Seven years later, NetForce was number 290 on the *Inc. 2000* list of the 500 fastest-growing firms. Its growth was partially subsidized by credit received from various lenders.

Obtaining a line of credit was not always easy, however. Some banks rejected Wald's credit applications because they thought that NetForce was too small. Later, banks spurned credit requests from NetForce because they thought that the firm was saddled with too many asset restrictions required by existing Small Business Administration loans.

In 1998, NetForce once again sought help from banks, as the firm was in desperate need of a larger line of credit. The negotiations shocked NetForce's comptroller, Sherri Holland. At one bank, where the salesperson had promised no hidden fees, she discovered that "receivables financing involved cash-management fees: $85 a month for a lock box, 40 cents per check deposited in the lock box, $15 a month for account processing, and $75 a month for the ability to check postings on-line." The requirement of a lock box meant that all of NetForce's accounts receivable payments would automatically go toward paying off the credit line, effectively transferring all control to the bank.

Understandably, Holland was unhappy with these conditions and turned down all offers. Finally, she sought out an investment bank, which eventually gave NetForce a $300,000 line of credit. This investment bank doesn't require a lock box, nor do its fees fluctuate based on a monthly accounts receivable review.

Wald is proud that now his business has finally passed the point of relying on federal and bank loans. "It makes you feel good," he says, "that you can finally graduate to that level of respect."

Source: Ilan Machari, "Who Needs a Bank Anyway?," *Inc.*, Vol. 22, No. 2 (February 2000), pp. 129–130.

Unfortunately, the cost of accepting major credit cards for payment over the Internet has increased. To deal with Internet fraud, small e-retailers are obtaining the services of firms that specialize in handling Internet credit card payments. For example, first-time entrepreneur Margaret Cobbs, founder of Velma Handbags in Redwood City, California, decided that it was too expensive for her online business to process credit card orders, so she employed CCNow, an Internet credit card service based in Delaware. CCNow has thwarted several attempts by customers to defraud Velma Handbags by using stolen credit cards. This protection, however, is expensive and CCNow collects 9 percent of every online credit sale made by Velma Handbags.[4]

Also, if a small firm makes credit sales online, it is subject to "chargebacks" whenever buyers dispute a transaction. Some credit card companies assess fines and threaten account termination if the number of chargebacks is excessive.

Four factors related to the entrepreneur's decision to extend credit are the type of business, credit policies of competitors, customers' income levels, and the availability of working capital.

TYPE OF BUSINESS Retailers of durable goods typically grant credit more freely than do small grocers who sell perishables. Indeed, most consumers find it necessary

to buy big-ticket items on an installment basis, and such a product's life span makes installment selling feasible.

CREDIT POLICIES OF COMPETITORS Unless a firm offers some compensating advantage, it is expected to be as generous as its competitors in extending credit. Wholesale hardware companies and retail furniture stores are examples of businesses that face stiff competition from credit sellers.

INCOME LEVEL OF CUSTOMERS The age and income level of a retailer's customers are significant factors in determining its credit policy. For example, a drugstore adjacent to a city high school would probably not extend credit to high school students, who are typically undesirable credit customers because of their lack of maturity and income.

AVAILABILITY OF WORKING CAPITAL There is no denying that credit sales increase the amount of working capital needed by the business doing the selling. Open-credit and installment accounts tie up money that may be needed to pay business expenses.

Types of Credit

consumer credit
financing granted by retailers to individuals who purchase for personal or family use

trade credit
financing provided by a supplier of inventory to a given company, which sets up an account payable for the amount

There are two broad classes of credit: consumer credit and trade credit. **Consumer credit** is granted by retailers to final consumers who purchase for personal or family use. A small business owner can sometimes use his or her personal consumer credit to purchase supplies and equipment for use in the business. **Trade credit** is extended by nonfinancial firms, such as manufacturers and wholesalers, to customers that are other business firms. Consumer credit and trade credit differ with respect to types of credit instruments used, sources for financing receivables, and terms of sale. Another important distinction is that credit insurance is available for trade credit only.

CONSUMER CREDIT The three major kinds of consumer credit accounts are open charge accounts, installment accounts, and revolving charge accounts. Many variations of these credit accounts are also used.

open charge account
a line of credit that allows the customer to obtain a product at the time of purchase, with payment due when billed

Open Charge Accounts When using an **open charge account,** a customer obtains possession of goods (or services) at the time of purchase, with payment due when billed. Stated terms typically call for payment at the end of the month, but it is customary to allow a longer period than that stated. There is no finance charge for this kind of credit if the balance on the account is paid in full at the end of the billing period. Customers are not generally required to make a down payment or to pledge collateral. Small accounts at department stores are good examples of open charge accounts.

installment account
a line of credit that requires a down payment, with the balance paid over a specified period of time

Installment Accounts An **installment account** is a vehicle for long-term consumer credit. A down payment is normally required, and annual finance charges can be 20 percent or more of the purchase price. Payment periods are commonly from 12 to 36 months, although automobile dealers often offer an extended payment period of 60 months. An installment account is useful for large purchases such as cars, washing machines, and televisions.

Revolving Charge Accounts A **revolving charge account** is a variation of the installment account. A seller grants a customer a line of credit, and charged purchases may not exceed the credit limit. A specified percentage of the outstanding balance must be paid monthly, forcing the customer to budget and limiting the amount of debt that can be carried. Finance charges are computed on the unpaid balance at the end of the month. Although credit cards offer this type of account, they are discussed separately in the next section because of their significance.

revolving charge account a line of credit on which the customer may charge purchases at any time, up to a preestablished limit

CREDIT CARDS Credit cards, frequently referred to as *plastic money,* have become a major source of retail credit. As just mentioned, credit cards are usually based on a revolving charge account system. Based on the sponsor, we can distinguish three basic types of credit cards: bank credit cards, entertainment credit cards, and retailer credit cards.

Bank Credit Cards The best known bank credit cards are MasterCard and VISA. Bank credit cards are widely accepted by retailers who want to offer credit but don't provide their own credit cards. Most small business retailers fit into this category. In return for a set fee (usually 2 to 5 percent of the purchase price) paid by the retailer, the bank takes the responsibility for making collections. Some banks charge annual membership fees to their cardholders. Also, cardholders are frequently able to receive cash up to the credit limit of their card.

http://www.mastercard.com
http://www.visa.com

Entertainment Credit Cards Well-known examples of entertainment credit cards are American Express and Diner's Club cards. These cards have traditionally charged an annual fee. Although originally used for services, these cards are now widely accepted for sales of merchandise. As with bank credit cards, the collection of charges on an entertainment credit card is the responsibility of the sponsoring agency.

http://www.americanexpress.com
http://www.dinersclub.com

Retailer Credit Cards Many companies—for example, department stores, oil companies, and telephone companies—issue their own credit cards for specific use in their outlets or for purchasing their products or services from other outlets. Customers are usually not charged annual fees or finance charges if their balance is paid each month.

TRADE CREDIT Business firms may sell goods subject to specified terms of sale, such as 2/10, net 30. This means that a 2 percent discount is given by the seller if the buyer pays within 10 days of the invoice date. Failure to take this discount makes the full amount of the invoice due in 30 days. For example, with these terms, a buyer paying for a $100,000 purchase within 10 days of the invoice date would save 2 percent, or $2,000.

Sales terms for trade credit depend on the product sold and the buyer's and the seller's circumstances. The credit period often varies directly with the length of the buyer's turnover period, which obviously depends on the type of product sold. The larger the order and the higher the credit rating of the buyer, the better the sales terms will be, assuming that individual terms are fixed for each buyer. The greater the financial strength and the more adequate and liquid the working capital of the seller, the more generous the seller's sales terms can be. Of course, no business can afford to allow competitors to outdo it in reasonable generosity of sales terms. In

many types of business, terms are so firmly set by tradition that a unique policy is difficult, if not impossible, for a small firm to implement.

Managing the Credit Process

5

Describe the activities involved in managing credit.

Unfortunately, many small firms pay little attention to their credit management systems until bad debts become a problem. Often, this is too late. Credit management should precede the first credit sale (in the form of a thorough screening process) and then continue throughout the credit cycle.

As mentioned previously, many small firms transfer all or part of the credit function to another party. For example, a small repair shop or retail clothing store that accepts VISA or MasterCard is transferring much of the credit risk; in effect, the fee that the business pays the credit card company covers the credit management process. Nevertheless, a number of small firms want to offer their own credit to their customers and, therefore, need an understanding of the credit function. Let's take a look at some of the major considerations in developing and operating a comprehensive credit management program for a small business.

Evaluation of Credit Applicants

In most retail stores, the first step in credit investigation is having the customer complete an application form. The information obtained on this form is used as the basis for examining an applicant's creditworthiness. Since the most important factor in determining a customer's credit limit is her or his ability to pay the obligation when it becomes due, it is crucial to evaluate the customer's financial resources, debt position, and income level. The amount of credit requested also requires careful consideration. Drugstore customers usually need only small amounts of credit. On the other hand, business customers of wholesalers and manufacturers typically expect large credit lines. In the special case of installment selling, the amount of credit should not exceed the repossession value of the goods sold. Automobile dealers follow this rule as a general practice.

THE FOUR CREDIT QUESTIONS In evaluating the credit status of applicants, a seller must answer the following questions:

1. Can the buyer pay as promised?
2. Will the buyer pay?
3. If so, when will the buyer pay?
4. If not, can the buyer be forced to pay?

The answers to these questions have to be based in part on the seller's estimate of the buyer's ability and willingness to pay. Such an estimate constitutes a judgment of the buyer's inherent creditworthiness. For credit to be approved, the answers to questions 1, 2, and 4 should be "yes" and the answer to question 3 should be "on schedule."

Every applicant is creditworthy to some degree; a decision to grant credit merely recognizes the buyer's credit standing. But the seller must consider the possibility that the buyer will be unable or unwilling to pay. When evaluating an applicant's credit status, therefore, the seller must decide how much risk of nonpayment to assume.

THE TRADITIONAL FIVE C'S OF CREDIT Ability to pay is evaluated in terms of the five C's of credit: character, capital, capacity, conditions, and collateral.

- *Character* refers to the fundamental integrity and honesty that should underlie all human and business relationships. For business customers, character is embodied in the business policies and ethical practices of the firm. Individual customers who are granted credit must be known to be morally responsible persons.
- *Capital* consists of the cash and other assets owned by the customer. A prospective business customer should have sufficient capital to underwrite planned operations, including an appropriate amount invested by the owner.
- *Capacity* refers to the customer's ability to conserve assets and faithfully and efficiently follow a financial plan. A business customer should utilize its invested capital wisely and capitalize to the fullest extent on business opportunities.
- *Conditions* refer to such factors as business cycles and changes in price levels, which may be either favorable or unfavorable to the payment of debts. For example, economic recession places a burden on both businesses' and consumers' abilities to pay their debts. Other adverse factors that might limit a customer's ability to pay include fires and other natural disasters, strong new competition, and labor problems.
- *Collateral* consists of designated security given as a pledge for fulfillment of an obligation. It is a secondary source for loan repayment in case the borrower's cash flows are insufficient for repaying a loan.

Sources of Credit Information

One of the most important, and most frequently neglected, sources of credit information is a customer's previous credit history. Properly analyzed, credit records show whether a business customer regularly takes cash discounts and, if not, whether the customer's account is typically slow. One small clothing retailer has every applicant reviewed by a Dun & Bradstreet–trained credit manager, who maintains a complete file of D&B credit reports on thousands of customers. Recent financial statements of customers are also on file. These reports, together with the retailer's own credit information, are the basis for decisions on credit sales, with heavy emphasis on the D&B credit reports. Nonretailing firms should similarly investigate credit applicants. The D&B Business Information Report costs less than $25 and provides a company's history and sales statistics.

http://www.dnb.com

Manufacturers and wholesalers can frequently use a firm's financial statements as an additional source of information. Obtaining maximum value from financial statements requires a careful ratio analysis, which will reveal a firm's working-capital position, profit-making potential, and general financial health (as discussed in Chapter 22).

Pertinent data may also be obtained from outsiders. For example, arrangements may be made with other sellers to exchange credit data. Such credit information exchanges are quite useful for learning about the sales and payment experiences others have had with the seller's own customers or credit applicants.

Another source of credit information for the small firm, particularly about commercial accounts, is the customer's banker. Some bankers willingly supply credit information about their depositors, considering this to be a service that helps those

firms or individuals obtain credit in amounts they can successfully handle. Other bankers believe that credit information is confidential and should not be disclosed.

trade-credit agencies
privately owned organizations that collect credit information on businesses

Organizations that may be consulted with reference to credit standings are trade-credit agencies and credit bureaus. **Trade-credit agencies** are privately owned and operated organizations that collect credit information on businesses only, not individual consumers. After analyzing and evaluating the data, trade-credit agencies make credit ratings available to client companies for a fee. Dun & Bradstreet, Inc. is a nationwide, general trade-credit agency. Manufacturers and wholesalers are especially interested in Dun & Bradstreet's reference book and credit reports. Available to subscribers only, the reference book covers most U.S. businesses and provides a credit rating, an evaluation of financial strength, and other key credit information on each firm.

credit bureaus
privately owned organizations that summarize a number of firms' credit experiences with particular individuals

Credit bureaus are the most common type of consumer reporting agency. These private companies maintain credit histories on individuals, based on reports from banks, mortgage companies, department stores, and other creditors. These companies make possible the exchange of credit information on persons with previous credit activity. Some credit bureaus do not require a business firm to be a member in order to get a credit report. The fee charged to nonmembers, however, is considerably higher than that charged to members. Most credit bureaus operate on one of the three online data-processing networks: Experian (formerly TRW Credit Data); Equifax, Inc.; or TransUnion Corporation.

http://www.experian.com
http://www.equifax.com
http://www.tuc.com

Obtaining credit data online is becoming increasingly popular. One example of a Web site containing this immediate and comparatively low-cost information is CreditFYI. The site is operated by Fair, Isaac, a New York Stock Exchange company with a history in credit scoring—rating applicants' creditworthiness. Based on data from Experian, it features reports on many small firms, specializing in companies with sales under $5 million. At a cost of under $15, each report provides key information for assessing a company's creditworthiness.[5] Figure 16-6 shows a hypothetical credit evaluation provided on the CreditFYI Web site. Another Internet site with useful credit and collection information is that of Creditworthy. This site includes a huge list of companies that provide goods and services to the credit industry.

http://www.creditfyi.com
http://www.creditworthy.com

Aging of Accounts Receivable

aging schedule
a categorization of accounts receivable based on the length of time they have been outstanding

Many small businesses can benefit from an **aging schedule,** which divides accounts receivable into categories based on the length of time they have been outstanding. Typically, some accounts are current and others are past due. Regular use of an aging schedule allows troublesome collection trends to be spotted so that appropriate actions can be taken. With experience, a small firm can estimate the probabilities of collecting accounts of various ages and use them to forecast cash conversion rates.

Figure 16-7 on page 416 presents a hypothetical aging schedule for accounts receivable. According to the schedule, four customers have overdue credit, totaling $200,000. Only customer 005 is current. Customer 003 has the largest amount overdue ($80,000). In fact, the schedule shows that customer 003 is overdue on all charges and has a past record of slow payment (indicated by a credit rating of C). Immediate attention must be given to collecting from this customer. Customer 002 should also be contacted, because, among overdue accounts, this customer has the largest amount ($110,000) in the "Not due" classification. Customer 002 could quickly have the largest amount overdue.

FIGURE 16-6 *Hypothetical Credit Evaluation*

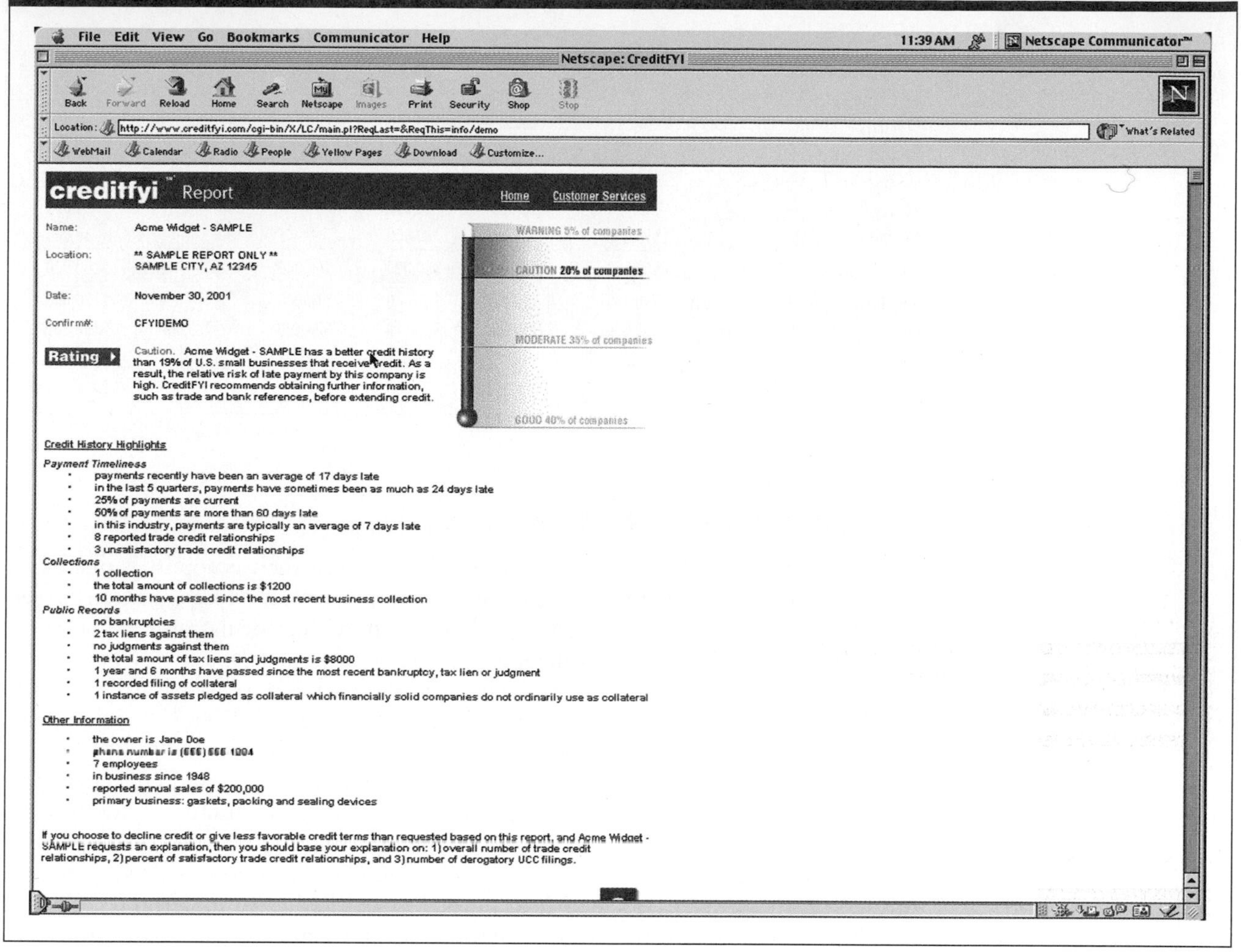

File Edit View Go Bookmarks Communicator Help 11:39 AM Netscape Communicator™

Netscape: CreditFYI

Back Forward Reload Home Search Netscape Images Print Security Shop Stop

Location: http://www.creditfyi.com/cgi-bin/X/LC/main.pl?ReqLast=&ReqThis=info/demo What's Related

WebMail Calendar Radio People Yellow Pages Download Customize...

creditfyi™ Report Home Customer Services

Name: Acme Widget - SAMPLE

Location: ** SAMPLE REPORT ONLY **
SAMPLE CITY, AZ 12345

Date: November 30, 2001

Confirm#: CFYIDEMO

Rating Caution. Acme Widget - SAMPLE has a better credit history than 19% of U.S. small businesses that receive credit. As a result, the relative risk of late payment by this company is high. CreditFYI recommends obtaining further information, such as trade and bank references, before extending credit.

WARNING 5% of companies
CAUTION **20% of companies**
MODERATE 35% of companies
GOOD 40% of companies

Credit History Highlights

Payment Timeliness

- payments recently have been an average of 17 days late
- in the last 5 quarters, payments have sometimes been as much as 24 days late
- 25% of payments are current
- 50% of payments are more than 60 days late
- in this industry, payments are typically an average of 7 days late
- 8 reported trade credit relationships
- 3 unsatisfactory trade credit relationships

Collections

- 1 collection
- the total amount of collections is $1200
- 10 months have passed since the most recent business collection

Public Records

- no bankruptcies
- 2 tax liens against them
- no judgments against them
- the total amount of tax liens and judgments is $8000
- 1 year and 6 months have passed since the most recent bankruptcy, tax lien or judgment
- 1 recorded filing of collateral
- 1 instance of assets pledged as collateral which financially solid companies do not ordinarily use as collateral

Other Information

- the owner is Jane Doe
- phone number is (666) 666 1904
- 7 employees
- in business since 1948
- reported annual sales of $200,000
- primary business: gaskets, packing and sealing devices

If you choose to decline credit or give less favorable credit terms than requested based on this report, and Acme Widget - SAMPLE requests an explanation, then you should base your explanation on: 1) overall number of trade credit relationships, 2) percent of satisfactory trade credit relationships, and 3) number of derogatory UCC filings.

Customers 001 and 004 require a special kind of analysis. Customer 001 has $10,000 more overdue than customer 004. However, customer 004's overdue credit of $40,000, which is 60 days past due, may well have a serious impact on the $100,000 not yet due ($10,000 in the beyond-discount period plus $90,000 still in the discount period). On the other hand, even though customer 001 has $50,000 of overdue credit, this customer's payment is overdue by only 15 days. Also, customer 001 has only $50,000 not yet due ($30,000 in the beyond-discount period plus $20,000 still in the discount period), compared to the $100,000 not yet due from customer 004. Both customers have an A credit rating. In conclusion, customer 001 is a better potential source of cash. Therefore, collection efforts should be focused on customer 004 rather than on customer 001, who may simply need a reminder of the overdue amount of $50,000.

FIGURE 16-7

Hypothetical Aging Schedule for Accounts Receivable

	CUSTOMER ACCOUNT NUMBER					
Account Status	**001**	**002**	**003**	**004**	**005**	**Total**
Days past due						
120 days	—	—	$50,000	—	—	$ 50,000
90 days	—	$ 10,000	—	—	—	10,000
60 days	—	—	—	$40,000	—	40,000
30 days	—	20,000	20,000	—	—	40,000
15 days	$50,000	—	10,000	—	—	60,000
Total overdue	$50,000	$ 30,000	$80,000	$40,000	$ 0	$200,000
Not due (beyond discount period)	$30,000	$ 10,000	$ 0	$10,000	$130,000	$180,000
Not due (still in discount period)	$20,000	$100,000	$ 0	$90,000	$220,000	$430,000
Credit rating	A	B	C	A	A	—

Billing and Collection Procedures

Timely notification of customers regarding the status of their accounts is one of the most effective methods of keeping credit accounts current. Most credit customers pay their bills on time if the creditor provides them with information verifying their credit balance. Failure on the seller's part to send invoices delays timely payments.

Overdue credit accounts tie up a seller's working capital, prevent further sales to the slow-paying customer, and lead to losses from bad debts. Even if a slow-paying customer is not lost, relations with this customer are strained for a time at least.

A firm extending credit must have adequate billing records and collection procedures if it expects prompt payments. Also, a personal acquaintance between seller and customer must not be allowed to tempt the seller into being less than businesslike in extending further credit and collecting overdue amounts. Given the seriousness of the problem, a small firm must decide whether to undertake collecting past-due accounts directly or turn the task over to an attorney or a collection agency.

Perhaps the most effective weapon in collecting past-due accounts is reminding the debtors that their credit standing may be impaired. Impairment is certain if the account is turned over to a collection agency. Delinquent customers will typically attempt to avoid damage to their credit standing, particularly when it would be known to the business community. This concern underlies and strengthens the various collection efforts of the seller.

A small firm should deal compassionately with delinquent customers. A collection technique that is too threatening not only may fail to work but also could cause the firm to lose the customer or become subject to legal action.

Many business firms have found that the most effective collection procedure consists of a series of steps, each somewhat more forceful than the preceding one. Although the procedure typically begins with a gentle written reminder, subsequent steps may include additional letters, telephone calls, registered letters, personal contacts, and referral to a collection agency or attorney. The timing of these steps may

IN THE TRENCHES | BUILDING CUSTOMER LOYALTY

STICK TO A FRIENDLY REMINDER

Using a customer-friendly approach to collecting accounts can help a small firm build strong client relationships. A friendly, relaxed appeal for payment is frequently better than the old "talk-tough" approach.

An early practitioner of this softer approach to collecting overdue accounts is Jack Renton, who was a credit manager for a construction firm in Australia. There he learned that "applying friendly, colorful reminder stickers to customers' invoices increased on-time payments substantially." Renton and his wife, Patience, began a part-time printing business selling these stickers. The stickers feature animal characters and have slogans like "friendly reminder," "we value your business," and "don't like to put the bite on you. . . ."

By the late 1960s, the business had become a full-time venture. Today, Jack's son, Peter, is president of Rentons' International Stationery, Inc. in Denver, Colorado. The company also sells other kinds of business-oriented stickers. "Most billings lack any type of relationship-building," says Peter Renton. "Companies spend a lot of money getting new customers, but never another dollar to keep them."

Beginning with a gentle reminder is a good way to avoid sending customers running in the opposite direction. And the colorful messages of sticker manufacturer Peter Renton help small businesses do just that.

Source: William Atkinson, "A Kinder, Gentler Way to Collect," *Nation's Business*, Vol. 87, No. 3 (March 1999), p. 43

http://www.rentons.com

be carefully standardized so that each one automatically follows the preceding one in a specified number of days.

Various ratios can be used to control expenses associated with credit sales. The best-known and most widely used expense ratio is the **bad-debt ratio**, which is computed by dividing the amount of bad debts by the total amount of credit sales. The bad-debt ratio reflects the efficiency of credit policies and procedures. A small firm may thus compare the effectiveness of its credit management with that of other firms. A relationship exists among bad-debt ratio, profitability, and size of the firm. Small profitable retailers have a much higher bad-debt ratio than large profitable retailers do. In general, the bad-debt losses of small firms range from a fraction of 1 percent of net sales to percentages large enough to put them out of business!

bad-debt ratio
the ratio of bad debts to credit sales

Credit Regulation

The use of credit is regulated by a variety of federal laws, as well as state laws that vary considerably from state to state. Prior to the passage of such legislation, consumers were often confused by credit agreements and were sometimes victims of credit abuse.

By far the most significant piece of credit legislation is the federal Consumer Credit Protection Act, which includes the 1968 Truth-in-Lending Act. Its two primary purposes are to ensure that consumers are informed about the terms of a credit agreement and to require creditors to specify how finance charges are computed. The act requires that a finance charge be stated as an annual percentage rate and that creditors specify their procedures for correcting billing mistakes.

Other federal legislation related to credit management includes the following:

- *The Fair Credit Billing Act* provides protection to credit customers in cases involving incorrect billing. A reasonable time period is allowed for billing errors to be corrected. The act does not cover installment credit.
- *The Fair Credit Reporting Act* gives certain rights to credit applicants regarding reports prepared by credit bureaus. A 1997 amendment to the act strengthened privacy provisions and defined more clearly the responsibilities and liabilities of businesses that provide information to credit reporting agencies.
- *The Equal Credit Opportunity Act* ensures that all consumers are given an equal chance to obtain credit. For example, a person is not required to reveal his or her sex, race, national origin, or religion to obtain credit.
- *The Fair Debt Collection Practices Act* bans the use of intimidation and deception in collection, requiring debt collectors to treat debtors fairly.

Pricing and credit decisions are of prime importance to a small firm because of their direct impact on its financial health. Many entrepreneurs learn to make the best decisions through experience; we hope that the concepts presented in this chapter will help smooth the trip.

Looking Back

1 Discuss the role of cost and demand factors in setting a price.

- The revenue of a firm is a direct reflection of two components: sales volume and price.
- Price must be sufficient to cover total cost plus some margin of profit.
- A firm should examine elasticity of demand—the relationship of price and quantity demanded—when setting a price.
- A product's competitive advantage is a demand factor in setting price.

2 Apply break-even analysis and markup pricing.

- Analyzing costs and revenue under different price assumptions identifies the break-even point, the quantity sold at which total costs equal total revenue.
- The usefulness of break-even analysis is enhanced by incorporating sales forecasts.
- Markup pricing is a generalized cost-plus system of pricing used by intermediaries with many products.

3 Identify specific pricing strategies.

- Penetration pricing and skimming pricing are short-term strategies used when new products are first introduced into the market.
- Follow-the-leader and variable pricing are special strategies that reflect the nature of the competition's pricing and concessions to customers.
- A price lining strategy simplifies choices for customers by offering a range of several distinct prices.
- State and federal laws must be considered in setting prices, as well as any impact that a price may have on other product line items.

4 Explain the benefits of credit, factors that affect credit extension, and types of credit.

- Credit offers potential benefits to both buyers and sellers.
- Type of business, credit policies of competitors, income level of customers, and availability of adequate working capital affect the decision to extend credit.
- The two broad classes of credit are consumer credit and trade credit.

5 Describe the activities involved in managing credit.

- Evaluating the credit status of applicants begins with the completion of an application form.
- A customer's willingness to pay is evaluated through the five C's of credit: character, capital, capacity, conditions, and collateral.

- Pertinent credit data can be obtained from several outside sources, including formal trade-credit agencies such as Dun & Bradstreet.
- An accounts receivable aging schedule can be used to improve credit collection.
- A small firm should establish a formal procedure for billing and collecting from charge customers.
- It is important that a small firm follow all relevant credit regulations.

KEY TERMS

price, p. 397
credit, p. 397
total cost, p. 398
total variable costs, p. 398
total fixed costs, p. 398
average pricing, p. 399
elasticity of demand, p. 400
elastic demand, p. 400
inelastic demand, p. 400
prestige pricing, p. 400
break-even point, p. 402
markup pricing, p. 404
penetration pricing strategy, p. 404
skimming price strategy, p. 405
follow-the-leader pricing strategy, p. 405
variable pricing strategy, p. 406
dynamic pricing strategy, p. 406
price lining strategy, p. 406
consumer credit, p. 410
trade credit, p. 410
open charge account, p. 410
installment account, p. 410
revolving charge account, p. 411
trade-credit agencies, p. 414
credit bureaus, p. 414
aging schedule, p. 414
bad-debt ratio, p. 417

DISCUSSION QUESTIONS

1. Why does average pricing sometimes result in a pricing mistake?
2. Explain the importance of total fixed and variable costs to the pricing decision.
3. How does the concept of elasticity of demand relate to prestige pricing? Give an example.
4. If a firm has fixed costs of $100,000 and variable costs per unit of $1, what is the break-even point in units, assuming a selling price of $5 per unit?
5. What is the difference between a penetration pricing strategy and a skimming price strategy? Under what circumstances would each be used?
6. If a small business conducts its break-even analysis properly and finds the break-even volume at a price of $10 to be 10,000 units, should it price its product at $10? Why or why not?
7. What are the major benefits of credit to buyers? What are its major benefits to sellers?
8. How does an open charge account differ from a revolving charge account?
9. What is meant by the terms 2/10, net 30? Does it pay to take discounts when they are offered?
10. What is the major purpose of aging accounts receivable? At what point in credit management should this activity be performed? Why?

You Make the Call

SITUATION 1

Steve Jones is the 35-year-old owner of a highly competitive small business, which supplies temporary office help. Like most businesspeople, he is always looking for ways to increase profit. However, the nature of his competition makes it very difficult to raise prices for the temps' services, while reducing their wages makes recruiting difficult. Jones has, nevertheless, found an area—bad debts—in which improvement should increase profits. A friend and business consultant met with Jones to advise him on credit management policies. Jones was pleased to get this friend's advice, as bad debts were costing him about 2 percent of sales. Currently, Jones has no system for managing credit.

Question 1 What advice would you give Jones regarding the screening of new credit customers?

Question 2 What action should Jones take to encourage current credit customers to pay their debts? Be specific.

Question 3 Jones has considered eliminating credit sales. What are the possible consequences of this decision?

SITUATION 2

Tom Anderson started his records storage business in the New York metropolitan area in 1991. His differentiation strategy was to offer competitive prices while providing state-of-art technology, easy access to his warehouse, and, of course, great service.

After opening the business, Anderson learned that most potential customers had already signed long-term storage contracts with competitors. These contracts included a removal fee for each box permanently removed from the storage company's warehouse, making it difficult for customers to consider switching.

Anderson believes that the survival of his company hinges on his view of what the essence of his business is. In other words, is he operating a storage company or a real estate business? He is convinced that he must answer this question before making any decision regarding pricing strategy.

Question 1 What do you think Anderson means when he asks, "Is my business storage or real estate? Why do you think he feels a need to ask this question prior to developing a pricing strategy?

Question 2 What pricing strategy would be effective in combatting the existing contractual relationships between potential customers and competitors?

Question 3 Assuming that business costs would allow Anderson to lower prices, what problems do you see with this approach?

Question 4 Do you believe his business could benefit from offering credit to customers? Why or why not?

SITUATION 3

Paul Bowlin owns and operates a tree removal, pruning, and spraying business in a large metropolitan area with a population of approximately 200,000. The business started in 1975 and has grown to the point where Bowlin uses one and sometimes two crews, with four or five employees on each crew. Pricing has always been an important tool in gaining business, but Bowlin realizes that there are ways to entice customers other than quoting the lowest price. For example, he provides careful cleanup of branches and leaves, takes out stumps below ground level, and waits until a customer is completely satisfied before taking payment. At the same time, he realizes his bids for tree removal jobs must cover his costs. In this industry, Bowlin faces intense price competition from operators with more sophisticated wood-processing equipment, such as chip grinders. Therefore, he is always open to suggestions about pricing strategy.

Question 1 What would the nature of this industry suggest about the elasticity of demand affecting Bowlin's pricing?

Question 2 What types of costs should Bowlin evaluate when he is determining his break-even point?

Question 3 What pricing strategies could Bowlin adopt to further his long-term success in this market?

Question 4 How can the high quality of Bowlin's work be used to justify somewhat higher price quotations?

EXPERIENTIAL EXERCISES

1. Interview a small business owner regarding his or her pricing strategy. Try to ascertain whether the strategy being used reflects the total fixed and variable costs of the business. Prepare a report on your findings.
2. Interview a small business owner regarding his or her policies for evaluating credit applicants. Summarize your findings in a report.
3. Interview the credit manager of a retail store about the benefits and drawbacks of extending credit to customers. Report your findings to the class.
4. Ask several small business owners in your community who extend credit to describe the credit management procedures they use to collect bad debts. Report your findings to the class.

EXPLORING THE WEB

1. Access the Web site for the Professional Pricing Society at **http://www.pricing-advisor.com**.
   a. Click About PPS to find out what the Professional Pricing Society is.
   b. Follow the link for Demos and Tools, and try out a couple of the demos. Which ones seem to be appropriate for small businesses?
   c. Choose Resource Center, and then click Software Resources. List five of the resources given here, and explain what pricing situation each is specifically targeted for.
2. Strategic Pricing Group (SPG) is a consulting firm that assists businesses in setting prices. Access its Web site at **http://www.strategicpricinggroup.com**.
   a. Under SPG Today, find out what approach the firm uses in pricing.
   b. Click on Test Yourself. Take the quiz, and see how well you know how to set pricing. Report your results.
   c. Follow the link to Articles, and read "Dynamic Pricing." Which companies commonly use this technique? What area will probably rely strongly on dynamic pricing in the future?
3. Check out **http://www.creditfyi.com**.
   a. View a sample report. What major items are contained in the report?
   b. Access Questions and Answers. How much does the service cost? How long does it take to receive results?
   c. Follow the link to Can CreditFYI Advise Me Whether to Extend Credit to a Small Business? Then click the link to Credit Tips. What are some considerations in deciding what level of credit risk you are willing to accept?
   d. List the four steps a small business owner should take to establish a credit management policy.

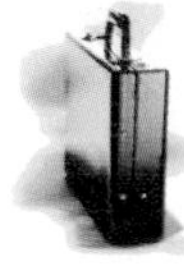

CASE 16

EBC COMPUTERS INC. (p. 683)

This case describes the business experiences of a Peruvian immigrant whose computer components business constantly strives to be the low-cost supplier to its customers.

Alternative Cases for Chapter 16:

Case 1, "Steve's Olympic Tees," p. 637
Case 2, "The Fantastic Catalogue Company," p. 641

chapter 17

PROMOTIONAL STRATEGIES

In the Spotlight

1-800-CONTACTS

Promoting a business is easier if the company name is easy to remember. Just ask Jonathan Coon, founder and CEO of 1-800-CONTACTS, a company he started in his college dorm room. Only 12 years after its start, the firm was the top contact lens retailer in the United States.

Coon studied marketing and business at Brigham Young University, eventually entering the MBA program, where he developed his business plan. Part of his business strategy was to use a creative toll-free telephone number. However, the number he wanted, 1-800-CONTACTS, was owned by someone else. Both Coon and cofounder John Nichols believed the number would be a valuable asset to their company, so they began a search to locate the owner.

No one answered the number, no matter what time Coon called. Finally, after hiring a private detective, Coon tracked him down. The owner asked for $500,000; Coon offered $500. They settled on $163,500 over five years. Coon and Nichols paid $10,000 upfront, and the owner financed the rest.

The two were shocked the first month, July 1995, when they took possession of the number. Without advertising, they received 2,000 calls, producing $38,000 in additional sales—more than doubling revenue from the month before.

Coon says many customers unintentionally call his company after seeing advertisements by other contact lens retailers; unable to remember the number, they assume it might be 1-800-CONTACTS. The

http://www.1800contacts.com

number is now the name of the company's Web site. The company, based just outside of Salt Lake City, Utah, attributes 40 percent of its revenues to Internet sales.

In 2000, Coon was named Retail Entrepreneur of the Year in the 14th Annual Ernst & Young Entrepreneur of the Year Awards competition. His experience shows that a simple phone number can be a key promotional tool. ◆

Source: Jim Hopkins, "Contact Lens Retailer Focused on Business Early On," *USA Today,* November 29, 2000, p. 6B.

Looking Ahead

After studying this chapter, you should be able to

1. *Describe the communication process and the factors determining a promotional mix.*
2. *Discuss methods of determining the appropriate level of promotional expenditure.*
3. *Describe personal selling activities.*
4. *Identify advertising options for a small business.*
5. *Describe sales promotional tools.*

The old adage "Build a better mousetrap and the world will beat a path to your door" suggests that innovation is the foundation of a successful marketing strategy. However, the narrow focus of the saying minimizes the roles of other vital marketing activities, such as promotion. Promotion informs customers about any new, improved "mousetrap" and how they can find the "door." Customers also must be persuaded that the new mousetrap is actually better than their old one. Clearly, entrepreneurs cannot rely on product innovation alone; they need some understanding of the promotional process in order to develop an effective marketing strategy for their particular "mousetrap."

Let's begin with a simple definition of *promotion.* **Promotion** consists of marketing communications that inform potential consumers about a firm or its product or service and try to persuade them to buy it. Small businesses use promotion in varying degrees; a given firm seldom uses all of the many promotional tools available. In order to simplify our discussion of the promotional process, we group the techniques discussed in this chapter into three traditional categories—personal selling, advertising, and using sales promotional tools.

promotion
marketing communications that inform and persuade consumers

Before examining the categories in the promotional process, let's first look at the basic process of communication that characterizes promotion. If an entrepreneur understands that promotion is just a special form of communication, he or she will be better able to grasp the entire process.

The Communication Process in Promotion

Describe the communication process and the factors determining a promotional mix.

Promotion is based on communication. In fact, promotion is wasted unless it effectively communicates a firm's message.

Communication is a process with identifiable components. As shown in Figure 17-1, every communication involves a source, a message, a channel, and a receiver. Each of us communicates in many ways each day, and these exchanges parallel small business communications. Part (a) in Figure 17-1 depicts a personal communication example—parents communicating with their daughter, who is away at college. Part (b) depicts a small business communication—a firm communicating with a customer.

As you can see, many similarities exist between the two. The receiver of the parents' message is their daughter. The parents, the source in this example, use three different channels for their message: an e-mail message, a personal conversation, and a special gift. The receiver of the message from the XYZ Company is the customer. The XYZ Company uses three message channels: a newspaper, a sales call, and a business gift. The parents' e-mail and the company's advertising both represent nonpersonal forms of communication—there is no face-to-face contact. The parents' visit to their daughter and the sales call made by the company's representative are personal forms of communication. Finally, the flowers and care package and the business gift are both special methods of communication. Thus, the promotional efforts of a small firm, like the communication between parents and

FIGURE 17-1

Similarity of Personal and Small Business Communication Processes

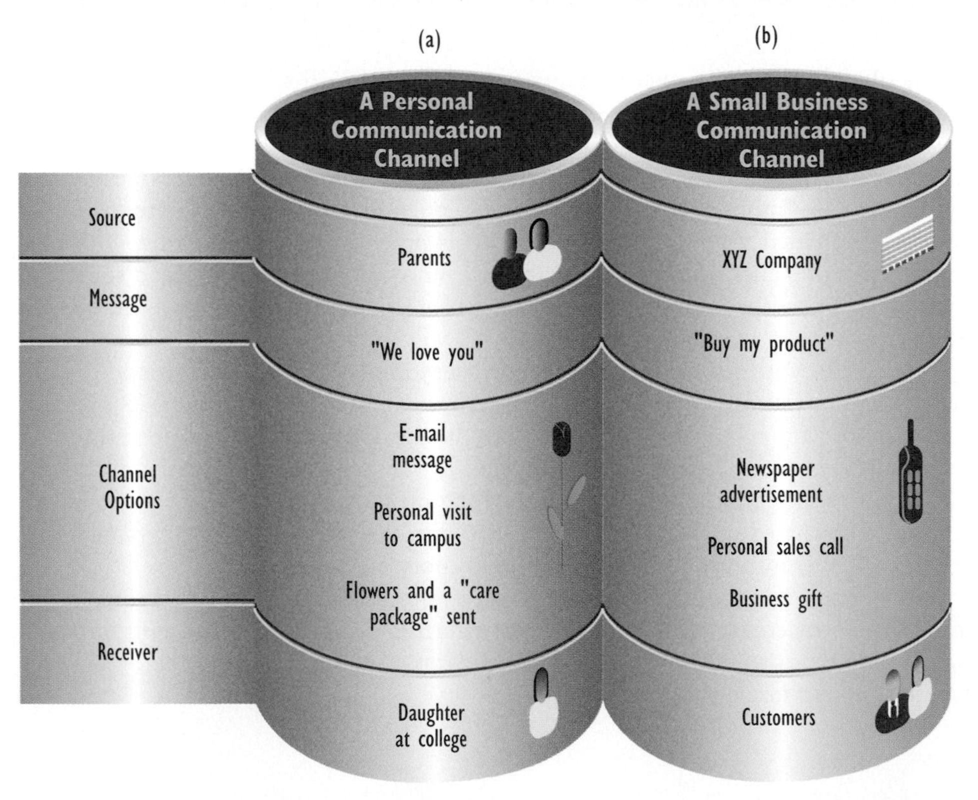

daughter, can be viewed simply as nonpersonal (advertising), personal (personal selling), and special forms of communication (sales promotion).

A term commonly used to denote a particular combination of promotional methods is *promotional mix*. A **promotional mix** describes the blend of nonpersonal, personal, and special forms of communication techniques used in a promotional campaign. The particular combination of the various promotional methods—advertising, personal selling, and sales promotional tools—is determined by many factors. One important factor is the geographical nature of the market to be reached. A widely dispersed market generally requires mass coverage through advertising, in contrast to the more costly individual contacts of personal selling. On the other hand, if the market is local or if the number of customers is relatively small, personal selling may be more feasible.

promotional mix
a blend of nonpersonal, personal, and special forms of communication aimed at a target market

Another factor is the size of the promotional budget. Small firms may not select certain forms of promotion because the costs are just too high. Television advertising, for example, is more expensive than radio advertising.

A third factor that heavily influences the promotional mix is the product's characteristics. If a product is of high unit value, such as a mobile home, personal selling will be a vital ingredient in the mix. Personal selling is also an effective method for promoting highly technical products, such as automobiles or street-sweeping machinery. On the other hand, nonpersonal advertising is more effective for a relatively inexpensive item, like razor blades.

There are, of course, many other considerations to be evaluated when developing a unique promotional mix. Nevertheless, promotional planning should always strive to begin with the optimum mix of techniques. The entrepreneur can then make any necessary adjustments—for example, by cutting back on the effort or seeking more funds to support the promotional plan.

Determining the Promotional Budget

Discuss methods of determining the appropriate level of promotional expenditure.

Unfortunately, no mathematical formula can answer the question "How much should a small business spend on promotion?" There are, however, four helpful common sense approaches to budgeting funds for small business promotion:

1. Allocating a percentage of sales
2. Deciding how much can be spared
3. Spending as much as the competition does
4. Determining what it will take to do the job

Allocating a Percentage of Sales

Often the simplest method of determining how much to budget for promotion is to earmark promotional dollars based on a percentage of sales. A firm's own past experiences should be evaluated to establish a promotion-to-sales ratio. If 2 percent of sales, for example, has historically been spent on promotion, the firm should budget 2 percent of forecasted sales for promotion. Secondary data on industry averages can be used for comparison. One source that reports what firms are doing with their advertising dollars is *Advertising Age*.

http://www.adage.com

A major shortcoming of this method is an inherent tendency to spend more on promotion when sales are increasing and less when they are declining. If promotion stimulates sales, then reducing promotional spending when sales are down is

illogical. Also, new firms have no historical sales figures on which to base their promotional budgets.

Deciding How Much Can Be Spared

Another piecemeal approach to promotional budgeting widely used by small firms is to spend whatever is left over when all other activities have been funded. The decision about promotional spending might be made only when a media representative sells an owner on a special deal that the business can afford. Such an approach to promotional spending should be avoided because it ignores promotional goals.

Spending as Much as the Competition Does

Sometimes, a small firm builds a promotional budget based on an analysis of competitors' budgets. The idea is by duplicating the promotional efforts of close competitors, the business will reach the same customers and will at least be spending as much as the competition. Obviously, if a competitor is a large business, this approach is not feasible. However, it can be used to react to short-run promotional tactics by small competitors. Unfortunately, this approach results in the copying of competitors' mistakes as well as their successes.

Determining What It Will Take to Do the Job

The preferred approach to estimating promotional expenditures is to decide what it will take to do the job. This method requires a comprehensive analysis of the market and the firm's goals. If reasonably accurate estimates are used, the total amount that needs to be spent can be determined.

In many cases, the best way for a small business to set promotional expenditures incorporates all four approaches. In other words, make a comparison of the four estimated amounts and set the promotional budget at a level that is somewhere between the maximum and minimum amounts. See Figure 17-2. After the budget has been determined, the entrepreneur must decide how dollars will be spent on the various promotional methods. Which methods are chosen depends on a number of factors. We now examine personal selling, a frequent choice for small firms.

Personal Selling in the Small Firm

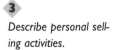

Describe personal selling activities.

personal selling
a sales presentation delivered in a one-on-one manner

Many products require **personal selling**—promotion delivered in a one-on-one environment. Personal selling includes the activities of both the inside salespeople of retail, wholesale, and service establishments and the outside sales representatives who call on business customers and final consumers. Frequently, the entrepreneur is the primary salesperson for a venture.

The Importance of Product Knowledge

Effective selling is built on a foundation of product knowledge. If a salesperson is well acquainted with a product's advantages, uses, and limitations, she or he can educate customers by successfully answering their questions and countering their objections. Most customers expect a salesperson to provide knowledgeable

FIGURE 17-2

Four-Step Method for Determining a Promotional Budget

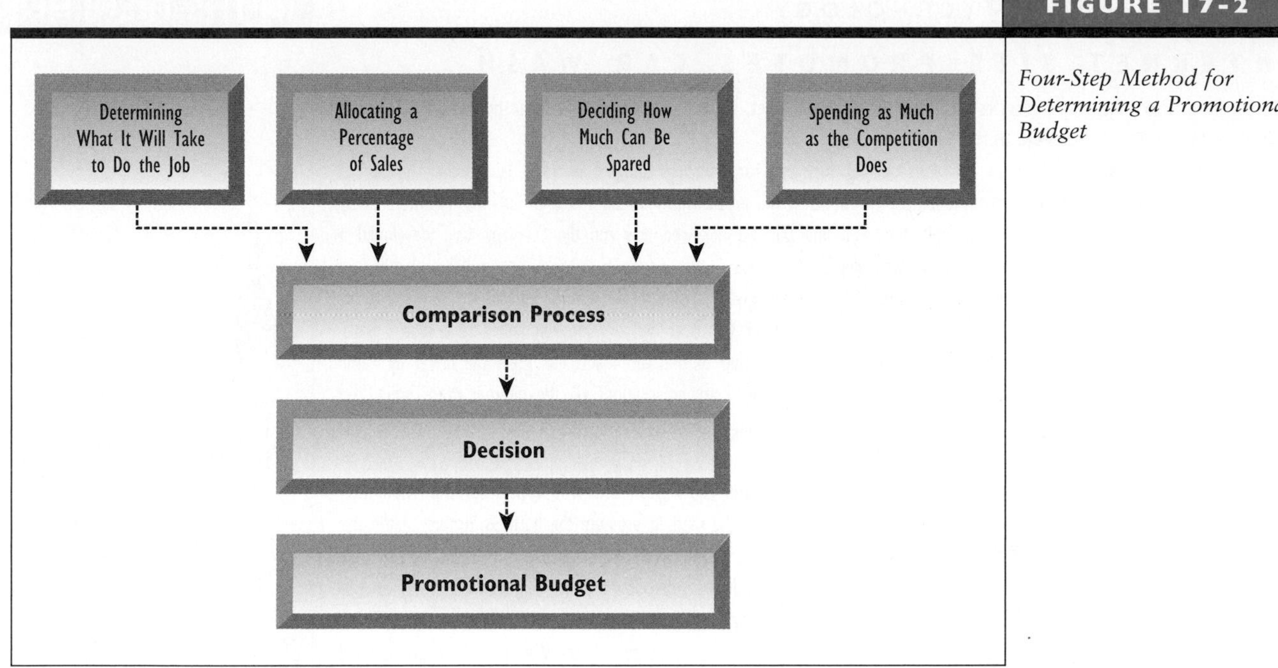

answers—whether the product is a camera, a coat, an automobile, paint, a machine tool, or office equipment. Customers are seldom experts on the products they buy; however, they can immediately sense a salesperson's knowledge or ignorance. Personal selling degenerates into mere order-taking when a salesperson lacks product knowledge.

The Sales Presentation

The heart of personal selling is the sales presentation to a prospective customer. At this crucial point, an order is either secured or lost. A preliminary step leading to an effective sales presentation is **prospecting**, a systematic process of continually looking for new customers.

prospecting
a systematic process of continually looking for new customers

USING PROSPECTING TECHNIQUES One of the most efficient prospecting techniques is obtaining personal referrals. Such referrals come from friends, customers, and other businesses. Initial contact with a potential customer is greatly facilitated when the salesperson is able to say, "You were referred to me by . . . ."

Another source of prospects is *impersonal referrals* from media publications, public records, and directories. Newspapers and magazines, particularly trade magazines, often identify prospects by reporting on new companies and new products. Wedding announcements in a newspaper can serve as impersonal referrals for a local bridal shop. Public records of property transactions and building permits can be impersonal referrals for, say, a garbage pick-up service, which might find prospective customers among those planning to build houses or apartment buildings.

Prospects can also be identified without referrals through *marketer-initiated contacts*. Telephone calls or mail surveys, for example, isolate prospects. In a market survey conducted to identify prospects for a small business, an author of this

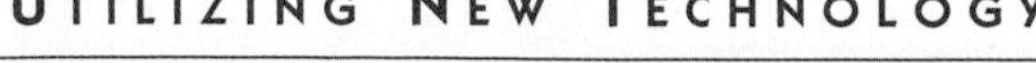

UTILIZING NEW TECHNOLOGY

IN THE TRENCHES

INTERNET SITE PROMOTES CAR WASH

Dot.com firms aren't the only businesses to benefit from the Internet. A traditional brick-and-mortar business can use this technology to promote and improve its operations.

Consider ScrubaDub, a full-service car wash offering fuel and car detailing. Founded in 1968 by Marshall Paisner in Natick, Massachusetts, the company currently operates 10 outlets in the northeastern United States. In an industry where many companies don't know their customers, Marshall's sons Bob and Dan Paisner, who now run the company, have developed a cutting-edge operation through their savvy use of technology.

When customers enroll in ScrubaDub's Car Care Club, they are given a windshield-mounted barcode. As soon as a car pulls into a ScrubaDub location, the barcode is scanned, and a computer screen at the car's location, linked to a central database via the Internet, flashes the customer's identity and other information so that attendants can greet the driver by name and recommend specific services. Accounting information is also exchanged among locations via the Internet every hour. "Use of the Internet for updating our database has saved us hundreds of hours of office work," says Bob.

The company Web site, which gets about 100 hits a day from both current and potential customers, is used to promote the business. Visitors to the site can learn about the Car Care Club, ScrubaDub's services and prices, how to buy coupon books, and how to find ScrubaDub locations; they can even play an online game to win a free car wash.

Bob, who is the CEO, also wants to use the Web to deliver promotional information to customers while they are getting their cars washed. ScrubaDub currently uses satellites to beam ads to monitors on each gas pump, but Bob has plans to use the Internet instead for these transmissions because it will permit more control through the main office. Bob says, "This technology can accelerate our growth and make new locations more productive."

Source: "Success, One Customer at a Time," Special Advertising Feature, *Inc.*, Vol. 22, No. 8 (June 2000), p. 113.

http://www.scrubadub.com

book used a mail questionnaire. The questionnaire, which asked technical questions about a service, concluded with the following statement: "If you would be interested in a service of this nature, please check the appropriate space below and your name will be added to the mailing list."

Finally, prospects can be identified by recording *customer-initiated contacts*. Inquiries by a potential customer that do not lead to a sale can still create a "hot prospect." Small furniture stores often require their salespeople to create a card for each person visiting the store. These prospects are then systematically contacted over the telephone or by e-mail. Records of these contacts are updated periodically. Firms with Web sites can follow up on visitors who have made inquiries.

Prospecting also includes consideration of whether a potential customer can be served by the company. For example, Fred Anderson who owns Anderson Landscaping Construction, in Lancaster, Massachusetts, does not make a pitch to potential customers until he qualifies each of them. With only five employees, Anderson knows that certain large jobs exceed his capacity to finish on time; therefore, sales efforts cease if he determines that the jobs are too large.[1]

PRACTICING THE SALES PRESENTATION Practicing always improves a salesperson's success rate; after all, "practice makes perfect." Prior to making a sales presentation, a salesperson should give his or her presentation in front of a spouse, a mirror, or a cassette recorder. Even better, he or she may want to use a camcorder to make a practice video.

The salesperson should be aware of possible customer objections to the product and be prepared to handle them. Most objections can be categorized as relating to (1) price, (2) product, (3) timing, (4) source, (5) service, or (6) need. Although there is no substitute for actual selling experience, salespeople find training helpful in learning how to deal with customers' objections. One sales textbook suggests the following techniques for dealing with customers' objections:[2]

- Convert the objection into the form of a question.
- Use third-party testimonials or experiences.
- Use the boomerang or positive conversion technique.
- Use comparisons.

The hypothetical conversations between a prospect and a salesperson in Figure 17-3 reflect these four techniques.

MAKING THE SALES PRESENTATION Salespeople must adapt their sales approach to customers' needs. A "canned" sales talk will not succeed with most buyers. For example, a person selling personal computers must demonstrate the capacity of the equipment to fill a customer's particular needs. Similarly, a boat salesperson must understand the special interests of particular customers and speak their language. Every sales objection must be answered explicitly and adequately.

Successful selling involves a number of psychological elements. Personal enthusiasm, friendliness, and persistence are required. Approximately 20 percent of all salespeople secure as much as 80 percent of all sales made because they bring these elements to the task of selling.

Some salespeople have special sales techniques that they use with success. One automobile salesperson, for example, offered free driving lessons to people who had never taken a driver's training course or who needed a few more lessons before they felt confident enough to take the required driving test. When such customers were ready to take the driving test, this salesperson would accompany them to the examination to provide moral support. Needless to say, these special efforts were greatly appreciated by new drivers who were in the market for cars.

Customer Goodwill and Relationship Selling

A salesperson must look beyond the immediate sale to building customer goodwill and creating satisfied customers who will patronize the company in the future. Selling effectiveness is enhanced when a salesperson displays a good appearance, has a pleasant personality, and uses professional etiquette in all contacts with customers. A salesperson can also build goodwill by listening carefully to the customer's point of view. Courtesy, attention to details, and genuine friendliness will help gain the customer's acceptance.

Of course, high ethical standards are of primary importance in creating customer goodwill. Such standards rule out any misrepresentation of the product and require confidential treatment of a customer's plans.

FIGURE 17-3 *Handling Customers' Objections*

TECHNIQUES: *Convert the objection into a question; use a third-party experience.*

Prospect: I want to think this proposition over.

Salesperson: I see, Ms. Prospect. You feel you should have a little time to think over my proposition. I can understand how you feel. Many people face the same question. The question is whether or not you have sufficient information at this point to make a decision. Isn't that correct?

Prospect: Yes.

Salesperson: Ms. Prospect, one of the things I have noticed in watching other business people, women and men, is that they don't assemble all the facts regarding an important subject, put them on their desk, and then go fishing for a week before making up their mind. They make their decision while the facts are fresh in their mind. *(Then tell a third-party story to illustrate the point and follow with the third party's testimony, if possible.)*

Ms. Prospect, if you understand my proposition clearly, now is the time to make up your mind, while I am still here to answer any of your questions. *(Close.)*

TECHNIQUE: *Use a testimonial.*

Prospect: I don't think I would ever use a set of fine china.

Salesperson: I can understand how you feel. You certainly wouldn't want to invest in something you would never use. A number of people I have called on in recent months have felt the same way. Do you happen to know Mary Ellen Brown? I called on her a month or two ago, and her grandmother happened to be there and sat through the demonstration. Mary Ellen expressed the same thought you just did: "I don't think I would ever use a set of fine china." But her grandmother made an interesting statement. She said "The time to have and use your fine china, besides when guests come, is when you are serving leftovers. Those leftovers, served on your best dishes and perhaps under candlelight, automatically taste better." She went on to say "And when you are just learning to cook, food tastes better when served in an attractive manner—our appetites often are controlled by what we see." Mary Ellen made the decision to get her fine china that evening. Later, she wrote me a letter saying . . . . *(Read testimonial and close.)*

TECHNIQUE: *Use positive conversion.*

Prospect: Your machine is much too heavy—it will cost more to install than those of your competitors.

Salesperson: Yes, Mr. Prospect, our machines are heavier. I can understand your concern because the installation costs are a bit higher. However, that extra weight will more than pay for itself. With a heavier machine, there is less vibration and consequently less wear and tear on the rest of your equipment. These reduced maintenance costs will more than make up for the additional weight and costs of installation. *(Close.)*

TECHNIQUE: *Use comparisons.*

Prospect: I have always used brand X oil in my car. Why should I change now?

Salesperson: Mr. Prospect, brand X oil has always been a good product, and I can understand how you feel. Why change from an old friend? Let's just compare brand X oil with our new polyglycol-based oil. *(Draw the following chart and explain each point.)*

	Old	New
Recommended Oil Change	Every 1,500 miles.	Every 12,000 miles—certainly more convenient.
Performance	Medium viscosity index; low corrosive qualities.	High viscosity index; completely noncorrosive (causes less wear and tear on the engine and transmission and thus gives longer life).
Ecological	Releases hydrocarbons and other particle emissions into the air.	Releases no hydrocarbons and has 90% fewer particle emissions (which are responsible for smell and smog).
Costs	With an oil change every 1,500 miles and an average cost of 85 cents per quart, the cost of oil per 12,000 miles equals \$6.80 (\$0.85 × 8 = \$6.80).	The oil needs to be changed only once every 12,000 miles, so the cost of oil per 12,000 miles equals \$2.30 (\$2.30 × 1 = \$2.30).

(Close.)

Source: Adapted from Robert E. Hite and Wesley J. Johnston, *Managing Salespeople: A Relationship Approach* (Cincinnati: South-Western, 1988), pp. D-5–D-7.

Cost Control in Personal Selling

Both economical and wasteful methods exist for achieving a given volume of sales. For example, routing traveling salespersons economically and making appointments prior to arrival can conserve time and transportation expenses. The cost of an outside sales call on a customer is likely to be considerable—perhaps hundreds of dollars—so efficient scheduling is crucial. Moreover, a salesperson for a manufacturing firm, say, can contribute to cost economy by stressing products whose increased sales would give the factory a more balanced production run. Similarly, a salesperson can increase profits by emphasizing high-margin products.

The Compensation Program for Salespeople

Salespeople are compensated in two ways for their efforts—financially and nonfinancially. A good compensation program allows its participants to work for both forms of reward, while recognizing that salespeople's goals may be different from entrepreneurs' goals. For example, an entrepreneur may seek nonfinancial rewards that are of little importance to salespeople.

NONFINANCIAL REWARDS Personal recognition and the satisfaction of reaching a sales quota are examples of nonfinancial rewards recognized by salespeople. Small retail businesses sometimes post the photograph of the top salesperson of the week or the month for all to see. Engraved plaques are also given as a more permanent record of sales achievements.

FINANCIAL REWARDS Typically, financial compensation is the more critical factor for salespeople. Two basic plans used for financial compensation are commissions and straight salary. Each plan has specific advantages and limitations for the small firm.

Most small businesses would prefer to use commissions as compensation, because such an approach is simple and directly related to productivity. Usually, a certain percentage of the sales generated by the salesperson represents his or her commission. A commission plan thereby incorporates a strong incentive into the selling activities—no sale, no commission! Also, with this type of plan, there is less drain on the firm's cash flow until a sale is made. Billy Ross, who owns a recreational vehicle (RV) dealership near Atlanta, Georgia, replaced a weekly salary plan for his salespeople with a compensation plan that is more motivational. Salespeople earn cash (up to a certain maximum amount) for each customer whose information is captured for a marketing database, plus a generous 20 percent commission on any RVs sold.[3]

The straight salary form of compensation provides salespeople with more security because their level of compensation is ensured, regardless of sales made. However, working for a straight salary can potentially reduce a salesperson's motivation.

Combining the two forms of compensation creates the most attractive plan for a small business. It is a common practice to structure combination plans so that salary represents the larger part of compensation for a new salesperson. As the salesperson gains experience, the ratio is adjusted to provide more money from commissions and less from salary.

ENTREPRENEURSHIP TODAY

IN THE TRENCHES

COMPENSATING SALESPEOPLE

A system for motivating salespeople may be successful but nevertheless need to be changed. Ron Farmer, CEO of US Signs, Inc. in Houston, Texas, came to that conclusion after realizing that his company's salespeople were making money—they were paid on commission—but the company was not!

The flaw in Farmer's system surfaced when projected growth didn't materialize. As Farmer described the problem, "It didn't matter how much the salespeople spent on overhead or selling expenses. They could spend the entire profit of a job making sure it got done right, and the company would have no profit at the end of the year."

Farmer reorganized the company into seven divisions with accountability through profit-and-loss statements. Salespeople are now compensated through salary plus a profitability bonus based on the divisional accounting system. Farmer believes the new system is working. US Signs' salespeople still exceed the average sales performance in the industry.

Source: Jill Hecht Maxwell, "For Every Sales Rep, a P&L," *Inc.,* Vol. 22, No. 18 (December 2000), p. 137.

http://www.ussigns.com

ADVERTISING PRACTICES FOR SMALL FIRMS

4

Identify advertising options for a small business.

advertising
the impersonal presentation of a business idea through mass media

Another significant promotional expenditure is advertising. **Advertising** is the impersonal presentation of an idea that is identified with a business sponsor. Ideas in advertising are communicated to consumers through media such as television, radio, magazines, newspapers, billboards, and the Internet.

Advertising Objectives

As its primary goal, advertising seeks to sell by informing, persuading, and reminding customers of the existence or superiority of a firm's product or service. To be successful, it must rest on a foundation of product quality and efficient service. It is important to remember that advertising can bring no more than temporary success to an otherwise inferior product. Advertising must always be viewed as a complement to a good product and never as a replacement for a bad product.

The entrepreneur must avoid creating false expectations with advertising, as such expectations can effectively reduce customer satisfaction. Advertising can accentuate a trend in the sale of an item or product line, but it seldom has the power to reverse a trend. It must, consequently, be able to reflect changes in customer needs and preferences.

At times, advertising may seem to be a waste of money. It is expensive and adds little utility to the product. But the primary alternative to advertising is personal selling, which is often more expensive and time-consuming.

product advertising
the presentation of a business idea designed to make potential customers aware of a specific product or service and create a desire for it

institutional advertising
the presentation of information about a particular firm, designed to enhance the firm's image

Types of Advertising

The two basic types of advertising are product advertising and institutional advertising. **Product advertising** is designed to make potential customers aware of a particular product or service and create a desire for it. **Institutional advertising,** on the

other hand, conveys information about the business itself. It is intended to keep the public aware of the company and enhance its image so that its product advertising will be more credible and effective.

The majority of small business advertising is of the product type. Small retailers' advertisements stress products almost exclusively—weekend specials in a supermarket, for example, or sportswear sold exclusively in a women's shop. It is important to note, however, that the same advertisement can convey both product and institutional themes. Furthermore, a firm may stress its product in newspaper advertisements, while using institutional advertising in the Yellow Pages. Decisions regarding the type of advertising to be used should be based on the nature of the business, industry practice, available media, and the objectives of the firm.

Frequency of Advertising

Determining how often to advertise is an important and highly complex issue for a small business. Obviously, advertising should be done regularly, and attempts to stimulate interest in a firm's products or services should be part of an ongoing promotional program. One-shot advertisements that are not part of a well-planned promotional effort lose much of their effectiveness in a short period. Deciding on the frequency of advertising involves a host of factors, both objective and subjective, and a wise entrepreneur will seek professional advice.

Of course, some noncontinuous advertising may be justified, such as advertising to prepare consumers for acceptance of a new product. Such advertising may also be used to suggest to customers new uses for established products or to promote special sales.

Where to Advertise

Most small firms restrict their advertising, either geographically or by customer type. Advertising media should reach—but not overreach—a firm's present or desired target market. From among the many media available, a small business entrepreneur must choose those that will provide the greatest return for the advertising dollar.

The most appropriate combination of advertising media depends on the type of business and its current circumstances. A real estate sales firm, for example, may rely almost exclusively on classified advertisements in the local newspaper, supplemented by institutional advertising in the Yellow Pages of the telephone directory. A transfer-and-storage firm may use a combination of radio, billboard, and Yellow Pages advertising to reach individuals planning to move household furniture. A small toy manufacturer may emphasize television advertisements and participation in trade fairs. A local retail store may concentrate on display advertisements in the local newspaper. The selection of media should be based not only on tradition but also on a careful evaluation of the various methods that are available to cover a firm's particular market.

The newest alternative media is Web advertising. Advertisers of all types have flocked to the Internet, hoping that the information superhighway will be the next great mass medium. The nature of Web advertising is examined in more detail in a later section.

A good way to build a media mix is to talk with representatives from each medium. A small firm will usually find these representatives willing to recommend an assortment of media, not just the ones they represent. Before meeting with these

representatives, the entrepreneur should learn about the strengths and weaknesses of each medium. Table 17-1 summarizes important facts about several traditional advertising media. Study this information carefully, noting the particular advantages and disadvantages of each medium.

Obtaining Assistance with Advertising

Most small businesses rely on others' expertise to create their promotional messages. Fortunately, there are several sources for this specialized assistance: advertising agencies, suppliers, trade associations, and advertising media.

Advertising agencies can provide the following services:

- Furnish design, artwork, and copy for specific advertisements and/or commercials
- Evaluate and recommend the advertising media with the greatest "pulling power"
- Evaluate the effectiveness of different advertising appeals
- Advise on sales promotions and merchandise displays
- Conduct market-sampling studies to evaluate product acceptance or determine the sales potential of a specific geographic area
- Furnish mailing lists

Since advertising agencies charge fees for their services, an entrepreneur must make sure that the return from those services will be greater than the fees paid. Quality advertising assistance can best be provided by a competent agency. For example, Flowers & Partners, an agency specializing in small business clients, offers a program called Underdog Advertising®. Of course, with the high level of computer

http://www.flowers-partners.com

TABLE 17-1 *Advantages and Disadvantages of Traditional Advertising Media*

Medium	Advantages	Disadvantages
Newspapers	Geographic selectivity and flexibility; short-term advertiser commitments; news value and immediacy; year-round readership; high individual market coverage; co-op and local tie-in availability; short lead time	Little demographic selectivity; limited color capabilities; low pass-along rate; may be expensive
Magazines	Good reproduction, especially for color; demographic selectivity; regional selectivity; local market selectivity; relatively long advertising life; high pass-along rate	Long-term advertiser commitments; slow audience buildup; limited demonstration capabilities; lack of urgency; long lead time
Radio	Low cost; immediacy of message; can be scheduled on short notice; relatively no seasonal change in audience; highly portable; short-term advertiser commitments; entertainment carryover	No visual treatment; short advertising life of message; high frequency required to generate comprehension and retention; distractions from background sound; commercial clutter
Television	Ability to reach a wide, diverse audience; low cost per thousand; creative opportunities for demonstration; immediacy of messages; entertainment carryover; demographic selectivity with cable stations	Short life of messages; some consumer skepticism about claims; high campaign cost; little demographic selectivity with network stations; long-term advertiser commitments; long lead times required for production; commercial clutter
Outdoor media	Repetition; moderate cost; flexibility; geographic selectivity	Short message; lack of demographic selectivity; high "noise" level distracting audience

Source: Charles W. Lamb, Jr., Joseph F. Hair, Jr., and Carl McDaniel, *Marketing* (Cincinnati: South-Western, 1998), p. 509.

IN THE TRENCHES

BUILDING CUSTOMER LOYALTY

A WINNING AD DOESN'T ALWAYS SELL

Bob Bowman, CEO of Outpost.com, learned from experience that an award-winning advertisement may get attention, but fail to attract paying customers. Back in 1998, when Outpost.com was a relatively unknown computer-selling site, the company hired a New York City ad agency to create some television spots. The spots won the agency a Grand Clio, the advertising industry's Oscar.

But the ads didn't do much for Outpost.com except attract viewers to its Web site. With gerbils being shot from cannons and wolves attacking a high school marching band, the ads increased site hits, but that's about all. "The second they ran, traffic would go up by 10,000 to 15,000," Bowman says. "We had a lot of visitors—but no buyers." The ad campaign generated some brand recognition, but little consumer awareness of what Outpost.com sold. "They didn't know that we sold computers," Bowman says. "They thought we sold clothes or didn't sell anything."

A year later, Outpost.com launched a new campaign full of information about the company. In this promotional effort, viewers were told, "Outpost.com sells computers and will ship them overnight." Site traffic from this campaign increased 40 percent, and, more importantly, visitors were buying!

Source: Anne Marie Borrego, "Wild Ads Make Web Stars," *Inc.*, Vol. 22, No. 2 (February 1, 2000), p. 66.

http://www.outpost.com

technology currently available, creating print advertising in-house is becoming increasingly common among small firms.

Other outside sources may assist in formulating and carrying out promotional programs. Suppliers often furnish display aids and even entire advertising programs to their dealers. Trade associations are also active in this area. In addition, the advertising media can provide some of the same services offered by an ad agency.

Web Advertising

The Internet has provided an entirely new way for small firms to advertise. With color graphics, two-way information exchanges, streaming video, and 24-hour availability, online advertising is challenging traditional media for promotional dollars. Web advertising allows advertisers to reach large numbers of global buyers in a timely manner, at less expense, and with more impact than many alternative forms of advertising.

Most large businesses have a presence on the Web, and more and more small firms are using Internet technology. The basic methods of Web promotion are (1) a corporate Web site, (2) banner ads and pop-ups, (3) e-mail, and (4) sponsorships and linkages.

CORPORATE WEB SITES A **Web site** is simply a location on the Internet where users can find information about a firm or its products on a home page and additional electronic pages. Web sites have done much to promote small businesses such as 1-800-CONTACTS, which was featured in this chapter's Spotlight. Figure 17-4 shows this firm's home page. Notice how the site promotes products with an offer of free shipping and also provides information about the company and its customer service.

Web site
a firm's location on the World Wide Web

FIGURE 17-4

Home Page of 1-800-CONTACTS

banner ads
advertisements that appear across a Web page, most often as moving rectangular strips

pop-up ads
advertisements that burst open on computer screens

BANNER ADS AND POP-UPS **Banner ads** are advertisements that appear across a Web page, most often as moving rectangular strips. In contrast, **pop-up ads** burst open on Web pages, but do not have movement. When viewers respond by clicking on an ad, they are automatically linked to the site providing the product or sales activity. These ads can be placed on search engine sites or on related Web pages. The effectiveness of this form of advertising has not been documented, but these ads may work well with a targeted campaign.

Unfortunately, online audiences often greet banner ads with little excitement. "A lot of Internet banner ads are like billboards on the side of the highway," says Martha Deevy of Charles Schwab & Co. "People drive right past them and don't bother to look."[4] Some research shows that click-through rates on banner ads have dropped from 30 percent when the first ads appeared in 1994 to 0.3 percent today.[5]

e-mail promotion
advertising delivered by means of electronic mail

DIRECT E-MAIL PROMOTION **E-mail promotion,** in which electronic mail is used to deliver a firm's message, provides a low-cost way to pinpoint customers and achieve response rates higher than those for banner ads. However, as more and more busi-

IN THE TRENCHES — UTILIZING NEW TECHNOLOGY

PROMOTING A DOT.COM VENTURE

Promotional dollars can bring visitors to a Web site, but do they guarantee orders? Ask Erik Stuebe, CEO of Blue Marlin Corporation. His wholesale company sells vintage baseball caps and apparel through better department stores and specialty retailers. On the advice of a Web developer, he invested $35,000 to launch a company Web site in the mid-1990s.

The site was designed as a baseball-history-lover's paradise, featuring "sparkling copy and thrilling animation to spin vivid, romantic yarns about the old minor, Negro, Cuban, and women's baseball leagues." The hope was that these stories would promote the products offered to customers who visited the site. The hits came, but by the end of 1998, the company had sold only $50,000 of merchandise.

Stuebe spent $15,000 a year for updates, but revenues never took off. Over 95 percent of site visitors didn't purchase anything. By 1999, Blue Marlin's online sales were only a small part of its revenues. Now, Stuebe says, he will put $500,000 originally budgeted for the Web site back into the wholesale business—a channel where customers can touch and feel the products. Blue Marlin's experience illustrates the uncertainty associated with this new type of advertising.

Source: Anne Marie Borrego, "Traffic Will Make You Rich," *Inc.*, Vol. 22, No. 2 (February 2000), p. 54.

http://www.bluemarlincorp.com

nesses use e-mail for this purpose, customer inboxes are becoming cluttered. And users are reluctant to open some e-mail messages, fearing computer viruses.

SPONSORSHIPS AND LINKAGES In **Web sponsorship,** a firm pays to be part of another organization's Web page. When the Web page includes a click-on link to the paying firm's site, there is said to be a **linkage.** Research shows that a significant number of online purchases originate from online links.

Web sponsorship
a type of advertising in which a firm pays another organization for the right to be part of that organization's Web page

linkage
a type of advertising agreement in which one firm pays another to include a click-on link on its site

Internet advertising is already facing an obstacle—blocking software from such companies as WebWasher, which has more than 4 million users worldwide.[6] As the name suggests, blocking software prevents ads from appearing on a viewer's Web page.

http://www.webwasher.com

SALES PROMOTIONAL TOOLS

5

Describe sales promotional tools.

Sales promotion serves as an inducement to buy a certain product while typically offering value to prospective customers. Generally, **sales promotion** includes any promotional technique, other than personal selling or advertising, that stimulates the purchase of a particular good or service.

sales promotion
an inclusive term for any promotional techniques that are neither personal selling nor advertising

Sales promotion should seldom comprise all the promotional efforts of a small business. Typically, it should be used in combination with personal selling and advertising. Popular sales promotional tools include specialties, contests, premiums, trade show exhibits, point-of-purchase displays, free merchandise, publicity, sampling, and coupons. The scope of this textbook does not allow discussion of all these tools. However, we will briefly examine specialties, trade show exhibits, and publicity.

Specialties

The most widely used specialty item is a calendar. Other popular specialty items are pens, key chains, coffee mugs, and shirts. Almost anything can be used as a specialty promotion, as long as each item is imprinted with the firm's name or other identifying slogan.

The distinguishing characteristic of specialties is their enduring nature and tangible value. Specialties are referred to as the "lasting medium." As functional products, they are worth something to recipients. Specialties can be used to promote a product directly or to create goodwill for a firm; they are excellent reminders of a firm's existence.

Finally, specialties are personal. They are distributed directly to the customer in a personal way; they can be used personally; and they have a personal message. A small business needs to retain its personal image, and entrepreneurs often use specialties to achieve this objective. More information on specialities is available on the Web site of the Promotional Products Association International at http://www.ppa.org.

http://www.ppa.org

Trade Show Exhibits

Advertising often cannot substitute for trial experiences with a product, and a customer's place of business is not always the best environment for product demonstrations. Trade show exhibits allow potential customers to get hands-on experience with a product.

Trade show exhibits are of particular value to manufacturers. The greatest benefit of these exhibits is the potential cost savings over personal selling. Trade show groups claim that the cost of an exhibit is less than one-fourth the cost of sales calls. Many small manufacturers agree that exhibits are more cost-effective than advertising. One leading trade publication, *Sales & Marketing Management,* offers some helpful tips regarding trade shows.[7]

http://www.salesandmarketing.com

- ***Create moving billboards.*** Smart exhibitors try to capture attendees' attention all over the trade show and the trade show city—not just at their booth. Give booth visitors handouts that amount to moving billboards. The most popular is a tote bag with your company name and logo that is then carried around the show. Also try sponsoring bus boards and cab boards that cruise the city during the trade show.
- ***Make the booth interactive.*** Games, contests, tests of skill, trivia challenges, and other interactive activities are effective ways of getting people into your booth. Make sure the prizes are worth winning; otherwise, the encounter may create a lasting negative impression.
- **Qualify leads immediately.** Ask all booth visitors to fill out a qualification card that includes questions on their interest in your product. If they stopped by the booth out of curiosity or simply to enter a drawing, that's fine. You just don't want to waste time following up on those who have no real interest in your product.
- ***Create a presence on the show floor.*** While this may be easier said than done, standing out in the crowd is a must. Some exhibitors hire celebrities, while others run exciting games. Whatever technique you decide to use, work hard at being extraordinary.

IN THE TRENCHES Entrepreneurship Today

SLASHING COSTS

Firms that depend on trade shows to promote their services have much to gain from cutting the costs associated with attending such shows. This was the motivation for Karetta Hubbard, co-founder of Hubbard & Revo-Cohen (HRC), a human resource consultancy in Vienna, Virginia, to devise a do-it-yourself blueprint for reducing her firm's trade show expenses.

"We have to participate in trade shows," she says. "That's where we sell our training software."

Hubbard was keenly aware of trade show costs, from the space itself to employee travel to the shipping of exhibit materials. She believed that thousands of dollars in annual savings would be possible if, instead of paying for specialty consultants, she could develop a notebook containing exhibitors' deadline rules and other custom information about each show.

The notebook includes checklists so that HRC can order what is needed for booths, as well as timelines so that HRC can ship goods well ahead of schedule. HRC did 18 trade shows in 1999 and saved more than $300 a show by bulk shipping early instead of using FedEx or UPS at the last minute. The notebook also provides reminders to make advance arrangements for booth necessities such as business card readers, Internet access, and refreshments. For example, a reminder that "in Chicago, you have to rely on union guys to bring your stuff into the building and switch on your electricity" prompts HRC to organize early so as to avoid a possible overtime charge by union members.

Source: Ilan Mochari, "Planning Conventions," *Inc.*, Vol. 22, No. 1 (January 2000), p. 93.

http://www.hrccentral.com

- ***Plan ahead.*** Just showing up isn't enough. Use the trade show as an opportunity to spend time with particularly important customers or prospects. This means planning well in advance to have the customer or prospect meet you at the booth for a special presentation or demonstration. Since major trade shows attract a large number of interested prospects, book as many meetings and make as many contacts as possible.
- ***Recruit customers.*** Make sure your marketing staff and salespeople don't stand around the booth talking to each other. Get them out in the aisles. Have them roam the convention hall passing out tote bags, buttons, or other premiums. Have them bring people to the booth for a serious demonstration.

Publicity

Of particular importance to small firms is **publicity**, which provides visibility for a business at little or no cost. Publicity can be used to promote both a product and a firm's image; it is a vital part of public relations for the small business. A good publicity program requires regular contacts with the news media.

publicity
information about a firm and its products or services that appears as a news item, usually free of charge

Although publicity is considered to be free advertising, this type of promotion is not always free. Examples of publicity efforts that entail some expense include involvement with school yearbooks and youth athletic programs. While the benefits are difficult to measure, publicity is nevertheless important to a small business and should be used at every opportunity.

Alexis Abramson, founder and chief executive of Mature Mart, has never spent a dollar on advertising. Her company, which specializes in products for elderly people, is promoted through editorials she writes for small-town newspapers. She has also made appearances on NBC's "Today Show." "Every time I appear with a few products, we get at least a 50 percent spike in sales for the items featured," Abramson says.[8]

When to Use Sales Promotion

A small firm can use sales promotion to accomplish various objectives. For example, small manufacturers can use it to stimulate channel members—retailers and wholesalers—to market their product. Wholesalers can use sales promotion to induce retailers to buy inventories earlier than they normally would, and retailers, with similar promotional tools, may be able to persuade customers to make a purchase.

Strategic Alliances and Sales Promotion

Joining with another firm to promote products is a form of a strategic alliance. For example, if a local dry cleaner and a nearby independent tailor had similar customers, they might share the cost of a coupon program, increasing the visibility of both firms without taking away each other's business. Small firms, however, are traditionally very independent and only recently have begun to recognize the benefits of cross-promotion.

Ideally, the discussions in this chapter have helped you understand the role that promotion plays in the marketing process. It is a complex activity, and entrepreneurs need to recognize their limitations in this area and seek professional advice when necessary.

LOOKING BACK

1 Describe the communication process and the factors determining a promotional mix.

- Every communication involves a source, a message, a channel, and a receiver.
- A promotional mix is a blend of nonpersonal, personal, and special forms of communication techniques.
- A promotional mix is influenced primarily by three important factors: the geographical nature of the market, the size of the promotional budget, and the product's characteristics.

2 Discuss methods of determining the appropriate level of promotional expenditure.

- Earmarking promotional dollars based on a percentage of sales is a simple method for determining expenditures.
- Spending only what can be spared is a widely used approach to promotional budgeting.
- Spending as much as the competition does is a way to react to short-run promotional tactics of competitors.
- The preferred approach to determining promotional expenditures is to decide what it will take to do the job, while factoring in elements used in the other methods.

3 Describe personal selling activities.

- A sales presentation is a process involving prospecting, practicing the presentation, and then making the presentation.
- Salespeople are compensated for their efforts in two ways—financially and nonfinancially.
- The two basic plans for financial compensation are commissions and straight salary.

4 Identify advertising options for a small business.

- Common advertising media include television, radio, magazines, newspapers, billboards, and the Internet.
- Product advertising is designed to promote a product or service, while institutional advertising conveys an idea regarding the business itself.
- A small firm must decide how often to advertise, where to advertise, and what the message will be.

5 Describe sales promotional tools.

- Sales promotion includes all promotional techniques other than personal selling and advertising.
- Typically, sales promotional tools should be used along with advertising and personal selling.
- Three widely used sales promotional tools are specialties, trade show exhibits, and publicity.

Key Terms

promotion, p. 423
promotional mix, p. 425
personal selling, p. 426
prospecting, p. 427
advertising, p. 432
product advertising, p. 432
institutional advertising, p. 432
Web site, p. 435
banner ads, p. 436
pop-up ads, p. 436
e-mail promotion, p. 436
Web sponsorship, p. 437
linkage, p. 437
sales promotion, p. 437
publicity, p. 439

Discussion Questions

1. Describe the parallel relationship that exists between a small business communication and a personal communication.
2. Discuss the advantages and disadvantages of each approach to budgeting funds for promotion.
3. Outline a system of prospecting that could be used by a small camera store. Incorporate all the techniques presented in this chapter.
4. Why are a salesperson's techniques for handling objections so important to a successful sales presentation?
5. Assume you have the opportunity to "sell" your course instructor on the idea of eliminating final examinations. Make a list of the objections you expect to hear from your instructor, and describe how you will handle each objection, using some of the techniques in Figure 17-3.
6. What are some nonfinancial rewards that could be offered to salespeople?
7. What are the advantages and disadvantages of compensating salespeople by salary? By commissions? What do you think is an acceptable compromise?
8. What are some approaches to advertising on the Web?
9. How do specialties differ from trade show exhibits and publicity? Be specific.
10. How can the concept of a strategic alliance be used in promotional strategy?

You Make the Call

SITUATION 1

The driving force behind Cannon Arp's new business was several bad experiences with his car—two speeding tickets and four minor fender-benders. Consequently, his insurance rates more than doubled, which resulted in Arp's idea to design and sell a bumper sticker that read "To Report Bad Driving, Call My Parents at . . . ." With a $200 investment, Arp printed 15,000 of the stickers, which contain space to write in the appropriate telephone number. He is now planning a promotion to support his strategy of distribution through auto parts stores.

Question 1 What role, if any, should personal selling have in Arp's total promotional plan?

Question 2 Arp is considering advertising in magazines. What do you think about this medium for promoting his product?

Question 3 Of what value might publicity be for selling Arp's stickers? Be specific.

SITUATION 2

Cheree Moore owns and operates a small business that supplies delicatessens with bulk containers of ready-made salads. When served in salad bars, the salads appear to have been freshly prepared from scratch at the delicatessen. Moore wants additional promotional exposure for her products and is considering using her fleet of trucks as rolling billboards. If the strategy is successful, she may even attempt to lease space on other trucks. Moore is concerned about the cost-effectiveness of the idea and whether the public will even notice the advertisements. She also wonders whether the image of her salad products might be hurt by this advertising medium.

Question 1 What suggestions can you offer that would help Moore make this decision?

Question 2 How could Moore go about determining the cost-effectiveness of this strategy?

Question 3 What additional factors should Moore evaluate before advertising on trucks?

SITUATION 3

Corinna Lathan is co-founder and CEO of AnthroTronix, which is currently located in the business incubator at the University of Maryland. Founded in July 1999, the company is a human factors engineering firm committed to optimizing interactions between people and technology.

With co-founder Jack M. Vice, Lathan is developing a Muppet-like robot for use as a therapeutic tool with children with speech, learning, and physical disabilities. The robot has been tested at a Maryland hospital, where the medical director says the kids using the device have shown measurable improvement. Here's how the robot, named JesterBot, works:

A child puts on leg- or armbands and a hat embedded with radio transceivers and sensors. By waving a hand, say, or nodding her head, she sends out radio signals that are interpreted by a central processing unit in the JesterBot. . . . During exercises, the JesterBot can gauge a child's range of motion, while electronically reporting the results of the session to a therapist via a data port hooked up to a PC.

To launch the product, the company needs additional funding, which it hopes to get soon.

Source: Nicole Ridgway, "Robo-Therapy," *Forbes,* Vol. 167, No. 11 (March 14, 2001), p. 216.

Question 1 When the product is ready to launch, what kinds of promotion should the company use? Why?

Question 2 What techniques might this firm use to set the promotional budget?

Question 3 In what way, if any, could Internet promotion help this business?

EXPERIENTIAL EXERCISES

1. Interview the owners of one or more small businesses to determine how they develop their promotional budget. Classify the owners' methods into one or more of the four approaches described in this chapter. Report your findings to the class.
2. Plan a sales presentation. With a classmate role-playing a potential buyer, make the presentation in class. Ask the other students to critique your technique.
3. Select a small business advertisement from a local newspaper, and evaluate its design and purpose.
4. Interview a media representative about advertising options for small businesses. Summarize your findings for the class.

EXPLORING THE WEB

1. The Web site at **http://www.allbusiness.com** offers a wealth of information on sales and marketing.
   a. How many trade shows should a startup business attend each year? Create a list of things to do to generate sales from trade shows.
   b. Cold calling may be the most difficult type of personal selling. List some do's and don'ts for success when using this type of selling. How many follow-up contacts are usually required before a sale is made?
   c. List five tips for building and maintaining a good sales team. What are eight characteristics of an excellent sales representative?
   d. What are the seven components of a sales campaign? How many of these are services provided through Allbusiness.com?
2. Examine the resources at **http://www.albertafirst.com**, a Web site that represents a partnership between industry and government of the Canadian province. Choose Small Business Guides, then Marketing for Small Business, and then click on Promotions and Advertising.
   a. List the four steps in developing a promotion plan.
   b. Print the promotional mix checklist.
   c. List three ways to measure the success of your promotion plan.
3. Ziff-Davis, a premier publisher in the computer industry, offers information on Web advertising on its site at **http://www.zdnet.com**. Choose the Business category, and then under the Small Business Guides, choose Marketing.
   a. Read one of the articles under Marketing Advice. Summarize in a paragraph the advice offered to small business owners.
   b. Read one of the Marketing Features articles. What specific suggestions are given for advertising on the Web?
   c. Examine the offerings under Marketing Products. What products will assist a small business in its online marketing efforts?

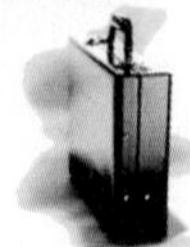

CASE 17

FLOWER GIRL (p. 686)

This case describes an entrepreneur's promotional strategy to keep her business in the public eye.

Alternative Cases for Chapter 17:

Case 1, "Steve's Olympic Tees," p. 637
Case 3, "HeadBlade Company," p. 645
Case 9, "ScrubaDub Auto Wash," p. 662

part

6

Small Business Management

chapter 18

Professional Management in the Growing Firm

In the Spotlight

Jessica's Wonders

Entrepreneurs often require outside managerial guidance to transform their dreams into profitable businesses. Jessica Nam, a linguistic anthropology major at Brown University, stumbled upon an entrepreneurial opportunity and used managerial assistance to make it a going concern.

One afternoon in 1998, Nam and a friend walked into a Providence, R.I., pizzeria. Next to the register was a pile of shrink-wrapped slices of dried-out old banana bread selling for $1.75 a piece. Says Nam: "I told the owner, 'Listen, I can bake banana bread better than that.' He says, 'Bring it in.' So I did." Pretty soon, the shop gave Nam a large corner of counter space, for which she designed impromptu display baskets—a first stab at marketing, and a glimpse of the path her enterprise would eventually follow.

Nam sought outside assistance from Brown University's entrepreneurship program. Through the program, she gained access to space, facilities, and guidance in a New York incubator.

In the spring of 1999, Nam entered Brown's student entrepreneur competition, where her strictly offline business model was a maverick amidst the deluge of 77 dot-com wannabes. Through this competition, Nam was fortunate enough to meet Steven Massarsky, a Brown alumnus and president of the New York City-based Business Incubation Group. Soon enough, Massarsky was providing Nam not only with a New York office space, sales, marketing, business models, and introductions to angel investors, but also with what he calls "mentor capital."

The incubation group helped Nam sharpen her business plan, tutored her on business topics such as

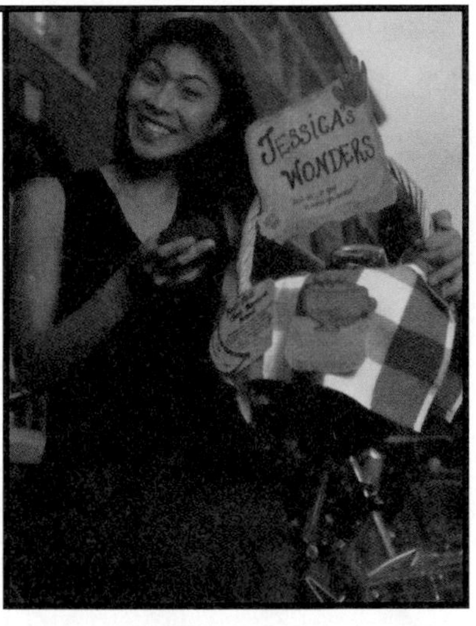

cash flow and inventory, and guided her in developing a salesforce. So, along with providing office space, phones, and computers, the group also helped her season her innovative business idea with business judgment, contacts, and know-how. ◆

Source: Benjamin L. Eisman, "Making Bread with Bread," *Executive Edge* (June-July 2000), p. 35.

http://www.bizincu.com

LOOKING AHEAD

After studying this chapter, you should be able to

1. *Discuss the distinctive features of small firm management.*
2. *Identify the various kinds of plans and approaches to planning.*
3. *Discuss the entrepreneur's leadership role.*
4. *Describe the nature and features of an organizational structure for small businesses.*
5. *Discuss the ways in which control is exercised in a small firm.*
6. *Describe the problem of time pressure and suggest solutions.*
7. *Explain the various types of outside management assistance.*

One need not be a manager to originate an idea for a business or prepare a business plan. Except for one-person operations, however, starting an enterprise requires a management process that integrates the efforts of a number of employees. An entrepreneur must move beyond the role of creator and provide direction for the business. This is absolutely necessary in order for production personnel, sales representatives, and support service personnel to work together effectively. This chapter considers the unique aspects of managing small firms, ways to improve methods of management, and managerial changes that are needed as firms grow.

DISTINCTIVE CHARACTERISTICS OF SMALL FIRM MANAGEMENT

Discuss the distinctive features of small firm management.

professional manager
a manager who uses systematic, analytical methods of management

As one entrepreneur commented, "Unless you thrive on chaos, a small company can be tough." Small firm operations are not always chaotic, of course, but small business owners face challenges that differ greatly from those of corporate executives. Furthermore, small companies experience change in their organizational and managerial needs as they move from point zero—their launching—to the point where they employ a full staff of **professional managers,** trained in the use of systematic, analytical managerial methods.

Professional-Level Management

There is, of course, much variation in the way business firms, as well as other organizations, are managed. Between the extremes of very unskilled and highly professional types of management lies a continuum. At the less professional end of this continuum are entrepreneurs and other managers who rely largely on past experience, rules of thumb, and personal whims in giving direction to their businesses. In most cases, their ideas of motivation are based on the way they were treated in earlier business or family relationships.

Other entrepreneurs and managers display much more professionalism. They are analytical and systematic in dealing with management problems and issues. Because they emphasize getting the facts and working out logical solutions, their approach is sometimes described as scientific in nature. The challenge for small firm managers is to develop as much professionalism as possible.

Founders as Managers

Founders of new firms are not always good organization members. As discussed in Chapter 1, they are creative, innovative, risk-taking individuals who have the courage to strike out on their own. Indeed, they are often propelled into entrepreneurship by precipitating events, sometimes involving their difficulty in fitting into conventional organizational roles. As a consequence, founders may fail to appreciate the value of good management practices. Understandably, their orientation frequently differs from that of professional managers.

Some entrepreneurs are professional in their approach to management, and some corporate managers are entrepreneurial in the sense of being innovative and willing to take risks. Nevertheless, a founder's less-than-professional management style often acts as a drag on business growth. Ideally, the founder is able to add a measure of professional management without sacrificing the entrepreneurial spirit and basic values that gave the business a successful start.

Managerial Weakness in Small Firms

Although some large corporations experience poor management, small businesses seem particularly vulnerable to this weakness. Many small firms are marginal or unprofitable businesses, struggling to survive from day to day. At best, they earn only a bare living for their owners. They operate, but to say that they are managed would be an exaggeration.

Consider American Dixie Group, Inc., founded by Lay Cooper in 1989 in Albany, New York to build the industrial machines used in food processing, packaging, and plastics making.[1] The business became successful, was praised for its problem-solving wizardry, and served customers like Nestlé and Campbell Soup. As

ENTREPRENEURSHIP TODAY

IN THE TRENCHES

FROM NERD TO MANAGER

The ability to create innovative products doesn't always go hand in hand with the ability to manage business operations. In some cases, for example, an entrepreneur's background is technical, requiring that he or she get additional training or experience in order to adapt to the managerial role. As one writer expressed it, "The U.S. economy is driven by nerds—a term that recently morphed from an insult to a quasi compliment."

"Nerd" bosses often engage in micromanaging, trying to do too much of the work themselves.

Don Spero confesses that he was a micromanager during his first years of running a business. A major technology of the company—Fusion Systems of Rockville, Maryland, which has interests in semiconductor-fabrication equipment—was based on Dr. Spero's postdoctoral research in physics. "I thought I couldn't manage unless I could do every job myself," Dr. Spero recalls.

After recognizing the drawbacks of his management style, Spero backed off and let others make decisions. He also made conscious efforts to transform himself into a real manager, by finding mentors among more seasoned CEOs and by listening to employees.

Today, after dividing and selling the company, Spero directs the University of Maryland Dingman Center for Entrepreneurship. His experiences as a nerd boss help him to educate aspiring student entrepreneurs about the dangers of micromanaging.

Source: Michaele Weissman, "Nerd Alert: How Smart Engineers Turn into Dumb Bosses," *The Wall Street Journal,* May 14, 2001, p. R14.

http://www.bmgt.umd.edu/dingman

long as the business remained small, with no more than two dozen employees in the shop and a half dozen or so projects in the pipeline, it apparently performed quite well. As it expanded, however, it ran into problems. Suppliers began griping about late payments, and customers became unhappy because of delayed deliveries and shoddy workmanship. In September 1998, American Dixie Group filed for bankruptcy; it had failed because it lacked professional management.

Managerial weaknesses of the type just described are all too typical of small firms. The good news, however, is that poor management is neither universal nor inevitable.

Constraints That Hamper Management

Managers of small firms, particularly new and growing companies, are constrained by conditions that do not trouble the average corporate executive—they must face the grim reality of small bank accounts and limited staff. A small firm often lacks the money for slick sales brochures, and it cannot afford much in the way of market research. The shortage of cash even makes it difficult to employ an adequate number of clerical employees. Such limitations are painfully apparent to large-firm managers who move into management positions in small firms.

A financial analyst at General Motors who became CEO of a smaller, entrepreneurial company described the drastic changes he faced:

You have to get used to moving the decimal points over a few places. At GM I was involved in billion-dollar analyses of new plants. Now I have to sign off on things like a trade show booth. For us it's a big deal.

Every thousand dollars means something. I had to make a decision whether I should lease a copier the other day. Can we afford to do it? Should we do it right now?[2]

Small firms typically lack adequate specialized professional staff. Most small business managers are generalists. Lacking the support of experienced specialists in such areas as market research, financial analysis, advertising, and human resources management, the manager of a small firm must make decisions in these areas without the expertise that is available in a larger business. This limitation may be partially overcome by using outside management assistance. But coping with a shortage of internal professional talent is part of the reality of managing entrepreneurial firms.

Firm Growth and Management

As a newly formed business becomes established and grows, its organizational structure and pattern of management change. To some extent, management in any organization must adapt to growth and change. However, the changes involved in the early growth stages of a new business are much more extensive than those that occur with the growth of a relatively mature business.

A number of experts have proposed models related to the growth stages of business firms.[3] These models typically describe four or five stages of growth and identify various management issues related to each stage. Figure 18-1 on page 450 shows four stages of organizational growth, characteristic of many small businesses. As firms progress from Stage 1 to Stage 4, they add layers of management and increase the formality of operations. Though some firms skip the first one or two stages by starting as larger businesses, thousands of small firms make their way through each of the stages pictured in Figure 18-1.

FIGURE 18-1 *Organizational Stages of Small Business Growth*

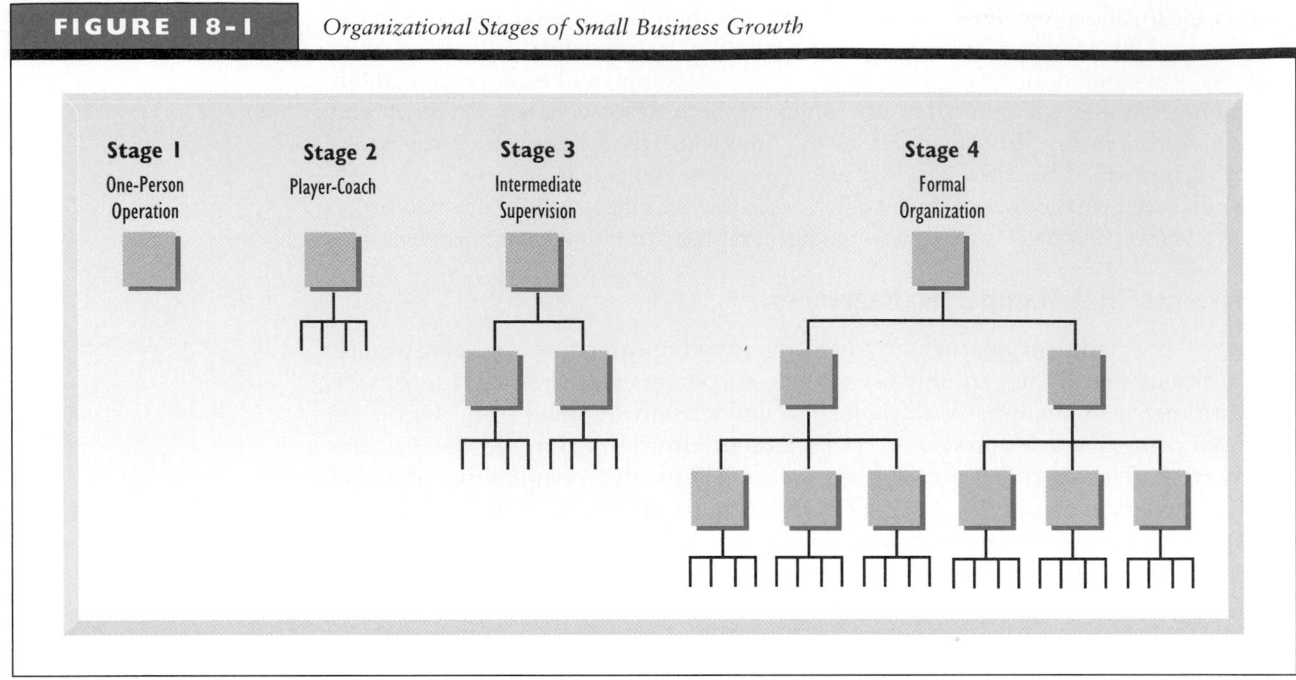

In Stage 1, the firm is simply a one-person operation. Some firms begin with a larger organization, but the one-person startup is by no means rare. Many businesses remain one-person operations indefinitely. In Stage 2, the entrepreneur becomes a player–coach, which implies continuing active participation in the operations of the business. In addition to performing the basic work—whether making the product, selling it, writing checks, or keeping records—the entrepreneur must also coordinate the efforts of others.

A major milestone is reached in Stage 3, when an intermediate level of supervision is added. In many ways, this is a turning point for the small firm, because the entrepreneur must rise above direct, hands-on management and work through an intervening layer of management. Stage 4, the stage of formal organization, involves more than increased size and multi-layered organization. The formalization of management entails adoption of written policies, preparation of plans and budgets, standardization of personnel practices, computerization of records, preparation of organization charts and job descriptions, scheduling of training conferences, institution of control procedures, and so on. While some formal management practices may be adopted prior to Stage 4, the steps shown in Figure 18-1 outline a typical pattern of development for successful firms. Flexibility and informality may be helpful when a firm is first started, but the firm's growth necessitates greater formality in planning and control. Tension often develops as the traditional easygoing patterns of management become dysfunctional. Great managerial skill is required of the entrepreneur in order to preserve a "family" atmosphere while introducing professional management.

As a firm moves from Stage 1 to Stage 4, the pattern of entrepreneurial activities changes. The entrepreneur becomes less of a doer and more of a manager. Managers who have strong doing skills often have weak managing skills. In 1986, with degrees in graphic arts, Steve Appel and Lee Whitehead started Nouveau

Contemporary Goods, a business that sells everything from quirky greeting cards to trendy furniture. In the beginning, they both supported themselves with other jobs. Their first store was a tiny gift store, which later moved to a much larger location in downtown Baltimore, Maryland. They have found running their business to be more difficult as it has grown.

http://www.nouveaubaltimore.com

They still struggle with inventory and payroll. They now have staff positions they never had before, like a full-time shipping-and-receiving employee and a full-time interior designer. They're still having trouble delegating responsibility and control. They're never out of debt. And their retail consultant, says Appel, has been exhorting them to "get a delivery service. Get a delivery service!"—instead of using their own employees and van.

They think it would be fun to have another store—in the Georgetown section of Washington, D.C., perhaps, or in Rehoboth Beach, Del. But they know they haven't come to grips with the growth they've experienced since 1996. "I think we really need to master this business because we don't have it mastered at all," says Appel.[4]

Small firms that are too hesitant to move through these organizational stages and acquire the necessary professional management limit their rate of growth. On the other hand, a small business may attempt to grow too quickly. If an entrepreneur's primary strength lies in product development or selling, for example, a quick move into Stage 4 may saddle the entrepreneur with managerial duties and rob the organization of his or her valuable entrepreneurial talents.

In his study of the origin and evolution of new businesses, Amar V. Bhide found that entrepreneurs play different roles in starting businesses than they play in building what he calls long-lived firms.[5] Likewise, the personal qualities involved in starting businesses differ from the qualities required to develop long-lived firms. This helps explain why so few ventures actually become established businesses with staying power. Therefore, growing a business requires maturation and adaptation on the part of the entrepreneur.

The Manager as Negotiator

In most small firms, as elsewhere, entrepreneurs and managers must personally interact with other individuals much of the time. Many personal contacts are outsiders, such as suppliers, customers, bankers, realtors, and providers of business services. Typically, the interests of the parties are in conflict, to some degree at least. A supplier, for example, wants to sell a product or service for the highest possible price, and the buyer wants to purchase it for the lowest possible price. To have a successful business, a manager must reach agreements that both meet the firm's requirements and contribute to good relationships over time.

Even within the business, the manager is involved in relationships that pit different perspectives and personal interests against one another. Subordinates, for example, frequently desire changes in their work assignments or feel that they are worth more to the company than their salary level indicates. Managers in different departments may compete for services offered by a steno pool, a maintenance department, or a computer services unit.

The process of developing workable solutions through discussions or interactions is termed **negotiation.** All of us are negotiators in our daily lives, both inside and outside our family relationships. Conflicting interests, desires, and demands require that we reconcile, or negotiate, the differences in order to live together peacefully.

negotiation
two-way communication process used to resolve differences in needs, goals, or ideas

Many people consider negotiation to be a win–lose game; that is, one party

FIGURE 18-2

Tips for Building Relationships

World-Class Tips:
Fifteen Statements That Will Help Build Solid Relationships
(or at Least Keep You Out of Deep Soup)

1. "I'm very pleased to meet you."
2. "Could you tell me more about your proposal?"
3. "I have a few more questions I'd like to ask you."
4. "We might be able to consider X if you could consider Y."
5. "Let me try to summarize where we stand now in our discussion."
6. "I'm very happy to see you again."
7. "Could you tell me more about your concerns?"
8. "Let me tell you where I have a concern."
9. "I feel disappointed that we haven't made more progress."
10. "I really appreciate the progress that we've made."
11. "Thank you."
12. "Can I answer any more questions about our organization or proposal?"
13. "What would it take for us to close this deal?"
14. "I've enjoyed doing business with you."
15. "I haven't talked to you since we signed the contract. I just wanted to follow up with you to see how things are working out."

Source: Reprinted from How to Negotiate Anything with Anyone, Anywhere Around the World. http://www.amacombooks.org

must win, and the other must lose. There is a problem, however, with this concept of negotiation. If both parties do not feel that they have won, the loser will go away with thoughts of getting even in subsequent negotiations. Such feelings do not contribute to good long-term relationships.

In contrast, other negotiators advocate a win–win strategy. A win–win negotiator tries to find a solution that will satisfy at least the basic interests of both parties.

Implementing a win–win strategy in relationships involves thinking about one's own interests and also exploring the interests of the other party. After clarifying the interests of the various parties and their needs, the negotiator can explore various alternatives to identify their overall fit, looking for a solution that will produce a workable plan for all. There are situations, of course, in which a win–win solution is impossible, but this type of solution should be pursued as frequently as possible.

A foundation for successful negotiating is created by developing strong relationships between the negotiating parties. In Figure 18-2, Frank L. Acuff provides examples of comments that contribute to cooperative relationships.

The Nature of Managerial Work

management functions
the activities of planning, leading, organizing, and controlling

Thus far, our discussion of the management process has been very general. Now it is time to look more closely at what managers do—how they plan, how they exercise leadership, how they organize, and how they control operations. These activities are called **management functions.**

Planning Activities

The preparation of a formal business plan for a new business, discussed in Chapter 8, is only the first phase of an ongoing planning process. This process guides production, marketing, and other activities on a month-to-month and year-to-year basis throughout the life of the business.

Identify the various kinds of plans and approaches to planning.

THE NEED FOR FORMAL PLANNING Most small business managers plan to some degree. However, the amount of planning they do is typically less than ideal. Also, what little planning there is tends to be haphazard and focused on specific, immediate issues—for example, how much inventory to purchase, whether to buy a new piece of equipment, and other questions of this type. Circumstances affect the degree to which formal planning is needed, but most businesses could function more profitably by increasing the amount of planning done by managers and making it more systematic.

The payoff from planning comes in several ways. First, the process of thinking through the issues confronting a firm and developing a plan to deal with those issues can improve productivity. Second, planning provides a focus for a firm: Managerial decisions over the course of the year can be guided by the annual plan, and employees can work consistently toward the same goal. Third, evidence of planning increases credibility with bankers, suppliers, and other outsiders.

TYPES OF PLANS A firm's basic path to the future is spelled out in a document called a **long-range plan,** or **strategic plan.** As noted in Chapter 2, strategy decisions concern such issues as niche markets and features that differentiate a firm from its competitors. A long-range plan provides a foundation for plans governing more specific activities.

long-range plan (strategic plan)
a firm's overall plan for the future

Short-range plans are action plans designed to deal with activities in production, marketing, and other areas over a period of one year or less. An important part of a short-range operating plan is the **budget**—a document that expresses future plans in monetary terms. A budget is usually prepared one year in advance, with a breakdown by quarters or months. (Budgeting is explained more fully in Chapter 23.)

short-range plan
a plan that governs a firm's operations for one year or less

budget
a document that expresses future plans in monetary terms

Other types of plans are less connected to the calendar and more concerned with the way things are done. **Business policies,** for example, are fundamental statements that serve as guides for managerial decision making. Examples of business policies are financial policies and personnel policies. A personnel policy may state, for example, that no employee may accept a gift from a supplier unless it is of nominal value.

business policies
basic statements that provide guidance for managerial decision making

Procedures are more specific plans and deal primarily with methodology—how something is to be done. In a furniture store, for example, a procedure might require any sale of furniture on credit to be approved by a credit manager prior to delivery to the customer. Once a work method is established, it may be standardized and referred to as a **standard operating procedure.**

procedures
specific work methods to be followed in business activities

standard operating procedure
an established method of conducting a business activity

PLANNING TIME Small business managers all too often succumb to the "tyranny of the urgent." Because they are busy putting out fires, they never get around to planning. Planning is easy to postpone and, therefore, easy for managers to ignore while concentrating on more urgent issues in such areas as production and sales. And, just as quarterbacks focusing on a receiver may be blindsided by blitzing linebackers, managers who have neglected to plan may be bowled over by competitors.

Some discipline is necessary in order to reap the benefits of planning. Time and a degree of seclusion must be provided if significant progress is to be made. Planning is primarily a mental process. It is seldom done effectively in an atmosphere of ringing telephones, rush orders, and urgent demands for decision making.

EMPLOYEE PARTICIPATION IN PLANNING Although a small firm owner should personally spend time planning, this responsibility may be delegated to some extent to the other members of the business. The larger the organization, the more important it is to delegate some planning to those most familiar with particular areas, as the owner can hardly specify in detail the program for each department.

The concept that the boss does the thinking and the employee does the work is outdated. Progressive managers have discovered that employees' ideas are often helpful in developing solutions to company problems. A salesperson, for example, is closer than his or her manager to the firm's customers and is usually better able to evaluate their needs and possible reactions.

Leading and Motivating

Discuss the entrepreneur's leadership role.

To be successful, an entrepreneur needs to create an atmosphere of cooperation and teamwork among all employees. The potential for good teamwork among employees in small firms is enhanced in some ways by the smallness of the enterprise.

PERSONAL INVOLVEMENT OF THE ENTREPRENEUR In most small firms, the owner-manager is not a faceless unknown, but an individual whom employees see and relate to in the course of their normal work schedules. If the employer-employee relationship is good, employees in small firms develop strong feelings of personal loyalty to their employer. This situation is entirely different from that of large corporations, where most employees never see the chief executive.

In very small firms—those with 20 or fewer employees—extensive interaction is typical. As a firm grows, the amount of personal contact an employee has with the owner naturally declines. Nevertheless, a significant personal relationship between the owner and employees is characteristic of most small businesses.

In a large corporation, the values of top-level executives must be filtered through many layers of management before they reach those who produce and sell the products. As a result, the influence of those at the top tends to be diluted by the process. In contrast, personnel in a small firm receive the leader's messages directly. This face-to-face contact facilitates their understanding of the leader's stand on integrity, customer service, and other important issues.

By creating an environment that encourages personal interaction, the leader of a small firm can get the best from his or her employees and also offer a strong inducement to prospective employees. Most professional managers prefer an organizational setting that minimizes office politics as a factor in getting ahead. By creating a friendly atmosphere that avoids the intrigue common in some organizations, an entrepreneur can build an environment that is very attractive to most employees and advantageous to the firm's productivity.

LEADERSHIP THAT BUILDS ENTHUSIASM Several decades ago, many managers were hard-nosed autocrats, giving orders and showing little concern for those who worked under them. Over the years, this style of leadership has given way to a gentler and more effective variety that emphasizes respect for all members of the organization and shows an appreciation for their potential.

Progressive managers frequently seek some degree of employee participation in decisions that affect personnel and work processes. In many cases, managers carry this leadership approach to a level called **empowerment.** The manager who uses empowerment goes beyond solicitation of employees' opinions and ideas by increasing their authority to act on their own and to make decisions about the processes they're involved with. Here is a description of worker empowerment at a small auto body shop called European Collision Center in Cambridge, Massachusetts:

empowerment
giving employees authority to make decisions or take actions on their own

Bodymen take "ownership" of a car while it's in the shop, staying with it start to finish. No one looks over their shoulders: "There are a set of parameters, then they have to be responsible," says owner Wayne Stevenson. Workers are cross-trained to take on new tasks and sent back to school yearly to keep skills up to date. Customers love what they get, and Stevenson's traffic has doubled every year for five years.[6]

Some companies carry employee participation a step further by creating self-managed **work teams.** Each work team is assigned a given task or operation; its members manage the task or operation without direct supervision and assume responsibility for the results. When work teams function properly, the number of supervisors needed decreases sharply.

work teams
groups of employees with freedom to function without close supervision

Management practices that include a high level of involvement by employees contribute to productivity and profits, according to research studies. Pfeffer and Veiga have explained the reasons for improved performance as follows:

Simply put, people work harder because of the increased involvement and commitment that comes from having more control and say in their work; people work smarter because they are encouraged to build skills and competence; and people work more responsibly because more responsibility is placed in hands of employees farther down in the organization. These practices work not because of some mystical process, but because they are grounded in sound social science principles that have been shown to be effective by a great deal of evidence. And, they make sense.[7]

EFFECTIVE COMMUNICATION Another key to a healthy organization is effective communication—that is, getting managers and employees to talk with each other and openly share problems and ideas. To some extent, the management hierarchy must be set aside so that personnel at all levels can speak freely with those higher up. The result is two-way communication—a far cry from the old-fashioned idea that managers give orders and employees simply carry them out. The need for good communication has been eloquently expressed as follows:

It's a no-brainer—you've got to talk, email, and kibitz with employees. The speed with which information moves through a company is critical to how well the mechanism works. Information is the oil that turns the gears.[8]

To communicate effectively, managers must tell employees where they stand, how the business is doing, and what the firm's plans are for the future. While negative feedback may be necessary at times, giving positive feedback to employees is the primary tool for establishing good human relations. Perhaps the most fundamental concept managers need to keep in mind is that employees are people, not machines. As people, they quickly detect insincerity but respond to honest efforts to treat them as mature, responsible individuals. In short, an atmosphere of trust and respect contributes greatly to good communication.

A small firm manager can adopt any of the following practical techniques for stimulating two-way communication:

- Periodic performance review sessions to discuss employees' ideas, questions, complaints, and job expectations
- Bulletin boards to keep employees informed about developments affecting them and/or the company
- Suggestion boxes to solicit employees' ideas
- Staff meetings to discuss problems and matters of general concern

These methods and others can be used to supplement the most basic of all channels for communication—the day-to-day interaction between each employee and his or her supervisor.

Creating an Organizational Structure

Describe the nature and features of an organizational structure for small businesses.

While an entrepreneur may give direction through personal leadership, she or he must also define the relationships among the firm's activities and among the individuals on the firm's payroll. Without some kind of organizational structure, operations eventually become chaotic and morale suffers.

THE UNPLANNED STRUCTURE In small companies, the organizational structure tends to evolve with little conscious planning. Certain employees begin performing particular functions when the company is new and retain those functions as it matures. Responsibilities for other functions are spread over a number of positions, even though they may have become crucial as a result of company growth.

This natural evolution is not all bad. Generally, a strong element of practicality characterizes these types of organizational arrangements. The structure is forged through the experience of working and growing, rather than being derived from a textbook or another firm's organizational chart. Unplanned structures are seldom perfect, however, and growth typically creates a need for organizational change. Periodically, therefore, the entrepreneur should examine structural relationships and make adjustments as needed for effective teamwork.

line organization
a simple organizational structure in which each person reports to one supervisor

chain of command
the official, vertical channel of communication in an organization

THE CHAIN OF COMMAND In a **line organization,** each person has one supervisor to whom he or she reports and looks for instructions. Thus, a single, specific chain of command exists, as illustrated in Figure 18-3. All employees are directly engaged in the firm's work—producing, selling, or performing office or financial duties. Most very small firms—for example, those with fewer than 10 employees—use this form of organization.

A **chain of command** implies superior–subordinate relationships with a downward flow of instructions, but it involves much more. It is also a channel for two-way communication. Although employees at the same level communicate among themselves, the chain of command is the official, vertical channel of communication.

An organizational problem occurs when managers or employees ignore formal lines of communication. In small firms, a climate of informality and flexibility makes it easy to short-circuit the chain of command. The president and founder of the business, for example, may absentmindedly give instructions to salespersons or plant employees instead of going through the sales manager or the production manager. Similarly, an employee who has worked with the entrepreneur from the start

FIGURE 18-3

Line Organization

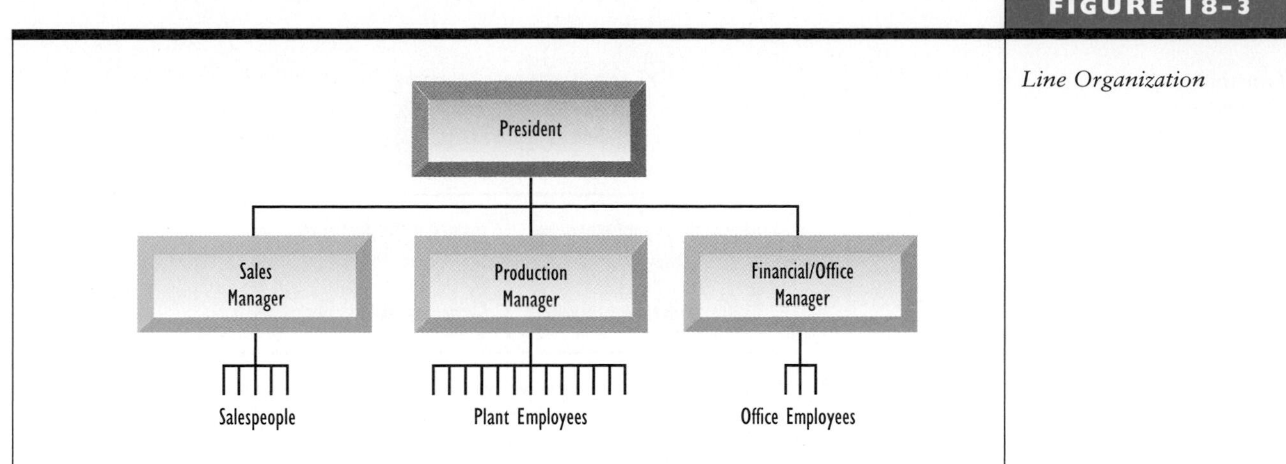

of the business tends to maintain a direct person-to-person relationship rather than observing newly instituted channels of communication.

As a practical matter, adherence to the chain of command can never be perfect. An organization in which the primary channel of communication was rigid would be bureaucratic and inefficient. Nevertheless, frequent and flagrant disregard of the chain of command quickly undermines the position of the bypassed manager.

A **line-and-staff organization** is similar to a line organization in that each person reports to a single supervisor. However, a line-and-staff structure also has staff specialists who perform specialized services or act as management advisors in specific areas (see Figure 18-4). Staff specialists may include a human resources manager, a production control technician, a quality control specialist, and an assistant to the president. Many small firms quickly grow to a size requiring some staff specialists. Consequently, the line-and-staff organization is widely used in small businesses.

line-and-staff organization
an organizational structure that includes staff specialists who assist management

Line activities are those that contribute directly to the primary objectives of a small firm. Typically, these are production and sales activities. **Staff activities,** on the other hand, are supporting activities. Although both types of activities are important, priority must be given to line activities—those that earn the customer's dollar. The owner-manager must insist that staff specialists function primarily as helpers and facilitators. Otherwise, confusion will dominate the firm's day-to-day operations, as employees receive directions from a variety of supervisors and staff specialists. **Unity of command**—that is, the situation in which each employee is receiving direction from only one boss—will be destroyed.

line activities
activities contributing directly to the primary objectives of a firm

staff activities
activities that support line activities

unity of command
a situation in which each employee's instructions come directly from only one immediate supervisor

INFORMAL GROUPS WITHIN THE ORGANIZATION The types of organizational structures just discussed address the formal relationships among members of an organization. All organizations, however, also have informal groups composed of people with something in common, such as jobs, hobbies, carpools, or affiliations with civic associations.

Although informal groups are not created by management, managers should observe them and evaluate their effect on the functioning of the total organization. An informal group, for example, may foster an attitude of working hard until the very end of the working day or doing the opposite—easing up and coasting for the

FIGURE 18-4

Line-and-Staff Organization

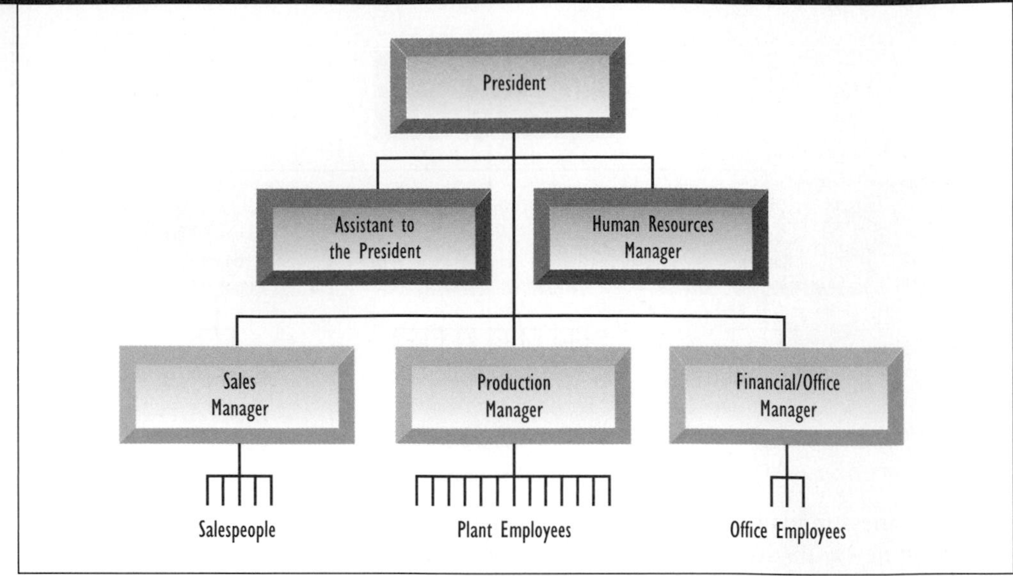

last half-hour. Ordinarily, no serious conflict arises between informal groups and the formal organization. Informal leaders often emerge who influence employee behavior. The wise manager understands the potentially positive contribution of informal groups and the inevitability of informal leadership.

Informal interaction among subordinates and managers can facilitate work performance and can also make life in the workplace more enjoyable for everyone. The value of compatible work groups to the individual became painfully clear to one college student working on a summer job:

I was employed as a forklift driver for one long, frustrating summer. Soon after being introduced to my work group, I knew I was in trouble. A clique had formed and, for some reason, resented college students. During lunch breaks and work breaks, I spent the whole time by myself. Each morning, I dreaded going to work. The job paid well, but I was miserable.[9]

span of control
the number of subordinates supervised by one manager

NUMBER OF SUBORDINATES The **span of control** is the number of employees who are supervised by a manager. Although some authorities have stated that six to eight people are all that one individual can supervise effectively, the optimum span of control is actually a variable that depends on a number of factors. Among these factors are the nature of the work and the manager's knowledge, energy, personality, and abilities. In addition, if the abilities of subordinates are better than average, the span of control may be broadened accordingly.

As a very small firm grows and adds employees, the entrepreneur's span of control is extended. The entrepreneur often has a tendency to stretch the span too far—to supervise not only the first five or six employees hired, but also all the employees added as time goes on. Eventually, a point is reached at which the attempted span exceeds the entrepreneur's reach, demanding more time and effort than he or she can devote to the business. It is at this point that the entrepreneur must establish in-

termediate levels of supervision and dedicate more time to management, moving beyond the role of player-coach.

DELEGATION OF AUTHORITY Through **delegation of authority,** a manager grants to subordinates the right to act or to make decisions. Turning over less important functions to subordinates by delegating authority frees the superior to perform more important tasks.

delegation of authority granting to subordinates the right to act or make decisions

Although failure to delegate may be found in any organization, it is often a special problem for entrepreneurs, given their backgrounds and personalities. Because they frequently must pay for mistakes made by subordinates, owners are inclined to keep a firm hold on the reins of leadership in order to protect the business.

Inability or unwillingness to delegate authority is manifested in numerous ways. For example, employees may find it necessary to clear even the most minor decisions with the boss. At any given time, a number of subordinates may be trying to get the attention of the owner to resolve some issue that they lack the authority to settle. This keeps the owner exceptionally busy—rushing from assisting a salesperson to helping iron out a production bottleneck to setting up a new filing system. Entrepreneurs often work long hours, and those who have difficulty delegating compound the problem, imposing on themselves even longer work hours.

Delegation of authority can help to free up time for the owner to enjoy a nonbusiness dimension to life and also lay a foundation for the firm's growth. Failure to delegate is the reason many firms never grow beyond a small-size business that can be directly supervised in detail by the owner. Consider the experience of one entrepreneur, who operated a small restaurant that achieved excellent profits. As a result of his success, he acquired a lease on another restaurant in the same area. During the first year of operating the second restaurant, the entrepreneur experienced constant headaches. Working long hours and trying to supervise both restaurants finally led him to give up the second one. This individual had never learned to delegate authority.

Stephen R. Covey has distinguished between what he calls "gofer" delegation and "stewardship" delegation.[10] Gofer delegation refers to work assignments in which the supervisor-delegator controls the details, telling subordinates to "go for this" or "go for that." This is not true delegation. Stewardship delegation, on the other hand, focuses on results and allows the individual receiving an assignment some latitude in carrying it out. Only stewardship delegation provides the benefits of delegation to both parties.

Exercising Control

Discuss the ways in which control is exercised in a small firm.

Despite good planning, organizations seldom function perfectly. As a result, managers must monitor operations to discover deviations from plans and to ensure that the firm is functioning as intended. Managerial activities that check on performance and correct it when necessary are part of the managerial control function; they serve to keep the business on course.

The control process begins with the establishment of standards. This is evidence of the connection between planning and control, for it is through planning and goal setting that control standards are established. Planners translate goals into norms (standards) by making them measurable. A goal to increase market share, for example, may be expressed as a projected dollar increase in sales volume for the coming year. Such an annual target may, in turn, be broken down into quarterly target

ENTREPRENEURSHIP AND ETHICS

DELEGATION FOR FAMILY REASONS

To keep up with the demands of a rapidly growing company, an entrepreneur may be tempted to neglect his or her family. Sometimes, delegating authority can provide a solution, allowing others to absorb some of the entrepreneur's pressures.

Heather Howitt, mother of a one-year-old son, is founder and CEO of Oregon Chai®, a firm that sells chai, a peppery-sweet mix of black tea, spices, and milk. She discovered the drink on a trip to the Himalayas while a student at University of California–Santa Cruz. In 1994, in Portland, Oregon, she started brewing the tea, and Oregon Chai was born. The business grew, and the drink has since become available in all 50 states. In fact, the business was ranked No. 18 on the *Inc. 500* in 2000.

To balance family life and entrepreneurship, Howitt found it necessary to delegate. To do so, she made some key hires, including a chief operating officer, who took over managing operations and finance. Also, she gave up making sales calls, allowing this task to be carried out by others.

Successful delegation has given her more time to spend with her son, allowing her, for example, to take a two-hour midday run with him in a nearby park. Afterwards, she may pass the baby and stroller along to a nanny, who will take him home, or to her sister-in-law, who is an intern in the company. At other times, she settles the baby into a crib in her own office. Through delegation, Howitt is better able to combine entrepreneurship and motherhood.

Source: From material from http://www.oregonchai.com; Thea Singer, "The Family Hour," *Inc. 500,* Vol. 22, No. 15 (2000), p. 106; and Anne Marie Borrego, "Oregon Chai," *Inc.,* Vol. 23, No. 1 (January 2001), p. 85.

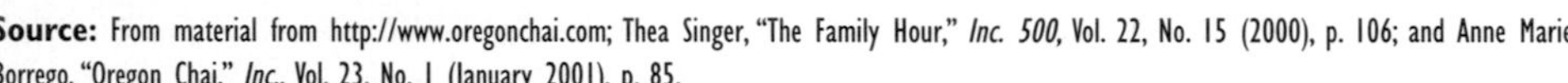

standards so that corrective action can be taken early if performance begins to fall below the projected amount.

Although this example specifically illustrates growth and sales standards, criteria for performance must be established in all areas of the business. In manufacturing, product specifications provide guidelines for meeting predetermined standards that regulate the manufacturing process: For example, a given dimension may be specified as 15 inches, with an error tolerance of plus or minus ¼ inch.

As Figure 18-5 shows, performance measurement occurs at various stages of the control process. Performance may be measured at the input stage (perhaps to determine the quality of materials purchased), during the process stage (perhaps to determine if the product being manufactured meets quality standards), and/or at the output stage (perhaps to check the quality of a completed product).

Corrective action is required when performance deviates significantly from the standard in an unfavorable direction. To prevent the deviation from recurring, such action must be accompanied by an analysis of the cause of the deviation. If the percentage of defective products increases, for example, a manager must determine whether the problem is caused by faulty raw materials, untrained workers, or some other factor. For a problem to be effectively controlled, corrective action must identify and deal with the real cause.

The cornerstone of financial control is the budget, which incorporates cost and performance standards. For salespeople, for example, an expense budget might in-

FIGURE 18-5 *Stages of the Control Process*

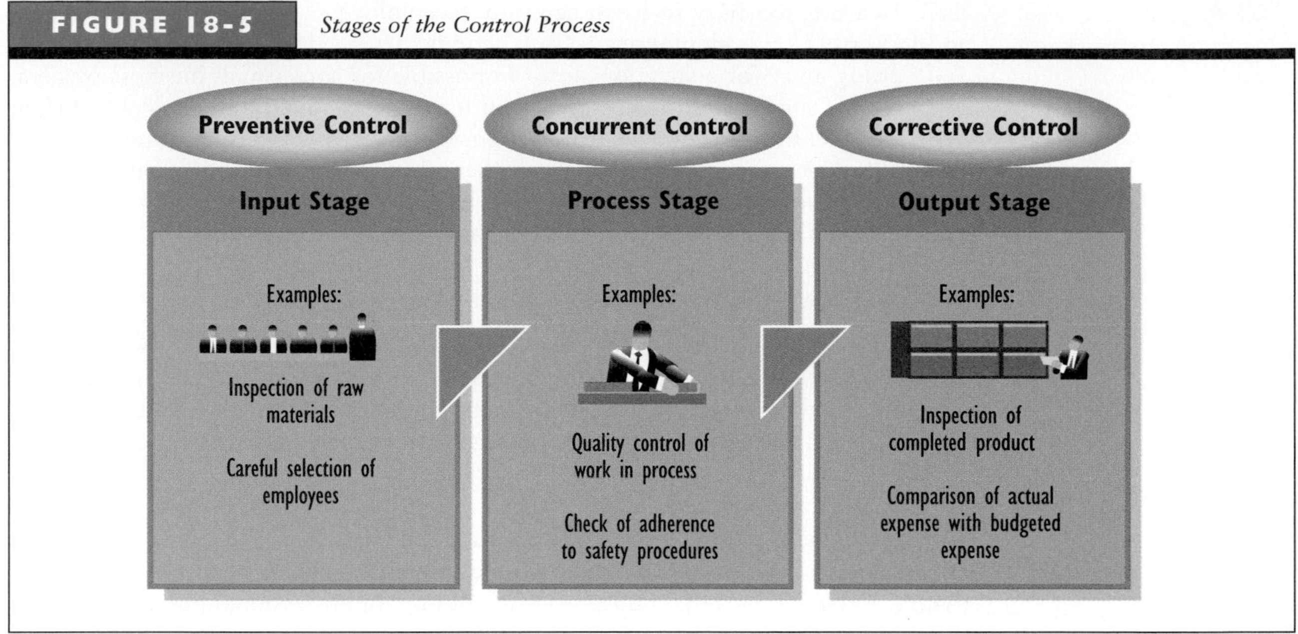

clude an item for travel expenses. At the end of a budget period, actual expenditures for travel would be compared with the budgeted amount. If there was a significant discrepancy, the matter would be investigated, the cause found, and the problem corrected. In this way, the budget can serve as a tool to control expenses.

Some very small businesses attempt to operate without a budget. However, even in these cases, the owners generally have a rough idea of what cost and performance should be, keep track of results, and investigate when results seem out of line.

Time Management

An owner-manager of a small firm spends much of the working day on the front line—meeting customers, solving problems, listening to employee complaints, talking with suppliers, and the like. She or he tackles such problems with the assistance of only a small staff. As a result, the owner-manager's energies and activities are diffused, and time becomes a scarce resource.

6
Describe the problem of time pressure and suggest solutions.

The Problem of Time Pressure

The hours worked by most new business owners are particularly long. Many owner-managers in small firms work from 60 to 80 hours per week. A frequent and unfortunate result of such a schedule is inefficient work performance. Owner-managers may be too busy to see sales representatives who could supply market information on new products and processes, too busy to read technical or trade literature that would tell them what others are doing and what improvements might be adapted to

their own use, too busy to listen carefully to employees' opinions and grievances, and too busy to give employees the instructions they need to do their jobs correctly.

Getting away for a vacation seems impossible for some small business owners. In extremely small firms, owners may find it necessary to close the business during their absence. Even in somewhat larger businesses, owners may fear that the firm will not function properly if they are not there. Unfortunately, keeping one's nose to the grindstone in this way may cost an entrepreneur dearly in terms of personal health, family relationships, and effectiveness in business leadership.

Time Savers for Busy Managers

Part of the solution to the problem of time pressure is application of the organizational practices discussed in the preceding section. For example, when possible, the manager should assign duties to subordinates who can work without close supervision. For such delegation to work, of course, a manager must first select and train qualified employees.

The greatest time saver is the effective use of time. Little will be accomplished if an individual flits from one task to another and back again. The first step in time management should be to survey how much time is normally spent on various activities. Relying on general impressions is not only unprofessional but also unscientific and likely to involve error. For a period of several days or (preferably) several weeks, the manager should record the amounts of time spent on various activities during the day. An analysis of these figures will reveal a pattern, indicating which projects and tasks consume the most time and which activities are responsible for wasted time. It will also reveal chronic time wasting due to excessive socializing, work on trivial matters, coffee breaks, and so on.

After eliminating practices that waste time, a manager can carefully plan his or her use of available time. A planned approach to a day's or week's work is much more effective than a haphazard do-whatever-comes-up-first approach. This is true even for small firm managers whose schedules are continually interrupted in unanticipated ways.

Many time management specialists recommend the use of a daily written plan of work activities. This plan may be a list of activities scribbled on a note pad or a formal computerized schedule, but it should reflect priorities. By classifying duties as first-, second-, or third-level priorities, a manager can identify and focus attention on the most crucial tasks.

Effective time management requires self-discipline. An individual may begin with good intentions but lapse into habitually attending to whatever he or she finds to do at the moment. Procrastination is a frequent thief of time. Many managers delay unpleasant and difficult tasks, retreating to trivial and less threatening activities and rationalizing that they are getting those duties out of the way in order to be able to concentrate better on the more important tasks.

Some managers devote much time to conferring with subordinates. These meetings often just happen and drag on without any serious attempt by the manager to control them. The manager should prepare an agenda for such meetings, set starting and ending times, limit discussion to key issues, and assign any necessary follow-up to specific individuals. In this way, the effectiveness of superior–subordinate conferences may be maximized and the manager's own time conserved, along with that of other staff members.

OUTSIDE MANAGEMENT ASSISTANCE

Explain the various types of outside management assistance.

Because entrepreneurs tend to be better doers than they are managers, they should consider the use of outside management assistance. Such outside assistance can supplement the manager's personal knowledge and the expertise of the few staff specialists on the company's payroll.

The Need for Outside Assistance

The typical entrepreneur not only is deficient in managerial skills but also lacks the opportunity to share ideas with peers. A survey of 210 small business owners revealed that 52 percent "frequently felt a sense of loneliness." Moreover, this group reported a much higher incidence of stress symptoms than did those who said they did not feel lonely.[11]

By using management consultants, entrepreneurs can overcome some of their managerial deficiencies and reduce their sense of isolation. Furthermore, by bringing an objective point of view and new ideas, supported by a broad knowledge of proven, successful, cost-saving methods, a consultant can help an insider directly involved in a business problem see the issues more clearly. The consultant can also help the manager improve decision making through better organization of fact gathering and the introduction of scientific techniques of analysis.

Sources of Management Assistance

Entrepreneurs seeking management assistance can turn to any number of sources, including business incubators, SBA programs, and management consultants. Other approaches the entrepreneur can take to obtain management help include consulting public and university libraries, attending evening classes at local colleges, and considering the suggestions of friends and customers.

BUSINESS INCUBATORS As discussed in Chapter 11 and this chapter's "In the Spotlight" feature, a business incubator is an organization that offers both space and managerial and clerical services to new businesses. There are now several hundred incubators in the United States, and the number is growing rapidly. Most of them involve the participation of governmental agencies and/or universities, although some have been launched as purely private endeavors. The primary motivation in establishing incubators has been a desire to encourage entrepreneurship and thereby contribute to economic development.

Often, individuals who wish to start businesses are deficient in pertinent knowledge and lacking in appropriate experience. In many cases, they need practical guidance in marketing, record keeping, management, and preparation of business plans. Business incubators offer new entrepreneurs on-site business expertise; the services available in an incubator are shown in Figure 18-6.

An incubator provides a supportive atmosphere for a business during the early months of its existence, when it is most fragile and vulnerable to external dangers and internal errors. If the incubator works as it should, the fledgling business gains strength quickly and, within a year or so, leaves the incubator setting.

Yvette Berke started Adapt Consulting, a firm that does environmental consulting, in an incubator in Thousand Oaks, California.[12] Locating in the incubator gave her access to conference rooms, a fax, a copier, the Internet, a kitchen, and teleconferencing equipment. Her firm advises businesses in the area of nonhazardous waste

FIGURE 18-6

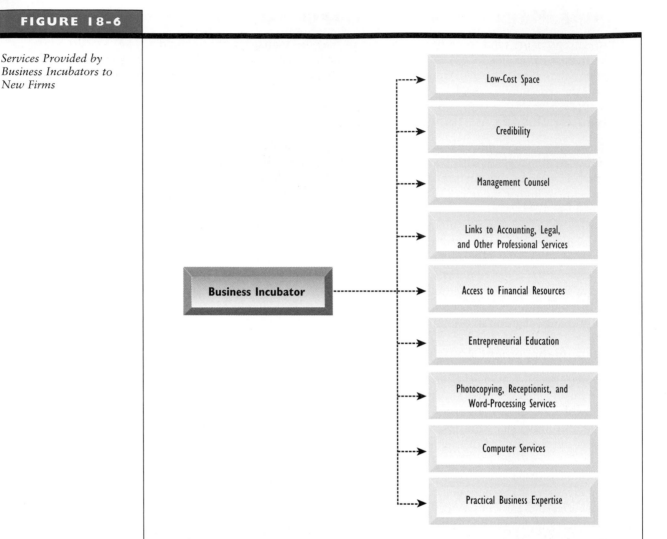

Services Provided by Business Incubators to New Firms

and helps them establish recycling and other programs. In addition to serving clients in the United States, Berke is now conducting business in Singapore, Malaysia, Sri Lanka, and other Pacific Rim countries.

Internet incubators, which provide beginning services to dot.com startups that are little more than an idea, are rapidly growing in number.[13] Like other incubators, they provide business advice, office services, and connections to financing. Most of them also provide seed capital in exchange for an equity stake in the business. One such incubator is eHatchery, a full-service incubator founded in 1999 in Atlanta, Georgia by entrepreneur Jeff Levy. Another is Idealab, which was created by entrepreneur Bill Gross in Pasadena, California in 1996.

http://www.ehatchery.com
http://www.idealab.com

STUDENT CONSULTING TEAMS Many colleges and universities have student consulting teams willing to assist small businesses. These teams of upper-class and graduate students, under the direction of a faculty member, work with owners of small firms in analyzing and devising solutions to their business problems.

The program has mutual benefits: It provides students with a practical view of business management and supplies small firms with answers to their problems. The students who participate are typically combined in teams that provide a diversity of academic background. Individual teams, for example, may include students specializing in management, marketing, accounting, and finance.

SERVICE CORPS OF RETIRED EXECUTIVES (SCORE) By appealing to any SBA field office, small business managers can obtain free management advice from a group called the **Service Corps of Retired Executives (SCORE).** SCORE is an organization of retired business executives who serve as consultants to small business managers on current problems. Functioning under the sponsorship of the SBA, SCORE provides an opportunity for retired executives to contribute to the business community and, in the process, help small business managers solve their problems. The relationship is thus mutually beneficial. By demonstrating the worth of consulting services, experiences with SCORE may encourage entrepreneurs to utilize paid consultants as their firms grow.

Service Corps of Retired Executives (SCORE)
an SBA-sponsored group of retired executives who give free advice to small businesses

Stories abound of SCORE's successfully assisting small firms. One entrepreneur, Peggy Harris, received counseling from a SCORE volunteer as she turned her crafts hobby into a business venture that involved teaching a no-sew technique for making drapes. Taking the advice of the SCORE counselor, Harris started a line of credit with a local bank before she needed money. When she later needed cash to produce a video of herself teaching the no-sew secrets, it was available.

IN THE TRENCHES ENTREPRENEURSHIP TODAY

SCORE ONE FOR THE MUDHOUSE CAFÉ

Ambitious individuals, eager to get into business for themselves, often lack the business know-how needed to get started. Lynelle and John Lawrence faced this dilemma when they returned to their home state of Virginia from Alaska with the dream of opening their own coffeehouse.

As they did research on their potential business, John waited tables at a local restaurant, and Lynelle worked a cart selling coffee in a downtown mall. A friend referred them to SCORE, where they met Joe Geller, who had worked in and owned restaurants as well as bed-and-breakfasts.

Geller's counseling proved invaluable to the Lawrences. He referred them to seminars on starting a business, and he met with them dozens of times, keeping them focused and keeping their morale up during the planning stage. Geller helped them prepare a detailed business plan and sent them to several banks for financing. Finally, they found a bank willing to extend a $60,000 loan for the coffeehouse, and the Mudhouse Café opened in 1995.

After the café opened, Geller continued to maintain contact with the Lawrences and provide encouragement to them. At times, he would even help wash dishes in the back!

Thanks to the guidance of a SCORE counselor, the business became successful. Today, it is not only a coffeehouse but also a cybercafé, with a room upstairs containing laptop computers and equipment for videoconferencing—a room that quickly caught on with students and faculty at the University of Virginia.

Source: J. Tol Broome, Jr., "SCORE's Impact on Small Firms," *Nation's Business,* Vol. 87, No. 1 (January 1999), pp. 41–43.

small business development centers (SBDCs)
university-affiliated centers offering consulting, education, and other support to small businesses

SMALL BUSINESS DEVELOPMENT CENTERS (SBDCs) Small business development centers (SBDCs), which are patterned after the Agricultural Extension Service, are affiliated with colleges or universities as a part of the SBA's overall program of assistance to small business. SBDCs provide direct consultation, continuing education, research assistance, and export services. One of their special priorities is to lend support to minority-owned firms. The staff typically includes faculty members, SCORE counselors, professional staff, and graduate student assistants. SBDC counselor John A. Boyd describes the type of assistance he provided to one entrepreneur:

Alice told me she had been a cook for 28 years in various restaurants (two totaled 21 years of service), and she wanted to start her own. As I worked through my list of standard questions, I began to find out that Alice had no particular target market in mind, had not yet developed a menu, only had a general idea about the price range, and had not considered the ambience or décor. She did, however, have a name, "Alice's Restaurant" (and you had to be an Arlo Guthrie fan to remember that).

In a case such as this, I work very slowly with the client. Initially, I avoid discussing finances or pro forma financial statements because many people are afraid of numbers. In addition, one cannot do meaningful projections before the target market is determined. I also do not intimidate the client with all of the questions on the list, but attempt to assign three to five as homework for our next meeting. After Alice settled on the target market, location, menu and pricing, we started on more esoteric concepts such as ambience and décor. Eventually, we developed pro forma financial statements. It took over a year, but Alice's Restaurant eventually opened.[14]

MANAGEMENT CONSULTANTS Management consultants serve small businesses as well as large corporations. Types of consultants range from large global firms to small one- and two-person operations. Small firm managers, however, are often reluctant to use outside advisors. Some of their reasons are reflected in the comments in Figure 18-7.

Some small businesses need analysis by consultants—especially businesses that have paid very little attention to their productivity. When Mario Arcari and Gregory Goldfarb started Hi-Tech Manufacturing in Schiller Park, Illinois, they were "just two guys and a shop making machine parts," as Arcari put it.[15] The business grew, but there were problems.

FIGURE 18-7

Ten Reasons Small Firm Managers Shun Outside Advice

1. "I can solve the problem myself."
2. "I don't want anyone throwing up roadblocks to my plans."
3. "Professional advisors should be used only as a last resort."
4. "An outsider could never understand my business."
5. "High-powered experts wouldn't be interested in my business."
6. "An advisor will raise a lot of issues I don't have time to bother with right now."
7. "I don't want to share any information with an outsider."
8. "Professional advisors cost too much."
9. "Our longtime attorney (or accountant or banker) is a friend and knows us best. We don't need anyone else."
10. "I'm unsure of how relationships with professional advisors work."

Source: Craig E. Aronoff and John L. Ward, "Why So Few Business Owners Get and Accept Good Advice," *Small Business Forum,* Vol. 14, No. 2 (Fall 1996), pp. 26–37.

Orders were processed on the fly. About 1% of all product material was left over as "scrap" and dumped or paid for out of Hi-Tech's pocket, costing thousands every year. There were no procedures to handle customer complaints. Machines went for months without maintenance checks. Imperfect parts—too long or short by fractions of an inch—were often shipped. Companies like Lockheed-Martin refused to talk to Hi-Tech until it had a quality-control program.[16]

http://www.cmcusa.org

By obtaining consulting help from the nonprofit Chicago Manufacturing Center, these entrepreneurs were able to eliminate many wasteful practices, reduce scrap, and increase customer satisfaction. The $15,000 consulting fee was easily recovered in the revenue resulting from the firm's improved performance.

To ensure client–provider satisfaction, the owner and the consultant should reach a mutual understanding on the nature of the assistance to be provided before it begins. Any consulting fees should be specified, and the particulars of the agreement should be put in writing. Fees are often quoted on a per diem basis and might easily range from $500 to $5,000 or more. Although the cost may seem high, it must be evaluated in terms of the expertise that it buys.

http://www.imcusa.org

Directories are available to help entrepreneurs find the right management consultant. One such directory is published by the Institute of Management Consultants, 521 Fifth Avenue, New York, NY 10175. The code of ethics to which institute members subscribe is an indication of their desire to foster professionalism in their work.

networking
the process of developing and engaging in mutually beneficial relationships

ENTREPRENEURIAL NETWORKS Entrepreneurs gain management assistance from peers through **networking**—the process of developing and engaging in mutually beneficial informal relationships. As business owners meet other business owners, they discover a commonality of interests that leads to an exchange of ideas and experiences. The settings for such meetings may be trade associations, civic clubs, fraternal organizations, or any other situation that brings businesspeople into contact with one another. Of course, the personal network of an entrepreneur is not limited to other entrepreneurs, but those individuals may be the most significant part of his or her network.

Entrepreneurs are linked by several kinds of ties—instrumental, affective, and moral. An *instrumental tie* is one formed when the parties engage in mutually rewarding activities—for example, exchanging useful ideas about certain business problems. An *affective tie* relates to emotional sentiments—for example, a shared vision about actions small businesses must take when faced with giant competitors or with the government. A *moral tie* involves some type of obligation—for example, a mutual commitment to the principle of private enterprise or to the importance of integrity in business transactions. In personal networks of entrepreneurs, affective and moral ties are believed to be stronger than instrumental ties.[17] This suggests that a sense of identity and self-respect may be a significant product of entrepreneurial networks.

OTHER BUSINESS AND PROFESSIONAL SERVICES A variety of business and professional groups provide management assistance. In many cases, such assistance is part of the business relationship. Sources of management advice include bankers, certified public accountants, attorneys, insurance agents, suppliers, trade associations, and chambers of commerce.

It takes initiative to draw on the management assistance available from such groups. For example, rather than confining his or her business relationship with a

FIGURE 19-1

Job Description for Stock Clerk in Retail Food Store

Title: Stock Clerk
Primary Function:
Supervision Receiv
Supervision Exerci

Duties:
1. Receive and store prod
2. Take products from sto
3. Provide information an
4. Monitor quantity of pr
5. Perform housekeeping d
6. Assist cashiers in baggi
7. Assist in other areas o

Duties listed
portant that job
a "that's not my
as it is in large l
tant. Engineers
may need to pin
In the proce
abilities, and oth
This statement o
job description.
the individual m
years of school.
Job descripti
other uses. For e
rection in trainin

job specification
a list of skills and abilities needed to perform a specific job

EVALUATING

Identify the steps to take in evaluating job applicants.

Recruitment act
needed to evalua
risk of taking a
ployer can take t

Step 1: Using

By using an app
termine whether
evaluation. Typi
Security number,
Although an
fully written to a
not seek inform

It is becoming increasingly difficult to obtain more than the basic facts concerning a person's background because of the potential for lawsuits brought against employers by disappointed applicants. Although reference checks on a prior employment record do not constitute infringements on privacy, the fact that third parties are often reluctant to divulge negative information limits the practical usefulness of reference checking.

For a fee, private investigation agencies or credit bureaus will supply an applicant's history (financial, criminal, employment, and so on). If an employer requests a credit report to establish an applicant's eligibility for employment, the Fair Credit Reporting Act requires that the applicant be notified in writing that such a report is being requested.

Step 4: Testing the Applicant

Many kinds of jobs lend themselves to performance testing. For example, an applicant for a secretarial or clerical position may be given a standardized keyboarding or word-processing test. With a little ingenuity, employers can improvise practical tests that are pertinent to many positions.

Psychological examinations may also be used by small businesses, but the results can be misleading because of difficulty in interpreting the tests or in adapting them to a particular business. In addition, the U.S. Supreme Court has upheld the Equal Employment Opportunity Commission's requirement that any test used in making employment decisions must be job-related.

validity
the extent to which a test assesses true job performance ability

reliability
the consistency of a test in measuring job performance ability

Useful tests of any kind must meet the criteria of **validity** and **reliability.** For a test to be valid, its results must correspond well with job performance; that is, the applicants with the best test scores must generally be the best employees. For a test to be reliable, it must provide consistent results when used at different times or by various individuals.

Step 5: Requiring Physical Examinations

A primary purpose of physical examinations is to evaluate the ability of applicants to meet the physical demands of specific jobs. By law, a conditional offer of employment must precede such an exam. Also, care must be taken to avoid discriminating against those who are physically disabled. The Americans with Disabilities Act requires employers to make "reasonable" adaptations to facilitate the employment of such individuals.

The law permits drug screening of applicants, and this can be included as part of the physical examination process. Since few small firms have staff physicians, most of them make arrangements with a local doctor or clinic to perform physical examinations.

TRAINING AND DEVELOPING EMPLOYEES

Describe the role of training for both managerial and nonmanagerial employees in a small firm.

Once an employee has been recruited and added to the payroll, the process of training and development must begin. The purpose of this process is to transform a new recruit into a well-trained technician, salesperson, manager, or other employee.

Purposes of Training and Development

One obvious purpose of training is to prepare a new recruit to perform the duties for which he or she has been hired. There are very few positions for which no training is required. If an employer fails to provide training, the new employee must learn by trial and error, which frequently wastes time, materials, and money.

Training to improve skills and knowledge should not be limited to new hires; the performance of current employees can often be improved through additional training. In view of the constant change in products, technology, policies, and procedures in the world of business, continual training is necessary to update knowledge and skills—in firms of all sizes. Only with such training can employees meet the changing demands being placed on them.

Both employers and employees have a stake in the advancement of qualified personnel to higher-level positions. Preparation for advancement usually involves developmental efforts—possibly of a different type than those needed to sharpen skills for current duties. Because personal development and advancement are prime concerns of able employees, a small business can profit from careful attention to this phase of the personnel program. Opportunities to grow and move up in an organization not only improve the morale of current employees but also serve as an inducement for potential applicants.

Orientation for New Personnel

The development process begins with an individual's first two or three days on the job. It is at this point that the new employee tends to feel lost and confused, confronted with a new physical layout, a different job title, unknown fellow employees, a different type of supervision, changed hours or work schedule, and/or a unique set of personnel policies and procedures. Any events that conflict with the newcomer's expectations are interpreted in light of his or her previous work experience, and these interpretations can either foster a strong commitment to the new employer or lead to feelings of alienation.

Recognizing the new employee's sensitivity at this point, the employer can contribute to a positive outcome through proper orientation. Taking steps to help the newcomer adjust will minimize her or his uneasiness in the new setting.

Some phases of the orientation can be accomplished by informal methods. Persistence Software, a 110-person company in San Mateo, California, uses bagels and muffins as a means of introducing newcomers to the rest of the staff.[5] On the first morning of work for a new employee, a tray of breakfast food is strategically placed near her or his desk. An e-mail invites everyone to come by and get acquainted.

http://www.persistence.com

Other phases of the orientation must be structured or formalized. In addition to explaining specific job duties, supervisors should outline the firm's policies and procedures in as much detail as possible. A clear explanation of performance criteria and the way in which an employee's work will be evaluated should be included in the discussion. The new employee should be encouraged to ask questions, and time should be taken to provide careful answers. The firm may facilitate the orientation process by providing a written list of company practices and procedures in the form of an employee handbook. The handbook may include information about work

hours, paydays, breaks, lunch hours, absences, holidays, names of supervisors, employee benefits, and so on. Since new employees are faced with an information overload at first, a follow-up orientation after a week or two is advisable.

Training to Improve Quality

Employee training is an integral part of comprehensive quality management programs. Although quality management is concerned with machines, materials, and measurements, it also focuses on human performance.

Training programs can be designed to promote higher-quality workmanship. The connection between effective quality management programs and employee training has been supported by a study of small manufacturing firms.[6]

Christian Kar, operator of Expresso Connection, an 11-store chain of drive-through coffee bars in Everett, Washington, found he was losing customers at the same time he was advertising for new ones. In an effort to keep the customers he already had, he beefed up training. New hires now spend a week learning how to use the equipment and prepare drinks. Later, they undergo another 40 hours of on-the-job training at a store. By improving customer service, the business almost doubled daily store revenues and increased per-store profits by 50 percent.[7]

To a considerable extent, training for quality performance is part of the ongoing supervisory role of all managers. In addition, special classes and seminars can be used to teach employees about the importance of quality control and ways in which to produce high-quality work.

Training of Nonmanagerial Employees

If a company has job descriptions or job specifications, these may be used to identify abilities or skills required for particular jobs. To a large extent, such requirements determine the appropriate type of training.

For all classes of employees, more training is accomplished on the job than through any other method. However, on-the-job training may be very haphazard unless it is conducted through planned, controlled procedures. One program designed to make on-the-job training more effective is known as **Job Instruction Training.** The steps in this program, shown in Figure 19-2, are intended to help supervisors become more effective in training nonmanagerial employees.

Job Instruction Training
a systematic step-by-step method for on-the-job training of nonmanagerial employees

Some small companies make an effort to help employees become acquainted with related jobs so that they can better understand the overall nature of the business. Danny O'Neill of The Roasterie, Inc., a wholesale coffee company in Kansas City, Missouri, describes the training given to a new sales representative: "He spent two days serving coffee in one of my customer's shops, then he was on the road helping with deliveries, and he'll also work in packaging and production."[8]

http://www.theroasterie.com

Development of Managerial and Professional Employees

A small business has a particularly strong need to develop managerial and professional employees. Whether the firm has only a few or many key positions, it must ensure that the individuals who hold these positions function effectively. Incumbents should be developed to the point that they can adequately carry out the responsibilities assigned to

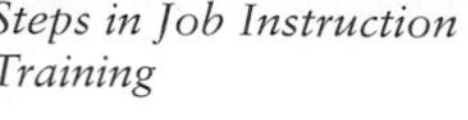

Steps in Job Instruction Training

PREPARE EMPLOYEES

- Put employees at ease.
- Place them in appropriate jobs.
- Find out what they know.
- Get them interested in learning.

PRESENT THE OPERATIONS

- Tell, show, and illustrate the task.
- Stress key points.
- Instruct clearly and completely.

TRY OUT PERFORMANCE

- Have employees perform the task.
- Have them tell, show, and explain.
- Ask employees questions and correct any errors.

FOLLOW UP

- Check on employees frequently.
- Tell them how to obtain help.
- Encourage questions.

them. Ideally, other staff members should be trained as potential replacements in case key individuals retire or leave for other reasons. Although an entrepreneur often postpones grooming a personal replacement, this step is crucial in ensuring a smooth transition in the firm's management.

Establishing a management training program requires serious consideration of the following factors:

- ***The need for training.*** What vacancies are expected? Who needs to be trained? What type of training and how much training are needed to meet the demands of the job description?
- ***A plan for training.*** How can the individuals be trained? Do they currently have enough responsibility to permit them to learn? Can they be assigned additional duties? Should they be given temporary assignments in other areas—for example, should they be shifted from production to sales? Would additional schooling be beneficial?
- ***A timetable for training.*** When should training begin? How much can be accomplished in the next six months or one year?
- ***Employee counseling.*** Do the individuals understand their need for training? Are they aware of their prospects within the firm? Has an understanding been reached as to the nature of training? Have the employees been consulted regularly about progress in their work and the problems confronting them? Have they been given the benefit of the owner's experience and insights without having decisions made for them?

Compensation and Incentives for Employees

4
Explain the various types of compensation plans, including the use of incentive plans.

Compensation is important to all employees, and small firms must acknowledge the role of the paycheck in attracting and motivating personnel. In addition, small firms can offer several nonfinancial incentives that appeal to both managerial and nonmanagerial employees.

Wage or Salary Levels

In general, small firms must be roughly competitive in wage or salary levels in order to attract well-qualified personnel. Wages or salaries paid to employees either are based on increments of time—such as an hour, a day, or a month—or vary with the output of the employees. Compensation based on time is most appropriate for jobs in which performance is not easily measured. Time-based compensation is also easier to understand and used more widely than incentive systems.

Financial Incentives

Incentive plans have been devised to motivate employees to increase their productivity. Incentive wages may constitute an employee's entire earnings or may supplement his or her regular wages or salary. The commission system often used to remunerate salespeople is one type of incentive compensation. In manufacturing, employees are sometimes paid according to the number of units they produce. Although many incentive plans apply to employees as individuals, such plans may involve the use of group incentives and team awards.

Some compensation systems go so far as to make employees partial owners. Key members of large firms are often offered stock options that enable them to share in the growing—or even skyrocketing—value of the company's stock. A number of small companies have likewise used stock as an incentive, especially during times of labor scarcity. One such firm is Aquatic and Wetland Company (AWC) of Boulder, Colorado, a 35-employee business that builds and rehabilitates fishing streams.[9] The firm's president, Jay Windell, offered an experienced, top-drawer construction manager a 10-percent ownership interest in order to make the job offer more attractive. "I don't think I would have got him without it," Windell said. Now Windell is considering providing ownership opportunities to all of AWC's employees. (Employee stock ownership plans are discussed further later in this section.)

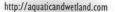

http://aquaticandwetland.com

General bonus or profit-sharing plans are especially important for managerial or other key personnel, although they may also include lower-level personnel. These plans provide employees with a "piece of the action" and may or may not involve assignment of shares of stock. Many profit-sharing plans simply entail distribution of a specified share of all profits or profits in excess of a target amount. Profit sharing serves more directly as a work-related incentive in small firms than in large firms, because the connection between individual performance and success can be more easily appreciated in a small firm.

Performance-based compensation plans must be designed carefully if they are to work successfully. Such plans should be devised with the aid of a consultant and/or public accounting firm. Some keys to developing effective bonus plans are identified in the following list:

1. ***Set attainable goals.*** Performance-based compensation plans work best when workers believe that they can meet the targets. Tying pay to broad, company-wide results leaves workers feeling frustrated and helpless.
2. ***Set meaningful goals.*** Managers neither motivate nor reward by setting targets employees can't comprehend. Complex financial measures or jargon-heavy benchmarks mean nothing to most people.
3. ***Bring workers in.*** Employees should have a say in developing the performance measures to be used and their advice solicited on ways to change work systems. Incentive plans should be phased in gradually so that employees have a chance to absorb them.
4. ***Keep targets moving.*** Performance-based plans must be continually adjusted to meet the changing needs of workers and customers. The life expectancy of a plan may be no more than three or four years.
5. ***Aim carefully.*** Managers should know what message they want to send; that is, they must make sure that the new plan doesn't reward the wrong behavior. Linking bonuses to plant safety, for example, could encourage coverups.[10]

Fringe Benefits

Fringe benefits, which include payments by the employer for such items as Social Security, vacations, holidays, health insurance, and retirement compensation, are expensive. According to a survey of 1996 compensation, the cost of fringe benefits amounted to 41.3 percent of payroll costs.[11] This means that for every dollar paid in wages, employers paid 41.3 cents for fringe benefits. (If the cost of fringe benefits were expressed as a percentage of total compensation costs—that is, payroll plus

fringe benefits
supplements to compensation, designed to be attractive and beneficial to employees

fringe benefits—the figure would obviously be lower than 41.3 percent.) In general, small firms are somewhat less generous than large firms in providing fringe benefits for their employees. Even so, the cost of such benefits is a substantial part of total labor costs for most small firms.

Though fringe benefits are expensive, a small firm cannot ignore them if it is to compete effectively for good employees. A small but growing number of small firms now use flexible benefit programs (or cafeteria plans), which allow employees to choose the types of fringe benefits they wish to receive.[12] All employees receive a core level of coverage, such as basic health insurance, and then are allowed to choose how an employer-specified amount is to be divided among additional options—for example, child care reimbursement, dental care, pension fund contributions, and additional health insurance.

For small firms that wish to avoid the detailed paperwork associated with administering cafeteria plans, outside help is available. Many small firms—including some with fewer than 25 employees—turn over the administration of their flexible benefit plans to outside consulting, payroll accounting, or insurance companies that provide such services for a monthly fee. In view of the increasing popularity of these plans and the wide availability of administrative services, it seems only a matter of time until many small firms will be offering flexible benefits.

The costs of fringe benefits have made some of them prohibitively expensive. A number of firms, however, have devised relatively inexpensive fringe benefits, tailored to their particular situation—benefits that make employment more attractive for their employees.[13]

- Autumn Harp, a manufacturer of skin-care products in Bristol, Vermont, gives many employees the opportunity to work one day a week at home.
- Half Price Books, a Dallas, Texas chain of discount book stores, offers employees the option of dressing casually—clothes need only be clean, untorn, and free of offensive slogans. (After a big debate, it was decided that shoes were required!)
- Kaufer Miller Communications, a Seattle, Washington communications agency, periodically rents a bus and takes its staff to a Mariners game or to play laser tag.
- Hot Topic, a chain of music-related apparel and accessories stores in Pomona, California, reimburses employees for tickets to rock concerts. To qualify for reimbursement, employees must bring back a report on the fashions the band and fans were wearing; that is, they must do some market research.

Employee Stock Ownership Plans

employee stock ownership plans (ESOPs) plans through which a firm is sold either in part or in total to its employees

Some small firms have created **employee stock ownership plans** (ESOPs), by which they give employees a share of ownership in the business.[14] These plans may be structured in a variety of ways. For example, a share of annual profits may be designated for the purchase of company stock, which is then placed in a trust for employees. When coupled with a commitment to employee participation in management of the company, ESOPs can motivate employees, resulting in improvements in productivity.

ESOPs also provide a way for owners to cash out and withdraw from a business without selling the firm to outsiders. (See Chapter 14 for discussion of this

topic.) The owner might sell equity to the firm's employees, who can borrow funds at attractive rates for this purpose. Tax advantages for both owners and employees have made ESOPs a popular option, despite the substantial costs and legal complexities involved in creating these plans.

Special Issues in Human Resource Management

So far, this chapter has dealt with the recruitment, selection, training, and compensation of employees. In addition to these primary activities, human resource management can encompass a number of other, more general issues. Several such issues—employee leasing, legal protection, labor unions, the formalizing of employer–employee relationships, and the need for a human resource manager—are the focus of this section.

5

Discuss the human resource issues of employee leasing, legal protection, labor unions, and the formalizing of employer–employee relationships.

Employee Leasing

Leasing equipment and property has long been an accepted alternative to buying them. **Employee leasing,** as surprising as it may seem, has become a common alternative to direct hiring. An estimated 2,500 or more employee-leasing companies, also known as **professional employment organizations (PEOs),** have emerged in recent years with the specific purpose of "renting" personnel to small businesses. For a fee of 1 to 5 percent of payroll, a PEO writes paychecks, pays payroll taxes, and files the necessary reports with government agencies. Although small firms using this service avoid a certain amount of paperwork, they do not usually escape the tasks of recruitment and selection. Typically, the employees of a small firm are simply shifted to the leasing company's payroll at some specified date. In most cases, the firm still determines who works, who gets promoted, and who gets time off.

employee leasing
the "renting" of personnel from an organization that handles paperwork and administers benefits for those employees

professional employment organization (PEO)
a personnel-leasing company that places employees on its own payroll and then "rents" them to employers on a permanent basis

http://www.napeo.org

Many employees like the leasing arrangement. It may allow small employers to provide better benefit packages, since leasing companies generally cover hundreds or thousands of employees and thus qualify for better rates. Of course, the small business must bear the cost of insurance and other benefits obtained through a leasing company, in addition to a basic service fee.

A note of caution about selecting a leasing company: As leasing companies have proliferated in recent years, a number of them have run into financial trouble and left employers liable for unpaid claims. Some states have enacted legislation to protect employer-clients, and more regulation is likely.

Another note of caution pertains to the application of government regulations to small businesses. Very small firms are often excluded from specific regulations. For example, firms with fewer than 15 employees are exempt from the Americans with Disabilities Act. When these employees officially become part of a large leasing organization, however, the small firm using the leased employees becomes subject to the law.

Legal Protection of Employees

Employees are afforded protection by a number of federal and state laws.[15] One of the most far-reaching statutes is the **Civil Rights Act,** originally enacted in 1964, and its amendments. This law, which applies to any employer of more than 15 people, prohibits discrimination on the basis of race, color, religion, sex, or national origin.

Civil Rights Act
legislation prohibiting discrimination based on race, color, religion, sex, or national origin

Other laws extend similar protection to the aged and handicapped. Any employment condition is covered, including hiring, firing, promotion, transfer, and compensation.

As newspaper headlines in recent years have made clear, the Civil Rights Act includes protection against sexual harassment. Given the growing attention to sexual harassment in our society, this issue must be addressed by small firms as well as large corporations. Education and prompt response to complaints are the best tools for avoiding the damage of sexual harassment and the possibility of liability claims. The following practical action steps have been expressly recommended for small businesses:

1. Establish clear and meaningful policies and procedures regarding sexual harassment in the workplace.
2. Meet with employees and supervisory personnel to discuss the policies.
3. Investigate any and all complaints of sexual harassment fairly and thoroughly.
4. Take timely and appropriate action against all violators.[16]

Occupational Safety and Health Act
legislation that regulates the safety of workplaces and work practices

Fair Labor Standards Act (FLSA)
federal law that establishes a minimum wage and provides for overtime pay

Family and Medical Leave Act
legislation that assures employees of unpaid leave for childbirth or other family needs

The health and safety of employees are protected by the **Occupational Safety and Health Act** of 1970. This law, which applies to business firms of any size involved in interstate commerce, created the Occupational Safety and Health Administration (OSHA) to establish and enforce necessary safety and health standards.

Compensation of employees is regulated by the minimum wage and overtime provisions of the **Fair Labor Standards Act (FLSA)**, as well as by other federal and state laws. The FLSA applies to employers involved in interstate commerce and having two or more employees; it sets the minimum wage (which is periodically updated by Congress) and specifies time-and-a-half pay for more than 40 hours per week.

The **Family and Medical Leave Act** of 1993 was passed and signed into law by President Clinton in February 1993. The law requires firms with 50 or more employees to allow workers as much as 12 weeks of unpaid leave for the adoption of a child, childbirth, or other specified family needs. The worker must have been employed by the firm for 12 months and have worked at least 1,250 hours. Furthermore, the employer must continue health-care coverage during the leave and guarantee that the employee can return to the same or a comparable job.

Labor Unions

Most entrepreneurs prefer to operate independently and to avoid unionization. Indeed, most small businesses are not unionized. To some extent, this results from the predominance of small business in services, where unionization is less common than in manufacturing. Also, unions typically focus their attention on large companies.

However, labor unions are not unknown in small firms. Many types of small firms—building and electrical contractors, for example—negotiate labor contracts and employ unionized personnel. The need to work with a union formalizes and, to some extent, complicates the relationship between a small firm and its employees.

If employees wish to bargain collectively, the law requires the employer to participate in such bargaining. The demand for labor union representation may arise from employees' dissatisfaction with the work environment and employment relationships. By following enlightened human resource policies, a small firm can minimize the likelihood of labor organization or improve the relationship between management and union.

IN THE TRENCHES ENTREPRENEURSHIP TODAY

USING EMPLOYEE COMMITTEES

As a small firm grows, it must decide how much formality to introduce into managing its human resources and when to introduce it. More rules and regulations are inevitable as size increases, but some firms try to preserve a less formal, more personal touch as long as possible.

Such avoidance of bureaucracy is evident in the management of Spectrum Signal Processing, Inc., a hardware and software designer in Burnaby, British Columbia. The firm has grown to 180 employees, but it still does not have a human resource department. Instead, it utilizes an employee committee, originally created to deal with specific employee dissatisfaction, to address such issues as performance appraisals, the employee handbook, company training, mentoring, and orientation. The committee, with a rotating membership of 12 employees, appears to be serving a transitional function for Spectrum as it moves from less to more formality as it grows.

Spectrum's positive human resource emphasis is evident in the following statement:

Our individual team members' personalities, capabilities and can-do attitudes make Spectrum what it is—a place where quality work is acknowledged and emphasized, and where all team members are empowered decision-makers!

This statement seems to say, "We are trying to avoid the bureaucracy that afflicts big business by empowering our employees through use of an employee committee."

Source: From material from http://www.spectrumsignal.com; and Christopher Caggiano, "Worker, Rule Thyself," *Inc.*, Vol. 21, No. 2 (February 1999), pp. 89–90.

http://www.spectrumsignal.com

Formalizing of Employer–Employee Relationships

As explained earlier in this chapter, the management system of small firms is typically less formal than that of larger ones. A degree of informality can, in fact, be a virtue in small organizations. As personnel are added, however, the benefits of informality decline and its costs increase. Large numbers of employees cannot be managed effectively without some system for regulating employer–employee relationships. This situation can be best understood in terms of a family relationship. House rules are generally unnecessary when only two people are living in the home. But when several children are added to the mix, Mom and Dad soon start sounding like a government regulatory agency.

Growth, then, produces pressures to formalize personnel policies and procedures. The question is how much formality and how soon—a decision that involves judgment. Some employee issues should be formalized from the very beginning; on the other hand, excessive regulation can become paralyzing.

One way to formalize employer–employee relationships is to prepare a personnel policy manual or employee handbook, which meets a communication need by letting employees know the firm's basic ground rules. It can also provide a basis for fairness and consistency in management decisions affecting employees. The content of an employee handbook may be as broad or as narrow as desired. It may include an expression of company philosophy—an overall view of what the company considers important, such as standards of excellence or quality considerations.

More specifically, personnel policies usually cover such topics as recruitment, selection, training, compensation, vacations, grievances, and discipline. Such policies should be written carefully, however, to avoid misunderstandings. In some states, an employee handbook is considered part of the employment contract.

Procedures relating to management of personnel may also be standardized. For example, a performance review system may be established and a timetable set up for reviews—perhaps an initial review after six months and subsequent reviews on an annual basis.

The Need for a Human Resource Manager

A firm with only a few employees cannot afford a full-time specialist to deal with personnel problems. Some of the more involved human resource techniques used in large businesses may be unnecessarily complicated for small businesses. As it grows in size, however, a small firm's personnel problems will increase in both number and complexity.

The point at which it becomes logical to hire a human resource manager cannot be specified precisely. In view of the increased overhead cost, the owner-manager of a growing business must decide whether circumstances would make it profitable to employ a personnel specialist. Hiring a part-time human resource manager—a retired personnel manager, for example—is a possible first step in some instances.

Conditions such as the following favor the appointment of a human resource manager in a small business:

- There are a substantial number of employees (100 or more is suggested as a guide).
- Employees are represented by a union.
- The labor turnover rate is high.
- The need for skilled or professional personnel creates problems in recruitment or selection.
- Supervisors or operative employees require considerable training.
- Employee morale is unsatisfactory.
- Competition for personnel is keen.

Until a human resource manager is hired, however, the owner-manager typically functions in that capacity. His or her decisions regarding employee selection and compensation, as well as other personnel issues, will have a direct impact on the operating success of the firm.

LOOKING BACK

1 Explain the importance of employee recruitment, and list some sources that can be useful in finding suitable applicants.

- Recruitment of good employees contributes to customer satisfaction and to profitability.
- Small firms can attract applicants by stressing unique work features and opportunities.
- Recruitment sources include walk-ins, schools, public and private employment agencies, executive search firms, employee referrals, the Internet, advertising, and temporary help agencies.

- The increasing diversity of the workforce requires a broadening of the scope of recruitment.
- Job descriptions outline the duties of the job; job specifications identify the skills needed by applicants.

2 Identify the steps to take in evaluating job applicants.

- In the first step, application forms help the employer obtain preliminary information from applicants. (Employers must avoid questions about sex, race, religion, color, national origin, age, and disabilities.)
- Additional evaluation steps are interviewing, checking references, and administering tests.
- The final evaluation step is often a physical examination, which may include drug screening.

3 Describe the role of training for both managerial and nonmanagerial employees in a small firm.

- Training enables employees to perform their jobs effectively and also prepares them for advancement.
- An orientation program helps introduce new employees to the firm and work environment.
- Training is one component of a firm's quality management program.
- Training and development programs are appropriate for both managerial and nonmanagerial employees.

4 Explain the various types of compensation plans, including the use of incentive plans.

- Small firms must be competitive in salary and wage levels.
- Daywork systems base compensation on increments of time.
- Incentive systems relate compensation to various measures of performance.
- On average, fringe benefit costs are equal to 41.3 percent of payroll costs.
- Employee stock ownership plans enable employees to own a share of the business.

5 Discuss the human resource issues of employee leasing, legal protection, labor unions, and the formalizing of employer–employee relationships.

- Small firms can reduce paperwork by transferring personnel to the payroll of a leasing company.
- Small businesses must observe laws prohibiting discrimination and protecting employee health and safety.
- Some small businesses must work with labor unions.
- As small firms grow, they must adopt more formal methods of human resource management.
- Employment of a human resource manager becomes necessary at some point as a firm continues to add employees.

KEY TERMS

headhunter, p. 475
workforce diversity, p. 477
job description, p. 477
job specification, p. 478
validity, p. 480
reliability, p. 480
Job Instruction Training, p. 482
fringe benefits, p. 485
employee stock ownership plans (ESOPs), p. 486
employee leasing, p. 487
professional employment organization (PEO), p. 487
Civil Rights Act, p. 487
Occupational Safety and Health Act, p. 488
Fair Labor Standards Act (FLSA), p. 488
Family and Medical Leave Act, p. 488

Discussion Questions

1. As a customer of small businesses, you can appreciate the importance of employees to their success. Describe one experience you had in which an employee's contribution to his or her employer's success was positive and one in which it was negative.
2. What factor or factors would make you cautious about going to work for a small business? Could these reasons for hesitation be overcome? How?
3. In what ways is the workforce becoming more diverse, and how do these changes affect recruitment by small firms?
4. Based on your own experience as an interviewee, what do you think is the most serious weakness in the interviewing process? How could it be remedied?
5. What steps and/or topics would you recommend for inclusion in the orientation program of a printing firm with 65 employees?
6. Choose a small business with which you are well acquainted. Determine whether adequate provisions have been made for replacement of key management personnel when it becomes necessary. Is the firm using any form of executive development?
7. What problems are involved in using incentive plans in a small firm? How would the nature of the work affect management's decision concerning the use of such a plan?
8. Is the use of a profit-sharing plan desirable in a small business? What might lessen such a plan's effectiveness in motivating employees?
9. How does employee leasing differ from using a temporary help agency? What are the greatest benefits of employee leasing?
10. Explain the impact of the Civil Rights Act and the Fair Labor Standards Act on human resource management.

You Make the Call

SITUATION 1

The following is an account of one employee's introduction to a new job:

It was my first job out of high school. After receiving a physical exam and a pamphlet on benefits, I was told by the manager about the dangers involved in the job. But it was the old-timers who explained what was really expected of me.

The company management never told me about the work environment or the unspoken rules. The old-timers let me know where to sleep and which supervisors to avoid. They told me how much work I was supposed to do and which shop steward to see if I had a problem.

Question 1 To what extent should a small firm use "old-timers" to help introduce new employees to the workplace? Is it inevitable that newcomers will look to old-timers to find out how things really work?

Question 2 How would you rate this firm's orientation effort? What are its strengths and weaknesses?

Question 3 Assume that this firm has fewer than 75 employees and no human resource manager. Could it possibly provide more extensive orientation than that described here? How? What low-cost improvements, if any, would you recommend?

SITUATION 2

Technical Products, Inc. distributes 15 percent of its profits quarterly to its eight employees. This money is invested for their benefit in a retirement plan and is fully vested after five years. An employee, therefore, has a claim to the retirement fund even if he or she leaves the company after five years of service.

The employees range in age from 25 to 59 and have worked for the company from 3 to 27 years. They seem to have recognized the value of the program. However, younger employees sometimes express a preference for cash over retirement benefits.

Question 1 What are the most important reasons for structuring the profit-sharing plan as a retirement program?

Question 2 What is the probable motivational impact of this compensation system?

Question 3 How will an employee's age affect the appeal of this plan? What other factors are likely to strengthen or lessen its motivational value? Should it be changed in any way?

SITUATION 3

Alibek Iskakov recently opened a small cafe, called Oasis, in Kokshetau, a city in Kazakhstan. The cafe, which is quite small, has seating for 20 customers and employs seven people.

Iskakov, the owner, has no experience in the restaurant business but has three years' experience in retailing and managing. He believes this experience will help him make intelligent decisions concerning management of the cafe. Iskakov oversees operations and assists wherever needed.

Zhanna Suleymenova was hired by Iskakov as an accountant and assistant manager. He hired her to be sure someone would always be at the

cafe. He expects her to do the accounting and to make suggestions that will help him operate the cafe efficiently. She is the key person in the operation, with sound accounting experience and a little food service experience.

The other employees are two cooks, two waitresses (who double as hostesses and bartenders), and a dishwasher.

Thus far, the cafe's operations have not run smoothly.

Source: This case was prepared by Dr. Aigul N. Toxanova and Yuliya L. Tkacheva, Kokshetau Institute of Economics and Management, Kokshetau, Kazakhstan.

Question 1 What is the most obvious weakness in the human resource management of this small cafe?

Question 2 Given that the restaurant has just opened, is it overstaffed or understaffed?

EXPERIENTIAL EXERCISES

1. Interview the director of the placement office for your college or university. Ask about the extent to which small firms use the office's services, and obtain the director's recommendations for improving college recruiting by small firms. Prepare a one-page summary of your findings.
2. Examine and evaluate the help-wanted section of a local newspaper. Summarize your conclusions and formulate some generalizations about small business advertising for personnel.
3. With another student, form an interviewer–interviewee team. Take turns posing as job applicants for a selected type of job vacancy. Critique each other's performance, using the interviewing principles outlined in this chapter.
4. With another student, take turns role-playing trainer and trainee. The student-trainer should select a simple task and teach it to the student-trainee, using the Job Instruction Training method outlined in Figure 19-2. Jointly critique the teaching performance after each episode.

EXPLORING THE WEB

1. Employment laws related to small businesses are published online at **http://www.dol.gov/asp/programs/handbook/main.htm**. Access the Overview, and look for answers to the following questions.
   a. What is the minimum wage and minimum age for employees?
   b. Companies with at least how many employees are required to offer up to 12 weeks of family leave?
   c. Are small businesses required to follow OSHA regulations for a hazard-free workplace?
   d. Is it legal to require employees to submit to lie detector tests?
2. Access the human resource (HR) material offered by IdeaCafe **http://www.ideacafe.com**.
   a. Outline the various human resource topics featured on this site.
   b. Select, read, and summarize the discussion of one of these topics.

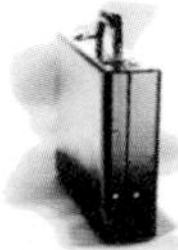

CASE 19

GIBSON MORTUARY (p. 691)

This case explores the human resource problems encountered by one small family business.

Alternative Cases for Chapter 19:

Case 7, "The Brown Family Business," p. 656
Case 9, "ScrubaDub Auto Wash," p. 662
Case 20, "Maricopa Ready Mix," p. 693

chapter 20

Quality Management and the Operations Process

In the VIDEO Spotlight

Ping Golf

John Solheim makes putters that sing—or is that ping? When the golf ball hits a Ping Putter, there is a ring—a ping. It is the sound of a novel golf club design that built a beautiful business. Karsten Manufacturing, maker of Ping golf clubs, started in a garage in 1959. Though it stayed there for seven years, today the Phoenix, Arizona–based company has nearly 900 employees working in 35 buildings on 30 acres, producing some of the world's best-loved products.

Karsten Solheim was a frustrated golfer, and he thought that if equipment was improved, everyone would have more fun playing the game. That insight started Karsten, with son John by his side, on a journey that would change his life and the game of golf.

When perfection is the goal, the concept of continuous improvement becomes a way of life and then a part of the corporate culture. Ping didn't become the world's largest manufacturer of putters by trying to be second best. To grow as this company has, you must have a big vision and high standards and, at the same time, commit to the details. It's the big goal of perfection that motivates everyone to reach for dozens of smaller goals that must be accomplished by hundreds of people every day. John says there is no quality control department because every employee is a quality control department of one, and each has the authority to send a product back for corrections or changes. Quality is not up to John; it's up to everyone. ◆

"There is always an easier route, but if you go that way, you won't be doing justice to your product."

—John Solheim

—Hattie Bryant, Producer, "Small Business School," The Series on PBS Stations, Worldnet, and the Web, http://smallbusinessschool.org

SmallBusinessSchool
the Series on PBS stations and the Web

Go to page 744 for More! on Ping Golf.

Looking Ahead

After studying this chapter, you should be able to

1. *Explain the key elements of total quality management (TQM) programs.*
2. *Discuss the nature of the operations process for both products and services.*
3. *Explain how reengineering and other methods of work improvement can increase productivity and make a firm more competitive.*
4. *Discuss the importance of purchasing and the nature of key purchasing policies.*
5. *Describe ways to control inventory and minimize inventory costs.*

Whether a business produces a product, a service, or both, it must use some kind of **operations process**, or **production process.** This process consists of the activities involved in creating value for customers and earning their dollars. A bakery, for example, begins its production process with the purchase of the ingredients needed to make bread, and a consulting firm first conducts research in order to produce advice for its customers. Small, entrepreneurial firms, as well as large corporations, must perform such work to serve their customers.

operations process (production process)
the activities that create value for customers through production of a firm's goods and services

In this chapter, we consider the ways in which small businesses can improve their operations by finding ways to increase quality and/or reduce operating costs. In their quest to improve operations, both bakeries and consulting firms strive to produce a higher-quality product (bread and advice, respectively) more economically. As quality performance is greatly valued by customers, it has the potential to serve as a particularly powerful competitive weapon for small businesses.

Quality Goals of Operations Management

Quality must be more than a slogan. Owners of successful small firms realize that quality management is serious business and that a strong commitment is essential for the realization of quality goals.

Explain the key elements of total quality management (TQM) programs.

Quality As a Competitive Tool

Quality may be defined as the characteristics of a product or service that bear on its ability to satisfy stated and implied needs. Quality obviously has many different aspects. For example, a restaurant's customers base their perceptions of its quality on the taste of the food, the attractiveness of the décor, the friendliness and promptness of the servers, the cleanliness of the silverware, the type of background music, and numerous other factors. The operations process establishes a level of quality as a product is produced or as a service is provided. Although costs and other considerations cannot be ignored, quality must remain a primary focus of a firm's operations.

quality
the features of a product or service that enable it to satisfy customers' needs

International competition is increasingly turning on quality differences. Automobile manufacturers in the United States, for example, now place greater emphasis on quality in their attempts to compete effectively with foreign producers. However, it is not solely big business that needs to make quality a major concern; the operations process of a small firm also deserves careful scrutiny. Many small firms have been slow to give adequate attention to the importance of producing

high-quality goods and services. In examining the operations process, therefore, small business managers must direct special attention to achieving superior product or service quality.

http://www.asq.org

total quality management (TQM) an all-encompassing management approach to providing high-quality products and services

The American Society for Quality (ASQ) has been the leading quality improvement organization in the United States for more than 50 years and has initiated many quality improvement methods used throughout the world. Among these is an approach known as **total quality management (TQM),** an aggressive effort by a firm to achieve superior quality. Total quality management implies an all-encompassing, quality-focused management approach to providing products and services that satisfy customer requirements. Firms that implement TQM programs are making quality a major goal.

Many businesses merely give lip service to achieving high quality standards; others have introduced quality programs that have failed. As Figure 20-1 shows, the most successful quality management efforts incorporate three elements—a focus on customers, a supportive organizational culture, and the use of appropriate tools and techniques.

The Customer Focus of Quality Management

A firm's quality management efforts should begin with a focus on the customers who purchase its products or services. Without such a focus, the quest for quality easily degenerates into an aimless search for some abstract, elusive ideal.

CUSTOMER EXPECTATIONS Quality is ultimately determined by the extent to which a product or service satisfies customers' needs and expectations. Customers have expectations regarding the quality of both products (durability and attractiveness, for example) and services (speed and accuracy, for example). A customer is concerned with *product quality* when purchasing a camera or a loaf of bread; the customer's primary concern is *service quality* when having an automobile repaired or tailoring done. Frequently, a customer expects some combination of product *and* service quality—when buying a lawnmower, a customer may be concerned with the performance of the lawnmower, knowledge and courtesy of the salesperson, credit terms offered, and terms of the warranty.

FIGURE 20-1

Essential Elements of Successful Quality Management

Customers often have in mind specific standards that are relevant to a product or service. In the following comments, customers revealed their expectations regarding three types of service businesses:

Automobile Repair Customers:

- Be competent. ("Fix it right the first time.")
- Explain things. ("Explain why I need the suggested repairs—provide an itemized list.")
- Be respectful. ("Don't treat me like I'm stupid.")

Hotel Customers:

- Provide a clean room. ("Don't have a deep-pile carpet that can't be completely cleaned. . . . You can literally see germs down there.")
- Provide a secure room. ("Have good bolts and a peephole on the door.")
- Treat me like a guest. ("It is almost like they're looking me over to decide whether they're going to let me have a room.")
- Keep your promises. ("They said the room would be ready, but it wasn't at the promised time.")

Equipment Repair Customers:

- Share my sense of urgency. ("Speed of response is important. One time I had to buy a second piece of equipment because of the huge down time with the first piece.")
- Be competent. ("Sometimes I'm quoting stuff from their instruction manuals to their own people, and they don't even know what it means.")
- Be prepared. ("Have all the parts ready.")[1]

A genuine concern for customer needs and customer satisfaction is a powerful force that energizes the total quality management effort of a business. When customer satisfaction is seen merely as a means of increasing profits, its effect on quality is negligible. When the customer becomes the focal point in quality efforts, however, real quality improvement occurs, and profits tend to grow as a result.

CUSTOMER FEEDBACK Attentive listening to customers' opinions can provide information about their level of satisfaction. Employees having direct contact with customers can serve as the eyes and ears of the business in evaluating existing quality levels and customer needs. Unfortunately, many managers are oblivious to the often subtle feedback from customers. Preoccupied with operating details, managers may not listen to, let alone solicit, customers' opinions. Employees having direct contact with customers—servers in a restaurant, for example—are seldom expected to obtain information about customers' quality expectations. Careful supervision and training of servers could make them more alert to consumers' tastes and attitudes and encourage them to report these reactions to management.

Experts now recommend that firms make aggressive efforts to involve and empower customers in efforts to improve quality.[2] The marketing research methods of observation, interviews, and customer surveys, as described in Chapter 9, can be used to investigate customers' views regarding quality. Some businesses, for example, provide comment cards for their customers to use in evaluating service or product quality.

Building Customer Loyalty

IN THE TRENCHES

BETTER VERSUS CHEAPER

The quality of a product or service should meet the desires and expectations of a firm's customers. The appropriate quality level depends, of course, on the kind of customers, the type of business, and the business strategy.

When Texas was hit by a recession in the mid-1980s, Carmelo Mauro, who runs Carmelo's Italian Restaurants in Houston and Austin, elected to go against the trend. Rather than lowering prices, he decided to compete on quality, increasing the number of menu items, using costlier ingredients, and raising prices!

"In no way could I compete with the large Italian-American pizza chains and their $3.99 buffets," Mauro says. "I marketed quality to attract a specific clientele, the only ones who could afford to eat out anymore and did not want to eat at a mass-volume restaurant."

Carmelo's is now recognized as a restaurant of exceptional quality. It was chosen by the National Pizza and Pasta Association as its 1993 "Pasta Maker of the Year." By emphasizing superior quality, Mauro was able to attract customers who appreciated the food and atmosphere associated with fine dining.

Source: From material from http://www.carmelositalrest.com; and Thomas Love, "Sometimes Better Is Better Than Cheaper," *Nation's Business*, Vol. 86, No. 4 (April 1998), p. 12.

http://www.carmelositalrest.com

Organizational Culture and Total Quality Management

organizational culture
the behaviors, beliefs, and values that characterize a particular firm

A crucial element of effective quality management is a supportive company culture. The values, beliefs, and traditional practices followed by members of a business firm may be described as the firm's **organizational culture.** Some firms are so concerned with quality levels that they will refund money if a service or product is unsatisfactory or will schedule overtime work to avoid disappointing a customer. Quality is a primary value in such a business's organizational culture. Quality management experts believe that a quality-oriented culture is necessary if a firm is to achieve outstanding success.

Time and training are required to build a TQM program that elicits the best efforts of everyone in the organization in producing a superior-quality product or service. A small business that adopts a total quality management philosophy commits itself to the pursuit of excellence in all aspects of its operations. Taking on such a dedication to quality on an organization-wide basis is sometimes described as a *cultural phenomenon.*

continuous quality improvement
a constant and dedicated effort to improve quality

benchmarking
the process of studying the products, services, and practices of other firms and using the insights gained to improve quality internally

Total quality management goes beyond merely ensuring that existing standards are met. Its objective is **continuous quality improvement,** an ongoing effort to improve quality. For example, if a production process has been improved to a level where there is only 1 defect in 100 products, the process must then be shifted to the next level and a new goal set of no more than 1 defect in 200 or even 500 products. The ultimate goal is zero defects—a goal that has been popularized by many quality improvement programs.

A firm's efforts toward continuous quality improvement may include **benchmarking,** which is the process of identifying the best products, services, and prac-

tices of other businesses, carefully studying those examples, and using any insights gained to improve one's own operations. A simple type of benchmarking occurs as owner-managers eat in competitors' restaurants or shop in competitors' stores. Benchmarking was used by Harry W. Schwartz Bookshops of Milwaukee, Wisconsin, a family business, in reacting to vigorous competition from bookstore chains.[3] Its managers visited book superstores, talked with other booksellers, watched customers shop, and even visited office supply superstores. By analyzing these other businesses, the managers were able to make substantial changes in their own operation, such as extending store hours, adopting a no-questions-asked return policy, bringing in authors for readings, providing comfortable chairs, and making freshly brewed coffee available to customers. The result was a more competitive and a more profitable business.

http://www.schwartzbooks.com

Tools and Techniques of Total Quality Management

The third element in effective quality management consists of the various tools, techniques, and procedures needed to ensure high-quality products and services. Once the focus is on the customer and the entire organization is committed to providing top-quality products and services, operating methodology becomes important. Implementing a quality management program requires developing practical procedures for training employees, inspecting products, and measuring progress toward quality goals. We will discuss three important areas—employee participation, the inspection process, and the use of statistical methods of quality management.

EMPLOYEE PARTICIPATION In most organizations, employee performance is a critical quality variable. Obviously, employees who work carefully produce better-quality products than those who work carelessly. The admonition "Never buy a car that was produced on a Friday or a Monday!" conveys the popular notion that workers lack commitment to their work and are especially careless prior to and immediately after a weekend away from work. The vital role of personnel in producing a high-quality product or service has led managers to seek ways to actively involve employees in quality management efforts.

Chapter 18 discussed the implementation of work teams and empowerment of employees as approaches to building employee involvement in the workplace. Many businesses have adopted these approaches as part of their TQM programs. Japanese firms are particularly noted for their use of work teams. Many self-managed work teams, both in Japan and in the United States, monitor the quality level of their work and take any steps necessary to continue operating at the proper quality level.

The quality circle is another technique that utilizes the contributions of employees in improving the quality of products and services. Originated by the Japanese, it is widely used by small firms in the United States and other parts of the world. A **quality circle** consists of a group of employees, usually a dozen or fewer. Such groups meet on company time, typically about once a week, to identify, analyze, and solve work-related problems, particularly those involving product or service quality. Quality circles can tap employees' potential to make enthusiastic and valuable contributions.

quality circle
a group of employees who meet regularly to discuss quality-related problems

THE INSPECTION PROCESS Management's traditional method of maintaining product quality has been **inspection,** which consists of scrutinizing a part or a product to determine whether or not it is acceptable. An inspector typically uses gauges to evaluate important quality variables. For effective quality control, the inspector must be

inspection
the examination of a product to determine whether it meets quality standards

honest, objective, and capable of resisting pressure from shop personnel to pass borderline cases.

Although the inspection process is usually discussed with reference to *product* quality, comparable steps can be used to evaluate *service* quality. Follow-up calls to customers of an auto repair shop, for example, might be used to measure the quality of the firm's repair services. Customers can be asked whether recent repairs were performed in a timely and satisfactory manner.

inspection standard
a specification of a desired quality level and allowable tolerances

In manufacturing, **inspection standards** consist of design tolerances that are set for every important quality variable. These tolerances indicate, in discrete terms, the variation allowable above and below the desired level of quality. Inspection standards must satisfy customer requirements for quality in finished products. Traditionally, inspection begins in the receiving room, where the condition and quantity of materials received from suppliers are checked. Inspection is also customary at critical processing points—for example, *before* any operation that might conceal existing defects and *after* any operation that might produce an excessive amount of defects. Of course, final inspection of finished products is of utmost importance.

Inspecting each item in every lot processed, called *100 percent inspection,* theoretically could be used to ensure the elimination of all bad materials and all defective products prior to shipment to customers. Such inspection goals are seldom reached, however, as this method of inspection is not only time-consuming, but also costly. Furthermore, inspectors often make honest errors in judgment, both in rejecting good items and in accepting bad items. Also, some types of inspection, such as opening a can of vegetables, destroy the product, making 100 percent inspection impractical.

attribute inspection
the determination of product acceptability based on whether it will or will not work

variable inspection
the determination of product acceptability based on a variable such as weight or length

In an inspection, either attributes or variables may be measured. **Attribute inspection** determines quality acceptability based on attributes that can be evaluated as being either present or absent. For example, a light bulb either lights or doesn't light; similarly, a water hose either leaks or doesn't leak.

Variable inspection, in contrast, determines quality acceptability based on where variables (such as weight) fall on a scale or continuum. For example, if a box of candy is to be sold as containing a minimum of one pound of candy, an inspector may judge the product acceptable if its weight falls within the range of 16 ounces to 16.5 ounces.

STATISTICAL METHODS OF QUALITY CONTROL The use of statistical methods can often make controlling product and service quality easier, less expensive, and more effective. As some knowledge of quantitative methods is necessary to develop a quality control method using statistical analysis, a properly qualified employee or outside consultant must be available. The savings made possible by use of an efficient statistical method can often justify the consulting fees required to devise a sound plan.

acceptance sampling
the use of a random, representative portion to determine the acceptability of an entire lot

Acceptance sampling involves taking random samples of products and measuring them against predetermined standards. Suppose, for example, that a small firm receives a shipment of 10,000 parts from a supplier. Rather than evaluate all 10,000 parts, the purchasing firm might check the acceptability of a small sample of parts and generalize about the acceptability of the entire order. The smaller the sample, the greater the risk of either accepting a defective lot or rejecting a good lot due to sampling error. A larger sample reduces this risk but increases the cost of inspection. A well-designed plan strikes a balance, simultaneously avoiding excessive inspection costs and minimizing the risk of accepting a bad lot or rejecting a good lot.

Statistical process control involves applying statistical techniques to control work processes. Items produced in a manufacturing process are not completely identical, although the variations are sometimes very small and the items may seem to be exactly alike. Careful measurement, however, can pinpoint differences. Usually, these differences can be plotted in the form of a normal curve, which aids in the application of statistical control techniques.

statistical process control
the use of statistical methods to assess quality during the operations process

The use of statistical analysis makes it possible to establish tolerance limits that allow for inherent variation due to chance. When measurements fall outside these tolerance limits, however, the quality controller knows that there is a problem and must then search for the cause. The problem might be caused by variations in raw materials, machine wear, or changes in employees' work practices. Consider, for example, a candy maker that is producing one-pound boxes of candy. Though the weight may vary slightly, each box must weigh at least 16 ounces. A study of the operations process has determined that the actual target weight must be 16.5 ounces, to allow for the normal variation between 16 and 17 ounces. During the production process, a box is weighed every 15 or 20 minutes. If the weight of a box falls outside the tolerance limits—below 16 or above 17 ounces—the quality controller must immediately try to find the problem and correct it.

A **control chart** graphically shows the limits for the process being controlled. As current data are entered, it is possible to tell whether a process is under control or out of control. Control charts may be used for either variable or attribute inspections. Continuing improvements in computer-based technology have advanced the use of statistical control processes in small firms.

control chart
a graphic illustration of the limits used in statistical process control

International Certification for Quality Management

A firm can obtain international recognition of its quality management program by meeting a series of standards, known as **ISO 9000**, developed by the International Organization for Standardization in Geneva, Switzerland. The certification process requires full documentation of a firm's quality management procedures, as well as an audit to ensure that the firm is operating in accordance with those procedures. In other words, the firm must show that it does what it says it does. ISO 9000 certification can give a business credibility with purchasers in other countries and thereby ease its entry into export markets. However, substantial costs are involved in obtaining certification.

ISO 9000
the standards governing international certification of a firm's quality management procedures

http://www.iso.ch

ISO 9000 certification is particularly valuable for small firms, because they usually lack a global image as producers of high-quality products. Buyers in other countries, especially in Europe, view this certification as an indicator of supplier reliability. Some large U.S. corporations, such as the Big Three automobile makers, require their domestic suppliers to conform to these standards. Small firms, therefore, may need ISO 9000 certification either to sell more easily in international markets or to meet the demands of their domestic customers.

Quality Management in Service Businesses

As discussed earlier, maintaining and improving quality are no less important for service businesses, such as motels, dry cleaners, accounting firms, and automobile repair shops, than for manufacturers. In fact, many firms offer a combination of tangible products and intangible services and effectively manage quality in both areas.

In recent years, the public has expressed growing dissatisfaction with the general quality of customer service. Studies by such groups as the Council of Better

Business Bureaus and the University of Michigan reveal that consumers find good service to be increasingly rare.[4] Part of this dissatisfaction may be explained by the practice among many large corporations of gearing the quality of service they provide to the profitability of the customer. Better customers get better service. Increasing customer dissatisfaction with poor service—exemplified by automated telephone answering systems that do not allow callers to speak to a live representative, long lines, and reluctance to respond to customer problems—opens the door for small service-oriented firms. Although some services are too costly to be used as powerful competitive weapons, much high-quality service simply requires attention to detail.

Measurement problems are always an issue in assessing the quality of a service. It is easier to measure the length of a piece of wood than the quality of motel accommodations. As noted earlier, however, methods can be devised for measuring the quality of services. For example, a motel manager might maintain a record of the number of problems with travelers' reservations, complaints about the cleanliness of rooms, and so on.

For many types of service firms, quality control constitutes the most important managerial responsibility. All that such firms sell is service, and their success depends on customers' perceptions of the quality of that service.

The Operations Process

2

Discuss the nature of the operations process for both products and services.

The operations, or production, process is necessary to get the job done—that is, to perform the work and create the quality expected by customers. Thus far, this chapter has discussed the way quality concerns drive operations management. Let's now turn to other important aspects of business operations.

The Nature of the Operations Process

operations management
planning and controlling the process of converting inputs into outputs

Operations management involves the planning and control of a conversion process. It includes acquiring inputs and then overseeing their transformation into products and services desired by customers. An operations process is required whether a firm produces a tangible product, such as clothing or bread, or an intangible service, such as dry cleaning or entertainment. The production process in clothing manufacturing, the baking process in a bakery, the cleaning process in dry cleaning, and the performance process in entertainment are all examples of an operations process.

Despite their differences, all operations processes are similar in that they change inputs into outputs. Inputs include money, raw materials, labor, equipment, information, and energy—all of which are combined in varying proportions, depending on the nature of the finished product or service. Outputs are the products and/or services that a business provides to its customers. Thus, the operations process may be described as a conversion process. As Figure 20-2 shows, the operations process converts inputs of various kinds into products, such as baked goods, or services, such as dry cleaning. A printing plant, for example, uses inputs such as paper, ink, the work of employees, printing presses, and electric power to produce printed material. Car wash facilities and motor freight firms, which are service businesses, also use operating systems to transform inputs into car-cleaning and freight-transporting services.

FIGURE 20-2

The Operations Process

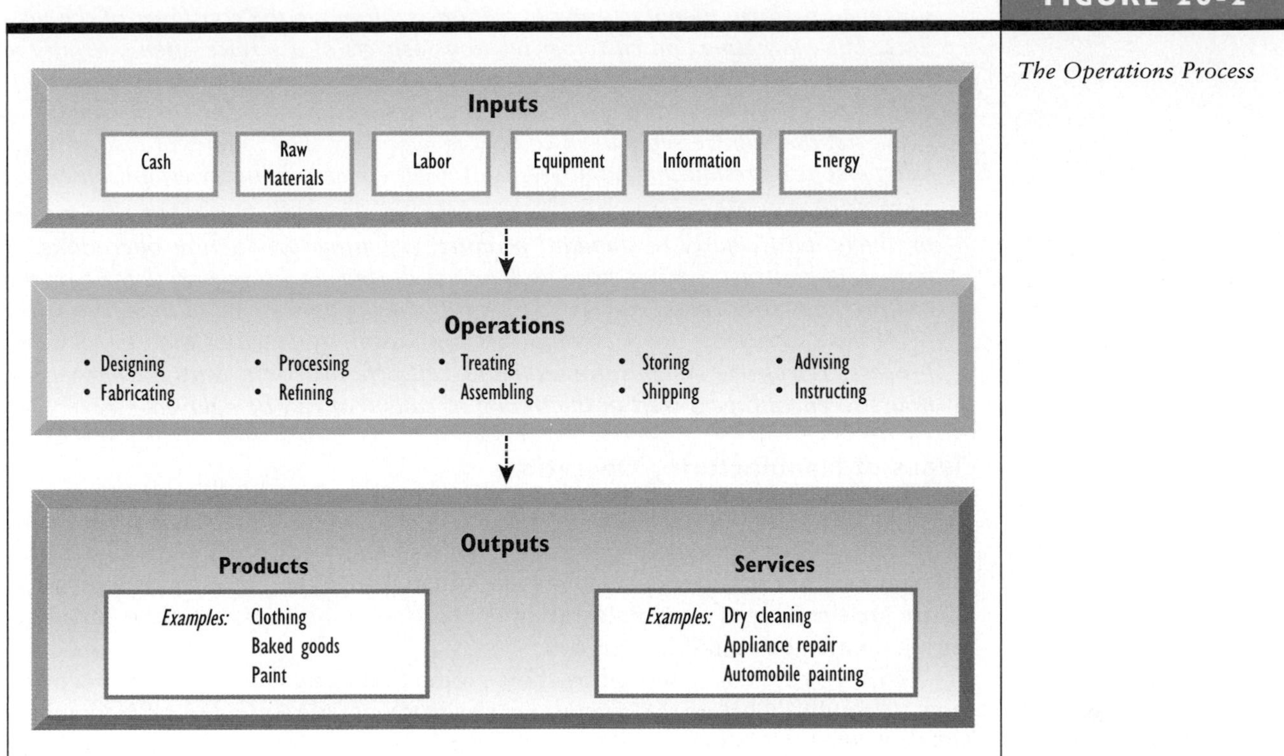

Manufacturing Versus Service Operations

The operations of product- and service-producing firms differ in a number of ways. One of the most obvious differences is that greater customer contact typically occurs in a service firm. In a beauty shop, for example, the customer is a participant in the operations process as well as a user of the service. James B. Dilworth has identified and summarized four areas of difference:

1. *Generally, productivity is more easily measured in manufacturing operations than in service operations because the former provides tangible products, whereas the products of service operations are usually intangible. A factory that produces automobile tires can readily count the number of tires produced in a day. Repair service operations may repair or replace portions of a tangible product, but their major service is the application of knowledge and skilled labor. Advisory services may provide only spoken words, an entirely intangible product and one very difficult to measure.*
2. *Quality standards are more difficult to establish and product quality is more difficult to evaluate in service operations. This difference is directly related to the previous one. Intangible products are more difficult to evaluate because they cannot be held, weighed, or measured. We can evaluate a repair to a tangible product by comparing the product's performance after the repair with its performance before the repair. It is more difficult to know the worth of a service such as legal defense. No one knows for certain how a judge or jury would have ruled had the attorney performed in some different manner.*

3. *Persons who provide services generally have contact with customers, whereas persons who perform manufacturing operations seldom see the consumer of the product. The marketing and customer relations aspects of a service often overlap the operations function. The doctor–patient relationship, for example, is often considered to be a very important component of the physician's services. In the service of hair care, the hairdresser–patron contact is necessary. The impact of discourteous salespersons or restaurant employees is of great concern in many establishments.*
4. *Manufacturing operations can accumulate or decrease inventory of finished products, particularly in standard product, repetitive production operations. A barber, in contrast, cannot store up haircuts during slack times so that he or she can provide service at an extremely high rate during peak demand time. Providers of services often try to overcome this limitation by leveling out the demand process. Telephone systems, for example, can offer discount rates during certain hours to encourage a shift in the timing of calls that can be delayed.*[5]

Types of Manufacturing Operations

Manufacturing operations differ in the degree to which they are repetitive. Some factories produce the same product day after day and week after week. Other production facilities have great flexibility and often change the products they produce. There are three types of manufacturing operations—job shops, repetitive manufacturing, and batch manufacturing.

job shops
a type of manufacturing operation in which short production runs are used to produce small quantities of unique items

repetitive manufacturing
a type of manufacturing operation in which long production runs are used to produce a large quantity of a standardized product

batch manufacturing
a type of manufacturing operation that is intermediate (between job shops and repetitive manufacturing) in volume and variety of products

Job shops are characterized by short production runs. Only one or a few products are produced before the general-purpose machines are shifted to a different production setup. Each job may be unique, requiring a special set of production steps to complete the finished item. Machine shops exemplify this type of operation.

Firms that produce one or relatively few standardized products use **repetitive manufacturing,** which is considered mass production as it involves long production runs. Repetitive manufacturing is associated with the assembly-line production of automobiles and other high-volume products. Highly specialized equipment can be employed, because it is used over and over again in manufacturing the same item. Few small business firms engage in repetitive manufacturing.

An intermediate type of production is called **batch manufacturing.** Batch manufacturing involves more variety (and less volume) than repetitive manufacturing but less variety (and more volume) than job shops. In batch manufacturing, one production run of 100 standardized units may be followed by a second production run of 100 units of another type of standardized product. A bottling plant that fills bottles with several varieties of soft drinks is engaging in batch manufacturing.

Operations Planning and Scheduling

In manufacturing, production planning and scheduling procedures are designed to achieve the orderly, sequential flow of products through a plant at a rate commensurate with scheduled deliveries to customers. In order for this objective to be reached, it is essential to avoid production bottlenecks and to utilize machines and personnel efficiently. Simple, informal control procedures are often used in small plants. If a procedure is simple and the output small, a manager can keep things moving smoothly with a minimum of paperwork. Eventually, however, any manufacturing organization experiencing growth will have to establish formal procedures to ensure production efficiency.

IN THE TRENCHES **Utilizing New Technology**

THE SCHEDULING TASK IN A DENTAL LABORATORY

The scheduling challenge for a dental laboratory is to develop a work program that fits the normal work hours of its employees and also meets the needs of its clients—the dentists and orthodontists using the laboratory's products. The process is complicated by the roller-coaster nature of demand for laboratory services, which has employees working overtime some days and sitting idle other days.

Over the years, Doug Kinnear of Kinnear Dental Laboratories, in Bellevue, Washington, has attempted to solve this problem with a variety of scheduling systems—booking by telephone, standardized turnaround times, pegboards, and customized calendars. With all of these approaches, Kinnear was dictating to clients when orders would be filled.

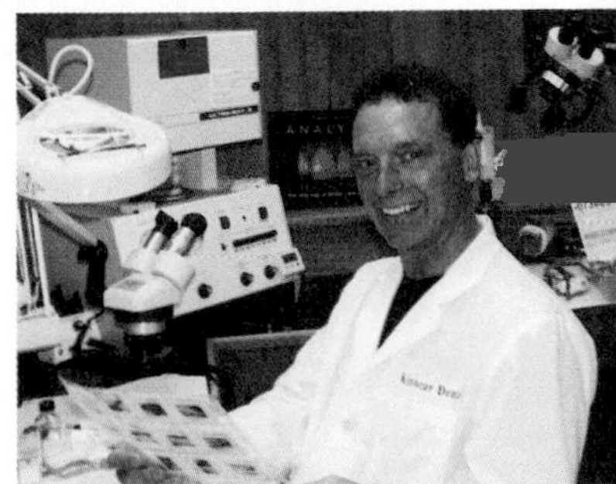

Then Kinnear discovered Jackrabbit.com, an online scheduling service that allows customers to schedule their own work. Instead of dictating a time to clients, Kinnear says, "Go ahead, pick a time." When clients log on to Kinnear's home page, they can click on an icon of a jackrabbit which activates a series of windows detailing the appointment process. Jackrabbit.com's software sends the client a confirming e-mail and updates the company's online scheduling book. The whole process, which takes only a few minutes, is a creative application of modern technology to solve a scheduling problem found in many production operations.

Source: From material from http://www.kinneardentallab.com; John Cook, "Make an Appointment, and Make It Fast," *Seattle Post-Intelligencer Reporter,* January 14, 2000; and Stephanie Izarek, "Making a Date," *Inc. Technology,* No. 3 (2000), p. 121.

http://www.kinneardentallab.com

Because service firms are so closely tied to their customers, they are limited in their ability to produce services and hold them in inventory for customers. An automobile repair shop must wait until a car arrives, and a beauty shop cannot function until a customer is available. A retail store can perform some of its services, such as transportation and storage, but it, too, must wait until the customer arrives to perform other services.

Part of the scheduling task for service firms relates to planning employees' working hours. Restaurants, for example, schedule the work of servers to coincide with variations in customer traffic. In a similar way, stores and medical clinics increase their staff to meet times of peak demand. Other strategies of service firms focus on scheduling customers. Appointment systems are used by many automobile repair shops and beauty shops, for example. Service firms such as dry cleaners and plumbers take requests for service and delay delivery until the work can be scheduled. Still other firms, such as banks and movie theaters, maintain a fixed schedule of services and tolerate some idle capacity. Some businesses attempt to spread out customer demand by offering incentives to use services at off-peak hours—examples include early-bird dinner specials at a restaurant and lower-price tickets for afternoon movies.

Plant Maintenance

Murphy's Law states that if anything can go wrong, it will. In operating systems that use tools and equipment, there is indeed much that can go wrong. The maintenance function is intended to correct malfunctions of equipment and, as far as possible, to prevent breakdowns from occurring.

THE ROLE OF MAINTENANCE Effective maintenance contributes directly to product and service quality and thus to customer satisfaction. Poor maintenance often creates problems for customers. A faulty shower or a reading lamp that doesn't work, for example, makes a motel stay less enjoyable for a traveler.

Equipment malfunctions and breakdowns not only cause problems for customers but also increase costs for the producing firm. Employees may be unproductive while repairs are being made, and expensive manufacturing equipment may stand idle when it should be producing. Furthermore, improperly maintained equipment wears out more rapidly and requires early replacement, thus adding to the overall costs of operation.

The nature of maintenance work obviously depends on the type of operations process and the type of equipment being used. In an office, for example, machines that require maintenance include computers, fax machines, typewriters, copiers, and related office equipment. Maintenance services are usually obtained on a contract basis—either by calling for repair personnel when a breakdown occurs and/or by scheduling periodic servicing. In manufacturing firms that use more complex and specialized equipment, plant maintenance is much more difficult and clearly requires the close attention of management. In small plants, maintenance work is often performed by regular production employees. As a firm expands its facilities, it may add specialized maintenance personnel and eventually create a maintenance department.

preventive maintenance activities intended to prevent machine breakdowns, injuries to people, and damage to facilities

corrective maintenance repairs necessary to restore equipment or a facility to good condition

TYPES OF MAINTENANCE Plant maintenance activities fall into two categories. **Preventive maintenance** consists of inspections and other activities intended to prevent machine breakdowns and damage to people and buildings. **Corrective maintenance** comprises both the major and the minor repairs necessary to restore equipment or a facility to good condition.

A small firm can ill afford to neglect preventive maintenance. A machine that is highly critical to the overall operation must be inspected and serviced regularly to preclude costly breakdowns.

Major repairs, which are a part of corrective maintenance, are unpredictable as to time of occurrence, repair time required, loss of output, and cost of downtime. Because of this unpredictability, some small manufacturers contract with outside service firms for major repair work.

Competitive Strength Through Improved Productivity

3

Explain how reengineering and other methods of work improvement can increase productivity and make a firm more competitive.

productivity the efficiency with which inputs are transformed into outputs

A society's standard of living depends, to some extent, on its **productivity**—the efficiency with which inputs are transformed into outputs. Similarly, the competitive strength of a particular business depends on its productivity. This section discusses approaches that can be used by small businesses to become more competitive through improved productivity.

The Importance of Improving Productivity

To remain competitive, a firm should continually try to improve its productivity. Improvement efforts vary greatly. Some involve major reorganizations or changes in technology, while others merely upgrade existing operations.

A business firm's productivity may be expressed as follows:

$$\text{Productivity} = \frac{\text{Outputs}}{\text{Inputs}} = \frac{\text{Products and/or services}}{\text{Labor} + \text{Energy} + \text{Cash} + \text{Raw materials} + \text{Equipment} + \text{Information}}$$

A firm improves its productivity by doing more with less—increasing outputs and/or decreasing inputs. This can be accomplished in many different ways. For example, a small restaurant may improve the pastry making of its chef by sending the chef to cooking school, buying better ingredients, getting a more efficient oven, or redesigning the kitchen.

At one time, productivity and quality were viewed as potentially conflicting, if not conflicting. However, production at a high quality level reduces scrap and rework. Therefore, quality improvements, automation, and other improvements in operations methods are all routes to better productivity.

Improving productivity in the labor-intensive service sector is especially difficult, since managers have less opportunity to take advantage of automation. Nevertheless, small service firms can find ways to become more efficient. At one time, for example, customers in barber shops wasted time waiting for barbers who took them on a first-come, first-served basis. To improve the system, many shops started using an appointment schedule. A drop-in customer can still get service immediately if a barber isn't busy or else sign up for the first convenient appointment. Such a system provides continuity in the barber's work schedule and reduces delays and frustration for customers.

Reengineering for Improved Productivity

In the early 1990s, Michael Hammer and James Champy described a method for restructuring companies to provide better service for customers. In their best-selling book, *Reengineering the Corporation,* Hammer and Champy defined **reengineering** as "the fundamental rethinking and radical redesign of business processes to achieve dramatic improvements in critical, contemporary measures of performance, such as cost, quality, service, and speed."[6]

reengineering
a fundamental restructuring to improve the operations process

Reengineering is concerned with improving the way in which a business operates, whether that business is large or small. Hammer and Champy concentrated their early analysis on large corporations such as Wal-Mart, Taco Bell, and Bell Atlantic, which redesigned their rigid bureaucratic structures to become more efficient. Firms that engage in reengineering seek fundamental improvements by asking questions about why they perform certain functions the way they do. They expect to make dramatic, radical changes rather than minimal adjustments to traditional operating methods. Reengineering involves careful analysis of the basic processes followed by a firm in creating goods and services for customers.

Reengineering's emphasis on basic processes is crucial and holds the potential for substantial improvements in operations. Like effective quality control efforts, it directs attention to activities that create value for the customer. Essentially, reengineering asks how the operations process can be better managed, even if it means eliminating traditional departmental lines and specialized job descriptions.

Utilizing New Technology

IN THE TRENCHES

IMPROVING PRODUCTIVITY IN TRUCKING

A small company can improve its bottom line by finding ways to operate more efficiently. In many cases, modern technology can give a helping hand.

Murray Kennedy and his wife, Linda, haul everything from computers to aircraft parts in their self-owned 18-wheel tractor-trailer. They can gross some $6,600 for a 3,000-mile one-way trip, but the key to better profitability lies in finding freight for the return drive.

For a number of years, the Kennedys have relied on Landstar, a logistics company, to find a return load. Eventually, they obtained a laptop computer with which to search Landstar's online network for available freight. But because they still had to pull over at truck stops in order to log in, they often missed the best deals.

Now, without leaving the truck, he [Murray] or Linda uses a cell phone equipped with customized software that lets them dial directly into Landstar's Web site. Kennedy bought the phone himself for $149, and pays only $15 a month to dial in. Using the number pad and a small screen, he recently used the system to locate a shipment of automotive parts in Charlotte, N.C. that needed to go to a Chrysler plant near his home. The search took him five minutes. Kennedy estimates that he could save a full day each trip because he no longer must wait for freight. The time savings could boost his revenues 20%.

Source: Rachel Harrison, "The Hands-On, Logged-On Worker," *Forbes,* Vol. 166, No. 12 (October 30, 2000), p. 138.

Operations Analysis

Improving productivity for an overall operation involves analyses of work flow, equipment, tooling, layout, working conditions, and individual jobs. For a specific manufacturing process, it means finding answers to questions such as these:

- Are the right machines being used?
- Can one employee operate two or more machines?
- Can automatic feeders or ejectors be used?
- Can power tools replace hand tools?
- Can the jigs and fixtures be improved?
- Is the workplace properly arranged?
- Is each operator's motion sequence effective?

Work methods can be analyzed for service or merchandising firms as well as for manufacturers. For example, a small plumbing company serving residential customers might examine its service vehicles to make sure they are equipped with the best possible assortment and arrangement of parts, tools, and supplies. In addition, the company might analyze the planning and routing of repair assignments to minimize unnecessary backtracking and wasting of time.

laws of motion economy
guidelines for increasing the efficiency of human movement and tool design

LAWS OF MOTION ECONOMY The **laws of motion economy** underlie any work improvement program—whether it is aimed at the overall operation of a plant or at a single task. These laws concern work arrangement, the use of the human hands and body, and the design and use of tools. Here's an example of one of these laws: If a worker makes motions simultaneously in opposite directions over similar paths, automaticity and rhythm develop naturally, and less fatigue is experienced.

motion study
an analysis of all the motions a worker makes to complete a given job

time study
the determination of the average time it takes a worker to complete a given task

METHODS OF WORK MEASUREMENT There are several ways to measure work in order to establish a performance standard. **Motion study** consists of detailed observation of all the actual movements a worker makes to complete a job under a given set of physical conditions. From this study, a skilled observer should be able to detect any wasted movements, which can then be corrected or eliminated. **Time study,** which follows motion study, typically involves use of a stopwatch to determine an average time for performing a given task.

Purchasing Policies and Practices

4
Discuss the importance of purchasing and the nature of key purchasing policies.

Although its importance varies with the type of business, **purchasing** constitutes a key part of operations management for most small businesses. Through purchasing, firms obtain materials, merchandise, equipment, and services to meet production and marketing goals. For example, manufacturing firms buy raw materials, merchandising firms purchase goods to be sold, and all types of firms obtain supplies.

purchasing
the process of obtaining materials, equipment, and services from outside suppliers

The Importance of Purchasing

The quality of a finished product depends on the quality of the raw materials used. If a product must be made with great precision and close tolerances, the manufacturer must acquire high-quality materials and component parts. Then, if the manufacturer uses a well-managed production process, excellent products will result. Similarly, the acquisition of high-quality merchandise makes a retailer's sales to customers easier and reduces the number of necessary markdowns and merchandise returns.

Purchasing also contributes to profitable operations by ensuring that goods are delivered when they are needed. Failure to receive materials, parts, or equipment on schedule can cause costly interruptions in production operations. In a retail business, failure to receive merchandise on schedule may mean a loss of sales and, possibly, a permanent loss of customers who were disappointed.

Another aspect of effective purchasing is securing the best possible price. Cost savings go directly to the bottom line, and purchasing practices that seek out the best prices can have a major impact on the financial health of a business.

Note, however, that the importance of the purchasing function varies according to the type of business. In a small, labor-intensive service business—such as an accounting firm—purchases of supplies are responsible for a very small part of the total operating costs. Such businesses are more concerned with labor costs than with the cost of supplies or other materials they may require in their operations process.

Purchasing Practices and Profitability

A small firm can increase the cost effectiveness of its purchasing activities by adopting appropriate purchasing practices. Through decisions related to making or buying, outsourcing, and other procurement issues, the firm's management can optimize both present and future earnings.

make-or-buy decision
a firm's choice between producing and purchasing component parts for its products

MAKING OR BUYING Many firms face **make-or-buy decisions.** Such decisions are especially important for small manufacturing firms that have the option of making or buying component parts for products they produce. A less obvious make-or-buy

choice exists with respect to certain services—for example, purchasing janitorial or car rental services versus providing for those needs internally. Some reasons for making component parts, rather than buying them, follow:

- More complete utilization of plant capacity permits more economical production.
- Supplies are assured, with fewer delays caused by design changes or difficulties with outside suppliers.
- A secret design may be protected.
- Expenses are reduced by an amount equivalent to transportation costs and the outside supplier's selling expense and profit.
- Closer coordination and control of the total production process may facilitate operations scheduling and control.
- Products produced may be of higher quality than those available from outside suppliers.

Some reasons for buying component parts, rather than making them, follow:

- An outside supplier's part may be cheaper because of the supplier's concentration on production of the part.
- Additional space, equipment, personnel skills, and working capital are not needed.
- Less diversified managerial experience and skills are required.
- Greater flexibility is provided, especially in the manufacture of a seasonal item.
- In-plant operations can concentrate on the firm's specialty—finished products and services.
- The risk of equipment obsolescence is transferred to outsiders.

The decision to make or buy should be based on long-run cost and profit optimization, as it may be expensive to reverse. Underlying cost differences need to be analyzed carefully, since small savings from either buying or making may greatly affect profit margins.

outsourcing
purchasing products or services that are outside the firm's area of competitive advantage

OUTSOURCING Buying products or services from other business firms is known as **outsourcing.** Although the preceding discussion of making or buying component parts related specifically to manufacturing, the concept can also be extended to procurement of a wide range of services. A small company, for example, may contract with outside suppliers to provide accounting services, payroll services, janitorial services, equipment repair services, and so on. A firm can often reduce costs by taking advantage of the economies of scale and the expertise of outside service providers, rather than trying to provide all such services in-house. Also, outside firms that specialize in specific areas usually provide better service in those areas.

Chapter 19 explained the practice of employee leasing through which a small firm transfers its employees to a leasing company, which then leases them back to the small firm. In effect, the small firm is outsourcing the payroll preparation process.

Outsourcing of services can be particularly helpful to a company looking to expand into an unfamiliar foreign environment—for example, a small U.S. firm wishing to start doing business in Great Britain. Commercial Angles, a business firm located in Northern England, is one of many firms offering its services to overseas clients via its Web site:

IN THE TRENCHES

ENTREPRENEURSHIP TODAY

OUTSOURCING THE RIGHT PROCESSES

In 1994, Cherie Serota and Jody Gardner, both executives at Henri Bendel, decided to launch an apparel business in Manhattan, to create stylish maternity clothes. They named the new business "Belly Basics."

Knowing they needed outside help, they began outsourcing various processes. For example, they knew they needed to be fully automated (with an electronic data interchange system) in order to interact with retail chains, so they outsourced technical back-office functions.

They also outsourced several functions they could have performed themselves, including some critical design tasks, for which they contracted with an outside designer. This proved to be an unwise decision, because it was the area in which their own skills were most applicable.

They backed off from this type of outsourcing quickly. "Now we won't outsource anything that has to do with anything creative," says Serota. They had learned to discriminate between critical functions they needed to perform personally and those that could be most readily outsourced.

Source: "Go Right to the Outsource," *Inc.,* Vol. 21, No. 2 (February 1999), p. 25.

Running an overseas operation in UK from your international base can be difficult using only your own resources. The consultants from Commercial Angles will complement your own expertise with our local knowledge and improve the efficiency of your operations in Great Britain. For an overview of our range of services please click here.

http://www.commercialangles.com

Small U.K. firms are also invited to take advantage of the *variety of services* provided by Commercial Angles, which include assistance with payroll, tax returns, accounting, debt collection, and import and export matters.

BUYING ON THE INTERNET In increasing numbers, small firms are buying on the Internet as an alternative method of purchasing. Many tasks that once required telephone calls or out-of-office time can now be accomplished simply and quickly on the Web. The changing purchasing environment has been described as follows:

In years past, small-business owners had scant buying power, little access to resources and information, and a dearth of applications to help them manage their businesses. The Internet has changed all that. Today's connected small-business owners can find themselves sitting happily as hundreds of suppliers, large and small, bid for their business. Instead of buying costly software packages, they can rent only the applications they need, and add more as the company grows. And they can outsource nearly any function—from business planning and human resources management to the purchase of office supplies.[7]

Even small farmers are beginning to investigate purchasing on the Internet as a way of reducing costs. Jerry Brightbill, who farms 4,200 acres near Cotton Center, Texas with his father and brother, visited a Web site called XSAg.com, looking for deals on farm supplies.[8] He found that he could often buy herbicides at 20 percent or more off the list price and eventually spent $40,000 during the year at this one

http://www.xsag.com

site. XSAg is only one of many Internet companies targeting the farm market. It seems probable that many of the nation's more than 2 million farmers, as well as millions of other small firms, will continue to increase their buying on the Internet.

DIVERSIFYING SOURCES OF SUPPLY Small firms often must decide whether it is desirable to use more than one supplier when purchasing a given item. The somewhat frustrating answer is "It all depends." For example, a business would rarely need more than one supplier when buying a few rolls of tape. However, several suppliers might be involved when a firm is buying a component part to be used in hundreds of products.

A small firm might prefer to concentrate purchases with one supplier for any of the following reasons:

- A particular supplier may be outstanding in its product quality.
- Concentrating purchases may lead to quantity discounts.
- Orders may be so small that it is impractical to divide them among several suppliers.
- The purchasing firm may, as a good customer, qualify for prompt treatment of rush orders and receive management advice, market information, and financial leniency in times of crisis.

Also, a small firm may be linked to a specific supplier by the very nature of its business—if it is a franchisee, for example. Typically, the franchise contract requires purchasing from the franchisor.

The following reasons favor diversifying rather than concentrating sources of supply:

- Shopping among suppliers enables the purchasing firm to locate the best source in terms of price, quality, and service.
- A supplier, knowing that competitors are getting some of its business, may try to provide better prices and service in order to obtain a larger piece of the purchasing pie.
- Diversifying supply sources for key products provides insurance against interruptions caused by strikes, fires, or similar problems with sole suppliers.

Some firms compromise by following a purchasing policy of concentrating enough purchases with a single supplier to justify special treatment and, at the same time, diversifying purchases sufficiently to maintain alternative sources of supply.

Relationships with Suppliers

Before choosing a supplier, a purchaser should be thoroughly familiar with the characteristics of the materials or merchandise to be purchased, including details of construction, quality and grade desired, intended use, maintenance or care required, and the importance of style features. In manufacturing, the purchaser must especially focus on how different grades and qualities of raw materials affect various manufacturing processes.

SELECTING SUPPLIERS A number of factors are relevant in deciding which suppliers to use on a continuing basis. Perhaps the most significant of these factors are price and quality. Price differences are clearly important to a firm's bottom line, if not offset by quality issues or other factors.

Quality differences are sometimes difficult to detect. For some types of materials, statistical controls can be applied to evaluate vendors' shipments. In this way, the purchaser can obtain an overall quality rating for various suppliers. The purchaser can often work with a supplier to upgrade quality. If satisfactory quality cannot be achieved, the purchaser clearly has a reason for dropping the supplier.

Supplier location becomes an especially important factor if a firm tries to keep inventory levels low, depending instead on rapid delivery of purchased items when they are needed. A supplier's overall reliability in providing goods and services is also significant. The purchaser must be able to depend on the supplier to meet delivery schedules and to respond promptly when emergency situations arise.

The services offered by a supplier must also be considered during the selection process. The extension of credit by suppliers provides a major portion of the working capital of many small firms. Some suppliers plan sales promotions, provide merchandising aids, and furnish management advice. During recessions, some small retailers have even received direct financial assistance from long-standing suppliers. Repair work for some types of products is another useful service offered by certain suppliers. A small industrial firm, for example, may select a particular supplier of a truck or diesel engine in large part because the supplier has a reliable service department.

BUILDING GOOD RELATIONSHIPS WITH SUPPLIERS Good relationships with suppliers are essential for firms of any size, but they are particularly important for small businesses. The small firm is only one among dozens, hundreds, or perhaps thousands buying from that supplier. And because the small firm's purchases are often small in volume, they may not be of concern to the supplier.

To implement a policy of fair play and to cultivate good relations with suppliers, a small firm should try to observe the following purchasing practices:

- Pay bills promptly.
- Give sales representatives a prompt, courteous hearing.
- Avoid abrupt cancellation of orders merely to gain a temporary advantage.
- Avoid attempts to browbeat the supplier into special concessions and/or unusual discounts.
- Cooperate with the supplier by making suggestions for product improvement and/or cost reduction, whenever possible.
- Provide courteous, reasonable explanations when rejecting bids, and make fair adjustments in the case of disputes.

If the volume of purchases is sufficiently large, small purchasers can build working partnerships with their suppliers. On the other hand, poor relationships with suppliers can be devastating for a small business in times of crisis. In the early 1990s, Howard and Phil's Western Wear of Santa Clarita, California, a family-owned chain of retail stores selling cowboy boots and attire, fell on hard times.[9] The fad for western wear was waning, and the 1994 California earthquake had damaged 12 of the firm's leading stores. As a result, suppliers tightened credit, and one supplier, Justin Boots, refused to deal with the company at all. The deterioration of supplier relationships played a major role in the firm's filing for bankruptcy in 1996. As one observer expressed it, "If you're a Western store and don't carry Justin Boots, you're sunk."

Although price can never be completely ignored, the development of cooperative relationships with qualified suppliers can pay substantial dividends to many

small firms. Small business buyers should remember that although it takes a long time to build good relationships with suppliers, those relationships can be damaged by one ill-timed, tactless act.

strategic alliance
an organizational relationship that links two independent business entities in a common endeavor

http://www.newpig.com

DEVELOPING STRATEGIC ALLIANCES Some small firms have found it advantageous to develop **strategic alliances** with suppliers. This form of partnering enables the buying and selling firms to work much more closely together than is customary in a simple contractual arrangement.

New Pig Corporation, a 300-employee company in Tipton, Pennsylvania, sought to improve its competitive strength by developing better working relationships with suppliers. This company produces sock-like materials used to soak up industrial spills and buys some element of each of the 3,000 different products it sells. New Pig's goals for partnering with its suppliers were to reduce the time it takes to introduce products, improve product quality, engage in joint problem solving, make joint adjustments to market conditions, and involve suppliers early in product development. One of the early benefits of the firm's collaboration with its suppliers was a change in a shipping method that resulted in savings of hundreds of thousands of dollars.[10]

Inventory Management and Operations

5

Describe ways to control inventory and minimize inventory costs.

Inventory management is not glamorous, but it can make the difference between success and failure for a small firm. The larger the inventory investment, the more vital proper inventory management is. Inventory management is particularly important in small retail or wholesale firms, as inventory typically represents a major financial investment by these firms.

Objectives of Inventory Management

Both purchasing and inventory management share the same objective: to have the right goods in the right quantities at the right time and place. As shown in Figure 20-3, achieving this general objective requires pursuing more specific subgoals of inventory control—ensuring continuous operations, maximizing sales, protecting assets, and minimizing inventory costs.

Ensuring continuous operations is particularly important in manufacturing, as delays caused by lack of materials or parts can be costly. Furthermore, sales can be maximized by completing production in a timely manner and by stocking an appropriate assortment of merchandise in retail stores and wholesale establishments. Protecting inventory against theft, shrinkage, and deterioration and optimizing investment costs likewise contribute to operational efficiency and business profits.

Inventory Cost Control

Maintaining inventory at an optimum level—the level that minimizes stockouts and eliminates excess inventory—saves money and contributes to operating profits. To determine the optimum level, managers must pay close attention to purchase quantities, because those quantities affect inventory levels. The ideal quantity of an item to purchase (at least some of which will be carried in inventory) is the number of items that minimizes total inventory costs, or the **economic order quantity** (EOQ).

economic order quantity (EOQ)
the quantity to purchase in order to minimize total inventory costs

If a firm could order merchandise or raw materials and carry inventory with no expenses other than the cost of the items, there would be no need to be concerned

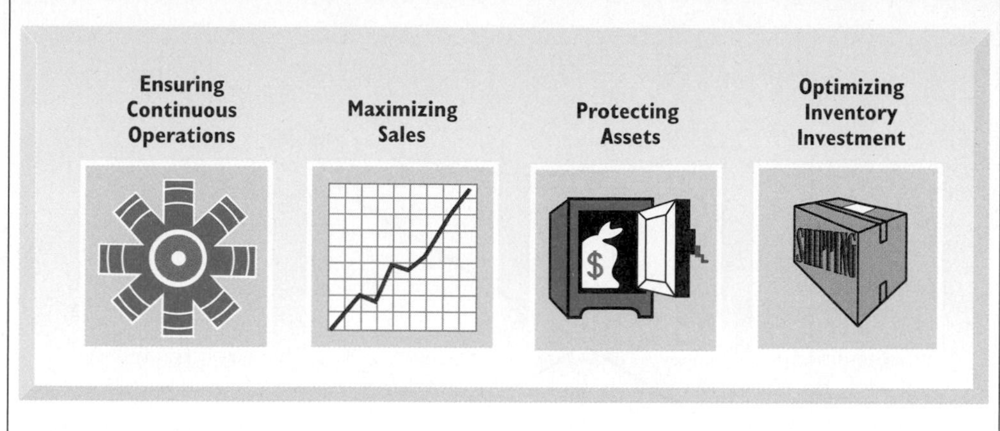

FIGURE 20-3

Objectives of Inventory Management

about what quantity to order at any given time. However, inventory costs are affected by both the costs of purchasing and the costs of carrying inventory—that is,

$$\text{Total inventory costs} = \text{Total carrying costs} + \text{Total ordering costs}$$

As noted earlier, carrying costs include storage costs, insurance premiums, the cost of money tied up in inventory, and losses due to spoilage or obsolescence. Carrying costs increase as inventories increase in size. Ordering costs, on the other hand, include expenses associated with preparing and processing purchase orders and expenses related to receiving and inspecting the purchased items. The cost of placing an order is a fixed cost; therefore, total ordering costs increase as a firm purchases smaller quantities more frequently. Quantity discounts, if available, favor the placement of larger orders.

The point labeled EOQ in Figure 20-4 on page 516 is the lowest point on the total costs curve; it coincides with the intersection of the carrying costs and ordering costs curves. In cases in which sufficient information on costs is available, this point can be calculated with some precision.[11] Even when the economic order quantity cannot be calculated with precision, a firm's goal must be to minimize both ordering costs and carrying costs.

ABC INVENTORY ANALYSIS Some inventory items are more valuable or more critical to a firm's operations than others. Therefore, those items have a greater effect on costs and profits. As a general rule, managers should attend most carefully to those inventory items entailing the largest investment.

One approach to inventory analysis, the **ABC method,** classifies inventory items into three categories based on value. The purpose of the ABC method is to focus managerial attention on the most important items. The number of categories could easily be expanded to four or more, if that seemed more appropriate for a particular firm.

ABC method
a system of classifying items in inventory by relative value

In the A category are a few high-value inventory items that account for the largest percentage of total dollars or are otherwise critical in the production process and, therefore, deserve close control. They might be monitored, for example, by an inventory system that keeps a running record of receipts, withdrawals, and balances

FIGURE 20-4

Graphic Portrayal of the Economic Order Quantity

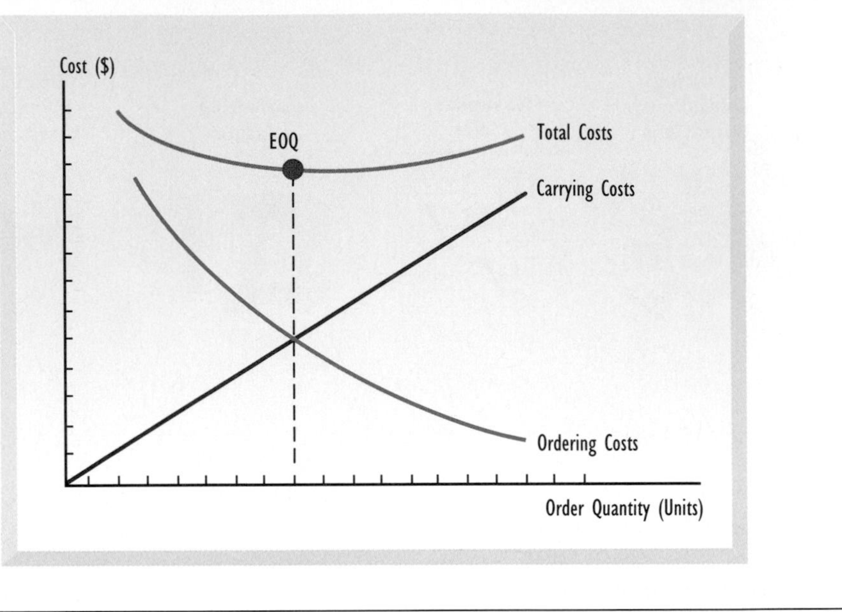

of each such item. In this way, a firm can avoid an unnecessarily heavy investment in costly inventory items. Category B items are less costly but deserve moderate managerial attention because they still make up a significant share of the firm's total inventory investment. Category C contains low-cost or noncritical items, such as paperclips in an office or nuts and bolts in a repair shop. The carrying costs of such items are not large enough to justify close control. These items might simply be checked periodically to ensure that a sufficient supply is available.

just-in-time inventory system
a method of reducing inventory levels to an absolute minimum

JUST-IN-TIME INVENTORY SYSTEM Optimizing inventory levels remains a goal of all operations managers. The **just-in-time inventory system** attempts to cut inventory carrying costs by reducing inventory to an absolute minimum. Popularized in Japan as *kanban,* the just-in-time system has led to cost reductions there and in other countries. New items are received, presumably, just as the last item of that type from existing inventory is placed into service. Many large U.S. firms have adopted some form of the just-in-time system for inventory management, and small businesses can also benefit from its use.

Adoption of a just-in-time system necessitates close cooperation with suppliers. Supplier locations, production schedules, and transportation schedules must be carefully considered, as they all affect a firm's ability to obtain materials quickly and in a predictable manner—a necessary condition for using a just-in-time inventory system.

The potential for failure is high in the just-in-time system. Out-of-stock situations, which arise when delays or mistakes occur, may result in interrupted production or unhappy customers. Most firms using the just-in-time inventory system maintain some safety stock (a reserve amount for use in emergency) to minimize difficulties of

this type. Although safety stock represents a compromise of the just-in-time philosophy, it protects a firm against large or unexpected withdrawals from inventory and delays in delivery of replacement items.

Inventory Record-Keeping Systems

The larger the business is, the greater the need for record keeping, but even a very small business needs a system for keeping tabs on its inventory. Because manufacturers are concerned with three broad categories of inventory (raw materials and supplies, work in process, and finished goods), their inventory records are more complex than those of wholesalers and retailers. Small firms should emphasize simplicity in their control methods. Too much control is as wasteful as it is unnecessary.

In most small businesses, inventory records are computerized. A large variety of software programs are available for this purpose; the manager, in consultation with the firm's accounting advisors, can select the software best suited for the particular business.

A **physical inventory system** depends on an actual count of items on hand. The counting is done in physical units such as pieces, gallons, and boxes. By using this method, a firm presumably gains an accurate record of its inventory level at a given point in time. Some businesses have an annual shutdown to count everything—a complete physical inventory. Others use **cycle counting,** scheduling different segments of the inventory for counting at different times during the year. This simplifies the inventorying process and makes it less of an ordeal for the business as a whole.

physical inventory system
a method that provides for periodic counting of items in inventory

cycle counting
a system of counting different segments of the physical inventory at different times during the year

A **perpetual inventory system** provides an ongoing, current record of inventory items. It does not require a physical count. However, a physical count of inventory should be made periodically to ensure the accuracy of the system and to make adjustments for such factors as theft.

perpetual inventory system
a method for keeping a running record of inventory

Any part of the operations process can damage a firm's sales and profit performance if it is not done well. Therefore, careful management is needed, not only in such often-highlighted areas as quality performance and cost-efficiency but also in such mundane areas as plant maintenance and inventory control. Achieving the goal of satisfactory customer service calls for fine-tuning a firm's basic operations.

Looking Back

1 Explain the key elements of total quality management (TQM) programs.

- Quality of products or services is a primary goal of the operations process.
- Quality management efforts are focused on meeting customer needs.
- Effective quality management requires an organizational culture that places a high value on quality.
- Quality management tools and techniques include employee involvement, quality circles, inspections, and statistical analysis.
- Service businesses can benefit from use of quality management programs.

2 Discuss the nature of the operations process for both products and services.

- Operations, or production, processes vary from one industry to another, but they all change inputs into outputs.
- Service and manufacturing operations typically differ in the extent of their contact with customers and the level of difficulty in establishing quality standards.
- The three types of manufacturing operations are job shops, repetitive manufacturing, and batch manufacturing.
- Operations management involves planning and scheduling activities that transform inputs into products or services.
- Proper plant maintenance is necessary for efficient operation and achievement of quality performance.
- Preventive maintenance is needed to minimize breakdowns in machinery; corrective maintenance is used to restore equipment to good condition.

3 Explain how reengineering and other methods of work improvement can increase productivity and make a firm more competitive.

- The competitive strength of a business depends on its level of productivity.
- Reengineering involves restructuring firms by redesigning their basic work processes.
- Laws of motion economy can be applied to make work easier and more efficient.
- Work may be analyzed through use of motion study and time study.

4 Discuss the importance of purchasing and the nature of key purchasing policies.

- Purchasing is important because it affects quality and profitability.
- A key decision for manufacturers is whether to make or buy components.
- In outsourcing, a small firm contracts with outside suppliers for accounting, repair, or other services and products.
- Small firms are doing more purchasing on the Internet, and many are finding bargains online.
- Decisions concerning diversifying sources of supply must take into account both the advantages and the disadvantages of having multiple suppliers.
- Purchasing policies may relate to concentrating or diversifying sources of supply.
- Careful selection of suppliers will identify those offering the best price, quality, and services.
- Paying bills promptly and dealing professionally with suppliers will help build good relationships, which in turn can bring benefits, such as training provided by a supplier.
- Strategic alliances enable small firms to work closely with their suppliers.

5 Describe ways to control inventory and minimize inventory costs.

- The calculation of economic order quantities, ABC inventory analysis, and the just-in-time inventory system can all help minimize inventory costs.
- Inventory record-keeping systems include the physical inventory method and the perpetual inventory method.

Key Terms

operations process (production process), p. 495
quality, p. 495
total quality management (TQM), p. 496
organizational culture, p. 498
continuous quality improvement, p. 498
benchmarking, p. 498
quality circle, p. 499
inspection, p. 499
inspection standard, p. 500
attribute inspection, p. 500
variable inspection, p. 500
acceptance sampling, p. 500
statistical process control, p. 501
control chart, p. 501
ISO 9000, p. 501
operations management, p. 502
job shops, p. 504
repetitive manufacturing, p. 504
batch manufacturing, p. 504
preventive maintenance, p. 506
corrective maintenance, p. 506
productivity, p. 506
reengineering, p. 507
laws of motion economy, p. 508
motion study, p. 509
time study, p. 509
purchasing, p. 509
make-or-buy decision, p. 509
outsourcing, p. 510
strategic alliance, p. 514
economic order quantity (EOQ), p. 514
ABC method, p. 515
just-in-time inventory system, p. 516
physical inventory system, p. 517
cycle counting, p. 517
perpetual inventory system, p. 517

Discussion Questions

1. Defend the customer focus of quality management.
2. Explain what is meant by total quality management.
3. A small manufacturer does not believe that statistical quality control charts and sampling plans are useful. Can traditional methods suffice? Can 100 percent inspection by final inspectors eliminate all defective products? Why or why not?
4. How do operations processes differ for manufacturing firms and service firms?
5. Customer demand for services is generally not uniform during a day, week, or other period of time. What strategies can be used by service firms to better match a firm's capacity to perform services to customer demand for services?
6. Explain the purpose and nature of reengineering.
7. Doing something rapidly and doing it well are often incompatible. How can quality improvement possibly contribute to productivity improvement?
8. What conditions make purchasing a particularly vital function in a small business? Can the owner-manager of a small firm safely delegate purchasing authority to a subordinate? Explain.
9. Under what conditions should a small manufacturer either make component parts or buy them from others?
10. Explain the basic concept underlying the calculation of an economic order quantity.

You Make the Call

SITUATION 1

The owner of two pizza restaurants in a city with a population of 150,000 is studying her firm's operations to be sure the firm is functioning as efficiently as possible. About 70 percent of the firm's sales represent dine-in business, and 30 percent come from deliveries. The owner has always attempted to produce a good-quality product and minimize the waiting time of customers both on- and off-premises.

A recent magazine article suggested that quality is now generally abundant and that quality differences in businesses are narrowing. The writer advocated placing emphasis on saving time for customers rather than producing a high-quality product. The owner is contemplating the implications of this article for the pizza business. Realizing that her attention should be focused, she wonders whether to concentrate primary managerial emphasis on delivery time.

Question 1 Is the writer of the article correct in believing that quality levels now are generally higher and that quality differences among businesses are minimal?

Question 2 What are the benefits and drawbacks of placing the firm's primary emphasis on minimizing customer waiting time?

Question 3 If you were advising the owner, what would you recommend?

SITUATION 2

Derek Dilworth, owner of a small manufacturing firm, is trying to rectify the firm's thin working capital situation by carefully managing payments to major suppliers. These suppliers extend credit for 30 days, and customers are expected to pay within that time period. However, the suppliers do not automatically refuse subsequent orders when a payment is a few days late. Dilworth's strategy is to delay payment of most invoices for 10 to 15 days beyond the due date. Although he is not meeting the "letter of the law," he believes that the suppliers will go along with him rather than lose future sales. This practice enables Dilworth's firm to operate with sufficient inventory, avoid costly interruptions in production, and reduce the likelihood of an overdraft at the bank.

Question 1 What are the ethical implications of Dilworth's payment practices?

Question 2 What impact, if any, might these practices have on the firm's supplier relationships? How serious would this impact be?

SITUATION 3

The owner of a small food products company was confronted with an inventory control problem involving differences of opinion among his subordinates. His accountant, with the concurrence of his general manager, had decided to "put some teeth" into the inventory control system by deducting inventory shortages from the pay of route drivers who distributed the firm's products to stores in their respective territories. Each driver was considered responsible for the inventory on his or her truck.

When the first "short" paychecks arrived, drivers were angry. Sharing their concern, their immediate supervisor, the regional manager, first went to the general manager and then, getting no satisfaction there, appealed to the owner. The regional manager argued that there was no question about the honesty of the drivers. He said that he personally had created the inventory control system the company was using, and he admitted that the system was complicated and susceptible to clerical mistakes by the driver and by the office. He pointed out that the system had never been studied by the general manager or the accountant, and he maintained that it was ethically wrong to make deductions from the small salaries of honest drivers for simple record-keeping errors.

Question 1 What is wrong, if anything, with the general manager's approach to making sure that drivers do not steal or act carelessly? Is some method of enforcement necessary to ensure careful adherence to the inventory control system?

Question 2 Is it wrong to deduct from drivers' paychecks shortages documented by inventory records?

Question 3 How should the owner resolve this dispute?

EXPERIENTIAL EXERCISES

1. Outline the operations process involved in your present educational program. Be sure to identify inputs, operations, and outputs.
2. Outline, in as much detail as possible, your customary practices in studying for a specific course. Evaluate the methods you use, and specify changes that might improve your productivity.
3. Using the ABC inventory analysis method, classify some of your personal possessions into three categories. Include at least two items in each category.
4. Interview the manager of a bookstore about the type of inventory control system used in the store. Write a report in which you explain the methods used to avoid buildup of excessive inventory and any use made of inventory turnover ratios (ratios that relate the dollar value of inventory to the volume of sales).

EXPLORING THE WEB

1. Small manufacturing firms have an excellent non-profit resource to help them become more productive and efficient. Check out the NIST Manufacturing Extension Partnership site at **http://www.mep.nist.gov**.
   a. Locate the MEP center nearest you.
   b. Under Manufacturing Hot Topics, read about "lean manufacturing." Write a definition for the term, explain how it differs from traditional manufacturing, and describe the benefits of being a "lean" firm.
   c. Read one of the success stories given on the MEP site. Describe the impact that MEP had on the company.
   d. Read the article in *Emerging Business* magazine (**http://www.ebmagz.com**) entitled "Mega-help for Small Manufacturers." Give a single example from the article on how a business was helped by MEP.
2. Inventory Control Management can easily be overlooked in a small business.
   a. Access the article entitled "The Benefits of Smart Inventory Management," published by *NationsBusiness* (**http://www.findarticles.com/m1154/6_87/54695720/p1/article.jhtml**). List the five suggestions given to entrepreneurs.
   b. Check out the selection of inventory control management software available for download from Zdnet.com. To do this, access **http://www.zdnet.com**, choose Downloads, choose Business and Finance, and follow the link to Inventory Systems. Compare the ratings, features, and prices of the items that have been downloaded more than 10,000 times. Print the page for the software that you would recommend to a small business trying to manage inventory. Explain your reasons for making this choice.
3. Access the Web site of the American Society for Quality at **http://www.asq.org**.
   a. Follow the link to Standards. How many countries subscribe to the standards set by ISO 9000?
   b. How do the ISO 9000 standards compare to those required for the prestigious Baldrige award?
   c. What other standards are defined here?
   d. Compare the resources offered at **http://www.isoregistered.com**. How is this Web site different from that of ASQ?

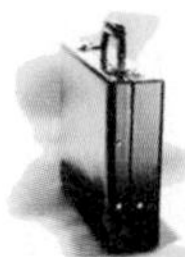

CASE 20

MARICOPA READY MIX (p. 693)

A small ready-mix concrete business adopts a global positioning system to improve productivity.

Alternative Cases for Chapter 20:

Case 9, "ScrubaDub Auto Wash," p. 662
Case 11, "Logan Beach," p. 669

chapter 21

Social and Ethical Issues

In the VIDEO Spotlight

Katz Deli

"You only get to keep what you give away."

—Marc Katz

In this episode of "Small Business School," the series on PBS stations, you will meet Marc Katz. Fifth-generation kosher butcher and founder of the Austin, Texas–based Katz Deli, Marc is called by some the "honorary mayor" of Austin. It seems as if everyone in Austin has eaten at Katz Deli, and many are aware of the owner's dedication to the community. When we contacted the Austin Chamber of Commerce for recommendations of business owners they would be proud to see on national television, the chamber representative said, "Marc Katz is a great example of a small business owner who works hard at his business and at making Austin a great place to live."

Marc grew up in the deli business in New York City, but he did not want to work for his family—he wanted to follow his own dreams. When he arrived in Austin, he went to work selling used cars until he could raise enough cash to get started in business. In 1978, with a partner and an instinct to buy a building where many other restaurants had failed, Marc began offering the first complete and authentic deli menu in Austin.

Katz Deli is a success because the food is loved by customers, and the customers are loved by Marc and the staff. Marc taught me that a signature restaurant is a place where customers are treated as valued friends and family. You'll see that he dresses up to go to work every day. He makes people feel as

Go to page 746 for More! on Katz Deli.

if they were visiting his home, where he had prepared a party for them.

Following the lead of big companies, Marc has always given to charities. For years, he has donated 10 percent of the gross receipts from his largest table to causes important to him, and this idea has been copied by over 150 restaurants in the United States. And even though every business owner I know is generous, Marc is my favorite example of a business owner who is in love with giving. ◆

—Hattie Bryant, Producer, "Small Business School," The Series on PBS Stations, Worldnet, and the Web, http://smallbusinessschool.org

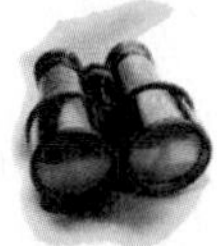

LOOKING AHEAD

After studying this chapter, you should be able to

1. *Identify the kinds of ethical issues in small businesses and explain the special vulnerability of small firms.*
2. *Describe practical approaches for building an ethical business.*
3. *Explain the impact of social responsibilities on small businesses.*
4. *Describe the special challenges of environmentalism and consumerism.*

In operating small businesses, owners and managers confront situations that require them to reflect on what is right and what is wrong. They must decide which course of action is ethical and what to do if it runs counter to the interests of the business.

Such decisions are often complicated by current developments in the business world. Businesses that operate across national boundaries, for example, must consider the ethical standards of other cultures, which may differ from those of their own country. And firms using the Internet face new types of ethical issues that have arisen in this technological age.

Fortunately, many small firms strive to achieve the highest standards of truthfulness, fairness, and trustworthiness in their business relationships. Although unethical practices receive much attention in the news media, many entrepreneurs and other leaders are people of principle whose integrity regulates their quest for profits.

ETHICS AND SMALL BUSINESS

Stories in the news media concerning insider trading, fraud, and bribery usually involve large corporations. However, ethical problems are clearly not confined to big businesses. In the less publicized day-to-day activities of small businesses, decision makers face ethical dilemmas and temptations to compromise principles for the sake of business or personal advantage.

Identify the kinds of ethical issues in small businesses and explain the special vulnerability of small firms.

Doing the Right Thing

ethical issues
questions of right and wrong

Ethical issues involve questions of right and wrong. Such questions go far beyond what is legal or illegal. Many situations call for decisions regarding what is honest, fair, and respectful.

Individuals who face ethical issues are sometimes tempted to place self-interest and personal financial gain ahead of the reasonable and legitimate interests of others. While self-interest is a legitimate force in human life, it can, when unchecked, lead to behavior that is patently unfair or harmful to others. To act ethically, an individual must consider the welfare of those around him or her.

In the short run, at least, honesty does not always pay—doing the right thing can be costly. In other situations, of course, honesty may be profitable for business. But most people who show great integrity in their business lives do not weigh the economic benefits to decide how ethical they can afford to be. Instead, they act ethically simply because it's the right thing to do.

In deciding upon a cause of action in a particular situation, some businesspeople ask this question: "How would I feel if my decision were reported in the daily newspaper?" A few simplify the question even further: "How well could I explain this to my mother?"

Kinds of Ethical Issues

In order to pinpoint the types of ethical issues that are most troublesome for small businesses, small business owners nationwide were asked the following question: "What is the most difficult ethical issue that you have faced in your work?" As might be expected, the question yielded a wide variety of responses, which have been grouped into the categories shown in Table 21-1.

These responses provide a rough idea of the kinds of ethical issues faced by owners of small businesses. As you can see in Table 21-1, the top category involves issues related to customers, clients, and competitors. The second category is concerned with management processes and relationships. Management relationship issues are especially disturbing because they reflect the moral fiber or culture of the firm, including weaknesses in managerial actions and commitments.

ETHICAL ISSUES IN BUSINESS OPERATIONS One glaring example of unethical behavior by small firm management is fraudulent reporting of income and expenses for income tax purposes. This conduct includes *skimming*—that is, concealing some income—as well as improperly claiming personal expenses as business expenses. We do not mean to imply that all or even most small firms engage in such practices. However, tax evasion does occur within small firms, and the practice is sufficiently widespread to be recognized as a general problem.

The Internal Revenue Service regularly uncovers cases of income tax fraud. For example, the John E. Long family, the largest promoter of country folk art shows in the nation, was forced to pay millions in back taxes, and four members of the family were given prison terms for tax law violations.[1] The Longs did not record the cash they collected for admission to their shows. Instead, they deposited into corporate accounts only checks received from such sources as booth rentals and magazine sales. Unfortunately for the Longs, the IRS discovered 2,000 unreported

TABLE 21-1 *Difficult Ethical Issues Facing Small Firms*

Issue	Number of Respondents	Responses
Relationships with customers, clients, and competitors (relationships with outside parties in the marketplace)	56	"Avoiding conflicts of interest when representing clients in the same field" "Putting old parts in a new device and selling it as new" "Lying to customers about test results"
Management processes and relationships (superior–subordinate relationships)	30	"Reporting to an unethical person" "Having to back up the owner/CEO's lies about business capability in order to win over an account and then lie more to complete the job" "Being asked by my superiors to do something that I know is not good for the company or its employees"
Employee obligations to employer (employee responsibilities and actions that in some way conflict with the best interests of the employer)	26	"Receiving kickbacks by awarding overpriced contracts or taking gratuities to give a subcontractor the contract" "Theft of corporate assets" "Getting people to do a full day's work"
Relationships with suppliers (practices and deceptions that tend to defraud suppliers)	18	"Vendors want a second chance to bid if their bid is out of line" "Software copyright issues" "The ordering of supplies when cash flows are low and bankruptcy may be coming"
Governmental obligations and relationships (compliance with governmental requirements and reporting to government agencies)	17	"Having to deal with so-called anti-discrimination laws which in fact force me to discriminate" "Bending state regulations" "Employing people who may not be legal [citizens] to work"
Human resource decisions (decisions relating to employment and promotion)	14	"Whether to lay off workers who [are] surplus to our needs and would have a problem finding work or to deeply cut executive pay and perks" "Sexual harassment" "Attempting to rate employees based on performance and not on personality"
Environmental and social responsibilities (business obligations to the environment and society)	5	"Whether to pay to have chemicals disposed of or just throw them in a dumpster" "Environmental safety versus cost to prevent accidents" "Environmental aspects of manufacturing"

Source: Justin Longenecker, Joseph A. McKinney, and Carlos W. Moore, "Ethical Attitudes, Issues, and Pressures in Small Business," paper presented at the International Council for Small Business Conference, Sydney, Australia, June 1995.

deposits that members of the family made into 37 different accounts. The Longs had reported that their business was losing money when, in fact, it was doing very well.

Cheating on taxes is only one type of unethical business practice. Questions of right and wrong permeate all areas of business decision making. Understanding the scope of the problem requires comprehending the ways in which ethical issues affect decisions in marketing, management, and finance.

When making marketing decisions, a business owner is confronted with a variety of ethical questions. For example, advertising content must sell the product or service but also tell "the truth, the whole truth, and nothing but the truth." Salespeople must walk a fine line between persuasion and deception. In some types

of small business, a salesperson might obtain contracts more easily by offering improper inducements to buyers or by joining with competitors in rigging bids.

In spite of such temptations, however, most people involved in marketing and direct selling (that is, face-to-face selling) are ethical in their business relationships. Criticisms of unethical conduct in direct selling point to such practices as pyramid schemes, bait-and-switch selling, and front-loading, in which new sales representatives are required to purchase large inventories, which they then must try to sell. A recent study of ethics in direct selling by Chonko, Loe, and Wotruba surveyed corporate officers in direct selling organizations.[2] The study reported that these executives evidenced generally high ethical standards; they were aware of opportunities to engage in unethical behavior but did not believe that such behavior contributed to success.

The level of managerial ethics in a firm is reflected in the respect or lack thereof given to employees. Through management decisions, an owner affects employees' personal and family lives. Issues of fairness, honesty, and impartiality surface in decisions and practices regarding hiring, promotions, salary increases, dismissals, layoffs, and work assignments. In communicating with employees, an owner may be truthful, vague, misleading, or totally dishonest. Some entrepreneurs treat outsiders with great courtesy but display demeaning behavior or attitudes toward subordinates, whom they regard as mere "underlings." Showing proper respect for subordinates as human beings and as valuable members of the team is an essential ingredient of strong ethical management.

Owners and managers also face ethical issues in reporting financial information. They must decide the extent to which they will be honest and candid. A firm has considerable discretion in reporting financial results. Financial reports can sometimes be misleading without being illegal. Owners should recognize that outsiders such as bankers, investors, and suppliers depend on a firm's financial reports to be accurate.

ETHICAL ISSUES AND EMPLOYEES In some cases, employees engage in unethical behavior at the expense of their employer. At the most basic level, they may fail in their ethical obligation to do "an honest day's work." Loafing on the job, working too slowly, and taking unjustified sick leave are all examples of such failure.

Other unethical behaviors are more flagrant. For example, some employees have feigned injuries and drawn fraudulent workers' compensation checks, thereby inflating their employer's insurance costs.

Employee theft and embezzlement cost employers millions of dollars each year. The products stolen include merchandise, tools, and equipment of the employer. In the case of embezzlement, of course, an employee steals money.

Employees of small firms sometimes face pressure from various sources to act in ways that conflict with their own sense of what is right and wrong. For example, a salesperson may feel pressured to compromise personal ethical standards in order to make a sale. Or an office employee may feel pressured by his or her boss to act unethically, perhaps by destroying documents. Such situations are guaranteed to produce an organizational culture that is soft on ethics.

Fortunately, most employees of small firms do not face such pressures. In a nationwide survey of individuals holding managerial and professional positions in small firms, respondents reported feeling the following degrees of pressure to act unethically:[3]

IN THE TRENCHES — ENTREPRENEURSHIP AND ETHICS

TELLING APPLICANTS THE TRUTH

The rollercoaster-like fortunes of many dot.com companies have highlighted some sensitive ethical issues. One of these is the hiring practices of troubled startups—that is, firms that are in immediate danger of going under. How honest can a firm on the edge of bankruptcy be in describing the firm to a prospective employee? The following account describes the experiences of Jeanne Romano, who lost her job soon after being hired.

She was 1 of 32 employees laid off when DeepCanyon.com, a Seattle startup that sold market research online, closed its doors earlier this month. As DeepCanyon's production vice-president, Romano had an employment contract, but it allowed the company to fire her without any penalties. . . .

Romano feels that DeepCanyon, which failed to get a second round of funding after being spun off from Hewlett-Packard earlier this year, handled the shutdown well. "Management was very open about our burn rate, about the deals that were, and weren't, in the making," she says. "Two months ago, they told us it was countdown time."

This firm and its management dealt honestly and fairly with employees. Job applicants received a realistic appraisal of bleak company prospects. Employees also received two weeks' notice of closing and two weeks' severance pay. A career counselor came in to discuss the local job scene, and the company manager established a Web site on which employees could post job résumés online. Even while teetering on the brink of bankruptcy, this firm refused to compromise its ethical principles.

Source: Jennifer Gill, "When Dot-Coms on a Deathbed Keep Hiring," *Business Week,* http://www.businessweek.com, October 24, 2000.

No pressure	67.2%
Slight pressure	29.0%
Extreme pressure	3.8%

While it is encouraging to note that two-thirds of the respondents reported an absence of pressure to compromise personal standards, the fact that one-third of the respondents experienced either slight or extreme pressure is disturbing. The stringency of a person's ethical standards is, of course, related to that individual's perception of pressure to act unethically. That is, a person with low ethical standards would probably encounter few situations that violated his or her standards. Conversely, a person with high ethical standards would find more situations that violated his or her personal norms. The ideal is to develop a business environment in which the best ethical practices are consistently and uniformly encouraged.

Internet Ethics

It is not surprising that issues of integrity, honesty, deception, and fraud are found on the Internet just as they are in traditional areas of commerce. The human beings who sell and buy on the Internet are some of the same people who populate malls and business firms. As in all business relationships, one quickly encounters questions of right and wrong.

One issue of general concern to Internet users is individual privacy. Some businesses and some consumers disagree about how private the identity of visitors to Web sites should be; some employers and some employees also differ in opinion as to how private e-mail messages should be.

As explained in Chapter 3, businesses can use "cookies" to collect data on patterns of usage related to a particular Internet address. In this way, a business may create a detailed profile of customers which it may then sell to other parties for profit. Businesses in the Internet industry—and even many of their customers—see the collection of personal information as helpful. A bookseller might, for example, welcome a customer back by name and tell him or her about a special book similar to those the customer ordered previously.

The extent to which an employer may monitor an employee's Internet activity is being hotly debated. According to a survey conducted by the Society of Financial Service, 44 percent of workers surveyed considered it seriously unethical for employers to monitor employee e-mail.[4] In their opinion, apparently, such a practice constitutes snooping and an invasion of their privacy. Employers, however, are concerned that employees may waste time dealing with personal e-mail, shopping online, and surfing the Internet.

The privacy issue is receiving attention from both legislators and business leaders. The probable result will be increased government regulation and also voluntary action by businesses. By 2000, as many as 100 businesses, including IBM and AT&T, had created a position of chief privacy officer to deal with privacy issues in their organizations.[5] Many firms have developed privacy policies—they either will not share personal data or will share it unless the customer takes the initiative to call or e-mail them. These policies are usually spelled out on firms' Web sites.

intellectual property original intellectual creations, including inventions, literary creations, and works of art, that are protected by patents or copyrights

Widespread use of the Internet has also focused attention on the issue of **intellectual property.** Traditionally, protection has been granted to original intellectual creations—whether inventions, literary works, or artistic products such as music—in the form of patents and copyrights. The law allows originators of such intellectual property to require compensation for its use. However, the Internet has made it easy for millions of users to copy intellectual property free of charge.

In the virtual world, journalists, photographers, filmmakers, authors, and musicians are referred to as content providers, a phrase that neatly sums up two problems: first, the fungible nature of this "content," and second, the dicey question of who pays these artists if everything they create can be reproduced free on the Net a hundred million times.[6]

Protection of intellectual property is a political as well as an ethical issue. Recent congressional hearings, lawsuits, and proposed legislation suggest that additions or changes to current laws are likely.

International Ethical Perspectives

Every country faces unethical business behavior within its borders, but some must deal with very serious forms of illegal business activity. In extreme cases, criminal gangs engage in business operations that might better be characterized as evil, rather than unethical. In the year 2000, for example, Italian authorities conducted raids in 28 cities, breaking up a criminal network of some 200 members in China, Russia, and Italy.[7] These gangs brought Chinese immigrants to Italy and forced them to

work 12 to 16 hours a day in textile, apparel, shoe, and leather factories for little or no pay. Other raids have discovered children as young as 11 years old laboring under sweatshop conditions. It is likely that isolated instances of extreme criminal behavior also occur in the United States. In addition, some U.S. companies have exploited labor in countries with weak labor laws in order to procure products at low costs. Acts of this kind must be condemned and targeted by law enforcement agencies.

Of more widespread concern in the area of global business ethics is the following question: Does a payment to a customs employee or to a well-connected, helpful individual in another country constitute a tip, extortion, a consulting fee, or a bribe? The answer may depend on the size of the payment and also on the individual's country of origin. Cultures differ in what they condone as ethical and condemn as unethical.

In operating abroad, then, U.S. businesspeople encounter ethical issues that are clouded by cultural differences.[8] Frequently, they simply apply U.S. standards to the situation. In some cases, however, this approach has been criticized for resulting in **ethical imperialism,** an arrogant attempt to impose U.S. standards on other societies. Some guidance is provided by restrictions specified in the Foreign Corrupt Practices Act, which makes it illegal for U.S. businesses to use bribery in their dealings anywhere in the world. (Some allowance is made for small "grease payments.") Regardless of local practices, U.S. firms must comply with such laws. Of course, "gray areas" exist, in which there are no obvious answers.

ethical imperialism
the belief that the ethical standards of one's own country can be applied universally

http://www.usdoj.gov/criminal/fraud/fcpa

Another viewpoint is embodied in the saying "When in Rome, do as the Romans do." This philosophy, which might be termed **ethical relativism,** is also troublesome, however, as it implies that anything goes if the local culture accepts it. Nicholas G. Moore, chairman of Coopers & Lybrand International, distinguished between business activities that reflect simple cultural differences and those, such as bribery, that are clearly unethical.[9]

ethical relativism
the belief that ethical standards are subject to local interpretation

But the gray areas are tougher to deal with. Think about the issues we deal with here in the United States, and then transplant them to foreign soil. Issues like diversity, the environment, child labor. We are much more sensitive to these issues. Still, the answers are very, very gray. And if they're gray here, they are really murky overseas. They require clear thinking and organizational support.[10]

To define its ethical landscape and work out its position on difficult issues, a small business must consider the nuances of its particular international environment. Training is also needed to ensure that each employee understands the firm's commitment to ethical behavior.

Vulnerability of Small Firms

Walking the straight and narrow may be more difficult and costly on Main Street than it is on Wall Street.[11] That is, small, privately held firms that are not part of the corporate world epitomized by Wall Street may face greater pressures than large businesses do to act unethically. For example, a lack of resources may make it difficult for owners of a small firm to resist extortion by public officials.

Professor William Baxter of the Stanford Law School notes that for such owners, delayed building permits or failed sanitation inspections can be "life-threatening events" that make them cave in to bribe demands. By contrast, he adds, "the local manager of Burger King is in a much better position" to tell these people to get lost.[12]

Because a small firm is at a disadvantage relative to larger competitors that have superior resources, the firm's owner may be tempted to rationalize bribery as a way of offsetting what seems to be a competitive disadvantage and securing an even playing field.

The struggle for survival can create extreme pressure to compromise ethical standards. In the early days of business life especially, a startup may be hanging by a thin thread. When *Inc.* surveyed the CEOs of companies on the 1995 and 1996 *Inc. 500* lists of rapidly growing companies, 14 percent said that bootstrapping (the scraping by and making do that are part of getting started), by definition, requires "unsavory business practices."[13] These practices range from delaying payment to a supplier to out-and-out lying.

http://www.letstalk.com

Nick Molina, referring to the early days of his company Let's Talk Cellular & Wireless, said, "Sometimes when you're backed up against the wall, your instincts take over, and you do what you have to do to survive."[14] When Molina sought to obtain space in the all-important Dadeland Mall in Miami, the leasing agent told him that his company needed to be "established" to be considered. So Molina manipulated financial reports to make his six-month-old firm look as though it had been in business for two years. Entrepreneurs in such difficult positions often try to rationalize their behavior by distinguishing between posturing (putting their "best foot forward") and lying.

The temptation for entrepreneurs to compromise ethical standards as they strive to earn profits is evident in the results of a study of entrepreneurial ethics.[15] In this study, entrepreneurs' views about various ethical issues were compared with those of other business managers and professionals. Respondents were presented with 16 vignettes, each describing a business decision having ethical overtones. They were asked to rate the degree to which they found each action compatible with their personal ethical views, using a 7-point scale from 1 (never acceptable) to 7 (always acceptable). Here is one of the vignettes: "An owner of a small firm obtained a free copy of a copyrighted computer software program from a business friend rather than spending $500 to obtain his own program from the software dealer."

For the most part, the respondents in this study, including entrepreneurs, expressed a moral stance. They condemned, in varying degrees, decisions that were ethically questionable as well as those that were clearly illegal. For all vignettes, the mean response rating for both entrepreneurs and other respondents was less than 4, thereby indicating some degree of disapproval. For nine of the sixteen vignettes, there were no significant differences between the responses of entrepreneurs and those of others. For the remaining seven vignettes, however, the responses of the entrepreneurs were significantly different. In five cases, the entrepreneurs appeared significantly less moral (less disapproving of questionable conduct) than the other respondents.[16] Each of these situations involved an opportunity to gain financially by taking a profit from someone else's pocket. For example, entrepreneurs were less severe in their condemnation of collusive bidding and duplicating copyrighted computer software without paying the manufacturer for its use.

Obviously, a special temptation exists for entrepreneurs who are strongly driven to earn profits. However, this finding must be kept in perspective. Even though the entrepreneurs appeared less moral than the other business respondents in their reactions to five ethical issues, the majority of the entrepreneurs were significantly *more* moral in their responses to two other issues that had no immediate impact on profit.[17] One of these issues involved an engineer's decision to keep quiet about a safety hazard that his employer had declined to correct.

Evidence shows, then, that most entrepreneurs display a general ethical sensitivity, but some are particularly vulnerable with regard to ethical issues that directly affect profits. While business pressures do not justify unethical behavior, they help explain the context in which the decisions are made. Decision making about ethical issues often calls for difficult choices on the part of the entrepreneur.

Building an Ethical Business

The goal of an ethically motivated entrepreneur is to have a business that operates honorably in all areas. This goal is not reached automatically, however. To achieve ethical performance, management must provide the kinds of leadership, culture, and instruction that support ethical behavior.

Describe practical approaches for building an ethical business.

Strong Underlying Values

The business practices that a firm's leaders or employees view as right or wrong reflect their **underlying values.** An individual's beliefs affect what that individual does on the job and how she or he acts toward customers and others. Of course, people sometimes engage in verbal posturing, speaking more ethically than they act. Thus, actual behavior provides the best clues to a person's underlying system of basic values. Behavior may reflect a commitment (or lack thereof) to honesty, respect, and truthfulness—that is, to integrity in all of its dimensions.

underlying values unarticulated ethical beliefs that provide a foundation for ethical behavior in a firm

Strongly held ethical values sometimes require tough choices. The most ethical and the most economical actions often differ, since taking the "right" course of action can be expensive. In such cases, an entrepreneur who has strong, widely recognized moral values will still do the right thing simply because it is the right thing to do.

Values that serve as a foundation for ethical behavior in business are based on personal views of the universe and the role of humankind in that universe. Such values, therefore, are part of basic philosophical and/or religious convictions. In the United States, Judeo-Christian values have traditionally served as the general body of beliefs underlying business behavior, although there are plenty of examples of ethical behavior based on principles derived from other religions. Since religious and/or philosophical values (or the lack thereof) are reflected in the business practices of firms of all sizes, a leader's personal commitment to certain basic values is an important determinant of the ethical climate in a small firm.

An observer of high-tech startups in Silicon Valley has commented on the significance of an entrepreneur's personal values:

I spent most of my career in Silicon Valley. I can tell you, even with the smallest high-technology companies, the product had to be good, the market had to be good, the people had to be good. But the one thing that was checked out most extensively by venture capitalists was the integrity of the management team. And if integrity wasn't there, it didn't matter how good the product was, how good the market was—they weren't funded.[18]

Entrepreneurs who are deeply committed to underlying ethical values operate their businesses in ways that reflect their personal interpretation of those values. After spending several years shuttling gamblers from Richmond, Virginia to Atlantic City, New Jersey, bus driver Tom Winston became convinced, on the basis of his religious faith, that he should no longer take poor people to gamble away what little money they had. So he resigned and started his own company, Universal Tours,

http://www.univertour.qpg.com

ENTREPRENEURSHIP AND ETHICS

PROFITS AND PRINCIPLES

Truitt Cathy has blended ethical principles with entrepreneurial flair in making his company, Chick-fil-A, into a major sandwich chain. In 1946, he started a tiny restaurant in Atlanta—so small that it contained only 10 counter stools and 4 tables! Cathy's business grew quickly, and now Chick-fil-A operates mall units and freestanding stores in 34 states.

Cathy's highly varied promotional efforts include major sports sponsorships and billboards featuring cows holding signs that read "Eat mor chickin." The former include the Chick-fil-A Charity Golf Championship, hosted by Nancy Lopez, and the Peach Bowl (football).

At the core of the business, however, is this stated corporate purpose, which reflects Cathy's deeply held ethical and religious convictions:

To glorify God by being a faithful steward of all that is entrusted to us. To have a positive influence on all who come in contact with Chick-fil-A.

Implementation of the firm's mission to act in a socially responsible way includes managerial emphasis on career opportunities for employees. This may explain Chick-fil-A's 5 to 6 percent turnover rate among restaurant operators versus an average rate of 35 percent in the fast-food industry. Externally, the company and Cathy have introduced such initiatives as creating foster homes for needy children, funding educational scholarships, and providing subsidies for poor children to attend summer camps. The business has prospered while managing humanely and underwriting efforts that contribute to the welfare of the community.

Source: See Bill Banks, "Road Called Fitting Tribute to Cathy's Life Journey," *The Atlanta Journal and Constitution,* April 15, 1999; Judith H. Dobrzynski, "Chicken Done to the Golden Rule," *New York Times,* April 3, 1996; and Fred Andrews, "Management: Ideas into Action," *New York Times,* December 29, 1999.

http://www.chick-fil-a.com

http://www.ukrops.com

which avoids the lucrative casino runs.[19] Another business that places the entrepreneur's personal values above dollars is Ukrop's Super Markets, a Richmond, Virginia–area supermarket chain that does not sell alcohol, that closes every Sunday, and that donates 10 percent of its profits to charity. *Fortune* magazine named Ukrop's to its list of the best 100 companies to work for in both 1999 and 2000. Ninety percent of its employees say they are proud of the company's involvement in the community.[20]

It seems apparent that a deep commitment to basic values affects business behavior and gives rise to ethical business principles that are widely appreciated and admired. Without a strong commitment to integrity on the part of small business leadership, ethical standards can easily be compromised.

Ethical Leadership

Entrepreneurs who care about ethical performance in their firms can use their influence as leaders and owners to urge and even insist that everyone in their firms display honesty and integrity in all operations. Ethical values are established by leaders in all organizations, and those at lower levels take their cues regarding proper behavior from the pronouncements and conduct of top-level management.

In a small organization, the ethical influence of a leader is more pronounced than it is in a large corporation, where leadership can become diffused. In a large

corporation, the chief executive has to exercise great care to make sure that her or his precepts are shared by those in the many and varied divisions and subsidiaries. Some corporate CEOs have professed great shock on discovering behavior at lower levels that conflicted sharply with their own espoused principles.

Leaders of large corporations are also responsible to stockholders, most of whom focus a great deal of attention on corporate profits. The management team is under pressure to deliver an increase in earnings per share year after year. The position of an entrepreneur is much simpler.

The opportunity for establishing high ethical standards is more apparent in small firms than in large ones. An entrepreneur who believes strongly in honesty and truthfulness can insist that those principles be followed throughout the organization. In effect, the founder or head of a small business can say, "My personal integrity is on the line, and I want you to do it this way!" Such statements are easily understood. And such a leader becomes even more effective when he or she backs up such statements with appropriate behavior. In fact, a leader's behavior has much greater influence on employees than his or her stated philosophy does.

In summary, the personal integrity of the founder or owner is the key to a firm's ethical performance. The dominant role of this one person (or the leadership team) gives that person (or the team) a powerful voice in the ethical performance of the small firm.

A Supportive Culture

Consistently strong ethical performance in a business requires a supportive organizational culture. Ideally, every manager and employee should instinctively resolve every ethical issue by simply doing the "right" thing. According to Shaun O'Malley, chairman emeritus of Price Waterhouse, an ethical culture requires an environment in which employees at every level are confident that the firm is fully committed to ethical conduct.

An ethical culture is one in which the company makes a good faith effort to meet its obligations to all its stakeholders—not just to its employees, but also to its customers, shareholders, the community and the environment. The list of stakeholders gets longer every day, and their interests often conflict, but they cannot be ignored.[21]

To a considerable degree, strong leadership helps build this understanding. As a small business grows, however, personal interactions between the owner and employees occur less and less, creating a need to articulate and reinforce ethical principles in ways that supplement the personal example of the entrepreneur.

The idealism and principles espoused by Rutledge & Company, a merchant bank in Greenwich, Connecticut, are reflected by a conference-room portrait that reminds employees "how to behave."[22] The portrait of an early business partner, V. P. "Bake" Baker (described as a "wonderfully principled man"), encourages today's members of the firm to follow such "Bake" principles as these:

1. Do the right thing. Right and wrong are powerful concepts. A handshake with a person who tries to do the right thing is more comforting than a ton of legal documents signed by a bad guy.
2. Stick to your principles. Hire people who want to live by them, teach them thoroughly, and insist on total commitment.
3. Principles are not for sale.

code of ethics
official standards of employee behavior formulated by a firm

At some point, the owner-manager of a firm should formulate a **code of ethics** similar to that of most large corporations. (See Figure 21-1 for an example of such a code.) This code should express the principles to be followed by employees of the firm and give examples of these principles in action. A code of ethics might, for example, prohibit acceptance of gifts or favors from suppliers but point out standard business courtesies, such as free lunches, that might be accepted without violating the policy.[23]

If a code of ethics is to be effective, employees must be aware of its nature and convinced of its importance. At the very least, each employee should read and sign it. As a firm grows larger, employee training becomes necessary to ensure that the code is well understood and taken seriously. It is also imperative, of course, that

FIGURE 21-1

Ethical Code of The Dwyer Group, Waco, Texas

CODE OF VALUES

We believe . . .

—in superior service to our customers, to our community, and to each other as members of The Dwyer Group family.
—in counting our blessings every day in every way.
—success is the result of clear, cooperative, positive thinking.
—loyalty adds meaning to our lives.
—management should seek out and recognize what people are doing right, and treat every associate with respect.
—challenges should be used as learning experiences.
—our Creator put us on this earth to succeed. We will accept our daily successes humbly, knowing that a higher power is guiding us.
—in the untapped potential of every human being. Every person we help achieve their potential fulfills our mission.
—we must re-earn our positions every day in every way.
—in building our country through the free enterprise system. We demonstrate this belief by continually attracting strong people in The Dwyer Group.

We live our Code of Values by . . .

INTEGRITY
—making only agreements we are willing, able and intend to keep.
—communicating any potentially broken agreements at the first appropriate opportunity to all parties concerned.
—looking to the system for correction and proposing all possible solutions if something is not working.
—operating in a responsible manner: "above the line."
—communicating honestly and with purpose.
—asking clarifying questions if we disagree or do not understand.
—never saying anything about anyone that we would not say to him or her.

RESPECT
—treating others as we would like to be treated.
—listening with the intent to understand what is being said and acknowledging that what is said is important to the speaker.
—responding in a timely fashion.
—speaking calmly, and respectfully, without profanity or sarcasm.
—acknowledging everyone as right from their own perspective.

CUSTOMER FOCUS
—continuously striving to maximize internal and external customer loyalty.
—making our best effort to understand and appreciate the customer's needs in every situation.

HAVING FUN IN THE PROCESS!

Source: Reprinted with permission of The Dwyer Group, Waco, Texas.

management operate in a manner consistent with its own principles and deal decisively with any infractions.

A code of ethics provides guidance by clarifying the rules and expressing the norms that employees are expected to follow. It provides support and gives encouragement to the majority who want to do the right thing.

In a large organization especially, there is a vast difference among people's abilities. They learn at different stages, they read at different levels, and their moral sensibilities develop at different rates. Consider, too, that some rules and laws are counterintuitive and that some employees may have come from a more freewheeling environment than others. Thus, it is important that clear guidelines exist for those who might need them.[24]

At a minimum, a code of ethics should establish a foundation for ethical conduct. With training and consistent management, a firm can then develop the level of understanding employees need to act in the spirit of the code in situations not covered by specific rules.

Better Business Bureaus

In any sizable community, all types of ethical and unethical business practices can be found. Some firms use highly questionable practices, such as bait advertising. In **bait advertising,** the seller lures customers in with a deceptive offer to sell a product at an attractive price, only to try to convince them to purchase more expensive products. Other firms are blatantly dishonest in the products or services they provide—for example, replacing auto parts that are perfectly good.

bait advertising
an insincere offer to sell a product or service at a very low price, used to lure customers in so that they can be switched later to a more expensive product or service

Because unethical operations reflect adversely on honest members of the business community, privately owned business firms in many cities have joined together to form Better Business Bureaus. The purpose of such organizations is to promote ethical conduct on the part of all business firms in the community.

Specifically, a Better Business Bureau's function is twofold: (1) It provides free buying guidelines and information a consumer should have about a company prior to completing a business transaction, and (2) it attempts to resolve questions or disputes concerning purchases. As a result, unethical business practices often decline in a community served by a Better Business Bureau.

http://www.bbb.org

The creation of Better Business Bureaus reflects an initiative on the part of independent firms to encourage ethical conduct within the business community. Although actions of this type and voluntary commitment to ethical performance within individual firms receive less press coverage than the ethical failures of some business leaders, such efforts to improve ethical performance contribute significantly to the effective functioning of the private enterprise system.

Social Responsibilities and Small Business

Explain the impact of social responsibilities on small businesses.

To most respondents, an ethical business is one that not only treats customers and employees honestly but also acts as a good citizen in its community. Some of the broader obligations of citizenship are described as social responsibilities.

The extent to which businesses have broad social responsibilities is controversial. Some argue that business firms, especially large corporations, should be expected simply to serve customers and earn profits, and that social expenditures are justified only if they enhance the firm's value. According to this view, good deeds

should be left to individual stockholders. Thus, the earnings of a business should flow to the owners (stockholders), who can decide for themselves whether and/or how to invest in various social causes. Small firms can also decide to minimize (or maximize) their contribution to the broader society.

Others regard some measure of social responsibility as a price of freedom to operate independently in a free economic system. They believe that the public has certain social expectations regarding business behavior, not all of which are required by law. Accordingly, they regard some social expenditures as proper even when they are costly. We must simply recognize that opinions differ as to the extent to which businesses are obligated to engage in a variety of socially desirable activities.

Do Small Firms Recognize Social Responsibilities?

social responsibility ethical obligations to customers, employees, and the general public

There is no single definition of **social responsibility**, but it is generally understood to include the obligations of a business to protect the interests of its customers, employees, suppliers, and the general public.

As you can see, social responsibilities go far beyond a firm's relationships with customers. Included are such diverse areas as the following:

- Environmental protection
- Consumerism
- Support of education, as in tuition scholarship assistance for employee dependents
- Compliance with governmental regulations
- Response to community needs, as in disaster relief and efforts to reduce poverty or increase social welfare
- Contributions to community organizations

The extent to which small businesses are sensitive to such issues varies. Some businesses emphasize environmentalism, minority contracting, and economic development, while others focus their attention on volunteerism, philanthropy, and day care for employees' dependents. Still others, of course, concentrate on serving customers and give only minimal attention to peripheral social issues.

http://www.partec.com

PAR Educational Technologies, a computer firm in Scottsdale, Arizona, expresses its concern for the community by sponsoring a volunteer program for its 65 employees.[25] Employees are invited (but not coerced) to choose from a variety of volunteer projects. One of these projects is Habitat for Humanity, through which the employees help build houses for low-income families.

Volunteer efforts may be useful in building team spirit and making the company a more attractive employer. It is clear, however, that volunteerism also draws on unselfish motivations. As Joel Barthelemy, president and CEO of PAR , said, "Both my parents have 'servant hearts,' and I may be influenced by that. . . . Volunteering also makes me feel good; it's more than just what's in it for Joel."[26] The Scottsdale Chamber of Commerce named PAR Technologies as its small business of the year in 1999.

Smaller businesses demonstrate a sense of social responsibility in special ways. Fuller's Plumbing Service of Chula Vista, California boasts a staff of five, including owner Steve Fuller.[27] In 1994, particularly touched by an article that described the needs of the homebound elderly, Fuller decided to help out the neediest individuals in his community. Fuller's plumbers now repair toilets and faucets, unclog stop-

IN THE TRENCHES ENTREPRENEURSHIP AND ETHICS

CHANGING THE WORLD ONE PAPER CLIP AT A TIME

Some small firms show their commitment to acting in a socially responsible way by contributing a portion of their business profits to social and charitable causes. Michael Hannigan and Sean Marx believed in the principle of social responsibility so strongly that they named their business "Give Something Back." Upon opening this Oakland, California, office supplies firm in 1991, they initially made sales calls out of Hannigan's living room.

In spite of its humble beginnings, Give Something Back hit $500,000 in sales in its first year. By the year 2000, it had reached a sales volume of over $20 million. Although it is still not a big-time company, its owners are definitely big-time givers! By 2001, their firm had contributed more than $1.5 million to charities. Some 57 percent of the firm's post-tax profits were contributed to charities in a three-year span in the late 1990s.

Small firms obviously differ in the extent of their generosity toward community needs. Hannigan and Marx are far more generous than the average small business owner. To make the company name fully descriptive, they might consider changing it from "Give Something Back" to "Give a Lot Back"!

Source: From material from http://www.givesomethingback.com; and Nathan Vardi, "The Profit Givers," *Forbes,* Vol. 166, No. 13 (November 13, 2000), pp. 133–134.

http://www.givesomethingback.com

pages, and fix water system leaks for low-income seniors and disabled people. Fuller's attitude is indicated by his comment "I like to think I owe a little bit back to the community that has supported us for 40 years. . . . That's why I think we can contribute our services to people in need."[28]

In 1998, Fuller was honored by the Points of Light Foundation of Washington, D.C., a nonpartisan organization devoted to promoting volunteerism.[29] The Daily Points of Light Award noted the connection between Fuller's plumbing work and a broader local network of service persons like mail carriers and trash collectors who check in regularly on the homebound.

http://www.pointsoflight.org

Given that small business owners have some awareness of their social obligations, how do they compare with big business CEOs in their view of social responsibility? The evidence is limited, but entrepreneurs who head small, growth-oriented companies seem to be more narrowly focused on profits and, therefore, less socially sensitive than do CEOs of large corporations. A study that compared small business entrepreneurs with large business CEOs concluded the following:

The entrepreneurial CEOs were found to be more economically driven and less socially oriented than their large-firm counterparts. Apparently, CSR [corporate social responsibility] is a luxury many small growth firms believe they cannot afford. Survival may be the first priority.[30]

In defense of small firm owners, we should note that they are spending their own money rather than corporate funds. It is, of course, easier to be generous when spending someone else's money. Furthermore, small business philanthropy often takes the form of personal contributions by business owners.

A few firms make meeting social needs a primary objective of their business. Some identify a particular social purpose or value and build a business to accomplish that purpose. Profit making may play a necessary, but secondary, role. Examples of such firms include the following:[31]

http://www.sustainableharvest.com

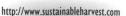

- **Sustainable Harvest Inc., Emeryville, California** (3 employees)
  Importer of organic coffees bought from family farms and cooperatives with which the company has formed a long-term relationship and to which the company provides a guaranteed minimum base price

http://www.wildplanet.com

- **Wild Planet Toys Inc., San Francisco, California** (40 employees)
  Manufacturer of nonsexist, nonviolent, imaginative toys

http://www.citysoft.com

- **CitySoft, Watertown, Massachusetts** (50 employees)
  Web developer with the mission of hiring its workforce from urban neighborhoods

Obviously, entrepreneurs differ in the importance they attach to social obligations. Most accept some degree of social responsibility, and some make substantial contributions to the larger community. Perhaps because of financial pressures, however, many are concerned about a possible trade-off between social responsibility and profits.

Social Responsibilities and Profit Making

Small firms, as well as large corporations, must reconcile their social obligations with the need to earn profits. Meeting the expectations of society can be expensive. Protective legislation, which varies from state to state and frequently changes, often increases the cost of doing business. Small firms must sometimes purchase new equipment or make costly changes in operations in order to protect the environment. For example, auto repair shops must incur additional costs to dispose of hazardous waste, such as old oil and filters. It is evident that acting in the public interest often requires the expenditure of money, with a consequent reduction in profits. There are limits, therefore, to what particular businesses can afford.

Fortunately, many types of socially responsible action can be consistent with a firm's long-term profit objective. Some degree of goodwill is earned by socially responsible behavior. A firm that consistently fulfills its social obligations makes itself a desirable member of the community and may attract customers because of that image. Conversely, a firm that scorns its social responsibilities may find itself the object of restrictive legislation and discover that its customers and employees lack loyalty to the business. Researchers Melissa Baucus and David Baucus of Utah State University compared the long-term performance of 67 corporations convicted of corporate wrongdoing with the performance of 188 other firms.[32] They found that the law-abiding firms experienced a significantly higher return on assets and on sales. To some extent, therefore, socially responsible practices may have a positive impact on profits.

Recognizing a social obligation does not change a profit-seeking business into a charitable organization. Earning a profit is absolutely essential. Without profits, a firm will not long be in a position to recognize its social responsibilities.

Challenges of Environmentalism and Consumerism

The social issues affecting businesses are numerous and diverse. Business firms are expected—at various times and by various groups—to help solve social problems in such areas as education, crime, ecology, and poverty. Two movements of immediate concern to small businesses are environmentalism and consumerism.

4

Describe the special challenges of environmentalism and consumerism.

Environmental Issues

In recent decades, deterioration of the environment has become a matter of widespread concern. **Environmentalism**—the effort to preserve and redeem the environment—thus directly affects all business organizations. One source of pollution has been the industrial discharge of waste into streams, contaminants into the air, and noise into the areas surrounding the operations.

environmentalism
the effort to protect and preserve the environment

The interests of small business owners and environmentalists are not necessarily—or uniformly—in conflict. Some business leaders, including many in small business, have consistently worked and acted for the cause of conservation. For example, many small firms have modernized their equipment and changed their procedures to reduce air and water pollution. Others have taken steps to landscape and otherwise improve the appearance of plant facilities. Some small businesses have actually been in a position to benefit from the general emphasis on ecology. For example, those firms whose products are harmless to the environment are generally preferred by customers over competitors whose products pollute. Also, some small firms are involved in servicing pollution-control equipment. Auto repair shops, for example, service pollution-control devices on automobile engines.

Other small firms, however, are adversely affected by efforts to protect the environment. Livestock feeding lots, cement plants, pet-food processors, and iron foundries are representative of industries that are especially vulnerable to extensive environmental regulation. The cost impact of such regulation on businesses of these types is often severe. Indeed, requiring improvements has forced the closure of some firms. Many small foundries, for example, have been obliged to close because of costly environmental controls.

It is ordinarily quite difficult for a small business to pass higher costs on to its customers; only in a very favorable market situation can a firm do so. The resulting economic hardships must, therefore, be recognized as a cost of environmental controls and evaluated accordingly. Requiring effective pollution control is especially hard on a small, marginal firm with obsolete equipment. In such a case, environmental regulation may simply hasten the inevitable closing of the firm.

Governmental regulations that originate at the state or local level pose particular problems for small businesses. State or local legislation may prove discriminatory by forcing on a local firm high costs that its competitors, located outside the regulated territory, do not have to pay. The immediate self-interest of a small firm, therefore, is best served by legislation that applies at the highest or most general level. Federal regulations apply to all U.S. firms and thus do not create competitive advantages among states and communities.

ENTREPRENEURSHIP AND ETHICS

IN THE TRENCHES

AN ENVIRONMENTALLY FRIENDLY DRY CLEANER

For half a century, dry cleaners have used perchloroethylene (perc) to clean clothes. Compared to other cleaning agents, perc is less likely to shrink or discolor clothes, and it permits clothes to be cleaned and dried in the same machine. The problem: Perc is toxic, potentially harmful to the environment, and subject to stringent disposal standards.

Out of a concern for the environment, a group of dry cleaners developed a new twist on an old business: a "green" dry cleaning solvent that removes grime without harming the environment. After a career at the Bank of New York, Chris Comfort moved to Denver in 1998 and opened Cleaner by Nature, a dry cleaning shop. Cleaner by Nature is representative of a group of dry cleaning shops that are profitably avoiding pollution of the environment.

Source: Stacy Kravetz, "Dry Cleaners' New Wrinkle: Going Green," *The Wall Street Journal,* June 3, 1998, p. B1.

http://www.cleanerbynature.com

Consumer Issues

consumerism
a movement that stresses the needs of consumers and the importance of serving them honestly and well

At one time, the accepted philosophy of business was expressed as "Let the buyer beware." In contrast, current business philosophy forces the seller to put more emphasis on meeting customers' expectations. Today's buyers expect to purchase products that are safe, reliable, durable, and honestly advertised. These expectations, which are the core of **consumerism,** have influenced various types of consumer legislation. The Magnuson-Moss Warranty Act, for example, imposes special restrictions on sellers, such as requiring that any written warranties be available for inspection rather than being hidden inside a package.

To some extent, small firms stand to gain from the consumer movement. Attention to customer needs and flexibility in meeting those needs have traditionally been strong assets of small businesses. Small firm managers have close relationships with their customers and thus are able to determine and respond to their needs. To the extent that these positive features have been realized in practice, consumerism has strengthened the position of small businesses.

Making a completely safe product and avoiding all errors in service are almost impossible goals to reach. Moreover, the growing complexity of products has made their production and servicing more difficult. To render satisfactory service today, a mechanic or repairperson must know a great deal more than he or she did two or three decades ago. Rising consumer expectations, therefore, provide a measure of risk as well as an opportunity for small firms. The quality of management in a small firm determines the extent to which it can realize opportunities and avoid threats to its success.

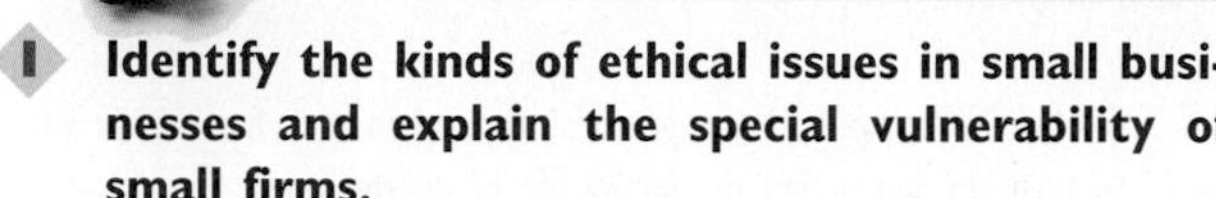

Looking Back

1 Identify the kinds of ethical issues in small businesses and explain the special vulnerability of small firms.

- Ethical issues go beyond what is legal or illegal to include more general questions of right and wrong.
- Income tax evasion by some small firms is an especially visible form of bad ethics.
- The most troublesome ethical issues for small businesses involve relationships with customers, clients, and competitors; management processes and relationships; and employees' obligations to their employers.
- Research shows that about one-third of the employees in small business experience some degree of pressure to act unethically in their jobs.
- Use of the Internet has highlighted ethical issues such as invasion of privacy and threats to intellectual property rights.
- Cultural differences complicate ethical decision making for small firms operating globally.
- The limited resources of small firms make them especially vulnerable to allowing or engaging in unethical practices.

2 Describe practical approaches for building an ethical business.

- The underlying values of business leaders and the behavioral examples of those leaders are powerful forces that affect ethical performance.
- An organizational culture that supports ethical performance is key to achieving ethical behavior among a firm's employees.
- Small firms should develop codes of ethics to provide guidance for their employees.
- Many small businesses join Better Business Bureaus to promote ethical conduct throughout the business community.

3 Explain the impact of social responsibilities on small businesses.

- Most small businesses recognize some social responsibilities, especially to their customers, employees, and community.
- Socially acceptable actions create goodwill in the community and attract customers.
- Some socially responsible practices are expensive, while others are cost-free.
- The need of small firms to remain profitable limits their ability to adopt costly social programs.

4 Describe the special challenges of environmentalism and consumerism.

- Many small businesses help protect the environment, and some contribute positively by providing environmental services.
- Some small firms, such as pet-food processors, are adversely affected by costly environmental regulations.
- By requiring the seller to meet consumer expectations, consumerism creates problems for some small businesses but provides opportunities for those businesses that serve their customers well.

Key Terms

ethical issues, p. 524
intellectual property, p. 528
ethical imperialism, p. 529
ethical relativism, p. 529
underlying values, p. 531
code of ethics, p. 534
bait advertising, p. 535
social responsibility, p. 536
environmentalism, p. 539
consumerism, p. 540

DISCUSSION QUESTIONS

1. The owner of a small business felt an obligation to pay $15,000 to a subcontractor, even though, because of an oversight, the subcontractor had never submitted a bill. How can willingness to pay under these circumstances be reconciled with the profit goal of a business in a free enterprise system?
2. What is skimming? How do you think owners of small firms might attempt to rationalize such a practice?
3. Give an example of an unethical business practice that you have personally encountered.
4. Based on your experience as an employee, customer, or observer of some particular small business, how would you rate its ethical performance? On what evidence or clues do you base your opinion?
5. Explain the connection between underlying values and ethical business behavior.
6. Give some examples of the practical application of a firm's basic commitment to supporting the family life of its employees.
7. To what extent do small business owners recognize their social responsibilities? Could you defend the position of those who say they have no social responsibility? If so, how?
8. Why might small business CEOs focus more attention on profit and less on social goals than large business CEOs do?
9. Give some examples of expenditures required on the part of small business firms to protect the environment.
10. Should all firms use biodegradable packaging? Would your answer be the same if you knew that using such packaging added 25 percent to the price of a product?

YOU MAKE THE CALL

SITUATION 1

Sally started her consulting business a year ago and has been doing very well. About a month ago, she decided she needed to hire someone to help her since she was getting busier and busier. After interviewing several candidates, she decided to hire the best one of the group, Mary. She called Mary on Monday to tell her she had gotten the job. They both agreed that she would start the following Monday and that Mary could come in and fill out all the hiring paperwork at that time.

On Tuesday of the same week, a friend of Sally's called her to say that she had found the perfect person for Sally. Sally explained that she had already hired someone, but the friend insisted. "Just meet this girl. Who knows, maybe you might want to hire her in the future!" Rather reluctantly, Sally consented. "Alright, if she can come in tomorrow, I'll meet with her, but that's all." "Oh, I'm so glad. I just know you're going to like her!" Sally's friend exclaimed.

And Sally did like her. She liked her a lot. Sally had met with Julie on Wednesday morning. She was everything that Sally had been looking for and more. In terms of experience, Julie far surpassed any of the candidates Sally had previously interviewed, including Mary. On top of that, she was willing to bring in clients of her own which would only increase business. All in all, Sally knew this was a win-win situation. But what about Mary? She had already given her word to Mary that she could start work on Monday.

Source: SBA Management Institute, "Business Ethics: The Foundation of Effective Leadership," http://www.onlinewbc.org, September 27, 2000.

Question 1 What decision on Sally's part would contribute most to the success of her business?

Question 2 What ethical reasoning would support hiring Mary?

Question 3 What ethical reasoning would support hiring Julie?

SITUATION 2

A software firm sells its product to retailers and dealers for resale to end users. It has been a slow year, and profits are running behind those of a year ago. One way to increase sales is to persuade dealers to stock more inventory. Exaggerating total product demand by presenting dealers with an extremely optimistic picture of the size and effectiveness of the company's promotional program would probably encourage dealers to build inventories larger and sooner than they would normally. The software itself is regarded as a good product, and the producer simply wishes to build sales by putting its best foot forward in this way.

Question 1 Is the software firm acting ethically if it attempts to increase sales in this way?

Question 2 If this approach is sound ethically, is it also good business?

Question 3 What course of action do you recommend? Why?

SITUATION 3

A self-employed commercial artist reports taxable income of $7,000. Actually, her income is considerably higher, but much of it takes the form of cash for small projects and thus is easy to conceal. She considers herself part of the "underground economy" and defends her behavior as a tactic that allows her small business to survive. If the business were to fail, she argues, the government would receive even less tax revenue.

Question 1 Is the need to survive a reasonable defense for the practice described here?

Question 2 If the practice of concealing income is widespread, as implied by the phrase "underground economy," is it really wrong?

EXPERIENTIAL EXERCISES

1. Examine a recent business periodical, and report briefly on some ethical problem in the news. Could this type of ethical problem occur in a small business? Explain.
2. Employees sometimes take sick leave when they are merely tired, and students sometimes miss class for the same reason. Separate into groups of four or five, and prepare a statement on the nature of the ethical issue (if any) in these practices.
3. Visit or telephone the nearest Better Business Bureau office to research the types of unethical business practices it has uncovered in the community and the ways in which it is attempting to support ethical practices. Report briefly on your findings.
4. Interview an entrepreneur or a small business manager to discover how consumerism affects her or his firm.

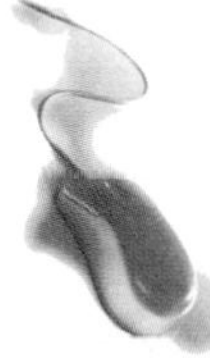

EXPLORING THE WEB

1. Ethical issues face both small businesses and large ones. One large company, Boeing, has its company ethics posted online at **http://www.boeing.com/companyoffices/aboutus/ethics/Index.htm**.
   a. Read over the Values and one or two topics under Ethics Policy and Procedure. How do these two documents work together?
   b. Would you say that the Ethics Policy and Procedure document is rather general or quite specific?
   c. Take the Ethics Challenge and report your score. Were you surprised at the result? In what areas are you weak (allow for the facts that you probably don't work in the industry and that you have not had any specific training)?
   d. An article in *Business Week* addresses the ethical climate for small businesses versus large ones (**http://www.businessweek.com/smallbiz/news/date/9810/e981005.htm**). According to the article, in what areas do small firms tend to act more ethically than large firms? In what areas do small companies have more trouble?
2. The increasing amount of advertising on the World Wide Web is subject to the same ethical concerns as advertising in other media. Access the Council of Better Business Bureau's Online Programs at **http://www.bbbonline.org**.
   a. Follow the link to the Reliability Program Requirements. List what a firm must do to earn the right to place on its Web page the Better Business Bureau's seal attesting to its commitment to ethical business practices.
   b. Examine the information on Online Privacy. What are the purposes of this program? Why is this such a key issue these days?
   c. Access the Frequently Asked Questions for BBBOnLine. What sorts of information may be stored in cookies?

3. To answer the following questions, access the Web site for the Center for Ethics and Business at **http://www.ethicsandbusiness.org**.
   a. Click on About Us and find out who sponsors this site. What approach to ethics is presented here?
   b. Follow the link to Toolbox and take the quiz that reveals your ethical style. Report your score, and describe your style of ethics, according to the quiz results.
   c. Access the Discussion Board and read some of the postings. On what ethical issues are people looking for advice?
   d. Would you feel comfortable posting an ethical issue raised at your company on this discussion board? Why or why not?

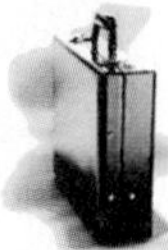

CASE 21

AFCO (p. 695)

This case describes a conflict between two brothers who were managers in a family-owned firm—a conflict that involves issues of fairness and of right and wrong.

Alternative Cases for Chapter 21:

Case 7, "The Brown Family Business," p. 656
Case 25, "When Everything Isn't Half Enough," p. 707

part

7

Financial Management in the Entrepreneurial Firm

chapter 22

Evaluating Financial Performance

In the VIDEO Spotlight

Theatrical Lighting

In this episode of "Small Business School," the series on PBS stations, you will meet Janet and David Milly, founders of Theatrical Lighting. Based in Huntsville, Alabama, with crews all over the country, Theatrical Lighting Systems lives up to its slogan, "We light the stars." Since 1981, it has been creating lighting magic for performers like Tony Bennett, Alabama, Emmylou Harris, Lee Greenwood, and many others, including David's favorite, Johnny Cash.

With 30 employees, the company is generating $5 million in annual sales. Revenues come from lighting sales and rentals and the design and installation of permanent lighting that integrates both house and theatrical lighting systems.

As a student at the University of Alabama at Huntsville, David booked entertainment and dances for his school. From his first booking of Earl Scruggs Review, a country-bluegrass band (of *Deliverance* fame), he knew this was what he wanted to do. But besides the band, David also had to book the lighting package for the show. He engaged Luna Tech, a sole proprietorship, and struck up a friendship with the owner. Within a couple years, they had a partnership. In 1975, they formed a corporation to protect themselves from the liability involved in manufacturing and creating pyrotechnic special effects. David became a 25 percent stockholder in the business, and in 1981 he negotiated a buyout of just the lighting division to go out on his own.

"I don't take risks. I make calculated investments."

—David Milly

Go to page 748 for More! on Theatrical Lighting.

Every department head provides David with a weekly "Flash" report; as the CFO, Janet compiles a simplified financial statement. They maintain a line of credit at a local bank; they use a small local CPA firm for closing statements, audits, and tax returns; and their suppliers love them. They have the habit of paying invoices on time or even before they're due. ◆

—Hattie Bryant, Producer, "Small Business School," The Series on PBS Stations, Worldnet, and the Web, http://smallbusinessschool.org

LOOKING AHEAD

After studying this chapter, you should be able to

1. *Identify the basic requirements for an accounting system.*
2. *Explain two alternative accounting options.*
3. *Describe the purpose of and procedures related to internal control.*
4. *Evaluate a firm's liquidity.*
5. *Assess a firm's operating profitability.*
6. *Measure a firm's use of debt or equity financing.*
7. *Evaluate the rate of return earned on the owners' investment.*

Managers must have accurate, meaningful, and timely information if they are to make good decisions. This is particularly true of financial information about a firm's operations. An inadequate accounting system is a primary factor in small business failures. Owner-managers of small firms sometimes believe that they have less need for financial information because of their personal involvement in day-to-day operations, but they are only deceiving themselves.

This chapter examines the basic elements of an effective accounting system. Then, suggestions are presented on how to use accounting data to draw conclusions about a firm's financial performance.

ACCOUNTING ACTIVITIES IN SMALL FIRMS

Rarely are small business owner-managers expert accountants—nor should they expect to be *or even want to be.* But every one of them should know enough about the accounting process, including financial statements, to recognize which accounting methods are best for their company.

Basic Requirements for Accounting Systems

Identify the basic requirements for an accounting system.

An accounting system structures the flow of financial information to provide a complete picture of a firm's financial activities. Conceivably, a few very small firms may not require formal financial statements. Most, however, need at least monthly financial statements, which should be computer-generated. The benefits of using a computer in developing financial information are so great and the costs so low that it makes absolutely no sense to do otherwise.

Regardless of its level of sophistication, an accounting system for a small business should accomplish the following objectives:

- Provide an accurate, thorough picture of operating results
- Permit a quick comparison of current data with prior years' operating results and budgetary goals
- Offer financial statements for use by management, bankers, and prospective creditors
- Facilitate prompt filing of reports and tax returns to regulatory and tax-collecting government agencies
- Reveal employee fraud, theft, waste, and record-keeping errors

THE RECORD-KEEPING SYSTEM An accounting system provides the framework for managerial control of a firm. Its effectiveness rests on a well-designed and well-managed record-keeping system. In addition to the financial statements intended for external use with bankers and investors, such as the balance sheet and the income statement, internal accounting records should be kept. The major types of internal accounting records are as follows:

- ***Accounts receivable records.*** Records of receivables are vital not only for making decisions on credit extension but also for billing accurately and maintaining good customer relations. An analysis of these records will reveal the effectiveness of a firm's credit and collection policies.
- ***Accounts payable records.*** Records of liabilities show what the firm owes to suppliers, facilitate the taking of cash discounts, and allow payments to be made when due.
- ***Inventory records.*** Adequate records are essential for the control and security of inventory items. Inventory records supply information for use in making purchases, maintaining adequate stock levels, and computing turnover ratios.
- ***Payroll records.*** Payroll records show the total salaries paid to employees and provide a base for computing and paying payroll taxes.
- ***Cash records.*** Carefully maintained records showing all receipts and disbursements are necessary to safeguard cash. They provide essential information about cash flows and cash balances.
- ***Fixed asset records.*** Fixed asset records show the original cost of each asset and the depreciation taken to date, along with other information such as the condition of the asset.
- ***Other accounting records.*** Among the other accounting records that are vital to the efficient operation of a small business are the insurance register (showing all policies in force), records of leaseholds, and records of the firm's investments outside its business.

COMPUTER SOFTWARE PACKAGES Software packages can be used to generate the required accounting records. Most computer software packages include the following features:

- A checkbook that automatically calculates a firm's cash balance, prints checks, and reconciles the account with the bank statement at month's end
- Automatic preparation of income statements, balance sheets, and statements of cash flows
- A cash budget that compares actual expenditures with budgeted expenditures
- Preparation of subsidiary journal accounts—accounts receivable, accounts payable, and other high-activity accounts

In addition, numerous software packages fulfill specialized accounting needs such as graphing, cash flow analysis, and tax preparation. Although the options are almost unlimited in terms of accounting software programs appropriate for use in a small firm, there are several leaders in the entry-level category. Ranging in cost from $100 to $300, they include

- *DacEasy*
  http://www.daceasy.com
- *Great Plains*
  http://www.greatplains.com
- *M.Y.O.B.*
  http://www.myob.com
- *Quick Books 2001*
  http://www.quickbooks.com
- *Peachtree*
  http://www.peachtree.com
- *Simply Accounting*
  http://www.accpac.com
- *Oracle Small Business Suite*
  http://www.oraclesmallbusiness.com

Although all these programs have been well tested and widely used, the small business owner should carefully consider the appropriateness of computer software or hardware before purchasing it. The chance of acquiring computer equipment or programs that do not fit a firm's needs is still significant.

OUTSIDE ACCOUNTING SERVICES Instead of having an employee or a member of the owner's family keep records, a firm may have its financial records kept by a certified public accountant or by a bookkeeping firm or service bureau that caters to small businesses. Very small firms often find it convenient to have the same person or agency keep their books and prepare their financial statements and tax returns.

Numerous small public accounting firms offer complete accounting services to small businesses. Such accounting firms usually offer their services at a lower cost than do larger accounting firms. However, larger accounting firms have begun paying closer attention to the accounting needs of small businesses, and, although their fees may be higher, discounts are usually available. Cost is, of course, an important consideration in selecting an accountant, but other major factors, such as whether the accountant has experience in the particular industry in which the entrepreneur is operating, should play a dominant role in this decision as well.

In some areas, mobile bookkeepers also serve small firms. Bringing to a firm's premises a mobile office that includes computer equipment, they obtain the necessary data and prepare the financial statements on site. Use of mobile bookkeeping can be a fast, inexpensive, and convenient approach to filling certain accounting needs.

Alternative Accounting Options

2

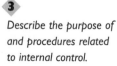

Explain two alternative accounting options.

Accounting records can be kept in just about any form as long as they provide users with needed data and meet legal requirements. Very small firms have some options when selecting accounting systems and accounting methods. Two such options—cash versus accrual accounting and single-entry versus double-entry systems—reflect the most basic issues in an accounting system.

CASH VERSUS ACCRUAL ACCOUNTING As discussed in Chapter 12, the major distinction between cash-basis and accrual-basis accounting is in the point at which a firm reports revenue and expenses. The cash method of accounting is easier to use; revenue and expenses are reported only when cash is received or a payment is made. In contrast, the accrual method of accounting reports revenue and expenses when they are incurred, regardless of when the cash is received or payment is made.

The cash method of accounting is sometimes selected by very small firms, as well as by firms with slow-moving receivables that want to help their cash flows by avoiding the payment of taxes on income not yet received. However, the cash method does not ultimately provide an accurate matching of revenue and expenses. The accrual method, although it involves more record keeping, is preferable because it provides a more realistic measure of profitability within an accounting period. The accrual method of accounting matches revenue against expenses incurred in obtaining that revenue. Alternating between a cash method and an accrual method of accounting is unacceptable, because it violates the accounting principle of consistency.

SINGLE-ENTRY VERSUS DOUBLE-ENTRY SYSTEMS A single-entry record-keeping system is occasionally still found in the very small business. It is not, however, a system recommended for firms that are striving to grow and achieve effective financial planning. A single-entry system neither incorporates a balance sheet nor directly generates an income statement. A **single-entry system** is basically a checkbook system of receipts and disbursements.

single-entry system
a checkbook system of accounting reflecting only receipts and disbursements

double-entry system
a self-balancing accounting system that uses journals and ledgers

Most introductory accounting textbooks provide information on setting up a **double-entry system.**[1] This type of accounting system provides a self-balancing mechanism in the form of two counterbalancing entries for each transaction recorded. It can be done with the record-keeping journals and ledgers found in most office supply retail stores. However, the relatively simple accounting software programs designed for small firms are preferable.

Internal Accounting Controls

3

Describe the purpose of and procedures related to internal control.

As already noted, an effective accounting system is vital to a firm's success. Without the information it provides, management cannot make informed decisions. However, the quality of a firm's accounting system is dependent on the effectiveness of the controls that exist within the firm. **Internal control** is a system of checks and balances that plays a key role in safeguarding a firm's assets and in enhancing the accuracy and reliability of its financial statements. The importance of internal control has long been recognized in large corporations. Some owners of smaller com-

panies, concerned about the cost or appropriateness of a system of internal control for a small company, don't appreciate its value—but they should.

internal control
a system of checks and balances that safeguards assets and enhances the accuracy and reliability of financial statements

Building internal controls may be difficult within a small company, but it is no less important than for a large company. The absence of internal controls significantly increases the chances not only of fraud and theft but also of bad decisions based on inaccurate and untimely accounting information. Effective internal controls are also necessary for an audit by independent accountants. Certified public accountants are unwilling to express an opinion about a firm's financial statements if the firm lacks adequate internal controls.

Although a complete description of an internal control system is beyond the scope of this textbook, it is important to understand the concept. An example of an internal control is separation of employees' duties so that the individual maintaining control over an asset is not the same person recording transactions in the accounting ledgers. That is, the employee who collects cash from customers should not be allowed to reconcile the bank statement. Here are some other examples of internal control:[2]

- Identifying the various types of transactions that require the owners' authorization
- Establishing a procedure to ensure that checks presented for signature are accompanied by complete supporting documentation
- Limiting access to accounting records
- Sending bank statements directly to the owner
- Safeguarding blank checks
- Requiring all employees to take regular vacations so that any irregularity is likely to be revealed
- Controlling access to the computer facilities

The importance of developing an effective system of internal control cannot be overemphasized. Extra effort may be needed to implement internal controls in a small company, in which business procedures may be informal and segregation of duties is difficult due to the limited number of employees. Even so, it is best to try to develop such controls. An accountant may be of assistance in minimizing the problems that can result from the absence of internal controls.

Assessment of Financial Performance

Once an effective accounting system is in place, a firm's owner must determine how to use the data it generates most productively. Mark Twain said of a person who doesn't read, "He who does not read is no better off than he who cannot read." An owner who has a good accounting system but doesn't use it is in the same situation. This section provides a framework for interpreting financial statements, designed to clarify these statements for individuals with varied accounting backgrounds and experience.

An owner needs to understand the financial effect—positive or negative—that management decisions may have. Ultimately, the results of operating decisions appear in a firm's financial statements.

The exact methods used to interpret financial statements can vary, with the perspective of the interpreter determining what areas are emphasized. For example, if a banker and an entrepreneur were analyzing the same financial statements, they

ENTREPRENEURSHIP TODAY

CONTROLLING CASH FLOW PROBLEMS

Effective internal controls can do more than prevent fraud—they can make a firm more efficient in its operations. Bob Martin owns and manages Martin Distribution, a sports novelty company. In its first three years of operation, it grew rapidly, amassing 25 employees and total assets of over $3 million. Then, although sales forecasts indicated continued growth, the company began to experience cash flow problems.

Martin hired a local CPA to study the situation. The accountant discovered the following problems:

- In the last three years, the average collection time on the firm's accounts receivable had increased from 30 days to 48 days, and the percentage of accounts receivable that were actually collected had decreased.
- Accounts receivable write-offs also increased during the same period by 67 percent.
- From the company's bank statements and deposit slips, the accountant determined that numerous deposits had been made by the company's office manager with a "less cash" notation. In addition, deposits were not being made on a regular basis.

A significant factor in the problem was a lack of internal controls, which contributed to relaxed credit policies, sloppy cash handling, and irregular bank deposits. To cover daily expenditures, cash was extracted from bank deposits.

might focus on different data. But whatever perspective is taken, the issues are fundamentally the same and are captured in the following four questions:

1. Does the firm have the capacity to meet its short-term (one year or less) financial commitments?
2. Is the firm producing adequate operating profits on its assets?
3. How is the firm financing its assets?
4. Are the owners (stockholders) receiving an acceptable return on their equity investment?

financial ratios
restatements of selected income statement and balance sheet data in relative terms

http://www.dnb.com
http://www.rmahq.org
http://www.standardandpoors.com

Answering these questions requires restating the data from the income statement and the balance sheet in relative terms, or **financial ratios.** Only in this way can comparisons be made with other firms, with industry averages, and across time. Typically, the industry averages or norms used for comparison purposes are those published by companies such as Dun & Bradstreet, Robert Morris Associates, or Standard & Poor's.[3] Table 22-1 shows the industry norms for the computer and software retailing industry, as reported by Robert Morris Associates, which compiles financial ratios for banks to use in their analyses of firms seeking loans. As shown in the table, the ratios are reported by firm size.

We can best demonstrate the use of financial ratios to evaluate a firm's performance by looking at the financial statements for Bates & Associates Leasing Company, presented in Chapter 12. For ease of reference, the firm's income statement and balance sheets are reproduced in Figures 22-1 on page 554 and 22-2 on page 555. Using these financial statements and relying on industry norms selected by the firm's management, we can answer the four questions about Bates's financial performance.

Can the Firm Meet Its Financial Commitments?

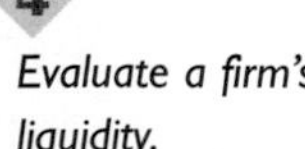
4
Evaluate a firm's liquidity.

A business—or a person, for that matter—that has a large sum of money relative to the amount of debt owed is described as highly liquid. More accurately, the **liquidity** of a business is the availability to the firm of cash to meet maturing debt obligations.

The solution to the problem was relatively simple. The accountant suggested implementing several controls:

- A thorough investigation of the creditworthiness of prospective customers before extending credit
- Controls to help ensure that sales orders would not be filled without prior credit approval
- Periodic reviews of credit limits for existing customers
- Cash deposited intact on a daily basis

After approximately three months, the percentage of accounts receivable collected increased significantly. Bad debts and returns decreased, and profit margins increased. In addition, strict accountability was established for cash collections and miscellaneous daily cash expenditures.

Source: Jack D. Baker and John A. Marts, "Internal Control for Protection and Profits," *Small Business Forum,* Vol. 8, No. 2 (Fall 1990), p. 32. Adapted with permission.

Measuring liquidity answers the question "Does the firm now have or will it have in the future the resources to pay creditors when debts come due?"

This question can be answered in two ways: (1) by comparing the firm's assets that are relatively liquid in nature with the debt coming due in the near term or (2) by examining the timeliness with which liquid assets are being converted into cash.

liquidity
the availability to a firm of cash to meet maturing debt obligations

TABLE 22-1

Financial Ratios for Retail Computer and Software Stores (Industry Code No. 5734)

	FIRM SIZE BY TOTAL ASSETS		
	Less than $500,000	$500,000 to $2 Million	$2 Million to $10 Million
Current ratio	1.0	1.4	1.2
Quick ratio	0.7	1.0	1.0
Accounts receivable turnover	15.4	8.5	6.3
Inventory turnover*	16.2	22.9	43.9
Operating income return on investment†	–1.53%	–6.08%	8.75%
Gross profit margin	41.2%	38.9%	29%
Operating profit margin	–0.3	–1.6	2.5
Fixed asset turnover	38.3	33.9	54.6
Total asset turnover	5.1	3.8	3.5
Debt/equity	4.5	3.1	4.1
Return on equity (before tax)	8.4%	13.4%	32.7%

*Based on cost of goods sold.
†Not reported in the RMA data, but computed by multiplying the operating profit margin times the total asset turnover.
Source: Adapted from RMA 2001–2002 *Annual Statement Studies* published by Robert Morris Associates, Philadelphia, Pa. Copyright Robert Morris Associates, 2001. Note: RMA cautions that the Studies be regarded only as a general guideline and not as an absolute industry norm. This is due to limited samples within categories, the categorization of companies by their primary Standard Industrial Classification (SIC) number only, and different methods of operations by companies within the same industry. For these reasons, RMA recommends that the figures be used only as general guidelines in addition to other methods of financial analysis.

FIGURE 22-1

Income Statement for Bates & Associates Leasing Company for the Year Ending December 31, 2002

Sales revenue		$850,000
Cost of goods sold		550,000
Gross profit on sales		$300,000
Operating expenses:		
Marketing expenses	$90,000	
General and administrative expenses	80,000	
Depreciation	30,000	
Total operating expenses		$200,000
Operating income		$100,000
Interest expense		20,000
Earnings before taxes		$ 80,000
Income tax (25%)		20,000
Net income		$ 60,000

MEASURING LIQUIDITY: APPROACH 1 The first approach to measuring liquidity is to compare cash and the assets that should be converted into cash within the year against the debt (liabilities) that is coming due and will be payable within the year. The liquid assets within a firm are its current assets, and the maturing debt consists of the current liabilities in the balance sheet. Thus, as discussed in Chapter 12, the current ratio estimates a company's relative liquidity:

$$\text{Current ratio} = \frac{\text{Current assets}}{\text{Current liabilities}}$$

Since the three primary current assets are cash, accounts receivable, and inventories, this measure of liquidity can be made more restrictive by excluding inventories, the least liquid of the current assets, in the numerator. The revised ratio is called the **acid-test ratio,** or **quick ratio:**

acid-test ratio (quick ratio)
a measure of a company's liquidity that excludes inventories

$$\text{Acid-test ratio} = \frac{\text{Cash} + \text{Accounts receivable}}{\text{Current liabilities}}$$

Using the data in Figure 22-2, let's compute the current ratio and the acid-test ratio for Bates & Associates Leasing Company.

$$\text{Current ratio} = \frac{\text{Current assets}}{\text{Current liabilities}} = \frac{\$350{,}000}{\$100{,}000} = 3.50$$

$$\text{Acid-test ratio} = \frac{\text{Cash} + \text{Accounts receivable}}{\text{Current liabilities}} = \frac{\$50{,}000 + \$80{,}000}{\$100{,}000} = 1.30$$

FIGURE 22-2

Balance Sheet for Bates & Associates Leasing Company for December 31, 2002

	2002
Assets	
Current assets:	
Cash	$ 50,000
Accounts receivable	80,000
Inventories	220,000
Total current assets	$350,000
Fixed assets:	
Gross plant and equipment	$890,000
Accumulated depreciation	(390,000)
Net plant and equipment	$500,000
Land	70,000
Total fixed assets	$570,000
TOTAL ASSETS	$920,000
Debt (Liabilities) and Equity	
Current liabilities:	
Accounts payable and accruals	$ 20,000
Short-term notes	80,000
Total current liabilities	$100,000
Long-term notes	200,000
Total liabilities	$300,000
Common stock	$300,000
Retained earnings	320,000
Total stockholders' equity	$620,000
TOTAL DEBT AND EQUITY	$920,000

These figures are then compared with the industry norms, or averages, of firms that management considers similar to Bates & Associates, which are as follows:

$$\text{Industry norm for current ratio} = 2.70$$

$$\text{Industry norm for acid-test ratio} = 1.25$$

In terms of the current ratio and the acid-test ratio, Bates & Associates is more liquid than the average firm in its industry. Bates has $3.50 in current assets for every $1 in current liabilities (debt), compared to $2.70 for a "typical" firm in the industry. The firm has $1.30 in cash and accounts receivable per $1 of current debt, compared to the industry norm of $1.25. Why does the current ratio suggest more liquidity than the acid-test ratio? Simply put, Bates has more inventories relative to current debt than most other firms. Which ratio should be given greater weight depends on the actual liquidity of the inventories. We'll return to this issue shortly.

MEASURING LIQUIDITY: APPROACH 2 The second view of liquidity examines a firm's ability to convert accounts receivable and inventory into cash on a timely basis. The ability to convert accounts receivable into cash may be measured by computing how

long it takes on average to collect the firm's receivables. In other words, how many days of sales are outstanding in the form of accounts receivable? This question can be answered by computing the **average collection period:**

average collection period
the average time it takes a firm to collect its accounts receivable

$$\text{Average collection period} = \frac{\text{Accounts receivable}}{\text{Daily credit sales}}$$

If we assume that all sales are credit sales, as opposed to cash sales, the average collection period in 2002 for Bates & Associates is 34.3 days:

$$\text{Average collection period} = \frac{\text{Accounts receivable}}{\text{Daily credit sales}}$$

$$= \frac{\$80{,}000}{\$850{,}000 \div 365} = 34.35$$

$$\text{Industry norm for average collection period} = 35$$

Comparing this value to the industry norm of 35 days, we find that Bates & Associates collects its receivables in about the same number of days as the average firm in the industry. It appears that its accounts receivable are of reasonable liquidity when viewed from the perspective of the length of time required to convert them into cash.

accounts receivable turnover
the number of times accounts receivable "roll over" during a year

We can reach the same conclusion by determining the **accounts receivable turnover**—that is, measuring the number of times that accounts receivable are "rolled over" during a year. Bates & Associates turns its receivables over 10.63 times a year:

$$\text{Accounts receivable turnover} = \frac{\text{Credit sales}}{\text{Accounts receivable}}$$

$$= \frac{\$850{,}000}{\$80{,}000} = 10.63$$

$$\text{Industry norm for accounts receivable turnover} = 10.43$$

We can also measure the accounts receivable turnover by dividing 365 days by the average collection period: 365 ÷ 34.35 = 10.63. Whether the average collection period or the accounts receivable turnover is used, the conclusion is the same: Bates & Associates is comparable to the average firm in the industry in terms of the collection of receivables.

To gain some insight into the liquidity of Bates's inventories, we now need to determine how many times the firm is turning over its inventories during the year. The **inventory turnover** is calculated as follows:

inventory turnover
the number of times inventories "roll over" during a year

$$\text{Inventory turnover} = \frac{\text{Cost of goods sold}}{\text{Inventory}}$$

Note that in this ratio sales are shown at the firm's cost, as opposed to the full market value when sold. Since the inventory (the denominator) is at cost, it is desirable

to measure sales (the numerator) on a cost basis also in order to avoid a biased answer.

The inventory turnover for Bates & Associates is calculated as follows:

$$\text{Inventory turnover} = \frac{\text{Cost of goods sold}}{\text{Inventory}}$$

$$= \frac{\$550{,}000}{\$220{,}000} = 2.50$$

$$\text{Industry norm for inventory turnover} = 4.00$$

This analysis reveals a significant problem for Bates & Associates. The firm is carrying excessive inventory, possibly even some obsolete inventory. It is generating only \$2.50 in sales at cost for every \$1 of inventory, compared to \$4.00 in sales at cost for the average firm. It is now more obvious why the current ratio made the firm look better than the acid-test ratio: Inventory is a larger component of current ratio for Bates than for other firms. So, Bates & Associates' current ratio is not totally comparable with the industry norm.

Is the Firm Producing Adequate Operating Profits on Its Assets?

Assess a firm's operating profitability.

Another question that is vitally important to a firm's investors is whether operating profits—profits that will be available for distribution to all the firm's investors—are sufficient relative to the total amount of assets invested. Figure 22-3 on page 558 provides an overview of the computation of the rate of return on all capital invested in a firm, both by creditors and by common stockholders. The total capital from various investors becomes the firm's total assets. These assets are invested for the express purpose of producing operating profits—profits that are then distributed to creditors and stockholders. A comparison of operating profits and total invested assets reveals the rate of return that is being earned on all the capital.

The profits—and, more importantly, cash flows—are then shared by each investor or investment group according to the terms of its investment agreement. Based on the amount of profits flowing to each investor, the rate of return on each investment can be computed.

MEASURING A FIRM'S RETURN ON INVESTMENT The first step in analyzing a firm's return on investment is finding the rate of return on the total invested capital (capital from all investors)—a rate of return that is independent of how the company is financed (debt versus equity). The rate is arrived at by calculating the **operating income return on investment** (OIROI), which compares a firm's operating income (earnings before interest and taxes) to its total invested capital or total assets. The operating income return on investment is computed as follows:

operating income return on investment (OIROI)
a measure of operating profits relative to total assets

$$\text{Operating income return on investment} = \frac{\text{Operating income}}{\text{Total assets}}$$

FIGURE 22-3

Return on Invested Capital: An Overview

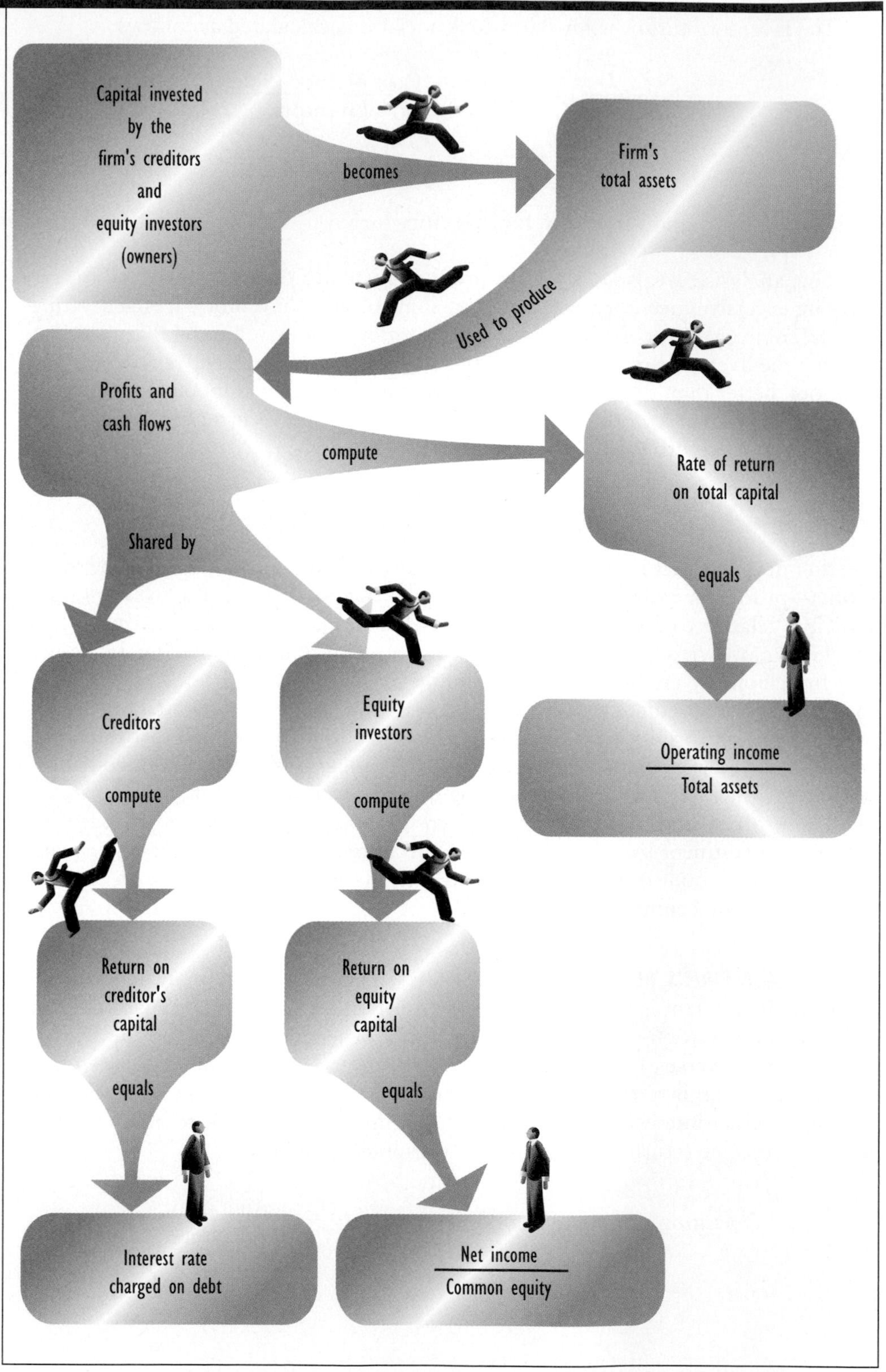

Capital invested by the firm's creditors and equity investors (owners)

becomes

Firm's total assets

Used to produce

Profits and cash flows

compute

Rate of return on total capital

equals

$$\frac{\text{Operating income}}{\text{Total assets}}$$

Shared by

Creditors

compute

Return on creditor's capital

equals

Interest rate charged on debt

Equity investors

compute

Return on equity capital

equals

$$\frac{\text{Net income}}{\text{Common equity}}$$

IN THE TRENCHES ENTREPRENEURSHIP TODAY

RATIO ANALYSIS CAN TELL AN IMPORTANT STORY

Until recently, Greg Smith, president and CEO of the Petra Technology Group, based in Corning, New York, rarely examined how his company compared with the rest of the industry. Why would he? Sales and profits of the company, a $1.5 million systems integrator, had grown every year since the company's inception in 1993.

But in 1998 sales flattened. Petra faced unprofitability for the first time. Though it was easy to attribute losses to the sales slump, Smith felt there was more to the story—he just couldn't pin down an answer. Was he overspending in ways he couldn't see?

Smith contacted Nancy Kirby of Kirby Beals Maier, a local accounting firm. Being familiar with private company growth issues, she suggested that Smith benchmark Petra's numbers against those of other IT-services companies of the same size. Specifically, she wanted Smith to examine payroll as a percentage of sales, which is crucial in an employee-dependent services company.

Smith quickly obtained two industry studies. One was from Robert Morris Associates, and the other from the Chalfin Group Inc., a consultancy in Metuchen, New Jersey, which Smith found through an Internet search.

That was only the beginning. Armed with industry-wide information, Smith quickly saw a problem. Payroll and related costs for his 15-employee business exceeded 60 percent of company sales—a ratio the Chalfin Group generally views as a red flag for companies trying to stay in the black. "At certain points, you have to face the music to remain profitable," Smith says. Part of facing the music for Smith meant reducing his head count by two and using contractors instead of staff employees.

At Kirby's prompting, Smith also checked Petra's ratio of current assets to current liabilities. It was 0.82—too low, in her view. "He had too much short-term debt," Kirby says. Most of the short-term debt was the result of having to pay down a $100,000 line of credit every year. Smith shifted the majority of his debt from a credit line to a seven-year note. Although a small line of credit may mean future cash flow troubles, Smith isn't worried: Petra bills biweekly, and its accounts receivable turn over ten times a year. In one study that Smith looked at, the average turnover of receivables was five times a year.

Smith used the numbers as guides rather than as absolutes. Most research groups recommend this approach in order to take into account the vagaries of individual businesses. "There are so many variables," says Robert Chalfin, president of the Chalfin Group. Chalfin adds that the survey process itself often skews information in favor of profitable companies. "They're happier to talk about their results," he says.

Smith has also become a lot more scrupulous in other areas, paying more attention to the company's weekly break-even point of $23,000 and charting sales in relation to it. He's learned that a big part of financial discipline is monitoring the simple things. "Losing money for a year is a good wake-up call," he says.

Source: Adapted from Ilan Mochari, "Significant Figures," at http://www.inc.com, July 1, 2000.

http://www.petragroup.com

The operating income return on investment for Bates & Associates for 2002 is as follows:

$$\text{Operating income return on investment} = \frac{\text{Operating income}}{\text{Total assets}}$$

$$= \frac{\$100{,}000}{\$920{,}000} = 0.1087, \text{ or } 10.87\%$$

Industry norm for operating income return on investment = 13.2%

It is evident that the firm's return on total invested capital is less than the average rate of return for the industry. For some reason, Bates & Associates is generating less operating income on each dollar of assets than are its competitors.

UNDERSTANDING THE RETURN-ON-INVESTMENT RESULTS The owners of Bates & Associates should not be satisfied with merely knowing that they are not earning a competitive return on the firm's assets. They should also want to know *why* the return is below average. To gain more understanding, the owners could separate the operating income return on investment into two important components: (1) the operating profit margin and (2) the total asset turnover.

operating profit margin the ratio of operating profits to sales, showing how well a firm manages its income statement

The **operating profit margin** is calculated as follows:

$$\text{Operating profit margin} = \frac{\text{Operating profits}}{\text{Sales}}$$

The operating profit margin shows how well a firm is managing its income statement—that is, how well a firm is managing the activities that affect its income. There are five factors, or driving forces, that affect the operating profit margin and, in turn, the operating income return on investment:

1. The number of units of product or service sold (volume)
2. The average selling price for each product or service unit (sales price)
3. The cost of manufacturing or acquiring the firm's product (cost of goods sold)
4. The ability to control general and administrative expenses (operating expenses)
5. The ability to control expenses in marketing and distributing the firm's product (operating expenses)

These influences should be apparent from an analysis of the income statement and consideration of what is involved in determining a firm's operating profits or income.

total asset turnover the ratio of sales to total assets, showing the efficiency with which a firm's assets are used to generate sales

The second component of a firm's operating income return on investment is the **total asset turnover,** which is calculated as follows:

$$\text{Total asset turnover} = \frac{\text{Sales}}{\text{Total assets}}$$

This financial ratio indicates how efficiently management is using the firm's assets to generate sales—that is, how well the firm is managing its balance sheet. If Company A can generate \$3 in sales with \$1 in assets while Company B generates \$2 in sales per asset dollar, then Company A is using its assets more efficiently in generating sales. This is a major determinant in the firm's return on investment.

By taking the product of the two foregoing financial ratios, we can restate the operating income return on investment:

$$\text{Operating income return on investment} = \frac{\text{Operating profits}}{\text{Sales}} \times \frac{\text{Sales}}{\text{Total assets}}$$

or

$$\text{OIROI} = \text{Operating profit margin} \times \text{Total asset turnover}$$

Separating the operating income return on investment into its two factors—the operating profit margin and total asset turnover—better isolates a firm's strengths and

weaknesses when it is attempting to identify ways to earn a competitive rate of return on its total invested capital.

Bates & Associates' operating profit margin and total asset turnover can be computed as follows:

$$\text{Operating profit margin} = \frac{\text{Operating profits}}{\text{Sales}}$$

$$= \frac{\$100{,}000}{\$850{,}000} = 0.1176, \text{ or } 11.76\%$$

$$\text{Total asset turnover} = \frac{\text{Sales}}{\text{Total assets}}$$

$$= \frac{\$850{,}000}{\$920{,}000} = 0.92$$

From data on industry norms,

$$\text{Industry norm for operating profit margin} = 11\%$$

$$\text{Industry norm for total asset turnover} = 1.20$$

Thus, for Bates & Associates,

$$\begin{matrix}\text{Operating income} \\ \text{return on investment}\end{matrix} = \begin{matrix}\text{Operating} \\ \text{profit margin}\end{matrix} \times \begin{matrix}\text{Total asset} \\ \text{turnover}\end{matrix}$$

or

$$\text{OIROI}_{\text{Bates}} = 0.1176 \times 0.92 = 0.1082, \text{ or } 10.82\%$$[4]

And for the industry,

$$\text{OIROI}_{\text{Ind}} = 0.11 \times 1.20 = 0.132, \text{ or } 13.2\%$$

Clearly, Bates & Associates is competitive when it comes to managing its income statement—keeping costs and expenses in line relative to sales—as reflected by the operating profit margin. In other words, its managers are performing satisfactorily in controlling the five driving forces of the operating profit margin. However, Bates & Associates' total asset turnover shows why its managers are less than competitive. The firm is not using its assets efficiently; the balance sheet is not being managed well. Bates's problem is that it generates $0.92 in sales per dollar of assets, while the competition produces $1.20 in sales from every dollar in assets.

The analysis should not stop here, however. It is clear that Bates's assets are not being used efficiently, but the next question should be "Which assets are the problem?" Is this firm overinvested in all assets or mainly in accounts receivable or inventory or fixed assets? To answer this question, we must examine the turnover ratio for each asset. The first two ratios—accounts receivable turnover and

fixed asset turnover a measure of the relationship of sales to fixed assets

inventory turnover—were calculated earlier. The third ratio, **fixed asset turnover,** is found by dividing sales by fixed assets. Thus, the three financial ratios are as follows:

Turnover Ratios			Bates & Associates	Industry Norm
Accounts receivable turnover	=	$\frac{\text{Credit sales}}{\text{Accounts receivable}}$	$\frac{\$850{,}000}{\$80{,}000} = 10.63$	10.43
Inventory turnover	=	$\frac{\text{Cost of goods sold}}{\text{Inventory}}$	$\frac{\$550{,}000}{\$220{,}000} = 2.50$	4.00
Fixed asset turnover	=	$\frac{\text{Sales}}{\text{Fixed assets}}$	$\frac{\$850{,}000}{\$570{,}000} = 1.49$	2.50

Bates's problems are now clearer. The firm has excessive inventories, as was evident earlier. Also, it is too heavily invested in fixed assets for the sales being produced. It appears that these two asset categories are not being managed well. Consequently, Bates & Associates is experiencing a lower-than-necessary operating income return on investment.

We have shown how to analyze a firm's ability to earn a satisfactory rate of return on its total investment capital. To this point, we have ignored the firm's decisions as to whether to use debt or equity financing and the consequence of such decisions on the owners' return on the equity investment. The analysis must now move to how the firm finances its investments.

How Is the Firm Financing Its Assets?

Measure a firm's use of debt or equity financing.

financial leverage the use of debt in financing a firm's assets

We'll return to the issue of profitability shortly. Now, however, let's consider how the firm is financed. Are the firm's assets financed to a greater extent by debt or by equity? Two ratios will be used to answer this question (although many others could be used). First, we must determine what percentage of the firm's assets is financed by debt—including both short-term and long-term debt. (The remaining percentage must be financed by equity.) As discussed in Chapter 13, the use of debt, or **financial leverage,** can increase a firm's return on equity, but with some risk involved. The debt ratio is calculated as follows:

$$\text{Debt ratio} = \frac{\text{Total debt}}{\text{Total assets}}$$

The same relationship can be stated as the *debt-equity ratio,* which is total debt divided by total equity, rather than total debt divided by total assets. Either ratio leads to the same conclusion.

For Bates & Associates in 2002, debt as a percentage of total assets is 33 percent, compared to an industry norm of 40 percent. The computation is as follows:

$$\text{Debt ratio} = \frac{\text{Total debt}}{\text{Total assets}}$$

$$= \frac{\$300{,}000}{\$920{,}000} = 0.33\text{, or } 33\%$$

$$\text{Industry norm for debt ratio} = 40\%$$

Thus, Bates & Associates uses somewhat less debt than the average firm in the industry, which means that it has less financial risk.

A second perspective on a firm's financing decisions can be gained by looking at the income statement. When a firm borrows money, it is required, at a minimum, to pay the interest on the debt. Thus, determining the amount of operating income available to pay the interest provides a firm with valuable information. Stated as a ratio, the computation shows the number of times the firm earns its interest. Thus, the **times interest earned ratio** is commonly used in examining a firm's debt position. This ratio is calculated as follows:

times interest earned ratio
the ratio of operating income to interest charges

$$\text{Times interest earned ratio} = \frac{\text{Operating income}}{\text{Interest expense}}$$

For Bates & Associates, the times interest earned ratio is as follows:

$$\text{Times interest earned ratio} = \frac{\text{Operating income}}{\text{Interest expense}}$$

$$= \frac{\$100{,}000}{\$20{,}000} = 5.00$$

Industry norm for times interest earned ratio = 4.00

Bates & Associates is better able to service its interest expense than most comparable firms. Remember, however, that interest is paid not with income but with cash. Also, the firm may be required to repay some of the debt principal as well as the interest. Thus, the times interest earned ratio is only a crude measure of a firm's capacity to service its debt. Nevertheless, it gives a general indication of the firm's debt capacity.

Are the Owners Receiving Adequate Return on Their Investment?

Evaluate the rate of return earned on the owners' investment.

The last question looks at the accounting return on the owners' investment, or **return on equity.** We must determine whether the earnings available to the firm's owners (or stockholders) are attractive when compared to the returns of owners of similar companies in the same industry. The return on the owners' equity capital can be measured as follows:

return on equity
the rate of return that owners earn on their investment

$$\text{Return on equity} = \frac{\text{Net income}}{\text{Common equity}}$$

The return on equity for Bates & Associates in 2002 is as follows:

$$\text{Return on equity} = \frac{\text{Net income}}{\text{Common equity}}$$

$$= \frac{\$60{,}000}{\$620{,}000} = 0.097, \text{ or } 9.7\%$$

Industry norm for return on equity = 12.5%

ENTREPRENEURSHIP TODAY

IN THE TRENCHES

IT TAKES MENTAL HEADGEAR TO USE FINANCIAL RATIOS

After graduating from college, Alan Wills and a friend established a firm to sell headgear and other accessories for winter sports. The idea originated from a class project they had worked on together. They first named the firm Do Rags but then later changed the name to Mental Headgear. After several years of operations, Wills bought out his partner with the idea of aggressively growing the business. At the time of the sale, the firm's financial statements were as shown on page 565.

What can be learned about Mental Headgear from the financial ratios?

1. The firm has $3.65 in current assets for every dollar in current debt, which means that the firm is relatively liquid by any standard.
2. Accounts receivable are collected every 68 days on average.
3. Inventory is turned over 5.55 times each year, or every 66 days.
4. The firm earns an operating income return on investment of about 24 percent by earning an 8 percent operating profit margin and by turning the firm's assets over almost three times per year. That is, for every $1 invested in the company, it earns $0.24—a relatively attractive return on investment but necessary to compensate Wills for the risk being taken.
5. The company is financed by about two-thirds debt and one-third owner's equity.
6. Wills's before tax return on equity is almost 66 percent, which represents a very high return on the owner's investment. This return, however, is a result of being in a relatively risky business and using a lot of debt financing. (Note that we have calculated the firm's return on equity on a before-tax basis. The firm is a Subchapter S corporation, and taxable income is reported by the owners on their personal tax return.)

While there is considerable risk in any small business, we can conclude, based on one year's information, that Mental Headgear *appears* to be a profitable opportunity for Wills.

Source: Personal communication with Alan Wills.

http://www.mentalheadgear.com

It appears that the owners of Bates & Associates are not receiving a return on their investment equivalent to that of owners of competing businesses. Why not? To answer this question, we have to understand the following:

1. The return on equity (ROE) will increase as the difference between the operating income return on investment (OIROI) and the interest rate paid for the use of debt financing *(i)* increases; that is, as (OIROI – *i*) increases, ROE increases.
2. As a firm's debt ratio (total debt ÷ total assets) increases, ROE will increase if OIROI is greater than *i*, but ROE will decrease if OIROI is less than *i*.

It is important for an entrepreneur to understand the foregoing relationships. Thus, you are encouraged to return to the illustrations in Chapter 13 (pages 323–327) of the effects on an owner's return on equity (net income ÷ common equity) of a firm's operating income return on investment (operating income ÷ total assets) and debt ratio (total debt ÷ total assets).

Balance Sheet

Current assets:		Current liabilities:	
Cash	$ 12,852	Accrued commissions payable	$ 20,176
Accounts receivable	272,706	Accounts payable	80,881
Sales rep receivables	2,676	Current notes payable	11,128
Payroll tax refund	325	Payroll taxes payable	4,919
Due from employees	1,645	Federal income tax payable	2,618
Bad checks receivable	549	Total current liabilities	$119,722
Inventory	146,452	Long-term notes payable	206,969
Total current assets	$ 437,205	Total liabilities	$326,691
Total fixed assets	$ 12,977	Stockholders' equity:	
Other assets:		Capital stock	$ 230
Other prepaid expenses	$ 12,867	Paid-in capital	145,590
Show exhibits	3,039	Retained earnings	(51,825)
Noncompete agreement	15,631	Prior period adjustments	(35,163)
Notes receivable	12,131	Current earnings	108,327
Total other assets	$ 43,668	Total stockholders' equity	$167,159
Total assets	$ 493,850	Total liabilities & equity	$493,850

Income Statement

Sales revenue	$1,470,344
Cost of goods sold	812,205
Gross profits on sales	$ 658,139
Operating expenses:	
Marketing expenses	$ 275,999
General and administrative expenses	265,616
Total operating expenses	$ 541,615
Operating income	$ 116,524
Other income	18,638
Interest expense	25,215

Financial Ratios

Current ratio	3.65
Acid-test ratio	2.43
Average collection period	67.70
Inventory turnover	5.55
Operating income return on investment	23.6%
Operating profit margin	7.9%
Total asset turnover	2.98
Fixed asset turnover	113.30
Debt ratio	0.66
Times interest earned ratio	4.62

In the case of Bates & Associates, we see that the firm has a lower return on equity in part because it is not as profitable in its operation as its competitors are. (Recall that the operating income return on investment was 10.87 percent for Bates & Associates, compared to 13.2 percent for the industry.) Also, Bates uses less debt than the average firm in the industry, causing its return on equity to be lower than that of other firms—provided, of course, that these firms are earning a return on their investments that exceeds the cost of debt (the interest rate). However, we should recognize that the use of less debt does reduce Bates's risk.

As a summary of financial ratios used in evaluating a firm's financial position, all ratios for Bates & Associates for 2002 are presented in Figure 22-4. The ratios are grouped by the issue being addressed: liquidity, operating profitability, financing, and owners' return on equity. Recall that the turnover ratios for accounts receivable and inventories are used for more than one purpose. These ratios have

FIGURE 22-4

Financial Ratio Analysis for Bates & Associates Leasing Company

Financial Ratios	Bates & Associates	Industry Norm
1. Firm liquidity		
Current ratio $= \dfrac{\text{Current assets}}{\text{Current liabilities}}$	$\dfrac{\$350{,}000}{\$100{,}000} = 3.50$	2.70
Acid-test ratio $= \dfrac{\text{Cash} + \text{Accounts receivable}}{\text{Current liabilities}}$	$\dfrac{\$50{,}000 + \$80{,}000}{\$100{,}000} = 1.30$	1.25
Average collection period $= \dfrac{\text{Accounts receivable}}{\text{Daily credit sales}}$	$\dfrac{\$80{,}000}{\$850{,}000 \div 365} = 34.35$	35.00
Accounts receivable turnover $= \dfrac{\text{Credit sales}}{\text{Accounts receivable}}$	$\dfrac{\$850{,}000}{\$80{,}000} = 10.63$	10.43
Inventory turnover $= \dfrac{\text{Cost of goods sold}}{\text{Inventory}}$	$\dfrac{\$550{,}000}{\$220{,}000} = 2.50$	4.00
2. Operating profitability		
Operating income return on investment $= \dfrac{\text{Operating income}}{\text{Total assets}}$	$\dfrac{\$100{,}000}{\$920{,}000} = 10.7\%$	13.2%
Operating profit margin $= \dfrac{\text{Operating profits}}{\text{Sales}}$	$\dfrac{\$100{,}000}{\$850{,}000} = 11.76\%$	11%
Total asset turnover $= \dfrac{\text{Sales}}{\text{Total assets}}$	$\dfrac{\$850{,}000}{\$920{,}000} = 0.92$	1.20
Accounts receivable turnover $= \dfrac{\text{Credit sales}}{\text{Accounts receivable}}$	$\dfrac{\$850{,}000}{\$80{,}000} = 10.63$	10.43
Inventory turnover $= \dfrac{\text{Cost of goods sold}}{\text{Inventory}}$	$\dfrac{\$550{,}000}{\$220{,}000} = 2.50$	4.00
Fixed asset turnover $= \dfrac{\text{Sales}}{\text{Fixed assets}}$	$\dfrac{\$850{,}000}{\$570{,}000} = 1.49$	1.58
3. Financing		
Debt ratio $= \dfrac{\text{Total debt}}{\text{Total assets}}$	$\dfrac{\$300{,}000}{\$920{,}000} = 33.00\%$	40%
Times interest earned ratio $= \dfrac{\text{Operating income}}{\text{Interest}}$	$\dfrac{\$100{,}000}{\$20{,}000} = \$5.00$	4.00
4. Return on equity		
Return on equity $= \dfrac{\text{Net income}}{\text{Common equity}}$	$\dfrac{\$60{,}000}{\$620{,}000} = 9.70\%$	12.5%

implications for both the firm's liquidity and its profitability; thus, they are listed in both areas. Note also that the figure shows both average collection period and accounts receivable turnover. Typically, only one of these ratios is used in analysis, since they represent different ways to measure the same thing. Presenting the ratios together, however, provides an overview of our discussion.

Looking Back

1 Identify the basic requirements for an accounting system.

- An accounting system structures the flow of financial information to provide a complete picture of financial activities.
- The system should be objective, follow generally accepted accounting principles, and supply information on a timely basis.
- In addition to the balance sheet and income statement, an accounting system should provide internal records that show accounts receivable, accounts payable, inventories, payroll, cash, and fixed assets, as well as insurance policies, leaseholds, and outside investments.

2 Explain two alternative accounting options.

- Accounting systems may use either cash or accrual methods and may be structured as either single-entry or double-entry systems.
- With the cash method of accounting, transactions are recorded only when cash is received or a payment is made; the accrual method of accounting matches revenue earned against expenses associated with it.
- A single-entry system is basically a checkbook system of receipts and disbursements; a double-entry system of accounting incorporates journals and ledgers and requires that each transaction be recorded twice.

3 Describe the purpose of and procedures related to internal control.

- Internal control refers to a system of checks and balances designed to safeguard a firm's assets and enhance the accuracy of financial statements.
- Some examples of internal control procedures are separation of employees' duties, limiting access to accounting records and computer facilities, and safeguarding blank checks.
- Building internal controls within a small business is difficult but important.

4 Evaluate a firm's liquidity.

- Liquidity is a firm's capacity to meet its short-term obligations.
- One way of measuring a firm's liquidity is to compare its liquid assets (cash, accounts receivable, and inventories) and its short-term debt, using the current ratio or the acid-test ratio.
- A second way to measure liquidity is to determine the time it takes to convert accounts receivable and inventories into cash, by computing the accounts receivable turnover and the inventory turnover.

5 Assess a firm's operating profitability.

- Operating profitability is evaluated by determining if the firm is earning a good return on its total assets, through computation of the operating income return on investment.
- The operating income return on investment can be separated into two components—the operating profit margin and the total asset turnover—to gain more insight into the firm's operating profitability.

6 Measure a firm's use of debt or equity financing.

- The debt ratio can be used to measure how much debt a firm uses in its financing mix.
- A firm's ability to cover interest charges on its debt can be measured by the times interest earned ratio.

7 Evaluate the rate of return earned on the owners' investment.

- Owners' return on investment (return on equity) is measured by dividing net income by the common equity invested in the business.
- The return on equity is a function of (1) the firm's operating income return on investment less the interest paid and (2) the amount of debt used relative to the amount of equity financing.

Key Terms

single-entry system, p. 550
double-entry system, p. 550
internal control, p. 551
financial ratios, p. 552
liquidity, p. 553
acid-test ratio (quick ratio), p. 554
average collection period, p. 556
accounts receivable turnover, p. 556
inventory turnover, p. 556
operating income return on investment (OIROI), p. 557
operating profit margin, p. 560
total asset turnover, p. 560
fixed asset turnover, p. 562
financial leverage, p. 562
times interest earned ratio, p. 563
return on equity, p. 563

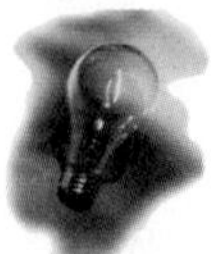

Discussion Questions

1. Explain the accounting concept that income is realized when earned, whether or not it has been received in cash.
2. Should entrepreneurs have an outside specialist set up an accounting system for their startup or do it themselves? Why?
3. What are the primary types of records required in a sound accounting system?
4. What are the major advantages of a double-entry accounting system over a single-entry system?
5. What is liquidity? Differentiate between the two approaches given in this chapter to measure liquidity.
6. Explain the following ratios:
   a. Operating profit margin
   b. Total asset turnover
   c. Times interest earned
7. What is the relationship among these ratios: operating income return on investment, operating profit margin, and total asset turnover?
8. What would be the difference between using operating profit and using net income when calculating a firm's return on investment?
9. What is financial leverage? When should it be used and when should it be avoided? Why?
10. What determines a firm's return on equity?

YOU MAKE THE CALL

SITUATION 1

In 2002, Carter Dalton purchased the Baugh Company. Although the firm has consistently earned profits, little cash has been available for other than business needs. Before purchasing Baugh, Dalton thought that cash flows were generally equal to profits plus depreciation. However, this does not seem to be the case. The industry norms for the financial ratios and the financial statements (in thousands) for the Baugh Company, 2001–2002, follow.

Balance Sheet (in thousands)

	2001	2002
ASSETS		
Current assets:		
Cash	$ 8	$ 10
Accounts receivable	15	20
Inventory	22	25
Total current assets	$45	$ 55
Fixed assets:		
Gross plant and equipment	$50	$ 55
Accumulated depreciation	15	20
Net fixed assets	$35	$ 35
Other assets	12	10
TOTAL ASSETS	$92	$100
DEBT (LIABILITIES) AND EQUITY		
Current liabilities:		
Accounts payable	$10	$ 12
Accruals	7	8
Short-term notes	5	5
Total current liabilities	$22	$ 25
Long-term liabilities	15	15
Total liabilities	$37	$ 40
Total stockholders' equity	55	60
TOTAL DEBT AND EQUITY	$92	$100

Income Statement, 2002 (in thousands)

Sales revenue		$175
Cost of goods sold		105
Gross profit on sales		$ 70
Operating expenses:		
Marketing expenses	$26	
General and administrative expenses	20	
Depreciation expense	5	
Total operating expenses		$ 51
Operating income		$ 19
Interest expense		3
Earnings before taxes		$ 16
Income tax		8
Net income		$ 8

Financial Ratios	Industry Norms
Current ratio	2.50
Acid-test ratio	1.50
Average collection period	30.00
Inventory turnover	6.00
Debt ratio	50.0%
Operating income return on investment	16.0%
Operating profit margin	8.0%
Total asset turnover	2.00
Fixed asset turnover	7.00
Times interest earned ratio	5.00
Return on equity	14.0%

Question 1 Why doesn't Dalton have cash for personal needs? (As part of your analysis, measure cash flows, as discussed in Chapter 12.)

Question 2 Evaluate the Baugh Company's financial performance, given the financial ratios for the industry.

SITUATION 2

The following financial statements are for the Cherokee Communications Corporation. The company provides pay phone service at many of the small convenience stores in the southwestern United States, primarily in Texas and New Mexico. The business was "meeting plan" until 2002, when a problem developed.

Balance Sheet

	2001	2002
ASSETS		
Current assets:		
Cash and cash equivalents	$ 668,778	$ 592,491
Accounts receivable	4,453,192	3,888,621
Inventories	137,036	112,699
Prepaid expenses and other current assets	411,990	407,274
Total current assets	$ 5,670,996	$ 5,001,085
Fixed assets:		
Property, plant and equipment (net)	$12,935,453	$16,466,001
Site licenses	1,941,467	3,771,571
Investments in affiliates	164,549	251,672
Total fixed assets	$15,041,469	$20,489,244
Other assets	681,754	455,488
TOTAL ASSETS	$21,394,219	$25,945,817
DEBT (LIABILITIES) AND EQUITY		
Current liabilities:		
Notes payable	$ 659,604	
Current portion of other notes payable	1,491,767	$ 3,320,197
Current portion of capital lease obligations	1,094,381	668,826
Accounts payable	310,358	835,384
Accrued telecommunications and other expenses	2,971,935	3,036,633
Income taxes payable	256,140	475,945
Total current liabilities	$ 6,784,185	$ 8,336,985

Long-term liabilities:		
Notes payable, less current portion	$ 6,605,835	$10,030,963
Capital lease obligations	780,593	56,219
Deferred income tax liability	342,359	306,021
Total long-term liabilities	$ 7,728,787	$10,393,203
Preferred stock	$ 2,400,000	$ 2,400,000
Common stockholders' equity:		
Common stock	$ 1,438,903	$ 1,438,903
Additional paid-in capital	10,630	10,630
Retained earnings	3,031,714	3,366,096
Total common stockholders' equity	$ 4,481,247	$ 4,815,629
TOTAL DEBT AND EQUITY	$ 21,394,219	$25,945,817

Income Statements for Cherokee Communications, Inc.

	2001	2002
Sales revenue:		
Pay phone coin calls	$14,036,665	$17,615,059
Automated operator, routed calls	17,049,394	15,932,154
Other	505,581	1,363,738
Total revenues	$31,591,640	$34,910,951
Operating expenses:		
Telephone charges	$ 7,851,842	$ 9,078,851
Commissions	4,909,445	5,627,288
Telecommunications fees	1,821,930	1,519,095
Depreciation and amortization	4,298,090	5,353,797
Field operations personnel	2,016,935	2,988,456
Chargebacks and doubtful accounts	1,104,896	1,111,857
General and administrative expenses	5,520,405	6,435,919
Total operating expenses	$27,523,543	$32,115,263
Operating income	$ 4,068,097	$ 2,795,688
Other income (expenses):		
Interest expense	$(1,631,416)	$(1,816,222)
Interest income	57,278	5,069
Losses on affiliates	(34,608)	(108,556)
Unusual gains	1,160,238	27,234
Total other income (expenses)	$ (448,508)	$(1,892,475)
Income before taxes	$ 3,619,589	$ 903,213
Provision for income taxes	1,399,140	424,831
Net income	$ 2,220,449	$ 478,382

Question 1 Using financial ratios, compare the firm's financial performance for 2001 and 2002.

Question 2 What do you think might have happened from 2001 to 2002?

SITUATION 3

Alibek Iskakov has opened a small cafe, Oasis, in Kokshetau, a city in Kazakhstan. A new business in operation for only a short period on a part-time basis in a less-developed country, it has small revenues. Nevertheless, ratio analysis can be used for a quick check on its status. The following amounts are given in tenge (1 dollar = 120 tenge), the Kazakhstan currency.

Balance Sheet

ASSETS	
Current assets:	
Cash	$ 22,000
Accounts receivable	2,500
Inventories	7,300
Prepaid expenses	6,500
Total current assets	$ 38,300
Fixed assets:	
Plant and equipment	$400,000
Accumulated depreciation	–400
Net plant and equipment	$399,600
TOTAL ASSETS	$437,900
DEBT (LIABILITIES) AND EQUITY	
Current liabilities:	
Accounts payable	$ 7,000
Income tax payable	5,500
Accrued wages and salaries	7,000
Total current liabilities	$ 19,500
Equity	418,400
TOTAL DEBT AND EQUITY	$437,900

Income Statement

Sales	$150,000
Cost of goods sold	80,000
Total revenues	$ 70,000
Operating expenses:	
Selling expenses	$ 5,000
General & administrative expenses	12,000
Other expenses	3,500
Total operating expenses	$ 20,500
Earnings before taxes	$ 49,500
Income tax (30%)	14,850
Net income	$ 34,650

Source: This case was prepared by Dr. Aigul N. Toxanova and Yuliya L. Tkacheva, Kokshetau Institute of Economics and Management, Kokshetau, Kazakhstan.

Question 1 Compute the firm's accounts receivable turnover. Do you think that this ratio is relevant for this business? Why or why not?

Question 2 What is the firm's operating income return on investment? Without the benefit of an industry norm for comparison, do you think that this is a good return on investment?

Question 3 What is the firm's return on equity? How does debt financing affect this return?

EXPERIENTIAL EXERCISES

1. Interview a local CPA who consults with small firms on small business accounting systems. Report to the class on the levels of accounting knowledge the CPA's clients appear to possess.
2. Contact several very small businesses and explain your interest in their accounting systems. Report to the class on their level of sophistication—for example, whether they use a single-entry system, a computer, or an outside professional.
3. Find out whether your public or university library subscribes to Robert Morris Associates or Dun & Bradstreet. If the library does not subscribe to either of these two financial services, ask whether it subscribes to another service that provides industry norms. When you find a source, select an industry and bring a copy of its ratios to class for discussion.
4. Locate a small company in your community that will allow you to perform a financial ratio analysis on its financial statements. You will need to decide which industry's data to use for comparative purposes and then find the norms in the library. You may need to promise the company's owners that you will change all names on statements to provide confidentiality.

EXPLORING THE WEB

1. The Kauffman Center for Entrepreneurial Leadership offers a free service called Business EKG to help small businesses see how they measure up according to industry benchmarks. Access the site at **http://www.BusinessEKG.com**. Use the example of Mental Headgear, given on pages 564–565 of this chapter.
   a. Begin the tutorial. Find the four-digit SIC code for manufacturers of hats.
   b. Continue to enter figures from the example. Assume that Mental Headgear has 25 employees and an annual growth rate of 10%.
   c. Print the results.
2. *PC Magazine's* Web site at **http://www.pcmag.com** offers independent reviews of software and hardware.
   a. Examine the reviews for accounting software. Choose View All Guides under Product Guides, and click Accounting. Print the list of product names and ratings.
   b. Read the review for the PC Editor's choice. What is the name of the software? How much does it cost? What features of the package are particularly good?
   c. Access the software company's Web site for the chosen product. If the company offers you a chance to test drive the software, use it and print a sample report.

CASE 22

ARTHO, INC. (p. 697)

This case requires the student to identify a company's financial strengths and weaknesses by using financial ratios and cash flow computations across time to compare the firm's performance to that of a similar firm.

Alternative Cases for Chapter 22:

Case 12, "Stegmart," p. 672
Case 13, "Calvert Toyota," p. 674

chapter 23

Managing the Firm's Assets

In the Spotlight

Integration Logic Inc.

Many entrepreneurs today spend so much time focusing on raising capital that they forget they have a business to run. Lance Miller and his partners, Phil Underhill and Mohammed Kabir, manage Integration Logic Inc. with a different philosophy. The company was started in the fall of 1998, when Miller combined his business experience with the technological skills of Underhill and Kabir. They began providing customizable productivity and e-commerce applications for Internet, intranet, and extranet users.

What distinguishes Integration Logic Inc. from other companies is that from the start it focused on techniques to control profitability and cash flows, rather than searching for investors to raise capital. Miller said, "We get scared when we look at companies that have raised money and are now burning through it in situations where their business fundamentals are still weak. At the end of the day, how many of them are still going to be around?"

Miller and his partners are keeping their sights set on long-term success and use three business fundamentals to help them reach their goals. First, the company must achieve and maintain profitability from day one. Second, cash flows must remain positive. Third, real company value must be created by building customer and product bases. ◆

Source: Jill Andresky Fraser, "Capital Steps," *Inc.*, Vol. 21, No. 5 (April 1999), pp. 119–120.

LOOKING AHEAD

After studying this chapter, you should be able to

1. *Describe the working-capital cycle of a small business.*
2. *Identify the important issues in managing a firm's cash flows.*
3. *Explain the key issues in managing accounts receivable, inventory, and accounts payable.*
4. *Discuss the techniques commonly used in making capital budgeting decisions.*
5. *Determine the appropriate cost of capital to be used in discounted cash flow techniques.*
6. *Describe the capital budgeting practices of small firms.*

Chapter 22 focused on managing a firm's income statement carefully—that is, managing expenses relative to the firm's level of sales. Owners and managers must also effectively administer the firm's balance sheet by managing both investments in working capital and long-term investments. This chapter considers the investment decisions of a firm, discussing first the management of working capital—that is, the management of short-term assets and liabilities—and then the process for making decisions on long-term investments, such as those for equipment and buildings.

THE WORKING-CAPITAL CYCLE

1 *Describe the working-capital cycle of a small business.*

working-capital management the management of current assets and current liabilities

Ask the owner of a small business about financial management and you will hear about the joys and tribulations of managing cash, accounts receivable, inventories, and accounts payable. **Working-capital management**—managing short-term assets (current assets) and short-term sources of financing (current liabilities)—is extremely important to most small firms. In fact, there may be no financial discipline that is more important, and yet more misunderstood. Good business opportunities can be irreparably damaged by ineffective management of a firm's short-term assets and liabilities.

The key issue in working-capital management is to avoid running out of cash. And understanding how to manage cash effectively requires knowledge of the working-capital cycle. "Business owners should be thinking about this issue from day one," says Stephen King, president of Virtual Growth, a New York City-based financial-consulting firm. Many entrepreneurs overlook effective cash management because they have other issues on their minds. "So long as more money seems to be coming into the business than going out, many company owners don't give cash management a second thought. And that leaves them vulnerable to all kinds of cash flow dangers."[1]

http://www.virtualgrowth.com

net operating working capital the sum of a firm's current assets (cash, accounts receivable, and inventories) less accounts payable and accruals

working-capital cycle the daily flow of resources through a firm's working-capital accounts

Net operating working capital consists primarily of three assets—cash, accounts receivable, and inventories—less two sources of short-term debt—accounts payable and accruals.[2] A firm's **working-capital cycle** is the flow of resources through these accounts as part of the firm's day-to-day operations. The steps in a firm's working-capital cycle are as follows:

Step 1. Purchase or produce inventory for sale, which increases accounts payable—assuming the purchase is a credit purchase—and increases inventories on hand.

Step 2. a. Sell the inventory for cash, which increases cash, or

b. Sell the inventory on credit, which increases accounts receivable.

Step 3. a. Pay the accounts payable, which decreases accounts payable and decreases cash.

b. Pay operating expenses and taxes, which decreases cash.

Step 4. Collect the accounts receivable when due, which decreases accounts receivable and increases cash.

Step 5. Begin the cycle again.

Figure 23-1 shows this cycle graphically.

Depending on the industry, the working-capital cycle may be long or short. For example, it is short and repeated quickly in the grocery business; it is longer and re-

FIGURE 23-1 *Working-Capital Cycle*

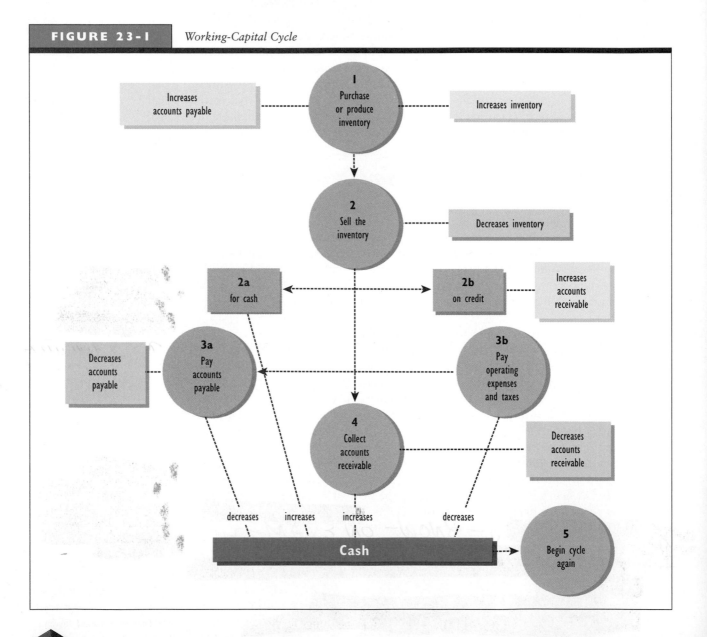

Increases accounts payable

1 Purchase or produce inventory

Increases inventory

2 Sell the inventory

Decreases inventory

2a for cash

2b on credit

Increases accounts receivable

Decreases accounts payable

3a Pay accounts payable

3b Pay operating expenses and taxes

4 Collect accounts receivable

Decreases accounts receivable

decreases increases increases decreases

Cash

5 Begin cycle again

peated more slowly in an automobile dealership. Whatever the industry, however, management should be working continuously to shorten the cycle.

The Timing and Size of Working-Capital Investments

It is imperative that owners of small companies understand the working-capital cycle, in terms of both the timing of investments and the size of the investment required (for example, the amounts necessary to maintain inventories and accounts receivable). The owner's failure to understand these relationships underlies many of the financial problems of small companies.

Figure 23-2 shows the chronological sequence of a hypothetical working-capital cycle. The time line reflects the order in which events unfold, beginning with an investment in inventory and ending with collection of accounts receivable. The key dates in the figure are as follows:

Day a. Inventory is ordered in anticipation of future sales.

Day b. Inventory is received.

Day c. Inventory is sold on credit.

Day d. Accounts payable come due and are paid.

Day e. Accounts receivable are collected.

The investing and financing implications of the working-capital cycle reflected in Figure 23-2 are as follows:

- Money is invested in inventory from day *b* to day *c*.
- The supplier provides financing for the inventories from day *b* to day *d*.
- Money is invested in accounts receivable from day *c* to day *e*.

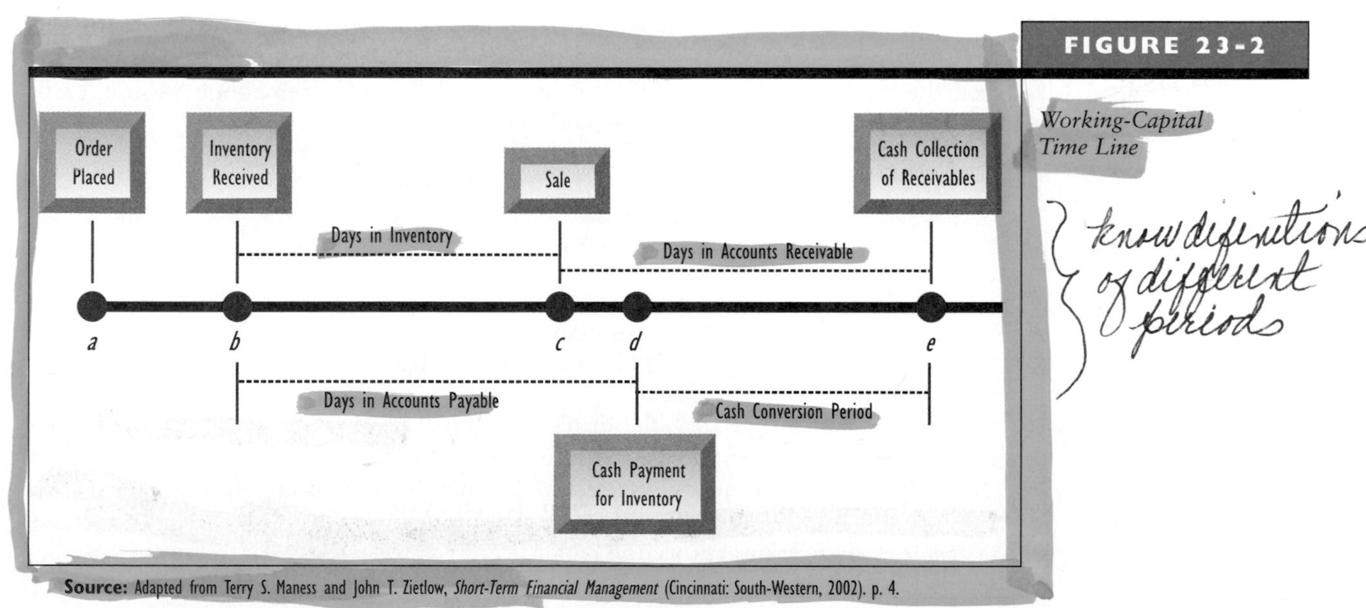

FIGURE 23-2

Working-Capital Time Line

Source: Adapted from Terry S. Maness and John T. Zietlow, *Short-Term Financial Management* (Cincinnati: South-Western, 2002). p. 4.

cash conversion period
the time required to convert paid-for inventories and accounts receivable into cash

- Financing of the firm's investment in accounts receivable must be provided from day *d* to day *e*. This time span, called the **cash conversion period,** represents the number of days required to complete the working-capital cycle, which ends with the conversion of accounts receivable into cash. During this period, the firm no longer has the benefit of supplier financing (accounts payable). The longer this period lasts, the greater the potential cash flow problems for the firm.

Examples of Working-Capital Management

Figure 23-3 offers two examples of working-capital management by firms with contrasting working-capital cycles: Pokey, Inc. and Quick Turn Company. On August 15, both firms buy inventory that they receive on August 31, but the similarity ends there. Pokey, Inc. must pay its supplier for the inventory on September 30, before eventually reselling it on October 15. It collects from its customers on November 30. As you can see, Pokey, Inc. must pay for the inventory two months prior to collecting from its customers. Its cash conversion period—the time required to convert the paid-for inventories and accounts receivable into cash—is 60 days. The firm's managers must find a way to finance this investment in inventories and accounts receivable, or else they will experience cash flow problems. Furthermore, although increased sales should produce higher profits, they will compound the cash flow problem.

Now consider Quick Turn Company's working-capital cycle, shown in the bottom portion of Figure 23-3. Compared to Pokey, Quick Turn Company has an enviable working-capital position. By the time Quick Turn must pay for its inventory purchases (October 31), it has sold its product (September 30) and collected from its customers (October 31). Thus, there is no cash conversion period because the supplier is essentially financing Quick Turn's working-capital needs.

To gain an even better understanding of the working-capital cycle, let's see what happens to Pokey's balance sheet and income statement. To do so, we will need more information about the firm's activities. A month-by-month listing of its activities and their effect on its balance sheet follow. Pay close attention to the firm's working capital, especially its cash balances.

July: Pokey, Inc. is a new company, having started operations in July with $1,000, financed by $300 in long-term debt and $700 in common stock. At the outset, the owner purchased $600 in fixed assets, leaving the remaining $400 in cash. At this point, the balance sheet would appear as follows:

Cash	$ 400
Fixed assets	600
TOTAL ASSETS	$1,000
Long-term debt	300
Common stock	700
TOTAL DEBT AND EQUITY	$1,000

August: On August 15, the firm's managers ordered $500 in inventory, which was received on August 31 (see Figure 23-3). The supplier allowed Pokey 30 days from the time the inventory was received to pay for the purchase; thus, inventories and accounts payable both increased by $500 when the inventory was received. As a result of these transactions, the balance sheet would appear as follows:

FIGURE 23-3

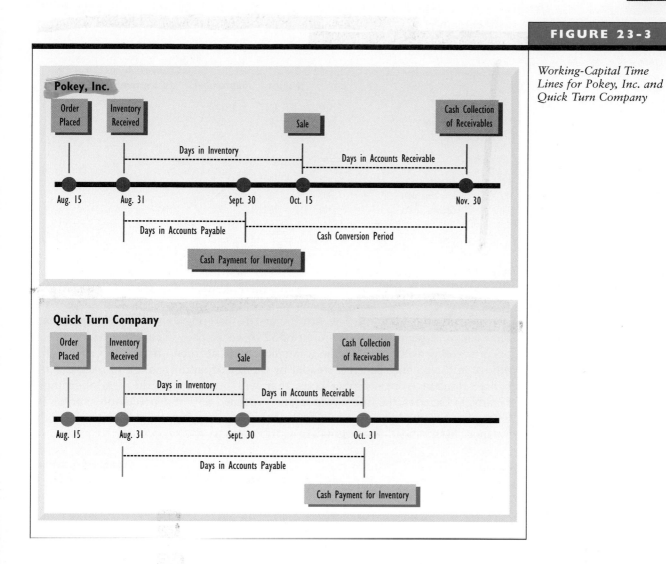

Working-Capital Time Lines for Pokey, Inc. and Quick Turn Company

	July	August	Changes: July to August
Cash	$ 400	$ 400	
Inventory	0	500	+$500
Fixed assets	600	600	
TOTAL ASSETS	$1,000	$1,500	
Accounts payable	$ 0	$ 500	+$500
Long-term debt	300	300	
Common stock	700	700	
TOTAL DEBT AND EQUITY	$1,000	$1,500	

So far, so good—no cash problems yet.

September: On September 30, the firm paid for the inventory; both cash and accounts payable decreased by $500.

	July	August	September	Changes: August to September
Cash	$ 400	$ 400	$ (100)	−$500
Inventory	0	500	500	
Fixed assets	600	600	600	
TOTAL ASSETS	$1,000	$1,500	$1,000	
Accounts payable	$ 0	$ 500	$ 0	−$500
Long-term debt	300	300	300	
Common stock	700	700	700	
TOTAL DEBT AND EQUITY	$1,000	$1,500	$1,000	

Now Pokey, Inc. has a cash flow problem in the form of a cash deficit of $100.

October: October was a busy month for Pokey. On October 15, merchandise was sold on credit for $900; sales (in the income statement) and accounts receivable increased by that amount. The firm incurred operating expenses (selling and administrative expenses) in the amount of $250, to be paid in early November; thus, operating expenses (in the income statement) and accrued operating expenses (liabilities in the balance sheet) increased by $250. (An additional $25 in accrued expenses resulted from accruing taxes that will be owed on the firm's earnings.) Finally, in October, the firm's accountants recorded $50 in depreciation expense (to be reported in the income statement), resulting in accumulated depreciation on the balance sheet of $50. The results are as follows:

	July	August	September	October	Changes: September to October
Cash	$ 400	$ 400	$ (100)	$ (100)	
Accounts receivable	0	0	0	900	+$900
Inventory	0	500	500	0	−500
Fixed assets	600	600	600	600	
Accumulated depreciation	0	0	0	(50)	−50
TOTAL ASSETS	$1,000	$1,500	$1,000	$1,350	
Accounts payable	$ 0	$ 500	$ 0	$ 0	
Accrued operating expenses	0	0	0	250	+$250
Income tax payable	0	0	0	25	+25
Long-term debt	300	300	300	300	
Common stock	700	700	700	700	
Retained earnings	0	0	0	75	+75
TOTAL DEBT AND EQUITY	$1,000	$1,500	$1,000	$1,350	

The October balance sheet shows all the activities just described, but there is one more change in the balance sheet: It now shows $75 in retained earnings, which had been $0 in the prior balance sheets. As you will see shortly, this amount represents the firm's income. Note also that Pokey, Inc. continues to be overdrawn by $100 on its cash. None of the events in October affected the firm's cash balance. All the transactions were the result of accruals recorded by the firm's accountant, off-

setting entries to the income statement. The relationship between the balance sheet and the income statement is as follows:

Change in the Balance Sheet	Effect on Income Statement	
Increase in accounts receivable of $900	Sales	$900
Decrease in inventories of $500	Cost of goods sold	$500
Increase in accrued operating expenses of $250	Operating expenses	$250
Increase in accumulated depreciation of $50	Depreciation expense	$50
Increase in accrued taxes of $25	Tax expense	$25

November: In November, the accrued expenses were paid, which resulted in a $250 decrease in cash along with an equal decrease in accrued expenses. At the end of November, the accounts receivable were collected, yielding a $900 increase in cash and a $900 decrease in accounts receivable. Thus, net cash increased by $650. The final series of balance sheets is as follows:

	July	August	September	October	November	Changes: October to November
Cash	$ 400	$ 400	$ (100)	$ (100)	$ 550	+$650
Accounts receivable	0	0	0	900	0	−900
Inventory	0	500	500	0	0	
Fixed assets	600	600	600	600	600	
Accumulated depreciation	0	0	0	(50)	(50)	
TOTAL ASSETS	$1,000	$1,500	$1,000	$1,350	$1,100	
Accounts payable	$ 0	$ 500	$ 0	$ 0	$ 0	
Accrued operating expenses	0	0	0	250	0	−$250
Income tax payable	0	0	0	25	25	
Long-term debt	300	300	300	300	300	
Common stock	700	700	700	700	700	
Retained earnings	0	0	0	75	75	
TOTAL DEBT AND EQUITY	$1,000	$1,500	$1,000	$1,350	$1,100	

As a result of the firm's activities, Pokey, Inc. reported $75 in profits for the period. The income statement for the period ending November 30 is as follows:

Sales revenue		$900
Cost of goods sold		500
Gross profit		$400
Operating expenses:		
Cash expense	$250	
Depreciation expense	50	
Total operating expenses		$300
Operating income		$100
Income tax (25%)		25
Net income		$ 75

The $75 in profits is reflected as retained earnings on the balance sheet to make the numbers match.

The somewhat contrived example of Pokey, Inc. illustrates an important point that deserves repeating: An owner of a small firm must understand the working-capital cycle of his or her firm. Although the business was profitable, Pokey ran out of cash in September and October (−$100) and didn't recover until November, when the accounts receivable were collected. This 60-day cash conversion period represents a critical time when the firm must find another source of financing if it is to survive. Moreover, when sales are ongoing throughout the year, the problem can be an unending one, unless financing is found to support the firm's sales. Also, as much as possible, a firm should arrange for sooner payment by customers (preferably in advance) and negotiate longer payment schedules with suppliers (preferably over several months).

An understanding of the working-capital cycle provides a basis for examining the primary components of working-capital management: cash flows, accounts receivable, inventory, and accounts payable.

Managing Cash Flows

2
Identify the important issues in managing a firm's cash flows.

It should be clear to you by now that the core of working-capital management is monitoring cash flows. Cash is constantly moving through a business. It flows in as customers pay for products or services, and it flows out as payments are made to suppliers. The typically uneven nature of cash inflows and outflows makes it imperative that they be properly understood and managed.

The Nature of Cash Flows

A firm's net cash flow may be determined quite simply by examining its bank account. Monthly cash deposits less checks written during the same period equal a firm's net cash flow. If deposits for a month add up to $100,000 and checks total $80,000, the firm has a net positive cash flow of $20,000. The cash balance at the end of the month is $20,000 higher than it was at the beginning of the month. Figure 23-4 graphically represents the flow of cash through a business; it includes not only the cash flows that arise as part of the firm's working-capital cycle (shown in Figure 23-1), but other cash flows as well, such as those from purchasing fixed assets and issuing stock. More specifically, cash sales, collection of accounts receivable, payment of expenses, and payment for inventory reflect the inflows and outflows of cash that relate to the working-capital cycle, while the other items in Figure 23-4 represent other, longer-term cash flows.

It is necessary in calculating net cash flow to distinguish between sales revenue and cash receipts—they are seldom the same. Revenue is recorded at the time a sale is made but does not affect cash flows at that time unless the sale is a cash sale. Cash receipts, on the other hand, are recorded when money actually flows into the firm, often a month or two after the sale. Similarly, it is necessary to distinguish between expenses and disbursements. Expenses occur when materials, labor, or other items are used. Payments (disbursements) for these expense items may be made later when checks are issued.

Net Cash Flow and Net Profit

In view of the distinguishing characteristics just noted, it should come as no surprise that net cash flow and net profit are different. Net cash flow is the difference between cash inflows and outflows. Net profit, in contrast, is the difference between

FIGURE 23-4

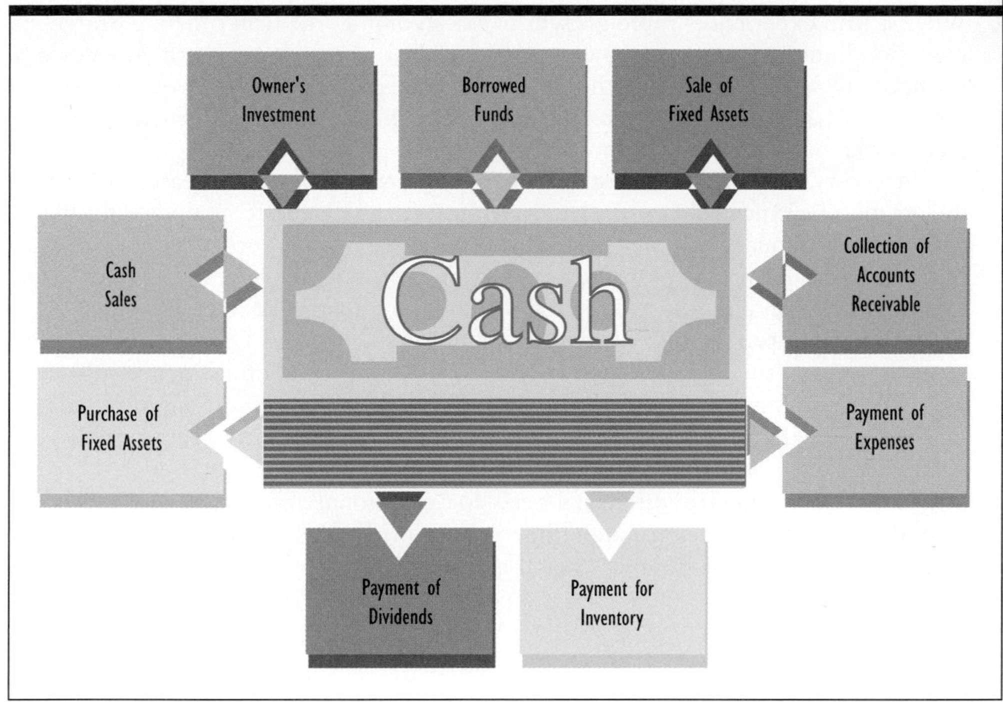

Flow of Cash Through a Business

revenue and expenses. Failure to understand this distinction can destroy a small firm's financial well-being.

One reason for the difference is the uneven timing of cash disbursements and the expensing of those disbursements. For example, the merchandise purchased by a retail store may be paid for (a cash disbursement) before it is sold (when it becomes recognized as a cost of goods sold). On the other hand, labor may be used (an expense) before a paycheck is written (a cash disbursement). In the case of a major cash outlay for a building or equipment, the disbursement shows up immediately as a cash outflow. However, it is recognized as an expense only as the building or equipment is depreciated over a period of years.

Similarly, the uneven timing of sales revenue and cash receipts occurs because of the extension of credit. When a sale is made, the transaction is recorded as revenue; the cash receipt is recorded when payment for the account receivable is received, often 30 or 60 days later. We observed this fact earlier as part of our discussion of the working-capital cycle.

Furthermore, some cash receipts are not revenue and never become revenue. When a firm borrows money from a bank, for example, it receives cash without receiving revenue. When the principal is repaid to the bank some months later, cash is disbursed. However, no expense is recorded, because the firm is merely returning money that was borrowed. Any interest paid to the bank on the loan would, of course, constitute both an expense when owed and a cash disbursement when paid.

It is imperative that small firms manage cash flows as carefully as they manage revenue, expenses, and profits. Otherwise, they may find themselves insolvent, while showing handsome paper profits. More businesses fail because of lack of cash than because of lack of profits.

The Growth Trap

growth trap
a cash shortage resulting from rapid growth

When a firm experiences rapid growth in sales volume, the firm's income statement may simultaneously reflect growing profits. However, rapid growth in sales and profits may be hazardous to the firm's cash. A **growth trap** can occur, because growth tends to soak up additional cash more rapidly than such cash can be generated in the form of additional profits.

Inventory, for example, must be expanded as sales volume increases; additional dollars must be expended for merchandise or raw materials to accommodate the higher level of sales. Similarly, accounts receivable must be expanded proportionally to meet the increased sales volume. Obviously, a growing, profitable business can quickly find itself in a financial bind—growing profitably, while going broke at the bank.

The growth problem is particularly acute for small firms. Quite simply, it's easier to increase a small firm's sales by 50 percent than those of a Fortune 500 firm. This fact, combined with the difficulty a small firm may have in obtaining funds externally, highlights the detrimental effect that rapid growth can have on small businesses if cash is not managed carefully.

In short, a high-growth firm's need for additional financing may exceed its available resources, even though the firm is profitable. Without additional resources, the firm's cash balances may decline sharply, leaving it in a precarious financial position.

Cash Budgeting

cash budget
a planning document strictly concerned with the receipt and payment of dollars

Cash budgets are tools for managing cash flows. These budgets are concerned specifically with dollars received and paid out. In contrast, income statements take items into consideration before they affect cash—for example, expenses that have been incurred but not yet paid and income earned but not yet received.

By using a cash budget, an entrepreneur can predict and plan the cash flows of a business. *No single planning document is more important in the life of a small company, either for avoiding cash flow problems when cash runs short or for anticipating short-term investment opportunities if excess cash becomes available.*

To better understand the process of preparing a cash budget, consider the example of the Chai Corporation, a manufacturer of containers. Its owner, Camaron Chai, wishes to develop a monthly cash budget for the next quarter (July through September) and has made the following forecasts.

- Historical and predicted sales:

Historical Sales		Predicted Sales	
April	$ 80,000	July	$130,000
May	100,000	August	130,000
June	120,000	September	120,000
		October	100,000

- Of the firm's sales dollars, 40 percent are collected the month of the sale, 30 percent one month after the sale, and the remaining 30 percent two months after the sale.
- Inventory is purchased one month before the sales month and is paid for in the month in which it is sold. Purchases equal 80 percent of projected sales for the next month.

- Cash expenses have been estimated for wages and salaries, rent, utilities, and tax payments, all of which are reflected in the cash budget.
- The firm's beginning cash balance for the budget period is $5,000. This amount should be maintained as a minimum cash balance.
- The firm has a $20,000 line of credit with its bank at an interest rate of 12 percent annually (1 percent monthly). The interest owed is to be paid monthly.
- Interest on a $40,000 bank note (with the principal due in December) is payable at an 8 percent annual rate for the three-month period ending in September.

Based on this information, Chai has used a computer spreadsheet to prepare a monthly cash budget for the three-month period ending September 30. Table 23-1 shows the results of her computations, which involved the following steps:

Step 1. Determine the amount of collections each month, based on the projected collection patterns.

Step 2. Estimate the amount and timing of the following cash disbursements:

a. Inventory purchases and payments. The amount of the purchases is shown in the boxed area of the table, with payments made one month later.

b. Rent, wages, taxes, utilities, and interest on the long-term note

c. Interest to be paid on any outstanding short-term borrowing. For example, the table shows that for the month of July the Chai Corporation will need to borrow $10,600 to prevent the firm's cash balance from falling below the $5,000 acceptable minimum. Assume that the money will be borrowed at the end of July and that the interest will be payable at the end of August. The amount of the interest in August is $106, or 1 percent of the $10,600 cumulative short-term debt outstanding at the end of July.

Step 3. Calculate the net change in cash (cash receipts less cash disbursements).

Step 4. Determine the beginning cash balance (ending cash balance from the prior month).

Step 5. Compute the cash balance before short-term borrowing (net change in cash for the month plus the cash balance at the beginning of the month).

Step 6. Calculate the short-term borrowing or repayment—the amount borrowed if there is a cash shortfall for the month or the amount repaid on any short-term debt outstanding.

Step 7. Compute the cumulative amount of short-term debt outstanding, which also determines the amount of interest to be paid in the following month.

As you can see in Table 23-1 on page 584, the firm does not achieve a positive cash flow until September. Short-term borrowing must be arranged, therefore, in both July and August. By preparing a cash budget, the Chai Corporation can anticipate these needs and avoid the nasty surprises that might otherwise occur.

A cash budget should anticipate occasions when a small business has idle funds or has generated unexpected excess funds. Taking advantage of the many short-term investment opportunities that are available, including certificates of deposit and money market certificates, can put excess cash to work for a firm.

TABLE 23-1

Three-Month Cash Budget for the Chai Corporation for July–September

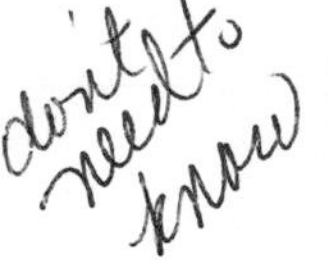

		May	June	July	August	September
	Monthly sales	$100,000	$120,000	$130,000	$130,000	$120,000
	Cash receipts:					
	Cash sales for month			$ 52,000	$ 52,000	$ 48,000
	1 month after sale			36,000	39,000	39,000
	2 months after sale			30,000	36,000	39,000
Step 1	Total collections			$118,000	$127,000	$126,000
	Purchases (80% of sales)		$104,000	$104,000	$ 96,000	$ 80,000
	Cash disbursements					
Step 2a	Payments on purchases			$104,000	$104,000	$ 96,000
Step 2b	Rent			3,000	3,000	3,000
Step 2b	Wages and salaries			18,000	18,000	16,000
Step 2b	Tax prepayment			1,000		
Step 2b	Utilities (2% of sales)			2,600	2,600	2,400
Step 2b	Interest on long-term note					800
Step 2c	Short-term interest (1% of short-term debt)				106	113
	Total cash disbursements			$128,600	$127,706	$118,313
Step 3	Net change in cash			−$ 10,600	−$ 706	$ 7,687
Step 4	Beginning cash balance			5,000	5,000	5,000
Step 5	Cash balance before borrowing			−$ 5,600	$ 4,294	$ 12,687
Step 6	Short-term borrowing (payments)			10,600	706	−7,687
	Ending cash balance			$ 5,000	$ 5,000	$ 5,000
Step 7	Cumulative short-term debt outstanding			$ 10,600	$ 11,306	$ 3,619

Managing Accounts Receivable

Explain the key issues in managing accounts receivable, inventory, and accounts payable.

Chapter 16 discussed the extension of credit by small firms and the managing and collecting of accounts receivable. This section considers the impact of credit decisions on working capital and particularly on cash flows. The most important factor in managing cash well within a small firm is the ability to collect accounts receivable quickly.

How Accounts Receivable Affect Cash

Granting credit to customers, although primarily a marketing decision, directly affects a firm's cash account. By selling on credit and thus allowing customers to delay payment, the selling firm delays the inflow of cash.

The total amount of customers' credit balances is carried on the balance sheet as accounts receivable—one of the firm's current assets. Of all noncash assets, accounts receivable are closest to becoming cash. Sometimes called *near cash*, or *receivables*, accounts receivable typically are collected and become cash within 30 to 60 days following a sale.

IN THE TRENCHES ENTREPRENEURSHIP TODAY

BATTEN DOWN THE HATCHES

Katie B. Tyler is no stranger to financial difficulties. Sixteen years ago, her interior construction company, Tyler II, in Charlotte, North Carolina, was hit by an economic slowdown. Business just stopped. She panicked, cut her salary in half, and drained the company's cash reserves to keep the business going. Her tactics worked, and the business has grown through the years.

Because the forecasts for 2001 were not positive, Tyler did not want to take any chances—she took steps to prepare for hard times. She made an agreement with her bank to double the company's credit line to $1 million. Internally, she increased the business development budget by 50 percent and promoted the office manager to client relations manager to ensure that current customers continued to be satisfied. Although the economic projections caused plans for a new $1 million headquarters to be delayed, Tyler is confident: "I plan to stay on a steady course and not panic."

Tyler's cool demeanor may not be characteristic of small business owners during an economic downturn. In fact, economists say that entrepreneurs are especially hard hit because they have fewer cash reserves than large companies, less access to credit markets, and less geographic diversity in global and domestic markets. To combat these added obstacles, entrepreneurs should thoroughly examine cash flows, operating costs, and overhead.

Source: Janin Friend, "Batten Down the Hatches," Business Week Online, http://www.businessweek.com, February 5, 2001.

The Life Cycle of Accounts Receivable

The receivables cycle begins with a credit sale. In most businesses, an invoice is then prepared and mailed to the purchaser. When the invoice is received, the purchaser processes it, prepares a check, and mails the check in payment to the seller.

Under ideal circumstances, each of these steps is taken in a timely manner. Obviously, delays can occur at any stage of this process. One small business owner found that the shipping clerk was batching invoices before sending them to the office for processing, thus delaying the preparation and mailing of invoices to customers. Of course, this practice also postponed the day on which the customers' money was received and deposited in the bank so that it could be used to pay bills. John Convoy, a cash flow consultant and former treasurer of several small firms, explains, "Most overdue receivables are unpaid because of problems in a company's organization. Your cash flow system is vulnerable at points where information gets transferred—between salespeople, operations departments, accounting clerks—because errors disrupt your ability to get paid promptly."[3]

Credit management policies, practices, and procedures affect the life cycle of receivables and the flow of cash from them. It is important for small business owners, when establishing credit policies, to consider cash flow requirements as well as the need to stimulate sales. A key goal of every business should be to minimize the average time it takes customers to pay their bills. By streamlining administrative procedures, a firm can facilitate the task of sending out bills, thereby generating cash more quickly. Here are some examples of credit management practices that can have a positive effect on a firm's cash flow:

- Minimize the time between shipping, invoicing, and sending notices on billings.
- Review previous credit experiences to determine impediments to cash flows, such as continued extension of credit to slow-paying or delinquent customers.

- Provide incentives for prompt payment by granting cash discounts or charging interest on delinquent accounts.
- Age accounts receivable on a monthly or even a weekly basis to identify quickly any delinquent accounts.
- Use the most effective methods for collecting overdue accounts. For example, prompt phone calls to overdue accounts can improve collections considerably.
- Use a **lock box**—a post office box for receiving remittances. If the firm's bank maintains the lock box to which customers send their payments, it can empty the box frequently and immediately deposit any checks received into the firm's account.

lock box
a post office box for receiving remittances from customers

Accounts Receivable Financing

Some small businesses speed up the cash flow from accounts receivable by borrowing against them. By financing receivables, these firms can often secure the use of their money 30 to 60 days earlier than would be possible otherwise. Although this practice was once concentrated largely in the garment business, it has expanded to many other types of small businesses, such as manufacturers, food processors, distributors, home building suppliers, and temporary employment agencies. Such financing is provided by commercial finance companies and by some banks.

Two types of accounts receivable financing are available. The first type uses a firm's **pledged accounts receivable** as collateral for a loan. Payments received from customers are forwarded to the lending institution to pay off the loan. In the second type of financing, a business sells its accounts receivable to a finance company, a practice known as **factoring.** The finance company thereby assumes the bad-debt risk associated with receivables it buys.

pledged accounts receivable
accounts receivable used as collateral for a loan

factoring
obtaining cash by selling accounts receivable to another firm

The obvious advantage of accounts receivable financing is the immediate cash flow it provides for firms that have limited working capital. As a secondary benefit, the volume of borrowing can be quickly expanded proportionally in order to match a firm's growth in sales and accounts receivable.

A drawback to this type of financing is its high cost. Rates typically run several points above the prime interest rate, and factors charge a fee to compensate them for their credit investigation activities and for the risk that customers may default in payment. Another weakness of accounts receivable financing is that pledging receivables may limit a firm's ability to borrow from a bank by removing a prime asset from its available collateral.

Managing Inventory

Inventory is a "necessary evil" in the financial management system. It is "necessary" because supply and demand cannot be managed to coincide precisely with day-to-day operations; it is an "evil" because it ties up funds that are not actively productive.

Reducing Inventory to Free Cash

Inventory is a bigger problem for some small businesses than for others. The inventory of many service firms, for example, consists of only a few supplies. A manufacturer, on the other hand, has several inventories—raw materials, work in process, and finished goods. Also, retailers and wholesalers, especially those with high in-

IN THE TRENCHES ENTREPRENEURSHIP TODAY

JUST-IN-TIME INVENTORY: GOOD FOR SMALL FIRMS TOO

The same principles that have increased efficiency in large-scale production are being applied effectively in smaller firms as well. Gamblin Artist's Oil Colors is one example of a small company that is benefiting from the concept of just-in-time manufacturing.

Gamblin, an oil paint manufacturer in Portland, Oregon, is owned and operated by Martha and Robert Gamblin. Twenty years ago, Robert, a painter, decided that someone should make paints with the artist in mind—and so he did. He started slowly, selling only three different colors of paint. Today, Gamblin Artist's Oil Colors sells 87 colors of oil paint all over the world.

With increased selection and production have come new questions about how to manage the inventory. The Gamblins hired Charlie Martin, a manufacturing consultant for the Oregon Manufacturing Extension Partnership, to introduce a more efficient inventory handling system.

The Gamblins had been making colors in batches of 1,200 tubes, which would remain in inventory for three to six months. With Martin's help, the Gamblins reduced their batch size to 500 tubes, while producing a single color at a time. The new manufacturing system also allowed the company to decrease the amount of time inventory is held to approximately six weeks. Thus, less cash is tied up in inventory at any one time. Since implementing the new system, the Gamblins have freed up about $200,000 in cash to grow the business and launch an advertising campaign.

Source: Jane Applegate, "Just-in-Time Manufacturing," http://www.entrepreneur.com, February 2000.

http://www.gamblincolors.com

ventory turnover rates such as firms in grocery distribution, are continually involved in solving inventory management problems.

Chapter 20 discussed several ideas related to purchasing and inventory management that are designed to minimize inventory-carrying costs and processing costs. The emphasis in this section is on practices that will minimize average inventory levels, thereby releasing funds for other applications. The correct minimum level of inventory is the level needed to maintain desired production schedules and/or a certain level of customer service. A concerted effort to manage inventory can trim inventory excess and pay handsome dividends.

Monitoring Inventory

One of the first steps in managing inventory is to discover what's in inventory and how long it's been there. Too often, items are purchased, warehoused, and essentially forgotten. A yearly inventory for accounting purposes is inadequate for proper inventory control. Items that are slow movers may sit in a retailer's inventory beyond the time when markdowns should have been applied.

Computers can provide assistance in inventory identification and control. Although physical inventories may still be required, their use will only serve to supplement the computerized system.

Controlling Stockpiles

Small business managers tend to overbuy inventory for several reasons. First, an entrepreneur's enthusiasm may lead him or her to forecast greater demand than is realistic. Second, the personalization of the business-customer relationship may

motivate a manager to stock everything customers want. Third, a price-conscious manager may be overly susceptible to a vendor's appeal to "buy now, because prices are going up."

Managers must exercise restraint when stockpiling. Improperly managed and uncontrolled stockpiling may greatly increase inventory-carrying costs and place a heavy drain on the funds of a small business.

Managing Accounts Payable

Cash flow management and accounts payable management are intertwined. As long as a payable is outstanding, the buying firm can keep cash equal to that amount in its own checking account. When payment is made, however, that firm's cash account is reduced accordingly.

Although payables are legal obligations, they can be paid at various times or even renegotiated in some cases. Therefore, financial management of accounts payable hinges on negotiation and timing.

Negotiation

Any business is subject to emergency situations and may find it necessary to ask creditors to postpone its payable obligations. Usually, creditors will cooperate in working out a solution because it's in their best interest for a client firm to succeed.

Timing

"Buy now, pay later" is the motto of many entrepreneurs. By buying on credit, a small business is using creditors' funds to supply short-term cash needs. The longer creditors' funds can be borrowed, the better. Payment, therefore, should be delayed as long as acceptable under the agreement.

Typically, accounts payable (trade credit) involve payment terms that include a cash discount. With trade-discount terms, paying later may be inappropriate. For example, terms of 3/10, net 30 offer a 3 percent potential discount. Table 23-2 shows the possible settlement costs over the credit period of 30 days. Note that for a $20,000 purchase, a settlement of only $19,400 is required if payment is made within the first 10 days ($20,000 less the 3 percent discount of $600). Between day 11 and day 30, the full settlement of $20,000 is required. After 30 days, the settlement cost may exceed the original amount, as late-payment fees are added.

The timing question then becomes "Should the account be paid on day 10 or day 30?" There is little reason to pay $19,400 on days 1 through 9, when the same amount will settle the account on day 10. Likewise, if payment is to be made after day 10, it makes sense to wait until day 30 to pay the $20,000.

TABLE 23-2

An Accounts Payable Timetable for Terms of 3/10, Net 30

Timetable (days after invoice date)	Settlement Costs for a $20,000 Purchase
Day 1 through 10	$19,400
Day 11 through 30	$20,000
Day 31 and thereafter	$20,000 + possible late penalty + deterioration in credit standing

By paying on the last day of the discount period, the buyer saves the amount of the discount offered. The other alternative of paying on day 30 allows the buyer to use the seller's money for an additional 20 days by forgoing the discount. As Table 23-2 shows, the buyer can use the seller's $19,400 for 20 days at a cost of $600. The annualized interest rate can be calculated as follows:

$$\text{Annualized interest rate} = \frac{\text{Days in year}}{\text{Net period} - \text{Cash discount period}} \times \frac{\text{Cash discount \%}}{100\% - \text{Cash discount \%}}$$

$$= \frac{365}{30 - 10} \times \frac{3\%}{100\% - 3\%}$$

$$= 18.25 \times 0.030928$$

$$= 0.564, \text{ or } 56.4\%$$

By failing to take a discount, a business typically pays a high rate for use of a supplier's money—56.4 percent per annum in this case. Payment on day 10 appears to be the most logical choice. Recall, however, that payment also affects cash flows. If funds are extremely short, a small firm may have to wait to pay until the last possible day in order to avoid an overdraft at the bank.

We now turn from management of a firm's working capital to management of its long-term assets—equipment and plant—or what is called *capital budgeting.*

Capital Budgeting

4 *Discuss the techniques commonly used in making capital budgeting decisions.*

capital budgeting analysis an analytical method that helps managers make decisions about long-term investments

Capital budgeting analysis helps managers make decisions about long-term investments. In order to develop a new product line, for example, a firm needs to expand its manufacturing capabilities and to buy the inventory required to make the product. That is, it makes investments today with an expectation of receiving profits or cash flows in the future, possibly over 10 or 20 years.

Some capital budgeting decisions that might be made by a small firm include the following:

- Develop and introduce a new product that shows promise but requires additional study and improvement.
- Replace a firm's delivery trucks with newer models.
- Expand sales activity into a new territory.
- Construct a new building.
- Hire several additional salespersons to intensify selling in the existing market.

Although the owner of a small business does not make long-term investment decisions frequently, capital budgeting is still important. Correct investment decisions will add value to the firm. An incorrect capital budgeting decision, on the other hand, may prove fatal to a small firm.

Capital Budgeting Techniques

The three major techniques for making capital budgeting decisions involve (1) accounting return on investment, (2) payback period, and (3) discounted cash flows, either net present value or internal rate of return. They all attempt to answer one basic question: Do the future benefits from an investment exceed the cost of making the investment? However, each technique addresses this general question by

focusing on a different specific question. The specific question each addresses can be stated as follows:

1. ***Accounting return on investment.*** How many dollars in average profits are generated per dollar of average investment?
2. ***Payback period.*** How long will it take to recover the original investment outlay?
3. ***Discounted cash flows.*** How does the present value of future benefits from the investment compare to the investment outlay?

Three simple rules are used in judging the merits of an investment. Although they may seem trite, the rules state in simple terms the best thinking about the attractiveness of an investment.

1. The investor prefers more cash rather than less cash.
2. The investor prefers cash sooner rather than later.
3. The investor prefers less risk rather than more risk.

With these criteria in mind, let's now look at each of the three capital budgeting techniques in detail.

accounting return on investment technique a capital budgeting technique that evaluates a capital expenditure based on the average annual after-tax profits relative to the average book value of an investment

ACCOUNTING RETURN ON INVESTMENT A small firm invests to earn profits. The **accounting return on investment technique** compares the average annual after-tax profits a firm expects to receive with the average book value of the investment:

$$\text{Accounting return on investment} = \frac{\text{Average annual after-tax profits per year}}{\text{Average book value of the investment}}$$

Average annual profits can be estimated by adding the after-tax profits expected over the life of the project and then dividing that amount by the number of years the project is expected to last. The average book value of an investment is equivalent to the average of the initial outlay and the estimated final projected salvage value. In making an accept–reject decision, the owner compares the calculated return to a minimum acceptable return, which is usually determined based on past experience.

To examine the use of the accounting return on investment technique, assume that you are contemplating buying a piece of equipment for $10,000 and depreciating it over four years to a book value of zero (it will have no salvage value). Further assume that you expect the investment to generate after-tax profits each year as follows:

Year	After-Tax Profits
1	$1,000
2	2,000
3	2,500
4	3,000

The accounting return on the proposed investment is calculated as follows:

$$\text{Accounting return on investment} = \frac{\left(\dfrac{\$1{,}000 + \$2{,}000 + \$2{,}500 + \$3{,}000}{4}\right)}{\left(\dfrac{\$10{,}000 + \$0}{2}\right)}$$

$$= \frac{\$2{,}125}{\$5{,}000} = 0.425, \text{ or } 42.5\%$$

For most people, a 42.5 percent profit rate would seem outstanding. Assuming the calculated accounting return on investment of 42.5 percent exceeds your minimum acceptable return, you will accept the project. If not, you will reject the investment—provided, of course, that you have confidence in the technique.

Although the accounting return on investment is easy to calculate, it has two major shortcomings. First, it is based on accounting profits rather than actual cash flows received. An investor should be more interested in the future cash produced by the investment than in the reported profits. Second, this technique ignores the time value of money. Thus, although popular, the accounting return on investment technique fails to satisfy any of the three rules concerning an investor's preference for receiving more cash sooner with less risk.

PAYBACK PERIOD The **payback period technique,** as the name suggests, measures how long it will take to recover the initial cash outlay of an investment. It deals with cash flows as opposed to accounting profits. The merits of a project are judged on whether the initial investment outlay can be recovered in less time than some maximum acceptable payback period. For example, an owner may not want to invest in any project that will require more than five years to recoup the original investment. Assume that the owner is studying an investment in equipment with an expected life of 10 years. The investment outlay will be $15,000, with the cost of the equipment depreciated on a straight-line basis, at $1,500 per year. If the owner makes the investment, the annual after-tax profits have been estimated to be as follows:

payback period technique
a capital budgeting technique that measures the amount of time it will take to recover the cash outlay of an investment

Years	After-Tax Profits
1–2	$1,000
3–6	2,000
7–10	2,500

To determine the after-tax cash flows from the investment, the owner merely adds back the depreciation of $1,500 each year to the profit. The reason for adding the depreciation to the profit is that it was deducted when the profits were calculated (as an accounting entry), even though it was not a cash outflow. The results, then, are as follows:

Years	After-Tax Cash Flows
1–2	$2,500
3–6	3,500
7–10	4,000

By the end of the second year, the owner will have recovered $5,000 of the investment outlay ($2,500 per year). By the end of the fourth year, another $7,000, or $12,000 in total, will have been recouped. The additional $3,000 can be recovered in the fifth year, when $3,500 is expected. Thus, it will take 4.86 years [4 years + ($3,000 ÷ $3,500)] to recover the investment. Since the maximum acceptable payback is less than 5 years, the owner will accept the investment.

Many managers and owners of companies use the payback period technique in evaluating investment decisions. Although it uses cash flows, rather than accounting profits, the payback period technique has two significant weaknesses. First, it does not consider the time value of money (cash is preferred sooner rather than

later). Second, it fails to consider the cash flows received after the payback period (more cash is preferred, rather than less).

DISCOUNTED CASH FLOWS Managers can avoid the deficiencies of the accounting return on investment and payback period techniques by using discounted cash flow analysis. Discounted cash flow techniques take into consideration the fact that cash received today is more valuable than cash received one year from now (time value of money). For example, interest can be earned on cash that is available for immediate investment; this is not true for cash to be received at some future date.

discounted cash flow (DCF) technique a capital budgeting technique that compares the present value of future cash flows with the cost of the initial investment

net present value (NPV) the present value of expected future cash flows less the initial investment outlay

internal rate of return (IRR) the rate of return a firm expects to earn on a project

Discounted cash flow (DCF) techniques compare the present value of future cash flows with the investment outlay. Such an analysis may take either of two forms: net present value or internal rate of return.

The **net present value** (**NPV**) method estimates the current value of the cash that will flow into the firm from the project in the future and deducts the amount of the initial outlay. To find the present value of expected future cash flows, we discount them back to the present at the firm's cost of capital, where the cost of capital is equal to the investors' required rate of return. If the net present value of the investment is positive (that is, if the present value of future cash flows discounted at the rate of return required to satisfy the firm's investors exceeds the initial outlay), the project is acceptable.

The **internal rate of return** (**IRR**) method estimates the rate of return that can be expected from a contemplated investment. For the investment outlay to be attractive, the internal rate of return must exceed the firm's cost of capital—the rate of return required to satisfy the firm's investors.

The use of DCF techniques is explained and illustrated in Appendix 23B at the end of this chapter. (Appendix 23A will familiarize you with the concept and application of time value of money.)

We have presented several approaches to evaluating investment opportunities. Discounted cash flow techniques can generally be trusted to provide a more reliable basis for decisions than can the accounting return on investment or the payback period technique. However, use of DCF techniques requires determination of the appropriate discount rate. The discount rate—often called the *cost of capital* or, more precisely, the *weighted cost of capital*—is an issue that deserves careful attention.

A Firm's Cost of Capital

Determine the appropriate cost of capital to be used in discounted cash flow techniques.

cost of capital the rate of return required to satisfy a firm's investors

opportunity cost the rate of return that could be earned on another investment of similar risk

The **cost of capital** is the rate of return a firm must earn on its investments in order to satisfy both its debt holders and its owners. An investment with a negative net present value—which means that the internal rate of return is below the cost of capital—will decrease the value of the firm and the owner's equity value. On the other hand, an investment with a positive net present value, or an internal rate of return above the cost of capital, will increase the owner's equity value.[4] Although determining a firm's cost of capital is extremely important for effective financial management, many small business owners are unaware of the concept.

MEASURING COST OF CAPITAL Calculation of a firm's cost of capital is based on the opportunity cost concept. The **opportunity cost** is the rate of return an owner could earn on another investment with similar risk. For example, a small business owner contemplating an expansion would want to know the rate of return that could be earned elsewhere with the same amount of risk. If the owner could earn a 15 per-

IN THE TRENCHES ENTREPRENEURSHIP AND ETHICS

IS IT A LEGAL OR A MORAL ISSUE?

Why should a man who has all the money he did be able to walk away from a million-dollar debt? They should make it illegal. If you have the funds to pay your debt, then you shouldn't be able to walk away.

Daniel Driscoll, who owns a $4-million general contracting company, is referring to money he lost in 1995, when he did some framing work for Coffee by George, a startup of drive-through coffee kiosks based in Boston.

The short-lived venture was founded by George Naddaff, best known as the entrepreneur responsible for Boston Chicken, the restaurant chain that in 1993 became one of the hottest public offerings ever. "When [Naddaff] realized that his concept wasn't going to be the next Boston Chicken," says Driscoll, "he pulled the plug on it."

After having invested about $5 million in the Coffee by George concept, Naddaff and his partners realized it wasn't going to work and decided to liquidate it. They ended up with an agreement to pay creditors roughly $0.30 on every dollar owed. Driscoll agreed to the payout. But he wasn't pleased.

Driscoll recognizes that what Naddaff did was perfectly legal; however, he believes he shouldn't have gotten off so easily. Given that Naddaff had the means—personally or through his other ventures—Driscoll thinks he should have taken responsibility for making good on his debts to his creditors. Some business owners agree with Driscoll, even if making good on what they owe means going beyond what the law requires.

Anyone starting a new company must face the chance that he or she will have to repay debt obligations if the firm gets into serious financial trouble. Therefore, you should give some thought to what you would do in such circumstances, based on your values. If you wait until the situation arises—and with any luck it never will—there is a real chance that you may compromise your beliefs.

Source: Jeffrey L. Seglin, "Brother, Can You Spare 30 Cents on the Dollar?" *Inc.*, Vol. 20, No. 5 (April 1998), p. 46.

cent return on the money by investing it elsewhere, then the expansion investment should not be made unless it is expected to earn at least 15 percent. The 15 percent rate of return is the opportunity cost of the money and, therefore, should be the cost of capital for the firm's equity investors.

The cost of capital should recognize all permanent sources of financing, including debt and ownership equity. That is, a **weighted cost of capital** is needed. For example, assume that a firm expects to finance future investments with 40 percent debt and 60 percent equity. Further assume that the opportunity cost of funds supplied by debt holders (that is, the current interest rate) is 10 percent. However, since the interest paid by a firm is tax deductible, the after-tax cost of the interest is reduced by the tax savings from the interest deduction. For instance, if the firm's tax rate is 25 percent, then the after-tax cost of the debt will be reduced by that amount. That is, the after-tax cost of a loan with a 10 percent interest rate is only 7.5 percent [10% × (1 − 0.25)]. And if the opportunity cost of the equity capital invested by the owners is thought to be 18 percent, the firm's weighted cost of capital is 13.8 percent.

weighted cost of capital
the cost of capital adjusted to reflect the relative costs of debt and equity financing

	Weight	Cost	Weighted Cost
Debt	40%	7.5%	3.0%
Equity	60	18.0	10.8
Total	100%		13.8%

The 13.8 percent rate becomes the discount rate used in present value analysis, assuming that future investments will be financed on average by 40 percent debt and 60 percent equity and that the riskiness of future investments will be similar to the riskiness of the firm's existing assets.

The greatest difficulty in measuring a firm's weighted cost of capital is estimating the cost of the owners' equity. Debt holders receive their rate of return mostly through the interest paid to them by the firm, and the cost estimation is relatively straightforward. The required return for the owners is another matter, however. Although some of their expected returns are in the form of dividends received, most are derived from the increase in the firm's value, or *capital gains*.

In measuring the cost of equity for a large publicly traded firm, an analyst uses market data to estimate the owners' required rate of return. However, since a small firm is owned either by a family or by a small group of investors, the owners should determine their own required rates of return. As long as the owners are informed about competitive rates in the marketplace, they can make appropriate judgments. For example, owners of smaller publicly traded firms (that is, the smallest 10 percent of the firms listed on the New York Stock Exchange) have earned an average annual rate of 16 percent on their investments for the past 75 years.[5] This fact suggests that owners of small privately owned companies should invest only if they can expect to earn a rate of return significantly exceeding 16 percent; after all, there is a lot more risk in investing in a small business whose stock is not regularly bought and sold than in a publicly traded firm. In fact, because of this additional risk, the required rate of return for an owner of a privately held firm should be at least 20 or 25 percent. However imprecise this approach may seem, making a good faith effort to recognize investors' (and owners') required rates of return is better than ignoring the problem, as is commonly done.

USING COST OF DEBT AS AN INVESTMENT CRITERION The weighted cost of capital may be fine in theory, but what if a company could borrow the entire amount needed for an investment in a new product line? Is it really necessary to use the weighted cost of capital, or can the decision simply be based on the cost of the debt providing the funding?

Consider the Young Corporation. The firm's owners believe they could earn a 14 percent rate of return by purchasing $50,000 worth of new equipment to expand the business. Although the firm tries to maintain a capital structure with equal amounts of debt and equity, it can borrow the entire $50,000 from the bank at an interest rate of 12 percent. Any time the return on the investment is greater than the cost of the debt financing, using debt will increase a firm's net income. In this case, the expected return on investment is 14 percent and the cost of debt financing is 12 percent. The increase in net income comes from the use of **favorable financial leverage,** investing at a rate of return that exceeds the interest rate on borrowed money.

favorable financial leverage
the benefit gained by investing at a rate of return that is greater than the interest rate on a loan

The owners of the firm have estimated the required rate of return for their funds to be 18 percent. However, since Young can finance the purchase totally by debt, the owners have decided to make the investment and finance it by borrowing the money from the bank at 12 percent.

The following year, Young's owners find another investment opportunity costing $50,000, but with an expected internal rate of return of 17 percent—better than the previous year's 14 percent. However, when they approach the bank for financing, they find the bank unwilling to lend the company any more money. In the words of the banker, "Young has used up all of its debt capacity." Before the bank

will agree to fund any more loans, the owners must either contribute more of their own money in the form of common equity or find new investors for the business.

What is the moral of the story for Young? Intuitively, we know that Young's owners made a mistake. Making the investment in the first year denied the firm the opportunity to make a better decision in the second year.

A more general conclusion is that a firm should never use a single cost of financing as the criterion for making capital budgeting decisions. When a firm uses debt, it implicitly uses up some of its debt capacity for future investments; only when it complements the use of debt with equity will it be able to continue to use more debt in the future. Thus, business owners should always use a weighted cost of capital that recognizes the need to blend equity with debt over time.

The Lack of Capital Budgeting Analysis

6

Describe the capital budgeting practices of small firms.

Historically, few small business owners have relied on any type of quantitative analysis in making capital budgeting decisions. Instead, the decision to buy new equipment or expand facilities has been based more on intuition and instinct than on economic analysis. And by those who do conduct some kind of quantitative analysis, rarely have discounted cash flow (DCF) techniques, either net present value or internal rate of return, been used.

We could easily conclude that small business owners are "uneducated" about theoretically sound financial methods. However, the cause of such limited use of DCF tools probably has more to do with the nature of the small firm itself than it does with the owners' unwillingness to learn. Several more important reasons exist, including the following:

- For many owners of small firms, the business is an extension of their lives—that is, business events affect them personally. The same is true in reverse: What happens to the owners personally affects their decisions about the firm. The firm and its owners are inseparable. We cannot fully understand decisions made about a firm without being aware of the personal events in the owners' lives. Consequently, nonfinancial variables may play a significant part in owners' decisions. For example, the desire to be viewed as a respected part of the community may be more important to an owner than the present value of a business decision.
- The undercapitalization and liquidity problems of a small firm can directly affect the decision-making process, and survival often becomes the top priority. Long-term planning is, therefore, not viewed by the owners as a high priority in the total scheme of things.
- The greater uncertainty of cash flows within a small firm makes long-term forecasting and planning seem unappealing and even a waste of time. The owners simply have no confidence in their ability to predict cash flows beyond two or three years. Thus, calculating the cash flows for the entire life of a project is viewed as a futile effort.
- The value of a closely held firm is less easily observed than that of a publicly held firm whose securities are actively traded in the marketplace. Therefore, the owner of a small firm may consider the market-value rule of maximizing net present values irrelevant. Estimating the cost of capital is also much more difficult for a small firm than for a large firm.

- The smaller size of a small firm's projects may make net present value computations less feasible in a practical sense. The time and expense required to analyze a capital investment are generally the same, whether the project is large or small. Therefore, it is relatively more costly for a small firm to conduct such a study.
- Management talent within a small firm is a scarce resource. Also, the owner-managers frequently have a technical background, as opposed to a business or finance orientation. The perspective of owners is influenced greatly by their backgrounds.

The foregoing characteristics of a small firm and its owners have a significant effect on the decision-making process within the firm. The result is often a short-term mind-set, caused partly by necessity and partly by choice. However, the owner of a small firm should make every effort to use discounted cash flow techniques and to be certain that contemplated investments will, in fact, provide returns that exceed the firm's cost of capital.

Looking Back

1 Describe the working-capital cycle of a small business.

- The working-capital cycle begins with the purchase of inventory and ends with the collection of accounts receivable.
- The cash conversion period is critical because it is the time period during which cash flow problems can arise and a firm can become illiquid.

2 Identify the important issues in managing a firm's cash flows.

- A firm's cash flows consist of cash flowing into a business (through sales revenue, borrowing, and so on) and cash flowing out of the business (through purchases, operating expenses, and so on).
- Profitable small companies sometimes encounter cash flow problems by failing to understand the working-capital cycle or failing to anticipate the negative consequences of growth.
- Cash inflows and outflows are reconciled in the cash budget, which involves forecasts of cash receipts and expenditures.

3 Explain the key issues in managing accounts receivable, inventory, and accounts payable.

- Granting credit to customers, primarily a marketing decision, directly affects a firm's cash account.
- A firm can improve its cash flows by speeding up collections from customers, minimizing inventories, and delaying payments to suppliers.
- Some small businesses speed up the cash flows from receivables by borrowing against them.
- A concerted effort to manage inventory can trim excess inventory and free cash for other uses.
- Accounts payable, a primary source of financing for small firms, directly affects a firm's cash flow situation.

4 Discuss the techniques commonly used in making capital budgeting decisions.

- Capital budgeting techniques attempt to determine whether future benefits from an investment will exceed the initial outlay.
- Capital budgeting techniques include accounting return on investment, the payback period, and the discounted cash flow techniques.
- The accounting return on investment technique has two significant shortcomings: (1) It is based on accounting profits rather than actual cash flows received, and (2) it ignores the time value of money.
- The payback period technique also has two major weaknesses: (1) It ignores the time value of money, and (2) it doesn't consider cash flows received after the payback period.
- The discounted cash flow techniques—net present value and internal rate of return—provide the best accept–reject decision criteria in capital budgeting analysis.

5 Determine the appropriate cost of capital to be used in discounted cash flow techniques.

- The cost of capital is the discount rate used in solving for a project's net present value.
- The cost of capital equals the investor's opportunity cost of funds.
- Few small firms make use of the concept of cost of capital.
- A firm should not use cost of debt as a substitute for the weighted cost-of-capital criterion in making investment decisions.

6 Describe the capital budgeting practices of small firms.

- Few small firms use any type of a discounted cash flow technique. In fact, most small companies do not use any formal analysis whatever.
- The very nature of small firms may explain, to some degree, why they seldom use the conceptually richer techniques for evaluating long-term investments.

KEY TERMS

working-capital management, p. 573
net operating working capital, p. 573
working-capital cycle, p. 573
cash conversion period, p. 576
growth trap, p. 582
cash budget, p. 582
lock box, p. 586
pledged accounts receivable, p. 586
factoring, p. 586
capital budgeting analysis, p. 589
accounting return on investment technique, p. 590
payback period technique, p. 591
discounted cash flow (DCF) technique, p. 592
net present value (NPV), p. 592
internal rate of return (IRR), p. 592
cost of capital, p. 592
opportunity cost, p. 592
weighted cost of capital, p. 593
favorable financial leverage, p. 594
compound value of a dollar, p. 601

DISCUSSION QUESTIONS

1. a. List the events in the working-capital cycle that directly affect cash and those that do not.
   b. What determines the length of a firm's cash conversion period?
2. a. What are some examples of cash receipts that are not sales revenue?
   b. Explain how expenses and cash disbursements during a month may be different.
3. How may a seller speed up the collection of accounts receivable? Give examples that may apply to various stages in the life cycle of receivables.
4. Suppose that a small firm could successfully shift to a just-in-time inventory system—an arrangement in which inventory is received just as it is needed. How would this affect the firm's working-capital management?
5. How do working-capital management and capital budgeting differ?
6. Compare the different techniques that can be used in capital budgeting analysis.
7. Could a firm conceivably make an investment that would increase its earnings but reduce the firm's value?
8. Define internal rate of return.
9. a. Find the accounting return on investment for a project that costs $10,000, will have no salvage value, and has expected annual after-tax profits of $1,000.
   b. Determine the payback period for a capital investment that costs $40,000 and has the following after-tax profits. (The project outlay of $40,000 will be depreciated on a straight-line basis to a zero salvage value.)

Year	After-Tax Profits
1	$4,000
2	5,000
3	6,000
4	6,500
5	6,500
6	6,000
7	5,000

10. a. Define cost of capital. Why is it important?
    b. Why is it necessary to compute a weighted cost of capital?

YOU MAKE THE CALL

SITUATION 1

A small firm specializing in the sale and installation of swimming pools was profitable but devoted very little attention to management of its working capital. It had, for example, never prepared or used a cash budget.

To be sure that money was available for payments as needed, the firm kept a minimum of $25,000 in a checking account. At times, this account grew larger; it totaled $43,000 at one time. The owner felt that this approach to cash management worked well for a small company because it eliminated all of the paperwork associated with cash budgeting. Moreover, it had enabled the firm to pay its bills in a timely manner.

Question 1 What are the advantages and weaknesses of the minimum-cash-balance practice?

Question 2 There is a saying "If it's not broke, don't fix it." In view of the firm's present success in paying bills promptly, should it be encouraged to use a cash budget? Be prepared to support your answer.

SITUATION 2

Ruston Manufacturing Company is a small firm selling entirely on a credit basis. It has experienced successful operation and earned modest profits.

Sales are made on the basis of net payment in 30 days. Collections from customers run approximately 70 percent in 30 days, 20 percent in 60 days, 7 percent in 90 days, and 3 percent bad debts.

The owner has considered the possibility of offering a cash discount for early payment. However, the practice seems costly and possibly unnecessary. As the owner puts it, "Why should I bribe customers to pay what they legally owe?"

Question 1 Is offering a cash discount the equivalent of a bribe?

Question 2 How would a cash discount policy relate to bad debts?

Question 3 What cash discount policy, if any, would you recommend?

Question 4 What other approaches might be used to improve cash flows from receivables?

SITUATION 3

Adrian Fudge of the Fudge Corporation has been engaged in the process of forecasting its financing needs over the fourth quarter (October–December) and has made the following forecasts of planned cash receipts and disbursements:

- Interest on a $75,000 bank note (due next March) is payable at an 8 percent annual rate in December for the three-month period just ended.
- The firm follows a policy of paying no cash dividends.
- Historical and predicted sales:

Historical		Predicted	
August	$150,000	October	$200,000
September	175,000	November	220,000
		December	180,000
		January	200,000

- The firm has a monthly rental expense of $5,000.
- Wages and salaries for the coming months are estimated at $25,000 per month.
- Of the firm's sales, 25 percent is collected in the month of the sale, 35 percent one month after the sale, and the remaining 40 percent two months after the sale.
- Merchandise is purchased one month before the sales month and is paid for in the month it is sold. Purchases equal 75 percent of sales. The firm's cost of goods sold is also 75 percent of sales.
- Tax prepayments are made quarterly, with a prepayment of $10,000 in October based on earnings for the quarter ended September 30.
- Utilities for the firm average 3 percent of sales and are paid in the month they are incurred.
- Depreciation expense is $20,000 annually.

Question 1 Prepare a monthly cash budget for the three-month period ending in December.

Question 2 If the firm's beginning cash balance for the budget period is $7,000, and this is its minimum desired balance, determine when and how much the firm will need to borrow during the budget period. The firm has a $50,000 line of credit with its bank, with interest (10 percent annual rate) paid monthly. For example, interest on a loan taken out at the end of September would be paid at the end of October and every month thereafter so long as the loan was outstanding.

SITUATION 4

Jack Griggs, owner of Griggs Oil Jobber, Inc., is considering a capital expenditure of $25,000 to invest in a new product line. The cost of the investment includes $15,000 for equipment and $10,000 in working capital (additional accounts receivable and inventories). The investment would have a five-year life, after which the equipment would have zero salvage value. The cost of the equipment would be depreciated over the five years on a straight-line basis. The working capital would need to be maintained for the

five years but could then be liquidated, with the firm recovering the full $10,000 in the last year. That is, all accounts receivable would be collected and the inventories liquidated. The projected income statements and after-tax cash flows for the next five years are as follows:

	YEARS					
	0	1	2	3	4	5
Sales revenue		$30,000	$35,000	$40,000	$40,000	$40,000
Cost of goods sold		18,000	21,000	24,000	24,000	24,000
Gross profit		$12,000	$14,000	$16,000	$16,000	$16,000
Operating expenses:						
Marketing		5,000	5,000	5,000	5,000	5,000
Depreciation		3,000	3,000	3,000	3,000	3,000
Operating income		$ 4,000	$ 6,000	$ 8,000	$ 8,000	$ 8,000
Taxes		1,000	1,500	2,000	2,000	2,000
Earnings after taxes		$ 3,000	$ 4,500	$ 6,000	$ 6,000	$ 6,000
Plus depreciation		3,000	3,000	3,000	3,000	3,000
Plus working capital						10,000
After-tax cash flows	−$25,000	$ 6,000	$ 7,500	$ 9,000	$ 9,000	$19,000
Book value of the investment:						
Working capital	$10,000	$10,000	$10,000	$10,000	$10,000	0
Equipment	15,000	12,000	9,000	6,000	3,000	0
Total book value	$25,000	$22,000	$19,000	$16,000	$13,000	0

(Note: You may want to use Appendix 23B to answer these questions.)

Question 1 Compute the project's accounting return on investment, payback period, net present value, and internal rate of return. The firm's weighted cost of capital is 16 percent.

Question 2 Should Griggs accept the project? Assume that he believes the project should have an accounting rate of return of 25 percent and a payback period of 2.5 years.

EXPERIENTIAL EXERCISES

1. Interview the owner of a small firm to determine the nature of the firm's working-capital time line. Try to estimate the cash conversion period.
2. Interview a small business owner or credit manager regarding the extension of credit and/or the collection of receivables in that firm. Summarize your findings in a report.
3. Identify a small firm in your community that has recently expanded. Interview the owner of the firm about the methods used in evaluating the expansion.
4. Either alone or with a classmate, approach an owner of a small company about getting data on a current problem or one the company encountered at some time in the past, to see whether you would reach the same decision as the owners did.

EXPLORING THE WEB

1. American Express, at **http://www.americanexpress.com**, offers resources for small businesses. Choose the Small Business tab and then click on the link for Learn from Online Business Resources. Click on Financial Management. Choose Manage Your Receivables and Collections under Interactive Tools.
   a. According to the article, what percentage of past-due accounts will never be collected?
   b. Take the quiz to test the effectiveness of your receivables policy. What areas of your receivables policy need to be improved?
   c. List 10 steps to effective collections.
   d. Read about collection laws. Jot down some that you were not aware of.
   e. List 7 tips for avoiding overdue accounts.
2. Go to **http://www.inc.com** and choose Finance & Capital to answer the following questions.
   a. Under Forecasting, read the article entitled "Forecasting and Cash Flow Budgeting." List the steps to creating a cash flow budget. What should you do with the budget once it has been created?
   b. Read the article "Prioritizing Bills When Money is Short." List the items that should be paid in order of importance.
   c. Access the article "Is Your Company at Risk?" List the key questions, and note which ones deal with cash flow issues.

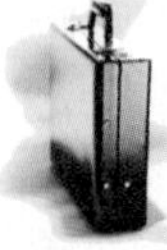

CASE 23

BARTON SALES AND SERVICE (p. 700)

This case looks at the financial performance of a small air-conditioning and heating services company, with emphasis on its working-capital policies.

Appendix 23A: Time Value of Money: Finding the Present Value of a Dollar

This appendix briefly explains the concept of time value of money—that is, a dollar today is worth more than a dollar received a year from now. To logically compare projects and financial strategies, we must move all cash flows back to the present.

The Departure Point

The starting point for finding the present value of future cash flows is represented in the following equation:

$$FV_n = PV(1 + i)^n$$

where

FV_n = future value of the investment at the end of n years
PV = present value or original amount invested at the beginning of the first year
i = annual interest (or discount) rate
n = number of years during which the compounding occurs

The above equation can be used to answer the following question: If you invested \$500 today (PV = \$500) at an annual interest rate of 8 percent ($i = 0.08$), how much money would you have (future value, or FV_n) in five years ($n = 5$)? If interest is compounded annually (interest is earned on the interest each new year), the answer is

$$FV_n = \$500(1 + 0.08)^5 = \$500(1.4693) = \$734.65$$

Thus, if you invested \$500 today at 8 percent, compounded annually, you would have \$734.65 at the end of five years. This procedure is called calculating the **compound value of a dollar.**

compound value of a dollar
the increasing value of a dollar over time resulting from interest earned both on the original dollar and on the interest received in prior periods

The Net Present Value of a Dollar

Determining the present value—that is, the value in today's dollars of a sum of money to be received in the future—involves reversing the compounding process just described. Restructuring the equation on page 601 to solve for the present value of a dollar yields

$$PV = \frac{FV_n}{(1 + i)^n}$$

which can be restated as

$$PV = FV_n \left[\frac{1}{(1 + i)^n}\right]$$

where PV is now the present value of a future sum of money, FV_n is the future value of the money to be received in year n, and i is the interest rate.

Thus, the present value of $1,200 to be received in seven years, assuming an interest rate of 10 percent, is

$$PV = FV_n \left[\frac{1}{(1 + i)^n}\right] = \$1{,}200 \left[\frac{1}{(1 + 0.10)^7}\right] = \$1{,}200(0.5132) = \$615.84$$

Rather than solving for the present value by using the above equation, we may instead use a financial calculator, such as a Texas Instruments BAII Plus. (*Note:* Other financial calculators are very similar in operation.) For this problem, we would find the present value by entering the following amounts and pressing the appropriate function keys:

Enter Amount	Press Key	
1200	FV	(for future value)
10	I/Y	(for discount rate)
7	N	(for number of years)
0	PMT	(for annual cash flows)

Press CPT (compute) and then PV (for present value) to get an answer of −$616. As in −$616, the calculator will always place a negative sign in front of the present value if the future value and annual payments are entered as positives. This negative sign can be disregarded. The calculator will give a positive answer if the other cash flows are entered as negatives.

Suppose that we want to calculate the present value of $2,000 to be received in 12 years, with an interest rate of 14 percent. Again using the TI BAII Plus calculator, the process is as follows:

Enter Amount	Press Key	
2000	FV	(for future value)
14	I/Y	(for discount rate)
12	N	(for number of years)
0	PMT	(for annual cash flows)

Press CPT (compute) and then PV (for present value) to get an answer of −$416. Therefore, the present value of $2,000 to be received in 12 years is $416 (disregard the negative sign), assuming an interest rate of 14 percent. In other words, we would be indifferent to whether we received $416 today or $2,000 in 12 years.

The Present Value of an Annuity

An annuity is a series of equal dollar payments for a specified number of years. That is, a 10-year annuity of $200 yields $200 each year for 10 years. Alternatively, we could say that an annuity involves depositing or investing an equal sum of money at the end of each year for a certain number of years and allowing it to grow at the stated interest rate.

The present value, PV, of a three-year annuity of $600 (received each year) at an interest rate of 13 percent can be determined as follows:

$$PV = \frac{\$600}{(1 + 0.13)^1} + \frac{\$600}{(1 + 0.13)^2} + \frac{\$600}{(1 + 0.13)^3}$$

We could solve the above equation manually, but it would involve quite a bit of effort. Using a financial calculator, we easily find the answer to be $1,417:

Enter Amount	Press Key	
13	I/Y	(for discount rate)
3	N	(for number of years)
600	PMT	(for annual cash flows)
0	FV	(for future value)

Press CPT (compute) and then PV (for present value) to get an answer of −$1,417.

Now let's find the present value of a cash flow that consists of a $1,400 payment every year (PMT) for five years (N) and an additional amount of $2,000 (FV) at the end of the four years. If the discount rate (I/Y) is 15 percent, the present value of this cash flow is $5,687, found as follows:

Enter Amount	Press Key	
15	I/Y	(for discount rate)
5	N	(for number of years)
1400	PMT	(for annual cash flows)
2000	FV	(for future value)

Press CPT (compute) and then PV (for present value) to get an answer of −$5,687.

We can use our understanding of finding the present value of future cash flows to conduct discounted cash flow analyses for capital budgeting decisions, as described in Appendix 23B.

Appendix 23B: Discounted Cash Flow Techniques: Computing a Project's Net Present Value and Internal Rate of Return

In Chapter 23, the application of discounted cash flow analysis to capital budgeting decisions was described. The two techniques commonly used—net present value and internal rate of return—were introduced. This appendix builds on that description and provides a more in-depth explanation of these two techniques.

Net Present Value

To measure a project's net present value (NPV), we estimate the value today of the dollars that will flow in from the project in the future and deduct the amount of the investment being made. That is, we discount the future after-tax cash flows back to their present value and then subtract the initial investment outlay. The computation can be represented as follows:

$$\text{Net present value} = \frac{\text{Present value of future}}{\text{after-tax cash flows}} - \frac{\text{Initial}}{\text{investment outlay}}$$

If the net present value of the investment is positive (that is, if the present value of future cash flows exceeds the initial outlay), we accept the project. Otherwise, we reject the investment.

The actual computation for finding the net present value follows:

$$NPV = \left[\frac{ACF_1}{(1+k)^1} + \frac{ACF_2}{(1+k)^2} + \frac{ACF_3}{(1+k)^3} + \cdots + \frac{ACF_n}{(1+k)^n}\right] - IO$$

where

NPV = net present value of the project
ACF_n = after-tax cash flows in year n
n = life of the project in years
k = discount rate (required rate of return)
IO = initial investment outlay

To see how to compute the net present value, assume that we are evaluating an investment in equipment that will cost $12,000. The equipment is expected to have a salvage value of $2,000 at the end of its projected life of five years. The investment is also expected to provide the following after-tax cash flows as a result of increased product sales:

Years	After-Tax Cash Flows
1	$1,500
2	2,500
3	4,000
4	4,000
5	3,000

These cash flows, plus the $2,000 in expected salvage value, can be represented graphically on a time line as follows. (Note that the after-tax cash flows in the fifth year include both the $3,000 cash flow from operating the project and the $2,000 expected salvage value.)

		Year 1	Year 2	Year 3	Year 4	Year 5
(Cash inflows)		$1,500	$2,500	$4,000	$4,000	$5,000
(Outlay)	$12,000					

Further assume that the firm's required rate of return—or cost of capital, as it is often called—is 14 percent. As explained in Chapter 23, a firm's *cost of capital*, which is used as the discount rate, is the rate the firm must earn to satisfy its investors. Given this information, we can compute the investment's net present value as follows:

$$\text{NPV} = \left[\frac{\$1{,}500}{(1 + 0.14)^1} + \frac{\$2{,}500}{(1 + 0.14)^2} + \frac{\$4{,}000}{(1 + 0.14)^3} + \frac{\$4{,}000}{(1 + 0.14)^4} + \frac{\$5{,}000}{(1 + 0.14)^5}\right] - \$12{,}000$$

A financial calculator can be used to solve for the net present value of the project. (Such computations are shown in Figure 23B-1 for a Hewlett Packard 17B II and for the Texas Instruments BAII Plus.) As noted in the figure, the net present value is −$1,095.

Since the net present value of the proposed investment is negative (that is, the present value of future cash flows is less than the cost of the investment), the investment should not be made. The negative net present value shows that the investment would not satisfy the firm's required rate of return of 14 percent. Only if the present value of future cash flows were greater than the $12,000 investment outlay would the firm's required rate of return be exceeded.

Internal Rate of Return

In the preceding example, we calculated the net present value and found it to be negative. Given the negative net present value, we concluded, rightfully, that the project would not earn the 14 percent required rate of return. The next logical step, however, would be to ask what rate would be earned, assuming our projections are

FIGURE 23B-1

Solving NPV Computations Using a Financial Calculator

PROBLEM Find the net present value of the project.

Years	Annual After-Tax Cash Flows
0	−$12,000
1	1,500
2	2,500
3	4,000
4	4,000
5	5,000

SOLUTION

Hewlett Packard 17B II

1. Select the FIN menu and then the CFLO menu; clear memory if FLOW(0) = ? does not appear.
2. Enter the investment outlay, CF_0, as follows: 12000 [+/−] [INPUT]
3. Enter the first year after-tax cash flows, CF_1, as follows: 1500 [INPUT]
4. Now the calculator will inquire if the $1,500 is for period 1 only. Press [INPUT] to indicate that the cash flow amount is for one year only.
5. Enter the remaining cash flow amounts, followed each time by [INPUT]. (Since $4,000 is expected for two years consecutively, to indicate two years of cash flows we could press [2] [INPUT].)
6. Press [EXIT] and then [CALC].
7. Enter 14 [I%] to indicate the discount rate.
8. Press [NPV] to find the project net present value of −$1,095.

Texas Instruments BAII Plus

1. Press [CF] to select the cash flow worksheet.
2. Press [2nd] [CLR Work] to clear memory.
3. Enter the investment outlay, CF_0, as follows: 12,000 [+/−] [ENTER]
4. Enter the first year after-tax cash flows, CF1, as follows: [↓] 1,500 [ENTER] [↓]
5. Enter the frequency number, F01. Key in "1" and press [ENTER] to indicate that the cash flow amount is for one year only.
6. Repeat steps 4 and 5 to enter the other cash flows. (Since $4,000 is expected for two years consecutively, to indicate two years of cash flows we could press 2 [ENTER].)
7. Press [NPV] 14 [ENTER] to indicate the discount rate of 14%.
8. Press [↓] [CPT] to compute the net present value of −$1,095.

on target. The internal rate of return (IRR) provides that answer by measuring the rate of return we expect to earn on the project.

To calculate the internal rate of return, we must find the discount rate that gives us a zero net present value. At that rate, the present value of future cash flows just

equals the investment outlay. For the previous example, we need to determine the discount rate that causes the present value of future cash flows to equal $12,000, the cost of the investment. In other words, we need to find the internal rate of return that satisfies the following condition:

$$\frac{\text{Present value of future}}{\text{after-tax cash flows}} - \frac{\text{Initial}}{\text{investment outlay}} = \$0$$

or

$$\frac{\text{Present value of future}}{\text{after-tax cash flows}} = \frac{\text{Initial}}{\text{investment outlay}}$$

If ACF_t is the after-tax cash flows received in year t, IO is the amount of the investment outlay, n is the life of the project in years, and the internal rate of return, IRR, is the discount rate, we have

$$\left[\frac{ACF_1}{(1 + IRR)^1}\right] + \frac{ACF_2}{(1 + IRR)^2} + \frac{ACF_3}{(1 + IRR)^3} + \cdots + \frac{ACF_t}{(1 + IRR)^n}) - IO = \$0$$

Thus, for the previous example, the equation for finding the IRR would be as follows:

$$\left[\frac{\$1{,}500}{(1+IRR)^1} + \frac{\$2{,}500}{(1+IRR)^2} + \frac{\$4{,}000}{(1+IRR)^3} + \frac{\$4{,}000}{(1+IRR)^4} + \frac{\$5{,}000}{(1+IRR)^5}\right] - \$12{,}000 = \$0$$

However, we cannot solve for the internal rate of return (IRR) directly from the above equation. We would have to try different internal rates of return until we eventually found the answer. Fortunately, a financial calculator will compute the answer for us.

To find the internal rate of return using either the Hewlett Packard 17B II or the Texas Instruments BAII Plus, repeat the steps taken in Figure 23B-1. Then, on either calculator, press IRR. The answer will be 10.74 percent. Of course, it would have been simpler to compute the IRR while the data were still in the calculator. An even better approach is to use a computer spreadsheet, such as Excel or Lotus, to solve the problem.

chapter 24

Risk and Insurance

In the Spotlight

T. Shipley

Thomas Shipley's firm, T. Shipley, is based in Altamonte Springs, Florida. The company sells business accessories, and a significant part of its revenues—30 percent to be exact—comes from orders placed on the firm's Web site. To be certain that the company's online transactions are as safe as possible, Shipley pays about $14,000 a year for a policy to insure the Web operations. The policy covers such costs as those that may result from hackers' attacking the firm's Web page.

Although Shipley has not had to file a claim on this policy, he is very happy that he has it. In Shipley's mind, the security he gains with the policy more than compensates for the additional expense. For him, the threat of a virus or other online risks is enough to warrant paying for the policy.

Insuring a company's Internet business is a new concept; most firms currently choose not to carry such insurance. But given some companies' unnerving experiences with hackers, the practice may become more popular in the future. ◆

Source: Ilan Mochari, "A Security Blanket for Your Web Site," *Inc.*, Vol. 22, No. 18 (December 2000), pp. 133–134.

http://www.tshipley.com

LOOKING AHEAD

After studying this chapter, you should be able to

1. *Define risk and explain the nature of risk.*
2. *Explain how risk management can be used in coping with business risks.*
3. *Describe the risks associated with different types of assets, both physical and human.*
4. *Explain the basic principles used in evaluating an insurance program and the fundamental requirements for obtaining insurance.*
5. *Identify the different types of insurance coverage.*

Because we live in a world of uncertainty, how we see risk is vitally important in almost all dimensions of our life. Risk must certainly be considered in making any business decisions. As sixth-century Greek poet and statesman Solon wrote,

There is risk in everything that one does, and no one knows where he will make his landfall when his enterprise is at its beginning. One man, trying to act effectively, fails to foresee something and falls into great and grim ruination, but to another man, one who is acting ineffectively, a god gives good fortune in everything and escape from his folly.[1]

While Solon gave more credit than we would to Zeus for the outcomes of ventures, his insight reminds us that little is new in this world, including the need to acknowledge and compensate as best we can for the risks we encounter. Peter Bernstein describes the importance of understanding the concept of risk as follows:

The revolutionary idea that defines the boundary between modern times and the past is the mastery of risk: the notion that the future is more than a whim of the gods and that men and women are not passive before nature. Until human beings discovered a way across that boundary, the future was a mirror of the past or the murky domain of oracles and soothsayers who held a monopoly over knowledge of anticipated events.[2]

Risk means different things to different people, depending on the context and on how they feel about taking chances. For a student, risk might be represented by the possibility of failing an exam. For a coal miner, risk might be represented by the chance of an explosion in the mine. For a retired person, risk could mean the likelihood of not being able to live comfortably on his or her fixed income. An entrepreneur's risk takes the form of the chance that a new venture will fail.

It is often said "Nothing is certain except death and taxes." Entrepreneurs might extend this adage: "Nothing is certain except death, taxes, and small business risks." Chapter 1 noted the moderate risk-taking propensities of entrepreneurs and their desire to exert some control over the risky situations in which they find themselves. In keeping with this desire, they seek to minimize business risks as much as possible. Our study of this important topic begins with a definition of risk.

What Is Risk?

1

Define risk and explain the nature of risk.

risk
the chance that a situation may end with loss or misfortune

market risk
the uncertainty associated with an investment decision

pure risk
the uncertainty associated with a situation where only loss or no loss can occur

Simply stated, **risk** is "a condition in which there is a possibility of an adverse deviation from a desired outcome that is expected or hoped for."[3] Applied to a business, risk translates into the possibility of losses associated with the assets and the earnings potential of the firm. Here, the term *assets* includes not only inventory and equipment but also such factors as the firm's employees and its reputation.

Business risks can be classified into two broad categories: market risk and pure risk. **Market risk** is the uncertainty associated with an investment decision. An entrepreneur who invests in a new business hopes for a gain but realizes that the eventual outcome may be a loss. Only after identifying the investment opportunity, developing strategies, and committing resources will she or he find out whether the final result is a gain or a loss.

Pure risk is used to describe a situation where only loss or no loss can occur—there is no potential gain. Owning property, for instance, creates the possibility of loss due to fire or severe weather; the only outcomes are loss or no loss. As a general rule, only pure risk is insurable. That is, insurance is not intended to protect investors from market risks, where the chances of both gain and loss exist. Later in the chapter, different categories of pure risk will be described, but for now, let's focus on risk management.

Risk Management

Explain how risk management can be used in coping with business risks.

risk management
ways of coping with risk that are designed to preserve assets and the earning power of a firm

Risk management consists of all efforts to preserve the assets and earning power of a business. Since risk management has grown out of insurance management, the two terms are often used interchangeably. However, risk management has a much broader meaning, covering both insurable and uninsurable risks and including non-insurance approaches to reducing all types of pure risks. Risk management involves more than trying to obtain the most insurance for each dollar spent; it is concerned with finding the best way possible to reduce the cost of handling risk. Insurance is only one of several approaches to minimizing the pure risks a firm encounters.

The Process of Risk Management

Five steps are required to implement risk management and its goal of preserving a firm's assets and earning power:[4]

Step 1: Identify risks. It is essential that a business owner be aware of the risks the firm faces. To reduce the chance of overlooking important risks, a business should adopt a systematic approach to identifying pure risks. Useful identification methods include insurance policy checklists, questionnaires, analysis of financial statements, and careful analysis of a firm's operations.

Step 2: Evaluate risks. Once the various risks have been identified, they must be evaluated in terms of the potential size of each loss and the probability that it will occur. At a minimum, risks should be classified into three groups: critical (loss could result in bankruptcy), important (loss would require investment of additional capital to continue operations), and unimportant (loss could easily be covered with current income or existing assets).

Step 3: Select methods to manage risk. The two basic ways to deal with risk are risk control and risk financing.

Risk control is designed to minimize loss through avoidance and/or reduction. **Risk avoidance** is achieved by choosing not to engage in a hazardous activity. For instance, the risk of losing critical computer records can be avoided by storing backup files at a different physical location. Keeping backup disks in the desk drawer in the same office as the computer will do little good if the desk is damaged by fire or water. **Risk reduction** focuses on lessening the frequency, severity, or unpredictability of losses. For example, a small firm needs to take every possible precaution to reduce the likelihood and severity of fires, including inspecting the safety of building construction, installing a completely automatic sprinkler system, providing an adequate water supply, and implementing a fire prevention program that keeps employees conscious of fire-safety measures. The building should be made of fire-resistant materials, and the electrical wiring should be adequate to carry the maximum load of electrical energy that will be imposed. Fire doors and insulation should be used where necessary.

risk control
minimizing potential losses by avoiding or reducing risk

risk avoidance
preventing risk by choosing not to engage in hazardous activities

risk reduction
lessening the frequency, severity, or unpredictability of losses

Risk financing, on the other hand, focuses on making funds available for losses that cannot be managed by risk control; it involves transferring the risk or retaining the risk. **Risk transfer** is accomplished largely through buying insurance but can also be achieved by making contractual arrangements that transfer the risk to others. Contractual arrangements, for example, can include subcontracting an activity or purchasing a surety bond to protect against employee fraud. **Risk retention** occurs when a firm does not take action to avoid, reduce, or transfer a risk and, thus, exposes itself to the risk. Retaining risk can be a conscious or unconscious decision and either voluntary or involuntary in nature. One common form of risk retention is **self-insurance,** in which part of a firm's earnings is designated as a cushion against possible future losses. Self-insurance can take a general or a specific form. In its general form, a part of the firm's earnings is earmarked for a contingency fund against possible future losses, regardless of the source. In its specific form, a self-insurance program designates funds to individual loss categories such as property, healthcare, or workers' compensation. Some firms have begun to rely heavily on self-insurance, particularly in the area of medical coverage for employees. However, we should point out that self-insurance is not affordable for every small firm. As a rule of thumb, a firm should have a net worth of at least $250,000 and at least 25 employees to be self-funded. Moreover, very few firms can practice unlimited self-insurance, especially when it comes to liability claims. Unless a small company has insurance to cover losses above a certain level, any large loss could put it out of business. Finally, self-insurance plans need to be approved and monitored to protect the interests of those covered.

risk financing
making funds available to cover losses that could not be managed by risk control

risk transfer
buying insurance or making contractual arrangements with others in order to transfer risk

risk retention
choosing—whether consciously or unconsciously, voluntarily or involuntarily—to manage risk internally

self-insurance
designating part of a firm's earnings as a cushion against possible future losses

In choosing the appropriate method for managing risk, the small business owner should consider the size of each potential loss, its probability of occurrence, and what resources would be available to cover the loss if it did occur. Table 24-1 shows the appropriate risk management techniques for potential losses of different probabilities (low frequency and high frequency) and sizes (low severity and high severity).

Step 4: Implement the decision. Once the decision has been made to use a particular technique or techniques to manage a firm's risks, this decision must be followed by action, such as purchasing insurance and/or setting aside backup funds to cope with any risks that have been retained. Failure to act—or even procrastination—could be a fatal error.

Step 5: Evaluate and review. Evaluation and review of the chosen risk management technique are essential because conditions change—new risks arise, and old ones disappear. Also, reviewing earlier decisions to use specific methods may identify mistakes made previously.

TABLE 24-1

Tools for Managing Risk

	High Frequency	Low Frequency
High Severity	• Risk avoidance • Risk reduction	• Self-insurance • Contractual agreements
Low Severity	• Risk reduction • Risk retention	• Risk retention

Note: To find a listing of the risk management tools appropriate for dealing with a potential loss, see the box corresponding to the severity and frequency of the potential loss.

Risk Management and the Small Firm

Regardless of the nature of a business, risk management is a serious issue, for small firms as well as large companies. Too often in the past, small businesses paid insufficient attention to analyzing potential risk. Today, such a situation is unthinkable. The small business owner must take an active role in managing the risks of her or his firm.

Risk management in a small firm differs from that in a large firm in several ways. First, insurance companies are not always eager to insure small firms and may even turn them down in some cases. Also, in a large firm, the responsibilities of risk management are frequently assigned to a specialized staff manager. It is more difficult for a small company to address risk management, because its risk manager is usually the owner, and the owner wears so many hats. Furthermore, risk management is not something that requires immediate attention—until something happens. Although small businesses have been slow to focus on managing risk, a prudent small business owner will take the time to identify the different types of risks faced by the firm and find ways to cope with them.

Classifying Risks by Type of Asset

Describe the risks associated with different types of assets, both physical and human.

As a practical matter, risks may be grouped according to the type of asset—physical or human—needing protection. Specifically, there are property-oriented risks, personnel-oriented risks, and customer-oriented risks. Figure 24-1 illustrates these risk categories and their components, with bankruptcy being the ultimate small business risk.

Property Risks

Property-oriented risks involve tangible and highly visible assets. When these physical assets are lost or destroyed, they are quickly missed. Fortunately, many property-oriented risks are insurable; they include fire, natural disasters, burglary and business swindles, and shoplifting.

FIRE Buildings, equipment, and inventory items can be totally or partially destroyed by fire. Of course, the degree of risk and potential for loss are different for each type of business. For example, industrial processes that are hazardous or that involve explosives, combustibles, or other flammable materials increase this particular risk.

Fire not only causes direct property loss but also interrupts business operations. Although a firm's operations may be halted, such fixed expenses as rent, supervisory salaries, and insurance fees continue.

FIGURE 24-1

The Wheel of Misfortune

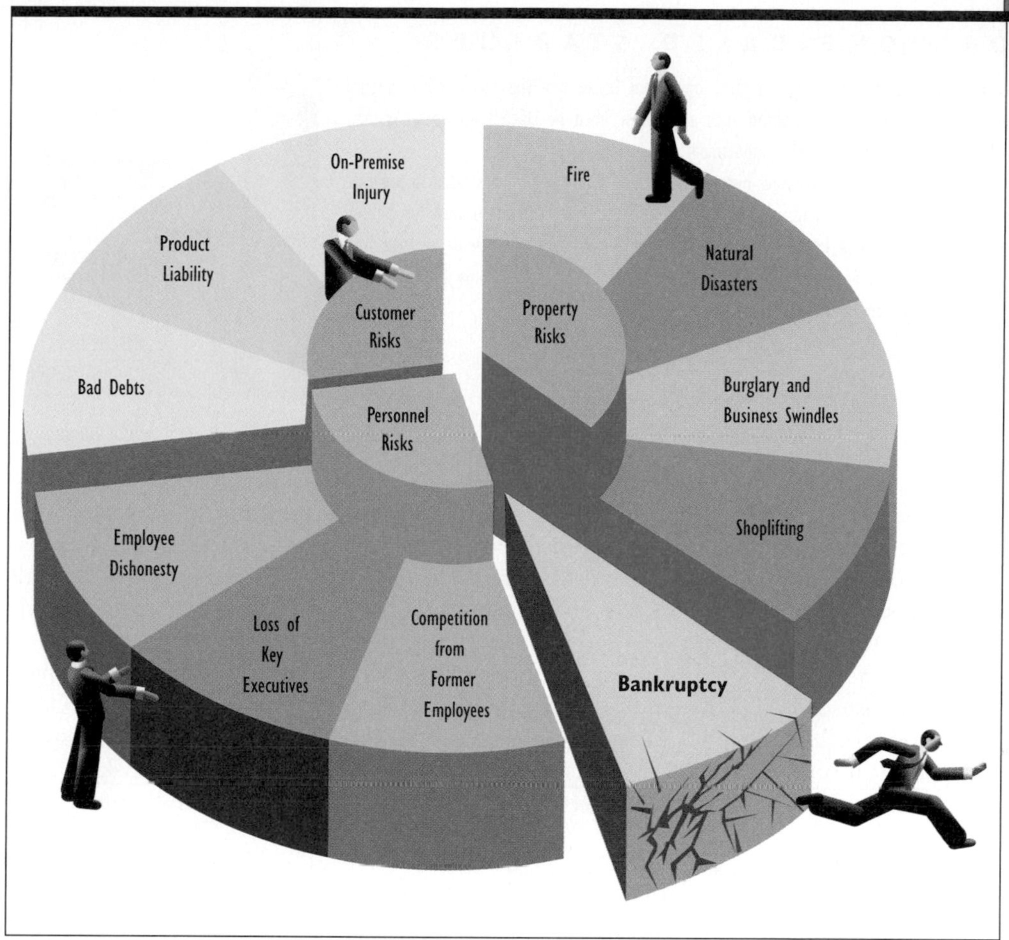

NATURAL DISASTERS Floods, hurricanes, tornadoes, and hail are often described as "acts of god" because of human limitations in foreseeing and controlling them. Like fire, natural disasters may interrupt business operations. Although a firm can take certain preventive measures to reduce a risk—for example, locating in an area not subject to flood damage—little can be done to avoid natural disasters. To minimize losses arising from business interruptions, a firm might, for example, have alternative sources of electric power, such as its own generators, for use in times of emergency.

Small businesses rely heavily on insurance in coping with natural disaster losses. Insurance may be purchased for flood damage to buildings, but only through a federal flood insurance program—and only in areas that have agreed to practice land-use management. Flood damage to movable property is insurable; for example, automobile policies usually provide insurance to cover flood damage to a vehicle. Similar insurance coverage can be acquired for losses incurred because of severe wind damage. In June 2001, Tropical Storm Allison struck the Houston, Texas area, resulting in over $1 billion in insurance claims, but that did not compare to the $16 billion in insurance losses resulting from Hurricane Andrew in 1992.

ENTREPRENEURSHIP TODAY

IN THE TRENCHES

INSURANCE FOR HOME-BASED STARTUPS

Home-based startups often have trouble getting insurance coverage for their operations because of the considerable amount of risk associated with the lack of a track record. Jon Feld experienced such a problem when he started Navigator Systems Inc., an information-technology consulting firm, in his 800-square-foot apartment.

Feld recalls that several insurers would not cover his operations because he did not have a business address separate from his home address. Determined to obtain both commercial insurance for the business and medical insurance for himself and his two employees, Feld persevered. He said, "We had a lot of misfires even though we were working with an insurance agent, which we thought would help us reach the right insurer quickly." It took the guidance of other home business owners coupled with the insurance agent's advice, to get coverage.

Source: Jill Andresky Fraser, "Getting the Right Insurance When You're Going Solo," *Inc.*, Vol. 21, No. 18, (December 1999) pp. 92–108.

BURGLARY AND BUSINESS SWINDLES The unauthorized entering of premises with the intent to commit a crime, such as the removal of cash or merchandise, is called burglary. Although insurance should be carried against losses from burglary, a small business may find it helpful to install a security alarm system or to arrange for private security services.

Business swindles cost firms thousands of dollars each year. Small firms are particularly susceptible to swindles such as bogus office-machine repairs, phony charity appeals, billing for listings in nonexistent directories, sales of advertising space in publications whose nature is misrepresented, and advance-fee deals. Risks of this kind are avoided only through alertness on the part of the business owner-manager.

SHOPLIFTING It is estimated that retailers lose $10 billion in merchandise each year—more than $25 million per day—to shoplifting. There are an estimated 23 million shoplifters in the United States today. Over 10 million people have been caught shoplifting in the last five years. Moreover, costs related to shoplifting are not limited to the loss of merchandise; hidden costs include the following:[5]

- The higher prices consumers have to pay for merchandise
- The added burden on the police and the courts
- The cost and inconvenience of security measures in retail stores
- The family problems that result from arrests on shoplifting charges
- The overall effect on the quality of life in a community

There are two types of shoplifters: professionals and nonprofessionals. Professional shoplifters—those for whom crime is a primary source of income—are much more skillful. Cleverly designed devices, such as clothing with large hidden pockets and shielded shopping bags for transporting merchandise with antitheft tags past detection gates, help the professional shoplifter conceal items both small and large.

Nonprofessional shoplifters steal goods that can be quickly and easily hidden inside clothing, a backpack, or a handbag. Shoplifting by these individuals is rarely about meeting physical needs. More often, the compulsion to steal arises from per-

sonal conflicts and emotional needs. Nonprofessional shoplifters usually know right from wrong and understand the potential consequences of their actions. They often don't need and sometimes don't use the items they steal. They usually have the money to pay for the item, rarely plan their theft in advance, and never try to sell the item for profit.

Precautionary measures that may be taken by small businesses to minimize shoplifting include the following:[6]

1. Train employees to be attentive. "Shoplifting is a constant problem for us," says Ed Sherman, owner of Sherman's Inc., a Tulsa, Oklahoma variety store. "It costs us a lot of money." Sherman's solution is to train employees in customer service. "An attentive sales force is the best deterrent to shoplifting," says Sherman, "because the shoplifter's first requirement is privacy."
2. Post signs around the store warning potential thieves that you will prosecute and then follow up on that threat. Katy Culmo, owner of By George, a women's clothing store in Austin, Texas, maintains that the best shoplifting defense is a strong offense. She cultivates a reputation for being hard on thieves. "An ambivalent approach makes you a target," Culmo says. Her clothes bear tags that sound an alarm if not removed at the cash register, and she trains her staff to catch and detain shoplifters.
3. Hang convex mirrors to eliminate blind aisles, and install alarms on emergency exits.
4. Display expensive items in security cases. Place "targeted" merchandise—those items most at risk—out of reach, near checkout stands. Howard Laves, owner of Benolds, a jewelry store in Austin, Texas, uses cameras and alarms to deter shoplifters. "We show expensive pieces one at a time," he says. When a thief is caught, Laves prosecutes.
5. Reduce clutter; arrange merchandise so that unexplained gaps on shelves can be easily detected.
6. Channel the flow of your customers past the cashier, and block off unused checkout stands.
7. Attend to the needs of your customers. Be visible, and be available.
8. Monitor fitting rooms and employee-only areas.
9. Consider using uniformed or plain-clothed store detectives, two-way mirrors, electronic sales tags, and video cameras.
10. Ask the police to do a "walk-through" of your store to pinpoint vulnerable areas.

http://www.benolds.com

In physical appearance, professional and nonprofessional shoplifters are undistinguishable from paying customers. Thus, reducing shoplifting by learning to recognize the profile of each type of shoplifter is not an easy task.

Personnel Risks

Personnel-oriented losses occur through the actions of employees. Employee theft, an illegal and intentional act against the business, is a major concern of many small firms. The sickness or injury of an employee can also give rise to a business loss. The three primary types of personnel-oriented risks are dishonesty of current employees, competition from former employees, and loss of key executives. Most employee-oriented risks are insurable.

EMPLOYEE DISHONESTY One of the more serious problems facing small businesses today is fraud and theft by employees. Employee theft accounts for 50 to 70 percent of all workplace crime. "If you have one or more employees, you're vulnerable," says Read Hayes, senior consultant at Loss Prevention Specialists in Winter Park, Florida.[7]

http://www.lossprevention.com

The extent and variety of such crimes are limitless, and objects include not only cash but also inventory items, tools, scrap materials, postage stamps, and the like. Possibilities exist for forgery, raising the amounts on checks, and other fraudulent practices. For example, a trusted bookkeeper could collude with an outsider to have presented for payment bogus invoices or invoices that are double or triple the correct amount. The bookkeeper could approve such invoices for payment, write a check, and secure the manager's signature. Two actual cases follow:

- An owner of a wholesale firm hired his wife's cousin, who had excellent credentials. The owner did not suspect any problems until the employee began changing his lifesyle—he bought a new house and sent his children to private schools, among other things. The employee was stealing inventory from the warehouse—$250,000 worth, to be exact. When discovered, the employee repaid the firm for a small part of the thefts (most of the money had been spent) and was dismissed from his job. Even though the owner's wife was furious that one of her own extended family members had stolen from them, she and her husband decided not to prosecute. But the emotional pain, not to mention the financial loss, was significant.
- A loan manager at a small bank was keeping the proceeds from collateral sold to pay delinquent debts and was writing off the loans as losses to the bank.

Small businesses are particularly vulnerable to employee fraud because owners generally do not have effective systems with which to monitor key workers who are given major responsibilities. A study based on experiences of members of the Association of Certified Fraud Examiners reports that the costliest abuses take place in companies with fewer than 100 employees. Joseph T. Wells, founder and chairman of the association, warns businesspeople against uncritically accepting the notion that most people are immune to the temptation to commit fraud. "[That] is probably the biggest myth of all about financial crimes," he says. "Fraud perpetrators come from all walks of life, all economic circumstances, and all social classes."[8]

http://www.cfenet.com

The best defenses against employee theft fall into a few general categories: (1) careful screening of applicants before they are hired, (2) effective internal controls to protect the firm's assets, and (3) safeguards, such as passwords, to prevent computer-related theft. Bonding employees—that is, purchasing from a bonding company insurance that will protect the purchasing firm against loss from employee fraud or embezzlement—is another way to counter the cost of employee dishonesty. However, a firm's most effective protection against employee fraud is to develop a comprehensive system of internal control. Some specific ways to defend against employee theft follow:[9]

- *Create a culture of honesty by establishing a written code of ethics and conduct. Train your employees in how to spot a problem and what to do about it. "If your corporate culture is one where people work hard and enjoy being a team, that's subtle social control," Hayes says. "If someone is doing something wrong, others will exert pressure on him to stop or will tell someone in authority. If, on the other hand, your culture is one of 'Get what you can get while you can get it,' there are going to be problems." Make sure managers lead by example and maintain a high level of integrity.*

- *Institute an employee screening program that will weed out potentially troublesome candidates.*
- *Do criminal background checks and drug testing on potential hires.*
- *Administer a standardized paper-and-pencil test (available from career counseling centers) that will indicate the respondent's level of integrity.*
- *Require keys and access cards for areas containing sensitive materials, and limit the number of employees who have them.*
- *Lock up laptops, cell phones, and other valuables at the end of the day.*

COMPETITION FROM FORMER EMPLOYEES Good employees are hard to find; they're even harder to keep. When a business experiences employee turnover—and it always will—there may be risks associated with former employees. Salespeople, beauticians, and other employees often take business with them when they leave. The risk is particularly acute with turnover of key executives, as they are likely candidates to start a competing business or to leave with trade secrets.

Most firms are very sensitive to the activities of former employees. Consider the following situation: You work for a firm that makes equipment and supplies used in oil fields. Through your job, you meet Hank Sorens, who owns a company that sells parts to your employer. You begin ordering parts from a second company owned by Sorens. In time, you and Sorens form your own corporation. You quit your job and begin competing with your former employer, who may elect to sue you and Sorens for misappropriating its manufacturing procedures and other alleged trade secrets. Courts have frequently awarded significant sums in such cases.

One common practice to reduce this kind of employee-oriented risk is to require employees to sign employment contracts that clearly set forth the employee's promise not to disclose certain information or use it to compete against the employer.

LOSS OF KEY EXECUTIVES Every successful small business has one or more key executives. These employees could be lost through death or through attraction to other employment. If key personnel cannot be successfully replaced, a small firm may suffer appreciably from the loss of their services.

In addition to valuable experience and skill, key executives may have specialized knowledge that is vital to the successful operation of a firm. Consider the case of a manufacturing firm executive who was killed in an auto accident at the age of 53. His processing operations involved the use of a secret chemical formula that he had personally devised and had divulged to no one because of his fear of losing the formula to competitors. Not even his family knew the formula. As a result of his sudden death, the firm went out of business within six months. Expensive special-purpose equipment had to be sold as junk. All that his widow salvaged was about $60,000 worth of bonds and the Florida residence that had been the couple's winter home.

At least two solutions are available to a small firm that may be faced with this situation. The first solution is purchasing life insurance, which is discussed later in this chapter. The second is developing replacement personnel. A potential replacement should be groomed for every key position, including the position of owner-manager.

Customer Risks

Customers are the source of profit for small businesses, but they are also the source of an ever-increasing amount of business risk. Much of this risk is attributable to on-premises injuries and product liability.

ON-PREMISES INJURIES Customers may initiate legal claims as a result of on-premises injuries. Because of high in-store traffic, this risk is particularly acute for small retailers. Personal injury liability may occur, for example, when a customer breaks an arm by slipping on icy steps while entering or leaving a store. An employer is, of course, at risk when employees suffer similar fates; but customers, because of their sheer numbers and lack of personal attachment to the business, make this risk more significant.

Another form of on-premises risk arises from inadequate security, which may result in robbery, assault, or other violent crimes. The number of on-premises liability cases involving violent crimes has increased dramatically during the past decade. Customers who are victims often look to the business to recover their losses.

Good management of this kind of customer-oriented risk requires a regular check of the premises for hazards. The concept of preventive maintenance applies to management of this risk factor.

PRODUCT LIABILITY Recent court decisions on product liability have broadened the scope of this form of risk. No reputable small business would intentionally produce or sell a product that would harm a customer, but good intentions are a weak defense in liability lawsuits.

A product liability suit may be filed when a customer becomes ill or sustains physical or property damage from using a product made or sold by a firm. Class action suits, together with individual suits, are now widely used by consumers in product liability cases. Some types of businesses operate in higher-risk markets than others. For example, the insulation business has been the target of numerous claims, based on the physical effects of asbestos on those exposed to it.

While risk management involves more than insurance, purchasing insurance is one of the main ways a small firm manages its risk. Let's now focus on this important component.

Insurance for the Small Business

Explain the basic principles used in evaluating an insurance program and the fundamental requirements for obtaining insurance.

Insurance provides one of the most important means for small firms to transfer business risks. A sound insurance program is imperative for the proper protection of a small business. Many small firms carry insufficient insurance protection—a fact that the entrepreneur often comes to realize only after a major loss. Good risk management requires careful study of insurance policies prior to a loss, rather than after a loss has occurred.

Small firms frequently pay significantly higher insurance premiums than do their larger counterparts. For example, at the beginning of 1999, health-care premiums increased by as much as 50 percent for some small companies. Small firms have always been more vulnerable to health-care premium increases, largely because their smaller number of employees poses a much greater actuarial risk to insurers. That may explain why Romano Brothers & Company received a notice of a 26 percent increase in its health-insurance premium. "Maybe it's because suddenly our employees have been having kids, so they have a lot more dependents to cover," says William Romano, owner of the family business. Also, small firms lag behind large companies in enrolling in managed-care plans, which are generally cheaper than traditional fee-for-service coverage.[10] Thus, small business owners are learning that, in order to keep insurance costs down, they must take an active role and become their own risk managers. They can no longer afford to sit back and wait for suggestions

IN THE TRENCHES ENTREPRENEURSHIP TODAY

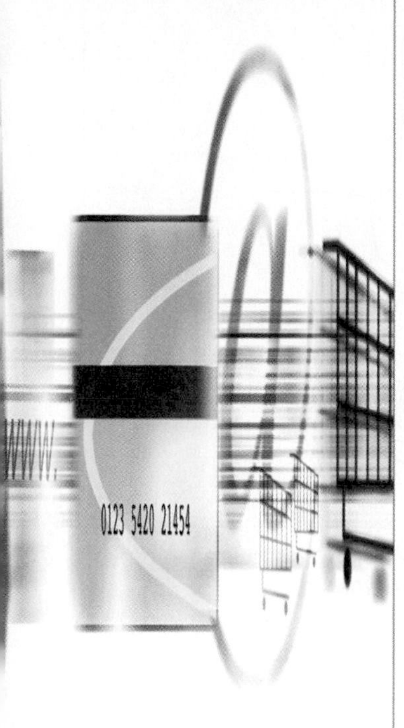

BUG YOUR BROKER

Keith Alper had reached the boiling point about his firm's insurance costs. His company, which had just under 60 employees, was spending $75,000 on policies. "We'd accumulated a lot of policies over the years, and at times we just paid our bills and didn't look at what we were paying for," says Alper, whose Creative Producers Group (CPG), based in St. Louis, produces videos and events for *Fortune 500* clients.

CPG's overspending on insurance could have been avoided if the firm had simply asked its broker a few basic questions and notified him of certain changes. For a whole year, CPG had been paying for coverage on four rental cars when it had only three. "When we asked, 'Why didn't you take that fourth car off the policy?' the answer was 'You didn't tell us to,'" says CPG director of finance and administration Lee Gerstenhaber.

After identifying the problem, Alper and Gerstenhaber grilled their broker on all insurance-related spending. They were stunned at what they found. In CPG's workers' compensation plan, several employees were in higher risk categories than they should have been because, initially, the company had made the mistake of basing such classifications on salary and position rather than on job activity. In other words, CPG executives who warranted a "clerical" classification for insurance purposes didn't get one, since the company wrongly assumed that the category was just for administrative staff.

CPG also asked the broker to translate all policies into "real English" and categorize each one as a "must," "should," or "shouldn't." One policy, known as bailee insurance, didn't survive the translation test. In real English, a bailee is a person to whom property is entrusted for a special purpose and a limited period. Alper's broker explained that although CPG technically was a bailee when it stored clients' property, the bailee policy was redundant with the company's general liability coverage and was therefore unnecessary.

CPG found its biggest cost savings simply by asking the broker for higher deductibles (and the resulting lower premiums) on rarely used policies. At CPG's request, the broker created a grid for each policy, including a sliding scale of premium and deductible rates and a history of claims. In both professional liability and general liability, for which the claims were few and far between, CPG got lower premiums. All told, the company saved $10,000 in annual insurance costs.

But even more important to CPG's managers has been the newfound discipline of reviewing policies annually. "We've learned to be proactive and ask questions," says Gerstenhaber, "as opposed to just blindly accepting what they give us."

Source: Ilan Mochari, "Bug Your Broker," *Inc.*, Vol. 22, No. 11 (August 2000), pp. 127–128.

http://www.getcreative.com

from insurance agents. Instead, they need to formulate and offer their own ideas, based on an understanding of the basic principles of a sound insurance program. (See Figure 24-2 on page 620.)

Basic Principles of a Sound Insurance Program

What kinds of risks can be covered by insurance? What types of coverage should be purchased? How much coverage is adequate? Unfortunately, there are no clear-cut answers to these questions. A reputable insurance agent can provide valuable assistance to a small firm in evaluating risks and designing proper protection plans, but an entrepreneur should become as knowledgeable as possible about what insurance is available. Basic principles in evaluating an insurance program include identifying business risks to be insured, limiting coverage to major potential losses, and relating premium costs to probability of loss.

IDENTIFYING INSURABLE BUSINESS RISKS Although the most common insurable risks were pointed out earlier, other less obvious risks may be revealed only by careful investigation. A small firm must first obtain risk coverages required by law or by

FIGURE 24-2

Risk-Taking Begins Early

SCHWADRON
"WE'RE STARTING FIRST-AID TRAINING, DAD. I NEED $150,000 FOR MALPRACTICE INSURANCE."

contract, such as workers' compensation insurance and automobile liability insurance. As part of the risk-identification process, plant and equipment should be reevaluated periodically by competent appraisers in order to ensure that adequate insurance coverage is maintained.

LIMITING COVERAGE TO MAJOR POTENTIAL LOSSES A small firm must determine the magnitude of loss that it could bear without serious financial difficulty. If the firm is sufficiently strong, it may decide to avoid purchasing unnecessary insurance by covering only those losses exceeding a specified minimum amount. It is important, of course, to guard against underestimating the severity of potential losses.

RELATING PREMIUM COSTS TO PROBABILITY OF LOSS Because insurance companies must collect enough premiums to pay the actual losses of insured parties, the cost of insurance must be proportional to the probability of occurrence of the insured event. As the loss becomes more certain, premium costs become so high that a firm may find that insurance is simply not worth the cost. Thus, insurance is most applicable and practical for *improbable* losses—that is, situations where the probability that the loss will occur is low, but the overall cost of the loss would be high. Larry Joiner, owner of West Coast Roofing and Waterproofing Company in Naples, Florida, reduced his insurance coverage by raising damage deductibles on his building and cutting back on vehicle-damage insurance. Because his roofing company could be swept away by a hurricane coming off the Gulf of Mexico, Joiner modified his coverage to use premium dollars where losses were likely to be most costly.

http://www.westcoastroofing.com

IN THE TRENCHES ENTREPRENEURSHIP TODAY

DON'T OVERLOOK THE POSSIBILITY OF DISABILITY

David Burros learned about disability insurance 10 years ago when his mother had a debilitating stroke that left her unable to continue the daily operations of the family antique shop. There was no one available to operate the business, and no financial resources to compensate for the loss.

David Burros is now a certified financial planner and CEO of Burros Consulting and Speaking, a personal and financial planning consulting firm in Denver. Because of his family's experience, he counsels his clients to protect their businesses with proper insurance before it is too late. As Burros contends, "Your greatest asset isn't your business but rather your ability to create wealth. You can lose everything else, and you'll get it all back again if you have the ability to work. That's why disability insurance is the first kind of insurance business owners should consider."

Burros recommends long-term disability insurance to guard against business loss resulting from a disability that lasts longer than 90 days. However, small business owners who cannot afford to purchase a disability policy that protects them until age 65 should consider, at the very least, a short-term policy.

Source: Claire Tristram, "For Good Measure," *Entrepreneur,* Vol. 27, No. 6 (June 1999), p. 38.

"You've got to be alert," says Joiner, "and you've got to care about these insurance details yourself."[11]

Requirements for Obtaining Insurance

Before an insurance company will be willing to underwrite possible losses, the particular risk and the insured firm must meet certain requirements. The risk must be calculable and exist in large numbers, the insured property must have commercial value, and the policyholder must have an insurable interest in the property or person insured.

- *The risk must be calculable.* The total overall loss arising from many insured risks can be calculated by means of actuarial tables. For example, the number of buildings that will suffer fire damage each year can be predicted with some accuracy. An insurance company can determine appropriate insurance rates only if the risks can be calculated.
- *The risk must exist in large numbers.* A particular risk must occur in sufficiently large numbers and be spread over a wide enough geographical area to permit the law of averages to work. A fire insurance company, for example, cannot afford to insure only one building or even all the buildings in a single town. It would have to insure multiple buildings in many towns and cities before it would be assured of an adequate, safe distribution of risk.
- *The insured property must have commercial value.* An item that possesses only sentimental value cannot be insured. For example, an old family photo that is of no value to the public may not be included among insured items whose value can be measured in monetary terms.
- *The policyholder must have an insurable interest in the property or person insured.* The purpose for insurance is reimbursement of actual loss, not creation of profit for the insured. For example, a firm could insure a building worth

$70,000 for $500,000, but it could collect only $70,000, the actual worth of the building, in case of loss. So, insuring for an amount higher than actual value is simply a waste of money, with no benefit to the insured. Similarly, a firm cannot obtain life insurance on its customers or suppliers.

Types of Insurance

5 *Identify the different types of insurance coverage.*

Several classifications of insurance and a variety of coverages are available from different insurance companies. Each purchaser of insurance should seek a balance among coverage, deductions, and premiums. Since the trend is toward higher and higher premiums for small businesses, the balancing act is becoming even more critical.

commercial property insurance
coverage that protects against losses associated with damage to or loss of property

COMMERCIAL PROPERTY COVERAGE **Commercial property insurance** provides protection from losses associated with damage to or loss of property. Causes of property loss that can be covered include fire, explosion, vandalism, broken glass, business interruption, and employee dishonesty.

business interruption insurance
coverage of lost income and certain other expenses while the business is being rebuilt

http://www.citylaundry.com

Most entrepreneurs recognize the need for protection against fire and maybe a few other, more traditional losses. However, few small business owners realize the value of business interruption insurance. **Business interruption insurance** protects firms during the period necessary to restore property damaged by an insured risk. Such coverage pays for lost income and certain other expenses of rebuilding the business. Standard property insurance will not, for example, cover payroll and other expenses that must be paid while a factory is being rebuilt. Other arrangements can also be made to minimize potential losses from the interruption of a firm's business. City Laundry and Drycleaning Company, a 50-year-old small business in Ohio, suffered $5 million in damage due to a fire. However, management had prepared a comprehensive disaster plan years earlier. Company employees had been trained in procedures to follow during such an emergency, and the company had agreements with other firms to transfer work in case of disruptions. Not only did City Laundry lease a new location and order new inventories within 24 hours after the fire; it was open for business at 7 A.M. the next business day. Despite the fire, revenues grew 9 percent that year and 12 percent the next.[12]

dishonesty insurance
coverage that protects against employees' crimes

Dishonesty insurance covers such traditional areas as fidelity bonds and crime insurance. Employees occupying positions of trust in handling company funds are customarily bonded as protection against their potential dishonesty. The informality and highly personal basis of employment in small firms make it difficult to realize the value of such insurance. Psychologically, employers can more easily accept the potential for money or other property to be lost through the dishonesty of persons other than employees, which can be covered by crime insurance.

coinsurance clause
part of an insurance policy that requires the insured to maintain a specific level of coverage or to assume a portion of any loss

Many commercial property policies contain a **coinsurance clause.** Under this clause, the insured agrees to maintain insurance equal to some specified percentage of the property value at the time of actual loss—80 percent is quite typical. In return, the insured is given a reduced rate. If the insured fails to maintain the 80 percent coverage, only part of the loss will be reimbursed. For instance, assume that the physical property of a business is valued at $50,000. If the business insures the property for $40,000 (or 80 percent of the property value) and incurs a fire loss of $20,000, the insurance company will pay the full amount of $20,000. However, if the business insures the property for only $30,000 (which is 75 percent of the specified minimum), the insurance company will pay only 75 percent of the loss, or $15,000.

SURETY BONDS **Surety bonds** insure against the failure of another firm or individual to fulfill a contractual obligation. They are frequently used in connection with construction contracts.

surety bonds
coverage that protects against another's failure to fulfill a contractual obligation

CREDIT INSURANCE **Credit insurance** protects businesses from abnormal bad-debt losses—for example, losses that result from a customer's insolvency due to tornado or flood losses, depressed industry conditions, business recession, or other factors. Credit insurance does not cover normal bad-debt losses that are predictable on the basis of business experience. Insurance companies compute the normal rate on the basis of industry experience and the loss record of the particular firm being insured.

credit insurance
coverage that protects against abnormal bad-debt losses

Credit insurance is available only to manufacturers and wholesalers, not to retailers. Thus, only trade credit may be insured. There are two reasons for this. The more important reason is the relative ease of analyzing business risks compared with analyzing consumer risks. The other reason is that retailers have a larger number of accounts receivable, which are smaller in dollar amount and provide greater risk diversification, so credit insurance is less acutely needed.

The credit standing of a small firm may be enhanced when it uses credit insurance. By showing bankers that steps have been taken to avoid unnecessary risks, the small firm might obtain more favorable consideration in securing bank credit.

Credit insurance policies typically provide for a collection service on bad accounts. Through the collection service, an insurance company makes available to a small firm legal talent and experience that might otherwise be unavailable. Although collection provisions vary, a common provision requires the insured to notify the insurance company within 90 days of the past-due status of an account and to turn it in for collection after 90 days. Collection efforts of insurance companies are generally considered superior to those of regular collection agencies.

Although the vast majority of policies provide general coverage, policies may be secured to cover individual accounts. A 10 percent or higher coinsurance requirement is included to limit coverage to approximately the replacement value of the merchandise. Higher percentages of coinsurance are required for inferior accounts in order to discourage reckless credit extension by insured firms. Accounts are classified according to ratings by Dun & Bradstreet or other recognized agencies, and premiums vary with these ratings.

http://www.dnb.com

COMMERCIAL LIABILITY INSURANCE Commercial liability insurance has two general classes: general liability and employer's liability/workers' compensation. **General liability insurance** covers businesses' liability to customers injured on the premises or injured off the premises by products sold to them. General liability insurance does not cover injury to a firm's own employees. However, employees using products such as machinery purchased from another manufacturer can bring suit under product liability laws against the equipment manufacturer.

general liability insurance
coverage that protects against lawsuits brought by customers

Employer's liability insurance is required by most states to insure employees. All states have workers' compensation laws. As the titles imply, **employer's liability insurance** provides protection for the insured business against lawsuits brought by employees who suffer injury, and **workers' compensation insurance** obligates the insurer to pay eligible employees for injury or illness related to employment.

employer's liability insurance
coverage that protects against lawsuits brought by employees who suffer injury

workers' compensation insurance
coverage that obligates the insurer to pay employees for injury or illness related to employment

KEY-PERSON INSURANCE By carrying **key-person insurance,** a small business can protect itself against the death of key personnel. Such insurance may be written on an individual or group basis. It is purchased by a firm, with the firm as the sole beneficiary.

key-person insurance
coverage that protects against the death of a firm's key personnel

ENTREPRENEURSHIP TODAY

IN THE TRENCHES

FRIENDSHIP INSURANCE

John Badovinac, director of disability sales for M Financial Group, contends that "if people understood how [disability] insurance benefits their company directly, there would be more interest." Dan VanderPloeg and Jerry Lanning would agree. VanderPloeg and Lanning are not only co-owners of VanderPloeg & Lanning Heating & Cooling Inc., they are also best friends—and they want to stay that way. For this reason, they purchased a disability buyout insurance policy that will enable one partner to buy the other's interest in the company for $500,000 should one of them become totally disabled. Mark Lilliedahl, sales manager of individual disability insurance at Provident Companies, stresses that "of all business insurance, buyout insurance is the most important, yet it is undersold. People don't know about it."

Source: Abby Livingston, "Covering Your Company Against Disability," *Nation's Business,* Vol. 86, No. 5 (May 1998), pp. 28, 30.

Most small business advisors suggest term insurance for key-person insurance policies, primarily because of lower premiums. How much key-person insurance to buy is more difficult to decide. Face values of such policies usually begin around $50,000 and may go as high as several million dollars.

DISABILITY INSURANCE One risk that small businesses do not normally consider is loss due to disability of a partner or other key employee of the company. Statistics, however, show that there is a 75 percent chance that one of two partners in their mid-30s will become disabled for at least three months before age 65. Although the risk of disability is much greater than the risk of death, partnerships are much more likely to purchase life insurance than disability insurance. In fact, 98 percent of partnerships and closely held corporations have a life insurance buyout agreement, but only 17 percent have disability insurance on partners or other key employees.[13]

disability insurance
coverage that protects against the disability of a firm's partner or other key employee

The most common type of **disability insurance** provides for the payment of a portion (typically two-thirds) of the disabled person's normal monthly income for a period of time after the disability occurs. However, it protects only the disabled person and not the business. Alternatively, partners can purchase disability buyout insurance. This type of disability insurance protects both partners by guaranteeing that the healthy partner will have enough cash for a buyout of the disabled partner without draining capital from the business.

Another option is key-person disability insurance, which replaces revenue lost because of the disability of a key employee. For example, if a firm's top salesperson, who brought in $5,000 a month, became disabled, this coverage would provide up to 125 percent replacement income for a year or more to give the firm time to recruit and train someone else.

Another type of disability insurance is designed to cover fixed overhead expenses, such as rent, utilities, employee salaries, and general office expenses, while an owner or other key employee recuperates. This type of insurance is especially well suited for a sole proprietorship, since the firm would have no income if the owner were unable to work.

LOOKING BACK

1 Define risk and explain the nature of risk.

- Risk is a condition in which there is a possibility of an adverse deviation from a desired outcome.
- Business risks can be classified into two broad categories: market risks and pure risks.
- Market risk is the uncertainty associated with an investment decision.
- Pure risk exists in a situation where only loss or no loss can occur.
- Only pure risk, as a general rule, is insurable.

2 Explain how risk management can be used in coping with business risks.

- Risk management is concerned with protection of the assets and the earning power of a business against accidental loss.
- Risk management involves identifying and evaluating the severity of risks, selecting methods for managing risk, implementing the decision, and reviewing and evaluating prior decisions.
- The two ways to manage business risks are risk control and risk financing. Risk control reduces or even aims to totally avoid the risk if the loss would be devastating to the firm, while risk financing involves transferring the risk to someone else or retaining the risk within the firm.

3 Describe the risks associated with different types of assets, both physical and human.

- From an asset-oriented perspective, insurable business risks can be categorized into property-oriented risks, personnel-oriented risks, and customer-oriented risks.
- Property-oriented risks involve tangible and highly visible assets.
- Personnel-oriented risks are related to the actions of employees.
- Customer-oriented risks are related to on-premises injuries and product liability.

4 Explain the basic principles used in evaluating an insurance program and the fundamental requirements for obtaining insurance.

- Basic principles of insurance include (1) identifying the business risks to be insured, (2) limiting coverage to major potential losses, and (3) relating the cost of premiums to the probability of loss.
- Fundamental requirements for obtaining insurance include the following: (1) the risk must be calculable, (2) the risk must exist in large numbers, (3) the insured property must have commercial value, and (4) the policyholder must have an insurable interest in the property or person insured.

5 Identify the different types of insurance coverage.

- Commercial property coverage provides protection against losses associated with damage to or loss of property.
- Surety bonds insure against the failure of another firm or individual to fulfill a contractual obligation.
- Credit insurance protects businesses from abnormal bad-debt losses.
- Commercial liability insurance includes general liability insurance, which covers business liability to customers injured on the premises or injured off the premises by products sold to them; employer's liability insurance, which provides protection against suits brought by employees who suffer injury; and workers' compensation insurance, which obligates the insurer to pay eligible employees for injury or illness related to employment.
- Key-person insurance provides protection against the death of key personnel in the firm.
- Disability insurance provides insurance benefits in the event that the owner or a key manager of a firm becomes disabled.

KEY TERMS

risk, p. 610
market risk, p. 610
pure risk, p. 610
risk management, p. 610
risk control, p. 611
risk avoidance, p. 611
risk reduction, p. 611
risk financing, p. 611
risk transfer, p. 611
risk retention, p. 611
self-insurance, p. 611
commercial property insurance, p. 622
business interruption insurance, p. 622
dishonesty insurance, p. 622
coinsurance clause, p. 622
surety bonds, p. 623
credit insurance, p. 623
general liability insurance, p. 623
employer's liability insurance, p. 623
workers' compensation insurance, p. 623
key-person insurance, p. 623
disability insurance, p. 624

Discussion Questions

1. What are the basic ways to cope with risk in a small business?
2. Which of the different classifications of business risks is the most difficult for the small firm to control? Why? Which is the least difficult to control? Why?
3. If you were shopping in a small retail store and somehow sustained an injury such as a broken arm, under what circumstances would you sue the store? Explain.
4. Do you think some firms are hesitant to enter into formal bankruptcy proceedings even though they might be able to save the business? Why?
5. Can a small firm safely assume that business risks will never turn into losses sufficient to bankrupt it? Why or why not?
6. When is it logical for a small business to utilize self-insurance?
7. List several approaches to combatting the danger of theft or fraud by employees and also by outsiders.
8. Under what conditions would purchasing life insurance on a business executive constitute little protection for a business? When is such life insurance helpful?
9. Are any kinds of business risks basically human risks? If so, who are the people involved?
10. Is the increase in liability claims and court awards of special concern to small manufacturers? Why?

You Make the Call

SITUATION 1

The Amigo Company manufactures motorized wheelchairs in its Bridgeport, Michigan plant, under the supervision of Alden Thieme. Alden is the brother of the firm's founder, Allen Thieme. The company has 100 employees and does $10 million in sales a year. Like many other firms, Amigo is faced with increased liability insurance costs. Although Alden is contemplating dropping all coverage, he realizes that the users of the firm's product are individuals who have already suffered physical and emotional pain. Therefore, if an accident occurred and resulted in a liability suit, a jury might be strongly tempted to favor the plaintiff. In fact, the company is currently facing litigation. A woman in an Amigo wheelchair was killed by a car on the street. Because the driver of the car had no insurance, Amigo was sued.

Question 1 Do you agree that the type of customer to whom the Amigo Company sells should influence its decision regarding insurance?

Question 2 In what way, if any, should the outcome of the current litigation affect Amigo's decision about renewing its insurance coverage?

Question 3 What options does Amigo have if it drops all insurance coverage? What is your recommendation?

SITUATION 2

Pansy Ellen Essman is a 42-year-old grandmother who is chairperson of a company that does $5 million in sales each year. Her company, Pansy Ellen Products, Inc., based in Atlanta, Georgia, grew out of a product idea that Essman had as she was bathing her squealing, squirming granddaughter in the bathroom tub. Her idea was to produce a sponge pillow that would cradle a child in the tub, thus freeing the caretaker's hands to clean the baby. From this initial product, the company expanded its product line to include nursery lamps, baby food organizers, strollers, and hook-on baby seats. Essman has seemingly managed her product mix risk well. However, she is concerned that other sources of business risk may have been ignored or slighted.

Question 1 What types of business risk do you think Essman might have overlooked? Be specific.

Question 2 Would a risk-retention insurance program be a good possibility for this company? Why or why not?

Question 3 What kinds of insurance coverage should this type of company carry?

SITUATION 3

H. Abbe International, owned by Herb Abbe, is a travel agency and freight forwarder located in downtown Minneapolis. When the building that housed the firm's offices suffered damage as a result of arson, the firm was forced to relocate its two computers and eleven employees. Moving into the offices of a client, Abbe worked from this temporary location for a month before returning to his regular offices. The disruption cost him about $70,000 in lost business and moving expenses. In addition, he had to lay off four employees.

Question 1 What are the major types of risk faced by a firm such as H. Abbe International? What kind of insurance will cover these risks?

Question 2 What kind of insurance would have helped Abbe cope with the loss resulting from arson? In purchasing this kind of insurance, what questions must be answered about the amount and terms?

Question 3 Would you have recommended that Abbe purchase insurance that would have covered the losses in this case?

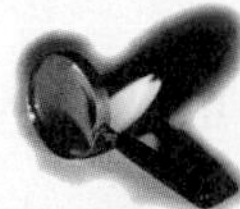

EXPERIENTIAL EXERCISES

1. Locate a recent issue of a business magazine in which you can read about new small business startups. Select one new firm that is marketing a product and another that is selling a service. Compare their situations relative to business risks. Report on your analysis to the class.
2. Contact a local small business owner and obtain his or her permission to conduct a risk analysis of the business. Report to the class on the business's situation in regard to risk and what preventive or protective actions you would suggest.
3. Arrange to interview the owner or one of the agents at a local insurance company. Determine in the interview the various types of coverage the company offers for small businesses. Write a report on your findings.
4. Assume that upon graduation you enter your family's business or obtain employment with an independent business in your hometown. Further assume that after five years of employment you leave to start your own competing business. Make a list of the considerations you would face regarding leaving the business with trade secrets.

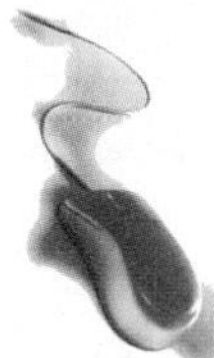

EXPLORING THE WEB

1. Access the SBA's site at **http://www.sba.gov**, and follow the link to Disaster Assistance. Choose General Information, and read the article entitled "Basic Facts About SBA Disaster Loan Programs."
   a. When and to whom does the SBA offer these loans?
   b. Why does the government offer loans instead of grants?
   c. What are the two types of loans offered, and what can the funds be used for?
   d. What are the typical interest rate and term for these loans?
2. The primary online source for information about health insurance is **http://www.ehealthinsurance.com**.
   a. Click on Small Business, and then follow the link to read Frequently Asked Questions (FAQs). After registering, list the two main types of health insurance and the benefits of each.
   b. Is it less expensive to purchase health insurance on the Web or from the insurance company?
   c. Work through getting a quote for a small business. What percentage must employers in your state contribute to health insurance premiums?
   d. Compare the features of the policies with the highest and lowest premiums. Print the comparison.

CASE 24

FOX MANUFACTURING (p. 704)

This case reviews the events and the owner's actions following the loss of a firm's manufacturing plant from a fire.

epilogue

Visualizing the End: Building a Legacy

In the Spotlight

The Bonneau Company

Exiting an entrepreneurial business often leads an entrepreneur to reflect on his or her achievements. Ed Bonneau arrived at this point as he was leaving a highly successful sunglass business. He had revolutionized the distribution of sunglasses in the United States and eventually dominated that market. While growing the firm, Bonneau had purchased Pennsylvania Optical (with its patents and contracts with Wal-Mart and Kmart) and industry giant Foster Grant (with its patents and manufacturing divisions).

Then Bonneau sold the business and walked away from it all. Reflecting on the transaction, he said, "It was hard for me to figure out what to do with all this money." From a business standpoint, his was a huge entrepreneurial success story.

However, in a comment on how he'd like to be remembered, Bonneau downplayed the money:

I would hope that they knew something else besides that I once ran the biggest sunglass company in the world. That's not the number one thing that I'd want to be known for. It's okay, but I'd much rather have that final assessment made by my kids and have them say, "He was a terrific dad." I never wanted to sacrifice my family or my church for my business.

And Bonneau's advice to younger entrepreneurs follows a similar theme:

Take God and your family with you when you go into business, and keep that balance in your life. Because when

you get to be 60 years old and you look back over your life, if all you have is the biggest sunglass company in the world and a pot full of money in the bank, . . . it won't be enough. Your life is going to be hollow, and you can't go back and redo it. ◆

Source: Personal communication with Ed Bonneau.

LOOKING AHEAD

After studying the epilogue, you should be able to

1. *Discuss the driving forces of entrepreneurial life and the process of exiting an entrepreneurial career.*
2. *Explain the concept of an entrepreneurial legacy and the challenges involved in crafting a worthy legacy.*

In the movie *Back to the Future,* do you remember the time vehicle that allowed the eccentric professor and his young companion to travel back to an earlier period and watch history unfolding?

In this epilogue, we ask you to undertake a similar process, without the aid of a time vehicle. As you begin to experience your entrepreneurial life, we want you to step back and think about it from the vantage point of closing out an entrepreneurial career—in other words, travel to the future to contemplate the past. Sound complicated? It's not. By looking at the future of your entrepreneurial career, you will be able to gain a broader perspective and avoid excessive preoccupation with the present. Such a step is particularly important for a fledgling entrepreneur, who faces a myriad of financial, marketing, and management issues and needs to distinguish between those that require short-term attention and those that will affect his or her legacy.

A new entrepreneur can develop a sense of perspective by reflecting on how his or her entrepreneurial life will look 20, 30, or 40 years from now. In the early years of a venture, the owner's primary concern is building a successful company. But things may look different when the entrepreneurial journey is ending. The last thing anyone wants to do is climb the ladder to success only to discover that it is leaning against the wrong wall!

LOOKING AHEAD TO THE END

Discuss the driving forces of entrepreneurial life and the process of exiting an entrepreneurial career.

Chapter 14 discussed the development of exit strategies—plans to harvest, or capture, the value created in a business. Looking ahead to the harvest is essential to maximizing financial returns and also to experiencing personal success. In this epilogue, we focus on the nonfinancial aspects of leaving an entrepreneurial venture behind.

As people complete any major undertaking—and especially as they come to the end of business or professional careers—they are prone to consider the value or meaning of their accomplishments. This is particularly true for those who have filled entrepreneurial roles. To some extent, family members and others involved in the leadership of an entrepreneurial firm are likely to share in such reflections. We urge you to undertake such a review prior to reaching the finish line.

How Entrepreneurs Exit

Exit routes vary. For example, a family business often grooms younger family members to take over leadership as the parent eases into retirement (see Chapter 7). This process may be smooth or difficult, but, if all goes well, the retiring leader eventually turns over the reins and then begins to critique his or her own performance record (often while worrying about the new, younger leadership).

Selling or merging the business may also thrust an owner into a post-entrepreneurial period of reflection. In some cases, the contract requires the ongoing participation of the seller. The limitations imposed by the buyer on the seller's leadership, however, frequently make such an arrangement little more than a part of the total compensation package for the business.

In recent years, the emergence of rapid-growth, high-tech Internet firms has allowed many young people to achieve the pinnacle of entrepreneurial success. Such success creates the option of cashing out at an early age and pursuing interests in other areas. Although youthful and older retirees may have some common concerns about exiting, here we will emphasize the more typical situation of entrepreneurs who, after spending years developing their businesses, simply come to the end of the entrepreneurial road.

Of course, business failure may also put an entrepreneur "on the street" again, or illness may cut short her or his career. The point is that no matter how an entrepreneur exits a venture, she or he is likely to feel the need to engage in an assessment of the entrepreneurial experience.

Driving Forces for Entrepreneurs

In Chapter 1, we pointed out that people are drawn to entrepreneurship by the prospect of such rewards as profit, independence, and personal fulfillment. Individually or in combination, these can be strong motivators. Involvement in other nonbusiness areas of life, such as family, community, church, and politics, may likewise be driving forces in the entrepreneur's life, creating tension between business and nonbusiness priorities.

PROFIT Obviously, money is a motivator for most people. Few can ignore the need to earn enough money to make ends meet. Some people are content to earn just enough money to get by on, while others strive to make a lot of money. The world of entrepreneurs consists of both types of people.

In a study of 287 entrepreneurs over a three-year period, Cooper and Artz found that entrepreneurs with primarily economic goals (that is, those with dollar signs in their eyes) were less satisfied than those with noneconomic goals.[1] This finding suggests possible drawbacks of concentrating solely on financial achievements.

Practicing entrepreneurs often voice doubts about the importance of focusing strictly on making money. An entrepreneur's letter to the editor of a business magazine reads as follows:

My philosophy is, what good is lots of money if I have only two weeks a year to enjoy it? I make enough money, and I enjoy every day—on my own terms.[2]

This comment and the study cited above raise questions about the adequacy of having profit as one's sole goal. Would becoming a multimillionaire be enough to allow you to take pride in your entrepreneurial achievements? In the Spotlight, Ed Bonneau answered the question with a resounding "No!"

THE EXCITEMENT OF THE WORK Entrepreneurial careers call for hard work. Especially at the beginning, startups seem to take over the entrepreneur's life, 24 hours a day, 7 days a week. Out of perceived necessity, the entrepreneur tends to become wrapped up in the business, struggling to avoid failure or to achieve success. Consider Bill and Frances Waugh, who founded a successful Mexican fast food restaurant business. By working more than 15 hours a day seven days a week, they eventually grew the business to more than 80 restaurants. To build the business, this couple devoted most of their waking hours to their chain of restaurants for a period of seven years!

Despite the hard work, the entrepreneurial world can be both interesting and exhilarating, with high rewards for good performance. If the work is fun, the long hours seem less punishing. Take, for example, Frank Carney, who co-founded Pizza Hut and then sold the company to PepsiCo. Eventually, he returned to entrepreneurship, acquiring a series of franchises from one of Pizza Hut's competitors, Papa John's International.

Today, Carney, 62, and his partners have 114 stores in Houston; Kansas City, Mo.; Wichita; Sacramento; and Honolulu—making him the company's second-largest franchise holder. "I'm an old guy tramping around in the trenches," he says. "But you do what's fun."[3]

Whether one works hard because the tasks are interesting or because they are necessary for survival, work can easily become the central focus of an entrepreneur's life.

If the thrill of the chase—the work itself—becomes a primary motivator, how will an entrepreneur be able to evaluate his or her life's work? What significance or meaning can be derived from the experience of starting and/or operating one's own business?

NONBUSINESS PRIORITIES As noted earlier, some entrepreneurs attach great value to areas of life outside the business. These also can become driving forces for entrepreneurs.

Many entrepreneurs, for example, use the business as a vehicle through which they contribute to the community. One entrepreneur, after exiting his business, realized that he should not have sold the business because it was his "base." He discovered that people defined him in terms of his being the owner of a successful business. He had used the company's resources—its profits and its personnel—to contribute to worthy private charities. For instance, when his alma mater undertook a fund-raising campaign, he made the firm's marketing staff available for designing promotional brochures.

Most entrepreneurs share a strong concern for family relationships—a concern that often exceeds their concern for the business itself. In those entrepreneurial endeavors that are family businesses (see Chapter 7), the interests of the family and the business are intertwined.

Although many growing businesses reduce family control over time, some are still viable family firms after many decades. Milliken and Company, for example, is a large textile firm that remains in the hands of the same family that started the business in the 19th century.[4] Roger Milliken, an 85-year-old executive, runs the company and strives diligently to keep ownership in the family. In recent years, he has added family members to the board of directors and used stockholder meetings and family forums to share the vision and maintain the loyalty of family members holding minority interests. In such cases, the business serves less as a provider of the family's economic needs and more as a preserver of the family name and heritage.

http://www.milliken.com

Surrendering Leadership

Handing entrepreneurial leadership to someone else is a major event in an entrepreneur's life. Its impact can easily be compared to that of getting married or divorced or losing a family member through death—the change may come as somewhat of a jolt.

An entrepreneur generally is heavily involved in business activities—making decisions, conferring with others, thinking about the future. Moving away from the entrepreneurial role brings a lull—for some, a quiet that seems deafening after a high-decibel business life. As one entrepreneur said, you can only play so many rounds of golf.

An entrepreneur is also the boss. Not only do entrepreneurs get their way; they also get deference. Lower-level personnel are solicitous of their opinions and, with some exceptions, respectful. For the entrepreneur, exiting usually brings a reduction in authority and status. By stepping down, entrepreneurs give up their built-in admiring—or at least acquiescent—audience.

Surrendering the reins of leadership brings a grinding halt to entrepreneurial life. The one-time entrepreneur must face the realities of normal life without the excitement and satisfaction that growing a business can bring. The beginning of post-entrepreneurial life is thus a natural occasion for reflecting on one's entrepreneurial career.

Looking Back at an Entrepreneurial Career

2 *Explain the concept of an entrepreneurial legacy and the challenges involved in crafting a worthy legacy.*

When an entrepreneur makes that final exit from the entrepreneurial stage, his or her business achievements become history. Reflecting on their lives and businesses at this point in their journeys, numerous entrepreneurs have come face to face with such questions as these: Was it a good trip? What kind of meaning does it hold for me now? Can I feel good about it? What are my disappointments? How did I make a difference? Such questions lead entrepreneurs to reassess their values, priorities, and commitments. By anticipating these questions, an entrepreneur can identify his or her most basic concerns early in the journey. Without such reflection, the entrepreneurial journey and its ending may prove disappointing.

Evaluating Accomplishments

Assessment of entrepreneurial performance requires establishing criteria. Obviously, no one standard can be applied. For example, a person who measured everything by the dollar sign would determine the degree of an entrepreneur's success by the size of his or her bank account.

The exiting entrepreneur will, at some point, think about achievements in terms of personal values and goals, rather than textbook criteria, popular culture, or financial rules of thumb. In all likelihood, a number of basic considerations will be relevant to the entrepreneur's sense of satisfaction.

In looking ahead to this time of looking back, one naturally thinks in terms of a legacy. A *legacy* consists of those things passed on or left behind. In a narrow sense, it describes material possessions bequeathed to one's heirs. In a broader sense, it refers to everything that one leaves behind—material items, good or bad family relationships, a record of integrity or avarice, a history of exploitation or contribution. An **entrepreneurial legacy** includes both tangible items and intangible qualities passed on not only to heirs but also to the broader society. One can appreciate then,

entrepreneurial legacy material assets and intangible qualities passed on to both heirs and society.

the seriousness with which the entrepreneur needs to consider the kind of legacy he or she is building.

In the following sections, we discuss the issues that seem important to many entrepreneurs and consider the experiences and ruminations of several people who have looked at entrepreneurial life from the inside.

Winning the Wrong Game

It's easy for entrepreneurs to get caught up in an activity trap, working harder and harder to keep up with the busy pace of life. Ultimately, such entrepreneurs may find their business accomplishments overshadowed by the neglect or sacrifice of something more important to them. It's possible to score points in the wrong game or win battles in the wrong war.

This type of entrepreneurial error produces a defective legacy, a sense that one's professional achievements are to some extent faulty. Consider what happens, for example, when the legitimate goal of earning money becomes a consuming passion. The CEO of a former *Inc. 500* company has critiqued the entrepreneurial experience in this way:

I believe that when our companies fail to satisfy our fundamental need to contribute to the community and instead exist predominantly to fill a bank account, then we lose our souls. Life is short. No one's gravestone reads, "He made a lot of money." Making a difference in your own life, your employees' lives, and your customers' lives is the real payoff.[5]

Ed Bonneau, who was featured in the Spotlight, expressed a similar sentiment:

You can measure wealth by counting your money. But it is more important to measure wealth by counting all the things you have that money can't *buy.*[6]

Entrepreneurs typically work—indeed, often must work—long hours, especially in the beginning. Sometimes, however, the obsession with work and the long hours become too extreme. Based on interviews with repeat entrepreneurs, Ilan Mochari summarizes their reports of early mistakes:

If they had it to do all over again, most of the group would have spent more time away from their first companies, hanging with the family, schmoozing up other CEOs, and pondering the long-term picture.[7]

One of the interviewees, Patrick Thean, CEO of MindBlazer, a provider of Web-based training, identified his error this way:

It was 24-7, and I had no time for you if you weren't in the company. . . . I didn't subscribe to the idea of a balanced life. I believe, though, that if I'd spent more time outside the company, things would've been much better.[8]

An excessive focus on money or work, then, can twist the entrepreneurial process. The outcome appears less satisfying and somehow less rewarding when the time for exit arrives.

Crafting a Worthy Legacy

An actor, athlete, or other performer ideally wants to make a final exit to the applause of an appreciative audience. In a similar way, an exiting entrepreneur enjoys having a "Well done!" tacked on to the final page of his or her entrepreneurial

exploits. And the entrepreneur's self-appraisal plays perhaps the most important part in that final assessment.

In entrepreneurial terms, what constitutes a worthy legacy? One issue is the nature of the endeavor itself. A business that operates within the law, provides jobs, and serves the public provides a good foundation for a satisfying entrepreneurial experience. Although a business that peddles pornography on the Internet might make a lot of money for its owner, most Americans would dismiss it as an unworthy enterprise because of its harmful, destructive character.

Within many individuals is a streak of nobility that gives them a genuine concern for the well-being of others. Their positive attitudes propel them toward endeavors of practical service to society.

Bernard Rapaport, a highly successful, principled, and generous entrepreneur, has stressed the importance of the means one takes to achieve a given end. "Whatever it is you want to achieve," he said, "*how* you achieve it is more important than *if* you achieve it." At 84 years of age, reflecting on life and legacy, he said, "What do I want to do? I want to save the world."[9]

Such idealism can guide an entrepreneur into many endeavors that are useful to our economic system. A few entrepreneurial ventures are specifically designed to meet the particular needs of society. One entrepreneur known to the authors has in his later years launched a firm whose primary objective is to provide good, low-cost housing to families that cannot otherwise afford it. His motivation for this venture, after earlier successful businesses, is personal concern for the needs of low-income families.

For most people looking back on entrepreneurship, satisfaction requires that their business have been constructive or positive in its impact—at the least, its effect should have been benign, causing no harm to the social order. In most cases, entrepreneurial businesses make positive contributions by providing jobs and services. A few make even greater contributions by addressing special needs in society.

The criteria by which one evaluates entrepreneurship are necessarily personal. Stephen R. Covey suggests that the most effective way "to begin with the end in mind" is to develop a personal mission statement or philosophy or creed.[10] Though individuals will have different mission statements because their goals and values will differ, widely shared values will underlie many of their judgments.

Perhaps the key to building a great entrepreneurial career is balance. Achieving the right blend of money, family, work, and other factors may allow the entrepreneur to avoid some otherwise troublesome problems. Sean Lyden points out the following risks of an unbalanced life:

- You risk burning out and sabotaging all that you have sacrificed for.
- You risk damaging relationships that are important to you and your business.
- You risk missing out on new money-making opportunities and ideas because you have tunnel vision.[11]

http://www.greatharvest.com

Pete and Laura Wakeman have attempted to develop a balanced entrepreneurial life in their operation of the Great Harvest Bread Company. In the process of running and growing the business of 137 franchised whole-wheat bakeries, they have created a life as well as a business.

In the early days of the business we had simple rules, but we followed them like religion. One was the two-day weekend. We never violated that, no matter what—it was a line we were afraid to cross, as though lightning would strike us down if we

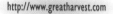

did. Combined, the two of us worked about 50 hours a week. We didn't talk about work at home; that was a rule. That's especially important. When we left the bakery, we were gone until we came back. In fact, for our first seven years in business we lived 17 miles out of town, the last 5 of those over gravel, and had no phone. No phone and a gravel road for seven years is a wonderful, wonderful thing for teaching the basic work–home separation habits.[12]

It may be difficult for most entrepreneurs to make such a sharp separation of work and family life. The Wakemans' example, however, highlights the importance of balancing significant values.

Beginning with the End in Mind

An entrepreneur builds a business, a life, and a legacy day by day, starting with the initial launch and proceeding through the months and years of operation that follow. A person exiting an entrepreneurial venture has completed the business part of his or her legacy—it must be constructed during the life of the business itself.

Therefore, as Covey said, an entrepreneur needs to "begin with the end in mind" and to keep that end in mind while making the innumerable operating decisions that follow. By selecting the proper values and wisely balancing their application, an entrepreneur can make a satisfying exit, leaving a positive and substantial legacy to heirs, employees, the community, and the broader society.

It is the authors' deepest hope that your journey as an entrepreneur will be a richly rewarding experience, not only in financial areas, but also, more importantly, in the things that matter most in life. Above all, we hope that your legacy will bring satisfaction to you and enhance the important relationships in your life. Go for it!

LOOKING BACK

1 Discuss the driving forces of entrepreneurial life and the process of exiting an entrepreneurial career.

- Entrepreneurs exit their business by passing leadership to their heirs, by selling or merging the business, or by giving up the business because the venture failed or because they are ill.
- Withdrawal from an enterprise entails major life changes.
- Driving forces in an entrepreneurial career include making money, enjoying the work itself, contributing to the community, and providing for one's family.

2 Explain the concept of an entrepreneurial legacy and the challenges involved in crafting a worthy legacy.

- An entrepreneur's legacy includes not only money and material possessions but also nonmaterial things such as personal relationships and values.
- Part of the legacy is the contribution of the business to the community.
- A worthy legacy includes a good balance of values and principles important to the entrepreneur. Errors in choosing or applying goals and values can create a defective legacy.
- Building a legacy is an ongoing process that begins at the launch of the firm and continues throughout its operating life.

KEY TERM

entrepreneurial legacy, p. 632

DISCUSSION QUESTIONS

1. How does the ultimate disposition of the firm—selling the business or passing it on to heirs—lead to differences in the exiting process?
2. What are some of the driving forces in an entrepreneurial life?
3. Why do you think some entrepreneurs describe their role as "fun"?
4. Why is conflict between business and family so common in entrepreneurial firms?
5. Explain the concept of entrepreneurial legacy.
6. Explain the following statement: "One can climb the ladder to success only to discover it is leaning against the wrong wall."
7. How would you describe a defective entrepreneurial legacy?
8. How does the type of business relate to one's legacy?
9. How is balance a key to building a good legacy? What things must be balanced?
10. What are some risks in an unbalanced entrepreneurial life?

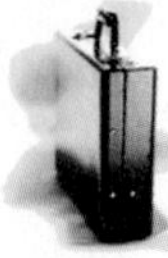

CASE 25

WHEN EVERYTHING ISN'T HALF ENOUGH (p. 707)

This case describes the experiences of an entrepreneur whose business success contrasts sharply with his troubled family relationships.

Alternative Case for Epilogue:
Case 7, "The Brown Family Business," p. 656

case 1

STEVE'S OLYMPIC TEES

JUMP-STARTING A BUSINESS

"I thought it was a great idea. After all, how often do the Olympics come to town?" mused Steve, as he pondered his decision to open a tee-shirt shop. Steve opened Steve's Tees in March 1996, a few months before the start of the 1996 Summer Olympic Games in Atlanta, Georgia.

Several years earlier, just after the announcement had been made that the Summer Olympic Games would be held in Atlanta, entrepreneurs began to make plans to capitalize on this monumental event. The Atlanta Olympic Committee had projected that more than 1.4 million people would come to the area over a 17-day period. The economic impact of the Olympics was estimated at more than $5.1 billion—the economic equivalent of 31 Super Bowl games! Further, an impact study, commissioned by the Atlanta Committee for the Olympic Games, projected that the economic benefit would be diffused into the surrounding region because many of its Olympic venues were in other areas of the state, including the cities of Athens, Buford, Conyers, and Savannah.

A major event like the Olympics has the potential to attract less-than-scrupulous business operators hoping to get rich quick. Therefore, prospective Olympic vendors had to complete an application and agree to meet specific requirements, as well as pay the required fees for retail space within a defined Olympic area. Vendors selling products with the Olympic logo were also required to obtain permission and to pay a fee for use of the logo.

Source: This case was prepared by Elisabeth J. Teal of Baylor University.

Steve had no desire to go through the Olympic bureaucracy to become an official Olympic vendor. However, he thought that he could still capitalize on the games—that they would provide a good chance for him to start a business. Why should big businesses, and people from outside the state, be the only ones to benefit from this once-in-a-lifetime opportunity? After all, a native—like Steve—should be in a better position than others to begin a business in the area.

STEVE'S BACKGROUND AND QUALIFICATIONS

Steve had grown up in the north Georgia town of Dahlonega, a small historic settlement in the foothills of the Appalachian Mountains. Atlanta, the state capital, was only about 55 miles to the southwest. In addition to being a thriving community, Dahlonega was also a favorite vacation spot for campers and hikers. The town was adjacent to the Chattahoochee National Forest, an area replete with wildlife, waterfalls, and native plants and trees. The first gold rush was sparked in Dahlonega in 1828, and visitors could still visit old gold mines and pan for gold in the cool mountain streams. Over the past few years, the downtown square had been revitalized and had become a thriving retail center, with coffee houses, unique restaurants, and boutiques selling local arts and crafts. Dahlonega was also the home of North Georgia College and State University, a four-year senior university within the Georgia system of colleges

and universities. The main university campus was situated on approximately 120 acres less than one mile from the downtown area of Dahlonega.

Steve's parents and grandparents had made substantial investments in the economic development of the community. In fact, long before it was accepted for a woman to be involved in business, Steve's grandmother had acquired residential real estate and undeveloped land located along a main thoroughfare in Dahlonega and adjacent to the university campus. During her lifetime, she had conducted a successful business providing rental housing for university students. The property had been passed to her heirs through her estate and was still owned by members of Steve's family, although the property was not all actively rented and managed as it had been in the past.

At first, Steve wasn't sure what type of business he wanted to open. Although he had considered several options, including a franchised yogurt shop and an independent pizza place, none of them seemed to capitalize sufficiently on his unique situation: the college town, the property adjacent to the university, and the upcoming Summer Olympics to be held just 55 miles south of Dahlonega in Atlanta.

Steve was a very bright individual, with a degree in physics from the University of South Carolina. When he had graduated from college, however, the job market for physics graduates was tight, and Steve ultimately accepted a management training position with a major regional bank. Steve was good with the bank's customers, was well liked by the other employees, and had demonstrated an ability to effectively manage many different tasks at one time.

However, after three years, Steve was bored with his job. He realized that he was solving the same problems over and over—only the names and faces changed. Steve also learned that "banker's hours" did not allow for as much free time as some nonbankers might believe. He found himself working most weekdays from 7:45 A.M. until about 6:00 P.M., and he was expected to attend an evening meeting of a community group such as the Chamber of Commerce or Rotary Club about once a week. He also had to work on the weekend from time to time, when the bank was involved in activities such as promoting a recently developed subdivision or opening a new branch location.

Steve began to dream of a job that would allow him to pursue a lifestyle more in keeping with his personal goals. He wished that he could come up with a business that would afford him greater flexibility with his time, let him be his own boss, and give him control over his own income.

One day, while having lunch with a friend at a sandwich shop near the campus, Steve noticed that every college student in the restaurant was wearing some type of jeans, khakis, or shorts and . . . a tee-shirt! Some of the shirts touted North Georgia College and college-related events, and others advertised music groups or professional sports teams, but they were all tee-shirts. "That's it!" Steve exclaimed to his friend Bob, who was calmly munching a ham and cheese sandwich. "A tee-shirt shop . . . next to the campus . . . selling tee-shirts, like the ones you see all around us . . . maybe even shirts about the Olympics. This could be good, Bob." For Steve, that moment at lunch was the inspiration for his business, which later became known as Steve's Tees.

The Development of Steve's Tees

Almost immediately, Steve began making arrangements to open his business. A vacant building from his grandmother's estate was selected as the location. Originally constructed in the 1940s as a residence, it was a wooden structure of about 1200 square feet, with a small parking area to its left. The land included about 100 feet of road frontage on a main street two blocks from campus.

Steve wanted his store to have a casual and relaxed atmosphere but did not want it associated in any way with tee-shirt shops that sold smoking supplies and novelty items such as black lights and posters. The quality of Steve's tee-shirts would be far superior to that of shirts sold in those types of shops, and he wanted the distinction to be clear to prospective customers.

Steve decided to use an art-gallery approach to displaying his merchandise. He thought it would be effective in suggesting the quality of the merchandise, as well as fairly inexpensive and easy to accomplish. He painted the walls of the interior display racks black and installed track lighting on the ceiling to highlight shirt racks attached to the walls. The house had a hardwood floor, and a bit of buffing gave it a clean and polished appearance. Steve purchased a large, oblong antique table which would support the cash register and provide space for completing sale transactions. He had a traditional-looking, painted,

wooden sign erected in front of the building, with "Steve's Tees" emblazoned on both sides.

Of the many tee-shirt suppliers in Atlanta, Steve identified three that sold top-quality, 100 percent cotton tee-shirts in unique designs. Unfortunately, one of these suppliers was not willing to sell the small quantities that Steve desired, and the second was unwilling to establish any type of trade credit for a new business. The third supplier was more flexible and agreed to provide shirts in lots of one dozen in assorted sizes which Steve could specify. This supplier offered credit terms of 2/10, net 30, so Steve decided to stock his store through this supplier and to supplement the stock, as needed, through the second supplier.

Steve personally selected each of the tee-shirts for the initial inventory. He wanted unique shirts that would appeal both to college students and to people in town and so focused on three main lines: heavyweight shirts in bright solid colors, cartoon designs licensed from Warner Brothers, and shirts with various Olympic logos. Most were screen-printed, although he also chose a few embroidered designs. To set the selling prices for the shirts, Steve marked each item up 100 percent. Thus, a tee-shirt with a wholesale cost of $8.00 would be priced at $16.00. That seemed like a big markup to Steve, and he hoped he wasn't setting prices too high. On the other hand, $16.00 seemed like a fair price for a quality tee-shirt.

Although Steve hoped that he would eventually be able to resign from his job at the bank and operate the store himself, he didn't think he should give up his job until he could determine whether the shop would provide sufficient income to support his family. Steve was pleased when he was able to convince Brent, his brother-in-law and a junior business major at the university, to manage the store for him. The hours of operation for the store were set at 11:00 A.M. to 6:00 P.M. Monday through Friday and 10:00 A.M. to 5:00 P.M. Saturday. The fact that the store's hours were determined by Brent's schedule seemed to Steve to be acceptable, if not ideal, since other students were also likely to be in class during the early morning hours.

The First Months of Operation

The official opening of Steve's Tees took place on March 1, 1996. In anticipation of the opening, Steve placed several ads in the student newspaper during the last week of February. He also placed a small classified ad in a weekly shopping guide that advertised various local businesses and individual items for sale. Steve inquired about advertising in the major Dahlonega newspaper, but when he learned that a small block ad would cost several hundred dollars each day it was run, he decided to wait to see if the business could afford such an advertising expenditure.

The first week the business was open, Steve's Tees had six customers, who purchased a total of two shirts. Steve was surprised that more people didn't come into the store that week, but he thought it was because the business was new and people were not yet aware that it was open. The second week was like the first, with just one or two customers coming into the store each day and a few shirts sold. Brent said that the customers, once they came into the store, seemed to like the shirts. In the hope of increasing the number of customers in the store, Brent began to ask his customers to tell their friends about the store and to bring them back with them.

Steve thought it was only a matter of time until the shop caught on with the students at the university. He was sure that the students would want to buy his quality tee-shirts if he could just get them into the store. Steve had to admit, however, that there were not as many student pedestrians in the area of the store as he had anticipated. Although the store was near campus, it was not in an area with other stores. Thus, most students only drove by the shop on their way to the university parking lots. Steve believed that advertising was the solution to his problem, and he continued to advertise in the student newspaper and the community shopping guide throughout the month of March.

April arrived, and Steve waited for customers, and sales, to increase. Surely the warmer weather would get those students out of their cars and dormitory rooms and into his store, buying his tee-shirts! As the weeks wore on, the store made a few more sales, but the sales volume did not come close to covering Brent's salary and the utility bill. Steve couldn't imagine what he would do if he had to pay rent on the building in addition to his other expenses. He began to wonder if he had been completely unrealistic to dream of quitting his job at the bank and supporting his family on the income from the business.

As May approached, Steve knew he needed to do something quickly to generate some business. Many students would be leaving for summer break, and,

based on the lack of response from the community, Steve didn't think the business could make it through a long, hot summer without the students. In an attempt to get more customers into the store, Steve decided to run a 25-percent-off sale. He made a big sale banner and draped it across the front of the wooden sign over the store.

Steve had not restocked his inventory since the store opened. Although the store could use some new inventory, he was hesitant to spend any more money on shirts that he might not be able to sell. Steve realized that he needed more customers, and more sales, if the business was to survive. But he was already spending as much money on advertising as he felt he could afford. Why weren't students coming into the store? What about the people in town? And, what about the anticipated economic impact of the Olympics? The only economic impact that Steve was feeling was a negative personal cash flow, from trying to keep the business afloat.

The Olympics were the source of another concern for Steve. He had expected the Olympic tee-shirts to be among his most popular items, yet he had sold only a few of them. Would sales pick up as the date of the Olympics drew closer? Or would people wait to purchase Olympic tee-shirts at official Olympic sites? Perhaps the Olympics would actually eliminate some potential customers, as students and townspeople left town to attend Olympic events.

Although Steve had been excited about the prospects for his business at first, he was beginning to have a sinking feeling that the business wasn't such a great idea after all. But what was the problem? What, if anything, could he do to jump-start this business? Right now, it appeared that the business was going nowhere very, very quickly.

QUESTIONS

1. What type of research could Steve have done to better prepare to open the business? In what ways would this research have helped him?
2. What was the problem with the advertising Steve used to introduce the new business to university students and to the local community? What type of advertising should have been used?
3. Evaluate Steve's choice of location for the business.
4. What recommendations would you give to Steve to "jump-start this business"? Do you think it is possible to make this a profitable business? Why or why not?

case

2

The Fantastic Catalogue Company

Gaining a Competitive Advantage in the Mail Order Market

It would be quite a wedding; the nuptials would take place in the stone chapel at the school from which the bride and groom had graduated. A reception for 400 guests would follow at the seaside home of the bride's parents. And from start to finish, the festivities would be imbued with Gatsby-esque elegance and style. Kathleen Mahoney, the bride herself, would see to that.

"I researched every aspect of it to the *n*th degree," she says, recalling the year of preparation. "I went haywire. I looked at 20 guest books, 20 bridesmaids' gifts, 20 different goblets, and so on. I wanted everything to be perfect."

Only the finest items would do, and finding them was frustrating. "There's a decentralized flow of information and goods in the wedding industry," Mahoney says. "There was no source for the upscale bride to find all the high-quality, tasteful wedding accessories she'd need." Her search took her to some 50 stores from Boston to San Francisco—gift shops, bridal boutiques, stationery stores.

All of which got her thinking. And by the time Mahoney and Ozzie Ayscue were married in June 1990, she had a new business on her hands. One-stop shopping for brides—the idea seemed irresistible. "It made intuitive sense to me, from my own experience," says Mahoney, 31. "I did some research with friends, and it made sense to everyone."

Source: Republished with permission of *Inc.* magazine, Goldhirsh Group, Inc., 38 Commercial Wharf, Boston, MA 02110. "Made to Order," Jay Finegan, May 1993, Vol. 14, No. 5. Reproduced by permission of the publisher via Copyright Clearance Center, Inc.

With 2.5 million weddings a year in the United States, a huge and lucrative market beckoned. The most promising targets, Mahoney reasoned, were career women, brides age 26 and up. They'd have the discretionary income to purchase topflight wedding goods but not the time to hunt for them.

How best to capitalize on the opportunity? She had dismissed a retail store as too limiting—hers was a national concept. A catalog, though, could put the products right at brides' fingertips. Mahoney was a catalog nut—she loved them. She didn't know the first thing about publishing one, she admits, but she figured she could learn.

The timing was fortunate. Mahoney was at American Express in Manhattan, in the direct-mail travel business. Ayscue was working for a travel-industry startup in San Francisco, where the couple had decided to settle. In late 1989, Mahoney left American Express and moved west, itching to take a crack at the catalog game.

It's no cakewalk to start a consumer catalog from scratch. Typically, retailers branch into mail order to augment established store-based operations. Other merchants tiptoe into the field by first advertising a few items in magazines. That's a cost-effective way of learning what sells while building a buyer file. Gradually, their product lines expand to fill full-blown catalogs. That's how Lands' End got started, for example.

One impediment to launching cold is capital. Catalogs inhale money. One might open a retail store for, say, $50,000, but that won't even get you off the

ground in the catalog trade. It can easily cost $150,000 or more to get that first book in the mail, and follow-on editions are needed to build a buyer file. First come production costs for photography, copywriting, layout, and design—the "creative" end of the business. Then come costs for list rental, photographic color separation, printing, fulfillment, data processing, and postage. And even before that first order comes in, a startup needs to stock most of the featured items.

Mind you, all that happens before you know if the phone will ever ring. What if all the recipients throw your catalog in the trash? By definition, a startup has zero name recognition. And with an estimated 9,000 consumer catalogs in the country, mailing hundreds of millions of copies, it's easy to get lost in the clutter. Given that saturation, catalogs are creeping into ever smaller niches, staking out tiny franchises in hopes of survival.

Even so, most of them don't last long. Industry lore is replete with tales of first-timers who sank $1 million or more into a black hole before calling it quits. The market is ruthless in weeding out the glut. According to Leslie Mackenzie, publisher of *The Directory of Mail Order Catalogs,* between 1,000 and 1,500 of them fail or cease operations every year.

It is a business, analysts stress, in which you must get everything right. For instance, you might have terrific merchandise, a superb shipping operation, and a good mailing list. But you drop the ball on the creative—the product photos and the copy don't quite click. In that case, says consultant Bill Nicolai, "you are toast. It's a very tricky business, but it's one where sharp entrepreneurs can find their way in."

As Mahoney mapped her plans, however, she felt confident. A private investor had promised her $1 million, for 30 percent of the company, plus a $500,000 loan. That would sustain business for two years or more. The wedding niche, moreover, seemed solid. "I knew in my heart it was a good idea, so I didn't do much formal market research other than some demographics," she says.

She presented her concept to Jeff Haggin, chairman of the MoreNow Corp., a catalog-production firm in Sausalito, Calif. Over the years, MoreNow had handled the creative work for many prominent catalogers—Smith & Hawken, Sierra Club, and dozens more. Haggin knew the industry cold, and he thought Mahoney's idea had real merit.

That's all she needed to hear. And thus was born, in February 1990, The Wedding Fantastic, Inc.

With that start date, the earliest Mahoney could mail her first catalog would be July. That wasn't optimal. The big wedding season is spring and summer, and she would miss most of it. But impatient to get something into the market, she plunged in, headquartered in her San Francisco apartment.

Ayscue pitched in and joined the company in July as copresident. Two years as an analyst with Morgan Stanley had given him strong number-crunching skills. He'd handle strategic planning, statistical analysis, and financial management, while Mahoney concentrated on merchandising and marketing. Working with list brokers, she identified between 3.5 million and 10 million rentable names that met her demographic profile. Industry wisdom has it that you must mail at least 100,000 books to get a reasonable response. To reach her target market, she rented 100,000 names from Bloomingdale's, Williams Sonoma, Victoria's Secret, Neiman-Marcus, and 16 other upscale catalogers. She also rented from bridal-magazine subscriber lists. "I wanted to reach not just brides but brides' mothers, aunts, and shower throwers," she says.

From each list she rented a "cell" of 5,000 names. As a rule, names rent for about a dime each for onetime use, with rates rising to 15¢ depending on the number of "selects." That is, a renter can request names based on such factors as the timing, frequency, and monetary value of the customers' catalog purchases. Mahoney shot for people who had ordered through the mail in the previous six months, a common select.

The use of competing cells is key. It allows a cataloger to see which lists work best, so that when more names are needed, one can mine deeper into good ones. Essentially, a cataloger cold calls people in their mailboxes, and on average only 1.66 percent of the prospects respond. In other words, for every 100 catalogs mailed to rented names, better than 98 yield no sales. And those who do respond place smaller orders than established buyers.

To succeed, a mail-order operator must build a buyer file so that repeat customers represent a substantial percentage of total circulation. That can take several years. In Mahoney's model, the critical mass would be reached in 1994, when, she calculated, 12 percent of the 7 million people receiving her catalog would be buyers. That's the point at which her busi-

ness would turn profitable. Her plan projected net sales that year of $12.5 million, with purchases averaging $95. That translates to more than 131,500 orders, enough that the company could amortize its costs over a far larger business base. General operating expenses, for example, would shrink from 41 percent of net sales in 1991 to 8 percent in 1994. Publicity expenses—creative work, color separation, printing, list rental—would drop from 89.5 percent of sales to 30 percent. And net income would rise from a 1991 loss of $837,000 to a positive $484,000.

Economies of scale work their magic all over the place once catalogs grow large, but reaching the magic number of 236,000 was, and remains, an ambitious goal. By comparison, Gump's, an old-line San Francisco gift cataloger, has a buyer file of about 100,000 names.

Pressing on, Mahoney contracted with MoreNow for production and arranged to have the book printed by Alden Press, a catalog specialty house in Elk Grove Village, Illinois. Fulfillment—everything from inventory storage to order taking to product packing—was farmed out to a small San Francisco company. United Parcel Service would handle deliveries.

Time was short. To get the catalog out in July, all the merchandise had to be selected and turned over to MoreNow by April 1, to start photography. It was a crash project, but Mahoney made it. Just three weeks after she and Ayscue exchanged vows, 100,000 copies of the inaugural edition of The Wedding Fantastic hit the mail.

It was very classy, a glossy, beautifully designed 32-pager featuring pretty much everything an upscale bride would need except a gown and a groom. Most items were the fruits of Mahoney's research for her own nuptials. There was a personalized Limoges porcelain ring box ($125), an heirloom-quality moiré hatbox ($298), a lace picture frame ($85), and even a sterling-silver service for the wedding cake (knife and server, $95 each).

The other half of the equation called for putting wedding gifts right in the catalog, to make it a complete wedding resource. They included some of Mahoney's personal favorites, among them a sterling ice-cream scoop ($95), a Zen rock garden ($48), and a birdhouse shaped like a Victorian manor ($145)—"mainstream products," she says, "but with a twist." In all, the catalog had 120 handpicked items.

Established catalogers know from experience how much inventory to carry. Startups don't know which items will be best-sellers and which will be dogs, and guessing wrong either way can be costly. "That's one of the hardest things we do," says Ayscue. "If you overstock, you are stuck with products. If you understock, you have to back-order and you might not make the sale." Going conservative, Mahoney went with a bare-bones inventory.

Competing not on price but on quality and uniqueness, she marked the products up 60 percent on average. On shipping and handling charges she aimed for break-even. The order form listed an 800 number and a fax number and allowed payment by check, money order, or credit card. On page three, a chatty "Dear brides" letter from Mahoney touted her commitment to top-quality goods and superb customer service, plus a full refund-exchange policy.

Getting that first book out was pricey. MoreNow's bill for the creative was $74,000—over $2,300 per page. Color separation added another $30,000. Alden charged $0.22 each for the 112,000 copies printed (there were some extras), and postage totaled $24,640. The combined in-the-mail cost came to $153,000, excluding list rental.

So handsome was the book that it won second prize that year in a new-catalog competition. "Even the most cynical of readers cannot help but be charmed by the catalog's sentimental approach to weddings," gushed trade journal *Catalog Age*.

The problem, however, was meager response, well below the 1.66 percent industry average for prospects. Response fell further when Mahoney "dropped" the second batch, 88,000, in September 1990, and further still when 127,000 went out in November. On the up side, however, the average order was $90, against an industry average of $61.

The new, updated spring edition hit the mail in three volleys, in February, March, and May of 1991. With 40 pages, it featured new items as well as top sellers from the first book. A total of 501,000 copies went out, half of them in May. With timing on the edition's side, the response rates climbed across the board. The new mailings generated sales of $917 per 1,000 catalogs, versus $547 for the first edition. Still, the response rate remained discouragingly below the industry standard, and the average order dipped to $81. "The wedding books were very narrowly targeted," Mahoney says now, "but we were taking a shotgun approach."

Needing something with broader appeal, she and Ayscue brought forth in September 1991 a brand-

new catalog—The Christmas Fantastic. Weddings were seasonal, so why not launch a sister publication for the hottest shopping time of the year?

Working again with MoreNow, they developed a 32-page version known in the trade as a "slim jim." By virtue of its dimensions, 6 inches by 11 inches, it was cheaper to print and mail. To give the new catalog a better product mix, Mahoney and her employee sidekick, Georgina Sanger, scoured gift shows all over the country and developed several exclusives with California artists.

As with the wedding catalog, the products in The Christmas Fantastic were eclectic and fairly expensive. The new book featured about 150 items, everything from personalized tree ornaments and stockings to a hand-painted "kitty privy" and a $795 "Grand Mr. President" desk set. There were books and CDs, festive party invitations, even a beer-brewing kit. Some old favorites encored—the silver ice-cream scoop, the Victorian birdhouse, and the Zen rock garden.

The company sent out a test quantity of 112,000 catalogs in three mailings (early returns provide a "product read" that removes some inventory guesswork), and this time it hit pay dirt. The response rate topped the national norm, orders averaged $97, and sales per 1,000 catalogs mailed hit $1,584, beating the industry standard by $566.

So compelling were the overall economics that Mahoney and Ayscue retooled, shifting entirely away from the bridal market and into the gift business. There will be no new The Wedding Fantastic this spring, although some of its products are featured in full-page ads in bridal magazines, and a leftover 10,000 copies are available for $3 each. Instead, they launched another new catalog—The Celebration Fantastic—and changed their name to the Fantastic Catalogue Company.

The newest book, a 32-page slim jim, is billed as a way to "celebrate life's special occasions with romance, whimsy and imagination!" While some core items remain—the birdhouse, for one—the new catalog is heavy on unusual gifts for Easter, Mother's Day, Father's Day, graduations, anniversaries, and new babies. Its 120 items include everything from a complete gourmet picnic hamper for six ($525) to donkey and elephant earrings for election years ($34). Like Mahoney's other books, it strikes an upscale and upbeat tone.

"We think now we are sending the right message to the right people," she says. "Our targeting is getting more refined."

If The Celebration Fantastic yields results comparable with the Christmas edition's, as Mahoney expects, she will have a strengthening, nonseasonal business and a more secure foothold in the $2-billion mail-order consumer gift market.

But as they say, that's a big if. Having virtually abandoned the wedding niche, she is stepping into a gift sector already sated with some 630 catalog companies, many of them large and resource rich. The Fantastic Catalogue Company has to establish itself fast. "We need to become the household name, the completely trusted brand name for this whole celebration segment," Mahoney says.

To do that she feels she has to expand quickly. She'd like to circulate a million copies of The Christmas Fantastic this fall to aggressively build her buyer file from its current 15,000 names. But with the initial financing of $1.5 million fast depleting, that hinges on raising $1.25 million or so by summer. And another $1 million will be needed in 1993 to move The Celebration Fantastic beyond the test phase.

As the company expands and Mahoney increasingly understands exactly who her customer is, she has begun to focus on servicing that customer better. Toward that end, she brought the company's fulfillment operations in-house early this year, a move that will require more employees and might produce as-yet-unseen complications.

QUESTIONS

1. Do you think Mahoney has correctly assessed the basic nature of the competition she faces? Why or why not?
2. What is the competitive advantage Mahoney is trying to create? Do you agree with this appeal? Why?
3. What market segmentation strategy is The Fantastic Catalogue Company following?
4. How can this firm use customer service to gain a competitive advantage?
5. Do you think Mahoney leaped before looking? What should she have done differently?

HeadBlade Company

Building a Business on the Web

When Todd Greene, 32, began losing his hair to male-pattern baldness in his 20s, he rejected the typical solutions: toupees, hair plugs, and the "comb-over" style. Instead, the computer artist and Web columnist began shaving his head. The bald look appealed to him, but the time-consuming—and often painful—process of shaving his pate with a conventional razor did not. So Greene invented a razor designed specifically for those men who opt to shave their heads before nature does the job for them.

Early in 1994, he tried to sell the concept to two large makers of men's grooming products, only to be rebuffed. But one rejection was particularly cutting. It came from the Schick division of Warner-Lambert Company, a $10.2 billion conglomerate based in Morris Plains, New Jersey. The tacky five-sentence form letter was actually stamped "Rejection."

"When I got that letter, I thought, I might as well work on this on my own," Greene says. "I knew I had a good idea because more and more people around the world are shaving their heads, and using a face razor to do it is very, very awkward. You're shaving areas that you can't see, the straight handle keeps your hand away from your head, and it takes 15 to 20 minutes to do it right. Now with HeadBlade, it takes me five minutes."

It was an impulsive beginning for the HeadBlade Company LLC. But then Greene tends to be an impulsive guy. Evidence: He met his wife, Danielle, by e-mail and married her three weeks later. It took him slightly longer—12 weeks to be exact—to take his product to market.

At 2.23 inches long, the HeadBlade resembles a miniature yellow Jet Ski and fastens loosely to the finger like a candy ring. I started out by making a clay model just to prove that the idea would work. That model raised a bunch of questions and I ripped the heck out of myself because there were so many design elements I hadn't thought of at first. I went through probably 15 prototypes, soldering them myself or baking them together. At one point, I made 25 test models and sent them out to people I knew who shaved their heads. I finally got their feedback and took their comments into account. For instance, some people said the finger ring wasn't big enough, so I went to jewelry stores to find out about average finger sizes and wound up making the hole adjustable. Overall, people told me that after two or three shaves they got used to the new razor and they liked the shave a lot better and found it was much easier.

During this time, I was working contract jobs out of my home and putting a lot of work into this design process, applying for my patents, and sending out prototypes. At one point, I thought I would license the design and I talked to a large company that was interested in the concept. However, they were moving very slowly, and I got scared that I would lose all control of the idea. I finally realized that it wasn't worth selling just as an idea because if I worked on actually producing a product, the value would go up tenfold.

Source: Based on Mike Hofman, "The Razor's Edge," *Inc.*, Vol. 22, No. 3 (March 2000), pp. 86–87; material on HeadBlade's Web site; and Karen E. Klein, "Small Business: New Trends and Help for Growing Companies," *Los Angeles Times*, January 5, 2000, Part C, p. 5.

I still feel that I could get a lot of benefit by teaming up with a larger company, with established retail distribution channels, and that's an idea I'm pursuing.

Greene's HeadBlade debuted for sale last June on a Web site he built himself.

I got funding from friends and relatives to do the design, the artwork, set up a Web site and start production. I went through six or seven mold-makers until I found a very talented guy who does Hollywood props and hired him to make the final models for me. It was expensive, but I wanted a high-quality product. My initial order was for 10,000. Setting the price point was tricky because I wanted it to be as inexpensive as possible, but I had to sell it for enough that it would be profitable initially.

He drummed up interest for the $15 item by posting messages on Web bulletin boards that catered to his target customers, which include balding men, hardcore athletes, members of the military, and aspiring bohemians. In the first week, Greene tallied sales of $300; these days, weekly receipts average $3,000.

Since the niche of people who shave is not exactly a staid, conservative market, I can get away with some alternative marketing, too. I have this old Honda CRX, and I put custom magnets on it and attached HeadBlades to the roof and the hood. I'm thinking about driving it around the country as part of a publicity tour this summer. Our Web site is getting 180,000 page views a month, and our December sales went over $25,000. We're still at the nickel-and-dime level, but we could support thousands of dollars of revenue online every day without having to expand, so we're ready to grow.

Building an organization will require creativity on Greene's part. He's raised only $150,000 in seed capital—not much for a business that manufactures and markets a consumer product. Even so, he claims, his goal is "to make the HeadBlade a household name, like Miracle Whip and Kleenex."

So far, Greene has proved himself to be an adept bootstrapper. Working from his home, he takes just-in-time delivery of razors from his supplier, tying up little capital in inventory. He passes shipping costs on to his customers.

I focused my main marketing efforts online and on getting free publicity. I sent out hundreds of press kits with a HeadBlade enclosed and the slogan "The Cure for the Common Comb-Over." Since June, we've been featured in 10 or 15 magazines, including Playboy, Sports Illustrated *and* Entertainment Weekly. *We made it into a couple of U.K. and Australian magazines as well. The only traditional advertising I've done has been a listing and an ad in a directory for collegiate-level swimmers, who shave their heads for competition. If I know [an article is] going to appear in a newspaper on the East Coast, I try to go to bed early so that I can be ready to answer the phone in the morning.*

Eager to retain his 90 percent equity stake—the rest is owned by friends and family—Greene has resisted bringing on employees, preferring to pay hired hands on an as-needed basis.

Hiring, Greene figures, means parting with equity cheaply. Either he'll have to raise money from investors, who will want sizable chunks of equity, or he'll have to compensate employees with shares. "He's making these decisions very carefully," says James R. Hunter, a client and business plan consultant. "He's an entrepreneur, but he's not dumb about his enthusiasm. He was convinced early on that he wanted to live from revenues." In fact, HeadBlade's income statement boasts enviable gross margins of 65 percent. Enviable, that is, assuming that there's a potential market of 10 million out there, which is what Greene hopes, though he admits that there are no hard numbers tracking what is, after all, just a hairstyle.

Even so, he reasons, mapping out the market could lead HeadBlade to other sources of revenues. "I don't know of anyone in the world who has a mailing list of guys who shave their heads," he says gleefully. "I'm building one with nearly 10,000 names so far. And think about China—all those Buddhist monks!"

QUESTIONS

1. What do you think about Greene's one-product marketing strategy? What other products, if any, could he offer in his online store?
2. Do you think his Web site (http://www.headblade.com) is a well-designed site? Why or why not?
3. What privacy does the HeadBlade Web site offer a visitor who is placing an order? Should this be a concern for the company?
4. What types of links to and alliances with other Web sites might benefit HeadBlade?

case

4

Sunny Designs, Inc.

An Adventure in China

To strengthen their businesses, increasing numbers of entrepreneurs are expanding into the international domain. One common motivation behind such moves is the hope of achieving gains in productivity by locating factories in countries where local conditions are favorable to these operations; however, this strategy is not without its drawbacks. Consider, for example, the case of Sunny Hwang, president of Sunny Designs, Inc., a manufacturer, importer, and wholesale distributor of wooden furniture with offices in Hayward, California. Hwang tells the story in his own words.

Cheap and good has been my motto in doing business. I started my business in a flea market as a retail vendor and then soon became a jobber, then a direct importer, and finally a manufacturer. To get better value, I delved into the original source—manufacturing in China.

China is one of the best places for the manufacturing of wooden furniture due to the cheap labor, materials, and other costs. I could hire approximately 20 workers in China for the wage of 1 in the United States. The cost of lumber is about half, and rent is about 20 percent compared to the U.S. There is also reasonable infrastructure available, such as transportation, electricity, and communication.

There are many cheap products available from Chinese factories; however, the quality is greatly lacking in many cases. Therefore, low prices alone are not sufficient justification for doing business in China. As a result, I contracted with an agent who hired several inspectors to control for the quality and delivery of our furniture products. Also, I established a partnership with a local Chinese manufacturer. However, none of these individuals were able to meet our needs.

After the partnership failed, I changed my business strategy by taking charge of my own factory. I hired my nephew, who was trained in the U.S., to oversee building a new factory and take care of purchases from other Chinese factories. Because of the different culture and expectations, it was always a challenge to get along with government officials, who happen to hold most of the properties in China. They are eager to attract overseas investors, but primarily to increase job availability for the local people.

We located our factory in a town near a large city where we had negotiated favorable terms with the local government officials. However, after the company was launched, their attitudes changed. They began demanding what we considered to be unreasonable requests and would interfere with management decisions. Even purchasing lumber became difficult due to a lack of supply chains. Advance payments would be requested by the suppliers for security, which was risky because the lumber shipments would frequently be delayed and even sometimes never delivered. Within six months, the venture failed.

The previous experience, while a failure financially, did provide us a better understanding about doing business in China. This time we found an opportunity to move to a building twice as large as the first one and containing equipment that we could

Source: As told by Sunny Hwang, May 25, 2001.

use. The total rent was only half the amount we had paid for the smaller building. This time we were very careful in negotiating strict terms with the government officials. Consequently, hiring qualified workers became much easier, without interference from the government officials and the local workers. Purchasing lumber also became much easier and cheaper by developing relationships of mutual trust with a limited number of agents. It takes time to acquire trust from the Chinese.

The final result has been a much-improved environment for doing business: we can now produce quality products more cheaply. It was a long and tedious journey, involving a lot of hard work, expense, and some tough lessons. But the adventure into China has proven to be a good one.

Sunny Hwang certainly recognizes the importance of knowing as much as possible about the challenges of doing business in a foreign country before getting involved there. An entrepreneur who is considering expanding into China—to connect with an outsourcing partner, to establish a production facility, or to reach a new market—should know the following key facts about the country:

- China's population of 1.3 billion people is the largest of any country in the world.
- China is the 3rd fastest-growing export market for small- and medium-size U.S. firms.
- Average income in China is approximately $725 per year, but disparities are great. Income in urban areas ranges from around $3,400 per year in Shanghai (China's wealthiest city) to the more typical $1,000 per year in other cities; income in rural areas is much lower.
- The Chinese software market is growing at an annual rate of 30 percent.
- Internet users increased fourfold in 1999 alone.
- The demand for consulting services in China is increasing, especially those related to information technology.
- China is entering the World Trade Organization (WTO), a development that has raised concerns about intellectual property protection. Its entry into the WTO may force more vigilant protection of intellectual property and a crackdown on counterfeiting.
- Many Chinese consumers have cell phones and regularly surf the Internet (especially in large urban centers such as Beijing, Shanghai, and Guangzhou).
- Counterfeit goods (including clothing, leather goods, software, and CDs) are readily available in China at a fraction of the cost of brand name items.
- Chinese merchants usually do business only with vendors with whom they have established relationships.

QUESTIONS

1. What is the primary force that motivated Hwang to internationalize? Did he make a good decision when he located his manufacturing facility in China? What other countries should have been considered? Why?
2. What strategy option did Hwang select for his China-based enterprise? Did he select the right strategy?
3. Given the details of the case and the key facts about China, assess the opportunities for U.S. firms in China. What features of the country should be particularly attractive to small businesses seeking to expand internationally?
4. What challenges to doing business in China did Hwang experience? Given the key facts about China, list issues that may present distinct problems for small U.S. firms doing business there.

case 5

STITCH CRAFT

BUYING A SMALL BUSINESS

Helen and Martha, recent graduates of the School of Fabric Design at Webster University, are interested in going into business in a field that will utilize their education. They both have been steady customers of Stitch Craft, a nationally franchised business, since it opened a year ago, and they both know Peggy and Susan, the owners. Helen and Martha have learned from Peggy that the store is doing quite well for having been in business only a year. Just the other day, while Martha was shopping in Stitch Craft, she was approached by Susan, who told her that she and Peggy were considering selling the business. Susan said the reason they wished to sell was that they had overextended themselves in terms of time availability and were having difficulties maintaining their homes, children, outside interests, and the business simultaneously. Since Helen and Martha had expressed an interest in the business and had experience in fabric design, Peggy and Susan thought they should be given the first chance to buy the business.

Helen and Martha are quite excited about this prospect and make an appointment to meet with Peggy and Susan. At this meeting, they are shown the entire business, from inventory procedures to ringing out the cash register at night. They are quite impressed and are eager to proceed with the takeover. When they discuss finances, Helen and Martha are told that, since the business is only one year old, Peggy and Susan are only asking them to assume the existing balance of the SBA loan and pay the invoice price of the inventory, plus $20,000 for the fixtures, leasehold improvements, and franchise fee. Helen and Martha don't know anything about finances, so they have come to you with a copy of Stitch Craft's income statement from last year (Figure C5-1), this month's balance sheet (Figure C5-2), and the following income statement for this month:

Sales	$6,750
Cost of goods	3,649
Gross margin	$3,101
Operating expense	6,001
Net income (loss)	($2,900)

Note: January/February sales are lowest in year. October/November sales are highest.

Other points that have come up in your discussion with Helen and Martha are that they have contacted the Stitch Craft Corporation, which granted Peggy and Susan the franchise, and were informed that they could indeed take over the remaining nine years of the franchise agreement. Martha also explained that the Stitch Craft brand is nationally known for quality and style, which accounts for its rapid acceptance in the Webster City market. Helen and Martha have given a great deal of thought to the store's current location, which is in a strip mall on the south end of town. The store's customers are mainly from the higher-income northwest section of town. Helen and Martha feel the store should be moved to a location that is closer to the market. If they buy the business, they plan to move the store at

Source: This case was prepared by Professor Carl Schweser of the University of Iowa.

the end of the current lease, which expires in two years. However, they have options to extend the lease for six years after the current lease expires should they decide not to move. The landlord has agreed to turn over Peggy and Susan's lease to Helen and Martha without alteration.

QUESTIONS

1. Your job is to review the current financial statements and all the data presented to you and make a recommendation on whether Helen and Martha should buy Stitch Craft.
2. What counteroffer would you recommend they make if you feel the current asking price is not attractive?

FIGURE C5-1

Stitch Craft Income Statement 2001

	Stitch Craft	Industry Data (% of Sales)
Sales		
Fabric	$144,376	82.0
Patterns/books	16,871	10.0
Sewing classes	6,932	7.0
Other	1,621	1.0
Total sales	$169,800	100.0
Cost of goods sold	79,300	51.0
Gross profit	$ 90,500	49.0
Expenses		
Wages	$ 30,600	14.0
Supplies	2,575	1.0
Rent	15,000	7.5
Utilities	2,880	1.5
Advertising	9,572	5.5
Displays	2,220	1.0
Travel	375	1.0
Phone	1,550	0.5
Services	1,875	0.5
Royalty fee (4.5% of sales)	7,436	4.5
Depreciation and amortization	4,128	2.0
Interest	7,185	1.0
Other	5,654	5.0
Total expenses	$ 91,050	45.0%
Income before taxes & owners' draw	($ 550)	4.0%

FIGURE C5-2

Stitch Craft Balance Sheet for January 31, 2002

Current assets:		
Cash on hand		$ 400
Cash in the bank		(1,245)
Accounts receivable		0
Inventory		
Fabrics	$20,372	
Notions	3,900	
Patterns/books	2,190	
Sewing machines	1,345	
		$27,807
Prepaid rent		1,250
Total current assets		$28,212
Fixed assets:		
Fixtures	$12,000	
Less accumulated depreciation	(1,300)	
		$10,700
Leasehold improvements	$11,760	
Less accumulated depreciation	(1,820)	
		$ 9,940
Franchise	$12,500	
Less amortization	(1,352)	
		$11,148
Total fixed assets		$31,788
TOTAL ASSETS		$60,000
Current liabilities:		
Accounts payable—trade	$21,873	
Withholdings payable	550	
Sales tax payable	202	
Total current liabilities		$22,625
Long-term liabilities:		
SBA loan—balance due		
($50,000 over 7 years @ 15%)		$46,025
Equity:		
Capital–Peggy Ralson	($ 275)	
Add current income/loss	(1,550)	
Training expense draw	(2,500)	
Plus other withdrawals	(0)	
New balance		($ 4,325)
Capital—Susan Keightly	($ 275)	
Add current income/loss	(1,550)	
Training expense draw	(2,500)	
Plus other withdrawals	(0)	
New balance		($ 4,325)
Total equity		(8,650)
TOTAL LIABILITIES AND EQUITY		$60,000

case 6

Universal Business Brokers

Franchise Networking

In the United States, the small business sector has flourished in recent years. By some estimates, roughly 70 percent of Americans dream of owning their own business at some point, yet only 15 percent actually attain business ownership. By the late 1990s, the number of small businesses in the United States approached 20 million, with roughly 20 percent of them for sale at any given time. In the past two decades, the small business sector has been invigorated by such trends as shifting immigration patterns and corporate downsizing.

In many ways, the process of selling a business is similar to that of selling real estate. Like realtors, business brokers solicit and generate listings of businesses for sale. They then advertise those listings, facilitate negotiations between sellers and buyers, and make sure that all the legal and technical requirements are fulfilled so that deals are successfully closed. Although prices and terms vary somewhat, the industry norm is a 10 percent commission on the sale price, paid to the broker by the seller at the closing of the deal.

Universal Business Brokers had started as a local office in Roanoke, Virginia. In the late 1990s, when that office had been operating for more than 15 years and Universal had been franchising for more than two years, the UBBSAT office in San Antonio was opened. In two short years of franchising, Universal had quickly expanded to become one of the largest business broker networks nationwide. With more than 60 offices, Universal was intensifying its franchising efforts in other parts of the country.

At the time of the UBBSAT startup, there were already two other Universal franchises in Texas. One was located in Dallas, and the other in Houston. At both franchises, business brokerage had been added as an adjunct to existing, related businesses. After becoming Universal franchises, both offices continued their prior operations, and they both continued using the trade names that they had established for themselves in their local markets instead of operating under the Universal Business Brokers name.

At Universal, the franchise operation was basically a two-person show. Mike Thompson, president, and Matt Walters, vice president, handled all franchise sales, franchisee and broker training and support, and franchise network development activities. Corporate headquarters was located adjacent to the original Roanoke brokerage office, in an office park. When no one was available at corporate headquarters, telephone calls were automatically forwarded to the brokerage office, where messages were taken for Mike and Matt. This practice gave corporate headquarters the appearance of being a larger operation than it actually was, while also keeping down costs and ensuring that the person answering the phone knew how to get in immediate touch with Mike or Matt in an emergency.

Like many other franchisors, Universal offered franchisees an established trade name, training, and support. Its up-front fees and subsequent charges to franchisees were low compared to the averages for all

Source: This case was prepared by Gary J. Castrogiovanni, University of Tulsa, and is used by permission of the author.

franchisors in all industries. At the network level, efforts to help franchisees control costs focused primarily on negotiating prices on stationery, printed forms, and other supplies. Benefits of network purchasing power were limited because business brokerage is a service business with no merchandise or major equipment expenditures.

Because confidentiality is a key concern in many business sales, there is no general multiple listing service, and co-broker arrangements are infrequent. Within the Universal network, however, there was a multiple listing arrangement. A person in Dallas wanting to buy a restaurant in Roanoke, for example, could go to the Universal office in Dallas to get basic details on the restaurants listed by the Universal office in Roanoke. If the buyer was sufficiently interested in one of those listings, he or she would be put in touch with a broker in the Roanoke office, who would take over the selling process at that point. If a deal were subsequently closed, the Roanoke office would share part of its commission with the Dallas office.

At the network level, Universal was aggressive in working out sales arrangements with other franchisors or firms offering distributorships or other business opportunities. This provided a secondary source of income to the local offices, in addition to the sale of existing businesses. A buyer interested in purchasing a gift shop, for example, might first be given information on the gift shops listed by the particular local office. If none of those listings appealed to that buyer, details on an available gift shop franchise could be presented. Then, if the buyer subsequently purchased that franchise, the franchisor would pay a commission to the local Universal office.

Within the Universal network, commissions charged to business sellers were the 10 percent industry standard, though there was a $10,000 minimum charged on sales of very small businesses (i.e., those with a selling price of less than $100,000), and the percentage was reduced for sales of larger ones (i.e., those with a sale price of $1,000,000 or more). When discussing the network-wide commission schedule with franchisees and their brokers, however, both Mike and Matt pointed out that some degree of flexibility might be desirable in order to close deals. It might be better, for example, to accept an $8,000 commission (i.e., something less than the $10,000 minimum) to get a deal closed, instead of letting that deal fall apart and ending up with no commission at all.

When commissions were received, they were split among the franchise office, the broker who had obtained the listing from the seller, and the broker who had worked with the buyer. (In some cases, the selling and buying broker were the same individual.) On a $10,000 commission, for example, the office would get $5,000 and the two brokers involved would get $2,500 each.

Local Market Conditions

George Stokes was a 48-year-old retired military officer who had taken a position as a marketing executive of a major corporation. When that position was eliminated in a corporate downsizing effort, George suddenly found himself unemployed for the first time in his life. His situation was not desperate, however, because his military pension, savings, and severance pay would provide a cushion until he found a new income source.

George and his wife, Helen, decided to go into business for themselves. During a month-long trip to Florida, they talked to several business brokers and checked out a number of businesses that were for sale. George and Helen also investigated various franchise acquisition opportunities. Eventually, they decided to buy a Universal franchise, and they chose the San Antonio territory because of its large market size. (Additional information about George and Helen, as well as details about the other key participants in the UBBSAT startup, is provided in Figure C6-1.)

With his franchise acquisition, George Stokes was granted exclusive rights to open Universal offices throughout the San Antonio metropolitan area. Centered around one of the largest cities in the United States, that local market consisted of nearly 125,000 small businesses. During any given year, an estimated 25,000 of them would be for sale.

The Yellow Pages and other directories indicated that there were roughly 50 business brokerages operating in the local market. That number was misleading, however, for several reasons. First, two large firms and several mid-sized operations dominated the market, while the other brokerages were relatively minor players. Second, there were many firms in related businesses, such as real estate and business consulting, offering business broker services in addition to their primary services. Third, because there was no licensing requirement for business brokers in the

FIGURE C6-1

Key Participants in the UBBSAT Startup

George Stokes Franchisee and office manager. Responsible for all aspects of the UBBSAT business, including startup operations, broker hiring and training, advertising, administrative details, financing, and ongoing operations.

Helen Stokes George's wife and franchisee partner. Responsible for bookkeeping, client relations, tracking brokerage sales through closing, and assisting George in administrative matters.

Glenn Digman Broker. Background in engineering (retired), currently a part-time real estate investor/landlord. Financially secure and thus working for UBBSAT because of personal interests more than for the income.

Tim Fischer Broker. Background in marketing and sales with some experience in business acquisitions. Former executive, "downsized" into early retirement.

Tommy Gates Broker. Background in various entrepreneurial and self-employment ventures including real estate, photography, and other service activities.

Scott Phillips Broker. Technical background in the chemical industry, recently laid off due to corporate downsizing. No source of income other than potential UBBSAT commissions.

Rick Price Broker. A former business broker who joined UBBSAT on a part-time basis while considering the acquisition of another Universal Business Brokers franchise in a different city.

Jenny Williams Broker. Background in various self-employment activities, working for UBBSAT as a way of exploring whether she was interested in being a business broker full-time, part-time, or not at all.

Mike Thompson President of Universal Business Brokers, the franchisor. Most actively involved in franchise sales, new franchisee training, initial new broker training within each franchise, and ongoing franchise support.

Matt Walters Vice president of Universal Business Brokers, the franchisor. Most actively involved in advanced franchisee training, advanced broker training, franchise support system development, and franchise network development.

state of Texas, just about anyone could start offering brokerage services at any time. And indeed, numerous individuals engaged in business broker activities on a temporary, part-time basis when opportunities arose for them to do so. Competition was intense. Whereas Universal commissions paralleled the 10 percent national norm, some rivals in the local market charged as little as 5 percent, with only a $2,000–$5,000 minimum. In addition to such differences in commissions, listing agreement terms and broker sales practices varied considerably as well. Unlike Universal, some competitors followed a "shared risk" arrangement, whereby business sellers would place their own business-for-sale ads or pay up-front advertising fees to the broker. That way, the broker would not lose money on a listing if the business could not be sold.

Under the Universal system, prospective buyers were required to meet face-to-face with a broker before they would be given business information beyond that which could be found in newspaper ads. At that meeting, the broker would attempt to establish a rapport with the buyer and gain an understanding of his or her needs and interests while explaining the importance of confidentiality and educating the buyer about the business sale process. In contrast, some competitors would not even have an initial meeting unless a buyer asked for one, choosing instead to simply fax a copy of all their listings to anyone who inquired about businesses for sale.

To establish a presence in the local market and to generate interest in particular listings, brokers found classified newspaper advertising to be essential—yet it was fairly expensive in the San Antonio area. One of the two major metropolitan newspapers had recently gone out of business, and the other had subsequently boosted its rates to advertisers. Consequently, the cost of city-wide newspaper advertising was above the national average.

This gave larger brokerages cost advantages on a per-listing basis, because they could advertise several similar businesses in a single ad. A broker with seven convenience store listings, for example, could reach prospective buyers of all seven with only one ad, whereas a broker with only one convenience store listing would incur approximately the same advertising costs. Additionally, brokerages with a variety of business listings could reach buyer prospects without

advertising each business or even each type. A buyer responding to a gift shop ad, for example, might end up buying an antique store or novelty shop that had not been advertised. Brokerages not having as wide a variety of listings, however, would not be able to direct buyers to such unadvertised alternatives.

The Franchise Startup

In August, George Stokes participated in a two-week training program for new franchisees at Universal's Roanoke office. During the first two days, he learned the basics of business brokering in a seminar that Mike Thompson gave periodically to new brokers. Then, over the next two days, George learned the fundamentals of running a business broker office and a Universal franchise. The rest of the two-week training period he spent working as a broker in the Roanoke office so that he could get some first-hand experience in brokerage operations.

During the next three months, George developed his business plan, found a suitable business location in San Antonio, and moved there with Helen. An aggressive, somewhat impatient, meticulous individual, George planned out every conceivable detail. He decided, for example, that the office would be located on the north side of town. It would serve the entire metropolitan area initially, but later would focus on northside businesses, after George opened three other offices—one each on the south, east, and west sides of town.

In late November, George began setting up the office, and he placed a "Help Wanted" newspaper ad for brokers. His startup plan called for five brokers, growing to eight brokers as the new office developed into an established operation. There was ample room for eight brokers. In fact, additional brokers could be squeezed in if desks were shared or one or two desks were placed in the storage/computer room. When he first saw the UBBSAT office, Mike Thompson remarked, "This is what a brokerage office should look like." He complimented George for "doing this right," instead of trying to cut corners as some other franchisees had done.

During the second week of December, Mike Thompson presented his two-day seminar for new brokers at the UBBSAT office. Aside from George, Helen, and Mike, one part-time and five full-time brokers were present: Glenn Digman, Tim Fischer, Tommy Gates, Scott Phillips, Rick Price, and Jenny Williams. To complement this two-day seminar, the brokers were given training manuals to study at home. During the seminar and again in the manuals, brokers were warned not to expect any income for four to six months because that was the average time needed for a broker to list a business, that listing to sell, the sale to close, and commission checks to be distributed. The brokers were required to sign documents stating that they were independent contractors, and that if they quit the office, they could not compete with UBBSAT for at least a year.

After the two-day training seminar, office operations began. The brokers spent two weeks in mid-December soliciting listings. Then the office closed down for a week surrounding Christmas. George viewed December primarily as a training and practice month, and thus he did not expect to see much progress. Then, full-scale UBBSAT operations were started during the first week in January.

QUESTIONS

1. What additional types of franchise evaluation should George and Helen Stokes have undertaken prior to making their decision?
2. Evaluate the training and other services of this franchisor.
3. What do you believe to be the biggest obstacle(s) to the success of this franchise?
4. What types of continued franchise support do you believe the franchisor should provide to George and Helen Stokes?

case

7

The Brown Family Business

Defining Work Opportunities for Family Members in a Family Firm

For 56 years, the Brown family has operated an agricultural products business in central Texas. As the business has grown, family leaders have attempted to preserve family relationships while operating the business in a profitable manner. At present, five members of the second generation, three members of the third generation, and one member of the fourth generation are active in the business. Other members of the family, of course, have ownership interests and a concern about the firm even though they are pursuing other careers.

In the interest of building the business and also preserving family harmony, the family has developed policies for entry and career opportunities for family members. The human resource policies governing family members are as follows:

Family Philosophy Concerning Family and Work Opportunities

1. A family working together as one unit will always be stronger than individuals or divided units.
2. Family is an "umbrella" that includes all direct descendants of P. and L. Brown and their spouses.
3. The Brown family believes that a career with Brown Bros. is only for those who
   - Believe in working for their success;
   - Believe that rewards they receive should come from the work they have done;
   - Believe in working for the company versus working for a paycheck; and
   - Believe that everyone must work to provide an equal and fair contribution for the good of the whole business.
4. While work opportunities and career opportunities with the family business will be communicated to all family members, there will be no guarantee of a job in the family business for any member of the family at any time.
5. A family member working in the family business, whether in a temporary or a long-term career position, will be offered work and career counseling by a supervisor or officer/family member (depending on the job level). However, the family member/employee is not guaranteed a job or a career position. His or her job performance and qualifications must be the primary factor in determining whether the family member will be allowed continued employment.
6. While the family business is principally agriculture-related, there are many jobs that both men and women can perform equally and safely.
7. Compensation will be based on comparable positions held by other employees.

Source: This case was prepared by Nancy B. Upton, founder of the Institute for Family Business, Baylor University.

TABLE C7-1

Criteria for a Career at Brown Bros.

	Mid-Management Positions	Upper-Management Positions
Personal:		
No criminal record	Required	Required
No substance abuse	Required	Required
Education:		
High school	Required	Required
College degree (2.5 on a 4-point system)	Recommended	Required
Work experience with others:		
While completing college	Recommended	Recommended
After completing college (one to three years)	Recommended	Required

Committee on Family Employee Development

1. Review, on an annual basis, policies for entry and recommend changes.
2. Receive notices of positions available and communicate them to all family members.
3. Review, on an annual basis, evaluations of family members' performance, training provided, outside training programs attended, and goals and development plans. Offer counseling to upper management when appropriate.
4. Committee composed of three persons—one of four Brown brothers in the business; one of seven non-operating Browns; one of the spouses of the eleven Browns.

The general criteria for having a career at Brown Bros. are given in Table C7-1.

QUESTIONS

1. What are the key ideas embodied in the statement of philosophy concerning family and work opportunities?
2. Evaluate each of the criteria specified for a management career in the firm. Which, if any, would you change or modify?
3. Evaluate the structure and functions of the committee on family employee development.

case

8

ROBINSON ASSOCIATES, INC.

BUSINESS PLAN FOR A NEW VENTURE

This case presents a business plan for a proposed management consulting firm. This plan was prepared by a graduate student in business who set up the firm to support himself both during and after his period of graduate study. A few details, such as name and location, have been changed, but the situation is real.

BUSINESS PLAN FOR DAVID R. ROBINSON MINNEAPOLIS, MINNESOTA

Scope of the Business

Personal. I plan to start a business consulting service in conjunction with USA Consultants (a nationwide business consulting firm).

History of USA Consultants. USA is over 30 years old. It originated in Boston and Atlanta. It started out as P. Miller Management Consultants. The name changed to USA in 1972. Paul Miller III is the current president of USA, which has over 160 consultants in more than 50 cities.

Specific Areas of Focus

Company (Brochure Available on Request)

1. Analysis Phase
2. Implementation Phase (selected examples)
   a. Marketing programs
   b. Organization planning
   c. Personnel training programs
   d. Cost reduction programs
   e. Loan package preparation
   f. Inventory control systems
   g. Financial control and reporting
   h. Mergers and acquisitions
   i. Strategic business planning
   j. Business evaluation

Source: This case was prepared by Philip R. Carpenter.

Personal. With my accounting background (CPA--inactive) and current experience consulting with small businesses, I would concentrate on:

1. Analysis phase
2. Implementation phase—especially on:
   a. Organization planning
   b. Loan package preparation
   c. Strategic business planning
   d. Financial control and reporting systems
3. USA continuing education programs in various areas in which I could update my skills.

Goals

Personal

1. I plan to begin the business July 1 and operate it part-time for three months. I will limit my hours to 32 per week. I will still be eligible for full-time benefits including health insurance and tuition remission. I will go into the business full-time starting October 1.

TABLE C8-1

Cash Flow Projections for David R. Robinson Family

	July	Aug.	Sept.	Oct.	Nov.	Dec.
Husband	$1,396	$1,396	$1,396	$ 0	$ 0	$ 0
Wife	$ 783	$ 783	$ 783	$ 783	$ 783	$ 783
USA	$ 0	$ 625	$ 935	$1,560	$2,500	$3,125
Subtotal	$2,179	$2,804	$3,114	$2,343	$3,283	$3,908
Expenses	$3,300	$3,300	$3,400	$3,500	$3,600	$3,700
Overage (Shortage)	($1,121)	($ 496)	($ 286)	($1,157)	($ 317)	$ 208

	Jan.	Feb.	Mar.	Apr.	May	June
Husband	$ 0	$ 0	$ 0	$ 0	$ 0	$ 0
Wife	$ 783	$ 783	$ 783	$ 0	$ 0	$ 0
USA	$2,500	$4,125	$4,125	$ 5,250	$6,375	$6,375
Other	$ 0	0	$ 0	$ 7,500	$ 0	$ 0
Subtotal	$3,283	$4,908	$4,908	$12,750	$6,375	$6,375
Expenses	$5,500	$3,800	$3,900	$ 4,000	$3,800	$3,900
Overage (Shortage)	($2,217)	$1,108	$1,008	$ 8,750	$2,575	$2,475

Summary of Overages (Shortages):

July	($1,121)
Aug.	($ 496)
Sept.	($ 286)
Oct.	($1,157)
Nov.	($ 317)
Dec.	$ 208
Jan.	($2,217)

2. I plan to continue pursuing a Ph.D. in business administration. This is entirely compatible with the consulting business. (See attached projected cash flow statements [Table C8-1].)

Financial. I plan to reach the following cumulative gross billing goals [Table C8-2]:

Six months	$ 22,500
Twelve months	$ 86,500
Eighteen months	$137,000
Twenty-four months	$191,000

Management Capability

See attached résumé [Figure C8-1].

Strong Points

1. Four years of consulting experience with Small Business Development Centers.
2. Admitted to Ph.D. program at the university in business administration. Major: Management; minor: International Business, with current G.P.A. of 4.0, out of possible 4.0.
3. Accepted by USA. USA advertised in *The Wall Street Journal, Inc.,* and *USA Today.* To date, they have received over 3,000 applications but approved only 158.
4. Education will be continued through schooling and USA's continuing education program.

Marketing

Competition

External:

1. Review of the Minneapolis–St. Paul *Webb's Directory* on management consultants shows no direct competition.

TABLE C8-2

Projected Billable Hours for First Year

	Hours	Billings	Compensation (@ 50%)
July	10	$ 1,250	$ 0
August	15	$ 1,875	$ 625
September	25	$ 3,125	$ 938
October	40	$ 5,000	$ 1,563
November	50	$ 6,250	$ 2,500
December	40	$ 5,000	$ 3,125
January*	55	$ 8,250	$ 2,500
February	55	$ 8,250	$ 4,125
March	70	$10,500	$ 4,125
April	85	$12,750	$ 5,250
May	85	$12,750	$ 6,375
June	75	$11,250	$ 6,375
Totals		$86,250	$37,501

*Pay review is conducted every six months—expect increase to $150/hour. After $50,000 in gross billings, consultant receives $7,500 deposit back. This should occur about the end of March.

2. Typically, consultants specialize in one to three areas. No firm can offer the wide range of services that USA can.

Internal: There are two other USA consultants in the Minneapolis–St. Paul area. One started his business in December of last year, and the second is just starting. Both are on the Minneapolis side of the river. There appears to be plenty of room in the market for a third USA consultant.

Customer Analysis. USA billing rates are $125/hour to $300/hour. These rates will preclude very small businesses from using my services in most cases. The firms that appear to be best suited for using a USA consultant would be firms with 30 to 400 employees. These firms can be identified through the use of *Webb's Directory* and various other publications.

Reaching the Customer. There are three primary methods to reach customers:

1. *Salesperson.* USA will assist the consultant in hiring and training.
2. *MAS services to small accounting firms.* USA works with accounting firms that do not have an MAS department to provide them with consulting services.
3. *Personal contacts.* Extensive contacts have been developed on both sides of the river and will be used to assist in identifying potential customers.

Market Trends. Many businesses today are downsizing. Typically, the person that businesses are outplacing is in middle management. Businesses will still have the same problems as before. Businesses will then turn to a consultant to assist in solving these problems.

Financial

Amount Needed:

$ 7,500	Initial deposit*
$ 1,000	Supplies**
$ 4,000	Working capital***
$12,500	Bank financing
$ 9,500	Personal collateral (certificate of deposit)
$22,000	Total

*To be refunded when $50,000 in gross billings have been achieved.

**Supplies include Webb's Directory, file cabinet, office supplies, shelving, business subscriptions, and business phone.

***See attached cash flow statement for details.

FIGURE C8-1 *Personal Résumé of David R. Robinson*

CAREER OBJECTIVE

To make optimal use of my organizational analysis and human relations abilities to become a skilled consultant to businesses. This will result in:

- More coordinated organizations
- Increased job satisfaction/productivity

QUALIFIED BY

Training and over 10 years' experience encompassing:

- Organizational skills
- Human relations
- Leadership skills
- Financial analysis
- Reporting

ACHIEVEMENTS

Organizational Skills

- Effectively worked with the Small Business Development Center (SBDC) director to present a highly rated conference on SBDCs for state and federal government personnel.
- Supervised and coordinated other staff accountants in the preparation of audited financial statements.
- Coordinated with volunteer personnel to achieve a very successful fund drive.
- Developed and presented in coordination with other area procurement specialists two highly rated seminars.

Human Relations

- Quickly developed an atmosphere of trust with established clients through careful consideration of their accounting and tax needs.
- Successfully assisted two business partners in planning, starting, and operating their own small business.
- Provided clear direction to several small businesses, which enabled them to successfully bid on government contracts.

Leadership Skills

- Effectively taught a government procurement seminar in a concise and clear manner to small business owners.
- Successfully started and developed a Procurement Assistance Center that helped local businesses obtain over $1,000,000 in government contracts in just over two years.

Financial Analysis

- Developed and successfully implemented annual budgets for the SBDC and Procurement Assistance Center for over two years.
- Thoroughly completed audits and prepared financial statements for corporations with assets up to $2,000,000.
- Developed an accounting system for the Chaplain Fund that provided more complete documentation and permitted audits to be completed in half the expected time.

Reporting

- Coordinated development of successful funding proposals for the local SBDC and Procurement Assistance Center.
- Thoroughly prepared two nominations for awards, one national and one state, which resulted in the nominees' receiving the rewards.
- Gathered information regarding a specific question by the Chaplain Fund council, then translated this information into a short, understandable format that permitted an immediate, well-informed decision.

EXPERIENCE

State University, Minnesota (June 1989–Present)
Procurement specialist/small business counselor/graduate assistant
Bellhaven Hospital (November 1987–May 1989)
Advanced staff auditor
Moore, Synder CPA, Inc. (December 1986–June 1987)
Staff accountant
Harry C. Reynolds & Co. (January 1985–November 1986)
Staff accountant
U.S. Army (1980–1984)
Fund custodian, Chaplain Fund, Illinois
Chapel activities specialist, Korea
Funds clerk, Chaplain Fund, Texas

EDUCATION

B.S. in accounting, State University, Ohio
M.A. in industrial/organizational psychology, State University, Minnesota
(thesis title: Comparative Psychological Characteristics of Entrepreneurs vs. Small Business Owners)

OTHER

Licensed as a CPA (inactive) in Minnesota.

QUESTIONS

1. Which part of this business plan would impress a potential investor most favorably?
2. What are the most serious concerns or questions a potential investor might have after reading this plan?
3. What additional information should be added to strengthen the plan?
4. What changes could be made in the format or wording of the plan to enhance its communication effectiveness?
5. As a banker, would you make a working-capital loan to this business? Why or why not?

case

9

ScrubaDub Auto Wash

Waxing Philosophical

Imagine charging more than competitors for a number of your services, yet maintaining a higher market share and profit margin. ScrubaDub Auto Wash, based in Natick, Massachusetts, does just that. With eight locations and sales of more than $5 million, ScrubaDub is the largest auto-wash chain in the Boston area. And the company has continued its growth—posting annual sales increases of 10 percent in recent years—despite a long-lasting and punishing recession in its home state.

"Nineteen ninety-two was an absolutely disastrous year for the economy in Massachusetts, but it was one of the best years we ever had," recounts Marshall Paisner, who owns and operates the chain with his wife, Elaine, and their sons, Dan and Bob.

Their secret? ScrubaDub combines an expertise in the science of cleaning cars with a flair for the art of marketing. The company has turned an otherwise mundane chore—getting the car washed—into a pleasant service interlude. Employees sweat the details that define the experience for customers, and the company tracks [customers'] buying habits to improve customer service and boost sales. ScrubaDub then backs up its work with guarantees, ensuring that customers are satisfied with the results.

In short, ScrubaDub's managers and employees think from the customer's point of view, says Paul M. Cole, vice president of marketing services at the Lexington, Massachusetts, office of Mercer Management Consulting Inc. The ScrubaDub staff looks beyond the moment to anticipate how customers will feel about the company's services and its long-term role in the community . . . from the performance guarantees to Halloween charity events. "They're looking for every opportunity to demonstrate concern for customers," Cole says.

Details and Data

Better yet, ScrubaDub didn't need the resources of an industry giant to create its marketing and service programs. Instead, the 100-plus employee company has focused on cutting overhead—by automating functions such as cash management—to free up funds to invest in labor, computer operations and customer service.

Here are seven lessons from the car-wash chain that might apply to your business as well:

Pay attention to the details. Just as the hospitality industry wants travelers to feel pampered, the Paisners want customers to view the car-wash service as a pleasant experience. The first clues to this service philosophy: flower beds decorate the entrance to the wash, neatly groomed employees greet customers courteously, and car owners receive little treats such as peanuts as they enter the cleaning tunnel.

Inside, the cars are cleaned by an equipment system the Paisners configured for the most effective treatment possible (as opposed to the standard systems used by some competitors) and scrubbed with a

Source: Jo-Ann Johnston, "Waxing Philosophical," *Small Business Reports,* Vol. 19, No. 6 (June 1994), pp. 14–19. Reprinted with permission.

soap that's exclusive to the chain. Meanwhile, any kids on board may be delighted to see cartoon characters like Garfield or Bart Simpson mounted on poles inside the tunnel. These familiar characters help calm children who are frightened when the washing machine descends on their family car—and thus allow their parents to relax. (Of course, kids like to be scared around Halloween, so then the chain decorates its tunnels like haunted houses.)

Once drivers emerge from the wash, they can go to a waiting room and get free coffee if they want the insides of their cars cleaned. Some customers—depending on the make of their car and the level of service they've chosen—have their wheels cleaned with a toothbrush. Others can go to the "satisfaction center," a final service checkpoint, for any extra attention they feel the car needs. The goal is to make sure customers feel well taken care of when they drive out of the lot.

Know the customer. ScrubaDub's marketing and service programs rely heavily on the tracking of customers' buying habits. For example, the company develops vehicle histories of its "club members," who spend $5.95 for a membership pass that entitles them to certain specials, such as a free wash after 10 paid cleanings. ScrubaDub uses a computer database to track the frequency of these customers' visits and the services purchased. Each time a member visits, an employee scans a bar-code sticker that's placed on the vehicle's window and logs information into the database.

Behind the scenes, the company analyzes the vehicle histories, along with other sales and profit data, to track buying habits and identify sales opportunities. To punch up its relatively slow business in the evening hours, for example, ScrubaDub introduced a "night wash" special with a $1 savings and doubled its volume. And if a review of the data shows that certain club members haven't been to the store for a while, the company sends out a "We miss you letter" to invite them back.

More recently, ScrubaDub has moved its vehicle histories out of the back office and onto the car-wash lot to improve its customer service. Now, when club members enter the car wash, sales advisors can call up their histories on a computer terminal. That way, they can address customers by name and remind them of services they've purchased before, such as an undercarriage wash, a special wax treatment, or a wheel cleaning.

What's more, employees can now use the histories to suggest service upgrades. If a customer usually gets a regular wash, for example, a sales advisor might recommend an undercarriage wash if the car has been coated by heavily salted roads. ScrubaDub counts on these special options to generate income above the base price of $5.95 (the average purchase above that level is $1.60), but it also wants employees to suggest only those services appropriate to the vehicle and the customer. The point-of-sale histories help guide the sales advisor to the customer's buying preferences.

Mine new prospects. ScrubaDub is always on the lookout for new prospects, using both mass-market means (such as radio jingles) and more targeted approaches to draw them in. New car buyers are obvious prospects, so the company works with local car dealers to distribute 30-day passes for free washes to their customers. To reach new home buyers, another target group, ScrubaDub uses an outside service to generate names from property-transfer records, then sends [those buyers] coupons for its services.

Last year, the company also launched a direct-mail campaign to reach people with $75,000 or more in income and homes close to one of its locations. The $30,000 mailing invited [those people] to become club members, who tend to be steady customers and purchase more add-on services. The mailing yielded more than 1,000 new members and generated a $45,000 return in its first year.

Fix the problems. If a customer believes the car wash has damaged his or her car in any way, the manager can spend up to $150 in labor or merchandise to fix the problem, no questions asked. Even if ScrubaDub is not at fault, the Paisners don't want customers driving away with a sour memory. When one customer's tire began to leak, for example, an employee spotted it, helped the customer change the tire and got the leaky one repaired. After a problem is fixed, says Elaine Paisner, ScrubaDub sends the customer "a little warm fuzzy" of flowers, cookies, or candy.

It also backs up its work with guarantees. Customers who purchase the basic wash can get a rewash if they're not satisfied, while club members are entitled to some added protection. In exchange for these customers' loyalty and investment,

ScrubaDub offers them a free replacement wash if it rains or snows within 24 hours after they've left the lot. With some of the more expensive treatments, customers are guaranteed a clean car for three days. If the driver goes through a puddle or parks under a flock of pigeons, the company will wash the car again for free.

The benefit of such guarantees? They help a company stay competitive by acknowledging that a bad service experience eats away at a customer's good will, says Christopher W. L. Hart, president of TQM Group, a Boston consulting firm. Of course, this forces a company to determine what services it can afford to guarantee and to improve operations so that mistakes are the exception. But the cost of fulfilling guarantees should be viewed as a marketing investment and a second chance to make a good impression, not as a loss. "View it as something to celebrate," says Hart.

Monitor customer satisfaction. The Paisners use a variety of feedback mechanisms to evaluate the quality of their service at the eight locations. These include comment cards available to all customers and special reports which the managers personally ask some drivers to fill out each month. In addition, ScrubaDub recently added a new service questionnaire for customers getting the insides of their cars cleaned. This feedback mechanism, which a ScrubaDub manager adopted from a noncompeting operator, allows the company to make sure its inside-cleaning service is as detailed as customers expect.

Together, these forms give ScrubaDub enough feedback to rate overall customer satisfaction and calculate it on an index ranging to 100. To supplement its own research, the company also employs an outside firm to send people through the car wash and generate professional "shoppers' reports" on their experiences.

Use training and incentives to ensure good service. If you want high-quality service, says Paisner, then get the message across with your hiring, training, and pay practices. His company tries to set itself apart from competitors by hiring well-groomed employees, for example, and Paisner believes you get what you ask for in the recruiting process. "If you expect clean-cut kids who are willing to wear shirts and ties, you're going to get them," he says.

Once hired, employees go through various training modules in a classroom setting—an unusual practice in the car-wash business—to make sure service will be consistent from location to location. New employees also must meet the approval of their coworkers, since the staff at each location is viewed as a team with its own sales and expense goals to meet.

Indeed, up to half of employees' pay is tied to such goals; the incentive-pay proportion for each individual varies according to the sales and management content of his or her job. (Managers' incentive pay is more heavily weighted toward incentives than that of employees who vacuum the cars.) The teams also compete for contest awards, based on specific sales goals and their satisfaction ratings from customer feedback mechanisms.

Finally, several employees from each location join an improvement team that meets regularly to discuss new ways to enhance customer service. Employees recently designed a new "QuickShine" program, aimed at 4 percent of customers, comprised of a wax treatment that's applied in 25 minutes and provides 90 days of protection.

Demonstrate respect for the community. One of the subtler ways ScrubaDub impresses customers is by being a good neighbor. In these days of environmental awareness, ScrubaDub reclaims some of the water used and treats the dirt that's eliminated for recycling as fill. And the company links its decorated Halloween tunnels—always a neighborhood attraction—to the problem of child poverty and homelessness. ScrubaDub donates a portion of its sales over a three-day period to nearby homeless shelters that use the cash to buy winter clothes for their young clients.

Continuous Improvements

There's a final lesson to be drawn from ScrubaDub's operations, says Cole of Mercer Management. As inventive as the company has been, the managers didn't always start from scratch in devising ways to improve their marketing and customer service. Instead, they adapted ideas from other industries for their own use. Doctors and dentists, for instance, use cartoon characters to make kids happier. And many industries, including airlines and long-distance telephone companies, use sophisticated databases to track customers' buying habits and create new marketing programs.

The important point is to foster curiosity and a constant desire to improve among employees—an objective that's well within reach of small companies. "Small business can be at the cutting edge. It doesn't require monolithic companies with huge resources and lines of MBAs," says Cole.

Paisner, for his part, believes that the companies best poised for long-term growth are those committed to keeping new ideas in the pipeline. "There's no such thing as staying the same anymore. You have to be prepared to improve all the time," he says.

QUESTIONS

1. Which type of marketing philosophy has ScrubaDub adopted? Do you think this is the best choice? Why or why not?
2. What methods of marketing research were used by ScrubaDub? What additional research could it do to better understand its customers?
3. Do you think the promotional activities of ScrubaDub could be improved and/or extended? Explain.
4. What kind of forecasting method do you believe would be most appropriate to estimate ScrubaDub's market potential?

case 10

CorrTech Systems, Inc.

A Large Company Seeks Small Partners

CorrTech Systems, Inc. is a large computer company. While CorrTech serves both corporate and personal customers, its business division provides products and services solely to corporate clients. Corporate clients demand a diverse line of products, including computers and networking products, along with extensive integration and consulting services. Thus, to serve these clients, CorrTech needs to have a full range of products and services.

The company strives to design and produce many of these products in-house. According to one of the firm's product managers, however, "CorrTech lacks the technical knowledge to develop all the products that its customers need. As a result, CorrTech has two choices: either restrict the scope of the business or go outside of the firm for non-core technologies." Because CorrTech wants to be able to fulfill all of its customers' needs, it looks for outside partners to fill out its product line.

CorrTech has an expressed preference for partnering with small companies. This preference is due to perceived problems in forming alliances with large firms and perceived advantages of partnering with small firms. CorrTech's desire to avoid forming alliances with firms that it considers to be direct competitors eliminates most large firms. According to the business division's counsel, "With big partners, we have overlap in customers and technologies. This makes the relationship much more complex." Small businesses, by contrast, generally have a very limited number of products. In addition, management does not consider small businesses to be competitors because they rarely sell to the same customers as CorrTech does.

Another perceived problem of partnering with large firms is that both partners may be reluctant to openly share ideas. According to one product manager, firms differentiate themselves by putting ideas—which come from a variety of sources—together in new ways: "When partnering with another large firm, both partners tend to be very cautious. Everyone is holding back. So these alliances don't work as well as when we partner with smaller firms." In contrast, CorrTech freely shares information with small partners.

CorrTech's small partners often have state-of-the-art products based on advanced technological knowledge. A purchasing manager for CorrTech notes that the firm usually gains more technological knowledge in its alliances than it shares. The ability to deliver products quickly to market is another perceived advantage of partnering with small firms. Also seen as favorable is the speed with which small firms are able to develop products in their areas of expertise. Small firms are also attractive because of their flexibility.

Management perceives alliances with small partners to be win–win situations. CorrTech is an attractive partner for small firms because it offers a

Source: This case was prepared by Patsy Norman of Baylor University. CorrTech Systems, Inc. is a fictitious name for a real company. This case is based on interviews with several managers in the company. These managers hold various positions and are involved in a number of aspects of CorrTech's alliances.

number of capabilities that smaller companies often lack. Most of the firm's managers echo the thoughts of the director of business development: "Small firms are attracted to CorrTech because of our marketing skills and distribution channel." The firm has a nationally recognized brand name and a large customer base. Its small partners, in contrast, often have no—or very small—sales forces; the large CorrTech sales force reaches customers that small firms may not be able to reach. A related issue is that small partners have limited capital to devote to marketing their products. Having their products sold by CorrTech's sales force offers a measure of credibility not otherwise available. Thus, a large firm can have a significant impact on a small partner's revenues. In addition to the sales impact, CorrTech is able to offer immediate financing to small partners who may otherwise lack easy access to capital.

While CorrTech prefers to partner with small firms, its managers are quick to acknowledge a number of issues that arise in these partnerships. Because the small firm's technologies and/or products are the primary reason for the partnership, high-quality products and/or technological skills are a prerequisite for consideration as a potential partner. In addition to a firm's technological skills, however, management looks at a number of other factors. In evaluating small companies, particularly new startups, CorrTech considers how long the company has been in business and assesses its financial stability by evaluating its financial backing. If a company is very young, the background and experience of the individuals involved are important considerations.

CorrTech is also concerned about the manufacturing and storage capacities of its small partners, as small firms may not be equipped to handle the volume of business that partnering with CorrTech usually brings. If a small firm lacks required manufacturing capacity, CorrTech's customers may be unable to get timely delivery of desired products. When a small firm is unable to store sufficient inventory, arrangements must be made for storage; in some cases, CorrTech must store the inventory. Obviously, CorrTech prefers to work with partners capable of handling storage on their own.

In setting up an alliance, CorrTech wants to be sure that its partner understands the requirements of the deal. According to one of CorrTech's development directors,

Small firms have different views of issues that are important. For example, service calls are critical at CorrTech. Some small partners do not put a priority on such calls. When CorrTech has relied on these partners, our customers have been unhappy with the level of support they receive. Based on these experiences, CorrTech must ensure that small firms know what CorrTech expects and that these firms have the capabilities to do what is expected of them.

Making an alliance work is never easy, but CorrTech managers acknowledge special problems with small partners. "Partners, especially small, entrepreneurial firms, tend to have very different cultures than CorrTech and are frustrated with our complexity." CorrTech is a large, bureaucratic organization, where decisions are made slowly and require a great deal of coordination. Another issue is the relative inexperience of many small firms; CorrTech's partners tend to have young workers and sometimes young management teams.

CorrTech's alliances range from "tactical" relationships, in which CorrTech sells a partner's products through its sales force, to more "strategic" relationships. In tactical relationships, CorrTech is not involved in developing or changing the partner's products. In strategic relationships, CorrTech becomes involved in joint development efforts with the partner. According to the firm's director of business development, joint development efforts that take advantage of a small firm's technological knowledge are better from CorrTech's perspective than purely tactical alliances: "We get less out of [tactical arrangements.]" In strategic arrangements, CorrTech's engineers work with the partner's engineers to develop new products. From CorrTech's perspective, the best partnerships are those that involve joint development and then allow CorrTech to actually manufacture the developed product.

Most of CorrTech's alliances are not meant to last forever. Many of CorrTech's managers note that, while they seek out small partners to fill gaps in the firm's product line, they continue to pursue the internal development of products similar to those of CorrTech's partners. In pursuing this internal

development, CorrTech is careful to separate employees who are working on internal development projects from those who work with alliance partners that have designed and produce potentially competing products. Development managers in charge of internal projects feel that they can do a better job of developing new products in-house. Unfortunately, the bureaucracy slows the development process, and CorrTech has been unable to complete many in-house projects in a timely manner.

Small partners are often concerned that CorrTech will take their knowledge and technology. To alleviate the concerns of one partner, CorrTech agreed to a five-year relationship. As the relationship progresses, the partners will gradually share more information and perform more activities on a joint basis. In the fourth year, CorrTech and its partner will decide whether to continue the relationship past the initial five-year period. In addition, the formal agreement addresses how intellectual property is to be handled both during and after the relationship. According to a product manager involved in the alliance, "It was like signing a prenuptial agreement."

QUESTIONS

1. Why does CorrTech favor small firms over large firms as alliance partners?
2. What does CorrTech seek from these small firms?
3. What benefits do the small firms derive from a partnership with CorrTech?
4. What risks do small firms face in entering into a partnership with CorrTech? What actions can firms take to address these risks?
5. Assume that Consolidated Components, a small business, decides to enter into an alliance with CorrTech. How should Consolidated Components attempt to structure the relationship?

case

11

Logan Beach

Sleepless in Chicago

It's the day before Virginia Lewey opens her first business, a cafe . . . called Logan Beach. And as she runs through her chores, the former lawyer is full of confidence.

"I have a little nagging feeling," she says, "that this isn't brain surgery."

But that evening, panic strikes. While preparing chicken salad at about 10 P.M., she notices that the chicken isn't sufficiently cooked. "My first day, and I kill people!" she says fretfully. She discards the salad and drops it from her opening menu. Not long afterward, the cafe's coffee maker, which she bought used, breaks down. And sometime around 3 A.M., the printer attached to her personal computer jams while printing the menus.

The next morning, Ms. Lewey arrives at the cafe at 6 o'clock to meet her milk supplier. He never appears.

Such are the trials of launching a new venture—an experience that can shatter anyone's illusions about the joys of owning a business.

Like many new owners, the 40-year-old Ms. Lewey chose entrepreneurship in the hope of finding a freer lifestyle. She gave up a six-figure income as a law partner and invested $28,000 to open Logan Beach this past summer. She dreamed of wearing jeans to work, blasting rock music, taking afternoon naps and luring a hip, bustling clientele by word-of-mouth.

Source: Barbara Marsh, "Sleepless in Chicago," *The Wall Street Journal,* October 15, 1993, p. R18. Reprinted by permission of *The Wall Street Journal,*

However, Ms. Lewey quickly discovered how surprisingly tough it is to run a small business. Her sales during the first seven days never rose above a trickle. On Friday night at the end of the first week, she counted five tables empty out of eight and confessed, "I thought there would be more people by now."

Ms. Lewey got off to a rocky start by opening before she had worked out all the kinks. Clark Wolf, a New York restaurant consultant, recommends that new owners first practice on their friends, inviting them in before the opening to try everything on the menu at a discounted price. This gives the owner a chance to train the staff, alert suppliers, develop efficient routines—and make the inevitable missteps without turning off the public.

Another problem is that Ms. Lewey ignored some marketing basics. Consultants find it incredible that Logan Beach lacks a visible sign. The cafe's name, painted on the front window, rises from ground level to waist height—ensuring that passing drivers can't see it. Moreover, the storefront itself is barely noticeable, being situated on a street that gets little foot traffic and is just off a square where vagrants tend to congregate.

Nevertheless, some say the cafe's best asset is Ms. Lewey herself. Customers remark on her warm, friendly manner. She chats as easily with the weekend yuppie crowd and their kids as she does with the Hispanic professionals grabbing a business lunch and the young hipsters who linger over evening coffee. If she can learn from her early errors, consultants say, she will improve her cafe's chance of success.

As it is for many new business owners, Ms. Lewey's opening date was a moving target. She originally aimed for May, but she misjudged the time required to remodel her 674-square-foot storefront. Inexperience slowed her down, as she herself pried out floor staples, combed secondhand shops for furnishings and experimented with the color scheme—first painting a navy stripe on the wall and then covering it with pale gold.

The final result? A striking, cozy spot with a high ceiling, wood floor, two couches, and local artists' works on the walls. There are 20 chairs and eight tables, each sporting a lamp and flowered tablecloth.

But the two months of remodeling delays cost Ms. Lewey $1,500 in rent for June and July, without any sales to offset the expense. She hoped that her opening week would change all that. Here's how the first couple of days went:

Friday, July 30. A city inspector visits Logan Beach—two weeks later than expected—and says she'll recommend Ms. Lewey for a business license. Thrilled, the new proprietor decides to open the next day, rather than wait however long it might take for written approval. Although restaurants often open with only such verbal approvals, consultants note that Ms. Lewey risked being closed down for operating without a license. (She has since received her license.)

Saturday, July 31. After her struggles with the chicken, the computer printer, and the coffee maker, and her fruitless wait for the milkman, Ms. Lewey opens her cafe at 10 A.M. Her menu lists a variety of specialty coffees and other beverages, muffins, bagels, fruit, sandwiches, and pastries, with prices ranging from $0.75 for milk to $4.25 for a sandwich of sliced turkey breast with cheese.

Within minutes, the cafe fills with professionals and their young children. Ms. Lewey is inundated with orders for chocolate milk and espresso drinks. She has no help: The friends she called yesterday, looking for volunteers, aren't here yet.

As the wait for service stretches uncomfortably, a friend in the crowd pitches in at the espresso machine. He doesn't know how to adjust the milk temperature, though, and serves the "hot cappuccino" lukewarm.

The milk supply dwindling, Ms. Lewey sends her friend's wife out for emergency provisions. But soon the counter is overflowing with duplicate items, for by the time the woman returns with her order, the volunteers are finally arriving with theirs. As everyone scrambles, both the groceries and the customers go unattended. This is hardly the way Ms. Lewey imagined her first half hour in business, and she later admits to feeling embarrassed about having been caught so off guard.

That evening, she notices that her coffee grinder isn't working properly. A volunteer figures he will remove its bean container to adjust the machine. But he doesn't know that he should first close the container's trap, where beans flow into the grinding mechanism. As he lifts the container, the cafe floor is showered with beans.

Sunday, August 1. Afternoon business is so slow that Ms. Lewey has little to do but sit listening to marketing tips from a local customer, retired from a retailing career.

But Ms. Lewey is skeptical. She dismisses as "hokey" such standard techniques as a highly publicized grand opening. Her advertising effort consists of a token $25 ad placed in a local community group's yearbook. Meanwhile, she is relying on an artist friend to donate his time designing fliers. She plans to sponsor a local theater's reading of "Waiting for Godot" in mid-August, though she doesn't expect to make such occasions regular events.

Monday, August 2. Ms. Lewey's early-morning commuter rush amounts to one woman. In a way, though, that's a blessing, because the machines aren't cooperating.

Ms. Lewey's first employee, Mary Lou Raiz, tests the faulty coffee maker. Scalding water sprays out of the top. In the meantime, the ice machine below the counter has stopped working. Ms. Lewey calls for servicing; two repairmen arrive promptly, tinker, and depart.

Later, during lunch, a customer points out that there are dark particles in his ice. Ms. Lewey theorizes that coffee grounds have fallen into the ice machine. At night, she looks more carefully and finds other grit in the machine that she can't identify. The coffee maker still isn't working, either.

Giving up on both, she decides to rely instead on a small coffee maker brought from home and her backup ice machine in the cafe's kitchen.

Tuesday, August 3. Operationally, the cafe starts to click. Ms. Raiz, a former truck-stop owner, has lunch fixings prepared by 7:30 A.M.—four hours earlier than on Monday. A caterer arrives for the first time. Now Ms. Lewey can add pasta salad, cold potato soup, gazpacho, and lemon and mocha dessert bars to the short menu.

Customers compliment her. Mario Ortiz, a coffee lover, can't say enough about the house blend. Mr. Ortiz's nephew David tries a cucumber-and-cream-cheese sandwich, then orders two more. Margaret McCombs, a real-estate agent who is reading as she eats, says she hates the rock music playing but will be back anyway because Ms. Lewey seems nice.

For the day, Ms. Lewey's cash-register total hits a new high of $279—and her spirits rise. She aims to average $1,000 a day within six weeks.

QUESTIONS

1. Which key location factors did Lewey ignore? Explain.
2. Was Lewey's decision to remodel wise? Why or why not?
3. What recommendations, regarding the cafe's facility and equipment, might have helped overcome some of the problems she experienced?

case 12

STEGMART

PROJECTING FINANCIAL REQUIREMENTS

Angela Martin is a sophomore English major attending Central State University, a small liberal arts college in Missouri. She is president of the journalism club, which is where she first met her dorm roommate and good friend Ashlie Stegemoller. Stegemoller is a junior computer science major. Martin and Stegemoller have been discussing the possibility of a new business venture. After months of brainstorming, they have agreed to start a venture that would offer students and local businesses help in preparing term papers and reports. Both young entrepreneurs recently attended a local seminar entitled "How to Start a New Business." From this experience, they realized the need for preparing pro forma financial statements to obtain necessary financing and also to help them better visualize the merits of the venture.

RESEARCH FINDINGS

Research indicates an unfulfilled demand for quality report-preparation services on campus. Market projections estimate a potential volume of 19,200 reports a year from Central State's students. Additionally, there are over 100 small businesses within two miles of the university that have indicated an interest in the service.

The majority of the students at Central State University are enrolled in classes that require two or three reports each semester, ranging from 5 to 50 pages in length. The venture's secondary target market consists of businesses in the nearby city of Emmett, Missouri, which has an SMA (Standard Metropolitan Area) population of approximately 150,000. There are two office building complexes within two miles of the university, each containing over 50 small businesses.

STATEMENT OF FINANCIAL ASSUMPTIONS

Drawing on their findings, Martin and Stegemoller have made the following observations:

1. Sales projections related to the preparation of student reports and term papers are based on the following assumptions:
   a. Eighty percent of the 12,000 students at the university, or 9,600 students, prepare at least two reports each 12-month period. This gives a projection of 19,200 reports (9,600 × 2 = 19,200).
   b. The firm will get 3 percent of the student market in the first year, which will increase to 5 percent and 7 percent in the following two years, respectively.
   c. Student reports will average 16 pages in length, for which the firm will receive $20 per report.
2. Revenue forecasts associated with the businesses needing the firm's services are based on the following assumptions:
   a. Sixty percent of the 100 local businesses will need at least 10 reports each 12-month period.

   b. The firm will obtain 6 percent of the business market in the first year, which will increase to 10 percent and 12 percent in the following two years, respectively.
   c. Business reports will average 30 pages in length, for which the firm will receive $40 per report.
3. On average, students will want one copy of their report in addition to the original; businesses will want five copies. The firm will charge $0.06 a page for copies.
4. Practically all copies of reports will be bound, for a charge of $1 per copy.
5. The effective income tax rate will be 20 percent.
6. The firm will extend credit to its business customers. Accounts receivable should be about 15 percent of annual business sales, and inventories should run about 12 percent of annual total sales. However, suppliers are expected to provide credit to the firm, which is estimated at 6 percent of annual sales.
7. The average cost of producing each report is estimated to be $12 in labor and $0.50 in materials.

Martin and Stegemoller have an option for a rent-free office in the university's student activities building. This arrangement was negotiated based on an understanding that they will provide the university with a special pricing schedule after 12 months of operation.

The initial operation will include two personal computers with word-processing, spreadsheet, and database software. One laser printer and two photocopying machines will also be needed. The total equipment costs will be as follows:

Computers	$12,000
Printers and copiers	$ 5,000
Total equipment costs	$17,000

The equipment will be depreciated on a straight-line basis over a five-year life expectancy.

Financing is expected to come from the following sources:

- As the founders, Martin and Stegemoller will each invest $2,000 in the business.
- Additional equity will be raised in the amount of $4,000 from an outside investor: $3,000 will be invested at startup and the remaining $1,000 at the conclusion of the first year of operations.
- The National Bank of Emmett has agreed to loan the firm $3,000, to be repaid within one year, but with the option to renew each year, provided the business is doing well. The interest rate is expected to be 9 percent.
- The $17,000 in equipment will be purchased with a down payment of $7,000; the remaining balance will be paid off at $2,000 in principal per year, plus interest due on the remaining balance at an interest rate of 10 percent.

QUESTION

Given the above information, help Martin and Stegemoller prepare pro forma income statements, balance sheets, and cash flow statements for the first three years of their operation.

case

13

Calvert Toyota

Structuring Financing for a Car Dealership

Mike Calvert has worked for the Metro Toyota dealership in Houston, Texas as the general manager for the past several years. Metro's present owner, Tom Gray, is interested in selling the dealership. While Calvert would like to buy the dealership, he does not have the necessary personal financing. As a result, he has approached a number of bankers to see if he could borrow the money for the purchase price. His only personal assets are shares of stock that he already owns in the dealership and some stock in a Chevrolet dealership where he had previously worked.

In an effort to secure financing to acquire the dealership, Calvert approached a banker with the following items: (1) the agreement between the seller and Calvert, the prospective buyer (Figure C13-1) and (2) the pro forma financial statements for the first year of operation if he acquires the business (Figures C13-2 and C13-3).

In order to understand how Calvert is proposing to structure the financing, you should be aware of the following:

1. There are two entities: the dealership and a real estate partnership. The dealership is the entity that will transact the day-to-day operations. The real estate partnership is a separate entity that will own the land and buildings associated with the business. Thus, the rent expense in the dealership's income statement (Figure C13-3) is actually the note payment to the real estate partnership. In turn, this rent income received by the partnership will be used to pay the note payments to the bank.
2. The income statement does not include a salary for Calvert.
3. Calvert will also be purchasing an insurance agency, which is not included in the financial statements. This agency will offer insurance coverage to customers. Historically, this operation has been very profitable.

QUESTIONS

1. Explain how the proposed financing for the dealership is to be structured, as represented in the agreement.
2. Is buying the dealership a good investment for Calvert? Explain.
3. If you were the banker, would you make the loan? Why or why not?
4. As the banker, how would you want to structure the loan? (Consider any problems with making the loan and how the loan could be structured to compensate for these deficiencies—if there are any.)
5. The pro forma statements prepared by Calvert assume that the note payments to the bank are amortized (equal payments each month). What changes should be made to the statements if the bank requires equal principal payments plus interest? (Assume a 12 percent interest rate.)

Source: Interview with Mike Calvert.

FIGURE C13-1

Legal Description of the Agreement

SALES AGREEMENT

This Agreement is entered into the day and year herein below set forth by and between METRO TOYOTA, INC., a Texas corporation, hereinafter referred to as "Seller," and MIKE CALVERT TOYOTA, INC., a Texas corporation, hereinafter referred to as "Purchaser."

WHEREAS, Seller is the owner of certain assets in connection with its business in Houston, Texas; and

WHEREAS, Purchaser desires to acquire such assets from Seller upon and pursuant to the terms and conditions set forth herein;

NOW, THEREFORE, in consideration of the mutual promises, covenants and agreements of Purchaser and Seller herein, Purchaser and Seller hereby agree as follows:

I.
Purchase and Sale

Seller hereby sells to Purchaser and Purchaser hereby purchases from Seller the following assets at the purchase price indicated:

Asset	Purchase Price
1. Accounts receivable	$ 104,000
2. Financing company receivables	$ 110,000
3. Inventory	$ 126,000
4. Parts	$ 360,000
5. Prepaid items	$ 25,000
6. Fixed assets	$ 475,000
Total	$1,200,000

Purchase Price

The purchase price for the assets set forth in Paragraph I shall be ONE MILLION TWO HUNDRED THOUSAND AND NO/100 DOLLARS ($1,200,000.00), which shall be allocated among the respective assets as set forth in Paragraph I. The purchase price shall be payable as follows:

(a) At the closing, Purchaser shall pay to Seller, by cashier's or certified check, the sum of $600,000.00; and

(b) The balance of the purchase price shall be fully satisfied by Purchaser's endorsement of and delivery to Seller at the closing of the following stock certificates:

  (i) One hundred thirty thousand (130,000) shares of the common stock of Gray Taylor, Inc., evidenced by certificate number 1472.

  (ii) Sixty-five thousand (65,000) shares of the preferred stock of Gray Taylor, Inc., evidenced by certificate number 423.

  (iii) Seventy-five thousand five hundred (75,500) shares of the common stock of Metro Toyota, Inc., evidenced by certificate number 10333.

  (iv) Two hundred fifty (250) shares of the common stock of Tom Gray Management Co., Inc., evidenced by certificate number 67230.

AGREEMENT FOR PURCHASE AND SALE OF REAL PROPERTY

THE STATE OF TEXAS §
COUNTY OF HARRIS §

This Agreement for Purchase and Sale of Real Property made the day and year herein below set forth by and between GC, LTD., a Texas Limited Partnership, whose sole General Partner is TOM GRAY, hereinafter referred to as "Seller," and MICHAEL R. CALVERT, TRUSTEE, hereinafter referred to as "Purchaser."

I.
Legal Description

1.01 The property consists of that one (1) certain 4.721 acre tract of land out of the J. Walters Survey, Abstract 874, Harris County, Texas, more particularly described by metes and bounds in the attached Exhibit "A," incorporated herein for all purposes, together with all of Seller's right, title and interest in and to adjacent streets, alleys, rights-of-way, accessions or reversions and all improvements located therein which, together, are herein designated as the "Property."

FIGURE C13-1

Legal Description of the Agreement (continued)

2.
Purchase and Sale

2.01 The purchase price for the Property shall be the sum of THREE MILLION AND NO/100 DOLLARS ($3,000,000.00).

2.02 Seller and Purchaser hereby agree that the purchase price shall be allocated among the land and improvements as follows:

Item	Amount
Land	$ 500,000
Buildings	1,850,000
Fences	30,000
Outdoor lighting fixtures	20,000
Lifts	75,000
8,000 gallon underground storage tank	10,000
Air compressor system	15,000
Concrete paving and parking areas	500,000
TOTAL	$3,000,000

3.
Payment of Purchase Price

3.01 The sum of the TWO MILLION TWO HUNDRED THOUSAND AND NO/100 DOLLARS ($2,200,000.00) shall be payable in cash at time of closing.

3.02 The balance of the purchase price shall be evidenced by a Promissory Note executed by Purchaser and payable to the order of Seller, containing the following provisions:

(a) Interest, at the same rate charged by Allied Bank of Texas, Houston, Harris County, Texas on the note to be executed by Purchaser described in Paragraph 3.03 hereof.

(b) Installments of principal and interest shall be due and payable monthly based upon a fifteen (15) year amortization with the principal balance of the Note, together with all accrued and unpaid interest thereon, being due and payable on or before the third anniversary date of the Note.

(c) Maker shall reserve the right to prepay all or any portion of the principal balance due, at any time, and from time to time, without penalty or fee.

(d) Such Note shall be secured by a Second Lien Deed of Trust to a Trustee ("Trustee") designated by Seller and shall be on State Bar of Texas form or other form mutually acceptable to Seller and Purchaser. Such Note shall be secondary, inferior and subordinate to the First Lien Note and Deed of Trust described in Paragraph 3.03 hereof.

3.03 A portion of the cash payable at closing shall be obtained by Purchaser through a loan from Allied Bank of Texas, Houston, Harris County, Texas, which shall be secured by the vendor's lien to be retained by Seller in the Deed to Purchaser and assigned to Allied Bank of Texas, together with a First Lien Deed of Trust on the Property.

CALVERT-DAVIS REAL ESTATE PARTNERSHIP
PRO FORMA BALANCE SHEET

Assets	
Land	$ 500,000
Buildings	1,850,000
Improvements	650,000
TOTAL ASSETS	$3,000,000
Liabilities	
Note payable—Allied Bank	$2,000,000
Note payable—GC, LTD.	800,000
Note payable—Calvert Toyota	200,000
	$3,000,000
Net worth	0
TOTAL LIABILITIES	$3,000,000

FIGURE C13-2

Calvert Toyota Pro Forma Balance Sheet

Assets		
Cash		$ 200,000
Accounts receivable:		
Service and parts	$ 95,000	
Warranty claims	7,000	
PDS	2,000	
Finance co. receivables—Current	335,000	
Total receivables		$ 439,000
Inventories:		
New vehicles—Toyota	$1,500,000	
Used vehicles	200,000	
Parts and accessories	360,000	
Gas, oil, and grease	15,000	
Body shop materials	5,000	
Sublet repairs	5,000	
Work in process—labor	26,000	
Total inventories		$2,111,000
Prepaid expenses		25,000
Total current assets		$2,775,000
Fixed assets		515,000
Other assets		200,000
TOTAL ASSETS		$3,490,000
Debt (Liabilities) and Equity		
Reserve for repossession losses	$ 225,000	
Vehicle inventory financing	1,625,000	
Current portion of long-term debt	155,000	
Total current liabilities		$2,005,000
Notes payables—capital loans	$ 860,000	
Other notes and contracts	25,000	
Total long-term debt		$ 885,000
Total liabilities		$2,890,000
NET WORTH		
Capital stock		600,000
TOTAL LIABILITIES AND EQUITY		$3,490,000

FIGURE C13-3

Calvert Toyota Pro Forma Income Statement

Total gross profit		$3,717,000
Departmental selling expenses:		
Sales commissions and incentives	$550,000	
Delivery expense	36,000	
Total selling expenses		$ 586,000
Departmental operating expenses:		
Advertising	$240,000	
Policy adjustments	20,000	
Floor plan interest	220,000	
Demos and company vehicles	50,000	
Personnel training	3,000	
Freight	3,000	
Supplies and small tools	30,000	
Laundry and uniforms	15,000	
Depreciation—equipment and vehicles	100,000	
Maintenance, repair, and rental equipment	10,000	
Miscellaneous expense	10,000	
Supervision salaries	478,000	
Salaries and wages	300,000	
Clerical salaries	180,000	
Vacation and time-off pay—production personnel	10,000	
Total operating expenses		$1,669,000
Total selling and operating expenses		2,255,000
Department profit (loss)		1,462,000
Overhead expenses:		
Rent and equipment	$420,000	
Payroll taxes	115,000	
Employee benefits	60,000	
Stationery and office supplies	30,000	
Data processing services	25,000	
Outside services	60,000	
Dues and subscriptions	12,000	
Telephone	32,000	
Legal and auditing	20,000	
Postage	3,000	
Travel and entertainment	12,000	
Heat, light, power, and water	50,000	
Other insurance	50,000	
Other taxes	25,000	
Total overhead expenses		$ 964,000
Total expenses		3,219,000
Net profit before bonuses		$ 498,000

case 14

The Bonneau Company

An Entrepreneur's Experience in Exiting His Firm

Ed Bonneau was the founder of The Bonneau Company and had been the owner for some 30 years. He described his decision to sell his company and his experiences during the harvesting process:

I thought about selling the firm five years before I did. At that time, a friend of mine in a similar business had cashed out. His decision caused me to reflect on selling my firm also. The same people who bought his firm talked to us about combining the two companies; it would have been a good deal. However, I was a year late in starting. As we progressed in those conversations, two things happened. First, our company hit a dip with a major account, so it decreased our profits a bit. They then came back with a much lower offering price. Second, their company also experienced a downturn for whatever reason. Thus, if I had started the year before, it would have been perfect—it was our most profitable year ever.

What really prompted me to sell was the terrible time we were having in the business. We were not having a good year to begin with—probably a break-even or loss year. Then an account went down, costing us $5 million. That loss was the wakeup call that prompted me to try to figure out a way to get out of the business. I really became serious about selling the company and harvesting my investment.

When we encountered the loss, I didn't think that the company was in the right position to sell at that time. I thought we had to hunker down and operate for a while to get out of a bad situation. We could then start thinking about a sale. However, Benson Eyecare contacted me about a possible sale. I said I was interested if they were willing to look at the company and consider the bad year an aberration—to look at the firm's value without the loss. They said they would do so.

Bonneau was asked if he considered other options for exiting besides selling.

I really didn't know what other options I had. An IPO was suggested to me a number of times over the years. However, nobody ever explained to me the upside of going public. I had some investment bankers come and look at our company to talk about going public; they said "Yeah, you can go public." They then asked me why I wanted to go public. I said "For one thing, I want some money out of the company. I have every dime I've got stuck in here." They responded that I couldn't do that. I asked what they meant. They said getting money out was not the purpose of going public. So I just quit thinking about it if I couldn't get something out of the firm. They said I could take a little, say $1 million. I wasn't interested in answering to other people about running the company if in fact I couldn't get any money out. Also, one of the disadvantages to me of going public would have been my competitors' gaining information about my company. When you have a very entrepreneurial company, that would really be distracting. They could know who your major accounts were and the volume

Source: Adapted from J. William Petty, John D. Martin, and John Kensinger, *Harvesting the Value of a Privately Held Company* (Morristown, NJ: Financial Executive Research Foundation, 1999).

you did; they could know some stuff they wouldn't otherwise know about your firm.

Bonneau offered the following description of how he determined the value of his company.

I don't know. They were the ones doing the valuation. I was just looking at the offer and negotiating with them in terms of what I thought the value of the company should be, but I didn't actually use a method to value the business. Neither did I have a value in mind in the beginning. When they approached us, I handled the negotiation through somebody else, and I didn't talk to them. They worked through the numbers, and only when they came back with their first offer did I start thinking in terms of what it should be; I started negotiating after the first offer. I thought the first offer was good, but we increased it a couple million dollars. But only when you sift through and read the fine print are you able to determine how good the offer is. It can be a big number, but you also have to consider the terms. The terms determine the eventual payout, and the likelihood of your receiving the value.

I was pleased with the value received. However, the value was bittersweet to me. I thought I was fortunate to get that amount of money for the company at the time. I knew that there was a previous point in time when the company was worth considerably more, but I was past that point—thus, the bittersweet. In looking at what had happened to the company, I thought we were fortunate to get what we did.

When asked to describe the harvesting process, Bonneau made the following comments.

I had gone through purchasing three companies, but they weren't anything like this. The complications of doing this deal were unbelievable to me, as well as the effort required to do it. All of my key people had to work on the sale, but they also had full-time regular jobs. We had to run the company during this time, and this was so demanding, while at the same time gathering all the needed information for the sale. Also, legal costs were way beyond what I had anticipated they would be, along with the madness of the communication in legal terms. My sitting on the sideline hearing things being discussed by attorneys for both sides was difficult because I didn't understand the points they were discussing or what the effects of those points were.

I ended up getting the value the company was worth. Also, I got free from the business. I didn't want a situation where I was still dependent on the firm's performance, because I didn't know whom I was selling to and that's always full of surprises. Also, there was certainly an emotional toll that took place during this process. Managing the business while at the same time trying to sell the company created a lot of stress. You then feel even more stress because you have a company that's been a close, family company and all that anxiety with all of the people in the company. You have the anxiety about what the future is going to be for personnel, and particularly your key personnel. You are having to keep business on an even keel when you don't even know yourself what the future's going to be after someone else buys the firm. Also, we had family involvement, which caused strain, because it meant something to members of our family who worked at the company, as well as to my wife and myself.

From my own perspective, I achieved my goals. I was satisfied that the time was right for me. I needed to get out and do something else. Our business had become very difficult and wasn't nearly as much fun as when we started. The subsequent events confirmed that the time was right.

QUESTIONS

1. Evaluate Bonneau's motivations and timing in exiting his firm.
2. Were Bonneau's impressions accurate about taking his firm public? Should he have more seriously considered going public?
3. How does Bonneau's experience in selling his company compare with what you studied in Chapter 14? Note some similarities and differences.

case

15

Professional Sports Authenticator

Growing an Internet Service Business

David Hall is no Mark McGwire. He wasn't even much of a Little League slugger. Yet Hall, 51, does have a pretty good eye.

He and his crack team at eight-year-old Professional Sports Authenticator (PSA), based in Newport Beach, Calif., can spot a phony 1991 Topps Sammy Sosa card. They can pick out a doctored 1953 Topps Mickey Mantle #82 by holding a magnifying glass to the card's edges. And they've shown a knack for turning that skill—the grading of collectible sports cards—into a fast-growing enterprise.

Hall chalks up some of PSA's success to the recent wave of sports-card trading on the Internet, which has made the company's card-authentication service all the more popular, because on-line buyers purchase cards sight unseen. Not content with the niche, however, Hall is swinging for more distant fences. PSA and its corporate parent, Collectors Universe, are trying to leverage the PSA brand in bold ventures linked to Internet auctions and, strange as it seems, DNA marking. Previously, they had scored a marketing coup: tying PSA's name to Mark McGwire and Sammy Sosa, the stars of the 1998 home-run derby.

The company can afford to think big. Owing to the hoopla surrounding McGwire and Sosa, PSA's card-grading business has been booming. Calls to its 800 number tripled during the home-run mania season, soaring from 600 to 1,800 in a four-week stretch. Two receptionists quit because they couldn't hack the volume. By year's end, claims Hall, the number of cards the company was grading—it evaluates a card's condition on a scale from one to 10—had increased almost fivefold, to roughly 80,000 cards a month.

"It just kind of exploded," says Hall, who's also chairman of Collectors Universe. Besides PSA, which has 35 employees, Collectors Universe runs a coin grading service, an Internet company featuring a wide assortment of collectibles-related Web sites, and a music collectibles business. Hall declines to provide PSA's revenues for past years but projects a total of $30 million in sales this year for all Collectors Universe businesses. However, given that PSA charged an average of $15 for each of the 370,000 cards the company says it graded last year, it's easy to do the math for that portion of the business. The card-grading business (covering football, basketball, hockey, and baseball cards) has apparently been very good to PSA.

Indeed, veteran sports-card dealers say the company has almost single-handedly created widespread demand for neutral third-party grading in the $700-million-a-year trade in collectible sports cards. Now few collectors would think of spending big money on a card that PSA hadn't inspected. "People who call our number or fax us, or E-mail us, are asking for one thing," says Levi Bleam, the owner of 707 Sports Cards, in Plumsteadville, Pa. "They're asking for PSA-graded cards."

Source: Republished with permission of *Inc.* magazine, Goldhirsh Group, Inc., 38 Commercial Wharf, Boston, MA 02110. "Ticket to the Show," Susan Hansen, April, 1999, Vol. 21, No. 5. Reproduced by permission of the publisher via Copyright Clearance Center, Inc.

Winning the kind of brand recognition PSA now commands hasn't come easy. A native Californian and a rare-coin nut from an early age, Hall founded Professional Coin Grading Service, one of PSA's sister companies, in 1986, before turning to sports cards. Hall was convinced that just as coin collectors relied on grading experts, sports-card hobbyists needed a way to be sure that the vintage cards they were buying were real and hadn't been recut or reglossed to hide decades of wear and tear. But convincing dealers was a different matter.

PSA president Stephen Rocchi remembers spending many a fruitless weekend at sports-card conventions trying to sell dealers on the need for third-party grading. The vast majority, he says, had zero interest in letting an outsider like PSA inspect—and potentially diminish the selling price of—their wares.

For its first three years, PSA lost an average of $10,000 a month and stayed afloat only through regular capital infusions from Hall's successful coin-grading business. Gradually, though, dealers began submitting their cards for PSA grading as more card buyers demanded it. By 1996 thousands of PSA-graded cards were circulating at sports-card shows, says Rocchi, and PSA was grading almost 10,000 cards a month.

Now, thanks in part to the wave of trading on the Internet, the demand for the company's services has snowballed even more. A sports-card buff jittery about on-line buying may be far less likely to balk if the 1915 "Shoeless" Joe Jackson he wants carries PSA's seal of approval. Consequently, dealers eager to sell on the Internet have first been shipping cards to PSA to grade, in ever-increasing numbers.

PSA, according to Web-commerce experts, is one of a handful of companies performing a vital new function: giving peace of mind to people making on-line, sight-unseen purchases. [Another] such business, Schiffman Grow & Co., an accounting firm based in Columbus, Ohio, inspects commercial Web sites, awarding some Internet entrepreneurs its seal of approval. Still another company, i-Escrow, based in San Mateo, Calif., offers a third-party escrow service. It holds on-line shoppers' payments in a bank account until the goods or services have been received. "In a lot of regards, the Internet is still the wild, wild West," says Michael Brader-Arje, founder and CEO of OpenSite Technologies, based in Research Triangle Park, N.C. Companies like PSA, he adds, are helping to make the new frontier far safer.

QUESTIONS

1. What kinds of customer service challenges do you see PSA potentially facing? Be specific.
2. What psychological factors related to PSA's customers might explain the success of its service?
3. Which product strategy options discussed in Chapter 12 might PSA pursue as it attempts to grow?

case 16

EBC Computers Inc.

A Rare Commodity

The Business Strategy

It's the kind of business nobody wants to run—selling an undifferentiated product in a crowded niche to price-conscious customers. But Edy Bedoya has spent a lifetime preparing for it.

Eduardo "Edy" Bedoya leans back in his office chair, wraps a telephone headset around his head, and punches in the number of one of his computer-component suppliers. He has received a bill that doesn't match the purchase order he placed the day before, and he wants to iron out the discrepancy. After a few jokes and a short discussion, the supplier agrees to lop a penny off the price of each of the 4,000 CD-ROMS in the order. Bedoya hangs up the phone and slips off his headset, satisfied.

It's a perplexing sight, watching the founder and owner of a $13-million business pick up the phone to save one penny per unit. After all, what's $40 to a computer reseller that's been growing at the rate of 30 percent a year? What matters most, Bedoya explains, is the principle. "I need to make sure that I can trust him," he says.

Such relentless vigilance saves EBC Computers Inc. a few thousand dollars a month. And without such vigilance, frankly, the business might not be around, let alone ranked among the nation's fastest-growing private companies. Eighty percent of EBC's business consists of selling computer parts to companies and techies who build their own machines. Bedoya says prices for such gizmos fall rapidly, sometimes several times a week. Even a one-day delay in a truckload container bound for EBC's shipping dock may cost him about $500 because of the falling value of the goods inside.

Given the ultra-competitive nature of the industry—last year, EBC eked out a net profit of 3 percent—Bedoya doesn't have the luxury of working a niche armed with a unique product. It helps that he has no illusions about the nature of what he's selling (a commodity) or the most effective strategy for selling lots of it (rock-bottom prices). Others might view EBC's positioning as more of a trap to be avoided than a strategy to be embraced. How low can EBC continue to go, after all, before Bedoya prices himself right out of existence? By balancing on such a thin bottom line, he risks taking a false step that could precipitate a serious tumble.

By nature, Bedoya operates a lean-to-the-bone business. Driving to work in Salt Lake City, he instinctively checks the price of gasoline at service stations. Later, he goes to the trouble of exchanging a few sickly tropical fish at Wal-Mart to save the $2.98 that he shelled out for each one. Even his sparsely furnished retail space is located in an industrial district rather than a mall with a lot of foot traffic. And, for the past two years, he has paid himself just $60,000 a year.

To maximize profit, Bedoya keeps his inventories bare and moves high volume. Each day, he monitors the number of computer chips (CPUs) and hard

drives in stock. Each day, he orders more, aiming to keep no more than a day and a half of CPUs and five to seven days' worth of hard drives on hand.

Immigrant Entrepreneur

Unlike many immigrants, Bedoya was raised in the middle class. His father is a lawyer in Peru; his mother, a social worker. And he was educated in Peru. But his first job in his adoptive country was cleaning toilets in a Peruvian restaurant for $2 an hour. (Minimum wage was then $3.35.) He moved up to dishwasher, working 12 to 16 hours a day, seven days a week, for three years. "I knew he was going to go places," says Hector Almeyda, the family friend who first put him up in Miami. "He was very hardworking."

When the restaurant closed down, a friend suggested he pick oranges. He climbed ladders and picked fruit for three months in Jupiter, Florida, working 10 hours a day and sleeping on a dirt floor with a blanket. It turned out to be a lucky career move.

In 1986, President Reagan signed a law granting amnesty to illegal aliens who had resided in the United States as of January 1, 1982. At the last minute, Congress also slipped in a special amnesty for farm workers who didn't meet the residency requirement. That provision—and his three months in the fields—qualified Bedoya for the amnesty program. He received a U.S. employment-authorization card, which allowed him to work legally, and began the slow process of securing his green card, or permanent residency. Although he became a U.S. citizen in 1998, he still carries around the employment card.

Around the same time, Bedoya heard about a school in Florida where he could take a two-week jewelry-repair course. After he completed the program, he divided his days between kitchens and jewelry stores. Besides doing repair work, he bought gold jewelry on the side, polished it up, and then sold it for twice what he had paid for it.

His life improved, but Bedoya still harbored dreams of becoming a lawyer like his father. Having joined the Mormon church, he was advised by a bishop to apply to Ricks College, a Mormon institution in Rexburg, Idaho. On New Year's Eve in 1988, he drove from Florida to Idaho, where it was so cold that his car didn't start again until April. Higher education was no more hospitable than the weather. "It would take me 30 minutes to read one page with a dictionary," he recalls. Fearing that he would never be fluent in English, Bedoya abandoned any notion of becoming a lawyer.

Starting the PC Business

When he returned to college, the school made an exception to its 20-hour limit on work study so that Bedoya could work 40 hours a week and still attend classes. He scored a work-study job in the computer lab, "though I didn't know anything about computers," he insists. There he befriended a couple of all-knowing techies. Within six months of his introduction to computers, he was building PCs in his dorm room and selling them to classmates. His girlfriend (now his wife), Colette, designed ads, which they plastered around campus.

After the couple graduated and moved to Salt Lake City, Bedoya worked the early shift at a software company's help desk so that he could spend the afternoon nurturing his business. "He had his day job and then would open up for business at 3 P.M., running it out of his basement," recalls Tony Tran, president of Traditional Technology Group Inc. in Los Angeles, one of Bedoya's first suppliers. "I was curious about him because I never saw anyone do business like that."

As business picked up—through word of mouth and small classified ads—customers grew impatient with the company's unusual hours. So, in 1993, Colette left her job as a customer service representative at a software company to care for their newborn son and to answer the business's phone. "Then it started to get really busy, and Colette sometimes didn't have time to eat," Bedoya says. So they hired a full-time baby-sitter and an employee. When Bedoya began thinking about leaving his job, Tran flew in from Los Angeles. "We were talking about it at 10 P.M. in his living room, and people would knock on the door looking for memory chips," Tran says. "I said, 'Edy, you can't live like this.' So the next day we started looking for a warehouse." In 1994, EBC's revenues reached about $575,000.

Tran also helped Bedoya work his way into a network of 50-odd suppliers, all of whom are Chinese Americans based in either Los Angeles or San Jose, California. The vendors buy directly from Taiwanese companies that make chips, laptops, mon-

itors, and other PC parts and act as brokers when retailers want to clear out inventory. The players in the network are constantly phoning, faxing, and e-mailing one another to buy and sell goods and trade gossip. Through the network, Bedoya gains access to intelligence and rumors, not only about prices but also about competitors who might be going under.

What matters more than the everyday haggling is the trust that develops among the network's members. Businesspeople like Bedoya need every advantage they can scrounge up just to squeeze out their slim profit. This is especially true in the Internet age, when computer distributors are selling at cost or actually giving away PCs. When Bedoya sells a fully configured PC—such systems account for about 20 percent of EBC's business—he marks it up $60 over what he paid for the components. Everyone in the network operates under similar constraints. Getting a deal now and again might be important, but even more so is maintaining good relations so that you don't get cut off. "To survive, you can't jerk people around, because the competition is really bad," says Tran.

Beyond pricing, suppliers have helped Bedoya finance EBC's growth without his taking on debt or soliciting investors. They grant him 30 days to pay for his order, instead of demanding cash on delivery. So Bedoya buys all he needs, sells the inventory within a week or two, and pays his bills on time. Assuming, of course, that his purchasing manager's instincts are on target.

The Future

Sometimes Bedoya wins, sometimes he loses, but as long as he averages out with a slim profit, he's not complaining. While other entrepreneurs might shun such a business—and for understandable reasons—it suits Bedoya just fine. Long ago, he says, he learned he could survive and even prosper if he was tenacious enough, relentless enough.

QUESTIONS

1. What risks are associated with Bedoya's using supplier financing? What other forms of debt should he consider?
2. Do you think that Bedoya's pricing strategy could be maintained if someone else replaced him one day at EBC? Why or why not?
3. Why is inventory turnover such a critical issue in his business?
4. What other target markets might EBC reach, enabling it to achieve higher gross margins on its computer products?

case 17

Flower Girl

Building Blocks of Successful Promotions

Nine years ago, when Karen Laich opened Flower Girl, a retail floral and gift shop in Bensalem, Pennsylvania, she didn't have much of a promotional budget. Still, she was determined to make the most of it.

First, she hired an artist to create a logo. Then she set out to reproduce that logo as much as possible. On her business stationery. On the sign in the shopping center parking lot where her store is located. On her delivery van. And on pens placed on her front counter.

"In a retail business," she explains, "pens left on the front counter will walk. I thought they might as well have our name and logo on them when they go." Laich also made certain to carry pens imprinted with her company's name wherever she went. She signed credit card receipts at restaurants and left a Flower Girl pen alongside the receipt. If she stood in line at the bank or dry cleaners and saw a person in front of her fumbling for something to write with, she offered a pen.

Next, Laich took advantage of some promotional opportunities many of her competitors overlook: product packaging. Many shops buy only white boxes and plain cellophane and tissue wrap, thinking it's a waste to imprint materials that are quickly discarded. Laich, however, feels differently. "Think of all the people who see the package," she points out. "Sometimes it's a neighbor who accepts the gift when the recipient isn't home. Other times it's a receptionist who holds the arrangement or box until the recipient comes back from lunch or a meeting. It's an easy way to let others know where the flowers come from."

In addition, the florist receives many orders for people who aren't current customers. "Seeing the Flower Girl name and logo prominently featured on all of the packaging and delivery materials is a cost-effective way for us to send a message that if you like what you see, we can do something similar for your family, friends and associates," Laich says.

As soon as the business could afford it, Laich turned to her promotional products counselor for uniforms for her staff. "I think it's critical in a retail business that customers can easily identify the staff from the shoppers," she says. "When you walk into Staples, if you need assistance, you know to look for someone dressed in red." Flower Girl colors are purple and white. Employees are given both long- and short-sleeved shirts in both colors, as well as jackets. This "uniformity" has worked in ways Laich never imagined. On a steady basis, walk-in new customers will ask where her other stores are located. "They think we're a franchise," she says, amazed. "It's the ultimate compliment to be perceived as so professional and polished that you're succeeding on a larger scale."

Flower Girl spreads the word about its services in a variety of ways. New residents in the community receive a "welcome to the neighborhood" mailing featuring a logoed refrigerator magnet and special introductory offer. Prospective business clients receive

Source: Cathy Cain, "Building Blocks of Successful Promotions," *Imprint* (Spring 1999), pp. 31–34.

a floral arrangement accompanied by promotional items they can use immediately, such as paper clips, pencils and letter openers. The store stays in touch with existing customers via newsletter and postcards and supplements its direct-mail activities with print advertising. To thank customers for referring new business, it sends an arrangement using an imprinted water bottle for a vase.

And to stretch her promotional budget—which today consists of about $30,000—even further, Laich makes good use of all the available resources. She cross-promotes her services constantly; every package that leaves the shop carries a piece of promotional literature about another product or service Flower Girl offers. During the month of December, walk-in customers are handed a calendar featuring a year of gift-giving ideas.

Is there a science to the success of Laich's promotional plan? "We're consistent," she says. "Several years ago, I attended a marketing seminar, and the presenter was a former consultant for McDonald's. He said that the management team at McDonald's knew its hamburgers were good, but not the best their customers would ever taste. It didn't matter, though, because McDonald's has been so consistent with its marketing that its customers know what to expect. We strive to operate the same way. When you order a certain arrangement for a certain price, it will always include certain items, whether you order it today or six months from now. There are no surprises that way, so our clients have come to trust and rely on our services. And that's why we've grown."

Laich cautions business managers to carefully monitor quality control when it comes to the reproduction of their logo in promotional marketing. "Whenever we work with a new graphic designer (or counselor), we provide a clean stat of our logo and ask to see an actual proof, not just a fax. Every service provider has different equipment and capabilities, and I want to make certain our image is consistently, professionally presented."

QUESTIONS

1. In what ways, if any, does Flower Girl's promotional plan build customer goodwill?
2. Would this business benefit from a Web site? How could a location on the Web be used to promote Flower Girl?
3. What type of strategic alliance could Flower Girl form to help promote the business? Be specific.

case

18

Central Engineering

How an Entrepreneur's Management Practices Hampered Decision Making

Henry and Jami Wolfram, a husband-and-wife team, owned and operated Central Engineering, a heating and air conditioning firm located in Huntsville, Alabama. The business prospered during the six years they owned it, and it served both residential and commercial accounts.

Organization Structure

Figure C18-1 shows the simple organization structure of the firm. Henry served as general operations manager. As the business grew, more and more responsibility fell on his shoulders. Although Jami assumed some of the burden by acting as treasurer and supervising the office work, Henry was personally involved in most of the key decisions. Henry's son, Jeff Wolfram, had started at Central Engineering as a worker on an installation crew. Later, he moved into the position of estimator-salesperson and acted as manager whenever his father was out of town.

The Bottleneck

An unfortunate consequence of Henry's growing workload was the creation of a bottleneck at the very top of the business. Since he was a key person, his judgment seemed indispensable to many actions. As a result, decisions were sometimes delayed, waiting for his attention. Others in the organization sometimes found themselves waiting in line to get a chance to talk with him. And Henry found himself rushed, with insufficient time to think carefully about some aspects of the business. In addition, he would have liked to devote a little more time to family, church, and personal interests.

Review of Customer Billing

One task that required Henry's attention was his personal review of invoices before they were sent to customers. When a management consultant asked why this was necessary, the following dialogue took place:

Henry: I really need to take a last look before bills are sent out. For example, on construction jobs there may be additions or extras that were included after we made the original bid.
Consultant: On regular service calls, is there a similar chance of an error?
Henry: That's right. For instance, maybe the worker left something off the work order. The worker may say he has done this and this and this, but, over here on the materials list, he has some items that don't match up or that are missing from what he said he's done.
Consultant: Can you tell me how many hours in a day or week are required for this?
Henry: Well, it cuts into a lot of time. This is part of another problem. The office is too open, with Jeff

Source: Personal communication; names have been disguised.

FIGURE C18-1 *Organization Structure of Central Engineering*

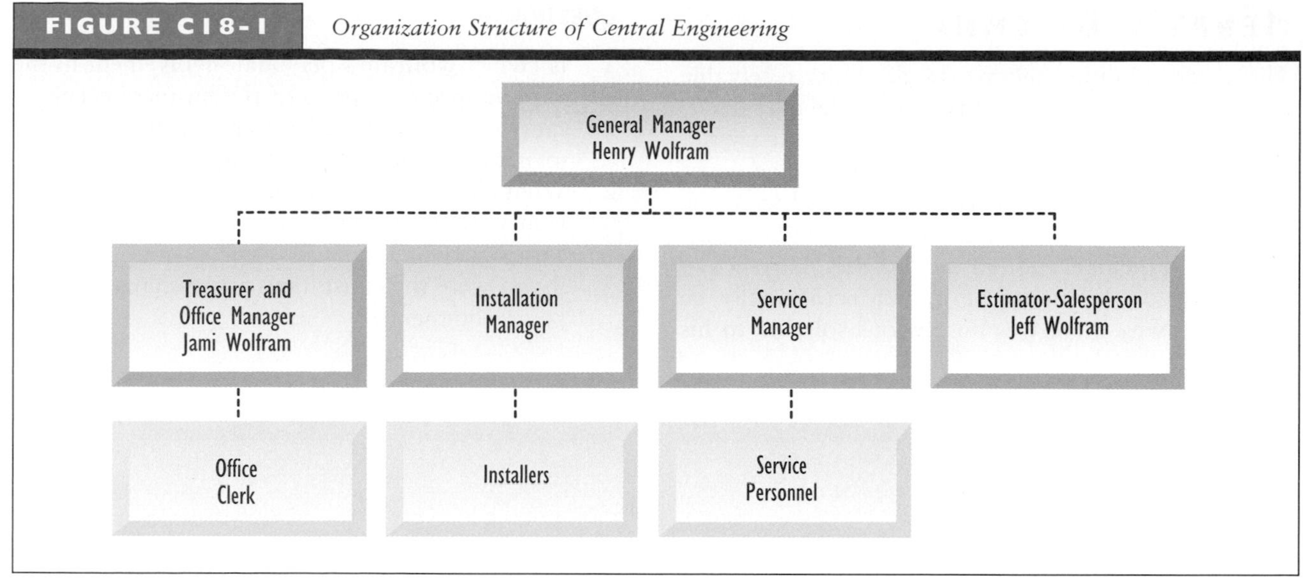

and his customers in the same office with me. I just don't have any place where I can concentrate on this type of work. I think that, when we get that physical arrangement changed, it will help some.

Consultant: So, how many hours a week does this take?

Henry: Sometimes, we stay here at night or come in Saturday to do this. But I suppose it might run 8 or 10 hours a week.

Consultant: Is there anybody else who could do this?

Henry: Well, on service calls, Jami can usually spot such discrepancies. She is getting enough experience that she can recognize them.

Consultant: What is Jeff's role? Could he do this?

Henry: He's an estimator and does sales work. He doesn't quite have the experience yet. Well, he might be close to being capable. But he's pretty busy. Also, I have a service manager who could catch a lot of these things when the orders are turned in. But he doesn't manage that carefully. I have a more aggressive manager in installation who is better at catching things like this.

The general theme in Henry's discussion with the management consultant was the difficulty of resolving the time-management problem. Henry recognized the burden this placed on him personally and on the business, but there seemed to be no obvious answer at this stage in the life of the firm.

Review of Accounts Payable

Henry also tried to look over all payments being made by accounts payable. His discussion with the management consultant regarding this function follows:

Henry: These payments need to be checked over because we may be charged too much on some bills.

Consultant: How does that happen?

Henry: On particular jobs, we may get special pricing. Say I'm working on a bid. I may pick up a phone and say to the supplier, "We need some special pricing. Here's what we're up against, and we need the special pricing to get this job." And if they give us the special pricing, we should pay accordingly.

Consultant: And you can't depend on them to bill you at that special price?

Henry: I don't think it's anything intentional. But they give it to their clerks to bill, and they may overlook the special pricing that was promised. So, if we don't catch it, we lose it.

Henry's Dilemma

The responsibilities relative to accounts receivable and accounts payable were typical of the overall situation. In many aspects of the business, Henry felt compelled to give his personal attention to the issues and the decisions that needed to be made. In a sense, he felt trapped by the very success and work that accompanied the operation of the business. He enjoyed the work, every minute of it, but occasionally he wondered why there was no obvious solution to his dilemma.

QUESTIONS

1. Is Henry Wolfram's personal involvement in the various specific aspects of the business necessary? Or is it a matter of habit or of simply enjoying doing business that way?
2. What changes would be necessary to extricate Henry from the checking of customer invoices before they are mailed?
3. If you were the consultant, what changes would you recommend?

case 19

Gibson Mortuary

Human Resource Problems in a Small Family Business

Gibson Mortuary was founded in 1929 and has become one of the best-known funeral homes in Tacoma, Washington. One of its most persistent problems over the years has been the recruitment and retention of qualified personnel.

Background of the Business

Gibson Mortuary is a family business headed by Ethel Gibson, who owns 51 percent of the stock. As an active executive in the business, Ethel is recognized as a community leader. She has served in various civic endeavors, been elected to the city council, and served one term as mayor.

The mortuary has built a reputation as one of the finest funeral homes in the state. The quality of its service over the years has been such that it continues to serve families over several generations. While large corporations have bought up many mortuaries in recent years, Gibson Mortuary continues to remain competitive as an independent family firm—a "family serving families." Funeral homes in general have recently become the target of public criticism, and books such as *The American Way of Death* reflect adversely on this type of business. Nevertheless, Gibson Mortuary has withstood this threat by its determined, consistent effort to provide the best possible customer service. In its most recent year, it conducted 375 funerals, which places it in the top 9 percent of all funeral homes in the nation when measured in terms of volume of business.

Source: Personal communication; names have been disguised.

Ethel's son, Max Gibson, entered the business after completing military service and became general manager of the firm. He is a licensed funeral director and embalmer. Both mother and son are active in the day-to-day management of the firm.

Recruitment and Retention Problem

Perhaps the most difficult problem facing Gibson Mortuary is the recruitment and retention of qualified personnel. The image of the industry has made it difficult to attract the right caliber of young people as employees. Many individuals are repelled by the idea of working for an organization in which they must face the fact of death daily. In addition, the challenges raised by social critics reflect poorly on the industry and conveyed to many people the impression that funeral homes are profiting from the misery of those who are bereaved.

One source of employees is walk-in applicants. Also, Gibson Mortuary works through local sales representatives who often know of people who might be considering a change in their careers.

As a small business, Gibson Mortuary presents fewer total opportunities than a larger company or even a funeral home chain. The fact that it is a family business also suggests to prospective employees that top management will remain in the family. It is apparent to all that the two top management spots are family positions. However, Ethel and Max (who is 49 years old) are the only family members

employed, so there is some hope for the future for nonfamily employees.

Training Problem

Gibson Mortuary uses two licensed embalmers—Max and another individual. The pressure of other managerial work has made it difficult for Max to devote sufficient time to this type of work.

Any individual interested in becoming a licensed embalmer has to attend mortuary college (mortuary science programs are part of some community-college programs) and serve a two-year apprenticeship. The apprenticeship can be served either prior to or after the college training. Gibson Mortuary advises most individuals to take the apprenticeship prior to the college training so that they can evaluate their own aptitude for this type of career.

Gibson Mortuary prefers its personnel to be competent in all phases of the business. The work involves not only embalming, but also making funeral arrangements with families and conducting funerals and burials. However, some part-time employees only assist in conducting funerals and do not perform preparatory work.

Personal Qualifications for Employment

All employees who meet the public and have any part in the funeral service need to be able to interact with others in a friendly and relaxed but dignified manner. The personalities of some individuals are much better suited to this than those of others. Ethel describes one of the problem personalities she had to deal with as follows:

In the first place, he didn't really look the part for our community here. He was short and stocky, too heavy for his height. His vest was too short, and he wore a big cowboy buckle! Can't you see that going over big in a mortuary! He wanted to stand at the door and greet people as they came. We do furnish suits, so we tried to polish off some of the rough edges.

But he was still too aggressive. He became upset with me because I wouldn't get him any business cards immediately. One day I had to send him to the printers, and he came back and said, "While I was there, I just told them to make some cards for me. I'll pay for them myself." I said to him, "Willis, you go right back there and cancel that order! When you are eligible for cards, I'll have them printed for you." We couldn't have him at that point scattering his cards with our name all over town.

Another young applicant made an impressive appearance but lacked polish. His grammar was so poor that he lacked the minimal skills necessary for any significant contact with the public.

Two characteristics of employment that discourage some applicants are the irregular hours and the constant interruptions that are part of the life of a funeral director. A funeral director might start to do one thing and then find it necessary to switch over to another, more urgent matter. Also, some night and weekend duty in the work schedule is required.

Solving the Human Resource Problems

Although Gibson Mortuary has not completely solved its need for qualified personnel, the business is working at it. While waiting for the right person to come along, Gibson Mortuary started another apprentice prior to any college training. In addition, it is following up on a former apprentice who worked during summer vacations while attending mortuary college. The business also employs a part-time minister as an extra driver. In these ways, Gibson Mortuary is getting along, but it still hopes to do a better job in personnel staffing.

QUESTIONS

1. Evaluate the human resource problems facing this firm. Which appears most serious?
2. How can Gibson Mortuary be more aggressive in recruitment? How can it make itself more attractive to prospective employees?
3. Does the fact that Gibson Mortuary is a family firm create a significant problem in recruitment? How can the firm overcome any problems that may exist in this area?
4. Assuming that you are the proper age to consider employment with Gibson Mortuary, what is the biggest question or problem you would have as a prospective employee? What, if anything, might the Gibsons do to deal with that type of question or problem?

case 20

Maricopa Ready Mix

Applying New Technology to Production Operations

As the CEO of Maricopa Ready Mix, a 10-month-old concrete supplier in Scottsdale, Arizona, David Hudder knows he ought to control his costs whenever possible. But as a 25-year veteran of the concrete industry, Hudder also knows there's only so much he can do.

The costs of the materials that he needs to make his product—water, cement, sand, gravel—are essentially fixed. The cost of the trucks that mix and deliver the concrete doesn't vary much either. Then there's the cost of driver hours, an expense that's traditionally controlled through efficient delivery scheduling. To maximize efficiency, a dispatcher needs constant knowledge of the fleet's whereabouts. But since most trucking companies still use a taxi-type dispatching system—a two-way radio combined with the driver's dashboard status box—such knowledge often proves elusive. "If a driver forgets to push a button, you don't know the status of the truck," says Hudder.

Which is why the CEO was incredulous when FMS Mobile Networking, a software vendor in Chandler, Arizona, showed him a demo for a new type of dispatching system—one that could lead to unheard-of scheduling efficiencies, which would in turn lead to cost savings for the 60-truck business. "We think it's as revolutionary as the two-way radio," Hudder says.

"It" is a product called Galileo (480-961-0409; www.fms-online.com; $2,000 to $2,600 per truck, plus monthly fees), a system that is currently available only in the Phoenix and Tucson areas and in Las Vegas and Houston. Using a satellite-based technology known as a global positioning system (GPS), Galileo allows a dispatcher to view in real time every Galileo-loaded truck within a 70-mile radius—without the drivers' having to do a thing. From sensors installed in the trucks' doors, dashboard, and cargo area, data is electronically transmitted to the dispatcher's computer via FMS's wireless network. And dispatchers get access to more than just mapped-location data: FMS's sensors can measure vehicle speed and battery voltage, as well as the length of time a driver spends at a location.

Galileo also has a tool that lets a dispatcher highlight a given area—say, a 10-block section of a city—on his screen and receive alerts whenever a truck leaves the area. The tool has been a boon to Hudder, because most of his customers don't accept concrete that's been mixing for more than 90 minutes. Now a dispatcher can monitor whether a truck's supply will make it to the next destination in an acceptable amount of time.

While quick to praise Galileo's capabilities, Hudder admits that he has yet to fully implement the product, which he purchased last spring. He expects to tie in the software with Maricopa's back-end systems for billings and payables by the end of the year. The delay, he says, stems from his basics-first approach. "There's a lot of training involved," admits Rich Rudow, FMS's CEO and president.

Rudow says his technicians can wire three or four trucks a day, so a 50-truck company—to which

Source: "Keep on Trucking," *Inc. Tech 1999,* Vol. 21, No. 17, p. 143.

he'd assign two technicians—would be done in a week. But it takes time for dispatchers and trucking executives to learn all of Galileo's features. FMS sends "corporate trainers" to spend a day or two with new customers and also provides phone support with personal backup.

For now, Hudder is thrilled with the cost savings he's realized. He notes that Galileo "has been a large factor" in Maricopa's productivity in two key metrics: yards of concrete produced per truck per day and yards of concrete produced per driver per hour. The company has been profitable since its fourth month, and Hudder anticipates revenues of $15 million this year. "We've only scratched the surface of what Galileo can do, and we're still light years ahead of anything available in the industry," he says.

QUESTIONS

1. How could David Hudder have improved the scheduling and operation of the truck fleet without using the Galileo global positioning system?
2. What are the principal difficulties involved in using Galileo, and how can these be overcome?
3. What long-term actions will be needed to maximize effective operation with the Galileo system?

case

21

AFCO

Ethical Issues in Family Business Relationships

In 1951, John and Sally Martin founded AFCO, a wholesaling firm in the construction industry. The firm grew beyond expectations, and sales exceeded $25 million by 1969. As a result, the Martin family prospered financially.

Beginning in 1961, the Martins' children started working for AFCO. The two oldest sons, David and Jess, along with their sister's husband, Jackson Faulkner, eventually assumed key managerial roles within the firm. The other children worked for the firm in operations and/or were beneficiaries of the firm's success through dividends on their stock. John Martin came to visualize the firm as a family effort that would benefit the family for generations to come.

In 1969, John Martin and Jackson Faulkner were killed in an airplane crash while flying in the company plane on business. The issue of firm leadership had to be resolved quickly for the sake of the firm's future. David and Jess, both in their late forties, were the obvious candidates. AFCO's board of directors, which included both family members and outsiders, eventually chose David, the older of the two sons, to be the firm's president.

Over time, conflicts and disagreements between David and Jess became increasingly frequent. Jess, who was the firm's vice president for sales, considered David to be uninformed about the firm's customers. And, whenever he approached David about a problem within the company, Jess felt that he was treated as the bearer of bad news. David, on the other hand, perceived Jess to be undermining his authority as president. At one point, David confronted Jess regarding actions that David considered to be no less than insubordination. He advised Jess that repeating such actions would result in his dismissal, even though they were brothers. When a similar event occurred sometime later, David met with the board and indicated that he planned to fire Jess. The board concurred, and Jess was subsequently terminated form the firm.

Jess was angered and hurt by David's decision, and he immediately appealed to other family members, especially their mother, to help settle the differences. Even though their mother agreed with Jess, efforts at reconciliation were unsuccessful.

In 1984, after about a year of bickering, David approached Jess and offered to buy his shares in the company for $1 per share. Jess rejected the offer but said he would sell at $1.75 per share—approximately $800,000 in total. David borrowed the money and bought Jess's shares.

At this time, David was expanding the company's operations through acquisitions of other firms. In 1988, at the peak of "merger mania," when financial groups were using heavy debt financing to buy companies, David was offered $20 per share for the firm. By this time, a large portion of the shares were held by employees in the form of an employee stock ownership plan. In a stockholders' meeting, a decision was made to sell the company because the price offered was too attractive to refuse.

When Jess learned about the sale, he was furious. Not only had David fired him, but he had now sold

Source: Personal communications with David and Jess Martin.

the shares that Jess had originally inherited for more than 10 times what Jess had received. Jess felt he had been robbed of his heritage by his own brother, who first took away his rightful place within the firm and now was making huge profits off "his" shares.

The conflict still has not been resolved. David does not think he has done anything wrong, either legally or ethically. Jess, however, continues to believe that he has been treated unfairly by a brother who placed his own personal welfare above that of the family. Meetings with independent mediators and counselors have yielded nothing in the way of reconciliation. Jess intends to continue pursuing the issue in every way possible, but David has decided that nothing can be gained from further discussion.

QUESTIONS

1. Did David act professionally and ethically in firing Jess?
2. Was David's purchase of shares from Jess at $1.75 each a fair deal?
3. Is Jess's complaint that he was "robbed" valid?
4. Evaluate the founders' record in building and managing the firm in the light of later developments.
5. Can you suggest a solution to the animosity and conflict that have developed in this family?

case

22

Artho, Inc.

Evaluating Financial Performance

Paul Carey is the owner of Artho, Inc., a firm that wholesales athletic equipment. He bought the firm almost 10 years ago, after being a high school coach for 12 years. Although it has taken a lot of his time, the business requires fewer hours than the long ones he experienced in coaching. He has also found that as the owner of Artho he can continue to be actively involved in the community.

While pleased with the business and with his performance, Carey has begun to question whether he has been managing the firm's financial resources as well as he could and should. He recently attended a seminar on "Financial Management for the Nonfinancial Executive." It was an eye opener for him. He had never really understood much of what the bankers said when they talked about Artho's financial performance.

Eager to use what he had learned at the seminar to evaluate his company, Carey asked his banker to acquire financial statements on a similar company so that Carey could compare his firm's performance with that of the other company. About a week later, the banker provided financial statements for what he labeled a "comparison firm."

The financial statements for Artho, Inc., beginning in 1997 and ending in 2001, are shown in Figures C22-1 and C22-2. Figures C22-3 and C22-4 show the financial data for the comparison firm.

QUESTIONS

1. Evaluate the two firms in terms of their financial performance over time (1997–2001) as it relates to (1) liquidity, (2) operating profitability, (3) financing the assets, and (4) the shareholders' (common equity) return on investment. (Note: Using a computer spreadsheet would be extremely helpful. In fact, looking up the financial statements for these two companies at **http://longenecker.swcollege.com** will save you some time in doing the assignment.)
2. Compare the two firms' financial performance. Discuss the firms' differences and similarities.
3. Compute the firms' cash flows and the financing from investors from 1997 to 2001; then compare the results. (Again, the computer spreadsheet available at **http://longenecker.swcollege.com** will be a real time saver in doing this exercise.)

FIGURE C22-1

Income Statements (in thousands) for Artho, Inc., 1997–2001

	1997	1998	1999	2000	2001
Sales revenue	$2,910	$2,890	$3,295	$3,512	$3,481
Cost of goods sold	1,799	1,695	1,938	2,084	2,108
Gross profit	$1,111	$1,195	$1,357	$1,428	$1,373
Selling, general and administrative expenses	807	770	890	1,000	1,066
Depreciation	27	35	32	35	40
Operating profit	$ 277	$ 390	$ 435	$ 393	$ 267
Interest expense	20	25	17	26	42
Earnings before taxes	$ 257	$ 365	$ 418	$ 367	$ 225
Income taxes	87	124	142	125	77
Net income	$ 170	$ 241	$ 276	$ 242	$ 148

FIGURE C22-2

Balance Sheets (in thousands) for Artho, Inc., 1997–2001

	1997	1998	1999	2000	2001
Assets					
Cash and equivalents	$ 104	$ 78	$ 84	$ 80	$ 232
Accounts receivable	418	457	642	637	591
Inventories	434	583	625	635	625
Prepaid expenses	24	22	30	—	20
Other current assets	79	55	66	121	156
Total current assets	$1,059	$1,195	$1,447	$1,473	$1,624
Gross plant and equipment	$ 196	$ 220	$ 283	$ 390	$ 436
Accumulated depreciation	69	104	136	171	211
Net plant, property and equipment	$ 127	$ 116	$ 147	$ 219	$ 225
Other assets	158	173	203	243	296
TOTAL ASSETS	$1,344	$1,484	$1,797	$1,935	$2,145
Liabilities and Equity					
Notes payable	$ 8	$ 26	$ 69	$ 41	$ 86
Accounts payable	281	138	171	166	176
Taxes payable	89	81	102	48	66
Accrued expenses	—	129	140	145	169
Other current liabilities	7	6	6	6	—
Total current liabilities	$ 385	$380	$ 488	$ 406	$ 497
Long-term debt	115	120	145	214	285
Deferred taxes	5	—	—	5	—
Total liabilities	$ 505	$ 500	$ 633	$ 625	$ 782
Equity:					
Common stock	$ 10	$ 10	$ 10	$ 10	$ 10
Capital surplus	60	60	60	60	60
Retained earnings	769	914	1,094	1,240	1,293
Common equity	$ 839	$ 984	$1,164	$1,310	$1,363
TOTAL LIABILITIES AND EQUITY	$1,344	$1,484	$1,797	$1,935	$2,145

FIGURE C22-3

Income Statements (in thousands) for the Comparison Company, 1997–2001

	1997	1998	1999	2000	2001
Sales	$3,412	$3,941	$3,798	$4,774	$5,983
Cost of goods sold	2,050	2,337	2,245	2,805	3,470
Gross profit	$1,362	$1,604	$1,553	$1,969	$2,513
Selling, general and administrative expenses	761	922	974	1,210	1,640
Depreciation	48	60	72	84	68
Operating profit	$ 553	$ 622	$ 507	$ 675	$ 805
Interest expense	31	27	16	24	39
Earnings before taxes	$ 521	$ 595	$ 491	$ 651	$ 766
Income taxes	177	202	167	221	260
Net income	$ 344	$ 393	$ 324	$ 430	$ 506

FIGURE C22-4

Balance Sheets (in thousands) for the Comparison Company, 1997–2001

	1997	1998	1999	2000	2001
Assets					
Cash and equivalents	$ 260	$ 291	$ 519	$ 216	$ 262
Accounts receivable	596	668	704	1,053	1,346
Inventories	471	593	615	630	931
Prepaid expenses	33	42	40	74	94
Other current assets	28	26	38	73	93
Total current assets	$1,388	$1,620	$1,916	$2,046	$2,726
Gross plant and equipment	$ 498	$ 590	$ 690	$ 923	$1,180
Accumulated depreciation	152	212	283	367	435
Net plant, property and equipment	$ 346	$ 378	$ 407	$ 556	$ 745
Other assets	139	189	195	542	580
TOTAL ASSETS	$1,873	$2,188	$2,518	$3,144	$4,051
Liabilities and Equity					
Notes payable	$ 110	$ 161	$ 228	$ 382	$ 577
Accounts payable	135	151	174	208	455
Taxes payable	42	17	38	36	79
Accrued expenses	134	139	161	345	480
Total current liabilities	$ 421	$ 468	$ 601	$ 971	$1,591
Long-term debt	69	15	12	11	10
Deferred taxes	27	30	18	18	2
Other liabilities	24	43	40	42	41
Total liabilities	$ 541	$ 556	$ 671	$1,042	$1,644
Equity:					
Common stock	$ 3	$ 3	$ 3	$ 3	$ 3
Capital surplus	94	94	94	94	94
Retained earnings	1,235	1,535	1,750	2,005	2,310
Common equity	1,332	1,632	1,847	2,102	2,407
TOTAL LIABILITIES AND EQUITY	$1,873	$2,188	$2,518	$3,144	$4,051

case

23

Barton Sales and Service

Managing a Firm's Working Capital

The owners of Barton Sales and Service, based in Little Rock, Arkansas, were John and Joyce Barton. John served as general manager, and Joyce as office manager. The firm sold General Electric, Carrier, and York air-conditioning and heating systems to both commercial and residential customers and serviced these and other types of systems. Although the business had operated successfully since the Bartons purchased it in 1996, it continued to experience working-capital problems.

Barton's Financial Structure

The firm had been profitable under the Bartons' ownership. Profits for 2001 were the highest for any year to date. Figure C23-1 shows the income statement for Barton Sales and Service for that year.

The balance sheet as of December 31, 2001, for Barton Sales and Service is shown in Figure C23-2. Note that the firm's equity was somewhat less than its total debt. However, $10,737 of the firm's liabilities was a long-term note payable to a stockholder. This note was issued at the time the Bartons purchased the business, with payments going to the former owner.

Barton's Cash Balance

A minimum cash balance is necessary in any business because of the uneven nature of cash inflows and outflows. John explained that they need a substantial amount in order to "feel comfortable." He believed that it might be possible to reduce the present balance by $5,000 to $10,000, but he stated that it gave them some "breathing room."

FIGURE C23-1

Barton Sales and Service Income Statement for the Year Ending December 31, 2001

Sales revenue	$727,679
Cost of goods sold	466,562
Gross profit	$261,117
Selling, general and administrative expenses (including officers' salaries)	189,031
Earnings before taxes	$ 72,086
Income tax	17,546
Net income	$ 54,540

FIGURE C23-2

Balance Sheet for Barton Sales and Service for December 31, 2001

Assets

Current assets:	
Cash	$ 28,789
Trade accounts receivable	56,753
Inventory	89,562
Prepaid expenses	4,415
Total current assets	$179,519
Loans to stockholders	41,832
Autos, trucks, and equipment, at cost, less accumulated depreciation of $36,841	24,985
Other assets: goodwill	16,500
TOTAL ASSETS	$262,836

Debt (Liabilities) and Equity

Current debt:	
Current maturities of long-term notes payable*	$ 26,403
Trade accounts payable	38,585
Accrued payroll taxes	2,173
Income tax payable	13,818
Other accrued expenses	4,001
Total current debt	$ 84,980
Long-term notes payable*	51,231
Total stockholders' equity	126,625
TOTAL DEBT AND EQUITY	$262,836

*Current and long-term portions of notes payable:

	Current	Long-Term	Total
• 10% note payable, secured by pickup, due in monthly installments of $200, including interest	$ 1,827	$ 1,367	$ 3,194
• 10% note payable, secured by equipment, due in monthly installments of $180, including interest	584	0	584
• 6% note payable, secured by inventory and equipment, due in monthly installments of $678, including interest	6,392	39,127	45,519
• 9% note payable to stockholder	0	10,737	10,737
• 12% note payable to bank in 30 days	17,600	0	17,600
	$26,403	$51,231	$77,634

Barton's Accounts Receivable

The trade accounts receivable at the end of 2001 were $56,753, but at some times during the year the accounts receivable were twice this amount. These accounts were not aged, so the firm had no specific knowledge of the number of overdue accounts. However, the firm had never experienced any significant loss from bad debts. The accounts receivable were thought, therefore, to be good accounts of a relatively recent nature.

Customers were given 30 days from the date of the invoice to pay the net amount. No cash discounts were offered. If payment was not received during the first 30 days, a second statement was mailed to the

customer and monthly carrying charges of 1/10 of 1 percent were added. The state usury law prohibited higher carrying charges.

On small residential jobs, the firm tried to collect from customers when work was completed. When a service representative finished repairing an air-conditioning system, for example, he or she presented a bill to the customer and attempted to obtain payment at that time. However, this was not always possible. On major items such as unit changeouts—which often ran as high as $2,500—billing was almost always necessary.

On new construction projects, the firm sometimes received partial payments prior to completion, which helped to minimize the amount tied up in receivables.

Barton's Inventory

Inventory accounted for a substantial portion of the firm's working capital. It consisted of the various heating and air-conditioning units, parts, and supplies used in the business.

The Bartons had no guidelines or industry standards to use in evaluating their overall inventory levels. They believed that there *might* be some excessive inventory, but, in the absence of a standard, this was basically an opinion. When pressed to estimate the amount that might be eliminated by careful control, John pegged it at 15 percent.

The firm used an annual physical inventory that coincided with the end of its fiscal year. Since the inventory level was known for only one time in the year, the income statement could be prepared only on an annual basis. There was no way of knowing how much of the inventory had been used at other points and, thus, no way to calculate profits. As a result, the Bartons lacked quarterly or monthly income statements to assist them in managing the business.

Barton Sales and Service was considering changing from a physical inventory to a perpetual inventory system, which would enable John to know the inventory levels of all items at all times. An inventory total could easily be computed for use in preparing statements. Shifting to a perpetual inventory system would require the purchase of proper file equipment, but the Bartons believed that that cost was not large enough to constitute a major barrier. A greater expense would be involved in the maintenance of the system—entering all incoming materials and all withdrawals. The Bartons estimated that this task would necessitate the work of one person on a half-time or three-fourths-time basis.

Barton's Note Payable to the Bank

Bank borrowing was the most costly form of credit. Barton Sales and Service paid the going rate, slightly above prime, and owed $17,600 on a 90-day renewable note. Usually, some of the principal was paid when the note was renewed. The total borrowing could probably be increased if necessary. There was no obvious pressure from the bank to reduce borrowing to zero. The amount borrowed during the year typically ranged from $10,000 to $25,000.

The Bartons had never explored the limits the bank might impose on borrowing, and there was no clearly specified line of credit. When additional funds were required, Joyce simply dropped by the bank, spoke with a bank officer, and signed a note for the appropriate amount.

Barton's Trade Accounts Payable

A significant amount of Barton's working capital came from its trade accounts payable. Although accounts payable at the end of 2001 were $38,585, the total payable varied over time and might be double this amount at another point in the year. Barton obtained from various dealers such supplies as expansion valves, copper tubing, sheet metal, electrical wire, and electrical conduit. Some suppliers offered a discount for cash (2/10, net 30), but Joyce felt that establishing credit was more important than saving a few dollars by taking a cash discount. By giving up the cash discount, the firm obtained the use of the money for 30 days. Although the Bartons could stretch the payment dates to 45 or even 60 days before being "put on C.O.D.," they found it unpleasant to delay payment more than 45 days because suppliers would begin calling and applying pressure for payment.

Their major suppliers (Carrier, General Electric, and York) used different terms of payment. Some large products could be obtained from Carrier on an arrangement known as "floor planning," meaning that the manufacturer would ship the products with-

out requiring immediate payment. The Bartons made payment only when the product was sold. If still unsold after 90 days, the product had to be returned or paid for. (It was shipped back on a company truck, so no expense was incurred in returning unsold items.) On items that were not floor-planned but were purchased from Carrier, Barton paid the net amount by the 10th of the month or was charged 18 percent interest on late payments.

Shipments from General Electric required payment at the bank soon after receipt of the products. If cash was not available at the time, further borrowing from the bank became necessary.

Purchases from York required net payment without discount within 30 days. However, if payment was not made within 30 days, interest at 18 percent per annum was added.

Can Good Profits Become Better?

Although Barton Sales and Service had earned a good profit in 2001, the Bartons wondered whether they were realizing the *greatest possible* profit. Slowness in the construction industry was affecting their business somewhat. They wanted to be sure they were meeting the challenging times as prudently as possible.

QUESTIONS

1. Evaluate the overall performance and financial structure of Barton Sales and Service.
2. What are the strengths and weaknesses in this firm's management of accounts receivable and inventory?
3. Should the firm reduce or expand the amount of its bank borrowing?
4. Evaluate Barton's management of trade accounts payable.
5. Calculate Barton's cash conversion period. Interpret your computation.
6. How can Barton Sales and Service improve its working-capital situation?

case

24

Fox Manufacturing

Responding to Disaster

The end of the workday on May 12 was like any other—or so Dale Fox thought when he closed up shop for the night. But 12 hours later, an electrical fire had destroyed Fox Manufacturing Inc.'s only plant, in Albuquerque, New Mexico. The damage exceeded $1.5 million.

"It was the largest fire New Mexico had seen in years. About 37 fire trucks were at the scene trying to put out the fire. We made local and national news," recalls Fox, president of the family-owned manufacturer and retailer of southwestern-style and contemporary furniture. The fire was especially devastating since all orders from the company's three showrooms were sent to the plant. Normally, the furniture was built and delivered 10 to 12 weeks later.

Such a disaster could force many companies out of business. But just eight weeks after the fire, the first piece of furniture rolled off the Fox assembly line in a brand new plant in a new building. The company even managed to increase sales that year. And now, just three years later, the company has emerged stronger than ever. Annual sales average between $3.5 million and $5 million.

How did Fox Manufacturing manage literally to rise from the ashes? It forged an aggressive recovery plan that focused not only on rebuilding the business, but also on using the untapped skills of employees and an intensive customer relations campaign. Indeed, with more than $1 million in unfilled orders at the time of the fire, Fox offered extra services to retain its customer base. Dale Fox also took advantage of his close relationships with his financial and legal experts to help manage the thicket of legal and insurance problems that arose after the fire.

Rising from the Ashes

Recovering from this disaster, and getting the company up and running again, was a particularly grueling experience for Fox and his employees. Having to complete the monumental task in just eight weeks added to the pressure. "We had no choice," says Fox. "Because we had more than $1 million in orders, we had to get back in production quickly so we wouldn't lose that business."

Fox found himself working up to 20 hours a day, seven days a week. One of his first tasks was finding a new building to house his manufacturing facility. Remodeling the old site—and the requisite tasks of clearing debris, rebuilding, and settling claims with the insurance company—would take too long and hold up the production of new furniture. At the same time, however, he had to quickly replace all the manufacturing equipment lost in the fire. He decided to hit the road, attending auctions and other sales across the country in search of manufacturing equipment, including sanders, glue machines, molding machines, and table saws. Unfortunately, all the company's hand-drawn furniture designs and cush-

Source: Don Nichols, "Back in Business," *Small Business Report*, Vol. 18, No. 3 (March 1993), pp. 55–60. Adapted by permission of publisher, from *Small Business Report*, March/1993 © 1993.

ion patterns also perished in the fire and had to be redrawn because no backup copies existed.

Tapping Employee Talent

Although Fox initially laid off most of his hourly workers, he put the company's 15 supervisors to work building new work tables that would be needed once manufacturing resumed. They did the work at an empty facility loaned to Fox by a friend. At the same time, the company's draftsmen—working in a rented garage—started redrawing the furniture designs, this time using a computer. (It took nearly a year to redraw all the designs lost in the fire.) To check frame configurations and measurements, they had to tear apart showroom furniture. A handful of hourly employees also started tearing apart cushions to redraw the patterns.

When Fox found the new building—the former home of a beer distributor—two weeks after the fire, he started rehiring the 65-plus hourly employees to help with the remodeling. Fox knew what construction skill—carpentry, plumbing, metalworking, or painting—each had to offer because the day he laid them off he had them fill out a form listing such skills. "If I had gone through the process of having contractors bid on the work, we never would have reopened as fast as we did. Plus, our employees needed the work to feed their families," says Fox.

Within five weeks of the fire, Fox had rehired most employees. The employees, who were paid the same hourly rate they earned before the fire, proved to be competent and cooperative. Like Fox, they often worked up to 20 hours a day because they were aware of their boss's ambitious timetable for reopening.

Staying in Close Contact with Customers

Fox's salespeople started calling customers the day of the fire to explain what had happened and assure them that the company planned to bounce back quickly. Just days later, Fox's two sons called the same customers to reinforce that message and let them know that the Fox family appreciated their patience. In subsequent weeks, customers received three or four more calls or letters that updated them on the company's progress. Fox even rented billboard space in Albuquerque to advertise that the company planned to be manufacturing furniture again soon.

"If we hadn't kept in such close contact with our customers, we probably would have lost 50 percent of the orders," Fox says. But Fox's strategy paid off handsomely; the company lost less than 3 percent of its prefire orders. That's an amazingly low percentage, especially since some customers had to wait up to 36 weeks for delivery, instead of the usual 10 to 12 weeks.

Customers had good reason to be patient: When they placed their orders, they were required to pay a 25 percent to 33 percent deposit. After the fire, as a goodwill gesture, the company agreed to pay them 1 percent per month on the deposited money until their orders were filled. To calculate his customers' interest, Fox started from the order date, not the fire date. And rather than simply deduct the interest from the final amount due, Fox wrote each customer a check, so they could see exactly how much money they had earned.

Because Fox also kept his suppliers informed, most of them continued filling the company's orders after the fire and told Fox not to worry about paying until his operation was in full swing again. "Factors were the only people we had any problem with," says Fox. "Once they found out about the fire, they wanted money that wasn't even due yet."

Relying Heavily on Professional Expertise

During a normal year, Fox pays his CPA and lawyer to handle such tasks as tax planning and consulting on leases, insurance, and operations. Together, their bills run about $25,000 to $30,000. The year of the fire, however, Fox Manufacturing's accounting bill topped $50,000; the legal bill was over $75,000. As far as Fox is concerned, it was money well spent: "Without their help, I couldn't have gotten back in business as quickly as I did."

Fox called his CPA and his lawyer as soon as he got news of the Saturday-morning fire. While the firemen battled the blaze, the three met with key management employees to develop a comeback plan. During subsequent weeks, his accountant and lawyer assumed so much responsibility for valuing lost assets and haggling with the insurance company that

Fox felt comfortable leaving the city to travel around the country buying manufacturing equipment.

One early decision was to apply for a $1 million loan to buy the new building. The CPA put together all the paperwork necessary for the bank to approve it—such as a financial analysis, a cash flow statement, and profit projections. He also played a key role in helping Fox's in-house accountant determine the value of the inventory, machinery, and work in progress destroyed in the fire, which totaled about $800,000.

His involvement lent credibility to the numbers that were generated and quelled any concerns or doubts that the insurance companies had. "It was very important to have an outside CPA firm verify the numbers. If we had tried to just throw some numbers together ourselves, we could have been in over our heads in arguments with insurance companies," Fox says.

Even so, settling insurance claims was difficult, and that's where Fox's lawyer earned his money. For example, what the insurance company thought it would cost to replace the old plant was less than half of what Fox claimed. One figure over which they disagreed was the cost of replacing the electrical wiring. The insurance company estimated that it would cost $30,000; Fox and his lawyer insisted it would cost $120,000. The lawyer had a local electrician familiar with the Fox plant verify that Fox's estimate was accurate. The insurance company finally settled the claim at Fox's value.

"Dealing with the insurance company was a constant battle. There are a lot of things they won't tell you unless you bring it up," Fox warns. Indeed, it was his lawyer, not the insurance company, who pointed out that Fox was entitled to $25,000 for the cost of cleaning away debris and $2,000 to replace shrubbery that was destroyed.

And, even after they settled the claim on Fox's business-interruption insurance, it took much longer than expected to get the final $750,000 payment. Fox finally had to call his insurance company with an ultimatum: "If I didn't get the check, I told them my lawyer and I were going to Santa Fe the next day to file a formal complaint with the insurance commissioner. I got the check."

Painfully aware that another disaster could strike at any time, Fox now takes risk management to a justified extreme. He doesn't leave anything to chance and takes numerous safety precautions that will make it easier for the company to rebound should it be dealt a similar setback again. What happened to Fox Manufacturing can happen to any company—other companies would do well to follow Dale Fox's lead.

QUESTION

What are some basic disaster precautions that Fox could have taken to minimize the loss incurred and the consequences of the disaster?

case

25

When Everything Isn't Half Enough

"You have 18 new messages." Norman Spencer looked at his watch, shook his head, and let out a sharp sigh. Was it possible that he had received 18 voice mail messages in the time he had spent at lunch and the gym? He'd only been gone for two hours. He dropped into his desk chair and unhappily poked at the number 1 key to let the messages play.

The first was from Tim Carson, chief trader at Arrowhead Capital Management, the San Francisco investment firm that Norman had founded and where he was owner, president, and CEO. After 22 years in business, Arrowhead had about $2.5 billion in assets under management and was well known on Wall Street as a top-notch boutique firm, specializing in the quantitative analysis of small and midcap technology stocks. Over the years, Norman had put together one of the best teams of "quant jocks" in the business. But that wasn't the only reason Arrowhead had soared, and he knew it. The new economy was the rising tide that lifted all ships.

"Hi, Norm, it's me," Tim said, "just giving you the noon update. We're off to a great start today—up a point and a half against the market. Another fantastic week for us. That ought to cheer you up—and hey, I'll check in again at the close."

Norman hit the delete key and leaned back. Like everything else lately, Tim's news had left him feeling numb. He gazed out over San Francisco Bay from his 34th-floor office and wondered why anyone really cared how his firm performed on any given day. The market went up and the market went down. Same story, year in and year out.

Second message. "Hello, Norm. Frank Keller here. I wanted to remind you that there's a Permanent Endowment Committee meeting next Monday night at 7:30. We're really going to need you there this time, Norm—your leadership, that is. It makes such a difference. . . ." Norm punched the delete button to cut Keller off. He was sick and tired of the Permanent Endowment Committee; he was sick and tired of being a trustee at his daughter's private high school—period. Serving on the board had once been a real kick for him. They'd turned around the school, doubled the endowment, built a science building, and raised teachers' salaries enough to make a difference. Now all Norm wanted to do was find a gracious way to quit.

"Third message, sent at 12:08 pm." At first there was silence. Then someone on the other end was breathing unevenly. Finally: "Uh, Dad, this is Danny. It's after 12. You were supposed to meet me and Mom at Dr. Blanton's at 11:30. We'll keep waiting." More silence, then Dan again, this time whispering: "Dad, I think you might have forgotten. You've been forgetting a lot lately. I'm worried about you. . . ."

Again, Norm hit the delete key. The last thing he needed was a 13-year-old kid worrying about him. And what the heck were he and his mother doing at

Source: Reprinted by permission of *Harvard Management Update.* From "When Everything Isn't Half Enough," by Suzy Wetlaufer, March/April 2000.

this Dr. Blanton's office in the middle of the day? They'd never mentioned any appointment to him. Or had they?

Norm cut off voice mail and reluctantly dialed home. First he'd have to deal with Dan's fretting, then Nancy's screeching. As it turned out, he got them both at once—on separate lines. The noise coming at him reminded Norman of everything he'd been going through for the past few months—half the world buzzing around him, wringing their hands and urging him to "get help" for his crankiness and insomnia; the other half marching back and forth, shouting at him to buck up and count his four million blessings.

Norman silently dropped the phone back into its cradle. He didn't have to listen. The truth was, he didn't have to do anything anymore. By every measure, Arrowhead was an unmitigated success. Yes, it had been tough at the beginning. Every start-up has its moments of difficulty, even its moments of staring straight into the headlights of failure. But these days, Arrowhead could boast 15 straight years of solid growth. The firm was making so much money now it felt illegal. No wonder so many breathless buyers were courting him, and dozens of potential institutional clients—some of them very major—were lined up at the door, clamoring to be let in.

As for his family, Norman didn't have to do anything else for them either. There was nothing left to buy. They had everything: the mansion in Pacific Heights, the yacht, and just for the heck of it, the new "cottage" in Nantucket. His 17-year-old daughter drove a BMW, his son was taking flying lessons in his own small plane, and recently his wife had found a new way to spend money: a personal feng shui adviser to help her redecorate the house—again.

And it wasn't as if Norman himself had been left out of the spoils. Over the past decade, he had accumulated every material possession a man could want. His whole life, he had wanted a 1965 Corvette. He owned several now. He'd wanted a pool. He had two—one inside the house and one outside. He'd wanted to dress well. His closet was now filled with suits made on Saville Row, most of which he never wore. These days, he didn't even know why he'd bought the stupid suits at $3,000 a pop. What a waste.

Norman gazed out his window again and felt a strange mix of defiance and sadness. I'm 48 years old, he told himself, and I've finally earned the right to say what I'm really thinking and to act the way I'm really feeling. I've finally earned the right not to answer every voice mail message, show up at every meeting, or remember every little detail about everyone's little life. I don't have to prove myself anymore. In fact, I don't even have to come into the office anymore. But I don't know what else to do. I just keep doing the same things I've always done—only now I do them without giving a damn. I wish the world would just go away.

Norman leaned back in his chair, covered his face in his hands, and, for the first time since he was a child, felt tears rise.

QUESTION

What is wrong with Norman Spencer, and how can he fix it?

Ph. 409-383-0000

SIBÔN
Beverage Corporation
P.O. Box 1927
202 Simmons Way
Jasper, Texas 75951-1927
1-800-755-0000

Fax: 409-383-0000

Executive Summary

The "New Age" beverage market is the result of a spectacular boom in demand for drinks that have nutritional value, are made from environmentally safe ingredients, and use water that comes from deep, clear, clean springs free of chemicals and pollutants. SIBÔN Beverage Corporation ("SIBÔN") will produce and market a full line of sparkling fruit drinks, flavored waters, and sports drinks of the highest quality and purity. These drinks have taste appeal similar to that of soft drinks, while using the most healthful fruit juices, natural sugars, and the purest spring water—the hallmark of the New Age drink market.

New Age beverages are relatively new in the $28 billion soft drink market, growing in sales from $117 million (wholesale) in 1987 to over $1 billion in 1998. The industry has grown tenfold in sales in less than 2 years, and demand has simply outpaced supply. The product is distinguished by rich natural fruit concentrates, spring waters, and all natural ingredients. A New Age drink is defined as a beverage that is perceived by consumers as (1) healthy, allowing consumers to feel good about themselves, and (2) a natural product, free of artificial ingredients, preservatives, and flavors.

SIBÔN projects gross sales and earnings as follows:

	1999	2000	2001
Gross sales	$1,446,731	$5,082,302	$8,095,825
Pre-tax income	($ 169,719)	$ 307,146	$1,261,782

SIBÔN proposes to finance its building and land, located in the Jasper Industrial Park, with an acceptable Jasper Bank, using a financial guarantee from the Jasper Economic Development Corporation (JEDC). The following business plan details SIBÔN's projected operations to support JEDC's guarantee.

Business Plan

HISTORY In 1990, David Rault, president of U.S. Aquarius, Inc., purchased 110 acres of land in Stewartstown, New Hampshire with the intent of building a plant to produce bottled pure spring water and sparkling fruit juice drinks.

For several years, Mr. Rault and his wife, Mary Jo, consulted geologists and hydrologists to determine the best way to secure a long-term supply of the purest spring water. In addition, the Raults spent time and money developing formulas for plain and sparkling water fruit drinks and an isotonic sports drink. They subsequently applied for and were issued a trademark for each of their products.

In 1994, Mr. Rault placed a purchase option on a defunct Coca-Cola bottling plant in Bunkie, Louisiana. The purchase of the 30,000-square-foot plant and

equipment gave rise to considerable obstacles. First, the equipment proved not to be satisfactory and was sold off to pay part of the debt incurred acquiring the property. In 1995, Mr. Rault and an investor attempted to finance the plant with a $2,000,000 loan. After 18 months of negotiation and over $125,000 in fees spent in an unsuccessful attempt to obtain the loan, the development was put on hold until proper financing could be arranged.

In 1998, Mr. Rault met with Kenneth R. Barnett of the Cypress Investment Group to determine if funding for the Company could be completed. After months of research and visits and discussions with people in the industry, the Cypress Investment Group made a commitment to raise the necessary funds to capitalize the Company and begin operations.

In February 1999, Mr. Barnett introduced a proposal to Robert J. Caskey, of Jasper, Texas, to relocate the company to Jasper, and in April 1999, SIBÔN Beverage Corporation was authorized by the state of Texas to begin operations.

PRODUCT DESIGN The product line will consist of

1. Aquaria, which is pure spring water from Buck Springs in Jasper, Texas.
2. SiBon, which is a carbonated natural fruit drink in four flavors, using pure fruit concentrates (not flavoring) and pure spring water. Since the carbonation is lighter than that of most sweetened competitors, SiBon uses less sweetener and has approximately 50 percent of the calories of a typical soft drink (68 calories per 12-ounce bottle). The Nutrasweet drink has only 2 calories per bottle.
3. Zingo, which is a lightly carbonated, fruit-flavored drink that tempts the palate by presenting a new taste in four flavors. Zingo will be as clear and pure as spring water.
4. Peppy-K, which is an isotonic sports drink bottled in four flavors with a new energy formula composed of a finely tuned balance of fruit juice flavors, vitamins and minerals, and electrolytes and carbohydrates. SiBôn is in negotiations with the inventor of the formula to license the Company with the exclusive worldwide right to market the formula in the beverage industry.

Aquaria and Peppy-K, packaged in plastic bottles to prevent breakage, will be targeted toward active people. SiBon and Zingo will be sold in glass bottles to prolong carbonation and retain flavor. Beverages in plastic bottles lose carbonation more quickly and tend to absorb the taste of the plastic. If market changes require a change in the containers, making the adaptation will simply be a matter of printing new labels—no changes will be required in the production equipment. If there is demand for flavors other than the present projected flavors, again making the adaptation will simply be a matter of changing the fruit concentrates and printing new labels.

The spring water used in production will come from Buck Springs in Jasper, Texas. These natural flowing springs have the purest water quality and were the prime reason for locating the plant in Jasper.

Quality control is of paramount concern to the Company in all aspects of its business, but particularly in regard to the springs. The water will be tested daily at

the springs, tested a second time when it is received at the bottling facility, and tested a final time as a finished product after bottling.

The Company has two sources for fruit concentrate. Both firms have a long history of dependably providing quality fruit concentrates to the beverage industry. One of the firms has provided assistance to the Company in developing formulas and samples for testing for over three years.

FORMULAS AND TRADEMARKS David Rault originated the formulas for Aquaria, SiBon, and Peppy-K, with the exception of the special energy-boosting formula for Peppy-K. He and his wife, Mary Jo, officially registered the labels as trademarks and have transferred all formulas and trademarks to SIBÔN Beverage Corporation.

MARKET ANALYSIS John C. Maxwell, Jr., *Beverage Industry* analyst, defines New Age beverages as nonalcoholic drinks containing natural ingredients without preservatives that are perceived by consumers as healthy alternatives to traditional soft drinks. Included are natural sodas, sparkling juices, and still or sparkling beverage waters that are either unflavored or flavored with juices or essences. According to Maxwell, "the New Age category is expected to grow in excess of 10 percent in volume in 2000 and should capture about 2 percent of the soft drink market." The premium-priced New Age market is expected to produce $1 billion in wholesale dollar sales in 2000, up from $117 million in 1990.

The Bottled Water Market report, a consumer survey of bottled water–purchasing behavior from Business Trend Analysts, Inc., indicates that health concerns and taste are the most important reasons for purchasing still and sparkling bottled water. Today's consumer is better educated and receives more information about his or her health than consumers at any other time in U.S. history. Consumers are demanding better products, packaging, and delivery systems to enhance their modern life-style.

Business Trend Analysts projects that bottled water production in the United States will increase annually by 9.6 percent between 1996 and 2006. SIBÔN is prepared to participate in this unprecedented expected growth of the New Age beverage market.

MARKET DEFINITION The Texas and Louisiana regional market for New Age beverages offers an unusual opportunity to produce and distribute a high-quality, fresh-tasting, sparkling fruit juice drink. Studies and reports by Beverage Marketing, the industry standard marketing research firm, and by *Beverage Industry* and *Beverage World*, the leading industry magazines, show high anticipated growth in the southeastern and southwestern United States for New Age beverages.

New Age beverages are sold in most retail outlets where soft drinks are sold—supermarkets, vending machines, convenience stores/gas marts/mom-and-pop operations, warehouse clubs, and restaurants.

Consumption of soft drinks, beer, wine, and liquor has consistently declined for the past eight years, according to all industry authorities. At the same time, the New Age category has been the fastest growing of any beverage category including bottled water, averaging over 40 percent annual growth since 1990. Most of the major players in beverages, particularly liquor producers, have tried to make inroads into this market, without much success. The reason is simply that consumers perceive

liquor as they do colas—high in sodium, high in calories, and not as thirst quenching as New Age products.

DISTRIBUTION New Age products are distributed through food brokers, beverage distributors, or directly by the manufacturer. Getting a new product on supermarket shelves requires a manufacturer or its representatives to pay slotting fees to reserve shelf space. In addition, expensive media campaigns are required, especially if a product is to be distributed on a national basis. However, grocery and supermarket sales represent only 20 percent of the market.

SIBÔN will distribute the majority of its products through beverage and food distributors, which will have an exclusive marketing area in which to represent the Company. For the past two years, Mr. Rault and Lloyd L. Simmons have been meeting with many distributors' representatives who are willing to sign an exclusive distribution agreement with the Company when it is ready to deliver the final product.

The Company has hired four regional district managers, located in Texas, Oklahoma, Louisiana, and Mississippi, who will begin taking distributor applications on September 1, 2001. SIBÔN has already received a letter of intent from two distributors that would require 17,500 cases per month of initial distribution. The projected break-even point is 18,600 cases per month. The following bottlers and distributors have expressed interest in distributing the Company's products as soon as possible:

Buck Springs	10,000 to 20,000 cases/month
Shreveport Beverage Distributors	7,500 cases/month

All American Bottling Corporation has 16 Royal Crown Cola bottling plants. This major bottler is seeking a fruit drink that will increase its profits. A list of its distribution centers follows.

States	Number of Sales Centers	Percentage of Area Covered
Alabama	2	12%
Georgia	1	4
Illinois	3	10
Indiana	2	20
Kentucky	3	50
Minnesota	3	65
Mississippi	5	70
North Dakota	2	10
Ohio	2	10
Oklahoma	1	18
South Dakota	2	65
Tennessee	5	65
Virginia	2	20
Washington, D.C.	2	100
West Virginia	3	30
Wisconsin	4	65

Areas in which All American has less than 50 percent coverage require additional distributors to deliver to areas and stores not served.

Additional direct-deliver distributors that have expressed interest in distributing Company products are as follows:

Tulsa 7-Up, northeast Oklahoma
Little Dixie Distributing, southeast Oklahoma
Lawton 7-Up, southwest Oklahoma
Pope Distributing, northwest Oklahoma
Clark Bottling/Distributing, central Mississippi, Louisiana, and western Kentucky

Food brokers that are interested in distributing Company products are

W. J. Jones, Oklahoma and the Texas panhandle
Acosta Sales, Alabama
Tennessee Valley Marketing, eastern Tennessee
J. A. Richardson, North Carolina and South Carolina

COMPETITION As with any consumer-oriented product, competition for sales requires dedicated focus and resources. The New Age beverage market is a highly competitive arena with premium-priced products. The competition is taken very seriously by all New Age beverage producers. The following competitive issues have been given careful consideration by the management of SiBôn:

- *Capital resources.* A well-capitalized company can weather market aberrations, miscalculations, and new competitive products in the marketplace. Major companies such as Coca-Cola, Pepsi, and Perrier are well positioned to participate in this market.
- *Technological advances.* New high-speed computerized bottling equipment has allowed bottlers to cut costs. New processing equipment has introduced innovative products to the market.
- *Distribution methods.* The largest producer of New Age beverages, Clearly Canadian, does not have any production facilities in the United States; all product sold in the United States is contract bottled. In management's opinion, problems and delays in filling orders result when the contract bottler is busy bottling its own product. When a company experiences extended delays in getting the product on the shelf for sale, market share is quickly eroded.
- *Marketing strategy.* Major competitors spend up to 8 to 9 percent of sales on advertising and marketing, trying to capture a larger share of this $1 billion market. The Company's initial strategy is to offer distributors what they want most—more profit per case sold (see SiBôn's marketing strategy).
- *Consumer acceptability.* A majority of consumers will purchase a new product because of the appeal of the label or a special advertising offer or coupon. It is extremely important to establish and maintain consumer confidence in the product. This is accomplished through eye-catching labels, bottles, and point-of-sale advertising.

MARKETING STRATEGY SiBôn's marketing strategy is to produce a superior spring water, sparkling fruit juice, and isotonic sports drink made with the purest spring water and the highest-quality fruit concentrates available. By providing distributors, wholesalers, and retailers with more profit per case sold and more service and support than they might expect, the Company will establish a strong regional distributor network by laying a foundation for national distribution.

COMPREHENSIVE PLAN The overall marketing plan for SiBôn's products is based on the following objectives:

1. Establish a financially strong, regional New Age beverage company by providing initial capital funding for the Company through private investor contributions
2. Work with the city and county of Jasper and the state of Texas to establish more jobs, an enhanced economic development, and a better community in which to work and play
3. Produce unique-tasting pure spring water and fruit concentrate products to meet today's health-conscious consumers' demands for a better alternative to colas
4. Create an exclusive distributor network that will participate in a greater share of the profits from retail sales and will therefore help the Company grow faster
5. Capture 1 percent of the regional market share in less than three years (estimated to be $7,600,000 in the third year)

PRODUCT STRATEGY The product strategy for the Company is to establish a wholesale distribution channel for SiBôn's products through beverage brokers and independent distributors servicing regional chain stores, convenience stores, grocers, health food stores, restaurants, institutional food service contractors, and other retailers operating in the southwestern and southeastern United States.

The Company will issue exclusive distributor agreements to qualified distributors to represent SiBôn's products in a specific territory or area. These distributors will be required to promote the products through local advertising, shelf locations in grocery stores and supermarkets, and point-of-sale advertisements in the form of display racks at the ends of aisles and cracker barrels filled with Company products.

Initially, there are no plans to advertise the products on billboards or through any other media such as television, radio, or newspaper. All advertising will be dedicated to assisting the exclusive distributor network in establishing product identification through point-of-sale displays, coupons, and in-store marketing samplers. Special promotions will be mainly by coupons and product sampling.

The formulas for Aquaria, SiBon, and Zingo are complete. Labels for the products are in the final design stage and have been approved by the Louisiana FDA. The way a product initially looks and feels is very important in appealing to consumers. Professional designers will assure the right product identity on an ongoing basis.

PUBLIC RELATIONS No public relations are anticipated initially. All efforts of management will be dedicated to providing support to distributors and the retailers selling the Company's products.

STRATEGY REVIEW A review of the corporation marketing strategy will be undertaken on a monthly basis and a report presented to the Board of Directors.

PRICING AND PROFITABILITY The prices for the Company's products will be determined first and foremost by competitive pricing of similar products in our marketing area. The Company will depend on its management and the distributor network to determine fair pricing.

It is projected that the net profit per case will be minimal for the first two years while the Company pays back the line of credit (see Financial Projections).

MARGIN STRUCTURE The margin of profit per case is different for each of SIBÔN's products.

	Aquaria	SiBon	Peppy-K	Zingo
Retail price	$16.56	$15.72	$15.36	$14.10
Wholesale price	12.42	11.79	11.52	10.58
Distributor price	10.42	9.79	9.52	8.58
Manufacturing cost	5.30	4.91	7.28	6.28
Gross margin	5.12	4.88	2.24	2.30

The retail margin will average 23 percent, or $3.25 per case; the distributor margin will average 18 percent, or $2.00 per case.

COSTS The estimated cost of manufacturing all Company products will be consistent. The cost of each product includes spring water, fruit flavor or concentrate, carbonation, Nutrasweet or high-fructose corn syrup, preservative, bottles, caps, and labels. Other expenses include labor, plant and equipment, general and administrative costs, bank-debt payback, and corporate overhead.

Some factors that may affect costs include the following (also see Financial Projections):

- Changes in product formulation
- A change in containers
- Freight rates for hauling spring water or delivering the product

LOCATION The plant site is located on five acres in the Jasper Industrial Park, at the intersection of Highway 190 and Highway 63 in the city of Jasper, Texas. It is approximately 140 miles northeast of Houston and 230 miles southeast of Dallas. Jasper's population is approaching 8,000 residents, the majority of whom are employed in the timber industry. The city and the county have a substantial semi-skilled labor force available for employment.

FACILITIES SIBÔN's plant will consist of three buildings:

1. ***Warehouse and production.*** A metal building that will contain 6,000 square feet of production area and 24,000 square feet of warehouse space
2. ***Office.*** A building containing 4,000 square feet of space that will house the corporate headquarters of SIBÔN

3. ***Bunkhouse.*** A 750-square-foot, two-room hotel in which truck drivers can stay overnight or catch a nap while their trucks are being loaded

LOGISTICS The plant site will be serviced mainly by trucks. Receipt of raw materials and delivery of Company products will be by truck on the main highways connecting Jasper with other major cities. Rail siding is not available or required.

PRODUCTION AND MANUFACTURING The processing of Aquaria, SiBon, Zingo, and Peppy-K simply requires the right bottling, labeling, and packaging equipment. Raw materials necessary for production are pure spring water, natural fruit flavors and concentrates, high-fructose corn syrup or Nutrasweet, and carbonation. Additionally, bottles, caps, and labels are required.

An agreement has been reached with Buck Springs in Jasper, Texas to supply pure spring water at an agreed contract price in 6,000-gallon tanker loads. An additional water supply is readily available in the surrounding Jasper area.

The fruit concentrates and flavorings will be supplied by Flavoring, A.B. of Sweden. Through its U.S. representative, David Packard, Flavoring, A.B. assisted Mr. Rault by providing samples for comparative testing of potential formulas for Company products. The Company will have a second supplier available to provide the concentrates and flavorings should they not be available from Flavoring, A.B.

Equipment Production equipment will include a completely automated bottling line capable of filling 400 bottles per minute, or approximately 250,000 cases per month, with an eight-hour shift. On the bottling line, pallets of bottles will be unpacked; bottles will then be washed, filled, labeled, capped, and packed in cartons and cases for shipping.

Technical Specifications All piping must be stainless steel, and all electrical wiring must be three phase. There are no hazardous materials in the manufacturing process. The plant meets all federal requirements with respect to clean air, water, toxic emissions, and noise abatement.

Inventory Requirements Inventory will be ordered in sufficient quantities to produce 60,000 cases of product per week. Lead times will vary from one week to eight weeks for delivery of the various raw materials. More inventory will have to be ordered during the high-volume months of April through September.

Production Standards Quality is controlled by assigning a batch number to each product manufactured. Test samples are made prior to mixing and during and after production runs. As product is delivered, numbers are matched by computer to keep accurate records and maintain quality control.

The Company's safety programs are based on National Soft Drink Association standards and OSHA regulations.

Integration (Make Versus Buy) The Company will produce all products for sale at the plant site, with the exception of 1- and 2.5-gallon bottles of spring water. An agreement has been reached with Buck Springs to produce these large-size bottles and attach the Aquaria label.

Employees Line employees include a forklift operator, uncaser, filler operator, syrup blender, caser, and packer. Staff employees include a production manager, computer operator/bookkeeper, and quality control person. Six to eight employees will work in the plant on each shift. They will all be trained by working on the job.

All hiring and screening will be done by David Rault and Lloyd Simmons. Each new employee will be given a physical, drug test, hepatitis shots, and reading and manual dexterity tests. All employees will be required to wear hard hats, ear plugs, back supports, and rubber boots to prevent injury.

Production procedures will use the team method, with all employees cross-trained for all skills. All employees will sign a nondisclosure agreement with regard to the formulas for all Company products.

Packaging The final steps in the manufacturing process are important in establishing the desired image for each product. SIBÔN's labels have eye-catching appeal, as do all point-of-sale materials and literature for distributors.

MANAGEMENT

Robert J. Caskey, Chairman of the Board, provides experience and direction to the Company and its officers.

Kenneth R. Barnett, President and CEO, is responsible for the overall financial and fiscal growth of the Company; he reports directly to the Chairman of the Board and the Board of Directors.

David Rault, Executive Vice President and COO, coordinates all production schedules, hires employees, orders all raw materials, and oversees shipping and receivables. He plans, develops, and establishes policies and objectives of the business organization in accordance with board directives and the corporation charter.

Lloyd L. Simmons, Vice President of Sales, manages all sales activities of the Company and directs staffing, training, and performance evaluations to develop and control the sales program. He coordinates sales territories, quotas, and goals and advises dealers, distributors, and clients concerning sales and advertising. He has over 32 years of experience in the beverage industry with major bottling companies in all phases of production and market analysis.

SHAREHOLDERS AND DIRECTORS Following is a list of the Company's shareholders.

Shareholders	Number of Shares
Robert J. Caskey, Director	38,000 (38%)
Kenneth R. Barnett, Director	20,000 (20%)
David Rault, Director	15,000 (15%)
Mary Jo Rault	15,000 (15%)
Frank Z. Johnston	10,000 (10%)
Shannon Caskey, Director	1,000 (1%)
Edward Soderstrom, Director	1,000 (1%)
Total Shares	100,000 (100%)

Financial Projections

SiBôn Beverage Corporation
Balance Sheet for July 31, 2001

Assets

Current assets:	
Cash	$ 176,760.27
Accounts receivable	250.00
Inventory	50,000.00
	$ 227,010.27
Fixed assets:	
Land*	$ 46,940.00
Building construction in progress*	563,666.68
Production equipment*	278,450.16
Furniture, fixtures, computer hardware and software	111,432.60
Automotive equipment	21,594.23
	$1,022,083.67
Other assets:	
Organization expense	$ 95,607.72
Financing costs	200,000.00
Formulas	25,000.00
Label design, trade names, and trademarks	21,057.70
	$ 341,665.42
TOTAL ASSETS	$1,590,759.36

Debt (Liabilities) and Equity

Current debt:	
Accrued interest	$ 3,402.52
Current portion of long-term debt	4,089.15
	$ 7,491.67
Long-term debt:†	
Note payable to First Bank & Trust East Texas under a $1,500,000 line of credit guaranteed by Robert J. Caskey; such guarantee secured by all real, personal, and intangible property other than a 2000 Plymouth Voyager	$1,330,000.00
Note payable to First Bank and Trust East Texas, payable in 36 equal monthly installments of $411.70, including interest thereon and commencing June 24, 2001, less the current portion of $4,089.15 secured by a 2000 Plymouth Voyager	8,398.56
	1,338,398.56
Total debt	$1,345,890.23
Equity:	
Capital stock, common $0.01 par value; 1,000,000 shares authorized; 100,000 shares issued and outstanding	$ 1,000.00
Paid in capital in excess of par value	249,000.00
Retained earnings	(5,130.87)
Total stockholders' equity	$ 244,869.13
TOTAL DEBT AND EQUITY	$1,590,759.36

*SiBôn Beverage Corporation was incorporated in the state of Texas on April 22, 2001 for the purpose of constructing a bottling plant in Jasper, Texas and then producing and marketing a full line of sparkling fruit drinks, flavored waters, and sports drinks under the trade names of SiBon, Aquaria, Zingo, and Peppy-K. It is expected that the plant will be fully completed and equipped and ready to run in September 2001, at a total cost of approximately $1,040,000, including land. Until such time as the plant becomes operational, virtually all costs are being capitalized.

†The note payable to First Bank and Trust East Texas bears interest at ½% over prime rate, payable quarterly on April 15, July 15, October 15, and January 15 of each year prior to maturity. The entire unpaid principal balance and accrued but unpaid interest owed, if not paid sooner, is due and payable on or before April 15, 2004.

The installment note payable to First Bank and Trust East Texas bears interest at 8%, for a total finance charge of $1,683.10, which together with principal of $13,138.10 is included in the original amount of the note. The first two payments on the installment note were timely made on July 31, 2001.

SIBÔN Beverage Corporation
Net Income by Quarter

		May–June 2001	Jul–Sept 2001	Oct–Dec 2001	Total
Cases Produced					
Aquaria	(16 oz.)	0	5,625	14,063	19,688
	(1.5 ltr.)	0	5,625	14,063	19,688
SiBon	(11 oz.)	0	13,125	39,375	52,500
	(23 oz.)	0	13,125	39,375	52,500
Peppy-K	(20 oz.)	0	0	2,813	2,813
	(36 oz.)	0	0	2,813	2,813
Zingo	(11 oz.)	0	0	0	0
	(23 oz.)	0	0	0	0
TOTAL CASES PRODUCED		0	37,500	112,500	150,000
Gross Sales					
Aquaria	(16 oz.)	0	$ 58,613	$ 146,531	$ 205,144
	(1.5 ltr.)	0	50,513	126,281	176,794
SiBon	(11 oz.)	0	124,950	374,850	499,800
	(23 oz.)	0	128,494	385,481	513,975
Peppy-K	(20 oz.)	0	0	26,775	26,775
	(36 oz.)	0	0	24,244	24,244
Zingo	(11 oz.)	0	0	0	0
	(23 oz.)	0	0	0	0
TOTAL GROSS SALES		0	$362,569	$1,084,163	$1,446,731
Less promotional allowances		0	(18,750)	(56,250)	(75,000)
Net Sales		0	$343,819	$1,027,913	$1,371,731
Cost of Sales (Schedule A)		0	$216,804	$ 660,902	$ 877,706
Gross Profit from Sales		0	$127,015	$ 367,010	$ 494,025
Selling, General and Administrative Expenses					
Salaries and wages		$ 28,500	$ 54,950	$ 79,350	$ 162,800
Payroll taxes		4,560	12,696	12,696	29,952
Commissions		0	3,000	9,000	12,000
Royalties		0	0	0	0
Office supplies		500	2,000	1,500	4,000
Insurance		1,500	9,900	9,900	21,300
Legal, accounting, and professional fees		102,000	15,000	15,000	132,000
Advertising		10,000	25,000	15,000	50,000
Postage, dues, and subscriptions		0	200	300	500
Freight out		0	18,750	56,250	75,000
Amortization		14,298	21,447	21,447	57,192
Travel and entertainment		7,000	21,000	37,500	65,500
Equipment rental		1,500	3,000	3,000	7,500
Research and development		0	5,000	0	5,000
Other taxes		0	0	0	0
Interest		3,688	21,344	10,469	35,500
Miscellaneous		0	2,500	3,000	5,500
TOTAL SELLING, G & A EXPENSE		$173,546	$215,787	$ 274,412	$ 663,744
Net Income Before Income Taxes		($173,546)	($ 88,772)	$ 92,598	($ 169,719)
Net Profit per Case		$ 0.00	$ 0.84	$ 1.12	$ 0.49
Income Tax		$ 0.00	$ 0.00	$ 0.00	$ 0.00
NET INCOME		($173,546)	($ 88,772)	$ 92,598	($ 169,719)

SIBÔN Beverage Corporation
Net Income by Quarter

		Jan–Mar 2002	Apr–June 2002	Jul–Sept 2002	Oct–Dec 2002	Total
Cases Produced						
Aquaria	(16 oz.)	11,156	17,719	22,313	14,438	65,625
	(1.5 ltr.)	11,156	17,719	22,313	14,438	65,625
SiBon	(11 oz.)	27,563	39,375	44,625	28,875	140,438
	(23 oz.)	27,563	39,375	44,625	28,875	140,438
Peppy-K	(20 oz.)	2,231	3,544	4,463	2,888	13,125
	(36 oz.)	2,231	3,544	4,463	2,888	13,125
Zingo	(11 oz.)	3,675	14,175	17,850	11,550	47,250
	(23 oz.)	3,675	14,175	17,850	11,550	47,250
TOTAL CASES PRODUCED		89,250	141,750	178,500	115,500	525,000
Gross Sales						
Aquaria	(16 oz.)	$116,248	$ 184,629	$ 232,496	$ 150,439	$ 683,813
	(1.5 ltr.)	100,183	159,114	200,366	129,649	589,313
SiBon	(11 oz.)	262,395	374,850	424,830	274,890	1,336,965
	(23 oz.)	269,837	385,481	436,879	282,686	1,374,833
Peppy-K	(20 oz.)	21,242	33,737	42,483	27,489	124,950
	(36 oz.)	19,233	30,547	38,467	24,890	113,138
Zingo	(11 oz.)	31,513	121,551	153,064	99,041	405,169
	(23 oz.)	35,127	136,222	171,539	110,996	454,073
TOTAL GROSS SALES		$855,968	$1,426,131	$1,700,123	$1,100,080	$5,082,302
Less promotional allowances		(44,625)	(70,875)	(89,250)	(57,750)	(262,500)
Net Sales		$811,343	$1,355,256	$1,610,873	$1,042,330	$4,819,802
Cost of Sales (Schedule A)		$520,261	$ 824,763	$ 975,793	$ 659,205	$2,980,022
Gross Profit from Sales		$291,082	$ 530,493	$ 635,080	$ 383,125	$1,839,780
Selling, General and Administrative Expenses						
Salaries and wages		$ 99,188	$ 99,188	$ 99,188	$ 99,188	$ 396,750
Payroll taxes		14,600	14,600	14,600	14,600	58,402
Commissions		8,211	13,041	16,422	10,626	48,300
Royalties		0	0	0	0	0
Office supplies		1,500	1,500	2,000	1,500	6,500
Insurance		9,900	8,100	9,900	9,900	37,800
Legal, accounting, and professional fees		15,000	15,000	15,000	15,000	60,000
Advertising		30,000	30,000	30,000	30,000	120,000
Postage, dues, and subscriptions		1,500	1,500	1,500	1,500	6,000
Freight out		44,625	70,875	89,250	57,750	262,500
Amortization		21,447	21,447	21,447	21,447	85,788
Travel and entertainment		45,000	45,000	45,000	45,000	180,000
Equipment rental		3,000	3,500	3,000	3,000	12,500
Research and development		7,500	7,500	7,500	7,500	30,000
Other taxes		1,000	0	0	0	1,000
Interest		16,500	10,875	0	0	27,375
Miscellaneous		7,500	7,500	7,500	7,500	30,000
TOTAL SELLING, G & A EXPENSE		$326,471	$ 349,626	$ 362,307	$ 324,511	$1,362,915
Net Income Before Income Taxes		($ 35,389)	$ 180,867	$ 272,773	$ 58,614	$ 307,146
Net Profit (Loss) per Case		($ 0.48)	$ 1.84	$ 1.52	$ 0.39	$ 0.68
Income Tax		$ 1,908	$ 36,173	$ 54,555	$ 14,374	$ 107,010
NET INCOME		($ 37,296)	$ 144,694	$ 218,218	$ 44,240	$ 200,136

SiBôn Beverage Corporation
Net Income by Quarter

		Jan–Mar 2003	Apr–June 2003	Jul–Sept 2003	Oct–Dec 2003	Total
Cases Produced						
Aquaria	(16 oz.)	18,063	28,688	36,125	23,375	106,250
	(1.5 ltr.)	18,063	28,688	36,125	23,375	106,250
SiBon	(11 oz.)	36,125	57,375	72,250	46,750	212,500
	(23 oz.)	36,125	57,375	72,250	46,750	212,500
Peppy-K	(20 oz.)	3,613	5,738	7,225	4,675	21,250
	(36 oz.)	3,613	5,738	7,225	4,675	21,250
Zingo	(11 oz.)	14,450	22,950	28,900	18,700	85,000
	(23 oz.)	14,450	22,950	28,900	18,700	85,000
TOTAL CASES PRODUCED		144,500	229,500	289,000	187,000	850,000
Gross Sales						
Aquaria	(16 oz.)	$ 188,211	$ 298,924	$ 376,423	$ 243,568	$1,107,125
	(1.5 ltr.)	162,201	257,614	324,403	209,908	954,125
SiBon	(11 oz.)	343,910	546,210	687,820	445,060	2,023,000
	(23 oz.)	353,664	561,701	707,328	457,683	2,080,375
Peppy-K	(20 oz.)	34,391	54,621	68,782	44,506	202,300
	(36 oz.)	31,140	49,457	62,280	40,299	183,175
Zingo	(11 oz.)	123,909	196,796	247,818	160,353	728,875
	(23 oz.)	138,865	220,550	277,729	179,707	816,850
TOTAL GROSS SALES		$1,376,290	$2,185,873	$2,752,581	$1,781,082	$8,095,825
Less promotional allowances		(72,250)	(114,750)	(144,500)	(93,500)	(425,000)
Net Sales		$1,304,040	$2,071,123	$2,608,081	$1,687,582	$7,670,825
Cost of Sales (Schedule A)		$ 804,936	$1,238,205	$1,537,205	$1,024,633	$4,604,979
Gross Profit from Sales		$ 499,104	$ 832,918	$1,070,876	$ 662,940	$3,065,846
Selling, General and Administrative Expenses						
Salaries and wages		$ 119,025	$ 119,025	$ 119,025	$ 119,025	$ 476,100
Payroll taxes		19,044	19,044	19,044	19,044	76,176
Commissions		15,028	23,868	30,056	19,448	88,400
Royalties		0	0	0	0	0
Office supplies		1,500	1,500	2,000	1,500	6,500
Insurance		9,900	9,900	9,900	9,900	39,600
Legal, accounting, and professional fees		7,500	7,500	10,000	7,500	32,500
Advertising		45,000	45,000	45,000	45,000	180,000
Postage, dues, and subscriptions		1,500	1,500	1,500	1,500	6,000
Freight out		72,250	114,750	144,500	93,500	425,000
Amortization		32,697	32,697	32,697	32,697	130,788
Travel and entertainment		60,000	60,000	60,000	60,000	240,000
Equipment rental		3,000	3,000	3,000	3,000	12,000
Research and development		7,500	7,500	7,500	7,500	30,000
Other taxes		1,000	0	0	0	1,000
Interest		0	0	0	0	0
Miscellaneous		15,000	15,000	15,000	15,000	60,000
TOTAL SELLING, G & A EXPENSE		$ 409,944	$ 460,284	$ 499,222	$ 434,614	$1,804,064
Net Income Before Income Taxes		$ 89,160	$ 372,634	$ 571,654	$ 228,334	$1,261,782
Net Profit per Case		$ 0.66	$ 1.59	$ 1.98	$ 1.13	$ 1.31
Income Tax		$ 2,290	$ 93,158	$ 142,913	$ 57,084	$ 315,445
NET INCOME		$ 66,870	$ 279,475	$ 428,740	$ 171,251	$ 946,336

Robert J. Caskey
Employment History

Robert J. Caskey has lived in Jasper, Texas for 41 years and has been an active participant and leader in the business, civic, cultural, and local communities. He has demonstrated expertise in management, planning, and implementation at Visador Company and on the Board of Directors of a number of corporations, hospitals, and institutions of higher learning.

A brief history of Mr. Caskey's business experience follows:

1955–1958 **El Paso Molding Company, Inc.**
Vice President and General Manager
Mr. Caskey managed 35 employees who made pre-hung door parts and finger-jointed moldings.

1958–1961 **Visador Mouldings, Inc.**
Vice President
As supervisor of 60 employees, Mr. Caskey began a lumber yard and kiln-drying system on behalf of the company.

1961–1966 **Visador Company** (a partnership)
Partner
Mr. Caskey was in charge of production, purchasing, and personnel; he later took on the added responsibility of credit manager for the company. During this period, Mr. Caskey was the designer of all plant expansion, and the company grew to over 200 employees.

1966–1993 **Visador Company** (a corporation)
President and Chief Executive Officer
Under Mr. Caskey's leadership, Visador's sales grew from $3 million to $48 million, while the company expanded to four manufacturing locations and four distribution centers with almost 700 employees.

Kenneth R. Barnett
Employment History

Mr. Barnett has been in the investment and financial planning industry in Houston, Texas for over 23 years. His experience includes representing key executives of Fortune 500 companies, professional athletes, professionals, and small business owners in virtually all areas of financial and investment management. He has a Bachelor of Science degree in Biology/Chemistry and is a Certified Financial Planner.

Some of Mr. Barnett's accomplishments follow:

- Held the position of Account Manager and Tax Shelter Management with Paine, Webber, Jackson & Curtis
- Founded and built the largest financial planning and consulting firm in Houston, Texas; provided total financial, investment, and estate planning for corporation executives, professional athletes, and entrepreneurs; negotiated and structured complex investment transactions in oil and gas, real estate, and private enterprise on behalf of clients
- Founded the fourth-largest single-family residential investment management company in Houston, Texas; structured and completed the registration of a

$50 million public limited partnership to provide mortgage funds on residential investment properties. The company had over 30 employees located in three states, with annual sales in excess of $15 million.

- Has evaluated over 150 investment, financial, and business proposals annually on behalf of clients, accountants, and attorneys

David Rault
Employment History

Academic Degrees: B.S., M.B.A.

1960–1962 **Loeb Rhodes**
Corporate Analyst
Evaluated existing companies controlled by Loeb Rhodes and new companies for acquisitions and mergers

1962–1972 **International Business Machines Corp.**
Branch Manager
Progressed from Systems Analyst to Salesman to Branch Manager, Federal Systems Division while at IBM; handled all specifications and bidding for main-frame computers; became the direct liaison for the company with the federal government, overseeing its purchases and installations

1972–1983 **Harbinger Homes**
President and Founder
Oversaw the building of over 5,000 homes and office distribution warehouses in the Greater Houston area

1984–1993 **Business Automation**
President and Founder
Supervised the selling and installation of multi-user computer systems. The company had an exclusive contract with Western Union to install and service all equipment in the state of Texas.

1993–Present **U.S. Aquarius, Inc.**
President
Created formulas, trademarks, and business plan to start a New Age beverage company

Mr. Rault's expertise is in evaluating, building, and managing companies through mergers, acquisitions, and liquidations and in assisting insolvent companies in getting back in the black. He has in-depth knowledge of the aerospace, wholesale liquor, food brokerage, food distribution, and insurance industries.

Lloyd L. Simmons
Employment History

Mr. Simmons has been in the beverage industry for 32 years. His employment has successfully progressed through the years in the following manner:

Pepsi Cola, Oklahoma
Started in production and was promoted to increasing responsibilities in the warehouse, vending service, and repair areas. Held the positions of Key Account

Manager, Merchandising Manager, Sales Manager, and General Sales Manager over five branches.

Oklahoma Beverage Distributors and Bottlers
Northeast Division Manager
Supervised six sales centers and the fountain supply company

Pepsi Cola, Arkansas
Division Manager

Bryant Beverage (Division of Mid-South Bottling)
Vice President
Managed all bottling and sales operations and two branch operations. His branch won the Highest Profit/Case and Highest Increased Market Share awards from Mid-South Bottling. Won the Cappy Award for the highest percentage increase in market share in the southeast region from Pepsi. Won the Kalab T. Branum (inventor of Pepsi) Award for quality assurance in production.

Arkansas Beverage (Division of Mid-South Bottling)
Vice President of Sales and Division Manager

Denver Coca-Cola
Division Manager
Managed the number one division in every area—product turnover, sales increase, fewest days of work missed, no job injuries, and sales record for a single month

Murray Distributing
Consultant to Paul Murray in acquiring Royal Crown plants

InterBevCo.
Operations Manager
Set up new plant. Promoted to Division Manager in Alabama

Willow Springs Bottled Water Company
Division Manager
Supervised sales of bottled water in four states and the wholesale division dealing with food and beverage brokers

Royal Crown Cola, Oklahoma
Franchisee/Owner with two partners
Sold the company to All American Bottling

U.S. Aquarius, Inc.
Vice President of Sales
Moved to Louisiana to start operations of new bottling plant

Cenla Water Company
Sales Manager
Supervised distribution of Kempwood bottled water in five Louisiana parishes

VIDEO Appendix

More!

In the VIDEO Spotlight

Cafe Pilon

Big Idea #1: Separate your ego from your business decisions.

Don't reinvent the wheel. Another common way of saying this is "If it ain't broke, don't fix it." The Souto family was in the espresso-roasting business in Cuba, but the biggest name in coffee in Cuba was Cafe Pilon. When the founder of Cafe Pilon was ready to retire, the Souto family offered to buy the business and then created growth by combining the companies to maximize efficiencies. And they never thought of replacing the Cafe Pilon name with Souto. What this teaches, I believe, is that business decisions should be made separate from egos. The Souto family preferred increased profits over seeing their own name on the package. Decades later, they acquired another competitor that carries a different name.

Think about it: Why doesn't every business owner do this?

Think back: How did the Soutos purchase Cafe Pilon?

Think about it: If the two families had been fierce, unfriendly competitors, do you think the Soutos could have purchased Cafe Pilon?

Think about it: What can be learned from this?

Big Idea #2: Acquiring the competition is a powerful way to build a business.

The Souto family has twice acquired its competitors. This strategy has made it the largest Cuban coffee roaster in the United States.

Think back: How was the Souto family able to make the takeovers work?

Big Idea #3: Employee loyalty springs from the Souto family's respect for the dignity of all people.

On a tour through the plant, Alberto introduced me to many people. You saw Jean-Paul, who runs the roasters, and Fernando, the taster and coffee buyer. These gentlemen have been at Cafe Pilon for years. The good small business owners I know are very close to their employees. They know the names of spouses and children and spend time asking about the welfare of an employee's family and extended family.

Jean-Paul even said, "They treat us like family." This is a meaningful compliment. It says to me that employees can go to the Soutos with more than work-related problems. This means that if Jean-Paul's child is in the school play, Jean-Paul should, of course, take time from work to go see the play. I hear this repeatedly from employees of small companies. Employees' feeling that they are all part of one big family is important to retention.

Think about it: Why do people work at a particular place?

Think about it: Why is employee loyalty important?

Think back: What are the ways Alberto demonstrates respect for employees?

Big Idea #4: Customization for customers is the way to fend off competition.

Cafe Pilon has two types of customers. It sells to retail outlets such as grocery stores and convenience stores, where customers purchase coffee in the sack and take it home to brew it themselves. It also sells to institutional customers, such as restaurants, cafes, coffee shops, hotels, and even hospitals, for whom it brews the coffee and serves it prepared. While the retail customers all have the same products on their shelves, institutional customers may ask for custom blends.

The competition doesn't know how Cafe Pilon makes its special blend for Versailles, and it would be difficult for them to find out. If Cafe Pilon were selling to Versailles what it sells in grocery stores, competitors could buy that product and analyze it. Unless an employee provides a sample of the coffee

grounds before brewing, competitors can only drink the finished product and try to guess how it was blended.

Think about it: Why does Cafe Pilon customize its blends for some customers, how does it do it, and how does this protect it against the competition?

Big Idea #5: Your reputation is your greatest asset.

It does not surprise me that Enrique said the most important lesson he learned from his father is "Your word is your bond."

Think about it: Why is this lesson so important for every person in business but even more critical for small business owners?

Big Idea #6: Capitalism is based on moral values and respect for the rule of law.

General rules govern business; and specific agreements are also entered into with suppliers, employees, and customers. While the Soutos use proper documentation in all their business relationships, they continue to rely on the handshake.

Think about it: Can business work if everyone involved in a relationship is working with only a written contract?

Big Idea # 7: The heart of democracy and human productivity is individual ownership of ideas, businesses, homes, and land.

The Souto family lost everything when Castro took over Cuba. They came to the United States where they started their business from scratch and were motivated to work very hard to create value for new customers. By doing so, they have been rewarded by our free-enterprise system.

Think about it: Do people who own their own home take more care to keep it attractive than do people who rent? Why?

Source: Hattie Bryant, Producer, "Small Business School," The Series on PBS Stations, Worldnet, and the Web, http://smallbusinessschool.org

More!

In the VIDEO Spotlight

Record Technology

Big Idea #1: Do one thing really well.

Record Technology's strategy to capture opportunity has always been to provide the highest-quality product in its niche. Experts agree that it makes the best vinyl records in the world. Don has never tried to be the funkiest or the fastest. Through thick and thin, real peaks and valleys, Record Technology has stayed true to its original mission. It'll never be the biggest, but it'll always be the best.

When the original owner, Bill Bauer, decided to start a business, he did his homework before deciding what kind of company he wanted to build. Through extensive research, he learned that there were plenty of record-pressing plants, but the end users told him no company was making flawless records. There is no reason to start a business when someone is already doing exactly what you want to do. Duplicating efforts or trying to copy a product or service never works in the long run.

Once you decide what your niche is going to be, stick to it. While it is tempting to try, you cannot be all things to all people. You cannot promise quality, low prices, and speed of delivery, for example—you must choose. Perhaps you can provide the lowest price and the fastest delivery, but you can't deliver high quality under that pressure. Or, you may be able to deliver quality and low price if you have all the time in the world to deliver. Or, you may be the quality provider with the highest prices and as-promised delivery.

Sometimes quality providers get in trouble missing deadlines. This happens to many professional service providers, such as attorneys, architects, and ad agencies. When Record Technology opened its doors, it announced that it would be *the* quality record-pressing company, and consistently over the years it has pleased customers with high-quality product and by meeting deadlines.

Don said, "Know what you do best, and do it. Try to block out the other extraneous things that might deter you from that focus. Competitors of ours try to be complete full service, and so they get into artwork and design and into printing and into package design and all these other different areas. If we did that, we would lose our quality focus and our quality reputation.

Think about it: Can a quality provider ever be the largest provider in its field?

Big Idea #2: Ask customers to inspire product development.

Big companies spend millions of dollars trying to find out what customers want. As small business owners, we often think we know what our customers are thinking because we work with them every day. On the other hand, most of us don't ask our customers the hard questions. Fear and lack of time are the biggest obstacles.

A small business owner who asks, "What would you like us to be doing that we're not now doing?" might actually have to change to meet customer needs. When Don was really scared that he might have to give in to the CD craze, he did the hard thing. He turned his total attention to his devoted customers and asked them what he could do to help them. He said they told him, "You have a great product. There's no better vinyl record manufactured anywhere in the world, but we feel it can be better." There were places making a thicker, heavier record. The typical record weighs about 110 grams, and some places were making phonograph records that were 180 grams, which is about 50 percent heavier. The customers were saying, "If we had an RTI pressing on a 180-gram record, that would be just great for us, because we could really sell that, and we would also be willing to pursue more licenses for product."

When Don's customers asked for a new product, he took action, but he didn't go so quickly that he sacrificed quality. He said, "It took us nine months of experimentation and tinkering and so forth to get the product to meet

our standards." Don had a "Name Our New Product" contest for the employees. The winning name turned out to be HQ-180, which, of course, stands for its high-quality and 180 grams in weight, just as the customers asked for.

Can't you just see all 37 employees watching the first HQ-180 being created? I can, and it gives me goose bumps. People love being challenged. Don said to his team, "Can we do this?" The answer was yes, the company is growing, and the HQ-180 is keeping Record Technology on the top of the heap.

Think about it: Do you want to wait to listen to your best customers until competitors with a new technology nearly eat your lunch?

Source: Hattie Bryant, Producer, "Small Business School," The Series on PBS Stations, Worldnet, and the Web, http://smallbusinessschool.org

More!

In the VIDEO Spotlight

Le Travel Store

Big Idea #1: Know what to change and what not to change.

For Bill and Joan, some things have never changed, while others have never stayed the same. What hasn't changed is their focus on the independent international traveler. They'll help any customer who wants to travel, but their focus is the independent traveler. This focus has dictated their product mix, their location, the types of employees they hire, and even the style of the business. When you enter the business, you feel it's independent, it's international, and it's travel.

What has changed over the years is the way Bill and Joan take care of these customers. They started by selling plane tickets, added backpacks, then a full-blown travel agency and a full line of travel products. They've been in three locations: a funky retail area, an upscale high-concept mall, and now a historic building.

Bill and Joan know how to change, what to change, and what not to change. Their focus, the independent international traveler, is a person who will never take a group tour. This person buys books and maps and dreams about adventure and is willing to face many obstacles on a trip. These travelers may not know for sure where they will sleep every night before they get on the airplane. On their own, they learn how to handle currency exchange, how to use public transportation, and how to ask for help. These are not people who want luxury and who expect to be pampered. Bill said when they first opened in Pacific Beach, their typical customer was about 24 years old with an old Volkswagen van. Today, that same person is between 45 and 50 years old and probably driving a Volvo.

The independent international traveler usually has more time and less money than does the traveler who wants a detailed package put together by a travel agent. Joan and Bill do so well serving the independent international traveler because they travel this way themselves. To sell and service these customers requires a great depth of understanding that can only be acquired from personal experience. The expression "You have to eat your own cooking" simply means that you should be your own best customer. Joan and Bill travel regularly, and they don't take tours. They always plan their own trips the same way they teach their customers to plan.

Think about it: Is the independent international traveler a market niche? Name some other travel industry niches.

Big Idea #2: A core product can take you through the thick and the thin.

Bill said the travel pack, which looks like a large backpack, has been critical to business success since they started selling it in the late 70s. The store has cultivated the image of the self-sufficient traveler. Thus, the simplicity of a backpack is in harmony with the philosophy of their core customers. Also, the Eagle Creek brand, which is manufactured in San Diego, continues to depend on Joan and Bill to test new products. Le Travel Store has been faithful to Eagle Creek and carries a full range of its products.

Think about it: What is the value of the manufacturer/retailer relationship?

Big Idea #3: Technology is just a small part of Le Travel Store's Internet strategy.

Since 1995, billions of dollars have been poured into Web-based retailers, and most of those companies have now disappeared because they thought it would be easy to acquire a customer using technology. Although many Web software applications have been developed and trillions of e-mails are being sent and received daily, it is still very difficult to convince a person to give you money over the

Web. Joan and Bill Keller have successfully accomplished what most have not been able to do—they are selling products via their well-designed Web site.

The roots of their success lie in the work they have been doing for decades. They came to the Web with insight about the international traveler and a long relationship with one of the best travel gear companies in the world. Le Travel Store is one of eight retailers Eagle Creek links to from its Web site.

Also, in 1995 Bill and Joan grabbed the domain name luggage.com. Given the combination of their own customer data base, Eagle Creek's Web site, luggage.com, and a presence at Yahoo.com, Le Travel Store is doing 60 percent of its total sales through the Web.

Think about it: When you visit a business's Web site, what causes you to make a purchase?

Special assignment: Go to http://letravelstore.com and see if you can describe why so many people are shopping at this site. Also, check out http://luggage.com. What happens when you arrive at this site?

Source: Hattie Bryant, Producer, "Small Business School," The Series on PBS Stations, Worldnet, and the Web, http://smallbusinessschool.org

More!

In the VIDEO Spotlight

FastSigns

Big Idea #1: To have a great company, recruit great people.

Gary and his partner opened the first FastSigns to tweak the business model and to serve as a shining example of what franchise owners can accomplish with their own companies. Gary's experience as a franchise owner in the past gave him insight into how to treat other owners. When I met Myra and Don Phillips and the other people attending training at FastSigns headquarters, I understood why this business is already successful and why it will continue to be so in the future.

Think about it: Why do you think Myra and Don Phillips are part of this company today?

Big Idea #2: Gary is recruiting owners from big business.

Today, this entrepreneur is enjoying great PR. The speed with which a person with the right idea at the right time can create a big company is remarkable. This country was founded by entrepreneurs, but most of this century has been dominated by the organization man. The rise of the professional manager has been documented by business writers everywhere. Hundreds of books have been written about how to be a manager. FastSigns is recruiting these professionals, people who are managing groups of people and who work in a huge company like Ford, Exxon, or American Airlines.

A "pure" entrepreneur is the man or woman who thinks of an idea and starts a business from scratch, not knowing if it will turn into a profitable business. A franchise owner is a hybrid of an entrepreneur and a manager. When a person buys a franchise, the idea has already been proven. Recall the banker who said that he has looked at the financials of many businesses through the years, and, when he looked at the financials of some of the FastSigns operations, he could see that FastSigns is a good idea. There is no risk involved in evaluating the basic idea.

Big business runs best when people follow the systems put in place, usually by someone else. The professional manager may have to put down his or her own money to buy into the business, and there is some risk that the location or the leadership will fail. But there is great comfort for the organization man in systems.

Gary has worked hard from day one to put systems in place that will ensure success. He's a systems man himself. You can tell when you hear him talk about opening the first store and how frustrating it was trying to get things done for customers before the systems were streamlined.

It's cool today to be able to say you own a business. Tapping into that trend and offering professional managers a chance to own a business that looks more like a big business than a small one, Gary has grown his company quickly. Once you have the product and the processes in place, all you need to grow a business is people.

Think about it: How does Gary court the men and women who already have good jobs in big companies?

Big Idea #3: School is always in session.

This is true for every growing company. If you want to build a company, you must be a teacher at heart or find someone to work for you who is. When I visited FastSigns, an initial training session was being held for new franchise owners. You may recall that Dr. John Hayes said if you buy a franchise, you must commit to ongoing training.

Before I thought of doing this television show, I made a living as a teacher. My customers were companies with 100 employees or less that were too small to have their own in-house instructors. I taught sales, customer service,

and leadership skills for managers. Our motto here at Small Business School is "Learn today, earn tomorrow," because we know that learning pays.

Not only do you increase your earning power when you learn, the learning process is invigorating. Learning to work on our Web site opened a whole new world for me.

Owners and employees need consistent exposure to fresh ideas. The Web is great, but you should also sign up for seminars and send employees off to different classes, then have them share what they learned with everyone back in the office.

A weekly or monthly lunch-and-learn works. Albert Black, another business owner featured on "Small Business School," is the greatest teacher I have ever met. The company he started from scratch will do $16 million in sales this year, and he says it is because he takes time to teach. Every Friday morning, he provides a hot breakfast and an "all-employee school session."

Think about it: What are some of the topics people in business should always be studying?

Source: Hattie Bryant, Producer, "Small Business School," The Series on PBS Stations, Worldnet, and the Web, http://smallbusinessschool.org

More!

In the VIDEO Spotlight

Sundance Catalog

Big Idea #1: The person with the idea may not be the best person to execute the idea.

When Robert Redford discovered that Harry Rosenthal had launched a successful catalog of children's items, he sought advice from Harry. In fact, Redford wanted to hire Harry, but Harry turned him down. Instead, Harry offered to write a business plan for the new business. He then told Redford that the current company did not have the right top executive in place to make the catalog a success. One person has to live, eat, and sleep the business when it is born, just as a newborn baby has to be watched carefully. You can't just leave the baby for a few hours when you feel like going to a movie. A new business is vulnerable and needs minute-by-minute leadership. Employees working a regular schedule could run a mature business like the lodge or the film festival, but they could not nurture a new company.

Many small business owners don't have enough money or an idea big enough to attract a talent like Harry, but this example shows that a person with experience can deliver dramatic results. I have seen many small companies full of great people, but it is rare for the owner to turn over the title of president from the get-go, as Redford did, which is part of the reason Harry subsequently joined Sundance.

Think about it: What does a small business owner need to do to attract talent?

Think back: Just from watching this episode, what do you think are Harry's strengths?

Big Idea #2: You can build a business faster with a brand than without one.

The success of the catalog started with the hit picture *Butch Cassidy and the Sundance Kid*. That film gave Robert Redford the money to purchase the land and lodge in Provo Canyon.

Most of us who start a business from scratch don't have brand recognition. Harry certainly did not have brand awareness when he started his children's products catalog. However, when he started the Sundance catalog, the lodge already existed, and soon the film festival also bore the name Sundance. As a result, the festival helps the catalog, the catalog helps the lodge, and the lodge helps the festival. With 12 million catalogs being mailed per year, the catalog is building brand awareness for all of Redford's enterprises.

A brand is a big idea, and a product is a specific item that in a way represents the brand. Think of IBM. It has been making products for decades, and some of those products have been marketplace hits and others haven't. However, through the years, the IBM brand has continued to stand for the same thing: the biggest technology company and reliability, consistency, and ethical business practices. An IBM employee could be fired for talking negatively about a competitive product.

The IBM ThinkPad, as a product, is sold as being light, easy, convenient, and flexible. With the IBM brand, the ThinkPad gets the rub-off of reliability. By promoting the brand, IBM can develop products that are sold under the same banner but that serve a very specific need.

Think about it: What is the Sundance brand known for?

Think about it: Can, or should, a very small business worry about brand?

Think about it: Name some brands you like, then name some of the brand's products.

Big Idea #3: Use a spokesperson with caution.

According to Harry Rosenthal, "The use of a spokesperson is a really complex topic. If it's perceived as nothing more than an advertising gimmick, it can actually bounce back and harm you after the early going. If depth

and reality are to be considered part of the image, as with Robert Redford, and you live up to that, then it can be very, very helpful. But in all cases, I think the advice I would give to people is that a spokesperson or a famous name or a famous brand gets people to try your product or service once. That's really all it gets you. If you deliver a good quality product or service at a good price and people are satisfied with the experience they have, then they will come back. And I don't know about all other businesses, but I can tell you that in the catalog business, all of the profitability really is based upon repeat customers. If they don't have a good experience, you won't have a successful business."

Some small business owners often use local celebrity endorsements or spokespersons. Think about car dealers and football players. Celebrity images attract attention, which is the single most important reason to use them. If you create a direct mail piece or a TV commercial to market your business and have a celebrity involved, more people will spend more time considering the message.

Think about it: Could Robert Redford's name hurt Sundance?

Source: Hattie Bryant, Producer, "Small Business School," The Series on PBS Stations, Worldnet, and the Web, http://smallbusinessschool.org

More!

In the VIDEO Spotlight

We'll Show You the Money

Big Idea #1: All money is not equal.

Most small business owners have never taken a business class. Since much of what they read in the paper or hear on "the street" about financing a business seems complicated and just too much trouble to bother with, they bootstrap their companies' growth, meaning they use profits to finance their growth ideas.

Frankly, most entrepreneurs start a business for freedom, and, as soon as they take money from a bank or some other source, they have to be accountable. Once your idea is bigger than your ability to use profits to achieve your goals or you commit to building a sustainable business, you should look at the alternatives.

There are basically just two ways to get money for your business ideas. You can borrow money (debt capital), or you can allow outsiders to buy a piece of your business (equity capital).

Think about it: Which companies on this tape use debt capital and which ones use equity capital?

Big Idea #2: Raising money pays.

All of these business owners went through fire to raise money, and it was an essential step for them to make their dreams come true. Jagged Edge now has a profitable Web site and has added three physical locations; Mickey Finn's installed micro-brewery equipment and quadrupled its dining space; Cross Timbers could not have produced one barrel of oil without investors; Boston Duck Tours became the hottest tourism ticket in Massachusetts; UroCor now has 300 employees; and The French Laundry is sold out two months in advance. None of these companies could be what they are today without OPM (other people's money).

Think about it: Other than the freedom issue we already discussed, why don't more small business owners seek OPM?

Big Idea #3: Bankers want to loan us money.

I heard Leonard Walker, senior vice president of small business financial products for Chase Bank, say, "Small business owners are sometimes impatient with bankers because we are very conservative. But it is not because we don't like an idea. It is because we are only going to earn 3 percent; for that small margin, we can't afford to make mistakes. Venture capitalists are looking for 100 percent return, and they can afford to make mistakes." Three business owners in this episode got bank loans.

The banker who consolidated Jagged Edge's debt said, "They brought me this amazing business plan." Lorie Davis's banker said, "She prepared a good package." Bill and Pat of Mickey Finn's had a good plan that included a competitive analysis, that is, numbers on brew pubs from the national study that Bill conducted. In addition, they had a bustling existing business (lines out the door). Bankers were fighting over making them a loan. (Remember, you can't expect a banker to hand you money without agreeing to a solid plan for the repayment.)

Bill and Pat did such a good job talking to bankers that they were able to eliminate those who only saw Mickey Finn's as a brew pub. They saw themselves as a central and critical meeting place for the town and invested in an upstairs party room that is now used during the day by many groups. The space is free to most of the town's organizations. Bill and Pat found a banker who is involved in the complete revitalization of Libertyville's historic business district, not a number cruncher who saw them as just another pub.

Think about it: What can you learn from Bill?

Big Idea #4: All venture capital is not equal.

Andy Wilson got funds from a venture capital firm, Fred Hoar talks about angel investors, and Thomas Keller

has 48 individual investors. Their deals are all alike because they all involve equity financing. But they all use a different type of investor. A venture capitalist is often investing and managing money that has been entrusted to him or her by others. Usually, the money comes from big corporations like insurance companies and pension funds; as Vince Occhipinti said, the venture firm typically has up to 10 years to provide "an outstanding rate of return." A good venture capitalist will not only provide financing, but also mentoring and key introductions to grow the business. Fred spoke of angel investors, who are simply wealthy individuals who loan money to entrepreneurs at a negotiated rate. Thomas had an attorney form a limited partnership to raise the money to buy out the owners of the location where we find The French Laundry today. After the partnership was formed, it could then get additional money from a traditional bank loan backed by the SBA.

Think about it: How does a business owner attract the attention of a venture capitalist?

Think back: What kind of product is Vince Occhipinti looking for?

Source: Hattie Bryant, Producer, "Small Business School," The Series on PBS Stations, Worldnet, and the Web, http://smallbusinessschool.org

More!

In the VIDEO Spotlight

NoUVIR

Big Idea #1: Sell to the person who cares the most.

NoUVIR uses a direct channel to sell its products to museums. This turns the lighting industry's standard practice on its head. The typical lighting manufacturer has sales reps who call on electrical contractors, lighting designers, general contractors, and architects. NoUVIR contacts the museum conservator, director, or curator directly because these people are responsible to their board of directors for the preservation of art and artifacts. Ruth Ellen told me their approach is so unique that more than one customer has told her, "You are not a lighting company—you are a museum company."

In discussions with Ruth Ellen that are not included in the video, I learned that she was surprised by many of the business practices she found in the lighting industry. For example, many manufacturers have multiple price lists. They sell the same product to an architect for one price, to a general contractor for another price, and to an electrical contractor for yet another price. Remember, lighting is often part of construction and becomes just one of the costs built in by the trade. Electrical contractors typically purchase lighting at a reduced price, but when invoices are presented to the customers, the full retail price is listed. The profit on the sale of lighting fixtures then subsidizes the contractor's labor costs.

The big obstacle then for NoUVIR is cutting through the clutter to reach the people who care about the art. The lighting industry focuses on lighting a room, while NoUVIR focuses on lighting the art. Ruth Ellen believes that when it comes to lighting, museums are "spending too much for too little."

There are 4200 museums in the United States, and NoUVIR knows it cannot have personal representation at every one of them. A catalog, a fun and informative Web site, and a direct mail plan puts its name in front of decision makers.

Think back: How does NoUVIR reach its target market, and how long is its sales cycle?

Big Idea #2: Shed new light on an old problem.

Ruth Ellen loves art, and, with her scientific background, she knows that she can help the museums of the world improve the way we all see art and artifacts. Jack Miller told me that you have two choices when trying to sell a product. You can make a generic product and sell it cheap or make a proprietary product and name your price as the only source. NoUVIR made the second choice and is doing very well.

Think back: What is NoUVIR's unique selling proposition?

Think about it: Who might be NoUVIR's biggest competitor?

Big Idea #3: Seek a patent to protect products you invent.

Jack explains that a patent is a monopoly that the government grants for a certain period of time, usually 17 to 20 years, which gives the patent owner the right to sue an infringer. He recommends that a product have more than one patent because big companies can see what an inventor is doing and can easily duplicate the product. The inventor usually isn't able to fight the big guy in court. If a product had three or more patents, it would be difficult for a big company to steal it away from the small business.

Think about it: Why is the patent process so slow?

Big Idea #4: Use trademarks and copyrights to protect your intellectual property.

A copyright can keep competitors from copying your product, and a trademark can keep them from stealing your name or logo. Ruth Ellen says the best way to protect yourself is to begin with a unique concept. NoUVIR stands for

"no uv and no ir." The created word is great to trademark because it is an invention and can be protected. Ordinary words are harder to trademark. You can, however, trademark the ordinary by giving it a special treatment. The company E-Poxy had the "E" in its name designed by an artist. You cannot trademark the word *epoxy,* but the owners of this company were able to trademark the special "E."

Think back: How long does the trademark process take?

Big Idea #5: Location, Location, Location.

This old real estate adage refers to property values and can be applied to businesses, as well. The cost of making things in California is high compared to other states. The environmental laws can be crushing, and taxes and utilities are among the highest in the country. The Millers had a vision, and they knew they did not want to invent something that had to be made in a factory; they wanted to build the products themselves. They also knew it would take a long time—years—to convince the museum community to install their systems. They needed every cost advantage they could get, so they moved to business-friendly Delaware.

Think about it: Would you move to find the best place to succeed at building a business?

Source: Hattie Bryant, Producer, "Small Business School," The Series on PBS Stations, Worldnet, and the Web, http://smallbusinessschool.org

More!

In the VIDEO Spotlight

Renegade Animation

Big Idea #1: Price it, then stick to your guns.

You may be tempted to take work just for the money. Darrell and Ashley would advise against that practice. They've built a solid business by saying no to projects that don't take advantage of their talents or that won't generate enough profit.

Most small business owners say yes to too many projects for instant cash flow or ego, or because they're not clear about what their goals are. Ashley and Darrell started Renegade with some cash in the bank. They found affordable office space, and they have kept their payroll under control. With this positioning, they don't have to do work just for the money. They both left Warner Bros. to start Renegade, and Darrell is a graduate of the prestigious Disney School of Animation. They don't need to take on work to build their personal self-esteem.

They know exactly what kind of work they want to do and at what price. Ashley said, "We do turn jobs down when we feel like they don't play to our strengths, because we have a feeling that eventually the client would not be happy with what we were giving them. And we would rather turn it down than have a bad experience, because they'll come back to us when they have something that is right. Some just don't have enough money to do what they want to do. And we're not going to take a loss on a job. And we're not going to cheap it out and have them be unhappy, because then we've lost them forever."

Think about it: Will this pricing strategy work for every small business owner?

Big Idea #2: Know the purpose of your business, and name it accordingly.

Renegade Animation's purpose is for Ashley and Darrell to use their talents to serve the customers who bring them fascinating and profitable projects. This may sound selfish, but consider their life experiences.

Neither one of them was happy in a big corporate environment. Having worked for over 20 years for the big studios, Darrell said, "The whole thing with [Renegade] has not been to make money. I didn't start by saying, 'You know what? I think we can make a lot of money. Let's go do this.' I did it because I wasn't happy where I was. I didn't like the alternatives out there once I left. Here we can kind of control our own destiny, and it's just more fun."

Darrell also said it makes him "crazy" to think about taking work that doesn't interest him. He says, "There's no point in taking a job that you're not interested in and having your work be crummy because you're going to do a bad job if you're not interested in it. The client's going to know you did a bad job, so they're not coming back to you. So if you're doing it just for the money, then you should forget it because you're not going to get any more work. That's a stupid way to operate."

This is not a bad business purpose, because as Ashley and Darrell please themselves, they create good work and customers are served. I have also found this philosophy in other companies created by people who have spent years in big companies.

Douglas Martin, writing for the *New York Times* on January 9, 2000, said, "Successful brands work by carving out a niche in our subconscious—what advertisers call a mind share." By choosing a name like Renegade Animation, Ashley and Darrell are building their brand around who they want you to think they are—rule-breakers, off-the-edge thinkers who certainly don't need your job to put food on their table.

If you agree with Roy Spence, an owner of the Austin, Texas ad agency GSD&M, that "the Jolly Green Giant and the Pillsbury Doughboy live in the same psychic space as Santa," then you can understand that with a name like Renegade Animation, Ashley and Darrell are saying, "We are out of the ordinary."

Renegade means "a person who deserts from a group or cause." When Ashley and Darrell "deserted" Warner Bros., they didn't exactly leave this huge organization high and dry. But, in many ways, their name still empowers them. Renegade Animation was started by two people who don't need the big guys and who are independent rebels out to do what they want to do when they want to do it. And, if you want to do business with them, be careful, because they can be outrageous.

Think about it: Do you think Ashley and Darrell could have been so successful had they not had a corporate experience?

Think about it: Does their business name impact their pricing strategy?

Think about it: Does their story give you any insight into your career path?

Source: Hattie Bryant, Producer, "Small Business School," The Series on PBS Stations, Worldnet, and the Web, http://smallbusinessschool.org

More!

In the VIDEO Spotlight

Gadabout Salon and Spa

Big Idea #1: Evolve. Remember Darwin?

Pam McNair started a hair salon decades ago, and she has stayed ahead of the curve. With five locations, 225 employees, and $11 million in sales, her latest growth has come from adding day-spa services. Gadabout offers dermabrasion, seaweed masks, stone therapy, the soft pack, and spa pedicures, in addition to traditional hair and nail care.

I had never heard of stone therapy, much less experienced it, until I visited Gadabout. While I am not a big spa customer, my point is that Pam is the first to offer almost any spa experience available. She is active in the spa trade association and is seen as a leader.

Gadabout was the first American spa to offer the soft pack, which is a machine that the client is placed in for relaxation. The client's body is covered with moisturizer, then wrapped in a waterproof blanket and lowered into warm water to float. When I tried this, my first thought was that I was getting into a coffin. Once I accepted the fact that I was in for something really unique, I was truly amazed by how good my spine felt.

Think about it: Could Pam grow a typical hair salon to Gadabout's current size?

Think back: Why is the day spa enjoying such growth as a sector within the industry?

Big Idea #2: People power trumps cash.

Pam started Gadabout because there were people who wanted to work for her. Rather than lose the opportunity to create a great place for these great people to work, Pam took a financial risk; she had to "find the financial wherewithal." For a young mother with no college education, she was brave. She instinctually knew that people are the most important part of a business and that with a quality workforce, she could figure out how to get the money.

Think about it: Where does startup money come from?

Big Idea #3: Build your team.

This is easier said than done. It's an old idea, but one of those basics you just can't ignore. If you have two or three people working in the same space, you must build a team. This is particularly difficult in the salon business, which attracts the artist personality. People study and train but see themselves as artists, as unique and irreplaceable.

Think back: How did Pam build a team?

Big Idea #4: When people feel good, they do good.

No matter what product or service you deliver, the people who deliver it have to feel good. Period. People who harbor resentment, anger, fear, or anxiety or who suffer from depression cannot provide a consistently high level of service.

Think back: According to Pam, what do people need in order to perform optimally?

Think about it: Is this psychobabble?

Think back: What is Pam's most important workplace goal?

Big Idea #5: Ongoing training keeps the team fit for heavy lifting.

Service is psychological heavy lifting. While construction workers haul brick and mortar, service providers haul emotions. Every employee at Gadabout has a set of skills and also has to deal with the feelings of clients. The interaction between a client and his or her service provider is intimate, and this intimacy is draining. Like a bartender, the hairdresser, massage therapist, and manicurist listen to people's problems all day long. Listening is part of the service and is appreciated by the client.

Think back: What kind of training has everyone at Gadabout just completed?

Big Idea #6: You work for your employees.

This idea works for Pam and can work for anyone with a service business dominated by women. I'm not saying that men don't want their bosses to be concerned for their total well-being, but women tend to be more interested in the intangibles of work than are men. Men seem to be able to do a job and separate it from their personal lives.

Jennifer, the director of spas, said that Pam is working for the employees rather than the employees working for Pam. She said this because she feels that she personally has become a better person in the Gadabout environment and attributes the positive change to Pam's ability to inspire people to be the best they can be. Jennifer gets the feeling that Pam goes home at night thinking about how she can help Jennifer. Pam doesn't care about what she can squeeze out of people, but rather what she can do to help them reach their potential.

Think back: List the roles Pam plays in the eyes of her employees.

Source: Hattie Bryant, Producer, "Small Business School," The Series on PBS Stations, Worldnet, and the Web, http://smallbusinessschool.org

More!

In the VIDEO Spotlight

Ping Golf

Big Idea #1: Work to achieve perfection.

While no business can ever be perfect, working toward perfection is a motivating goal. And having perfection as a goal attracts employees who find inspiration in a place where they are recognized for their hard work. Many people flourish in this type of environment and would be unhappy and frustrated if they worked in a place where the leadership is more motivated by money than by process.

It is hard. If it were easy, everyone would do it. For Ping Golf, the idea of striving for perfection sprang from the engineer-founder and his son, John. They were simply not interested in the status quo when they invented their first putter, and John is still not interested in it. You can run a successful business with the goal of doing everything as it has always been done. However, if you are fascinated by progress, having the goal to strive for perfection is a good one.

Think back: What did director of engineering, John Bliss, say about being at Ping?

Big Idea #2: Give every person in the company quality control responsibility.

You heard John say, "We don't have inspectors as such. Everybody is considered an inspector. Anybody can reject a club throughout the system at any time." This is a bold statement giving every employee the power to shut down the plant if something isn't right. This owner's attitude makes every person at Ping feel valued. And that feeling translates into a sense of pride, which is the reason I think this business is so profitable.

Think about it: Is quality important in every business?

Big Idea #3: Worry about the product or service first, then think about the money.

At the very end of this episode, John said he and his father never worried about making money; instead, they worried about making a great product, and the money followed. I am sure there are plenty of business owners who start their businesses with the question "How do I make money?" However, what I have experienced is that once people have enough money to be comfortable, they get bored with just making money and become more intrigued with innovating, creating a brand, making a mark, or changing the world. Karsten had a paycheck when he started his invention process; he was more interested in improving his own golf game than in making money. Having spent time with John and many employees of Ping, I believe John and think he is a great mentor for any business owner. It is ok not to have money as the driving force.

Think about it: Why does making money seem to be the priority of most business owners?

Big Idea #4: Going up against the establishment takes a steel backbone.

Ping putters were outlawed soon after the Solheims brought their invention to the marketplace. The United States Golf Association prohibited professionals from using the odd putters in competition. The association argued that they simply didn't meet established regulations.

Think about it: Why was USGA approval important?

Big Idea #5: Being first is bad and good.

Creating a new and unusual putter got the attention of the USGA, throwing Ping into expensive and energy-draining legal battles, and that was bad. However, the company's novel idea for fitting clubs to customers proved to be all good. Ping was the first company to build clubs based on custom fitting done by golf pros. The Solheims

believe that every person is different and needs custom fitting of golf clubs to fully enjoy playing the game. Many companies do this now, but Ping did it first.

In addition to building the clubs, Ping keeps a record of each customer's clubs and etches a personal serial number onto each club. If a club is damaged or lost, Ping can rebuild it exactly like the original. This gives Ping a terrific service advantage over any company that is not able to capture the contact information for the customer.

Think about it: Before the widespread use of computers, what kinds of systems would a company have had to have in place to pull off custom fitting?

Big Idea #6: To sell a high-end product, find an existing network of experts.

The Solheims went to the golf pros who run golf shops at country clubs and offered to teach them how to fit clubs; they then offered them exclusive marketing rights. This means you won't find Ping clubs in a place where a professional golfer is not available to do the fitting.

To keep the pros motivated, Ping offers ongoing training in Phoenix, provides the tools for custom fitting, has invested in a Web site designed to help the golf pro sell clubs, does extensive marketing campaigns around golf events, and stands behind a quality product.

Think about it: What other companies depend on experts to sell their products?

Source: Hattie Bryant, Producer, "Small Business School," The Series on PBS Stations, Worldnet, and the Web, http://smallbusinessschool.org

More!

In the VIDEO Spotlight

Katz Deli

Big Idea #1: Giving comes back to the giver.

Marc says, "You only get to keep what you give away." All of us expect to earn profits from our businesses and to enjoy the fruits of our labor. We think, too, that the bottom line is managed by increasing sales and by controlling costs, but that is only partly true. When we're small, we're usually afraid to be generous because we need every penny to fund our growth. Marc says his commitment to charities has taught him that giving pays. He points out that he does not model himself as much after the small business owners his size, but after big business. He even asked me, "Why do you think big corporations have foundations and give millions away through many programs, from matching employee donations to paying for the T-shirts worn by Little Leaguers?"

The mayor of Austin says he cannot imagine the community without the involvement of Marc Katz. Marc has organized fundraising benefits that have helped to raise thousands of dollars for a variety of community organizations such as hospice services in Austin, KUT Public Radio, Pediatric AIDS League, Diverse Arts, and more.

Want your business to grow? Find ways to give yourself and your services away. Take action to be a catalyst for good. As Marc says, you keep what you have by giving it away. Many charities get cash, food, a free meeting location, and even free promotion from Marc. He is most proud that he originated the AIDS Services dining program. The biggest table in the restaurant is dedicated to raising money to help people with AIDS. Ten percent of every bill generated by that table goes to AIDS research and other services. When other restaurateurs heard about Marc's idea, they started doing it too. Now some 150 restaurants are involved with the program.

Think about it: Can Marc really make money by giving it away? How?

Think about it: What is Marc's business justification for his generosity?

Big Idea #2: We're all in the people business.

When we were looking for interesting business owners in Austin, Texas, one of the places we called was the Austin Chamber of Commerce. They told me, "Marc Katz is the unofficial mayor of Austin." Marc took me for a ride around town in his vintage Cadillac, and many people waved hello to him. He has a big smile for everyone, and he knows the names of many of his customers. Marc also told me that fellow restaurant owners make the mistake of complaining about dishwasher turnover and many don't even know their dishwashers' names. Marc believes it is his responsibility as the owner to make sure that employees are appreciated and that customers are coddled.

Think about it: Why is driving a yellow Cadillac convertible good for Marc's business?

Think about it: Marc says that he is in the people business and that he owns a signature restaurant. What do you think he means?

Think beyond: If you had your own restaurant, how would you put your signature on it?

Big Idea #3: Multiple revenue streams improve efficiency.

Revenues come from the deli food and beverages, the downstairs bar, the gift shop, the upstairs bar, the cover charge for live band performances, the upstairs patio for dining, the rent on the buildings he owns, and a growing takeout business that is fueled by Internet orders. Marc explains that each revenue source is interdependent on the others. Like any good business owner, Marc calculates the dollars generated by each of these activities separately. If you can't measure it, you can't manage it and you don't

know if you're making a profit. Being on popular 6th Street in Austin, where college students go to enjoy the night life, Marc's operation hours were always long, but, when he decided to stay open 24 hours, sales increased more than expected.

Think about it: Will increasing sales always increase profits?

Think about it: Why is it smart to have multiple revenue streams?

Big Idea #4: If you believe in a location, buy it.

The decision to own or lease a space is a tough one for business owners and has to be considered on a case by case basis. However, most of the owners we have studied have been in business for years, and generally they encourage real estate ownership. The location Katz is in today proved to be bad for many previous restaurant owners. Knowing that other restaurants had failed in the location, Marc still bought the building.

Think about it: Why is Marc succeeding where others failed?

Big Idea #5: Doing what you know and love can make you rich.

Marc is a wealthy man today. He started with third-generation knowledge of how to make deli food. He had experience working for his father. However, he did not have startup money from his father.

Think back: What do you see in this episode that tells you Marc Katz loves his business?

Think about it: When does the wealth come?

Source: Hattie Bryant, Producer, "Small Business School," The Series on PBS Stations, Worldnet, and the Web, http://smallbusinessschool.org

More!

In the VIDEO Spotlight

Theatrical Lighting

Big Idea #1: Bundle products and services.

In their popular book *Blur: The Speed of Change in the Connected Economy,* Christopher Meyer and Stan Davis insist that we should forget trying to sell a product without a service or a service without a product. Since 1976, David Milly has been bundling products and services.

Think back: What does the business offer its customers?

Think back: What did David say the company does?

Think about it: What does he mean by "asset management"?

Think beyond: Name other businesses who bundle products and services. Can you think of a business you would like to start? How would you bundle a product with a service?

Big Idea #2: A clear, simple mission is better than a contrived one.

David's mission statement is "To make money doing lights." When I first heard him say this, I was a bit shocked at this rather short, curt phrase. Then it dawned on me that most people in this industry love show business. They would "do lights" for free, just to hang around the musicians. As people get older, they start taking on more responsibility. They have children to feed, clothe, and educate; they have a mortgage. Now, they have to grow up and bring home the bacon.

Think about it: Why does this mission statement work so well for David, although it might backfire at Johnson & Johnson?

Think beyond: What type of mission statement would attract you to work in a specific company? What kind of mission statement would you write for a business you might want to start?

Big Idea #3: Treat vendors just as you treat your best customers.

Janet says, "Vendors are our support system." Every source you access is part of your supply chain, and we all know the chain is only as strong as its weakest link. I was surprised to learn that Janet pays vendors early, as this is an unusual business practice.

Think about it: Why is this strategy so useful?

Think about it: Why don't more companies pay ahead of schedule?

Big Idea #4: Get on the scales.

The only way to know how you're doing is to constantly measure your progress. Many small business owners prefer to not look at their numbers, because sometimes the truth hurts. I believe it is human nature to avoid negative feedback. When I know my business is having problems, I work hard to make changes and hope that action will give me the right results. At the same time, I might ignore the most recent financial statement.

Think back: How does David know what is going on in his business?

Think about it: Why is it good for department managers to be involved in this process?

Big Idea #5: Many people want a family feeling at work.

Much has been written about the trend of work being more like home than home is. With the divorce rate and with the number of Americans living alone on the rise (caused by people's living longer, women's economic power, young people's delaying marriage), work becomes the place where a new family forms. Also, with more and more businesses conducting onsite training where people

learn communication skills, work groups may be better at solving personal problems that arise than are family groups. Janet told me that she may be the CFO, but she is also a mother figure.

In *Love 'Em or Lose 'Em: Getting Good People to Stay,* Beverly L. Kaye and Sharon Jordan-Evans write about the simple truth that people stay where they are loved. This is a simple idea but difficult to execute. It is one of the most powerful competitive edges we have as small business owners. The big guys may cut bigger checks, but we small business owners buy loyalty with our bigger hearts.

Think about it: Do you think people like being able to bring personal problems to a responsible person in the workplace to seek advice and even get a short-term fix?

Big Idea #6: Stop doing and start leading.

David said, "I'm not a lighting guy. I'm a businessman."

Think about it: Why is this mind-set so important?

Think about it: What did David need most to make the shift from lighting guy to businessman?

Big Idea #7: Use mail and the Web to keep your name in front of customers and prospects.

We all thought the Web was going to eliminate paper. David says that although they have had a Web site since 1994 that provides information and service to customers, customers still ask for a physical catalog.

Think about it: Why is a physical catalog still in demand?

Source: Hattie Bryant, Producer, "Small Business School," The Series on PBS Stations, Worldnet, and the Web, http://smallbusinessschool.org

Photo Credits

pp. 2, 28, 56, 144, 240, 320, 396, 472, 494, 522, 546, Photos taken from the video footage created by "Small Business School," The series on PBS stations and the Web; **p. 4,** Courtesy, Jonathan F. Johnson; **p. 6,** Courtesy, Auntie Anne's Pretzels; **p. 9,** © Johnny Hart; **p. 12,** © Wide World; **p. 15,** Courtesy, Adrienne Landau; **p. 16,** Courtesy, Cindy Rowe Auto Glass; **p. 21,** Courtesy, Meyer Technologies; **p. 40,** Courtesy, Coactive Connector; **p. 49,** Courtesy, National Airlines; **p. 61,** Courtesy, Three Dog Bakery; **p. 62,** © PhotoDisc; **p. 68,** © Susan Van Etten; **p. 69,** Walkabout Travel Gear; **p. 70,** Courtesy, VeriSign, Inc.; **p. 71,** Courtesy, Namesecure; **p. 73,** Courtesy, Shoe.buy.com; **p. 74,** Courtesy, Hire Quality, Inc.; **p. 88,** © Edward Santalone; **p. 91,** Courtesy, Baazee.com; **p. 100,** © Keren Su/Corbis; **p. 103,** © Susan Van Etten; **p. 107,** © PhotoDisc; **p. 118,** Courtesy, Glow Dog, Inc.; **p. 124,** © 2001 Brian Smith; **p. 133,** Courtesy, Cecelia Levine; **p. 138,** Courtesy, Zhao Chiang; **p. 147,** Courtesy, International Franchise Association; **p. 150,** Courtesy, Two Men and a Truck; **p. 158,** Courtesy, Curves for Women; **p. 160,** Courtesy, PostNet; **p. 166,** Courtesy, Frieda Caplan; **p. 169,** Courtesy, Heather D. Blease; **p. 176,** Courtesy, Peter Pan Bus Lines; **p. 183,** Courtesy, Tom and Mike Jennison; **p. 190,** Courtesy, Application Technologies; **p. 216,** © James McGoon/BBH Exhibits; **p. 219,** Courtesy, Maxine Clark; **p. 222,** Courtesy, Bite Footwear; **p. 233,** Courtesy, Amy Ratekin; **p. 248,** © Ed Kashi/Corbis; **p. 256,** Reproduced with permission from Crain's Chicago Business 2001. Photographer: John R. Boehm; **p. 258,** © PhotoDisc; **p. 260,** Courtesy, Razorfish, Inc.; **p. 262,** © Susan Van Etten; **p. 270,** Courtesy, Shannon Entin; **p. 274,** Courtesy, Eastex Farms; **p. 282,** Courtesy, Sally Odegaard; **p. 290,** Courtesy, Linda Nespole, Hi-Shear Technology; **p. 331,** © 2001 Edward Caldwell. All Rights Reserved; **p. 346,** Courtesy, Maggie Etheridge; **p. 368,** Photo by Thom Thompson; **p. 382,** Courtesy, Brett Herbst; **p. 385, top right,** Courtesy, Adweek; **bottom right,** Photography by Photonics Graphics; **p. 386,** © Parker Clayton, Smith Photography; **p. 390,** © Norman Y. Lono; **p. 401,** Courtesy, Eric Schechter; **p. 405,** Courtesy, E. Kelly Hanson; **p. 409,** Courtesy, Tommy Wald/NetForce Technologies; **p. 415,** Courtesy, CrediFYI; **p. 417,** Courtesy, Rentons' International Stationery; **p. 422,** Courtesy, 1-800-CONTACTS; **p. 427,** Courtesy, Bob and Dan Paisner; **p. 432,** Courtesy, Ron Farmer, US Signs, Houston; **p. 435,** © Cherry Kim Photography; **p. 436,** Courtesy, 1-800-CONTACTS; **p. 437,** © Rich Ashley; **p. 439,** Courtesy of Scendis; **p. 446,** Courtesy, Jessica Nam; **p. 460,** © Kathy Cheney; **p. 465,** Courtesy, Mudhouse Café; **p. 477,** © Susan Van Etten; **p. 489,** © Arc Rajtar/Spectrum Signal Processing, Inc.; p. 498, Courtesy, Carmelo Mauro; **p. 505,** Courtesy, Doug Kinnear; **p. 508,** Courtesy, Murray and Linda Kennedy; **p. 511,** Courtesy, Belly Basics; **p. 527,** Courtesy, Formerly Deep Canyon; **p. 532,** © Susan Van Etten; **p. 537,** Courtesy, Give Something Back; **p. 572,** © Cherry Kim Photography; **p. 608,** © Gregg Matthews; **p. 620,** © Harley Schwadron/Cartoon Features Syndicate; **p. 624,** © Susan Van Etten; **p. 628,** Courtesy, Ed Bonneau

Endnotes

Chapter 1

1. Todd D. Maddocks, "Best of the Best," *Business Start-Ups,* Vol. 12, No. 6 (June 2000), pp. 59–60.

2. Thomas Kellner, "He Keeps His Ear to the Ground," *Forbes,* Vol. 164, No. 12 (November 15, 1999), pp. 204–206. Reprinted by permission of Forbes Magazine © 2001 Forbes Inc.

3. *Ibid.,* p. 204.

4. *Ibid.,* p. 205.

5. *Ibid.,* p. 206.

6. From material from http://www.auntieannes.com.

7. Kemp Powers, "Entrepreneurs: Upward Spiral," *Forbes,* Vol. 166, No. 4 (August 7, 2000), pp. 104–106; and from material from http://www.rotozip.com.

8. *Ibid.,* p. 105.

9. "Main Street Enters Mainstream," *USA Today,* Nov. 16, 1999.

10. "Importing Can Help a Firm Expand and Diversify," *Nation's Business,* Vol. 83, No. 1 (January 1995), p. 11.

11. Jere W. Glover, "Labor Day 2000: A Small Business Celebration," *The Small Business Advocate* (Washington: U.S. Small Business Administration), September 2000, p. 3.

12. Thomas J. Stanley and William D. Danko, *The Millionaire Next Door* (New York: Simon & Schuster, 1996), p. 227.

13. "Poll: Most Like Being Own Boss," *USA Today,* May 6, 1991. For a scholarly study confirming the importance of a quest for independence as a motivational factor, see Marco Virarelli, "The Birth of New Enterprises," *Small Business Economics,* Vol. 3, No. 3 (September 1991), pp. 215–223.

14. Russell M. Knight, "Entrepreneurship in Canada," paper presented at the annual conference of the International Council for Small Business, Asilomar, California, June 22–25, 1980.

15. Colleen Mastony, "Micro-entrepreneurs," *Forbes,* Vol. 162, No. 13 (December 14, 1998), p. 88.

16. *Ibid.*

17. Daniel Roth, "The Ray Kroc of Pigsties," *Forbes 400* (Special Issue), Vol. 10, No. 3 (October 13, 1997), pp. 115–120.

18. Norman R. Smith, *The Entrepreneur and His Firm: The Relationship Between Type of Man and Type of Company* (East Lansing: Bureau of Business and Economic Research, Michigan State University, 1967). See also Norman R. Smith and John B. Miner, "Type of Entrepreneur, Type of Firm, and Managerial Motivation: Implications for Organizational Life Cycle Theory," *Strategic Management Journal,* Vol. 4, No. 4 (October-December 1983), pp. 325–340; and Carolyn Y. Woo, Arnold C. Cooper, and William C. Dunkelberg, "The Development and Interpretation of Entrepreneurial Typologies," *Journal of Business Venturing,* Vol. 6, No. 2 (March 1991), pp. 93–114.

19. "Women Increase Standing as Business Owners," *USA Today,* June 29, 1999, p. 1B.

20. "Fixing Windshields Shatters Expectations," *USA Today,* September 27, 1999, p. 6B.

21. *Ibid.*

22. See "Thinking About Tomorrow," *The Wall Street Journal,* May 24, 1999, p. R-30; and James Worsham, "The Flip Side of Downsizing," *Nation's Business,* Vol. 84, No. 10 (October 1996), pp. 18–25.

23. Michael Barrier, "Building Your Customer Portfolio," *Nation's Business,* Vol. 84, No. 12 (December 1996), pp. 45–46.

24. Jeffrey A. Timmons, *New Venture Creation,* 4th ed. (Burr Ridge, IL: Irwin, 1994), p. 5.

25. Cited in Gary M. Stern, "Young Entrepreneurs Make Their Mark," *Nation's Business,* Vol. 84, No. 8 (August 1996), pp. 49–51.

26. Robert Johnson, "Teen Tycoon," *The Wall Street Journal* (May 22, 2000), p. R8.

27. Personal communication with Jayson Meyer, August 2001.

28. J. B. Rotter, "Generalized Expectancies for Internal Versus External Control of Reinforcement," *Psychological Monographs,* 1966a. A more recent review is given in Robert H. Brockhaus, Sr., and Pamela S. Horwitz, "The Psychology of the Entrepreneur," in Donald L. Sexton and Raymond W. Smilor (eds.), *The Art and Science of Entrepreneurship* (Cambridge, MA: Ballinger, 1986), pp. 25–48.

29. Roberta Maynard, "Sliding into Home," *Nation's Business,* Vol. 86, No. 1 (January 1998), p. 52.

Chapter 2

1. James C. Collins and Jerry I. Porras, *Built to Last: Successful Habits of Visionary Companies* (New York: Harper Business, 1994), pp. 22–28.

2. Gayle Sato Stodder, "New Wave," *Entrepreneur,* Vol. 25, No. 1 (January 1997), pp. 98–102.

3. Laura Johannes, "Fiesty Mom-and-Pops of Gotham Strike Back at Drugstore Chains, *The Wall Street Journal,* March 20, 2000, p. A1.

4. John Grossmann, "Running Out of Time," *Inc.,* Vol. 19, No. 2 (February 1997), pp. 62–73.

5. Regis McKenna, "1997 Marketing Masters Awards," *Inc.,* Vol. 19, No. 18 (December 1997), pp. 135–136.

6. Thomas Bartlett, "Mobile Business on Roll," *Waco Tribune-Herald,* April 6, 1997, p. 7C.

7. Karl H. Vesper, *New Venture Strategies,* rev. ed. (Englewood Cliffs, NJ: Prentice-Hall, 1990), p. 192.

8. For a rigorous study of this subject, see Suresh Kotha and Anil Nair, "Strategy and Environment as Determinants of Performance: Evidence from the Japanese Machine Tool Industry," *Strategic Management Journal,* Vol. 16, No. 7 (October 1995), pp. 497–518.

9. Rona Kobell, "Funeral Industry Adapts to Change," *The Houston Chronicle,* October 8, 2000, p. B7; and "Business Opportunities in Space," *Fortune,* Vol. 137, No. 1 (January 12, 1998), pp. 46–47.

10. "Discarded Tires, Once a Nightmare, Are Where Ecologists Dream to Tread," *The Wall Street Journal,* April 24, 2000, p. B17.

11. William A. Sahlman, "How to Write a Great Business Plan," *Harvard Business Review,* Vol. 75, No. 4 (July-August 1997), pp. 103–104.

12. Karen Stevens and Dale Kurschner, "That Vroom! You Hear May Not Be a Harley," *Business Week* (October 20, 1997), p. 159; Lillian Zier Martell, "Wichita, Kan., Offers Tax Break to Keep Motorcycle Maker from Relocating," *The Wichita Eagle,* October 20, 1999, p. C1; and "Big Dog Motorcycles Announces Sales Growth and First Profitable 6-Month Period," press release, July 25, 2000.

13. Gary Hamel, "Strategy as Revolution," *Harvard Business Review,* Vol. 74, No. 4 (July-August 1996), p. 80.

14. Peter Drucker, *Innovation and Entrepreneurship* (New York: Harper Business, 1993), p. 35.

15. Peter F. Drucker, "The Discipline of Innovation," *Harvard Business Review,* Vol. 76, No. 6 (November-December 1998), p. 149.

16. Faith Keenan, "Warehouse Trouble," *Business Week,* November 20, 2000, pp. EB124, EB126.

17. "Micros Systems, Inc.," *Standard and Poor's Stock Report,* Vol. 2 (April 1998); Kate Bohner Lewis, "Thou Better Not Steal," *Forbes,* Vol. 154, No. 11 (November 7, 1994), pp. 216–217; and material from http://www.micros.com.

18. Karl H. Vesper, "New Venture Ideas: Do Not Overlook Experience Factor," in William A. Sahlman and Howard H. Stevensen (eds.), *The Entrepreneurial Venture* (Boston: Harvard Business School Publications, 1992), p. 75.

19. James P. Sterba, "Here's Why Asians Are All Hopped Up About Frog Farming," *The Wall Street Journal,* March 27, 2001, pp. A1, A8.

20. Joshua Harris Praeger, "Behind the Suction Cup Industry, a Very Sticky Rivalry," *The Wall Street Journal,* April 7, 1998, pp. B1–B2.

21. *Ibid.*

22. John Case, "How to Launch an *Inc. 500* Company," *Inc.,* Vol. 14, No. 10 (October 1992), p. 91.

23. John Pierson, "There's Much Ado About Composting in the Round," *The Wall Street Journal,* December 2, 1992, p. B1.

24. Personal telephone conversation with Wee Care Academy, November 30, 2000; and Cynthia E. Griffin, "Wee the People," *Entrepreneur,* Vol. 22, No. 8 (July 1994), p. 213.

25. Michael Barrier, "A Global Reach for Small Firms," *Nation's Business,* Vol. 82, No. 4 (April 1994), p. 66.

26. "City Family," *Ulrich's International Periodicals Directory,* 2000, Vol. 5 (New Providence, NJ: R. R. Bowker Publishing, 2000); and Jeffrey A. Tannenbaum, "New Magazine Targeting Poor Instead of Wealthy," *The Wall Street Journal,* November 7, 1994, p. B1.

27. Roberta Maynard, "Rich Niches," *Nation's Business,* Vol. 81, No. 11 (November 1993), p. 39; and material from http://www.atlanticpublicationsgrp.com, November 30, 2000.

28. Amar Bhide, "How Entrepreneurs Craft Strategies That Work," *Harvard Business Review,* Vol. 72, No. 2 (March-April 1992), p. 154.

29. Michael Barrier, "Ties That Bind," *Nation's Business,* Vol. 85, No. 8 (August 1997), pp. 12–18.

30. Barrier, *op. cit.;* and Donna Fenn, "A Bigger Wheel," *Inc.,* Vol. 22, No. 16 (November 2000), pp. 78–88.

31. Michael E. Porter, *Competitive Advantage* (New York: Free Press, 1985), p. 5.

32. Erika Kotite, "Watch Your Back," *Entrepreneur,* Vol. 22, No. 8 (August 1994), pp. 112–117.

33. David J. Collis and Cynthia A. Montgomery, "Competing on Resources: Strategy in the 1990s," *Harvard Business Review,* Vol. 73, No. 4 (July-August 1995), pp. 118–128.

34. For example, see Richard Hall, "A Framework Linking Intangible Resources and Capabilities to Sustainable Competitive Advantage," *Strategic Management Journal,* Vol. 14, No. 8 (November 1993), pp. 607–618; Steven Maijoor and Arjen van Witteloostujin, "An Empirical Test of the Resource-Based Theory: Strategic Regulation in the Dutch Audit Industry," *Strategic Management Journal,* Vol. 17, No. 7 (July 1996), pp. 549–569; Christine Oliver, "Sustainable Competitive Advantage: Combining Institutional and Resource-Based Views," *Strategic Management Journal,* Vol. 18, No. 9 (October 1997), pp. 697–713; and Thomas C. Powell and Anne Dent-Micallef, "Information Technology as Competitive Advantage," *Strategic Management Journal,* Vol. 18, No. 5 (May 1997), pp. 375–405.

35. David J. Collis, "How Valuable Are Organizational Capabilities?" *Strategic Management Journal,* Vol. 15 (Winter 1994), pp. 143–152.

36. Ian C. MacMillan, "Controlling Competitive Dynamics by Taking Strategic Initiative," *Academy of Management Executive,* Vol. 2, No. 2 (May 1988), pp. 111–112.

37. Rodney Ho, "Beanie Babies Bears Down in Suit Against Religious Firm," *The Wall Street Journal,*

October 12, 1999, p. B2.

38. Rodney Ho, "Best Cellars Inc. Doesn't Think Imitation Is Flattering," *The Wall Street Journal,* April 18, 2000, p. B2.

39. Fenn, *op. cit.*

40. Patrick Kelly, "The Mystery of the Empty Truck," *Inc.,* Vol. 19, No. 14 (October 1997), pp. 35–36.

Chapter 3

1. "Seed Money," *Inc. Technology,* Vol. 21, No. 17 (1999), pp. 72–73.

2. Norm Brodsky, "An Internet Model That Works," *Inc.,* Vol. 23, No. 6 (May 2001), p. 25.

3. "Adventure Capitalism," *Inc. Technology,* Vol. 21, No. 17 (1999), pp. 88–89.

4. Thomas W. Leigh, "eCRM Is the Customer Thing!," *Careers in Professional Selling* (Waco, TX: Baylor University, 2000), p. 28.

5. Ellen Neuborne, "Why E-Tail Will Click," *Business Week,* No. 3691 (July 24, 2000), p. EB14.

6. Jackie Ross, "Bidding for Business," *MyBusiness,* January/February 2001, pp. 52–53.

7. Shawn Tully, "The B2B Tool That Really Is Changing the World," *Fortune,* Vol. 141, No. 6 (March 20, 2000), p. 133.

8. Robert McGarvey, "Lonely," *Business Start-Ups,* Vol. 12, No. 6 (June 2000), p. 22.

9. Aron Benon, "Affiliations Can Pay Off," *MyBusiness,* January/February 2001, p. 54.

10. Leigh Buchanan, "Make Way for Duck Links," *Inc. Technology,* Vol. 21, No. 17 (1999), p. 14.

11. Robert A. Mamis, "The Name Game," *Inc., The State of Small Business 2000,* May 16, 2000, p. 144.

12. *Ibid.*

13. "Here Lies the Guts of the Web," *Inc. Technology,* Vol. 22, No. 13 (2000), p. 28.

14. Rick Edler, "Razzle-Dazzle Makes Web Sites Great," *Inc.,* Vol. 22, No. 2 (February 2000), p. 60.

15. David S. Bernstein, "We've Been Hacked," *Inc. Technology,* Vol. 22, No. 3 (2000), p. 111.

16. Article posted on http://www.fraud.org/internet/99final.htm, February 16, 2000, National Consumers League.

17. Elizabeth Weise, "Cookies Sound Sweet, but They Watch Your Every Move," *USA Today,* June 27, 2000, p. 17E.

Chapter 4

1. Gerald P. O'Driscoll Jr., Kim R. Holmes, and Melanie Kirkpatrick, "Who's Free, Who's Not," *The Wall Street Journal,* November 1, 2000, p. A26.

2. *Ibid.*

3. Patricia Phillips McDougall and Benjamin M. Oviatt, "A Framework for Understanding Accelerated International Entrepreneurship," in A. M. Rugman & R. W. Wright (Eds.), *Research in Global Strategic Management,* Vol. 7 (Stamford, CT: JAI Press, 1996), pp. 23–40.

4. Erkko Autio, Harry J. Sapienza, and James G. Almeida, "Effects of Age at Entry, Knowledge Intensity, and Imitability on International Growth," *Academy of Management Journal,* Vol. 43, No. 5 (October 2000), pp. 909–924.

5. *Ibid.*

6. Timothy Aeppel, "Two Partners Find an Unlikely New Niche Inside Commercial Jets," *The Wall Street Journal,* January 15, 1999, p. B1.

7. James F. Foley, *The Global Entrepreneur: Taking Your Business International* (Chicago: Dearborn Financial Publishing, 1999), p. 5.

8. Michael A. Hitt, R. Duane Ireland, and Robert E. Hoskisson, *Strategic Management: Competitiveness and Globalization* (Cincinnati: South-Western, 2001), p. 209.

9. Karen E. Klein, "The Bumpy Road to Global Trade," *Business Week,* October 9, 2000, p. 32.

10. John Grossman, "Great Leap into China," *Inc.,* Vol. 21, No. 15 (October 15, 1999), p. 29.

11. Raymond Vernon, "International Investment and International Trade in the Product Cycle," *Quarterly Journal of Economics,* Vol. 80, No. 2 (May 1966), pp. 190–207.

12. Gordon B. Baty, *Entrepreneurship for the Nineties* (Englewood Cliffs, NJ: Prentice Hall, 1990), p. 166.

13. Rodney C. Shrader, Benjamin M. Oviatt, and Patricia Phillips McDougall, "How New Ventures Exploit Trade-Offs Among International Risk Factors: Lessons for the Accelerated Internationalization of the 21st Century," *Academy of Management Journal,* Vol. 43, No. 6 (December 2000), pp. 1227–1247.

14. Scott Doggett, "Your Company," *Los Angeles Times,* October 11, 2000, p. C6.

15. Patricia P. McDougall, Rodney C. Shrader, and Benjamin M. Oviatt, "International Entrepreneurs: Risk Takers or Risk Managers?" in Sue Birley and Daniel F. Muzyka (Eds.), *Mastering Entrepreneurship* (London: Financial Times/Prentice Hall, 2000), pp. 246–250.

16. David Birch, "Thinking About Tomorrow," *The Wall Street Journal,* May 24, 1999, p. R30.

17. *Ibid.*

18. Hugh Pope, "Why Are the World's IBMs Putting Down Roots in the Desert? A: Dubai," *The Wall Street Journal,* January 23, 2001, p. A18.

19. John B. Cullen, *Multinational Management: A Strategic Approach* (Cincinnati: South-Western, 1999), p. 204.

20. Shrader, Oviatt, and McDougall, *op. cit.*

21. U.S. Small Business Administration, "The Facts About Small Business 1999," http://www.sba.gov/library/oitreport/archive/oitnov99report.html, October 26, 2001.

22. Klein, *op. cit.*

23. James A. Wolff and Timothy L. Pett, "Internationalization of Small Firms: An Examination of Export Competitive Patterns, Firm Size, and Export Performance," *Journal of Small Business Management,* Vol. 38, No. 2 (April 2000), p. 35.

24. Karen E. Klein, *op. cit.*

25. James Flanigan, "Globalization in a Nutshell," *Los Angeles Times,* May 31, 2000, p. C1.

26. Roberta Maynard, "Trade Links via the Internet," *Nation's Business,* Vol. 85, No. 12 (December 1997), pp. 51–53.

27. Robert Johnson, "Toy Web Site Collects Fans, Profits with Action Figures," *The Wall Street Journal,* June 27, 2000, p. B2.

28. Melanie Warner, "Going Pro on eBay," *Fortune,* Vol. 141, No. 7 (April 3, 2000), pp. 250–252.

29. Maria Atanasov, "Taking Her Business on the Road," *Fortune,* Vol. 137, No. 7 (April 13, 1998), pp. 159–160.

30. Michael A. Hitt and R. Duane Ireland, "The Intersection of Entrepreneurship and Strategic Management Research," in D. L Sexton and H. Landstrom (Eds.), *The Blackwell Handbook of Entrepreneurship* (Oxford, UK: Blackwell Publishers, 2000), pp. 45–63.

31. Doggett, *op. cit.*

32. U.S. Small Business Administration, *Breaking into the Trade Game: A Small Business Guide to Exporting* (Washington, DC: U.S. Small Business Administration and AT&T, 1994), p. 105.

33. Leslie Gourse, "Speed Kills: For Some Chains, Quality, Not Quantity, Is the Better Way," *Success,* Vol. 44, No. 8 (October 1997), pp. 98–101.

34. From material from http://www.mooneyfarms.com/about_us.htm, February 12, 2001.

35. *Ibid.*

36. U.S. Small Business Administration, "Breaking into the Trade Game: A Small Business Guide to Exporting," http://www.sba.gov/oit/info/Guide-To-Exporting/trad8.html.

Chapter 5

1. Rekha Balu, "Starting Your Startup," *Fast Company,* Vol. 31 (January/February 2000), p. 81.

2. Amar Bhide, "Bootstrap Finance: The Art of Start-Ups," *Harvard Business Review,* November-December 1992, pp. 109–117.

3. Emily Barker, "Hot Startups: The Young and the Caloric," *Inc.,* Vol. 21, No. 10 (July 1999), p. 37.

4. Samuel Fromartz, "How to Get Your First Great Idea," *Inc.,* Vol. 20, No. 5 (April 1998), p. 91.

5. Marc Ballon, "Hot Startups: Petal Pushers," *Inc.,* Vol. 21, No. 10 (July 1999), p. 36.

6. Donna Fenn, "Grand Plans," *Inc.,* Vol. 21, No. 11 (August 1999), pp. 44–45.

7. *Ibid.,* p. 45.

8. *Ibid.,* p. 46.

9. Personal communication with Bill Waugh and Burger Street management.

10. Dennis Rodkin, "Leap of Faith," *Entrepreneur,* Vol. 26, No. 2 (February 1998), pp. 150–155.

11. Peter Weaver, "New Owners Take Stock," *Business Advisor,* January-February 2001, pp. 12–15.

12. Jill Andresky Fraser, "Business for Sale: Florida Fuel Delivery Service," *Inc.,* Vol. 22, No. 10 (July 2000), p. 148.

13. If you are not familiar with the concept of discounting cash flows to their present value, read Appendix 23B.

14. Leslie Brokaw, "The Truth About Start-Ups," *Inc.,* Vol. 15, No. 3 (March 1993), pp. 56–64.

15. Personal communication with DeWayne Eidson.

16. Paul Reynolds, "The Truth About Start-Ups," *Inc.,* Vol. 17, No. 12 (February 1995), p. 24.

Chapter 6

1. Richard Landesberg, "A New Career for You Might Start at Franchise U.," *Success Magazine,* http://www.successmagazine.com, July-August 2000.

2. From material from http://www.FranchiseRegistry.com/Partnership.asp, November 11, 2000.

3. See Cecilia M. Falbe and Dianne H. B. Welch, "NAFTA and Franchising: A Comparison of Franchisor Perceptions of Characteristics Associated with Franchisee Success and Failure in Canada, Mexico, and the United States," *Journal of Business Venturing,* Vol. 13, No. 2 (March 1998), pp. 151–171.

4. James H. Amos, Jr., "Trends and Developments in International Franchising," *The Franchising Handbook* (American Management Association: New York, 1993), p. 463.

5. Roberta Maynard, "Choosing a Franchise," *Nation's Business,* Vol. 84, No. 10 (October 1996), p. 62R.

Chapter 7

1. These comments appeared in the Letters section of *Inc.,* Vol. 19, No. 10 (July 1997), p. 17.

2. Richard Heller, "Folk Fortune," *Forbes,* Vol. 166, No. 6 (September 4, 2000), pp. 66–69.

3. Daniel L. McConaughy, "Family CEOs vs. Non-Family CEOs in the Family-Controlled Firm: An Examination of the Level and Sensitivity of Pay to Performance," *Family Business Review,* Vol. 13, No. 2 (June 2000), pp. 121–131.

4. The quotation is taken from an advertising letter that the Wilkirson-Hatch-Bailey Funeral Home in Waco, Texas sent out in February, 1998.

5. Peter Davis, "Realizing the Potential of the Family Business," *Organizational Dynamics,* Vol. 12 (Summer 1983), pp. 53–54.

6. John Robben, "Have Toys, Will Travel: My Father's Journey," *Family Business,* Vol. 4, No. 1 (Winter 1993), p. 63.

7. Ivan Lansberg, "Narcissism: The Hidden Cost of Success," *Family Business,* Vol. 11, No. 3 (Summer 2000), pp. 15–16.

8. W. Gibb Dyer, Jr., *Cultural Change in Family Firms* (San Francisco: Jossey-Bass, 1986), Chapter 2.

9. Stephanie Armour, "Couple of Heads for Business," *USA Today,* June 18, 1999, pp. 1B–2B.

10. James Samuelson, "Solomonic Solution," *Forbes,* Vol. 157, No. 5 (March 11, 1996), pp. 80–82.

11. Katy Danco, *From the Other Side of the Bed: A Woman Looks at Life in the Family Business* (Cleveland: Center for Family Business, 1981), p. 21.

12. John L. Ward, "Growing the Family Business: Special Challenges and Best Practices," *Family Business Review,* Vol. 10, No. 4 (December 1997), pp. 323–337.

13. Nancy Upton, *Transferring Management in a Family-Owned Business* (Washington, DC: U.S. Small Business Administration, 1991), p. 6.

14. For a discussion of mentoring in the family firm, see John Boyd, Nancy Upton, and Michelle Wircenski, "Mentoring in Family Firms: A Reflective Analysis of Senior Executives' Perceptions," *Family Business Review,* Vol. 12, No. 4 (December, 1999), pp. 299–309.

15. For an earlier extended treatment of this topic, see Justin G. Longenecker and John E. Schoen, "Management Succession in the Family Business," *Journal of Small Business Management,* Vol. 16 (July 1978), pp. 1–6.

16. Colette Dumas, "Integrating the Daughter into Family Business Management," *Entrepreneurship Theory and Practice,* Vol. 16, No. 4 (Summer 1992), p. 47.

Chapter 8

1. Jack Stack, "Stay the Course," *Inc.,* Vol. 19, No. 8 (June 1997), pp. 41–42.

2. Amar Bhide, *The Origin and Evolution of New Businesses* (New York: Oxford University Press, 2000), p. 70.

3. Mark Stevens, "Seven Steps to a Well-Prepared Business Plan," *Executive Female,* Vol. 18, No. 2 (March 1995), p. 30.

4. Ellyn E. Spragins, "How to Write a Business Plan That Will Get You in the Door," *Inc. Guide to Small Business Management,* pp. 6–8.

5. William Sahlman, "How to Write a Great Business Plan," *Harvard Business Review,* Vol. 75, No. 4 (July-August 1997), pp. 98–108.

6. Kenneth Blanchard and Spencer Johnson, *The One-Minute Manager* (New York: William Morrow, 1982).

7. Personal conversation with Tim Smith, March 2001.

8. Stanley R. Rich and David E. Gumpert, *Business Plans That Win $$$: Lessons from the MIT Enterprise Forum* (New York: Harper & Row, 1985), p. 22.

9. *Ibid.,* p. 23.

10. Adapted from Philip Thurston, "Should Smaller Companies Make Formal Plans?" *Harvard Business Review* (September-October 1983), p. 163.

11. Bhide, *op cit.,* p. 53.

12. Arthur Andersen and Company, *An Entrepreneur's Guide to Developing a Business Plan* (Chicago: Author, 1990).

13. Sahlman, *op cit.*

14. Rhonda M. Abrams, *The Successful Business Plan: Secrets and Strategies,* 2nd ed. (Grants Pass, OR: Oasis Press, 1993).

15. Jill Andresky Fraser, "Who Can Help Out with a Business Plan?" *Inc.,* Vol. 21, No. 8 (June 1999), pp. 115–117.

Chapter 9

1. William Bak, "Read All About It," *Entrepreneur,* Vol. 22, No. 1 (January 1994), pp. 50–53.

2. Cheryl Abrams, "The Quick 'N Natural Soup Entrepreneur," *In Business,* Vol. 20, No. 3 (May-June 1998), pp. 32–33.

3. Jim Hopkins, "Entrepreneur 101: Competition," *USA Today,* February 14, 2001, p. 6B.

4. Gayle Sato Strodder, "Right Off Target," *Entrepreneur,* Vol. 22, No. 10 (October 1994), p. 56.

5. Michael Porter, *Competitive Advantage* (New York: Free Press, 1985), p. 5.

6. Alan Naditz, "Desktop Sleuthing," *Independent Business,* Vol. 9, No. 1 (January-February 1998), p. 24.

Chapter 10

1. Simon Stockley, "Building and Maintaining the Entrepreneurial Team—A Critical Competence for Venture Growth," in Sue Birley and Daniel F. Muzyka (Eds.), *Mastering Entrepreneurship: The Complete MBA Companion in Entrepreneurship* (London: Financial Times–Prentice Hall, 2000), pp. 206–212.

2. Michael Barrier, "Creator of Habits," *Nation's Business,* Vol. 81, No. 11 (November 1993), p. 64.

3. "The *Inc.* Fax Poll: Are Partners Bad for Business?" *Inc.,* Vol. 14, No. 2 (February 1992), p. 24.

4. Joshua Hyatt, "Reconcilable Differences," *Inc.,* Vol. 13, No. 4 (April 1991), p. 87.

5. Lori Ioannou, "Can't We Get Along," *Fortune,* Vol. 138, No. 11 (December 7, 1998), p. 244[E].

6. *Ibid.*

7. Jim Hopkins, "Goals, Risks Can Help You Decide Legal Structure," *USA Today,* December 18, 2000, p. 5B.

8. *Ibid.*

9. Laura Saunders, "Freedom Day for Small Business," *Forbes,* Vol. 163, No. 4 (February 22, 1999), pp. 128, 130.

10. Jill Andresky Fraser, "Perfect Form," *Inc.,* Vol. 19, No. 18 (December 1997), pp. 155–157.

11. Christopher Caggiano, "Hotlinks," *Inc.,* Vol. 21, No. 14 (October 1999), pp. 72–81.

12. Dianne Cyr, "High Tech, High Impact: Creating Canada's Competitive Advantage Through Technology Alliances," *Academy of Management Executive,* Vol. 13, No. 2 (May 1999), p. 18; and http://www.alitech.com.

13. Mike Hoffman, "Dear Max: Drop Dead. Love, Go Card," *Inc.,* Vol. 19, No. 5 (April 1997), p. 28.

14. Ilan Mochari, "Fishing for Big-Name Partners," *Inc.,* Vol. 22, No. 6 (May 2000), p. 163.

15. Caggiano, *op. cit.*

16. Arie Y. Lewin, "Putting the S-Word Back in Alliances," *Financial Times,* November 1, 1999, p. 12.

17. Gardner W. Heidrick, "Selecting Outside Directors," *Family Business Review,* Vol. 1, No. 3 (Fall 1988), p. 271.

18. Jill Andresky Fraser, "Building the Board," *Inc.,* Vol. 21, No. 16 (November 1999), p. 132.

19. Harold W. Fox, "Growing Concerns: Quasi-Boards—Useful Small Business Confidants," *Harvard Business Review,* Vol. 60, No. 1 (January-February 1982), p. 164.

20. Fred A. Tillman, "Commentary on Legal Liability: Organizing the Advisory Council," *Family Business Review,* Vol. 1, No. 3 (Fall 1988), pp. 287–288.

Chapter 11

1. For a more comprehensive treatment of relocation issues, see Rick Mullin, "Site Selection," *Journal of Business Strategy,* May-June 1996, pp. 26–39.

2. From material from http://www.hatworld.com, August 6, 2001.

3. Michael Selz, "Odd Jobs," *The Wall Street Journal,* May 22, 1997, p. 12.

4. Wyoming Department of Revenue, http://revenue.state.wy.us, February 6, 2001.

5. "What Are Oregon Enterprise Zones?" http://www.econ.state.or.us/enterthezones/whatare.html, March 3, 2001.

6. "What Are Empowerment Zones and Enterprise Communities?" http://www.hud.gov/whatezec.cfm, March 8, 2001.

7. Randy Fitzgerald, "It's Your Business," *Reader's Digest,* Vol. 153, No. 915 (July 1998), p. 183.

8. Susan Hansen, "Wooden Bowl Maker Barks Up Wrong Trees," *Inc.,* Vol. 22, No. 1 (January 2000), p. 36.

9. Debra Cash, "There's No Office Like Home," *Inc. Technology,* Vol. 20, No. 4 (1998), p. 36.

10. American Association of Home-Based Businesses, http://www.aahbb.org, March 8, 2001.

11. John Grossmann, "Meeting's at 9. I'll Be the One in Slippers," *Inc.: The State of Small Business* (Special Issue), Vol. 20, No. 7 (1998), p. 47.

12. Nichole L. Torres, "No Place Like Home," *Start-ups,* Vol. 12, No. 9 (September 2000), p. 40.

13. Grossmann, *op. cit.*

14. Luisa Kroll, "Entrepreneur Moms," *Forbes,* Vol. 161, No. 10 (May 18, 1998), p. 85.

15. Cynthia E. Griffin, "Kidding Around," *Entrepreneur,* Vol. 24, No. 9 (September, 1996), pp. 56–59.

16. Michael Haritan, "Divide Your Territory," *Independent Business,* Vol. 8, No. 4 (July-August 1997), p. 14.

17. Cynthia E. Griffin, "Home Improvement," *Entrepreneur,* Vol. 24, No. 9 (September 1996), pp. 106–107.

18. Griffin, *op. cit.*

19. Alan Naditz, "Now Hear This!" *Independent Business,* Vol. 9, No. 2 (March-April 1998), p. 22.

20. Roberta Maynard, "Could Your Shop Use a Face-Lift?" *Nation's Business,* Vol. 82, No. 8 (August 1994), p. 47.

Chapter 12

1. Linda Elkins, "Real Numbers Don't Deceive," *Nation's Business,* Vol. 85, No. 3 (March 1997), pp. 51–52.

2. *Ibid.*

3. Investors look to financial projections to determine the sales level necessary for the firm to break even. A firm's break-even point, while important from a financial perspective, is also important to pricing its products or services. The issue of pricing is discussed in Chapter 16.

4. Elkins, *op. cit.*

Chapter 13

1. Jill Andresky Fraser, "The Start-Up Years," *Inc. 500* (Special Issue), 1997, p. 28.

2. Jeffrey E. Sohl, "The Early Stage Equity Markets in the United States," *Venture Capital: An International Journal of Entrepreneurial Finance,* Vol. 1, No. 2 (1999), pp. 101–120.

3. Jeffrey E. Sohl, "The State of the United States Angel Market," report prepared for the Advanced Technology Program, Department of Commerce, September 2001.

4. *The State of Small Business: A Report of the President, 1988,* Appendix B, Office of Advocacy, U.S. Small Business Administration, Washington, DC, 1988; John Freear, Jeffrey E. Sohl, and William E. Wetzel, Jr., *Creating New Capital Markets for Emerging Ventures,* SBAHQ-95-M-1062, report prepared for the Office of Advocacy, U.S. Small Business Administration, Washington, DC, June 1996.

5. Sohl, "The State of the United States Angel Market," *op. cit.*

6. Jill Andresky Fraser, "Money Hunt—Plans for Growth," *Inc.,* Vol. 23, No. 3 (March 2001), p. 56.

7. The ratio of current assets to current liabilities is called the current ratio. The ratio of total debt to total assets is called the debt ratio. These ratios are discussed in Chapter 12.

8. Personal interview with Bill Bailey, former owner of Cherokee Communications.

9. Jill Andresky Fraser, "The Art of the Covenant," *Inc.,* Vol. 19, No. 8 (August 1997), p. 99.

10. Venture Economics/National Venture Capital Association, "Venture Capital Investment Activity Returns to 1999 Levels," May 2, 2001 news release.

11. Jim Hopkins, "Corporate Giants Bankroll Start-Ups," *USA Today,* March 29, 2001, p. 1B.

Chapter 14

1. Arthur Andersen/MassMutual, *American Family Business Survey* (Houston: Arthur Andersen Center for Family Business, 1998).

2. M. Wright, S. Thompson, K. Robbie, and P. Wong, "Management Buy-Outs in the Short and Long Term," in N. C. Churchill, J. Katz, B. Kirchhoff, K. Vesper, and W. Wetzel, Jr. (Eds.), *Frontiers of Entrepreneurship Research* (Wellesley, MA: Babson College, 1992), pp. 302–316.

3. Lisa D. Stein, presentation at the National Forum for Women in Finance, sponsored by the Financial Women's Association of New York, *Fortune,* and the Financial Executive Institute, New York, September 16–17, 1998.

4. S. R. Holmburg, "Value Creation and Capture: Entrepreneurship Harvest and IPO Strategies," in N. C. Churchill, W. D. Bygrave, J. C. Covin, D. L. Sexton, D. P. Slevin, K. H. Vesper, and W. E. Wetzel, Jr. (Eds.), *Frontiers of Entrepreneurship Research* (Wellesley, MA: Babson College, 1991), pp. 191–204.

5. Wayne H. Mikkelson, M. Megan Partch, and Kshitij Shah, "Ownership and Operating Performance of Companies That Go Public," *Journal of Financial Economics,* Vol. 44, No. 3 (1997), pp. 281–307.

6. Stein, *op. cit.*

7. L. Brokaw, "The First Day of the Rest of Your Life," *Inc.,* Vol. 15, No. 5 (1993), p. 144.

8. Nancy B. Upton and J. William Petty, "Funding Options for Transferring the Family-Held Firm: A Comparative Analysis," Working Paper, Baylor University, Waco, TX, 1998.

9. The quotes in this part of the chapter are taken from personal interviews conducted as part of a research study on harvesting, sponsored by the Financial Executive Research Foundation and cited in J. William Petty, John D. Martin, and John Kensinger, *Harvesting the Value of a Privately Held Company* (Morristown, NJ: Financial Executive Research Foundation, 1999). To acquire a copy of the book, write the Financial Executive Research Foundation, Inc., P.O. Box 1938, Morristown, NJ 07962-1938, or call 973-898-4600.

Chapter 15

1. Thomas O. Jones and W. Earl Sasser, Jr., "Why Satisfied Customers Defect," *Harvard Business Review,* Vol. 73, No. 6 (November-December 1995), p. 90.

2. Jerry Fisher, "The Secret's Out," *Entrepreneur,* Vol. 26, No. 5 (May 1998), p. 118.

3. Ralph Kinney Bennett, "What Ever Happened to Service?" *Reader's Digest,* December 1998, pp. 104-109.

4. Roberta Maynard, "The Heat Is On," *Nation's Business,* Vol. 85, No. 10 (October 1997), pp. 18–19.

5. Maxine Lans Retsky, "The ABC's of Protecting Your Package," *Marketing News,* October 9, 1995, p. 12.

6. Something Ventured: An Entrepreneurial Approach to Small Business Management, Episode 115 of a telecourse produced by INTELECOM (818-796-7300).

Chapter 16

1. Chris J. Ketron, "Paying the Price," *Inc.* "Letters to the Editor" feature, Vol. 22, No. 10 (July 2000), p. 25. This letter was from Chris J. Ketron, owner, Gallery House Furniture, Bristol, VA.

2. For an excellent discussion of price setting, see Charles W. Lamb, Jr., Joseph H. Hair, Jr., and Carl McDaniel, *Principles of Marketing* (Cincinnati: South-Western, 1998), Chapter 21.

3. David Streitfeld, "On the Web, Price Tags Blur," *The Washington Post,* September 27, 2000, p. A01.

4. Susan Greco, "The Fraud Bogeyman," http://www.inc.com/articles, February 1, 2001.

5. From material from http://www.creditfyi.com, March 16, 2001.

Chapter 17

1. "The Secrets to Marketing and Sales Success," http://www.smallbizpartners.com/success, May 29, 2001.

2. Robert E. Hite and Wesley J. Johnston, *Managing Salespeople: A Relationship Approach* (Cincinnati: South-Western, 1998), p. 5.

3. Shane McLaughlin, "Paying Cash for Contacts," *Inc.,* Vol. 20, No. 11 (November 1998), p. 107.

4. George Anders, "Internet Advertising, Just Like Its Medium, Is Pushing Boundaries," *The Wall Street Journal,* November 30, 1998, p. A1.

5. Heather Green and Ben Elgin, "Do E-ads Have a Future?" *Business Week E.biz,* January 22, 2001, p. 48.

6. Michelle Kessler, "Software Boots Online Ads Off PC," *USA Today,* April 17, 2001, p. 1B.

7. Adapted from "Ways to Win Business at a Major Trade Show," *Sales & Marketing Management* (February 1996), p. 39.

8. Morgan Murphy, "Guilt Trip," *Forbes,* Vol. 164, No. 2, (July 26, 1999), p. 92.

Chapter 18

1. William W. Horne, "Machine Maker Unhinged by Sales Emphasis," *Inc.,* Vol. 21, No. 3 (March 1999), p. 25.

2. Curtis Wozniak, "Pulling a Mandl," *Forbes,* Vol. 158, No. 10 (October 21, 1996), pp. 18–20.

3. The best-known model is found in Neil C. Churchill and Virginia L. Lewis, "The Five Stages of Small Business Growth," *Harvard Business Review,* Vol. 83, No. 3 (May-June 1983), pp. 30–50. Another study was conducted by Kathleen M. Watson and Gerhard R. Plaschka, "Entrepreneurial Firms: An Examination of Organizational Structure and Management Roles Across Life Cycle Stages," paper presented at the United States Association for Small Business and Entrepreneurship Annual Conference, Baltimore, Maryland, October 13–16, 1993.

4. Sharon Nelton, "Coming to Grips with Growth," *Nation's Business,* Vol. 86, No. 2 (February 1998), pp. 26–32.

5. Amar V. Bhide, *The Origin and Evolution of New Businesses* (New York: Oxford University Press, 2000), p. 315.

6. "Special Report: Rethinking Work," *Business Week,* October 17, 1994, p. 77.

7. Jeffrey Pfeffer and John F. Veiga, "Putting People First for Organizational Success," *Academy of Management Executive,* Vol. 13, No. 2 (May 1999), p. 40.

8. Rodes Fishburne, "More Survival Advice: Communicate," *Forbes ASAP,* April 3, 2000, p. 120.

9. Personal communication from a student of one of the authors.

10. Stephen R. Covey, *The 7 Habits of Highly Effective People* (New York: Simon & Schuster, 1990), pp. 173–179.

11. David E. Gumpert and David P. Boyd, "The Loneliness of the Small Business Owner," *Harvard Business Review,* Vol. 62, No. 6 (November-December 1984), p. 19.

12. Grace Ertel, "An Incubator for Green Start-Ups," *In Business,* Vol. 18, No. 3 (May-June 1996), pp. 21–22.

13. Morten T. Hansen, Henry W. Chesbrough, Nitin Nohria, and Donald N. Sull, "Networked Incubators: Hothouses of the New Economy," *Harvard Business Review,* Vol. 78, No. 5 (September-October 2000), pp. 74–82.

14. John A. Boyd, "A Business Advisor's Guide to Counseling Theories," *Small Business Forum,* Vol. 11, No. 1 (Spring 1993), pp. 52–54.

15. Joanne Gordon, "Calling Dr. Demetria," *Forbes,* Vol. 165, No. 14 (June 12, 2000), p. 212.

16. *Ibid.*

17. Bengt Johannisson and Rein Peterson, *The Personal Networks of Entrepreneurs,* paper presented at the Third Canadian Conference, International Council for Small Business, Toronto, Canada, May 23–25, 1984.

18. Howard Scott, "Getting Help from Your Accountant," *IB Magazine,* Vol. 3, No. 3 (May-June 1992), p. 38.

Chapter 19

1. Karen Southwick, "To Survive," *Forbes ASAP,* April 3, 2000, p. 118.

2. Robert L. Mathis and John H. Jackson, *Human Resource Management* (Cincinnati: South-Western College Publishing, 2000), p. 143.

3. Rochelle Sharpe and Felicia Morton, "Summer Help Wanted: Foreigners Please Apply," *Business Week,* No. 3691 (July 24, 2000), p. 32.

4. Diane P. Burley, "Making Job Descriptions Pay," *Independent Business,* Vol. 5, No. 2 (March-April 1994), pp. 54–56.

5. "Do I Know You?" *Inc. 500,* 1999, p. 211.

6. Gaylen N. Chandler and Glenn M. McEvoy, "Human Resource Management, TQM, and Firm Performance in Small and Medium-Size Enterprises," *Entrepreneurship Theory and Practice,* Vol. 25, No. 1 (Fall 2000), pp. 43–57.

7. Emily Barker, "Hi-test Education," *Inc.,* Vol. 23, No. 10 (July 2001), pp. 81–82.

8. Susan St. John, "More Bang for Your Training Dollars," *Independent Business,* Vol. 10, No. 6 (November-December 1999), p. 17.

9. Rodney Ho and Dan Morse, "Small Business Chiefs Loosen the Reins," *The Wall Street Journal,* December 14, 1998, p. A-2.

10. "Bonus Pay: Buzzword or Bonanza?" *Business Week,* November 14, 1994, pp. 62–63.

11. Stephen Blakely, "Company-Paid Costs Decline Slightly," *Nation's Business,* Vol. 86, No. 2 (February 1998), p. 40.

12. George Bohlander, Scott Snell, and Arthur Sherman, *Managing Human Resources,* 12th ed. (Cincinnati: South-Western College Publishing, 2001), pp. 438–439.

13. Christopher Caggiano, "Perks You Can Afford," *Inc.,* Vol. 19, No. 16 (November 1997), pp. 107–108.

14. Get more information about ESOPs on the Web site of the National Center for Employee Ownership at http://www.nceo.org.

15. For more detailed information on laws protecting employees, see Bohlander, Snell, and Sherman, *op. cit.*

16. Robert K. Robinson, William T. Jackson, Geralyn McClure Franklin, and Diana Hensley, "U.S. Sexual

Harassment Law: Implications for Small Businesses," *Journal of Small Business Management,* Vol. 36, No. 2 (April 1998), p. 7.

Chapter 20

1. Adapted from Leonard L. Berry, A. Parasuraman, and Valarie A. Zeithaml, "Improving Service Quality in America: Lessons Learned," *Academy of Management Executive,* Vol. 8, No. 2 (May 1994), p. 36.

2. Anthony W. Ulwick, "Turn Customer Input into Innovation," *Harvard Business Review,* Vol. 8, No. 1 (January 2002), pp. 91–97.

3. Tom Ehrenfeld, "The New and Improved American Small Business," *Inc.,* Vol. 17, No. 1 (January 1995), pp. 34–48.

4. Diane Brady, "Why Service Stinks," *Business Week,* October 23, 2000, p. 120.

5. James B. Dilworth, *Operations Management: Providing Value in Goods and Services,* 3rd ed. (Orlando, FL: The Dryden Press, 2000), pp. 12–13.

6. Michael Hammer and James Champy, *Reengineering the Corporation* (New York: HarperCollins, 1994), p. 32.

7. "Big Help for the Little Guy," *Fortune Technology Guide,* Vol. 142, No. 12 (Winter 2001), p. 208.

8. "E-I-E-I-E-Farming," *Business Week,* May 1, 2000, p. 202.

9. Mike Hofman, "Western Wear Retailer Unhorsed by Suppliers," *Inc.,* Vol. 21, No. 16 (November 1999), p. 27.

10. Roberta Maynard, "Striking the Right Match," *Nation's Business,* Vol. 84, No. 5 (May 1996), p. 19.

11. For formulas and calculations related to determining the economic order quantity, see an operations management textbook, such as Dilworth, *op. cit.,* pp. 416–420.

Chapter 21

1. Janet Novack, "You Know Who You Are, and So Do We," *Forbes,* Vol. 153, No. 8 (April 11, 1994), pp. 88–92.

2. Lawrence B. Chonko, Terry W. Loe, and Thomas R. Wotruba, "Direct Selling Ethics at the Top: An Industry Audit and Status Report," paper under review for publication, 2001.

3. Justin G. Longenecker, Joseph A. McKinney, and Carlos W. Moore, "Ethical Attitudes, Issues, and Pressures in Small Business," paper presented at the International Council for Small Business Conference, Sydney, Australia, June 1995.

4. Del Jones, "Poll: More Workers Value E-Mail, Voice-Mail Privacy," *USA Today,* March 27, 2000, p. 1B.

5. Pamela Mendels, "The Rise of the Chief Privacy Officer," *Business Week,* http://www.businessweek.com, December 14, 2000.

6. Carl M. Cannon, "Ambushed," *Forbes ASAP,* February 19, 2001, p. 50.

7. Gail Edmondson, Kate Carlisle, Inka Resch, Karen Nickel Anhalt, and Heidi Dawley, "Workers in Bondage," *Business Week,* November 27, 2000, pp. 146–162.

8. For a general review of this topic, see Steven L. Wartick and Donna J. Wood, *International Business and Society* (Malden, Massachusetts: Blackwell, 1998).

9. Nicholas G. Moore, "Ethics: The Way to Do Business," The Sears Lectureship in Business Ethics, Bentley College, Waltham, MA, February 9, 1998.

10. *Ibid.*

11. This possibility is advanced by Michael Allen in "Small-Business Jungle," *The Wall Street Journal,* June 10, 1988, p. 19R.

12. *Ibid.*

13. Jeffrey L. Seglin, "True Lies," *Inc. 500* (Special Issue), 1998, pp. 136–142.

14. *Ibid.*

15. Justin G. Longenecker, Joseph A. McKinney, and Carlos W. Moore, "Egoism and Independence: Entrepreneurial Ethics," *Organizational Dynamics,* Vol. 16, No. 3 (Winter 1988), pp. 64–72.

16. These differences were significant at the .05 level.

17. These differences were significant at the .05 level.

18. Moore, *op. cit.*

19. Jan Cienski, "Faith Jostles with Profits for Some Christian Businesses," *Waco Tribune-Herald,* May 24, 1997.

20. *Ibid.;* and "The Best 100 Companies to Work For," *Fortune,* Vol. 143, No. 1 (January 8, 2001), pp. 148–168.

21. Shaun F. O'Malley, "Ethical Cultures—Corporate and Personal," *Ethics Journal* (Ethics Resource Center, Washington, DC), Winter 1995, p. 9.

22. John Rutledge, "The Portrait on My Office Wall," *Forbes,* Vol. 158, No. 15 (December 30, 1996), p. 78.

23. Sample codes of ethics can be obtained from the Ethics Resource Center, Inc., 1025 Connecticut Avenue, N.W., Washington, DC 22036.

24. Francis J. Daly, "Rules and Values Are Ethical Allies," *Center for Business Ethics News* (Bentley College, Waltham, Massachusetts), Vol. 6, No. 2 (Summer 1998), p. 7.

25. Harvey Meyer, "Helping Employees to Help Others," *Nation's Business,* Vol. 87, No. 3 (March 1999), pp. 48–51; and Jane Larson, "2 E. Valley Businesses Win Awards," *The Arizona Republic,* June 9, 1999, p. E2.

26. Meyer, *op. cit.,* p. 50.

27. Michael Kinsman, "Corporate Caring," *The San Diego Union-Tribune,* December 15, 1997, p. C-1.

28. *Ibid.*

29. "Daily Points of Light Award Winner," October 27, 1998 (The Points of Light Foundation, 1400 I Street NW, Suite 800, Washington, DC 20005).

30. Kenneth E. Aupperle, F. Bruce Simmons III, and William Acar, "An Empirical Investigation into How

Entrepreneurs View Their Social Responsibilities," paper presented at the Academy of Management Meetings, San Francisco, California, August 1990.

31. Thea Singer, "Can Business Still Save the World?," *Inc.,* Vol. 23, No. 5 (April 2001), p. 65.

32. Priscilla Elsass, "The Cost of Illegal Business Practices," *Academy of Management Executive,* Vol. 12, No. 1 (1998), pp. 87–88.

Chapter 22

1. See, for example, Charles Horngren and Tom Harrison, *Principles of Accounting,* 4th ed. (Englewood Cliffs, N.J.: Prentice-Hall, Inc., 2001).

2. Jack D. Baker and John A. Marts, "Internal Control for Protection and Profits," *Small Business Forum,* Vol. 8, No. 2 (Fall 1990), p. 29.

3. For example, Dun & Bradstreet publishes annually a set of 14 key financial ratios for 125 lines of business. RMA, the Association of Bank Loan and Credit Officers, publishes a set of 16 key ratios for over 350 types of businesses. In both cases, the ratios are classified by industry and by firm size to provide a basis for more meaningful comparisons.

4. When we computed Bates's operating income return on investment earlier, we found it to be be 10.87 percent. Now it is 10.85 percent. The difference is the result of rounding.

Chapter 23

1. Jill Andresky Fraser, "The Art of Cash Management," *Inc.,* Vol. 20, No. 14 (October, 1998), p. 124.

2. Accruals are not considered in terms of managing working capital. Accrued expenses, although shown as a short-term liability, primarily result from the accountant's effort to match revenues and expenses. There is little that could be done to "manage accruals."

3. "Cash Flow: Who's in Charge," *Inc.,* Vol. 15, No. 11 (November 1993), p. 140.

4. If a project has a positive (negative) net present value, it will always have an internal rate of return above (below) the cost of capital.

5. Roger G. Ibbotson and Rex A. Sinquefield, *Stocks, Bonds, Bills and Inflation: 2000 Yearbook* (Chicago: Dow Jones–Irwin, 2001).

Chapter 24

1. Translated by Arthur W. H. Adkins from the Greek text of Solon's poem "Prosperity, Justice and the Hazards of Life," in M. L. West (Ed.), *Iambi et Elegi Gracci ante Alexandrum Canttati,* Vol. 2 (Oxford: Clarendon Press, 1972).

2. Peter Bernstein, *Against the Gods, the Remarkable Story of Risk* (New York: John Wiley & Sons, Inc. 1998), p. 1.

3. Emmett J. Vaughan and Theresa M. Vaughan, *Fundamentals of Risk and Insurance,* 8th ed. (New York: John Wiley & Sons, 1998), p. 5.

4. *Ibid.*

5. From material from http://www.shopliftersalternative.org, May 2001.

6. Joe Dacy II, "They Come to Steal," *Independent Business,* Vol. 3, No. 5 (September-October 1992), pp. 24–29.

7. Pamela Rohland, "Caught in the Act," *Business Start-Ups,* Vol. 12, No. 6 (June 2000).

8. Robert T. Gray "Clamping Down on Worker Crime," *Nation's Business,* Vol. 85, No. 4 (April 1997), pp. 44–45.

9. Rohland, *op.cit.*

10. These observations and the quote come from Dale D. Buss, "Small Firms Are Hit Hard by Rising Health Premiums," *The Wall Street Journal,* November 17, 1998, p. B2.

11. John S. de Mott, "Think Like a Risk Manager," *Nation's Business,* Vol. 83, No. 6 (June 1995), pp. 30–31.

12. Michael Barrier, "Opportunity's Many Faces," *Nation's Business,* Vol. 85, No. 3 (March 1997), pp. 38–39.

13. Abby Livingston, "Insuring Your Earning Power," *Nation's Business,* Vol. 85, No. 4 (April 1997), pp. 75–76.

Epilogue

1. Arnold C. Cooper and Kendall W. Artz, "Determinants of Satisfaction for Entrepreneurs," *Journal of Business Venturing,* Vol. 10 (1995), pp. 439–457.

2. Stephanie Fitz Ariel, "Letters," *Inc.,* Vol. 22, No. 16 (November 2000), p. 22.

3. Jim Hopkins, "Serial Entrepreneur Strikes Again at Age 70," *USA Today,* August 15, 2000, pp. 1B–2B.

4. Brigid McMenamin, "Close-Knit," *Forbes,* Vol. 166, No. 16 (December 25, 2000), pp. 134–137.

5. Paul Rerucha, Letters, *Inc.,* Vol. 22, No. 16 (November 2000), p. 22.

6. Personal interview with Ed Bonneau.

7. Ilan Mochari, "What Would You Do Differently?" *Inc.,* Vol. 23, No. 3 (March 2001), p. 65.

8. *Ibid.,* p. 67.

9. Personal interview with Bernard Rapaport.

10. Stephen R. Covey, *The Seven Habits of Highly Effective People* (New York: Simon and Schuster, 1989), pp. 106–142.

11. Sean M. Lyden, "Perfect Balance," *Start-Ups,* January 2001, p. 42.

12. Pete Wakeman, "The Good Life: How to Get It," *Inc.,* Vol. 23, No. 2 (February 2001), p. 47.

Note: Updated information on the Web addresses listed can be found on our Web site at http://longenecker.swcollege.com.

A.L.I. Technologies, Inc. **http://www.alitech.com**
Adams Manufacturing **http://www.adamsmfg.com**
Advertising Age **http://www.adage.com**
Alvaka Networks **http://www.alvaka.com**
Amazon.com **http://www.amazon.com**
American Association of Home-Based Businesses **http://www.aahbb.org**
American Cedar, Inc. **http://www.americancedar.com**
American Express **http://www.americanexpress.com**
American Society for Quality **http://www.asq.org**
APL Logistics **http://www.apllogistics.com**
Aquatic and Wetland Company **http://www.aquaticandwetland.com**
Atlantic Publication Group, Inc. **http://www.atlanticpublicationgrp.com**
Auntie Anne's **http://www.auntieannes.com**

Baazee.com **http://www.baazee.com**
Basic Guide to Exporting, A **http://www.unzo.com/basicguide**
BBH Exhibits, Inc. **http://www.bbhinc.net**
Benolds **http://www.benolds.com**
Best Cellars, Inc. **http://www.bestcellars.com**
Better Business Bureau **http://www.bbb.org**
Big Dog Motorcycles **http://www.bigdogmotorcycles.com**
Big Emerging Markets, U.S. Department of Commerce **http://www.ita.doc.gov/bems**
Bite Footwear **http://www.bitefootwear.com**
Blue Marlin Corporation **http://www.bluemarlincorp.com**
Blue Note **http://www.bluenote.net**
Bo Peep Productions **http://www.bopeepproductions.com**
BooksonBiz.com **http://www.booksonbiz.com**
Boston Book Company **http://www.rarebook.com**
Bplans.com **http://www.bplans.com**
British Franchising Association **http://www.british-franchise.org**
Build-A-Bear Workshops **http://www.buildabear.com**
Business Incubation Group **http://www.bizincu.com**
Business Marketing Group, Inc. **http://www.bmginc.com**
Business Mediation Associates **http://www.business-mediation.com**

Cambria Environmental Technology **http://www.cambria-environment.com**
CareerBuilder, Inc. **http://www.careerbuilder.com**
Carmelo's Italian Restaurants **http://www.carmelositalrest.com**
CCI Triad **http://www.ccitriad.com**
Celestis **http://www.celestis.com**
Certified Business Brokers **http://www.certifiedbb.com**
Certified Fraud Examiners **http://www.cfenet.com**
Chicago Manufacturing Center **http://www.cmcusa.org**
Chick-fil-A **http://www.chick-fil-a.com**
Cindy Rowe Auto Glass **http://www.cindyrowe.com**
City Laundry and Drycleaning Company **http://www.citylaundry.com**
CitySoft **http://www.citysoft.com**
Clean Air Gardening Company **http://www.cleanairgardening.com**
Cleaner by Nature **http://www.cleanerbynature.com**
Coactive Networks **http://www.coactive.com**
Cold Stone Creamery **http://www.coldstonecreamery.com**
Commercial Angles **http://www.commercialangles.com**
Consumer Product Safety Commission **http://www.cpsc.gov**
Creative Producers Group **http://www.getcreative.com**
Credit FYI **http://www.creditfyi.com**
Creditworthy **http://www.creditworthy.com**
Curves for Women **http://www.curvesforwomen.com**
CypherWire **http://www.cypherwire.com**

Dahlgren & Co. **http://www.sunflowerseed.com**
Dain Rauscher Inc. **http://www.dainrauscher.com**
DataMark **http://www.data-mark.com**
Delaware Valley Reinvestment Fund **http://www.efgp.org**
Delia's **http://www.delias.com**
Dell Computer Corporation **http://www.dell.com**
Department of Commerce **http://www.unzco.com/basicguide**
Diner's Club **http://www.dinersclub.com**
Dodge-Regupol, Inc. **http://www.regupol.com**
Dun & Bradstreet **http://www.dnb.com**
Dunkin' Donuts **http://www.dunkindonuts.com**

E-Stamp Corporation **http://www.stamps.com**
Eastex Farms **http://www.tx-marketeers.com/Eastexfarms**
eBay **http://www.ebay.com**
Edler Group **http://www.edlergroup.com**
eHatchery **http://www.ehatchery.com**
Entertainment Earth **http://www.entertainmentearth.com**
Entex Information Services **http://www.entex.com**
Entrepreneur Magazine **http://www.entrepreneurmag.com**
Equifax, Inc. **http://www.equifax.com**
Euromoney Magazine **http://www.euromoney.com**
Ex Officio Inc. **http://www.exofficio.com**
Experian **http://www.experian.com**

FastSigns **http://fastsigns.com**
Federal Trade Commission **http://www.ftc.gov**
FitnessLink **http://www.fitnesslink.com**
Fizzion **http://www.fizzion.com**
Florist.com **http://www.florist.com**
Flowers & Partners **http://www.flowers-partners.com**
Foreign Corrupt Practices Act **http://www.usdoj.gov/criminal/fraud/fcpa**
Franchise Connections **http://www.franchiseconnections.com**
FreeMarkets, Inc. **http://www.freemarkets.com**
Frieda's, Inc. **http://www.friedas.com**
FullArmor Corporation **http://www.fullarmor.com**
FunMail **http://www.wemailsmiles.com**

Gamblin Artist's Oil Colors **http://www.gamblincolors.com**
Garden-ville **http://www.garden-ville.com**
GEMdesign **http://www.gemdesign.bigstep.com**
Give Something Back **http://www.givesomethingback.com**

Glow Dog, Inc. **http://www.glowdog.com**
GoCard **http://www.gocard.com**
Golden Circle Loan Guarantee Fund **http://www.ci.des-moines.ia.us**
Great American Merchandise and Events **http://www.duckrace.com**
Great Harvest Bread Company **http://www.greatharvest.com**
GreenMan Technologies, Inc. **http://www.greenman-tech.com**
Grunder Landscaping Company **http://www.grunderlandscaping.com**

Harry W. Schwartz Bookshops **http://www.schwartzbooks.com**
Hatteras Yachts, Inc. **http://www.hatterasyachts.com**
HeadBlade **http://www.headblade.com**
Heritage Partners **http://www.heritagepartnersinc.com**
Hi-Shear Technology **http://www.hstc.com**
Hicks, Muse, Tate, & Furst **http://www.bus.utexas.edu/HMTFcenter**
Hire Quality, Inc. **http://www.hirequality.com**
HolyBears, Inc. **http://www.holybears.com**
HotJobs.com **http://www.hotjobs.com**
Hubbard & Revo-Cohen **http://www.hrccentral.com**

IBM **http://www.ibm.com**
Idealab **http://www.idealab.com**
Ikea **http://www.ikea.com**
Image Stream Internet Solutions **http://www.imagestream-is.com**
Inc. Magazine **http://www.inc.com**
Institute of Management Consultants **http://www.imcusa.org**
Integrated Management Resources **http://www.integratedmanagementresources.com**
Integrity Industries, Inc. **http://www.integrityindustries.com**
International Franchise Association **http://www.franchise.org**
International Franchising **http://www.franchiseintl.com**
International Organization for Standardization **http://www.iso.ch**
Internet Corporation for Assigned Names and Numbers **http://www.icann.org**
Internet Fraud Watch **http://www.fraud.org**
InterNic **http://www.internic.net**

Johnson Research & Development **http://www.supersoaker.com**

KaBloom, Ltd. **http://www.kabloom.com**
Ken's Hatchery and Fish Farms **http://www.kens-fishfarm.com**
Kinnear Dental Laboratories **http://www.kinneardentallab.com**
Kirkham Motorsports **http://www.kirkhammotorsports.com**
Kwik Kopy Printing **http://www.kwikkopy.com**

Landstar **http://www.landstar.com**
Le Travel Store **http://letravelstore.com**
Let's Talk Cellular & Wireless **http://www.letstalk.com**
Library of Congress **http://www.loc.gov**
Loranger Manufacturing Corporation **http://www.loranger-mfg.com**
Lori Bonn Design, Inc. **http://www.loribonn.com**
Loss Prevention Specialists **http://www.lossprevention.com**

MasterCard **http://www.mastercard.com**
Mayfield Fund **http://www.mayfield.com**
McDonald's **http://www.mcdonalds.com**
Mental Headgear **http://www.mentalheadgear.com**
Mergerstat **http://www.mergerstat.com**
Meyer Technologies, Inc. **http://www.meyertechnologies.com**
MICROS Systems, Inc. **http://www.micros.com**
Microsoft **http://www.microsoft.com**
Milliken and Company **http://www.milliken.com**
MindPrime, Inc. **http://www.mindprime.com**
MIT Enterprise Forum **http://web.mit.edu/entforum/www**
Monster.com **http://www.monster.com**
Mooney Farms **http://www.mooneyfarms.com**
MSS Global **http://www.mssretail.com**

NameLab **http://www.namelab.com**
Namesecure **http://www.namesecure.com**
National Association of Professional Employer Organizations **http://www.napeo.org**
Navigator Systems Inc. **http://www.navigatorsystems.com**
Net Perceptions **http://www.netperceptions.com**
NetForce Technologies **http://www.netforce-tech.com**
NetReflector InstantSurvey **http://www.netreflector.com**
Network Solutions **http://www.netsol.com**
New Pig Corporation **http://www.newpig.com**
North American Industry Classification System **http://www.naics.com**
North American Securities Administrators Association **http://www.nasaa.org**
Nouveau Contemporary Goods **http:// www.nouveaubaltimore.com**

OffRoad Capital **http://www.offroadcapital.com**
1-800-CONTACTS **http://www.1800contacts.com**
Oracle Small Business **http://www.oraclesmallbusiness.com**
Oregon Chai **http://www.oregonchai.com**
Outpost.com **http://www.outpost.com**

PAR Educational Technologies **http://www.partec.com**
PC Connection **http://www.pcconnection.com**
Peace Frogs **http://www.peacefrogs.com**
Peachtree **http://www.peachtree.com**
Persistence Software **http://www.persistence.com**
Peter Pan Bus Lines **http://www.peterpan-bus.com**
Petra Technology Group **http://www.petragroup.com**
Physician Sales and Service, Inc. **http://www.pssd.com**

Playcentric.com http://www.playcentric.com
Points of Light Foundation http://www.pointsoflight.org
PostNet http://www.postnet.net
Power Paper Ltd. http://www.powerpaper.com
Prairie Frontier http://www.prairiefrontier.com
Presto Galaxy Suction Cups, Inc. http://www.suctioncupsinc.com
Promotional Products Association International http://www.ppa.org
ProWorth http://www.proworth.com

QuickBooks http://www.quickbooks.com
QuickFarm Incorporated http://www.quickfarm.com

Raging Bull http://www.raging bull.lycos.com
Razorfish http://www.razorfish.com
RB Rubber Products, Inc. http://www.rbrubber.com
Record Technology http://recordtech.com
Rentons' International Stationery, Inc. http://www.rentons.com
Robert Morris Associates http://www.rmahq.org
Roto Zip Tool Corporation http://www.rotozip.com

Sales & Marketing Management http://www.salesandmarketing.com
SBA, Office of International Trade http://www.sba.gov/oit
ScrubaDub http://www.scrubadub.com
Securities and Exchange Commission http://www.sec.gov/info/smallbus
Sewell Village Cadillac http://www.sewell.com
Ships-for-sale.com http://www.ships-for-sale.com
Shoebuy.com http://www.shoebuy.com
Small Business Administration http://www.sba.gov
"Small Business School," The Series http://smallbusinessschool.org
Southwest Securities http://www.southwestsecurities.com
SOYOUWANNA.com http://www.soyouwanna.com
Spectrum Signal Processing, Inc. http://www.spectrumsignal.com
Sportsline.com http://www.sportsline.com
Spun.com http://www.spun.com
Staffcentrix http://www.staffcentrix.com
Standard & Poor's http://www.standardandpoors.com
StockMaster.com Inc. http://www.stockmaster.com
Subway http://www.subway.com
Sudbury Soup Company http://www.sudburysoup.com
Sun Tzu Security http://www.suntzu.net
Sundance Catalog http://sundancecatalog.com
SurveySite, Inc. http://www.surveysite.com
Sustainable Harvest Inc. http://www.sustainableharvest.com
Sutter Hill Ventures http://www.sutterhillventures.com
Synergy Investment http://www.synergyinv.com

T. Shipley http://www.tshipley.com
Taco Cabana http://www.tacocabana.com
Talent Plus http://www.talentplus.com
Technology Capital Network http://www.tcnmit.org
The Franchise Company http://www.thefranchisecompany.com
The MAiZE http://www.cornfieldmaize.com
The Roasterie, Inc. http:// www.theroasterie.com
Three Dog Bakery http://www.threedog.com
TradePort http://www.tradeport.org
TransUnion Corporation http://www.tuc.com
Triple Crown Sports http://triplecrownsports.com
Two Men and a Truck http://www.twomen.com
Ty Inc. http://www.ty.com

U.S. Patent and Trademark Office http://www.uspto.gov
Ukrop's Super Markets http://www.ukrops.com
Universal Tours http://www.univertour.qpg.com
University of Maryland Dingman Center for Entrepreneurship http://www.bmgt.umd.edu/dingman
US Signs, Inc. http://www.ussigns.com
UTStarcom, Inc. http://www.utstar.com

Vellus Products Inc. http://www.vellus.com
Virtual Growth http://www.virtualgrowth.com
VISA http://www.visa.com

Wal-Mart Stores, Inc. http://www.walmart.com
Walkabout Travel Gear http://walkabouttravelgear.com
Wall Street Journal http://www.startup.wsj.com
WebWasher http://www.webwasher.com
Wee Care Academy, Inc. http://www.weecareinc.com
West Coast Roofing and Waterproofing Company http://www.westcoastroofing.com
Wild Planet Toys Inc. http://www.wildplanet.com
Wilkirson-Hatch-Bailey http://www.wilkirsonhatchbailey.com
World Trade Magazine http://www.worldtrademag.com

XSAg.com http://www.xsag.com

Zane's Cycles http://www.zanescycles.com
Zero Stage Capital http://www.zerostage.com

ABC method a system of classifying items in inventory by relative value.

acceptance sampling the use of a random, representative portion to determine the acceptability of an entire lot.

accounting return on investment technique a capital budgeting technique that evaluates a capital expenditure based on the average annual after-tax profits relative to the average book value of an investment.

accounts payable (trade credit) financing provided by a supplier of inventory to a given company.

accounts receivable the amount of credit extended to customers that is currently outstanding.

accounts receivable turnover the number of times accounts receivable "roll over" during a year.

accrual-basis accounting a method of accounting that matches revenues when they are earned against the expenses associated with those revenues, no matter when they are paid.

accrued expenses short-term liabilities that have been incurred but not paid.

accumulated depreciation total depreciation expense taken over the assets' life.

acid-test ratio (quick ratio) a measure of a company's liquidity that excludes inventories.

administrative entrepreneur an entrepreneur who oversees the operation of an ongoing business.

advertising the impersonal presentation of a business idea through mass media.

advisory council a group that functions like a board of directors but acts only in an advisory capacity.

affiliation a form of Web site linkage whereby other Web sites gain visitors from the sponsoring firm.

after-tax cash flows from operations cash flows generated from operating a business, calculated by adding back to net income depreciation expense and interest expense.

agency power the ability of any one partner to legally bind the other partners.

agents/brokers intermediaries that do not take title to the goods they distribute.

aging schedule a categorization of accounts receivable based on the length of time they have been outstanding.

area developers individuals or firms that obtain the legal right to open several franchised outlets in a given area.

artisan entrepreneur a person with primarily technical skills and little business knowledge who starts a business.

asset-based loan a line of credit secured by working-capital assets.

asset-based valuation approach the determination of the value of a business by estimating the value of its assets.

attitude an enduring opinion based on knowledge, feeling, and behavioral tendency.

attractive small firm a small firm that provides substantial profits to its owner.

attribute inspection the determination of product acceptability based on whether it will or will not work.

auction sites Web-based businesses offering participants the ability to list products for bidding.

average collection period the average time it takes a firm to collect its accounts receivable.

average pricing an approach in which total cost for a given period is divided by quantity sold in that period to set a price.

bad-debt ratio the ratio of bad debts to credit sales.

bait advertising an insincere offer to sell a product or service at a very low price, used to lure customers in so that they can be switched later to a more expensive product or service.

balance sheet a financial report showing a firm's assets, liabilities, and owners' equity at a specific point in time.

banner ads advertisements that appear across a Web page, most often as moving rectangular strips.

batch manufacturing a type of manufacturing operation that is intermediate (between job shops and repetitive manufacturing) in volume and variety of products.

benchmarking the process of studying the products, services, and practices of other firms and using the insights gained to improve quality internally.

benefit variables specific characteristics that distinguish market segments according to the benefits sought by customers.

bill of lading a document indicating that a product has been shipped and the title to that product has been transferred.

board of directors the governing body of a corporation, elected by the stockholders.

brand a verbal and/or symbolic means of identifying a product.

break-even point sales volume at which total sales revenue equals total costs.

breakdown process (chain-ratio method) a forecasting method that begins with a macro-level variable and works down to the sales forecast.

brick-and-mortar store the traditional physical store from which businesses have historically operated.

budget a document that expresses future plans in monetary terms.

build-up LBO a leveraged buyout involving the purchase of a group of similar companies with the intent of making the firms into one larger company.

build-up process a forecasting method in which all potential buyers in the various submarkets are identified and then the estimated demand is added up.

business format franchising a franchise arrangement whereby the franchisee obtains an entire marketing system and ongoing management guidance from the franchisor.

business incubator a facility that provides shared space, services, and management assistance to new businesses.

business interruption insurance coverage of lost income and certain other expenses while the business is being rebuilt.

business model a group of shared characteristics, behaviors, and goals that a firm follows in a particular business situation.

business plan a document that sets out the basic idea underlying a business and related startup considerations.

business policies basic statements that provide guidance for managerial decision making.

business-to-business (B2B) model a business model based on selling to business customers electronically.

business-to-consumer (B2C) model a business model based on selling to final consumers electronically.

bust-up LBO a leveraged buyout involving the purchase of a company with the intent of selling off its assets.

buyout purchasing an existing business.

C corporation an ordinary corporation, taxed by the federal government as a separate legal entity.

capital budgeting analysis an analytical method that helps managers make decisions about long-term investments.

capital gains and losses gains and losses incurred from sales of property that are not a part of the firm's regular business operations.

cash-basis accounting a method of accounting that reports transactions only when cash is received or a payment is made.

cash budget a planning document strictly concerned with the receipt and payment of dollars.

cash conversion period the time required to convert paid-for inventories and accounts receivable into cash.

cash flow–based valuation approach the determination of the value of a business by comparing the expected and required rates of return on the investment.

cash flows from assets after-tax cash flows generated from operations less the firm's investments in assets.

cash flows from financing cash flows generated by payments made to or received by a firm's investors or creditors.

chain of command the official, vertical channel of communication in an organization.

channel of distribution the system of relationships established to guide the movement of a product.

chattel mortgage a loan for which items of inventory or other moveable property serve as collateral.

Civil Rights Act legislation prohibiting discrimination based on race, color, religion, sex, or national origin.

code of ethics official standards of employee behavior formulated by a firm.

cognitive dissonance the anxiety that occurs when a customer has second thoughts immediately following a purchase.

coinsurance clause part of an insurance policy that requires the insured to maintain a specific level of coverage or to assume a portion of any loss.

commercial property insurance coverage that protects against losses associated with damage to or loss of property.

common carriers transportation intermediaries available for hire to the general public.

community-based financial institution a lender that provides financing to small businesses in low-income communities for the purpose of encouraging economic development.

competitive advantage a benefit that exists when a firm has a product or service that is seen by its target market as better than those of competitors.

compound value of a dollar the increasing value of a dollar over time resulting from interest earned both on the original dollar and on the interest received in prior periods.

consumer credit financing granted by retailers to individuals who purchase for personal or family use.

consumerism a movement that stresses the needs of consumers and the importance of serving them honestly and well.

content/information-based model a business model in which the Web site provides information but not the ability to buy or sell products and services.

continuous quality improvement a constant and dedicated effort to improve quality.

contract carriers transportation intermediaries that contract with individual shippers.

control chart a graphic illustration of the limits used in statistical process control.

cookie a data file that is electronically sent to the customer's computer when other requested materials are downloaded from an Internet Web site.

copyright the exclusive right of a creator to reproduce, publish, perform, display, or sell his or her own works.

core competencies those resources and capabilities that provide a firm with a competitive advantage over its rivals.

corporate charter a document that establishes a corporation's existence.

corporate refugee a person who leaves big business to go into business for himself or herself.

corporation a business organization that exists as a legal entity and provides limited liability to its owners.

corrective maintenance repairs necessary to restore equipment or a facility to good condition.

cost-based strategy a plan of action that requires a firm to be the lowest-cost producer within its market.

cost of capital investors' and owners' required rate of return on their investment.

cost of goods sold the cost of producing or acquiring goods or services to be sold by a firm.

counterfeit activity the unauthorized use of intellectual property.

credit an agreement between a buyer and a seller that provides for delayed payment for a product or service.

credit bureaus privately owned organizations that summarize a number of firms' credit experiences with particular individuals.

credit insurance coverage that protects against abnormal bad-debt losses.

cross-border acquisition purchase by a business in one country of a company located in another country.

cultural configuration the total culture of a family firm, consisting of the firm's business, family, and governance patterns.

culture behavioral patterns and values that characterize a group of consumers in a target market.

current assets (gross working capital) assets that can be converted into cash within a company's operating cycle.

current debt (short-term liabilities) borrowed money that must be repaid within 12 months.

current ratio a measure of a company's relative liquidity, determined by dividing current assets by current liabilities.

customer profile a description of potential customers in a target market.

cybercrime criminal activity on the Internet.

cycle counting a system of counting different segments of the physical inventory at different times during the year.

D

debt capital business financing provided by creditors.

debt ratio a measure of the fraction of a firm's assets that are financed by debt, determined by dividing total debt by total assets.

delegation of authority granting to subordinates the right to act or make decisions.

demographic variables specific characteristics that describe customers and their purchasing power.

depreciable assets assets whose value declines, or depreciates, over time.

depreciation expense costs related to a fixed asset, such as a building or equipment, distributed over its useful life.

design patent registered protection for the appearance of a product and its inseparable parts.

differentiation-based strategy a plan of action designed to provide a product or service with unique attributes that are valued by consumers.

direct channel a distribution system without intermediaries.

direct forecasting a forecasting method in which sales is the predicting variable.

direct loan money provided directly by the Small Business Administration.

disability insurance coverage that protects against the disability of a firm's partner or other key employee.

disclosure document a detailed statement provided to a prospective franchisee, containing such information as the franchisor's finances, experience, size, and involvement in litigation.

discounted cash flow (DCF) technique a capital budgeting technique that compares the present value of future cash flows with the cost of the initial investment.

dishonesty insurance coverage that protects against employees' crimes.

distribution physically moving products and establishing intermediary relationships to support such movement.

double-entry system a self-balancing accounting system that uses journals and ledgers.

dual distribution a distribution system that involves more than one channel.

due diligence the exercise of prudence, such as would be expected of a reasonable person, in the careful evaluation of a business opportunity.

dynamic pricing strategy charging more than the standard price when the customer's profile suggests that the higher price will be accepted.

e-commerce the paperless exchange of business information via the Internet.

e-mail promotion advertising delivered by means of electronic mail.

earnings before interest, taxes, depreciation, and amortization (EBITDA) a company's earnings before subtraction of interest expense, taxes, and noncash expenses, such as depreciation and amortization.

earnings multiple a ratio determined by dividing a firm's value by its annual earnings; also called *value-to-earnings ratio*.

economic order quantity (EOQ) the quantity to purchase in order to minimize total inventory costs.

economic risk the probability that a government will mismanage its economy and thereby change the business environment in ways that hinder the performance of firms operating there.

economies of scale efficiencies that result from expansion of production.

elastic demand demand that changes significantly when there is a change in the price of the product.

elasticity of demand the degree to which a change in price affects the quantity demanded.

Electronic Customer Relationship Marketing (eCRM) an electronically based system that emphasizes customer relationships.

employee leasing the "renting" of personnel from an organization that handles paperwork and administers benefits for those employees.

employee stock ownership plan (ESOP) a method by which a firm is sold either in part or in total to its employees.

employer's liability insurance coverage that protects against lawsuits brought by employees who suffer injury.

empowerment giving employees authority to make decisions or take actions on their own.

Empowerment Zone/Enterprise Communities (EZ/EC) a program of the federal government that provides financial support to local communities for the purpose of economic advancement.

enterprise zones state-designated areas that are established to bring jobs to economically deprived regions through regulatory and tax incentives.

entrepreneur a person who starts and/or operates a business.

entrepreneurial opportunity a value-creating innovation with market potential.

entrepreneurial team two or more people who work together as entrepreneurs.

environmentalism the effort to protect and preserve the environment.

equipment loan an installment loan from a seller of machinery used by a business.

ethical imperialism the belief that the ethical standards of one's own country can be applied universally.

ethical issues questions of right and wrong.

ethical relativism the belief that ethical standards are subject to local interpretation.

European Union (EU) an organization whose purpose is to ensure free trade among member countries.

evaluative criteria the features of a product or service that customers use to compare brands.

evoked set a group of brands that a customer is both aware of and willing to consider as a solution to a purchase problem.

exchange rates the value of one country's currency relative to that of another country.

executive summary a section of the business plan that conveys a clear and concise overall picture of the proposed venture.

exiting (harvesting) the process used by entrepreneurs and investors to reap the value of a business when they get out of it.

expense-based model a business model that focuses on reducing costs.

experience curve efficiencies per-unit savings gained from the repeated production of the same good.

exporting selling products produced in the home country to customers in another country.

external equity capital that comes from the owners' investment in a firm.

external locus of control a belief that one's life is controlled more by luck or fate than by one's own efforts.

factoring obtaining cash by selling accounts receivable to another firm.

Fair Labor Standards Act (FLSA) federal law that establishes a minimum wage and provides for overtime pay.

Family and Medical Leave Act legislation that assures employees of unpaid leave for childbirth or other family needs.

family business a company in which two or more members of the same family share ownership or work together in its operation.

family council an organized group of family members who gather periodically to discuss family-related business issues.

family retreat a gathering of family members, usually at a remote location, to discuss family business matters.

favorable financial leverage the benefit gained by investing at a rate of return that is greater than the interest rate on a loan.

financial acquisition a purchase in which the value of the business is based on the stand-alone cash-generating potential of the firm being acquired.

financial leverage the use of debt in financing a firm's assets.

financial plan a section of the business plan that provides an account of the new firm's financial needs and sources of financing and a projection of its revenues, costs, and profits.

financial ratios restatements of selected income statement and balance sheet data in relative terms.

financial statements (accounting statements) reports of a firm's financial performance and resources, including an income statement and a balance sheet.

financing costs the amount of interest owed to lenders on borrowed money.

firewall a combination of hardware and software designed to keep unauthorized outsiders from tampering with a computer system.

fixed asset turnover a measure of the relationship of sales to fixed assets.

fixed assets relatively permanent assets intended for use in the business, such as plant and equipment.

focus strategy a plan of action that isolates an enterprise from competitors and other market forces by targeting a restricted market segment.

follow-the-leader pricing strategy using a particular competitor as a model in setting prices.

foreign licensing allowing a company in another country to purchase the right to manufacture and sell a company's products in international markets.

foreign refugee a person who leaves her or his native country and becomes an entrepreneur in a new country.

founder an entrepreneur who brings a new firm into existence.

franchise the privileges conveyed in a franchise contract.

franchise contract the legal agreement between franchisor and franchisee.

franchisee an entrepreneur whose power is limited by a contractual relationship with a franchisor.

franchising a marketing system involving a legal agreement, whereby the franchisee conducts business according to terms specified by the franchisor.

franchisor the party in a franchise contract that specifies the methods to be followed and the terms to be met by the other party.

free-flow pattern a flexible retail store layout that is visually appealing and gives customers freedom of movement.

fringe benefits supplements to compensation, designed to be attractive and beneficial to employees.

general environment the broad environment, encompassing factors that influence most businesses in a society.

general liability insurance coverage that protects against lawsuits brought by customers.

general partner a partner in a limited partnership who has unlimited personal liability.

general-purpose equipment machines that serve many functions in the production process.

globalization the expansion of international business, promoted by converging market preferences, falling trade barriers, and the integration of national economies.

greenfield venture a wholly owned subsidiary formed "from scratch" in another country.

grid pattern a block-like retail store layout that provides for good merchandise exposure and simplifies security and cleaning.

gross fixed assets original cost of depreciable assets before any depreciation expense has been taken.

gross profit sales less the cost of goods sold.

growth-based model a business model that focuses on customer growth for profitability.

growth trap a cash shortage resulting from rapid growth.

guaranty loan money provided by a private lender, with the Small Business Administration guaranteeing repayment.

headhunter a search firm that locates qualified candidates for executive positions.

high-potential venture (gazelle) a small firm that has great prospects for growth.

hits Internet connections made to a Web site.

home-based business a business that maintains its primary facility in the residence of its owner.

importing selling goods produced in another country to buyers in the home country.

income statement (profit and loss statement) a financial report showing the profit or loss from a firm's operations over a given period of time.

indirect channel a distribution system with one or more intermediaries.

indirect forecasting a forecasting method in which variables are related to sales to project future sales.

industry environment the combined forces that directly impact a given firm and its competitors.

inelastic demand demand that does not change significantly when there is a change in the price of the product.

informal venture capital funds provided by wealthy private individuals (business angels) to high-risk ventures.

initial public offering (IPO) the first sale of shares of a company's stock to the public.

inspection the examination of a product to determine whether it meets quality standards.

inspection standard a specification of a desired quality level and allowable tolerances.

installment account a line of credit that requires a down payment, with the balance paid over a specified period of time.

institutional advertising the presentation of information about a particular firm, designed to enhance the firm's image.

intangible resources those organizational resources that are invisible and difficult to quantify.

intellectual property original intellectual creations, including inventions, literary creations, and works of art, that are protected by patents or copyrights.

internal control a system of checks and balances that safeguards assets and enhances the accuracy and reliability of financial statements.

internal equity capital that comes from retaining profits within a firm.

internal locus of control a belief that one's success depends on one's own efforts.

internal rate of return (IRR) the rate of return a firm expects to earn on a project.

international franchising selling a standard package of products, systems, and management services to a company in another country.

international strategic alliance a combination of the efforts and/or assets of companies in different countries for the sake of pooling resources and sharing the risks of an enterprise.

Internet a huge, loosely connected computer network that links smaller networks all over the world, through modems, phone lines, satellite links, and other communication channels.

inventory a firm's raw materials and products held in anticipation of eventual sale.

inventory turnover the number of times inventories "roll over" during a year.

ISO 9000 the standards governing international certification of a firm's quality management procedures.

job description a written summary of the duties required by a specific job.

Job Instruction Training a systematic step-by-step method for on-the-job training of nonmanagerial employees.

job shops a type of manufacturing operation in which short production runs are used to produce small quantities of unique items.

job specification a list of skills and abilities needed to perform a specific job.

just-in-time inventory system a method of reducing inventory levels to an absolute minimum.

key-person insurance coverage that protects against the death of a firm's key personnel.

laws of motion economy guidelines for increasing the efficiency of human movement and tool design.

learning effects insights, gained from experience, that lead to improved work performance.

legal entity a business organization that is recognized by the law as having a separate legal existence.

letter of credit an agreement issued by a bank to honor a draft or other demand for payment when specified conditions are met.

leveraged buyout (LBO) a purchase heavily financed with debt, where the potential cash flow of the target company is expected to be sufficient to meet debt repayments.

LIBOR (London InterBank Offered Rate) the interest rate charged by London banks on loans to other London banks.

licensee the company buying licensing rights.

licensor the company selling licensing rights.

limited liability the restriction of an owner's legal financial responsibilities to the amount invested in the business.

limited liability company a corporation in which stockholders have limited liability but pay personal income taxes on business profits.

limited partner a partner in a limited partnership who is not active in its management and has limited personal liability.

limited partnership a partnership with at least one general partner and one or more limited partners.

line activities activities contributing directly to the primary objectives of a firm.

line-and-staff organization an organizational structure that includes staff specialists who assist management.

line of credit an informal agreement between a borrower and a bank as to the maximum amount of funds the bank will provide at any one time.

line organization a simple organizational structure in which each person reports to one supervisor.

linkage a type of advertising agreement in which one firm pays another to include a click-on link on its site.

liquidation value technique the determination of the value of a business by estimating the money available if the firm were to liquidate its assets.

liquidity the availability to a firm of cash to meet maturing debt obligations.

loan covenants bank-imposed restrictions on a borrower that enhance the chances of timely repayment.

lock box a post office box for receiving remittances from customers.

long-range plan (strategic plan) a firm's overall plan for the future.

long-term debt loans from banks or other sources with repayment terms of more than 12 months.

make-or-buy decision a firm's choice between producing and purchasing component parts for its products.

management buyout (MBO) a leveraged buyout in which the firm's top managers become significant shareholders in the acquired firm.

management functions the activities of planning, leading, organizing, and controlling.

management plan a section of the business plan that describes a new firm's organizational structure and the backgrounds of its key players.

management team managers and other key persons who give a company its general direction.

market a group of customers or potential customers who have purchasing power and unsatisfied needs.

market analysis an evaluation process that encompasses market segmentation, marketing research, and sales forecasting.

market-comparable valuation approach the determination of the value of a business based on the sale prices of comparable firms.

market risk the uncertainty associated with an investment decision.

market segmentation the division of a market into several smaller groups with similar needs.

marketing mix the combination of product, pricing, promotion, and distribution activities.

marketing plan a section of the business plan that describes the user benefits of the product or service and the type of market that exists.

marketing research the gathering, processing, reporting, and interpreting of market information.

markup pricing applying a percentage to a product's cost to obtain its selling price.

master licensee an independent firm or individual acting as a sales agent with the responsibility for finding new franchisees within a specified territory.

matchmakers specialized brokers who bring together buyers and sellers of businesses.

mentoring guiding and supporting the work and development of a new or less-experienced organization member.

merchant middlemen intermediaries that take title to the goods they distribute.

microbusiness a small firm that provides minimal profits to its owner.

mission statement a concise written description of a firm's philosophy.

modified book value technique the determination of the value of a business by adjusting book value to re-

flect differences between the historical cost and the current value of the assets.

Moore's Law the theory that computing power doubles every 18 months.

mortgage a long-term loan from a creditor for which real estate is pledged as collateral.

motion study an analysis of all the motions a worker makes to complete a given job.

motivations forces that organize and give direction to the tension caused by unsatisfied needs.

multiple-unit ownership holding by a single franchisee of more than one franchise from the same company.

multisegmentation strategy a strategy that recognizes different preferences of individual market segments and develops a unique marketing mix for each.

needs the starting point for all behavior.

negotiation two-way communication process used to resolve differences in needs, goals, or ideas.

net fixed assets gross fixed assets less accumulated depreciation.

net income available to owners (net income) income that may be distributed to the owners or reinvested in the company.

net present value (NPV) the present value of expected future cash flows less the initial investment outlay.

net operating working capital the sum of a firm's current assets (cash, accounts receivable, and inventories) less accounts payable and accruals.

networking the process of developing and engaging in mutually beneficial relationships.

normalized earnings earnings that have been adjusted for unusual items, such as fire damage.

North American Free Trade Agreement (NAFTA) an agreement ensuring free trade between the United States, Canada, and Mexico.

Occupational Safety and Health Act legislation that regulates the safety of workplaces and work practices.

open charge account a line of credit that allows the customer to obtain a product at the time of purchase, with payment due when billed.

operating expenses costs related to marketing and distributing a firm's product or service, general administrative expenses, and depreciation expense.

operating income earnings before interest and taxes are paid.

operating income return on investment (OIROI) a measure of operating profits relative to total assets.

operating plan a section of the business plan that offers information on how a product will be produced or a service provided, including descriptions of the new firm's facilities, labor, raw materials, and processing requirements.

operating profit margin the ratio of operating profits to sales, showing how well a firm manages its income statement.

operating working capital money invested in current assets less accounts payable and accruals.

operations management planning and controlling the process of converting inputs into outputs.

operations process (production process) the activities that create value for customers through production of a firm's goods and services.

opinion leader a group leader who plays a key communications role.

opportunistic entrepreneur a person with both sophisticated managerial skills and technical knowledge who starts a business.

opportunity cost the rate of return that could be earned on another investment of similar risk.

ordinary income income earned in the ordinary course of business, including any salary.

organizational capabilities the integration of several organizational resources that are deployed together to the firm's advantage.

organizational culture the behaviors, beliefs, and values that characterize a particular firm.

organizational resources basic inputs that a firm uses to conduct its business.

other assets assets other than current assets and fixed assets, such as patents, copyrights, and goodwill.

outsourcing purchasing products or services that are outside the firm's area of competitive advantage.

owners' equity owners' investments in a company, plus profits retained in the firm.

paradox of attraction the concept that an attractive industry opportunity is likely to draw multiple new entrants, diminishing its attractiveness.

partnership a legal entity formed by two or more co-owners to carry on a business for profit.

partnership agreement a document that states explicitly the rights and duties of partners.

patent the registered, exclusive right of an inventor to make, use, or sell an invention.

payback period technique a capital budgeting technique that measures the amount of time it will take to recover the cash outlay of an investment.

penetration pricing strategy setting lower than normal prices to hasten market acceptance of a product or service or to increase market share.

percentage-of-sales technique a method of forecasting asset investments and financing requirements.

perception the individual processes that give meaning to the stimuli confronting consumers.

perceptual categorization the process of grouping similar things so as to manage huge quantities of incoming stimuli.

perpetual inventory system a method for keeping a running record of inventory.

personal selling a sales presentation delivered in a one-on-one manner.

physical distribution (logistics) the activities of distribution involved in the physical relocation of products.

physical inventory system a method that provides for periodic counting of items in inventory.

piggyback franchising the operation of a retail franchise within the physical facilities of a host store.

plant patent registered protection for any distinct and new variety of plant.

pledged accounts receivable accounts receivable used as collateral for a loan.

political risk the potential for political forces in a country to negatively affect the performance of businesses operating within its borders.

pop-up ads advertisements that burst open on computer screens.

pre-emptive right the right of stockholders to buy new shares of stock before they are offered to the public.

precipitating event an event, such as losing a job, that moves an individual to become an entrepreneur.

prestige pricing setting a high price to convey an image of high quality or uniqueness.

preventive maintenance activities intended to prevent machine breakdowns, injuries to people, and damage to facilities.

price a specification of what a seller requires in exchange for transferring ownership or use of a product or service.

price lining strategy setting a range of several distinct merchandise price levels.

primary data new market information that is gathered by the firm conducting the research.

prime rate the interest rate charged by a commercial bank on loans to its most creditworthy customers.

private carriers lines of transport owned by the shippers.

private equity money provided by venture capitalists or private investors.

private placement the sale of a firm's capital stock to selected individuals.

pro forma financial statements statements that project a firm's financial performance and condition.

procedures specific work methods to be followed in business activities.

process layout a factory design that groups similar machines together.

product a total bundle of satisfaction—a service, a good, or both—offered to consumers in an exchange transaction.

product advertising the presentation of a business idea designed to make potential customers aware of a specific product or service and create a desire for it.

product and trade name franchising a franchise agreement granting the right to use a widely recognized product or name.

product item the lowest common denominator in the product mix—the individual item.

product layout a factory design that arranges machines according to their roles in the production process.

product line the sum of related individual product items.

product mix a firm's total product lines.

product mix consistency the similarity of product lines in a product mix.

product strategy the way the product component of the marketing mix is used to achieve a firm's objectives.

productivity the efficiency with which inputs are transformed into outputs.

products and/or services plan a section of the business plan that describes the product and/or service to be provided and explains its merits.

professional employment organization (PEO) a personnel-leasing company that places employees on its own payroll and then "rents" them to employers on a permanent basis.

professional manager a manager who uses systematic, analytical methods of management.

profit retention the reinvestment of profits in a firm.

promotion marketing communications that inform and persuade consumers.

promotional mix a blend of nonpersonal, personal, and special forms of communication aimed at a target market.

prospecting a systematic process of continually looking for new customers.

prospectus a marketing document used to solicit investors' monies.

publicity information about a firm and its products or services that appears as a news item, usually free of charge.

purchasing the process of obtaining materials, equipment, and services from outside suppliers.

pure risk the uncertainty associated with a situation where only loss or no loss can occur.

quality the features of a product or service that enable it to satisfy customers' needs.

quality circle a group of employees who meet regularly to discuss quality-related problems.

real estate mortgage a long-term loan with real property held as collateral.

reengineering a fundamental restructuring to improve the operations process.

reference groups groups that an individual allows to influence his or her behavior.

refugee a person who becomes an entrepreneur to escape an undesirable situation.

reliability the consistency of a test in measuring job performance ability.

repetitive manufacturing a type of manufacturing operation in which long production runs are used to produce a large quantity of a standardized product.

replacement value technique the determination of the value of a business by estimating the cost of replacing the firm's assets.

retained earnings profits less withdrawals (dividends).

return on equity the rate of return that owners earn on their investment.

revenue-based model a business model that focuses on generating, maintaining, and increasing revenues.

revolving charge account a line of credit on which the customer may charge purchases at any time, up to a preestablished limit.

revolving credit agreement a legal commitment by a bank to lend up to a maximum amount.

risk the chance that a situation may end with loss or misfortune.

risk avoidance preventing risk by choosing not to engage in hazardous activities.

risk control minimizing potential losses by avoiding or reducing risk.

risk financing making funds available to cover losses that could not be managed by risk control.

risk management ways of coping with risk that are designed to preserve assets and the earning power of a firm.

risk reduction lessening the frequency, severity, or unpredictability of losses.

risk retention choosing—whether consciously or unconsciously, voluntarily or involuntarily—to manage risk internally.

risk transfer buying insurance or making contractual arrangements with others in order to transfer risk.

royalties fees paid by the licensee to the licensor for each unit produced under a licensing contract.

S corporation (Subchapter S corporation) a type of corporation that is taxed by the federal government as a partnership.

sales forecast a prediction of how much of a product or service will be purchased within a market during a specified time period.

sales promotion an inclusive term for any promotional techniques that are neither personal selling nor advertising.

secondary data market information that has been previously compiled.

Section 1244 stock stock that offers some tax benefit to the stockholder in the case of corporate failure.

segmentation variables the parameters used to distinguish one form of market behavior from another.

self-insurance designating part of a firm's earnings as a cushion against possible future losses.

self-service layout a type of retail store design that gives customers direct access to merchandise.

serendipity the faculty for making desirable discoveries by accident.

Service Corps of Retired Executives (SCORE) an SBA-sponsored group of retired executives who give free advice to small businesses.

service mark a legal term indicating the exclusive right to use a brand to identify a service.

short-range plan a plan that governs a firm's operations for one year or less.

short-term notes cash amounts borrowed from a bank or other lending sources that must be repaid within a short period of time.

single-entry system a checkbook system of accounting reflecting only receipts and disbursements.

single-segmentation strategy a strategy that recognizes the existence of several distinct market segments but focuses on only the most profitable segment.

skimming price strategy setting very high prices for a limited period before reducing them to more competitive levels.

small business development centers (SBDCs) university-affiliated centers offering consulting, education, and other support to small businesses.

Small Business Innovative Research (SBIR) a government program that helps finance companies that plan to transform laboratory research into marketable products.

small business investment companies (SBICs) privately owned banks, regulated by the Small Business Administration, that supply capital to small businesses.

small business marketing business activities that identify a target market, determine that market's potential, and prepare, communicate, and deliver a bundle of satisfaction to that market.

social responsibility ethical obligations to customers, employees, and the general public.

sole proprietorship a business owned by one person.

span of control the number of subordinates supervised by one manager.

special-purpose equipment machines designed to serve specialized functions in the production process.

spontaneous financing short-term debts, such as accounts payable, that automatically increase in proportion to a firm's sales.

staff activities activities that support line activities.

stages in succession phases in the process of transferring leadership from parent to child in a family business.

standard operating procedure an established method of conducting a business activity.

startup creating a new business from scratch.

statistical process control the use of statistical methods to assess quality during the operations process.

stock certificate a document specifying the number of shares owned by a stockholder.

strategic acquisition a purchase in which the value of the business is based on both the firm's stand-alone characteristics and the synergies that the buyer thinks can be created.

strategic alliance an organizational relationship that links two or more independent business entities in a common endeavor.

strategic decision a decision regarding the direction a firm will take in relating to its customers and competitors.

strategy a plan of action that coordinates the resources and commitments of an organization to achieve superior performance.

surety bonds coverage that protects against another's failure to fulfill a contractual obligation.

sustainable competitive advantage a value-creating industry position that is likely to endure over time.

sustainable growth growth that can be financed from cash flows generated from operating the business.

SWOT analysis a type of assessment that provides a concise overview of a firm's strategic situation.

tangible resources those organizational resources that are visible and easy to measure.

tariffs taxes charged on imported goods.

term loan money loaned for a five- to ten-year term, corresponding to the length of time the investment will bring in profits.

time study the determination of the average time it takes a worker to complete a given task.

times interest earned ratio the ratio of operating income to interest charges.

total asset turnover the ratio of sales to total assets, showing the efficiency with which a firm's assets are used to generate sales.

total cost the sum of cost of goods sold, selling expenses, and overhead costs.

total fixed costs costs that remain constant as the quantity produced or sold varies.

total quality management (TQM) an all-encompassing management approach to providing high-quality products and services.

total variable costs costs that vary with the quantity produced or sold.

trade-credit agencies privately owned organizations that collect credit information on businesses.

trade dress elements of a firm's distinctive image not protected by a trademark, patent, or copyright.

trade intermediary an agency that distributes a company's products on a contract basis to customers in another country.

trade mission a trip organized to help small business owners make direct contact with potential buyers abroad.

trademark an identifying feature used to distinguish a manufacturer's product.

transaction-based model a business model in which the Web site provides a mechanism for buying or selling products or services.

transfer of ownership distribution of ownership of the family business to the next generation.

24/7 e-tailing electronic retailing providing round-the-clock access to products and services.

Type A ideas startup ideas centered around providing customers with an existing product not available in their market.

Type B ideas startup ideas, involving new technology, centered around providing customers with a new product.

Type C ideas startup ideas centered around providing customers with an improved product.

underlying values unarticulated ethical beliefs that provide a foundation for ethical behavior in a firm.

Uniform Franchise Offering Circular (UFOC) a document accepted by the Federal Trade Commission as satisfying its franchise disclosure requirements.

unity of command a situation in which each employee's instructions come directly from only one immediate supervisor.

unlimited liability liability on the part of an owner that extends beyond the owner's investment in the business.

unsegmented strategy (mass marketing) a strategy that defines the total market as the target market.

utility patent registered protection for a new process or a product's function.

validity the extent to which a test assesses true job performance ability.

valuation multiple a multiple of a firm's earnings, used to value the company.

variable inspection the determination of product acceptability based on a variable such as weight or length.

variable pricing strategy setting more than one price for a good or service in order to offer price concessions to certain customers.

venture capitalist an investor or investment group that commits money to new business ventures.

warranty a promise that a product will perform at a certain level or meet certain standards.

Web site a firm's location on the World Wide Web.

Web sponsorship a type of advertising in which a firm pays another organization for the right to be part of that organization's Web page.

weighted cost of capital the cost of capital adjusted to reflect the relative costs of debt and equity financing.

work teams groups of employees with freedom to function without close supervision.

workers' compensation insurance coverage that obligates the insurer to pay employees for injury or illness related to employment.

workforce diversity differences among employees in terms of such dimensions as gender, age, and race.

working-capital cycle the daily flow of resources through a firm's working-capital accounts.

working-capital management the management of current assets and current liabilities.

World Wide Web (WWW) a system of Internet servers accessible with browsers, which navigate via hypertext links.

zoning ordinances local laws regulating land use.

INDEX

INDEX